Financial
PAYMENT TABLES
FOR
CANADIAN MORTGAGES

All tables are computed on the basis of nominal
annual interest rates compounded semiannually, in
order to conform to Canadian Law.

PUBLICATION NO. 42, REVISED
SEPTEMBER 1986

*Computed and
Published by*

FINANCIAL
PUBLISHING
COMPANY

82 Brookline Avenue
Boston, Massachusetts 02215
(617) 262-4040

PUBLICATION NO. 42, REVISED
COPYRIGHT © 1974, 1983, 1986 BY
FINANCIAL PUBLISHING COMPANY

PRINTED IN THE
UNITED STATES OF AMERICA

ISBN 0-87600-042-1

TABLE OF CONTENTS

Page

7%

MONTHLY PAYMENT
NECESSARY TO AMORTIZE A LOAN

TERM AMOUNT	1 YEAR	1½ YEARS	2 YEARS	2½ YEARS	3 YEARS	3½ YEARS	4 YEARS	4½ YEARS	5 YEARS
$ 25	2.17	1.47	1.12	.91	.78	.68	.60	.54	.50
50	4.33	2.94	2.24	1.82	1.55	1.35	1.20	1.08	.99
75	6.49	4.40	3.36	2.73	2.32	2.02	1.80	1.62	1.49
100	8.65	5.87	4.48	3.64	3.09	2.69	2.39	2.16	1.98
200	17.30	11.73	8.95	7.28	6.17	5.38	4.78	4.32	3.96
300	25.95	17.60	13.42	10.92	9.25	8.07	7.17	6.48	5.93
400	34.60	23.46	17.90	14.56	12.34	10.75	9.56	8.64	7.91
500	43.25	29.32	22.37	18.20	15.42	13.44	11.95	10.80	9.88
600	51.89	35.19	26.84	21.84	18.50	16.13	14.34	12.96	11.86
700	60.54	41.05	31.31	25.48	21.59	18.81	16.73	15.12	13.83
800	69.19	46.92	35.79	29.11	24.67	21.50	19.12	17.28	15.81
900	77.84	52.78	40.26	32.75	27.75	24.19	21.51	19.44	17.78
1000	86.49	58.64	44.73	36.39	30.84	26.87	23.90	21.60	19.76
2000	172.97	117.28	89.46	72.78	61.67	53.74	47.80	43.19	39.51
3000	259.45	175.92	134.19	109.16	92.50	80.61	71.70	64.79	59.27
4000	345.93	234.56	178.91	145.55	123.33	107.48	95.60	86.38	79.02
5000	432.41	293.20	223.64	181.94	154.16	134.35	119.50	107.98	98.78
6000	518.89	351.84	268.37	218.32	184.99	161.21	143.40	129.57	118.53
7000	605.37	410.48	313.10	254.71	215.82	188.08	167.30	151.17	138.28
8000	691.85	469.12	357.82	291.10	246.66	214.95	191.20	172.76	158.04
9000	778.33	527.76	402.55	327.48	277.49	241.82	215.10	194.36	177.79
10000	864.81	586.40	447.28	363.87	308.32	268.69	239.00	215.95	197.55
15000	1297.22	879.60	670.91	545.80	462.48	403.03	358.50	323.93	296.32
20000	1729.62	1172.80	894.55	727.73	616.63	537.37	478.00	431.90	395.09
25000	2162.02	1465.99	1118.19	909.67	770.79	671.71	597.50	539.88	493.86
30000	2594.43	1759.19	1341.82	1091.60	924.95	806.05	717.00	647.85	592.63
35000	3026.83	2052.39	1565.46	1273.53	1079.10	940.39	836.50	755.82	691.40
36000	3113.31	2111.03	1610.19	1309.92	1109.94	967.26	860.40	777.42	711.15
37000	3199.79	2169.67	1654.91	1346.30	1140.77	994.13	884.30	799.01	730.91
38000	3286.27	2228.31	1699.64	1382.69	1171.60	1020.99	908.20	820.61	750.66
39000	3372.75	2286.95	1744.37	1419.08	1202.43	1047.87	932.10	842.20	770.41
40000	3459.23	2345.59	1789.10	1455.46	1233.26	1074.73	956.00	863.80	790.17
41000	3545.71	2404.23	1833.82	1491.85	1264.09	1101.60	979.90	885.39	809.92
42000	3632.19	2462.87	1878.55	1528.24	1294.92	1128.47	1003.80	906.99	829.68
43000	3718.67	2521.51	1923.28	1564.62	1325.76	1155.34	1027.70	928.58	849.43
44000	3805.15	2580.15	1968.01	1601.01	1356.59	1182.21	1051.60	950.18	869.18
45000	3891.64	2638.79	2012.73	1637.40	1387.42	1209.07	1075.50	971.77	888.94
46000	3978.12	2697.43	2057.46	1673.78	1418.25	1235.94	1099.40	993.37	908.69
47000	4064.60	2756.07	2102.19	1710.17	1449.08	1262.81	1123.30	1014.96	928.45
48000	4151.08	2814.71	2146.91	1746.56	1479.91	1289.68	1147.20	1036.56	948.20
49000	4237.56	2873.34	2191.64	1782.94	1510.74	1316.55	1171.10	1058.15	967.95
50000	4324.04	2931.98	2236.37	1819.33	1541.58	1343.42	1195.00	1079.75	987.71
51000	4410.52	2990.62	2281.10	1855.72	1572.41	1370.28	1218.90	1101.34	1007.46
52000	4497.00	3049.26	2325.82	1892.10	1603.24	1397.15	1242.80	1122.94	1027.22
53000	4583.48	3107.90	2370.55	1928.49	1634.07	1424.02	1266.70	1144.53	1046.97
54000	4669.96	3166.54	2415.28	1964.87	1664.90	1450.89	1290.60	1166.13	1066.73
55000	4756.44	3225.18	2460.01	2001.26	1695.73	1477.76	1314.50	1187.72	1086.48
56000	4842.92	3283.82	2504.73	2037.65	1726.56	1504.62	1338.40	1209.32	1106.23
57000	4929.40	3342.46	2549.46	2074.03	1757.40	1531.49	1362.30	1230.91	1125.99
58000	5015.88	3401.10	2594.19	2110.42	1788.23	1558.36	1386.20	1252.51	1145.74
59000	5102.36	3459.74	2638.91	2146.81	1819.06	1585.23	1410.10	1274.10	1165.50
60000	5188.85	3518.38	2683.64	2183.19	1849.89	1612.10	1434.00	1295.70	1185.25
61000	5275.33	3577.02	2728.37	2219.58	1880.72	1638.97	1457.90	1317.29	1205.00
62000	5361.81	3635.66	2773.10	2255.97	1911.55	1665.83	1481.80	1338.89	1224.76
63000	5448.29	3694.30	2817.82	2292.35	1942.38	1692.70	1505.70	1360.48	1244.51
64000	5534.77	3752.94	2862.55	2328.74	1973.22	1719.57	1529.60	1382.08	1264.27
65000	5621.25	3811.58	2907.28	2365.13	2004.05	1746.44	1553.50	1403.67	1284.02
66000	5707.73	3870.22	2952.01	2401.51	2034.88	1773.31	1577.40	1425.27	1303.77
67000	5794.21	3928.86	2996.73	2437.90	2065.71	1800.17	1601.30	1446.86	1323.53
68000	5880.69	3987.50	3041.46	2474.29	2096.54	1827.04	1625.20	1468.45	1343.28
69000	5967.17	4046.14	3086.19	2510.67	2127.37	1853.91	1649.10	1490.05	1363.04
70000	6053.65	4104.78	3130.91	2547.06	2158.20	1880.78	1673.00	1511.64	1382.79
75000	6486.06	4397.97	3354.55	2728.99	2312.36	2015.12	1792.50	1619.62	1481.56
80000	6918.46	4691.17	3578.19	2910.92	2466.52	2149.46	1912.00	1727.59	1580.33
100000	8648.07	5863.96	4472.73	3638.65	3083.15	2686.83	2389.99	2159.49	1975.41

4

MONTHLY PAYMENT 7%
NECESSARY TO AMORTIZE A LOAN

TERM AMOUNT	6 YEARS	7 YEARS	8 YEARS	9 YEARS	10 YEARS	11 YEARS	12 YEARS	13 YEARS	14 YEARS
$ 25	.43	.38	.34	.32	.29	.28	.26	.25	.24
50	.86	.76	.68	.63	.58	.55	.52	.49	.47
75	1.28	1.13	1.02	.94	.87	.82	.77	.73	.70
100	1.71	1.51	1.36	1.25	1.16	1.09	1.03	.98	.93
200	3.41	3.01	2.72	2.50	2.32	2.17	2.05	1.95	1.86
300	5.11	4.52	4.08	3.74	3.47	3.25	3.07	2.92	2.79
400	6.81	6.02	5.44	4.99	4.63	4.34	4.10	3.90	3.72
500	8.51	7.53	6.80	6.23	5.78	5.42	5.12	4.87	4.65
600	10.21	9.03	8.16	7.48	6.94	6.50	6.14	5.84	5.58
700	11.91	10.54	9.51	8.72	8.10	7.59	7.17	6.81	6.51
800	13.61	12.04	10.87	9.97	9.25	8.67	8.19	7.79	7.44
900	15.31	13.54	12.23	11.22	10.41	9.75	9.21	8.76	8.37
1000	17.01	15.05	13.59	12.46	11.56	10.84	10.24	9.73	9.30
2000	34.01	30.09	27.17	24.92	23.12	21.67	20.47	19.46	18.60
3000	51.01	45.14	40.76	37.37	34.68	32.50	30.70	29.19	27.90
4000	68.01	60.18	54.34	49.83	46.24	43.33	40.93	38.91	37.20
5000	85.01	75.22	67.93	62.28	57.80	54.16	51.16	48.64	46.50
6000	102.01	90.27	81.51	74.74	69.36	65.00	61.39	58.37	55.80
7000	119.01	105.31	95.09	87.19	80.92	75.83	71.62	68.09	65.10
8000	136.01	120.36	108.68	99.65	92.48	86.66	81.85	77.82	74.40
9000	153.01	135.40	122.26	112.11	104.04	97.49	92.08	87.55	83.70
10000	170.02	150.44	135.85	124.56	115.60	108.32	102.31	97.27	93.00
15000	255.02	225.66	203.77	186.84	173.40	162.48	153.46	145.91	139.49
20000	340.03	300.88	271.69	249.12	231.19	216.64	204.62	194.54	185.99
25000	425.03	376.10	339.61	311.40	288.99	270.80	255.77	243.17	232.48
30000	510.04	451.32	407.53	373.68	346.79	324.96	306.92	291.81	278.98
35000	595.04	526.54	475.45	435.95	404.58	379.12	358.08	340.44	325.47
36000	612.04	541.58	489.03	448.41	416.14	389.95	368.31	350.17	334.77
37000	629.04	556.63	502.61	460.87	427.70	400.78	378.54	359.89	344.07
38000	646.04	571.67	516.20	473.32	439.26	411.61	388.77	369.62	353.37
39000	663.05	586.72	529.78	485.78	450.82	422.44	399.00	379.35	362.67
40000	680.05	601.76	543.37	498.23	462.38	433.28	409.23	389.07	371.97
41000	697.05	616.80	556.95	510.69	473.94	444.11	419.46	398.80	381.27
42000	714.05	631.85	570.53	523.14	485.50	454.94	429.69	408.53	390.57
43000	731.05	646.89	584.12	535.60	497.06	465.77	439.92	418.25	399.87
44000	748.05	661.94	597.70	548.06	508.62	476.60	450.15	427.98	409.16
45000	765.05	676.98	611.29	560.51	520.18	487.43	460.38	437.71	418.46
46000	782.05	692.02	624.87	572.97	531.74	498.27	470.61	447.43	427.76
47000	799.05	707.07	638.45	585.42	543.30	509.10	480.84	457.16	437.06
48000	816.06	722.11	652.04	597.88	554.86	519.93	491.07	466.89	446.36
49000	833.06	737.15	665.62	610.33	566.42	530.76	501.30	476.61	455.66
50000	850.06	752.20	679.21	622.79	577.97	541.59	511.54	486.34	464.96
51000	867.06	767.24	692.79	635.25	589.53	552.43	521.77	496.07	474.26
52000	884.06	782.29	706.37	647.70	601.09	563.26	532.00	505.79	483.56
53000	901.06	797.33	719.96	660.16	612.65	574.09	542.23	515.52	492.86
54000	918.06	812.37	733.54	672.61	624.21	584.92	552.46	525.25	502.15
55000	935.06	827.42	747.13	685.07	635.77	595.75	562.69	534.97	511.45
56000	952.06	842.46	760.71	697.52	647.33	606.58	572.92	544.70	520.75
57000	969.06	857.51	774.29	709.98	658.89	617.42	583.15	554.43	530.05
58000	986.07	872.55	787.88	722.44	670.45	628.25	593.38	564.15	539.35
59000	1003.07	887.59	801.46	734.89	682.01	639.08	603.61	573.88	548.65
60000	1020.07	902.64	815.05	747.35	693.57	649.91	613.84	583.61	557.95
61000	1037.07	917.68	828.63	759.80	705.13	660.74	624.07	593.33	567.25
62000	1054.07	932.72	842.21	772.26	716.69	671.57	634.30	603.06	576.55
63000	1071.07	947.77	855.80	784.71	728.25	682.41	644.53	612.79	585.85
64000	1088.07	962.81	869.38	797.17	739.81	693.24	654.76	622.51	595.15
65000	1105.07	977.86	882.97	809.63	751.37	704.07	664.99	632.24	604.44
66000	1122.07	992.90	896.55	822.08	762.93	714.90	675.23	641.97	613.74
67000	1139.08	1007.94	910.13	834.54	774.48	725.73	685.46	651.69	623.04
68000	1156.08	1022.99	923.72	846.99	786.04	736.57	695.69	661.42	632.34
69000	1173.08	1038.03	937.30	859.45	797.60	747.40	705.92	671.15	641.64
70000	1190.08	1053.08	950.89	871.90	809.16	758.23	716.15	680.87	650.94
75000	1275.08	1128.29	1018.81	934.18	866.96	812.39	767.30	729.51	697.44
80000	1360.09	1203.51	1086.73	996.46	924.76	866.55	818.45	778.14	743.93
100000	1700.11	1504.39	1358.41	1245.58	1155.94	1083.18	1023.07	972.67	929.91

5

7%

MONTHLY PAYMENT
NECESSARY TO AMORTIZE A LOAN

TERM AMOUNT	15 YEARS	16 YEARS	17 YEARS	18 YEARS	19 YEARS	20 YEARS	21 YEARS	22 YEARS	23 YEARS
$ 25	.23	.22	.21	.21	.20	.20	.19	.19	.19
50	.45	.44	.42	.41	.40	.39	.38	.37	.37
75	.67	.65	.63	.61	.60	.58	.57	.56	.55
100	.90	.87	.84	.81	.79	.77	.76	.74	.73
200	1.79	1.73	1.67	1.62	1.58	1.54	1.51	1.48	1.45
300	2.68	2.59	2.51	2.43	2.37	2.31	2.26	2.22	2.18
400	3.58	3.45	3.34	3.24	3.16	3.08	3.01	2.95	2.90
500	4.47	4.31	4.17	4.05	3.95	3.85	3.77	3.69	3.62
600	5.36	5.17	5.01	4.86	4.73	4.62	4.52	4.43	4.35
700	6.26	6.04	5.84	5.67	5.52	5.39	5.27	5.17	5.07
800	7.15	6.90	6.68	6.48	6.31	6.16	6.02	5.90	5.79
900	8.04	7.76	7.51	7.29	7.10	6.93	6.78	6.64	6.52
1000	8.94	8.62	8.34	8.10	7.89	7.70	7.53	7.38	7.24
2000	17.87	17.24	16.68	16.20	15.77	15.39	15.05	14.75	14.48
3000	26.80	25.85	25.02	24.30	23.65	23.08	22.58	22.12	21.72
4000	35.73	34.47	33.36	32.39	31.54	30.78	30.10	29.50	28.95
5000	44.67	43.08	41.70	40.49	39.42	38.47	37.63	36.87	36.19
6000	53.60	51.70	50.04	48.59	47.30	46.16	45.15	44.24	43.43
7000	62.53	60.31	58.38	56.68	55.18	53.86	52.67	51.61	50.66
8000	71.46	68.93	66.72	64.78	63.07	61.55	60.20	58.99	57.90
9000	80.40	77.54	75.06	72.88	70.95	69.24	67.72	66.36	65.14
10000	89.33	86.16	83.40	80.97	78.83	76.94	75.25	73.73	72.38
15000	133.99	129.24	125.09	121.46	118.25	115.40	112.87	110.60	108.56
20000	178.65	172.31	166.79	161.94	157.66	153.87	150.49	147.46	144.75
25000	223.32	215.39	208.48	202.42	197.08	192.33	188.11	184.33	180.93
30000	267.98	258.47	250.18	242.91	236.49	230.80	225.73	221.19	217.12
35000	312.64	301.55	291.88	283.39	275.90	269.26	263.35	258.05	253.30
36000	321.57	310.16	300.21	291.49	283.79	276.96	270.87	265.43	260.54
37000	330.51	318.78	308.55	299.58	291.67	284.65	278.40	272.80	267.77
38000	339.44	327.39	316.89	307.68	299.55	292.34	285.92	280.17	275.01
39000	348.37	336.01	325.23	315.78	307.44	300.04	293.44	287.54	282.25
40000	357.30	344.62	333.57	323.87	315.32	307.73	300.97	294.92	289.49
41000	366.24	353.24	341.91	331.97	323.20	315.42	308.49	302.29	296.72
42000	375.17	361.85	350.25	340.07	331.08	323.12	316.02	309.66	303.96
43000	384.10	370.47	358.59	348.16	338.97	330.81	323.54	317.04	311.20
44000	393.03	379.08	366.93	356.26	346.85	338.50	331.06	324.41	318.43
45000	401.97	387.70	375.27	364.36	354.73	346.19	338.59	331.78	325.67
46000	410.90	396.32	383.61	372.46	362.62	353.89	346.11	339.15	332.91
47000	419.83	404.93	391.94	380.55	370.50	361.58	353.64	346.53	340.14
48000	428.76	413.55	400.28	388.65	378.38	369.27	361.16	353.90	347.38
49000	437.70	422.16	408.62	396.75	386.26	376.97	368.68	361.27	354.62
50000	446.63	430.78	416.96	404.84	394.15	384.66	376.21	368.65	361.86
51000	455.56	439.39	425.30	412.94	402.03	392.35	383.73	376.02	369.09
52000	464.49	448.01	433.64	421.04	409.91	400.05	391.26	383.39	376.33
53000	473.43	456.62	441.98	429.13	417.80	407.74	398.78	390.76	383.57
54000	482.36	465.24	450.32	437.23	425.68	415.43	406.30	398.14	390.80
55000	491.29	473.85	458.66	445.33	433.56	423.13	413.83	405.51	398.04
56000	500.22	482.47	467.00	453.42	441.44	430.82	421.35	412.88	405.28
57000	509.16	491.09	475.34	461.52	449.33	438.51	428.88	420.26	412.51
58000	518.09	499.70	483.68	469.62	457.21	446.21	436.40	427.63	419.75
59000	527.02	508.32	492.01	477.71	465.09	453.90	443.92	435.00	426.99
60000	535.95	516.93	500.35	485.81	472.98	461.59	451.45	442.37	434.23
61000	544.89	525.55	508.69	493.91	480.86	469.28	458.97	449.75	441.46
62000	553.82	534.16	517.03	502.00	488.74	476.98	466.50	457.12	448.70
63000	562.75	542.78	525.37	510.10	496.62	484.67	474.02	464.49	455.94
64000	571.68	551.39	533.71	518.20	504.51	492.36	481.54	471.87	463.17
65000	580.62	560.01	542.05	526.29	512.39	500.06	489.07	479.24	470.41
66000	589.55	568.62	550.39	534.39	520.27	507.75	496.59	486.61	477.65
67000	598.48	577.24	558.73	542.49	528.15	515.44	504.12	493.98	484.88
68000	607.41	585.86	567.07	550.58	536.04	523.14	511.64	501.36	492.12
69000	616.35	594.47	575.41	558.68	543.92	530.83	519.16	508.73	499.36
70000	625.28	603.09	583.75	566.78	551.80	538.52	526.69	516.10	506.60
75000	669.94	646.16	625.44	607.26	591.22	576.99	564.31	552.97	542.78
80000	714.60	689.24	667.14	647.74	630.63	615.45	601.93	589.83	578.97
100000	893.25	861.55	833.92	809.68	788.29	769.32	752.41	737.29	723.71

6

MONTHLY PAYMENT 7%
NECESSARY TO AMORTIZE A LOAN

TERM AMOUNT	24 YEARS	25 YEARS	26 YEARS	27 YEARS	28 YEARS	29 YEARS	30 YEARS	35 YEARS	40 YEARS
$ 25	.18	.18	.18	.18	.17	.17	.17	.16	.16
50	.36	.36	.35	.35	.34	.34	.33	.32	.31
75	.54	.53	.52	.52	.51	.50	.50	.48	.47
100	.72	.71	.70	.69	.68	.67	.66	.64	.62
200	1.43	1.41	1.39	1.37	1.35	1.34	1.32	1.27	1.23
300	2.14	2.11	2.08	2.05	2.02	2.00	1.98	1.90	1.85
400	2.85	2.81	2.77	2.73	2.70	2.67	2.64	2.53	2.46
500	3.56	3.51	3.46	3.41	3.37	3.33	3.30	3.16	3.08
600	4.27	4.21	4.15	4.09	4.04	4.00	3.96	3.80	3.69
700	4.99	4.91	4.84	4.77	4.72	4.66	4.62	4.43	4.30
800	5.70	5.61	5.53	5.46	5.39	5.33	5.27	5.06	4.92
900	6.41	6.31	6.22	6.14	6.06	5.99	5.93	5.69	5.53
1000	7.12	7.01	6.91	6.82	6.74	6.66	6.59	6.32	6.15
2000	14.23	14.01	13.81	13.63	13.47	13.31	13.18	12.64	12.29
3000	21.35	21.02	20.72	20.44	20.20	19.97	19.76	18.96	18.43
4000	28.46	28.02	27.62	27.26	26.93	26.62	26.35	25.28	24.57
5000	35.58	35.03	34.53	34.07	33.66	33.28	32.94	31.60	30.71
6000	42.69	42.03	41.43	40.88	40.39	39.93	39.52	37.92	36.86
7000	49.81	49.03	48.33	47.70	47.12	46.59	46.11	44.24	43.00
8000	56.92	56.04	55.24	54.51	53.85	53.24	52.69	50.55	49.14
9000	64.04	63.04	62.14	61.32	60.58	59.90	59.28	56.87	55.28
10000	71.15	70.05	69.05	68.14	67.31	66.55	65.87	63.19	61.42
15000	106.73	105.07	103.57	102.20	100.96	99.83	98.80	94.78	92.13
20000	142.30	140.09	138.09	136.27	134.61	133.10	131.73	126.38	122.84
25000	177.87	175.11	172.61	170.33	168.26	166.38	164.66	157.97	153.55
30000	213.45	210.13	207.13	204.40	201.92	199.65	197.59	189.56	184.26
35000	249.02	245.15	241.65	238.46	235.57	232.93	230.52	221.16	214.97
36000	256.13	252.15	248.55	245.28	242.30	239.58	237.10	227.48	221.11
37000	263.25	259.16	255.45	252.09	249.03	246.24	243.69	233.79	227.25
38000	270.36	266.16	262.36	258.90	255.76	252.89	250.27	240.11	233.40
39000	277.48	273.17	269.26	265.72	262.49	259.55	256.86	246.43	239.54
40000	284.59	280.17	276.17	272.53	269.22	266.20	263.45	252.75	245.68
41000	291.71	287.18	283.07	279.34	275.95	272.86	270.03	259.07	251.82
42000	298.82	294.18	289.97	286.16	282.68	279.51	276.62	265.39	257.96
43000	305.94	301.18	296.88	292.97	289.41	286.17	283.20	271.71	264.10
44000	313.05	308.19	303.78	299.78	296.14	292.82	289.79	278.02	270.25
45000	320.17	315.19	310.69	306.60	302.87	299.48	296.38	284.34	276.39
46000	327.28	322.20	317.59	313.41	309.60	306.13	302.96	290.66	282.53
47000	334.40	329.20	324.49	320.22	316.33	312.79	309.55	296.98	288.67
48000	341.51	336.20	331.40	327.03	323.06	319.44	316.13	303.30	294.81
49000	348.62	343.21	338.30	333.85	329.79	326.10	322.72	309.62	300.96
50000	355.74	350.21	345.21	340.66	336.52	332.75	329.31	315.94	307.10
51000	362.85	357.22	352.11	347.47	343.25	339.41	335.89	322.26	313.24
52000	369.97	364.22	359.01	354.29	349.99	346.06	342.48	328.57	319.38
53000	377.08	371.23	365.92	361.10	356.72	352.72	349.06	334.89	325.52
54000	384.20	378.23	372.82	367.91	363.45	359.37	355.65	341.21	331.66
55000	391.31	385.23	379.73	374.73	370.18	366.03	362.24	347.53	337.81
56000	398.43	392.24	386.63	381.54	376.91	372.68	368.82	353.85	343.95
57000	405.54	399.24	393.54	388.35	383.64	379.34	375.41	360.17	350.09
58000	412.66	406.25	400.44	395.17	390.37	385.99	381.99	366.49	356.23
59000	419.77	413.25	407.34	401.98	397.10	392.65	388.58	372.80	362.37
60000	426.89	420.25	414.25	408.79	403.83	399.30	395.17	379.12	368.52
61000	434.00	427.26	421.15	415.61	410.56	405.96	401.75	385.44	374.66
62000	441.12	434.26	428.06	422.42	417.29	412.61	408.34	391.76	380.80
63000	448.23	441.27	434.96	429.23	424.02	419.27	414.93	398.08	386.94
64000	455.34	448.27	441.86	436.04	430.75	425.92	421.51	404.40	393.08
65000	462.46	455.28	448.77	442.86	437.48	432.58	428.10	410.72	399.22
66000	469.57	462.28	455.67	449.67	444.21	439.23	434.68	417.03	405.37
67000	476.69	469.28	462.58	456.48	450.94	445.89	441.27	423.35	411.51
68000	483.80	476.29	469.48	463.30	457.67	452.54	447.86	429.67	417.65
69000	490.92	483.29	476.38	470.11	464.40	459.20	454.44	435.99	423.79
70000	498.03	490.30	483.29	476.92	471.13	465.85	461.03	442.31	429.93
75000	533.61	525.32	517.81	510.99	504.78	499.13	493.96	473.90	460.64
80000	569.18	560.34	552.33	545.05	538.44	532.40	526.89	505.50	491.35
100000	711.47	700.42	690.41	681.32	673.04	665.50	658.61	631.87	614.19

7

MONTHLY PAYMENT
NECESSARY TO AMORTIZE A LOAN

TERM AMOUNT	1 YEAR	1½ YEARS	2 YEARS	2½ YEARS	3 YEARS	3½ YEARS	4 YEARS	4½ YEARS	5 YEARS
$ 25	2.17	1.47	1.13	.92	.78	.68	.61	.55	.50
50	4.33	2.94	2.25	1.83	1.55	1.35	1.21	1.09	1.00
75	6.50	4.41	3.37	2.74	2.33	2.03	1.81	1.63	1.50
100	8.66	5.88	4.49	3.65	3.10	2.70	2.41	2.18	1.99
200	17.32	11.75	8.97	7.30	6.19	5.40	4.81	4.35	3.98
300	25.98	17.63	13.46	10.95	9.29	8.10	7.21	6.52	5.97
400	34.64	23.50	17.94	14.60	12.38	10.80	9.61	8.69	7.95
500	43.30	29.38	22.42	18.25	15.48	13.50	12.01	10.86	9.94
600	51.96	35.25	26.91	21.90	18.57	16.19	14.41	13.03	11.93
700	60.62	41.13	31.39	25.55	21.66	18.89	16.81	15.20	13.91
800	69.28	47.00	35.87	29.20	24.76	21.59	19.22	17.37	15.90
900	77.94	52.88	40.36	32.85	27.85	24.29	21.62	19.54	17.89
1000	86.60	58.75	44.84	36.50	30.95	26.99	24.02	21.71	19.87
2000	173.19	117.50	89.68	73.00	61.89	53.97	48.03	43.42	39.74
3000	259.78	176.25	134.52	109.50	92.83	80.95	72.04	65.13	59.61
4000	346.38	235.00	179.35	145.99	123.77	107.93	96.06	86.84	79.48
5000	432.97	293.75	224.19	182.49	154.72	134.91	120.07	108.55	99.35
6000	519.56	352.50	269.03	218.99	185.66	161.89	144.08	130.26	119.22
7000	606.15	411.25	313.87	255.48	216.60	188.87	168.09	151.96	139.09
8000	692.75	470.00	358.70	291.98	247.54	215.85	192.11	173.67	158.95
9000	779.34	528.75	403.54	328.48	278.49	242.83	216.12	195.38	178.82
10000	865.93	587.50	448.38	364.97	309.43	269.81	240.13	217.09	198.69
15000	1298.89	881.25	672.57	547.46	464.14	404.71	360.19	325.63	298.04
20000	1731.86	1175.00	896.75	729.94	618.85	539.61	480.26	434.17	397.38
25000	2164.82	1468.75	1120.94	912.43	773.57	674.51	600.32	542.72	496.72
30000	2597.78	1762.50	1345.13	1094.91	928.28	809.41	720.38	651.26	596.07
35000	3030.75	2056.25	1569.31	1277.40	1082.99	944.31	840.45	759.80	695.41
36000	3117.34	2115.00	1614.15	1313.89	1113.93	971.29	864.46	781.51	715.28
37000	3203.93	2173.75	1658.99	1350.39	1144.88	998.27	888.47	803.22	735.15
38000	3290.52	2232.50	1703.83	1386.89	1175.82	1025.25	912.48	824.93	755.01
39000	3377.12	2291.25	1748.66	1423.38	1206.76	1052.23	936.50	846.64	774.88
40000	3463.71	2350.00	1793.50	1459.88	1237.70	1079.21	960.51	868.34	794.75
41000	3550.30	2408.75	1838.34	1496.38	1268.65	1106.19	984.52	890.05	814.62
42000	3636.89	2467.50	1883.17	1532.87	1299.59	1133.17	1008.53	911.76	834.49
43000	3723.49	2526.25	1928.01	1569.37	1330.53	1160.15	1032.55	933.47	854.36
44000	3810.08	2585.00	1972.85	1605.87	1361.47	1187.13	1056.56	955.18	874.23
45000	3896.67	2643.75	2017.69	1642.37	1392.42	1214.11	1080.57	976.89	894.10
46000	3983.27	2702.50	2062.52	1678.86	1423.36	1241.09	1104.58	998.59	913.96
47000	4069.86	2761.25	2107.36	1715.36	1454.30	1268.07	1128.60	1020.30	933.83
48000	4156.45	2820.00	2152.20	1751.86	1485.24	1295.05	1152.61	1042.01	953.70
49000	4243.04	2878.75	2197.04	1788.35	1516.19	1322.03	1176.62	1063.72	973.57
50000	4329.64	2937.50	2241.87	1824.85	1547.13	1349.01	1200.63	1085.43	993.44
51000	4416.23	2996.25	2286.71	1861.35	1578.07	1375.99	1224.65	1107.14	1013.31
52000	4502.82	3055.00	2331.55	1897.84	1609.01	1402.97	1248.66	1128.85	1033.18
53000	4589.41	3113.75	2376.39	1934.34	1639.96	1429.95	1272.67	1150.55	1053.04
54000	4676.01	3172.50	2421.22	1970.84	1670.90	1456.93	1296.68	1172.26	1072.91
55000	4762.60	3231.25	2466.06	2007.33	1701.84	1483.91	1320.70	1193.97	1092.78
56000	4849.19	3290.00	2510.90	2043.83	1732.78	1510.89	1344.71	1215.68	1112.65
57000	4935.78	3348.75	2555.74	2080.33	1763.73	1537.87	1368.72	1237.39	1132.52
58000	5022.38	3407.50	2600.57	2116.83	1794.67	1564.85	1392.73	1259.10	1152.39
59000	5108.97	3466.25	2645.41	2153.32	1825.61	1591.83	1416.75	1280.80	1172.26
60000	5195.56	3525.00	2690.25	2189.82	1856.55	1618.81	1440.76	1302.51	1192.13
61000	5282.15	3583.75	2735.08	2226.32	1887.49	1645.79	1464.77	1324.22	1211.99
62000	5368.75	3642.50	2779.92	2262.81	1918.44	1672.77	1488.78	1345.93	1231.86
63000	5455.34	3701.25	2824.76	2299.31	1949.38	1699.75	1512.80	1367.64	1251.73
64000	5541.93	3760.00	2869.60	2335.81	1980.32	1726.73	1536.81	1389.35	1271.60
65000	5628.53	3818.75	2914.43	2372.30	2011.26	1753.71	1560.82	1411.06	1291.47
66000	5715.12	3877.50	2959.27	2408.80	2042.21	1780.69	1584.84	1432.76	1311.34
67000	5801.71	3936.25	3004.11	2445.30	2073.15	1807.67	1608.85	1454.47	1331.21
68000	5888.30	3995.00	3048.95	2481.79	2104.09	1834.65	1632.86	1476.18	1351.07
69000	5974.90	4053.75	3093.78	2518.29	2135.03	1861.63	1656.87	1497.89	1370.94
70000	6061.49	4112.50	3138.62	2554.79	2165.98	1888.61	1680.89	1519.60	1390.81
75000	6494.45	4406.25	3362.81	2737.27	2320.69	2023.51	1800.95	1628.14	1490.16
80000	6927.41	4700.00	3586.99	2919.76	2475.40	2158.41	1921.01	1736.68	1589.50
100000	8659.27	5875.00	4483.74	3649.70	3094.25	2698.01	2401.26	2170.85	1986.87

MONTHLY PAYMENT 7¼%
NECESSARY TO AMORTIZE A LOAN

TERM AMOUNT	6 YEARS	7 YEARS	8 YEARS	9 YEARS	10 YEARS	11 YEARS	12 YEARS	13 YEARS	14 YEARS
$ 25	.43	.38	.35	.32	.30	.28	.26	.25	.24
50	.86	.76	.69	.63	.59	.55	.52	.50	.48
75	1.29	1.14	1.03	.95	.88	.83	.78	.74	.71
100	1.72	1.52	1.38	1.26	1.17	1.10	1.04	.99	.95
200	3.43	3.04	2.75	2.52	2.34	2.20	2.08	1.98	1.89
300	5.14	4.55	4.12	3.78	3.51	3.29	3.11	2.96	2.83
400	6.85	6.07	5.49	5.04	4.68	4.39	4.15	3.95	3.78
500	8.56	7.59	6.86	6.29	5.85	5.48	5.19	4.93	4.72
600	10.28	9.10	8.23	7.55	7.02	6.58	6.22	5.92	5.66
700	11.99	10.62	9.60	8.81	8.18	7.68	7.26	6.91	6.61
800	13.70	12.14	10.97	10.07	9.35	8.77	8.29	7.89	7.55
900	15.41	13.65	12.34	11.33	10.52	9.87	9.33	8.88	8.49
1000	17.12	15.17	13.71	12.58	11.69	10.96	10.37	9.86	9.44
2000	34.24	30.33	27.41	25.16	23.37	21.92	20.73	19.72	18.87
3000	51.36	45.49	41.12	37.74	35.06	32.88	31.09	29.58	28.30
4000	68.48	60.66	54.82	50.32	46.74	43.84	41.45	39.44	37.74
5000	85.59	75.82	68.53	62.90	58.43	54.80	51.81	49.30	47.17
6000	102.71	90.98	82.23	75.48	70.11	65.76	62.17	59.15	56.60
7000	119.83	106.14	95.94	88.06	81.80	76.72	72.53	69.01	66.03
8000	136.95	121.31	109.64	100.64	93.48	87.68	82.89	78.87	75.47
9000	154.06	136.47	123.35	113.21	105.17	98.64	93.25	88.73	84.90
10000	171.18	151.63	137.05	125.79	116.85	109.60	103.61	98.59	94.33
15000	256.77	227.44	205.58	188.69	175.27	164.39	155.41	147.88	141.50
20000	342.36	303.26	274.10	251.58	233.70	219.19	207.21	197.17	188.66
25000	427.95	379.07	342.63	314.47	292.12	273.98	259.01	246.46	235.83
30000	513.54	454.88	411.15	377.37	350.54	328.78	310.81	295.75	282.99
35000	599.12	530.70	479.68	440.26	408.97	383.57	362.61	345.05	330.15
36000	616.24	545.86	493.38	452.84	420.65	394.53	372.97	354.90	339.59
37000	633.36	561.02	507.09	465.42	432.34	405.49	383.33	364.76	349.02
38000	650.48	576.18	520.79	478.00	444.02	416.45	393.69	374.62	358.45
39000	667.59	591.35	534.50	490.58	455.70	427.41	404.05	384.48	367.89
40000	684.71	606.51	548.20	503.16	467.39	438.37	414.41	394.34	377.32
41000	701.83	621.67	561.91	515.73	479.07	449.33	424.77	404.20	386.75
42000	718.95	636.83	575.61	528.31	490.76	460.29	435.13	414.05	396.18
43000	736.07	652.00	589.32	540.89	502.44	471.25	445.49	423.91	405.62
44000	753.18	667.16	603.02	553.47	514.13	482.21	455.85	433.77	415.05
45000	770.30	682.32	616.73	566.05	525.81	493.17	466.21	443.63	424.48
46000	787.42	697.49	630.43	578.63	537.50	504.13	476.57	453.49	433.92
47000	804.54	712.65	644.14	591.21	549.18	515.08	486.93	463.35	443.35
48000	821.65	727.81	657.84	603.79	560.87	526.04	497.29	473.20	452.78
49000	838.77	742.97	671.55	616.36	572.55	537.00	507.65	483.06	462.21
50000	855.89	758.14	685.25	628.94	584.24	547.96	518.01	492.92	471.65
51000	873.01	773.30	698.96	641.52	595.92	558.92	528.37	502.78	481.08
52000	890.12	788.46	712.66	654.10	607.60	569.88	538.73	512.64	490.51
53000	907.24	803.62	726.37	666.68	619.29	580.84	549.09	522.50	499.94
54000	924.36	818.79	740.07	679.26	630.97	591.80	559.45	532.35	509.38
55000	941.48	833.95	753.78	691.84	642.66	602.76	569.81	542.21	518.81
56000	958.60	849.11	767.48	704.42	654.34	613.72	580.17	552.07	528.24
57000	975.71	864.27	781.19	716.99	666.03	624.68	590.53	561.93	537.68
58000	992.83	879.44	794.89	729.57	677.71	635.64	600.89	571.79	547.11
59000	1009.95	894.60	808.60	742.15	689.40	646.59	611.25	581.65	556.54
60000	1027.07	909.76	822.30	754.73	701.08	657.55	621.61	591.50	565.97
61000	1044.18	924.92	836.01	767.31	712.77	668.51	631.97	601.36	575.41
62000	1061.30	940.09	849.71	779.89	724.45	679.47	642.33	611.22	584.84
63000	1078.42	955.25	863.41	792.47	736.14	690.43	652.69	621.08	594.27
64000	1095.54	970.41	877.12	805.05	747.82	701.39	663.05	630.94	603.71
65000	1112.65	985.57	890.82	817.62	759.50	712.35	673.41	640.80	613.14
66000	1129.77	1000.74	904.53	830.20	771.19	723.31	683.77	650.65	622.57
67000	1146.89	1015.90	918.23	842.78	782.87	734.27	694.13	660.51	632.00
68000	1164.01	1031.06	931.94	855.36	794.56	745.23	704.49	670.37	641.44
69000	1181.13	1046.23	945.64	867.94	806.24	756.19	714.85	680.23	650.87
70000	1198.24	1061.39	959.35	880.52	817.93	767.14	725.21	690.09	660.30
75000	1283.83	1137.20	1027.87	943.41	876.35	821.94	777.01	739.38	707.47
80000	1369.42	1213.01	1096.40	1006.31	934.77	876.74	828.81	788.67	754.63
100000	1711.77	1516.27	1370.50	1257.88	1168.47	1095.92	1036.02	985.84	943.29

9

7¼%
MONTHLY PAYMENT
NECESSARY TO AMORTIZE A LOAN

TERM AMOUNT	15 YEARS	16 YEARS	17 YEARS	18 YEARS	19 YEARS	20 YEARS	21 YEARS	22 YEARS	23 YEARS
$ 25	.23	.22	.22	.21	.21	.20	.20	.19	.19
50	.46	.44	.43	.42	.41	.40	.39	.38	.37
75	.69	.66	.64	.62	.61	.59	.58	.57	.56
100	.91	.88	.85	.83	.81	.79	.77	.76	.74
200	1.82	1.76	1.70	1.65	1.61	1.57	1.54	1.51	1.48
300	2.73	2.63	2.55	2.48	2.41	2.36	2.31	2.26	2.22
400	3.63	3.51	3.40	3.30	3.22	3.14	3.07	3.01	2.96
500	4.54	4.38	4.24	4.12	4.02	3.92	3.84	3.77	3.70
600	5.45	5.26	5.09	4.95	4.82	4.71	4.61	4.52	4.44
700	6.35	6.13	5.94	5.77	5.62	5.49	5.38	5.27	5.18
800	7.26	7.01	6.79	6.60	6.43	6.28	6.14	6.02	5.92
900	8.17	7.88	7.64	7.42	7.23	7.06	6.91	6.78	6.65
1000	9.07	8.76	8.48	8.24	8.03	7.84	7.68	7.53	7.39
2000	18.14	17.51	16.96	16.48	16.06	15.68	15.35	15.05	14.78
3000	27.21	26.27	25.44	24.72	24.09	23.52	23.02	22.57	22.17
4000	36.28	35.02	33.92	32.96	32.11	31.36	30.69	30.09	29.56
5000	45.35	43.77	42.40	41.20	40.14	39.20	38.36	37.62	36.95
6000	54.42	52.53	50.88	49.44	48.17	47.04	46.04	45.14	44.34
7000	63.48	61.28	59.36	57.68	56.19	54.88	53.71	52.66	51.72
8000	72.55	70.03	67.84	65.91	64.22	62.72	61.38	60.18	59.11
9000	81.62	78.79	76.32	74.15	72.25	70.56	69.05	67.71	66.50
10000	90.69	87.54	84.80	82.39	80.27	78.39	76.72	75.23	73.89
15000	136.03	131.31	127.19	123.59	120.41	117.59	115.08	112.84	110.83
20000	181.37	175.07	169.59	164.78	160.54	156.78	153.44	150.45	147.77
25000	226.71	218.84	211.98	205.97	200.67	195.98	191.80	188.07	184.72
30000	272.06	262.61	254.38	247.17	240.81	235.17	230.16	225.68	221.66
35000	317.40	306.37	296.77	288.36	280.94	274.37	268.52	263.29	258.60
36000	326.47	315.13	305.25	296.60	288.97	282.21	276.19	270.81	265.99
37000	335.53	323.88	313.73	304.84	297.00	290.05	283.86	278.34	273.38
38000	344.60	332.63	322.21	313.08	305.02	297.89	291.53	285.86	280.77
39000	353.67	341.39	330.69	321.31	313.05	305.72	299.21	293.38	288.16
40000	362.74	350.14	339.17	329.55	321.08	313.56	306.88	300.90	295.54
41000	371.81	358.89	347.65	337.79	329.10	321.40	314.55	308.43	302.93
42000	380.88	367.65	356.13	346.03	337.13	329.24	322.22	315.95	310.32
43000	389.94	376.40	364.61	354.27	345.16	337.08	329.89	323.47	317.71
44000	399.01	385.15	373.08	362.51	353.18	344.92	337.57	330.99	325.10
45000	408.08	393.91	381.56	370.75	361.21	352.76	345.24	338.52	332.49
46000	417.15	402.66	390.04	378.98	369.24	360.60	352.91	346.04	339.88
47000	426.22	411.41	398.52	387.22	377.26	368.44	360.58	353.56	347.26
48000	435.29	420.17	407.00	395.46	385.29	376.28	368.25	361.08	354.65
49000	444.35	428.92	415.48	403.70	393.32	384.11	375.92	368.61	362.04
50000	453.42	437.67	423.96	411.94	401.34	391.95	383.60	376.13	369.43
51000	462.49	446.43	432.44	420.18	409.37	399.79	391.27	383.65	376.82
52000	471.56	455.18	440.92	428.42	417.40	407.63	398.94	391.17	384.21
53000	480.63	463.93	449.40	436.66	425.42	415.47	406.61	398.70	391.59
54000	489.70	472.69	457.88	444.89	433.45	423.31	414.28	406.22	398.98
55000	498.76	481.44	466.35	453.13	441.48	431.15	421.96	413.74	406.37
56000	507.83	490.19	474.83	461.37	449.50	438.99	429.63	421.26	413.76
57000	516.90	498.95	483.31	469.61	457.53	446.83	437.30	428.78	421.15
58000	525.97	507.70	491.79	477.85	465.56	454.67	444.97	436.31	428.54
59000	535.04	516.45	500.27	486.09	473.58	462.50	452.64	443.83	435.93
60000	544.11	525.21	508.75	494.33	481.61	470.34	460.31	451.35	443.31
61000	553.17	533.96	517.23	502.57	489.64	478.18	467.99	458.87	450.70
62000	562.24	542.71	525.71	510.80	497.66	486.02	475.66	466.40	458.09
63000	571.31	551.47	534.19	519.04	505.69	493.86	483.33	473.92	465.48
64000	580.38	560.22	542.67	527.28	513.72	501.70	491.00	481.44	472.87
65000	589.45	568.97	551.15	535.52	521.74	509.54	498.67	488.96	480.26
66000	598.52	577.73	559.62	543.76	529.77	517.38	506.35	496.49	487.65
67000	607.58	586.48	568.10	552.00	537.80	525.22	514.02	504.01	495.03
68000	616.65	595.23	576.58	560.24	545.82	533.06	521.69	511.53	502.42
69000	625.72	603.99	585.06	568.47	553.85	540.89	529.36	519.05	509.81
70000	634.79	612.74	593.54	576.71	561.88	548.73	537.03	526.58	517.20
75000	680.13	656.51	635.94	617.91	602.01	587.93	575.39	564.19	554.14
80000	725.47	700.27	678.33	659.10	642.15	627.12	613.75	601.80	591.08
100000	906.84	875.34	847.91	823.87	802.68	783.90	767.19	752.25	738.85

10

MONTHLY PAYMENT 7¼%
NECESSARY TO AMORTIZE A LOAN

TERM AMOUNT	24 YEARS	25 YEARS	26 YEARS	27 YEARS	28 YEARS	29 YEARS	30 YEARS	35 YEARS	40 YEARS
$ 25	.19	.18	.18	.18	.18	.18	.17	.17	.16
50	.37	.36	.36	.35	.35	.35	.34	.33	.32
75	.55	.54	.53	.53	.52	.52	.51	.49	.48
100	.73	.72	.71	.70	.69	.69	.68	.65	.64
200	1.46	1.44	1.42	1.40	1.38	1.37	1.35	1.30	1.27
300	2.19	2.15	2.12	2.10	2.07	2.05	2.03	1.95	1.90
400	2.91	2.87	2.83	2.79	2.76	2.73	2.70	2.60	2.53
500	3.64	3.58	3.54	3.49	3.45	3.41	3.38	3.25	3.16
600	4.37	4.30	4.24	4.19	4.14	4.09	4.05	3.90	3.80
700	5.09	5.02	4.95	4.89	4.83	4.78	4.73	4.55	4.43
800	5.82	5.73	5.65	5.58	5.52	5.46	5.40	5.20	5.06
900	6.55	6.45	6.36	6.28	6.21	6.14	6.08	5.85	5.69
1000	7.27	7.16	7.07	6.98	6.90	6.82	6.75	6.49	6.32
2000	14.54	14.32	14.13	13.95	13.70	13.04	13.50	12.98	12.64
3000	21.81	21.48	21.19	20.92	20.68	20.45	20.25	19.47	18.96
4000	29.08	28.64	28.25	27.89	27.57	27.27	27.00	25.96	25.28
5000	36.34	35.80	35.31	34.86	34.46	34.09	33.75	32.45	31.60
6000	43.61	42.96	42.37	41.83	41.35	40.90	40.50	38.94	37.92
7000	50.88	50.12	49.43	48.81	48.24	47.72	47.25	45.43	44.23
8000	58.15	57.28	56.49	55.78	55.13	54.54	54.00	51.92	50.55
9000	65.42	64.44	63.55	62.75	62.02	61.35	60.75	58.41	56.87
10000	72.68	71.60	70.61	69.72	68.91	68.17	67.50	64.89	63.19
15000	109.02	107.39	105.92	104.58	103.36	102.25	101.24	97.34	94.78
20000	145.36	143.19	141.22	139.44	137.81	136.34	134.99	129.78	126.37
25000	181.70	178.98	176.52	174.29	172.27	170.42	168.74	162.23	157.96
30000	218.04	214.78	211.83	209.15	206.72	204.50	202.48	194.67	189.56
35000	254.38	250.58	247.13	244.01	241.17	238.59	236.23	227.12	221.15
36000	261.65	257.74	254.19	250.98	248.06	245.40	242.98	233.61	227.47
37000	268.92	264.89	261.25	257.95	254.95	252.22	249.73	240.10	233.78
38000	276.19	272.05	268.31	264.92	261.84	259.04	256.48	246.59	240.10
39000	283.46	279.21	275.38	271.90	268.73	265.85	263.23	253.08	246.42
40000	290.72	286.37	282.44	278.87	275.62	272.67	269.97	259.56	252.74
41000	297.99	293.53	289.50	285.84	282.51	279.49	276.72	266.05	259.06
42000	305.26	300.69	296.56	292.81	289.40	286.30	283.47	272.54	265.38
43000	312.53	307.85	303.62	299.78	296.29	293.12	290.22	279.03	271.69
44000	319.79	315.01	310.68	306.75	303.18	299.94	296.97	285.52	278.01
45000	327.06	322.17	317.74	313.72	310.08	306.75	303.72	292.01	284.33
46000	334.33	329.33	324.80	320.70	316.97	313.57	310.47	298.50	290.65
47000	341.60	336.49	331.86	327.67	323.86	320.39	317.22	304.99	296.97
48000	348.87	343.65	338.92	334.64	330.75	327.20	323.97	311.48	303.29
49000	356.13	350.81	345.98	341.61	337.64	334.02	330.72	317.97	309.60
50000	363.40	357.96	353.04	348.58	344.53	340.84	337.47	324.45	315.92
51000	370.67	365.12	360.10	355.55	351.42	347.65	344.22	330.94	322.24
52000	377.94	372.28	367.17	362.53	358.31	354.47	350.97	337.43	328.56
53000	385.21	379.44	374.23	369.50	365.20	361.29	357.71	343.92	334.88
54000	392.47	386.60	381.29	376.47	372.09	368.10	364.46	350.41	341.20
55000	399.74	393.76	388.35	383.44	378.98	374.92	371.21	356.90	347.51
56000	407.01	400.92	395.41	390.41	385.87	381.73	377.96	363.39	353.83
57000	414.28	408.08	402.47	397.38	392.76	388.55	384.71	369.88	360.15
58000	421.55	415.24	409.53	404.35	399.65	395.37	391.46	376.37	366.47
59000	428.81	422.40	416.59	411.33	406.54	402.18	398.21	382.86	372.79
60000	436.08	429.56	423.65	418.30	413.43	409.00	404.96	389.34	379.11
61000	443.35	436.72	430.71	425.27	420.32	415.82	411.71	395.83	385.42
62000	450.62	443.87	437.77	432.24	427.21	422.63	418.46	402.32	391.74
63000	457.89	451.03	444.83	439.21	434.10	429.45	425.21	408.81	398.06
64000	465.15	458.19	451.90	446.18	440.99	436.27	431.96	415.30	404.38
65000	472.42	465.35	458.96	453.16	447.88	443.08	438.71	421.79	410.70
66000	479.69	472.51	466.02	460.13	454.77	449.90	445.46	428.28	417.02
67000	486.96	479.67	473.08	467.10	461.67	456.72	452.20	434.77	423.33
68000	494.23	486.83	480.14	474.07	468.56	463.53	458.95	441.26	429.65
69000	501.49	493.99	487.20	481.04	475.45	470.35	465.70	447.75	435.97
70000	508.76	501.15	494.26	488.01	482.34	477.17	472.45	454.23	442.29
75000	545.10	536.94	529.56	522.87	516.79	511.25	506.20	486.68	473.88
80000	581.44	572.74	564.87	557.73	551.24	545.33	539.94	519.12	505.47
100000	726.80	715.92	706.08	697.16	689.05	681.67	674.93	648.90	631.84

7½% MONTHLY PAYMENT
NECESSARY TO AMORTIZE A LOAN

TERM AMOUNT	1 YEAR	1½ YEARS	2 YEARS	2½ YEARS	3 YEARS	3½ YEARS	4 YEARS	4½ YEARS	5 YEARS
$ 25	2.17	1.48	1.13	.92	.78	.68	.61	.55	.50
50	4.34	2.95	2.25	1.84	1.56	1.36	1.21	1.10	1.00
75	6.51	4.42	3.38	2.75	2.33	2.04	1.81	1.64	1.50
100	8.68	5.89	4.50	3.67	3.11	2.71	2.42	2.19	2.00
200	17.35	11.78	8.99	7.33	6.22	5.42	4.83	4.37	4.00
300	26.02	17.66	13.49	10.99	9.32	8.13	7.24	6.55	6.00
400	34.69	23.55	17.98	14.65	12.43	10.84	9.66	8.73	8.00
500	43.36	29.44	22.48	18.31	15.53	13.55	12.07	10.92	10.00
600	52.03	35.32	26.97	21.97	18.64	16.26	14.48	13.10	12.00
700	60.70	41.21	31.47	25.63	21.74	18.97	16.89	15.28	13.99
800	69.37	47.09	35.96	29.29	24.85	21.68	19.31	17.46	15.99
900	78.04	52.98	40.46	32.95	27.95	24.39	21.72	19.65	17.99
1000	86.71	58.87	44.95	36.61	31.06	27.10	24.13	21.83	19.99
2000	173.41	117.73	89.90	73.22	62.11	54.19	48.26	43.65	39.97
3000	260.12	176.59	134.85	109.83	93.17	81.28	72.38	65.47	59.96
4000	346.82	235.45	179.80	146.43	124.22	108.37	96.51	87.29	79.94
5000	433.53	294.31	224.74	183.04	155.27	135.47	120.63	109.12	99.92
6000	520.23	353.17	269.69	219.65	186.33	162.56	144.76	130.94	119.91
7000	606.94	412.03	314.64	256.26	217.38	189.65	168.88	152.76	139.89
8000	693.64	470.89	359.59	292.86	248.43	216.74	193.01	174.58	159.87
9000	780.35	529.75	404.53	329.47	279.49	243.83	217.13	196.41	179.86
10000	867.05	588.61	449.48	366.08	310.54	270.93	241.26	218.23	199.84
15000	1300.57	882.91	674.22	549.12	465.81	406.39	361.89	327.34	299.76
20000	1734.10	1177.21	898.96	732.15	621.08	541.85	482.51	436.45	399.68
25000	2167.62	1471.51	1123.69	915.19	776.35	677.31	603.14	545.56	499.59
30000	2601.14	1765.81	1348.43	1098.23	931.61	812.77	723.77	654.67	599.51
35000	3034.66	2060.11	1573.17	1281.26	1086.88	948.23	844.40	763.79	699.43
36000	3121.37	2118.97	1618.12	1317.87	1117.94	975.32	868.52	785.61	719.41
37000	3208.07	2177.83	1663.06	1354.48	1148.99	1002.41	892.65	807.43	739.40
38000	3294.78	2236.69	1708.01	1391.09	1180.04	1029.50	916.77	829.25	759.38
39000	3381.48	2295.55	1752.96	1427.69	1211.10	1056.59	940.90	851.08	779.36
40000	3468.19	2354.41	1797.91	1464.30	1242.15	1083.69	965.02	872.90	799.35
41000	3554.89	2413.27	1842.85	1500.91	1273.20	1110.78	989.15	894.72	819.33
42000	3641.60	2472.13	1887.80	1537.52	1304.26	1137.87	1013.27	916.54	839.31
43000	3728.30	2531.00	1932.75	1574.12	1335.31	1164.96	1037.40	938.37	859.30
44000	3815.00	2589.86	1977.70	1610.73	1366.36	1192.05	1061.53	960.19	879.28
45000	3901.71	2648.72	2022.64	1647.34	1397.42	1219.15	1085.65	982.01	899.26
46000	3988.41	2707.58	2067.59	1683.95	1428.47	1246.24	1109.78	1003.83	919.25
47000	4075.12	2766.44	2112.54	1720.55	1459.53	1273.33	1133.90	1025.65	939.23
48000	4161.82	2825.30	2157.49	1757.16	1490.58	1300.42	1158.03	1047.48	959.22
49000	4248.53	2884.16	2202.43	1793.77	1521.63	1327.51	1182.15	1069.30	979.20
50000	4335.23	2943.02	2247.38	1830.38	1552.69	1354.61	1206.28	1091.12	999.18
51000	4421.94	3001.88	2292.33	1866.98	1583.74	1381.70	1230.40	1112.94	1019.17
52000	4508.64	3060.74	2337.28	1903.59	1614.79	1408.79	1254.53	1134.77	1039.15
53000	4595.35	3119.60	2382.22	1940.20	1645.85	1435.88	1278.65	1156.59	1059.13
54000	4682.05	3178.46	2427.17	1976.81	1676.90	1462.97	1302.78	1178.41	1079.12
55000	4768.75	3237.32	2472.12	2013.41	1707.95	1490.07	1326.91	1200.23	1099.10
56000	4855.46	3296.18	2517.07	2050.02	1739.01	1517.16	1351.03	1222.06	1119.08
57000	4942.16	3355.04	2562.01	2086.63	1770.06	1544.25	1375.16	1243.88	1139.07
58000	5028.87	3413.90	2606.96	2123.24	1801.12	1571.34	1399.28	1265.70	1159.05
59000	5115.57	3472.76	2651.91	2159.84	1832.17	1598.43	1423.41	1287.52	1179.03
60000	5202.28	3531.62	2696.86	2196.45	1863.22	1625.53	1447.53	1309.34	1199.02
61000	5288.98	3590.48	2741.80	2233.06	1894.28	1652.62	1471.66	1331.17	1219.00
62000	5375.69	3649.34	2786.75	2269.66	1925.33	1679.71	1495.78	1352.99	1238.99
63000	5462.39	3708.20	2831.70	2306.27	1956.38	1706.80	1519.91	1374.81	1258.97
64000	5549.09	3767.06	2876.65	2342.88	1987.44	1733.89	1544.04	1396.63	1278.95
65000	5635.80	3825.92	2921.59	2379.49	2018.49	1760.99	1568.16	1418.46	1298.94
66000	5722.50	3884.78	2966.54	2416.09	2049.54	1788.08	1592.29	1440.28	1318.92
67000	5809.21	3943.64	3011.49	2452.70	2080.60	1815.17	1616.41	1462.10	1338.90
68000	5895.91	4002.50	3056.44	2489.31	2111.65	1842.26	1640.54	1483.92	1358.89
69000	5982.62	4061.36	3101.38	2525.92	2142.71	1869.35	1664.66	1505.75	1378.87
70000	6069.32	4120.22	3146.33	2562.52	2173.76	1896.45	1688.79	1527.57	1398.85
75000	6502.84	4414.52	3371.07	2745.56	2329.03	2031.91	1809.42	1636.68	1498.77
80000	6936.37	4708.82	3595.81	2928.60	2484.30	2167.37	1930.04	1745.79	1598.69
100000	8670.46	5886.03	4494.76	3660.75	3105.37	2709.21	2412.55	2182.24	1998.36

12

MONTHLY PAYMENT 7½%
NECESSARY TO AMORTIZE A LOAN

TERM AMOUNT	6 YEARS	7 YEARS	8 YEARS	9 YEARS	10 YEARS	11 YEARS	12 YEARS	13 YEARS	14 YEARS
$ 25	.44	.39	.35	.32	.30	.28	.27	.25	.24
50	.87	.77	.70	.64	.60	.56	.53	.50	.48
75	1.30	1.15	1.04	.96	.89	.84	.79	.75	.72
100	1.73	1.53	1.39	1.28	1.19	1.11	1.05	1.00	.96
200	3.45	3.06	2.77	2.55	2.37	2.22	2.10	2.00	1.92
300	5.18	4.59	4.15	3.82	3.55	3.33	3.15	3.00	2.88
400	6.90	6.12	5.54	5.09	4.73	4.44	4.20	4.00	3.83
500	8.62	7.65	6.92	6.36	5.91	5.55	5.25	5.00	4.79
600	10.35	9.17	8.30	7.63	7.09	6.66	6.30	6.00	5.75
700	12.07	10.70	9.68	8.90	8.27	7.77	7.35	7.00	6.70
800	13.79	12.23	11.07	10.17	9.45	8.87	8.40	8.00	7.66
900	15.52	13.76	12.45	11.44	10.63	9.98	9.45	9.00	8.62
1000	17.24	15.29	13.83	12.71	11.82	11.09	10.50	10.00	9.57
2000	34.47	30.57	27.66	25.41	23.63	22.18	20.99	19.99	19.14
3000	51.71	45.85	41.48	38.11	35.44	33.27	31.48	29.98	28.71
4000	68.94	61.13	55.31	50.81	47.25	44.35	41.97	39.97	38.27
5000	86.18	76.41	69.14	63.52	59.06	55.44	52.46	49.96	47.84
6000	103.41	91.70	82.96	76.22	70.87	66.53	62.95	59.95	57.41
7000	120.65	106.98	96.79	88.92	82.68	77.62	73.44	69.94	66.98
8000	137.88	122.26	110.62	101.62	94.49	88.70	83.93	79.93	76.54
9000	155.12	137.54	124.44	114.33	106.30	99.79	94.42	89.92	86.11
10000	172.35	152.82	138.27	127.03	118.11	110.88	104.91	99.91	95.68
15000	258.53	229.23	207.40	190.54	177.16	166.31	157.36	149.87	143.52
20000	344.70	305.64	276.53	254.05	236.21	221.75	209.81	199.82	191.35
25000	430.87	382.05	345.66	317.56	295.27	277.19	262.27	249.77	239.19
30000	517.05	458.46	414.79	381.08	354.32	332.62	314.72	299.73	287.03
35000	603.22	534.87	483.93	444.59	413.37	388.06	367.17	349.68	334.87
36000	620.45	550.15	497.75	457.29	425.18	399.14	377.66	359.67	344.43
37000	637.69	565.43	511.58	469.99	436.99	410.23	388.15	369.66	354.00
38000	654.92	580.71	525.40	482.70	448.80	421.32	398.64	379.66	363.57
39000	672.16	595.99	539.23	495.40	460.61	432.41	409.13	389.65	373.14
40000	689.39	611.28	553.06	508.10	472.42	443.49	419.62	399.64	382.70
41000	706.63	626.56	566.88	520.80	484.23	454.58	430.11	409.63	392.27
42000	723.86	641.84	580.71	533.51	496.04	465.67	440.60	419.62	401.84
43000	741.10	657.12	594.54	546.21	507.86	476.76	451.09	429.61	411.41
44000	758.33	672.40	608.36	558.91	519.67	487.84	461.58	439.60	420.97
45000	775.57	687.69	622.19	571.61	531.48	498.93	472.07	449.59	430.54
46000	792.80	702.97	636.02	584.31	543.29	510.02	482.56	459.58	440.11
47000	810.04	718.25	649.84	597.02	555.10	521.10	493.05	469.57	449.68
48000	827.27	733.53	663.67	609.72	566.91	532.19	503.54	479.56	459.24
49000	844.50	748.81	677.49	622.42	578.72	543.28	514.04	489.55	468.81
50000	861.74	764.09	691.32	635.12	590.53	554.37	524.53	499.54	478.38
51000	878.97	779.38	705.15	647.83	602.34	565.45	535.02	509.54	487.95
52000	896.21	794.66	718.97	660.53	614.15	576.54	545.51	519.53	497.51
53000	913.44	809.94	732.80	673.23	625.96	587.63	556.00	529.52	507.08
54000	930.68	825.22	746.63	685.93	637.77	598.71	566.49	539.51	516.65
55000	947.91	840.50	760.45	698.64	649.58	609.80	576.98	549.50	526.22
56000	965.15	855.79	774.28	711.34	661.39	620.89	587.47	559.49	535.78
57000	982.38	871.07	788.10	724.04	673.20	631.98	597.96	569.48	545.35
58000	999.62	886.35	801.93	736.74	685.01	643.06	608.45	579.47	554.92
59000	1016.85	901.63	815.76	749.45	696.82	654.15	618.94	589.46	564.49
60000	1034.09	916.91	829.58	762.15	708.63	665.24	629.43	599.45	574.05
61000	1051.32	932.19	843.41	774.85	720.44	676.33	639.92	609.44	583.62
62000	1068.56	947.48	857.24	787.55	732.25	687.41	650.41	619.43	593.19
63000	1085.79	962.76	871.06	800.26	744.06	698.50	660.90	629.43	602.76
64000	1103.02	978.04	884.89	812.96	755.87	709.59	671.39	639.42	612.32
65000	1120.26	993.32	898.72	825.66	767.69	720.67	681.88	649.41	621.89
66000	1137.49	1008.60	912.54	838.36	779.50	731.76	692.37	659.40	631.46
67000	1154.73	1023.89	926.37	851.06	791.31	742.85	702.86	669.39	641.03
68000	1171.96	1039.17	940.19	863.77	803.12	753.94	713.35	679.38	650.59
69000	1189.20	1054.45	954.02	876.47	814.93	765.02	723.84	689.37	660.16
70000	1206.43	1069.73	967.85	889.17	826.74	776.11	734.33	699.36	669.73
75000	1292.61	1146.14	1036.98	952.68	885.79	831.55	786.79	749.31	717.57
80000	1378.78	1222.55	1106.11	1016.20	944.84	886.98	839.24	799.27	765.40
100000	1723.47	1528.18	1382.64	1270.24	1181.05	1108.73	1049.05	999.08	956.75

7½%
MONTHLY PAYMENT
NECESSARY TO AMORTIZE A LOAN

TERM AMOUNT	15 YEARS	16 YEARS	17 YEARS	18 YEARS	19 YEARS	20 YEARS	21 YEARS	22 YEARS	23 YEARS
$ 25	.24	.23	.22	.21	.21	.20	.20	.20	.19
50	.47	.45	.44	.42	.41	.40	.40	.39	.38
75	.70	.67	.65	.63	.62	.60	.59	.58	.57
100	.93	.89	.87	.84	.82	.80	.79	.77	.76
200	1.85	1.78	1.73	1.68	1.64	1.60	1.57	1.54	1.51
300	2.77	2.67	2.59	2.52	2.46	2.40	2.35	2.31	2.27
400	3.69	3.56	3.45	3.36	3.27	3.20	3.13	3.07	3.02
500	4.61	4.45	4.32	4.20	4.09	4.00	3.92	3.84	3.78
600	5.53	5.34	5.18	5.03	4.91	4.80	4.70	4.61	4.53
700	6.45	6.23	6.04	5.87	5.73	5.60	5.48	5.38	5.28
800	7.37	7.12	6.90	6.71	6.54	6.39	6.26	6.14	6.04
900	8.29	8.01	7.76	7.55	7.36	7.19	7.04	6.91	6.79
1000	9.21	8.90	8.63	8.39	8.18	7.99	7.83	7.68	7.55
2000	18.42	17.79	17.25	16.77	16.35	15.98	15.65	15.35	15.09
3000	27.62	26.68	25.87	25.15	24.52	23.96	23.47	23.03	22.63
4000	36.83	35.57	34.49	33.53	32.69	31.95	31.29	30.70	30.17
5000	46.03	44.47	43.11	41.91	40.86	39.94	39.11	38.37	37.71
6000	55.24	53.36	51.73	50.30	49.04	47.92	46.93	46.05	45.25
7000	64.44	62.25	60.35	58.68	57.21	55.91	54.75	53.72	52.79
8000	73.65	71.14	68.97	67.06	65.38	63.89	62.57	61.39	60.33
9000	82.85	80.04	77.59	75.44	73.55	71.88	70.39	69.07	67.88
10000	92.06	88.93	86.21	83.82	81.72	79.87	78.21	76.74	75.42
15000	138.08	133.39	129.31	125.73	122.58	119.80	117.32	115.11	113.12
20000	184.11	177.85	172.41	167.64	163.44	159.73	156.42	153.47	150.83
25000	230.13	222.31	215.51	209.55	204.30	199.66	195.53	191.84	188.54
30000	276.16	266.77	258.61	251.46	245.16	239.59	234.63	230.21	226.24
35000	322.18	311.23	301.71	293.37	286.02	279.52	273.73	268.57	263.95
36000	331.39	320.13	310.33	301.75	294.19	287.50	281.55	276.25	271.49
37000	340.60	329.02	318.95	310.13	302.36	295.49	289.38	283.92	279.03
38000	349.80	337.91	327.57	318.51	310.53	303.47	297.20	291.59	286.57
39000	359.01	346.80	336.19	326.89	318.71	311.46	305.02	299.27	294.11
40000	368.21	355.70	344.81	335.27	326.88	319.45	312.84	306.94	301.65
41000	377.42	364.59	353.43	343.66	335.05	327.43	320.66	314.61	309.20
42000	386.62	373.48	362.05	352.04	343.22	335.42	328.48	322.29	316.74
43000	395.83	382.37	370.67	360.42	351.39	343.40	336.30	329.96	324.28
44000	405.03	391.26	379.29	368.80	359.57	351.39	344.12	337.63	331.82
45000	414.24	400.16	387.91	377.18	367.74	359.38	351.94	345.31	339.36
46000	423.44	409.05	396.53	385.57	375.91	367.36	359.76	352.98	346.90
47000	432.65	417.94	405.15	393.95	384.08	375.35	367.58	360.65	354.44
48000	441.85	426.83	413.77	402.33	392.25	383.33	375.40	368.33	361.98
49000	451.06	435.73	422.39	410.71	400.42	391.32	383.22	376.00	369.53
50000	460.26	444.62	431.01	419.09	408.60	399.31	391.05	383.67	377.07
51000	469.47	453.51	439.63	427.47	416.77	407.29	398.87	391.35	384.61
52000	478.67	462.40	448.25	435.86	424.94	415.28	406.69	399.02	392.15
53000	487.88	471.30	456.87	444.24	433.11	423.26	414.51	406.69	399.69
54000	497.08	480.19	465.49	452.62	441.28	431.25	422.33	414.37	407.23
55000	506.29	489.08	474.11	461.00	449.46	439.24	430.15	422.04	414.77
56000	515.49	497.97	482.73	469.38	457.63	447.22	437.97	429.71	422.31
57000	524.70	506.86	491.35	477.76	465.80	455.21	445.79	437.39	429.86
58000	533.90	515.76	499.97	486.15	473.97	463.19	453.61	445.06	437.40
59000	543.11	524.65	508.59	494.53	482.14	471.18	461.43	452.73	444.94
60000	552.31	533.54	517.21	502.91	490.31	479.17	469.25	460.41	452.48
61000	561.52	542.43	525.83	511.29	498.49	487.15	477.07	468.08	460.02
62000	570.72	551.33	534.45	519.67	506.66	495.14	484.90	475.75	467.56
63000	579.93	560.22	543.07	528.05	514.83	503.12	492.72	483.43	475.10
64000	589.13	569.11	551.69	536.44	523.00	511.11	500.54	491.10	482.64
65000	598.34	578.00	560.31	544.82	531.17	519.10	508.36	498.77	490.19
66000	607.54	586.89	568.93	553.20	539.35	527.08	516.18	506.45	497.73
67000	616.75	595.79	577.55	561.58	547.52	535.07	524.00	514.12	505.27
68000	625.95	604.68	586.17	569.96	555.69	543.05	531.82	521.79	512.81
69000	635.16	613.57	594.79	578.35	563.86	551.04	539.64	529.47	520.35
70000	644.36	622.46	603.41	586.73	572.03	559.03	547.46	537.14	527.89
75000	690.39	666.93	646.51	628.64	612.89	598.96	586.57	575.51	565.60
80000	736.42	711.39	689.61	670.54	653.75	638.89	625.67	613.87	603.30
100000	920.52	889.23	862.01	838.18	817.19	798.61	782.09	767.34	754.13

14

MONTHLY PAYMENT 7½%
NECESSARY TO AMORTIZE A LOAN

TERM AMOUNT	24 YEARS	25 YEARS	26 YEARS	27 YEARS	28 YEARS	29 YEARS	30 YEARS	35 YEARS	40 YEARS
$ 25	.19	.19	.19	.18	.18	.18	.18	.17	.17
50	.38	.37	.37	.36	.36	.35	.35	.34	.33
75	.56	.55	.55	.54	.53	.53	.52	.50	.49
100	.75	.74	.73	.72	.71	.70	.70	.67	.65
200	1.49	1.47	1.45	1.43	1.42	1.40	1.39	1.34	1.30
300	2.23	2.20	2.17	2.14	2.12	2.10	2.08	2.00	1.95
400	2.97	2.93	2.89	2.86	2.83	2.80	2.77	2.67	2.60
500	3.72	3.66	3.61	3.57	3.53	3.49	3.46	3.34	3.25
600	4.46	4.39	4.34	4.28	4.24	4.19	4.15	4.00	3.90
700	5.20	5.13	5.06	5.00	4.94	4.89	4.84	4.67	4.55
800	5.94	5.86	5.78	5.71	5.65	5.59	5.54	5.33	5.20
900	6.69	6.59	6.50	6.42	6.35	6.29	6.23	6.00	5.85
1000	7.43	7.32	7.22	7.14	7.06	6.98	6.92	6.67	6.50
2000	14.85	14.64	14.44	14.27	14.11	13.96	13.83	13.33	13.00
3000	22.27	21.95	21.66	21.40	21.16	20.94	20.75	19.99	19.49
4000	29.70	29.27	28.88	28.53	28.21	27.92	27.66	26.65	25.99
5000	37.12	36.58	36.10	35.66	35.26	34.90	34.57	33.31	32.49
6000	44.54	43.90	43.32	42.79	42.32	41.88	41.49	39.97	38.98
7000	51.96	51.21	50.54	49.92	49.37	48.86	48.40	46.63	45.48
8000	59.39	58.53	57.76	57.06	56.42	55.84	55.32	53.29	51.97
9000	66.81	65.84	64.97	64.19	63.47	62.82	62.23	59.95	58.47
10000	74.23	73.16	72.19	71.32	70.52	69.80	69.14	66.61	64.97
15000	111.34	109.74	108.29	106.98	105.78	104.70	103.71	99.92	97.45
20000	148.46	146.32	144.38	142.63	141.04	139.60	138.28	133.22	129.93
25000	185.57	182.89	180.48	178.29	176.30	174.50	172.85	166.52	162.41
30000	222.68	219.47	216.57	213.95	211.56	209.39	207.42	199.83	194.89
35000	259.79	256.05	252.67	249.60	246.82	244.29	241.99	233.13	227.37
36000	267.22	263.36	259.88	256.73	253.87	251.27	248.90	239.79	233.87
37000	274.64	270.68	267.10	263.86	260.93	258.25	255.82	246.45	240.36
38000	282.06	278.00	274.32	271.00	267.98	265.23	262.73	253.11	246.86
39000	289.48	285.31	281.54	278.13	275.03	272.21	269.65	259.77	253.36
40000	296.91	292.63	288.76	285.26	282.08	279.19	276.56	266.44	259.85
41000	304.33	299.94	295.98	292.39	289.13	286.17	283.47	273.10	266.35
42000	311.75	307.26	303.20	299.52	296.18	293.15	290.39	279.76	272.85
43000	319.17	314.57	310.42	306.65	303.24	300.13	297.30	286.42	279.34
44000	326.60	321.89	317.64	313.78	310.29	307.11	304.21	293.08	285.84
45000	334.02	329.20	324.85	320.92	317.34	314.09	311.13	299.74	292.33
46000	341.44	336.52	332.07	328.05	324.39	321.07	318.04	306.40	298.83
47000	348.86	343.84	339.29	335.18	331.44	328.05	324.96	313.06	305.33
48000	356.29	351.15	346.51	342.31	338.50	335.03	331.87	319.72	311.82
49000	363.71	358.47	353.73	349.44	345.55	342.01	338.78	326.38	318.32
50000	371.13	365.78	360.95	356.57	352.60	348.99	345.70	333.04	324.81
51000	378.55	373.10	368.17	363.70	359.65	355.97	352.61	339.70	331.31
52000	385.98	380.41	375.39	370.83	366.70	362.95	359.53	346.36	337.81
53000	393.40	387.73	382.61	377.97	373.76	369.93	366.44	353.03	344.30
54000	400.82	395.04	389.82	385.10	380.81	376.91	373.35	359.69	350.80
55000	408.24	402.36	397.04	392.23	387.86	383.89	380.27	366.35	357.30
56000	415.67	409.68	404.26	399.36	394.91	390.87	387.18	373.01	363.79
57000	423.09	416.99	411.48	406.49	401.96	397.85	394.10	379.67	370.29
58000	430.51	424.31	418.70	413.62	409.01	404.83	401.01	386.33	376.78
59000	437.93	431.62	425.92	420.75	416.07	411.80	407.92	392.99	383.28
60000	445.36	438.94	433.14	427.89	423.12	418.78	414.84	399.65	389.78
61000	452.78	446.25	440.36	435.02	430.17	425.76	421.75	406.31	396.27
62000	460.20	453.57	447.58	442.15	437.22	432.74	428.66	412.97	402.77
63000	467.62	460.88	454.79	449.28	444.27	439.72	435.58	419.63	409.27
64000	475.05	468.20	462.01	456.41	451.33	446.70	442.49	426.29	415.76
65000	482.47	475.52	469.23	463.54	458.38	453.68	449.41	432.95	422.26
66000	489.89	482.83	476.45	470.67	465.43	460.66	456.32	439.62	428.75
67000	497.31	490.15	483.67	477.80	472.48	467.64	463.23	446.28	435.25
68000	504.74	497.46	490.89	484.94	479.53	474.62	470.15	452.94	441.75
69000	512.16	504.78	498.11	492.07	486.59	481.60	477.06	459.60	448.24
70000	519.58	512.09	505.33	499.20	493.64	488.58	483.98	466.26	454.74
75000	556.70	548.67	541.42	534.86	528.90	523.48	518.54	499.56	487.22
80000	593.81	585.25	577.52	570.51	564.16	558.38	553.11	532.87	519.70
100000	742.26	731.56	721.89	713.14	705.19	697.97	691.39	666.08	649.62

7¾% MONTHLY PAYMENT
NECESSARY TO AMORTIZE A LOAN

TERM AMOUNT	1 YEAR	1½ YEARS	2 YEARS	2½ YEARS	3 YEARS	3½ YEARS	4 YEARS	4½ YEARS	5 YEARS
$ 25	2.18	1.48	1.13	.92	.78	.69	.61	.55	.51
50	4.35	2.95	2.26	1.84	1.56	1.37	1.22	1.10	1.01
75	6.52	4.43	3.38	2.76	2.34	2.05	1.82	1.65	1.51
100	8.69	5.90	4.51	3.68	3.12	2.73	2.43	2.20	2.01
200	17.37	11.80	9.02	7.35	6.24	5.45	4.85	4.39	4.02
300	26.05	17.70	13.52	11.02	9.35	8.17	7.28	6.59	6.03
400	34.73	23.59	18.03	14.69	12.47	10.89	9.70	8.78	8.04
500	43.41	29.49	22.53	18.36	15.59	13.61	12.12	10.97	10.05
600	52.09	35.39	27.04	22.04	18.70	16.33	14.55	13.17	12.06
700	60.78	41.28	31.55	25.71	21.82	19.05	16.97	15.36	14.07
800	69.46	47.18	36.05	29.38	24.94	21.77	19.40	17.55	16.08
900	78.14	53.08	40.56	33.05	28.05	24.49	21.82	19.75	18.09
1000	86.82	58.98	45.06	36.72	31.17	27.21	24.24	21.94	20.10
2000	173.64	117.95	90.12	73.44	62.33	54.41	48.48	43.88	40.20
3000	260.45	176.92	135.18	110.16	93.50	81.62	72.72	65.81	60.30
4000	347.27	235.89	180.24	146.88	124.66	108.82	96.96	87.75	80.40
5000	434.09	294.86	225.29	183.60	155.83	136.03	121.20	109.69	100.50
6000	520.90	353.83	270.35	220.31	186.99	163.23	145.44	131.62	120.60
7000	607.72	412.80	315.41	257.03	218.16	190.43	169.67	153.56	140.70
8000	694.54	471.77	360.47	293.75	249.32	217.64	193.91	175.50	160.79
9000	781.35	530.74	405.52	330.47	280.49	244.84	218.15	197.43	180.89
10000	868.17	589.71	450.58	367.19	311.65	272.05	242.39	219.37	200.99
15000	1302.25	884.56	675.87	550.78	467.48	408.07	363.58	329.05	301.49
20000	1736.33	1179.42	901.16	734.37	623.30	544.09	484.78	438.73	401.98
25000	2170.42	1474.27	1126.45	917.96	779.13	680.11	605.97	548.42	502.47
30000	2604.50	1769.12	1351.74	1101.55	934.95	816.13	727.16	658.10	602.97
35000	3038.58	2063.97	1577.02	1285.14	1090.78	952.15	848.35	767.78	703.46
36000	3125.40	2122.95	1622.08	1321.85	1121.94	979.35	872.59	789.72	723.56
37000	3212.21	2181.92	1667.14	1358.57	1153.11	1006.56	896.83	811.65	743.66
38000	3299.03	2240.89	1712.20	1395.29	1184.27	1033.76	921.07	833.59	763.76
39000	3385.84	2299.86	1757.26	1432.01	1215.44	1060.97	945.31	855.53	783.85
40000	3472.66	2358.83	1802.31	1468.73	1246.60	1088.17	969.55	877.46	803.95
41000	3559.48	2417.80	1847.37	1505.44	1277.77	1115.38	993.79	899.40	824.05
42000	3646.29	2476.77	1892.43	1542.16	1308.93	1142.58	1018.02	921.34	844.15
43000	3733.11	2535.74	1937.49	1578.88	1340.10	1169.78	1042.26	943.27	864.25
44000	3819.93	2594.71	1982.54	1615.60	1371.26	1196.99	1066.50	965.21	884.35
45000	3906.74	2653.68	2027.60	1652.32	1402.43	1224.19	1090.74	987.14	904.45
46000	3993.56	2712.65	2072.66	1689.03	1433.59	1251.40	1114.98	1009.08	924.55
47000	4080.38	2771.62	2117.72	1725.75	1464.76	1278.60	1139.22	1031.01	944.64
48000	4167.19	2830.59	2162.77	1762.47	1495.92	1305.80	1163.46	1052.95	964.74
49000	4254.01	2889.56	2207.83	1799.19	1527.09	1333.01	1187.69	1074.89	984.84
50000	4340.83	2948.53	2252.89	1835.91	1558.25	1360.21	1211.93	1096.83	1004.94
51000	4427.64	3007.50	2297.95	1872.62	1589.42	1387.42	1236.17	1118.76	1025.04
52000	4514.46	3066.47	2343.01	1909.34	1620.58	1414.62	1260.41	1140.70	1045.14
53000	4601.27	3125.45	2388.06	1946.06	1651.75	1441.82	1284.65	1162.64	1065.23
54000	4688.09	3184.42	2433.12	1982.78	1682.91	1469.03	1308.89	1184.57	1085.33
55000	4774.91	3243.39	2478.18	2019.50	1714.08	1496.23	1333.13	1206.51	1105.43
56000	4861.72	3302.36	2523.24	2056.21	1745.24	1523.44	1357.36	1228.45	1125.53
57000	4948.54	3361.33	2568.29	2092.93	1776.41	1550.64	1381.60	1250.38	1145.63
58000	5035.36	3420.30	2613.35	2129.65	1807.57	1577.85	1405.84	1272.32	1165.73
59000	5122.17	3479.27	2658.41	2166.37	1838.74	1605.05	1430.08	1294.25	1185.83
60000	5208.99	3538.24	2703.47	2203.09	1869.90	1632.25	1454.32	1316.19	1205.93
61000	5295.81	3597.21	2748.53	2239.80	1901.07	1659.46	1478.56	1338.13	1226.03
62000	5382.62	3656.18	2793.58	2276.52	1932.23	1686.66	1502.80	1360.06	1246.13
63000	5469.44	3715.15	2838.64	2313.24	1963.40	1713.87	1527.03	1382.00	1266.22
64000	5556.26	3774.12	2883.70	2349.96	1994.56	1741.07	1551.27	1403.94	1286.32
65000	5643.07	3833.09	2928.76	2386.68	2025.73	1768.27	1575.51	1425.87	1306.42
66000	5729.89	3892.06	2973.81	2423.39	2056.89	1795.48	1599.75	1447.81	1326.52
67000	5816.70	3951.03	3018.87	2460.11	2088.05	1822.68	1623.99	1469.75	1346.62
68000	5903.52	4010.00	3063.93	2496.83	2119.22	1849.89	1648.23	1491.68	1366.72
69000	5990.34	4068.97	3108.99	2533.55	2150.38	1877.09	1672.47	1513.62	1386.82
70000	6077.15	4127.94	3154.04	2570.27	2181.55	1904.30	1696.70	1535.56	1406.91
75000	6511.24	4422.80	3379.33	2753.86	2337.37	2040.32	1817.90	1645.24	1507.41
80000	6945.32	4717.65	3604.62	2937.45	2493.20	2176.34	1939.09	1754.92	1607.90
100000	8681.65	5897.06	4505.78	3671.81	3116.50	2720.42	2423.86	2193.65	2009.88

16

TERM AMOUNT	6 YEARS	7 YEARS	8 YEARS	9 YEARS	10 YEARS	11 YEARS	12 YEARS	13 YEARS	14 YEARS
$ 25	.44	.39	.35	.33	.30	.29	.27	.26	.25
50	.87	.78	.70	.65	.60	.57	.54	.51	.49
75	1.31	1.16	1.05	.97	.90	.85	.80	.76	.73
100	1.74	1.55	1.40	1.29	1.20	1.13	1.07	1.02	.98
200	3.48	3.09	2.79	2.57	2.39	2.25	2.13	2.03	1.95
300	5.21	4.63	4.19	3.85	3.59	3.37	3.19	3.04	2.92
400	6.95	6.17	5.58	5.14	4.78	4.49	4.25	4.05	3.89
500	8.68	7.71	6.98	6.42	5.97	5.61	5.32	5.07	4.86
600	10.42	9.25	8.37	7.70	7.17	6.73	6.38	6.08	5.83
700	12.15	10.79	9.77	8.98	8.36	7.86	7.44	7.09	6.80
800	13.89	12.33	11.16	10.27	9.55	8.98	8.50	8.10	7.77
900	15.62	13.87	12.56	11.55	10.75	10.10	9.56	9.12	8.74
1000	17.36	15.41	13.95	12.83	11.94	11.22	10.63	10.13	9.71
2000	34.71	30.81	27.90	25.66	23.88	22.44	21.25	20.25	19.41
3000	52.06	46.21	41.85	38.48	35.82	33.66	31.87	30.38	29.11
4000	69.41	61.61	55.80	51.31	47.75	44.87	42.49	40.50	38.82
5000	86.77	77.01	69.75	64.14	59.69	56.09	53.11	50.63	48.52
6000	104.12	92.41	83.69	76.96	71.63	67.30	63.73	60.75	58.22
7000	121.47	107.81	97.64	89.79	83.56	78.52	74.36	70.87	67.93
8000	138.82	123.22	111.59	102.62	95.50	89.73	84.98	81.00	77.63
9000	156.17	138.62	125.54	115.44	107.44	100.95	95.60	91.12	87.33
10000	173.53	154.02	139.49	128.27	119.37	112.17	106.22	101.25	97.04
15000	260.29	231.03	209.23	192.40	179.06	168.25	159.33	151.87	145.55
20000	347.05	308.03	278.97	256.54	238.74	224.33	212.43	202.49	194.07
25000	433.81	385.04	348.71	320.67	298.43	280.41	265.54	253.11	242.58
30000	520.57	462.05	418.45	384.80	358.11	336.49	318.65	303.73	291.10
35000	607.33	539.05	488.19	448.94	417.80	392.57	371.76	354.35	339.61
36000	624.68	554.46	502.14	461.76	429.74	403.78	382.38	364.47	349.31
37000	642.03	569.86	516.09	474.59	441.67	415.00	393.00	374.60	359.02
38000	659.38	585.26	530.04	487.42	453.61	426.21	403.62	384.72	368.72
39000	676.73	600.66	543.99	500.24	465.55	437.43	414.24	394.85	378.42
40000	694.09	616.06	557.93	513.07	477.48	448.65	424.86	404.97	388.13
41000	711.44	631.46	571.88	525.89	489.42	459.86	435.49	415.09	397.83
42000	728.79	646.86	585.83	538.72	501.36	471.08	446.11	425.22	407.53
43000	746.14	662.27	599.78	551.55	513.29	482.29	456.73	435.34	417.23
44000	763.49	677.67	613.73	564.37	525.23	493.51	467.35	445.47	426.94
45000	780.85	693.07	627.67	577.20	537.17	504.73	477.97	455.59	436.64
46000	798.20	708.47	641.62	590.03	549.11	515.94	488.59	465.71	446.34
47000	815.55	723.87	655.57	602.85	561.04	527.16	499.21	475.84	456.05
48000	832.90	739.27	669.52	615.68	572.98	538.37	509.84	485.96	465.75
49000	850.26	754.67	683.47	628.51	584.92	549.59	520.46	496.09	475.45
50000	867.61	770.08	697.42	641.33	596.85	560.81	531.08	506.21	485.16
51000	884.96	785.48	711.36	654.16	608.79	572.02	541.70	516.33	494.86
52000	902.31	800.88	725.31	666.99	620.73	583.24	552.32	526.46	504.56
53000	919.66	816.28	739.26	679.81	632.66	594.45	562.94	536.58	514.26
54000	937.02	831.68	753.21	692.64	644.60	605.67	573.56	546.71	523.97
55000	954.37	847.08	767.16	705.47	656.54	616.89	584.19	556.83	533.67
56000	971.72	862.48	781.10	718.29	668.47	628.10	594.81	566.95	543.37
57000	989.07	877.89	795.05	731.12	680.41	639.32	605.43	577.08	553.08
58000	1006.42	893.29	809.00	743.95	692.35	650.53	616.05	587.20	562.78
59000	1023.78	908.69	822.95	756.77	704.29	661.75	626.67	597.33	572.48
60000	1041.13	924.09	836.90	769.60	716.22	672.97	637.29	607.45	582.19
61000	1058.48	939.49	850.85	782.43	728.16	684.18	647.91	617.58	591.89
62000	1075.83	954.89	864.79	795.25	740.10	695.40	658.54	627.70	601.59
63000	1093.18	970.29	878.74	808.08	752.03	706.61	669.16	637.82	611.29
64000	1110.54	985.69	892.69	820.91	763.97	717.83	679.78	647.95	621.00
65000	1127.89	1001.10	906.64	833.73	775.91	729.05	690.40	658.07	630.70
66000	1145.24	1016.50	920.59	846.56	787.84	740.26	701.02	668.20	640.40
67000	1162.59	1031.90	934.54	859.39	799.78	751.48	711.64	678.32	650.11
68000	1179.94	1047.30	948.48	872.21	811.72	762.69	722.26	688.44	659.81
69000	1197.30	1062.70	962.43	885.04	823.66	773.91	732.89	698.57	669.51
70000	1214.65	1078.10	976.38	897.87	835.59	785.13	743.51	708.69	679.22
75000	1301.41	1155.11	1046.12	962.00	895.28	841.21	796.62	759.31	727.73
80000	1388.17	1232.12	1115.86	1026.13	954.96	897.29	849.72	809.93	776.25
100000	1735.21	1540.15	1394.83	1282.66	1193.70	1121.61	1062.15	1012.42	970.31

7¾%

MONTHLY PAYMENT
NECESSARY TO AMORTIZE A LOAN

TERM AMOUNT	15 YEARS	16 YEARS	17 YEARS	18 YEARS	19 YEARS	20 YEARS	21 YEARS	22 YEARS	23 YEARS
$ 25	.24	.23	.22	.22	.21	.21	.20	.20	.20
50	.47	.46	.44	.43	.42	.41	.40	.40	.39
75	.71	.68	.66	.64	.63	.62	.60	.59	.58
100	.94	.91	.88	.86	.84	.82	.80	.79	.77
200	1.87	1.81	1.76	1.71	1.67	1.63	1.60	1.57	1.54
300	2.81	2.71	2.63	2.56	2.50	2.45	2.40	2.35	2.31
400	3.74	3.62	3.51	3.42	3.33	3.26	3.19	3.14	3.08
500	4.68	4.52	4.39	4.27	4.16	4.07	3.99	3.92	3.85
600	5.61	5.42	5.26	5.12	5.00	4.89	4.79	4.70	4.62
700	6.55	6.33	6.14	5.97	5.83	5.70	5.58	5.48	5.39
800	7.48	7.23	7.01	6.83	6.66	6.51	6.38	6.27	6.16
900	8.41	8.13	7.89	7.68	7.49	7.33	7.18	7.05	6.93
1000	9.35	9.04	8.77	8.53	8.32	8.14	7.98	7.83	7.70
2000	18.69	18.07	17.53	17.06	16.64	16.27	15.95	15.66	15.40
3000	28.03	27.10	26.29	25.58	24.96	24.41	23.92	23.48	23.09
4000	37.38	36.13	35.05	34.11	33.28	32.54	31.89	31.31	30.79
5000	46.72	45.17	43.82	42.63	41.60	40.68	39.86	39.13	38.48
6000	56.06	54.20	52.58	51.16	49.91	48.81	47.83	46.96	46.18
7000	65.41	63.23	61.34	59.69	58.23	56.94	55.80	54.78	53.87
8000	74.75	72.26	70.10	68.21	66.55	65.08	63.77	62.61	61.57
9000	84.09	81.29	78.86	76.74	74.87	73.21	71.74	70.43	69.26
10000	93.43	90.33	87.63	85.26	83.19	81.35	79.72	78.26	76.96
15000	140.15	135.49	131.44	127.89	124.78	122.02	119.57	117.39	115.43
20000	186.86	180.65	175.25	170.52	166.37	162.69	159.43	156.51	153.91
25000	233.58	225.81	219.06	213.15	207.96	203.36	199.28	195.64	192.39
30000	280.29	270.97	262.87	255.78	249.55	244.03	239.14	234.77	230.86
35000	327.01	316.13	306.68	298.41	291.14	284.70	278.99	273.90	269.34
36000	336.35	325.16	315.44	306.94	299.45	292.84	286.96	281.72	277.03
37000	345.69	334.20	324.20	315.46	307.77	300.97	294.93	289.55	284.73
38000	355.03	343.23	332.97	323.99	316.09	309.11	302.90	297.37	292.42
39000	364.38	352.26	341.73	332.51	324.41	317.24	310.87	305.20	300.12
40000	373.72	361.29	350.49	341.04	332.73	325.37	318.85	313.02	307.82
41000	383.06	370.32	359.25	349.57	341.04	333.51	326.82	320.85	315.51
42000	392.41	379.36	368.01	358.09	349.36	341.64	334.79	328.67	323.21
43000	401.75	388.39	376.78	366.62	357.68	349.78	342.76	336.50	330.90
44000	411.09	397.42	385.54	375.14	366.00	357.91	350.73	344.33	338.60
45000	420.43	406.45	394.30	383.67	374.32	366.05	358.70	352.15	346.29
46000	429.78	415.48	403.06	392.20	382.63	374.18	366.67	359.98	353.99
47000	439.12	424.52	411.82	400.72	390.95	382.31	374.64	367.80	361.68
48000	448.46	433.55	420.59	409.25	399.27	390.45	382.61	375.63	369.38
49000	457.81	442.58	429.35	417.77	407.59	398.58	390.58	383.45	377.07
50000	467.15	451.61	438.11	426.30	415.91	406.72	398.56	391.28	384.77
51000	476.49	460.65	446.87	434.82	424.22	414.85	406.53	399.10	392.46
52000	485.83	469.68	455.64	443.35	432.54	422.98	414.50	406.93	400.16
53000	495.18	478.71	464.40	451.88	440.86	431.12	422.47	414.76	407.85
54000	504.52	487.74	473.16	460.40	449.18	439.25	430.44	422.58	415.55
55000	513.86	496.77	481.92	468.93	457.50	447.39	438.41	430.41	423.24
56000	523.21	505.81	490.68	477.45	465.81	455.52	446.38	438.23	430.94
57000	532.55	514.84	499.45	485.98	474.13	463.66	454.35	446.06	438.63
58000	541.89	523.87	508.21	494.51	482.45	471.79	462.32	453.88	446.33
59000	551.23	532.90	516.97	503.03	490.77	479.92	470.29	461.71	454.03
60000	560.58	541.94	525.73	511.56	499.09	488.06	478.27	469.53	461.72
61000	569.92	550.97	534.49	520.08	507.40	496.19	486.24	477.36	469.42
62000	579.26	560.00	543.26	528.61	515.72	504.33	494.21	485.18	477.11
63000	588.61	569.03	552.02	537.13	524.04	512.46	502.18	493.01	484.81
64000	597.95	578.06	560.78	545.66	532.36	520.60	510.15	500.84	492.50
65000	607.29	587.10	569.54	554.19	540.68	528.73	518.12	508.66	500.20
66000	616.63	596.13	578.30	562.71	548.99	536.86	526.09	516.49	507.89
67000	625.98	605.16	587.07	571.24	557.31	545.00	534.06	524.31	515.59
68000	635.32	614.19	595.83	579.76	565.63	553.13	542.03	532.14	523.28
69000	644.66	623.22	604.59	588.29	573.95	561.27	550.00	539.96	530.98
70000	654.01	632.26	613.35	596.82	582.27	569.40	557.98	547.79	538.67
75000	700.72	677.42	657.16	639.45	623.86	610.07	597.83	586.92	577.15
80000	747.43	722.58	700.97	682.07	665.45	650.74	637.69	626.04	615.63
100000	934.29	903.22	876.22	852.59	831.81	813.43	797.11	782.55	769.53

18

TERM AMOUNT	24 YEARS	25 YEARS	26 YEARS	27 YEARS	28 YEARS	29 YEARS	30 YEARS	35 YEARS	40 YEARS
$ 25	.19	.19	.19	.19	.19	.18	.18	.18	.17
50	.38	.38	.37	.37	.37	.36	.36	.35	.34
75	.57	.57	.56	.55	.55	.54	.54	.52	.51
100	.76	.75	.74	.73	.73	.72	.71	.69	.67
200	1.52	1.50	1.48	1.46	1.45	1.43	1.42	1.37	1.34
300	2.28	2.25	2.22	2.19	2.17	2.15	2.13	2.06	2.01
400	3.04	2.99	2.96	2.92	2.89	2.86	2.84	2.74	2.68
500	3.79	3.74	3.69	3.65	3.61	3.58	3.54	3.42	3.34
600	4.55	4.49	4.43	4.38	4.33	4.29	4.25	4.11	4.01
700	5.31	5.24	5.17	5.11	5.06	5.01	4.96	4.79	4.68
800	6.07	5.98	5.91	5.84	5.78	5.72	5.67	5.47	5.35
900	6.83	6.73	6.65	6.57	6.50	6.43	6.38	6.16	6.01
1000	7.58	7.48	7.38	7.30	7.22	7.15	7.08	6.84	6.68
2000	15.16	14.95	14.76	14.59	14.43	14.29	14.16	13.67	13.36
3000	22.74	22.42	22.14	21.88	21.65	21.44	21.24	20.51	20.03
4000	30.32	29.90	29.52	29.17	28.86	28.58	28.32	27.34	26.71
5000	37.90	37.37	36.90	36.47	36.08	35.73	35.40	34.17	33.38
6000	45.48	44.84	44.27	43.76	43.29	42.87	42.48	41.01	40.06
7000	53.05	52.32	51.65	51.05	50.51	50.01	49.56	47.84	46.73
8000	60.63	59.79	59.03	58.34	57.72	57.16	56.64	54.68	53.41
9000	68.21	67.26	66.41	65.64	64.94	64.30	63.72	61.51	60.08
10000	75.79	74.74	73.79	72.93	72.15	71.45	70.80	68.34	66.76
15000	113.68	112.10	110.68	109.39	108.23	107.17	106.20	102.51	100.13
20000	151.57	149.47	147.57	145.85	144.30	142.89	141.60	136.68	133.51
25000	189.46	186.84	184.46	182.32	180.37	178.61	177.00	170.85	166.89
30000	227.36	224.20	221.35	218.78	216.45	214.33	212.40	205.02	200.26
35000	265.25	261.57	258.25	255.24	252.52	250.05	247.80	239.19	233.64
36000	272.83	269.04	265.62	262.53	259.73	257.19	254.88	246.02	240.32
37000	280.41	276.51	273.00	269.83	266.95	264.34	261.96	252.86	246.99
38000	287.98	283.99	280.38	277.12	274.16	271.48	269.04	259.69	253.67
39000	295.56	291.46	287.76	284.41	281.38	278.62	276.12	266.53	260.34
40000	303.14	298.93	295.14	291.70	288.59	285.77	283.20	273.36	267.02
41000	310.72	306.41	302.52	299.00	295.81	292.91	290.28	280.19	273.69
42000	318.30	313.88	309.89	306.29	303.02	300.06	297.36	287.03	280.37
43000	325.88	321.35	317.27	313.58	310.24	307.20	304.44	293.86	287.04
44000	333.45	328.83	324.65	320.87	317.45	314.34	311.52	300.70	293.72
45000	341.03	336.30	332.03	328.17	324.67	321.49	318.60	307.53	300.39
46000	348.61	343.77	339.41	335.46	331.88	328.63	325.68	314.36	307.07
47000	356.19	351.25	346.79	342.75	339.10	335.78	332.76	321.20	313.74
48000	363.77	358.72	354.16	350.04	346.31	342.92	339.84	328.03	320.42
49000	371.35	366.19	361.54	357.34	353.52	350.06	346.92	334.86	327.10
50000	378.92	373.67	368.92	364.63	360.74	357.21	354.00	341.70	333.77
51000	386.50	381.14	376.30	371.92	367.95	364.35	361.08	348.53	340.45
52000	394.08	388.61	383.68	379.21	375.17	371.50	368.16	355.37	347.12
53000	401.66	396.09	391.05	386.51	382.38	378.64	375.24	362.20	353.80
54000	409.24	403.56	398.43	393.80	389.60	385.78	382.32	369.03	360.47
55000	416.82	411.03	405.81	401.09	396.81	392.93	389.40	375.87	367.15
56000	424.40	418.50	413.19	408.38	404.03	400.07	396.48	382.70	373.82
57000	431.97	425.98	420.57	415.68	411.24	407.22	403.56	389.54	380.50
58000	439.55	433.45	427.95	422.97	418.46	414.36	410.64	396.37	387.17
59000	447.13	440.92	435.32	430.26	425.67	421.50	417.72	403.20	393.85
60000	454.71	448.40	442.70	437.55	432.89	428.65	424.79	410.04	400.52
61000	462.29	455.87	450.08	444.85	440.10	435.79	431.87	416.87	407.20
62000	469.87	463.34	457.46	452.14	447.32	442.94	438.95	423.71	413.87
63000	477.44	470.82	464.84	459.43	454.53	450.08	446.03	430.54	420.55
64000	485.02	478.29	472.22	466.72	461.74	457.22	453.11	437.37	427.23
65000	492.60	485.76	479.59	474.02	468.96	464.37	460.19	444.21	433.90
66000	500.18	493.24	486.97	481.31	476.17	471.51	467.27	451.04	440.58
67000	507.76	500.71	494.35	488.60	483.39	478.66	474.35	457.87	447.25
68000	515.34	508.18	501.73	495.89	490.60	485.80	481.43	464.71	453.93
69000	522.91	515.66	509.11	503.19	497.82	492.95	488.51	471.54	460.60
70000	530.49	523.13	516.49	510.48	505.03	500.09	495.59	478.38	467.28
75000	568.38	560.50	553.38	546.94	541.11	535.81	530.99	512.55	500.65
80000	606.28	597.86	590.27	583.40	577.18	571.53	566.39	546.71	534.03
100000	757.84	747.33	737.84	729.25	721.47	714.41	707.99	683.39	667.54

8%

MONTHLY PAYMENT
NECESSARY TO AMORTIZE A LOAN

TERM AMOUNT	1 YEAR	1½ YEARS	2 YEARS	2½ YEARS	3 YEARS	3½ YEARS	4 YEARS	4½ YEARS	5 YEARS
$ 25	2.18	1.48	1.13	.93	.79	.69	.61	.56	.51
50	4.35	2.96	2.26	1.85	1.57	1.37	1.22	1.11	1.02
75	6.52	4.44	3.39	2.77	2.35	2.05	1.83	1.66	1.52
100	8.70	5.91	4.52	3.69	3.13	2.74	2.44	2.21	2.03
200	17.39	11.82	9.04	7.37	6.26	5.47	4.88	4.42	4.05
300	26.08	17.73	13.56	11.05	9.39	8.20	7.31	6.62	6.07
400	34.78	23.64	18.07	14.74	12.52	10.93	9.75	8.83	8.09
500	43.47	29.55	22.59	18.42	15.64	13.66	12.18	11.03	10.11
600	52.16	35.45	27.11	22.10	18.77	16.39	14.62	13.24	12.13
700	60.85	41.36	31.62	25.79	21.90	19.13	17.05	15.44	14.15
800	69.55	47.27	36.14	29.47	25.03	21.86	19.49	17.65	16.18
900	78.24	53.18	40.66	33.15	28.15	24.59	21.92	19.85	18.20
1000	86.93	59.09	45.17	36.83	31.28	27.32	24.36	22.06	20.22
2000	173.86	118.17	90.34	73.66	62.56	54.64	48.71	44.11	40.43
3000	260.79	177.25	135.51	110.49	93.83	81.95	73.06	66.16	60.65
4000	347.72	236.33	180.68	147.32	125.11	109.27	97.41	88.21	80.86
5000	434.65	295.41	225.84	184.15	156.39	136.59	121.76	110.26	101.08
6000	521.57	354.49	271.01	220.98	187.66	163.90	146.12	132.31	*21.29
7000	608.50	413.57	316.18	257.81	218.94	191.22	170.47	154.36	141.50
8000	695.43	472.65	361.35	294.63	250.22	218.54	194.82	176.41	161.72
9000	782.36	531.73	406.52	331.46	281.49	245.85	219.17	198.46	181.93
10000	869.29	590.81	451.68	368.29	312.77	273.17	243.52	220.51	202.15
15000	1303.93	886.22	677.52	552.44	469.15	409.75	365.28	330.77	303.22
20000	1738.57	1181.62	903.36	736.58	625.53	546.33	487.04	441.02	404.29
25000	2173.21	1477.03	1129.20	920.72	781.91	682.92	608.80	551.27	505.36
30000	2607.85	1772.43	1355.04	1104.87	938.30	819.50	730.56	661.53	606.43
35000	3042.49	2067.84	1580.88	1289.01	1094.68	956.08	852.32	771.78	707.50
36000	3129.42	2126.92	1626.05	1325.84	1125.95	983.40	876.67	793.83	727.71
37000	3216.35	2186.00	1671.22	1362.67	1157.23	1010.71	901.02	815.88	747.93
38000	3303.28	2245.08	1716.39	1399.50	1188.51	1038.03	925.38	837.93	768.14
39000	3390.21	2304.16	1761.56	1436.33	1219.78	1065.35	949.73	859.99	788.36
40000	3477.14	2363.24	1806.72	1473.15	1251.06	1092.66	974.08	882.04	808.57
41000	3564.06	2422.32	1851.89	1509.98	1282.34	1119.98	998.43	904.09	828.79
42000	3650.99	2481.40	1897.06	1546.81	1313.61	1147.30	1022.78	926.14	849.00
43000	3737.92	2540.48	1942.23	1583.64	1344.89	1174.61	1047.14	948.19	869.21
44000	3824.85	2599.57	1987.39	1620.47	1376.16	1201.93	1071.49	970.24	889.43
45000	3911.78	2658.65	2032.56	1657.30	1407.44	1229.25	1095.84	992.29	909.64
46000	3998.70	2717.73	2077.73	1694.13	1438.72	1256.56	1120.19	1014.34	929.86
47000	4085.63	2776.81	2122.90	1730.95	1469.99	1283.88	1144.54	1036.39	950.07
48000	4172.56	2835.89	2168.07	1767.78	1501.27	1311.20	1168.89	1058.44	970.28
49000	4259.49	2894.97	2213.23	1804.61	1532.55	1338.51	1193.25	1080.49	990.50
50000	4346.42	2954.05	2258.40	1841.44	1563.82	1365.83	1217.60	1102.54	1010.71
51000	4433.35	3013.13	2303.57	1878.27	1595.10	1393.14	1241.95	1124.60	1030.93
52000	4520.27	3072.21	2348.74	1915.10	1626.38	1420.46	1266.30	1146.65	1051.14
53000	4607.20	3131.29	2393.91	1951.93	1657.65	1447.78	1290.65	1168.70	1071.36
54000	4694.13	3190.37	2439.07	1988.76	1688.93	1475.09	1315.01	1190.75	1091.57
55000	4781.06	3249.46	2484.24	2025.58	1720.20	1502.41	1339.36	1212.80	1111.78
56000	4867.99	3308.54	2529.41	2062.41	1751.48	1529.73	1363.71	1234.85	1132.00
57000	4954.92	3367.62	2574.58	2099.24	1782.76	1557.04	1388.06	1256.90	1152.21
58000	5041.84	3426.70	2619.75	2136.07	1814.03	1584.36	1412.41	1278.95	1172.43
59000	5128.77	3485.78	2664.91	2172.90	1845.31	1611.68	1436.77	1301.00	1192.64
60000	5215.70	3544.86	2710.08	2209.73	1876.59	1638.99	1461.12	1323.05	1212.85
61000	5302.63	3603.94	2755.25	2246.56	1907.86	1666.31	1485.47	1345.10	1233.07
62000	5389.56	3663.02	2800.42	2283.39	1939.14	1693.63	1509.82	1367.15	1253.28
63000	5476.49	3722.10	2845.59	2320.21	1970.42	1720.94	1534.17	1389.20	1273.50
64000	5563.41	3781.18	2890.75	2357.04	2001.69	1748.26	1558.52	1411.26	1293.71
65000	5650.34	3840.26	2935.92	2393.87	2032.97	1775.58	1582.88	1433.31	1313.93
66000	5737.27	3899.35	2981.09	2430.70	2064.24	1802.89	1607.23	1455.36	1334.14
67000	5824.20	3958.43	3026.26	2467.53	2095.52	1830.21	1631.58	1477.41	1354.35
68000	5911.13	4017.51	3071.43	2504.36	2126.80	1857.52	1655.93	1499.46	1374.57
69000	5998.05	4076.59	3116.59	2541.19	2158.07	1884.84	1680.28	1521.51	1394.78
70000	6084.98	4135.67	3161.76	2578.02	2189.35	1912.16	1704.64	1543.56	1415.00
75000	6519.62	4431.07	3387.60	2762.16	2345.73	2048.74	1826.40	1653.81	1516.07
80000	6954.27	4726.48	3613.44	2946.30	2502.11	2185.32	1948.15	1764.07	1617.14
100000	8692.83	5908.10	4516.80	3682.88	3127.64	2731.65	2435.19	2205.08	2021.42

20

MONTHLY PAYMENT
NECESSARY TO AMORTIZE A LOAN

8%

TERM AMOUNT	6 YEARS	7 YEARS	8 YEARS	9 YEARS	10 YEARS	11 YEARS	12 YEARS	13 YEARS	14 YEARS
$ 25	.44	.39	.36	.33	.31	.29	.27	.26	.25
50	.88	.78	.71	.65	.61	.57	.54	.52	.50
75	1.32	1.17	1.06	.98	.91	.86	.81	.77	.74
100	1.75	1.56	1.41	1.30	1.21	1.14	1.08	1.03	.99
200	3.50	3.11	2.82	2.60	2.42	2.27	2.16	2.06	1.97
300	5.25	4.66	4.23	3.89	3.62	3.41	3.23	3.08	2.96
400	6.99	6.21	5.63	5.19	4.83	4.54	4.31	4.11	3.94
500	8.74	7.77	7.04	6.48	6.04	5.68	5.38	5.13	4.92
600	10.49	9.32	8.45	7.78	7.24	6.81	6.46	6.16	5.91
700	12.23	10.87	9.85	9.07	8.45	7.95	7.53	7.19	6.89
800	13.98	12.42	11.26	10.37	9.66	9.08	8.61	8.21	7.88
900	15.73	13.97	12.67	11.66	10.86	10.22	9.68	9.24	8.86
1000	17.47	15.53	14.08	12.96	12.07	11.35	10.76	10.26	9.84
2000	34.94	31.05	28.15	25.91	24.13	22.70	21.51	20.52	19.68
3000	52.41	46.57	42.22	38.86	36.20	34.04	32.26	30.78	29.52
4000	69.88	62.09	56.29	51.81	48.26	45.39	43.02	41.04	39.36
5000	87.35	77.61	70.36	64.76	60.33	56.73	53.77	51.30	49.20
6000	104.82	93.13	84.43	77.71	72.39	68.08	64.52	61.55	59.04
7000	122.29	108.66	98.50	90.66	84.45	79.42	75.28	71.81	68.88
8000	139.76	124.18	112.57	103.62	96.52	90.77	86.03	82.07	78.72
9000	157.23	139.70	126.64	116.57	108.58	102.11	96.78	92.33	88.56
10000	174.70	155.22	140.71	129.52	120.65	113.46	107.54	102.59	98.40
15000	262.05	232.83	211.06	194.28	180.97	170.19	161.30	153.88	147.60
20000	349.40	310.43	281.42	259.03	241.29	226.91	215.07	205.17	196.79
25000	436.75	388.04	351.77	323.79	301.61	283.64	268.84	256.46	245.99
30000	524.10	465.65	422.12	388.55	361.93	340.37	322.60	307.75	295.19
35000	611.45	543.26	492.48	453.30	422.25	397.10	376.37	359.04	344.38
36000	628.92	558.78	506.55	466.25	434.31	408.44	387.12	369.30	354.22
37000	646.39	574.30	520.62	479.20	446.38	419.79	397.88	379.56	364.06
38000	663.86	589.82	534.69	492.16	458.44	431.13	408.63	389.82	373.90
39000	681.33	605.34	548.76	505.11	470.50	442.48	419.38	400.08	383.74
40000	698.80	620.86	562.83	518.06	482.57	453.82	430.14	410.33	393.58
41000	716.26	636.38	576.90	531.01	494.63	465.17	440.89	420.59	403.42
42000	733.73	651.91	590.97	543.96	506.70	476.52	451.64	430.85	413.26
43000	751.20	667.43	605.04	556.91	518.76	487.86	462.40	441.11	423.10
44000	768.67	682.95	619.11	569.86	530.82	499.21	473.15	451.37	432.94
45000	786.14	698.47	633.18	582.82	542.89	510.55	483.90	461.63	442.78
46000	803.61	713.99	647.25	595.77	554.95	521.90	494.66	471.88	452.62
47000	821.08	729.51	661.32	608.72	567.02	533.24	505.41	482.14	462.46
48000	838.55	745.03	675.39	621.67	579.08	544.59	516.16	492.40	472.30
49000	856.02	760.56	689.46	634.62	591.15	555.93	526.92	502.66	482.14
50000	873.49	776.08	703.54	647.57	603.21	567.28	537.67	512.92	491.98
51000	890.96	791.60	717.61	660.52	615.27	578.62	548.42	523.17	501.82
52000	908.43	807.12	731.68	673.47	627.34	589.97	559.18	533.43	511.65
53000	925.90	822.64	745.75	686.43	639.40	601.32	569.93	543.69	521.49
54000	943.37	838.16	759.82	699.38	651.47	612.66	580.68	553.95	531.33
55000	960.84	853.68	773.89	712.33	663.53	624.01	591.44	564.21	541.17
56000	978.31	869.21	787.96	725.28	675.59	635.35	602.19	574.47	551.01
57000	995.78	884.73	802.03	738.23	687.66	646.70	612.94	584.72	560.85
58000	1013.25	900.25	816.10	751.18	699.72	658.04	623.70	594.98	570.69
59000	1030.72	915.77	830.17	764.13	711.79	669.39	634.45	605.24	580.53
60000	1048.19	931.29	844.24	777.09	723.85	680.73	645.20	615.50	590.37
61000	1065.66	946.81	858.31	790.04	735.91	692.08	655.96	625.76	600.21
62000	1083.13	962.33	872.38	802.99	747.98	703.43	666.71	636.02	610.05
63000	1100.60	977.86	886.45	815.94	760.04	714.77	677.46	646.27	619.89
64000	1118.07	993.38	900.52	828.89	772.11	726.12	688.22	656.53	629.73
65000	1135.54	1008.90	914.59	841.84	784.17	737.46	698.97	666.79	639.57
66000	1153.01	1024.42	928.67	854.79	796.23	748.81	709.72	677.05	649.41
67000	1170.48	1039.94	942.74	867.75	808.30	760.15	720.48	687.31	659.25
68000	1187.95	1055.46	956.81	880.70	820.36	771.50	731.23	697.56	669.09
69000	1205.42	1070.98	970.88	893.65	832.43	782.84	741.98	707.82	678.93
70000	1222.89	1086.51	984.95	906.60	844.49	794.19	752.73	718.08	688.76
75000	1310.24	1164.11	1055.30	971.36	904.81	850.92	806.50	769.37	737.96
80000	1397.59	1241.72	1125.65	1036.11	965.13	907.64	860.27	820.66	787.16
100000	1746.98	1552.15	1407.07	1295.14	1206.41	1134.55	1075.33	1025.83	983.95

21

8% MONTHLY PAYMENT
NECESSARY TO AMORTIZE A LOAN

TERM AMOUNT	15 YEARS	16 YEARS	17 YEARS	18 YEARS	19 YEARS	20 YEARS	21 YEARS	22 YEARS	23 YEARS
$ 25	.24	.23	.23	.22	.22	.21	.21	.20	.20
50	.48	.46	.45	.44	.43	.42	.41	.40	.40
75	.72	.69	.67	.66	.64	.63	.61	.60	.59
100	.95	.92	.90	.87	.85	.83	.82	.80	.79
200	1.90	1.84	1.79	1.74	1.70	1.66	1.63	1.60	1.58
300	2.85	2.76	2.68	2.61	2.54	2.49	2.44	2.40	2.36
400	3.80	3.67	3.57	3.47	3.39	3.32	3.25	3.20	3.15
500	4.75	4.59	4.46	4.34	4.24	4.15	4.07	3.99	3.93
600	5.69	5.51	5.35	5.21	5.08	4.98	4.88	4.79	4.72
700	6.64	6.43	6.24	6.07	5.93	5.80	5.69	5.59	5.50
800	7.59	7.34	7.13	6.94	6.78	6.63	6.50	6.39	6.29
900	8.54	8.26	8.02	7.81	7.62	7.46	7.32	7.19	7.07
1000	9.49	9.18	8.91	8.68	8.47	8.29	8.13	7.98	7.86
2000	18.97	18.35	17.82	17.35	16.94	16.57	16.25	15.96	15.71
3000	28.45	27.52	26.72	26.02	25.40	24.86	24.37	23.94	23.56
4000	37.93	36.70	35.63	34.69	33.87	33.14	32.49	31.92	31.41
5000	47.41	45.87	44.53	43.36	42.33	41.42	40.62	39.90	39.26
6000	56.89	55.04	53.44	52.03	50.80	49.71	48.74	47.88	47.11
7000	66.38	64.22	62.34	60.70	59.26	57.99	56.86	55.86	54.96
8000	75.86	73.39	71.25	69.37	67.73	66.27	64.98	63.84	62.81
9000	85.34	82.56	80.15	78.04	76.19	74.56	73.11	71.81	70.66
10000	94.82	91.74	89.06	86.72	84.66	82.84	81.23	79.79	78.51
15000	142.23	137.60	133.58	130.07	126.98	124.26	121.84	119.69	117.76
20000	189.64	183.47	178.11	173.43	169.31	165.68	162.45	159.58	157.01
25000	237.04	229.33	222.63	216.78	211.64	207.09	203.06	199.47	196.27
30000	284.45	275.20	267.16	260.14	253.96	248.51	243.68	239.37	235.52
35000	331.86	321.06	311.69	303.49	296.29	289.93	284.29	279.26	274.77
36000	341.34	330.23	320.59	312.16	304.76	298.21	292.41	287.24	282.62
37000	350.82	339.41	329.50	320.83	313.22	306.50	300.53	295.22	290.47
38000	360.30	348.58	338.40	329.51	321.69	314.78	308.65	303.20	298.32
39000	369.78	357.75	347.31	338.18	330.15	323.06	316.78	311.18	306.17
40000	379.27	366.93	356.21	346.85	338.62	331.35	324.90	319.16	314.02
41000	388.75	376.10	365.12	355.52	347.08	339.63	333.02	327.14	321.88
42000	398.23	385.27	374.02	364.19	355.55	347.92	341.14	335.11	329.73
43000	407.71	394.45	382.93	372.86	364.01	356.20	349.27	343.09	337.58
44000	417.19	403.62	391.83	381.53	372.48	364.48	357.39	351.07	345.43
45000	426.67	412.79	400.74	390.20	380.94	372.77	365.51	359.05	353.28
46000	436.16	421.97	409.64	398.87	389.41	381.05	373.63	367.03	361.13
47000	445.64	431.14	418.55	407.55	397.87	389.33	381.76	375.01	368.98
48000	455.12	440.31	427.45	416.22	406.34	397.62	389.88	382.99	376.83
49000	464.60	449.48	436.36	424.89	414.81	405.90	398.00	390.97	384.68
50000	474.08	458.66	445.26	433.56	423.27	414.18	406.12	398.94	392.53
51000	483.56	467.83	454.17	442.23	431.74	422.47	414.25	406.92	400.38
52000	493.04	477.00	463.07	450.90	440.20	430.75	422.37	414.90	408.23
53000	502.53	486.18	471.98	459.57	448.67	439.03	430.49	422.88	416.08
54000	512.01	495.35	480.88	468.24	457.13	447.32	438.61	430.86	423.93
55000	521.49	504.52	489.79	476.91	465.60	455.60	446.73	438.84	431.78
56000	530.97	513.70	498.69	485.58	474.06	463.89	454.86	446.82	439.63
57000	540.45	522.87	507.60	494.26	482.53	472.17	462.98	454.80	447.48
58000	549.93	532.04	516.51	502.93	490.99	480.45	471.10	462.77	455.33
59000	559.42	541.21	525.41	511.60	499.46	488.74	479.22	470.75	463.18
60000	568.90	550.39	534.32	520.27	507.92	497.02	487.35	478.73	471.03
61000	578.38	559.56	543.22	528.94	516.39	505.30	495.47	486.71	478.89
62000	587.86	568.73	552.13	537.61	524.85	513.59	503.59	494.69	486.74
63000	597.34	577.91	561.03	546.28	533.32	521.87	511.71	502.67	494.59
64000	606.82	587.08	569.94	554.95	541.78	530.15	519.84	510.65	502.44
65000	616.30	596.25	578.84	563.62	550.25	538.44	527.96	518.63	510.29
66000	625.79	605.43	587.75	572.30	558.72	546.72	536.08	526.61	518.14
67000	635.27	614.60	596.65	580.97	567.18	555.00	544.20	534.58	525.99
68000	644.75	623.77	605.56	589.64	575.65	563.29	552.33	542.56	533.84
69000	654.23	632.95	614.46	598.31	584.11	571.57	560.45	550.54	541.69
70000	663.71	642.12	623.37	606.98	592.58	579.86	568.57	558.52	549.54
75000	711.12	687.98	667.89	650.33	634.90	621.27	609.18	598.41	588.79
80000	758.53	733.85	712.42	693.69	677.23	662.69	649.79	638.31	628.04
100000	948.16	917.31	890.52	867.11	846.54	828.36	812.24	797.88	785.05

22

MONTHLY PAYMENT 8%
NECESSARY TO AMORTIZE A LOAN

TERM AMOUNT	24 YEARS	25 YEARS	26 YEARS	27 YEARS	28 YEARS	29 YEARS	30 YEARS	35 YEARS	40 YEARS
$ 25	.20	.20	.19	.19	.19	.19	.19	.18	.18
50	.39	.39	.38	.38	.37	.37	.37	.36	.35
75	.59	.58	.57	.56	.56	.55	.55	.53	.52
100	.78	.77	.76	.75	.74	.74	.73	.71	.69
200	1.55	1.53	1.51	1.50	1.48	1.47	1.45	1.41	1.38
300	2.33	2.29	2.27	2.24	2.22	2.20	2.18	2.11	2.06
400	3.10	3.06	3.02	2.99	2.96	2.93	2.90	2.81	2.75
500	3.87	3.82	3.77	3.73	3.69	3.66	3.63	3.51	3.43
600	4.65	4.58	4.53	4.48	4.43	4.39	4.35	4.21	4.12
700	5.42	5.35	5.28	5.22	5.17	5.12	5.08	4.91	4.80
800	6.19	6.11	6.04	5.97	5.91	5.85	5.80	5.61	5.49
900	6.97	6.87	6.79	6.71	6.65	6.58	6.53	6.31	6.18
1000	7.74	7.64	7.54	7.46	7.38	7.31	7.25	7.01	6.86
2000	15.48	15.27	15.08	14.91	14.76	14.62	14.50	14.02	13.72
3000	23.21	22.90	22.62	22.37	22.14	21.93	21.75	21.03	20.57
4000	30.95	30.53	30.16	29.82	29.52	29.24	28.99	28.04	27.43
5000	38.68	38.17	37.70	37.28	36.90	36.55	36.24	35.05	34.28
6000	46.42	45.80	45.24	44.73	44.28	43.86	43.49	42.05	41.14
7000	54.15	53.43	52.78	52.19	51.66	51.17	50.73	49.06	47.99
8000	61.89	61.06	60.32	59.64	59.04	58.48	57.98	56.07	54.85
9000	69.62	68.69	67.86	67.10	66.41	65.79	65.23	63.08	61.71
10000	77.36	76.33	75.39	74.55	73.79	73.10	72.48	70.09	68.56
15000	116.04	114.49	113.09	111.83	110.69	109.65	108.71	105.13	102.84
20000	154.71	152.65	150.78	149.10	147.58	146.20	144.95	140.17	137.12
25000	193.39	190.81	188.48	186.38	184.47	182.75	181.18	175.21	171.40
30000	232.07	228.97	226.17	223.65	221.37	219.30	217.42	210.25	205.67
35000	270.75	267.13	263.87	260.93	258.26	255.85	253.65	245.29	239.95
36000	278.48	274.76	271.41	268.38	265.64	263.16	260.90	252.30	246.81
37000	286.22	282.39	278.95	275.84	273.02	270.47	268.15	259.31	253.66
38000	293.95	293.03	286.49	283.29	280.40	277.78	275.40	266.32	260.52
39000	301.69	297.66	294.03	290.75	287.78	285.09	282.64	273.33	267.37
40000	309.42	305.29	301.56	298.20	295.16	292.40	289.89	280.34	274.23
41000	317.16	312.92	309.10	305.66	302.53	299.71	297.14	287.34	281.09
42000	324.90	320.55	316.64	313.11	309.91	307.02	304.38	294.35	287.94
43000	332.63	328.19	324.18	320.56	317.29	314.33	311.63	301.36	294.80
44000	340.37	335.82	331.72	328.02	324.67	321.63	318.88	308.37	301.65
45000	348.10	343.45	339.26	335.47	332.05	328.94	326.12	315.38	308.51
46000	355.84	351.08	346.80	342.93	339.43	336.25	333.37	322.39	315.36
47000	363.57	358.72	354.34	350.38	346.81	343.56	340.62	329.39	322.22
48000	371.31	366.35	361.88	357.84	354.19	350.87	347.87	336.40	329.07
49000	379.04	373.98	369.42	365.29	361.56	358.18	355.11	343.41	335.93
50000	386.78	381.61	376.95	372.75	368.94	365.49	362.36	350.42	342.79
51000	394.52	389.24	384.49	380.20	376.32	372.80	369.61	357.43	349.64
52000	402.25	396.88	392.03	387.66	383.70	380.11	376.85	364.43	356.50
53000	409.99	404.51	399.57	395.11	391.08	387.42	384.10	371.44	363.35
54000	417.72	412.14	407.11	402.57	398.46	394.73	391.35	378.45	370.21
55000	425.46	419.77	414.65	410.02	405.84	402.04	398.60	385.46	377.06
56000	433.19	427.40	422.19	417.48	413.22	409.35	405.84	392.47	383.92
57000	440.93	435.04	429.73	424.93	420.59	416.66	413.09	399.48	390.78
58000	448.66	442.67	437.27	432.39	427.97	423.97	420.34	406.48	397.63
59000	456.40	450.30	444.81	439.84	435.35	431.28	427.58	413.49	404.49
60000	464.13	457.93	452.34	447.30	442.73	438.59	434.83	420.50	411.34
61000	471.87	465.57	459.88	454.75	450.11	445.90	442.08	427.51	418.20
62000	479.61	473.20	467.42	462.21	457.49	453.21	449.33	434.52	425.05
63000	487.34	480.83	474.96	469.66	464.87	460.52	456.57	441.53	431.91
64000	495.08	488.46	482.50	477.12	472.25	467.83	463.82	448.53	438.76
65000	502.81	496.09	490.04	484.57	479.63	475.14	471.07	455.54	445.62
66000	510.55	503.73	497.58	492.03	487.00	482.45	478.31	462.55	452.48
67000	518.28	511.36	505.12	499.48	494.38	489.76	485.56	469.56	459.33
68000	526.02	518.99	512.66	506.94	501.76	497.07	492.81	476.57	466.19
69000	533.75	526.62	520.20	514.39	509.14	504.38	500.06	483.58	473.04
70000	541.49	534.25	527.73	521.85	516.52	511.69	507.30	490.58	479.90
75000	580.17	572.42	565.43	559.12	553.41	548.24	543.54	525.62	514.18
80000	618.84	610.58	603.12	596.40	590.31	584.79	579.77	560.67	548.45
100000	773.55	763.22	753.90	745.49	737.88	730.98	724.72	700.83	685.57

23

8¼%

MONTHLY PAYMENT
NECESSARY TO AMORTIZE A LOAN

TERM AMOUNT	1 YEAR	1½ YEARS	2 YEARS	2½ YEARS	3 YEARS	3½ YEARS	4 YEARS	4½ YEARS	5 YEARS
$ 25	2.18	1.48	1.14	.93	.79	.69	.62	.56	.51
50	4.36	2.96	2.27	1.85	1.57	1.38	1.23	1.11	1.02
75	6.53	4.44	3.40	2.78	2.36	2.06	1.84	1.67	1.53
100	8.71	5.92	4.53	3.70	3.14	2.75	2.45	2.22	2.04
200	17.41	11.84	9.06	7.39	6.28	5.49	4.90	4.44	4.07
300	26.12	17.76	13.59	11.09	9.42	8.23	7.34	6.65	6.10
400	34.82	23.68	18.12	14.78	12.56	10.98	9.79	8.87	8.14
500	43.53	29.60	22.64	18.47	15.70	13.72	12.24	11.09	10.17
600	52.23	35.52	27.17	22.17	18.84	16.46	14.68	13.30	12.20
700	60.93	41.44	31.70	25.86	21.98	19.21	17.13	15.52	14.24
800	69.64	47.36	36.23	29.56	25.12	21.95	19.58	17.74	16.27
900	78.34	53.28	40.76	33.25	28.25	24.69	22.02	19.95	18.30
1000	87.05	59.20	45.28	36.94	31.39	27.43	24.47	22.17	20.33
2000	174.09	118.39	90.56	73.88	62.78	54.86	48.94	44.34	40.66
3000	261.13	177.58	135.84	110.82	94.17	82.29	73.40	66.50	60.99
4000	348.17	236.77	181.12	147.76	125.56	109.72	97.87	88.67	81.32
5000	435.21	295.96	226.40	184.70	156.94	137.15	122.33	110.83	101.65
6000	522.25	355.15	271.67	221.64	188.33	164.58	146.80	133.00	121.98
7000	609.29	414.34	316.95	258.58	219.72	192.01	171.26	155.16	142.31
8000	696.33	473.54	362.23	295.52	251.11	219.44	195.73	177.33	162.64
9000	783.37	532.73	407.51	332.46	282.50	246.87	220.19	199.49	182.97
10000	870.41	591.92	452.79	369.40	313.88	274.29	244.66	221.66	203.30
15000	1305.61	887.87	679.18	554.10	470.82	411.44	366.99	332.49	304.95
20000	1740.81	1183.83	905.57	738.80	627.76	548.58	489.31	443.31	406.60
25000	2176.01	1479.79	1131.96	923.49	784.70	685.73	611.64	554.14	508.25
30000	2611.21	1775.74	1358.35	1108.19	941.64	822.87	733.97	664.97	609.90
35000	3046.41	2071.70	1584.74	1292.89	1098.58	960.02	856.29	775.79	711.55
36000	3133.45	2130.89	1630.02	1329.83	1129.97	987.45	880.76	797.96	731.88
37000	3220.49	2190.08	1675.30	1366.77	1161.36	1014.88	905.22	820.12	752.21
38000	3307.53	2249.27	1720.58	1403.71	1192.75	1042.31	929.69	842.29	772.54
39000	3394.57	2308.46	1765.86	1440.65	1224.13	1069.73	954.15	864.45	792.87
40000	3481.61	2367.66	1811.13	1477.59	1255.52	1097.16	978.62	886.62	813.20
41000	3568.65	2426.85	1856.41	1514.52	1286.91	1124.59	1003.09	908.79	833.53
42000	3655.69	2486.04	1901.69	1551.46	1318.30	1152.02	1027.55	930.95	853.86
43000	3742.73	2545.23	1946.97	1588.40	1349.69	1179.45	1052.02	953.12	874.19
44000	3829.77	2604.42	1992.25	1625.34	1381.07	1206.88	1076.48	975.28	894.52
45000	3916.81	2663.61	2037.53	1662.28	1412.46	1234.31	1100.95	997.45	914.85
46000	4003.85	2722.80	2082.80	1699.22	1443.85	1261.74	1125.41	1019.61	935.18
47000	4090.89	2781.99	2128.08	1736.16	1475.24	1289.17	1149.88	1041.78	955.51
48000	4177.93	2841.19	2173.36	1773.10	1506.62	1316.59	1174.34	1063.94	975.84
49000	4264.97	2900.38	2218.64	1810.04	1538.01	1344.02	1198.81	1086.11	996.17
50000	4352.01	2959.57	2263.92	1846.98	1569.40	1371.45	1223.27	1108.27	1016.50
51000	4439.05	3018.76	2309.20	1883.92	1600.79	1398.88	1247.74	1130.44	1036.83
52000	4526.09	3077.95	2354.47	1920.86	1632.18	1426.31	1272.20	1152.60	1057.16
53000	4613.13	3137.14	2399.75	1957.80	1663.56	1453.74	1296.67	1174.77	1077.49
54000	4700.17	3196.33	2445.03	1994.74	1694.95	1481.17	1321.14	1196.94	1097.82
55000	4787.21	3255.53	2490.31	2031.68	1726.34	1508.60	1345.60	1219.10	1118.15
56000	4874.25	3314.72	2535.59	2068.62	1757.73	1536.03	1370.07	1241.27	1138.48
57000	4961.29	3373.91	2580.86	2105.56	1789.12	1563.46	1394.53	1263.43	1158.81
58000	5048.33	3433.10	2626.14	2142.50	1820.50	1590.88	1419.00	1285.60	1179.14
59000	5135.37	3492.29	2671.42	2179.44	1851.89	1618.31	1443.46	1307.76	1199.47
60000	5222.41	3551.48	2716.70	2216.38	1883.28	1645.74	1467.93	1329.93	1219.80
61000	5309.45	3610.67	2761.98	2253.31	1914.67	1673.17	1492.39	1352.09	1240.13
62000	5396.49	3669.86	2807.26	2290.25	1946.06	1700.60	1516.86	1374.26	1260.46
63000	5483.53	3729.06	2852.53	2327.19	1977.44	1728.03	1541.32	1396.42	1280.79
64000	5570.57	3788.25	2897.81	2364.13	2008.83	1755.46	1565.79	1418.59	1301.12
65000	5657.61	3847.44	2943.09	2401.07	2040.22	1782.89	1590.25	1440.75	1321.45
66000	5744.65	3906.63	2988.37	2438.01	2071.61	1810.32	1614.72	1462.92	1341.78
67000	5831.69	3965.82	3033.65	2474.95	2102.99	1837.74	1639.19	1485.09	1362.11
68000	5918.73	4025.01	3078.93	2511.89	2134.38	1865.17	1663.65	1507.25	1382.44
69000	6005.77	4084.20	3124.20	2548.83	2165.77	1892.60	1688.12	1529.42	1402.77
70000	6092.81	4143.39	3169.48	2585.77	2197.16	1920.03	1712.58	1551.58	1423.10
75000	6528.01	4439.35	3395.87	2770.47	2354.10	2057.18	1834.91	1662.41	1524.75
80000	6963.21	4735.31	3622.26	2955.17	2511.04	2194.32	1957.24	1773.24	1626.40
100000	8704.01	5919.13	4527.83	3693.96	3138.80	2742.90	2446.54	2216.54	2032.99

24

MONTHLY PAYMENT

NECESSARY TO AMORTIZE A LOAN

8¼%

TERM AMOUNT	6 YEARS	7 YEARS	8 YEARS	9 YEARS	10 YEARS	11 YEARS	12 YEARS	13 YEARS	14 YEARS
$ 25	.44	.40	.36	.33	.31	.29	.28	.26	.25
50	.88	.79	.71	.66	.61	.58	.55	.52	.50
75	1.32	1.18	1.07	.99	.92	.87	.82	.78	.75
100	1.76	1.57	1.42	1.31	1.22	1.15	1.09	1.04	1.00
200	3.52	3.13	2.84	2.62	2.44	2.30	2.18	2.08	2.00
300	5.28	4.70	4.26	3.93	3.66	3.45	3.27	3.12	3.00
400	7.04	6.26	5.68	5.24	4.88	4.60	4.36	4.16	4.00
500	8.80	7.83	7.10	6.54	6.10	5.74	5.45	5.20	4.99
600	10.56	9.39	8.52	7.85	7.32	6.89	6.54	6.24	5.99
700	12.32	10.95	9.94	9.16	8.54	8.04	7.63	7.28	6.99
800	14.08	12.52	11.36	10.47	9.76	9.19	8.71	8.32	7.99
900	15.83	14.08	12.78	11.77	10.98	10.33	9.80	9.36	8.98
1000	17.59	15.65	14.20	13.08	12.20	11.48	10.89	10.40	9.98
2000	35.18	31.29	28.39	26.16	24.30	22.96	21.78	20.79	19.96
3000	52.77	46.93	42.59	39.24	36.58	34.43	32.66	31.18	29.94
4000	70.36	62.57	56.78	52.31	48.77	45.91	43.55	41.58	39.91
5000	87.94	78.21	70.97	65.39	60.96	57.38	54.43	51.97	49.89
6000	105.53	93.86	85.17	78.47	73.16	68.86	65.32	62.36	59.87
7000	123.12	109.50	99.36	91.54	85.35	80.33	76.21	72.76	69.84
8000	140.71	125.14	113.55	104.62	97.54	91.81	87.09	83.15	79.82
9000	158.30	140.78	127.75	117.70	109.73	103.29	97.98	93.54	89.80
10000	175.88	156.42	141.94	130.77	121.92	114.76	108.86	103.94	99.77
15000	263.82	234.63	212.91	196.16	182.88	172.14	163.29	155.90	149.66
20000	351.76	312.84	283.88	261.54	243.84	229.52	217.72	207.87	199.54
25000	439.70	391.05	354.84	326.92	304.80	286.90	272.15	259.83	249.42
30000	527.64	469.26	425.81	392.31	365.76	344.27	326.58	311.80	299.31
35000	615.58	547.47	496.78	457.69	426.72	401.65	381.01	363.77	349.19
36000	633.17	563.11	510.97	470.77	438.91	413.13	391.90	374.16	359.17
37000	650.75	578.76	525.16	483.84	451.10	424.60	402.78	384.55	369.14
38000	668.34	594.40	539.36	496.92	463.30	436.08	413.67	394.95	379.12
39000	685.93	610.04	553.55	510.00	475.49	447.56	424.55	405.34	389.10
40000	703.52	625.68	567.75	523.07	487.68	459.03	435.44	415.73	399.07
41000	721.11	641.32	581.94	536.15	499.87	470.51	446.32	426.12	409.05
42000	738.69	656.97	596.13	549.23	512.06	481.98	457.21	436.52	419.03
43000	756.28	672.61	610.33	562.30	524.25	493.46	468.10	446.91	429.00
44000	773.87	688.25	624.52	575.38	536.45	504.93	478.98	457.30	438.98
45000	791.46	703.89	638.71	588.46	548.64	516.41	489.87	467.70	448.96
46000	809.04	719.53	652.91	601.53	560.83	527.89	500.75	478.09	458.93
47000	826.63	735.17	667.10	614.61	573.02	539.36	511.64	488.48	468.91
48000	844.22	750.82	681.29	627.69	585.21	550.84	522.53	498.88	478.89
49000	861.81	766.46	695.49	640.76	597.41	562.31	533.41	509.27	488.86
50000	879.40	782.10	709.68	653.84	609.60	573.79	544.30	519.66	498.84
51000	896.98	797.74	723.87	666.92	621.79	585.26	555.18	530.06	508.82
52000	914.57	813.38	738.07	679.99	633.98	596.74	566.07	540.45	518.79
53000	932.16	829.03	752.26	693.07	646.17	608.22	576.96	550.84	528.77
54000	949.75	844.67	766.45	706.15	658.36	619.69	587.84	561.24	538.75
55000	967.34	860.31	780.65	719.22	670.56	631.17	598.73	571.63	548.72
56000	984.92	875.95	794.84	732.30	682.75	642.64	609.61	582.02	558.70
57000	1002.51	891.59	809.03	745.38	694.94	654.12	620.50	592.42	568.68
58000	1020.10	907.24	823.23	758.45	707.13	665.59	631.38	602.81	578.65
59000	1037.69	922.88	837.42	771.53	719.32	677.07	642.27	613.20	588.63
60000	1055.27	938.52	851.62	784.61	731.52	688.54	653.16	623.59	598.61
61000	1072.86	954.16	865.81	797.68	743.71	700.02	664.04	633.99	608.58
62000	1090.45	969.80	880.00	810.76	755.90	711.50	674.93	644.38	618.56
63000	1108.04	985.45	894.20	823.84	768.09	722.97	685.81	654.77	628.54
64000	1125.63	1001.09	908.39	836.91	780.28	734.45	696.70	665.17	638.51
65000	1143.21	1016.73	922.58	849.99	792.48	745.92	707.59	675.56	648.49
66000	1160.80	1032.37	936.78	863.07	804.67	757.40	718.47	685.95	658.47
67000	1178.39	1048.01	950.97	876.14	816.86	768.87	729.36	696.35	668.44
68000	1195.98	1063.65	965.16	889.22	829.05	780.35	740.24	706.74	678.42
69000	1213.56	1079.30	979.36	902.30	841.24	791.83	751.13	717.13	688.40
70000	1231.15	1094.94	993.55	915.37	853.43	803.30	762.01	727.53	698.37
75000	1319.09	1173.15	1064.52	980.76	914.39	860.68	816.44	779.49	748.26
80000	1407.03	1251.36	1135.49	1046.14	975.35	918.06	870.87	831.46	798.14
100000	1758.79	1564.20	1419.36	1307.67	1219.19	1147.57	1088.59	1039.32	997.67

8¼%   MONTHLY PAYMENT
NECESSARY TO AMORTIZE A LOAN

TERM AMOUNT	15 YEARS	16 YEARS	17 YEARS	18 YEARS	19 YEARS	20 YEARS	21 YEARS	22 YEARS	23 YEARS
$ 25	.25	.24	.23	.23	.22	.22	.21	.21	.21
50	.49	.47	.46	.45	.44	.43	.42	.41	.41
75	.73	.70	.68	.67	.65	.64	.63	.61	.61
100	.97	.94	.91	.89	.87	.85	.83	.82	.81
200	1.93	1.87	1.81	1.77	1.73	1.69	1.66	1.63	1.61
300	2.89	2.80	2.72	2.65	2.59	2.54	2.49	2.44	2.41
400	3.85	3.73	3.62	3.53	3.45	3.38	3.31	3.26	3.21
500	4.82	4.66	4.53	4.41	4.31	4.22	4.14	4.07	4.01
600	5.78	5.59	5.43	5.30	5.17	5.07	4.97	4.88	4.81
700	6.74	6.53	6.34	6.18	6.03	5.91	5.80	5.70	5.61
800	7.70	7.46	7.24	7.06	6.90	6.75	6.62	6.51	6.41
900	8.66	8.39	8.15	7.94	7.76	7.60	7.45	7.32	7.21
1000	9.63	9.32	9.05	8.82	8.62	8.44	8.28	8.14	8.01
2000	19.25	18.63	18.10	17.64	17.23	16.87	16.55	16.27	16.02
3000	28.87	27.95	27.15	26.46	25.85	25.31	24.83	24.40	24.03
4000	38.49	37.26	36.20	35.27	34.46	33.74	33.10	32.54	32.03
5000	48.11	46.58	45.25	44.09	43.07	42.18	41.38	40.67	40.04
6000	57.73	55.89	54.30	52.91	51.69	50.61	49.65	48.80	48.05
7000	67.35	65.21	63.35	61.73	60.30	59.04	57.93	56.94	56.05
8000	76.97	74.52	72.40	70.54	68.91	67.48	66.20	65.07	64.06
9000	86.59	83.84	81.45	79.36	77.53	75.91	74.48	73.20	72.07
10000	96.22	93.15	90.50	88.18	86.14	84.35	82.75	81.34	80.07
15000	144.32	139.73	135.74	132.26	129.21	126.52	124.13	122.00	120.11
20000	192.43	186.30	180.99	176.35	172.28	168.69	165.50	162.67	160.14
25000	240.53	232.88	226.24	220.44	215.35	210.86	206.88	203.34	200.18
30000	288.64	279.45	271.48	264.52	258.42	253.03	248.25	244.00	240.21
35000	336.74	326.03	316.73	308.61	301.48	295.20	289.63	284.67	280.25
36000	346.36	335.34	325.78	317.43	310.10	303.63	297.90	292.80	288.25
37000	355.99	344.66	334.83	326.25	318.71	312.06	306.17	300.94	296.26
38000	365.61	353.97	343.88	335.06	327.32	320.50	314.45	309.07	304.27
39000	375.23	363.29	352.93	343.88	335.94	328.93	322.72	317.20	312.28
40000	384.85	372.60	361.97	352.70	344.55	337.37	331.00	325.34	320.28
41000	394.47	381.92	371.02	361.51	353.17	345.80	339.27	333.47	328.29
42000	404.09	391.23	380.07	370.33	361.78	354.23	347.55	341.60	336.30
43000	413.71	400.54	389.12	379.15	370.39	362.67	355.82	349.74	344.30
44000	423.33	409.86	398.17	387.97	379.01	371.10	364.10	357.87	352.31
45000	432.95	419.17	407.22	396.78	387.62	379.54	372.37	366.00	360.32
46000	442.58	428.49	416.27	405.60	396.23	387.97	380.65	374.14	368.32
47000	452.20	437.80	425.32	414.42	404.85	396.40	388.92	382.27	376.33
48000	461.82	447.12	434.37	423.24	413.46	404.84	397.20	390.40	384.34
49000	471.44	456.43	443.42	432.05	422.08	413.27	405.47	398.54	392.34
50000	481.06	465.75	452.47	440.87	430.69	421.71	413.75	406.67	400.35
51000	490.68	475.06	461.52	449.69	439.30	430.14	422.02	414.80	408.36
52000	500.30	484.38	470.57	458.50	447.92	438.57	430.30	422.94	416.37
53000	509.92	493.69	479.61	467.32	456.53	447.01	438.57	431.07	424.37
54000	519.54	503.01	488.66	476.14	465.14	455.44	446.85	439.20	432.38
55000	529.17	512.32	497.71	484.96	473.76	463.88	455.12	447.34	440.39
56000	538.79	521.64	506.76	493.77	482.37	472.31	463.40	455.47	448.39
57000	548.41	530.95	515.81	502.59	490.98	480.75	471.67	463.60	456.40
58000	558.03	540.27	524.86	511.41	499.60	489.18	479.95	471.74	464.41
59000	567.65	549.58	533.91	520.23	508.21	497.61	488.22	479.87	472.41
60000	577.27	558.90	542.96	529.04	516.83	506.05	496.50	488.00	480.42
61000	586.89	568.21	552.01	537.86	525.44	514.48	504.77	496.14	488.43
62000	596.51	577.53	561.06	546.68	534.05	522.92	513.05	504.27	496.43
63000	606.13	586.84	570.11	555.50	542.67	531.35	521.32	512.40	504.44
64000	615.76	596.16	579.16	564.31	551.28	539.78	529.60	520.54	512.45
65000	625.38	605.47	588.21	573.13	559.89	548.22	537.87	528.67	520.46
66000	635.00	614.79	597.25	581.95	568.51	556.65	546.15	536.80	528.46
67000	644.62	624.10	606.30	590.76	577.12	565.09	554.42	544.93	536.47
68000	654.24	633.42	615.35	599.58	585.74	573.52	562.70	553.07	544.48
69000	663.86	642.73	624.40	608.40	594.35	501.95	570.97	561.20	552.48
70000	673.48	652.05	633.45	617.22	602.96	590.39	579.25	569.33	560.49
75000	721.59	698.62	678.70	661.30	646.03	632.56	620.62	610.00	600.52
80000	769.69	745.20	723.94	705.39	689.05	674.73	661.99	650.67	640.56
100000	962.12	931.49	904.93	881.74	861.37	843.41	827.49	813.33	800.70

26

MONTHLY PAYMENT 8¼%
NECESSARY TO AMORTIZE A LOAN

TERM AMOUNT	24 YEARS	25 YEARS	26 YEARS	27 YEARS	28 YEARS	29 YEARS	30 YEARS	35 YEARS	40 YEARS
$ 25	.20	.20	.20	.20	.19	.19	.19	.18	.18
50	.40	.39	.39	.39	.38	.38	.38	.36	.36
75	.60	.59	.58	.58	.57	.57	.57	.54	.53
100	.79	.78	.78	.77	.76	.75	.75	.72	.71
200	1.58	1.56	1.55	1.53	1.51	1.50	1.49	1.44	1.41
300	2.37	2.34	2.32	2.29	2.27	2.25	2.23	2.16	2.12
400	3.16	3.12	3.09	3.05	3.02	3.00	2.97	2.88	2.82
500	3.95	3.90	3.86	3.81	3.78	3.74	3.71	3.60	3.52
600	4.74	4.68	4.63	4.58	4.53	4.49	4.45	4.32	4.23
700	5.53	5.46	5.40	5.34	5.29	5.24	5.20	5.03	4.93
800	6.32	6.24	6.17	6.10	6.04	5.99	5.94	5.75	5.63
900	7.11	7.02	6.94	6.86	6.79	6.73	6.68	6.47	6.34
1000	7.90	7.80	7.71	7.62	7.55	7.48	7.42	7.19	7.04
2000	15.79	15.59	15.41	15.24	15.09	14.96	14.84	14.37	14.08
3000	23.69	23.38	23.11	22.86	22.64	22.44	22.25	21.56	21.12
4000	31.58	31.17	30.81	30.48	30.18	29.91	29.67	28.74	28.15
5000	39.47	38.97	38.51	38.10	37.73	37.39	37.08	35.92	35.19
6000	47.37	46.76	46.21	45.72	45.27	44.87	44.50	43.11	42.23
7000	55.26	54.55	53.91	53.33	52.81	52.34	51.91	50.29	49.26
8000	63.16	62.34	61.61	60.95	60.36	59.82	59.33	57.48	56.30
9000	71.05	70.14	69.31	68.57	67.90	67.30	66.75	64.66	63.34
10000	78.94	77.93	77.01	76.19	75.45	74.77	74.16	71.84	70.38
15000	118.41	116.89	115.52	114.28	113.17	112.16	111.24	107.76	105.56
20000	157.88	155.85	154.02	152.38	150.89	149.54	148.32	143.68	140.75
25000	197.35	194.81	192.53	190.47	188.61	186.92	185.40	179.60	175.93
30000	236.82	233.77	231.03	228.56	226.33	224.31	222.47	215.52	211.12
35000	276.29	272.74	269.54	266.65	264.05	261.69	259.55	251.44	246.30
36000	284.18	280.53	277.24	274.27	271.59	269.17	266.97	258.62	253.34
37000	292.08	288.32	284.94	281.89	279.14	276.64	274.38	265.81	260.38
38000	299.97	296.11	292.64	289.51	286.68	284.12	281.80	272.99	267.41
39000	307.86	303.90	300.34	297.13	294.23	291.60	289.22	280.18	274.45
40000	315.76	311.70	308.04	304.75	301.77	299.07	296.63	287.36	281.49
41000	323.65	319.49	315.74	312.37	309.31	306.55	304.05	294.54	288.52
42000	331.55	327.28	323.44	319.98	316.86	314.03	311.46	301.73	295.56
43000	339.44	335.07	331.15	327.60	324.40	321.50	318.88	308.91	302.60
44000	347.33	342.87	338.85	335.22	331.95	328.98	326.29	316.10	309.64
45000	355.23	350.66	346.55	342.84	339.49	336.46	333.71	323.28	316.67
46000	363.12	358.45	354.25	350.46	347.03	343.93	341.12	330.46	323.71
47000	371.01	366.24	361.95	358.08	354.58	351.41	348.54	337.65	330.75
48000	378.91	374.03	369.65	365.70	362.12	358.89	355.96	344.83	337.78
49000	386.80	381.83	377.35	373.31	369.67	366.36	363.37	352.01	344.82
50000	394.70	389.62	385.05	380.93	377.21	373.84	370.79	359.20	351.86
51000	402.59	397.41	392.75	388.55	384.75	381.32	378.20	366.38	358.89
52000	410.48	405.20	400.45	396.17	392.30	388.80	385.62	373.57	365.93
53000	418.38	413.00	408.15	403.79	399.84	396.27	393.03	380.75	372.97
54000	426.27	420.79	415.86	411.41	407.39	403.75	400.45	387.93	380.01
55000	434.16	428.58	423.56	419.03	414.93	411.23	407.87	395.12	387.04
56000	442.06	436.37	431.26	426.64	422.48	418.70	415.28	402.30	394.08
57000	449.95	444.17	438.96	434.26	430.02	426.18	422.70	409.49	401.12
58000	457.85	451.96	446.66	441.88	437.56	433.66	430.11	416.67	408.15
59000	465.74	459.75	454.36	449.50	445.11	441.13	437.53	423.85	415.19
60000	473.63	467.54	462.06	457.12	452.65	448.61	444.94	431.04	422.23
61000	481.53	475.33	469.76	464.74	460.20	456.09	452.36	438.22	429.27
62000	489.42	483.13	477.46	472.36	467.74	463.56	459.78	445.40	436.30
63000	497.32	490.92	485.16	479.97	475.28	471.04	467.19	452.59	443.34
64000	505.21	498.71	492.86	487.59	482.83	478.52	474.61	459.77	450.38
65000	513.10	506.50	500.57	495.21	490.37	485.99	482.02	466.96	457.41
66000	521.00	514.30	508.27	502.83	497.92	493.47	489.44	474.14	464.45
67000	528.89	522.09	515.97	510.45	505.46	500.95	496.85	481.32	471.49
68000	536.78	529.88	523.67	518.07	513.00	508.42	504.27	488.51	478.52
69000	544.68	537.67	531.37	525.68	520.55	515.90	511.68	495.69	485.56
70000	552.57	545.47	539.07	533.30	528.09	523.38	519.10	502.88	492.60
75000	592.04	584.43	577.57	571.40	565.81	560.76	556.18	538.80	527.78
80000	631.51	623.39	616.08	609.49	603.53	598.14	593.26	574.71	562.97
100000	789.39	779.23	770.10	761.86	754.42	747.68	741.57	718.39	703.71

27

8½%
MONTHLY PAYMENT
NECESSARY TO AMORTIZE A LOAN

TERM AMOUNT	1 YEAR	1½ YEARS	2 YEARS	2½ YEARS	3 YEARS	3½ YEARS	4 YEARS	4½ YEARS	5 YEARS
$ 25	2.18	1.49	1.14	.93	.79	.69	.62	.56	.52
50	4.36	2.97	2.27	1.86	1.58	.98	1.23	1.12	1.03
75	6.54	4.45	3.41	2.78	2.37	2.07	1.85	1.68	1.54
100	8.72	5.94	4.54	3.71	3.15	2.76	2.46	2.23	2.05
200	17.44	11.87	9.08	7.42	6.30	5.51	4.92	4.46	4.09
300	26.15	17.80	13.62	11.12	9.45	8.27	7.38	6.69	6.14
400	34.87	23.73	18.16	14.83	12.60	11.02	9.84	8.92	8.18
500	43.58	29.66	22.70	18.53	15.75	13.78	12.29	11.15	10.23
600	52.30	35.59	27.24	22.24	18.90	16.53	14.75	13.37	12.27
700	61.01	41.52	31.78	25.94	22.05	19.28	17.21	15.60	14.32
800	69.73	47.45	36.32	29.65	25.20	22.04	19.67	17.83	16.36
900	78.44	53.38	40.85	33.35	28.35	24.79	22.13	20.06	18.41
1000	87.16	59.31	45.39	37.06	31.50	27.55	24.58	22.29	20.45
2000	174.31	118.61	90.78	74.11	63.00	55.09	49.16	44.57	40.90
3000	261.46	177.91	136.17	111.16	94.50	82.63	73.74	66.85	61.34
4000	348.61	237.21	181.56	148.21	126.00	110.17	98.32	89.13	81.79
5000	435.76	296.51	226.95	185.26	157.50	137.71	122.90	111.41	102.23
6000	522.92	355.81	272.34	222.31	189.00	165.25	147.48	133.69	122.68
7000	610.07	415.12	317.73	259.36	220.50	192.80	172.06	155.97	143.13
8000	697.22	474.42	363.11	296.41	252.00	220.34	196.64	178.25	163.57
9000	784.37	533.72	408.50	333.46	283.50	247.88	221.22	200.53	184.02
10000	871.52	593.02	453.89	370.51	315.00	275.42	245.80	222.81	204.46
15000	1307.28	889.53	680.83	555.76	472.50	413.13	368.69	334.21	306.69
20000	1743.04	1186.04	907.78	741.01	630.00	550.84	491.59	445.61	408.92
25000	2178.80	1482.55	1134.72	926.26	787.49	688.55	614.48	557.01	511.15
30000	2614.56	1779.05	1361.66	1111.52	944.99	826.25	737.38	668.41	613.38
35000	3050.32	2075.56	1588.61	1296.77	1102.49	963.96	860.27	779.81	715.61
36000	3137.47	2134.86	1633.99	1333.82	1133.99	991.50	884.85	802.09	736.06
37000	3224.62	2194.17	1679.38	1370.87	1165.49	1019.04	909.43	824.37	756.50
38000	3311.78	2253.47	1724.77	1407.92	1196.99	1046.59	934.01	846.65	776.95
39000	3398.93	2312.77	1770.16	1444.97	1228.49	1074.13	958.59	868.93	797.39
40000	3486.08	2372.07	1815.55	1482.02	1259.99	1101.67	983.17	891.21	817.84
41000	3573.23	2431.37	1860.94	1519.07	1291.49	1129.21	1007.75	913.49	838.29
42000	3660.38	2490.67	1906.33	1556.12	1322.99	1156.75	1032.33	935.77	858.73
43000	3747.53	2549.98	1951.71	1593.17	1354.49	1184.29	1056.91	958.05	879.18
44000	3834.69	2609.28	1997.10	1630.22	1385.99	1211.84	1081.48	980.33	899.62
45000	3921.84	2668.58	2042.49	1667.27	1417.49	1239.38	1106.06	1002.61	920.07
46000	4008.99	2727.88	2087.88	1704.32	1448.99	1266.92	1130.64	1024.90	940.52
47000	4096.14	2787.18	2133.27	1741.37	1480.49	1294.46	1155.22	1047.18	960.96
48000	4183.29	2846.48	2178.66	1778.42	1511.99	1322.00	1179.80	1069.46	981.41
49000	4270.45	2905.79	2224.05	1815.47	1543.49	1349.54	1204.38	1091.74	1001.85
50000	4357.60	2965.09	2269.43	1852.52	1574.98	1377.09	1228.96	1114.02	1022.30
51000	4444.75	3024.39	2314.82	1889.57	1606.48	1404.63	1253.54	1136.30	1042.75
52000	4531.90	3083.69	2360.21	1926.62	1637.98	1432.17	1278.12	1158.58	1063.19
53000	4619.05	3142.99	2405.60	1963.68	1669.48	1459.71	1302.70	1180.86	1083.64
54000	4706.21	3202.29	2450.99	2000.73	1700.98	1487.25	1327.28	1203.14	1104.08
55000	4793.36	3261.60	2496.38	2037.78	1732.48	1514.79	1351.85	1225.42	1124.53
56000	4880.51	3320.90	2541.77	2074.83	1763.98	1542.33	1376.43	1247.70	1144.97
57000	4967.66	3380.20	2587.15	2111.88	1795.48	1569.88	1401.01	1269.98	1165.42
58000	5054.81	3439.50	2632.54	2148.93	1826.98	1597.42	1425.59	1292.26	1185.87
59000	5141.96	3498.80	2677.93	2185.98	1858.48	1624.96	1450.17	1314.54	1206.31
60000	5229.12	3558.10	2723.32	2223.03	1889.98	1652.50	1474.75	1336.82	1226.76
61000	5316.27	3617.41	2768.71	2260.08	1921.48	1680.04	1499.33	1359.10	1247.20
62000	5403.42	3676.71	2814.10	2297.13	1952.98	1707.58	1523.91	1381.38	1267.65
63000	5490.57	3736.01	2859.49	2334.18	1984.48	1735.13	1548.49	1403.66	1288.10
64000	5577.72	3795.31	2904.87	2371.23	2015.98	1762.67	1573.07	1425.94	1308.54
65000	5664.88	3854.61	2950.26	2408.28	2047.48	1790.21	1597.65	1448.22	1328.99
66000	5752.03	3913.91	2995.65	2445.33	2078.98	1817.75	1622.22	1470.50	1349.43
67000	5839.18	3973.21	3041.04	2482.38	2110.48	1845.29	1646.80	1492.78	1369.88
68000	5926.33	4032.52	3086.43	2519.43	2141.98	1872.83	1671.38	1515.06	1390.33
69000	6013.48	4091.82	3131.82	2556.48	2173.48	1900.38	1695.96	1537.34	1410.77
70000	6100.63	4151.12	3177.21	2593.53	2204.98	1927.92	1720.54	1559.62	1431.22
75000	6536.39	4447.63	3404.15	2778.78	2362.47	2065.63	1843.44	1671.02	1533.45
80000	6972.15	4744.14	3631.09	2964.04	2519.97	2203.33	1966.33	1782.42	1635.68
100000	8715.19	5930.17	4538.86	3705.04	3149.96	2754.17	2457.91	2228.03	2044.59

28

MONTHLY PAYMENT 8½%
NECESSARY TO AMORTIZE A LOAN

TERM AMOUNT	6 YEARS	7 YEARS	8 YEARS	9 YEARS	10 YEARS	11 YEARS	12 YEARS	13 YEARS	14 YEARS
$ 25	.45	.40	.36	.34	.31	.30	.28	.27	.26
50	.89	.79	.72	.67	.62	.59	.56	.53	.51
75	1.33	1.19	1.08	1.00	.93	.88	.83	.79	.76
100	1.78	1.58	1.44	1.33	1.24	1.17	1.11	1.06	1.02
200	3.55	3.16	2.87	2.65	2.47	2.33	2.21	2.11	2.03
300	5.32	4.73	4.30	3.97	3.70	3.49	3.31	3.16	3.04
400	7.09	6.31	5.73	5.29	4.93	4.65	4.41	4.22	4.05
500	8.86	7.89	7.16	6.61	6.17	5.81	5.51	5.27	5.06
600	10.63	9.46	8.60	7.93	7.40	6.97	6.62	6.32	6.07
700	12.40	11.04	10.03	9.25	8.63	8.13	7.72	7.38	7.09
800	14.17	12.62	11.46	10.57	9.86	9.29	8.82	8.43	8.10
900	15.94	14.19	12.89	11.89	11.09	10.45	9.92	9.48	9.11
1000	17.71	15.77	14.32	13.21	12.33	11.61	11.02	10.53	10.12
2000	35.42	31.53	28.64	26.41	24.65	23.22	22.04	21.06	20.23
3000	53.12	47.29	42.96	39.61	36.97	34.82	33.06	31.59	30.35
4000	70.83	63.06	57.27	52.82	49.29	46.43	44.08	42.12	40.46
5000	88.54	78.82	71.59	66.02	61.61	58.04	55.10	52.65	50.58
6000	106.24	94.58	85.91	79.22	73.93	69.64	66.12	63.18	60.69
7000	123.95	110.34	100.22	92.42	86.25	81.25	77.14	73.71	70.81
8000	141.65	126.11	114.54	105.63	98.57	92.86	88.16	84.24	80.92
9000	159.36	141.87	128.86	118.83	110.89	104.46	99.18	94.77	91.04
10000	177.07	157.63	143.17	132.03	123.21	116.07	110.20	105.29	101.15
15000	265.60	236.45	214.76	198.04	184.81	174.10	165.29	157.94	151.73
20000	354.13	315.26	286.34	264.06	246.41	232.14	220.39	210.58	202.30
25000	442.66	394.08	357.93	330.07	308.01	290.17	275.48	263.23	252.88
30000	531.19	472.89	429.51	396.08	369.61	348.20	330.58	315.87	303.45
35000	619.72	551.70	501.10	462.09	431.21	406.23	385.68	368.52	354.02
36000	637.43	567.47	515.41	475.30	443.53	417.84	396.69	379.05	364.14
37000	655.14	583.23	529.73	488.50	455.85	429.45	407.71	389.57	374.25
38000	672.84	598.99	544.05	501.70	468.17	441.05	418.73	400.10	384.37
39000	690.55	614.75	558.36	514.91	480.49	452.66	429.75	410.63	394.48
40000	708.25	630.52	572.68	528.11	492.81	464.27	440.77	421.16	404.60
41000	725.96	646.28	587.00	541.31	505.13	475.87	451.79	431.69	414.71
42000	743.67	662.04	601.31	554.51	517.45	487.48	462.81	442.22	424.83
43000	761.37	677.81	615.63	567.72	529.78	499.09	473.83	452.75	434.94
44000	779.08	693.57	629.95	580.92	542.10	510.69	484.85	463.28	445.06
45000	796.79	709.33	644.27	594.12	554.42	522.30	495.87	473.81	455.17
46000	814.49	725.09	658.58	607.32	566.74	533.90	506.89	484.33	465.29
47000	832.20	740.86	672.90	620.53	579.06	545.51	517.91	494.86	475.40
48000	849.90	756.62	687.22	633.73	591.38	557.12	528.92	505.39	485.52
49000	867.61	772.38	701.53	646.93	603.70	568.72	539.94	515.92	495.63
50000	885.32	788.15	715.85	660.13	616.02	580.33	550.96	526.45	505.75
51000	903.02	803.91	730.17	673.34	628.34	591.94	561.98	536.98	515.86
52000	920.73	819.67	744.48	686.54	640.66	603.54	573.00	547.51	525.98
53000	938.44	835.43	758.80	699.74	652.98	615.15	584.02	558.04	536.09
54000	956.14	851.20	773.12	712.94	665.30	626.76	595.04	568.57	546.21
55000	973.85	866.96	787.43	726.15	677.62	638.36	606.06	579.09	556.32
56000	991.55	882.72	801.75	739.35	689.94	649.97	617.08	589.62	566.43
57000	1009.26	898.48	816.07	752.55	702.26	661.58	628.10	600.15	576.55
58000	1026.97	914.25	830.38	765.75	714.58	673.18	639.12	610.68	586.66
59000	1044.67	930.01	844.70	778.96	726.90	684.79	650.14	621.21	596.78
60000	1062.38	945.77	859.02	792.16	739.22	696.40	661.15	631.74	606.89
61000	1080.09	961.54	873.34	805.36	751.54	708.00	672.17	642.27	617.01
62000	1097.79	977.30	887.65	818.56	763.86	719.61	683.19	652.80	627.12
63000	1115.50	993.06	901.97	831.77	776.18	731.22	694.21	663.33	637.24
64000	1133.20	1008.82	916.29	844.97	788.50	742.82	705.23	673.85	647.35
65000	1150.91	1024.59	930.60	858.17	800.82	754.43	716.25	684.38	657.47
66000	1168.62	1040.35	944.92	871.37	813.14	766.04	727.27	694.91	667.58
67000	1186.32	1056.11	959.24	884.58	825.46	777.64	738.29	705.44	677.70
68000	1204.03	1071.88	973.55	897.78	837.78	789.25	749.31	715.97	687.81
69000	1221.74	1087.64	987.87	910.98	850.10	800.85	760.33	726.50	697.93
70000	1239.44	1103.40	1002.19	924.18	862.42	812.46	771.35	737.03	708.04
75000	1327.97	1182.22	1073.77	990.20	924.02	870.49	826.44	789.67	758.62
80000	1416.50	1261.03	1145.36	1056.21	985.62	928.53	881.54	842.32	809.19
100000	1770.63	1576.29	1431.69	1320.26	1232.03	1160.66	1101.92	1052.90	1011.49

29

8½% MONTHLY PAYMENT
NECESSARY TO AMORTIZE A LOAN

TERM AMOUNT	15 YEARS	16 YEARS	17 YEARS	18 YEARS	19 YEARS	20 YEARS	21 YEARS	22 YEARS	23 YEARS
$ 25	.25	.24	.23	.23	.22	.22	.22	.21	.21
50	.49	.48	.46	.45	.44	.43	.43	.42	.41
75	.74	.71	.69	.68	.66	.65	.64	.63	.62
100	.98	.95	.92	.90	.88	.86	.85	.83	.82
200	1.96	1.90	1.84	1.80	1.76	1.72	1.69	1.66	1.64
300	2.93	2.84	2.76	2.69	2.63	2.58	2.53	2.49	2.45
400	3.91	3.79	3.68	3.59	3.51	3.44	3.38	3.32	3.27
500	4.89	4.73	4.60	4.49	4.39	4.30	4.22	4.15	4.09
600	5.86	5.68	5.52	5.38	5.26	5.16	5.06	4.98	4.90
700	6.84	6.63	6.44	6.28	6.14	6.01	5.90	5.81	5.72
800	7.81	7.57	7.36	7.18	7.02	6.87	6.75	6.64	6.54
900	8.79	8.52	8.28	8.07	7.89	7.73	7.59	7.47	7.35
1000	9.77	9.46	9.20	8.97	8.77	8.59	8.43	8.29	8.17
2000	19.53	18.92	18.39	17.93	17.53	17.18	16.86	16.58	16.33
3000	29.29	28.38	27.59	26.90	26.29	25.76	25.29	24.87	24.50
4000	39.05	37.84	36.78	35.86	35.05	34.35	33.72	33.16	32.66
5000	48.81	47.29	45.98	44.83	43.82	42.93	42.15	41.45	40.83
6000	58.57	56.75	55.17	53.79	52.58	51.52	50.58	49.74	48.99
7000	68.34	66.21	64.36	62.76	61.35	60.10	59.00	58.03	57.16
8000	78.10	75.67	73.56	71.72	70.11	68.69	67.43	66.32	65.32
9000	87.86	85.12	82.75	80.69	78.87	77.28	75.86	74.61	73.49
10000	97.62	94.58	91.95	89.65	87.64	85.86	84.29	82.89	81.65
15000	146.43	141.87	137.92	134.47	131.45	128.79	126.43	124.34	122.47
20000	195.24	189.16	183.89	179.30	175.27	171.72	168.57	165.78	163.30
25000	244.04	236.45	229.86	224.12	219.08	214.64	210.72	207.23	204.12
30000	292.85	283.74	275.83	268.94	262.90	257.57	252.86	248.67	244.94
35000	341.66	331.02	321.80	313.76	306.71	300.50	295.00	290.12	285.76
36000	351.42	340.48	331.00	322.73	315.48	309.09	303.43	298.41	293.93
37000	361.18	349.94	340.19	331.69	324.24	317.67	311.86	306.69	302.09
38000	370.94	359.40	349.39	340.66	333.00	326.26	320.29	314.98	310.26
39000	380.71	368.85	358.58	349.62	341.77	334.84	328.72	323.27	318.42
40000	390.47	378.31	367.78	358.59	350.53	343.43	337.14	331.56	326.59
41000	400.23	387.77	376.97	367.55	359.29	352.01	345.57	339.85	334.75
42000	409.99	397.23	386.16	376.52	368.06	360.60	354.00	348.14	342.91
43000	419.75	406.68	395.36	385.48	376.82	369.19	362.43	356.43	351.08
44000	429.51	416.14	404.55	394.45	385.58	377.77	370.86	364.72	359.24
45000	439.28	425.60	413.75	403.41	394.35	386.36	379.29	373.01	367.41
46000	449.04	435.06	422.94	412.38	403.11	394.94	387.72	381.30	375.57
47000	458.80	444.52	432.14	421.34	411.87	403.53	396.14	389.58	383.74
48000	468.56	453.97	441.33	430.30	420.63	412.11	404.57	397.87	391.90
49000	478.32	463.43	450.52	439.27	429.40	420.70	413.00	406.16	400.07
50000	488.08	472.89	459.72	448.23	438.16	429.28	421.43	414.45	408.23
51000	497.85	482.35	468.91	457.20	446.92	437.87	429.86	422.74	416.40
52000	507.61	491.80	478.11	466.16	455.69	446.46	438.29	431.03	424.56
53000	517.37	501.26	487.30	475.13	464.45	455.04	446.71	439.32	432.72
54000	527.13	510.72	496.50	484.09	473.21	463.63	455.14	447.61	440.89
55000	536.89	520.18	505.69	493.06	481.98	472.21	463.57	455.90	449.05
56000	546.65	529.63	514.88	502.02	490.74	480.80	472.00	464.18	457.22
57000	556.41	539.09	524.08	510.99	499.50	489.38	480.43	472.47	465.38
58000	566.18	548.55	533.27	519.95	508.27	497.97	488.86	480.76	473.55
59000	575.94	558.01	542.47	528.91	517.03	506.55	497.29	489.05	481.71
60000	585.70	567.47	551.66	537.88	525.79	515.14	505.71	497.34	489.88
61000	595.46	576.92	560.86	546.84	534.56	523.73	514.14	505.63	498.04
62000	605.22	586.38	570.05	555.81	543.32	532.31	522.57	513.92	506.21
63000	614.98	595.84	579.24	564.77	552.08	540.90	531.00	522.21	514.37
64000	624.75	605.30	588.44	573.74	560.84	549.48	539.43	530.50	522.53
65000	634.51	614.75	597.63	582.70	569.61	558.07	547.86	538.78	530.70
66000	644.27	624.21	606.83	591.67	578.37	566.65	556.28	547.07	538.86
67000	654.03	633.67	616.02	600.63	587.13	575.24	564.71	555.36	547.03
68000	663.79	643.13	625.22	609.60	595.90	583.83	573.14	563.65	555.19
69000	673.55	652.58	634.41	618.56	604.66	592.41	581.57	571.94	563.36
70000	683.32	662.04	643.60	627.52	613.42	601.00	590.00	580.23	571.52
75000	732.12	709.33	689.58	672.35	657.24	643.92	632.14	621.67	612.34
80000	780.93	756.62	735.55	717.17	701.05	686.85	674.28	663.12	653.17
100000	976.16	945.77	919.43	896.46	876.32	858.56	842.85	828.90	816.46

30

TERM AMOUNT	24 YEARS	25 YEARS	26 YEARS	27 YEARS	28 YEARS	29 YEARS	30 YEARS	35 YEARS	40 YEARS
$ 25	.21	.20	.20	.20	.20	.20	.19	.19	.19
50	.41	.40	.40	.39	.39	.39	.38	.37	.37
75	.61	.60	.60	.59	.59	.58	.58	.57	.55
100	.81	.80	.79	.78	.78	.77	.76	.74	.73
200	1.62	1.60	1.58	1.56	1.55	1.53	1.52	1.48	1.45
300	2.42	2.39	2.36	2.34	2.32	2.30	2.28	2.21	2.17
400	3.23	3.19	3.15	3.12	3.09	3.06	3.04	2.95	2.89
500	4.03	3.98	3.94	3.90	3.86	3.83	3.80	3.69	3.61
600	4.84	4.78	4.72	4.68	4.63	4.59	4.56	4.42	4.34
700	5.64	5.57	5.51	5.45	5.40	5.36	5.31	5.16	5.06
800	6.45	6.37	6.30	6.23	6.17	6.12	6.07	5.89	5.78
900	7.25	7.16	7.08	7.01	6.94	6.89	6.83	6.63	6.50
1000	8.06	7.96	7.87	7.79	7.72	7.65	7.59	7.37	7.22
2000	16.11	15.91	15.73	15.57	15.43	15.29	15.18	14.73	14.44
3000	24.16	23.87	23.60	23.36	23.14	22.94	22.76	22.09	21.66
4000	32.22	31.82	31.46	31.14	30.85	30.58	30.35	29.45	28.88
5000	40.27	39.77	39.33	38.92	38.56	38.23	37.93	36.81	36.10
6000	48.32	47.73	47.19	46.71	46.27	45.87	45.52	44.17	43.32
7000	56.38	55.68	55.05	54.49	53.98	53.52	53.10	51.53	50.54
8000	64.43	63.63	62.92	62.27	61.69	61.16	60.69	58.89	57.76
9000	72.48	71.59	70.78	70.06	69.40	68.81	68.27	66.25	64.98
10000	80.54	79.54	78.65	77.84	77.11	76.45	75.86	73.61	72.20
15000	120.80	119.31	117.97	116.76	115.67	114.68	113.79	110.41	108.30
20000	161.07	159.08	157.29	155.67	154.22	152.90	151.71	147.22	144.40
25000	201.34	198.85	196.61	194.59	192.77	191.13	189.64	184.02	180.49
30000	241.60	238.61	235.93	233.51	231.33	229.35	227.57	220.82	216.59
35000	281.87	278.38	275.25	272.42	269.88	267.58	265.49	257.63	252.69
36000	289.92	286.34	283.11	280.21	277.59	275.22	273.08	264.99	259.91
37000	297.98	294.29	290.98	287.99	285.30	282.87	280.66	272.35	267.13
38000	306.03	302.24	298.84	295.78	293.01	290.51	288.25	279.71	274.35
39000	314.08	310.20	306.70	303.56	300.72	298.16	295.84	287.07	281.57
40000	322.14	318.15	314.57	311.34	308.43	305.80	303.42	294.43	288.79
41000	330.19	326.10	322.43	319.13	316.14	313.45	311.01	301.79	296.01
42000	338.24	334.06	330.30	326.91	323.85	321.09	318.59	309.15	303.23
43000	346.30	342.01	338.16	334.69	331.56	328.74	326.18	316.51	310.45
44000	354.35	349.96	346.02	342.48	339.27	336.38	333.76	323.87	317.66
45000	362.40	357.92	353.89	350.26	346.99	344.03	341.35	331.23	324.88
46000	370.46	365.87	361.75	358.04	354.70	351.67	348.93	338.59	332.10
47000	378.51	373.83	369.62	365.83	362.41	359.32	356.52	345.95	339.32
48000	386.56	381.78	377.48	373.61	370.12	366.96	364.10	353.32	346.54
49000	394.62	389.73	385.34	381.39	377.83	374.61	371.69	360.68	353.76
50000	402.67	397.69	393.21	389.18	385.54	382.25	379.27	368.04	360.98
51000	410.72	405.64	401.07	396.96	393.25	389.90	386.86	375.40	368.20
52000	418.78	413.59	408.94	404.74	400.96	397.54	394.45	382.76	375.42
53000	426.83	421.55	416.80	412.53	408.67	405.19	402.03	390.12	382.64
54000	434.88	429.50	424.66	420.31	416.38	412.83	409.62	397.48	389.86
55000	442.94	437.45	432.53	428.09	424.09	420.48	417.20	404.84	397.08
56000	450.99	445.41	440.39	435.88	431.80	428.12	424.79	412.20	404.30
57000	459.04	453.36	448.26	443.66	439.51	435.76	432.37	419.56	411.52
58000	467.10	461.32	456.12	451.44	447.22	443.41	439.96	426.92	418.74
59000	475.15	469.27	463.99	459.23	454.93	451.05	447.54	434.28	425.96
60000	483.20	477.22	471.85	467.01	462.65	458.70	455.13	441.64	433.18
61000	491.26	485.18	479.71	474.79	470.36	466.34	462.71	449.00	440.40
62000	499.31	493.13	487.58	482.58	478.07	473.99	470.30	456.36	447.62
63000	507.36	501.08	495.44	490.36	485.78	481.63	477.88	463.72	454.84
64000	515.42	509.04	503.31	498.14	493.49	489.28	485.47	471.09	462.06
65000	523.47	516.99	511.17	505.93	501.20	496.92	493.06	478.45	469.28
66000	531.52	524.94	519.03	513.71	508.91	504.57	500.64	485.81	476.49
67000	539.58	532.90	526.90	521.49	516.62	512.21	508.23	493.17	483.71
68000	547.63	540.85	534.76	529.28	524.33	519.86	515.81	500.53	490.93
69000	555.68	548.81	542.63	537.06	532.04	527.50	523.40	507.89	498.15
70000	563.74	556.76	550.49	544.84	539.75	535.15	530.98	515.25	505.37
75000	604.00	596.53	589.81	583.76	578.31	573.37	568.91	552.05	541.47
80000	644.27	636.30	629.13	622.68	616.86	611.60	606.84	588.86	577.57
100000	805.34	795.37	786.41	778.35	771.07	764.50	758.54	736.07	721.96

8¾% MONTHLY PAYMENT
NECESSARY TO AMORTIZE A LOAN

TERM AMOUNT	1 YEAR	1½ YEARS	2 YEARS	2½ YEARS	3 YEARS	3½ YEARS	4 YEARS	4½ YEARS	5 YEARS
$ 25	2.19	1.49	1.14	.93	.80	.70	.62	.56	.52
50	4.37	2.98	2.28	1.86	1.59	1.39	1.24	1.12	1.03
75	6.55	4.46	3.42	2.79	2.38	2.08	1.86	1.68	1.55
100	8.73	5.95	4.55	3.72	3.17	2.77	2.47	2.24	2.06
200	17.46	11.89	9.10	7.44	6.33	5.54	4.94	4.48	4.12
300	26.18	17.83	13.65	11.15	9.49	8.30	7.41	6.72	6.17
400	34.91	23.77	18.20	14.87	12.65	11.07	9.88	8.96	8.23
500	43.64	29.71	22.75	18.59	15.81	13.83	12.35	11.20	10.29
600	52.36	35.65	27.30	22.30	18.97	16.60	14.82	13.44	12.34
700	61.09	41.59	31.85	26.02	22.13	19.36	17.29	15.68	14.40
800	69.82	47.53	36.40	29.73	25.29	22.13	19.76	17.92	16.45
900	78.54	53.48	40.95	33.45	28.46	24.89	22.23	20.16	18.51
1000	87.27	59.42	45.50	37.17	31.62	27.66	24.70	22.40	20.57
2000	174.53	118.83	91.00	74.33	63.23	55.31	49.39	44.80	41.13
3000	261.80	178.24	136.50	111.49	94.84	82.97	74.08	67.19	61.69
4000	349.06	237.65	182.00	148.65	126.45	110.62	98.78	89.59	82.25
5000	436.32	297.07	227.50	185.81	158.06	138.28	123.47	111.98	102.82
6000	523.59	356.48	273.00	222.97	189.67	165.93	148.16	134.38	123.38
7000	610.85	415.89	318.50	260.13	221.28	193.59	172.86	156.77	143.94
8000	698.11	475.30	364.00	297.30	252.90	221.24	197.55	179.17	164.50
9000	785.38	534.71	409.50	334.46	284.51	248.89	222.24	201.56	185.06
10000	872.64	594.13	454.99	371.62	316.12	276.55	246.94	223.96	205.63
15000	1308.96	891.19	682.49	557.43	474.18	414.82	370.40	335.93	308.44
20000	1745.28	1188.25	909.98	743.23	632.23	553.09	493.87	447.91	411.25
25000	2181.60	1485.31	1137.48	929.04	790.29	691.37	617.33	559.89	514.06
30000	2617.91	1782.37	1364.97	1114.85	948.35	829.64	740.80	671.86	616.87
35000	3054.23	2079.43	1592.47	1300.65	1106.40	967.91	864.26	783.84	719.68
36000	3141.49	2138.84	1637.97	1337.81	1138.02	995.56	888.95	806.24	740.24
37000	3228.76	2198.25	1683.47	1374.97	1169.63	1023.22	913.65	828.63	760.81
38000	3316.02	2257.66	1728.97	1412.14	1201.24	1050.87	938.34	851.03	781.37
39000	3403.29	2317.07	1774.47	1449.30	1232.85	1078.53	963.03	873.42	801.93
40000	3490.55	2376.49	1819.96	1486.46	1264.46	1106.18	987.73	895.82	822.49
41000	3577.81	2435.90	1865.46	1523.62	1296.07	1133.84	1012.42	918.21	843.05
42000	3665.08	2495.31	1910.96	1560.78	1327.68	1161.49	1037.11	940.61	863.62
43000	3752.34	2554.72	1956.46	1597.94	1359.30	1189.14	1061.80	963.00	884.18
44000	3839.60	2614.13	2001.96	1635.10	1390.91	1216.80	1086.50	985.40	904.74
45000	3926.87	2673.55	2047.46	1672.27	1422.52	1244.45	1111.19	1007.79	925.30
46000	4014.13	2732.96	2092.96	1709.43	1454.13	1272.11	1135.88	1030.19	945.86
47000	4101.39	2792.37	2138.46	1746.59	1485.74	1299.76	1160.58	1052.58	966.43
48000	4188.66	2851.78	2183.96	1783.75	1517.35	1327.42	1185.27	1074.98	986.99
49000	4275.92	2911.19	2229.45	1820.91	1548.96	1355.07	1209.96	1097.37	1007.55
50000	4363.19	2970.61	2274.95	1858.07	1580.58	1382.73	1234.66	1119.77	1028.11
51000	4450.45	3030.02	2320.45	1895.23	1612.19	1410.38	1259.35	1142.17	1048.68
52000	4537.71	3089.43	2365.95	1932.39	1643.80	1438.03	1284.04	1164.56	1069.24
53000	4624.98	3148.84	2411.45	1969.56	1675.41	1465.69	1308.74	1186.96	1089.80
54000	4712.24	3208.25	2456.95	2006.72	1707.02	1493.34	1333.43	1209.35	1110.36
55000	4799.50	3267.67	2502.45	2043.88	1738.63	1521.00	1358.12	1231.75	1130.92
56000	4886.77	3327.08	2547.95	2081.04	1770.24	1548.65	1382.81	1254.14	1151.49
57000	4974.03	3386.49	2593.45	2118.20	1801.86	1576.31	1407.51	1276.54	1172.05
58000	5061.29	3445.90	2638.95	2155.36	1833.47	1603.96	1432.20	1298.93	1192.61
59000	5148.56	3505.31	2684.44	2192.52	1865.08	1631.62	1456.89	1321.33	1213.17
60000	5235.82	3564.73	2729.94	2229.69	1896.69	1659.27	1481.59	1343.72	1233.74
61000	5323.09	3624.14	2775.44	2266.85	1928.30	1686.92	1506.28	1366.12	1254.30
62000	5410.35	3683.55	2820.94	2304.01	1959.91	1714.58	1530.97	1388.51	1274.86
63000	5497.61	3742.96	2866.44	2341.17	1991.52	1742.23	1555.66	1410.91	1295.42
64000	5584.88	3802.37	2911.94	2378.33	2023.13	1769.89	1580.36	1433.30	1315.98
65000	5672.14	3861.79	2957.44	2415.49	2054.75	1797.54	1605.05	1455.70	1336.55
66000	5759.40	3921.20	3002.94	2452.65	2086.36	1825.20	1629.74	1478.09	1357.11
67000	5846.67	3980.61	3048.44	2489.82	2117.97	1852.85	1654.44	1500.49	1377.67
68000	5933.93	4040.02	3093.94	2526.98	2149.58	1880.51	1679.13	1522.89	1398.23
69000	6021.19	4099.43	3139.43	2564.14	2181.19	1908.16	1703.82	1545.28	1418.79
70000	6108.46	4158.85	3184.93	2601.30	2212.80	1935.81	1728.52	1567.68	1439.36
75000	6544.78	4455.91	3412.43	2787.11	2370.86	2074.09	1851.98	1679.65	1542.17
80000	6981.09	4752.97	3639.92	2972.91	2528.92	2212.36	1975.45	1791.63	1644.98
100000	8726.37	5941.21	4549.90	3716.14	3161.15	2765.45	2469.31	2239.53	2056.22

32

MONTHLY PAYMENT 8¾%
NECESSARY TO AMORTIZE A LOAN

TERM AMOUNT	6 YEARS	7 YEARS	8 YEARS	9 YEARS	10 YEARS	11 YEARS	12 YEARS	13 YEARS	14 YEARS
$ 25	.45	.40	.37	.34	.32	.30	.28	.27	.26
50	.90	.80	.73	.67	.63	.59	.56	.54	.52
75	1.34	1.20	1.09	1.00	.94	.89	.84	.80	.77
100	1.79	1.59	1.45	1.34	1.25	1.18	1.12	1.07	1.03
200	3.57	3.18	2.89	2.67	2.49	2.35	2.24	2.14	2.06
300	5.35	4.77	4.34	4.00	3.74	3.53	3.35	3.20	3.08
400	7.14	6.36	5.78	5.34	4.98	4.70	4.47	4.27	4.11
500	8.92	7.95	7.23	6.67	6.23	5.87	5.58	5.34	5.13
600	10.70	9.54	8.67	8.00	7.47	7.05	6.70	6.40	6.16
700	12.48	11.12	10.11	9.34	8.72	8.22	7.81	7.47	7.18
800	14.27	12.71	11.56	10.67	9.96	9.40	8.93	8.54	8.21
900	16.05	14.30	13.00	12.00	11.21	10.57	10.04	9.60	9.23
1000	17.83	15.89	14.45	13.33	12.45	11.74	11.16	10.67	10.26
2000	35.66	31.77	28.89	26.66	24.90	23.48	22.31	21.34	20.51
3000	53.48	47.66	43.33	39.99	37.35	35.22	33.46	32.00	30.77
4000	71.31	63.54	57.77	53.32	49.80	46.96	44.62	42.67	41.02
5000	89.13	79.43	72.21	66.65	62.25	58.70	55.77	53.33	51.27
6000	106.96	95.31	86.65	79.98	74.70	70.43	66.92	64.00	61.53
7000	124.78	111.19	101.09	93.31	87.15	82.17	78.08	74.66	71.78
8000	142.61	127.08	115.53	106.64	99.60	93.91	89.23	85.33	82.04
9000	160.43	142.96	129.97	119.97	112.05	105.65	100.38	95.99	92.29
10000	178.26	158.85	144.41	133.30	124.50	117.39	111.54	106.66	102.54
15000	267.38	238.27	216.62	199.94	186.74	176.08	167.30	159.99	153.81
20000	356.51	317.69	288.82	266.59	248.99	234.77	223.07	213.31	205.08
25000	445.63	397.11	361.02	333.23	311.24	293.46	278.84	266.64	256.35
30000	534.76	476.53	433.23	399.88	373.48	352.15	334.60	319.97	307.62
35000	623.88	555.95	505.43	466.52	435.73	410.84	390.37	373.30	358.89
36000	641.71	571.83	519.87	479.85	448.18	422.58	401.52	383.96	369.14
37000	659.53	587.72	534.31	493.18	460.63	434.31	412.67	394.63	379.40
38000	677.36	603.60	548.75	506.51	473.08	446.05	423.83	405.29	389.65
39000	695.18	619.49	563.20	519.84	485.53	457.79	434.98	415.96	399.90
40000	713.01	635.37	577.64	533.17	497.97	469.53	446.13	426.62	410.16
41000	730.83	651.25	592.08	546.49	510.42	481.27	457.29	437.29	420.41
42000	748.66	667.14	606.52	559.82	522.87	493.00	468.44	447.95	430.66
43000	766.48	683.02	620.96	573.15	535.32	504.74	479.59	458.62	440.92
44000	784.31	698.91	635.40	586.48	547.77	516.48	490.75	469.28	451.17
45000	802.13	714.79	649.84	599.81	560.22	528.22	501.90	479.95	461.43
46000	819.96	730.67	664.28	613.14	572.67	539.96	513.05	490.61	471.68
47000	837.78	746.56	678.72	626.47	585.12	551.69	524.21	501.28	481.93
48000	855.61	762.44	693.16	639.80	597.57	563.43	535.36	511.95	492.19
49000	873.43	778.33	707.60	653.13	610.02	575.17	546.51	522.61	502.44
50000	891.26	794.21	722.04	666.46	622.47	586.91	557.67	533.28	512.69
51000	909.08	810.09	736.48	679.78	634.92	598.65	568.82	543.94	522.95
52000	926.91	825.98	750.93	693.11	647.37	610.38	579.97	554.61	533.20
53000	944.73	841.86	765.37	706.44	659.81	622.12	591.13	565.27	543.46
54000	962.56	857.75	779.81	719.77	672.26	633.86	602.28	575.94	553.71
55000	980.38	873.63	794.25	733.10	684.71	645.60	613.43	586.60	563.96
56000	998.21	889.52	808.69	746.43	697.16	657.34	624.59	597.27	574.22
57000	1016.03	905.40	823.13	759.76	709.61	669.07	635.74	607.93	584.47
58000	1033.86	921.28	837.57	773.09	722.06	680.81	646.89	618.60	594.72
59000	1051.68	937.17	852.01	786.42	734.51	692.55	658.04	629.27	604.98
60000	1069.51	953.05	866.45	799.75	746.96	704.29	669.20	639.93	615.23
61000	1087.33	968.94	880.89	813.07	759.41	716.03	680.35	650.60	625.49
62000	1105.16	984.82	895.33	826.40	771.86	727.76	691.50	661.26	635.74
63000	1122.98	1000.70	909.77	839.73	784.31	739.50	702.66	671.93	645.99
64000	1140.81	1016.59	924.21	853.06	796.76	751.24	713.81	682.59	656.25
65000	1158.63	1032.47	938.66	866.39	809.21	762.98	724.96	693.26	666.50
66000	1176.46	1048.36	953.10	879.72	821.65	774.72	736.12	703.92	676.76
67000	1194.28	1064.24	967.54	893.05	834.10	786.46	747.27	714.59	687.01
68000	1212.11	1080.12	981.98	906.38	846.55	798.19	758.42	725.25	697.26
69000	1229.93	1096.01	996.42	919.71	859.00	809.93	769.58	735.92	707.52
70000	1247.76	1111.89	1010.86	933.04	871.45	821.67	780.73	746.59	717.77
75000	1336.88	1191.31	1083.06	999.68	933.70	880.36	836.50	799.91	769.04
80000	1426.01	1270.73	1155.27	1066.33	995.94	939.05	892.26	853.24	820.31
100000	1782.51	1588.42	1444.08	1332.91	1244.93	1173.81	1115.33	1066.55	1025.38

33

8¾%

MONTHLY PAYMENT
NECESSARY TO AMORTIZE A LOAN

TERM AMOUNT	15 YEARS	16 YEARS	17 YEARS	18 YEARS	19 YEARS	20 YEARS	21 YEARS	22 YEARS	23 YEARS
$ 25	.25	.25	.24	.23	.23	.22	.22	.22	.21
50	.50	.49	.47	.46	.45	.44	.43	.43	.42
75	.75	.73	.71	.69	.67	.66	.65	.64	.63
100	1.00	.97	.94	.92	.90	.88	.86	.85	.84
200	1.99	1.93	1.87	1.83	1.79	1.75	1.72	1.69	1.67
300	2.98	2.89	2.81	2.74	2.68	2.63	2.58	2.54	2.50
400	3.97	3.85	3.74	3.65	3.57	3.50	3.44	3.38	3.33
500	4.96	4.81	4.68	4.56	4.46	4.37	4.30	4.23	4.17
600	5.95	5.77	5.61	5.47	5.35	5.25	5.15	5.07	5.00
700	6.94	6.73	6.54	6.38	6.24	6.12	6.01	5.92	5.83
800	7.93	7.69	7.48	7.30	7.14	7.00	6.87	6.76	6.66
900	8.92	8.65	8.41	8.21	8.03	7.87	7.73	7.61	7.50
1000	9.91	9.61	9.35	9.12	8.92	8.74	8.59	8.45	8.33
2000	19.81	19.21	18.69	18.23	17.83	17.48	17.17	16.90	16.65
3000	29.71	28.81	28.03	27.34	26.75	26.22	25.75	25.34	24.97
4000	39.62	38.41	37.37	36.46	35.66	34.96	34.34	33.79	33.30
5000	49.52	48.01	46.71	45.57	44.57	43.70	42.92	42.23	41.62
6000	59.42	57.61	56.05	54.68	53.49	52.43	51.50	50.68	49.94
7000	69.33	67.21	65.39	63.79	62.40	61.17	60.09	59.12	58.27
8000	79.23	76.82	74.73	72.91	71.31	69.91	68.67	67.57	66.59
9000	89.13	86.42	84.07	82.02	80.23	78.65	77.25	76.02	74.91
10000	99.03	96.02	93.41	91.13	89.14	87.39	85.84	84.46	83.24
15000	148.55	144.03	140.11	136.70	133.71	131.08	128.75	126.69	124.85
20000	198.06	192.03	186.81	182.26	178.28	174.77	171.67	168.92	166.47
25000	247.58	240.04	233.51	227.83	222.84	218.46	214.59	211.15	208.09
30000	297.09	288.05	280.21	273.39	267.41	262.15	257.50	253.38	249.70
35000	346.61	336.05	326.92	318.95	311.98	305.84	300.42	295.60	291.32
36000	356.51	345.65	336.26	328.07	320.89	314.58	309.00	304.05	299.64
37000	366.41	355.26	345.60	337.18	329.81	323.32	317.58	312.49	307.97
38000	376.32	364.86	354.94	346.29	338.72	332.06	326.17	320.94	316.29
39000	386.22	374.46	364.28	355.41	347.64	340.80	334.75	329.39	324.61
40000	396.12	384.06	373.62	364.52	356.55	349.53	343.33	337.83	332.94
41000	406.03	393.66	382.96	373.63	365.46	358.27	351.92	346.28	341.26
42000	415.93	403.26	392.30	382.74	374.38	367.01	360.50	354.72	349.58
43000	425.83	412.86	401.64	391.86	383.29	375.75	369.08	363.17	357.90
44000	435.73	422.47	410.98	400.97	392.20	384.49	377.67	371.61	366.23
45000	445.64	432.07	420.32	410.08	401.12	393.22	386.25	380.06	374.55
46000	455.54	441.67	429.66	419.20	410.03	401.96	394.83	388.51	382.87
47000	465.44	451.27	439.00	428.31	418.94	410.70	403.42	396.95	391.20
48000	475.35	460.87	448.34	437.42	427.86	419.44	412.00	405.40	399.52
49000	485.25	470.47	457.68	446.53	436.77	428.18	420.58	413.84	407.84
50000	495.15	480.07	467.02	455.65	445.68	436.92	429.17	422.29	416.17
51000	505.06	489.68	476.36	464.76	454.60	445.65	437.75	430.73	424.49
52000	514.96	499.28	485.70	473.87	463.51	454.39	446.33	439.18	432.81
53000	524.86	508.88	495.04	482.99	472.43	463.13	454.91	447.63	441.14
54000	534.76	518.48	504.38	492.10	481.34	471.87	463.50	456.07	449.46
55000	544.67	528.08	513.72	501.21	490.25	480.61	472.08	464.52	457.78
56000	554.57	537.68	523.06	510.32	499.17	489.35	480.66	472.96	466.11
57000	564.47	547.28	532.40	519.44	508.08	498.08	489.25	481.41	474.43
58000	574.38	556.89	541.74	528.55	516.99	506.82	497.83	489.85	482.75
59000	584.28	566.49	551.08	537.66	525.91	515.56	506.41	498.30	491.08
60000	594.18	576.09	560.42	546.78	534.82	524.30	515.00	506.75	499.40
61000	604.08	585.69	569.76	555.89	543.73	533.04	523.58	515.19	507.72
62000	613.99	595.29	579.10	565.00	552.65	541.77	532.16	523.64	516.05
63000	623.89	604.89	588.44	574.11	561.56	550.51	540.75	532.08	524.37
64000	633.79	614.49	597.78	583.23	570.48	559.25	549.33	540.53	532.69
65000	643.70	624.10	607.12	592.34	579.39	567.99	557.91	548.97	541.02
66000	653.60	633.70	616.47	601.45	588.30	576.73	566.50	557.42	549.34
67000	663.50	643.30	625.81	610.57	597.22	585.47	575.08	565.87	557.66
68000	673.41	652.90	635.15	619.68	606.13	594.20	583.66	574.31	565.99
69000	683.31	662.50	644.49	628.79	615.04	602.94	592.25	582.76	574.31
70000	693.21	672.10	653.83	637.90	623.96	611.68	600.83	591.20	582.63
75000	742.73	720.11	700.53	683.47	668.52	655.37	643.75	633.43	624.25
80000	792.24	768.12	747.23	729.03	713.09	699.06	686.66	675.66	665.87
100000	990.30	960.14	934.04	911.29	891.36	873.83	858.33	844.57	832.33

34

MONTHLY PAYMENT 8¾%
NECESSARY TO AMORTIZE A LOAN

TERM AMOUNT	24 YEARS	25 YEARS	26 YEARS	27 YEARS	28 YEARS	29 YEARS	30 YEARS	35 YEARS	40 YEARS
$ 25	.21	.21	.21	.20	.20	.20	.20	.19	.19
50	.42	.41	.41	.40	.40	.40	.39	.38	.38
75	.62	.61	.61	.60	.60	.59	.59	.57	.56
100	.83	.82	.81	.80	.80	.79	.78	.76	.75
200	1.65	1.63	1.61	1.59	1.58	1.57	1.56	1.51	1.49
300	2.47	2.44	2.41	2.39	2.37	2.35	2.33	2.27	2.23
400	3.29	3.25	3.22	3.18	3.16	3.13	3.11	3.02	2.97
500	4.11	4.06	4.02	3.98	3.94	3.91	3.88	3.77	3.71
600	4.93	4.87	4.82	4.77	4.73	4.69	4.66	4.53	4.45
700	5.75	5.69	5.62	5.57	5.52	5.47	5.43	5.28	5.19
800	6.58	6.50	6.43	6.36	6.31	6.26	6.21	6.04	5.93
900	7.40	7.31	7.23	7.16	7.10	7.04	6.99	6.79	6.67
1000	8.22	8.12	8.03	7.95	7.88	7.82	7.76	7.54	7.41
2000	16.43	16.24	16.06	15.90	15.70	15.63	15.52	15.08	14.81
3000	24.66	24.35	24.09	23.85	23.64	23.45	23.27	22.62	22.21
4000	32.86	32.47	32.12	31.80	31.52	31.26	31.03	30.16	29.62
5000	41.07	40.59	40.15	39.75	39.40	39.08	38.79	37.70	37.02
6000	49.29	48.70	48.18	47.70	47.28	46.89	46.54	45.24	44.42
7000	57.50	56.82	56.20	55.65	55.15	54.70	54.30	52.77	51.83
8000	65.72	64.93	64.23	63.60	63.03	62.52	62.06	60.31	59.23
9000	73.93	73.05	72.26	71.55	70.91	70.33	69.81	67.85	66.63
10000	82.14	81.17	80.29	79.50	78.79	78.15	77.57	75.39	74.04
15000	123.21	121.75	120.43	119.25	118.18	117.22	116.35	113.08	111.05
20000	164.28	162.33	160.57	158.99	157.57	156.29	155.13	150.77	148.07
25000	205.35	202.91	200.71	198.74	196.96	195.36	193.91	188.47	185.08
30000	246.42	243.49	240.86	238.49	236.36	234.43	232.69	226.16	222.10
35000	287.49	284.07	281.00	278.24	275.75	273.50	271.48	263.85	259.11
36000	295.71	292.19	289.03	286.19	283.63	281.32	279.23	271.39	266.51
37000	303.92	300.30	297.05	294.14	291.51	289.13	286.99	278.93	273.92
38000	312.14	308.42	305.08	302.08	299.38	296.95	294.74	286.47	281.32
39000	320.35	316.53	313.11	310.03	307.26	304.76	302.50	294.01	288.72
40000	328.56	324.65	321.14	317.98	315.14	312.58	310.26	301.54	296.13
41000	336.78	332.77	329.17	325.93	323.02	320.39	318.01	309.08	303.53
42000	344.99	340.88	337.20	333.88	330.90	328.20	325.77	316.62	310.93
43000	353.21	349.00	345.23	341.83	338.78	336.02	333.53	324.16	318.33
44000	361.42	357.12	353.25	349.78	346.65	343.83	341.28	331.70	325.74
45000	369.63	365.23	361.28	357.73	354.53	351.65	349.04	339.24	333.14
46000	377.85	373.35	369.31	365.68	362.41	359.46	356.79	346.78	340.54
47000	386.06	381.46	377.34	373.63	370.29	367.28	364.55	354.31	347.95
48000	394.28	389.58	385.37	381.58	378.17	375.09	372.31	361.85	355.35
49000	402.49	397.70	393.40	389.53	386.05	382.90	380.06	369.39	362.75
50000	410.70	405.81	401.42	397.48	393.92	390.72	387.82	376.93	370.16
51000	418.92	413.93	409.45	405.43	401.80	398.53	395.58	384.47	377.56
52000	427.13	422.04	417.48	413.38	409.68	406.35	403.33	392.01	384.96
53000	435.35	430.16	425.51	421.33	417.56	414.16	411.09	399.54	392.36
54000	443.56	438.28	433.54	429.28	425.44	421.97	418.85	407.08	399.77
55000	451.77	446.39	441.57	437.23	433.32	429.79	426.60	414.62	407.17
56000	459.99	454.51	449.59	445.18	441.19	437.60	434.36	422.16	414.57
57000	468.20	462.63	457.62	453.12	449.07	445.42	442.11	429.70	421.98
58000	476.41	470.74	465.65	461.07	456.95	453.23	449.87	437.24	429.38
59000	484.63	478.86	473.68	469.02	464.83	461.05	457.63	444.78	436.78
60000	492.84	486.97	481.71	476.97	472.71	468.86	465.38	452.31	444.19
61000	501.06	495.09	489.74	484.92	480.59	476.67	473.14	459.85	451.59
62000	509.27	503.21	497.76	492.87	488.47	484.49	480.90	467.39	458.99
63000	517.48	511.32	505.79	500.82	496.34	492.30	488.65	474.93	466.39
64000	525.70	519.44	513.82	508.77	504.22	500.12	496.41	482.47	473.80
65000	533.91	527.55	521.85	516.72	512.10	507.93	504.16	490.01	481.20
66000	542.13	535.67	529.88	524.67	519.98	515.75	511.92	497.55	488.60
67000	550.34	543.79	537.91	532.62	527.86	523.56	519.68	505.08	496.01
68000	558.55	551.90	545.93	540.57	535.74	531.37	527.43	512.62	503.41
69000	566.77	560.02	553.96	548.52	543.61	539.19	535.19	520.16	510.81
70000	574.98	568.13	561.99	556.47	551.49	547.00	542.95	527.70	518.22
75000	616.05	608.72	602.13	596.22	590.88	586.07	581.73	565.39	555.23
80000	657.12	649.30	642.28	635.96	630.28	625.15	620.51	603.08	592.25
100000	821.40	811.62	802.84	794.95	787.84	781.43	775.64	753.85	740.31

35

9%

MONTHLY PAYMENT
NECESSARY TO AMORTIZE A LOAN

TERM AMOUNT	1 YEAR	1½ YEARS	2 YEARS	2½ YEARS	3 YEARS	3½ YEARS	4 YEARS	4½ YEARS	5 YEARS
$ 25	2.19	1.49	1.15	.94	.80	.70	.63	.57	.52
50	4.37	2.98	2.29	1.87	1.59	1.39	1.25	1.13	1.04
75	6.56	4.47	3.43	2.80	2.38	2.09	1.87	1.69	1.56
100	8.74	5.96	4.57	3.73	3.18	2.78	2.49	2.26	2.07
200	17.48	11.91	9.13	7.46	6.35	5.56	4.97	4.51	4.14
300	26.22	17.86	13.69	11.19	9.52	8.34	7.45	6.76	6.21
400	34.96	23.81	18.25	14.91	12.69	11.11	9.93	9.01	8.28
500	43.69	29.77	22.81	18.64	15.87	13.89	12.41	11.26	10.34
600	52.43	35.72	27.37	22.37	19.04	16.67	14.89	13.51	12.41
700	61.17	41.67	31.93	26.10	22.21	19.44	17.37	15.76	14.48
800	69.91	47.62	36.49	29.82	25.38	22.22	19.85	18.01	16.55
900	78.64	53.58	41.05	33.55	28.56	25.00	22.33	20.26	18.62
1000	87.38	59.53	45.61	37.28	31.73	27.77	24.81	22.52	20.68
2000	174.76	119.05	91.22	74.55	63.45	55.54	49.62	45.03	41.36
3000	262.13	178.57	136.83	111.82	95.18	83.31	74.43	67.54	62.04
4000	349.51	238.09	182.44	149.09	126.90	111.07	99.23	90.05	82.72
5000	436.88	297.62	228.05	186.37	158.62	138.84	124.04	112.56	103.40
6000	524.26	357.14	273.66	223.64	190.35	166.61	148.85	135.07	124.08
7000	611.63	416.66	319.27	260.91	222.07	194.38	173.65	157.58	144.76
8000	699.01	476.18	364.88	298.18	253.79	222.14	198.46	180.09	165.43
9000	786.38	535.71	410.49	335.46	285.52	249.91	223.27	202.60	186.11
10000	873.76	595.23	456.10	372.73	317.24	277.68	248.08	225.11	206.79
15000	1310.63	892.84	684.15	559.09	475.86	416.52	372.11	337.66	310.19
20000	1747.51	1190.45	912.19	745.45	634.47	555.35	496.15	450.22	413.58
25000	2184.39	1488.07	1140.24	931.81	793.09	694.19	620.18	562.77	516.97
30000	2621.26	1785.68	1368.29	1118.18	951.71	833.03	744.22	675.32	620.37
35000	3058.14	2083.29	1596.33	1304.54	1110.32	971.86	868.25	787.88	723.76
36000	3145.52	2142.81	1641.94	1341.81	1142.05	999.63	893.06	810.39	744.44
37000	3232.89	2202.33	1687.55	1379.08	1173.77	1027.40	917.87	832.90	765.12
38000	3320.27	2261.86	1733.16	1416.36	1205.49	1055.17	942.68	855.41	785.80
39000	3407.64	2321.38	1778.77	1453.63	1237.22	1082.93	967.48	877.92	806.48
40000	3495.02	2380.90	1824.38	1490.90	1268.94	1110.70	992.29	900.43	827.15
41000	3582.39	2440.42	1869.99	1528.17	1300.66	1138.47	1017.10	922.94	847.83
42000	3669.77	2499.95	1915.60	1565.45	1332.39	1166.24	1041.90	945.45	868.51
43000	3757.14	2559.47	1961.21	1602.72	1364.11	1194.00	1066.71	967.96	889.19
44000	3844.52	2618.99	2006.82	1639.99	1395.83	1221.77	1091.52	990.47	909.87
45000	3931.89	2678.51	2052.43	1677.26	1427.56	1249.54	1116.33	1012.98	930.55
46000	4019.27	2738.04	2098.04	1714.54	1459.28	1277.31	1141.13	1035.49	951.23
47000	4106.65	2797.56	2143.65	1751.81	1491.00	1305.07	1165.94	1058.00	971.91
48000	4194.02	2857.08	2189.26	1789.08	1522.73	1332.84	1190.75	1080.51	992.58
49000	4281.40	2916.60	2234.87	1826.35	1554.45	1360.61	1215.55	1103.03	1013.26
50000	4368.77	2976.13	2280.48	1863.62	1586.17	1388.37	1240.36	1125.54	1033.94
51000	4456.15	3035.65	2326.09	1900.90	1617.90	1416.14	1265.17	1148.05	1054.62
52000	4543.52	3095.17	2371.69	1938.17	1649.62	1443.91	1289.98	1170.56	1075.30
53000	4630.90	3154.69	2417.30	1975.44	1681.34	1471.68	1314.78	1193.07	1095.98
54000	4718.27	3214.21	2462.91	2012.71	1713.07	1499.44	1339.59	1215.58	1116.66
55000	4805.65	3273.74	2508.52	2049.99	1744.79	1527.21	1364.40	1238.09	1137.34
56000	4893.02	3333.26	2554.13	2087.26	1776.51	1554.98	1389.20	1260.60	1158.01
57000	4980.40	3392.78	2599.74	2124.53	1808.24	1582.75	1414.01	1283.11	1178.69
58000	5067.77	3452.30	2645.35	2161.80	1839.96	1610.51	1438.82	1305.62	1199.37
59000	5155.15	3511.83	2690.96	2199.08	1871.68	1638.28	1463.63	1328.13	1220.05
60000	5242.52	3571.35	2736.57	2236.35	1903.41	1666.05	1488.43	1350.64	1240.73
61000	5329.90	3630.87	2782.18	2273.62	1935.13	1693.82	1513.24	1373.15	1261.41
62000	5417.28	3690.39	2827.79	2310.89	1966.85	1721.58	1538.05	1395.66	1282.09
63000	5504.65	3749.92	2873.40	2348.17	1998.58	1749.35	1562.85	1418.17	1302.76
64000	5592.03	3809.44	2919.01	2385.44	2030.30	1777.12	1587.66	1440.68	1323.44
65000	5679.40	3868.96	2964.62	2422.71	2062.02	1804.89	1612.47	1463.20	1344.12
66000	5766.78	3928.48	3010.23	2459.98	2093.75	1832.65	1637.28	1485.71	1364.80
67000	5854.15	3988.01	3055.84	2497.26	2125.47	1860.42	1662.08	1508.22	1385.48
68000	5941.53	4047.53	3101.45	2534.53	2157.19	1888.19	1686.89	1530.73	1406.16
69000	6028.90	4107.05	3147.05	2571.80	2188.92	1915.96	1711.70	1553.24	1426.84
70000	6116.28	4166.57	3192.66	2609.07	2220.64	1943.72	1736.50	1575.75	1447.52
75000	6553.15	4464.19	3420.71	2795.43	2379.26	2082.56	1860.54	1688.30	1550.91
80000	6990.03	4761.80	3648.76	2981.80	2537.87	2221.40	1984.57	1800.85	1654.30
100000	8737.54	5952.25	4560.95	3727.24	3172.34	2776.74	2480.72	2251.07	2067.88

MONTHLY PAYMENT   9%
NECESSARY TO AMORTIZE A LOAN

TERM AMOUNT	6 YEARS	7 YEARS	8 YEARS	9 YEARS	10 YEARS	11 YEARS	12 YEARS	13 YEARS	14 YEARS
$ 25	.45	.41	.37	.34	.32	.30	.29	.28	.26
50	.90	.81	.73	.68	.63	.60	.57	.55	.52
75	1.35	1.21	1.10	1.01	.95	.90	.85	.82	.78
100	1.80	1.61	1.46	1.35	1.26	1.19	1.13	1.09	1.04
200	3.59	3.21	2.92	2.70	2.52	2.38	2.26	2.17	2.08
300	5.39	4.81	4.37	4.04	3.78	3.57	3.39	3.25	3.12
400	7.18	6.41	5.83	5.39	5.04	4.75	4.52	4.33	4.16
500	8.98	8.01	7.29	6.73	6.29	5.94	5.65	5.41	5.20
600	10.77	9.61	8.74	8.08	7.55	7.13	6.78	6.49	6.24
700	12.57	11.21	10.20	9.42	8.81	8.31	7.91	7.57	7.28
800	14.36	12.81	11.66	10.77	10.07	9.50	9.04	8.65	8.32
900	16.15	14.41	13.11	12.12	11.33	10.69	10.16	9.73	9.36
1000	17.95	16.01	14.57	13.46	12.58	11.88	11.29	10.81	10.40
2000	35.89	32.02	29.14	26.92	25.16	23.75	22.50	21.61	20.79
3000	53.84	48.02	43.70	40.37	37.74	35.62	33.87	32.41	31.19
4000	71.78	64.03	58.27	53.83	50.32	47.49	45.16	43.22	41.58
5000	89.73	80.03	72.83	67.29	62.90	59.36	56.44	54.02	51.97
6000	107.67	96.04	87.40	80.74	75.48	71.23	67.73	64.82	62.37
7000	125.61	112.05	101.96	94.20	88.06	83.10	79.02	75.62	72.76
8000	143.56	128.05	116.53	107.65	100.64	94.97	90.31	86.43	83.15
9000	161.50	144.06	131.09	121.11	113.21	106.84	101.60	97.23	93.55
10000	179.45	160.06	145.66	134.57	125.79	118.71	112.88	108.03	103.94
15000	269.17	240.09	218.48	201.85	188.69	178.06	169.32	162.05	155.91
20000	358.89	320.12	291.31	269.13	251.58	237.41	225.76	216.06	207.88
25000	448.61	400.15	364.13	336.41	314.48	296.76	282.20	270.07	259.84
30000	538.33	480.18	436.96	403.69	377.37	356.11	338.64	324.09	311.81
35000	628.05	560.21	509.78	470.97	440.26	415.46	395.08	378.10	363.78
36000	645.99	576.22	524.35	484.42	452.84	427.34	406.37	388.90	374.17
37000	663.94	592.22	538.92	497.88	465.42	439.21	417.66	399.71	384.57
38000	681.88	608.23	553.48	511.33	478.00	451.08	428.95	410.51	394.96
39000	699.83	624.23	568.05	524.79	490.58	462.95	440.24	421.31	405.35
40000	717.77	640.24	582.61	538.25	503.16	474.82	451.52	432.11	415.75
41000	735.71	656.24	597.18	551.70	515.74	486.69	462.81	442.92	426.14
42000	753.66	672.25	611.74	565.16	528.32	498.56	474.10	453.72	436.54
43000	771.60	688.26	626.31	578.61	540.90	510.43	485.39	464.52	446.93
44000	789.55	704.26	640.87	592.07	553.47	522.30	496.68	475.33	457.32
45000	807.49	720.27	655.44	605.53	566.05	534.17	507.96	486.13	467.72
46000	825.43	736.27	670.00	618.98	578.63	546.04	519.25	496.93	478.11
47000	843.38	752.28	684.57	632.44	591.21	557.91	530.54	507.73	488.50
48000	861.32	768.29	699.13	645.89	603.79	569.78	541.83	518.54	498.90
49000	879.27	784.29	713.70	659.35	616.37	581.65	553.12	529.34	509.29
50000	897.21	800.30	728.26	672.81	628.95	593.52	564.40	540.14	519.68
51000	915.16	816.30	742.83	686.26	641.53	605.39	575.69	550.94	530.08
52000	933.10	832.31	757.39	699.72	654.11	617.26	586.98	561.75	540.47
53000	951.04	848.31	771.96	713.17	666.68	629.13	598.27	572.55	550.87
54000	968.99	864.32	786.52	726.63	679.26	641.00	609.56	583.35	561.26
55000	986.93	880.33	801.09	740.09	691.84	652.87	620.84	594.16	571.65
56000	1004.88	896.33	815.65	753.54	704.42	664.74	632.13	604.96	582.05
57000	1022.82	912.34	830.22	767.00	717.00	676.61	643.42	615.76	592.44
58000	1040.76	928.34	844.78	780.45	729.58	688.48	654.71	626.56	602.83
59000	1058.71	944.35	859.35	793.91	742.16	700.35	666.00	637.37	613.23
60000	1076.65	960.36	873.91	807.37	754.74	712.22	677.28	648.17	623.62
61000	1094.60	976.36	888.48	820.82	767.32	724.09	688.57	658.97	634.01
62000	1112.54	992.37	903.04	834.28	779.89	735.96	699.86	669.78	644.41
63000	1130.48	1008.37	917.61	847.73	792.47	747.83	711.15	680.58	654.80
64000	1148.43	1024.38	932.17	861.19	805.05	759.70	722.44	691.38	665.19
65000	1166.37	1040.38	946.74	874.65	817.63	771.57	733.72	702.18	675.59
66000	1184.32	1056.39	961.30	888.10	830.21	783.44	745.01	712.99	685.98
67000	1202.26	1072.40	975.87	901.56	842.79	795.31	756.30	723.79	696.38
68000	1220.21	1088.40	990.43	915.01	855.37	807.18	767.59	734.59	706.77
69000	1238.15	1104.41	1005.00	928.47	867.95	819.05	778.88	745.39	717.16
70000	1256.06	1120.41	1019.56	941.93	880.52	830.92	790.16	756.20	727.56
75000	1345.81	1200.44	1092.39	1009.21	943.42	890.28	846.60	810.21	779.52
80000	1435.54	1280.47	1165.22	1076.49	1006.31	949.63	903.04	864.22	831.49
100000	1794.42	1600.59	1456.52	1345.61	1257.89	1187.03	1128.80	1080.28	1039.36

9% MONTHLY PAYMENT
NECESSARY TO AMORTIZE A LOAN

TERM AMOUNT	15 YEARS	16 YEARS	17 YEARS	18 YEARS	19 YEARS	20 YEARS	21 YEARS	22 YEARS	23 YEARS
$ 25	.26	.25	.24	.24	.23	.23	.22	.22	.22
50	.51	.49	.48	.47	.46	.45	.44	.44	.43
75	.76	.74	.72	.70	.68	.67	.66	.65	.64
100	1.01	.98	.95	.93	.91	.89	.88	.87	.85
200	2.01	1.95	1.90	1.86	1.82	1.78	1.75	1.73	1.70
300	3.02	2.93	2.85	2.78	2.72	2.67	2.63	2.59	2.55
400	4.02	3.90	3.80	3.71	3.63	3.56	3.50	3.45	3.40
500	5.03	4.88	4.75	4.64	4.54	4.45	4.37	4.31	4.25
600	6.03	5.85	5.70	5.56	5.44	5.34	5.25	5.17	5.09
700	7.04	6.83	6.65	6.49	6.35	6.23	6.12	6.03	5.94
800	8.04	7.80	7.59	7.41	7.26	7.12	7.00	6.89	6.79
900	9.05	8.78	8.54	8.34	8.16	8.01	7.87	7.75	7.64
1000	10.05	9.75	9.49	9.27	9.07	8.90	8.74	8.61	8.49
2000	20.10	19.50	18.98	18.53	18.14	17.79	17.48	17.21	16.97
3000	30.14	29.24	28.47	27.79	27.20	26.68	26.22	25.82	25.45
4000	40.19	38.99	37.95	37.05	36.27	35.57	34.96	34.42	33.94
5000	50.23	48.74	47.44	46.32	45.33	44.46	43.70	43.02	42.42
6000	60.28	58.48	56.93	55.58	54.40	53.36	52.44	51.63	50.90
7000	70.32	68.23	66.42	64.84	63.46	62.25	61.18	60.23	59.39
8000	80.37	77.97	75.90	74.10	72.53	71.14	69.92	68.83	67.87
9000	90.41	87.72	85.39	83.36	81.59	80.03	78.66	77.44	76.35
10000	100.46	97.47	94.88	92.63	90.66	88.92	87.39	86.04	84.84
15000	150.68	146.20	142.31	138.94	135.98	133.38	131.09	129.06	127.25
20000	200.91	194.93	189.75	185.25	181.31	177.84	174.78	172.08	169.67
25000	251.13	243.66	237.19	231.56	226.63	222.30	218.48	215.09	212.08
30000	301.36	292.39	284.62	277.87	271.96	266.76	262.17	258.11	254.50
35000	351.59	341.12	332.06	324.18	317.28	311.22	305.87	301.13	296.91
36000	361.63	350.86	341.55	333.44	326.35	320.11	314.61	309.73	305.40
37000	371.68	360.61	351.03	342.70	335.41	329.01	323.35	318.34	313.88
38000	381.72	370.35	360.52	351.97	344.48	337.90	332.09	326.94	322.36
39000	391.77	380.10	370.01	361.23	353.54	346.79	340.83	335.54	330.85
40000	401.81	389.85	379.50	370.49	362.61	355.68	349.56	344.15	339.33
41000	411.86	399.59	388.98	379.75	371.67	364.57	358.30	352.75	347.81
42000	421.90	409.34	398.47	389.01	380.74	373.46	367.04	361.35	356.29
43000	431.95	419.08	407.96	398.28	389.80	382.36	375.78	369.96	364.78
44000	441.99	428.83	417.45	407.54	398.87	391.25	384.52	378.56	373.26
45000	452.04	438.58	426.93	416.80	407.93	400.14	393.26	387.16	381.74
46000	462.08	448.32	436.42	426.06	417.00	409.03	402.00	395.77	390.23
47000	472.13	458.07	445.91	435.32	426.06	417.92	410.74	404.37	398.71
48000	482.17	467.81	455.39	444.59	435.13	426.82	419.48	412.97	407.19
49000	492.22	477.56	464.88	453.85	444.19	435.71	428.22	421.58	415.68
50000	502.26	487.31	474.37	463.11	453.26	444.60	436.95	430.18	424.16
51000	512.31	497.05	483.86	472.37	462.33	453.49	445.69	438.78	432.64
52000	522.35	506.80	493.34	481.64	471.39	462.38	454.43	447.39	441.13
53000	532.40	516.54	502.83	490.90	480.46	471.28	463.17	455.99	449.61
54000	542.45	526.29	512.32	500.16	489.52	480.17	471.91	464.59	458.09
55000	552.49	536.04	521.81	509.42	498.59	489.06	480.65	473.20	466.57
56000	562.54	545.78	531.29	518.68	507.65	497.95	489.39	481.80	475.06
57000	572.58	555.53	540.78	527.95	516.72	506.84	498.13	490.41	483.54
58000	582.63	565.27	550.27	537.21	525.78	515.73	506.87	499.01	492.02
59000	592.67	575.02	559.75	546.47	534.85	524.63	515.61	507.61	500.51
60000	602.72	584.77	569.24	555.73	543.91	533.52	524.34	516.22	508.99
61000	612.76	594.51	578.73	564.99	552.98	542.41	533.08	524.82	517.47
62000	622.81	604.26	588.22	574.26	562.04	551.30	541.82	533.42	525.96
63000	632.85	614.00	597.70	583.52	571.11	560.19	550.56	542.03	534.44
64000	642.90	623.75	607.19	592.78	580.17	569.09	559.30	550.63	542.92
65000	652.94	633.50	616.68	602.04	589.24	577.98	568.04	559.23	551.41
66000	662.99	643.24	626.17	611.30	598.30	586.87	576.78	567.84	559.89
67000	673.03	652.99	635.65	620.57	607.37	595.76	585.52	576.44	568.37
68000	683.08	662.73	645.14	629.83	616.43	604.65	594.26	585.04	576.86
69000	693.12	672.48	654.63	639.09	625.50	613.55	603.00	593.65	585.34
70000	703.17	682.23	664.12	648.35	634.56	622.44	611.73	602.25	593.82
75000	753.39	730.96	711.55	694.66	679.89	666.90	655.43	645.27	636.24
80000	803.62	779.69	758.99	740.97	725.21	711.36	699.12	688.29	678.65
100000	1004.52	974.61	948.73	926.22	906.51	889.19	873.90	860.36	848.31

38

TERM AMOUNT	24 YEARS	25 YEARS	26 YEARS	27 YEARS	28 YEARS	29 YEARS	30 YEARS	35 YEARS	40 YEARS
$ 25	.21	.21	.21	.21	.21	.20	.20	.20	.19
50	.42	.42	.41	.41	.41	.40	.40	.39	.38
75	.63	.63	.62	.61	.61	.60	.60	.58	.57
100	.84	.83	.82	.82	.81	.80	.80	.78	.76
200	1.68	1.66	1.64	1.63	1.61	1.60	1.59	1.55	1.52
300	2.52	2.49	2.46	2.44	2.42	2.40	2.38	2.32	2.28
400	3.36	3.32	3.28	3.25	3.22	3.20	3.18	3.09	3.04
500	4.19	4.14	4.10	4.06	4.03	4.00	3.97	3.86	3.80
600	5.03	4.97	4.92	4.87	4.83	4.80	4.76	4.64	4.56
700	5.87	5.80	5.74	5.69	5.64	5.59	5.55	5.41	5.32
800	6.71	6.63	6.56	6.50	6.44	6.39	6.35	6.18	6.07
900	7.54	7.46	7.38	7.31	7.25	7.19	7.14	6.95	6.83
1000	8.38	8.28	8.20	8.12	8.06	7.99	7.93	7.72	7.59
2000	16.76	16.55	16.39	16.24	16.10	15.97	15.86	15.44	15.18
3000	25.13	24.84	24.59	24.35	24.15	23.96	23.79	23.16	22.77
4000	33.51	33.12	32.78	32.47	32.19	31.94	31.72	30.87	30.35
5000	41.88	41.40	40.97	40.59	40.24	39.93	39.65	38.59	37.94
6000	50.26	49.68	49.17	48.70	48.29	47.91	47.57	46.31	45.53
7000	58.64	57.96	57.36	56.82	56.34	55.90	55.50	54.03	53.12
8000	67.01	66.24	65.56	64.94	64.38	63.88	63.43	61.74	60.70
9000	75.39	74.52	73.75	73.05	72.43	71.87	71.36	69.46	68.29
10000	83.76	82.80	81.94	81.17	80.48	79.85	79.29	77.18	75.88
15000	125.64	124.20	122.91	121.75	120.71	119.78	118.93	115.77	113.82
20000	167.52	165.60	163.88	162.34	160.95	159.70	158.57	154.35	151.75
25000	209.40	207.00	204.85	202.92	201.19	199.62	198.21	192.94	189.69
30000	251.28	248.40	245.82	243.50	241.42	239.55	237.85	231.53	227.63
35000	293.16	289.80	286.79	284.09	281.66	279.47	277.50	270.11	265.56
36000	301.53	298.08	294.98	292.20	289.71	287.46	285.42	277.83	273.15
37000	309.91	306.36	303.18	300.32	297.75	295.44	293.35	285.55	280.74
38000	318.28	314.64	311.37	308.44	305.80	303.42	301.28	293.27	288.33
39000	326.66	322.92	319.56	316.55	313.85	311.41	309.21	300.98	295.91
40000	335.03	331.20	327.76	324.67	321.89	319.39	317.14	308.70	303.50
41000	343.41	339.48	335.95	332.79	329.94	327.38	325.07	316.42	311.09
42000	351.79	347.76	344.15	340.90	337.99	335.36	332.99	324.14	318.68
43000	360.16	356.04	352.34	349.02	346.04	343.35	340.92	331.85	326.26
44000	368.54	364.32	360.53	357.14	354.08	351.33	348.85	339.57	333.85
45000	376.91	372.59	368.73	365.25	362.13	359.32	356.78	347.29	341.44
46000	385.29	380.87	376.92	373.37	370.18	367.30	364.71	355.00	349.03
47000	393.66	389.15	385.11	381.49	378.23	375.29	372.64	362.72	356.61
48000	402.04	397.43	393.31	389.60	386.27	383.27	380.56	370.44	364.20
49000	410.42	405.71	401.50	397.72	394.32	391.26	388.49	378.16	371.79
50000	418.79	413.99	409.70	405.84	402.37	399.24	396.42	385.87	379.38
51000	427.17	422.27	417.89	413.95	410.41	407.23	404.35	393.59	386.96
52000	435.54	430.55	426.08	422.07	418.46	415.21	412.28	401.31	394.55
53000	443.92	438.83	434.28	430.19	426.51	423.20	420.21	409.03	402.14
54000	452.29	447.11	442.47	438.30	434.56	431.18	428.13	416.74	409.72
55000	460.67	455.39	450.66	446.42	442.60	439.17	436.06	424.46	417.31
56000	469.05	463.67	458.86	454.54	450.65	447.15	443.99	432.18	424.90
57000	477.42	471.95	467.05	462.65	458.70	455.13	451.92	439.90	432.49
58000	485.80	480.23	475.25	470.77	466.75	463.12	459.85	447.61	440.07
59000	494.17	488.51	483.44	478.89	474.79	471.10	467.78	455.33	447.66
60000	502.55	496.79	491.63	487.00	482.84	479.09	475.70	463.05	455.25
61000	510.92	505.07	499.83	495.12	490.89	487.07	483.63	470.77	462.84
62000	519.30	513.35	508.02	503.24	498.93	495.06	491.56	478.48	470.42
63000	527.68	521.63	516.22	511.35	506.98	503.04	499.49	486.20	478.01
64000	536.05	529.91	524.41	519.47	515.03	511.03	507.42	493.92	485.60
65000	544.43	538.19	532.60	527.59	523.08	519.01	515.35	501.64	493.19
66000	552.80	546.47	540.80	535.70	531.12	527.00	523.27	509.35	500.77
67000	561.18	554.75	548.99	543.82	539.17	534.98	531.20	517.07	508.36
68000	569.55	563.03	557.18	551.94	547.22	542.97	539.13	524.79	515.95
69000	577.93	571.31	565.38	560.05	555.27	550.95	547.06	532.50	523.54
70000	586.31	579.59	573.57	568.17	563.31	558.94	554.99	540.22	531.12
75000	628.18	620.99	614.54	608.75	603.55	598.86	594.63	578.81	569.06
80000	670.06	662.39	655.51	649.34	643.78	638.78	634.27	617.40	607.00
100000	837.58	827.98	819.39	811.67	804.73	798.48	792.84	771.74	758.75

39

9¼% MONTHLY PAYMENT
NECESSARY TO AMORTIZE A LOAN

TERM AMOUNT	1 YEAR	1½ YEARS	2 YEARS	2½ YEARS	3 YEARS	3½ YEARS	4 YEARS	4½ YEARS	5 YEARS
$ 25	2.19	1.50	1.15	.94	.80	.70	.63	.57	.52
50	4.38	2.99	2.29	1.87	1.60	1.40	1.25	1.14	1.04
75	6.57	4.48	3.43	2.81	2.39	2.10	1.87	1.70	1.56
100	8.75	5.97	4.58	3.74	3.19	2.79	2.50	2.27	2.08
200	17.50	11.93	9.15	7.48	6.37	5.58	4.99	4.53	4.16
300	26.25	17.89	13.72	11.22	9.56	8.37	7.48	6.79	6.24
400	35.00	23.86	18.29	14.96	12.74	11.16	9.97	9.06	8.32
500	43.75	29.82	22.86	18.70	15.92	13.95	12.47	11.32	10.40
600	52.50	35.78	27.44	22.44	19.11	16.73	14.96	13.58	12.48
700	61.25	41.75	32.01	26.17	22.29	19.52	17.45	15.84	14.56
800	69.99	47.71	36.58	29.91	25.47	22.31	19.94	18.11	16.64
900	78.74	53.67	41.15	33.65	28.66	25.10	22.43	20.37	18.72
1000	87.49	59.64	45.72	37.39	31.84	27.89	24.93	22.63	20.80
2000	174.98	119.27	91.44	74.77	63.68	55.77	49.85	45.26	41.60
3000	262.47	178.90	137.16	112.16	95.51	83.65	74.77	67.88	62.39
4000	349.95	238.54	182.88	149.54	127.35	111.53	99.69	90.51	83.19
5000	437.44	298.17	228.60	186.92	159.18	139.41	124.61	113.14	103.98
6000	524.93	357.80	274.32	224.31	191.02	167.29	149.53	135.76	124.78
7000	612.41	417.43	320.04	261.69	222.85	195.17	174.46	158.39	145.57
8000	699.90	477.07	365.76	299.07	254.69	223.05	199.38	181.01	166.37
9000	787.39	536.70	411.48	336.46	286.52	250.93	224.30	203.64	187.17
10000	874.88	596.33	457.20	373.84	318.36	278.81	249.22	226.27	207.96
15000	1312.31	894.50	685.80	560.76	477.54	418.21	373.83	339.40	311.94
20000	1749.75	1192.66	914.40	747.68	636.71	557.62	498.43	452.53	415.92
25000	2187.18	1490.82	1143.00	934.59	795.89	697.02	623.04	565.66	519.89
30000	2624.62	1788.99	1371.60	1121.51	955.07	836.42	747.65	678.79	623.87
35000	3062.05	2087.15	1600.20	1308.43	1114.24	975.82	872.26	791.92	727.85
36000	3149.54	2146.79	1645.92	1345.81	1146.08	1003.70	897.18	814.55	748.65
37000	3237.02	2206.42	1691.64	1383.20	1177.92	1031.58	922.10	837.17	769.44
38000	3324.51	2266.05	1737.36	1420.58	1209.75	1059.47	947.02	859.80	790.24
39000	3412.00	2325.68	1783.08	1457.96	1241.59	1087.35	971.94	882.43	811.03
40000	3499.49	2385.32	1828.80	1495.35	1273.42	1115.23	996.86	905.05	831.83
41000	3586.97	2444.95	1874.52	1532.73	1305.26	1143.11	1021.78	927.68	852.62
42000	3674.46	2504.58	1920.24	1570.11	1337.09	1170.99	1046.71	950.30	873.42
43000	3761.95	2564.22	1965.96	1607.50	1368.93	1198.87	1071.63	972.93	894.21
44000	3849.43	2623.85	2011.68	1644.88	1400.76	1226.75	1096.55	995.56	915.01
45000	3936.92	2683.48	2057.40	1682.26	1432.60	1254.63	1121.47	1018.18	935.81
46000	4024.41	2743.11	2103.12	1719.65	1464.43	1282.51	1146.39	1040.81	956.60
47000	4111.89	2802.75	2148.84	1757.03	1496.27	1310.39	1171.31	1063.44	977.40
48000	4199.38	2862.38	2194.56	1794.41	1528.10	1338.27	1196.23	1086.06	998.19
49000	4286.87	2922.01	2240.28	1831.80	1559.94	1366.15	1221.16	1108.69	1018.99
50000	4374.36	2981.64	2286.00	1869.18	1591.78	1394.03	1246.08	1131.31	1039.78
51000	4461.84	3041.28	2331.72	1906.57	1623.61	1421.91	1271.00	1153.94	1060.58
52000	4549.33	3100.91	2377.44	1943.95	1655.45	1449.79	1295.92	1176.57	1081.37
53000	4636.82	3160.54	2423.16	1981.33	1687.28	1477.67	1320.84	1199.19	1102.17
54000	4724.30	3220.18	2468.88	2018.72	1719.12	1505.55	1345.76	1221.82	1122.97
55000	4811.79	3279.81	2514.60	2056.10	1750.95	1533.43	1370.68	1244.44	1143.76
56000	4899.28	3339.44	2560.32	2093.48	1782.79	1561.32	1395.61	1267.07	1164.56
57000	4986.76	3399.07	2606.04	2130.87	1814.62	1589.20	1420.53	1289.70	1185.35
58000	5074.25	3458.71	2651.76	2168.25	1846.46	1617.08	1445.45	1312.32	1206.15
59000	5161.74	3518.34	2697.48	2205.63	1878.29	1644.96	1470.37	1334.95	1226.94
60000	5249.23	3577.97	2743.20	2243.02	1910.13	1672.84	1495.29	1357.58	1247.74
61000	5336.71	3637.61	2788.92	2280.40	1941.96	1700.72	1520.21	1380.20	1268.53
62000	5424.20	3697.24	2834.64	2317.78	1973.80	1728.60	1545.13	1402.83	1289.33
63000	5511.69	3756.87	2880.36	2355.17	2005.64	1756.48	1570.06	1425.45	1310.13
64000	5599.17	3816.50	2926.08	2392.55	2037.47	1784.36	1594.98	1448.08	1330.92
65000	5686.66	3876.14	2971.80	2429.93	2069.31	1812.24	1619.90	1470.71	1351.72
66000	5774.15	3935.77	3017.52	2467.32	2101.14	1840.12	1644.82	1493.33	1372.51
67000	5861.63	3995.40	3063.24	2504.70	2132.98	1868.00	1669.74	1515.96	1393.31
68000	5949.12	4055.03	3108.96	2542.09	2164.81	1895.88	1694.66	1538.58	1414.10
69000	6036.61	4114.67	3154.68	2579.47	2196.65	1923.76	1719.58	1561.21	1434.90
70000	6124.10	4174.30	3200.40	2616.85	2228.48	1951.64	1744.51	1583.84	1455.69
75000	6561.53	4472.46	3429.00	2803.77	2387.66	2091.05	1869.11	1696.97	1559.67
80000	6998.97	4770.63	3657.60	2990.69	2546.84	2230.45	1993.72	1810.10	1663.65
100000	8748.71	5963.28	4572.00	3738.36	3183.55	2788.06	2492.15	2262.62	2079.56

MONTHLY PAYMENT 9¼%
NECESSARY TO AMORTIZE A LOAN

TERM AMOUNT	6 YEARS	7 YEARS	8 YEARS	9 YEARS	10 YEARS	11 YEARS	12 YEARS	13 YEARS	14 YEARS
$ 25	.46	.41	.37	.34	.32	.31	.29	.28	.27
50	.91	.81	.74	.68	.64	.61	.58	.55	.53
75	1.36	1.21	1.11	1.02	.96	.91	.86	.83	.80
100	1.81	1.62	1.47	1.36	1.28	1.21	1.15	1.10	1.06
200	3.62	3.23	2.94	2.72	2.55	2.41	2.29	2.19	2.11
300	5.42	4.84	4.41	4.08	3.82	3.61	3.43	3.29	3.17
400	7.23	6.46	5.88	5.44	5.09	4.81	4.57	4.38	4.22
500	9.04	8.07	7.35	6.80	6.36	6.01	5.72	5.48	5.27
600	10.84	9.68	8.82	8.16	7.63	7.21	6.86	6.57	6.33
700	12.65	11.29	10.29	9.51	8.90	8.41	8.00	7.66	7.38
800	14.46	12.91	11.76	10.87	10.17	9.61	9.14	8.76	8.43
900	16.26	14.52	13.23	12.23	11.44	10.81	10.29	9.85	9.49
1000	18.07	16.13	14.69	13.59	12.71	12.01	11.43	10.95	10.54
2000	36.13	32.26	29.38	27.17	25.42	24.01	22.85	21.89	21.07
3000	54.20	48.39	44.07	40.76	38.13	36.01	34.28	32.83	31.61
4000	72.26	64.52	58.76	54.34	50.84	48.02	45.70	43.77	42.14
5000	90.32	80.64	73.45	67.92	63.55	60.02	57.12	54.71	52.68
6000	108.39	96.77	88.14	81.51	76.26	72.02	68.55	65.65	63.21
7000	126.45	112.90	102.83	95.09	88.97	84.03	79.97	76.59	73.74
8000	144.51	129.03	117.52	108.67	101.68	96.03	91.39	87.53	84.28
9000	162.58	145.16	132.21	122.26	114.39	108.03	102.82	98.47	94.81
10000	180.64	161.28	146.90	135.84	127.10	120.04	114.24	109.41	105.35
15000	270.96	241.92	220.35	203.76	190.64	180.05	171.36	164.12	158.02
20000	361.28	322.56	293.80	271.68	254.19	240.07	228.48	218.82	210.69
25000	451.59	403.20	367.25	339.59	317.73	300.08	285.59	273.53	263.36
30000	541.91	483.84	440.70	407.51	381.28	360.10	342.71	328.23	316.03
35000	632.23	564.48	514.15	475.43	444.82	420.12	399.83	382.93	368.70
36000	650.29	580.61	528.84	489.01	457.53	432.12	411.25	393.87	379.24
37000	668.36	596.74	543.53	502.60	470.24	444.12	422.67	404.82	389.77
38000	686.42	612.87	558.22	516.18	482.95	456.13	434.10	415.76	400.31
39000	704.48	629.00	572.91	529.76	495.66	468.13	445.52	426.70	410.84
40000	722.55	645.12	587.60	543.35	508.37	480.13	456.95	437.64	421.37
41000	740.61	661.25	602.29	556.93	521.08	492.13	468.37	448.58	431.91
42000	758.68	677.38	616.98	570.51	533.79	504.14	479.79	459.52	442.44
43000	776.74	693.51	631.67	584.10	546.50	516.14	491.22	470.46	452.98
44000	794.80	709.64	646.36	597.68	559.20	528.14	502.64	481.40	463.51
45000	812.87	725.76	661.05	611.26	571.91	540.15	514.06	492.34	474.04
46000	830.93	741.89	675.74	624.85	584.62	552.15	525.49	503.28	484.58
47000	848.99	758.02	690.43	638.43	597.33	564.15	536.91	514.22	495.11
48000	867.06	774.15	705.12	652.02	610.04	576.16	548.33	525.16	505.65
49000	885.12	790.28	719.81	665.60	622.75	588.16	559.76	536.11	516.18
50000	903.18	806.40	734.50	679.18	635.46	600.16	571.18	547.05	526.72
51000	921.25	822.53	749.19	692.77	648.17	612.17	582.60	557.99	537.25
52000	939.31	838.66	763.88	706.35	660.88	624.17	594.03	568.93	547.78
53000	957.38	854.79	778.57	719.93	673.59	636.17	605.45	579.87	558.32
54000	975.44	870.92	793.26	733.52	686.30	648.18	616.87	590.81	568.85
55000	993.50	887.04	807.95	747.10	699.00	660.18	628.30	601.75	579.39
56000	1011.57	903.17	822.64	760.68	711.71	672.18	639.72	612.69	589.92
57000	1029.63	919.30	837.33	774.27	724.42	684.19	651.14	623.63	600.46
58000	1047.69	935.43	852.02	787.85	737.13	696.19	662.57	634.57	610.99
59000	1065.76	951.56	866.71	801.43	749.84	708.19	673.99	645.51	621.52
60000	1083.82	967.68	881.40	815.02	762.55	720.19	685.42	656.45	632.06
61000	1101.88	983.81	896.09	828.60	775.26	732.20	696.84	667.40	642.59
62000	1119.95	999.94	910.78	842.19	787.97	744.20	708.26	678.34	653.13
63000	1138.01	1016.07	925.47	855.77	800.68	756.20	719.69	689.28	663.66
64000	1156.07	1032.20	940.16	869.35	813.39	768.21	731.11	700.22	674.19
65000	1174.14	1048.32	954.85	882.94	826.10	780.21	742.53	711.16	684.73
66000	1192.20	1064.45	969.54	896.52	838.80	792.21	753.96	722.10	695.26
67000	1210.27	1080.58	984.23	910.10	851.51	804.22	765.38	733.04	705.80
68000	1228.33	1096.71	998.92	923.69	864.22	816.22	776.80	743.98	716.33
69000	1246.39	1112.84	1013.61	937.27	876.93	828.22	788.23	754.92	726.87
70000	1264.46	1128.96	1028.30	950.85	889.64	840.23	799.65	765.86	737.40
75000	1354.77	1209.60	1101.75	1018.77	953.19	900.24	856.77	820.57	790.07
80000	1445.09	1290.24	1175.20	1086.69	1016.73	960.26	913.89	875.27	842.74
100000	1806.36	1612.80	1469.00	1358.36	1270.91	1200.32	1142.36	1094.09	1053.43

41

9¼%

MONTHLY PAYMENT
NECESSARY TO AMORTIZE A LOAN

TERM AMOUNT	15 YEARS	16 YEARS	17 YEARS	18 YEARS	19 YEARS	20 YEARS	21 YEARS	22 YEARS	23 YEARS
$ 25	.26	.25	.25	.24	.24	.23	.23	.22	.22
50	.51	.50	.49	.48	.47	.46	.45	.44	.44
75	.77	.75	.73	.71	.70	.68	.67	.66	.65
100	1.02	.99	.97	.95	.93	.91	.89	.88	.87
200	2.04	1.98	1.93	1.89	1.85	1.81	1.78	1.76	1.73
300	3.06	2.97	2.90	2.83	2.77	2.72	2.67	2.63	2.60
400	4.08	3.96	3.86	3.77	3.69	3.62	3.56	3.51	3.46
500	5.10	4.95	4.82	4.71	4.61	4.53	4.45	4.39	4.33
600	6.12	5.94	5.79	5.65	5.54	5.43	5.34	5.26	5.19
700	7.14	6.93	6.75	6.59	6.46	6.34	6.23	6.14	6.06
800	8.16	7.92	7.71	7.53	7.38	7.24	7.12	7.01	6.92
900	9.17	8.91	8.68	8.48	8.30	8.15	8.01	7.89	7.78
1000	10.19	9.90	9.64	9.42	9.22	9.05	8.90	8.77	8.65
2000	20.38	19.79	19.28	18.83	18.44	18.10	17.80	17.53	17.29
3000	30.57	29.68	28.91	28.24	27.66	27.14	26.69	26.29	25.94
4000	40.76	39.57	38.55	37.65	36.88	36.19	35.59	35.05	34.58
5000	50.95	49.46	48.18	47.07	46.09	45.24	44.48	43.82	43.23
6000	61.13	59.35	57.82	56.48	55.31	54.28	53.38	52.58	51.87
7000	71.32	69.25	67.45	65.89	64.53	63.33	62.28	61.34	60.51
8000	81.51	79.14	77.09	75.30	73.75	72.38	71.17	70.10	69.16
9000	91.70	89.03	86.72	84.72	82.96	81.42	80.07	78.87	77.80
10000	101.89	98.92	96.36	94.13	92.18	90.47	88.96	87.63	86.45
15000	152.83	148.38	144.53	141.19	138.27	135.70	133.44	131.44	129.67
20000	203.77	197.84	192.71	188.25	184.36	180.94	177.92	175.25	172.89
25000	254.71	247.29	240.89	235.31	230.45	226.17	222.40	219.07	216.11
30000	305.65	296.75	289.06	282.38	276.53	271.40	266.88	262.88	259.33
35000	356.60	346.21	337.24	329.44	322.62	316.64	311.36	306.69	302.55
36000	366.78	356.10	346.87	338.85	331.84	325.68	320.25	315.45	311.19
37000	376.97	365.99	356.51	348.26	341.06	334.73	329.15	324.21	319.83
38000	387.16	375.88	366.14	357.67	350.27	343.78	338.05	332.98	328.48
39000	397.35	385.78	375.78	367.09	359.49	352.82	346.94	341.74	337.12
40000	407.54	395.67	385.41	376.50	368.71	361.87	355.84	350.50	345.77
41000	417.73	405.56	395.05	385.91	377.93	370.92	364.73	359.26	354.41
42000	427.91	415.45	404.68	395.32	387.14	379.96	373.63	368.03	363.05
43000	438.10	425.34	414.32	404.74	396.36	389.01	382.53	376.79	371.70
44000	448.29	435.23	423.95	414.15	405.58	398.06	391.42	385.55	380.34
45000	458.48	445.13	433.59	423.56	414.80	407.10	400.32	394.31	388.99
46000	468.67	455.02	443.22	432.97	424.01	416.15	409.21	403.08	397.63
47000	478.86	464.91	452.86	442.39	433.23	425.20	418.11	411.84	406.27
48000	489.04	474.80	462.50	451.80	442.45	434.24	427.00	420.60	414.92
49000	499.23	484.69	472.13	461.21	451.67	443.29	435.90	429.36	423.56
50000	509.42	494.58	481.77	470.62	460.89	452.33	444.80	438.13	432.21
51000	519.61	504.48	491.40	480.04	470.10	461.38	453.69	446.89	440.85
52000	529.80	514.37	501.04	489.45	479.32	470.43	462.59	455.65	449.49
53000	539.98	524.26	510.67	498.86	488.54	479.47	471.48	464.41	458.14
54000	550.17	534.15	520.31	508.27	497.76	488.52	480.38	473.18	466.78
55000	560.36	544.04	529.94	517.68	506.97	497.57	489.28	481.94	475.43
56000	570.55	553.93	539.58	527.10	516.19	506.61	498.17	490.70	484.07
57000	580.74	563.82	549.21	536.51	525.41	515.66	507.07	499.46	492.71
58000	590.93	573.72	558.85	545.92	534.63	524.71	515.96	508.23	501.36
59000	601.11	583.61	568.48	555.33	543.84	533.75	524.86	516.99	510.00
60000	611.30	593.50	578.12	564.75	553.06	542.80	533.75	525.75	518.65
61000	621.49	603.39	587.75	574.16	562.28	551.85	542.65	534.51	527.29
62000	631.68	613.28	597.39	583.57	571.50	560.89	551.55	543.28	535.93
63000	641.87	623.17	607.02	592.98	580.71	569.94	560.44	552.04	544.58
64000	652.06	633.07	616.66	602.40	589.93	578.99	569.34	560.80	553.22
65000	662.24	642.96	626.29	611.81	599.15	588.03	578.23	569.56	561.87
66000	672.43	652.85	635.93	621.22	608.37	597.08	587.13	578.32	570.51
67000	682.62	662.74	645.56	630.63	617.58	606.13	596.03	587.09	579.15
68000	692.81	672.63	655.20	640.05	626.80	615.17	604.92	595.85	587.80
69000	703.00	682.52	664.83	649.46	636.02	624.22	613.82	604.61	596.44
70000	713.19	692.41	674.47	658.87	645.24	633.27	622.71	613.37	605.09
75000	764.13	741.87	722.65	705.93	691.33	678.50	667.19	657.19	648.31
80000	815.07	791.33	770.82	752.99	737.41	723.73	711.67	701.00	691.53
100000	1018.83	989.16	963.53	941.24	921.77	904.66	889.59	876.25	864.41

42

MONTHLY PAYMENT 9¼%
NECESSARY TO AMORTIZE A LOAN

TERM AMOUNT	24 YEARS	25 YEARS	26 YEARS	27 YEARS	28 YEARS	29 YEARS	30 YEARS	35 YEARS	40 YEARS
$ 25	.22	.22	.21	.21	.21	.21	.21	.20	.20
50	.43	.43	.42	.42	.42	.42	.41	.40	.39
75	.65	.64	.63	.63	.62	.62	.61	.60	.59
100	.86	.85	.84	.84	.83	.83	.82	.79	.78
200	1.71	1.69	1.68	1.66	1.65	1.64	1.63	1.58	1.56
300	2.57	2.54	2.51	2.49	2.47	2.45	2.44	2.37	2.34
400	3.42	3.38	3.35	3.32	3.29	3.27	3.25	3.16	3.11
500	4.27	4.23	4.19	4.15	4.11	4.08	4.06	3.95	3.89
600	5.13	5.07	5.02	4.98	4.94	4.90	4.87	4.74	4.67
700	5.98	5.92	5.86	5.80	5.76	5.71	5.68	5.53	5.45
800	6.84	6.76	6.69	6.63	6.58	6.53	6.49	6.32	6.22
900	7.69	7.61	7.53	7.46	7.40	7.35	7.30	7.11	7.00
1000	8.54	8.45	8.37	8.29	8.22	8.16	8.11	7.90	7.78
2000	17.08	16.89	16.73	16.57	16.44	16.32	16.21	15.80	15.55
3000	25.62	25.34	25.09	24.86	24.66	24.47	24.31	23.70	23.32
4000	34.16	33.78	33.45	33.14	32.87	32.63	32.41	31.59	31.10
5000	42.70	42.23	41.81	41.43	41.09	40.79	40.51	39.49	38.87
6000	51.24	50.67	50.17	49.71	49.31	48.94	48.61	47.39	46.64
7000	59.78	59.12	58.53	58.00	57.53	57.10	56.71	55.29	54.41
8000	68.31	67.56	66.89	66.28	65.74	65.26	64.82	63.18	62.19
9000	76.85	76.01	75.25	74.57	73.96	73.41	72.92	71.08	69.96
10000	85.39	84.45	83.61	82.85	82.18	81.57	81.02	78.98	77.73
15000	128.08	126.67	125.41	124.28	123.26	122.35	121.53	118.46	116.59
20000	170.78	168.89	167.21	165.70	164.35	163.13	162.03	157.95	155.46
25000	213.47	211.12	209.01	207.13	205.43	203.91	202.54	197.44	194.32
30000	256.16	253.34	250.82	248.55	246.52	244.69	243.05	236.92	233.18
35000	298.86	295.56	292.62	289.98	287.61	285.47	283.55	276.41	272.05
36000	307.39	304.01	300.98	298.26	295.82	293.63	291.66	284.31	279.82
37000	315.93	312.45	309.34	306.55	304.04	301.79	299.76	292.20	287.59
38000	324.47	320.90	317.70	314.83	312.26	309.94	307.86	300.10	295.37
39000	333.01	329.34	326.06	323.12	320.48	318.10	315.96	308.00	303.14
40000	341.55	337.78	334.42	331.40	328.69	326.26	324.06	315.90	310.91
41000	350.09	346.23	342.78	339.69	336.91	334.41	332.16	323.79	318.68
42000	358.63	354.67	351.14	347.97	345.13	342.57	340.26	331.69	326.46
43000	367.16	363.12	359.50	356.26	353.34	350.73	348.37	339.59	334.23
44000	375.70	371.56	367.86	364.54	361.56	358.88	356.47	347.49	342.00
45000	384.24	380.01	376.22	372.83	369.78	367.04	364.57	355.38	349.77
46000	392.78	388.45	384.58	381.11	378.00	375.19	372.67	363.28	357.55
47000	401.32	396.90	392.94	389.40	386.21	383.35	380.77	371.18	365.32
48000	409.86	405.34	401.30	397.68	394.43	391.51	388.87	379.07	373.09
49000	418.40	413.79	409.66	405.97	402.65	399.66	396.97	386.97	380.87
50000	426.93	422.23	418.02	414.25	410.86	407.82	405.08	394.87	388.64
51000	435.47	430.67	426.38	422.54	419.08	415.98	413.18	402.77	396.41
52000	444.01	439.12	434.74	430.82	427.30	424.13	421.28	410.66	404.18
53000	452.55	447.56	443.10	439.11	435.52	432.29	429.38	418.56	411.96
54000	461.09	456.01	451.46	447.39	443.73	440.44	437.48	426.46	419.73
55000	469.63	464.45	459.82	455.68	451.95	448.60	445.58	434.36	427.50
56000	478.17	472.90	468.18	463.96	460.17	456.76	453.68	442.25	435.27
57000	486.70	481.34	476.54	472.25	468.38	464.91	461.79	450.15	443.05
58000	495.24	489.79	484.90	480.53	476.60	473.07	469.89	458.05	450.82
59000	503.78	498.23	493.27	488.81	484.82	481.23	477.99	465.94	458.59
60000	512.32	506.67	501.63	497.10	493.04	489.38	486.09	473.84	466.36
61000	520.86	515.12	509.99	505.38	501.25	497.54	494.19	481.74	474.14
62000	529.40	523.56	518.35	513.67	509.47	505.69	502.29	489.64	481.91
63000	537.94	532.01	526.71	521.95	517.69	513.85	510.39	497.53	489.68
64000	546.47	540.45	535.07	530.24	525.91	522.01	518.50	505.43	497.45
65000	555.01	548.90	543.43	538.52	534.12	530.16	526.60	513.33	505.23
66000	563.55	557.34	551.79	546.81	542.34	538.32	534.70	521.23	513.00
67000	572.09	565.79	560.15	555.09	550.56	546.48	542.80	529.12	520.77
68000	580.63	574.23	568.51	563.38	558.77	554.63	550.90	537.02	528.55
69000	589.17	582.68	576.87	571.66	566.99	562.79	559.00	544.92	536.32
70000	597.71	591.12	585.23	579.95	575.21	570.94	567.10	552.81	544.09
75000	640.40	633.34	627.03	621.37	616.29	611.73	607.61	592.30	582.95
80000	683.09	675.56	668.83	662.80	657.38	652.51	648.12	631.79	621.82
100000	853.86	844.45	836.04	828.50	821.72	815.63	810.15	789.73	777.27

43

9½% MONTHLY PAYMENT
NECESSARY TO AMORTIZE A LOAN

TERM AMOUNT	1 YEAR	1½ YEARS	2 YEARS	2½ YEARS	3 YEARS	3½ YEARS	4 YEARS	4½ YEARS	5 YEARS
$ 25	2.19	1.50	1.15	.94	.80	.70	.63	.57	.53
50	4.38	2.99	2.30	1.88	1.60	1.40	1.26	1.14	1.05
75	6.57	4.49	3.44	2.82	2.40	2.10	1.88	1.71	1.57
100	8.76	5.98	4.59	3.75	3.20	2.80	2.51	2.28	2.10
200	17.52	11.95	9.17	7.50	6.39	5.60	5.01	4.55	4.19
300	26.28	17.93	13.75	11.25	9.59	8.40	7.52	6.83	6.28
400	35.04	23.90	18.34	15.00	12.78	11.20	10.02	9.10	8.37
500	43.80	29.88	22.92	18.75	15.98	14.00	12.52	11.38	10.46
600	52.56	35.85	27.50	22.50	19.17	16.80	15.03	13.65	12.55
700	61.32	41.83	32.09	26.25	22.37	19.60	17.53	15.92	14.64
800	70.08	47.80	36.67	30.00	25.56	22.40	20.03	18.20	16.74
900	78.84	53.77	41.25	33.75	28.76	25.20	22.54	20.47	18.83
1000	87.60	59.75	45.84	37.50	31.95	28.00	25.04	22.75	20.92
2000	175.20	119.49	91.67	74.99	63.90	55.99	50.08	45.49	41.83
3000	262.80	179.23	137.50	112.49	95.85	83.99	75.11	68.23	62.74
4000	350.40	238.98	183.33	149.98	127.80	111.98	100.15	90.97	83.66
5000	438.00	298.72	229.16	187.48	159.74	139.97	125.18	113.71	104.57
6000	525.60	358.46	274.99	224.97	191.69	167.97	150.22	136.46	125.48
7000	613.20	418.21	320.82	262.47	223.64	195.96	175.26	159.20	146.39
8000	700.79	477.95	366.65	299.96	255.59	223.96	200.29	181.94	167.31
9000	788.39	537.69	412.48	337.46	287.53	251.95	225.33	204.68	188.22
10000	875.99	597.44	458.31	374.95	319.48	279.94	250.36	227.42	209.13
15000	1313.99	896.15	687.46	562.43	479.22	419.91	375.54	341.13	313.70
20000	1751.98	1194.87	916.61	749.90	638.96	559.88	500.72	454.84	418.26
25000	2189.97	1493.58	1145.77	937.37	798.69	699.85	625.90	568.55	522.82
30000	2627.97	1792.30	1374.92	1124.85	958.43	839.82	751.08	682.26	627.39
35000	3065.96	2091.02	1604.07	1312.32	1118.17	979.79	876.26	795.97	731.95
36000	3153.56	2150.76	1649.90	1349.82	1150.12	1007.78	901.30	818.72	752.86
37000	3241.16	2210.50	1695.73	1387.31	1182.07	1035.78	926.34	841.46	773.77
38000	3328.75	2270.25	1741.56	1424.81	1214.01	1063.77	951.37	864.20	794.69
39000	3416.35	2329.99	1787.39	1462.30	1245.96	1091.76	976.41	886.94	815.60
40000	3503.95	2389.73	1833.22	1499.80	1277.91	1119.76	1001.44	909.68	836.51
41000	3591.55	2449.48	1879.05	1537.29	1309.86	1147.75	1026.48	932.43	857.42
42000	3679.15	2509.22	1924.88	1574.79	1341.80	1175.75	1051.52	955.17	878.34
43000	3766.75	2568.96	1970.71	1612.28	1373.75	1203.74	1076.55	977.91	899.25
44000	3854.35	2628.71	2016.54	1649.77	1405.70	1231.73	1101.59	1000.65	920.16
45000	3941.95	2688.45	2062.37	1687.27	1437.65	1259.73	1126.62	1023.39	941.08
46000	4029.54	2748.19	2108.21	1724.76	1469.59	1287.72	1151.66	1046.14	961.99
47000	4117.14	2807.94	2154.04	1762.26	1501.54	1315.72	1176.70	1068.88	982.90
48000	4204.74	2867.68	2199.87	1799.75	1533.49	1343.71	1201.73	1091.62	1003.81
49000	4292.34	2927.42	2245.70	1837.25	1565.44	1371.70	1226.77	1114.36	1024.73
50000	4379.94	2987.16	2291.53	1874.74	1597.38	1399.70	1251.80	1137.10	1045.64
51000	4467.54	3046.91	2337.36	1912.24	1629.33	1427.69	1276.84	1159.85	1066.55
52000	4555.14	3106.65	2383.19	1949.73	1661.28	1455.68	1301.87	1182.59	1087.46
53000	4642.73	3166.39	2429.02	1987.23	1693.23	1483.68	1326.91	1205.33	1108.38
54000	4730.33	3226.14	2474.85	2024.72	1725.18	1511.67	1351.95	1228.07	1129.29
55000	4817.93	3285.88	2520.68	2062.22	1757.12	1539.67	1376.98	1250.81	1150.20
56000	4905.53	3345.62	2566.51	2099.71	1789.07	1567.66	1402.02	1273.56	1171.11
57000	4993.13	3405.37	2612.34	2137.21	1821.02	1595.65	1427.05	1296.30	1192.03
58000	5080.73	3465.11	2658.17	2174.70	1852.97	1623.65	1452.09	1319.04	1212.94
59000	5168.33	3524.85	2704.00	2212.20	1884.91	1651.64	1477.13	1341.78	1233.85
60000	5255.93	3584.60	2749.83	2249.69	1916.86	1679.64	1502.16	1364.52	1254.77
61000	5343.52	3644.34	2795.66	2287.19	1948.81	1707.63	1527.20	1387.26	1275.68
62000	5431.12	3704.08	2841.49	2324.68	1980.76	1735.62	1552.23	1410.01	1296.59
63000	5518.72	3763.83	2887.32	2362.18	2012.70	1763.62	1577.27	1432.75	1317.50
64000	5606.32	3823.57	2933.15	2399.67	2044.65	1791.61	1602.31	1455.49	1338.42
65000	5693.92	3883.31	2978.98	2437.16	2076.60	1819.60	1627.34	1478.23	1359.33
66000	5781.52	3943.06	3024.81	2474.66	2108.55	1847.60	1652.38	1500.97	1380.24
67000	5869.12	4002.80	3070.64	2512.15	2140.49	1875.59	1677.41	1523.72	1401.15
68000	5956.71	4062.54	3116.48	2549.65	2172.44	1903.59	1702.45	1546.46	1422.07
69000	6044.31	4122.29	3162.31	2587.14	2204.39	1931.58	1727.49	1569.20	1442.98
70000	6131.91	4182.03	3208.14	2624.64	2236.34	1959.57	1752.52	1591.94	1463.89
75000	6569.91	4480.74	3437.29	2812.11	2396.07	2099.54	1877.70	1705.65	1568.46
80000	7007.90	4779.46	3666.44	2999.59	2555.81	2239.51	2002.88	1819.36	1673.02
100000	8759.87	5974.32	4583.05	3749.48	3194.76	2799.39	2503.60	2274.20	2091.27

44

MONTHLY PAYMENT 9½%
NECESSARY TO AMORTIZE A LOAN

TERM AMOUNT	6 YEARS	7 YEARS	8 YEARS	9 YEARS	10 YEARS	11 YEARS	12 YEARS	13 YEARS	14 YEARS
$ 25	.46	.41	.38	.35	.33	.31	.29	.28	.27
50	.91	.82	.75	.69	.65	.61	.58	.56	.54
75	1.37	1.22	1.12	1.03	.97	.92	.87	.84	.81
100	1.82	1.63	1.49	1.38	1.29	1.22	1.16	1.11	1.07
200	3.64	3.26	2.97	2.75	2.57	2.43	2.32	2.22	2.14
300	5.46	4.88	4.45	4.12	3.86	3.65	3.47	3.33	3.21
400	7.28	6.51	5.93	5.49	5.14	4.86	4.63	4.44	4.28
500	9.10	8.13	7.41	6.86	6.42	6.07	5.78	5.54	5.34
600	10.92	9.76	8.89	8.23	7.71	7.29	6.94	6.65	6.41
700	12.73	11.38	10.38	9.60	8.99	8.50	8.10	7.76	7.48
800	14.55	13.01	11.86	10.97	10.28	9.71	9.25	8.87	8.55
900	16.37	14.63	13.34	12.35	11.56	10.93	10.41	9.98	9.61
1000	18.19	16.26	14.82	13.72	12.84	12.14	11.56	11.08	10.68
2000	36.37	32.51	29.64	27.43	25.68	24.28	23.12	22.16	21.36
3000	54.56	48.76	44.45	41.14	38.52	36.42	34.68	33.24	32.03
4000	72.74	65.01	59.27	54.85	51.36	48.55	46.24	44.32	42.71
5000	90.92	81.26	74.08	68.56	64.20	60.69	57.80	55.40	53.38
6000	109.11	97.51	88.90	82.27	77.04	72.83	69.36	66.48	64.06
7000	127.29	113.76	103.71	95.99	89.88	84.96	80.92	77.56	74.73
8000	145.47	130.01	118.53	109.70	102.72	97.10	92.48	88.64	85.41
9000	163.66	146.26	133.34	123.41	115.56	109.24	104.04	99.72	96.09
10000	181.84	162.51	148.16	137.12	128.40	121.37	115.60	110.80	106.76
15000	272.76	243.76	222.23	205.68	192.60	182.06	173.40	166.20	160.14
20000	363.67	325.02	296.31	274.24	256.80	242.74	231.20	221.60	213.52
25000	454.59	406.27	370.39	342.80	321.00	303.42	289.00	277.00	266.90
30000	545.51	487.52	444.46	411.35	385.20	364.11	346.80	332.40	320.27
35000	636.42	568.77	518.54	479.91	449.40	424.79	404.60	387.79	373.65
36000	654.61	585.02	533.36	493.62	462.24	436.93	416.16	398.87	384.33
37000	672.79	601.28	548.17	507.34	475.08	449.06	427.71	409.95	395.00
38000	690.97	617.53	562.99	521.05	487.92	461.20	439.27	421.03	405.68
39000	709.16	633.78	577.80	534.76	500.76	473.34	450.83	432.11	416.36
40000	727.34	650.03	592.62	548.47	513.60	485.47	462.39	443.19	427.03
41000	745.52	666.28	607.43	562.18	526.44	497.61	473.95	454.27	437.71
42000	763.71	682.53	622.25	575.89	539.28	509.75	485.51	465.35	448.38
43000	781.89	698.78	637.06	589.61	552.12	521.88	497.07	476.43	459.06
44000	800.07	715.03	651.88	603.32	564.96	534.02	508.63	487.51	469.73
45000	818.26	731.28	666.69	617.03	577.80	546.16	520.19	498.59	480.41
46000	836.44	747.53	681.51	630.74	590.64	558.29	531.75	509.67	491.08
47000	854.62	763.78	696.32	644.45	603.48	570.43	543.31	520.75	501.76
48000	872.81	780.03	711.14	658.16	616.32	582.57	554.87	531.83	512.44
49000	890.99	796.28	725.96	671.88	629.16	594.70	566.43	542.91	523.11
50000	909.17	812.53	740.77	685.59	642.00	606.84	577.99	553.99	533.79
51000	927.36	828.78	755.59	699.30	654.84	618.98	589.55	565.07	544.46
52000	945.54	845.03	770.40	713.01	667.68	631.11	601.11	576.15	555.14
53000	963.73	861.28	785.22	726.72	680.52	643.25	612.67	587.23	565.81
54000	981.91	877.53	800.03	740.43	693.36	655.39	624.23	598.31	576.49
55000	1000.09	893.79	814.85	754.15	706.20	667.52	635.79	609.39	587.17
56000	1018.28	910.04	829.66	767.86	719.04	679.66	647.35	620.47	597.84
57000	1036.46	926.29	844.48	781.57	731.88	691.80	658.91	631.55	608.52
58000	1054.64	942.54	859.29	795.28	744.72	703.93	670.47	642.63	619.19
59000	1072.83	958.79	874.11	808.99	757.56	716.07	682.03	653.71	629.87
60000	1091.01	975.04	888.92	822.70	770.40	728.21	693.59	664.79	640.54
61000	1109.19	991.29	903.74	836.42	783.24	740.34	705.15	675.87	651.22
62000	1127.38	1007.54	918.55	850.13	796.08	752.48	716.71	686.95	661.89
63000	1145.56	1023.79	933.37	863.84	808.92	764.62	728.27	698.02	672.57
64000	1163.74	1040.04	948.18	877.55	821.76	776.75	739.83	709.10	683.25
65000	1181.93	1056.29	963.00	891.26	834.60	788.89	751.39	720.18	693.92
66000	1200.11	1072.54	977.82	904.97	847.44	801.03	762.95	731.26	704.60
67000	1218.29	1088.79	992.63	918.69	860.28	813.16	774.51	742.34	715.27
68000	1236.48	1105.04	1007.45	932.40	873.12	825.30	786.07	753.42	725.95
69000	1254.66	1121.29	1022.26	946.11	885.96	837.44	797.63	764.50	736.62
70000	1272.84	1137.54	1037.08	959.82	898.80	849.57	809.19	775.58	747.30
75000	1363.76	1218.80	1111.15	1028.38	963.00	910.26	866.98	830.98	800.68
80000	1454.68	1300.05	1185.23	1096.94	1027.20	970.94	924.78	886.38	854.06
100000	1818.34	1625.06	1481.54	1371.17	1284.00	1213.68	1155.98	1107.97	1067.57

45

9½%

MONTHLY PAYMENT
NECESSARY TO AMORTIZE A LOAN

TERM AMOUNT	15 YEARS	16 YEARS	17 YEARS	18 YEARS	19 YEARS	20 YEARS	21 YEARS	22 YEARS	23 YEARS
$ 25	.26	.26	.25	.24	.24	.24	.23	.23	.23
50	.52	.51	.49	.48	.47	.47	.46	.45	.45
75	.78	.76	.74	.72	.71	.70	.68	.67	.67
100	1.04	1.01	.98	.96	.94	.93	.91	.90	.89
200	2.07	2.01	1.96	1.92	1.88	1.85	1.82	1.79	1.77
300	3.10	3.02	2.94	2.87	2.82	2.77	2.72	2.68	2.65
400	4.14	4.02	3.92	3.83	3.75	3.69	3.63	3.57	3.53
500	5.17	5.02	4.90	4.79	4.69	4.61	4.53	4.47	4.41
600	6.20	6.03	5.88	5.74	5.63	5.53	5.44	5.36	5.29
700	7.24	7.03	6.85	6.70	6.56	6.45	6.34	6.25	6.17
800	8.27	8.04	7.83	7.66	7.50	7.37	7.25	7.14	7.05
900	9.30	9.04	8.81	8.61	8.44	8.29	8.15	8.04	7.93
1000	10.34	10.04	9.79	9.57	9.38	9.21	9.06	8.93	8.81
2000	20.67	20.08	19.57	19.13	18.75	18.41	18.11	17.85	17.62
3000	31.00	30.12	29.36	28.70	28.12	27.61	27.17	26.77	26.42
4000	41.33	40.16	39.14	38.26	37.49	36.81	36.22	35.69	35.23
5000	51.67	50.20	48.93	47.82	46.86	46.02	45.27	44.62	44.03
6000	62.00	60.23	58.71	57.39	56.23	55.22	54.33	53.54	52.84
7000	72.33	70.27	68.49	66.95	65.60	64.42	63.38	62.46	61.65
8000	82.66	80.31	78.28	76.51	74.97	73.62	72.43	71.38	70.45
9000	93.00	90.35	88.06	86.08	84.34	82.83	81.49	80.31	79.26
10000	103.33	100.39	97.85	95.64	93.72	92.03	90.54	89.23	88.06
15000	154.99	150.58	146.77	143.46	140.57	138.04	135.81	133.84	132.09
20000	206.65	200.77	195.69	191.28	187.43	184.05	181.08	178.45	176.12
25000	258.31	250.96	244.61	239.09	234.28	230.06	226.35	223.06	220.15
30000	309.97	301.15	293.53	286.91	281.14	276.07	271.62	267.68	264.18
35000	361.63	351.34	342.45	334.73	327.99	322.09	316.88	312.29	308.21
36000	371.97	361.37	352.23	344.29	337.36	331.29	325.94	321.21	317.02
37000	382.30	371.41	362.02	353.86	346.74	340.49	334.99	330.13	325.83
38000	392.63	381.45	371.80	363.42	356.11	349.69	344.05	339.05	334.63
39000	402.96	391.49	381.58	372.98	365.48	358.89	353.10	347.98	343.44
40000	413.30	401.53	391.37	382.55	374.85	368.10	362.15	356.90	352.24
41000	423.63	411.56	401.15	392.11	384.22	377.30	371.21	365.82	361.05
42000	433.96	421.60	410.94	401.67	393.59	386.50	380.26	374.74	369.86
43000	444.29	431.64	420.72	411.24	402.96	395.70	389.31	383.67	378.66
44000	454.62	441.68	430.50	420.80	412.33	404.91	398.37	392.59	387.47
45000	464.96	451.72	440.29	430.37	421.70	414.11	407.42	401.51	396.27
46000	475.29	461.75	450.07	439.93	431.08	423.31	416.47	410.43	405.08
47000	485.62	471.79	459.86	449.49	440.45	432.51	425.53	419.36	413.89
48000	495.95	481.83	469.64	459.06	449.82	441.72	434.58	428.28	422.69
49000	506.29	491.87	479.42	468.62	459.19	450.92	443.64	437.20	431.50
50000	516.62	501.91	489.21	478.18	468.56	460.12	452.69	446.12	440.30
51000	526.95	511.94	498.99	487.75	477.93	469.32	461.74	455.05	449.11
52000	537.28	521.98	508.78	497.31	487.30	478.52	470.80	463.97	457.91
53000	547.61	532.02	518.56	506.87	496.67	487.73	479.85	472.89	466.72
54000	557.95	542.06	528.34	516.44	506.04	496.93	488.90	481.81	475.53
55000	568.28	552.10	538.13	526.00	515.42	506.13	497.96	490.74	484.33
56000	578.61	562.13	547.91	535.56	524.79	515.33	507.01	499.66	493.14
57000	588.94	572.17	557.70	545.13	534.16	524.54	516.07	508.58	501.94
58000	599.28	582.21	567.48	554.69	543.53	533.74	525.12	517.50	510.75
59000	609.61	592.25	577.26	564.26	552.90	542.94	534.17	526.42	519.56
60000	619.94	602.29	587.05	573.82	562.27	552.14	543.23	535.35	528.36
61000	630.27	612.32	596.83	583.38	571.64	561.35	552.28	544.27	537.17
62000	640.61	622.36	606.62	592.95	581.01	570.55	561.33	553.19	545.97
63000	650.94	632.40	616.40	602.51	590.38	579.75	570.39	562.11	554.78
64000	661.27	642.44	626.18	612.07	599.75	588.95	579.44	571.04	563.59
65000	671.60	652.48	635.97	621.64	609.13	598.15	588.49	579.96	572.39
66000	681.93	662.51	645.75	631.20	618.50	607.36	597.55	588.88	581.20
67000	692.27	672.55	655.54	640.76	627.87	616.56	606.60	597.80	590.00
68000	702.60	682.59	665.32	650.33	637.24	625.76	615.66	606.73	598.81
69000	712.93	692.63	675.11	659.89	646.61	634.96	624.71	615.65	607.62
70000	723.26	702.67	684.89	669.45	655.98	644.17	633.76	624.57	616.42
75000	774.92	752.86	733.81	717.27	702.84	690.18	679.03	669.18	660.45
80000	826.59	803.05	782.73	765.09	749.69	736.19	724.30	713.79	704.48
100000	1033.23	1003.81	978.41	956.36	937.11	920.24	905.37	892.24	880.60

46

MONTHLY PAYMENT $9\frac{1}{2}$%
NECESSARY TO AMORTIZE A LOAN

TERM AMOUNT	24 YEARS	25 YEARS	26 YEARS	27 YEARS	28 YEARS	29 YEARS	30 YEARS	35 YEARS	40 YEARS
$ 25	.22	.22	.22	.22	.21	.21	.21	.21	.20
50	.44	.44	.43	.43	.42	.42	.42	.41	.40
75	.66	.65	.64	.64	.63	.63	.63	.61	.60
100	.88	.87	.86	.85	.84	.84	.83	.81	.80
200	1.75	1.73	1.71	1.70	1.68	1.67	1.66	1.62	1.60
300	2.62	2.59	2.56	2.54	2.52	2.50	2.49	2.43	2.39
400	3.49	3.45	3.42	3.39	3.36	3.34	3.32	3.24	3.19
500	4.36	4.31	4.27	4.23	4.20	4.17	4.14	4.04	3.98
600	5.23	5.17	5.12	5.08	5.04	5.00	4.97	4.85	4.78
700	6.10	6.03	5.97	5.92	5.88	5.84	5.80	5.66	5.58
800	6.97	6.89	6.83	6.77	6.72	6.67	6.63	6.47	6.37
900	7.84	7.75	7.68	7.61	7.55	7.50	7.45	7.28	7.17
1000	8.71	8.62	8.53	8.46	8.39	8.33	8.28	8.08	7.96
2000	17.41	17.23	17.06	16.91	16.78	16.66	16.55	16.16	15.92
3000	26.11	25.84	25.59	25.37	25.17	24.99	24.83	24.24	23.88
4000	34.81	34.45	34.12	33.82	33.56	33.32	33.11	32.32	31.84
5000	43.52	43.06	42.64	42.28	41.95	41.65	41.38	40.40	39.80
6000	52.22	51.67	51.17	50.73	50.33	49.98	49.66	48.47	47.76
7000	60.92	60.28	59.70	59.18	58.72	58.31	57.93	56.55	55.72
8000	69.62	68.89	68.23	67.64	67.11	66.64	66.21	64.63	63.67
9000	78.33	77.50	76.76	76.09	75.50	74.96	74.48	72.71	71.63
10000	87.03	86.11	85.28	84.55	83.89	83.29	82.76	80.79	79.59
15000	130.54	129.16	127.92	126.82	125.83	124.94	124.14	121.18	119.39
20000	174.05	172.21	170.56	169.09	167.77	166.58	165.52	161.57	159.18
25000	217.57	215.26	213.20	211.36	209.71	208.23	206.89	201.96	198.97
30000	261.08	258.31	255.84	253.63	251.65	249.87	248.27	242.35	238.77
35000	304.59	301.36	298.48	295.90	293.59	291.52	289.65	282.74	278.56
36000	313.29	309.97	307.01	304.36	301.98	299.84	297.92	290.82	286.52
37000	322.00	318.59	315.54	312.81	310.37	308.17	306.20	298.89	294.48
38000	330.70	327.20	324.07	321.27	318.76	316.50	314.48	306.97	302.44
39000	339.40	335.81	332.59	329.72	327.14	324.83	322.75	315.05	310.39
40000	348.10	344.42	341.12	338.17	335.53	333.16	331.03	323.13	318.35
41000	356.81	353.03	349.65	346.63	343.92	341.49	339.30	331.21	326.31
42000	365.51	361.64	358.18	355.08	352.31	349.82	347.58	339.28	334.27
43000	374.21	370.25	366.71	363.54	360.70	358.15	355.85	347.36	342.23
44000	382.91	378.86	375.23	371.99	369.08	366.48	364.13	355.44	350.19
45000	391.62	387.47	383.76	380.45	377.47	374.80	372.40	363.52	358.15
46000	400.32	396.08	392.29	388.90	385.86	383.13	380.68	371.60	366.11
47000	409.02	404.69	400.82	397.35	394.25	391.46	388.96	379.68	374.06
48000	417.72	413.30	409.35	405.81	402.64	399.79	397.23	387.75	382.02
49000	426.43	421.91	417.87	414.26	411.03	408.12	405.51	395.83	389.98
50000	435.13	430.52	426.40	422.72	419.41	416.45	413.78	403.91	397.94
51000	443.83	439.13	434.93	431.17	427.80	424.78	422.06	411.99	405.90
52000	452.53	447.74	443.46	439.63	436.19	433.11	430.33	420.07	413.86
53000	461.24	456.35	451.99	448.08	444.58	441.43	438.61	428.14	421.82
54000	469.94	464.96	460.51	456.53	452.97	449.76	446.88	436.22	429.78
55000	478.64	473.57	469.04	464.99	461.35	458.09	455.16	444.30	437.73
56000	487.34	482.18	477.57	473.44	469.74	466.42	463.44	452.38	445.69
57000	496.05	490.79	486.10	481.90	478.13	474.75	471.71	460.46	453.65
58000	504.75	499.40	494.62	490.35	486.52	483.08	479.99	468.53	461.61
59000	513.45	508.01	503.15	498.80	494.91	491.41	488.26	476.61	469.57
60000	522.15	516.62	511.68	507.26	503.30	499.74	496.54	484.69	477.53
61000	530.86	525.23	520.21	515.71	511.68	508.07	504.81	492.77	485.49
62000	539.56	533.84	528.74	524.17	520.07	516.39	513.09	500.85	493.44
63000	548.26	542.45	537.26	532.62	528.46	524.72	521.36	508.92	501.40
64000	556.96	551.06	545.79	541.08	536.85	533.05	529.64	517.00	509.36
65000	565.67	559.67	554.32	549.53	545.24	541.38	537.92	525.08	517.32
66000	574.37	568.28	562.85	557.98	553.62	549.71	546.19	533.16	525.28
67000	583.07	576.89	571.38	566.44	562.01	558.04	554.47	541.24	533.24
68000	591.77	585.50	579.90	574.89	570.40	566.37	562.74	549.32	541.20
69000	600.48	594.11	588.43	583.35	578.79	574.70	571.02	557.39	549.16
70000	609.18	602.72	596.96	591.80	587.18	583.03	579.29	565.47	557.11
75000	652.69	645.78	639.60	634.07	629.12	624.67	620.67	605.86	596.91
80000	696.20	688.83	682.24	676.34	671.06	666.31	662.05	646.25	636.70
100000	870.25	861.03	852.80	845.43	838.82	832.89	827.56	807.81	795.88

47

9¾% MONTHLY PAYMENT
NECESSARY TO AMORTIZE A LOAN

TERM AMOUNT	1 YEAR	1½ YEARS	2 YEARS	2½ YEARS	3 YEARS	3½ YEARS	4 YEARS	4½ YEARS	5 YEARS
$ 25	2.20	1.50	1.15	.95	.81	.71	.63	.58	.53
50	4.39	3.00	2.30	1.89	1.61	1.41	1.26	1.15	1.06
75	6.58	4.49	3.45	2.83	2.41	2.11	1.89	1.72	1.58
100	8.78	5.99	4.60	3.77	3.21	2.82	2.52	2.29	2.11
200	17.55	11.98	9.19	7.53	6.42	5.63	5.04	4.58	4.21
300	26.32	17.96	13.79	11.29	9.62	8.44	7.55	6.86	6.31
400	35.09	23.95	18.38	15.05	12.83	11.25	10.07	9.15	8.42
500	43.86	29.93	22.98	18.81	16.03	14.06	12.58	11.43	10.52
600	52.63	35.92	27.57	22.57	19.24	16.87	15.10	13.72	12.62
700	61.40	41.90	32.16	26.33	22.45	19.68	17.61	16.01	14.73
800	70.17	47.89	36.76	30.09	25.65	22.49	20.13	18.29	16.83
900	78.94	53.87	41.35	33.85	28.86	25.30	22.64	20.58	18.93
1000	87.72	59.86	45.95	37.61	32.06	28.11	25.16	22.86	21.04
2000	175.43	119.71	91.89	75.22	64.12	56.22	50.31	45.72	42.07
3000	263.14	179.57	137.83	112.82	96.18	84.33	75.46	68.58	63.10
4000	350.85	239.42	183.77	150.43	128.24	112.43	100.61	91.44	84.13
5000	438.56	299.27	229.71	188.04	160.30	140.54	125.76	114.29	105.16
6000	526.27	359.13	275.65	225.64	192.36	168.65	150.91	137.15	126.19
7000	613.98	418.98	321.59	263.25	224.42	196.76	176.06	160.01	147.22
8000	701.69	478.83	367.53	300.85	256.48	224.86	201.21	182.87	168.25
9000	789.40	538.69	413.47	338.46	288.54	252.97	226.36	205.73	189.28
10000	877.11	598.54	459.42	376.07	320.60	281.08	251.51	228.58	210.31
15000	1315.66	897.81	689.12	564.10	480.90	421.61	377.27	342.87	315.46
20000	1754.21	1197.08	918.83	752.13	641.20	562.15	503.02	457.16	420.61
25000	2192.76	1496.35	1148.53	940.16	801.50	702.69	628.77	571.45	525.76
30000	2631.31	1795.61	1378.24	1128.19	961.80	843.22	754.53	685.74	630.91
35000	3069.87	2094.88	1607.94	1316.22	1122.10	983.76	880.28	800.03	736.06
36000	3157.58	2154.73	1653.88	1353.82	1154.16	1011.87	905.43	822.89	757.09
37000	3245.29	2214.59	1699.82	1391.43	1186.22	1039.98	930.58	845.75	778.12
38000	3333.00	2274.44	1745.76	1429.04	1218.28	1068.08	955.73	868.61	799.15
39000	3420.71	2334.30	1791.71	1466.64	1250.34	1096.19	980.88	891.47	820.18
40000	3508.42	2394.15	1837.65	1504.25	1282.40	1124.30	1006.03	914.32	841.21
41000	3596.13	2454.00	1883.59	1541.85	1314.46	1152.40	1031.18	937.18	862.24
42000	3683.84	2513.86	1929.53	1579.46	1346.52	1180.51	1056.33	960.04	883.27
43000	3771.55	2573.71	1975.47	1617.07	1378.58	1208.62	1081.48	982.90	904.30
44000	3859.26	2633.56	2021.41	1654.67	1410.64	1236.73	1106.63	1005.76	925.33
45000	3946.97	2693.42	2067.35	1692.28	1442.70	1264.83	1131.79	1028.61	946.36
46000	4034.68	2753.27	2113.29	1729.88	1474.76	1292.94	1156.94	1051.47	967.39
47000	4122.39	2813.12	2159.23	1767.49	1506.82	1321.05	1182.09	1074.33	988.42
48000	4210.10	2872.98	2205.17	1805.10	1538.88	1349.16	1207.24	1097.19	1009.45
49000	4297.81	2932.83	2251.12	1842.70	1570.94	1377.26	1232.39	1120.05	1030.48
50000	4385.52	2992.69	2297.06	1880.31	1603.00	1405.37	1257.54	1142.90	1051.51
51000	4473.23	3052.54	2343.00	1917.91	1635.06	1433.48	1282.69	1165.76	1072.54
52000	4560.94	3112.39	2388.94	1955.52	1667.12	1461.59	1307.84	1188.62	1093.57
53000	4648.65	3172.25	2434.88	1993.13	1699.18	1489.69	1332.99	1211.48	1114.60
54000	4736.36	3232.10	2480.82	2030.73	1731.24	1517.80	1358.14	1234.34	1135.63
55000	4824.07	3291.95	2526.76	2068.34	1763.30	1545.91	1383.29	1257.19	1156.66
56000	4911.78	3351.81	2572.70	2105.95	1795.36	1574.01	1408.44	1280.05	1177.69
57000	4999.49	3411.66	2618.64	2143.55	1827.42	1602.12	1433.59	1302.91	1198.72
58000	5087.20	3471.51	2664.58	2181.16	1859.48	1630.23	1458.74	1325.77	1219.75
59000	5174.91	3531.37	2710.53	2218.76	1891.54	1658.34	1483.90	1348.63	1240.78
60000	5262.62	3591.22	2756.47	2256.37	1923.60	1686.44	1509.05	1371.48	1261.81
61000	5350.33	3651.08	2802.41	2293.98	1955.66	1714.55	1534.20	1394.34	1282.84
62000	5438.04	3710.93	2848.35	2331.58	1987.72	1742.66	1559.35	1417.20	1303.87
63000	5525.75	3770.78	2894.29	2369.19	2019.78	1770.77	1584.50	1440.06	1324.90
64000	5613.46	3830.64	2940.23	2406.79	2051.84	1798.87	1609.65	1462.92	1345.93
65000	5701.17	3890.49	2986.17	2444.40	2083.90	1826.98	1634.80	1485.77	1366.96
66000	5788.88	3950.34	3032.11	2482.01	2115.96	1855.09	1659.95	1508.63	1387.99
67000	5876.59	4010.20	3078.05	2519.61	2148.02	1883.20	1685.10	1531.49	1409.02
68000	5964.30	4070.05	3124.00	2557.22	2180.08	1911.30	1710.25	1554.35	1430.05
69000	6052.02	4129.90	3169.94	2594.82	2212.14	1939.41	1735.40	1577.21	1451.08
70000	6139.73	4189.76	3215.88	2632.43	2244.20	1967.52	1760.55	1600.06	1472.11
75000	6578.28	4489.03	3445.58	2820.46	2404.50	2108.05	1886.31	1714.35	1577.26
80000	7016.83	4788.29	3675.29	3008.49	2564.80	2248.59	2012.06	1828.64	1682.41
100000	8771.03	5985.37	4594.11	3760.61	3206.00	2810.74	2515.07	2285.80	2103.01

48

MONTHLY PAYMENT 9¾%
NECESSARY TO AMORTIZE A LOAN

TERM AMOUNT	6 YEARS	7 YEARS	8 YEARS	9 YEARS	10 YEARS	11 YEARS	12 YEARS	13 YEARS	14 YEARS
$ 25	.46	.41	.38	.35	.33	.31	.30	.29	.28
50	.92	.82	.75	.70	.65	.62	.59	.57	.55
75	1.38	1.23	1.13	1.04	.98	.93	.88	.85	.82
100	1.84	1.64	1.50	1.39	1.30	1.23	1.17	1.13	1.09
200	3.67	3.28	2.99	2.77	2.60	2.46	2.34	2.25	2.17
300	5.50	4.92	4.49	4.16	3.90	3.69	3.51	3.37	3.25
400	7.33	6.55	5.98	5.54	5.19	4.91	4.68	4.49	4.33
500	9.16	8.19	7.48	6.93	6.49	6.14	5.85	5.61	5.41
600	10.99	9.83	8.97	8.31	7.79	7.37	7.02	6.74	6.50
700	12.82	11.47	10.46	9.69	9.08	8.59	8.19	7.86	7.58
800	14.65	13.10	11.96	11.08	10.38	9.82	9.36	8.98	8.66
900	16.48	14.74	13.45	12.46	11.68	11.05	10.53	10.10	9.74
1000	18.31	16.38	14.95	13.85	12.98	12.28	11.70	11.22	10.82
2000	36.61	32.75	29.89	27.69	25.95	24.56	23.40	22.44	21.64
3000	54.92	49.13	44.83	41.53	38.92	36.82	35.09	33.66	32.46
4000	73.22	65.50	59.77	55.37	51.89	49.09	46.79	44.88	43.28
5000	91.52	81.87	74.71	69.21	64.86	61.36	58.49	56.10	54.09
6000	109.83	98.25	89.65	83.05	77.83	73.63	70.18	67.32	64.91
7000	128.13	114.62	104.59	96.89	90.80	85.90	81.88	78.54	75.73
8000	146.43	130.99	119.53	110.73	103.78	98.17	93.58	89.76	86.55
9000	164.74	147.37	134.48	124.57	116.75	110.44	105.27	100.98	97.37
10000	183.04	163.74	149.42	138.41	129.72	122.71	116.97	112.20	108.18
15000	274.56	245.61	224.12	207.61	194.58	184.07	175.45	168.29	162.27
20000	366.08	327.48	298.83	276.81	259.43	245.42	233.94	224.39	216.36
25000	457.59	409.34	373.53	346.01	324.29	306.78	292.42	280.49	270.45
30000	549.11	491.21	448.24	415.21	389.15	368.13	350.90	336.58	324.54
35000	640.63	573.08	522.94	484.41	454.00	429.49	409.39	392.68	378.63
36000	658.93	589.45	537.89	498.25	466.97	441.76	421.08	403.90	389.45
37000	677.24	605.83	552.83	512.10	479.94	454.03	432.78	415.12	400.27
38000	695.54	622.20	567.77	525.94	492.92	466.30	444.48	426.34	411.08
39000	713.84	638.57	582.71	539.78	505.89	478.57	456.17	437.56	421.90
40000	732.15	654.95	597.65	553.62	518.86	490.84	467.87	448.78	432.72
41000	750.45	671.32	612.59	567.46	531.83	503.11	479.57	460.00	443.54
42000	768.75	687.69	627.53	581.30	544.80	515.38	491.26	471.22	454.36
43000	787.06	704.07	642.47	595.14	557.77	527.65	502.96	482.43	465.17
44000	805.36	720.44	657.41	608.98	570.74	539.92	514.66	493.65	475.99
45000	823.66	736.81	672.36	622.82	583.72	552.20	526.35	504.87	486.81
46000	841.97	753.19	687.30	636.66	596.69	564.47	538.05	516.09	497.63
47000	860.27	769.56	702.24	650.50	609.66	576.74	549.75	527.31	508.45
48000	878.58	785.93	717.18	664.34	622.63	589.01	561.44	538.53	519.26
49000	896.88	802.31	732.12	678.18	635.60	601.28	573.14	549.75	530.08
50000	915.18	818.68	747.06	692.00	648.57	613.55	584.84	560.97	540.90
51000	933.49	835.05	762.00	705.86	661.54	625.82	596.53	572.19	551.72
52000	951.79	851.43	776.94	719.70	674.51	638.09	608.23	583.41	562.53
53000	970.09	867.80	791.88	733.54	687.49	650.36	619.93	594.63	573.35
54000	988.40	884.18	806.83	747.38	700.46	662.63	631.62	605.85	584.17
55000	1006.70	900.55	821.77	761.22	713.43	674.90	643.32	617.07	594.99
56000	1025.00	916.92	836.71	775.06	726.40	687.18	655.02	628.29	605.81
57000	1043.31	933.30	851.65	788.90	739.37	699.45	666.71	639.50	616.62
58000	1061.61	949.67	866.59	802.74	752.34	711.72	678.41	650.72	627.44
59000	1079.91	966.04	881.53	816.58	765.31	723.99	690.11	661.94	638.26
60000	1098.22	982.42	896.47	830.42	778.29	736.26	701.80	673.16	649.08
61000	1116.52	998.79	911.41	844.26	791.26	748.53	713.50	684.38	659.90
62000	1134.83	1015.16	926.35	858.10	804.23	760.80	725.20	695.60	670.71
63000	1153.13	1031.54	941.30	871.94	817.20	773.07	736.89	706.82	681.53
64000	1171.43	1047.91	956.24	885.78	830.17	785.34	748.59	718.04	692.35
65000	1189.74	1064.28	971.18	899.62	843.14	797.61	760.29	729.26	703.17
66000	1208.04	1080.66	986.12	913.46	856.11	809.88	771.98	740.48	713.98
67000	1226.34	1097.03	1001.06	927.30	869.09	822.16	783.68	751.70	724.80
68000	1244.65	1113.40	1016.00	941.14	882.06	834.43	795.38	762.92	735.62
69000	1262.95	1129.78	1030.94	954.98	895.03	846.70	807.07	774.14	746.44
70000	1281.25	1146.15	1045.88	968.82	908.00	858.97	818.77	785.36	757.26
75000	1372.77	1228.02	1120.59	1038.03	972.86	920.32	877.25	841.45	811.35
80000	1464.29	1309.89	1195.29	1107.23	1037.71	981.68	935.74	897.55	865.44
100000	1830.36	1637.36	1494.12	1384.03	1297.14	1227.10	1169.67	1121.93	1081.79

49

9¾% MONTHLY PAYMENT
NECESSARY TO AMORTIZE A LOAN

TERM AMOUNT	15 YEARS	16 YEARS	17 YEARS	18 YEARS	19 YEARS	20 YEARS	21 YEARS	22 YEARS	23 YEARS
$ 25	.27	.26	.25	.25	.24	.24	.24	.23	.23
50	.53	.51	.50	.49	.48	.47	.47	.46	.45
75	.79	.77	.75	.73	.72	.71	.70	.69	.68
100	1.05	1.02	1.00	.98	.96	.94	.93	.91	.90
200	2.10	2.04	1.99	1.95	1.91	1.88	1.85	1.82	1.80
300	3.15	3.06	2.99	2.92	2.86	2.81	2.77	2.73	2.70
400	4.20	4.08	3.98	3.89	3.82	3.75	3.69	3.64	3.59
500	5.24	5.10	4.97	4.86	4.77	4.68	4.61	4.55	4.49
600	6.29	6.12	5.97	5.83	5.72	5.62	5.53	5.45	5.39
700	7.34	7.13	6.96	6.81	6.67	6.56	6.45	6.36	6.28
800	8.39	8.15	7.95	7.78	7.63	7.49	7.38	7.27	7.18
900	9.43	9.17	8.95	8.75	8.58	8.43	8.30	8.18	8.08
1000	10.48	10.19	9.94	9.72	9.53	9.36	9.22	9.09	8.97
2000	20.96	20.38	19.87	19.44	19.06	18.72	18.43	18.17	17.94
3000	31.44	30.56	29.81	29.15	28.58	28.08	27.64	27.25	26.91
4000	41.91	40.75	39.74	38.87	38.11	37.44	36.86	36.34	35.88
5000	52.39	50.93	49.67	48.58	47.63	46.80	46.07	45.42	44.85
6000	62.87	61.12	59.61	58.30	57.16	56.16	55.28	54.50	53.82
7000	73.34	71.30	69.54	68.01	66.68	65.52	64.49	63.59	62.79
8000	83.82	81.49	79.48	77.73	76.21	74.88	73.71	72.67	71.76
9000	94.30	91.67	89.41	87.45	85.73	84.24	82.92	81.75	80.73
10000	104.78	101.86	99.34	97.16	95.26	93.59	92.13	90.84	89.69
15000	157.16	152.78	149.01	145.74	142.89	140.39	138.19	136.25	134.54
20000	209.55	203.71	198.68	194.32	190.52	187.18	184.26	181.67	179.38
25000	261.93	254.64	248.35	242.90	238.14	233.98	230.32	227.09	224.23
30000	314.32	305.56	298.02	291.48	285.77	280.77	276.38	272.50	269.07
35000	366.70	356.49	347.69	340.05	333.40	327.57	322.44	317.92	313.92
36000	377.18	366.68	357.62	349.77	342.92	336.93	331.66	327.00	322.89
37000	387.66	376.86	367.56	359.49	352.45	346.29	340.87	336.09	331.86
38000	398.13	387.05	377.49	369.20	361.98	355.65	350.08	345.17	340.82
39000	408.61	397.23	387.42	378.92	371.50	365.01	359.29	354.25	349.79
40000	419.09	407.42	397.36	388.63	381.03	374.36	368.51	363.34	358.76
41000	429.56	417.60	407.29	398.35	390.55	383.72	377.72	372.42	367.73
42000	440.04	427.79	417.23	408.06	400.08	393.08	386.93	381.50	376.70
43000	450.52	437.97	427.16	417.78	409.60	402.44	396.14	390.59	385.67
44000	461.00	448.16	437.09	427.50	419.13	411.80	405.36	399.67	394.64
45000	471.47	458.34	447.03	437.21	428.65	421.16	414.57	408.75	403.61
46000	481.95	468.53	456.96	446.93	438.18	430.52	423.78	417.84	412.58
47000	492.43	478.72	466.89	456.64	447.71	439.88	432.99	426.92	421.55
48000	502.90	488.90	476.83	466.36	457.23	449.24	442.21	436.00	430.51
49000	513.38	499.09	486.76	476.07	466.76	458.60	451.42	445.09	439.48
50000	523.86	509.27	496.70	485.79	476.28	467.95	460.63	454.17	448.45
51000	534.34	519.46	506.63	495.51	485.81	477.31	469.84	463.25	457.42
52000	544.81	529.64	516.56	505.22	495.33	486.67	479.06	472.34	466.39
53000	555.29	539.83	526.50	514.94	504.86	496.03	488.27	481.42	475.36
54000	565.77	550.01	536.43	524.65	514.38	505.39	497.48	490.50	484.33
55000	576.24	560.20	546.37	534.37	523.91	514.75	506.70	499.59	493.30
56000	586.72	570.38	556.30	544.08	533.44	524.11	515.91	508.67	502.27
57000	597.20	580.57	566.23	553.80	542.96	533.47	525.12	517.75	511.23
58000	607.67	590.75	576.17	563.52	552.49	542.83	534.33	526.84	520.20
59000	618.15	600.94	586.10	573.23	562.01	552.19	543.55	535.92	529.17
60000	628.63	611.12	596.03	582.95	571.54	561.54	552.76	545.00	538.14
61000	639.11	621.31	605.97	592.66	581.06	570.90	561.97	554.09	547.11
62000	649.58	631.49	615.90	602.38	590.59	580.26	571.18	563.17	556.08
63000	660.06	641.68	625.84	612.09	600.11	589.62	580.40	572.25	565.05
64000	670.54	651.87	635.77	621.81	609.64	598.98	589.61	581.34	574.02
65000	681.01	662.05	645.70	631.53	619.17	608.34	598.82	590.42	582.99
66000	691.49	672.24	655.64	641.24	628.69	617.70	608.03	599.50	591.95
67000	701.97	682.42	665.57	650.96	638.22	627.06	617.25	608.59	600.92
68000	712.45	692.61	675.50	660.67	647.74	636.42	626.46	617.67	609.89
69000	722.92	702.79	685.44	670.39	657.27	645.78	635.67	626.75	618.86
70000	733.40	712.98	695.37	680.10	666.79	655.13	644.88	635.84	627.83
75000	785.78	763.90	745.04	728.68	714.42	701.93	690.95	681.25	672.58
80000	838.17	814.83	794.71	777.26	762.05	748.72	737.01	726.67	717.52
100000	1047.71	1018.54	993.39	971.58	952.56	935.90	921.26	908.34	896.90

MONTHLY PAYMENT
NECESSARY TO AMORTIZE A LOAN

9¾%

TERM AMOUNT	24 YEARS	25 YEARS	26 YEARS	27 YEARS	28 YEARS	29 YEARS	30 YEARS	35 YEARS	40 YEARS
$ 25	.23	.22	.22	.22	.22	.22	.22	.21	.21
50	.45	.44	.44	.44	.43	.43	.43	.42	.41
75	.67	.66	.66	.65	.65	.64	.64	.62	.62
100	.89	.88	.87	.87	.86	.86	.85	.83	.82
200	1.78	1.76	1.74	1.73	1.72	1.71	1.70	1.66	1.63
300	2.67	2.64	2.61	2.59	2.57	2.56	2.54	2.48	2.45
400	3.55	3.52	3.48	3.45	3.43	3.41	3.39	3.31	3.26
500	4.44	4.39	4.35	4.32	4.29	4.26	4.23	4.13	4.08
600	5.33	5.27	5.22	5.18	5.14	5.11	5.08	4.96	4.89
700	6.21	6.15	6.09	6.04	6.00	5.96	5.92	5.79	5.71
800	7.10	7.03	6.96	6.90	6.85	6.81	6.77	6.61	6.52
900	7.99	7.90	7.83	7.77	7.71	7.66	7.61	7.44	7.34
1000	8.87	8.78	8.70	8.63	8.57	8.51	8.46	8.26	8.15
2000	17.74	17.56	17.40	17.25	17.13	17.01	16.91	16.52	16.30
3000	26.61	26.34	26.09	25.88	25.69	25.51	25.36	24.78	24.44
4000	35.47	35.11	34.79	34.50	34.25	34.01	33.81	33.04	32.59
5000	44.34	43.89	43.49	43.13	42.81	42.52	42.26	41.30	40.73
6000	53.21	52.67	52.18	51.75	51.37	51.02	50.71	49.56	48.88
7000	62.08	61.44	60.88	60.38	59.93	59.52	59.16	57.82	57.02
8000	70.94	70.22	69.58	69.00	68.49	68.02	67.61	66.08	65.17
9000	79.81	79.00	78.27	77.63	77.05	76.53	76.06	74.34	73.31
10000	88.68	87.78	86.97	86.25	85.61	85.03	84.51	82.60	81.46
15000	133.02	131.66	130.45	129.37	128.41	127.54	126.76	123.90	122.19
20000	177.35	175.55	173.94	172.50	171.21	170.05	169.02	165.20	162.91
25000	221.69	219.43	217.42	215.62	214.01	212.57	211.27	206.50	203.64
30000	266.03	263.32	260.90	258.74	256.81	255.08	253.52	247.80	244.37
35000	310.36	307.20	304.38	301.87	299.61	297.59	295.78	289.10	285.10
36000	319.23	315.98	313.08	310.49	308.17	306.09	304.23	297.36	293.24
37000	328.10	324.76	321.78	319.11	316.73	314.60	312.68	305.62	301.39
38000	336.97	333.53	330.47	327.74	325.29	323.10	321.13	313.88	309.53
39000	345.83	342.31	339.17	336.36	333.85	331.60	329.58	322.14	317.68
40000	354.70	351.09	347.87	344.99	342.41	340.10	338.03	330.40	325.82
41000	363.57	359.87	356.56	353.61	350.97	348.61	346.48	338.66	333.97
42000	372.44	368.64	365.26	362.24	359.53	357.11	354.93	346.92	342.12
43000	381.30	377.42	373.96	370.86	368.09	365.61	363.38	355.18	350.26
44000	390.17	386.20	382.65	379.49	376.65	374.11	371.83	363.44	358.41
45000	399.04	394.97	391.35	388.11	385.21	382.62	380.28	371.70	366.55
46000	407.91	403.75	400.05	396.74	393.77	391.12	388.73	379.96	374.70
47000	416.77	412.53	408.74	405.36	402.33	399.62	397.19	388.22	382.84
48000	425.64	421.30	417.44	413.98	410.89	408.12	405.64	396.47	390.99
49000	434.51	430.08	426.14	422.61	419.45	416.63	414.09	404.73	399.13
50000	443.38	438.86	434.83	431.23	428.01	425.13	422.54	412.99	407.28
51000	452.24	447.64	443.53	439.86	436.57	433.63	430.99	421.25	415.43
52000	461.11	456.41	452.22	448.48	445.13	442.13	439.44	429.51	423.57
53000	469.98	465.19	460.92	457.11	453.69	450.63	447.89	437.77	431.72
54000	478.85	473.97	469.62	465.73	462.25	459.14	456.34	446.03	439.86
55000	487.71	482.74	478.31	474.36	470.81	467.64	464.79	454.29	448.01
56000	496.58	491.52	487.01	482.98	479.37	476.14	473.24	462.55	456.15
57000	505.45	500.30	495.71	491.61	487.93	484.64	481.69	470.81	464.30
58000	514.31	509.08	504.40	500.23	496.50	493.15	490.14	479.07	472.44
59000	523.18	517.85	513.10	508.85	505.06	501.65	498.59	487.33	480.59
60000	532.05	526.63	521.80	517.48	513.62	510.15	507.04	495.59	488.73
61000	540.92	535.41	530.49	526.10	522.18	518.65	515.49	503.85	496.88
62000	549.78	544.18	539.19	534.73	530.74	527.16	523.94	512.11	505.03
63000	558.65	552.96	547.89	543.35	539.30	535.66	532.40	520.37	513.17
64000	567.52	561.74	556.58	551.98	547.86	544.16	540.85	528.63	521.32
65000	576.39	570.52	565.28	560.60	556.42	552.66	549.30	536.89	529.46
66000	585.25	579.29	573.98	569.23	564.98	561.17	557.75	545.15	537.61
67000	594.12	588.07	582.67	577.85	573.54	569.67	566.20	553.41	545.75
68000	602.99	596.85	591.37	586.48	582.10	578.17	574.65	561.67	553.90
69000	611.86	605.62	600.07	595.10	590.66	586.67	583.10	569.93	562.04
70000	620.72	614.40	608.76	603.73	599.22	595.18	591.55	578.19	570.19
75000	665.06	658.29	652.24	646.85	642.02	637.69	633.80	619.49	610.92
80000	709.40	702.17	695.73	689.97	684.82	680.20	676.06	660.79	651.64
100000	886.75	877.71	869.66	862.46	856.02	850.25	845.07	825.98	814.55

10% MONTHLY PAYMENT
NECESSARY TO AMORTIZE A LOAN

TERM / AMOUNT	1 YEAR	1½ YEARS	2 YEARS	2½ YEARS	3 YEARS	3½ YEARS	4 YEARS	4½ YEARS	5 YEARS
$ 25	2.20	1.50	1.16	.95	.81	.71	.64	.58	.53
50	4.40	3.00	2.31	1.89	1.61	1.42	1.27	1.15	1.06
75	6.59	4.50	3.46	2.83	2.42	2.12	1.90	1.73	1.59
100	8.79	6.00	4.61	3.78	3.22	2.83	2.53	2.30	2.12
200	17.57	12.00	9.22	7.55	6.44	5.65	5.06	4.60	4.23
300	26.35	17.99	13.82	11.32	9.66	8.47	7.58	6.90	6.35
400	35.13	23.99	18.43	15.09	12.87	11.29	10.11	9.19	8.46
500	43.92	29.99	23.03	18.86	16.09	14.12	12.64	11.49	10.58
600	52.70	35.98	27.64	22.64	19.31	16.94	15.16	13.79	12.69
700	61.48	41.98	32.24	26.41	22.53	19.76	17.69	16.09	14.81
800	70.26	47.98	36.85	30.18	25.74	22.58	20.22	18.38	16.92
900	79.04	53.97	41.45	33.95	28.96	25.40	22.74	20.68	19.04
1000	87.83	59.97	46.06	37.72	32.18	28.23	25.27	22.98	21.15
2000	175.65	119.93	92.11	75.44	64.35	56.45	50.54	45.95	42.30
3000	263.47	179.90	138.16	113.16	96.52	84.67	75.80	68.93	63.45
4000	351.29	239.86	184.21	150.87	128.69	112.89	101.07	91.90	84.60
5000	439.11	299.83	230.26	188.59	160.87	141.11	126.33	114.88	105.74
6000	526.94	359.79	276.31	226.31	193.04	169.33	151.60	137.85	126.89
7000	614.76	419.75	322.37	264.03	225.21	197.55	176.86	160.82	148.04
8000	702.58	479.72	368.42	301.74	257.38	225.77	202.13	183.80	169.19
9000	790.40	539.68	414.47	339.46	289.56	253.99	227.40	206.77	190.33
10000	878.22	599.65	460.52	377.18	321.73	282.21	252.66	229.75	211.48
15000	1317.33	899.47	690.78	565.77	482.59	423.32	378.99	344.62	317.22
20000	1756.44	1199.29	921.04	754.35	643.45	564.42	505.32	459.49	422.96
25000	2195.55	1499.11	1151.30	942.94	804.31	705.53	631.64	574.36	528.70
30000	2634.66	1798.93	1381.55	1131.53	965.18	846.63	757.97	689.23	634.44
35000	3073.77	2098.75	1611.81	1320.12	1126.04	987.74	884.30	804.10	740.17
36000	3161.59	2158.71	1657.86	1357.83	1158.21	1015.96	909.57	827.08	761.32
37000	3249.41	2218.67	1703.92	1395.55	1190.38	1044.18	934.83	850.05	782.47
38000	3337.24	2278.64	1749.97	1433.27	1222.55	1072.40	960.10	873.03	803.62
39000	3425.06	2338.60	1796.02	1470.99	1254.73	1100.62	985.36	896.00	824.77
40000	3512.88	2398.57	1842.07	1508.70	1286.90	1128.84	1010.63	918.98	845.91
41000	3600.70	2458.53	1888.12	1546.42	1319.07	1157.06	1035.89	941.95	867.06
42000	3688.52	2518.49	1934.17	1584.14	1351.24	1185.28	1061.16	964.92	888.21
43000	3776.35	2578.46	1980.23	1621.86	1383.42	1213.51	1086.43	987.90	909.36
44000	3864.17	2638.42	2026.28	1659.57	1415.59	1241.73	1111.69	1010.87	930.50
45000	3951.99	2698.39	2072.33	1697.29	1447.76	1269.95	1136.96	1033.85	951.65
46000	4039.81	2758.35	2118.38	1735.01	1479.93	1298.17	1162.22	1056.82	972.80
47000	4127.63	2818.31	2164.43	1772.73	1512.11	1326.39	1187.49	1079.80	993.95
48000	4215.46	2878.28	2210.48	1810.44	1544.28	1354.61	1212.75	1102.77	1015.09
49000	4303.28	2938.24	2256.54	1848.16	1576.45	1382.83	1238.02	1125.74	1036.24
50000	4391.10	2998.21	2302.59	1885.88	1608.62	1411.05	1263.28	1148.72	1057.39
51000	4478.92	3058.17	2348.64	1923.60	1640.79	1439.27	1288.55	1171.69	1078.54
52000	4566.74	3118.13	2394.69	1961.31	1672.97	1467.49	1313.82	1194.67	1099.69
53000	4654.56	3178.10	2440.74	1999.03	1705.14	1495.72	1339.08	1217.64	1120.83
54000	4742.39	3238.06	2486.79	2036.75	1737.31	1523.94	1364.35	1240.61	1141.98
55000	4830.21	3298.03	2532.85	2074.47	1769.48	1552.16	1389.61	1263.59	1163.13
56000	4918.03	3357.99	2578.90	2112.18	1801.66	1580.38	1414.88	1286.56	1184.28
57000	5005.85	3417.95	2624.95	2149.90	1833.83	1608.60	1440.14	1309.54	1205.42
58000	5093.67	3477.92	2671.00	2187.62	1866.00	1636.82	1465.41	1332.51	1226.57
59000	5181.50	3537.88	2717.05	2225.34	1898.17	1665.04	1490.68	1355.49	1247.72
60000	5269.32	3597.85	2763.10	2263.05	1930.35	1693.26	1515.94	1378.46	1268.87
61000	5357.14	3657.81	2809.16	2300.77	1962.52	1721.48	1541.21	1401.43	1290.01
62000	5444.96	3717.77	2855.21	2338.49	1994.69	1749.70	1566.47	1424.41	1311.16
63000	5532.78	3777.74	2901.26	2376.21	2026.86	1777.92	1591.74	1447.38	1332.31
64000	5620.61	3837.70	2947.31	2413.92	2059.04	1806.15	1617.00	1470.36	1353.46
65000	5708.43	3897.67	2993.36	2451.64	2091.21	1834.37	1642.27	1493.33	1374.61
66000	5796.25	3957.63	3039.41	2489.36	2123.38	1862.59	1667.53	1516.31	1395.75
67000	5884.07	4017.59	3085.47	2527.08	2155.55	1890.81	1692.80	1539.28	1416.90
68000	5971.89	4077.56	3131.52	2564.79	2187.72	1919.03	1718.07	1562.25	1438.05
69000	6059.71	4137.52	3177.57	2602.51	2219.90	1947.25	1743.33	1585.23	1459.20
70000	6147.54	4197.49	3223.62	2640.23	2252.07	1975.47	1768.60	1608.20	1480.34
75000	6586.65	4497.31	3453.88	2828.82	2412.93	2116.58	1894.92	1723.07	1586.08
80000	7025.76	4797.13	3684.14	3017.40	2573.79	2257.68	2021.25	1837.95	1691.82
100000	8782.19	5996.41	4605.17	3771.75	3217.24	2822.10	2526.56	2297.43	2114.77

52

TERM AMOUNT	6 YEARS	7 YEARS	8 YEARS	9 YEARS	10 YEARS	11 YEARS	12 YEARS	13 YEARS	14 YEARS
$ 25	.47	.42	.38	.35	.33	.32	.30	.29	.28
50	.93	.83	.76	.70	.66	.63	.60	.57	.55
75	1.39	1.24	1.14	1.05	.99	.94	.89	.86	.83
100	1.85	1.65	1.51	1.40	1.32	1.25	1.19	1.14	1.10
200	3.69	3.30	3.02	2.80	2.63	2.49	2.37	2.28	2.20
300	5.53	4.95	4.53	4.20	3.94	3.73	3.56	3.41	3.29
400	7.37	6.60	6.03	5.59	5.25	4.97	4.74	4.55	4.39
500	9.22	8.25	7.54	6.99	6.56	6.21	5.92	5.68	5.49
600	11.06	9.90	9.05	8.39	7.87	7.45	7.11	6.82	6.58
700	12.90	11.55	10.55	9.78	9.18	8.69	8.29	7.96	7.68
800	14.74	13.20	12.06	11.18	10.49	9.93	9.47	9.09	8.77
900	16.59	14.85	13.57	12.58	11.80	11.17	10.66	10.23	9.87
1000	18.43	16.50	15.07	13.97	13.11	12.41	11.84	11.36	10.97
2000	36.85	33.00	30.14	27.94	26.21	24.82	23.67	22.72	21.93
3000	55.28	49.50	45.21	41.91	39.32	37.22	35.51	34.08	32.89
4000	73.70	65.99	60.27	55.88	52.42	49.63	47.34	45.44	43.85
5000	92.13	82.49	75.34	69.85	65.52	62.03	59.18	56.80	54.81
6000	110.55	98.99	90.41	83.82	78.63	74.44	71.01	68.16	65.77
7000	128.97	115.48	105.48	97.79	91.73	86.85	82.84	79.52	76.73
8000	147.40	131.98	120.54	111.76	104.83	99.25	94.68	90.88	87.69
9000	165.82	148.48	135.61	125.73	117.94	111.66	106.51	102.24	98.65
10000	184.25	164.97	150.68	139.70	131.04	124.06	118.35	113.60	109.61
15000	276.37	247.46	226.02	209.55	196.56	186.09	177.52	170.40	164.42
20000	368.49	329.94	301.35	279.39	262.07	248.12	236.69	227.20	219.22
25000	460.61	412.43	376.69	349.24	327.59	310.15	295.86	284.00	274.03
30000	552.73	494.91	452.03	419.09	393.11	372.18	355.03	340.79	328.83
35000	644.85	577.40	527.36	488.94	458.62	434.21	414.20	397.59	383.64
36000	663.27	593.89	542.43	502.90	471.73	446.61	426.04	408.95	394.60
37000	681.69	610.39	557.50	516.87	484.83	459.02	437.87	420.31	405.56
38000	700.12	626.89	572.57	530.84	497.93	471.42	449.71	431.67	416.52
39000	718.54	643.38	587.63	544.81	511.04	483.83	461.54	443.03	427.48
40000	736.97	659.88	602.70	558.78	524.14	496.24	473.38	454.39	438.44
41000	755.39	676.38	617.77	572.75	537.24	508.64	485.21	465.75	449.40
42000	773.81	692.87	632.84	586.72	550.35	521.05	497.04	477.11	460.36
43000	792.24	709.37	647.90	600.69	563.45	533.45	508.88	488.47	471.32
44000	810.66	725.87	662.97	614.66	576.55	545.86	520.71	499.83	482.28
45000	829.09	742.37	678.04	628.63	589.66	558.26	532.55	511.19	493.25
46000	847.51	758.86	693.11	642.60	602.76	570.67	544.38	522.55	504.21
47000	865.93	775.36	708.17	656.57	615.86	583.08	556.22	533.91	515.17
48000	884.36	791.86	723.24	670.54	628.97	595.48	568.05	545.27	526.13
49000	902.78	808.35	738.31	684.51	642.07	607.89	579.88	556.63	537.09
50000	921.21	824.85	753.37	698.48	655.17	620.29	591.72	567.99	548.05
51000	939.63	841.35	768.44	712.45	668.28	632.70	603.55	579.35	559.01
52000	958.06	857.84	783.51	726.42	681.38	645.10	615.39	590.71	569.97
53000	976.48	874.34	798.58	740.39	694.48	657.51	627.22	602.07	580.93
54000	994.90	890.84	813.64	754.35	707.59	669.92	639.06	613.43	591.89
55000	1013.33	907.33	828.71	768.32	720.69	682.32	650.89	624.79	602.85
56000	1031.75	923.83	843.78	782.29	733.79	694.73	662.72	636.14	613.82
57000	1050.18	940.33	858.85	796.26	746.90	707.13	674.56	647.50	624.78
58000	1068.60	956.83	873.91	810.23	760.00	719.54	686.39	658.86	635.74
59000	1087.02	973.32	888.98	824.20	773.10	731.94	698.23	670.22	646.70
60000	1105.45	989.82	904.05	838.17	786.21	744.35	710.06	681.58	657.66
61000	1123.87	1006.32	919.12	852.14	799.31	756.76	721.90	692.94	668.62
62000	1142.30	1022.81	934.18	866.11	812.41	769.16	733.73	704.30	679.58
63000	1160.72	1039.31	949.25	880.08	825.52	781.57	745.56	715.66	690.54
64000	1179.14	1055.81	964.32	894.05	838.62	793.97	757.40	727.02	701.50
65000	1197.57	1072.30	979.39	908.02	851.72	806.38	769.23	738.38	712.46
66000	1215.99	1088.80	994.45	921.99	864.83	818.78	781.07	749.74	723.42
67000	1234.42	1105.30	1009.52	935.96	877.93	831.19	792.90	761.10	734.39
68000	1252.84	1121.79	1024.59	949.93	891.03	843.60	804.74	772.46	745.35
69000	1271.26	1138.29	1039.66	963.90	904.14	856.00	816.57	783.82	756.31
70000	1289.69	1154.79	1054.72	977.87	917.24	868.41	828.40	795.18	767.27
75000	1381.81	1237.27	1130.06	1047.71	982.76	930.44	887.58	851.98	822.07
80000	1473.93	1319.76	1205.40	1117.56	1048.27	992.47	946.75	908.78	876.88
100000	1842.41	1649.70	1506.74	1396.95	1310.34	1240.58	1183.43	1135.97	1096.10

53

10% MONTHLY PAYMENT
NECESSARY TO AMORTIZE A LOAN

TERM / AMOUNT	15 YEARS	16 YEARS	17 YEARS	18 YEARS	19 YEARS	20 YEARS	21 YEARS	22 YEARS	23 YEARS
$ 25	.27	.26	.26	.25	.25	.24	.24	.24	.23
50	.54	.52	.51	.50	.49	.48	.47	.47	.46
75	.80	.78	.76	.75	.73	.72	.71	.70	.69
100	1.07	1.04	1.01	.99	.97	.96	.94	.93	.92
200	2.13	2.07	2.02	1.98	1.94	1.91	1.88	1.85	1.83
300	3.19	3.11	3.03	2.97	2.91	2.86	2.82	2.78	2.74
400	4.25	4.14	4.04	3.95	3.88	3.81	3.75	3.70	3.66
500	5.32	5.17	5.05	4.94	4.85	4.76	4.69	4.63	4.57
600	6.38	6.21	6.06	5.93	5.81	5.71	5.63	5.55	5.48
700	7.44	7.24	7.06	6.91	6.78	6.67	6.57	6.48	6.40
800	8.50	8.27	8.07	7.90	7.75	7.62	7.50	7.40	7.31
900	9.57	9.31	9.08	8.89	8.72	8.57	8.44	8.33	8.22
1000	10.63	10.34	10.09	9.87	9.69	9.52	9.38	9.25	9.14
2000	21.25	20.67	20.17	19.74	19.37	19.04	18.75	18.50	18.27
3000	31.87	31.01	30.26	29.61	29.05	28.55	28.12	27.74	27.40
4000	42.50	41.34	40.34	39.48	38.73	38.07	37.49	36.99	36.54
5000	53.12	51.67	50.43	49.35	48.41	47.59	46.87	46.23	45.67
6000	63.74	62.01	60.51	59.22	58.09	57.10	56.24	55.48	54.80
7000	74.36	72.34	70.60	69.09	67.77	66.62	65.61	64.72	63.94
8000	84.99	82.67	80.68	78.96	77.45	76.14	74.98	73.97	73.07
9000	95.61	93.01	90.77	88.82	87.13	85.65	84.36	83.21	82.20
10000	106.23	103.34	100.85	98.69	96.81	95.17	93.73	92.46	91.33
15000	159.35	155.01	151.27	148.04	145.22	142.75	140.59	138.68	137.00
20000	212.46	206.67	201.69	197.38	193.62	190.34	187.45	184.91	182.66
25000	265.57	258.34	252.12	246.72	242.03	237.92	234.31	231.14	228.33
30000	318.69	310.01	302.54	296.07	290.43	285.50	281.18	277.36	273.99
35000	371.80	361.68	352.96	345.41	338.84	333.09	328.04	323.59	319.66
36000	382.42	372.01	363.05	355.28	348.52	342.60	337.41	332.83	328.79
37000	393.04	382.34	373.13	365.15	358.20	352.12	346.78	342.08	337.92
38000	403.67	392.68	383.22	375.02	367.88	361.64	356.16	351.32	347.06
39000	414.29	403.01	393.30	384.89	377.56	371.15	365.53	360.57	356.19
40000	424.91	413.34	403.38	394.76	387.24	380.67	374.90	369.82	365.32
41000	435.54	423.68	413.47	404.62	396.92	390.19	384.27	379.06	374.45
42000	446.16	434.01	423.55	414.49	406.60	399.70	393.64	388.31	383.59
43000	456.78	444.35	433.64	424.36	416.29	409.22	403.02	397.55	392.72
44000	467.40	454.68	443.72	434.23	425.97	418.74	412.39	406.80	401.85
45000	478.03	465.01	453.81	444.10	435.65	428.25	421.76	416.04	410.99
46000	488.65	475.35	463.89	453.97	445.33	437.77	431.13	425.29	420.12
47000	499.27	485.68	473.98	463.84	455.01	447.29	440.51	434.53	429.25
48000	509.89	496.01	484.06	473.71	464.69	456.80	449.88	443.78	438.38
49000	520.52	506.35	494.14	483.57	474.37	466.32	459.25	453.02	447.52
50000	531.14	516.68	504.23	493.44	484.05	475.84	468.62	462.27	456.65
51000	541.76	527.01	514.31	503.31	493.73	485.35	478.00	471.51	465.78
52000	552.39	537.35	524.40	513.18	503.41	494.87	487.37	480.76	474.92
53000	563.01	547.68	534.48	523.05	513.09	504.39	496.74	490.00	484.05
54000	573.63	558.01	544.57	532.92	522.78	513.90	506.11	499.25	493.18
55000	584.25	568.35	554.65	542.79	532.46	523.42	515.49	508.49	502.31
56000	594.88	578.68	564.74	552.66	542.14	532.94	524.86	517.74	511.45
57000	605.50	589.01	574.82	562.52	551.82	542.45	534.23	526.98	520.58
58000	616.12	599.35	584.90	572.39	561.50	551.97	543.60	536.23	529.71
59000	626.74	609.68	594.99	582.26	571.18	561.49	552.98	545.48	538.85
60000	637.37	620.01	605.07	592.13	580.86	571.00	562.35	554.72	547.98
61000	647.99	630.35	615.16	602.00	590.54	580.52	571.72	563.97	557.11
62000	658.61	640.68	625.24	611.87	600.22	590.04	581.09	573.21	566.25
63000	669.24	651.02	635.33	621.74	609.90	599.55	590.46	582.46	575.38
64000	679.86	661.35	645.41	631.61	619.58	609.07	599.84	591.70	584.51
65000	690.48	671.68	655.50	641.47	629.27	618.59	609.21	600.95	593.64
66000	701.10	682.02	665.58	651.34	638.95	628.10	618.58	610.19	602.78
67000	711.73	692.35	675.66	661.21	648.63	637.62	627.95	619.44	611.91
68000	722.35	702.68	685.75	671.08	658.31	647.14	637.33	628.68	621.04
69000	732.97	713.02	695.83	680.95	667.99	656.65	646.70	637.93	630.18
70000	743.59	723.35	705.92	690.82	677.67	666.17	656.07	647.17	639.31
75000	796.71	775.02	756.34	740.16	726.00	713.75	702.93	693.40	684.97
80000	849.82	826.68	806.76	789.51	774.48	761.34	749.80	739.63	730.64
100000	1062.27	1033.35	1008.45	986.88	968.10	951.67	937.24	924.53	913.30

54

MONTHLY PAYMENT **10%**
NECESSARY TO AMORTIZE A LOAN

TERM AMOUNT	24 YEARS	25 YEARS	26 YEARS	27 YEARS	28 YEARS	29 YEARS	30 YEARS	35 YEARS	40 YEARS
$ 25	.23	.23	.23	.22	.22	.22	.22	.22	.21
50	.46	.45	.45	.44	.44	.44	.44	.43	.42
75	.68	.68	.67	.66	.66	.66	.65	.64	.63
100	.91	.90	.89	.88	.88	.87	.87	.85	.84
200	1.81	1.79	1.78	1.76	1.75	1.74	1.73	1.69	1.67
300	2.71	2.69	2.66	2.64	2.62	2.61	2.59	2.54	2.50
400	3.62	3.58	3.55	3.52	3.50	3.48	3.46	3.38	3.34
500	4.52	4.48	4.44	4.40	4.37	4.34	4.32	4.23	4.17
600	5.42	5.37	5.32	5.28	5.24	5.21	5.18	5.07	5.00
700	6.33	6.27	6.21	6.16	6.12	6.08	6.04	5.91	5.84
800	7.23	7.16	7.10	7.04	6.99	6.95	6.91	6.76	6.67
900	8.13	8.06	7.98	7.92	7.86	7.81	7.77	7.60	7.50
1000	9.04	8.95	8.87	8.80	8.74	8.68	8.63	8.45	8.34
2000	18.07	17.89	17.74	17.60	17.47	17.36	17.26	16.89	16.67
3000	27.10	26.84	26.60	26.39	26.20	26.04	25.89	25.33	25.00
4000	36.14	35.78	35.47	35.19	34.94	34.71	34.51	33.77	33.34
5000	45.17	44.73	44.34	43.98	43.67	43.39	43.14	42.22	41.67
6000	54.20	53.67	53.20	52.78	52.40	52.07	51.77	50.66	50.00
7000	63.24	62.62	62.07	61.58	61.14	60.74	60.39	59.10	58.34
8000	72.27	71.56	70.93	70.37	69.87	69.42	69.02	67.54	66.67
9000	81.30	80.51	79.80	79.17	78.60	78.10	77.65	75.99	75.00
10000	90.34	89.45	88.67	87.96	87.34	86.77	86.27	84.43	83.33
15000	135.50	134.18	133.00	131.94	131.00	130.16	129.41	126.64	125.00
20000	180.67	178.90	177.33	175.92	174.67	173.54	172.54	168.85	166.66
25000	225.84	223.63	221.66	219.90	218.33	216.93	215.67	211.06	208.33
30000	271.00	268.35	265.99	263.88	262.00	260.31	258.81	253.27	249.99
35000	316.17	313.08	310.32	307.86	305.66	303.70	301.94	295.49	291.66
36000	325.20	322.02	319.19	316.66	314.40	312.38	310.57	303.93	299.99
37000	334.24	330.97	328.05	325.45	323.13	321.05	319.19	312.37	308.33
38000	343.27	339.91	336.92	334.25	331.86	329.73	327.82	320.81	316.66
39000	352.30	348.86	345.78	343.04	340.60	338.41	336.45	329.26	324.99
40000	361.34	357.80	354.65	351.84	349.33	347.08	345.07	337.70	333.32
41000	370.37	366.74	363.52	360.64	358.06	355.76	353.70	346.14	341.66
42000	379.40	375.69	372.38	369.43	366.80	364.44	362.33	354.58	349.99
43000	388.44	384.63	381.25	378.23	375.53	373.12	370.95	363.02	358.32
44000	397.47	393.58	390.11	387.02	384.26	381.79	379.58	371.47	366.66
45000	406.50	402.52	398.98	395.82	393.00	390.47	388.21	379.91	374.99
46000	415.54	411.47	407.85	404.62	401.73	399.15	396.83	388.35	383.32
47000	424.57	420.41	416.71	413.41	410.46	407.82	405.46	396.79	391.66
48000	433.60	429.36	425.58	422.21	419.20	416.50	414.09	405.24	399.99
49000	442.64	438.30	434.45	431.00	427.93	425.18	422.71	413.68	408.32
50000	451.67	447.25	443.31	439.80	436.66	433.85	431.34	422.12	416.65
51000	460.70	456.19	452.18	448.60	445.39	442.53	439.97	430.56	424.99
52000	469.74	465.14	461.04	457.39	454.13	451.21	448.59	439.01	433.32
53000	478.77	474.08	469.91	466.19	462.86	459.89	457.22	447.45	441.65
54000	487.80	483.03	478.78	474.98	471.59	468.56	465.85	455.89	449.99
55000	496.84	491.97	487.64	483.78	480.33	477.24	474.47	464.33	458.32
56000	505.87	500.92	496.51	492.57	489.06	485.92	483.10	472.77	466.65
57000	514.90	509.86	505.37	501.37	497.79	494.59	491.73	481.22	474.98
58000	523.94	518.81	514.24	510.17	506.53	503.27	500.35	489.66	483.32
59000	532.97	527.75	523.11	518.96	515.26	511.95	508.98	498.10	491.65
60000	542.00	536.70	531.97	527.76	523.99	520.62	517.61	506.54	499.98
61000	551.04	545.64	540.84	536.55	532.73	529.30	526.23	514.99	508.32
62000	560.07	554.59	549.70	545.35	541.46	537.98	534.86	523.43	516.65
63000	569.10	563.53	558.57	554.15	550.19	546.66	543.49	531.87	524.98
64000	578.14	572.48	567.44	562.94	558.93	555.33	552.11	540.31	533.32
65000	587.17	581.42	576.30	571.74	567.66	564.01	560.74	548.76	541.65
66000	596.20	590.37	585.17	580.53	576.39	572.69	569.37	557.20	549.98
67000	605.24	599.31	594.04	589.33	585.13	581.36	577.99	565.64	558.31
68000	614.27	608.26	602.90	598.13	593.86	590.04	586.62	574.08	566.65
69000	623.30	617.20	611.77	606.92	602.59	598.72	595.25	582.52	574.98
70000	632.34	626.15	620.63	615.72	611.32	607.39	603.87	590.97	583.31
75000	677.50	670.87	664.96	659.70	654.99	650.78	647.01	633.18	624.98
80000	722.67	715.59	709.29	703.68	698.66	694.16	690.14	675.39	666.64
100000	903.34	894.49	886.62	879.59	873.32	867.70	862.67	844.24	833.30

55

10¼%   MONTHLY PAYMENT
NECESSARY TO AMORTIZE A LOAN

TERM AMOUNT	1 YEAR	1½ YEARS	2 YEARS	2½ YEARS	3 YEARS	3½ YEARS	4 YEARS	4½ YEARS	5 YEARS
$ 25	2.20	1.51	1.16	.95	.81	.71	.64	.58	.54
50	4.40	3.01	2.31	1.90	1.62	1.42	1.27	1.16	1.07
75	6.60	4.51	3.47	2.84	2.43	2.13	1.91	1.74	1.60
100	8.80	6.01	4.62	3.79	3.23	2.84	2.54	2.31	2.13
200	17.59	12.02	9.24	7.57	6.46	5.67	5.08	4.62	4.26
300	26.39	18.03	13.85	11.35	9.69	8.51	7.62	6.93	6.38
400	35.18	24.03	18.47	15.14	12.92	11.34	10.16	9.24	8.51
500	43.97	30.04	23.09	18.92	16.15	14.17	12.70	11.55	10.64
600	52.77	36.05	27.70	22.70	19.38	17.01	15.23	13.86	12.76
700	61.56	42.06	32.32	26.49	22.60	19.84	17.77	16.17	14.89
800	70.35	48.06	36.93	30.27	25.83	22.67	20.31	18.48	17.02
900	79.15	54.07	41.55	34.05	29.06	25.51	22.85	20.79	19.14
1000	87.94	60.08	46.17	37.83	32.29	28.34	25.39	23.10	21.27
2000	175.87	120.15	92.33	75.66	64.57	56.67	50.77	46.19	42.54
3000	263.81	180.23	138.49	113.49	96.86	85.01	76.15	69.28	63.80
4000	351.74	240.30	184.65	151.32	129.14	113.34	101.53	92.37	85.07
5000	439.67	300.38	230.82	189.15	161.43	141.68	126.91	115.46	106.33
6000	527.61	360.45	276.98	226.98	193.71	170.01	152.29	138.55	127.60
7000	615.54	420.53	323.14	264.81	226.00	198.35	177.67	161.64	148.86
8000	703.47	480.60	369.30	302.64	258.28	226.68	203.05	184.73	170.13
9000	791.41	540.68	415.47	340.47	290.57	255.02	228.43	207.82	191.40
10000	879.34	600.75	461.63	378.29	322.85	283.35	253.81	230.91	212.66
15000	1319.01	901.12	692.44	567.44	484.28	425.03	380.72	346.37	318.99
20000	1758.67	1201.49	923.25	756.58	645.70	566.70	507.62	461.82	425.32
25000	2198.34	1501.87	1154.06	945.73	807.13	708.37	634.52	577.27	531.65
30000	2638.01	1802.24	1384.88	1134.87	968.55	850.05	761.43	692.73	637.97
35000	3077.68	2102.61	1615.69	1324.02	1129.98	991.72	888.33	808.18	744.30
36000	3165.61	2162.69	1661.85	1361.85	1162.26	1020.06	913.71	831.27	765.57
37000	3253.54	2222.76	1708.01	1399.68	1194.55	1048.39	939.09	854.36	786.83
38000	3341.48	2282.83	1754.17	1437.51	1226.83	1076.72	964.47	877.45	808.10
39000	3429.41	2342.91	1800.34	1475.33	1259.12	1105.06	989.85	900.54	829.36
40000	3517.34	2402.98	1846.50	1513.16	1291.40	1133.39	1015.23	923.64	850.63
41000	3605.28	2463.06	1892.66	1550.99	1323.69	1161.73	1040.61	946.73	871.90
42000	3693.21	2523.13	1938.82	1588.82	1355.97	1190.06	1065.99	969.82	893.16
43000	3781.14	2583.21	1984.99	1626.65	1388.26	1218.40	1091.38	992.91	914.43
44000	3869.08	2643.28	2031.15	1664.48	1420.54	1246.73	1116.76	1016.00	935.69
45000	3957.01	2703.36	2077.31	1702.31	1452.83	1275.07	1142.14	1039.09	956.96
46000	4044.94	2763.43	2123.47	1740.14	1485.11	1303.40	1167.52	1062.18	978.22
47000	4132.88	2823.50	2169.64	1777.97	1517.40	1331.74	1192.90	1085.27	999.49
48000	4220.81	2883.58	2215.80	1815.79	1549.68	1360.07	1218.28	1108.36	1020.75
49000	4308.74	2943.65	2261.96	1853.62	1581.97	1388.41	1243.66	1131.45	1042.02
50000	4396.68	3003.73	2308.12	1891.45	1614.25	1416.74	1269.04	1154.54	1063.29
51000	4484.61	3063.80	2354.28	1929.28	1646.54	1445.08	1294.42	1177.63	1084.55
52000	4572.54	3123.88	2400.45	1967.11	1678.82	1473.41	1319.80	1200.72	1105.82
53000	4660.48	3183.95	2446.61	2004.94	1711.11	1501.75	1345.18	1223.81	1127.08
54000	4748.41	3244.03	2492.77	2042.77	1743.39	1530.08	1370.56	1246.91	1148.35
55000	4836.34	3304.10	2538.93	2080.60	1775.67	1558.42	1395.94	1270.00	1169.61
56000	4924.28	3364.17	2585.10	2118.43	1807.96	1586.75	1421.32	1293.09	1190.88
57000	5012.21	3424.25	2631.26	2156.26	1840.24	1615.08	1446.71	1316.18	1212.15
58000	5100.14	3484.32	2677.42	2194.08	1872.53	1643.42	1472.09	1339.27	1233.41
59000	5188.08	3544.40	2723.58	2231.91	1904.81	1671.75	1497.47	1362.36	1254.68
60000	5276.01	3604.47	2769.75	2269.74	1937.10	1700.09	1522.85	1385.45	1275.94
61000	5363.94	3664.55	2815.91	2307.57	1969.38	1728.42	1548.23	1408.54	1297.21
62000	5451.88	3724.62	2862.07	2345.40	2001.67	1756.76	1573.61	1431.63	1318.47
63000	5539.81	3784.70	2908.23	2383.23	2033.95	1785.09	1598.99	1454.72	1339.74
64000	5627.75	3844.77	2954.40	2421.06	2066.24	1813.43	1624.37	1477.81	1361.00
65000	5715.68	3904.84	3000.56	2458.89	2098.52	1841.76	1649.75	1500.90	1382.27
66000	5803.61	3964.92	3046.72	2496.72	2130.81	1870.10	1675.13	1523.99	1403.54
67000	5891.55	4024.99	3092.88	2534.55	2163.09	1898.43	1700.51	1547.09	1424.80
68000	5979.48	4085.07	3139.04	2572.37	2195.38	1926.77	1725.89	1570.18	1446.07
69000	6067.41	4145.14	3185.21	2610.20	2227.66	1955.10	1751.27	1593.27	1467.33
70000	6155.35	4205.22	3231.37	2648.03	2259.95	1983.44	1776.65	1616.36	1488.60
75000	6595.01	4505.59	3462.18	2837.18	2421.37	2125.11	1903.56	1731.81	1594.93
80000	7034.68	4805.96	3692.99	3026.32	2582.80	2266.78	2030.46	1847.27	1701.25
100000	8793.35	6007.45	4616.24	3782.90	3228.50	2833.48	2538.08	2309.08	2126.57

56

MONTHLY PAYMENT 10¼%
NECESSARY TO AMORTIZE A LOAN

TERM AMOUNT	6 YEARS	7 YEARS	8 YEARS	9 YEARS	10 YEARS	11 YEARS	12 YEARS	13 YEARS	14 YEARS
$ 25	.47	.42	.38	.36	.34	.32	.30	.29	.28
50	.93	.84	.76	.71	.67	.63	.60	.58	.56
75	1.40	1.25	1.14	1.06	1.00	.95	.90	.87	.84
100	1.86	1.67	1.52	1.41	1.33	1.26	1.20	1.16	1.12
200	3.71	3.33	3.04	2.82	2.65	2.51	2.40	2.31	2.23
300	5.57	4.99	4.56	4.23	3.98	3.77	3.60	3.46	3.34
400	7.42	6.65	6.08	5.64	5.30	5.02	4.79	4.61	4.45
500	9.28	8.32	7.60	7.05	6.62	6.28	5.99	5.76	5.56
600	11.13	9.98	9.12	8.46	7.95	7.53	7.19	6.91	6.67
700	12.99	11.64	10.64	9.87	9.27	8.78	8.39	8.06	7.78
800	14.84	13.30	12.16	11.28	10.59	10.04	9.58	9.21	8.89
900	16.70	14.96	13.68	12.69	11.92	11.29	10.78	10.36	10.00
1000	18.55	16.63	15.20	14.10	13.24	12.55	11.98	11.51	11.11
2000	37.09	33.25	30.39	28.20	26.48	25.09	23.95	23.01	22.21
3000	55.64	49.87	45.59	42.30	39.71	37.63	35.92	34.51	33.32
4000	74.18	66.49	60.78	56.40	52.95	50.17	47.90	46.01	44.42
5000	92.73	83.11	75.98	70.50	66.18	62.71	59.87	57.51	55.53
6000	111.27	99.73	91.17	84.60	79.42	75.25	71.84	69.01	66.63
7000	129.82	116.35	106.36	98.70	92.66	87.79	83.81	80.51	77.74
8000	148.36	132.97	121.56	112.80	105.89	100.33	95.79	92.01	88.84
9000	166.91	149.59	136.75	126.90	119.13	112.88	107.76	103.51	99.95
10000	185.45	166.21	151.95	141.00	132.36	125.42	119.73	115.01	111.05
15000	278.18	249.32	227.92	211.49	198.54	188.12	179.59	172.52	166.58
20000	370.90	332.42	303.89	281.99	264.72	250.83	239.46	230.02	222.10
25000	463.63	415.52	379.86	352.48	330.90	313.54	299.32	287.52	277.62
30000	556.35	498.63	455.83	422.98	397.08	376.24	359.18	345.03	333.15
35000	649.08	581.73	531.80	493.47	463.26	438.95	419.05	402.53	388.67
36000	667.62	598.35	546.99	507.57	476.50	451.49	431.02	414.03	399.77
37000	686.17	614.97	562.19	521.67	489.74	464.03	442.99	425.53	410.88
38000	704.71	631.59	577.38	535.77	502.97	476.57	454.96	437.03	421.98
39000	723.26	648.21	592.58	549.87	516.21	489.11	466.94	448.53	433.09
40000	741.80	664.83	607.77	563.97	529.44	501.65	478.91	460.03	444.19
41000	760.34	681.45	622.96	578.07	542.68	514.20	490.88	471.53	455.30
42000	778.89	698.07	638.16	592.17	555.92	526.74	502.85	483.04	466.40
43000	797.43	714.69	653.35	606.27	569.15	539.28	514.83	494.54	477.51
44000	815.98	731.32	668.55	620.37	582.39	551.82	526.80	506.04	488.61
45000	834.52	747.94	683.74	634.47	595.62	564.36	538.77	517.54	499.72
46000	853.07	764.56	698.94	648.56	608.86	576.90	550.74	529.04	510.82
47000	871.61	781.18	714.13	662.66	622.10	589.44	562.72	540.54	521.93
48000	890.16	797.80	729.32	676.76	635.33	601.98	574.69	552.04	533.03
49000	908.70	814.42	744.52	690.86	648.57	614.53	586.66	563.54	544.14
50000	927.25	831.04	759.71	704.96	661.80	627.07	598.63	575.04	555.24
51000	945.79	847.66	774.91	719.06	675.04	639.61	610.61	586.54	566.34
52000	964.34	864.28	790.10	733.16	688.28	652.15	622.58	598.04	577.45
53000	982.88	880.90	805.29	747.26	701.51	664.69	634.55	609.54	588.55
54000	1001.43	897.52	820.49	761.36	714.75	677.23	646.52	621.04	599.66
55000	1019.97	914.14	835.68	775.45	727.98	689.77	658.50	632.55	610.76
56000	1038.52	930.76	850.88	789.56	741.22	702.31	670.47	644.05	621.87
57000	1057.06	947.38	866.07	803.66	754.46	714.86	682.44	655.55	632.97
58000	1075.61	964.00	881.27	817.75	767.69	727.40	694.42	667.05	644.08
59000	1094.15	980.63	896.46	831.85	780.93	739.94	706.39	678.55	655.18
60000	1112.70	997.25	911.65	845.95	794.16	752.48	718.36	690.05	666.29
61000	1131.24	1013.87	926.85	860.05	807.40	765.02	730.33	701.55	677.39
62000	1149.79	1030.49	942.04	874.15	820.64	777.56	742.31	713.05	688.50
63000	1168.33	1047.11	957.24	888.25	833.87	790.10	754.28	724.55	699.60
64000	1186.88	1063.73	972.43	902.35	847.11	802.64	766.25	736.05	710.71
65000	1205.42	1080.35	987.62	916.45	860.34	815.19	778.22	747.55	721.81
66000	1223.97	1096.97	1002.82	930.55	873.58	827.73	790.20	759.05	732.92
67000	1242.51	1113.59	1018.01	944.65	886.82	840.27	802.17	770.55	744.02
68000	1261.06	1130.21	1033.21	958.75	900.05	852.81	814.14	782.05	755.12
69000	1279.60	1146.83	1048.40	972.84	913.29	865.35	826.11	793.56	766.23
70000	1298.15	1163.45	1063.59	986.94	926.52	877.89	838.09	805.06	777.33
75000	1390.87	1246.56	1139.57	1057.44	992.70	940.60	897.95	862.56	832.86
80000	1483.59	1329.66	1215.54	1127.94	1058.88	1003.30	957.81	920.06	888.38
100000	1854.49	1662.07	1519.42	1409.92	1323.60	1254.13	1197.26	1150.08	1110.48

10¼% MONTHLY PAYMENT
NECESSARY TO AMORTIZE A LOAN

TERM AMOUNT	15 YEARS	16 YEARS	17 YEARS	18 YEARS	19 YEARS	20 YEARS	21 YEARS	22 YEARS	23 YEARS
$ 25	.27	.27	.26	.26	.25	.25	.24	.24	.24
50	.54	.53	.52	.51	.50	.49	.48	.48	.47
75	.81	.79	.77	.76	.74	.73	.72	.71	.70
100	1.08	1.05	1.03	1.01	.99	.97	.96	.95	.93
200	2.16	2.10	2.05	2.01	1.97	1.94	1.91	1.89	1.86
300	3.24	3.15	3.08	3.01	2.96	2.91	2.86	2.83	2.79
400	4.31	4.20	4.10	4.01	3.94	3.88	3.82	3.77	3.72
500	5.39	5.25	5.12	5.02	4.92	4.84	4.77	4.71	4.65
600	6.47	6.29	6.15	6.02	5.91	5.81	5.72	5.65	5.58
700	7.54	7.34	7.17	7.02	6.89	6.78	6.68	6.59	6.51
800	8.62	8.39	8.19	8.02	7.87	7.75	7.63	7.53	7.44
900	9.70	9.44	9.22	9.03	8.86	8.71	8.58	8.47	8.37
1000	10.77	10.49	10.24	10.03	9.84	9.68	9.54	9.41	9.30
2000	21.54	20.97	20.48	20.05	19.68	19.36	19.07	18.82	18.60
3000	32.31	31.45	30.71	30.07	29.52	29.03	28.60	28.23	27.90
4000	43.08	41.94	40.95	40.10	39.35	38.71	38.14	37.64	37.20
5000	53.85	52.42	51.19	50.12	49.19	48.38	47.67	47.05	46.49
6000	64.62	62.90	61.42	60.14	59.03	58.06	57.20	56.45	55.79
7000	75.39	73.38	71.66	70.16	68.87	67.73	66.74	65.86	65.09
8000	86.16	83.87	81.89	80.19	78.70	77.41	76.27	75.27	74.39
9000	96.93	94.35	92.13	90.21	88.54	87.08	85.80	84.68	83.69
10000	107.70	104.83	102.37	100.23	98.38	96.76	95.34	94.09	92.98
15000	161.54	157.24	153.55	150.35	147.56	145.13	143.00	141.13	139.47
20000	215.39	209.66	204.73	200.46	196.75	193.51	190.67	188.17	185.96
25000	269.23	262.07	255.91	250.57	245.94	241.89	238.33	235.21	232.45
30000	323.08	314.48	307.09	300.69	295.12	290.26	286.00	282.25	278.94
35000	376.93	366.89	358.27	350.80	344.31	338.64	333.67	329.29	325.43
36000	387.69	377.38	368.50	360.82	354.15	348.31	343.20	338.70	334.73
37000	398.46	387.86	378.74	370.85	363.98	357.99	352.73	348.11	344.02
38000	409.23	398.34	388.97	380.87	373.82	367.66	362.27	357.51	353.32
39000	420.00	408.82	399.21	390.89	383.66	377.34	371.80	366.92	362.62
40000	430.77	419.31	409.45	400.91	393.49	387.01	381.33	376.33	371.92
41000	441.54	429.79	419.68	410.94	403.33	396.69	390.86	385.74	381.22
42000	452.31	440.27	429.92	420.96	413.17	406.36	400.40	395.15	390.51
43000	463.08	450.75	440.15	430.98	423.01	416.04	409.93	404.56	399.81
44000	473.85	461.24	450.39	441.00	432.84	425.72	419.46	413.96	409.11
45000	484.62	471.72	460.63	451.03	442.68	435.39	429.00	423.37	418.41
46000	495.39	482.20	470.86	461.05	452.52	445.07	438.53	432.78	427.71
47000	506.15	492.68	481.10	471.07	462.36	454.74	448.06	442.19	437.00
48000	516.92	503.17	491.33	481.10	472.19	464.42	457.60	451.60	446.30
49000	527.69	513.65	501.57	491.12	482.03	474.09	467.13	461.00	455.60
50000	538.46	524.13	511.81	501.14	491.87	483.77	476.66	470.41	464.90
51000	549.23	534.61	522.04	511.16	501.70	493.44	486.20	479.82	474.19
52000	560.00	545.10	532.28	521.19	511.54	503.12	495.73	489.23	483.49
53000	570.77	555.58	542.51	531.21	521.38	512.79	505.26	498.64	492.79
54000	581.54	566.06	552.75	541.23	531.22	522.47	514.80	508.05	502.09
55000	592.31	576.54	562.99	551.25	541.05	532.14	524.33	517.45	511.39
56000	603.08	587.03	573.22	561.28	550.89	541.82	533.86	526.86	520.68
57000	613.85	597.51	583.46	571.30	560.73	551.49	543.40	536.27	529.98
58000	624.62	607.99	593.69	581.32	570.57	561.17	552.93	545.68	539.28
59000	635.38	618.47	603.93	591.35	580.40	570.84	562.46	555.09	548.58
60000	646.15	628.96	614.17	601.37	590.24	580.52	571.99	564.49	557.87
61000	656.92	639.44	624.40	611.39	600.08	590.19	581.53	573.90	567.17
62000	667.69	649.92	634.64	621.41	609.91	599.87	591.06	583.31	576.47
63000	678.46	660.40	644.87	631.44	619.75	609.54	600.59	592.72	585.77
64000	689.23	670.89	655.11	641.46	629.59	619.22	610.13	602.13	595.07
65000	700.00	681.37	665.35	651.48	639.43	628.90	619.66	611.53	604.36
66000	710.77	691.85	675.58	661.50	649.26	638.57	629.19	620.94	613.66
67000	721.54	702.33	685.82	671.53	659.10	648.25	638.73	630.35	622.96
68000	732.31	712.82	696.05	681.55	668.94	657.92	648.26	639.76	632.26
69000	743.08	723.30	706.29	691.57	678.77	667.60	657.79	649.17	641.56
70000	753.85	733.78	716.53	701.60	688.61	677.27	667.33	658.58	650.85
75000	807.69	786.19	767.71	751.71	737.80	725.65	714.99	705.62	697.34
80000	861.54	838.61	818.89	801.82	786.98	774.02	762.66	752.66	743.83
100000	1076.92	1048.26	1023.61	1002.28	983.73	967.53	953.32	940.82	929.79

58

MONTHLY PAYMENT 10¼%
NECESSARY TO AMORTIZE A LOAN

TERM AMOUNT	24 YEARS	25 YEARS	26 YEARS	27 YEARS	28 YEARS	29 YEARS	30 YEARS	35 YEARS	40 YEARS
$ 25	.24	.23	.23	.23	.23	.23	.23	.22	.22
50	.47	.46	.46	.45	.45	.45	.45	.44	.43
75	.70	.69	.68	.68	.67	.67	.67	.65	.64
100	.93	.92	.91	.90	.90	.89	.89	.87	.86
200	1.85	1.83	1.81	1.80	1.79	1.78	1.77	1.73	1.71
300	2.77	2.74	2.72	2.70	2.68	2.66	2.65	2.59	2.56
400	3.69	3.65	3.62	3.59	3.57	3.55	3.53	3.46	3.41
500	4.61	4.56	4.52	4.49	4.46	4.43	4.41	4.32	4.27
600	5.53	5.47	5.43	5.39	5.35	5.32	5.29	5.18	5.12
700	6.45	6.38	6.33	6.28	6.24	6.20	6.17	6.04	5.97
800	7.37	7.30	7.23	7.18	7.13	7.09	7.05	6.91	6.82
900	8.29	8.21	8.14	8.08	8.02	7.97	7.93	7.77	7.67
1000	9.21	9.12	9.04	8.97	8.91	8.86	8.81	8.63	8.53
2000	18.41	18.23	18.08	17.94	17.82	17.71	17.61	17.26	17.05
3000	27.61	27.35	27.11	26.91	26.73	26.56	26.42	25.88	25.57
4000	36.81	36.46	36.15	35.88	35.63	35.41	35.22	34.51	34.09
5000	46.01	45.57	45.19	44.85	44.54	44.27	44.02	43.13	42.61
6000	55.21	54.69	54.22	53.81	53.45	53.12	52.83	51.76	51.13
7000	64.41	63.80	63.26	62.78	62.35	61.97	61.63	60.38	59.65
8000	73.61	72.91	72.30	71.75	71.26	70.82	70.43	69.01	68.17
9000	82.81	82.03	81.33	80.72	80.17	79.68	79.24	77.64	76.69
10000	92.01	91.14	90.37	89.69	89.08	88.53	88.04	86.26	85.22
15000	138.01	136.71	135.55	134.53	133.61	132.79	132.06	129.39	127.82
20000	184.01	182.28	180.74	179.37	178.15	177.05	176.08	172.52	170.43
25000	230.01	227.85	225.92	224.21	222.68	221.32	220.10	215.65	213.03
30000	276.01	273.41	271.10	269.05	267.22	265.58	264.11	258.77	255.64
35000	322.01	318.98	316.29	313.89	311.75	309.84	308.13	301.90	298.24
36000	331.21	328.10	325.32	322.86	320.66	318.69	316.94	310.53	306.76
37000	340.41	337.21	334.36	331.83	329.56	327.55	325.74	319.15	315.29
38000	349.61	346.32	343.40	340.79	338.47	336.40	334.54	327.78	323.81
39000	358.81	355.44	352.43	349.76	347.38	345.25	343.35	336.40	332.33
40000	368.01	364.55	361.47	358.73	356.29	354.10	352.15	345.03	340.85
41000	377.21	373.66	370.51	367.70	365.19	362.95	360.95	353.66	349.37
42000	386.41	382.78	379.54	376.67	374.10	371.81	369.76	362.28	357.89
43000	395.61	391.89	388.58	385.64	383.01	380.66	378.56	370.91	366.41
44000	404.81	401.00	397.62	394.60	391.91	389.51	387.36	379.53	374.93
45000	414.01	410.12	406.65	403.57	400.82	398.36	396.17	388.16	383.45
46000	423.21	419.23	415.69	412.54	409.73	407.22	404.97	396.78	391.98
47000	432.41	428.35	424.73	421.51	418.64	416.07	413.77	405.41	400.50
48000	441.61	437.46	433.76	430.48	427.54	424.92	422.58	414.03	409.02
49000	450.82	446.57	442.80	439.44	436.45	433.77	431.38	422.66	417.54
50000	460.02	455.69	451.84	448.41	445.36	442.63	440.19	431.29	426.06
51000	469.22	464.80	460.87	457.38	454.26	451.48	448.99	439.91	434.58
52000	478.42	473.91	469.91	466.35	463.17	460.33	457.79	448.54	443.10
53000	487.62	483.03	478.95	475.32	472.08	469.18	466.60	457.16	451.62
54000	496.82	492.14	487.98	484.28	480.98	478.04	475.40	465.79	460.14
55000	506.02	501.25	497.02	493.25	489.89	486.89	484.20	474.41	468.67
56000	515.22	510.37	506.06	502.22	498.80	495.74	493.01	483.04	477.19
57000	524.42	519.48	515.09	511.19	507.71	504.59	501.81	491.67	485.71
58000	533.62	528.60	524.13	520.16	516.61	513.45	510.61	500.29	494.23
59000	542.82	537.71	533.17	529.13	525.52	522.30	519.42	508.92	502.75
60000	552.02	546.82	542.20	538.09	534.43	531.15	528.22	517.54	511.27
61000	561.22	555.94	551.24	547.06	543.33	540.00	537.03	526.17	519.79
62000	570.42	565.05	560.28	556.03	552.24	548.86	545.83	534.79	528.31
63000	579.62	574.16	569.31	565.00	561.15	557.71	554.63	543.42	536.83
64000	588.82	583.28	578.35	573.97	570.05	566.56	563.44	552.04	545.36
65000	598.02	592.39	587.39	582.93	578.96	575.41	572.24	560.67	553.88
66000	607.22	601.50	596.42	591.90	587.87	584.27	581.04	569.30	562.40
67000	616.42	610.62	605.46	600.87	596.78	593.12	589.85	577.92	570.92
68000	625.62	619.73	614.50	609.84	605.68	601.97	598.65	586.55	579.44
69000	634.82	628.84	623.53	618.81	614.59	610.82	607.45	595.17	587.96
70000	644.02	637.96	632.57	627.77	623.50	619.68	616.26	603.80	596.48
75000	690.02	683.53	677.75	672.62	668.03	663.94	660.28	646.93	639.09
80000	736.02	729.09	722.94	717.46	712.57	708.20	704.29	690.05	681.69
100000	920.03	911.37	903.67	896.82	890.71	885.25	880.37	862.57	852.11

59

10½% MONTHLY PAYMENT
NECESSARY TO AMORTIZE A LOAN

TERM AMOUNT	1 YEAR	1½ YEARS	2 YEARS	2½ YEARS	3 YEARS	3½ YEARS	4 YEARS	4½ YEARS	5 YEARS
$ 25	2.21	1.51	1.16	.95	.81	.72	.64	.59	.54
50	4.41	3.01	2.32	1.90	1.62	1.43	1.28	1.17	1.07
75	6.61	4.52	3.48	2.85	2.43	2.14	1.92	1.75	1.61
100	8.81	6.02	4.63	3.80	3.24	2.85	2.55	2.33	2.14
200	17.61	12.04	9.26	7.59	6.48	5.69	5.10	4.65	4.28
300	26.42	18.06	13.89	11.39	9.72	8.54	7.65	6.97	6.42
400	35.22	24.08	18.51	15.18	12.96	11.38	10.20	9.29	8.56
500	44.03	30.10	23.14	18.98	16.20	14.23	12.75	11.61	10.70
600	52.83	36.12	27.77	22.77	19.44	17.07	15.30	13.93	12.84
700	61.64	42.13	32.40	26.56	22.68	19.92	17.85	16.25	14.97
800	70.44	48.15	37.02	30.36	25.92	22.76	20.40	18.57	17.11
900	79.25	54.17	41.65	34.15	29.16	25.61	22.95	20.89	19.25
1000	88.05	60.19	46.28	37.95	32.40	28.45	25.50	23.21	21.39
2000	176.09	120.37	92.55	75.89	64.80	56.90	51.00	46.42	42.77
3000	264.14	180.56	138.82	113.83	97.20	85.35	76.49	69.63	64.16
4000	352.18	240.74	185.10	151.77	129.60	113.80	101.99	92.83	85.54
5000	440.23	300.93	231.37	189.71	161.99	142.25	127.49	116.04	106.92
6000	528.27	361.11	277.64	227.65	194.39	170.70	152.98	139.25	128.31
7000	616.32	421.30	323.92	265.59	226.79	199.15	178.48	162.46	149.69
8000	704.36	481.48	370.19	303.53	259.19	227.59	203.97	185.66	171.08
9000	792.41	541.67	416.46	341.47	291.58	256.04	229.47	208.87	192.46
10000	880.45	601.85	462.74	379.41	323.98	284.49	254.97	232.08	213.84
15000	1320.68	902.78	694.10	569.11	485.97	426.74	382.45	348.12	320.76
20000	1760.90	1203.70	925.47	758.82	647.96	568.98	509.93	464.15	427.68
25000	2201.13	1504.63	1156.83	948.52	809.94	711.22	637.41	580.19	534.60
30000	2641.35	1805.55	1388.20	1138.22	971.93	853.47	764.89	696.23	641.52
35000	3081.58	2106.48	1619.56	1327.92	1133.92	995.71	892.37	812.27	748.44
36000	3169.62	2166.66	1665.84	1365.86	1166.32	1024.16	917.86	835.47	769.82
37000	3257.67	2226.85	1712.11	1403.80	1198.72	1052.61	943.36	858.68	791.21
38000	3345.71	2287.03	1758.38	1441.75	1231.11	1081.06	968.85	881.89	812.59
39000	3433.76	2347.22	1804.65	1479.69	1263.51	1109.50	994.35	905.10	833.97
40000	3521.80	2407.40	1850.93	1517.63	1295.91	1137.95	1019.85	928.30	855.36
41000	3609.85	2467.59	1897.20	1555.57	1328.31	1166.40	1045.34	951.51	876.74
42000	3697.89	2527.77	1943.47	1593.51	1360.70	1194.85	1070.84	974.72	898.12
43000	3785.94	2587.96	1989.75	1631.45	1393.10	1223.30	1096.33	997.93	919.51
44000	3873.98	2648.14	2036.02	1669.39	1425.50	1251.75	1121.83	1021.13	940.89
45000	3962.03	2708.33	2082.29	1707.33	1457.90	1280.20	1147.33	1044.34	962.28
46000	4050.07	2768.51	2128.57	1745.27	1490.29	1308.64	1172.82	1067.55	983.66
47000	4138.12	2828.69	2174.84	1783.21	1522.69	1337.09	1198.32	1090.76	1005.04
48000	4226.16	2888.88	2221.11	1821.15	1555.09	1365.54	1223.81	1113.96	1026.43
49000	4314.21	2949.06	2267.39	1859.09	1587.49	1393.99	1249.31	1137.17	1047.81
50000	4402.25	3009.25	2313.66	1897.03	1619.88	1422.44	1274.81	1160.38	1069.20
51000	4490.30	3069.43	2359.93	1934.97	1652.28	1450.89	1300.30	1183.59	1090.58
52000	4578.34	3129.62	2406.20	1972.91	1684.68	1479.34	1325.80	1206.79	1111.96
53000	4666.39	3189.80	2452.48	2010.85	1717.08	1507.79	1351.29	1230.00	1133.35
54000	4754.43	3249.99	2498.75	2048.79	1749.47	1536.23	1376.79	1253.21	1154.73
55000	4842.48	3310.17	2545.02	2086.73	1781.87	1564.68	1402.29	1276.42	1176.11
56000	4930.52	3370.36	2591.30	2124.67	1814.27	1593.13	1427.78	1299.62	1197.50
57000	5018.57	3430.54	2637.57	2162.62	1846.67	1621.58	1453.28	1322.83	1218.88
58000	5106.61	3490.73	2683.84	2200.56	1879.07	1650.03	1478.77	1346.04	1240.27
59000	5194.66	3550.91	2730.12	2238.50	1911.46	1678.48	1504.27	1369.25	1261.65
60000	5282.70	3611.10	2776.39	2276.44	1943.86	1706.93	1529.77	1392.45	1283.03
61000	5370.75	3671.28	2822.66	2314.38	1976.26	1735.37	1555.26	1415.66	1304.42
62000	5458.79	3731.47	2868.94	2352.32	2008.66	1763.82	1580.76	1438.87	1325.80
63000	5546.84	3791.65	2915.21	2390.26	2041.05	1792.27	1606.25	1462.08	1347.18
64000	5634.88	3851.84	2961.48	2428.20	2073.45	1820.72	1631.75	1485.28	1368.57
65000	5722.93	3912.02	3007.75	2466.14	2105.85	1849.17	1657.25	1508.49	1389.95
66000	5810.97	3972.21	3054.03	2504.08	2138.25	1877.62	1682.74	1531.70	1411.34
67000	5899.02	4032.39	3100.30	2542.02	2170.64	1906.07	1708.24	1554.91	1432.72
68000	5987.06	4092.58	3146.57	2579.96	2203.04	1934.52	1733.73	1578.11	1454.10
69000	6075.11	4152.76	3192.85	2617.90	2235.44	1962.96	1759.23	1601.32	1475.49
70000	6163.15	4212.95	3239.12	2655.84	2267.84	1991.41	1784.73	1624.53	1496.87
75000	6603.38	4513.87	3470.49	2845.54	2429.82	2133.66	1912.21	1740.57	1603.79
80000	7043.60	4814.80	3701.85	3035.25	2591.81	2275.90	2039.69	1856.60	1710.71
100000	8804.50	6018.49	4627.31	3794.06	3239.76	2844.87	2549.61	2320.75	2138.39

60

MONTHLY PAYMENT 10½%
NECESSARY TO AMORTIZE A LOAN

TERM AMOUNT	6 YEARS	7 YEARS	8 YEARS	9 YEARS	10 YEARS	11 YEARS	12 YEARS	13 YEARS	14 YEARS
$ 25	.47	.42	.39	.36	.34	.32	.31	.30	.29
50	.94	.84	.77	.72	.67	.64	.61	.59	.57
75	1.40	1.26	1.15	1.07	1.01	.96	.91	.88	.85
100	1.87	1.68	1.54	1.43	1.34	1.27	1.22	1.17	1.13
200	3.74	3.35	3.07	2.85	2.68	2.54	2.43	2.33	2.25
300	5.60	5.03	4.60	4.27	4.02	3.81	3.64	3.50	3.38
400	7.47	6.70	6.13	5.70	5.35	5.08	4.85	4.66	4.50
500	9.34	8.38	7.67	7.12	6.69	6.34	6.06	5.83	5.63
600	11.20	10.05	9.20	8.54	8.03	7.61	7.27	6.99	6.75
700	13.07	11.73	10.73	9.97	9.36	8.88	8.48	8.15	7.88
800	14.94	13.40	12.26	11.39	10.70	10.15	9.69	9.32	9.00
900	16.80	15.08	13.79	12.81	12.04	11.41	10.91	10.48	10.13
1000	18.67	16.75	15.33	14.23	13.37	12.68	12.12	11.65	11.25
2000	37.34	33.49	30.66	28.46	26.74	25.36	24.23	23.29	22.50
3000	56.00	50.24	45.97	42.69	40.11	38.04	36.34	34.93	33.75
4000	74.67	66.98	61.29	56.92	53.48	50.71	48.45	46.58	45.00
5000	93.34	83.73	76.61	71.15	66.85	63.39	60.56	58.22	56.25
6000	112.00	100.47	91.93	85.38	80.22	76.07	72.67	69.86	67.50
7000	130.67	117.22	107.25	99.61	93.59	88.75	84.79	81.50	78.75
8000	149.33	133.96	122.58	113.84	106.96	101.42	96.90	93.15	90.00
9000	168.00	150.71	137.90	128.07	120.33	114.10	109.01	104.79	101.25
10000	186.67	167.45	153.22	142.30	133.70	126.78	121.12	116.43	112.50
15000	280.00	251.18	229.83	213.45	200.54	190.17	181.68	174.64	168.74
20000	373.33	334.90	306.43	284.59	267.39	253.55	242.24	232.86	224.99
25000	466.66	418.63	383.04	355.74	334.23	316.94	302.79	291.07	281.24
30000	559.99	502.35	459.65	426.89	401.08	380.33	363.35	349.28	337.48
35000	653.32	586.08	536.25	498.03	467.93	443.71	423.91	407.49	393.73
36000	671.98	602.82	551.57	512.26	481.30	456.39	436.02	419.14	404.98
37000	690.65	619.57	566.90	526.49	494.66	469.07	448.13	430.78	416.23
38000	709.31	636.31	582.22	540.72	508.03	481.74	460.25	442.42	427.48
39000	727.98	653.06	597.54	554.95	521.40	494.42	472.36	454.06	438.73
40000	746.65	669.80	612.86	569.18	534.77	507.10	484.47	465.71	449.98
41000	765.31	686.54	628.18	583.41	548.14	519.78	496.58	477.35	461.23
42000	783.98	703.29	643.50	597.64	561.51	532.45	508.69	488.99	472.47
43000	802.64	720.03	658.82	611.87	574.88	545.13	520.80	500.63	483.72
44000	821.31	736.78	674.14	626.10	588.25	557.81	532.92	512.28	494.97
45000	839.98	753.52	689.47	640.33	601.62	570.49	545.03	523.92	506.22
46000	858.64	770.27	704.79	654.56	614.99	583.16	557.14	535.56	517.47
47000	877.31	787.01	720.11	668.78	628.36	595.84	569.25	547.20	528.72
48000	895.97	803.76	735.43	683.01	641.73	608.52	581.36	558.85	539.97
49000	914.64	820.50	750.75	697.24	655.09	621.20	593.47	570.49	551.22
50000	933.31	837.25	766.07	711.47	668.46	633.87	605.58	582.13	562.47
51000	951.97	853.99	781.39	725.70	681.83	646.55	617.70	593.77	573.72
52000	970.64	870.74	796.72	739.93	695.20	659.23	629.81	605.42	584.97
53000	989.31	887.48	812.04	754.16	708.57	671.91	641.92	617.06	596.22
54000	1007.97	904.23	827.36	768.39	721.94	684.58	654.03	628.70	607.47
55000	1026.64	920.97	842.68	782.62	735.31	697.26	666.14	640.35	618.72
56000	1045.30	937.72	858.00	796.85	748.68	709.94	678.25	651.99	629.96
57000	1063.97	954.46	873.32	811.08	762.05	722.61	690.37	663.63	641.21
58000	1082.64	971.21	888.64	825.31	775.42	735.29	702.48	675.27	652.46
59000	1101.30	987.95	903.96	839.54	788.79	747.97	714.59	686.92	663.71
60000	1119.97	1004.70	919.29	853.77	802.16	760.65	726.70	698.56	674.96
61000	1138.63	1021.44	934.61	868.00	815.52	773.32	738.81	710.20	686.21
62000	1157.30	1038.19	949.93	882.22	828.89	786.00	750.92	721.84	697.46
63000	1175.97	1054.93	965.25	896.45	842.26	798.68	763.04	733.49	708.71
64000	1194.63	1071.68	980.57	910.68	855.63	811.36	775.15	745.13	719.96
65000	1213.30	1088.42	995.89	924.91	869.00	824.03	787.26	756.77	731.21
66000	1231.96	1105.17	1011.21	939.14	882.37	836.71	799.37	768.41	742.46
67000	1250.63	1121.91	1026.54	953.37	895.74	849.39	811.48	780.06	753.71
68000	1269.30	1138.66	1041.86	967.60	909.11	862.07	823.59	791.70	764.96
69000	1287.96	1155.40	1057.18	981.83	922.48	874.74	835.70	803.34	776.21
70000	1306.63	1172.15	1072.50	996.06	935.85	887.42	847.82	814.98	787.45
75000	1399.96	1255.87	1149.11	1067.21	1002.69	950.81	908.37	873.20	843.70
80000	1493.29	1339.60	1225.71	1138.35	1069.54	1014.19	968.93	931.41	899.95
100000	1866.61	1674.49	1532.14	1422.94	1336.92	1267.74	1211.16	1164.26	1124.93

61

10½%   MONTHLY PAYMENT
NECESSARY TO AMORTIZE A LOAN

TERM AMOUNT	15 YEARS	16 YEARS	17 YEARS	18 YEARS	19 YEARS	20 YEARS	21 YEARS	22 YEARS	23 YEARS
$ 25	.28	.27	.26	.26	.25	.25	.25	.24	.24
50	.55	.54	.52	.51	.50	.50	.49	.48	.48
75	.82	.80	.78	.77	.75	.74	.73	.72	.71
100	1.10	1.07	1.04	1.02	1.00	.99	.97	.96	.95
200	2.19	2.13	2.08	2.04	2.00	1.97	1.94	1.92	1.90
300	3.28	3.19	3.12	3.06	3.00	2.96	2.91	2.88	2.84
400	4.37	4.26	4.16	4.08	4.00	3.94	3.88	3.83	3.79
500	5.46	5.32	5.20	5.09	5.00	4.92	4.85	4.79	4.74
600	6.55	6.38	6.24	6.11	6.00	5.91	5.82	5.75	5.68
700	7.65	7.45	7.28	7.13	7.00	6.89	6.79	6.71	6.63
800	8.74	8.51	8.32	8.15	8.00	7.87	7.76	7.66	7.58
900	9.83	9.57	9.35	9.16	9.00	8.86	8.73	8.62	8.52
1000	10.92	10.64	10.39	10.18	10.00	9.84	9.70	9.58	9.47
2000	21.84	21.27	20.78	20.36	19.99	19.67	19.39	19.15	18.93
3000	32.75	31.90	31.17	30.54	29.99	29.51	29.09	28.72	28.40
4000	43.67	42.53	41.56	40.72	39.98	39.34	38.78	38.29	37.86
5000	54.59	53.17	51.95	50.89	49.98	49.18	48.48	47.86	47.32
6000	65.50	63.80	62.34	61.07	59.97	59.01	58.17	57.44	56.79
7000	76.42	74.43	72.72	71.25	69.97	68.85	67.87	67.01	66.25
8000	87.34	85.06	83.11	81.43	79.96	78.68	77.56	76.58	75.71
9000	98.25	95.70	93.50	91.60	89.96	88.52	87.26	86.15	85.18
10000	109.17	106.33	103.89	101.78	99.95	98.35	96.95	95.72	94.64
15000	163.75	159.49	155.83	152.67	149.92	147.53	145.43	143.58	141.96
20000	218.33	212.65	207.77	203.56	199.89	196.70	193.90	191.44	189.28
25000	272.92	265.81	259.71	254.44	249.87	245.87	242.38	239.30	236.60
30000	327.50	318.98	311.66	305.33	299.84	295.05	290.85	287.16	283.92
35000	382.08	372.14	363.60	356.22	349.81	344.22	339.33	335.02	331.23
36000	393.00	382.77	373.99	366.40	359.81	354.06	349.02	344.60	340.70
37000	403.91	393.40	384.38	376.57	369.80	363.89	358.72	354.17	350.16
38000	414.83	404.04	394.76	386.75	379.79	373.72	368.41	363.74	359.63
39000	425.74	414.67	405.15	396.93	389.79	383.56	378.10	373.31	369.09
40000	436.66	425.30	415.54	407.11	399.78	393.39	387.80	382.88	378.55
41000	447.58	435.93	425.93	417.29	409.78	403.23	397.49	392.46	388.02
42000	458.49	446.57	436.32	427.46	419.77	413.06	407.19	402.03	397.48
43000	469.41	457.20	446.71	437.64	429.77	422.90	416.88	411.60	406.94
44000	480.33	467.83	457.09	447.82	439.76	432.73	426.58	421.17	416.41
45000	491.24	478.46	467.48	458.00	449.75	442.57	436.27	430.74	425.87
46000	502.16	489.09	477.87	468.17	459.75	452.40	445.97	440.32	435.33
47000	513.08	499.73	488.26	478.35	469.74	462.24	455.66	449.89	444.80
48000	523.99	510.36	498.65	488.53	479.74	472.07	465.36	459.46	454.26
49000	534.91	520.99	509.04	498.71	489.73	481.91	475.05	469.03	463.73
50000	545.83	531.62	519.42	508.88	499.73	491.74	484.75	478.60	473.19
51000	556.74	542.26	529.81	519.06	509.72	501.58	494.44	488.18	482.65
52000	567.66	552.89	540.20	529.24	519.72	511.41	504.14	497.75	492.12
53000	578.57	563.52	550.59	539.42	529.71	521.25	513.83	507.32	501.58
54000	589.49	574.15	560.98	549.59	539.71	531.08	523.53	516.89	511.04
55000	600.41	584.79	571.37	559.77	549.70	540.92	533.22	526.46	520.51
56000	611.32	595.42	581.76	569.95	559.70	550.75	542.92	536.04	529.97
57000	622.24	606.05	592.14	580.13	569.69	560.58	552.61	545.61	539.44
58000	633.16	616.68	602.53	590.30	579.68	570.42	562.31	555.18	548.90
59000	644.07	627.32	612.92	600.48	589.68	580.25	572.00	564.75	558.36
60000	654.99	637.95	623.31	610.66	599.67	590.09	581.70	574.32	567.83
61000	665.91	648.58	633.70	620.84	609.67	599.92	591.39	583.90	577.29
62000	676.82	659.21	644.09	631.01	619.66	609.76	601.09	593.47	586.75
63000	687.74	669.85	654.47	641.19	629.66	619.59	610.78	603.04	596.22
64000	698.65	680.48	664.86	651.37	639.65	629.43	620.48	612.61	605.68
65000	709.57	691.11	675.25	661.55	649.64	639.26	630.17	622.18	615.14
66000	720.49	701.74	685.64	671.72	659.64	649.10	639.87	631.76	624.61
67000	731.40	712.37	696.03	681.90	669.63	658.93	649.56	641.33	634.07
68000	742.32	723.01	706.42	692.08	679.63	668.77	659.26	650.90	643.54
69000	753.24	733.64	716.80	702.26	689.62	678.60	668.95	660.47	653.00
70000	764.15	744.27	727.19	712.43	699.62	688.44	678.65	670.04	662.46
75000	818.74	797.43	779.13	763.32	749.59	737.61	727.12	717.90	709.78
80000	873.32	850.60	831.08	814.21	799.56	786.78	775.59	765.76	757.10
100000	1091.65	1063.24	1038.84	1017.76	999.45	983.48	969.49	957.20	946.37

MONTHLY PAYMENT 10½%
NECESSARY TO AMORTIZE A LOAN

TERM AMOUNT	24 YEARS	25 YEARS	26 YEARS	27 YEARS	28 YEARS	29 YEARS	30 YEARS	35 YEARS	40 YEARS
$ 25	.24	.24	.24	.23	.23	.23	.23	.23	.22
50	.47	.47	.47	.46	.46	.46	.45	.45	.44
75	.71	.70	.70	.69	.69	.68	.68	.67	.66
100	.94	.93	.93	.92	.91	.91	.90	.89	.88
200	1.88	1.86	1.85	1.83	1.82	1.81	1.80	1.77	1.75
300	2.82	2.79	2.77	2.75	2.73	2.71	2.70	2.65	2.62
400	3.75	3.72	3.69	3.66	3.64	3.62	3.60	3.53	3.49
500	4.69	4.65	4.61	4.58	4.55	4.52	4.50	4.41	4.36
600	5.63	5.57	5.53	5.49	5.45	5.42	5.39	5.29	5.23
700	6.56	6.50	6.45	6.40	6.36	6.33	6.29	6.17	6.10
800	7.50	7.43	7.37	7.32	7.27	7.23	7.19	7.05	6.97
900	8.44	8.36	8.29	8.23	8.18	8.13	8.09	7.93	7.84
1000	9.37	9.29	9.21	9.15	9.09	9.03	8.99	8.81	8.71
2000	18.74	18.57	18.42	18.29	18.17	18.06	17.97	17.62	17.42
3000	28.11	27.85	27.63	27.43	27.25	27.09	26.95	26.43	26.13
4000	37.48	37.14	36.84	36.57	36.33	36.12	35.93	35.24	34.84
5000	46.85	46.42	46.05	45.71	45.41	45.15	44.91	44.05	43.55
6000	56.21	55.70	55.25	54.85	54.50	54.18	53.89	52.86	52.26
7000	65.58	64.99	64.46	63.99	63.58	63.21	62.87	61.67	60.97
8000	74.95	74.27	73.67	73.14	72.66	72.24	71.86	70.48	69.68
9000	84.32	83.55	82.88	82.28	81.74	81.26	80.84	79.29	78.39
10000	93.69	92.84	92.09	91.42	90.82	90.29	89.82	88.10	87.10
15000	140.53	139.25	138.13	137.12	136.23	135.44	134.73	132.15	130.65
20000	187.37	185.67	184.17	182.83	181.64	180.58	179.63	176.20	174.20
25000	234.21	232.09	230.21	228.54	227.05	225.72	224.54	220.25	217.75
30000	281.05	278.50	276.25	274.24	272.46	270.87	269.45	264.29	261.30
35000	327.89	324.92	322.29	319.95	317.87	316.01	314.35	308.34	304.85
36000	337.25	334.20	331.50	329.09	326.95	325.04	323.34	317.15	313.56
37000	346.62	343.49	340.71	338.23	336.03	334.07	332.32	325.96	322.27
38000	355.99	352.77	349.91	347.37	345.11	343.10	341.30	334.77	330.98
39000	365.36	362.05	359.12	356.52	354.20	352.13	350.28	343.58	339.69
40000	374.73	371.34	368.33	365.66	363.28	361.16	359.26	352.39	348.40
41000	384.09	380.62	377.54	374.80	372.36	370.18	368.24	361.20	357.11
42000	393.46	389.90	386.75	383.94	381.44	379.21	377.22	370.01	365.82
43000	402.83	399.19	395.95	393.08	390.52	388.24	386.21	378.82	374.53
44000	412.20	408.47	405.16	402.22	399.60	397.27	395.19	387.63	383.24
45000	421.57	417.75	414.37	411.36	408.69	406.30	404.17	396.44	391.95
46000	430.93	427.04	423.58	420.50	417.77	415.33	413.15	405.25	400.66
47000	440.30	436.32	432.79	429.65	426.85	424.36	422.13	414.06	409.37
48000	449.67	445.60	441.99	438.79	435.93	433.39	431.11	422.87	418.08
49000	459.04	454.89	451.20	447.93	445.01	442.41	440.09	431.68	426.79
50000	468.41	464.17	460.41	457.07	454.10	451.44	449.08	440.49	435.50
51000	477.77	473.45	469.62	466.21	463.18	460.47	458.06	449.30	444.21
52000	487.14	482.74	478.83	475.35	472.26	469.50	467.04	458.11	452.91
53000	496.51	492.02	488.04	484.49	481.34	478.53	476.02	466.92	461.62
54000	505.88	501.30	497.24	493.64	490.42	487.56	485.00	475.73	470.33
55000	515.25	510.59	506.45	502.78	499.50	496.59	493.98	484.54	479.04
56000	524.61	519.87	515.66	511.92	508.59	505.62	502.96	493.35	487.75
57000	533.98	529.15	524.87	521.06	517.67	514.64	511.94	502.16	496.46
58000	543.35	538.44	534.08	530.20	526.75	523.67	520.93	510.96	505.17
59000	552.72	547.72	543.28	539.34	535.83	532.70	529.91	519.77	513.88
60000	562.09	557.00	552.49	548.48	544.91	541.73	538.89	528.58	522.59
61000	571.45	566.29	561.70	557.62	554.00	550.76	547.87	537.39	531.30
62000	580.82	575.57	570.91	566.77	563.08	559.79	556.85	546.20	540.01
63000	590.19	584.85	580.12	575.91	572.16	568.82	565.83	555.01	548.72
64000	599.56	594.14	589.32	585.05	581.24	577.85	574.81	563.82	557.43
65000	608.93	603.42	598.53	594.19	590.32	586.87	583.80	572.63	566.14
66000	618.29	612.70	607.74	603.33	599.40	595.90	592.78	581.44	574.85
67000	627.66	621.99	616.95	612.47	608.49	604.93	601.76	590.25	583.56
68000	637.03	631.27	626.16	621.61	617.57	613.96	610.74	599.06	592.27
69000	646.40	640.55	635.37	630.75	626.65	622.99	619.72	607.87	600.98
70000	655.77	649.84	644.57	639.90	635.73	632.02	628.70	616.68	609.69
75000	702.61	696.25	690.61	685.60	681.14	677.16	673.61	660.73	653.24
80000	749.45	742.67	736.65	731.31	726.55	722.31	718.52	704.78	696.79
100000	936.81	928.33	920.82	914.14	908.19	902.88	898.15	880.97	870.99

10¾% MONTHLY PAYMENT
NECESSARY TO AMORTIZE A LOAN

TERM AMOUNT	1 YEAR	1½ YEARS	2 YEARS	2½ YEARS	3 YEARS	3½ YEARS	4 YEARS	4½ YEARS	5 YEARS
$ 25	2.21	1.51	1.16	.96	.82	.72	.65	.59	.54
50	4.41	3.02	2.32	1.91	1.63	1.43	1.29	1.17	1.08
75	6.62	4.53	3.48	2.86	2.44	2.15	1.93	1.75	1.62
100	8.82	6.03	4.64	3.81	3.26	2.86	2.57	2.34	2.16
200	17.64	12.06	9.28	7.62	6.51	5.72	5.13	4.67	4.31
300	26.45	18.09	13.92	11.42	9.76	8.57	7.69	7.00	6.46
400	35.27	24.12	18.56	15.23	13.01	11.43	10.25	9.33	8.61
500	44.08	30.15	23.20	19.03	16.26	14.29	12.81	11.67	10.76
600	52.90	36.18	27.84	22.84	19.51	17.14	15.37	14.00	12.91
700	61.71	42.21	32.47	26.64	22.76	20.00	17.93	16.33	15.06
800	70.53	48.24	37.11	30.45	26.01	22.86	20.49	18.66	17.21
900	79.35	54.27	41.75	34.25	29.26	25.71	23.06	21.00	19.36
1000	88.16	60.30	46.39	38.06	32.52	28.57	25.62	23.33	21.51
2000	176.32	120.60	92.77	76.11	65.03	57.13	51.23	46.65	43.01
3000	264.47	180.89	139.16	114.16	97.54	85.69	76.84	69.98	64.51
4000	352.63	241.19	185.54	152.21	130.05	114.26	102.45	93.30	86.01
5000	440.79	301.48	231.92	190.27	162.56	142.82	128.06	116.63	107.52
6000	528.94	361.78	278.31	228.32	195.07	171.38	153.67	139.95	129.02
7000	617.10	422.07	324.69	266.37	227.58	199.94	179.29	163.28	150.52
8000	705.26	482.37	371.08	304.42	260.09	228.51	204.90	186.60	172.02
9000	793.41	542.66	417.46	342.47	292.60	257.07	230.51	209.92	193.53
10000	881.57	602.96	463.84	380.53	325.11	285.63	256.12	233.25	215.03
15000	1322.35	904.44	695.76	570.79	487.66	428.45	384.18	349.87	322.54
20000	1763.13	1205.91	927.68	761.05	650.21	571.26	512.24	466.49	430.05
25000	2203.92	1507.39	1159.60	951.31	812.76	714.07	640.29	583.12	537.56
30000	2644.70	1808.87	1391.52	1141.57	975.32	856.89	768.35	699.74	645.07
35000	3085.48	2110.34	1623.44	1331.83	1137.87	999.70	896.41	816.36	752.58
36000	3173.64	2170.64	1669.82	1369.88	1170.38	1028.27	922.02	833.68	774.09
37000	3261.79	2230.93	1716.21	1407.94	1202.89	1056.83	947.63	863.01	795.59
38000	3349.95	2291.23	1762.59	1445.99	1235.40	1085.39	973.24	886.33	817.09
39000	3438.11	2351.52	1808.98	1484.04	1267.91	1113.95	998.85	909.66	838.59
40000	3526.26	2411.82	1855.36	1522.09	1300.42	1142.52	1024.47	932.98	860.10
41000	3614.42	2472.11	1901.74	1560.14	1332.93	1171.08	1050.08	956.31	881.60
42000	3702.58	2532.41	1948.13	1598.20	1365.44	1199.64	1075.69	979.63	903.10
43000	3790.73	2592.70	1994.51	1636.25	1397.95	1228.21	1101.30	1002.96	924.60
44000	3878.89	2653.00	2040.89	1674.30	1430.46	1256.77	1126.91	1026.28	946.10
45000	3967.05	2713.30	2087.28	1712.35	1462.97	1285.33	1152.52	1049.60	967.61
46000	4055.20	2773.59	2133.66	1750.41	1495.48	1313.89	1178.14	1072.93	989.11
47000	4143.36	2833.89	2180.05	1788.46	1527.99	1342.46	1203.75	1096.25	1010.61
48000	4231.51	2894.18	2226.43	1826.51	1560.50	1371.02	1229.36	1119.58	1032.11
49000	4319.67	2954.48	2272.81	1864.56	1593.01	1399.58	1254.97	1142.90	1053.62
50000	4407.83	3014.77	2319.20	1902.61	1625.52	1428.14	1280.58	1166.23	1075.12
51000	4495.98	3075.07	2365.58	1940.67	1658.04	1456.71	1306.19	1189.55	1096.62
52000	4584.14	3135.36	2411.97	1978.72	1690.55	1485.27	1331.80	1212.88	1118.12
53000	4672.30	3195.66	2458.35	2016.77	1723.06	1513.83	1357.42	1236.20	1139.62
54000	4760.45	3255.95	2504.73	2054.82	1755.57	1542.40	1383.03	1259.52	1161.13
55000	4848.61	3316.25	2551.12	2092.88	1788.08	1570.96	1408.64	1282.85	1182.63
56000	4936.77	3376.54	2597.50	2130.93	1820.59	1599.52	1434.25	1306.17	1204.13
57000	5024.92	3436.84	2643.88	2168.98	1853.10	1628.08	1459.86	1329.50	1225.63
58000	5113.08	3497.13	2690.27	2207.03	1885.61	1656.65	1485.47	1352.82	1247.14
59000	5201.24	3557.43	2736.65	2245.08	1918.12	1685.21	1511.08	1376.15	1268.64
60000	5289.39	3617.73	2783.04	2283.14	1950.63	1713.77	1536.70	1399.47	1290.14
61000	5377.55	3678.02	2829.42	2321.19	1983.14	1742.34	1562.31	1422.80	1311.64
62000	5465.71	3738.32	2875.80	2359.24	2015.65	1770.90	1587.92	1446.12	1333.14
63000	5553.86	3798.61	2922.19	2397.29	2048.16	1799.46	1613.53	1469.44	1354.65
64000	5642.02	3858.91	2968.57	2435.34	2080.67	1828.02	1639.14	1492.77	1376.15
65000	5730.17	3919.20	3014.96	2473.40	2113.18	1856.59	1664.75	1516.09	1397.65
66000	5818.33	3979.50	3061.34	2511.45	2145.69	1885.15	1690.37	1539.42	1419.15
67000	5906.49	4039.79	3107.72	2549.50	2178.20	1913.71	1715.98	1562.74	1440.66
68000	5994.64	4100.09	3154.11	2587.55	2210.71	1942.28	1741.59	1586.07	1462.16
69000	6082.80	4160.38	3200.49	2625.61	2243.22	1970.84	1767.20	1609.39	1483.66
70000	6170.96	4220.68	3246.87	2663.66	2275.73	1999.40	1792.81	1632.72	1505.16
75000	6611.74	4522.16	3478.79	2853.92	2438.28	2142.21	1920.87	1749.34	1612.67
80000	7052.52	4823.63	3710.71	3044.18	2600.84	2285.03	2048.93	1865.96	1720.19
100000	8815.65	6029.54	4638.39	3805.22	3251.04	2856.28	2561.16	2332.45	2150.23

64

TERM AMOUNT	6 YEARS	7 YEARS	8 YEARS	9 YEARS	10 YEARS	11 YEARS	12 YEARS	13 YEARS	14 YEARS
$ 25	.47	.43	.39	.36	.34	.33	.31	.30	.29
50	.94	.85	.78	.72	.68	.65	.62	.59	.57
75	1.41	1.27	1.16	1.08	1.02	.97	.92	.89	.86
100	1.88	1.69	1.55	1.44	1.36	1.29	1.23	1.18	1.14
200	3.76	3.38	3.09	2.88	2.71	2.57	2.46	2.36	2.28
300	5.64	5.07	4.64	4.31	4.06	3.85	3.68	3.54	3.42
400	7.52	6.75	6.18	5.75	5.41	5.13	4.91	4.72	4.56
500	9.40	8.44	7.73	7.19	6.76	6.41	6.13	5.90	5.70
600	11.28	10.13	9.27	8.62	8.11	7.69	7.36	7.08	6.84
700	13.16	11.81	10.82	10.06	9.46	8.97	8.58	8.25	7.98
800	15.04	13.50	12.36	11.49	10.81	10.26	9.81	9.43	9.12
900	16.91	15.19	13.91	12.93	12.16	11.54	11.03	10.61	10.26
1000	18.79	16.87	15.45	14.37	13.51	12.82	12.26	11.70	11.40
2000	37.58	33.74	30.90	28.73	27.01	25.63	24.51	23.58	22.79
3000	56.37	50.61	46.35	43.09	40.51	38.45	36.76	35.36	34.19
4000	75.16	67.48	61.80	57.45	54.02	51.26	49.01	47.15	45.58
5000	93.94	84.35	77.25	71.81	67.52	64.08	61.26	58.93	56.98
6000	112.73	101.22	92.70	86.17	81.02	76.89	73.51	70.72	68.37
7000	131.52	118.09	108.15	100.53	94.53	89.70	85.76	82.50	79.77
8000	150.31	134.96	123.60	114.89	108.03	102.52	98.02	94.29	91.16
9000	169.09	151.83	139.05	129.25	121.53	115.33	110.27	106.07	102.56
10000	187.88	168.70	154.50	143.61	135.03	128.15	122.52	117.86	113.95
15000	281.82	253.05	231.74	215.41	202.55	192.22	183.77	176.78	170.92
20000	375.76	337.39	308.99	287.21	270.06	256.29	245.03	235.71	227.90
25000	469.69	421.74	386.23	359.01	337.58	320.36	306.29	294.63	284.87
30000	563.63	506.09	463.48	430.81	405.09	384.43	367.54	353.56	341.84
35000	657.57	590.44	540.72	502.61	472.61	448.50	428.80	412.48	398.82
36000	676.36	607.31	556.17	516.97	486.11	461.31	441.05	424.27	410.21
37000	695.14	624.18	571.62	531.33	499.61	474.13	453.30	436.05	421.61
38000	713.93	641.04	587.07	545.69	513.12	486.94	465.55	447.84	433.00
39000	732.72	657.91	602.52	560.05	526.62	499.76	477.80	459.62	444.39
40000	751.51	674.78	617.97	574.41	540.12	512.57	490.06	471.41	455.79
41000	770.29	691.65	633.42	588.77	553.63	525.38	502.31	483.19	467.18
42000	789.08	708.52	648.86	603.13	567.13	538.20	514.56	494.98	478.58
43000	807.87	725.39	664.31	617.49	580.63	551.01	526.81	506.76	489.97
44000	826.66	742.26	679.76	631.85	594.13	563.83	539.06	518.55	501.37
45000	845.44	759.13	695.21	646.21	607.64	576.64	551.31	530.33	512.76
46000	864.23	776.00	710.66	660.57	621.14	589.45	563.56	542.12	524.16
47000	883.02	792.87	726.11	674.93	634.64	602.27	575.81	553.90	535.55
48000	901.81	809.74	741.56	689.29	648.15	615.08	588.07	565.69	546.95
49000	920.59	826.61	757.01	703.65	661.65	627.90	600.32	577.47	558.34
50000	939.38	843.48	772.46	718.01	675.15	640.71	612.57	589.26	569.74
51000	958.17	860.35	787.91	732.37	688.66	653.52	624.82	601.04	581.13
52000	976.96	877.22	803.35	746.73	702.16	666.34	637.07	612.83	592.52
53000	995.74	894.09	818.80	761.09	715.66	679.15	649.32	624.61	603.92
54000	1014.53	910.96	834.25	775.45	729.16	691.97	661.57	636.40	615.31
55000	1033.32	927.83	849.70	789.81	742.67	704.78	673.82	648.18	626.71
56000	1052.11	944.70	865.15	804.17	756.17	717.60	686.08	659.97	638.10
57000	1070.89	961.56	880.60	818.53	769.67	730.41	698.33	671.75	649.50
58000	1089.68	978.43	896.05	832.89	783.18	743.22	710.58	683.54	660.89
59000	1108.47	995.30	911.50	847.25	796.68	756.04	722.83	695.33	672.29
60000	1127.26	1012.17	926.95	861.61	810.18	768.85	735.08	707.11	683.68
61000	1146.05	1029.04	942.40	875.97	823.68	781.67	747.33	718.90	695.08
62000	1164.83	1045.91	957.84	890.33	837.19	794.48	759.58	730.68	706.47
63000	1183.62	1062.78	973.29	904.69	850.69	807.29	771.84	742.47	717.87
64000	1202.41	1079.65	988.74	919.05	864.19	820.11	784.09	754.25	729.26
65000	1221.20	1096.52	1004.19	933.41	877.70	832.92	796.34	766.04	740.65
66000	1239.98	1113.39	1019.64	947.77	891.20	845.74	808.59	777.82	752.05
67000	1258.77	1130.26	1035.09	962.13	904.70	858.55	820.84	789.61	763.44
68000	1277.56	1147.13	1050.54	976.49	918.21	871.36	833.09	801.39	774.84
69000	1296.35	1164.00	1065.99	990.85	931.71	884.18	845.34	813.18	786.23
70000	1315.13	1180.87	1081.44	1005.21	945.21	896.99	857.59	824.96	797.63
75000	1409.07	1265.21	1158.68	1077.01	1012.73	961.06	918.85	883.89	854.60
80000	1503.01	1349.56	1235.93	1148.81	1080.24	1025.13	980.11	942.81	911.57
100000	1878.76	1686.95	1544.91	1436.01	1350.30	1281.42	1225.13	1178.51	1139.47

10¾% MONTHLY PAYMENT
NECESSARY TO AMORTIZE A LOAN

TERM AMOUNT	15 YEARS	16 YEARS	17 YEARS	18 YEARS	19 YEARS	20 YEARS	21 YEARS	22 YEARS	23 YEARS
$ 25	.28	.27	.27	.26	.26	.25	.25	.25	.25
50	.56	.54	.53	.52	.51	.50	.50	.49	.49
75	.83	.81	.80	.78	.77	.75	.74	.74	.73
100	1.11	1.08	1.06	1.04	1.02	1.00	.99	.98	.97
200	2.22	2.16	2.11	2.07	2.04	2.00	1.98	1.95	1.93
300	3.32	3.24	3.17	3.10	3.05	3.00	2.96	2.93	2.89
400	4.43	4.32	4.22	4.14	4.07	4.00	3.95	3.90	3.86
500	5.54	5.40	5.28	5.17	5.08	5.00	4.93	4.87	4.82
600	6.64	6.47	6.33	6.20	6.10	6.00	5.92	5.85	5.78
700	7.75	7.55	7.38	7.24	7.11	7.00	6.91	6.82	6.75
800	8.86	8.63	8.44	8.27	8.13	8.00	7.89	7.79	7.71
900	9.96	9.71	9.49	9.30	9.14	9.00	8.88	8.77	8.67
1000	11.07	10.79	10.55	10.34	10.16	10.00	9.86	9.74	9.64
2000	22.13	21.57	21.09	20.67	20.31	20.00	19.72	19.48	19.27
3000	33.20	32.35	31.63	31.00	30.46	29.99	29.58	29.22	28.90
4000	44.26	43.14	42.17	41.34	40.62	39.99	39.43	38.95	38.53
5000	55.33	53.92	52.71	51.67	50.77	49.98	49.29	48.69	48.16
6000	66.39	64.70	63.25	62.00	60.92	59.98	59.15	58.43	57.79
7000	77.46	75.49	73.80	72.34	71.07	69.97	69.01	68.16	67.42
8000	88.52	86.27	84.34	82.67	81.23	79.97	78.86	77.90	77.05
9000	99.59	97.05	94.88	93.00	91.38	89.96	88.72	87.64	86.68
10000	110.65	107.84	105.42	103.34	101.53	99.96	98.58	97.37	96.31
15000	165.97	161.75	158.13	155.00	152.29	149.93	147.87	146.06	144.46
20000	221.29	215.67	210.84	206.67	203.06	199.91	197.15	194.74	192.61
25000	276.62	269.58	263.55	258.34	253.82	249.88	246.44	243.42	240.77
30000	331.94	323.50	316.25	310.00	304.58	299.86	295.73	292.11	288.92
35000	387.26	377.41	368.96	361.67	355.34	349.83	345.02	340.79	337.07
36000	398.33	388.20	379.50	372.00	365.50	359.83	354.83	350.53	346.70
37000	409.39	398.98	390.05	382.34	375.65	369.82	364.73	360.26	356.33
38000	420.45	409.76	400.59	392.67	385.80	379.82	374.59	370.00	365.96
39000	431.52	420.54	411.13	403.00	395.95	389.82	384.45	379.74	375.59
40000	442.58	431.33	421.67	413.34	406.11	399.81	394.30	389.47	385.22
41000	453.65	442.11	432.21	423.67	416.26	409.81	404.16	399.21	394.85
42000	464.71	452.89	442.75	434.00	426.41	419.80	414.02	408.95	404.48
43000	475.78	463.68	453.30	444.34	436.56	429.80	423.88	418.68	414.11
44000	486.84	474.46	463.84	454.67	446.72	439.79	433.73	428.42	423.74
45000	497.91	485.24	474.38	465.00	456.87	449.79	443.59	438.16	433.38
46000	508.97	496.03	484.92	475.34	467.02	459.78	453.45	447.89	443.01
47000	520.03	506.81	495.46	485.67	477.18	469.78	463.31	457.63	452.64
48000	531.10	517.59	506.00	496.00	487.33	479.77	473.16	467.37	462.27
49000	542.16	528.38	516.55	506.34	497.48	489.77	483.02	477.10	471.90
50000	553.23	539.16	527.09	516.67	507.63	499.76	492.88	486.84	481.53
51000	564.29	549.94	537.63	527.00	517.79	509.76	502.74	496.58	491.16
52000	575.36	560.72	548.17	537.34	527.94	519.75	512.59	506.31	500.79
53000	586.42	571.51	558.71	547.67	538.09	529.75	522.45	516.05	510.42
54000	597.49	582.29	569.25	558.00	548.24	539.74	532.31	525.79	520.05
55000	608.55	593.07	579.80	568.34	558.40	549.74	542.17	535.52	529.68
56000	619.61	603.86	590.34	578.67	568.55	559.73	552.02	545.26	539.31
57000	630.68	614.64	600.88	589.00	578.70	569.73	561.88	555.00	548.94
58000	641.74	625.42	611.42	599.34	588.85	579.72	571.74	564.73	558.57
59000	652.81	636.21	621.96	609.67	599.01	589.72	581.60	574.47	568.20
60000	663.87	646.99	632.50	620.00	609.16	599.71	591.45	584.21	577.83
61000	674.94	657.77	643.04	630.34	619.31	609.71	601.31	593.94	587.46
62000	686.00	668.56	653.59	640.67	629.46	619.70	611.17	603.68	597.09
63000	697.07	679.34	664.13	651.00	639.62	629.70	621.03	613.42	606.72
64000	708.13	690.12	674.67	661.33	649.77	639.69	630.88	623.15	616.35
65000	719.19	700.90	685.21	671.67	659.92	649.69	640.74	632.89	625.98
66000	730.26	711.69	695.75	682.00	670.07	659.68	650.60	642.63	635.61
67000	741.32	722.47	706.29	692.33	680.23	669.68	660.46	652.36	645.25
68000	752.39	733.25	716.84	702.67	690.38	679.67	670.31	662.10	654.88
69000	763.45	744.04	727.38	713.00	700.53	689.67	680.17	671.84	664.51
70000	774.52	754.82	737.92	723.33	710.68	699.66	690.03	681.57	674.14
75000	829.84	808.74	790.63	775.00	761.45	749.64	739.32	730.26	722.29
80000	885.16	862.65	843.34	826.67	812.21	799.62	788.60	778.94	770.44
100000	1106.45	1078.31	1054.17	1033.33	1015.26	999.52	985.75	973.68	963.05

66

MONTHLY PAYMENT 10¾%
NECESSARY TO AMORTIZE A LOAN

TERM AMOUNT	24 YEARS	25 YEARS	26 YEARS	27 YEARS	28 YEARS	29 YEARS	30 YEARS	35 YEARS	40 YEARS
$ 25	.24	.24	.24	.24	.24	.24	.23	.23	.23
50	.48	.48	.47	.47	.47	.47	.46	.45	.45
75	.72	.71	.71	.70	.70	.70	.69	.68	.67
100	.96	.95	.94	.94	.93	.93	.92	.90	.89
200	1.91	1.90	1.88	1.87	1.86	1.85	1.84	1.80	1.78
300	2.87	2.84	2.82	2.80	2.78	2.77	2.75	2.70	2.67
400	3.82	3.79	3.76	3.73	3.71	3.69	3.67	3.60	3.56
500	4.77	4.73	4.70	4.66	4.63	4.61	4.59	4.50	4.45
600	5.73	5.68	5.63	5.59	5.56	5.53	5.50	5.40	5.34
700	6.68	6.62	6.57	6.53	6.49	6.45	6.42	6.30	6.23
800	7.63	7.57	7.51	7.46	7.41	7.37	7.33	7.20	7.12
900	8.59	8.51	8.45	8.39	8.34	8.29	8.25	8.10	8.01
1000	9.54	9.46	9.39	9.32	9.26	9.21	9.17	9.00	8.90
2000	19.08	18.91	18.77	18.64	18.52	18.42	18.33	17.99	17.80
3000	28.62	28.37	28.15	27.95	27.78	27.62	27.49	26.99	26.70
4000	38.15	37.82	37.53	37.27	37.03	36.83	36.65	35.98	35.60
5000	47.69	47.27	46.91	46.58	46.29	46.03	45.81	44.98	44.50
6000	57.23	56.73	56.29	55.90	55.55	55.24	54.97	53.97	53.40
7000	66.76	66.18	65.67	65.21	64.81	64.45	64.13	62.97	62.30
8000	76.30	75.64	75.05	74.53	74.06	73.65	73.29	71.96	71.20
9000	85.84	85.09	84.43	83.84	83.32	82.86	82.45	80.95	80.10
10000	95.37	94.54	93.81	93.16	92.58	92.06	91.61	89.95	89.00
15000	143.06	141.81	140.71	139.73	138.87	138.09	137.41	134.92	133.49
20000	190.74	189.08	187.61	186.31	185.15	184.12	183.21	179.89	177.99
25000	238.42	236.35	234.52	232.89	231.44	230.15	229.01	224.86	222.48
30000	286.11	283.62	281.42	279.46	277.73	276.18	274.81	269.84	266.98
35000	333.79	330.89	328.32	326.04	324.02	322.21	320.61	314.81	311.47
36000	343.33	340.34	337.70	335.36	333.27	331.42	329.77	323.80	320.37
37000	352.86	349.80	347.08	344.67	342.53	340.62	338.93	332.80	329.27
38000	362.40	359.25	356.46	353.99	351.79	349.83	348.09	341.79	338.17
39000	371.94	368.71	365.84	363.30	361.05	359.04	357.25	350.79	347.07
40000	381.47	378.16	375.22	372.62	370.30	368.24	366.41	359.78	355.97
41000	391.01	387.61	384.60	381.93	379.56	377.45	375.57	368.77	364.87
42000	400.55	397.07	393.98	391.25	388.82	386.65	384.73	377.77	373.77
43000	410.08	406.52	403.36	400.56	398.07	395.86	393.89	386.76	382.66
44000	419.62	415.98	412.75	409.88	407.33	405.07	403.05	395.76	391.56
45000	429.16	425.43	422.13	419.19	416.59	414.27	412.21	404.75	400.46
46000	438.69	434.88	431.51	428.51	425.85	423.48	421.37	413.75	409.36
47000	448.23	444.34	440.89	437.83	435.10	432.68	430.53	422.74	418.26
48000	457.77	453.79	450.27	447.14	444.36	441.89	439.69	431.74	427.16
49000	467.30	463.24	459.65	456.46	453.62	451.09	448.85	440.73	436.06
50000	476.84	472.70	469.03	465.77	462.88	460.30	458.01	449.72	444.96
51000	486.38	482.15	478.41	475.09	472.13	469.51	467.17	458.72	453.86
52000	495.91	491.61	487.79	484.40	481.39	478.71	476.33	467.71	462.76
53000	505.45	501.06	497.17	493.72	490.65	487.92	485.49	476.71	471.65
54000	514.99	510.51	506.55	503.03	499.91	497.12	494.65	485.70	480.55
55000	524.52	519.97	515.93	512.35	509.16	506.33	503.81	494.70	489.45
56000	534.06	529.42	525.31	521.66	518.42	515.54	512.97	503.69	498.35
57000	543.60	538.88	534.69	530.98	527.68	524.74	522.13	512.68	507.25
58000	553.14	548.33	544.07	540.29	536.94	533.95	531.29	521.68	516.15
59000	562.67	557.78	553.45	549.61	546.19	543.15	540.45	530.67	525.05
60000	572.21	567.24	562.83	558.92	555.45	552.36	549.61	539.67	533.95
61000	581.75	576.69	572.21	568.24	564.71	561.57	558.77	548.66	542.85
62000	591.28	586.14	581.59	577.56	573.97	570.77	567.93	557.66	551.75
63000	600.82	595.60	590.97	586.87	583.22	579.98	577.09	566.65	560.65
64000	610.36	605.05	600.35	596.19	592.48	589.18	586.25	575.65	569.54
65000	619.89	614.51	609.74	605.50	601.74	598.39	595.41	584.64	578.44
66000	629.43	623.96	619.12	614.82	611.00	607.60	604.57	593.63	587.34
67000	638.97	633.41	628.50	624.13	620.25	616.80	613.73	602.63	596.24
68000	648.50	642.87	637.88	633.45	629.51	626.01	622.89	611.62	605.14
69000	658.04	652.32	647.26	642.76	638.77	635.21	632.05	620.62	614.04
70000	667.58	661.78	656.64	652.08	648.03	644.42	641.21	629.61	622.94
75000	715.26	709.04	703.54	698.65	694.31	690.45	687.01	674.58	667.43
80000	762.94	756.31	750.44	745.23	740.60	736.48	732.81	719.56	711.93
100000	953.68	945.39	938.05	931.54	925.75	920.60	916.01	899.44	889.91

11% MONTHLY PAYMENT
NECESSARY TO AMORTIZE A LOAN

TERM AMOUNT	1 YEAR	1½ YEARS	2 YEARS	2½ YEARS	3 YEARS	3½ YEARS	4 YEARS	4½ YEARS	5 YEARS
$ 25	2.21	1.52	1.17	.96	.82	.72	.65	.59	.55
50	4.42	3.03	2.33	1.91	1.64	1.44	1.29	1.18	1.09
75	6.63	4.54	3.49	2.87	2.45	2.16	1.93	1.76	1.63
100	8.83	6.05	4.65	3.82	3.27	2.87	2.58	2.35	2.17
200	17.66	12.09	9.30	7.64	6.53	5.74	5.15	4.69	4.33
300	26.49	18.13	13.95	11.45	9.79	8.61	7.72	7.04	6.49
400	35.31	24.17	18.60	15.27	13.05	11.48	10.30	9.38	8.65
500	44.14	30.21	23.25	19.09	16.32	14.34	12.87	11.73	10.82
600	52.97	36.25	27.90	22.90	19.58	17.21	15.44	14.07	12.98
700	61.79	42.29	32.55	26.72	22.84	20.08	18.01	16.41	15.14
800	70.62	48.33	37.20	30.54	26.10	22.95	20.59	18.76	17.30
900	79.45	54.37	41.85	34.35	29.37	25.81	23.16	21.10	19.46
1000	88.27	60.41	46.50	38.17	32.63	28.68	25.73	23.45	21.63
2000	176.54	120.82	92.99	76.33	65.25	57.36	51.46	46.89	43.25
3000	264.81	181.22	139.49	114.50	97.87	86.04	77.19	70.33	64.87
4000	353.08	241.63	185.98	152.66	130.50	114.71	102.91	93.77	86.49
5000	441.34	302.03	232.48	190.82	163.12	143.39	128.64	117.21	108.11
6000	529.61	362.44	278.97	228.99	195.74	172.07	154.37	140.65	129.73
7000	617.88	422.85	325.47	267.15	228.37	200.74	180.10	164.10	151.35
8000	706.15	483.25	371.96	305.32	260.99	229.42	205.82	187.54	172.97
9000	794.42	543.66	418.46	343.48	293.61	258.10	231.55	210.98	194.59
10000	882.68	604.06	464.95	381.64	326.24	286.78	257.28	234.42	216.21
15000	1324.02	906.09	697.43	572.46	489.35	430.16	385.91	351.63	324.32
20000	1765.36	1208.12	929.90	763.28	652.47	573.55	514.55	468.84	432.42
25000	2206.70	1510.15	1162.37	954.10	815.59	716.93	643.19	586.05	540.53
30000	2648.04	1812.18	1394.85	1144.92	978.70	860.32	771.82	703.25	648.63
35000	3089.38	2114.21	1627.32	1335.74	1141.82	1003.70	900.46	820.46	756.74
36000	3177.65	2174.61	1673.81	1373.91	1174.44	1032.38	926.19	843.90	778.36
37000	3265.92	2235.02	1720.31	1412.07	1207.07	1061.06	951.91	867.35	799.98
38000	3354.19	2295.43	1766.80	1450.23	1239.69	1089.73	977.64	890.79	821.60
39000	3442.45	2355.83	1813.30	1488.40	1272.31	1118.41	1003.37	914.23	843.22
40000	3530.72	2416.24	1859.79	1526.56	1304.94	1147.09	1029.09	937.67	864.84
41000	3618.99	2476.64	1906.29	1564.73	1337.56	1175.76	1054.82	961.11	886.46
42000	3707.26	2537.05	1952.78	1602.89	1370.18	1204.44	1080.55	984.55	908.09
43000	3795.53	2597.45	1999.28	1641.05	1402.81	1233.12	1106.28	1008.00	929.71
44000	3883.79	2657.86	2045.77	1679.22	1435.43	1261.80	1132.00	1031.44	951.33
45000	3972.06	2718.27	2092.27	1717.38	1468.05	1290.47	1157.73	1054.88	972.95
46000	4060.33	2778.67	2138.76	1755.55	1500.68	1319.15	1183.46	1078.32	994.57
47000	4148.60	2839.08	2185.25	1793.71	1533.30	1347.83	1209.18	1101.76	1016.19
48000	4236.87	2899.48	2231.75	1831.87	1565.92	1376.50	1234.91	1125.20	1037.81
49000	4325.13	2959.89	2278.24	1870.04	1598.55	1405.18	1260.64	1148.64	1059.43
50000	4413.40	3020.29	2324.74	1908.20	1631.17	1433.86	1286.37	1172.09	1081.05
51000	4501.67	3080.70	2371.23	1946.36	1663.79	1462.54	1312.09	1195.53	1102.67
52000	4589.94	3141.11	2417.73	1984.53	1696.42	1491.21	1337.82	1218.97	1124.30
53000	4678.20	3201.51	2464.22	2022.69	1729.04	1519.89	1363.55	1242.41	1145.92
54000	4766.47	3261.92	2510.72	2060.86	1761.66	1548.57	1389.28	1265.85	1167.54
55000	4854.74	3322.32	2557.21	2099.02	1794.29	1577.24	1415.00	1289.29	1189.16
56000	4943.01	3382.73	2603.71	2137.18	1826.91	1605.92	1440.73	1312.74	1210.78
57000	5031.28	3443.14	2650.20	2175.35	1859.53	1634.60	1466.46	1336.18	1232.40
58000	5119.54	3503.54	2696.70	2213.51	1892.16	1663.27	1492.18	1359.62	1254.02
59000	5207.81	3563.95	2743.19	2251.68	1924.78	1691.95	1517.91	1383.06	1275.64
60000	5296.08	3624.35	2789.69	2289.84	1957.40	1720.63	1543.64	1406.50	1297.26
61000	5384.35	3684.76	2836.18	2328.00	1990.03	1749.31	1569.37	1429.94	1318.88
62000	5472.62	3745.16	2882.67	2366.17	2022.65	1777.98	1595.09	1453.39	1340.51
63000	5560.88	3805.57	2929.17	2404.33	2055.27	1806.66	1620.82	1476.83	1362.13
64000	5649.15	3865.98	2975.66	2442.50	2087.90	1835.34	1646.55	1500.27	1383.75
65000	5737.42	3926.38	3022.16	2480.66	2120.52	1864.01	1672.27	1523.71	1405.37
66000	5825.69	3986.79	3068.65	2518.82	2153.14	1892.69	1698.00	1547.15	1426.99
67000	5913.96	4047.19	3115.15	2556.99	2185.77	1921.37	1723.73	1570.59	1448.61
68000	6002.22	4107.60	3161.64	2595.15	2218.39	1950.05	1749.46	1594.04	1470.23
69000	6090.49	4168.00	3208.14	2633.32	2251.01	1978.72	1775.18	1617.48	1491.85
70000	6178.76	4228.41	3254.63	2671.48	2283.64	2007.40	1800.91	1640.92	1513.47
75000	6620.10	4530.44	3487.11	2862.30	2446.75	2150.78	1929.55	1758.13	1621.58
80000	7061.44	4832.47	3719.58	3053.12	2609.87	2294.17	2058.18	1875.34	1729.68
100000	8826.80	6040.58	4649.47	3816.40	3262.34	2867.71	2572.73	2344.17	2162.10

68

TERM / AMOUNT	6 YEARS	7 YEARS	8 YEARS	9 YEARS	10 YEARS	11 YEARS	12 YEARS	13 YEARS	14 YEARS
$ 25	.48	.43	.39	.37	.35	.33	.31	.30	.29
50	.95	.85	.78	.73	.69	.65	.62	.60	.58
75	1.42	1.28	1.17	1.09	1.03	.98	.93	.90	.87
100	1.90	1.70	1.56	1.45	1.37	1.30	1.24	1.20	1.16
200	3.79	3.40	3.12	2.90	2.73	2.60	2.48	2.39	2.31
300	5.68	5.10	4.68	4.35	4.10	3.89	3.72	3.58	3.47
400	7.57	6.80	6.24	5.80	5.46	5.19	4.96	4.78	4.62
500	9.46	8.50	7.79	7.25	6.82	6.48	6.20	5.97	5.78
600	11.35	10.20	9.35	8.70	8.19	7.78	7.44	7.16	6.93
700	13.24	11.90	10.91	10.15	9.55	9.07	8.68	8.35	8.08
800	15.13	13.60	12.47	11.60	10.91	10.37	9.92	9.55	9.24
900	17.02	15.30	14.02	13.05	12.28	11.66	11.16	10.74	10.39
1000	18.91	17.00	15.58	14.50	13.64	12.96	12.40	11.93	11.55
2000	37.82	33.99	31.16	28.99	27.28	25.91	24.79	23.86	23.09
3000	56.73	50.99	46.74	43.48	40.92	38.86	37.18	35.79	34.63
4000	75.64	67.98	62.31	57.97	54.55	51.81	49.57	47.72	46.17
5000	94.55	84.98	77.89	72.46	68.19	64.76	61.96	59.65	57.71
6000	113.46	101.97	93.47	86.95	81.83	77.71	74.35	71.57	69.25
7000	132.37	118.97	109.05	101.44	95.47	90.67	86.75	83.50	80.79
8000	151.28	135.96	124.62	115.94	109.10	103.62	99.14	95.43	92.33
9000	170.19	152.96	140.20	130.43	122.74	116.57	111.53	107.36	103.87
10000	189.10	169.95	155.78	144.92	136.38	129.52	123.92	119.29	115.41
15000	283.65	254.92	233.66	217.38	204.56	194.28	185.88	178.93	173.12
20000	378.19	339.89	311.55	289.83	272.75	259.03	247.84	238.57	230.82
25000	472.74	424.87	389.43	362.29	340.94	323.79	309.80	298.21	288.52
30000	567.29	509.84	467.32	434.75	409.12	388.55	371.75	357.85	346.23
35000	661.83	594.81	545.21	507.20	477.31	453.31	433.71	417.50	403.93
36000	680.74	611.81	560.78	521.69	490.95	466.26	446.10	429.42	415.47
37000	699.65	628.80	576.36	536.18	504.58	479.21	458.49	441.35	427.01
38000	718.56	645.79	591.94	550.68	518.22	492.16	470.89	453.28	438.55
39000	737.47	662.79	607.51	565.17	531.86	505.11	483.28	465.21	450.09
40000	756.38	679.78	623.09	579.66	545.50	518.06	495.67	477.14	461.63
41000	775.29	696.78	638.67	594.15	559.13	531.02	508.06	489.07	473.17
42000	794.20	713.77	654.25	608.64	572.77	543.97	520.45	500.99	484.71
43000	813.11	730.77	669.82	623.13	586.41	556.92	532.84	512.92	496.25
44000	832.02	747.76	685.40	637.62	600.05	569.87	545.24	524.85	507.79
45000	850.93	764.76	700.98	652.12	613.68	582.82	557.63	536.78	519.34
46000	869.84	781.75	716.55	666.61	627.32	595.77	570.02	548.71	530.88
47000	888.75	798.74	732.13	681.10	640.96	608.73	582.41	560.64	542.42
48000	907.66	815.74	747.71	695.59	654.59	621.68	594.80	572.56	553.96
49000	926.56	832.73	763.29	710.08	668.23	634.63	607.19	584.49	565.50
50000	945.47	849.73	778.86	724.57	681.87	647.58	619.59	596.42	577.04
51000	964.38	866.72	794.44	739.06	695.51	660.53	631.98	608.35	588.58
52000	983.29	883.72	810.02	753.56	709.14	673.48	644.37	620.28	600.12
53000	1002.20	900.71	825.59	768.05	722.78	686.43	656.76	632.21	611.66
54000	1021.11	917.71	841.17	782.54	736.42	699.39	669.15	644.13	623.20
55000	1040.02	934.70	856.75	797.03	750.06	712.34	681.54	656.06	634.74
56000	1058.93	951.69	872.33	811.52	763.69	725.29	693.94	667.99	646.28
57000	1077.84	968.69	887.90	826.01	777.33	738.24	706.33	679.92	657.82
58000	1096.75	985.68	903.48	840.50	790.97	751.19	718.72	691.85	669.36
59000	1115.66	1002.68	919.06	854.99	804.60	764.14	731.11	703.78	680.91
60000	1134.57	1019.67	934.63	869.49	818.24	777.09	743.50	715.70	692.45
61000	1153.48	1036.67	950.21	883.98	831.88	790.05	755.89	727.63	703.99
62000	1172.39	1053.66	965.79	898.47	845.52	803.00	768.29	739.56	715.53
63000	1191.30	1070.66	981.37	912.96	859.15	815.95	780.68	751.49	727.07
64000	1210.21	1087.65	996.94	927.45	872.79	828.90	793.07	763.42	738.61
65000	1229.11	1104.64	1012.52	941.94	886.43	841.85	805.46	775.35	750.15
66000	1248.02	1121.64	1028.10	956.43	900.07	854.80	817.85	787.27	761.69
67000	1266.93	1138.63	1043.67	970.93	913.70	867.75	830.24	799.20	773.23
68000	1285.84	1155.63	1059.25	985.42	927.34	880.71	842.63	811.13	784.77
69000	1304.75	1172.62	1074.83	999.91	940.98	893.66	855.03	823.06	796.31
70000	1323.66	1189.62	1090.41	1014.40	954.62	906.61	867.42	834.99	807.85
75000	1418.21	1274.59	1168.29	1086.86	1022.80	971.37	929.38	894.63	865.56
80000	1512.76	1359.56	1246.18	1159.31	1090.99	1036.12	991.33	954.27	923.26
100000	1890.94	1699.45	1557.72	1449.14	1363.73	1295.15	1239.17	1192.84	1154.07

11% MONTHLY PAYMENT
NECESSARY TO AMORTIZE A LOAN

TERM AMOUNT	15 YEARS	16 YEARS	17 YEARS	18 YEARS	19 YEARS	20 YEARS	21 YEARS	22 YEARS	23 YEARS
$ 25	.29	.28	.27	.27	.26	.26	.26	.25	.25
50	.57	.55	.54	.53	.52	.51	.51	.50	.49
75	.85	.83	.81	.79	.78	.77	.76	.75	.74
100	1.13	1.10	1.07	1.05	1.04	1.02	1.01	1.00	.98
200	2.25	2.19	2.14	2.10	2.07	2.04	2.01	1.99	1.96
300	3.37	3.29	3.21	3.15	3.10	3.05	3.01	2.98	2.94
400	4.49	4.38	4.28	4.20	4.13	4.07	4.01	3.97	3.92
500	5.61	5.47	5.35	5.25	5.16	5.08	5.02	4.96	4.90
600	6.73	6.57	6.42	6.30	6.19	6.10	6.02	5.95	5.88
700	7.85	7.66	7.49	7.35	7.22	7.11	7.02	6.94	6.86
800	8.98	8.75	8.56	8.40	8.25	8.13	8.02	7.93	7.84
900	10.10	9.85	9.63	9.45	9.29	9.15	9.02	8.92	8.82
1000	11.22	10.94	10.70	10.49	10.32	10.16	10.03	9.91	9.80
2000	22.43	21.87	21.40	20.98	20.63	20.32	20.05	19.81	19.60
3000	33.64	32.81	32.09	31.47	30.94	30.47	30.07	29.71	29.40
4000	44.86	43.74	42.79	41.96	41.25	40.63	40.09	39.61	39.20
5000	56.07	54.68	53.48	52.45	51.56	50.79	50.11	49.52	49.00
6000	67.28	65.61	64.18	62.94	61.87	60.94	60.13	59.42	58.79
7000	78.50	76.55	74.87	73.43	72.19	71.10	70.15	69.32	68.59
8000	89.71	87.48	85.57	83.92	82.50	81.26	80.17	79.22	78.39
9000	100.92	98.42	96.27	94.41	92.81	91.41	90.19	89.13	88.19
10000	112.14	109.35	106.96	104.90	103.12	101.57	100.21	99.03	97.99
15000	168.20	164.02	160.44	157.35	154.68	152.35	150.32	148.54	146.98
20000	224.27	218.70	213.92	209.80	206.24	203.13	200.42	198.05	195.97
25000	280.34	273.37	267.40	262.25	257.79	253.91	250.53	247.56	244.96
30000	336.40	328.04	320.88	314.70	309.35	304.70	300.63	297.07	293.95
35000	392.47	382.71	374.35	367.15	360.91	355.48	350.74	346.59	342.94
36000	403.68	393.65	385.05	377.64	371.22	365.64	360.76	356.49	352.74
37000	414.90	404.58	395.75	388.13	381.53	375.79	370.78	366.39	362.53
38000	426.11	415.52	406.44	398.62	391.84	385.95	380.80	376.29	372.33
39000	437.32	426.45	417.14	409.11	402.15	396.10	390.82	386.20	382.13
40000	448.54	437.39	427.83	419.60	412.47	406.26	400.84	396.10	391.93
41000	459.75	448.32	438.53	430.09	422.78	416.42	410.86	406.00	401.73
42000	470.96	459.26	449.22	440.58	433.09	426.57	420.89	415.90	411.52
43000	482.18	470.19	459.92	451.07	443.40	436.73	430.91	425.80	421.32
44000	493.39	481.13	470.62	461.56	453.71	446.89	440.93	435.71	431.12
45000	504.60	492.06	481.31	472.05	464.02	457.04	450.95	445.61	440.92
46000	515.82	502.99	492.01	482.54	474.33	467.20	460.97	455.51	450.72
47000	527.03	513.93	502.70	493.03	484.65	477.36	470.99	465.41	460.52
48000	538.24	524.86	513.40	503.52	494.96	487.51	481.01	475.32	470.31
49000	549.46	535.80	524.09	514.01	505.27	497.67	491.03	485.22	480.11
50000	560.67	546.73	534.79	524.50	515.58	507.82	501.05	495.12	489.91
51000	571.88	557.67	545.49	534.99	525.89	517.98	511.07	505.02	499.71
52000	583.10	568.60	556.18	545.48	536.20	528.14	521.09	514.93	509.51
53000	594.31	579.54	566.88	555.97	546.52	538.29	531.12	524.83	519.30
54000	605.52	590.47	577.57	566.46	556.83	548.45	541.14	534.73	529.10
55000	616.73	601.41	588.27	576.95	567.14	558.61	551.16	544.63	538.90
56000	627.95	612.34	598.96	587.44	577.45	568.76	561.18	554.53	548.70
57000	639.16	623.27	609.66	597.93	587.76	578.92	571.20	564.44	558.50
58000	650.37	634.21	620.36	608.42	598.07	589.08	581.22	574.34	568.29
59000	661.59	645.14	631.05	618.91	608.38	599.23	591.24	584.24	578.09
60000	672.80	656.08	641.75	629.40	618.70	609.39	601.26	594.14	587.89
61000	684.01	667.01	652.44	639.88	629.01	619.55	611.28	604.05	597.69
62000	695.23	677.95	663.14	650.37	639.32	629.70	621.30	613.95	607.49
63000	706.44	688.88	673.83	660.86	649.63	639.86	631.33	623.85	617.28
64000	717.65	699.82	684.53	671.35	659.94	650.01	641.35	633.75	627.08
65000	728.87	710.75	695.23	681.84	670.25	660.17	651.37	643.66	636.88
66000	740.08	721.69	705.92	692.33	680.57	670.33	661.39	653.56	646.68
67000	751.29	732.62	716.62	702.82	690.88	680.48	671.41	663.46	656.48
68000	762.51	743.55	727.31	713.31	701.19	690.64	681.43	673.36	666.28
69000	773.72	754.49	738.01	723.80	711.50	700.80	691.45	683.26	676.07
70000	784.93	765.42	748.70	734.29	721.81	710.95	701.47	693.17	685.87
75000	841.00	820.10	802.18	786.74	773.37	761.73	751.58	742.68	734.86
80000	897.07	874.77	855.66	839.19	824.93	812.52	801.68	792.19	783.85
100000	1121.33	1093.46	1069.58	1048.99	1031.16	1015.64	1002.10	990.24	979.81

TERM AMOUNT	24 YEARS	25 YEARS	26 YEARS	27 YEARS	28 YEARS	29 YEARS	30 YEARS	35 YEARS	40 YEARS
$ 25	.25	.25	.24	.24	.24	.24	.24	.23	.23
50	.49	.49	.48	.48	.48	.47	.47	.46	.46
75	.73	.73	.72	.72	.71	.71	.71	.69	.69
100	.98	.97	.96	.95	.95	.94	.94	.92	.91
200	1.95	1.93	1.92	1.90	1.89	1.88	1.87	1.84	1.82
300	2.92	2.89	2.87	2.85	2.84	2.82	2.81	2.76	2.73
400	3.89	3.86	3.83	3.80	3.78	3.76	3.74	3.68	3.64
500	4.86	4.82	4.78	4.75	4.72	4.70	4.67	4.59	4.55
600	5.83	5.78	5.74	5.70	5.67	5.64	5.61	5.51	5.46
700	6.80	6.74	6.69	6.65	6.61	6.57	6.54	6.43	6.37
800	7.77	7.71	7.65	7.60	7.55	7.51	7.48	7.35	7.28
900	8.74	8.67	8.60	8.55	8.50	8.45	8.41	8.27	8.18
1000	9.71	9.63	9.56	9.50	9.44	9.39	9.34	9.18	9.09
2000	19.42	19.26	19.11	18.99	18.87	18.77	18.68	18.36	18.18
3000	29.12	28.88	28.67	28.48	28.31	28.16	28.02	27.54	27.27
4000	38.83	38.51	38.22	37.97	37.74	37.54	37.36	36.72	36.36
5000	48.54	48.13	47.77	47.46	47.17	46.92	46.70	45.90	45.45
6000	58.24	57.76	57.33	56.95	56.61	56.31	56.04	55.08	54.54
7000	67.95	67.38	66.88	66.44	66.04	65.69	65.38	64.26	63.63
8000	77.66	77.01	76.43	75.93	75.48	75.08	74.72	73.44	72.72
9000	87.36	86.63	85.99	85.42	84.91	84.46	84.06	82.62	81.80
10000	97.07	96.26	95.54	94.91	94.34	93.84	93.40	91.80	90.89
15000	145.60	144.38	143.31	142.36	141.51	140.76	140.10	137.70	136.34
20000	194.13	192.51	191.08	189.81	188.68	187.68	186.79	183.60	181.78
25000	242.66	240.64	238.85	237.26	235.85	234.60	233.49	229.50	227.22
30000	291.19	288.76	286.61	284.71	283.02	281.52	280.19	275.40	272.67
35000	339.73	336.89	334.38	332.16	330.19	328.44	326.88	321.30	318.11
36000	349.43	346.52	343.94	341.65	339.62	337.82	336.22	330.48	327.20
37000	359.14	356.14	353.49	351.14	349.06	347.21	345.56	339.66	336.29
38000	368.84	365.77	363.04	360.63	358.49	356.59	354.90	348.84	345.38
39000	378.55	375.39	372.60	370.12	367.93	365.98	364.24	358.02	354.47
40000	388.26	385.02	382.15	379.61	377.36	375.36	373.58	367.19	363.56
41000	397.96	394.64	391.70	389.10	386.79	384.74	382.92	376.37	372.65
42000	407.67	404.27	401.26	398.59	396.23	394.13	392.26	385.55	381.73
43000	417.38	413.89	410.81	408.08	405.66	403.51	401.60	394.73	390.82
44000	427.08	423.52	420.37	417.57	415.10	412.90	410.94	403.91	399.91
45000	436.79	433.14	429.92	427.06	424.53	422.28	420.28	413.09	409.00
46000	446.49	442.77	439.47	436.55	433.96	431.66	429.62	422.27	418.09
47000	456.20	452.39	449.03	446.04	443.40	441.05	438.96	431.45	427.18
48000	465.91	462.02	458.58	455.53	452.83	450.43	448.30	440.63	436.27
49000	475.61	471.64	468.13	465.02	462.27	459.81	457.63	449.81	445.36
50000	485.32	481.27	477.69	474.51	471.70	469.20	466.97	458.99	454.44
51000	495.03	490.89	487.24	484.00	481.13	478.58	476.31	468.17	463.53
52000	504.73	500.52	496.79	493.49	490.57	487.97	485.65	477.35	472.62
53000	514.44	510.15	506.35	502.99	500.00	497.35	494.99	486.53	481.71
54000	524.15	519.77	515.90	512.48	509.43	506.73	504.33	495.71	490.80
55000	533.85	529.40	525.46	521.97	518.87	516.12	513.67	504.89	499.89
56000	543.56	539.02	535.01	531.46	528.30	525.50	523.01	514.07	508.98
57000	553.26	548.65	544.56	540.95	537.74	534.89	532.35	523.25	518.07
58000	562.97	558.27	554.12	550.44	547.17	544.27	541.69	532.43	527.16
59000	572.68	567.90	563.67	559.93	556.60	553.65	551.03	541.61	536.24
60000	582.38	577.52	573.22	569.42	566.04	563.04	560.37	550.79	545.33
61000	592.09	587.15	582.78	578.91	575.47	572.42	569.71	559.97	554.42
62000	601.80	596.77	592.33	588.40	584.91	581.80	579.05	569.15	563.51
63000	611.50	606.40	601.89	597.89	594.34	591.19	588.39	578.33	572.60
64000	621.21	616.02	611.44	607.38	603.77	600.57	597.73	587.51	581.69
65000	630.91	625.65	620.99	616.87	613.21	609.96	607.06	596.69	590.78
66000	640.62	635.27	630.55	626.36	622.64	619.34	616.40	605.87	599.87
67000	650.33	644.90	640.10	635.85	632.08	628.72	625.74	615.05	608.95
68000	660.03	654.52	649.65	645.34	641.51	638.11	635.08	624.23	618.04
69000	669.74	664.15	659.21	654.83	650.94	647.49	644.42	633.41	627.13
70000	679.45	673.78	668.76	664.32	660.38	656.88	653.76	642.59	636.22
75000	727.98	721.90	716.53	711.77	707.55	703.80	700.46	688.49	681.66
80000	776.51	770.03	764.30	759.22	754.72	750.71	747.16	734.38	727.11
100000	970.64	962.53	955.37	949.00	943.39	938.39	933.94	917.98	908.88

11¼% MONTHLY PAYMENT
NECESSARY TO AMORTIZE A LOAN

TERM AMOUNT	1 YEAR	1½ YEARS	2 YEARS	2½ YEARS	3 YEARS	3½ YEARS	4 YEARS	4½ YEARS	5 YEARS
$ 25	2.21	1.52	1.17	.96	.82	.72	.65	.59	.55
50	4.42	3.03	2.34	1.92	1.64	1.44	1.30	1.18	1.09
75	6.63	4.54	3.50	2.88	2.46	2.16	1.94	1.77	1.64
100	8.84	6.06	4.67	3.83	3.28	2.88	2.59	2.36	2.18
200	17.68	12.11	9.33	7.66	6.55	5.76	5.17	4.72	4.35
300	26.52	18.16	13.99	11.49	9.83	8.64	7.76	7.07	6.53
400	35.36	24.21	18.65	15.32	13.10	11.52	10.34	9.43	8.70
500	44.19	30.26	23.31	19.14	16.37	14.40	12.93	11.78	10.87
600	53.03	36.31	27.97	22.97	19.65	17.28	15.51	14.14	13.05
700	61.87	42.37	32.63	26.80	22.92	20.16	18.10	16.50	15.22
800	70.71	48.42	37.29	30.63	26.19	23.04	20.68	18.85	17.40
900	79.55	54.47	41.95	34.45	29.47	25.92	23.26	21.21	19.57
1000	88.38	60.52	46.61	38.28	32.74	28.80	25.85	23.56	21.74
2000	176.76	121.04	93.22	76.56	65.48	57.59	51.69	47.12	43.48
3000	265.14	181.55	139.82	114.83	98.21	86.38	77.53	70.68	65.22
4000	353.52	242.07	186.43	153.11	130.95	115.17	103.38	94.24	86.96
5000	441.90	302.59	233.03	191.38	163.69	143.96	129.22	117.80	108.70
6000	530.28	363.10	279.64	229.66	196.42	172.75	155.06	141.36	130.44
7000	618.66	423.62	326.24	267.94	229.16	201.55	180.91	164.92	152.18
8000	707.04	484.14	372.85	306.21	261.90	230.34	206.75	188.48	173.92
9000	795.42	544.65	419.45	344.49	294.63	259.13	232.59	212.04	195.66
10000	883.80	605.17	466.06	382.76	327.37	287.92	258.44	235.60	217.40
15000	1325.70	907.75	699.09	574.14	491.05	431.88	387.65	353.39	326.10
20000	1767.59	1210.33	932.12	765.52	654.73	575.83	516.87	471.19	434.80
25000	2209.49	1512.91	1165.14	956.90	818.41	719.79	646.08	588.98	543.50
30000	2651.39	1815.49	1398.17	1148.28	982.10	863.75	775.30	706.78	652.20
35000	3093.28	2118.07	1631.20	1339.66	1145.78	1007.71	904.51	824.57	760.90
36000	3181.66	2178.59	1677.80	1377.93	1178.51	1036.50	930.36	848.13	782.64
37000	3270.04	2239.11	1724.41	1416.21	1211.25	1065.29	956.20	871.69	804.38
38000	3358.42	2299.62	1771.02	1454.48	1243.99	1094.08	982.04	895.25	826.12
39000	3446.80	2360.14	1817.62	1492.76	1276.72	1122.87	1007.89	918.81	847.86
40000	3535.18	2420.66	1864.23	1531.03	1309.46	1151.66	1033.73	942.37	869.60
41000	3623.56	2481.17	1910.83	1569.31	1342.20	1180.46	1059.57	965.93	891.34
42000	3711.94	2541.69	1957.44	1607.59	1374.93	1209.25	1085.42	989.49	913.08
43000	3800.32	2602.20	2004.04	1645.86	1407.67	1238.04	1111.26	1013.04	934.82
44000	3888.70	2662.72	2050.65	1684.14	1440.41	1266.83	1137.10	1036.60	956.56
45000	3977.08	2723.24	2097.25	1722.41	1473.14	1295.62	1162.95	1060.16	978.30
46000	4065.45	2783.75	2143.86	1760.69	1505.88	1324.41	1188.79	1083.72	1000.04
47000	4153.83	2844.27	2190.47	1798.96	1538.61	1353.20	1214.63	1107.28	1021.78
48000	4242.21	2904.79	2237.07	1837.24	1571.35	1382.00	1240.47	1130.84	1043.52
49000	4330.59	2965.30	2283.68	1875.52	1604.09	1410.79	1266.32	1154.40	1065.26
50000	4418.97	3025.82	2330.28	1913.79	1636.82	1439.58	1292.16	1177.96	1087.00
51000	4507.35	3086.33	2376.89	1952.07	1669.56	1468.37	1318.00	1201.52	1108.74
52000	4595.73	3146.85	2423.49	1990.34	1702.30	1497.16	1343.85	1225.08	1130.48
53000	4684.11	3207.37	2470.10	2028.62	1735.03	1525.95	1369.69	1248.63	1152.22
54000	4772.49	3267.88	2516.70	2066.90	1767.77	1554.75	1395.53	1272.19	1173.96
55000	4860.87	3328.40	2563.31	2105.17	1800.51	1583.54	1421.38	1295.75	1195.70
56000	4949.25	3388.92	2609.92	2143.45	1833.24	1612.33	1447.22	1319.31	1217.44
57000	5037.63	3449.43	2656.52	2181.72	1865.98	1641.12	1473.06	1342.87	1239.18
58000	5126.01	3509.95	2703.13	2220.00	1898.71	1669.91	1498.91	1366.43	1260.92
59000	5214.39	3570.46	2749.73	2258.27	1931.45	1698.70	1524.75	1389.99	1282.66
60000	5302.77	3630.98	2796.34	2296.55	1964.19	1727.49	1550.59	1413.55	1304.40
61000	5391.15	3691.50	2842.94	2334.83	1996.92	1756.29	1576.44	1437.11	1326.14
62000	5479.52	3752.01	2889.55	2373.10	2029.66	1785.08	1602.28	1460.67	1347.88
63000	5567.90	3812.53	2936.15	2411.38	2062.40	1813.87	1628.12	1484.23	1369.62
64000	5656.28	3873.05	2982.76	2449.65	2095.13	1842.66	1653.96	1507.78	1391.36
65000	5744.66	3933.56	3029.36	2487.93	2127.87	1871.45	1679.81	1531.34	1413.10
66000	5833.04	3994.08	3075.97	2526.20	2160.61	1900.24	1705.65	1554.90	1434.84
67000	5921.42	4054.59	3122.58	2564.48	2193.34	1929.03	1731.49	1578.46	1456.58
68000	6009.80	4115.11	3169.18	2602.76	2226.08	1957.83	1757.34	1602.02	1478.32
69000	6098.18	4175.63	3215.79	2641.03	2258.81	1986.62	1783.18	1625.58	1500.06
70000	6186.56	4236.14	3262.39	2679.31	2291.55	2015.41	1809.02	1649.14	1521.80
75000	6628.46	4538.72	3495.42	2870.69	2455.23	2159.37	1938.24	1766.93	1630.50
80000	7070.35	4841.31	3728.45	3062.06	2618.91	2303.32	2067.45	1884.73	1739.20
100000	8837.94	6051.63	4660.56	3827.58	3273.64	2879.15	2584.32	2355.91	2174.00

72

MONTHLY PAYMENT 11¼%
NECESSARY TO AMORTIZE A LOAN

TERM AMOUNT	6 YEARS	7 YEARS	8 YEARS	9 YEARS	10 YEARS	11 YEARS	12 YEARS	13 YEARS	14 YEARS
$ 25	.48	.43	.40	.37	.35	.33	.32	.31	.30
50	.96	.86	.79	.74	.69	.66	.63	.61	.59
75	1.43	1.29	1.18	1.10	1.04	.99	.94	.91	.88
100	1.91	1.72	1.58	1.47	1.38	1.31	1.26	1.21	1.17
200	3.81	3.43	3.15	2.93	2.76	2.62	2.51	2.42	2.34
300	5.71	5.14	4.72	4.39	4.14	3.93	3.76	3.63	3.51
400	7.62	6.85	6.29	5.85	5.51	5.24	5.02	4.83	4.68
500	9.52	8.56	7.86	7.32	6.89	6.55	6.27	6.04	5.85
600	11.42	10.28	9.43	8.78	8.27	7.86	7.52	7.25	7.02
700	13.33	11.99	11.00	10.24	9.65	9.17	8.78	8.46	8.19
800	15.23	13.70	12.57	11.70	11.02	10.48	10.03	9.66	9.35
900	17.13	15.41	14.14	13.17	12.40	11.79	11.28	10.87	10.52
1000	19.04	17.12	15.71	14.63	13.78	13.09	12.54	12.08	11.69
2000	38.07	34.24	31.42	29.25	27.55	26.18	25.07	24.15	23.38
3000	57.10	51.36	47.12	43.87	41.32	39.27	37.60	36.22	35.07
4000	76.13	68.48	62.83	58.50	55.09	52.36	50.14	48.29	46.75
5000	95.16	85.60	78.53	73.12	68.87	65.45	62.67	60.37	58.44
6000	114.19	102.72	94.24	87.74	82.64	78.54	75.20	72.44	70.13
7000	133.23	119.84	109.95	102.37	96.41	91.63	87.73	84.51	81.82
8000	152.26	136.96	125.65	116.99	110.18	104.72	100.27	96.58	93.50
9000	171.29	154.08	141.36	131.61	123.95	117.81	112.80	108.66	105.19
10000	190.32	171.20	157.06	146.24	137.73	130.90	125.33	120.73	116.88
15000	285.48	256.80	235.59	219.35	206.59	196.35	187.99	181.09	175.32
20000	380.64	342.40	314.12	292.47	275.45	261.79	250.66	241.45	233.75
25000	475.79	428.00	392.65	365.58	344.31	327.24	313.32	301.81	292.19
30000	570.95	513.60	471.18	438.70	413.17	392.69	375.98	362.17	350.63
35000	666.11	599.20	549.71	511.81	482.03	458.14	438.65	422.53	409.07
36000	685.14	616.32	565.41	526.44	495.80	471.23	451.18	434.61	420.75
37000	704.17	633.44	581.12	541.06	509.58	484.32	463.71	446.68	432.44
38000	723.20	650.56	596.82	555.68	523.35	497.41	476.24	458.75	444.13
39000	742.24	667.68	612.53	570.31	537.12	510.49	488.78	470.82	455.82
40000	761.27	684.80	628.24	584.93	550.89	523.58	501.31	482.90	467.50
41000	780.30	701.92	643.94	599.55	564.67	536.67	513.84	494.97	479.19
42000	799.33	719.04	659.65	614.18	578.44	549.76	526.38	507.04	490.88
43000	818.36	736.16	675.35	628.80	592.21	562.85	538.91	519.11	502.57
44000	837.39	753.28	691.06	643.42	605.98	575.94	551.44	531.19	514.25
45000	856.42	770.40	706.76	658.05	619.75	589.03	563.97	543.26	525.94
46000	875.46	787.52	722.47	672.67	633.53	602.12	576.51	555.33	537.63
47000	894.49	804.64	738.18	687.29	647.30	615.21	589.04	567.40	549.32
48000	913.52	821.76	753.88	701.91	661.07	628.30	601.57	579.47	561.00
49000	932.55	838.88	769.59	716.54	674.84	641.39	614.10	591.55	572.69
50000	951.58	856.00	785.29	731.16	688.61	654.48	626.64	603.62	584.38
51000	970.61	873.12	801.00	745.78	702.39	667.57	639.17	615.69	596.07
52000	989.65	890.24	816.70	760.41	716.16	680.66	651.70	627.76	607.75
53000	1008.68	907.36	832.41	775.03	729.93	693.75	664.23	639.84	619.44
54000	1027.71	924.48	848.12	789.65	743.70	706.84	676.77	651.91	631.13
55000	1046.74	941.60	863.82	804.28	757.48	719.93	689.30	663.98	642.82
56000	1065.77	958.72	879.53	818.90	771.25	733.02	701.83	676.05	654.50
57000	1084.80	975.84	895.23	833.52	785.02	746.11	714.36	688.12	666.19
58000	1103.83	992.96	910.94	848.15	798.79	759.19	726.90	700.20	677.88
59000	1122.87	1010.08	926.64	862.77	812.56	772.28	739.43	712.27	689.57
60000	1141.90	1027.19	942.35	877.39	826.34	785.37	751.96	724.34	701.25
61000	1160.93	1044.31	958.06	892.02	840.11	798.46	764.49	736.41	712.94
62000	1179.96	1061.43	973.76	906.64	853.88	811.55	777.03	748.49	724.63
63000	1198.99	1078.55	989.47	921.26	867.65	824.64	789.56	760.56	736.32
64000	1218.02	1095.67	1005.17	935.88	881.43	837.73	802.09	772.63	748.00
65000	1237.06	1112.79	1020.88	950.51	895.20	850.82	814.63	784.70	759.69
66000	1256.09	1129.91	1036.58	965.13	908.97	863.91	827.16	796.78	771.38
67000	1275.12	1147.03	1052.29	979.75	922.74	877.00	839.69	808.85	783.07
68000	1294.15	1164.15	1068.00	994.38	936.51	890.09	852.22	820.92	794.75
69000	1313.18	1181.27	1083.70	1009.00	950.29	903.18	864.76	832.99	806.44
70000	1332.21	1198.39	1099.41	1023.62	964.06	916.27	877.29	845.06	818.13
75000	1427.37	1283.99	1177.94	1096.74	1032.92	981.72	939.95	905.43	876.57
80000	1522.53	1369.59	1256.47	1169.85	1101.78	1047.16	1002.61	965.79	935.00
100000	1903.16	1711.99	1570.58	1462.32	1377.22	1308.95	1253.27	1207.23	1168.75

73

11¼% MONTHLY PAYMENT
NECESSARY TO AMORTIZE A LOAN

TERM AMOUNT	15 YEARS	16 YEARS	17 YEARS	18 YEARS	19 YEARS	20 YEARS	21 YEARS	22 YEARS	23 YEARS
$ 25	.29	.28	.28	.27	.27	.26	.26	.26	.25
50	.57	.56	.55	.54	.53	.52	.51	.51	.50
75	.86	.84	.82	.80	.79	.78	.77	.76	.75
100	1.14	1.11	1.09	1.07	1.05	1.04	1.02	1.01	1.00
200	2.28	2.22	2.18	2.13	2.10	2.07	2.04	2.02	2.00
300	3.41	3.33	3.26	3.20	3.15	3.10	3.06	3.03	2.99
400	4.55	4.44	4.35	4.26	4.19	4.13	4.08	4.03	3.99
500	5.69	5.55	5.43	5.33	5.24	5.16	5.10	5.04	4.99
600	6.82	6.66	6.52	6.39	6.29	6.20	6.12	6.05	5.98
700	7.96	7.77	7.60	7.46	7.33	7.23	7.13	7.05	6.98
800	9.10	8.87	8.69	8.52	8.38	8.26	8.15	8.06	7.98
900	10.23	9.98	9.77	9.59	9.43	9.29	9.17	9.07	8.97
1000	11.37	11.09	10.86	10.65	10.48	10.32	10.19	10.07	9.97
2000	22.73	22.18	21.71	21.30	20.95	20.64	20.38	20.14	19.94
3000	34.09	33.27	32.56	31.95	31.42	30.96	30.56	30.21	29.90
4000	45.46	44.35	43.41	42.59	41.89	41.28	40.75	40.28	39.87
5000	56.82	55.44	54.26	53.24	52.36	51.60	50.93	50.35	49.84
6000	68.18	66.53	65.11	63.89	62.83	61.92	61.12	60.42	59.80
7000	79.55	77.61	75.96	74.54	73.30	72.23	71.30	70.49	69.77
8000	90.91	88.70	86.81	85.18	83.78	82.55	81.49	80.56	79.74
9000	102.27	99.79	97.66	95.83	94.25	92.87	91.67	90.62	89.70
10000	113.63	110.87	108.51	106.48	104.72	103.19	101.86	100.69	99.67
15000	170.45	166.31	162.76	159.71	157.07	154.78	152.78	151.04	149.50
20000	227.26	221.74	217.02	212.95	209.43	206.38	203.71	201.38	199.34
25000	284.08	277.18	271.27	266.19	261.79	257.97	254.64	251.72	249.17
30000	340.89	332.61	325.52	319.42	314.14	309.56	305.56	302.07	299.00
35000	397.71	388.04	379.78	372.66	366.50	361.15	356.49	352.41	348.84
36000	409.07	399.13	390.63	383.31	376.97	371.47	366.68	362.48	358.80
37000	420.43	410.22	401.48	393.95	387.44	381.79	376.86	372.55	368.77
38000	431.79	421.30	412.33	404.60	397.91	392.11	387.05	382.62	378.73
39000	443.16	432.39	423.18	415.25	408.39	402.43	397.23	392.69	388.70
40000	454.52	443.48	434.03	425.89	418.86	412.75	407.42	402.76	398.67
41000	465.88	454.57	444.88	436.54	429.33	423.06	417.60	412.82	408.63
42000	477.25	465.65	455.73	447.19	439.80	433.38	427.79	422.89	418.60
43000	488.61	476.74	466.58	457.84	450.27	443.70	437.97	432.96	428.57
44000	499.97	487.83	477.43	468.48	460.74	454.02	448.16	443.03	438.53
45000	511.33	498.91	488.28	479.13	471.21	464.34	458.34	453.10	448.50
46000	522.70	510.00	499.13	489.78	481.69	474.66	468.53	463.17	458.47
47000	534.06	521.09	509.98	500.42	492.16	484.98	478.71	473.24	468.43
48000	545.42	532.17	520.83	511.07	502.63	495.29	488.90	483.31	478.40
49000	556.79	543.26	531.68	521.72	513.10	505.61	499.08	493.37	488.37
50000	568.15	554.35	542.53	532.37	523.57	515.93	509.27	503.44	498.33
51000	579.51	565.43	553.38	543.01	534.04	526.25	519.45	513.51	508.30
52000	590.87	576.52	564.24	553.66	544.51	536.57	529.64	523.58	518.27
53000	602.24	587.61	575.09	564.31	554.98	546.89	539.83	533.65	528.23
54000	613.60	598.69	585.94	574.96	565.46	557.20	550.01	543.72	538.20
55000	624.96	609.78	596.79	585.60	575.93	567.52	560.20	553.79	548.17
56000	636.33	620.87	607.64	596.25	586.40	577.84	570.38	563.86	558.13
57000	647.69	631.95	618.49	606.90	596.87	588.16	580.57	573.93	568.10
58000	659.05	643.04	629.34	617.54	607.34	598.48	590.75	583.99	578.07
59000	670.41	654.13	640.19	628.19	617.81	608.80	600.94	594.06	588.03
60000	681.78	665.22	651.04	638.84	628.28	619.12	611.12	604.13	598.00
61000	693.14	676.30	661.89	649.49	638.76	629.43	621.31	614.20	607.97
62000	704.50	687.39	672.74	660.13	649.23	639.75	631.49	624.27	617.93
63000	715.87	698.48	683.59	670.78	659.70	650.07	641.68	634.34	627.90
64000	727.23	709.56	694.44	681.43	670.17	660.39	651.86	644.41	637.87
65000	738.59	720.65	705.29	692.07	680.64	670.71	662.05	654.48	647.83
66000	749.95	731.74	716.14	702.72	691.11	681.03	672.23	664.54	657.80
67000	761.32	742.82	726.99	713.37	701.58	691.35	682.42	674.61	667.77
68000	772.68	753.91	737.84	724.02	712.05	701.66	692.60	684.68	677.73
69000	784.04	765.00	748.70	734.66	722.53	711.98	702.79	694.75	687.70
70000	795.41	776.08	759.55	745.31	733.00	722.30	712.98	704.82	697.67
75000	852.22	831.52	813.80	798.55	785.35	773.89	763.90	755.16	747.50
80000	909.03	886.95	868.05	851.78	837.71	825.49	814.83	805.51	797.33
100000	1136.29	1108.69	1085.06	1064.73	1047.14	1031.86	1018.53	1006.88	996.66

74

MONTHLY PAYMENT 11¼%
NECESSARY TO AMORTIZE A LOAN

TERM AMOUNT	24 YEARS	25 YEARS	26 YEARS	27 YEARS	28 YEARS	29 YEARS	30 YEARS	35 YEARS	40 YEARS
$ 25	.25	.25	.25	.25	.25	.24	.24	.24	.24
50	.50	.49	.49	.49	.49	.48	.48	.47	.47
75	.75	.74	.73	.73	.73	.72	.72	.71	.70
100	.99	.98	.98	.97	.97	.96	.96	.94	.93
200	1.98	1.96	1.95	1.94	1.93	1.92	1.91	1.88	1.86
300	2.97	2.94	2.92	2.90	2.89	2.87	2.86	2.81	2.79
400	3.96	3.92	3.90	3.87	3.85	3.83	3.81	3.75	3.72
500	4.94	4.90	4.87	4.84	4.81	4.79	4.76	4.69	4.64
600	5.93	5.88	5.84	5.80	5.77	5.74	5.72	5.62	5.57
700	6.92	6.86	6.81	6.77	6.73	6.70	6.67	6.56	6.50
800	7.91	7.84	7.79	7.74	7.69	7.66	7.62	7.50	7.43
900	8.89	8.82	8.76	8.70	8.66	8.61	8.57	8.43	8.36
1000	9.88	9.80	9.73	9.67	9.62	9.57	9.52	9.37	9.28
2000	19.76	19.60	19.46	19.34	19.23	19.13	19.04	18.74	18.56
3000	29.64	29.40	29.19	29.00	28.84	28.69	28.56	28.10	27.84
4000	39.51	39.20	38.92	38.67	38.45	38.26	38.08	37.47	37.12
5000	49.39	48.99	48.64	48.33	48.06	47.82	47.60	46.83	46.40
6000	59.27	58.79	58.37	58.00	57.67	57.38	57.12	56.20	55.68
7000	69.14	68.59	68.10	67.67	67.28	66.94	66.64	65.56	64.96
8000	79.02	78.39	77.83	77.33	76.89	76.51	76.16	74.93	74.24
9000	88.90	88.18	87.55	87.00	86.51	86.07	85.68	84.30	83.52
10000	98.77	97.98	97.28	96.66	96.12	95.63	95.20	93.66	92.79
15000	148.16	146.97	145.92	144.99	144.17	143.44	142.80	140.49	139.19
20000	197.54	195.96	194.56	193.32	192.23	191.26	190.39	187.32	185.58
25000	246.92	244.94	243.20	241.65	240.28	239.07	237.99	234.15	231.98
30000	296.31	293.93	291.83	289.98	288.34	286.88	285.59	280.98	278.37
35000	345.69	342.92	340.47	338.31	336.39	334.70	333.19	327.80	324.77
36000	355.57	352.72	350.20	347.98	346.01	344.26	342.71	337.17	334.05
37000	365.44	362.51	359.93	357.64	355.62	353.82	352.23	346.54	343.33
38000	375.32	372.31	369.66	367.31	365.23	363.38	361.75	355.90	352.61
39000	385.20	382.11	379.38	376.97	374.84	372.95	371.27	365.27	361.89
40000	395.07	391.91	389.11	386.64	384.45	382.51	380.78	374.63	371.16
41000	404.95	401.70	398.84	396.30	394.06	392.07	390.30	384.00	380.44
42000	414.83	411.50	408.57	405.97	403.67	401.63	399.82	393.36	389.72
43000	424.70	421.30	418.29	415.64	413.28	411.20	409.34	402.73	399.00
44000	434.58	431.10	428.02	425.30	422.89	420.76	418.86	412.10	408.28
45000	444.46	440.89	437.75	434.97	432.51	430.32	428.38	421.46	417.56
46000	454.33	450.69	447.48	444.63	442.12	439.88	437.90	430.83	426.84
47000	464.21	460.49	457.20	454.30	451.73	449.45	447.42	440.19	436.12
48000	474.09	470.29	466.93	463.97	461.34	459.01	456.94	449.56	445.40
49000	483.96	480.08	476.66	473.63	470.95	468.57	466.46	458.92	454.68
50000	493.84	489.88	486.39	483.30	480.56	478.13	475.98	468.29	463.95
51000	503.72	499.68	496.12	492.96	490.17	487.70	485.50	477.66	473.23
52000	513.59	509.48	505.84	502.63	499.78	497.26	495.02	487.02	482.51
53000	523.47	519.28	515.57	512.30	509.39	506.82	504.54	496.39	491.79
54000	533.35	529.07	525.30	521.96	519.01	516.38	514.06	505.75	501.07
55000	543.22	538.87	535.03	531.63	528.62	525.95	523.58	515.12	510.35
56000	553.10	548.67	544.75	541.29	538.23	535.51	533.10	524.48	519.63
57000	562.98	558.47	554.48	550.96	547.84	545.07	542.62	533.85	528.91
58000	572.85	568.26	564.21	560.62	557.45	554.63	552.14	543.22	538.19
59000	582.73	578.06	573.94	570.29	567.06	564.20	561.65	552.58	547.47
60000	592.61	587.86	583.66	579.96	576.67	573.76	571.17	561.95	556.74
61000	602.49	597.66	593.39	589.62	586.28	583.32	580.69	571.31	566.02
62000	612.36	607.45	603.12	599.29	595.89	592.88	590.21	580.68	575.30
63000	622.24	617.25	612.85	608.95	605.51	602.45	599.73	590.04	584.58
64000	632.12	627.05	622.57	618.62	615.12	612.01	609.25	599.41	593.86
65000	641.99	636.85	632.30	628.29	624.73	621.57	618.77	608.78	603.14
66000	651.87	646.64	642.03	637.95	634.34	631.14	628.29	618.14	612.42
67000	661.75	656.44	651.76	647.62	643.95	640.70	637.81	627.51	621.70
68000	671.62	666.24	661.49	657.28	653.56	650.26	647.33	636.87	630.98
69000	681.50	676.04	671.21	666.95	663.17	659.82	656.85	646.24	640.26
70000	691.38	685.83	680.94	676.61	672.78	669.39	666.37	655.60	649.53
75000	740.76	734.82	729.58	724.94	720.84	717.20	713.97	702.43	695.93
80000	790.14	783.81	778.22	773.27	768.89	765.01	761.56	749.26	742.32
100000	987.68	979.76	972.77	966.59	961.12	956.26	951.95	936.58	927.90

11½% MONTHLY PAYMENT
NECESSARY TO AMORTIZE A LOAN

TERM AMOUNT	1 YEAR	1½ YEARS	2 YEARS	2½ YEARS	3 YEARS	3½ YEARS	4 YEARS	4½ YEARS	5 YEARS
$ 25	2.22	1.52	1.17	.96	.83	.73	.65	.60	.55
50	4.43	3.04	2.34	1.92	1.65	1.45	1.30	1.19	1.10
75	6.64	4.55	3.51	2.88	2.47	2.17	1.95	1.78	1.64
100	8.85	6.07	4.68	3.84	3.29	2.90	2.60	2.37	2.19
200	17.70	12.13	9.35	7.68	6.57	5.79	5.20	4.74	4.38
300	26.55	18.19	14.02	11.52	9.86	8.68	7.79	7.11	6.56
400	35.40	24.26	18.69	15.36	13.14	11.57	10.39	9.48	8.75
500	44.25	30.32	23.36	19.20	16.43	14.46	12.98	11.84	10.93
600	53.10	36.38	28.03	23.04	19.71	17.35	15.58	14.21	13.12
700	61.95	42.44	32.71	26.88	23.00	20.24	18.18	16.58	15.31
800	70.80	48.51	37.38	30.72	26.28	23.13	20.77	18.95	17.49
900	79.65	54.57	42.05	34.55	29.57	26.02	23.37	21.31	19.68
1000	88.50	60.63	46.72	38.39	32.85	28.91	25.96	23.68	21.86
2000	176.99	121.26	93.44	76.78	65.70	57.82	51.92	47.36	43.72
3000	265.48	181.89	140.15	115.17	98.55	86.72	77.88	71.04	65.58
4000	353.97	242.51	186.87	153.56	131.40	115.63	103.84	94.71	87.44
5000	442.46	303.14	233.59	191.94	164.25	144.54	129.80	118.39	109.30
6000	530.95	363.77	280.30	230.33	197.10	173.44	155.76	142.07	131.16
7000	619.44	424.39	327.02	268.72	229.95	202.35	181.72	165.74	153.02
8000	707.93	485.02	373.74	307.11	262.80	231.25	207.68	189.42	174.88
9000	796.42	545.65	420.45	345.49	295.65	260.16	233.64	213.10	196.74
10000	884.91	606.27	467.17	383.88	328.50	289.07	259.60	236.77	218.60
15000	1327.37	909.41	700.75	575.82	492.75	433.60	389.39	355.16	327.89
20000	1769.82	1212.54	934.33	767.76	657.00	578.13	519.19	473.54	437.19
25000	2212.27	1515.67	1167.92	959.70	821.24	722.66	648.99	591.92	546.48
30000	2654.73	1818.81	1401.50	1151.63	985.49	867.19	778.78	710.31	655.78
35000	3097.18	2121.94	1635.08	1343.57	1149.74	1011.72	908.58	828.69	765.08
36000	3185.67	2182.57	1681.80	1381.96	1182.59	1040.62	934.54	852.37	786.94
37000	3274.16	2243.19	1728.51	1420.35	1215.44	1069.53	960.50	876.04	808.80
38000	3362.65	2303.82	1775.23	1458.74	1248.29	1098.44	986.45	899.72	830.65
39000	3451.14	2364.45	1821.95	1497.12	1281.14	1127.34	1012.41	923.40	852.51
40000	3539.63	2425.07	1868.66	1535.51	1313.99	1156.25	1038.37	947.07	874.37
41000	3628.13	2485.70	1915.38	1573.90	1346.84	1185.15	1064.33	970.75	896.23
42000	3716.62	2546.33	1962.10	1612.29	1379.69	1214.06	1090.29	994.43	918.09
43000	3805.11	2606.95	2008.81	1650.67	1412.54	1242.97	1116.25	1018.10	939.95
44000	3893.60	2667.58	2055.53	1689.06	1445.38	1271.87	1142.21	1041.78	961.81
45000	3982.09	2728.21	2102.25	1727.45	1478.23	1300.78	1168.17	1065.46	983.67
46000	4070.58	2788.83	2148.96	1765.84	1511.08	1329.68	1194.13	1089.13	1005.53
47000	4159.07	2849.46	2195.68	1804.22	1543.93	1358.59	1220.09	1112.81	1027.39
48000	4247.56	2910.09	2242.39	1842.61	1576.78	1387.50	1246.05	1136.49	1049.25
49000	4336.05	2970.71	2289.11	1881.00	1609.63	1416.40	1272.01	1160.16	1071.11
50000	4424.54	3031.34	2335.83	1919.39	1642.48	1445.31	1297.97	1183.84	1092.96
51000	4513.03	3091.97	2382.54	1957.78	1675.33	1474.21	1323.92	1207.52	1114.82
52000	4601.52	3152.59	2429.26	1996.16	1708.18	1503.12	1349.88	1231.19	1136.68
53000	4690.01	3213.22	2475.98	2034.55	1741.03	1532.03	1375.84	1254.87	1158.54
54000	4778.51	3273.85	2522.69	2072.94	1773.88	1560.93	1401.80	1278.55	1180.40
55000	4867.00	3334.47	2569.41	2111.33	1806.73	1589.84	1427.76	1302.22	1202.26
56000	4955.49	3395.10	2616.13	2149.71	1839.58	1618.74	1453.72	1325.90	1224.12
57000	5043.98	3455.73	2662.84	2188.10	1872.43	1647.65	1479.68	1349.58	1245.98
58000	5132.47	3516.35	2709.56	2226.49	1905.28	1676.56	1505.64	1373.25	1267.84
59000	5220.96	3576.98	2756.28	2264.88	1938.13	1705.46	1531.60	1396.93	1289.70
60000	5309.45	3637.61	2802.99	2303.26	1970.98	1734.37	1557.56	1420.61	1311.56
61000	5397.94	3698.23	2849.71	2341.65	2003.83	1763.28	1583.52	1444.28	1333.42
62000	5486.43	3758.86	2896.43	2380.04	2036.68	1792.18	1609.48	1467.96	1355.28
63000	5574.92	3819.49	2943.14	2418.43	2069.53	1821.09	1635.43	1491.64	1377.13
64000	5663.41	3880.12	2989.86	2456.81	2102.38	1849.99	1661.39	1515.31	1398.99
65000	5751.90	3940.74	3036.57	2495.20	2135.23	1878.90	1687.35	1538.99	1420.85
66000	5840.39	4001.37	3083.29	2533.59	2168.07	1907.81	1713.31	1562.67	1442.71
67000	5928.88	4062.00	3130.01	2571.98	2200.92	1936.71	1739.27	1586.34	1464.57
68000	6017.38	4122.62	3176.72	2610.37	2233.77	1965.62	1765.23	1610.02	1486.43
69000	6105.87	4183.25	3223.44	2648.75	2266.62	1994.52	1791.19	1633.70	1508.29
70000	6194.36	4243.88	3270.16	2687.14	2299.47	2023.43	1817.15	1657.37	1530.15
75000	6636.81	4547.01	3503.74	2879.08	2463.72	2167.96	1946.95	1775.76	1639.44
80000	7079.26	4850.14	3737.32	3071.02	2627.97	2312.49	2076.74	1894.14	1748.74
100000	8849.08	6062.68	4671.65	3838.77	3284.96	2890.61	2595.93	2367.67	2185.92

76

MONTHLY PAYMENT 11½%
NECESSARY TO AMORTIZE A LOAN

TERM AMOUNT	6 YEARS	7 YEARS	8 YEARS	9 YEARS	10 YEARS	11 YEARS	12 YEARS	13 YEARS	14 YEARS
$ 25	.48	.44	.40	.37	.35	.34	.32	.31	.30
50	.96	.87	.80	.74	.70	.67	.64	.62	.60
75	1.44	1.30	1.19	1.11	1.05	1.00	.96	.92	.89
100	1.92	1.73	1.59	1.48	1.40	1.33	1.27	1.23	1.19
200	3.84	3.45	3.17	2.96	2.79	2.65	2.54	2.45	2.37
300	5.75	5.18	4.76	4.43	4.18	3.97	3.81	3.67	3.56
400	7.67	6.90	6.34	5.91	5.57	5.30	5.07	4.89	4.74
500	9.58	8.63	7.92	7.38	6.96	6.62	6.34	6.11	5.92
600	11.50	10.35	9.51	8.86	8.35	7.94	7.61	7.34	7.11
700	13.41	12.08	11.09	10.33	9.74	9.26	8.88	8.56	8.29
800	15.33	13.80	12.67	11.81	11.13	10.59	10.14	9.78	9.47
900	17.24	15.53	14.26	13.28	12.52	11.91	11.41	11.00	10.66
1000	19.16	17.25	15.84	14.76	13.91	13.23	12.68	12.22	11.84
2000	38.31	34.50	31.67	29.52	27.82	26.46	25.35	24.44	23.68
3000	57.47	51.74	47.51	44.27	41.73	39.69	38.03	36.66	35.51
4000	76.62	68.99	63.34	59.03	55.64	52.92	50.70	48.87	47.35
5000	95.78	86.23	79.18	73.78	69.54	66.15	63.38	61.09	59.18
6000	114.93	103.48	95.01	88.54	83.45	79.37	76.05	73.31	71.02
7000	134.08	120.72	110.85	103.29	97.36	92.60	88.72	85.52	82.85
8000	153.24	137.97	126.68	118.05	111.27	105.83	101.40	97.74	94.69
9000	172.39	155.22	142.52	132.80	125.17	119.06	114.07	109.96	106.52
10000	191.55	172.46	158.35	147.56	139.08	132.29	126.75	122.17	118.36
15000	287.32	258.69	237.53	221.34	208.62	198.43	190.12	183.26	177.53
20000	383.09	344.92	316.70	295.11	278.16	264.57	253.49	244.34	236.71
25000	478.86	431.15	395.87	368.89	347.70	330.71	316.86	305.43	295.88
30000	574.63	517.37	475.05	442.67	417.24	396.85	380.23	366.51	355.06
35000	670.40	603.60	554.22	516.44	486.77	462.99	443.60	427.60	414.23
36000	689.55	620.85	570.06	531.20	500.68	476.22	456.28	439.81	426.07
37000	708.70	638.09	585.89	545.95	514.59	489.44	468.95	452.03	437.90
38000	727.86	655.34	601.73	560.71	528.50	502.67	481.63	464.25	449.74
39000	747.01	672.58	617.56	575.47	542.40	515.90	494.30	476.46	461.57
40000	766.17	689.83	633.40	590.22	556.31	529.13	506.98	488.68	473.41
41000	785.32	707.07	649.23	604.98	570.22	542.36	519.65	500.90	485.24
42000	804.47	724.32	665.07	619.73	584.13	555.58	532.32	513.12	497.08
43000	823.63	741.57	680.90	634.49	598.03	568.81	545.00	525.33	508.91
44000	842.78	758.81	696.74	649.24	611.94	582.04	557.67	537.55	520.75
45000	861.94	776.06	712.57	664.00	625.85	595.27	570.35	549.77	532.58
46000	881.09	793.30	728.41	678.75	639.76	608.50	583.02	561.98	544.42
47000	900.24	810.55	744.24	693.51	653.67	621.72	595.70	574.20	556.25
48000	919.40	827.79	760.08	708.26	667.57	634.95	608.37	586.42	568.09
49000	938.55	845.04	775.91	723.02	681.48	648.18	621.04	598.63	579.92
50000	957.71	862.29	791.74	737.78	695.39	661.41	633.72	610.85	591.76
51000	976.86	879.53	807.58	752.53	709.30	674.64	646.39	623.07	603.59
52000	996.01	896.78	823.41	767.29	723.20	687.87	659.07	635.28	615.43
53000	1015.17	914.02	839.25	782.04	737.11	701.09	671.74	647.50	627.26
54000	1034.32	931.27	855.08	796.80	751.02	714.32	684.42	659.72	639.10
55000	1053.48	948.51	870.92	811.55	764.93	727.55	697.09	671.94	650.93
56000	1072.63	965.76	886.75	826.31	778.83	740.78	709.76	684.15	662.77
57000	1091.78	983.00	902.59	841.06	792.74	754.01	722.44	696.37	674.60
58000	1110.94	1000.25	918.42	855.82	806.65	767.23	735.11	708.59	686.44
59000	1130.09	1017.50	934.26	870.57	820.56	780.46	747.79	720.80	698.27
60000	1149.25	1034.74	950.09	885.33	834.47	793.69	760.46	733.02	710.11
61000	1168.40	1051.99	965.93	900.08	848.37	806.92	773.14	745.24	721.94
62000	1187.56	1069.23	981.76	914.84	862.28	820.15	785.81	757.45	733.78
63000	1206.71	1086.48	997.60	929.60	876.19	833.38	798.48	769.67	745.61
64000	1225.86	1103.72	1013.43	944.35	890.10	846.60	811.16	781.89	757.45
65000	1245.02	1120.97	1029.27	959.11	904.00	859.83	823.83	794.10	769.28
66000	1264.17	1138.21	1045.10	973.86	917.91	873.06	836.51	806.32	781.12
67000	1283.33	1155.46	1060.94	988.62	931.82	886.29	849.18	818.54	792.95
68000	1302.48	1172.71	1076.77	1003.37	945.73	899.51	861.86	830.76	804.79
69000	1321.63	1189.95	1092.61	1018.13	959.63	912.74	874.53	842.97	816.62
70000	1340.79	1207.20	1108.44	1032.88	973.54	925.97	887.20	855.19	828.46
75000	1436.56	1293.43	1187.61	1106.66	1043.08	992.11	950.58	916.27	887.63
80000	1532.33	1379.65	1266.79	1180.44	1112.62	1058.25	1013.95	977.36	946.81
100000	1915.41	1724.57	1583.48	1475.55	1390.77	1322.81	1267.43	1221.70	1183.51

11½%   MONTHLY PAYMENT
NECESSARY TO AMORTIZE A LOAN

TERM / AMOUNT	15 YEARS	16 YEARS	17 YEARS	18 YEARS	19 YEARS	20 YEARS	21 YEARS	22 YEARS	23 YEARS
$ 25	.29	.29	.28	.28	.27	.27	.26	.26	.26
50	.58	.57	.56	.55	.54	.53	.52	.52	.51
75	.87	.85	.83	.82	.80	.79	.78	.77	.77
100	1.16	1.13	1.11	1.09	1.07	1.05	1.04	1.03	1.02
200	2.31	2.25	2.21	2.17	2.13	2.10	2.08	2.05	2.03
300	3.46	3.38	3.31	3.25	3.19	3.15	3.11	3.08	3.05
400	4.61	4.50	4.41	4.33	4.26	4.20	4.15	4.10	4.06
500	5.76	5.62	5.51	5.41	5.32	5.25	5.18	5.12	5.07
600	6.91	6.75	6.61	6.49	6.38	6.29	6.22	6.15	6.09
700	8.06	7.87	7.71	7.57	7.45	7.34	7.25	7.17	7.10
800	9.22	9.00	8.81	8.65	8.51	8.39	8.29	8.19	8.11
900	10.37	10.12	9.91	9.73	9.57	9.44	9.32	9.22	9.13
1000	11.52	11.24	11.01	10.81	10.64	10.49	10.36	10.24	10.14
2000	23.03	22.48	22.02	21.62	21.27	20.97	20.71	20.48	20.28
3000	34.54	33.72	33.02	32.42	31.90	31.45	31.06	30.71	30.41
4000	46.06	44.96	44.03	43.23	42.53	41.93	41.41	40.95	40.55
5000	57.57	56.20	55.04	54.03	53.16	52.41	51.76	51.19	50.68
6000	69.08	67.44	66.04	64.84	63.80	62.89	62.11	61.42	60.82
7000	80.60	78.68	77.05	75.64	74.43	73.38	72.46	71.66	70.96
8000	92.11	89.92	88.06	86.45	85.06	83.86	82.81	81.89	81.09
9000	103.62	101.16	99.06	97.25	95.69	94.34	93.16	92.13	91.23
10000	115.14	112.40	110.07	108.06	106.32	104.82	103.51	102.37	101.36
15000	172.70	168.60	165.10	162.09	159.48	157.23	155.26	153.55	152.04
20000	230.27	224.80	220.13	216.11	212.64	209.63	207.01	204.73	202.72
25000	287.84	281.00	275.16	270.14	265.80	262.04	258.77	255.91	253.40
30000	345.40	337.20	330.19	324.17	318.96	314.45	310.52	307.09	304.08
35000	402.97	393.40	385.22	378.19	372.12	366.86	362.27	358.27	354.76
36000	414.48	404.64	396.23	389.00	382.75	377.34	372.62	368.50	364.90
37000	425.99	415.88	407.24	399.81	393.39	387.82	382.97	378.74	375.03
38000	437.51	427.12	418.24	410.61	404.02	398.30	393.32	388.98	385.17
39000	449.02	438.36	429.25	421.42	414.65	408.78	403.67	399.21	395.30
40000	460.53	449.60	440.26	432.22	425.28	419.26	414.02	409.45	405.44
41000	472.05	460.84	451.26	443.03	435.91	429.74	424.37	419.68	415.58
42000	483.56	472.08	462.27	453.83	446.55	440.23	434.72	429.92	425.71
43000	495.07	483.32	473.27	464.64	457.18	450.71	445.07	440.16	435.85
44000	506.59	494.56	484.28	475.44	467.81	461.19	455.43	450.39	445.98
45000	518.10	505.80	495.29	486.25	478.44	471.67	465.78	460.63	456.12
46000	529.61	517.04	506.29	497.05	489.07	482.15	476.13	470.86	466.26
47000	541.13	528.28	517.30	507.86	499.71	492.63	486.48	481.10	476.39
48000	552.64	539.52	528.31	518.67	510.34	503.11	496.83	491.34	486.53
49000	564.15	550.76	539.31	529.47	520.97	513.60	507.18	501.57	496.66
50000	575.67	562.00	550.32	540.28	531.60	524.08	517.53	511.81	506.80
51000	587.18	573.24	561.32	551.08	542.23	534.56	527.88	522.04	516.94
52000	598.69	584.48	572.33	561.89	552.87	545.04	538.23	532.28	527.07
53000	610.20	595.72	583.34	572.69	563.50	555.52	548.58	542.52	537.21
54000	621.72	606.96	594.34	583.50	574.13	566.00	558.93	552.75	547.34
55000	633.23	618.20	605.35	594.30	584.76	576.49	569.28	562.99	557.48
56000	644.74	629.44	616.36	605.11	595.39	586.97	579.63	573.22	567.61
57000	656.26	640.68	627.36	615.91	606.03	597.45	589.98	583.46	577.75
58000	667.77	651.92	638.37	626.72	616.66	607.93	600.33	593.70	587.89
59000	679.28	663.16	649.37	637.52	627.29	618.41	610.68	603.93	598.02
60000	690.80	674.40	660.38	648.33	637.92	628.89	621.03	614.17	608.16
61000	702.31	685.64	671.39	659.14	648.55	639.37	631.38	624.40	618.29
62000	713.82	696.88	682.39	669.94	659.19	649.86	641.73	634.64	628.43
63000	725.34	708.12	693.40	680.75	669.82	660.34	652.08	644.88	638.57
64000	736.85	719.36	704.41	691.55	680.45	670.82	662.43	655.11	648.70
65000	748.36	730.60	715.41	702.36	691.08	681.30	672.78	665.35	658.84
66000	759.88	741.84	726.42	713.16	701.71	691.78	683.14	675.58	668.97
67000	771.39	753.08	737.42	723.97	712.34	702.26	693.49	685.82	679.11
68000	782.90	764.32	748.43	734.77	722.98	712.74	703.84	696.06	689.25
69000	794.42	775.56	759.44	745.58	733.61	723.23	714.19	706.29	699.38
70000	805.93	786.80	770.44	756.38	744.24	733.71	724.54	716.53	709.52
75000	863.50	843.00	825.47	810.41	797.40	786.11	776.29	767.71	760.20
80000	921.06	899.20	880.51	864.44	850.56	838.52	828.04	818.89	810.88
100000	1151.33	1123.99	1100.63	1080.55	1063.20	1048.15	1035.05	1023.61	1013.59

MONTHLY PAYMENT 11½%
NECESSARY TO AMORTIZE A LOAN

TERM AMOUNT	24 YEARS	25 YEARS	26 YEARS	27 YEARS	28 YEARS	29 YEARS	30 YEARS	35 YEARS	40 YEARS
$ 25	.26	.25	.25	.25	.25	.25	.25	.24	.24
50	.51	.50	.50	.50	.49	.49	.49	.48	.48
75	.76	.75	.75	.74	.74	.74	.73	.72	.72
100	1.01	1.00	1.00	.99	.98	.98	.98	.96	.95
200	2.01	2.00	1.99	1.97	1.96	1.95	1.95	1.92	1.90
300	3.02	3.00	2.98	2.96	2.94	2.93	2.92	2.87	2.85
400	4.02	3.99	3.97	3.94	3.92	3.90	3.89	3.83	3.79
500	5.03	4.99	4.96	4.93	4.90	4.88	4.86	4.78	4.74
600	6.03	5.99	5.95	5.91	5.88	5.85	5.83	5.74	5.69
700	7.04	6.98	6.94	6.89	6.86	6.82	6.80	6.69	6.63
800	8.04	7.98	7.93	7.88	7.84	7.80	7.77	7.65	7.58
900	9.05	8.98	8.92	8.86	8.82	8.77	8.74	8.60	8.53
1000	10.05	9.98	9.91	9.85	9.79	9.75	9.71	9.56	9.47
2000	20.10	19.95	19.81	19.69	19.58	19.49	19.41	19.11	18.94
3000	30.15	29.92	29.71	29.53	29.37	29.23	29.11	28.66	28.41
4000	40.20	39.89	39.61	39.37	39.16	38.97	38.81	38.21	37.88
5000	50.24	49.86	49.52	49.22	48.95	48.72	48.51	47.77	47.35
6000	60.29	59.83	59.42	59.06	58.74	58.46	58.21	57.32	56.82
7000	70.34	69.80	69.32	68.90	68.53	68.20	67.91	66.87	66.29
8000	80.39	79.77	79.22	78.74	78.32	77.94	77.61	76.42	75.76
9000	90.44	89.74	89.13	88.59	88.11	87.68	87.31	85.98	85.23
10000	100.48	99.71	99.03	98.43	97.90	97.43	97.01	95.53	94.70
15000	150.72	149.56	148.54	147.64	146.84	146.14	145.51	143.29	142.05
20000	200.96	199.42	198.05	196.85	195.79	194.85	194.01	191.05	189.40
25000	251.20	249.27	247.57	246.06	244.73	243.56	242.51	238.81	236.75
30000	301.44	299.12	297.08	295.27	293.68	292.27	291.01	286.57	284.09
35000	351.68	348.98	346.59	344.48	342.62	340.98	339.52	334.33	331.44
36000	361.73	358.95	356.49	354.33	352.41	350.72	349.22	343.89	340.91
37000	371.78	368.92	366.40	364.17	362.20	360.46	358.92	353.44	350.38
38000	381.83	378.89	376.30	374.01	371.99	370.20	368.62	362.99	359.85
39000	391.88	388.86	386.20	383.85	381.78	379.94	378.32	372.54	369.32
40000	401.92	398.83	396.10	393.70	391.57	389.69	388.02	382.09	378.79
41000	411.97	408.80	406.01	403.54	401.36	399.43	397.72	391.65	388.26
42000	422.02	418.77	415.91	413.38	411.15	409.17	407.42	401.20	397.73
43000	432.07	428.74	425.81	423.22	420.94	418.91	417.12	410.75	407.20
44000	442.11	438.71	435.71	433.07	430.72	428.65	426.82	420.30	416.67
45000	452.16	448.68	445.61	442.91	440.51	438.40	436.52	429.86	426.14
46000	462.21	458.65	455.52	452.75	450.30	448.14	446.22	439.41	435.61
47000	472.26	468.62	465.42	462.59	460.09	457.88	455.92	448.96	445.08
48000	482.31	478.59	475.32	472.43	469.88	467.62	465.62	458.51	454.55
49000	492.35	488.56	485.22	482.28	479.67	477.36	475.32	468.06	464.02
50000	502.40	498.54	495.13	492.12	489.46	487.11	485.02	477.62	473.49
51000	512.45	508.51	505.03	501.96	499.25	496.85	494.72	487.17	482.95
52000	522.50	518.48	514.93	511.80	509.04	506.59	504.42	496.72	492.42
53000	532.55	528.45	524.83	521.65	518.83	516.33	514.12	506.27	501.89
54000	542.59	538.42	534.74	531.49	528.62	526.07	523.82	515.83	511.36
55000	552.64	548.39	544.64	541.33	538.40	535.82	533.52	525.38	520.83
56000	562.69	558.36	554.54	551.17	548.19	545.56	543.22	534.93	530.30
57000	572.74	568.33	564.44	561.01	557.98	555.30	552.92	544.48	539.77
58000	582.79	578.30	574.35	570.86	567.77	565.04	562.62	554.04	549.24
59000	592.83	588.27	584.25	580.70	577.56	574.78	572.32	563.59	558.71
60000	602.88	598.24	594.15	590.54	587.35	584.53	582.02	573.14	568.18
61000	612.93	608.21	604.05	600.38	597.14	594.27	591.72	582.69	577.65
62000	622.98	618.18	613.96	610.23	606.93	604.01	601.42	592.24	587.12
63000	633.03	628.15	623.86	620.07	616.72	613.75	611.12	601.80	596.59
64000	643.07	638.12	633.76	629.91	626.51	623.49	620.82	611.35	606.06
65000	653.12	648.09	643.66	639.75	636.30	633.24	630.52	620.90	615.53
66000	663.17	658.06	653.57	649.60	646.08	642.98	640.22	630.45	625.00
67000	673.22	668.04	663.47	659.44	655.87	652.72	649.93	640.01	634.47
68000	683.27	678.01	673.37	669.28	665.66	662.46	659.63	649.56	643.94
69000	693.31	687.98	683.27	679.12	675.45	672.20	669.33	659.11	653.41
70000	703.36	697.95	693.18	688.96	685.24	681.95	679.03	668.66	662.88
75000	753.60	747.80	742.69	738.18	734.19	730.66	727.53	716.42	710.23
80000	803.84	797.65	792.20	787.39	783.13	779.37	776.03	764.18	757.57
100000	1004.80	997.07	990.25	984.23	978.91	974.21	970.04	955.23	946.97

79

11¾% MONTHLY PAYMENT
NECESSARY TO AMORTIZE A LOAN

TERM AMOUNT	1 YEAR	1½ YEARS	2 YEARS	2½ YEARS	3 YEARS	3½ YEARS	4 YEARS	4½ YEARS	5 YEARS
$ 25	2.22	1.52	1.18	.97	.83	.73	.66	.60	.55
50	4.44	3.04	2.35	1.93	1.65	1.46	1.31	1.19	1.10
75	6.65	4.56	3.52	2.89	2.48	2.18	1.96	1.79	1.65
100	8.87	6.08	4.69	3.85	3.30	2.91	2.61	2.38	2.20
200	17.73	12.15	9.37	7.70	6.60	5.81	5.22	4.76	4.40
300	26.59	18.23	14.05	11.55	9.89	8.71	7.83	7.14	6.60
400	35.45	24.30	18.74	15.40	13.19	11.61	10.44	9.52	8.80
500	44.31	30.37	23.42	19.25	16.49	14.52	13.04	11.90	10.99
600	53.17	36.45	28.10	23.10	19.78	17.42	15.65	14.28	13.19
700	62.03	42.52	32.78	26.95	23.08	20.32	18.26	16.66	15.39
800	70.89	48.59	37.47	30.80	26.38	23.22	20.87	19.04	17.59
900	79.75	54.67	42.15	34.65	29.67	26.12	23.47	21.42	19.79
1000	88.61	60.74	46.83	38.50	32.97	29.03	26.08	23.80	21.98
2000	177.21	121.48	93.66	77.00	65.93	58.05	52.16	47.59	43.96
3000	265.81	182.22	140.49	115.50	98.89	87.07	78.23	71.39	65.94
4000	354.41	242.95	187.31	154.00	131.86	116.09	104.31	95.18	87.92
5000	443.02	303.69	234.14	192.50	164.82	145.11	130.38	118.98	109.90
6000	531.62	364.43	280.97	231.00	197.78	174.13	156.46	142.77	131.88
7000	620.22	425.17	327.80	269.50	230.74	203.15	182.53	166.57	153.86
8000	708.82	485.90	374.62	308.00	263.71	232.17	208.61	190.36	175.83
9000	797.42	546.64	421.45	346.50	296.67	261.19	234.68	214.16	197.81
10000	886.03	607.38	468.28	385.00	329.63	290.21	260.76	237.95	219.79
15000	1329.04	911.06	702.42	577.50	494.45	435.32	391.14	356.92	329.69
20000	1772.05	1214.75	936.55	770.00	659.26	580.42	521.51	475.90	439.58
25000	2215.06	1518.43	1170.69	962.50	824.08	725.53	651.89	594.87	549.47
30000	2658.07	1822.12	1404.83	1154.99	988.89	870.63	782.27	713.84	659.37
35000	3101.08	2125.81	1638.96	1347.49	1153.70	1015.73	912.65	832.81	769.26
36000	3189.68	2186.54	1685.79	1385.99	1186.67	1044.75	938.72	856.61	791.24
37000	3278.28	2247.28	1732.62	1424.49	1219.63	1073.77	964.80	880.40	813.22
38000	3366.89	2308.02	1779.45	1462.99	1252.59	1102.80	990.87	904.20	835.20
39000	3455.49	2368.76	1826.27	1501.49	1285.56	1131.82	1016.95	927.99	857.17
40000	3544.09	2429.49	1873.10	1539.99	1318.52	1160.84	1043.02	951.79	879.15
41000	3632.69	2490.23	1919.93	1578.49	1351.48	1189.86	1069.10	975.58	901.13
42000	3721.29	2550.97	1966.76	1616.99	1384.44	1218.88	1095.18	999.38	923.11
43000	3809.90	2611.70	2013.58	1655.49	1417.41	1247.90	1121.25	1023.17	945.09
44000	3898.50	2672.44	2060.41	1693.99	1450.37	1276.92	1147.33	1046.97	967.07
45000	3987.10	2733.18	2107.24	1732.49	1483.33	1305.94	1173.40	1070.76	989.05
46000	4075.70	2793.92	2154.07	1770.99	1516.30	1334.96	1199.48	1094.56	1011.03
47000	4164.30	2854.65	2200.89	1809.49	1549.26	1363.98	1225.55	1118.35	1033.00
48000	4252.91	2915.39	2247.72	1847.99	1582.22	1393.00	1251.63	1142.14	1054.98
49000	4341.51	2976.13	2294.55	1886.49	1615.18	1422.02	1277.70	1165.94	1076.96
50000	4430.11	3036.86	2341.38	1924.99	1648.15	1451.05	1303.78	1189.73	1098.94
51000	4518.71	3097.60	2388.20	1963.49	1681.11	1480.07	1329.85	1213.53	1120.92
52000	4607.31	3158.34	2435.03	2001.99	1714.07	1509.09	1355.93	1237.32	1142.90
53000	4695.92	3219.08	2481.86	2040.49	1747.03	1538.11	1382.01	1261.12	1164.88
54000	4784.52	3279.81	2528.69	2078.99	1780.00	1567.13	1408.08	1284.91	1186.85
55000	4873.12	3340.55	2575.51	2117.49	1812.96	1596.15	1434.16	1308.71	1208.83
56000	4961.72	3401.29	2622.34	2155.99	1845.92	1625.17	1460.23	1332.50	1230.81
57000	5050.33	3462.03	2669.17	2194.48	1878.89	1654.19	1486.31	1356.30	1252.79
58000	5138.93	3522.76	2715.99	2232.98	1911.85	1683.21	1512.38	1380.09	1274.77
59000	5227.53	3583.50	2762.82	2271.48	1944.81	1712.23	1538.46	1403.88	1296.75
60000	5316.13	3644.24	2809.65	2309.98	1977.77	1741.25	1564.53	1427.68	1318.73
61000	5404.73	3704.97	2856.48	2348.48	2010.74	1770.27	1590.61	1451.47	1340.71
62000	5493.34	3765.71	2903.30	2386.98	2043.70	1799.29	1616.68	1475.27	1362.68
63000	5581.94	3826.45	2950.13	2425.48	2076.66	1828.32	1642.76	1499.06	1384.66
64000	5670.54	3887.19	2996.96	2463.98	2109.63	1857.34	1668.84	1522.86	1406.64
65000	5759.14	3947.92	3043.79	2502.48	2142.59	1886.36	1694.91	1546.65	1428.62
66000	5847.74	4008.66	3090.61	2540.98	2175.55	1915.38	1720.99	1570.45	1450.60
67000	5936.35	4069.40	3137.44	2579.48	2208.51	1944.40	1747.06	1594.24	1472.58
68000	6024.95	4130.13	3184.27	2617.98	2241.48	1973.42	1773.14	1618.04	1494.56
69000	6113.55	4190.87	3231.10	2656.48	2274.44	2002.44	1799.21	1641.83	1516.54
70000	6202.15	4251.61	3277.92	2694.98	2307.40	2031.46	1825.29	1665.62	1538.51
75000	6645.16	4555.29	3512.06	2887.48	2472.22	2176.57	1955.67	1784.60	1648.41
80000	7088.17	4858.98	3746.20	3079.98	2637.03	2321.67	2086.04	1903.57	1758.30
100000	8860.22	6073.72	4682.75	3849.97	3296.29	2902.09	2607.55	2379.46	2197.87

MONTHLY PAYMENT 11¾%
NECESSARY TO AMORTIZE A LOAN

TERM AMOUNT	6 YEARS	7 YEARS	8 YEARS	9 YEARS	10 YEARS	11 YEARS	12 YEARS	13 YEARS	14 YEARS
$ 25	.49	.44	.40	.38	.36	.34	.33	.31	.30
50	.97	.87	.80	.75	.71	.67	.65	.62	.60
75	1.45	1.31	1.20	1.12	1.06	1.01	.97	.93	.90
100	1.93	1.74	1.60	1.49	1.41	1.34	1.29	1.24	1.20
200	3.86	3.48	3.20	2.98	2.81	2.68	2.57	2.48	2.40
300	5.79	5.22	4.79	4.47	4.22	4.02	3.85	3.71	3.60
400	7.72	6.95	6.39	5.96	5.62	5.35	5.13	4.95	4.80
500	9.64	8.69	7.99	7.45	7.03	6.69	6.41	6.19	6.00
600	11.57	10.43	9.58	8.94	8.43	8.03	7.69	7.42	7.19
700	13.50	12.17	11.18	10.43	9.84	9.36	8.98	8.66	8.39
800	15.43	13.90	12.78	11.92	11.24	10.70	10.26	9.89	9.59
900	17.35	15.64	14.37	13.40	12.64	12.04	11.54	11.13	10.79
1000	19.28	17.38	15.97	14.89	14.05	13.37	12.82	12.37	11.99
2000	38.56	34.75	31.93	29.78	28.09	26.74	25.64	24.73	23.97
3000	57.84	52.12	47.90	44.67	42.14	40.11	38.45	37.09	35.95
4000	77.11	69.49	63.86	59.56	56.18	53.47	51.27	49.45	47.94
5000	96.39	86.86	79.83	74.45	70.22	66.84	64.09	61.82	59.92
6000	115.67	104.24	95.79	89.33	84.27	80.21	76.90	74.18	71.90
7000	134.94	121.61	111.76	104.22	98.31	93.58	89.72	86.54	83.89
8000	154.22	138.98	127.72	119.11	112.35	106.94	102.54	98.90	95.87
9000	173.50	156.35	143.68	134.00	126.40	120.31	115.35	111.27	107.85
10000	192.77	173.72	159.65	148.89	140.44	133.68	128.17	123.63	119.84
15000	289.16	260.58	239.47	223.33	210.66	200.51	192.25	185.44	179.75
20000	385.54	347.44	319.29	297.77	280.88	267.35	256.34	247.25	239.67
25000	481.93	434.30	399.11	372.21	351.10	334.19	320.42	309.06	299.59
30000	578.31	521.16	478.93	446.65	421.32	401.02	384.50	370.87	359.50
35000	674.69	608.02	558.76	521.09	491.53	467.86	448.59	432.68	419.42
36000	693.97	625.39	574.72	535.98	505.58	481.23	461.40	445.05	431.40
37000	713.25	642.76	590.68	550.87	519.62	494.59	474.22	457.41	443.39
38000	732.53	660.13	606.65	565.76	533.67	507.96	487.04	469.77	455.37
39000	751.80	677.50	622.61	580.64	547.71	521.33	499.85	482.13	467.35
40000	771.08	694.88	638.58	595.53	561.75	534.70	512.67	494.49	479.34
41000	790.36	712.25	654.54	610.42	575.80	548.06	525.48	506.86	491.32
42000	809.63	729.62	670.51	625.31	589.84	561.43	538.30	519.22	503.30
43000	828.91	746.99	686.47	640.20	603.88	574.80	551.12	531.58	515.29
44000	848.19	764.36	702.43	655.09	617.93	588.17	563.93	543.94	527.27
45000	867.46	781.73	718.40	669.97	631.97	601.53	576.75	556.31	539.25
46000	886.74	799.11	734.36	684.86	646.01	614.90	589.57	568.67	551.24
47000	906.02	816.48	750.33	699.75	660.06	628.27	602.38	581.03	563.22
48000	925.29	833.85	766.29	714.64	674.10	641.63	615.20	593.39	575.20
49000	944.57	851.22	782.26	729.53	688.15	655.00	628.02	605.75	587.19
50000	963.85	868.59	798.22	744.41	702.19	668.37	640.83	618.12	599.17
51000	983.12	885.97	814.18	759.30	716.23	681.74	653.65	630.48	611.15
52000	1002.40	903.34	830.15	774.19	730.28	695.10	666.47	642.84	623.14
53000	1021.68	920.71	846.11	789.08	744.32	708.47	679.28	655.20	635.12
54000	1040.96	938.08	862.08	803.97	758.36	721.84	692.10	667.57	647.10
55000	1060.23	955.45	878.04	818.86	772.41	735.21	704.92	679.93	659.08
56000	1079.51	972.82	894.01	833.74	786.45	748.57	717.73	692.29	671.07
57000	1098.79	990.20	909.97	848.63	800.50	761.94	730.55	704.65	683.05
58000	1118.06	1007.57	925.93	863.52	814.54	775.31	743.37	717.01	695.03
59000	1137.34	1024.94	941.90	878.41	828.58	788.67	756.18	729.38	707.02
60000	1156.62	1042.31	957.86	893.30	842.63	802.04	769.00	741.74	719.00
61000	1175.89	1059.68	973.83	908.18	856.67	815.41	781.82	754.10	730.98
62000	1195.17	1077.05	989.79	923.07	870.71	828.78	794.63	766.46	742.97
63000	1214.45	1094.43	1005.76	937.96	884.76	842.14	807.45	778.83	754.95
64000	1233.72	1111.80	1021.72	952.85	898.80	855.51	820.27	791.19	766.93
65000	1253.00	1129.17	1037.68	967.74	912.85	868.88	833.08	803.55	778.92
66000	1272.28	1146.54	1053.65	982.63	926.89	882.25	845.90	815.91	790.90
67000	1291.55	1163.91	1069.61	997.51	940.93	895.61	858.72	828.27	802.88
68000	1310.83	1181.29	1085.58	1012.40	954.98	908.98	871.53	840.64	814.87
69000	1330.11	1198.66	1101.54	1027.29	969.02	922.35	884.35	853.00	826.85
70000	1349.38	1216.03	1117.51	1042.18	983.06	935.71	897.17	865.36	838.83
75000	1445.77	1302.89	1197.33	1116.62	1053.28	1002.55	961.25	927.17	898.75
80000	1542.15	1389.75	1277.15	1191.06	1123.50	1069.39	1025.33	988.98	958.67
100000	1927.69	1737.18	1596.43	1488.82	1404.37	1336.73	1281.66	1236.23	1198.33

81

11¾% MONTHLY PAYMENT
NECESSARY TO AMORTIZE A LOAN

TERM AMOUNT	15 YEARS	16 YEARS	17 YEARS	18 YEARS	19 YEARS	20 YEARS	21 YEARS	22 YEARS	23 YEARS
$ 25	.30	.29	.28	.28	.27	.27	.27	.27	.26
50	.59	.57	.56	.55	.54	.54	.53	.53	.52
75	.88	.86	.84	.83	.81	.80	.79	.79	.78
100	1.17	1.14	1.12	1.10	1.08	1.07	1.06	1.05	1.04
200	2.34	2.28	2.24	2.20	2.16	2.13	2.11	2.09	2.07
300	3.50	3.42	3.35	3.29	3.24	3.20	3.16	3.13	3.10
400	4.67	4.56	4.47	4.39	4.32	4.26	4.21	4.17	4.13
500	5.84	5.70	5.59	5.49	5.40	5.33	5.26	5.21	5.16
600	7.00	6.84	6.70	6.58	6.48	6.39	6.31	6.25	6.19
700	8.17	7.98	7.82	7.68	7.56	7.46	7.37	7.29	7.22
800	9.34	9.12	8.94	8.78	8.64	8.52	8.42	8.33	8.25
900	10.50	10.26	10.05	9.87	9.72	9.59	9.47	9.37	9.28
1000	11.67	11.40	11.17	10.97	10.80	10.65	10.52	10.41	10.31
2000	23.33	22.79	22.33	21.93	21.59	21.30	21.04	20.81	20.62
3000	35.00	34.19	33.49	32.90	32.39	31.94	31.55	31.22	30.92
4000	46.66	45.58	44.66	43.86	43.18	42.59	42.07	41.62	41.23
5000	58.33	56.97	55.82	54.83	53.97	53.23	52.59	52.03	51.53
6000	69.99	68.37	66.98	65.79	64.77	63.88	63.10	62.43	61.84
7000	81.65	79.76	78.14	76.76	75.56	74.52	73.62	72.83	72.15
8000	93.32	91.15	89.31	87.72	86.35	85.17	84.14	83.24	82.45
9000	104.98	102.55	100.47	98.68	97.15	95.81	94.65	93.64	92.76
10000	116.65	113.94	111.63	109.65	107.94	106.46	105.17	104.05	103.06
15000	174.97	170.91	167.45	164.47	161.91	159.68	157.75	156.07	154.59
20000	233.29	227.88	223.26	219.29	215.87	212.91	210.33	208.09	206.12
25000	291.61	284.85	279.07	274.12	269.84	266.14	262.92	260.11	257.65
30000	349.93	341.82	334.89	328.94	323.81	319.36	315.50	312.13	309.18
35000	408.25	398.79	390.70	383.76	377.77	372.59	368.08	364.15	360.71
36000	419.92	410.18	401.86	394.72	388.57	383.23	378.60	374.55	371.02
37000	431.58	421.57	413.03	405.69	399.36	393.88	389.11	384.96	381.33
38000	443.25	432.97	424.19	416.65	410.15	404.52	399.63	395.36	391.63
39000	454.91	444.36	435.35	427.62	420.95	415.17	410.15	405.77	401.94
40000	466.58	455.75	446.51	438.58	431.74	425.81	420.66	416.17	412.24
41000	478.24	467.15	457.68	449.55	442.53	436.46	431.18	426.58	422.55
42000	489.90	478.54	468.84	460.51	453.33	447.10	441.69	436.98	432.86
43000	501.57	489.93	480.00	471.47	464.12	457.75	452.21	447.38	443.16
44000	513.23	501.33	491.16	482.44	474.91	468.39	462.73	457.79	453.47
45000	524.90	512.72	502.33	493.40	485.71	479.04	473.24	468.19	463.77
46000	536.56	524.12	513.49	504.37	496.50	489.68	483.76	478.60	474.08
47000	548.23	535.51	524.65	515.33	507.29	500.33	494.28	489.00	484.39
48000	559.89	546.90	535.82	526.30	518.09	510.97	504.79	499.40	494.69
49000	571.55	558.30	546.98	537.26	528.88	521.62	515.31	509.81	505.00
50000	583.22	569.69	558.14	548.23	539.67	532.27	525.83	520.21	515.30
51000	594.88	581.08	569.30	559.19	550.47	542.91	536.34	530.62	525.61
52000	606.55	592.48	580.47	570.15	561.26	553.56	546.86	541.02	535.92
53000	618.21	603.87	591.63	581.12	572.05	564.20	557.38	551.42	546.22
54000	629.88	615.27	602.79	592.08	582.85	574.85	567.89	561.83	556.53
55000	641.54	626.66	613.95	603.05	593.64	585.49	578.41	572.23	566.83
56000	653.20	638.05	625.12	614.01	604.43	596.14	588.92	582.64	577.14
57000	664.87	649.45	636.28	624.98	615.23	606.78	599.44	593.04	587.45
58000	676.53	660.84	647.44	635.94	626.02	617.43	609.96	603.45	597.75
59000	688.20	672.23	658.61	646.91	636.81	628.07	620.47	613.85	608.06
60000	699.86	683.63	669.77	657.87	647.61	638.72	630.99	624.25	618.36
61000	711.53	695.02	680.93	668.83	658.40	649.36	641.51	634.66	628.67
62000	723.19	706.42	692.09	679.80	669.19	660.01	652.02	645.06	638.98
63000	734.85	717.81	703.26	690.76	679.99	670.65	662.54	655.47	649.28
64000	746.52	729.20	714.42	701.73	690.78	681.30	673.06	665.87	659.59
65000	758.18	740.60	725.58	712.69	701.57	691.94	683.57	676.27	669.89
66000	769.85	751.99	736.74	723.66	712.37	702.59	694.09	686.68	680.20
67000	781.51	763.38	747.91	734.62	723.16	713.23	704.61	697.08	690.51
68000	793.18	774.78	759.07	745.59	733.95	723.88	715.12	707.49	700.81
69000	804.84	786.17	770.23	756.55	744.75	734.52	725.64	717.89	711.12
70000	816.50	797.57	781.40	767.51	755.54	745.17	736.15	728.30	721.42
75000	874.83	854.53	837.21	822.34	809.51	798.40	788.74	780.32	772.95
80000	933.15	911.50	893.02	877.16	863.47	851.62	841.32	832.34	824.48
100000	1166.43	1139.38	1116.28	1096.45	1079.34	1064.53	1051.65	1040.42	1030.60

MONTHLY PAYMENT 11¾%
NECESSARY TO AMORTIZE A LOAN

TERM AMOUNT	24 YEARS	25 YEARS	26 YEARS	27 YEARS	28 YEARS	29 YEARS	30 YEARS	35 YEARS	40 YEARS
$ 25	.26	.26	.26	.26	.25	.25	.25	.25	.25
50	.52	.51	.51	.51	.50	.50	.50	.49	.49
75	.77	.77	.76	.76	.75	.75	.75	.74	.73
100	1.03	1.02	1.01	1.01	1.00	1.00	.99	.98	.97
200	2.05	2.03	2.02	2.01	2.00	1.99	1.98	1.95	1.94
300	3.07	3.05	3.03	3.01	3.00	2.98	2.97	2.93	2.90
400	4.09	4.06	4.04	4.01	3.99	3.97	3.96	3.90	3.87
500	5.11	5.08	5.04	5.01	4.99	4.97	4.95	4.87	4.84
600	6.14	6.09	6.05	6.02	5.99	5.96	5.93	5.85	5.80
700	7.16	7.11	7.06	7.02	6.98	6.95	6.92	6.82	6.77
800	8.18	8.12	8.07	8.02	7.98	7.94	7.91	7.80	7.73
900	9.20	9.13	9.08	9.02	8.98	8.93	8.90	8.77	8.70
1000	10.22	10.15	10.08	10.02	9.97	9.93	9.89	9.74	9.67
2000	20.44	20.29	20.16	20.04	19.94	19.85	19.77	19.48	19.33
3000	30.66	30.44	30.24	30.06	29.91	29.77	29.65	29.22	28.99
4000	40.88	40.58	40.32	40.08	39.88	39.69	39.53	38.96	38.65
5000	51.10	50.73	50.39	50.10	49.84	49.62	49.41	48.70	48.31
6000	61.32	60.87	60.47	60.12	59.81	59.54	59.30	58.44	57.97
7000	71.54	71.02	70.55	70.14	69.78	69.46	69.18	68.18	67.63
8000	81.76	81.16	80.63	80.16	79.75	79.38	79.06	77.92	77.29
9000	91.98	91.30	90.71	90.18	89.71	89.30	88.94	87.66	86.95
10000	102.20	101.45	100.78	100.20	99.68	99.23	98.82	97.40	96.61
15000	153.30	152.17	151.17	150.30	149.52	148.84	148.23	146.09	144.91
20000	204.40	202.89	201.56	200.39	199.36	198.45	197.64	194.79	193.22
25000	255.50	253.62	251.95	250.49	249.20	248.06	247.05	243.49	241.52
30000	306.60	304.34	302.34	300.59	299.04	297.67	296.46	292.18	289.82
35000	357.70	355.06	352.73	350.69	348.88	347.28	345.87	340.88	338.13
36000	367.92	365.20	362.81	360.70	358.84	357.20	355.75	350.62	347.79
37000	378.14	375.35	372.89	370.72	368.81	367.12	365.63	360.36	357.45
38000	388.36	385.49	382.97	380.74	378.78	377.05	375.51	370.10	367.11
39000	398.58	395.64	393.05	390.76	388.75	386.97	385.39	379.84	376.77
40000	408.80	405.78	403.12	400.78	398.72	396.89	395.28	389.58	386.43
41000	419.02	415.93	413.20	410.80	408.68	406.81	405.16	399.32	396.09
42000	429.24	426.07	423.28	420.82	418.65	416.73	415.04	409.06	405.75
43000	439.46	436.22	433.36	430.84	428.62	426.66	424.92	418.79	415.41
44000	449.68	446.36	443.44	440.86	438.59	436.58	434.80	428.53	425.07
45000	459.90	456.50	453.51	450.88	448.55	446.50	444.68	438.27	434.73
46000	470.12	466.65	463.59	460.90	458.52	456.42	454.57	448.01	444.39
47000	480.34	476.79	473.67	470.92	468.49	466.35	464.45	457.75	454.05
48000	490.56	486.94	483.75	480.94	478.46	476.27	474.33	467.49	463.71
49000	500.78	497.08	493.83	490.96	488.43	486.19	484.21	477.23	473.37
50000	511.00	507.23	503.90	500.98	498.39	496.11	494.09	486.97	483.03
51000	521.22	517.37	513.98	511.00	508.36	506.03	503.98	496.71	492.70
52000	531.44	527.52	524.06	521.02	518.33	515.96	513.86	506.45	502.36
53000	541.66	537.66	534.14	531.03	528.30	525.88	523.74	516.19	512.02
54000	551.88	547.80	544.22	541.05	538.26	535.80	533.62	525.93	521.68
55000	562.10	557.95	554.29	551.07	548.23	545.72	543.50	535.67	531.34
56000	572.32	568.09	564.37	561.09	558.20	555.64	553.38	545.41	541.00
57000	582.54	578.24	574.45	571.11	568.17	565.57	563.27	555.14	550.66
58000	592.76	588.38	584.53	581.13	578.14	575.49	573.15	564.88	560.32
59000	602.98	598.53	594.61	591.15	588.10	585.41	583.03	574.62	569.98
60000	613.20	608.67	604.68	601.17	598.07	595.33	592.91	584.36	579.64
61000	623.42	618.82	614.76	611.19	608.04	605.26	602.79	594.10	589.30
62000	633.64	628.96	624.84	621.21	618.01	615.18	612.67	603.84	598.96
63000	643.86	639.10	634.92	631.23	627.97	625.10	622.56	613.58	608.62
64000	654.08	649.25	645.00	641.25	637.94	635.02	632.44	623.32	618.28
65000	664.30	659.39	655.07	651.27	647.91	644.94	642.32	633.06	627.94
66000	674.52	669.54	665.15	661.29	657.88	654.87	652.20	642.80	637.60
67000	684.74	679.68	675.23	671.31	667.85	664.79	662.08	652.54	647.26
68000	694.96	689.83	685.31	681.33	677.81	674.71	671.97	662.28	656.93
69000	705.18	699.97	695.39	691.35	687.78	684.63	681.85	672.02	666.59
70000	715.40	710.12	705.46	701.37	697.75	694.55	691.73	681.76	676.25
75000	766.50	760.84	755.85	751.46	747.59	744.17	741.14	730.45	724.55
80000	817.60	811.56	806.24	801.56	797.43	793.78	790.55	779.15	772.85
100000	1022.00	1014.45	1007.80	1001.95	996.78	992.22	988.18	973.93	966.06

83

12% MONTHLY PAYMENT
NECESSARY TO AMORTIZE A LOAN

TERM AMOUNT	1 YEAR	1½ YEARS	2 YEARS	2½ YEARS	3 YEARS	3½ YEARS	4 YEARS	4½ YEARS	5 YEARS
$ 25	2.22	1.53	1.18	.97	.83	.73	.66	.60	.56
50	4.44	3.05	2.35	1.94	1.66	1.46	1.31	1.20	1.11
75	6.66	4.57	3.53	2.90	2.49	2.19	1.97	1.80	1.66
100	8.88	6.09	4.70	3.87	3.31	2.92	2.62	2.40	2.21
200	17.75	12.17	9.39	7.73	6.62	5.83	5.24	4.79	4.42
300	26.62	18.26	14.09	11.59	9.93	8.75	7.86	7.18	6.63
400	35.49	24.34	18.78	15.45	13.24	11.66	10.48	9.57	8.84
500	44.36	30.43	23.47	19.31	16.54	14.57	13.10	11.96	11.05
600	53.23	36.51	28.17	23.17	19.85	17.49	15.72	14.35	13.26
700	62.10	42.60	32.86	27.03	23.16	20.40	18.34	16.74	15.47
800	70.98	48.68	37.56	30.89	26.47	23.31	20.96	19.14	17.68
900	79.85	54.77	42.25	34.76	29.77	26.23	23.58	21.53	19.89
1000	88.72	60.85	46.94	38.62	33.08	29.14	26.20	23.92	22.10
2000	177.43	121.70	93.88	77.23	66.16	58.28	52.39	47.83	44.20
3000	266.15	182.55	140.82	115.84	99.23	87.41	78.58	71.74	66.30
4000	354.86	243.40	187.76	154.45	132.31	116.55	104.77	95.66	88.40
5000	443.57	304.24	234.70	193.06	165.39	145.68	130.96	119.57	110.50
6000	532.29	365.09	281.64	231.68	198.46	174.82	157.16	143.48	132.60
7000	621.00	425.94	328.57	270.29	231.54	203.95	183.35	167.39	154.69
8000	709.71	486.79	375.51	308.90	264.61	233.09	209.54	191.31	176.79
9000	798.43	547.63	422.45	347.51	297.69	262.23	235.73	215.22	198.89
10000	887.14	608.48	469.39	386.12	330.77	291.36	261.92	239.13	220.99
15000	1330.71	912.72	704.08	579.18	496.15	437.04	392.88	358.69	331.48
20000	1774.27	1216.96	938.77	772.24	661.53	582.72	523.84	478.26	441.97
25000	2217.84	1521.20	1173.47	965.30	826.91	728.40	654.80	597.82	552.47
30000	2661.41	1825.44	1408.16	1158.36	992.29	874.08	785.76	717.38	662.96
35000	3104.98	2129.67	1642.85	1351.41	1157.67	1019.75	916.72	836.95	773.45
36000	3193.69	2190.52	1689.79	1390.03	1190.75	1048.89	942.91	860.86	795.55
37000	3282.40	2251.37	1736.73	1428.64	1223.83	1078.03	969.11	884.77	817.65
38000	3371.12	2312.22	1783.66	1467.25	1256.90	1107.16	995.30	908.69	839.75
39000	3459.83	2373.06	1830.60	1505.86	1289.98	1136.30	1021.49	932.60	861.84
40000	3548.54	2433.91	1877.54	1544.47	1323.05	1165.43	1047.68	956.51	883.94
41000	3637.26	2494.76	1924.48	1583.09	1356.13	1194.57	1073.87	980.42	906.04
42000	3725.97	2555.61	1971.42	1621.70	1389.21	1223.70	1100.07	1004.34	928.14
43000	3814.68	2616.46	2018.36	1660.31	1422.28	1252.84	1126.26	1028.25	950.24
44000	3903.40	2677.30	2065.30	1698.92	1455.36	1281.98	1152.45	1052.16	972.34
45000	3992.11	2738.15	2112.23	1737.53	1488.44	1311.11	1178.64	1076.07	994.44
46000	4080.82	2799.00	2159.17	1776.14	1521.51	1340.25	1204.83	1099.99	1016.53
47000	4169.54	2859.85	2206.11	1814.76	1554.59	1369.38	1231.03	1123.90	1038.63
48000	4258.25	2920.69	2253.05	1853.37	1587.66	1398.52	1257.22	1147.81	1060.73
49000	4346.96	2981.54	2299.99	1891.98	1620.74	1427.65	1283.41	1171.73	1082.83
50000	4435.68	3042.39	2346.93	1930.59	1653.82	1456.79	1309.60	1195.64	1104.93
51000	4524.39	3103.24	2393.86	1969.20	1686.89	1485.93	1335.79	1219.55	1127.03
52000	4613.10	3164.08	2440.80	2007.81	1719.97	1515.06	1361.99	1243.46	1149.12
53000	4701.82	3224.93	2487.74	2046.43	1753.05	1544.20	1388.18	1267.38	1171.22
54000	4790.53	3285.78	2534.68	2085.04	1786.12	1573.33	1414.37	1291.29	1193.32
55000	4879.24	3346.63	2581.62	2123.65	1819.20	1602.47	1440.56	1315.20	1215.42
56000	4967.96	3407.47	2628.56	2162.26	1852.27	1631.60	1466.75	1339.11	1237.52
57000	5056.67	3468.32	2675.49	2200.87	1885.35	1660.74	1492.95	1363.03	1259.62
58000	5145.38	3529.17	2722.43	2239.48	1918.43	1689.88	1519.14	1386.94	1281.72
59000	5234.10	3590.02	2769.37	2278.10	1951.50	1719.01	1545.33	1410.85	1303.81
60000	5322.81	3650.87	2816.31	2316.71	1984.58	1748.15	1571.52	1434.76	1325.91
61000	5411.52	3711.71	2863.25	2355.32	2017.66	1777.28	1597.71	1458.68	1348.01
62000	5500.24	3772.56	2910.19	2393.93	2050.73	1806.42	1623.91	1482.59	1370.11
63000	5588.95	3833.41	2957.13	2432.54	2083.81	1835.55	1650.10	1506.50	1392.21
64000	5677.67	3894.26	3004.06	2471.15	2116.88	1864.69	1676.29	1530.42	1414.31
65000	5766.38	3955.10	3051.00	2509.77	2149.96	1893.83	1702.48	1554.33	1436.40
66000	5855.09	4015.95	3097.94	2548.38	2183.04	1922.96	1728.67	1578.24	1458.50
67000	5943.81	4076.80	3144.88	2586.99	2216.11	1952.10	1754.87	1602.15	1480.60
68000	6032.52	4137.65	3191.82	2625.60	2249.19	1981.23	1781.06	1626.07	1502.70
69000	6121.23	4198.49	3238.76	2664.21	2282.27	2010.37	1807.25	1649.98	1524.80
70000	6209.95	4259.34	3285.69	2702.82	2315.34	2039.50	1833.44	1673.89	1546.90
75000	6653.51	4563.58	3520.39	2895.88	2480.72	2185.18	1964.40	1793.45	1657.39
80000	7097.08	4867.82	3755.08	3088.94	2646.10	2330.86	2095.36	1913.02	1767.88
100000	8871.35	6084.77	4693.85	3861.18	3307.63	2913.57	2619.20	2391.27	2209.85

MONTHLY PAYMENT 12%
NECESSARY TO AMORTIZE A LOAN

TERM AMOUNT	6 YEARS	7 YEARS	8 YEARS	9 YEARS	10 YEARS	11 YEARS	12 YEARS	13 YEARS	14 YEARS
$ 25	.49	.44	.41	.38	.36	.34	.33	.32	.31
50	.97	.88	.81	.76	.71	.68	.65	.63	.61
75	1.46	1.32	1.21	1.13	1.07	1.02	.98	.94	.91
100	1.94	1.75	1.61	1.51	1.42	1.36	1.30	1.26	1.22
200	3.88	3.50	3.22	3.01	2.84	2.71	2.60	2.51	2.43
300	5.82	5.25	4.83	4.51	4.26	4.06	3.89	3.76	3.64
400	7.76	7.00	6.44	6.01	5.68	5.41	5.19	5.01	4.86
500	9.70	8.75	8.05	7.52	7.10	6.76	6.48	6.26	6.07
600	11.64	10.50	9.66	9.02	8.51	8.11	7.78	7.51	7.28
700	13.58	12.25	11.27	10.52	9.93	9.46	9.08	8.76	8.50
800	15.52	14.00	12.88	12.02	11.35	10.81	10.37	10.01	9.71
900	17.46	15.75	14.49	13.52	12.77	12.16	11.67	11.26	10.92
1000	19.40	17.50	16.10	15.03	14.19	13.51	12.96	12.51	12.14
2000	38.80	35.00	32.19	30.05	28.37	27.02	25.92	25.02	24.27
3000	58.20	52.50	48.29	45.07	42.55	40.53	38.88	37.53	36.40
4000	77.60	70.00	64.38	60.09	56.73	54.03	51.84	50.04	48.53
5000	97.00	87.50	80.48	75.11	70.91	67.54	64.80	62.55	60.67
6000	116.40	104.99	96.57	90.13	85.09	81.05	77.76	75.05	72.80
7000	135.80	122.49	112.66	105.16	99.27	94.55	90.72	87.56	84.93
8000	155.20	139.99	128.76	120.18	113.45	108.06	103.68	100.07	97.06
9000	174.60	157.49	144.85	135.20	127.63	121.57	116.64	112.58	109.20
10000	194.00	174.99	160.95	150.22	141.81	135.08	129.60	125.09	121.33
15000	291.00	262.48	241.42	225.33	212.71	202.61	194.40	187.63	181.99
20000	388.00	349.97	321.89	300.43	283.61	270.15	259.20	250.17	242.65
25000	485.00	437.46	402.36	375.54	354.51	337.68	323.99	312.71	303.31
30000	582.00	524.95	482.83	450.65	425.41	405.22	388.79	375.25	363.97
35000	679.00	612.45	563.30	525.76	496.31	472.75	453.59	437.79	424.63
36000	698.40	629.94	579.40	540.78	510.49	486.26	466.55	450.30	436.77
37000	717.80	647.44	595.49	555.80	524.67	499.77	479.51	462.81	448.90
38000	737.20	664.94	611.59	570.82	538.86	513.27	492.47	475.32	461.03
39000	756.60	682.44	627.68	585.84	553.04	526.78	505.43	487.83	473.16
40000	776.00	699.94	643.77	600.86	567.22	540.29	518.39	500.33	485.29
41000	795.40	717.44	659.87	615.89	581.40	553.80	531.35	512.84	497.43
42000	814.80	734.93	675.96	630.91	595.58	567.30	544.30	525.35	509.56
43000	834.20	752.43	692.06	645.93	609.76	580.81	557.26	537.86	521.69
44000	853.60	769.93	708.15	660.95	623.94	594.32	570.22	550.37	533.82
45000	873.00	787.43	724.25	675.97	638.12	607.82	583.18	562.88	545.96
46000	892.40	804.93	740.34	690.99	652.30	621.33	596.14	575.38	558.09
47000	911.80	822.43	756.43	706.01	666.48	634.84	609.10	587.89	570.22
48000	931.20	839.92	772.53	721.04	680.66	648.34	622.06	600.40	582.35
49000	950.60	857.42	788.62	736.06	694.84	661.85	635.02	612.91	594.48
50000	970.00	874.92	804.72	751.08	709.02	675.36	647.98	625.42	606.62
51000	989.40	892.42	820.81	766.10	723.20	688.87	660.94	637.92	618.75
52000	1008.80	909.92	836.90	781.12	737.38	702.37	673.90	650.43	630.88
53000	1028.20	927.42	853.00	796.14	751.56	715.88	686.86	662.94	643.01
54000	1047.60	944.91	869.09	811.16	765.74	729.39	699.82	675.45	655.15
55000	1067.00	962.41	885.19	826.19	779.92	742.89	712.78	687.96	667.28
56000	1086.40	979.91	901.28	841.21	794.10	756.40	725.74	700.47	679.41
57000	1105.80	997.41	917.38	856.23	808.28	769.91	738.70	712.97	691.54
58000	1125.20	1014.91	933.47	871.25	822.46	783.42	751.66	725.48	703.67
59000	1144.60	1032.41	949.56	886.27	836.64	796.92	764.62	737.99	715.81
60000	1164.00	1049.90	965.66	901.29	850.82	810.43	777.58	750.50	727.94
61000	1183.40	1067.40	981.75	916.31	865.00	823.94	790.54	763.01	740.07
62000	1202.80	1084.90	997.85	931.34	879.18	837.44	803.50	775.52	752.20
63000	1222.20	1102.40	1013.94	946.36	893.36	850.95	816.45	788.02	764.34
64000	1241.60	1119.90	1030.04	961.38	907.54	864.46	829.41	800.53	776.47
65000	1261.00	1137.40	1046.13	976.40	921.72	877.96	842.37	813.04	788.60
66000	1280.40	1154.89	1062.22	991.42	935.90	891.47	855.33	825.55	800.73
67000	1299.80	1172.39	1078.32	1006.44	950.08	904.98	868.29	838.06	812.86
68000	1319.20	1189.89	1094.41	1021.47	964.26	918.49	881.25	850.56	825.00
69000	1338.60	1207.39	1110.51	1036.49	978.44	931.99	894.21	863.07	837.13
70000	1358.00	1224.89	1126.60	1051.51	992.62	945.50	907.17	875.58	849.26
75000	1455.00	1312.38	1207.07	1126.62	1063.53	1013.04	971.97	938.12	909.92
80000	1552.00	1399.87	1287.54	1201.72	1134.43	1080.57	1036.77	1000.66	970.58
100000	1940.00	1749.84	1609.43	1502.15	1418.03	1350.71	1295.96	1250.83	1213.23

MONTHLY PAYMENT
NECESSARY TO AMORTIZE A LOAN

TERM AMOUNT	15 YEARS	16 YEARS	17 YEARS	18 YEARS	19 YEARS	20 YEARS	21 YEARS	22 YEARS	23 YEARS
$ 25	.30	.29	.29	.28	.28	.28	.27	.27	.27
50	.60	.58	.57	.56	.55	.55	.54	.53	.53
75	.89	.87	.85	.84	.83	.82	.81	.80	.79
100	1.19	1.16	1.14	1.12	1.10	1.09	1.07	1.06	1.05
200	2.37	2.31	2.27	2.23	2.20	2.17	2.14	2.12	2.10
300	3.55	3.47	3.40	3.34	3.29	3.25	3.21	3.18	3.15
400	4.73	4.62	4.53	4.45	4.39	4.33	4.28	4.23	4.20
500	5.91	5.78	5.66	5.57	5.48	5.41	5.35	5.29	5.24
600	7.09	6.93	6.80	6.68	6.58	6.49	6.41	6.35	6.29
700	8.28	8.09	7.93	7.79	7.67	7.57	7.48	7.41	7.34
800	9.46	9.24	9.06	8.90	8.77	8.65	8.55	8.46	8.39
900	10.64	10.40	10.19	10.02	9.87	9.73	9.62	9.52	9.43
1000	11.82	11.55	11.32	11.13	10.96	10.81	10.69	10.58	10.48
2000	23.64	23.10	22.64	22.25	21.92	21.62	21.37	21.15	20.96
3000	35.45	34.65	33.96	33.38	32.87	32.43	32.05	31.72	31.44
4000	47.27	46.20	45.28	44.50	43.83	43.24	42.74	42.30	41.91
5000	59.09	57.75	56.60	55.63	54.78	54.05	53.42	52.87	52.39
6000	70.90	69.29	67.92	66.75	65.74	64.86	64.10	63.44	62.87
7000	82.72	80.84	79.24	77.87	76.69	75.67	74.79	74.02	73.34
8000	94.53	92.39	90.56	89.00	87.65	86.48	85.47	84.59	83.82
9000	106.35	103.94	101.88	100.12	98.61	97.29	96.15	95.16	94.30
10000	118.17	115.49	113.20	111.25	109.56	108.10	106.84	105.74	104.77
15000	177.25	173.23	169.80	166.87	164.34	162.15	160.25	158.60	157.16
20000	236.33	230.97	226.40	222.49	219.12	216.20	213.67	211.47	209.54
25000	295.41	288.71	283.00	278.11	273.89	270.25	267.08	264.33	261.93
30000	354.49	346.45	339.60	333.73	328.67	324.30	320.50	317.20	314.31
35000	413.57	404.20	396.20	389.35	383.45	378.35	373.92	370.06	366.69
36000	425.38	415.74	407.52	400.48	394.41	389.16	384.60	380.63	377.17
37000	437.20	427.29	418.84	411.60	405.36	399.97	395.28	391.21	387.65
38000	449.02	438.84	430.16	422.72	416.32	410.78	405.97	401.78	398.13
39000	460.83	450.39	441.48	433.85	427.27	421.58	416.65	412.35	408.60
40000	472.65	461.94	452.80	444.97	438.23	432.39	427.33	422.93	419.08
41000	484.46	473.48	464.12	456.10	449.18	443.20	438.02	433.50	429.56
42000	496.28	485.03	475.44	467.22	460.14	454.01	448.70	444.07	440.03
43000	508.10	496.58	486.76	478.34	471.09	464.82	459.38	454.64	450.51
44000	519.91	508.13	498.08	489.47	482.05	475.63	470.07	465.22	460.99
45000	531.73	519.68	509.40	500.59	493.01	486.44	480.75	475.79	471.46
46000	543.55	531.23	520.72	511.72	503.96	497.25	491.43	486.36	481.94
47000	555.36	542.77	532.04	522.84	514.92	508.06	502.11	496.94	492.42
48000	567.18	554.32	543.36	533.97	525.87	518.87	512.80	507.51	502.89
49000	578.99	565.87	554.68	545.09	536.83	529.68	523.48	518.08	513.37
50000	590.81	577.42	566.00	556.21	547.78	540.49	534.16	528.66	523.85
51000	602.63	588.97	577.32	567.34	558.74	551.30	544.85	539.23	534.32
52000	614.44	600.52	588.64	578.46	569.69	562.11	555.53	549.80	544.80
53000	626.26	612.06	599.96	589.59	580.65	572.92	566.21	560.37	555.28
54000	638.07	623.61	611.28	600.71	591.61	583.73	576.90	570.95	565.76
55000	649.89	635.16	622.60	611.84	602.56	594.54	587.58	581.52	576.23
56000	661.71	646.71	633.92	622.96	613.52	605.35	598.26	592.09	586.71
57000	673.52	658.26	645.24	634.08	624.47	616.16	608.95	602.67	597.19
58000	685.34	669.81	656.56	645.21	635.43	626.97	619.63	613.24	607.66
59000	697.15	681.35	667.88	656.33	646.38	637.78	630.31	623.81	618.14
60000	708.97	692.90	679.20	667.46	657.34	648.59	641.00	634.39	628.62
61000	720.79	704.45	690.52	678.58	668.29	659.40	651.68	644.96	639.09
62000	732.60	716.00	701.84	689.70	679.25	670.21	662.36	655.53	649.57
63000	744.42	727.55	713.16	700.83	690.21	681.02	673.05	666.10	660.05
64000	756.24	739.10	724.48	711.95	701.16	691.83	683.73	676.68	670.52
65000	768.05	750.64	735.80	723.08	712.12	702.64	694.41	687.25	681.00
66000	779.87	762.19	747.12	734.20	723.07	713.45	705.10	697.82	691.48
67000	791.68	773.74	758.44	745.33	734.03	724.26	715.78	708.40	701.95
68000	803.50	785.29	769.76	756.45	744.98	735.07	726.46	718.97	712.43
69000	815.32	796.84	781.08	767.57	755.94	745.88	737.14	729.54	722.91
70000	827.13	808.39	792.40	778.70	766.89	756.69	747.83	740.12	733.38
75000	886.21	866.13	849.00	834.32	821.67	810.74	801.24	792.98	785.77
80000	945.29	923.87	905.60	889.94	876.45	864.78	854.66	845.85	838.15
100000	1181.61	1154.83	1132.00	1112.42	1095.56	1080.98	1068.32	1057.31	1047.69

MONTHLY PAYMENT

NECESSARY TO AMORTIZE A LOAN

12%

TERM AMOUNT	24 YEARS	25 YEARS	26 YEARS	27 YEARS	28 YEARS	29 YEARS	30 YEARS	35 YEARS	40 YEARS
$ 25	.26	.26	.26	.26	.26	.26	.26	.25	.25
50	.52	.52	.52	.51	.51	.51	.51	.50	.50
75	.78	.78	.77	.77	.77	.76	.76	.75	.74
100	1.04	1.04	1.03	1.02	1.02	1.02	1.01	1.00	.99
200	2.08	2.07	2.06	2.04	2.03	2.03	2.02	1.99	1.98
300	3.12	3.10	3.08	3.06	3.05	3.04	3.02	2.98	2.96
400	4.16	4.13	4.11	4.08	4.06	4.05	4.03	3.98	3.95
500	5.20	5.16	5.13	5.10	5.08	5.06	5.04	4.97	4.93
600	6.24	6.20	6.16	6.12	6.09	6.07	6.04	5.96	5.92
700	7.28	7.23	7.18	7.14	7.11	7.08	7.05	6.95	6.90
800	8.32	8.26	8.21	8.16	8.12	8.09	8.06	7.95	7.89
900	9.36	9.29	9.23	9.18	9.14	9.10	9.06	8.94	8.87
1000	10.40	10.32	10.26	10.20	10.15	10.11	10.07	9.93	9.86
2000	20.79	20.64	20.51	20.40	20.30	20.21	20.13	19.86	19.71
3000	31.18	30.96	30.77	30.60	30.45	30.31	30.20	29.79	29.56
4000	41.58	41.28	41.02	40.79	40.59	40.42	40.26	39.71	39.41
5000	51.97	51.60	51.28	50.99	50.74	50.52	50.32	49.64	49.26
6000	62.36	61.92	61.53	61.19	60.89	60.62	60.39	59.57	59.12
7000	72.75	72.24	71.78	71.39	71.03	70.73	70.45	69.49	68.97
8000	83.15	82.56	82.04	81.58	81.18	80.83	80.52	79.42	78.82
9000	93.54	92.88	92.29	91.78	91.33	90.93	90.58	89.35	88.67
10000	103.93	103.19	102.55	101.98	101.48	101.03	100.64	99.27	98.52
15000	155.90	154.79	153.82	152.96	152.21	151.55	150.96	148.91	147.78
20000	207.86	206.38	205.09	203.95	202.95	202.06	201.28	198.54	197.04
25000	259.82	257.98	256.36	254.94	253.68	252.58	251.60	248.18	246.30
30000	311.79	309.57	307.63	305.92	304.42	303.09	301.92	297.81	295.56
35000	363.75	361.17	358.90	356.91	355.15	353.61	352.24	347.44	344.82
36000	374.14	371.49	369.16	367.11	365.30	363.71	362.30	357.37	354.67
37000	384.54	381.81	379.41	377.30	375.45	373.81	372.37	367.30	364.53
38000	394.93	392.13	389.67	387.50	385.60	383.92	382.43	377.22	374.38
39000	405.32	402.45	399.92	397.70	395.74	394.02	392.50	387.15	384.23
40000	415.71	412.76	410.17	407.90	405.89	404.12	402.56	397.08	394.08
41000	426.11	423.08	420.43	418.09	416.04	414.22	412.62	407.01	403.93
42000	436.50	433.40	430.68	428.29	426.18	424.33	422.69	416.93	413.79
43000	446.89	443.72	440.94	438.49	436.33	434.43	432.75	426.86	423.64
44000	457.29	454.04	451.19	448.69	446.48	444.53	442.82	436.79	433.49
45000	467.68	464.36	461.45	458.88	456.63	454.64	452.88	446.71	443.34
46000	478.07	474.68	471.70	469.08	466.77	464.74	462.94	456.64	453.19
47000	488.46	485.00	481.95	479.28	476.92	474.84	473.01	466.57	463.05
48000	498.86	495.32	492.21	489.48	487.07	484.94	483.07	476.49	472.90
49000	509.25	505.64	502.46	499.67	497.21	495.05	493.13	486.42	482.75
50000	519.64	515.95	512.72	509.87	507.36	505.15	503.20	496.35	492.60
51000	530.03	526.27	522.97	520.07	517.51	515.25	513.26	506.27	502.45
52000	540.43	536.59	533.23	530.26	527.66	525.36	523.33	516.20	512.30
53000	550.82	546.91	543.48	540.46	537.80	535.46	533.39	526.13	522.16
54000	561.21	557.23	553.73	550.66	547.95	545.56	543.45	536.05	532.01
55000	571.61	567.55	563.99	560.86	558.10	555.67	553.52	545.98	541.86
56000	582.00	577.87	574.24	571.05	568.24	565.77	563.58	555.91	551.71
57000	592.39	588.19	584.50	581.25	578.39	575.87	573.65	565.83	561.56
58000	602.78	598.51	594.75	591.45	588.54	585.97	583.71	575.76	571.42
59000	613.18	608.83	605.01	601.65	598.69	596.08	593.77	585.69	581.27
60000	623.57	619.14	615.26	611.84	608.83	606.18	603.84	595.61	591.12
61000	633.96	629.46	625.51	622.04	618.98	616.28	613.90	605.54	600.97
62000	644.35	639.78	635.77	632.24	629.13	626.39	623.97	615.47	610.82
63000	654.75	650.10	646.02	642.43	639.27	636.49	634.03	625.40	620.68
64000	665.14	660.42	656.28	652.63	649.42	646.59	644.09	635.32	630.53
65000	675.53	670.74	666.53	662.83	659.57	656.69	654.16	645.25	640.38
66000	685.93	681.06	676.79	673.03	669.72	666.80	664.22	655.18	650.23
67000	696.32	691.38	687.04	683.22	679.86	676.90	674.28	665.10	660.08
68000	706.71	701.70	697.29	693.42	690.01	687.00	684.35	675.03	669.94
69000	717.10	712.02	707.55	703.62	700.16	697.11	694.41	684.96	679.79
70000	727.50	722.33	717.80	713.82	710.30	707.21	704.48	694.88	689.64
75000	779.46	773.93	769.07	764.80	761.04	757.72	754.80	744.52	738.93
80000	831.42	825.52	820.34	815.79	811.78	808.24	805.11	794.15	788.16
100000	1039.28	1031.90	1025.43	1019.73	1014.72	1010.30	1006.39	992.69	985.20

87

12¼% MONTHLY PAYMENT
NECESSARY TO AMORTIZE A LOAN

TERM AMOUNT	1 YEAR	1½ YEARS	2 YEARS	2½ YEARS	3 YEARS	3½ YEARS	4 YEARS	4½ YEARS	5 YEARS
$ 25	2.23	1.53	1.18	.97	.83	.74	.66	.61	.56
50	4.45	3.05	2.36	1.94	1.66	1.47	1.32	1.21	1.12
75	6.67	4.58	3.53	2.91	2.49	2.20	1.98	1.81	1.67
100	8.89	6.10	4.71	3.88	3.32	2.93	2.64	2.41	2.23
200	17.77	12.20	9.41	7.75	6.64	5.86	5.27	4.81	4.45
300	26.65	18.29	14.12	11.62	9.96	8.78	7.90	7.21	6.67
400	35.53	24.39	18.82	15.49	13.28	11.71	10.53	9.62	8.89
500	44.42	30.48	23.53	19.37	16.60	14.63	13.16	12.02	11.11
600	53.30	36.58	28.23	23.24	19.92	17.56	15.79	14.42	13.34
700	62.18	42.68	32.94	27.11	23.24	20.48	18.42	16.83	15.56
800	71.06	48.77	37.64	30.98	26.56	23.41	21.05	19.23	17.78
900	79.95	54.87	42.35	34.86	29.88	26.33	23.68	21.63	20.00
1000	88.83	60.96	47.05	38.73	33.19	29.26	26.31	24.04	22.22
2000	177.65	121.92	94.10	77.45	66.38	58.51	52.62	48.07	44.44
3000	266.48	182.88	141.15	116.18	99.57	87.76	78.93	72.10	66.66
4000	355.30	243.84	188.20	154.90	132.76	117.01	105.24	96.13	88.88
5000	444.13	304.80	235.25	193.62	165.95	146.26	131.55	120.16	111.10
6000	532.95	365.75	282.30	232.35	199.14	175.51	157.86	144.19	133.32
7000	621.78	426.71	329.35	271.07	232.33	204.76	184.17	168.22	155.53
8000	710.60	487.67	376.40	309.80	265.52	234.01	210.47	192.25	177.75
9000	799.43	548.63	423.45	348.52	298.71	263.26	236.78	216.28	199.97
10000	888.25	609.59	470.50	387.24	331.90	292.51	263.09	240.31	222.19
15000	1332.38	914.38	705.75	580.86	497.85	438.77	394.63	360.47	333.28
20000	1776.50	1219.17	940.99	774.48	663.80	585.02	526.18	480.62	444.37
25000	2220.62	1523.96	1176.24	968.10	829.75	731.27	657.72	600.78	555.47
30000	2664.75	1828.75	1411.49	1161.72	995.70	877.53	789.26	720.93	666.56
35000	3108.87	2133.54	1646.74	1355.34	1161.65	1023.78	920.81	841.09	777.65
36000	3197.70	2194.50	1693.79	1394.06	1194.84	1053.03	947.11	865.12	799.87
37000	3286.52	2255.46	1740.84	1432.79	1228.03	1082.28	973.42	889.15	822.09
38000	3375.35	2316.42	1787.88	1471.51	1261.22	1111.53	999.73	913.18	844.31
39000	3464.17	2377.37	1834.93	1510.24	1294.41	1140.78	1026.04	937.21	866.53
40000	3552.99	2438.33	1881.98	1548.96	1327.60	1170.03	1052.35	961.24	888.74
41000	3641.82	2499.29	1929.03	1587.68	1360.79	1199.29	1078.66	985.28	910.96
42000	3730.64	2560.25	1976.08	1626.41	1393.97	1228.54	1104.97	1009.31	933.18
43000	3819.47	2621.21	2023.13	1665.13	1427.16	1257.79	1131.27	1033.34	955.40
44000	3908.29	2682.16	2070.18	1703.86	1460.35	1287.04	1157.58	1057.37	977.62
45000	3997.12	2743.12	2117.23	1742.58	1493.54	1316.29	1183.89	1081.40	999.84
46000	4085.94	2804.08	2164.28	1781.30	1526.73	1345.54	1210.20	1105.43	1022.05
47000	4174.77	2865.04	2211.33	1820.03	1559.92	1374.79	1236.51	1129.46	1044.27
48000	4263.59	2926.00	2258.38	1858.75	1593.11	1404.04	1262.82	1153.49	1066.49
49000	4352.42	2986.96	2305.43	1897.47	1626.30	1433.29	1289.13	1177.52	1088.71
50000	4441.24	3047.91	2352.48	1936.20	1659.49	1462.54	1315.43	1201.55	1110.93
51000	4530.07	3108.87	2399.53	1974.92	1692.68	1491.79	1341.74	1225.59	1133.15
52000	4618.89	3169.83	2446.58	2013.65	1725.87	1521.04	1368.05	1249.62	1155.37
53000	4707.72	3230.79	2493.63	2052.37	1759.06	1550.29	1394.36	1273.65	1177.58
54000	4796.54	3291.75	2540.68	2091.09	1792.25	1579.55	1420.67	1297.68	1199.80
55000	4885.37	3352.70	2587.73	2129.82	1825.44	1608.80	1446.98	1321.71	1222.02
56000	4974.19	3413.66	2634.78	2168.54	1858.63	1638.05	1473.29	1345.74	1244.24
57000	5063.02	3474.62	2681.82	2207.27	1891.82	1667.30	1499.60	1369.77	1266.46
58000	5151.84	3535.58	2728.87	2245.99	1925.01	1696.55	1525.90	1393.80	1288.68
59000	5240.66	3596.54	2775.92	2284.71	1958.20	1725.80	1552.21	1417.83	1310.90
60000	5329.49	3657.50	2822.97	2323.44	1991.39	1755.05	1578.52	1441.86	1333.11
61000	5418.31	3718.45	2870.02	2362.16	2024.58	1784.30	1604.83	1465.89	1355.33
62000	5507.14	3779.41	2917.07	2400.88	2057.77	1813.55	1631.14	1489.93	1377.55
63000	5595.96	3840.37	2964.12	2439.61	2090.96	1842.80	1657.45	1513.96	1399.77
64000	5684.79	3901.33	3011.17	2478.33	2124.15	1872.05	1683.76	1537.99	1421.99
65000	5773.61	3962.29	3058.22	2517.06	2157.34	1901.30	1710.06	1562.02	1444.21
66000	5862.44	4023.24	3105.27	2555.78	2190.53	1930.55	1736.37	1586.05	1466.42
67000	5951.26	4084.20	3152.32	2594.50	2223.72	1959.80	1762.68	1610.08	1488.64
68000	6040.09	4145.16	3199.37	2633.23	2256.91	1989.06	1788.99	1634.11	1510.86
69000	6128.91	4206.12	3246.42	2671.95	2290.10	2018.31	1815.30	1658.14	1533.08
70000	6217.74	4267.08	3293.47	2710.68	2323.29	2047.56	1841.61	1682.17	1555.30
75000	6661.86	4571.87	3528.71	2904.29	2489.24	2193.81	1973.15	1802.33	1666.39
80000	7105.98	4876.66	3763.96	3097.91	2655.19	2340.06	2104.69	1922.48	1777.48
100000	8882.48	6095.82	4704.95	3872.39	3318.98	2925.08	2630.86	2403.10	2221.85

88

MONTHLY PAYMENT 12¼%
NECESSARY TO AMORTIZE A LOAN

TERM AMOUNT	6 YEARS	7 YEARS	8 YEARS	9 YEARS	10 YEARS	11 YEARS	12 YEARS	13 YEARS	14 YEARS
$ 25	.49	.45	.41	.38	.36	.35	.33	.32	.31
50	.98	.89	.82	.76	.72	.69	.66	.64	.62
75	1.47	1.33	1.22	1.14	1.08	1.03	.99	.95	.93
100	1.96	1.77	1.63	1.52	1.44	1.37	1.32	1.27	1.23
200	3.91	3.53	3.25	3.04	2.87	2.73	2.63	2.54	2.46
300	5.86	5.29	4.87	4.55	4.30	4.10	3.94	3.80	3.69
400	7.81	7.06	6.49	6.07	5.73	5.46	5.25	5.07	4.92
500	9.77	8.82	8.12	7.58	7.16	6.83	6.56	6.33	6.15
600	11.72	10.58	9.74	9.10	8.60	8.19	7.87	7.60	7.37
700	13.67	12.34	11.36	10.61	10.03	9.56	9.18	8.86	8.60
800	15.62	14.11	12.98	12.13	11.46	10.92	10.49	10.13	9.83
900	17.58	15.87	14.61	13.64	12.89	12.29	11.80	11.39	11.06
1000	19.53	17.63	16.23	15.16	14.32	13.65	13.11	12.66	12.29
2000	39.05	35.26	32.45	30.32	28.64	27.30	26.21	25.31	24.57
3000	58.58	52.88	48.68	45.47	42.96	40.95	39.31	37.97	36.85
4000	78.10	70.51	64.90	60.63	57.27	54.59	52.42	50.62	49.13
5000	97.62	88.13	81.13	75.78	71.59	68.24	65.52	63.28	61.41
6000	117.15	105.76	97.35	90.94	85.91	81.89	78.62	75.93	73.70
7000	136.67	123.38	113.58	106.09	100.23	95.54	91.73	88.59	85.98
8000	156.19	141.01	129.80	121.25	114.54	109.18	104.83	101.24	98.26
9000	175.72	158.63	146.03	136.40	128.86	122.83	117.93	113.90	110.54
10000	195.24	176.26	162.25	151.56	143.18	136.48	131.04	126.55	122.82
15000	292.86	264.38	243.37	227.33	214.77	204.72	196.55	189.83	184.23
20000	390.47	352.51	324.50	303.11	286.35	272.95	262.07	253.10	245.64
25000	488.09	440.64	405.62	378.89	357.94	341.19	327.58	316.38	307.05
30000	585.71	528.76	486.74	454.66	429.53	409.43	393.10	379.65	368.46
35000	683.33	616.89	567.87	530.44	501.11	477.67	458.61	442.93	429.87
36000	702.85	634.51	584.09	545.59	515.43	491.31	471.72	455.58	442.15
37000	722.37	652.14	600.32	560.75	529.75	504.96	484.82	468.24	454.43
38000	741.90	669.76	616.54	575.90	544.07	518.61	497.92	480.89	466.72
39000	761.42	687.39	632.76	591.06	558.38	532.26	511.03	493.55	479.00
40000	780.94	705.01	648.99	606.22	572.70	545.90	524.13	506.20	491.28
41000	800.47	722.64	665.21	621.37	587.02	559.55	537.23	518.86	503.56
42000	819.99	740.27	681.44	636.53	601.34	573.20	550.33	531.51	515.84
43000	839.51	757.89	697.66	651.68	615.65	586.85	563.44	544.16	528.13
44000	859.04	775.52	713.89	666.84	629.97	600.49	576.54	556.82	540.41
45000	878.56	793.14	730.11	681.99	644.29	614.14	589.64	569.47	552.69
46000	898.08	810.77	746.34	697.15	658.60	627.79	602.75	582.13	564.97
47000	917.61	828.39	762.56	712.30	672.92	641.44	615.85	594.78	577.25
48000	937.13	846.02	778.79	727.46	687.24	655.08	628.95	607.44	589.53
49000	956.65	863.64	795.01	742.61	701.56	668.73	642.06	620.09	601.82
50000	976.18	881.27	811.24	757.77	715.87	682.38	655.16	632.75	614.10
51000	995.70	898.89	827.46	772.92	730.19	696.03	668.26	645.40	626.38
52000	1015.23	916.52	843.68	788.08	744.51	709.67	681.37	658.06	638.66
53000	1034.75	934.14	859.91	803.23	758.83	723.32	694.47	670.71	650.94
54000	1054.27	951.77	876.13	818.39	773.14	736.97	707.57	683.37	663.23
55000	1073.80	969.39	892.36	833.54	787.46	750.62	720.67	696.02	675.51
56000	1093.32	987.02	908.58	848.70	801.78	764.26	733.78	708.68	687.79
57000	1112.84	1004.64	924.81	863.85	816.10	777.91	746.88	721.33	700.07
58000	1132.37	1022.27	941.03	879.01	830.41	791.56	759.98	733.99	712.35
59000	1151.89	1039.89	957.26	894.17	844.73	805.21	773.09	746.64	724.64
60000	1171.41	1057.52	973.48	909.32	859.05	818.85	786.19	759.30	736.92
61000	1190.94	1075.15	989.71	924.48	873.37	832.50	799.29	771.95	749.20
62000	1210.46	1092.77	1005.93	939.63	887.68	846.15	812.40	784.61	761.48
63000	1229.98	1110.40	1022.16	954.79	902.00	859.80	825.50	797.26	773.76
64000	1249.51	1128.02	1038.38	969.94	916.32	873.44	838.60	809.92	786.04
65000	1269.03	1145.65	1054.60	985.10	930.64	887.09	851.71	822.57	798.33
66000	1288.55	1163.27	1070.83	1000.25	944.95	900.74	864.81	835.23	810.61
67000	1308.08	1180.90	1087.05	1015.41	959.27	914.38	877.91	847.88	822.89
68000	1327.60	1198.52	1103.28	1030.56	973.59	928.03	891.01	860.54	835.17
69000	1347.12	1216.15	1119.50	1045.72	987.90	941.68	904.12	873.19	847.45
70000	1366.65	1233.77	1135.73	1060.87	1002.22	955.33	917.22	885.85	859.74
75000	1464.26	1321.90	1216.85	1136.65	1073.81	1023.56	982.74	949.12	921.14
80000	1561.88	1410.02	1297.97	1212.43	1145.40	1091.80	1048.25	1012.40	982.55
100000	1952.35	1762.53	1622.47	1515.53	1431.74	1364.75	1310.31	1265.49	1228.19

MONTHLY PAYMENT
NECESSARY TO AMORTIZE A LOAN

TERM AMOUNT	15 YEARS	16 YEARS	17 YEARS	18 YEARS	19 YEARS	20 YEARS	21 YEARS	22 YEARS	23 YEARS
$ 25	.30	.30	.29	.29	.28	.28	.28	.27	.27
50	.60	.59	.58	.57	.56	.55	.55	.54	.54
75	.90	.88	.87	.85	.84	.83	.82	.81	.80
100	1.20	1.18	1.15	1.13	1.12	1.10	1.09	1.08	1.07
200	2.40	2.35	2.30	2.26	2.23	2.20	2.18	2.15	2.13
300	3.60	3.52	3.45	3.39	3.34	3.30	3.26	3.23	3.20
400	4.79	4.69	4.60	4.52	4.45	4.40	4.35	4.30	4.26
500	5.99	5.86	5.74	5.65	5.56	5.49	5.43	5.38	5.33
600	7.19	7.03	6.89	6.78	6.68	6.59	6.52	6.45	6.39
700	8.38	8.20	8.04	7.90	7.79	7.69	7.60	7.52	7.46
800	9.58	9.37	9.19	9.03	8.90	8.79	8.69	8.60	8.52
900	10.78	10.54	10.34	10.16	10.01	9.88	9.77	9.67	9.59
1000	11.97	11.71	11.48	11.29	11.12	10.98	10.86	10.75	10.65
2000	23.94	23.41	22.96	22.57	22.24	21.96	21.71	21.49	21.30
3000	35.91	35.12	34.44	33.86	33.36	32.93	32.56	32.23	31.95
4000	47.88	46.82	45.92	45.14	44.48	43.91	43.41	42.98	42.60
5000	59.85	58.52	57.39	56.43	55.60	54.88	54.26	53.72	53.25
6000	71.82	70.23	68.87	67.71	66.72	65.86	65.11	64.46	63.90
7000	83.79	81.93	80.35	79.00	77.83	76.83	75.96	75.20	74.54
8000	95.75	93.63	91.83	90.28	88.95	87.81	86.81	85.95	85.19
9000	107.72	105.34	103.31	101.57	100.07	98.78	97.66	96.69	95.84
10000	119.69	117.04	114.78	112.85	111.19	109.76	108.51	107.43	106.49
15000	179.53	175.56	172.17	169.28	166.78	164.63	162.77	161.14	159.73
20000	239.38	234.08	229.56	225.70	222.38	219.51	217.02	214.86	212.97
25000	299.22	292.59	286.95	282.12	277.97	274.38	271.27	268.57	266.22
30000	359.06	351.11	344.34	338.55	333.56	329.26	325.53	322.28	319.46
35000	418.91	409.63	401.73	394.97	389.15	384.13	379.78	376.00	372.70
36000	430.88	421.33	413.21	406.25	400.27	395.11	390.63	386.74	383.35
37000	442.84	433.04	424.69	417.54	411.39	406.08	401.48	397.48	394.00
38000	454.81	444.74	436.17	428.82	422.51	417.06	412.33	408.22	404.65
39000	466.78	456.45	447.64	440.11	433.63	428.03	423.18	418.97	415.30
40000	478.75	468.15	459.12	451.39	444.75	439.01	434.03	429.71	425.94
41000	490.72	479.85	470.60	462.68	455.87	449.98	444.88	440.45	436.59
42000	502.69	491.56	482.08	473.96	466.98	460.96	455.73	451.20	447.24
43000	514.66	503.26	493.56	485.25	478.10	471.93	466.58	461.94	457.89
44000	526.62	514.96	505.03	496.53	489.22	482.91	477.44	472.68	468.54
45000	538.59	526.67	516.51	507.82	500.34	493.88	488.29	483.42	479.19
46000	550.56	538.37	527.99	519.10	511.46	504.86	499.14	494.17	489.83
47000	562.53	550.07	539.47	530.39	522.58	515.83	509.99	504.91	500.48
48000	574.50	561.78	550.95	541.67	533.69	526.81	520.84	515.65	511.13
49000	586.47	573.48	562.42	552.96	544.81	537.78	531.69	526.39	521.78
50000	598.44	585.18	573.90	564.24	555.93	548.76	542.54	537.14	532.43
51000	610.40	596.89	585.38	575.53	567.05	559.73	553.39	547.88	543.08
52000	622.37	608.59	596.86	586.81	578.17	570.71	564.24	558.62	553.73
53000	634.34	620.30	608.33	598.09	589.29	581.68	575.09	569.36	564.37
54000	646.31	632.00	619.81	609.38	600.41	592.66	585.94	580.11	575.02
55000	658.28	643.70	631.29	620.66	611.52	603.63	596.79	590.85	585.67
56000	670.25	655.41	642.77	631.95	622.64	614.61	607.64	601.59	596.32
57000	682.22	667.11	654.25	643.23	633.76	625.58	618.49	612.33	606.97
58000	694.19	678.81	665.72	654.52	644.88	636.56	629.35	623.08	617.62
59000	706.15	690.52	677.20	665.80	656.00	647.53	640.20	633.82	628.26
60000	718.12	702.22	688.68	677.09	667.12	658.51	651.05	644.56	638.91
61000	730.09	713.92	700.16	688.37	678.24	669.48	661.90	655.31	649.56
62000	742.06	725.63	711.64	699.66	689.35	680.46	672.75	666.05	660.21
63000	754.03	737.33	723.11	710.94	700.47	691.43	683.60	676.79	670.86
64000	766.00	749.03	734.59	722.23	711.59	702.41	694.45	687.53	681.51
65000	777.97	760.74	746.07	733.51	722.71	713.38	705.30	698.28	692.16
66000	789.93	772.44	757.55	744.80	733.83	724.36	716.15	709.02	702.80
67000	801.90	784.15	769.03	756.08	744.95	735.33	727.00	719.76	713.45
68000	813.87	795.85	780.50	767.37	756.07	746.31	737.85	730.50	724.10
69000	825.84	807.55	791.98	778.65	767.18	757.28	748.70	741.25	734.75
70000	837.81	819.26	803.46	789.93	778.30	768.26	759.55	751.99	745.40
75000	897.65	877.77	860.85	846.36	833.90	823.13	813.81	805.70	798.64
80000	957.49	936.29	918.24	902.78	889.49	878.01	868.06	859.42	851.88
100000	1196.87	1170.36	1147.80	1128.48	1111.86	1097.51	1085.07	1074.27	1064.85

MONTHLY PAYMENT 12¼%
NECESSARY TO AMORTIZE A LOAN

TERM AMOUNT	24 YEARS	25 YEARS	26 YEARS	27 YEARS	28 YEARS	29 YEARS	30 YEARS	35 YEARS	40 YEARS
$ 25	.27	.27	.27	.26	.26	.26	.26	.26	.26
50	.53	.53	.53	.52	.52	.52	.52	.51	.51
75	.80	.79	.79	.78	.78	.78	.77	.76	.76
100	1.06	1.05	1.05	1.04	1.04	1.03	1.03	1.02	1.01
200	2.12	2.10	2.09	2.08	2.07	2.06	2.05	2.03	2.01
300	3.17	3.15	3.13	3.12	3.10	3.09	3.08	3.04	3.02
400	4.23	4.20	4.18	4.16	4.14	4.12	4.10	4.05	4.02
500	5.29	5.25	5.22	5.19	5.17	5.15	5.13	5.06	5.03
600	6.34	6.30	6.26	6.23	6.20	6.18	6.15	6.07	6.03
700	7.40	7.35	7.31	7.27	7.23	7.20	7.18	7.09	7.04
800	8.46	8.40	8.35	8.31	8.27	8.23	8.20	8.10	8.04
900	9.51	9.45	9.39	9.34	9.30	9.26	9.23	9.11	9.04
1000	10.57	10.50	10.44	10.38	10.33	10.29	10.25	10.12	10.05
2000	21.14	20.99	20.87	20.76	20.66	20.57	20.50	20.23	20.09
3000	31.70	31.49	31.30	31.13	30.99	30.86	30.74	30.35	30.14
4000	42.27	41.98	41.73	41.51	41.31	41.14	40.99	40.46	40.18
5000	52.84	52.48	52.16	51.88	51.64	51.43	51.24	50.58	50.22
6000	63.40	62.97	62.59	62.26	61.97	61.71	61.48	60.69	60.27
7000	73.97	73.46	73.02	72.64	72.30	72.00	71.73	70.81	70.31
8000	84.53	83.96	83.45	83.01	82.62	82.28	81.98	80.92	80.35
9000	95.10	94.45	93.89	93.39	92.95	92.56	92.22	91.04	90.40
10000	105.67	104.95	104.32	103.76	103.28	102.85	102.47	101.15	100.44
15000	158.50	157.42	156.47	155.64	154.91	154.27	153.70	151.73	150.66
20000	211.33	209.89	208.63	207.52	206.55	205.69	204.94	202.30	200.88
25000	264.16	262.36	260.78	259.40	258.18	257.11	256.17	252.88	251.09
30000	316.99	314.83	312.94	311.28	309.82	308.53	307.40	303.45	301.31
35000	369.82	367.30	365.10	363.16	361.46	359.96	358.63	354.02	351.53
36000	380.39	377.80	375.53	373.53	371.78	370.24	368.88	364.14	361.57
37000	390.96	388.29	385.96	383.91	382.11	380.52	379.13	374.25	371.62
38000	401.52	398.79	396.39	394.29	392.44	390.81	389.37	384.37	381.66
39000	412.09	409.28	406.82	404.66	402.76	401.09	399.62	394.48	391.70
40000	422.65	419.78	417.25	415.04	413.09	411.38	409.87	404.60	401.75
41000	433.22	430.27	427.68	425.41	423.42	421.66	420.11	414.71	411.79
42000	443.79	440.76	438.12	435.79	433.75	431.95	430.36	424.83	421.83
43000	454.35	451.26	448.55	446.17	444.07	442.23	440.61	434.94	431.88
44000	464.92	461.75	458.98	456.54	454.40	452.51	450.85	445.06	441.92
45000	475.49	472.25	469.41	466.92	464.73	462.80	461.10	455.17	451.96
46000	486.05	482.74	479.84	477.29	475.05	473.08	471.35	465.29	462.01
47000	496.62	493.24	490.27	487.67	485.38	483.37	481.59	475.40	472.05
48000	507.18	503.73	500.70	498.04	495.71	493.65	491.84	485.52	482.09
49000	517.75	514.22	511.13	508.42	506.04	503.94	502.09	495.63	492.14
50000	528.32	524.72	521.56	518.80	516.36	514.22	512.33	505.75	502.18
51000	538.88	535.21	532.00	529.17	526.69	524.50	522.58	515.86	512.23
52000	549.45	545.71	542.43	539.55	537.02	534.79	532.83	525.98	522.27
53000	560.02	556.20	552.86	549.92	547.34	545.07	543.07	536.09	532.31
54000	570.58	566.70	563.29	560.30	557.67	555.36	553.32	546.20	542.36
55000	581.15	577.19	573.72	570.68	568.00	565.64	563.57	556.32	552.40
56000	591.71	587.68	584.15	581.05	578.33	575.93	573.81	566.43	562.44
57000	602.28	598.18	594.58	591.43	588.65	586.21	584.06	576.55	572.49
58000	612.85	608.67	605.01	601.80	598.98	596.49	594.31	586.66	582.53
59000	623.41	619.17	615.45	612.18	609.31	606.78	604.55	596.78	592.57
60000	633.98	629.66	625.88	622.55	619.63	617.06	614.80	606.89	602.62
61000	644.55	640.16	636.31	632.93	629.96	627.35	625.05	617.01	612.66
62000	655.11	650.65	646.74	643.31	640.29	637.63	635.29	627.12	622.70
63000	665.68	661.14	657.17	653.68	650.62	647.92	645.54	637.24	632.75
64000	676.24	671.64	667.60	664.06	660.94	658.20	655.79	647.35	642.79
65000	686.81	682.13	678.03	674.43	671.27	668.48	666.03	657.47	652.84
66000	697.38	692.63	688.46	684.81	681.60	678.77	676.28	667.58	662.88
67000	707.94	703.12	698.89	695.18	691.92	689.05	686.53	677.70	672.92
68000	718.51	713.62	709.33	705.56	702.25	699.34	696.77	687.81	682.97
69000	729.07	724.11	719.76	715.94	712.58	709.62	707.02	697.93	693.01
70000	739.64	734.60	730.19	726.31	722.91	719.91	717.26	708.04	703.05
75000	792.47	787.08	782.34	778.19	774.54	771.33	768.50	758.62	753.27
80000	845.30	839.55	834.50	830.07	826.18	822.75	819.73	809.19	803.49
100000	1056.63	1049.43	1043.12	1037.59	1032.72	1028.44	1024.66	1011.49	1004.36

91

12½% MONTHLY PAYMENT
NECESSARY TO AMORTIZE A LOAN

TERM AMOUNT	1 YEAR	1½ YEARS	2 YEARS	2½ YEARS	3 YEARS	3½ YEARS	4 YEARS	4½ YEARS	5 YEARS
$ 25	2.23	1.53	1.18	.98	.84	.74	.67	.61	.56
50	4.45	3.06	2.36	1.95	1.67	1.47	1.33	1.21	1.12
75	6.68	4.59	3.54	2.92	2.50	2.21	1.99	1.82	1.68
100	8.90	6.11	4.72	3.89	3.34	2.94	2.65	2.42	2.24
200	17.79	12.22	9.44	7.77	6.67	5.88	5.29	4.83	4.47
300	26.69	18.33	14.15	11.66	10.00	8.81	7.93	7.25	6.71
400	35.58	24.43	18.87	15.54	13.33	11.75	10.58	9.66	8.94
500	44.47	30.54	23.59	19.42	16.66	14.69	13.22	12.08	11.17
600	53.37	36.65	28.30	23.31	19.99	17.62	15.86	14.49	13.41
700	62.26	42.75	33.02	27.19	23.32	20.56	18.50	16.91	15.64
800	71.15	48.86	37.73	31.07	26.65	23.50	21.15	19.32	17.88
900	80.05	54.97	42.45	34.96	29.98	26.43	23.79	21.74	20.11
1000	88.94	61.07	47.17	38.84	33.31	29.37	26.43	24.15	22.34
2000	177.88	122.14	94.33	77.68	66.61	58.74	52.86	48.30	44.68
3000	266.81	183.21	141.49	116.51	99.92	88.10	79.28	72.45	67.02
4000	355.75	244.28	188.65	155.35	133.22	117.47	105.71	96.60	89.36
5000	444.69	305.35	235.81	194.19	166.52	146.83	132.13	120.75	111.70
6000	533.62	366.42	282.97	233.02	199.83	176.20	158.56	144.90	134.04
7000	622.56	427.49	330.13	271.86	233.13	205.57	184.98	169.05	156.38
8000	711.49	488.55	377.29	310.69	266.43	234.93	211.41	193.20	178.71
9000	800.43	549.62	424.45	349.53	299.74	264.30	237.83	217.35	201.05
10000	889.37	610.69	471.61	388.37	333.04	293.66	264.26	241.50	223.39
15000	1334.05	916.03	707.41	582.55	499.56	440.49	396.39	362.25	335.09
20000	1778.73	1221.38	943.22	776.73	666.07	587.32	528.51	483.00	446.78
25000	2223.41	1526.72	1179.02	970.91	832.59	734.15	660.64	603.74	558.47
30000	2668.09	1832.06	1414.82	1165.09	999.11	880.98	792.77	724.49	670.17
35000	3112.77	2137.41	1650.62	1359.27	1165.62	1027.81	924.90	845.24	781.86
36000	3201.70	2198.48	1697.79	1398.10	1198.93	1057.18	951.32	869.39	804.20
37000	3290.64	2259.55	1744.95	1436.94	1232.23	1086.54	977.75	893.54	826.54
38000	3379.57	2320.61	1792.11	1475.78	1265.53	1115.91	1004.17	917.69	848.88
39000	3468.51	2381.68	1839.27	1514.61	1298.84	1145.28	1030.60	941.84	871.22
40000	3557.45	2442.75	1886.43	1553.45	1332.14	1174.64	1057.02	965.99	893.55
41000	3646.38	2503.82	1933.59	1592.29	1365.44	1204.01	1083.45	990.14	915.89
42000	3735.32	2564.89	1980.75	1631.12	1398.75	1233.37	1109.87	1014.29	938.23
43000	3824.25	2625.96	2027.91	1669.96	1432.05	1262.74	1136.30	1038.43	960.57
44000	3913.19	2687.03	2075.07	1708.79	1465.35	1292.11	1162.72	1062.58	982.91
45000	4002.13	2748.09	2122.23	1747.63	1498.66	1321.47	1189.15	1086.73	1005.25
46000	4091.06	2809.16	2169.39	1786.47	1531.96	1350.84	1215.58	1110.88	1027.59
47000	4180.00	2870.23	2216.55	1825.30	1565.26	1380.20	1242.00	1135.03	1049.93
48000	4268.93	2931.30	2263.71	1864.14	1598.57	1409.57	1268.43	1159.18	1072.26
49000	4357.87	2992.37	2310.87	1902.97	1631.87	1438.94	1294.85	1183.33	1094.60
50000	4446.81	3053.44	2358.03	1941.81	1665.18	1468.30	1321.28	1207.48	1116.94
51000	4535.74	3114.51	2405.19	1980.65	1698.48	1497.67	1347.70	1231.63	1139.28
52000	4624.68	3175.58	2452.35	2019.48	1731.78	1527.03	1374.13	1255.78	1161.62
53000	4713.61	3236.64	2499.51	2058.32	1765.09	1556.40	1400.55	1279.93	1183.96
54000	4802.55	3297.71	2546.68	2097.15	1798.39	1585.77	1426.98	1304.08	1206.30
55000	4891.49	3358.78	2593.84	2135.99	1831.69	1615.13	1453.40	1328.23	1228.64
56000	4980.42	3419.85	2641.00	2174.83	1865.00	1644.50	1479.83	1352.38	1250.97
57000	5069.36	3480.92	2688.16	2213.66	1898.30	1673.86	1506.26	1376.53	1273.31
58000	5158.29	3541.99	2735.32	2252.50	1931.60	1703.23	1532.68	1400.68	1295.65
59000	5247.23	3603.06	2782.48	2291.33	1964.91	1732.60	1559.11	1424.83	1317.99
60000	5336.17	3664.12	2829.64	2330.17	1998.21	1761.96	1585.53	1448.98	1340.33
61000	5425.10	3725.19	2876.80	2369.01	2031.51	1791.33	1611.96	1473.13	1362.67
62000	5514.04	3786.26	2923.96	2407.84	2064.82	1820.69	1638.38	1497.28	1385.01
63000	5602.97	3847.33	2971.12	2446.68	2098.12	1850.06	1664.81	1521.43	1407.35
64000	5691.91	3908.40	3018.28	2485.52	2131.42	1879.43	1691.23	1545.57	1429.68
65000	5780.85	3969.47	3065.44	2524.35	2164.73	1908.79	1717.66	1569.72	1452.02
66000	5869.78	4030.54	3112.60	2563.19	2198.03	1938.16	1744.08	1593.87	1474.36
67000	5958.72	4091.61	3159.76	2602.02	2231.33	1967.52	1770.51	1618.02	1496.70
68000	6047.65	4152.67	3206.92	2640.86	2264.64	1996.89	1796.94	1642.17	1519.04
69000	6136.59	4213.74	3254.08	2679.70	2297.94	2026.25	1823.36	1666.32	1541.38
70000	6225.53	4274.81	3301.24	2718.53	2331.24	2055.62	1849.79	1690.47	1563.72
75000	6670.21	4580.15	3537.05	2912.71	2497.76	2202.45	1981.91	1811.22	1675.41
80000	7114.89	4885.50	3772.85	3106.89	2664.28	2349.28	2114.04	1931.97	1787.10
100000	8893.61	6106.87	4716.06	3883.61	3330.35	2936.60	2642.55	2414.96	2233.88

92

MONTHLY PAYMENT 12½%
NECESSARY TO AMORTIZE A LOAN

TERM AMOUNT	6 YEARS	7 YEARS	8 YEARS	9 YEARS	10 YEARS	11 YEARS	12 YEARS	13 YEARS	14 YEARS
$ 25	.50	.45	.41	.39	.37	.35	.34	.33	.32
50	.99	.89	.82	.77	.73	.69	.67	.65	.63
75	1.48	1.34	1.23	1.15	1.09	1.04	1.00	.97	.94
100	1.97	1.78	1.64	1.53	1.45	1.38	1.33	1.29	1.25
200	3.93	3.56	3.28	3.06	2.90	2.76	2.65	2.57	2.49
300	5.90	5.33	4.91	4.59	4.34	4.14	3.98	3.85	3.73
400	7.86	7.11	6.55	6.12	5.79	5.52	5.30	5.13	4.98
500	9.83	8.88	8.18	7.65	7.23	6.90	6.63	6.41	6.22
600	11.79	10.66	9.82	9.18	8.68	8.28	7.95	7.69	7.46
700	13.76	12.43	11.45	10.71	10.12	9.66	9.28	8.97	8.71
800	15.72	14.21	13.09	12.24	11.57	11.04	10.60	10.25	9.95
900	17.69	15.98	14.72	13.77	13.01	12.41	11.93	11.53	11.19
1000	19.65	17.76	16.36	15.29	14.46	13.79	13.25	12.81	12.44
2000	39.30	35.51	32.72	30.58	28.92	27.58	26.50	25.61	24.87
3000	58.95	53.26	49.07	45.87	43.37	41.37	39.75	38.41	37.30
4000	78.59	71.02	65.43	61.16	57.83	55.16	52.99	51.21	49.73
5000	98.24	88.77	81.78	76.45	72.28	68.95	66.24	64.02	62.17
6000	117.89	106.52	98.14	91.74	86.74	82.74	79.49	76.82	74.60
7000	137.54	124.27	114.49	107.03	101.19	96.52	92.74	89.62	87.03
8000	157.18	142.03	130.85	122.32	115.65	110.31	105.98	102.42	99.46
9000	176.83	159.78	147.20	137.61	130.10	124.10	119.23	115.22	111.89
10000	196.48	177.53	163.56	152.90	144.56	137.89	132.48	128.03	124.33
15000	294.71	266.29	245.34	229.35	216.83	206.83	198.71	192.04	186.49
20000	392.95	355.06	327.11	305.80	289.11	275.77	264.95	256.05	248.65
25000	491.19	443.82	408.89	382.24	361.38	344.72	331.19	320.06	310.81
30000	589.42	532.58	490.67	458.69	433.66	413.66	397.42	384.07	372.97
35000	687.66	621.34	572.44	535.14	505.93	482.60	463.66	448.08	435.13
36000	707.31	639.10	588.80	550.43	520.39	496.39	476.91	460.88	447.56
37000	726.95	656.85	605.16	565.72	534.84	510.18	490.15	473.69	460.00
38000	746.60	674.60	621.51	581.01	549.30	523.97	503.40	486.49	472.43
39000	766.25	692.36	637.87	596.30	563.75	537.75	516.65	499.29	484.86
40000	785.90	710.11	654.22	611.59	578.21	551.54	529.90	512.09	497.29
41000	805.54	727.86	670.58	626.88	592.66	565.33	543.14	524.89	509.72
42000	825.19	745.61	686.93	642.17	607.12	579.12	556.39	537.70	522.16
43000	844.84	763.37	703.29	657.45	621.57	592.91	569.64	550.50	534.59
44000	864.48	781.12	719.64	672.74	636.03	606.70	582.88	563.30	547.02
45000	884.13	798.87	736.00	688.03	650.48	620.48	596.13	576.10	559.45
46000	903.78	816.62	752.35	703.32	664.94	634.27	609.38	588.91	571.89
47000	923.43	834.38	768.71	718.61	679.39	648.06	622.63	601.71	584.32
48000	943.07	852.13	785.07	733.90	693.85	661.85	635.87	614.51	596.75
49000	962.72	869.88	801.42	749.19	708.30	675.64	649.12	627.31	609.18
50000	982.37	887.63	817.78	764.48	722.76	689.43	662.37	640.11	621.61
51000	1002.01	905.39	834.13	779.77	737.21	703.21	675.62	652.92	634.05
52000	1021.66	923.14	850.49	795.06	751.67	717.00	688.86	665.72	646.48
53000	1041.31	940.89	866.84	810.35	766.12	730.79	702.11	678.52	658.91
54000	1060.96	958.64	883.20	825.64	780.58	744.58	715.36	691.32	671.34
55000	1080.60	976.40	899.55	840.93	795.03	758.37	728.60	704.13	683.78
56000	1100.25	994.15	915.91	856.22	809.49	772.16	741.85	716.93	696.21
57000	1119.90	1011.90	932.26	871.51	823.94	785.95	755.10	729.73	708.64
58000	1139.55	1029.65	948.62	886.80	838.40	799.73	768.35	742.53	721.07
59000	1159.19	1047.41	964.97	902.09	852.85	813.52	781.59	755.33	733.50
60000	1178.84	1065.16	981.33	917.38	867.31	827.31	794.84	768.14	745.94
61000	1198.49	1082.91	997.69	932.67	881.76	841.10	808.09	780.94	758.37
62000	1218.13	1100.66	1014.04	947.96	896.22	854.89	821.34	793.74	770.80
63000	1237.78	1118.42	1030.40	963.25	910.67	868.68	834.58	806.54	783.23
64000	1257.43	1136.17	1046.75	978.53	925.13	882.46	847.83	819.34	795.66
65000	1277.08	1153.92	1063.11	993.82	939.58	896.25	861.08	832.15	808.10
66000	1296.72	1171.67	1079.46	1009.11	954.04	910.04	874.32	844.95	820.53
67000	1316.37	1189.43	1095.82	1024.40	968.49	923.83	887.57	857.75	832.96
68000	1336.02	1207.18	1112.17	1039.69	982.95	937.62	900.82	870.55	845.39
69000	1355.67	1224.93	1128.53	1054.98	997.40	951.41	914.07	883.36	857.83
70000	1375.31	1242.68	1144.88	1070.27	1011.86	965.20	927.31	896.16	870.26
75000	1473.55	1331.45	1226.66	1146.72	1084.13	1034.14	993.55	960.17	932.42
80000	1571.79	1420.21	1308.44	1223.17	1156.41	1103.08	1059.79	1024.18	994.58
100000	1964.73	1775.26	1635.55	1528.96	1445.51	1378.85	1324.73	1280.22	1243.22

93

12½% MONTHLY PAYMENT
NECESSARY TO AMORTIZE A LOAN

TERM AMOUNT	15 YEARS	16 YEARS	17 YEARS	18 YEARS	19 YEARS	20 YEARS	21 YEARS	22 YEARS	23 YEARS
$ 25	.31	.30	.30	.29	.29	.28	.28	.28	.28
50	.61	.60	.59	.58	.57	.56	.56	.55	.55
75	.91	.89	.88	.86	.85	.84	.83	.82	.82
100	1.22	1.19	1.17	1.15	1.13	1.12	1.11	1.10	1.09
200	2.43	2.38	2.33	2.29	2.26	2.23	2.21	2.19	2.17
300	3.64	3.56	3.50	3.44	3.39	3.35	3.31	3.28	3.25
400	4.85	4.75	4.66	4.58	4.52	4.46	4.41	4.37	4.33
500	6.07	5.93	5.82	5.73	5.65	5.58	5.51	5.46	5.42
600	7.28	7.12	6.99	6.87	6.77	6.69	6.62	6.55	6.50
700	8.49	8.31	8.15	8.02	7.90	7.80	7.72	7.64	7.58
800	9.70	9.49	9.31	9.16	9.03	8.92	8.82	8.74	8.66
900	10.91	10.68	10.48	10.31	10.16	10.03	9.92	9.83	9.74
1000	12.13	11.86	11.64	11.45	11.29	11.15	11.02	10.92	10.83
2000	24.25	23.72	23.28	22.90	22.57	22.29	22.04	21.83	21.65
3000	36.37	35.58	34.91	34.34	33.85	33.43	33.06	32.74	32.47
4000	48.49	47.44	46.55	45.79	45.13	44.57	44.08	43.66	43.29
5000	60.61	59.30	58.19	57.23	56.42	55.71	55.10	54.57	54.11
6000	72.74	71.16	69.82	68.68	67.70	66.85	66.12	65.48	64.93
7000	84.86	83.02	81.46	80.13	78.98	77.99	77.14	76.40	75.75
8000	96.98	94.88	93.10	91.57	90.26	89.13	88.16	87.31	86.57
9000	109.10	106.74	104.73	103.02	101.55	100.27	99.18	98.22	97.39
10000	121.22	118.60	116.37	114.46	112.83	111.42	110.19	109.13	108.21
15000	181.83	177.90	174.55	171.69	169.24	167.12	165.29	163.70	162.32
20000	242.44	237.20	232.74	228.92	225.65	222.83	220.38	218.26	216.42
25000	303.05	296.50	290.92	286.15	282.06	278.53	275.48	272.83	270.52
30000	363.66	355.79	349.10	343.38	338.47	334.24	330.57	327.39	324.63
35000	424.27	415.09	407.29	400.61	394.88	389.94	385.67	381.96	378.73
36000	436.39	426.95	418.92	412.06	406.17	401.08	396.69	392.87	389.55
37000	448.51	438.81	430.56	423.51	417.45	412.22	407.71	403.79	400.37
38000	460.64	450.67	442.20	434.95	428.73	423.37	418.72	414.70	411.20
39000	472.76	462.53	453.83	446.40	440.01	434.51	429.74	425.61	422.02
40000	484.88	474.39	465.47	457.84	451.30	445.65	440.76	436.52	432.84
41000	497.00	486.25	477.11	469.29	462.58	456.79	451.78	447.44	443.66
42000	509.12	498.11	488.74	480.74	473.86	467.93	462.80	458.35	454.48
43000	521.24	509.97	500.38	492.18	485.14	479.07	473.82	469.26	465.30
44000	533.37	521.83	512.02	503.63	496.42	490.21	484.84	480.18	476.12
45000	545.49	533.69	523.65	515.07	507.71	501.35	495.86	491.09	486.94
46000	557.61	545.55	535.29	526.52	518.99	512.49	506.88	502.00	497.76
47000	569.73	557.41	546.93	537.97	530.27	523.64	517.90	512.91	508.58
48000	581.85	569.27	558.56	549.41	541.55	534.78	528.91	523.83	519.40
49000	593.98	581.13	570.20	560.86	552.84	545.92	539.93	534.74	530.22
50000	606.10	592.99	581.84	572.30	564.12	557.06	550.95	545.65	541.04
51000	618.22	604.85	593.47	583.75	575.40	568.20	561.97	556.57	551.87
52000	630.34	616.71	605.11	595.20	586.68	579.34	572.99	567.48	562.69
53000	642.46	628.56	616.75	606.64	597.96	590.48	584.01	578.39	573.51
54000	654.59	640.42	628.38	618.09	609.25	601.62	595.03	589.31	584.33
55000	666.71	652.28	640.02	629.53	620.53	612.76	606.05	600.22	595.15
56000	678.83	664.14	651.66	640.98	631.81	623.91	617.07	611.13	605.97
57000	690.95	676.00	663.29	652.43	643.09	635.05	628.08	622.04	616.79
58000	703.07	687.86	674.93	663.87	654.38	646.19	639.10	632.96	627.61
59000	715.19	699.72	686.57	675.32	665.66	657.33	650.12	643.87	638.43
60000	727.32	711.58	698.20	686.76	676.94	668.47	661.14	654.78	649.25
61000	739.44	723.44	709.84	698.21	688.22	679.61	672.16	665.70	660.07
62000	751.56	735.30	721.48	709.66	699.50	690.75	683.18	676.61	670.89
63000	763.68	747.16	733.11	721.10	710.79	701.89	694.20	687.52	681.71
64000	775.80	759.02	744.75	732.55	722.07	713.03	705.22	698.44	692.54
65000	787.93	770.88	756.39	743.99	733.35	724.18	716.24	709.35	703.36
66000	800.05	782.74	768.02	755.44	744.63	735.32	727.26	720.26	714.18
67000	812.17	794.60	779.66	766.89	755.92	746.46	738.27	731.17	725.00
68000	824.29	806.46	791.30	778.33	767.20	757.60	749.29	742.09	735.82
69000	836.41	818.32	802.93	789.78	778.48	768.74	760.31	753.00	746.64
70000	848.53	830.18	814.57	801.22	789.76	779.88	771.33	763.91	757.46
75000	909.14	889.48	872.75	858.45	846.17	835.59	826.43	818.48	811.56
80000	969.75	948.77	930.93	915.68	902.59	891.29	881.52	873.04	865.67
100000	1212.19	1185.97	1163.67	1144.60	1128.23	1114.11	1101.90	1091.30	1082.08

MONTHLY PAYMENT 12½%
NECESSARY TO AMORTIZE A LOAN

TERM AMOUNT	24 YEARS	25 YEARS	26 YEARS	27 YEARS	28 YEARS	29 YEARS	30 YEARS	35 YEARS	40 YEARS
$ 25	.27	.27	.27	.27	.27	.27	.27	.26	.26
50	.54	.54	.54	.53	.53	.53	.53	.52	.52
75	.81	.81	.80	.80	.79	.79	.79	.78	.77
100	1.08	1.07	1.07	1.06	1.06	1.05	1.05	1.04	1.03
200	2.15	2.14	2.13	2.12	2.11	2.10	2.09	2.07	2.05
300	3.23	3.21	3.19	3.17	3.16	3.14	3.13	3.10	3.08
400	4.30	4.27	4.25	4.23	4.21	4.19	4.18	4.13	4.10
500	5.38	5.34	5.31	5.28	5.26	5.24	5.22	5.16	5.12
600	6.45	6.41	6.37	6.34	6.31	6.28	6.26	6.19	6.15
700	7.52	7.47	7.43	7.39	7.36	7.33	7.31	7.22	7.17
800	8.60	8.54	8.49	8.45	8.41	8.38	8.35	8.25	8.19
900	9.67	9.61	9.55	9.50	9.46	9.42	9.39	9.28	9.22
1000	10.75	10.68	10.61	10.56	10.51	10.47	10.43	10.31	10.24
2000	21.49	21.35	21.22	21.11	21.02	20.94	20.86	20.61	20.48
3000	32.23	32.02	31.83	31.67	31.53	31.40	31.29	30.91	30.71
4000	42.97	42.69	42.44	42.22	42.04	41.87	41.72	41.22	40.95
5000	53.71	53.36	53.05	52.78	52.54	52.34	52.15	51.52	51.18
6000	64.45	64.03	63.66	63.33	63.05	62.80	62.58	61.82	61.42
7000	75.19	74.70	74.27	73.89	73.56	73.27	73.01	72.13	71.65
8000	85.93	85.37	84.88	84.44	84.07	83.74	83.44	82.43	81.89
9000	96.67	96.04	95.48	95.00	94.57	94.20	93.87	92.73	92.12
10000	107.41	106.71	106.09	105.55	105.08	104.67	104.30	103.04	102.36
15000	161.11	160.06	159.14	158.33	157.62	157.00	156.45	154.55	153.54
20000	214.81	213.41	212.18	211.10	210.16	209.33	208.60	206.07	204.71
25000	268.52	266.76	265.23	263.88	262.70	261.66	260.75	257.59	255.89
30000	322.22	320.11	318.27	316.65	315.24	313.99	312.90	309.10	307.07
35000	375.92	373.46	371.31	369.43	367.78	366.33	365.05	360.62	358.25
36000	386.66	384.13	381.92	379.98	378.28	376.79	375.48	370.92	368.48
37000	397.40	394.80	392.53	390.54	388.79	387.26	385.91	381.22	378.72
38000	408.14	405.47	403.14	401.09	399.30	397.72	396.34	391.53	388.95
39000	418.88	416.14	413.75	411.65	409.81	408.19	406.77	401.83	399.19
40000	429.62	426.81	424.36	422.20	420.32	418.66	417.20	412.13	409.42
41000	440.36	437.48	434.97	432.76	430.82	429.12	427.63	422.44	419.66
42000	451.10	448.15	445.57	443.31	441.33	439.59	438.06	432.74	429.89
43000	461.84	458.82	456.18	453.87	451.84	450.06	448.49	443.04	440.13
44000	472.58	469.49	466.79	464.42	462.35	460.52	458.92	453.35	450.36
45000	483.32	480.17	477.40	474.98	472.85	470.99	469.35	463.65	460.60
46000	494.06	490.84	488.01	485.53	483.36	481.45	479.78	473.95	470.84
47000	504.81	501.51	498.62	496.09	493.87	491.92	490.21	484.26	481.07
48000	515.55	512.18	509.23	506.64	504.38	502.39	500.64	494.56	491.31
49000	526.29	522.85	519.84	517.20	514.89	512.85	511.07	504.86	501.54
50000	537.03	533.52	530.45	527.75	525.39	523.32	521.50	515.17	511.78
51000	547.77	544.19	541.05	538.31	535.90	533.79	531.93	525.47	522.01
52000	558.51	554.86	551.66	548.86	546.41	544.25	542.36	535.77	532.25
53000	569.25	565.53	562.27	559.42	556.92	554.72	552.79	546.08	542.48
54000	579.99	576.20	572.88	569.97	567.42	565.18	563.22	556.38	552.72
55000	590.73	586.87	583.49	580.53	577.93	575.65	573.65	566.68	562.95
56000	601.47	597.54	594.10	591.08	588.44	586.12	584.07	576.99	573.19
57000	612.21	608.21	604.71	601.64	598.95	596.58	594.50	587.29	583.43
58000	622.95	618.88	615.32	612.19	609.46	607.05	604.93	597.59	593.66
59000	633.69	629.55	625.92	622.75	619.96	617.52	615.36	607.89	603.90
60000	644.43	640.22	636.53	633.30	630.47	627.98	625.79	618.20	614.13
61000	655.17	650.89	647.14	643.86	640.98	638.45	636.22	628.50	624.37
62000	665.91	661.56	657.75	654.41	651.49	648.91	646.65	638.80	634.60
63000	676.65	672.23	668.36	664.97	661.99	659.38	657.08	649.11	644.84
64000	687.39	682.90	678.97	675.52	672.50	669.85	667.51	659.41	655.07
65000	698.13	693.57	689.58	686.08	683.01	680.31	677.94	669.71	665.31
66000	708.87	704.24	700.19	696.63	693.52	690.78	688.37	680.02	675.54
67000	719.61	714.91	710.80	707.19	704.03	701.25	698.80	690.32	685.78
68000	730.35	725.58	721.40	717.74	714.53	711.71	709.23	700.62	696.02
69000	741.09	736.25	732.01	728.30	725.04	722.18	719.66	710.93	706.25
70000	751.83	746.92	742.62	738.85	735.55	732.65	730.09	721.23	716.49
75000	805.54	800.27	795.67	791.63	788.09	784.98	782.24	772.75	767.66
80000	859.24	853.62	848.71	844.40	840.63	837.31	834.39	824.26	818.84
100000	1074.05	1067.03	1060.89	1055.50	1050.78	1046.63	1042.99	1030.33	1023.55

12¾% MONTHLY PAYMENT
NECESSARY TO AMORTIZE A LOAN

TERM AMOUNT	1 YEAR	1½ YEARS	2 YEARS	2½ YEARS	3 YEARS	3½ YEARS	4 YEARS	4½ YEARS	5 YEARS
$ 25	2.23	1.53	1.19	.98	.84	.74	.67	.61	.57
50	4.46	3.06	2.37	1.95	1.68	1.48	1.33	1.22	1.13
75	6.68	4.59	3.55	2.93	2.51	2.22	2.00	1.83	1.69
100	8.91	6.12	4.73	3.90	3.35	2.95	2.66	2.43	2.25
200	17.81	12.24	9.46	7.79	6.69	5.90	5.31	4.86	4.50
300	26.72	18.36	14.19	11.69	10.03	8.85	7.97	7.29	6.74
400	35.62	24.48	18.91	15.58	13.37	11.80	10.62	9.71	8.99
500	44.53	30.59	23.64	19.48	16.71	14.75	13.28	12.14	11.23
600	53.43	36.71	28.37	23.37	20.06	17.69	15.93	14.57	13.48
700	62.34	42.83	33.10	27.27	23.40	20.64	18.58	16.99	15.73
800	71.24	48.95	37.82	31.16	26.74	23.59	21.24	19.42	17.97
900	80.15	55.07	42.55	35.06	30.08	26.54	23.89	21.85	20.22
1000	89.05	61.18	47.28	38.95	33.42	29.49	26.55	24.27	22.46
2000	178.10	122.36	94.55	77.90	66.84	58.97	53.09	48.54	44.92
3000	267.15	183.54	141.82	116.85	100.26	88.45	79.63	72.81	67.38
4000	356.19	244.72	189.09	155.80	133.67	117.93	106.17	97.08	89.84
5000	445.24	305.90	236.36	194.75	167.09	147.41	132.72	121.35	112.30
6000	534.29	367.08	283.64	233.70	200.51	176.89	159.26	145.61	134.76
7000	623.34	428.26	330.91	272.64	233.93	206.37	185.80	169.88	157.22
8000	712.38	489.44	378.18	311.59	267.34	235.86	212.34	194.15	179.68
9000	801.43	550.62	425.45	350.54	300.76	265.34	238.89	218.42	202.14
10000	890.48	611.80	472.72	389.49	334.18	294.82	265.43	242.69	224.60
15000	1335.71	917.69	709.08	584.23	501.26	442.22	398.14	364.03	336.89
20000	1780.95	1223.59	945.44	778.97	668.35	589.63	530.85	485.37	449.19
25000	2226.19	1529.48	1181.80	973.72	835.43	737.04	663.57	606.71	561.49
30000	2671.42	1835.38	1418.16	1168.46	1002.52	884.44	796.28	728.05	673.78
35000	3116.66	2141.28	1654.51	1363.20	1169.61	1031.85	928.99	849.40	786.08
36000	3205.71	2202.46	1701.79	1402.15	1203.02	1061.33	955.53	873.66	808.54
37000	3294.75	2263.63	1749.06	1441.10	1236.44	1090.81	982.08	897.93	831.00
38000	3383.80	2324.81	1796.33	1480.04	1269.86	1120.29	1008.62	922.20	853.46
39000	3472.85	2385.99	1843.60	1518.99	1303.27	1149.78	1035.16	946.47	875.92
40000	3561.89	2447.17	1890.87	1557.94	1336.69	1179.26	1061.70	970.74	898.38
41000	3650.94	2508.35	1938.14	1596.89	1370.11	1208.74	1088.25	995.00	920.84
42000	3739.99	2569.53	1985.42	1635.84	1403.53	1238.22	1114.79	1019.27	943.29
43000	3829.04	2630.71	2032.69	1674.79	1436.94	1267.70	1141.33	1043.54	965.75
44000	3918.08	2691.89	2079.96	1713.74	1470.36	1297.18	1167.87	1067.81	988.21
45000	4007.13	2753.07	2127.23	1752.68	1503.78	1326.66	1194.42	1092.08	1010.67
46000	4096.18	2814.25	2174.50	1791.63	1537.19	1356.14	1220.96	1116.35	1033.13
47000	4185.23	2875.43	2221.77	1830.58	1570.61	1385.63	1247.50	1140.61	1055.59
48000	4274.27	2936.61	2269.05	1869.53	1604.03	1415.11	1274.04	1164.88	1078.05
49000	4363.32	2997.78	2316.32	1908.48	1637.45	1444.59	1300.59	1189.15	1100.51
50000	4452.37	3058.96	2363.59	1947.43	1670.86	1474.07	1327.13	1213.42	1122.97
51000	4541.41	3120.14	2410.86	1986.37	1704.28	1503.55	1353.67	1237.69	1145.43
52000	4630.46	3181.32	2458.13	2025.32	1737.70	1533.03	1380.21	1261.96	1167.89
53000	4719.51	3242.50	2505.41	2064.27	1771.11	1562.51	1406.76	1286.22	1190.35
54000	4808.56	3303.68	2552.68	2103.22	1804.53	1591.99	1433.30	1310.49	1212.81
55000	4897.60	3364.86	2599.95	2142.17	1837.95	1621.48	1459.84	1334.76	1235.27
56000	4986.65	3426.04	2647.22	2181.12	1871.37	1650.96	1486.38	1359.03	1257.72
57000	5075.70	3487.22	2694.49	2220.06	1904.78	1680.44	1512.93	1383.30	1280.18
58000	5164.74	3548.40	2741.76	2259.01	1938.20	1709.92	1539.47	1407.57	1302.64
59000	5253.79	3609.58	2789.04	2297.96	1971.62	1739.40	1566.01	1431.83	1325.10
60000	5342.84	3670.76	2836.31	2336.91	2005.03	1768.88	1592.55	1456.10	1347.56
61000	5431.89	3731.93	2883.58	2375.86	2038.45	1798.36	1619.10	1480.37	1370.02
62000	5520.93	3793.11	2930.85	2414.81	2071.87	1827.85	1645.64	1504.64	1392.48
63000	5609.98	3854.29	2978.12	2453.76	2105.29	1857.33	1672.18	1528.91	1414.94
64000	5699.03	3915.47	3025.39	2492.70	2138.70	1886.81	1698.72	1553.18	1437.40
65000	5788.08	3976.65	3072.67	2531.65	2172.12	1916.29	1725.27	1577.44	1459.86
66000	5877.12	4037.83	3119.94	2570.60	2205.54	1945.77	1751.81	1601.71	1482.32
67000	5966.17	4099.01	3167.21	2609.55	2238.95	1975.25	1778.35	1625.98	1504.78
68000	6055.22	4160.19	3214.48	2648.50	2272.37	2004.73	1804.89	1650.25	1527.24
69000	6144.26	4221.37	3261.75	2687.45	2305.79	2034.21	1831.44	1674.52	1549.70
70000	6233.31	4282.55	3309.02	2726.39	2339.21	2063.70	1857.98	1698.79	1572.15
75000	6678.55	4588.44	3545.38	2921.14	2506.29	2211.10	1990.69	1820.13	1684.45
80000	7123.78	4894.34	3781.74	3115.88	2673.38	2358.51	2123.40	1941.47	1796.75
100000	8904.73	6117.92	4727.17	3894.85	3341.72	2948.13	2654.25	2426.83	2245.93

96

MONTHLY PAYMENT 12¾%
NECESSARY TO AMORTIZE A LOAN

TERM AMOUNT	6 YEARS	7 YEARS	8 YEARS	9 YEARS	10 YEARS	11 YEARS	12 YEARS	13 YEARS	14 YEARS
$ 25	.50	.45	.42	.39	.37	.35	.34	.33	.32
50	.99	.90	.83	.78	.73	.70	.67	.65	.63
75	1.49	1.35	1.24	1.16	1.10	1.05	1.01	.98	.95
100	1.98	1.79	1.65	1.55	1.46	1.40	1.34	1.30	1.26
200	3.96	3.58	3.30	3.09	2.92	2.79	2.68	2.60	2.52
300	5.94	5.37	4.95	4.63	4.38	4.18	4.02	3.89	3.78
400	7.91	7.16	6.60	6.17	5.84	5.58	5.36	5.19	5.04
500	9.89	8.95	8.25	7.72	7.30	6.97	6.70	6.48	6.30
600	11.87	10.73	9.90	9.26	8.76	8.36	8.04	7.78	7.55
700	13.84	12.52	11.55	10.80	10.22	9.76	9.38	9.07	8.81
800	15.82	14.31	13.19	12.34	11.68	11.15	10.72	10.37	10.07
900	17.80	16.10	14.84	13.89	13.14	12.54	12.06	11.66	11.33
1000	19.78	17.89	16.49	15.43	14.60	13.93	13.40	12.96	12.59
2000	39.55	35.77	32.98	30.85	29.19	27.86	26.79	25.91	25.17
3000	59.32	53.65	49.47	46.28	43.78	41.79	40.18	38.86	37.75
4000	79.09	71.53	65.95	61.70	58.38	55.72	53.57	51.81	50.34
5000	98.86	89.41	82.44	77.13	72.97	69.65	66.97	64.76	62.92
6000	118.63	107.29	98.93	92.55	87.56	83.58	80.36	77.71	75.50
7000	138.40	125.17	115.41	107.97	102.16	97.51	93.75	90.66	88.09
8000	158.18	143.05	131.90	123.40	116.75	111.44	107.14	103.61	100.67
9000	177.95	160.93	148.39	138.82	131.34	125.37	120.53	116.56	113.25
10000	197.72	178.81	164.87	154.25	145.94	139.30	133.93	129.51	125.84
15000	296.58	268.21	247.31	231.37	218.90	208.95	200.89	194.26	188.75
20000	395.43	357.61	329.74	308.49	291.87	278.60	267.85	259.01	251.67
25000	494.29	447.01	412.17	385.61	364.84	348.25	334.81	323.76	314.58
30000	593.15	536.41	494.61	462.73	437.80	417.90	401.77	388.51	377.50
35000	692.00	625.81	577.04	539.85	510.77	487.55	468.73	453.26	440.42
36000	711.77	643.69	593.53	555.28	525.36	501.48	482.12	466.21	453.00
37000	731.55	661.57	610.01	570.70	539.95	515.41	495.51	479.16	465.58
38000	751.32	679.45	626.50	586.13	554.55	529.34	508.90	492.11	478.17
39000	771.09	697.34	642.99	601.55	569.14	543.27	522.30	505.06	490.75
40000	790.86	715.22	659.47	616.98	583.73	557.20	535.69	518.01	503.33
41000	810.63	733.10	675.96	632.40	598.33	571.13	549.08	530.96	515.92
42000	830.40	750.98	692.45	647.82	612.92	585.06	562.47	543.91	528.50
43000	850.17	768.86	708.93	663.25	627.51	598.99	575.86	556.86	541.08
44000	869.94	786.74	725.42	678.67	642.11	612.92	589.26	569.81	553.66
45000	889.72	804.62	741.91	694.10	656.70	626.85	602.65	582.76	566.25
46000	909.49	822.50	758.39	709.52	671.29	640.78	616.04	595.71	578.83
47000	929.26	840.38	774.88	724.95	685.89	654.71	629.43	608.66	591.41
48000	949.03	858.26	791.37	740.37	700.48	668.64	642.82	621.61	604.00
49000	968.80	876.14	807.85	755.79	715.07	682.57	656.22	634.56	616.58
50000	988.57	894.02	824.34	771.22	729.67	696.50	669.61	647.51	629.16
51000	1008.34	911.90	840.83	786.64	744.26	710.43	683.00	660.46	641.75
52000	1028.12	929.78	857.31	802.07	758.85	724.36	696.39	673.41	654.33
53000	1047.89	947.66	873.80	817.49	773.45	738.29	709.78	686.36	666.91
54000	1067.66	965.54	890.29	832.92	788.04	752.22	723.18	699.31	679.50
55000	1087.43	983.42	906.77	848.34	802.63	766.15	736.57	712.26	692.08
56000	1107.20	1001.30	923.26	863.76	817.23	780.08	749.96	725.21	704.66
57000	1126.97	1019.18	939.75	879.19	831.82	794.01	763.35	738.16	717.25
58000	1146.74	1037.06	956.23	894.61	846.41	807.94	776.74	751.11	729.83
59000	1166.52	1054.94	972.72	910.04	861.01	821.87	790.14	764.06	742.41
60000	1186.29	1072.82	989.21	925.46	875.60	835.80	803.53	777.01	755.00
61000	1206.06	1090.70	1005.69	940.89	890.19	849.73	816.92	789.96	767.58
62000	1225.83	1108.58	1022.18	956.31	904.79	863.66	830.31	802.91	780.16
63000	1245.60	1126.46	1038.67	971.73	919.38	877.59	843.71	815.86	792.75
64000	1265.37	1144.34	1055.15	987.16	933.97	891.52	857.10	828.81	805.33
65000	1285.14	1162.22	1071.64	1002.58	948.57	905.45	870.49	841.76	817.91
66000	1304.91	1180.10	1088.13	1018.01	963.16	919.38	883.88	854.71	830.49
67000	1324.69	1197.98	1104.61	1033.43	977.75	933.31	897.27	867.66	843.08
68000	1344.46	1215.86	1121.10	1048.86	992.35	947.24	910.67	880.61	855.66
69000	1364.23	1233.74	1137.59	1064.28	1006.94	961.17	924.06	893.56	868.24
70000	1384.00	1251.62	1154.07	1079.70	1021.53	975.10	937.45	906.51	880.83
75000	1482.86	1341.02	1236.51	1156.83	1094.50	1044.75	1004.41	971.27	943.74
80000	1581.71	1430.43	1318.94	1233.95	1167.46	1114.40	1071.37	1036.02	1006.66
100000	1977.14	1788.03	1648.67	1542.43	1459.33	1393.00	1339.21	1295.02	1258.32

12¾% MONTHLY PAYMENT
NECESSARY TO AMORTIZE A LOAN

TERM AMOUNT	15 YEARS	16 YEARS	17 YEARS	18 YEARS	19 YEARS	20 YEARS	21 YEARS	22 YEARS	23 YEARS
$ 25	.31	.31	.30	.30	.29	.29	.28	.28	.28
50	.62	.61	.59	.59	.58	.57	.56	.56	.55
75	.93	.91	.89	.88	.86	.85	.84	.84	.83
100	1.23	1.21	1.18	1.17	1.15	1.14	1.12	1.11	1.10
200	2.46	2.41	2.36	2.33	2.29	2.27	2.24	2.22	2.20
300	3.69	3.61	3.54	3.49	3.44	3.40	3.36	3.33	3.30
400	4.92	4.81	4.72	4.65	4.58	4.53	4.48	4.44	4.40
500	6.14	6.01	5.90	5.81	5.73	5.66	5.60	5.55	5.50
600	7.37	7.21	7.08	6.97	6.87	6.79	6.72	6.66	6.60
700	8.60	8.42	8.26	8.13	8.02	7.92	7.84	7.76	7.70
800	9.83	9.62	9.44	9.29	9.16	9.05	8.96	8.87	8.80
900	11.05	10.82	10.62	10.45	10.31	10.18	10.07	9.98	9.90
1000	12.28	12.02	11.80	11.61	11.45	11.31	11.19	11.09	11.00
2000	24.56	24.04	23.60	23.22	22.90	22.62	22.38	22.17	21.99
3000	36.83	36.05	35.39	34.83	34.35	33.93	33.57	33.26	32.99
4000	49.11	48.07	47.19	46.44	45.79	45.24	44.76	44.34	43.98
5000	61.38	60.09	58.99	58.04	57.24	56.54	55.94	55.43	54.97
6000	73.66	72.10	70.78	69.65	68.69	67.85	67.13	66.51	65.97
7000	85.94	84.12	82.58	81.26	80.13	79.16	78.32	77.59	76.96
8000	98.21	96.14	94.37	92.87	91.58	90.47	89.51	88.68	87.96
9000	110.49	108.15	106.17	104.48	103.03	101.78	100.70	99.76	98.95
10000	122.76	120.17	117.97	116.08	114.47	113.08	111.88	110.85	109.94
15000	184.14	180.25	176.95	174.12	171.71	169.62	167.82	166.27	164.91
20000	245.52	240.33	235.93	232.16	228.94	226.16	223.76	221.69	219.88
25000	306.90	300.41	294.91	290.20	286.17	282.70	279.70	277.11	274.85
30000	368.28	360.50	353.89	348.24	343.41	339.24	335.64	332.53	329.82
35000	429.66	420.58	412.87	406.28	400.64	395.78	391.58	387.95	384.79
36000	441.93	432.59	424.66	417.89	412.09	407.09	402.77	399.03	395.78
37000	454.21	444.61	436.46	429.50	423.53	418.40	413.96	410.11	406.78
38000	466.48	456.63	448.25	441.11	434.98	429.70	425.15	421.20	417.77
39000	478.76	468.64	460.05	452.72	446.43	441.01	436.33	432.28	428.76
40000	491.04	480.66	471.85	464.32	457.87	452.32	447.52	443.37	439.76
41000	503.31	492.68	483.64	475.93	469.32	463.63	458.71	454.45	450.75
42000	515.59	504.69	495.44	487.54	480.77	474.93	469.90	465.53	461.74
43000	527.86	516.71	507.23	499.15	492.21	486.24	481.09	476.62	472.74
44000	540.14	528.72	519.03	510.76	503.66	497.55	492.27	487.70	483.73
45000	552.41	540.74	530.83	522.36	515.11	508.86	503.46	498.79	494.73
46000	564.69	552.76	542.62	533.97	526.55	520.17	514.65	509.87	505.72
47000	576.97	564.77	554.42	545.58	538.00	531.47	525.84	520.95	516.71
48000	589.24	576.79	566.22	557.19	549.45	542.78	537.02	532.04	527.71
49000	601.52	588.81	578.01	568.80	560.89	554.09	548.21	543.12	538.70
50000	613.79	600.82	589.81	580.40	572.34	565.40	559.40	554.21	549.70
51000	626.07	612.84	601.60	592.01	583.79	576.70	570.59	565.29	560.69
52000	638.35	624.86	613.40	603.62	595.23	588.01	581.78	576.37	571.68
53000	650.62	636.87	625.20	615.23	606.68	599.32	592.96	587.46	582.68
54000	662.90	648.89	636.99	626.84	618.13	610.63	604.15	598.54	593.67
55000	675.17	660.90	648.79	638.44	629.57	621.94	615.34	609.63	604.66
56000	687.45	672.92	660.58	650.05	641.02	633.24	626.53	620.71	615.66
57000	699.72	684.94	672.38	661.66	652.47	644.55	637.72	631.79	626.65
58000	712.00	696.95	684.18	673.27	663.91	655.86	648.90	642.88	637.65
59000	724.28	708.97	695.97	684.88	675.36	667.17	660.09	653.96	648.64
60000	736.55	720.99	707.77	696.48	686.81	678.48	671.28	665.05	659.63
61000	748.83	733.00	719.56	708.09	698.25	689.78	682.47	676.13	670.63
62000	761.10	745.02	731.36	719.70	709.70	701.09	693.66	687.21	681.62
63000	773.38	757.03	743.16	731.31	721.15	712.40	704.84	698.30	692.61
64000	785.65	769.05	754.95	742.92	732.59	723.71	716.03	709.38	703.61
65000	797.93	781.07	766.75	754.52	744.04	735.01	727.22	720.45	714.60
66000	810.21	793.08	778.54	766.13	755.49	746.32	738.41	731.55	725.60
67000	822.48	805.10	790.34	777.74	766.93	757.63	749.60	742.63	736.59
68000	834.76	817.12	802.14	789.35	778.38	768.94	760.78	753.72	747.58
69000	847.03	829.13	813.93	800.96	789.83	780.25	771.97	764.80	758.58
70000	859.31	841.15	825.73	812.56	801.27	791.55	783.16	775.89	769.57
75000	920.69	901.23	884.71	870.60	858.51	848.09	839.10	831.31	824.54
80000	982.07	961.31	943.69	928.64	915.74	904.63	895.04	886.73	879.51
100000	1227.58	1201.64	1179.61	1160.80	1144.67	1130.79	1118.80	1108.41	1099.39

MONTHLY PAYMENT 12¾%
NECESSARY TO AMORTIZE A LOAN

TERM AMOUNT	24 YEARS	25 YEARS	26 YEARS	27 YEARS	28 YEARS	29 YEARS	30 YEARS	35 YEARS	40 YEARS
$ 25	.28	.28	.27	.27	.27	.27	.27	.27	.27
50	.55	.55	.54	.54	.54	.54	.54	.53	.53
75	.82	.82	.81	.81	.81	.80	.80	.79	.79
100	1.10	1.09	1.08	1.08	1.07	1.07	1.07	1.05	1.05
200	2.19	2.17	2.16	2.15	2.14	2.13	2.13	2.10	2.09
300	3.28	3.26	3.24	3.23	3.21	3.20	3.19	3.15	3.13
400	4.37	4.34	4.32	4.30	4.28	4.26	4.25	4.20	4.18
500	5.46	5.43	5.40	5.37	5.35	5.33	5.31	5.25	5.22
600	6.55	6.51	6.48	6.45	6.42	6.39	6.37	6.30	6.26
700	7.65	7.60	7.56	7.52	7.49	7.46	7.43	7.35	7.30
800	8.74	8.68	8.63	8.59	8.56	8.52	8.50	8.40	8.35
900	9.83	9.77	9.71	9.67	9.63	9.59	9.56	9.45	9.30
1000	10.92	10.85	10.79	10.74	10.69	10.05	10.62	10.50	10.43
2000	21.84	21.70	21.58	21.47	21.38	21.30	21.23	20.99	20.86
3000	32.75	32.55	32.37	32.21	32.07	31.95	31.85	31.48	31.29
4000	43.67	43.39	43.15	42.94	42.76	42.60	42.46	41.97	41.72
5000	54.58	54.24	53.94	53.68	53.45	53.25	53.07	52.46	52.14
6000	65.50	65.09	64.73	64.41	64.14	63.90	63.69	62.96	62.57
7000	76.41	75.93	75.51	75.15	74.83	74.55	74.30	73.45	73.00
8000	87.33	86.78	86.30	85.88	85.52	85.20	84.91	83.94	83.43
9000	98.24	97.63	97.09	96.62	96.21	95.84	95.53	94.43	93.85
10000	109.16	108.47	107.88	107.35	106.89	106.49	106.14	104.92	104.28
15000	163.73	162.71	161.81	161.03	160.34	159.74	159.21	157.38	156.42
20000	218.31	216.94	215.75	214.70	213.78	212.98	212.28	209.84	208.56
25000	272.89	271.18	269.68	268.37	267.23	266.23	265.35	262.30	260.70
30000	327.46	325.41	323.62	322.05	320.67	319.47	318.41	314.76	312.83
35000	382.04	379.64	377.55	375.72	374.12	372.71	371.48	367.22	364.97
36000	392.96	390.49	388.34	386.46	384.81	383.36	382.09	377.72	375.40
37000	403.87	401.34	399.13	397.19	395.50	394.01	392.71	388.21	385.83
38000	414.79	412.18	409.91	407.93	406.19	404.66	403.32	398.70	396.25
39000	425.70	423.03	420.70	418.66	416.87	415.31	413.94	409.19	406.68
40000	436.62	433.88	431.49	429.40	427.56	425.96	424.55	419.68	417.11
41000	447.53	444.73	442.27	440.13	438.25	436.61	435.16	430.18	427.54
42000	458.45	455.57	453.06	450.86	448.94	447.26	445.78	440.67	437.96
43000	469.36	466.42	463.85	461.60	459.63	457.90	456.39	451.16	448.39
44000	480.28	477.27	474.64	472.33	470.32	468.55	467.00	461.65	458.82
45000	491.19	488.11	485.42	483.07	481.01	479.20	477.62	472.14	469.25
46000	502.11	498.96	496.21	493.80	491.70	489.85	488.23	482.64	479.67
47000	513.02	509.81	507.00	504.54	502.39	500.50	498.84	493.13	490.10
48000	523.94	520.65	517.78	515.27	513.08	511.15	509.46	503.62	500.53
49000	534.85	531.50	528.57	526.01	523.76	521.80	520.07	514.11	510.96
50000	545.77	542.35	539.36	536.74	534.45	532.45	530.69	524.60	521.39
51000	556.69	553.19	550.14	547.48	545.14	543.10	541.30	535.10	531.81
52000	567.60	564.04	560.93	558.21	555.83	553.74	551.91	545.59	542.24
53000	578.52	574.89	571.72	568.95	566.52	564.39	562.53	556.08	552.67
54000	589.43	585.73	582.51	579.68	577.21	575.04	573.14	566.57	563.10
55000	600.35	596.58	593.29	590.42	587.90	585.69	583.75	577.06	573.52
56000	611.26	607.43	604.08	601.15	598.59	596.34	594.37	587.56	583.95
57000	622.18	618.27	614.87	611.89	609.28	606.99	604.98	598.05	594.38
58000	633.09	629.12	625.65	622.62	619.97	617.64	615.59	608.54	604.81
59000	644.01	639.97	636.44	633.36	630.65	628.29	626.21	619.03	615.23
60000	654.92	650.82	647.23	644.09	641.34	638.93	636.82	629.52	625.66
61000	665.84	661.66	658.02	654.83	652.03	649.58	647.43	640.02	636.09
62000	676.75	672.51	668.80	665.56	662.72	660.23	658.05	650.51	646.52
63000	687.67	683.36	679.59	676.29	673.41	670.88	668.66	661.00	656.94
64000	698.58	694.20	690.38	687.03	684.10	681.53	679.28	671.49	667.37
65000	709.50	705.05	701.16	697.76	694.79	692.18	689.89	681.98	677.80
66000	720.41	715.90	711.95	708.50	705.48	702.83	700.50	692.48	688.23
67000	731.33	726.74	722.74	719.23	716.17	713.48	711.12	702.97	698.65
68000	742.25	737.59	733.52	729.97	726.86	724.13	721.73	713.46	709.08
69000	753.16	748.44	744.31	740.70	737.54	734.77	732.34	723.95	719.51
70000	764.08	759.28	755.10	751.44	748.23	745.42	742.96	734.44	729.94
75000	818.65	813.52	809.03	805.11	801.68	798.67	796.03	786.90	782.08
80000	873.23	867.75	862.97	858.79	855.12	851.91	849.09	839.36	834.21
100000	1091.53	1084.69	1078.71	1073.48	1068.90	1064.89	1061.37	1049.20	1042.77

13% MONTHLY PAYMENT
NECESSARY TO AMORTIZE A LOAN

TERM AMOUNT	1 YEAR	1½ YEARS	2 YEARS	2½ YEARS	3 YEARS	3½ YEARS	4 YEARS	4½ YEARS	5 YEARS
$ 25	2.23	1.54	1.19	.98	.84	.74	.67	.61	.57
50	4.46	3.07	2.37	1.96	1.68	1.48	1.34	1.22	1.13
75	6.69	4.60	3.56	2.93	2.52	2.22	2.00	1.83	1.70
100	8.92	6.13	4.74	3.91	3.36	2.96	2.67	2.44	2.26
200	17.84	12.26	9.48	7.82	6.71	5.92	5.34	4.88	4.52
300	26.75	18.39	14.22	11.72	10.06	8.88	8.00	7.32	6.78
400	35.67	24.52	18.96	15.63	13.42	11.84	10.67	9.76	9.04
500	44.58	30.65	23.70	19.54	16.77	14.80	13.33	12.20	11.30
600	53.50	36.78	28.43	23.44	20.12	17.76	16.00	14.64	13.55
700	62.42	42.91	33.17	27.35	23.48	20.72	18.67	17.08	15.81
800	71.33	49.04	37.91	31.25	26.83	23.68	21.33	19.51	18.07
900	80.25	55.17	42.65	35.16	30.18	26.64	24.00	21.95	20.33
1000	89.16	61.29	47.39	39.07	33.54	29.60	26.66	24.39	22.59
2000	178.32	122.58	94.77	78.13	67.07	59.20	53.32	48.78	45.17
3000	267.48	183.87	142.15	117.19	100.60	88.80	79.98	73.17	67.75
4000	356.64	245.16	189.54	156.25	134.13	118.39	106.64	97.55	90.33
5000	445.80	306.45	236.92	195.31	167.66	147.99	133.30	121.94	112.91
6000	534.96	367.74	284.30	234.37	201.19	177.59	159.96	146.33	135.49
7000	624.11	429.03	331.69	273.43	234.72	207.18	186.62	170.72	158.07
8000	713.27	490.32	379.07	312.49	268.25	236.78	213.28	195.10	180.65
9000	802.43	551.61	426.45	351.55	301.78	266.38	239.94	219.49	203.23
10000	891.59	612.90	473.83	390.61	335.32	295.97	266.60	243.88	225.81
15000	1337.38	919.35	710.75	585.92	502.97	443.96	399.90	365.81	338.71
20000	1783.17	1225.80	947.66	781.22	670.63	591.94	533.20	487.75	451.61
25000	2228.97	1532.25	1184.58	976.53	838.28	739.92	666.50	609.69	564.51
30000	2674.76	1838.70	1421.49	1171.83	1005.94	887.91	799.80	731.62	677.41
35000	3120.55	2145.14	1658.41	1367.13	1173.59	1035.89	933.09	853.56	790.31
36000	3209.71	2206.43	1705.79	1406.19	1207.12	1065.49	959.75	877.95	812.89
37000	3298.87	2267.72	1753.17	1445.26	1240.65	1095.09	986.41	902.33	835.47
38000	3388.03	2329.01	1800.55	1484.32	1274.18	1124.68	1013.07	926.72	858.05
39000	3477.18	2390.30	1847.94	1523.38	1307.71	1154.28	1039.73	951.11	880.63
40000	3566.34	2451.59	1895.32	1562.44	1341.25	1183.88	1066.39	975.50	903.21
41000	3655.50	2512.88	1942.70	1601.50	1374.78	1213.47	1093.05	999.88	925.79
42000	3744.66	2574.17	1990.09	1640.56	1408.31	1243.07	1119.71	1024.27	948.37
43000	3833.82	2635.46	2037.47	1679.62	1441.84	1272.67	1146.37	1048.66	970.95
44000	3922.98	2696.75	2084.85	1718.68	1475.37	1302.26	1173.03	1073.04	993.53
45000	4012.13	2758.04	2132.23	1757.74	1508.90	1331.86	1199.69	1097.43	1016.11
46000	4101.29	2819.33	2179.62	1796.80	1542.43	1361.46	1226.35	1121.82	1038.69
47000	4190.45	2880.62	2227.00	1835.86	1575.96	1391.05	1253.01	1146.21	1061.27
48000	4279.61	2941.91	2274.38	1874.92	1609.49	1420.65	1279.67	1170.59	1083.85
49000	4368.77	3003.20	2321.77	1913.98	1643.03	1450.25	1306.33	1194.98	1106.43
50000	4457.93	3064.49	2369.15	1953.05	1676.56	1479.84	1332.99	1219.37	1129.01
51000	4547.09	3125.78	2416.53	1992.11	1710.09	1509.44	1359.65	1243.76	1151.59
52000	4636.24	3187.07	2463.91	2031.17	1743.62	1539.04	1386.31	1268.14	1174.17
53000	4725.40	3248.36	2511.30	2070.23	1777.15	1568.64	1412.97	1292.53	1196.75
54000	4814.56	3309.65	2558.68	2109.29	1810.68	1598.23	1439.63	1316.92	1219.33
55000	4903.72	3370.94	2606.06	2148.35	1844.21	1627.83	1466.29	1341.30	1241.91
56000	4992.88	3432.23	2653.45	2187.41	1877.74	1657.43	1492.95	1365.69	1264.49
57000	5082.04	3493.52	2700.83	2226.47	1911.27	1687.02	1519.61	1390.08	1287.07
58000	5171.19	3554.81	2748.21	2265.53	1944.81	1716.62	1546.27	1414.47	1309.65
59000	5260.35	3616.10	2795.60	2304.59	1978.34	1746.22	1572.93	1438.85	1332.23
60000	5349.51	3677.39	2842.98	2343.65	2011.87	1775.81	1599.59	1463.24	1354.81
61000	5438.67	3738.68	2890.36	2382.71	2045.40	1805.41	1626.25	1487.63	1377.39
62000	5527.83	3799.97	2937.74	2421.78	2078.93	1835.01	1652.91	1512.02	1399.97
63000	5616.99	3861.25	2985.13	2460.84	2112.46	1864.60	1679.57	1536.40	1422.55
64000	5706.15	3922.54	3032.51	2499.90	2145.99	1894.20	1706.23	1560.79	1445.13
65000	5795.30	3983.83	3079.89	2538.96	2179.52	1923.80	1732.88	1585.18	1467.71
66000	5884.46	4045.12	3127.28	2578.02	2213.05	1953.39	1759.54	1609.56	1490.29
67000	5973.62	4106.41	3174.66	2617.08	2246.58	1982.99	1786.20	1633.95	1512.87
68000	6062.78	4167.70	3222.04	2656.14	2280.12	2012.59	1812.86	1658.34	1535.45
69000	6151.94	4228.99	3269.42	2695.20	2313.65	2042.18	1839.52	1682.73	1558.03
70000	6241.10	4290.28	3316.81	2734.26	2347.18	2071.78	1866.18	1707.11	1580.61
75000	6686.89	4596.73	3553.72	2929.57	2514.83	2219.76	1999.48	1829.05	1693.51
80000	7132.68	4903.18	3790.64	3124.87	2682.49	2367.75	2132.78	1950.99	1806.41
100000	8915.85	6128.97	4738.29	3906.09	3353.11	2959.68	2665.97	2438.73	2258.01

100

MONTHLY PAYMENT 13%
NECESSARY TO AMORTIZE A LOAN

TERM AMOUNT	6 YEARS	7 YEARS	8 YEARS	9 YEARS	10 YEARS	11 YEARS	12 YEARS	13 YEARS	14 YEARS
$ 25	.50	.46	.42	.39	.37	.36	.34	.33	.32
50	1.00	.91	.84	.78	.74	.71	.68	.66	.64
75	1.50	1.36	1.25	1.17	1.11	1.06	1.02	.99	.96
100	1.99	1.81	1.67	1.56	1.48	1.41	1.36	1.31	1.28
200	3.98	3.61	3.33	3.12	2.95	2.82	2.71	2.62	2.55
300	5.97	5.41	4.99	4.67	4.42	4.23	4.07	3.93	3.83
400	7.96	7.21	6.65	6.23	5.90	5.63	5.42	5.24	5.10
500	9.95	9.01	8.31	7.78	7.37	7.04	6.77	6.55	6.37
600	11.94	10.81	9.98	9.34	8.84	8.45	8.13	7.86	7.65
700	13.93	12.61	11.64	10.90	10.32	9.86	9.48	9.17	8.92
800	15.92	14.41	13.30	12.45	11.79	11.26	10.83	10.48	10.19
900	17.91	16.21	14.96	14.01	13.26	12.67	12.19	11.79	11.47
1000	19.90	18.01	16.62	15.56	14.74	14.08	13.54	13.10	12.74
2000	39.80	36.02	33.24	31.12	29.47	28.15	27.08	26.20	25.47
3000	59.69	54.03	49.86	46.68	44.20	42.22	40.62	39.30	38.21
4000	79.59	72.04	66.48	62.24	58.93	56.29	54.15	52.40	50.94
5000	99.48	90.05	83.10	77.80	73.66	70.37	67.69	65.50	63.68
6000	119.38	108.05	99.72	93.36	88.40	84.44	81.23	78.60	76.41
7000	139.28	126.06	116.33	108.92	103.13	98.51	94.77	91.70	89.15
8000	159.17	144.07	132.95	124.48	117.86	112.58	108.30	104.79	101.88
9000	179.07	162.08	149.57	140.04	132.59	126.65	121.84	117.89	114.62
10000	198.96	180.09	166.19	155.60	147.32	140.73	135.38	130.99	127.35
15000	298.44	270.13	249.28	233.40	220.98	211.09	203.07	196.49	191.03
20000	397.92	360.17	332.37	311.20	294.64	281.45	270.75	261.98	254.70
25000	497.40	450.21	415.46	388.99	368.30	351.81	338.44	327.47	318.38
30000	596.88	540.25	498.56	466.79	441.96	422.17	406.13	392.97	382.05
35000	696.36	630.30	581.65	544.59	515.62	492.53	473.82	458.46	445.72
36000	716.25	648.30	598.27	560.15	530.36	506.60	487.35	471.56	458.46
37000	736.15	666.31	614.88	575.71	545.09	520.67	500.89	484.66	471.19
38000	756.04	684.32	631.50	591.27	559.82	534.74	514.43	497.76	483.93
39000	775.94	702.33	648.12	606.83	574.55	548.82	527.97	510.86	496.66
40000	795.84	720.34	664.74	622.39	589.28	562.89	541.50	523.95	509.40
41000	815.73	738.35	681.36	637.95	604.02	576.96	555.04	537.05	522.13
42000	835.63	756.35	697.98	653.51	618.75	591.03	568.58	550.15	534.87
43000	855.52	774.36	714.59	669.06	633.48	605.10	582.12	563.25	547.60
44000	875.42	792.37	731.21	684.62	648.21	619.18	595.65	576.35	560.34
45000	895.32	810.38	747.83	700.18	662.94	633.25	609.19	589.45	573.07
46000	915.21	828.39	764.45	715.74	677.68	647.32	622.73	602.55	585.81
47000	935.11	846.40	781.07	731.30	692.41	661.39	636.27	615.64	598.54
48000	955.00	864.40	797.69	746.86	707.14	675.46	649.80	628.74	611.28
49000	974.90	882.41	814.30	762.42	721.87	689.54	663.34	641.84	624.01
50000	994.79	900.42	830.92	777.98	736.60	703.61	676.88	654.94	636.75
51000	1014.69	918.43	847.54	793.54	751.33	717.68	690.42	668.04	649.48
52000	1034.59	936.44	864.16	809.10	766.07	731.75	703.95	681.14	662.22
53000	1054.48	954.45	880.78	824.66	780.80	745.83	717.49	694.24	674.95
54000	1074.38	972.45	897.40	840.22	795.53	759.90	731.03	707.34	687.69
55000	1094.27	990.46	914.01	855.78	810.26	773.97	744.57	720.43	700.42
56000	1114.17	1008.47	930.63	871.34	824.99	788.04	758.10	733.53	713.16
57000	1134.06	1026.48	947.25	886.90	839.73	802.11	771.64	746.63	725.89
58000	1153.96	1044.49	963.87	902.46	854.46	816.19	785.18	759.73	738.63
59000	1173.86	1062.50	980.49	918.02	869.19	830.26	798.72	772.83	751.36
60000	1193.75	1080.50	997.11	933.58	883.92	844.33	812.25	785.93	764.09
61000	1213.65	1098.51	1013.72	949.14	898.65	858.40	825.79	799.03	776.83
62000	1233.54	1116.52	1030.34	964.70	913.39	872.47	839.33	812.13	789.56
63000	1253.44	1134.53	1046.96	980.26	928.12	886.55	852.87	825.22	802.30
64000	1273.34	1152.54	1063.58	995.81	942.85	900.62	866.40	838.32	815.03
65000	1293.23	1170.55	1080.20	1011.37	957.58	914.69	879.94	851.42	827.77
66000	1313.13	1188.55	1096.82	1026.93	972.31	928.76	893.48	864.52	840.50
67000	1333.02	1206.56	1113.44	1042.49	987.05	942.83	907.02	877.62	853.24
68000	1352.92	1224.57	1130.05	1058.05	1001.78	956.91	920.55	890.72	865.97
69000	1372.81	1242.58	1146.67	1073.61	1016.51	970.98	934.09	903.82	878.71
70000	1392.71	1260.59	1163.29	1089.17	1031.24	985.05	947.63	916.92	891.44
75000	1492.19	1350.63	1246.38	1166.97	1104.90	1055.41	1015.31	982.41	955.12
80000	1591.67	1440.67	1329.47	1244.77	1178.56	1125.77	1083.00	1047.90	1018.79
100000	1989.58	1800.84	1661.84	1555.96	1473.20	1407.21	1353.75	1309.88	1273.49

13% MONTHLY PAYMENT
NECESSARY TO AMORTIZE A LOAN

TERM AMOUNT	15 YEARS	16 YEARS	17 YEARS	18 YEARS	19 YEARS	20 YEARS	21 YEARS	22 YEARS	23 YEARS
$ 25	.32	.31	.30	.30	.30	.29	.29	.29	.28
50	.63	.61	.60	.59	.59	.58	.57	.57	.56
75	.94	.92	.90	.89	.88	.87	.86	.85	.84
100	1.25	1.22	1.20	1.18	1.17	1.15	1.14	1.13	1.12
200	2.49	2.44	2.40	2.36	2.33	2.30	2.28	2.26	2.24
300	3.73	3.66	3.59	3.54	3.49	3.45	3.41	3.38	3.36
400	4.98	4.87	4.79	4.71	4.65	4.60	4.55	4.51	4.47
500	6.22	6.09	5.98	5.89	5.81	5.74	5.68	5.63	5.59
600	7.46	7.31	7.18	7.07	6.97	6.89	6.82	6.76	6.71
700	8.71	8.53	8.37	8.24	8.13	8.04	7.96	7.88	7.82
800	9.95	9.74	9.57	9.42	9.29	9.19	9.09	9.01	8.94
900	11.19	10.96	10.77	10.60	10.46	10.33	10.23	10.14	10.06
1000	12.44	12.18	11.96	11.78	11.62	11.48	11.36	11.26	11.17
2000	24.87	24.35	23.92	23.55	23.23	22.96	22.72	22.52	22.34
3000	37.30	36.53	35.87	35.32	34.84	34.43	34.08	33.77	33.51
4000	49.73	48.70	47.83	47.09	46.45	45.91	45.44	45.03	44.67
5000	62.16	60.87	59.79	58.86	58.06	57.38	56.79	56.28	55.84
6000	74.59	73.05	71.74	70.63	69.68	68.86	68.15	67.54	67.01
7000	87.02	85.22	83.70	82.40	81.29	80.33	79.51	78.80	78.18
8000	99.45	97.40	95.65	94.17	92.90	91.81	90.87	90.05	89.34
9000	111.88	109.57	107.61	105.94	104.51	103.28	102.22	101.31	100.51
10000	124.31	121.74	119.57	117.71	116.12	114.76	113.58	112.56	111.68
15000	186.46	182.61	179.35	176.57	174.18	172.13	170.37	168.84	167.52
20000	248.61	243.48	239.13	235.42	232.24	229.51	227.16	225.12	223.35
25000	310.76	304.35	298.91	294.27	290.30	286.89	283.94	281.40	279.19
30000	372.92	365.22	358.69	353.13	348.36	344.26	340.73	337.68	335.03
35000	435.07	426.09	418.47	411.98	406.42	401.64	397.52	393.96	390.87
36000	447.50	438.26	430.43	423.75	418.03	413.12	408.88	405.21	402.03
37000	459.93	450.43	442.38	435.52	429.64	424.59	420.24	416.47	413.20
38000	472.36	462.61	454.34	447.29	441.25	436.07	431.59	427.72	424.37
39000	484.79	474.78	466.30	459.06	452.87	447.54	442.95	438.98	435.54
40000	497.22	486.96	478.25	470.83	464.48	459.02	454.31	450.24	446.70
41000	509.65	499.13	490.21	482.60	476.09	470.49	465.67	461.49	457.87
42000	522.08	511.30	502.16	494.37	487.70	481.97	477.02	472.75	469.04
43000	534.51	523.48	514.12	506.14	499.31	493.44	488.38	484.00	480.21
44000	546.94	535.65	526.08	517.91	510.93	504.92	499.74	495.26	491.37
45000	559.37	547.82	538.03	529.69	522.54	516.39	511.10	506.51	502.54
46000	571.80	560.00	549.99	541.46	534.15	527.87	522.45	517.77	513.71
47000	584.23	572.17	561.94	553.23	545.76	539.34	533.81	529.03	524.88
48000	596.66	584.35	573.90	565.00	557.37	550.82	545.17	540.28	536.04
49000	609.09	596.52	585.86	576.77	568.98	562.29	556.53	551.54	547.21
50000	621.52	608.69	597.81	588.54	580.60	573.77	567.88	562.79	558.38
51000	633.95	620.87	609.77	600.31	592.21	585.25	579.24	574.05	569.55
52000	646.38	633.04	621.73	612.08	603.82	596.72	590.60	585.30	580.71
53000	658.81	645.21	633.68	623.85	615.43	608.20	601.96	596.56	591.88
54000	671.25	657.39	645.64	635.62	627.04	619.67	613.31	607.82	603.05
55000	683.68	669.56	657.59	647.39	638.66	631.15	624.67	619.07	614.22
56000	696.11	681.74	669.55	659.16	650.27	642.62	636.03	630.33	625.38
57000	708.54	693.91	681.51	670.93	661.88	654.10	647.39	641.58	636.55
58000	720.97	706.08	693.46	682.70	673.49	665.57	658.74	652.84	647.72
59000	733.40	718.26	705.42	694.47	685.10	677.05	670.10	664.09	658.89
60000	745.83	730.43	717.38	706.25	696.71	688.52	681.46	675.35	670.05
61000	758.26	742.61	729.33	718.02	708.33	700.00	692.82	686.61	681.22
62000	770.69	754.78	741.29	729.79	719.94	711.47	704.17	697.86	692.39
63000	783.12	766.95	753.24	741.56	731.55	722.95	715.53	709.12	703.56
64000	795.55	779.13	765.20	753.33	743.16	734.42	726.89	720.37	714.72
65000	807.98	791.30	777.16	765.10	754.77	745.90	738.25	731.63	725.89
66000	820.41	803.47	789.11	776.87	766.39	757.38	749.60	742.88	737.06
67000	832.84	815.65	801.07	788.64	778.00	768.85	760.96	754.14	748.23
68000	845.27	827.82	813.02	800.41	789.61	780.33	772.32	765.40	759.39
69000	857.70	840.00	824.98	812.18	801.22	791.80	783.68	776.65	770.56
70000	870.13	852.17	836.94	823.95	812.83	803.28	795.03	787.91	781.73
75000	932.28	913.04	896.72	882.81	870.89	860.65	851.82	844.19	837.57
80000	994.43	973.91	956.50	941.66	928.95	918.03	908.61	900.47	893.40
100000	1243.04	1217.38	1195.62	1177.00	1161.19	1147.54	1135.76	1125.58	1116.75

102

MONTHLY PAYMENT 13%
NECESSARY TO AMORTIZE A LOAN

TERM AMOUNT	24 YEARS	25 YEARS	26 YEARS	27 YEARS	28 YEARS	29 YEARS	30 YEARS	35 YEARS	40 YEARS
$ 25	.28	.28	.28	.28	.28	.28	.27	.27	.27
50	.56	.56	.55	.55	.55	.55	.54	.54	.54
75	.84	.83	.83	.82	.82	.82	.81	.81	.80
100	1.11	1.11	1.10	1.10	1.09	1.09	1.08	1.07	1.07
200	2.22	2.21	2.20	2.19	2.18	2.17	2.16	2.14	2.13
300	3.33	3.31	3.29	3.28	3.27	3.25	3.24	3.21	3.19
400	4.44	4.41	4.39	4.37	4.35	4.34	4.32	4.28	4.25
500	5.55	5.52	5.49	5.46	5.44	5.42	5.40	5.35	5.31
600	6.66	6.62	6.58	6.55	6.53	6.50	6.48	6.41	6.38
700	7.77	7.72	7.68	7.65	7.61	7.59	7.56	7.48	7.44
800	8.88	8.82	8.78	8.74	8.70	8.67	8.64	8.55	8.50
900	9.99	9.93	9.87	9.83	9.79	9.75	9.72	9.62	9.56
1000	11.10	11.03	10.97	10.92	10.88	10.84	10.80	10.69	10.62
2000	22.19	22.05	21.94	21.84	21.75	21.67	21.60	21.37	21.24
3000	33.28	33.08	32.90	32.75	32.62	32.50	32.40	32.05	31.86
4000	44.37	44.10	43.87	43.67	43.49	43.33	43.20	42.73	42.48
5000	55.46	55.13	54.83	54.58	54.36	54.16	53.99	53.41	53.10
6000	66.55	66.15	65.80	65.50	65.23	65.00	64.79	64.09	63.72
7000	77.64	77.17	76.77	76.41	76.10	75.83	75.59	74.77	74.34
8000	88.73	88.20	87.73	87.33	86.97	86.66	86.39	85.45	84.96
9000	99.82	99.22	98.70	98.24	97.84	97.49	97.19	96.14	95.58
10000	110.91	110.25	109.66	109.16	108.71	108.32	107.98	106.82	106.20
15000	166.37	165.37	164.49	163.73	163.07	162.48	161.97	160.22	159.30
20000	221.82	220.49	219.32	218.31	217.42	216.64	215.96	213.63	212.40
25000	277.28	275.61	274.15	272.88	271.77	270.80	269.95	267.03	265.50
30000	332.73	330.73	328.98	327.46	326.13	324.96	323.94	320.44	318.60
35000	388.18	385.85	383.81	382.03	380.48	379.12	377.93	373.84	371.70
36000	399.27	396.87	394.78	392.95	391.35	389.95	388.73	384.53	382.32
37000	410.37	407.90	405.74	403.86	402.22	400.79	399.53	395.21	392.94
38000	421.46	418.92	416.71	414.78	413.09	411.62	410.32	405.89	403.56
39000	432.55	429.94	427.68	425.69	423.96	422.45	421.12	416.57	414.18
40000	443.64	440.97	438.64	436.61	434.83	433.28	431.92	427.25	424.80
41000	454.73	451.99	449.61	447.52	445.70	444.11	442.72	437.93	435.42
42000	465.82	463.02	460.57	458.44	456.58	454.94	453.52	448.61	446.04
43000	476.91	474.04	471.54	469.35	467.45	465.78	464.31	459.29	456.66
44000	488.00	485.06	482.50	480.27	478.32	476.61	475.11	469.97	467.28
45000	499.09	496.09	493.47	491.19	489.19	487.44	485.91	480.66	477.90
46000	510.18	507.11	504.44	502.10	500.06	498.27	496.71	491.34	488.52
47000	521.27	518.14	515.40	513.02	510.93	509.10	507.51	502.02	499.14
48000	532.36	529.16	526.37	523.93	521.80	519.94	518.30	512.70	509.76
49000	543.45	540.18	537.33	534.85	532.67	530.77	529.10	523.38	520.38
50000	554.55	551.21	548.30	545.76	543.54	541.60	539.90	534.06	531.00
51000	565.64	562.23	559.27	556.68	554.41	552.43	550.70	544.74	541.62
52000	576.73	573.26	570.23	567.59	565.28	563.26	561.49	555.42	552.24
53000	587.82	584.28	581.20	578.51	576.15	574.10	572.29	566.11	562.86
54000	598.91	595.31	592.16	589.42	587.02	584.93	583.09	576.79	573.48
55000	610.00	606.33	603.13	600.34	597.90	595.76	593.89	587.47	584.10
56000	621.09	617.35	614.10	611.25	608.77	606.59	604.69	598.15	594.72
57000	632.18	628.38	625.06	622.17	619.64	617.42	615.48	608.83	605.34
58000	643.27	639.40	636.03	633.08	630.51	628.25	626.28	619.51	615.96
59000	654.36	650.43	646.99	644.00	641.38	639.09	637.08	630.19	626.58
60000	665.45	661.45	657.96	654.91	652.25	649.92	647.88	640.87	637.20
61000	676.54	672.47	668.92	665.83	663.12	660.75	658.68	651.55	647.82
62000	687.64	683.50	679.89	676.74	673.99	671.58	669.47	662.24	658.44
63000	698.73	694.52	690.86	687.66	684.86	682.41	680.27	672.92	669.06
64000	709.82	705.55	701.82	698.57	695.73	693.25	691.07	683.60	679.68
65000	720.91	716.57	712.79	709.49	706.60	704.08	701.87	694.28	690.30
66000	732.00	727.59	723.75	720.40	717.47	714.91	712.67	704.96	700.92
67000	743.09	738.62	734.72	731.32	728.34	725.74	723.46	715.64	711.54
68000	754.18	749.64	745.69	742.23	739.21	736.57	734.26	726.32	722.16
69000	765.27	760.67	756.65	753.15	750.09	747.41	745.06	737.00	732.78
70000	776.36	771.69	767.62	764.06	760.96	758.24	755.86	747.68	743.40
75000	831.82	826.81	822.45	818.64	815.31	812.40	809.85	801.09	796.50
80000	887.27	881.93	877.28	873.21	869.66	866.56	863.84	854.50	849.60
100000	1109.09	1102.41	1096.59	1091.52	1087.08	1083.19	1079.79	1068.12	1062.00

103

13¼% MONTHLY PAYMENT
NECESSARY TO AMORTIZE A LOAN

TERM AMOUNT	1 YEAR	1½ YEARS	2 YEARS	2½ YEARS	3 YEARS	3½ YEARS	4 YEARS	4½ YEARS	5 YEARS
$ 25	2.24	1.54	1.19	.98	.85	.75	.67	.62	.57
50	4.47	3.08	2.38	1.96	1.69	1.49	1.34	1.23	1.14
75	6.70	4.61	3.57	2.94	2.53	2.23	2.01	1.84	1.71
100	8.93	6.15	4.75	3.92	3.37	2.98	2.68	2.46	2.28
200	17.86	12.29	9.50	7.84	6.73	5.95	5.36	4.91	4.55
300	26.79	18.43	14.25	11.76	10.10	8.92	8.04	7.36	6.82
400	35.71	24.57	19.00	15.67	13.46	11.89	10.72	9.81	9.09
500	44.64	30.71	23.75	19.59	16.83	14.86	13.39	12.26	11.36
600	53.57	36.85	28.50	23.51	20.19	17.83	16.07	14.71	13.63
700	62.49	42.99	33.25	27.43	23.56	20.80	18.75	17.16	15.90
800	71.42	49.13	38.00	31.34	26.92	23.77	21.43	19.61	18.17
900	80.35	55.27	42.75	35.26	30.29	26.75	24.10	22.06	20.44
1000	89.27	61.41	47.50	39.18	33.65	29.72	26.78	24.51	22.71
2000	178.54	122.81	94.99	78.35	67.30	59.43	53.56	49.02	45.41
3000	267.81	184.21	142.49	117.52	100.94	89.14	80.34	73.52	68.11
4000	357.08	245.61	189.98	156.70	134.59	118.85	107.11	98.03	90.81
5000	446.35	307.01	237.48	195.87	168.23	148.57	133.89	122.54	113.51
6000	535.62	368.41	284.97	235.04	201.88	178.28	160.67	147.04	136.21
7000	624.89	429.81	332.46	274.22	235.52	207.99	187.44	171.55	158.91
8000	714.16	491.21	379.96	313.39	269.17	237.70	214.22	196.06	181.61
9000	803.43	552.61	427.45	352.56	302.81	267.42	241.00	220.56	204.31
10000	892.70	614.01	474.95	391.74	336.46	297.13	267.78	245.07	227.02
15000	1339.05	921.01	712.42	587.60	504.68	445.69	401.66	367.60	340.52
20000	1785.40	1228.01	949.89	783.47	672.91	594.25	535.55	490.13	454.03
25000	2231.75	1535.01	1187.36	979.34	841.13	742.82	669.43	612.67	567.53
30000	2678.09	1842.01	1424.83	1175.20	1009.36	891.38	803.32	735.20	681.04
35000	3124.44	2149.01	1662.30	1371.07	1177.58	1039.94	937.20	857.73	794.54
36000	3213.71	2210.41	1709.79	1410.24	1211.23	1069.65	963.98	882.24	817.24
37000	3302.98	2271.81	1757.29	1449.42	1244.87	1099.37	990.76	906.74	839.95
38000	3392.25	2333.21	1804.78	1488.59	1278.52	1129.08	1017.53	931.25	862.65
39000	3481.52	2394.61	1852.28	1527.76	1312.16	1158.79	1044.31	955.76	885.35
40000	3570.79	2456.01	1899.77	1566.94	1345.81	1188.50	1071.09	980.26	908.05
41000	3660.06	2517.41	1947.26	1606.11	1379.45	1218.22	1097.87	1004.77	930.75
42000	3749.33	2578.81	1994.76	1645.28	1413.10	1247.93	1124.64	1029.28	953.45
43000	3838.60	2640.21	2042.25	1684.46	1446.74	1277.64	1151.42	1053.78	976.15
44000	3927.87	2701.61	2089.75	1723.63	1480.39	1307.35	1178.20	1078.29	998.85
45000	4017.14	2763.01	2137.24	1762.80	1514.03	1337.07	1204.97	1102.80	1021.55
46000	4106.41	2824.41	2184.73	1801.98	1547.68	1366.78	1231.75	1127.30	1044.26
47000	4195.68	2885.81	2232.23	1841.15	1581.32	1396.49	1258.53	1151.81	1066.96
48000	4284.95	2947.21	2279.72	1880.32	1614.97	1426.20	1285.31	1176.32	1089.66
49000	4374.22	3008.61	2327.22	1919.50	1648.61	1455.92	1312.09	1200.82	1112.36
50000	4463.49	3070.01	2374.71	1958.67	1682.26	1485.63	1338.86	1225.33	1135.06
51000	4552.76	3131.42	2422.20	1997.84	1715.90	1515.34	1365.64	1249.84	1157.76
52000	4642.02	3192.82	2469.70	2037.02	1749.55	1545.05	1392.41	1274.34	1180.46
53000	4731.29	3254.22	2517.19	2076.19	1783.19	1574.76	1419.19	1298.85	1203.16
54000	4820.56	3315.62	2564.69	2115.36	1816.84	1604.48	1445.97	1323.35	1225.86
55000	4909.83	3377.02	2612.18	2154.54	1850.48	1634.19	1472.75	1347.86	1248.57
56000	4999.10	3438.42	2659.68	2193.71	1884.13	1663.90	1499.52	1372.37	1271.27
57000	5088.37	3499.82	2707.17	2232.88	1917.77	1693.61	1526.30	1396.87	1293.97
58000	5177.64	3561.22	2754.66	2272.06	1951.42	1723.33	1553.08	1421.38	1316.67
59000	5266.91	3622.62	2802.16	2311.23	1985.06	1753.04	1579.85	1445.89	1339.37
60000	5356.18	3684.02	2849.65	2350.40	2018.71	1782.75	1606.63	1470.39	1362.07
61000	5445.45	3745.42	2897.15	2389.58	2052.35	1812.46	1633.41	1494.90	1384.77
62000	5534.72	3806.82	2944.64	2428.75	2086.00	1842.18	1660.18	1519.41	1407.47
63000	5623.99	3868.22	2992.13	2467.92	2119.64	1871.89	1686.96	1543.91	1430.17
64000	5713.26	3929.62	3039.63	2507.10	2153.29	1901.60	1713.74	1568.42	1452.87
65000	5802.53	3991.02	3087.12	2546.27	2186.93	1931.31	1740.52	1592.93	1475.58
66000	5891.80	4052.42	3134.62	2585.44	2220.58	1961.03	1767.29	1617.43	1498.28
67000	5981.07	4113.82	3182.11	2624.62	2254.22	1990.74	1794.07	1641.94	1520.98
68000	6070.34	4175.22	3229.60	2663.79	2287.87	2020.45	1820.85	1666.45	1543.68
69000	6159.61	4236.62	3277.10	2702.96	2321.51	2050.16	1847.62	1690.95	1566.38
70000	6248.88	4298.02	3324.59	2742.14	2355.16	2079.88	1874.40	1715.46	1589.08
75000	6695.23	4605.02	3562.06	2938.00	2523.38	2228.44	2008.29	1837.99	1702.59
80000	7141.57	4912.02	3799.53	3133.87	2691.61	2377.00	2142.17	1960.52	1816.09
100000	8926.97	6140.02	4749.42	3917.33	3364.51	2971.25	2677.71	2450.65	2270.11

104

MONTHLY PAYMENT 13¼%
NECESSARY TO AMORTIZE A LOAN

TERM AMOUNT	6 YEARS	7 YEARS	8 YEARS	9 YEARS	10 YEARS	11 YEARS	12 YEARS	13 YEARS	14 YEARS
$ 25	.51	.46	42	40	.38	.36	.35	.34	.33
50	1.01	.91	.84	.79	.75	.72	.69	.67	.65
75	1.51	1.37	1.26	1.18	1.12	1.07	1.03	1.00	.97
100	2.01	1.82	1.68	1.57	1.49	1.43	1.37	1.33	1.29
200	4.01	3.63	3.36	3.14	2.98	2.85	2.74	2.65	2.58
300	6.01	5.45	5.03	4.71	4.47	4.27	4.11	3.98	3.87
400	8.01	7.26	6.71	6.28	5.95	5.69	5.48	5.30	5.16
500	10.02	9.07	8.38	7.85	7.44	7.11	6.85	6.63	6.45
600	12.02	10.89	10.06	9.42	8.93	8.53	8.22	7.95	7.74
700	14.02	12.70	11.73	10.99	10.41	9.96	9.58	9.28	9.03
800	16.02	14.51	13.41	12.56	11.90	11.38	10.95	10.60	10.31
900	18.02	16.33	15.08	14.13	13.39	12.80	12.32	11.93	11.60
1000	20.03	18.14	16.76	15.70	14.80	14.22	13.69	13.25	12.89
2000	40.05	36.28	33.51	31.40	29.75	28.43	27.37	26.50	25.78
3000	60.07	54.42	50.26	47.09	44.62	42.65	41.06	39.75	38.67
4000	80.09	72.55	67.01	62.79	59.49	56.86	54.74	53.00	51.55
5000	100.11	90.69	83.76	78.48	74.36	71.08	68.42	66.24	64.44
6000	120.13	108.83	100.51	94.18	89.23	85.29	82.11	79.49	77.33
7000	140.15	126.96	117.26	109.87	104.10	99.51	95.79	92.74	90.21
8000	160.17	145.10	134.01	125.57	118.97	113.72	109.47	105.99	103.10
9000	180.19	163.24	150.76	141.26	133.85	127.94	123.16	119.24	115.99
10000	200.21	181.37	167.51	156.96	148.72	142.15	136.84	132.48	128.88
15000	300.31	272.06	251.26	235.43	223.07	213.23	205.26	198.72	193.31
20000	400.42	362.74	335.01	313.91	297.43	284.30	273.67	264.96	257.75
25000	500.52	453.42	418.77	392.39	371.79	355.37	342.09	331.20	322.18
30000	600.62	544.11	502.52	470.86	446.14	426.45	410.51	397.44	386.62
35000	700.72	634.79	586.27	549.34	520.50	497.52	478.93	463.68	451.05
36000	720.74	652.93	603.02	565.03	535.37	511.74	492.61	476.93	463.94
37000	740.76	671.07	619.77	580.73	550.24	525.95	506.29	490.18	476.83
38000	760.78	689.20	636.52	596.42	565.11	540.17	519.98	503.43	489.72
39000	780.81	707.34	653.27	612.12	579.98	554.38	533.66	516.67	502.60
40000	800.83	725.48	670.02	627.81	594.85	568.60	547.34	529.92	515.49
41000	820.85	743.61	686.77	643.51	609.72	582.81	561.03	543.17	528.38
42000	840.87	761.75	703.52	659.21	624.60	597.02	574.71	556.42	541.26
43000	860.89	779.89	720.28	674.90	639.47	611.24	588.39	569.67	554.15
44000	880.91	798.02	737.03	690.60	654.34	625.45	602.08	582.91	567.04
45000	900.93	816.16	753.78	706.29	669.21	639.67	615.76	596.16	579.93
46000	920.95	834.30	770.53	721.99	684.08	653.88	629.44	609.41	592.81
47000	940.97	852.43	787.28	737.68	698.95	668.10	643.13	622.66	605.70
48000	960.99	870.57	804.03	753.38	713.82	682.31	656.81	635.91	618.59
49000	981.01	888.71	820.78	769.07	728.69	696.53	670.49	649.15	631.47
50000	1001.03	906.84	837.53	784.77	743.57	710.74	684.18	662.40	644.36
51000	1021.05	924.98	854.28	800.46	758.44	724.96	697.86	675.65	657.25
52000	1041.07	943.12	871.03	816.16	773.31	739.17	711.55	688.90	670.14
53000	1061.09	961.25	887.78	831.85	788.18	753.39	725.23	702.15	683.02
54000	1081.11	979.39	904.53	847.55	803.05	767.60	738.91	715.39	695.91
55000	1101.13	997.53	921.28	863.24	817.92	781.82	752.60	728.64	708.80
56000	1121.15	1015.66	938.03	878.94	832.79	796.03	766.28	741.89	721.68
57000	1141.17	1033.80	954.78	894.63	847.66	810.25	779.96	755.14	734.57
58000	1161.20	1051.94	971.53	910.33	862.53	824.46	793.65	768.38	747.46
59000	1181.22	1070.07	988.28	926.02	877.41	838.68	807.33	781.63	760.35
60000	1201.24	1088.21	1005.03	941.72	892.28	852.89	821.01	794.88	773.23
61000	1221.26	1106.35	1021.78	957.41	907.15	867.10	834.70	808.13	786.12
62000	1241.28	1124.48	1038.53	973.11	922.02	881.32	848.38	821.38	799.01
63000	1261.30	1142.62	1055.28	988.81	936.89	895.53	862.06	834.62	811.89
64000	1281.32	1160.76	1072.04	1004.50	951.76	909.75	875.75	847.87	824.78
65000	1301.34	1178.89	1088.79	1020.20	966.63	923.96	889.43	861.12	837.67
66000	1321.36	1197.03	1105.54	1035.89	981.50	938.18	903.11	874.37	850.56
67000	1341.38	1215.17	1122.29	1051.59	996.38	952.39	916.80	887.62	863.44
68000	1361.40	1233.31	1139.04	1067.28	1011.25	966.61	930.48	900.86	876.33
69000	1381.42	1251.44	1155.79	1082.98	1026.12	980.82	944.16	914.11	889.22
70000	1401.44	1269.58	1172.54	1098.67	1040.99	995.04	957.85	927.36	902.10
75000	1501.54	1360.26	1256.29	1177.15	1115.35	1066.11	1026.26	993.60	966.54
80000	1601.65	1450.95	1340.04	1255.62	1189.70	1137.19	1094.68	1059.84	1030.98
100000	2002.06	1813.68	1675.05	1569.53	1487.13	1421.48	1368.35	1324.80	1288.72

13¼% MONTHLY PAYMENT
NECESSARY TO AMORTIZE A LOAN

TERM AMOUNT	15 YEARS	16 YEARS	17 YEARS	18 YEARS	19 YEARS	20 YEARS	21 YEARS	22 YEARS	23 YEARS
$ 25	.32	.31	.31	.30	.30	.30	.29	.29	.29
50	.63	.62	.61	.60	.59	.59	.58	.58	.57
75	.95	.93	.91	.90	.89	.88	.87	.86	.86
100	1.26	1.24	1.22	1.20	1.18	1.17	1.16	1.15	1.14
200	2.52	2.47	2.43	2.39	2.36	2.33	2.31	2.29	2.27
300	3.78	3.70	3.64	3.59	3.54	3.50	3.46	3.43	3.41
400	5.04	4.94	4.85	4.78	4.72	4.66	4.62	4.58	4.54
500	6.30	6.17	6.06	5.97	5.89	5.83	5.77	5.72	5.68
600	7.56	7.40	7.28	7.17	7.07	6.99	6.92	6.86	6.81
700	8.81	8.64	8.49	8.36	8.25	8.16	8.07	8.00	7.94
800	10.07	9.87	9.70	9.55	9.43	9.32	9.23	9.15	9.08
900	11.33	11.10	10.91	10.75	10.60	10.48	10.38	10.29	10.21
1000	12.59	12.34	12.12	11.94	11.78	11.65	11.53	11.43	11.35
2000	25.18	24.67	24.24	23.87	23.56	23.29	23.06	22.86	22.69
3000	37.76	37.00	36.36	35.81	35.34	34.94	34.59	34.29	34.03
4000	50.35	49.33	48.47	47.74	47.12	46.58	46.12	45.72	45.37
5000	62.93	61.66	60.59	59.68	58.89	58.22	57.64	57.15	56.71
6000	75.52	74.00	72.71	71.61	70.67	69.87	69.17	68.57	68.06
7000	88.10	86.33	84.82	83.54	82.45	81.51	80.70	80.00	79.40
8000	100.69	98.66	96.94	95.48	94.23	93.15	92.23	91.43	90.74
9000	113.28	110.99	109.06	107.41	106.00	104.80	103.76	102.86	102.08
10000	125.86	123.32	121.17	119.35	117.78	116.44	115.28	114.29	113.42
15000	188.79	184.98	181.76	179.02	176.67	174.66	172.92	171.43	170.13
20000	251.72	246.64	242.34	238.69	235.56	232.87	230.56	228.57	226.84
25000	314.65	308.30	302.93	298.36	294.45	291.09	288.20	285.71	283.55
30000	377.57	369.96	363.51	358.03	353.33	349.31	345.84	342.85	340.26
35000	440.50	431.62	424.10	417.70	412.22	407.53	403.48	399.99	396.97
36000	453.09	443.95	436.22	429.63	424.00	419.17	415.01	411.42	408.31
37000	465.67	456.28	448.33	441.56	435.78	430.81	426.54	422.85	419.65
38000	478.26	468.62	460.45	453.50	447.56	442.46	438.07	434.27	430.99
39000	490.84	480.95	472.57	465.43	459.33	454.10	449.59	445.70	442.34
40000	503.43	493.28	484.68	477.37	471.11	465.74	461.12	457.13	453.68
41000	516.02	505.61	496.80	489.30	482.89	477.39	472.65	468.56	465.02
42000	528.60	517.94	508.92	501.24	494.67	489.03	484.18	479.99	476.36
43000	541.19	530.28	521.03	513.17	506.44	500.67	495.70	491.42	487.70
44000	553.77	542.61	533.15	525.10	518.22	512.32	507.23	502.84	499.04
45000	566.36	554.94	545.27	537.04	530.00	523.96	518.76	514.27	510.39
46000	578.94	567.27	557.39	548.97	541.78	535.60	530.29	525.70	521.73
47000	591.53	579.60	569.50	560.91	553.55	547.25	541.82	537.13	533.07
48000	604.12	591.93	581.62	572.84	565.33	558.89	553.34	548.56	544.41
49000	616.70	604.27	593.74	584.77	577.11	570.53	564.87	559.98	555.75
50000	629.29	616.60	605.85	596.71	588.89	582.18	576.40	571.41	567.10
51000	641.87	628.93	617.97	608.64	600.67	593.82	587.93	582.84	578.44
52000	654.46	641.26	630.09	620.58	612.44	605.46	599.46	594.27	589.78
53000	667.04	653.59	642.20	632.51	624.22	617.11	610.98	605.70	601.12
54000	679.63	665.93	654.32	644.44	636.00	628.75	622.51	617.12	612.46
55000	692.22	678.26	666.44	656.38	647.78	640.39	634.04	628.55	623.80
56000	704.80	690.59	678.56	668.31	659.55	652.04	645.57	639.98	635.15
57000	717.39	702.92	690.67	680.25	671.33	663.68	657.10	651.41	646.49
58000	729.97	715.25	702.79	692.18	683.11	675.32	668.62	662.84	657.83
59000	742.56	727.59	714.91	704.11	694.89	686.97	680.15	674.27	669.17
60000	755.14	739.92	727.02	716.05	706.66	698.61	691.68	685.69	680.51
61000	767.73	752.25	739.14	727.98	718.44	710.26	703.21	697.12	691.86
62000	780.31	764.58	751.26	739.92	730.22	721.90	714.73	708.55	703.20
63000	792.90	776.91	763.37	751.85	742.00	733.54	726.26	719.98	714.54
64000	805.49	789.24	775.49	763.78	753.78	745.19	737.79	731.41	725.88
65000	818.07	801.58	787.61	775.72	765.55	756.83	749.32	742.83	737.22
66000	830.66	813.91	799.73	787.65	777.33	768.47	760.85	754.26	748.56
67000	843.24	826.24	811.84	799.59	789.11	780.12	772.37	765.69	759.91
68000	855.83	838.57	823.96	811.52	800.89	791.76	783.90	777.12	771.25
69000	868.41	850.90	836.08	823.45	812.66	803.40	795.43	788.55	782.59
70000	881.00	863.24	848.19	835.39	824.44	815.05	806.96	799.97	793.93
75000	943.93	924.90	908.78	895.06	883.33	873.26	864.60	857.12	850.64
80000	1006.86	986.55	969.36	954.73	942.22	931.48	922.24	914.26	907.35
100000	1258.57	1233.19	1211.70	1193.41	1177.77	1164.35	1152.79	1142.82	1134.19

TERM AMOUNT	24 YEARS	25 YEARS	26 YEARS	27 YEARS	28 YEARS	29 YEARS	30 YEARS	35 YEARS	40 YEARS
$ 25	.29	.29	.28	.28	.28	.28	.28	.28	.28
50	.57	.57	.56	.56	.56	.56	.55	.55	.55
75	.85	.85	.84	.84	.83	.83	.83	.82	.82
100	1.13	1.13	1.12	1.11	1.11	1.11	1.10	1.09	1.09
200	2.26	2.25	2.23	2.22	2.22	2.21	2.20	2.18	2.17
300	3.39	3.37	3.35	3.33	3.32	3.31	3.30	3.27	3.25
400	4.51	4.49	4.46	4.44	4.43	4.41	4.40	4.35	4.33
500	5.64	5.61	5.58	5.55	5.53	5.51	5.50	5.44	5.41
600	6.77	6.73	6.69	6.66	6.64	6.61	6.59	6.53	6.49
700	7.89	7.85	7.81	7.77	7.74	7.72	7.69	7.61	7.57
800	9.02	8.97	8.92	8.88	8.85	8.82	8.79	8.70	8.66
900	10.15	10.09	10.04	9.99	9.95	9.92	9.80	9.79	9.74
1000	11.27	11.21	11.15	11.10	11.06	11.02	10.99	10.88	10.82
2000	22.54	22.41	22.30	22.20	22.11	22.04	21.97	21.75	21.63
3000	33.81	33.61	33.44	33.29	33.16	33.05	32.95	32.62	32.44
4000	45.07	44.81	44.59	44.39	44.22	44.07	43.94	43.49	43.26
5000	56.34	56.01	55.73	55.49	55.27	55.08	54.92	54.36	54.07
6000	67.61	67.22	66.88	66.58	66.32	66.10	65.90	65.23	64.88
7000	78.87	78.42	78.02	77.68	77.38	77.11	76.88	76.10	75.69
8000	90.14	89.62	89.17	88.77	88.43	88.13	87.87	86.97	86.51
9000	101.41	100.82	100.31	99.87	99.48	99.14	98.85	97.84	97.32
10000	112.67	112.02	111.46	110.97	110.54	110.16	109.83	108.71	108.13
15000	169.01	168.03	167.18	166.45	165.80	165.24	164.74	163.06	162.19
20000	225.34	224.04	222.91	221.93	221.07	220.31	219.66	217.42	216.26
25000	281.68	280.05	278.64	277.41	276.33	275.39	274.57	271.77	270.32
30000	338.01	336.06	334.36	332.89	331.60	330.47	329.48	326.12	324.38
35000	394.35	392.07	390.09	388.37	386.86	385.55	384.40	380.48	378.44
36000	405.62	403.27	401.24	399.46	397.91	396.56	395.38	391.35	389.26
37000	416.88	414.48	412.38	410.56	408.97	407.58	406.36	402.22	400.07
38000	428.15	425.68	423.53	421.65	420.02	418.59	417.34	413.09	410.88
39000	439.42	436.88	434.67	432.75	431.07	429.61	428.33	423.96	421.69
40000	450.68	448.08	445.82	443.85	442.13	440.62	439.31	434.83	432.51
41000	461.95	459.28	456.96	454.94	453.18	451.64	450.29	445.70	443.32
42000	473.22	470.49	468.11	466.04	464.23	462.65	461.28	456.57	454.13
43000	484.48	481.69	479.25	477.13	475.28	473.67	472.26	467.44	464.94
44000	495.75	492.89	490.40	488.23	486.34	484.69	483.24	478.31	475.76
45000	507.02	504.09	501.54	499.33	497.39	495.70	494.22	489.18	486.57
46000	518.28	515.29	512.69	510.42	508.44	506.72	505.21	500.05	497.38
47000	529.55	526.49	523.84	521.52	519.50	517.73	516.19	510.92	508.19
48000	540.82	537.70	534.98	532.61	530.55	528.75	527.17	521.79	519.01
49000	552.09	548.90	546.13	543.71	541.60	539.76	538.15	532.66	529.82
50000	563.35	560.10	557.27	554.81	552.66	550.78	549.14	543.53	540.63
51000	574.62	571.30	568.42	565.90	563.71	561.79	560.12	554.41	551.44
52000	585.89	582.50	579.56	577.00	574.76	572.81	571.10	565.28	562.26
53000	597.15	593.71	590.71	588.09	585.81	583.82	582.08	576.15	573.07
54000	608.42	604.91	601.85	599.19	596.87	594.84	593.07	587.02	583.88
55000	619.69	616.11	613.00	610.29	607.92	605.86	604.05	597.89	594.69
56000	630.95	627.31	624.14	621.38	618.97	616.87	615.03	608.76	605.51
57000	642.22	638.51	635.29	632.48	630.03	627.89	626.01	619.63	616.32
58000	653.49	649.72	646.43	643.57	641.08	638.90	637.00	630.50	627.13
59000	664.75	660.92	657.58	654.67	652.13	649.92	647.98	641.37	637.94
60000	676.02	672.12	668.72	665.77	663.19	660.93	658.96	652.24	648.76
61000	687.29	683.32	679.87	676.86	674.24	671.95	669.95	663.11	659.57
62000	698.56	694.52	691.02	687.96	685.29	682.96	680.93	673.98	670.38
63000	709.82	705.73	702.16	699.05	696.34	693.98	691.91	684.85	681.19
64000	721.09	716.93	713.31	710.15	707.40	704.99	702.89	695.72	692.01
65000	732.36	728.13	724.45	721.25	718.45	716.01	713.88	706.59	702.82
66000	743.62	739.33	735.60	732.34	729.50	727.03	724.86	717.46	713.63
67000	754.89	750.53	746.74	743.44	740.56	738.04	735.84	728.33	724.44
68000	766.16	761.73	757.89	754.53	751.61	749.06	746.82	739.21	735.26
69000	777.42	772.94	769.03	765.63	762.66	760.07	757.81	750.08	746.07
70000	788.69	784.14	780.18	776.73	773.72	771.09	768.79	760.95	756.88
75000	845.03	840.15	835.90	832.21	828.98	826.16	823.70	815.30	810.94
80000	901.36	896.16	891.63	887.69	884.25	881.24	878.62	869.65	865.01
100000	1126.70	1120.20	1114.54	1109.61	1105.31	1101.55	1098.27	1087.06	1081.26

13½% MONTHLY PAYMENT
NECESSARY TO AMORTIZE A LOAN

TERM AMOUNT	1 YEAR	1½ YEARS	2 YEARS	2½ YEARS	3 YEARS	3½ YEARS	4 YEARS	4½ YEARS	5 YEARS
$ 25	2.24	1.54	1.20	.99	.85	.75	.68	.62	.58
50	4.47	3.08	2.39	1.97	1.69	1.50	1.35	1.24	1.15
75	6.71	4.62	3.58	2.95	2.54	2.24	2.02	1.85	1.72
100	8.94	6.16	4.77	3.93	3.38	2.99	2.69	2.47	2.29
200	17.88	12.31	9.53	7.86	6.76	5.97	5.38	4.93	4.57
300	26.82	18.46	14.29	11.79	10.13	8.95	8.07	7.39	6.85
400	35.76	24.61	19.05	15.72	13.51	11.94	10.76	9.86	9.13
500	44.70	30.76	23.81	19.65	16.88	14.92	13.45	12.32	11.42
600	53.63	36.91	28.57	23.58	20.26	17.90	16.14	14.78	13.70
700	62.57	43.06	33.33	27.51	23.64	20.88	18.83	17.24	15.98
800	71.51	49.21	38.09	31.43	27.01	23.87	21.52	19.71	18.26
900	80.45	55.36	42.85	35.36	30.39	26.85	24.21	22.17	20.55
1000	89.39	61.52	47.61	39.29	33.76	29.83	26.90	24.63	22.83
2000	178.77	123.03	95.22	78.58	67.52	59.66	53.79	49.26	45.65
3000	268.15	184.54	142.82	117.86	101.28	89.49	80.69	73.88	68.47
4000	357.53	246.05	190.43	157.15	135.04	119.32	107.58	98.51	91.29
5000	446.91	307.56	238.03	196.43	168.80	149.15	134.48	123.13	114.12
6000	536.29	369.07	285.64	235.72	202.56	178.97	161.37	147.76	136.94
7000	625.67	430.58	333.24	275.01	236.32	208.80	188.27	172.39	159.76
8000	715.05	492.09	380.85	314.29	270.08	238.63	215.16	197.01	182.58
9000	804.43	553.60	428.45	353.58	303.84	268.46	242.06	221.64	205.41
10000	893.81	615.11	476.06	392.86	337.60	298.29	268.95	246.26	228.23
15000	1340.72	922.67	714.09	589.29	506.39	447.43	403.43	369.39	342.34
20000	1787.62	1230.22	952.11	785.72	675.19	596.57	537.90	492.52	456.45
25000	2234.52	1537.77	1190.14	982.15	843.98	745.71	672.37	615.65	570.56
30000	2681.43	1845.33	1428.17	1178.58	1012.78	894.85	806.85	738.78	684.68
35000	3128.33	2152.88	1666.19	1375.01	1181.57	1043.99	941.32	861.91	798.79
36000	3217.71	2214.39	1713.80	1414.30	1215.33	1073.82	968.21	886.54	821.61
37000	3307.09	2275.90	1761.40	1453.58	1249.09	1103.65	995.11	911.16	844.43
38000	3396.47	2337.41	1809.01	1492.87	1282.85	1133.48	1022.00	935.79	867.26
39000	3485.85	2398.92	1856.61	1532.15	1316.61	1163.31	1048.90	960.41	890.08
40000	3575.23	2460.43	1904.22	1571.44	1350.37	1193.14	1075.79	985.04	912.90
41000	3664.62	2521.94	1951.83	1610.72	1384.13	1222.96	1102.69	1009.67	935.72
42000	3754.00	2583.46	1999.43	1650.01	1417.89	1252.79	1129.58	1034.29	958.54
43000	3843.38	2644.97	2047.04	1689.30	1451.65	1282.62	1156.48	1058.92	981.37
44000	3932.76	2706.48	2094.64	1728.58	1485.41	1312.45	1183.37	1083.54	1004.19
45000	4022.14	2767.99	2142.25	1767.87	1519.17	1342.28	1210.27	1108.17	1027.01
46000	4111.52	2829.50	2189.85	1807.15	1552.93	1372.10	1237.16	1132.80	1049.83
47000	4200.90	2891.01	2237.46	1846.44	1586.68	1401.93	1264.05	1157.42	1072.66
48000	4290.28	2952.52	2285.06	1885.73	1620.44	1431.76	1290.95	1182.05	1095.48
49000	4379.66	3014.03	2332.67	1925.01	1654.20	1461.59	1317.84	1206.67	1118.30
50000	4469.04	3075.54	2380.27	1964.30	1687.96	1491.42	1344.74	1231.30	1141.12
51000	4558.42	3137.05	2427.88	2003.58	1721.72	1521.25	1371.63	1255.93	1163.95
52000	4647.80	3198.56	2475.48	2042.87	1755.48	1551.07	1398.53	1280.55	1186.77
53000	4737.18	3260.01	2523.09	2082.15	1789.24	1580.90	1425.42	1305.18	1209.59
54000	4826.57	3321.58	2570.70	2121.44	1823.00	1610.73	1452.32	1329.80	1232.41
55000	4915.95	3383.09	2618.30	2160.73	1856.76	1640.56	1479.21	1354.43	1255.24
56000	5005.33	3444.61	2665.91	2200.01	1890.52	1670.39	1506.11	1379.05	1278.06
57000	5094.71	3506.12	2713.51	2239.30	1924.28	1700.22	1533.00	1403.68	1300.88
58000	5184.09	3567.63	2761.12	2278.58	1958.04	1730.04	1559.90	1428.31	1323.70
59000	5273.47	3629.14	2808.72	2317.87	1991.79	1759.87	1586.79	1452.93	1346.53
60000	5362.85	3690.65	2856.33	2357.16	2025.55	1789.70	1613.69	1477.56	1369.35
61000	5452.23	3752.16	2903.93	2396.44	2059.31	1819.53	1640.58	1502.18	1392.17
62000	5541.61	3813.67	2951.54	2435.73	2093.07	1849.36	1667.48	1526.81	1414.99
63000	5630.99	3875.18	2999.14	2475.01	2126.83	1879.19	1694.37	1551.44	1437.81
64000	5720.37	3936.69	3046.75	2514.30	2160.59	1909.01	1721.26	1576.06	1460.64
65000	5809.75	3998.20	3094.35	2553.59	2194.35	1938.84	1748.16	1600.69	1483.46
66000	5899.13	4059.71	3141.96	2592.87	2228.11	1968.67	1775.05	1625.31	1506.28
67000	5988.52	4121.22	3189.57	2632.16	2261.87	1998.50	1801.95	1649.94	1529.10
68000	6077.90	4182.73	3237.17	2671.44	2295.63	2028.33	1828.84	1674.57	1551.93
69000	6167.28	4244.24	3284.78	2710.73	2329.39	2058.15	1855.74	1699.19	1574.75
70000	6256.66	4305.76	3332.38	2750.01	2363.14	2087.98	1882.63	1723.82	1597.57
75000	6703.56	4613.31	3570.41	2946.44	2531.94	2237.12	2017.11	1846.95	1711.68
80000	7150.46	4920.86	3808.44	3142.87	2700.74	2386.27	2151.58	1970.08	1825.80
100000	8938.08	6151.08	4760.54	3928.59	3375.92	2982.83	2689.47	2462.59	2282.24

108

TERM AMOUNT	6 YEARS	7 YEARS	8 YEARS	9 YEARS	10 YEARS	11 YEARS	12 YEARS	13 YEARS	14 YEARS
$ 25	.51	.46	.43	.40	.38	.36	.35	.34	.33
50	1.01	.92	.85	.80	.76	.72	.70	.67	.66
75	1.52	1.37	1.27	1.19	1.13	1.08	1.04	1.01	.98
100	2.02	1.83	1.69	1.59	1.51	1.44	1.39	1.34	1.31
200	4.03	3.66	3.38	3.17	3.01	2.88	2.77	2.68	2.61
300	6.05	5.48	5.07	4.75	4.51	4.31	4.15	4.02	3.92
400	8.06	7.31	6.76	6.34	6.01	5.75	5.54	5.36	5.22
500	10.08	9.14	8.45	7.92	7.51	7.18	6.92	6.70	6.53
600	12.09	10.96	10.13	9.50	9.01	8.62	8.30	8.04	7.83
700	14.11	12.79	11.82	11.09	10.51	10.06	9.69	9.38	9.13
800	16.12	14.62	13.51	12.67	12.01	11.49	11.07	10.72	10.44
900	18.14	16.44	15.20	14.25	13.51	12.93	12.45	12.06	11.74
1000	20.15	18.27	16.89	15.84	15.02	14.36	13.84	13.40	13.05
2000	40.30	36.54	33.77	31.67	30.03	28.72	27.67	26.80	26.09
3000	60.44	54.80	50.65	47.50	45.04	43.08	41.50	40.20	39.13
4000	80.59	73.07	67.54	63.33	60.05	57.44	55.33	53.60	52.17
5000	100.73	91.33	84.42	79.16	75.06	71.79	69.16	66.99	65.21
6000	120.88	109.60	101.30	94.99	90.07	86.15	82.99	80.39	78.25
7000	141.02	127.86	118.19	110.83	105.08	100.51	96.82	93.79	91.29
8000	161.17	146.13	135.07	126.66	120.09	114.87	110.65	107.19	104.33
9000	181.32	164.40	151.95	142.49	135.10	129.23	124.48	120.58	117.37
10000	201.46	182.66	168.84	158.32	150.11	143.58	138.31	133.98	130.41
15000	302.19	273.99	253.25	237.48	225.17	215.37	207.46	200.97	195.61
20000	402.92	365.32	337.67	316.63	300.22	287.16	276.61	267.96	260.81
25000	503.64	456.64	422.08	395.79	375.28	358.95	345.76	334.95	326.01
30000	604.37	547.97	506.50	474.95	450.33	430.74	414.91	401.94	391.21
35000	705.10	639.30	590.91	554.11	525.39	502.53	484.06	468.93	456.41
36000	725.25	657.57	607.79	569.94	540.40	516.89	497.89	482.32	469.45
37000	745.39	675.83	624.68	585.77	555.41	531.25	511.72	495.72	482.49
38000	765.54	694.10	641.56	601.60	570.42	545.61	525.55	509.12	495.53
39000	785.68	712.36	658.44	617.43	585.43	559.97	539.38	522.52	508.57
40000	805.83	730.63	675.33	633.26	600.44	574.32	553.21	535.91	521.61
41000	825.97	748.89	692.21	649.09	615.45	588.68	567.04	549.31	534.65
42000	846.12	767.16	709.09	664.93	630.47	603.04	580.87	562.71	547.69
43000	866.26	785.42	725.97	680.76	645.48	617.40	594.70	576.11	560.73
44000	886.41	803.69	742.86	696.59	660.49	631.76	608.53	589.51	573.77
45000	906.56	821.96	759.74	712.42	675.50	646.11	622.36	602.90	586.81
46000	926.70	840.22	776.62	728.25	690.51	660.47	636.19	616.30	599.85
47000	946.85	858.49	793.51	744.08	705.52	674.83	650.02	629.70	612.89
48000	966.99	876.75	810.39	759.91	720.53	689.19	663.85	643.10	625.93
49000	987.14	895.02	827.27	775.75	735.54	703.55	677.68	656.49	638.97
50000	1007.28	913.28	844.16	791.58	750.55	717.90	691.51	669.89	652.01
51000	1027.43	931.55	861.04	807.41	765.56	732.26	705.34	683.29	665.05
52000	1047.57	949.82	877.92	823.24	780.57	746.62	719.17	696.69	678.09
53000	1067.72	968.08	894.80	839.07	795.59	760.98	733.00	710.09	691.13
54000	1087.87	986.35	911.69	854.90	810.60	775.34	746.83	723.48	704.17
55000	1108.01	1004.61	928.57	870.73	825.61	789.69	760.66	736.88	717.21
56000	1128.16	1022.88	945.45	886.57	840.62	804.05	774.49	750.28	730.25
57000	1148.30	1041.14	962.34	902.40	855.63	818.41	788.32	763.68	743.29
58000	1168.45	1059.41	979.22	918.23	870.64	832.77	802.15	777.07	756.33
59000	1188.59	1077.67	996.10	934.06	885.65	847.13	815.98	790.47	769.37
60000	1208.74	1095.94	1012.99	949.89	900.66	861.48	829.81	803.87	782.41
61000	1228.88	1114.21	1029.87	965.72	915.67	875.84	843.64	817.27	795.45
62000	1249.03	1132.47	1046.75	981.55	930.68	890.20	857.47	830.67	808.49
63000	1269.18	1150.74	1063.63	997.39	945.70	904.56	871.30	844.06	821.53
64000	1289.32	1169.00	1080.52	1013.22	960.71	918.92	885.13	857.46	834.57
65000	1309.47	1187.27	1097.40	1029.05	975.72	933.27	898.96	870.86	847.61
66000	1329.61	1205.53	1114.28	1044.88	990.73	947.63	912.79	884.26	860.65
67000	1349.76	1223.80	1131.17	1060.71	1005.74	961.99	926.62	897.65	873.69
68000	1369.90	1242.06	1148.05	1076.54	1020.75	976.35	940.45	911.05	886.73
69000	1390.05	1260.33	1164.93	1092.37	1035.76	990.71	954.28	924.45	899.77
70000	1410.19	1278.60	1181.82	1108.21	1050.77	1005.06	968.11	937.85	912.81
75000	1510.92	1369.92	1266.23	1187.36	1125.83	1076.85	1037.26	1004.84	978.01
80000	1611.65	1461.25	1350.65	1266.52	1200.88	1148.64	1106.41	1071.82	1043.21
100000	2014.56	1826.56	1688.31	1583.15	1501.10	1435.80	1383.01	1339.78	1304.01

13½% MONTHLY PAYMENT
NECESSARY TO AMORTIZE A LOAN

TERM AMOUNT	15 YEARS	16 YEARS	17 YEARS	18 YEARS	19 YEARS	20 YEARS	21 YEARS	22 YEARS	23 YEARS
$ 25	.32	.32	.31	.31	.30	.30	.30	.30	.29
50	.64	.63	.62	.61	.60	.60	.59	.59	.58
75	.96	.94	.93	.91	.90	.89	.88	.88	.87
100	1.28	1.25	1.23	1.21	1.20	1.19	1.17	1.17	1.16
200	2.55	2.50	2.46	2.42	2.39	2.37	2.34	2.33	2.31
300	3.83	3.75	3.69	3.63	3.59	3.55	3.51	3.49	3.46
400	5.10	5.00	4.92	4.84	4.78	4.73	4.68	4.65	4.61
500	6.38	6.25	6.14	6.05	5.98	5.91	5.85	5.81	5.76
600	7.65	7.50	7.37	7.26	7.17	7.09	7.02	6.97	6.92
700	8.92	8.75	8.60	8.47	8.37	8.27	8.19	8.13	8.07
800	10.20	10.00	9.83	9.68	9.56	9.45	9.36	9.29	9.22
900	11.47	11.25	11.06	10.89	10.75	10.64	10.53	10.45	10.37
1000	12.75	12.50	12.28	12.10	11.95	11.82	11.70	11.61	11.52
2000	25.49	24.99	24.56	24.20	23.89	23.63	23.40	23.21	23.04
3000	38.23	37.48	36.84	36.30	35.84	35.44	35.10	34.81	34.56
4000	50.97	49.97	49.12	48.40	47.78	47.25	46.80	46.41	46.07
5000	63.71	62.46	61.40	60.50	59.73	59.07	58.50	58.01	57.59
6000	76.45	74.95	73.68	72.59	71.67	70.88	70.20	69.61	69.11
7000	89.20	87.44	85.95	84.69	83.61	82.69	81.90	81.21	80.62
8000	101.94	99.93	98.23	96.79	95.56	94.50	93.60	92.81	92.14
9000	114.68	112.42	110.51	108.89	107.50	106.32	105.29	104.42	103.66
10000	127.42	124.91	122.79	120.99	119.45	118.13	116.99	116.02	115.17
15000	191.13	187.36	184.18	181.48	179.17	177.19	175.49	174.02	172.76
20000	254.84	249.82	245.57	241.97	238.89	236.25	233.98	232.03	230.34
25000	318.54	312.27	306.97	302.46	298.61	295.31	292.48	290.03	287.92
30000	382.25	374.72	368.36	362.95	358.33	354.37	350.97	348.04	345.51
35000	445.96	437.18	429.75	423.44	418.05	413.43	409.47	406.05	403.09
36000	458.70	449.67	442.03	435.54	429.99	425.25	421.16	417.65	414.61
37000	471.44	462.16	454.31	447.64	441.94	437.06	432.86	429.25	426.12
38000	484.18	474.65	466.59	459.73	453.88	448.87	444.56	440.85	437.64
39000	496.93	487.14	478.86	471.83	465.83	460.68	456.26	452.45	449.16
40000	509.67	499.63	491.14	483.93	477.77	472.50	467.96	464.05	460.68
41000	522.41	512.12	503.42	496.03	489.72	484.31	479.66	475.65	472.19
42000	535.15	524.61	515.70	508.13	501.66	496.12	491.36	487.25	483.71
43000	547.89	537.10	527.98	520.22	513.60	507.93	503.06	498.85	495.23
44000	560.63	549.59	540.26	532.32	525.55	519.74	514.76	510.46	506.74
45000	573.37	562.08	552.54	544.42	537.49	531.56	526.45	522.06	518.26
46000	586.12	574.57	564.81	556.52	549.44	543.37	538.15	533.66	529.78
47000	598.86	587.07	577.09	568.62	561.38	555.18	549.85	545.26	541.29
48000	611.60	599.56	589.37	580.71	573.32	566.99	561.55	556.86	552.81
49000	624.34	612.05	601.65	592.81	585.27	578.81	573.25	568.46	564.33
50000	637.08	624.54	613.93	604.91	597.21	590.62	584.95	580.06	575.84
51000	649.82	637.03	626.21	617.01	609.16	602.43	596.65	591.66	587.36
52000	662.57	649.52	638.48	629.11	621.10	614.24	608.35	603.27	598.88
53000	675.31	662.01	650.76	641.20	633.05	626.05	620.05	614.87	610.39
54000	688.05	674.50	663.04	653.30	644.99	637.87	631.74	626.47	621.91
55000	700.79	686.99	675.32	665.40	656.93	649.68	643.44	638.07	633.43
56000	713.53	699.48	687.60	677.50	668.88	661.49	655.14	649.67	644.94
57000	726.27	711.97	699.88	689.60	680.82	673.30	666.84	661.27	656.46
58000	739.02	724.46	712.16	701.70	692.77	685.12	678.54	672.87	667.98
59000	751.76	736.95	724.43	713.79	704.71	696.93	690.24	684.47	679.49
60000	764.50	749.44	736.71	725.89	716.65	708.74	701.94	696.07	691.01
61000	777.24	761.93	748.99	737.99	728.60	720.55	713.64	707.68	702.53
62000	789.98	774.42	761.27	750.09	740.54	732.36	725.34	719.28	714.04
63000	802.72	786.92	773.55	762.19	752.49	744.18	737.03	730.88	725.56
64000	815.46	799.41	785.83	774.28	764.43	755.99	748.73	742.48	737.08
65000	828.21	811.90	798.10	786.38	776.38	767.80	760.43	754.08	748.59
66000	840.95	824.39	810.38	798.48	788.32	779.61	772.13	765.68	760.11
67000	853.69	836.88	822.66	810.58	800.26	791.43	783.83	777.28	771.63
68000	866.43	849.37	834.94	822.68	812.21	803.24	795.53	788.88	783.14
69000	879.17	861.86	847.22	834.77	824.15	815.05	807.23	800.49	794.66
70000	891.91	874.35	859.50	846.87	836.10	826.86	818.93	812.09	806.18
75000	955.62	936.80	920.89	907.36	895.82	885.92	877.42	870.09	863.76
80000	1019.33	999.26	982.28	967.85	955.54	944.99	935.92	928.10	921.35
100000	1274.16	1249.07	1227.85	1209.82	1194.42	1181.23	1169.89	1160.12	1151.68

MONTHLY PAYMENT 13½%
NECESSARY TO AMORTIZE A LOAN

TERM AMOUNT	24 YEARS	25 YEARS	26 YEARS	27 YEARS	28 YEARS	29 YEARS	30 YEARS	35 YEARS	40 YEARS
$ 25	.29	.29	.29	.29	.29	.28	.28	.28	.28
50	.58	.57	.57	.57	.57	.57	.56	.56	.56
75	.86	.86	.85	.85	.85	.84	.84	.83	.83
100	1.15	1.14	1.14	1.13	1.13	1.12	1.12	1.11	1.11
200	2.29	2.28	2.27	2.26	2.25	2.24	2.24	2.22	2.21
300	3.44	3.42	3.40	3.39	3.38	3.36	3.36	3.32	3.31
400	4.58	4.56	4.54	4.52	4.50	4.48	4.47	4.43	4.41
500	5.73	5.70	5.67	5.64	5.62	5.60	5.59	5.54	5.51
600	6.87	6.83	6.80	6.77	6.75	6.72	6.71	6.64	6.61
700	8.02	7.97	7.93	7.90	7.87	7.84	7.82	7.75	7.71
800	9.16	9.11	9.07	9.03	8.99	8.96	8.94	8.85	8.81
900	10.30	10.25	10.20	10.15	10.12	10.08	10.06	9.96	9.91
1000	11.45	11.39	11.33	11.28	11.24	11.20	11.17	11.07	11.01
2000	22.89	22.77	22.66	22.56	22.48	22.40	22.34	22.13	22.02
3000	34.34	34.15	33.98	33.84	33.71	33.60	33.51	33.19	33.02
4000	45.78	45.53	45.31	45.11	44.95	44.80	44.68	44.25	44.03
5000	57.22	56.91	56.63	56.39	56.18	56.00	55.84	55.31	55.03
6000	68.67	68.29	67.96	67.67	67.42	67.20	67.01	66.37	66.04
7000	80.11	79.67	79.28	78.95	78.66	78.40	78.18	77.43	77.04
8000	91.55	91.05	90.61	90.22	89.89	89.60	89.35	88.49	88.05
9000	103.00	102.43	101.93	101.50	101.13	100.80	100.52	99.55	99.05
10000	114.44	113.81	113.26	112.78	112.36	112.00	111.68	110.61	110.06
15000	171.66	170.71	169.88	169.17	168.54	168.00	167.52	165.91	165.08
20000	228.88	227.61	226.51	225.55	224.72	223.99	223.36	221.21	220.11
25000	286.10	284.51	283.14	281.94	280.90	279.99	279.20	276.51	275.14
30000	343.32	341.41	339.76	338.33	337.08	335.99	335.04	331.82	330.16
35000	400.53	398.32	396.39	394.72	393.26	391.99	390.88	387.12	385.19
36000	411.98	409.70	407.72	405.99	404.49	403.19	402.05	398.18	396.19
37000	423.42	421.08	419.04	417.27	415.73	414.39	413.21	409.24	407.20
38000	434.86	432.46	430.37	428.55	426.96	425.59	424.38	420.30	418.20
39000	446.31	443.84	441.69	439.83	438.20	436.78	435.55	431.36	429.21
40000	457.75	455.22	453.02	451.10	449.44	447.98	446.72	442.42	440.21
41000	469.20	466.60	464.34	462.38	460.67	459.18	457.89	453.48	451.22
42000	480.64	477.98	475.67	473.66	471.91	470.38	469.05	464.54	462.22
43000	492.08	489.36	486.99	484.94	483.14	481.58	480.22	475.60	473.23
44000	503.53	500.74	498.32	496.21	494.38	492.78	491.39	486.66	484.24
45000	514.97	512.12	509.64	507.49	505.62	503.98	502.56	497.72	495.24
46000	526.41	523.50	520.97	518.77	516.85	515.18	513.72	508.78	506.25
47000	537.86	534.88	532.29	530.04	528.09	526.38	524.89	519.84	517.25
48000	549.30	546.26	543.62	541.32	539.32	537.58	536.06	530.90	528.26
49000	560.75	557.64	554.94	552.60	550.56	548.78	547.23	541.96	539.26
50000	572.19	569.02	566.27	563.88	561.79	559.98	558.40	553.02	550.27
51000	583.63	580.40	577.60	575.15	573.03	571.18	569.56	564.08	561.27
52000	595.08	591.78	588.92	586.43	584.27	582.38	580.73	575.14	572.28
53000	606.52	603.16	600.25	597.71	595.50	593.58	591.90	586.20	583.28
54000	617.96	614.54	611.57	608.99	606.74	604.78	603.07	597.26	594.29
55000	629.41	625.92	622.90	620.26	617.97	615.98	614.24	608.32	605.29
56000	640.85	637.30	634.22	631.54	629.21	627.18	625.40	619.38	616.30
57000	652.29	648.68	645.55	642.82	640.44	638.38	636.57	630.44	627.30
58000	663.74	660.06	656.87	654.10	651.68	649.58	647.74	641.50	638.31
59000	675.18	671.44	668.20	665.37	662.92	660.77	658.91	652.57	649.31
60000	686.63	682.82	679.52	676.65	674.15	671.97	670.07	663.63	660.32
61000	698.07	694.20	690.85	687.93	685.39	683.17	681.24	674.69	671.32
62000	709.51	705.59	702.17	699.21	696.62	694.37	692.41	685.75	682.33
63000	720.96	716.97	713.50	710.48	707.86	705.57	703.58	696.81	693.33
64000	732.40	728.35	724.82	721.76	719.10	716.77	714.75	707.87	704.34
65000	743.84	739.73	736.15	733.04	730.33	727.97	725.91	718.93	715.35
66000	755.29	751.11	747.47	744.32	741.57	739.17	737.08	729.99	726.35
67000	766.73	762.49	758.80	755.59	752.80	750.37	748.25	741.05	737.36
68000	778.18	773.87	770.13	766.87	764.04	761.57	759.42	752.11	748.36
69000	789.62	785.25	781.45	778.15	775.27	772.77	770.58	763.17	759.37
70000	801.06	796.63	792.78	789.43	786.51	783.97	781.75	774.23	770.37
75000	858.28	853.53	849.40	845.81	842.69	839.97	837.59	829.53	825.40
80000	915.50	910.43	906.03	902.20	898.87	895.96	893.43	884.83	880.42
100000	1144.37	1138.04	1132.53	1127.75	1123.58	1119.95	1116.79	1106.04	1100.53

111

13¾% MONTHLY PAYMENT
NECESSARY TO AMORTIZE A LOAN

TERM AMOUNT	1 YEAR	1½ YEARS	2 YEARS	2½ YEARS	3 YEARS	3½ YEARS	4 YEARS	4½ YEARS	5 YEARS
$ 25	2.24	1.55	1.20	.99	.85	.75	.68	.62	.58
50	4.48	3.09	2.39	1.97	1.70	1.50	1.36	1.24	1.15
75	6.72	4.63	3.58	2.96	2.55	2.25	2.03	1.86	1.73
100	8.95	6.17	4.78	3.94	3.39	3.00	2.71	2.48	2.30
200	17.90	12.33	9.55	7.88	6.78	5.99	5.41	4.95	4.59
300	26.85	18.49	14.32	11.82	10.17	8.99	8.11	7.43	6.89
400	35.80	24.65	19.09	15.76	13.55	11.98	10.81	9.90	9.18
500	44.75	30.82	23.86	19.70	16.94	14.98	13.51	12.38	11.48
600	53.70	36.98	28.64	23.64	20.33	17.97	16.21	14.85	13.77
700	62.65	43.14	33.41	27.58	23.72	20.97	18.91	17.33	16.07
800	71.60	49.30	38.18	31.52	27.10	23.96	21.61	19.80	18.36
900	80.55	55.46	42.95	35.46	30.49	26.95	24.32	22.28	20.65
1000	89.50	61.63	47.72	39.40	33.88	29.95	27.02	24.75	22.95
2000	178.99	123.25	95.44	78.80	67.75	59.89	54.03	49.50	45.89
3000	268.48	184.87	143.16	118.20	101.63	89.84	81.04	74.24	68.84
4000	357.97	246.49	190.87	157.60	135.50	119.78	108.05	98.99	91.78
5000	447.46	308.11	238.59	197.00	169.37	149.73	135.07	123.73	114.72
6000	536.96	369.73	286.31	236.40	203.25	179.67	162.08	148.48	137.67
7000	626.45	431.35	334.02	275.79	237.12	209.61	189.09	173.22	160.61
8000	715.94	492.98	381.74	315.19	270.99	239.56	216.10	197.97	183.56
9000	805.43	554.60	429.46	354.59	304.87	269.50	243.12	222.71	206.50
10000	894.92	616.22	477.17	393.99	338.74	299.45	270.13	247.46	229.44
15000	1342.38	924.32	715.76	590.98	508.11	449.17	405.19	371.19	344.16
20000	1789.84	1232.43	954.34	787.97	677.47	598.89	540.25	494.92	458.88
25000	2237.30	1540.54	1192.92	984.97	846.84	748.61	675.32	618.64	573.60
30000	2684.76	1848.64	1431.51	1181.96	1016.21	898.33	810.38	742.37	688.32
35000	3132.22	2156.75	1670.09	1378.95	1185.57	1048.05	945.44	866.10	803.04
36000	3221.71	2218.37	1717.81	1418.35	1219.45	1078.00	972.45	890.84	825.99
37000	3311.20	2279.99	1765.52	1457.75	1253.32	1107.94	999.47	915.59	848.93
38000	3400.70	2341.61	1813.24	1497.15	1287.19	1137.88	1026.48	940.34	871.87
39000	3490.19	2403.23	1860.96	1536.55	1321.07	1167.83	1053.49	965.08	894.82
40000	3579.68	2464.86	1908.67	1575.94	1354.94	1197.77	1080.50	989.83	917.76
41000	3669.17	2526.48	1956.39	1615.34	1388.81	1227.72	1107.52	1014.57	940.71
42000	3758.66	2588.10	2004.11	1654.74	1422.69	1257.66	1134.53	1039.32	963.65
43000	3848.15	2649.72	2051.82	1694.14	1456.56	1287.61	1161.54	1064.06	986.59
44000	3937.65	2711.34	2099.54	1733.54	1490.43	1317.55	1188.55	1088.81	1009.54
45000	4027.14	2772.96	2147.26	1772.94	1524.31	1347.49	1215.57	1113.55	1032.48
46000	4116.63	2834.58	2194.97	1812.34	1558.18	1377.44	1242.58	1138.30	1055.42
47000	4206.12	2896.20	2242.69	1851.73	1592.05	1407.38	1269.59	1163.04	1078.37
48000	4295.61	2957.83	2290.41	1891.13	1625.93	1437.33	1296.60	1187.79	1101.31
49000	4385.11	3019.45	2338.12	1930.53	1659.80	1467.27	1323.61	1212.54	1124.26
50000	4474.60	3081.07	2385.84	1969.93	1693.67	1497.22	1350.63	1237.28	1147.20
51000	4564.09	3142.69	2433.56	2009.33	1727.55	1527.16	1377.64	1262.03	1170.14
52000	4653.58	3204.31	2481.27	2048.73	1761.42	1557.10	1404.65	1286.77	1193.09
53000	4743.07	3265.93	2528.99	2088.12	1795.29	1587.05	1431.66	1311.52	1216.03
54000	4832.57	3327.55	2576.71	2127.52	1829.17	1616.99	1458.68	1336.26	1238.98
55000	4922.06	3389.17	2624.42	2166.92	1863.04	1646.94	1485.69	1361.01	1261.92
56000	5011.55	3450.80	2672.14	2206.32	1896.91	1676.88	1512.70	1385.75	1284.86
57000	5101.04	3512.42	2719.86	2245.72	1930.79	1706.82	1539.71	1410.50	1307.81
58000	5190.53	3574.04	2767.57	2285.12	1964.66	1736.77	1566.73	1435.25	1330.75
59000	5280.02	3635.66	2815.29	2324.52	1998.53	1766.71	1593.74	1459.99	1353.70
60000	5369.52	3697.28	2863.01	2363.91	2032.41	1796.66	1620.75	1484.74	1376.64
61000	5459.01	3758.90	2910.72	2403.31	2066.28	1826.60	1647.76	1509.48	1399.58
62000	5548.50	3820.52	2958.44	2442.71	2100.15	1856.55	1674.78	1534.23	1422.53
63000	5637.99	3882.14	3006.16	2482.11	2134.03	1886.49	1701.79	1558.97	1445.47
64000	5727.48	3943.77	3053.87	2521.51	2167.90	1916.43	1728.80	1583.72	1468.42
65000	5816.98	4005.39	3101.59	2560.91	2201.77	1946.38	1755.81	1608.46	1491.36
66000	5906.47	4067.01	3149.31	2600.30	2235.65	1976.32	1782.83	1633.21	1514.30
67000	5995.96	4128.63	3197.02	2639.70	2269.52	2006.27	1809.84	1657.96	1537.25
68000	6085.45	4190.25	3244.74	2679.10	2303.39	2036.21	1836.85	1682.70	1560.19
69000	6174.94	4251.87	3292.46	2718.50	2337.27	2066.16	1863.86	1707.45	1583.13
70000	6264.43	4313.49	3340.17	2757.90	2371.14	2096.10	1890.88	1732.19	1606.08
75000	6711.89	4621.60	3578.76	2954.89	2540.51	2245.82	2025.94	1855.92	1720.80
80000	7159.35	4929.71	3817.34	3151.88	2709.87	2395.54	2161.00	1979.65	1835.52
100000	8949.19	6162.13	4771.67	3939.85	3387.34	2994.43	2701.25	2474.56	2294.40

MONTHLY PAYMENT 13¾%
NECESSARY TO AMORTIZE A LOAN

TERM AMOUNT	6 YEARS	7 YEARS	8 YEARS	9 YEARS	10 YEARS	11 YEARS	12 YEARS	13 YEARS	14 YEARS
$ 25	.51	.46	.43	.40	.38	.37	.35	.34	.33
50	1.02	.92	.86	.80	.76	.73	.70	.68	.66
75	1.53	1.38	1.28	1.20	1.14	1.09	1.05	1.02	.99
100	2.03	1.84	1.71	1.60	1.52	1.46	1.40	1.36	1.32
200	4.06	3.68	3.41	3.20	3.04	2.91	2.80	2.71	2.64
300	6.09	5.52	5.11	4.80	4.55	4.36	4.20	4.07	3.96
400	8.11	7.36	6.81	6.39	6.07	5.81	5.60	5.42	5.28
500	10.14	9.20	8.51	7.99	7.58	7.26	6.99	6.78	6.60
600	12.17	11.04	10.21	9.59	9.10	8.71	8.39	8.13	7.92
700	14.19	12.88	11.92	11.18	10.61	10.16	9.79	9.49	9.24
800	16.22	14.72	13.62	12.78	12.13	11.61	11.19	10.84	10.56
900	18.25	16.56	15.32	14.38	13.64	13.06	12.58	12.20	11.88
1000	20.28	18.40	17.02	15.97	15.16	14.51	13.98	13.55	13.20
2000	40.55	36.79	34.04	31.94	30.31	29.01	27.96	27.10	26.39
3000	60.82	55.19	51.05	47.91	45.46	43.51	41.94	40.65	39.59
4000	81.09	73.58	68.07	63.88	60.61	58.01	55.91	54.20	52.78
5000	101.36	91.98	85.08	79.85	75.76	72.51	69.89	67.75	65.97
6000	121.63	110.37	102.10	95.81	90.91	87.02	83.87	81.29	79.17
7000	141.90	128.77	119.12	111.78	106.06	101.52	97.85	94.84	92.36
8000	162.17	147.16	136.13	127.75	121.21	116.02	111.82	108.39	105.55
9000	182.44	165.56	153.15	143.72	136.37	130.52	125.80	121.94	118.75
10000	202.71	183.95	170.16	159.69	151.52	145.02	139.78	135.49	131.94
15000	304.07	275.93	255.24	239.53	227.27	217.53	209.66	203.23	197.91
20000	405.42	367.90	340.32	319.37	303.03	290.04	279.55	270.97	263.88
25000	506.78	459.87	425.40	399.21	378.79	362.55	349.44	338.71	329.85
30000	608.13	551.85	510.48	479.05	454.54	435.06	419.32	406.45	395.81
35000	709.49	643.82	595.56	558.89	530.30	507.57	489.21	474.19	461.78
36000	729.76	662.22	612.58	574.86	545.45	522.07	503.18	487.74	474.98
37000	750.03	680.61	629.60	590.82	560.60	536.57	517.16	501.29	488.17
38000	770.30	699.01	646.61	606.79	575.75	551.07	531.14	514.84	501.36
39000	790.57	717.40	663.63	622.76	590.90	565.57	545.12	528.38	514.56
40000	810.84	735.80	680.64	638.73	606.05	580.08	559.09	541.93	527.75
41000	831.11	754.19	697.66	654.70	621.21	594.58	573.07	555.48	540.94
42000	851.38	772.58	714.68	670.66	636.36	609.08	587.05	569.03	554.14
43000	871.65	790.98	731.69	686.63	651.51	623.58	601.03	582.58	567.33
44000	891.93	809.37	748.71	702.60	666.66	638.08	615.00	596.12	580.52
45000	912.20	827.77	765.72	718.57	681.81	652.58	628.98	609.67	593.72
46000	932.47	846.16	782.74	734.54	696.96	667.09	642.96	623.22	606.91
47000	952.74	864.56	799.76	750.51	712.11	681.59	656.93	636.77	620.10
48000	973.01	882.95	816.77	766.47	727.26	696.09	670.91	650.32	633.30
49000	993.28	901.35	833.79	782.44	742.42	710.59	684.89	663.87	646.49
50000	1013.55	919.74	850.80	798.41	757.57	725.09	698.87	677.41	659.69
51000	1033.82	938.14	867.82	814.38	772.72	739.59	712.84	690.96	672.88
52000	1054.09	956.53	884.83	830.35	787.87	754.10	726.82	704.51	686.07
53000	1074.36	974.93	901.85	846.31	803.02	768.60	740.80	718.06	699.27
54000	1094.63	993.32	918.87	862.28	818.17	783.10	754.77	731.61	712.46
55000	1114.91	1011.72	935.88	878.25	833.32	797.60	768.75	745.15	725.65
56000	1135.18	1030.11	952.90	894.22	848.47	812.10	782.73	758.70	738.85
57000	1155.45	1048.51	969.91	910.19	863.63	826.61	796.71	772.25	752.04
58000	1175.72	1066.90	986.93	926.15	878.78	841.11	810.68	785.80	765.24
59000	1195.99	1085.30	1003.95	942.12	893.93	855.61	824.66	799.35	778.43
60000	1216.26	1103.69	1020.96	958.09	909.08	870.11	838.64	812.90	791.62
61000	1236.53	1122.09	1037.98	974.06	924.23	884.61	852.61	826.44	804.82
62000	1256.80	1140.48	1054.99	990.03	939.38	899.11	866.59	839.99	818.01
63000	1277.07	1158.87	1072.01	1005.99	954.53	913.62	880.57	853.54	831.20
64000	1297.34	1177.27	1089.03	1021.96	969.68	928.12	894.55	867.09	844.40
65000	1317.62	1195.66	1106.04	1037.93	984.83	942.62	908.52	880.64	857.59
66000	1337.89	1214.06	1123.06	1053.90	999.99	957.12	922.50	894.18	870.78
67000	1358.16	1232.45	1140.07	1069.87	1015.14	971.62	936.48	907.73	883.98
68000	1378.43	1250.85	1157.09	1085.84	1030.29	986.12	950.46	921.28	897.17
69000	1398.70	1269.24	1174.11	1101.80	1045.44	1000.63	964.43	934.83	910.37
70000	1418.97	1287.64	1191.12	1117.77	1060.59	1015.13	978.41	948.38	923.56
75000	1520.32	1379.61	1276.20	1197.61	1136.35	1087.64	1048.30	1016.12	989.53
80000	1621.68	1471.59	1361.28	1277.45	1212.10	1160.15	1118.18	1083.86	1055.49
100000	2027.10	1839.48	1701.60	1596.81	1515.13	1450.18	1397.73	1354.82	1319.37

113

13¾% MONTHLY PAYMENT
NECESSARY TO AMORTIZE A LOAN

TERM AMOUNT	15 YEARS	16 YEARS	17 YEARS	18 YEARS	19 YEARS	20 YEARS	21 YEARS	22 YEARS	23 YEARS
$ 25	.33	.32	.32	.31	.31	.30	.30	.30	.30
50	.65	.64	.63	.62	.61	.60	.60	.59	.59
75	.97	.95	.94	.92	.91	.90	.90	.89	.88
100	1.29	1.27	1.25	1.23	1.22	1.20	1.19	1.18	1.17
200	2.58	2.54	2.49	2.46	2.43	2.40	2.38	2.36	2.34
300	3.87	3.80	3.74	3.68	3.64	3.60	3.57	3.54	3.51
400	5.16	5.07	4.98	4.91	4.85	4.80	4.75	4.71	4.68
500	6.45	6.33	6.23	6.14	6.06	6.00	5.94	5.89	5.85
600	7.74	7.60	7.47	7.36	7.27	7.19	7.13	7.07	7.02
700	9.03	8.86	8.71	8.59	8.48	8.39	8.31	8.25	8.19
800	10.32	10.13	9.96	9.82	9.69	9.59	9.50	9.42	9.36
900	11.61	11.39	11.20	11.04	10.91	10.79	10.69	10.60	10.53
1000	12.90	12.66	12.45	12.27	12.12	11.99	11.88	11.78	11.70
2000	25.80	25.31	24.89	24.53	24.23	23.97	23.75	23.55	23.39
3000	38.70	37.96	37.33	36.79	36.34	35.95	35.62	35.33	35.08
4000	51.60	50.61	49.77	49.06	48.45	47.93	47.49	47.10	46.77
5000	64.50	63.26	62.21	61.32	60.56	59.91	59.36	58.88	58.47
6000	77.39	75.91	74.65	73.58	72.67	71.90	71.23	70.65	70.16
7000	90.29	88.56	87.09	85.84	84.78	83.88	83.10	82.43	81.85
8000	103.19	101.21	99.53	98.11	96.90	95.86	94.97	94.20	93.54
9000	116.09	113.86	111.97	110.37	109.01	107.84	106.84	105.98	105.24
10000	128.99	126.51	124.41	122.63	121.12	119.82	118.71	117.75	116.93
15000	193.48	189.76	186.61	183.95	181.67	179.73	178.06	176.63	175.39
20000	257.97	253.01	248.82	245.26	242.23	239.64	237.41	235.50	233.85
25000	322.46	316.26	311.02	306.58	302.79	299.55	296.77	294.37	292.31
30000	386.95	379.51	373.22	367.89	363.34	359.46	356.12	353.25	350.77
35000	451.44	442.76	435.43	429.20	423.90	419.36	415.47	412.12	409.23
36000	464.34	455.41	447.87	441.47	436.01	431.35	427.34	423.90	420.93
37000	477.24	468.06	460.31	453.73	448.12	443.33	439.21	435.67	432.62
38000	490.13	480.71	472.75	465.99	460.23	455.31	451.08	447.45	444.31
39000	503.03	493.36	485.19	478.25	472.35	467.29	462.95	459.22	456.00
40000	515.93	506.01	497.63	490.52	484.46	479.27	474.82	471.00	467.70
41000	528.83	518.66	510.07	502.78	496.57	491.25	486.69	482.77	479.39
42000	541.73	531.31	522.51	515.04	508.68	503.24	498.57	494.55	491.08
43000	554.62	543.96	534.95	527.31	520.79	515.22	510.44	506.32	502.77
44000	567.52	556.61	547.39	539.57	532.90	527.20	522.31	518.10	514.47
45000	580.42	569.26	559.83	551.83	545.01	539.18	534.18	529.87	526.16
46000	593.32	581.91	572.27	564.09	557.12	551.16	546.05	541.65	537.85
47000	606.22	594.56	584.71	576.36	569.24	563.14	557.92	553.42	549.54
48000	619.11	607.21	597.15	588.62	581.35	575.13	569.79	565.20	561.23
49000	632.01	619.86	609.59	600.88	593.46	587.11	581.66	576.97	572.93
50000	644.91	632.51	622.03	613.15	605.57	599.09	593.53	588.74	584.62
51000	657.81	645.16	634.48	625.41	617.68	611.07	605.40	600.52	596.31
52000	670.71	657.81	646.92	637.67	629.79	623.05	617.27	612.29	608.00
53000	683.60	670.46	659.36	649.93	641.90	635.03	629.14	624.07	619.70
54000	696.50	683.11	671.80	662.20	654.02	647.02	641.01	635.84	631.39
55000	709.40	695.76	684.24	674.46	666.13	659.00	652.88	647.62	643.08
56000	722.30	708.41	696.68	686.72	678.24	670.98	664.75	659.39	654.77
57000	735.20	721.06	709.12	698.99	690.35	682.96	676.62	671.17	666.47
58000	748.10	733.71	721.56	711.25	702.46	694.94	688.49	682.94	678.16
59000	760.99	746.36	734.00	723.51	714.57	706.92	700.36	694.72	689.85
60000	773.89	759.01	746.44	735.77	726.68	718.91	712.23	706.49	701.54
61000	786.79	771.66	758.88	748.04	738.79	730.89	724.10	718.27	713.23
62000	799.69	784.31	771.32	760.30	750.91	742.87	735.97	730.04	724.93
63000	812.59	796.96	783.76	772.56	763.02	754.85	747.85	741.82	736.62
64000	825.48	809.61	796.20	784.83	775.13	766.83	759.72	753.59	748.31
65000	838.38	822.26	808.64	797.09	787.24	778.82	771.59	765.37	760.00
66000	851.28	834.91	821.08	809.35	799.35	790.80	783.46	777.14	771.70
67000	864.18	847.56	833.52	821.61	811.46	802.78	795.33	788.92	783.39
68000	877.08	860.21	845.97	833.88	823.57	814.76	807.20	800.69	795.08
69000	889.97	872.86	858.41	846.14	835.68	826.74	819.07	812.47	806.77
70000	902.87	885.51	870.85	858.40	847.80	838.72	830.94	824.24	818.46
75000	967.36	948.76	933.05	919.72	908.35	898.63	890.29	883.11	876.93
80000	1031.85	1012.01	995.25	981.03	968.91	958.54	949.64	941.99	935.39
100000	1289.82	1265.01	1244.06	1226.29	1211.14	1198.17	1187.05	1177.48	1169.23

114

MONTHLY PAYMENT 13¾%
NECESSARY TO AMORTIZE A LOAN

TERM AMOUNT	24 YEARS	25 YEARS	26 YEARS	27 YEARS	28 YEARS	29 YEARS	30 YEARS	35 YEARS	40 YEARS
$ 25	.30	.29	.29	.29	.29	.29	.29	.29	.28
50	.59	.58	.58	.58	.58	.57	.57	.57	.56
75	.88	.87	.87	.86	.86	.86	.86	.85	.84
100	1.17	1.16	1.16	1.15	1.15	1.14	1.14	1.13	1.12
200	2.33	2.32	2.31	2.30	2.29	2.28	2.28	2.26	2.24
300	3.49	3.47	3.46	3.44	3.43	3.42	3.41	3.38	3.36
400	4.65	4.63	4.61	4.59	4.57	4.56	4.55	4.51	4.48
500	5.82	5.78	5.76	5.73	5.71	5.70	5.68	5.63	5.60
600	6.98	6.94	6.91	6.88	6.86	6.84	6.82	6.76	6.72
700	8.14	8.10	8.06	8.03	8.00	7.97	7.95	7.88	7.84
800	9.30	9.25	9.21	9.17	9.14	9.11	9.09	9.01	8.96
900	10.46	10.41	10.36	10.32	10.28	10.25	10.22	10.13	10.08
1000	11.63	11.56	11.51	11.46	11.42	11.39	11.36	11.26	11.20
2000	23.25	23.12	23.02	22.92	22.84	22.77	22.71	22.51	22.40
3000	34.87	34.68	34.52	34.38	34.26	34.16	34.07	33.76	33.60
4000	46.49	46.24	46.03	45.84	45.68	45.54	45.42	45.01	44.80
5000	58.11	57.80	57.53	57.30	57.10	56.92	56.77	56.26	56.00
6000	69.73	69.36	69.04	68.76	68.52	68.31	68.13	67.51	67.19
7000	81.35	80.92	80.55	80.22	79.94	79.69	79.48	78.76	78.39
8000	92.97	92.48	92.05	91.68	91.36	91.08	90.83	90.01	89.59
9000	104.59	104.04	103.56	103.14	102.78	102.46	102.19	101.26	100.79
10000	116.21	115.60	115.06	114.60	114.20	113.84	113.54	112.51	111.99
15000	174.32	173.39	172.59	171.90	171.29	170.76	170.31	168.76	167.98
20000	232.42	231.19	230.12	229.19	228.39	227.68	227.07	225.01	223.97
25000	290.53	288.99	287.65	286.49	285.48	284.60	283.84	281.26	279.96
30000	348.63	346.78	345.18	343.79	342.58	341.52	340.61	337.52	335.95
35000	406.74	404.58	402.71	401.08	399.67	398.44	397.37	393.77	391.94
36000	418.36	416.14	414.21	412.54	411.09	409.83	408.73	405.02	403.14
37000	429.98	427.70	425.72	424.00	422.51	421.21	420.08	416.27	414.33
38000	441.60	439.26	437.23	435.46	433.93	432.60	431.43	427.52	425.53
39000	453.22	450.82	448.73	446.92	445.35	443.98	442.79	438.77	436.73
40000	464.84	462.38	460.24	458.38	456.77	455.36	454.14	450.02	447.93
41000	476.47	473.94	471.74	469.84	468.19	466.75	465.50	461.27	459.13
42000	488.09	485.49	483.25	481.30	479.60	478.13	476.85	472.52	470.32
43000	499.71	497.05	494.75	492.76	491.02	489.51	488.20	483.77	481.52
44000	511.33	508.61	506.26	504.22	502.44	500.90	499.56	495.02	492.72
45000	522.95	520.17	517.77	515.68	513.86	512.28	510.91	506.27	503.92
46000	534.57	531.73	529.27	527.14	525.28	523.67	522.26	517.52	515.12
47000	546.19	543.29	540.78	538.60	536.70	535.05	533.62	528.77	526.32
48000	557.81	554.85	552.28	550.05	548.12	546.43	544.97	540.02	537.51
49000	569.43	566.41	563.79	561.51	559.54	557.82	556.32	551.27	548.71
50000	581.05	577.97	575.29	572.97	570.96	569.20	567.68	562.52	559.91
51000	592.68	589.53	586.80	584.43	582.38	580.59	579.03	573.77	571.11
52000	604.30	601.09	598.31	595.89	593.79	591.97	590.38	585.02	582.31
53000	615.92	612.65	609.81	607.35	605.21	603.35	601.74	596.27	593.50
54000	627.54	624.21	621.32	618.81	616.63	614.74	613.09	607.52	604.70
55000	639.16	635.77	632.82	630.27	628.05	626.12	624.44	618.78	615.90
56000	650.78	647.32	644.33	641.73	639.47	637.51	635.80	630.03	627.10
57000	662.40	658.88	655.84	653.19	650.89	648.89	647.15	641.28	638.30
58000	674.02	670.44	667.34	664.65	662.31	660.27	658.50	652.53	649.49
59000	685.64	682.00	678.85	676.11	673.73	671.66	669.86	663.78	660.69
60000	697.26	693.56	690.35	687.57	685.15	683.04	681.21	675.03	671.89
61000	708.89	705.12	701.86	699.03	696.57	694.43	692.56	686.28	683.09
62000	720.51	716.68	713.36	710.49	707.99	705.81	703.92	697.53	694.29
63000	732.13	728.24	724.87	721.95	719.40	717.19	715.27	708.78	705.48
64000	743.75	739.80	736.38	733.40	730.82	728.58	726.62	720.03	716.68
65000	755.37	751.36	747.88	744.86	742.24	739.96	737.98	731.28	727.88
66000	766.99	762.92	759.39	756.32	753.66	751.35	749.33	742.53	739.08
67000	778.61	774.48	770.89	767.78	765.08	762.73	760.68	753.78	750.28
68000	790.23	786.04	782.40	779.24	776.50	774.11	772.04	765.03	761.47
69000	801.85	797.60	793.90	790.70	787.92	785.50	783.39	776.28	772.67
70000	813.47	809.15	805.41	802.16	799.34	796.88	794.74	787.53	783.87
75000	871.58	866.95	862.94	859.46	856.43	853.80	851.51	843.78	839.86
80000	929.68	924.75	920.47	916.75	913.53	910.72	908.28	900.03	895.85
100000	1162.10	1155.93	1150.58	1145.94	1141.91	1138.40	1135.35	1125.04	1119.81

14% MONTHLY PAYMENT
NECESSARY TO AMORTIZE A LOAN

TERM AMOUNT	1 YEAR	1½ YEARS	2 YEARS	2½ YEARS	3 YEARS	3½ YEARS	4 YEARS	4½ YEARS	5 YEARS
$ 25	2.25	1.55	1.20	.99	.85	.76	.68	.63	.58
50	4.49	3.09	2.40	1.98	1.70	1.51	1.36	1.25	1.16
75	6.73	4.63	3.59	2.97	2.55	2.26	2.04	1.87	1.73
100	8.97	6.18	4.79	3.96	3.40	3.01	2.72	2.49	2.31
200	17.93	12.35	9.57	7.91	6.80	6.02	5.43	4.98	4.62
300	26.89	18.52	14.35	11.86	10.20	9.02	8.14	7.46	6.92
400	35.85	24.70	19.14	15.81	13.60	12.03	10.86	9.95	9.23
500	44.81	30.87	23.92	19.76	17.00	15.04	13.57	12.44	11.54
600	53.77	37.04	28.70	23.71	20.40	18.04	16.28	14.92	13.84
700	62.73	43.22	33.48	27.66	23.80	21.05	19.00	17.41	16.15
800	71.69	49.39	38.27	31.61	27.20	24.05	21.71	19.90	18.46
900	80.65	55.56	43.05	35.57	30.59	27.06	24.42	22.38	20.76
1000	89.61	61.74	47.83	39.52	33.99	30.07	27.14	24.87	23.07
2000	179.21	123.47	95.66	79.03	67.98	60.13	54.27	49.74	46.14
3000	268.81	185.20	143.49	118.54	101.97	90.19	81.40	74.60	69.20
4000	358.42	246.93	191.32	158.05	135.96	120.25	108.53	99.47	92.27
5000	448.02	308.66	239.15	197.56	169.94	150.31	135.66	124.33	115.33
6000	537.62	370.40	286.97	237.07	203.93	180.37	162.79	149.20	138.40
7000	627.23	432.13	334.80	276.58	237.92	210.43	189.92	174.06	161.46
8000	716.83	493.86	382.63	316.09	271.91	240.49	217.05	198.93	184.53
9000	806.43	555.59	430.46	355.61	305.89	270.55	244.18	223.79	207.60
10000	896.03	617.32	478.29	395.12	339.88	300.61	271.31	248.66	230.66
15000	1344.05	925.98	717.43	592.67	509.82	450.91	406.96	372.99	345.99
20000	1792.06	1234.64	956.57	790.23	679.76	601.21	542.61	497.31	461.32
25000	2240.08	1543.30	1195.71	987.78	849.70	751.51	678.26	621.64	576.65
30000	2688.09	1851.96	1434.85	1185.34	1019.64	901.81	813.92	745.97	691.98
35000	3136.11	2160.62	1673.99	1382.90	1189.57	1052.12	949.57	870.29	807.30
36000	3225.71	2222.35	1721.81	1422.41	1223.56	1082.18	976.70	895.16	830.37
37000	3315.31	2284.08	1769.64	1461.92	1257.55	1112.24	1003.83	920.02	853.44
38000	3404.92	2345.81	1817.47	1501.43	1291.54	1142.30	1030.96	944.89	876.50
39000	3494.52	2407.54	1865.30	1540.94	1325.53	1172.36	1058.09	969.75	899.57
40000	3584.12	2469.28	1913.13	1580.45	1359.51	1202.42	1085.22	994.62	922.63
41000	3673.72	2531.01	1960.96	1619.96	1393.50	1232.48	1112.35	1019.49	945.70
42000	3763.33	2592.74	2008.78	1659.48	1427.49	1262.54	1139.48	1044.35	968.76
43000	3852.93	2654.47	2056.61	1698.99	1461.48	1292.60	1166.61	1069.22	991.83
44000	3942.53	2716.20	2104.44	1738.50	1495.46	1322.66	1193.74	1094.08	1014.90
45000	4032.14	2777.94	2152.27	1778.01	1529.45	1352.72	1220.87	1118.95	1037.96
46000	4121.74	2839.67	2200.10	1817.52	1563.44	1382.78	1248.00	1143.81	1061.03
47000	4211.34	2901.40	2247.92	1857.03	1597.43	1412.84	1275.13	1168.68	1084.09
48000	4300.95	2963.13	2295.75	1896.54	1631.41	1442.90	1302.26	1193.54	1107.16
49000	4390.55	3024.86	2343.58	1936.05	1665.40	1472.96	1329.39	1218.41	1130.22
50000	4480.15	3086.59	2391.41	1975.56	1699.39	1503.02	1356.52	1243.27	1153.29
51000	4569.75	3148.33	2439.24	2015.08	1733.38	1533.08	1383.66	1268.14	1176.35
52000	4659.36	3210.06	2487.06	2054.59	1767.37	1563.14	1410.79	1293.00	1199.42
53000	4748.96	3271.79	2534.89	2094.10	1801.35	1593.20	1437.92	1317.87	1222.49
54000	4838.56	3333.52	2582.72	2133.61	1835.34	1623.26	1465.05	1342.74	1245.55
55000	4928.17	3395.25	2630.55	2173.12	1869.33	1653.32	1492.18	1367.60	1268.62
56000	5017.77	3456.99	2678.38	2212.63	1903.32	1683.38	1519.31	1392.47	1291.68
57000	5107.37	3518.72	2726.20	2252.14	1937.30	1713.44	1546.44	1417.33	1314.75
58000	5196.97	3580.45	2774.03	2291.65	1971.29	1743.50	1573.57	1442.20	1337.81
59000	5286.58	3642.18	2821.86	2331.17	2005.28	1773.56	1600.70	1467.06	1360.88
60000	5376.18	3703.91	2869.69	2370.68	2039.27	1803.62	1627.83	1491.93	1383.95
61000	5465.78	3765.64	2917.52	2410.19	2073.25	1833.68	1654.96	1516.79	1407.01
62000	5555.39	3827.38	2965.34	2449.70	2107.24	1863.74	1682.09	1541.66	1430.08
63000	5644.99	3889.11	3013.17	2489.21	2141.23	1893.80	1709.22	1566.52	1453.14
64000	5734.59	3950.84	3061.00	2528.72	2175.22	1923.86	1736.35	1591.39	1476.21
65000	5824.20	4012.57	3108.83	2568.23	2209.21	1953.93	1763.48	1616.25	1499.27
66000	5913.80	4074.30	3156.66	2607.74	2243.19	1983.99	1790.61	1641.12	1522.34
67000	6003.40	4136.03	3204.48	2647.26	2277.18	2014.05	1817.74	1665.99	1545.41
68000	6093.00	4197.77	3252.31	2686.77	2311.17	2044.11	1844.87	1690.85	1568.47
69000	6182.61	4259.50	3300.14	2726.28	2345.16	2074.17	1872.00	1715.72	1591.54
70000	6272.21	4321.23	3347.97	2765.79	2379.14	2104.23	1899.13	1740.58	1614.60
75000	6720.22	4629.89	3587.11	2963.34	2549.08	2254.53	2034.78	1864.91	1729.93
80000	7168.24	4938.55	3826.25	3160.90	2719.02	2404.83	2170.44	1989.24	1845.26
100000	8960.30	6173.18	4782.81	3951.12	3398.77	3006.04	2713.04	2486.54	2306.57

MONTHLY PAYMENT 14%
NECESSARY TO AMORTIZE A LOAN

TERM AMOUNT	6 YEARS	7 YEARS	8 YEARS	9 YEARS	10 YEARS	11 YEARS	12 YEARS	13 YEARS	14 YEARS
$ 25	.51	.47	.43	.41	.39	.37	.36	.35	.34
50	1.02	.93	.86	.81	.77	.74	.71	.69	.67
75	1.53	1.39	1.29	1.21	1.15	1.10	1.06	1.03	1.01
100	2.04	1.86	1.72	1.62	1.53	1.47	1.42	1.37	1.34
200	4.08	3.71	3.43	3.23	3.06	2.93	2.83	2.74	2.67
300	6.12	5.56	5.15	4.84	4.59	4.40	4.24	4.11	4.01
400	8.16	7.41	6.86	6.45	6.12	5.86	5.65	5.48	5.34
500	10.20	9.27	8.58	8.06	7.65	7.33	7.07	6.85	6.68
600	12.24	11.12	10.29	9.67	9.18	8.79	8.48	8.22	8.01
700	14.28	12.97	12.01	11.28	10.71	10.26	9.89	9.59	9.35
800	16.32	14.82	13.72	12.89	12.24	11.72	11.30	10.96	10.68
900	18.36	16.68	15.44	14.50	13.77	13.19	12.72	12.33	12.02
1000	20.40	18.53	17.15	16.11	15.30	14.65	14.13	13.70	13.35
2000	40.80	37.05	34.30	32.22	30.59	29.30	28.25	27.40	26.70
3000	61.19	55.58	51.45	48.32	45.88	43.94	42.38	41.10	40.05
4000	81.59	74.10	68.60	64.43	61.17	58.59	56.50	54.80	53.40
5000	101.99	92.63	85.75	80.53	76.47	73.24	70.63	68.50	66.74
6000	122.38	111.15	102.90	96.64	91.76	87.88	84.75	82.20	80.09
7000	142.78	129.68	120.05	112.74	107.05	102.53	98.88	95.90	93.44
8000	163.18	148.20	137.20	128.85	122.34	117.17	113.00	109.60	106.79
9000	183.57	166.72	154.35	144.95	137.63	131.82	127.13	123.30	120.14
10000	203.97	185.25	171.50	161.06	152.93	146.47	141.25	137.00	133.48
15000	305.95	277.87	257.24	241.58	229.39	219.70	211.88	205.49	200.22
20000	407.94	370.49	342.99	322.11	305.85	292.93	282.50	273.99	266.96
25000	509.92	463.11	428.74	402.64	382.31	366.16	353.13	342.49	333.70
30000	611.90	555.73	514.48	483.16	458.77	439.39	423.75	410.98	400.44
35000	713.89	648.36	600.23	563.69	535.23	512.62	494.38	479.48	467.18
36000	734.28	666.88	617.38	579.79	550.52	527.26	508.50	493.18	480.53
37000	754.68	685.40	634.53	595.90	565.81	541.91	522.63	506.88	493.87
38000	775.08	703.93	651.68	612.00	581.10	556.56	536.75	520.57	507.22
39000	795.47	722.45	668.83	628.11	596.39	571.20	550.88	534.27	520.57
40000	815.87	740.98	685.98	644.21	611.69	585.85	565.00	547.97	533.92
41000	836.27	759.50	703.13	660.32	626.98	600.49	579.13	561.67	547.26
42000	856.66	778.03	720.28	676.42	642.27	615.14	593.25	575.37	560.61
43000	877.06	796.55	737.43	692.53	657.56	629.79	607.38	589.07	573.96
44000	897.45	815.07	754.58	708.63	672.85	644.43	621.50	602.77	587.31
45000	917.85	833.60	771.72	724.74	688.15	659.08	635.63	616.47	600.66
46000	938.25	852.12	788.87	740.84	703.44	673.72	649.75	630.17	614.00
47000	958.64	870.65	806.02	756.95	718.73	688.37	663.88	643.87	627.35
48000	979.04	889.17	823.17	773.06	734.02	703.02	678.00	657.57	640.70
49000	999.44	907.70	840.32	789.16	749.31	717.66	692.13	671.27	654.05
50000	1019.83	926.22	857.47	805.27	764.61	732.31	706.25	684.97	667.39
51000	1040.23	944.74	874.62	821.37	779.90	746.95	720.38	698.66	680.74
52000	1060.63	963.27	891.77	837.48	795.19	761.60	734.50	712.36	694.09
53000	1081.02	981.79	908.92	853.58	810.48	776.25	748.63	726.06	707.44
54000	1101.42	1000.32	926.07	869.69	825.77	790.89	762.75	739.76	720.79
55000	1121.82	1018.84	943.22	885.79	841.07	805.54	776.88	753.46	734.13
56000	1142.21	1037.37	960.37	901.90	856.36	820.18	791.00	767.16	747.48
57000	1162.61	1055.89	977.52	918.00	871.65	834.83	805.13	780.86	760.83
58000	1183.01	1074.41	994.67	934.11	886.94	849.48	819.25	794.56	774.18
59000	1203.40	1092.94	1011.82	950.21	902.23	864.12	833.38	808.26	787.53
60000	1223.80	1111.46	1028.96	966.32	917.53	878.77	847.50	821.96	800.87
61000	1244.20	1129.99	1046.11	982.42	932.82	893.42	861.63	835.66	814.22
62000	1264.59	1148.51	1063.26	998.53	948.11	908.06	875.75	849.36	827.57
63000	1284.99	1167.04	1080.41	1014.63	963.40	922.71	889.88	863.05	840.92
64000	1305.39	1185.56	1097.56	1030.74	978.69	937.35	904.00	876.75	854.26
65000	1325.78	1204.08	1114.71	1046.84	993.99	952.00	918.13	890.45	867.61
66000	1346.18	1222.61	1131.86	1062.95	1009.28	966.65	932.25	904.15	880.96
67000	1366.58	1241.13	1149.01	1079.05	1024.57	981.29	946.38	917.85	894.31
68000	1386.97	1259.66	1166.16	1095.16	1039.86	995.94	960.50	931.55	907.66
69000	1407.37	1278.18	1183.31	1111.26	1055.15	1010.58	974.63	945.25	921.00
70000	1427.77	1296.71	1200.46	1127.37	1070.45	1025.23	988.75	958.95	934.35
75000	1529.75	1389.33	1286.20	1207.90	1146.91	1098.46	1059.38	1027.45	1001.09
80000	1631.73	1481.95	1371.95	1288.42	1223.37	1171.69	1130.00	1095.94	1067.83
100000	2039.66	1852.44	1714.94	1610.53	1529.21	1464.61	1412.50	1369.93	1334.78

14%

MONTHLY PAYMENT
NECESSARY TO AMORTIZE A LOAN

TERM AMOUNT	15 YEARS	16 YEARS	17 YEARS	18 YEARS	19 YEARS	20 YEARS	21 YEARS	22 YEARS	23 YEARS
$ 25	.33	.33	.32	.32	.31	.31	.31	.30	.30
50	.66	.65	.64	.63	.62	.61	.61	.60	.60
75	.98	.97	.95	.94	.93	.92	.91	.90	.90
100	1.31	1.29	1.27	1.25	1.23	1.22	1.21	1.20	1.19
200	2.62	2.57	2.53	2.49	2.46	2.44	2.41	2.39	2.38
300	3.92	3.85	3.79	3.73	3.69	3.65	3.62	3.59	3.57
400	5.23	5.13	5.05	4.98	4.92	4.87	4.82	4.78	4.75
500	6.53	6.41	6.31	6.22	6.14	6.08	6.03	5.98	5.94
600	7.84	7.69	7.57	7.46	7.37	7.30	7.23	7.17	7.13
700	9.14	8.97	8.83	8.70	8.60	8.51	8.43	8.37	8.31
800	10.45	10.25	10.09	9.95	9.83	9.73	9.64	9.56	9.50
900	11.75	11.53	11.35	11.19	11.06	10.94	10.84	10.76	10.69
1000	13.06	12.82	12.61	12.43	12.28	12.16	12.05	11.95	11.87
2000	26.12	25.63	25.21	24.86	24.56	24.31	24.09	23.90	23.74
3000	39.17	38.44	37.82	37.29	36.84	36.46	36.13	35.85	35.61
4000	52.23	51.25	50.42	49.72	49.12	48.61	48.18	47.80	47.48
5000	65.28	64.06	63.02	62.15	61.40	60.76	60.22	59.75	59.35
6000	78.34	76.87	75.63	74.57	73.68	72.92	72.26	71.70	71.22
7000	91.39	89.68	88.23	87.00	85.96	85.07	84.30	83.65	83.08
8000	104.45	102.49	100.83	99.43	98.24	97.22	96.35	95.60	94.95
9000	117.50	115.30	113.44	111.86	110.52	109.37	108.39	107.55	106.82
10000	130.56	128.11	126.04	124.29	122.80	121.52	120.43	119.50	118.69
15000	195.83	192.16	189.06	186.43	184.19	182.28	180.65	179.24	178.03
20000	261.11	256.21	252.07	248.57	245.59	243.04	240.86	238.99	237.37
25000	326.39	320.26	315.09	310.71	306.98	303.80	301.07	298.73	296.71
30000	391.66	384.31	378.11	372.85	368.38	364.56	361.29	358.48	356.06
35000	456.94	448.36	441.12	434.99	429.77	425.32	421.50	418.22	415.40
36000	470.00	461.17	453.73	447.42	442.05	437.47	433.54	430.17	427.27
37000	483.05	473.98	466.33	459.85	454.33	449.62	445.58	442.12	439.14
38000	496.11	486.79	478.93	472.28	466.61	461.77	457.63	454.07	451.00
39000	509.16	499.60	491.54	484.70	478.89	473.92	469.67	466.02	462.87
40000	522.22	512.41	504.14	497.13	491.17	486.08	481.71	477.97	474.74
41000	535.27	525.22	516.74	509.56	503.45	498.23	493.76	489.91	486.61
42000	548.33	538.03	529.35	521.99	515.73	510.38	505.80	501.86	498.48
43000	561.38	550.84	541.95	534.42	528.01	522.53	517.84	513.81	510.35
44000	574.44	563.65	554.55	546.84	540.28	534.68	529.88	525.76	522.21
45000	587.49	576.46	567.16	559.27	552.56	546.83	541.93	537.71	534.08
46000	600.55	589.27	579.76	571.70	564.84	558.99	553.97	549.66	545.95
47000	613.60	602.08	592.36	584.13	577.12	571.14	566.01	561.61	557.82
48000	626.66	614.89	604.97	596.56	589.40	583.29	578.05	573.56	569.69
49000	639.71	627.70	617.57	608.99	601.68	595.44	590.10	585.51	581.56
50000	652.77	640.51	630.17	621.41	613.96	607.59	602.14	597.46	593.42
51000	665.83	653.32	642.78	633.84	626.24	619.74	614.18	609.41	605.29
52000	678.88	666.13	655.38	646.27	638.52	631.90	626.23	621.35	617.16
53000	691.94	678.94	667.98	658.70	650.80	644.05	638.27	633.30	629.03
54000	704.99	691.75	680.59	671.13	663.08	656.20	650.31	645.25	640.90
55000	718.05	704.56	693.19	683.55	675.35	668.35	662.35	657.20	652.77
56000	731.10	717.37	705.79	695.98	687.63	680.50	674.40	669.15	664.63
57000	744.16	730.18	718.40	708.41	699.91	692.66	686.44	681.10	676.50
58000	757.21	742.99	731.00	720.84	712.19	704.81	698.48	693.05	688.37
59000	770.27	755.80	743.60	733.27	724.47	716.96	710.52	705.00	700.24
60000	783.32	768.61	756.21	745.69	736.75	729.11	722.57	716.95	712.11
61000	796.38	781.42	768.81	758.12	749.03	741.26	734.61	728.90	723.98
62000	809.43	794.23	781.41	770.55	761.31	753.41	746.65	740.84	735.84
63000	822.49	807.04	794.02	782.98	773.59	765.57	758.69	752.79	747.71
64000	835.54	819.85	806.62	795.41	785.87	777.72	770.74	764.74	759.58
65000	848.60	832.66	819.22	807.84	798.15	789.87	782.78	776.69	771.45
66000	861.65	845.47	831.83	820.26	810.42	802.02	794.82	788.64	783.32
67000	874.71	858.28	844.43	832.69	822.70	814.17	806.87	800.59	795.19
68000	887.77	871.09	857.03	845.12	834.98	826.32	818.91	812.54	807.06
69000	900.82	883.90	869.64	857.55	847.26	838.48	830.95	824.49	818.92
70000	913.88	896.71	882.24	869.98	859.54	850.63	842.99	836.44	830.79
75000	979.15	960.76	945.26	932.12	920.94	911.39	903.21	896.18	890.13
80000	1044.43	1024.81	1008.27	994.26	982.33	972.15	963.42	955.93	949.48
100000	1305.53	1281.02	1260.34	1242.82	1227.91	1215.18	1204.27	1194.91	1186.84

118

MONTHLY PAYMENT   **14%**
NECESSARY TO AMORTIZE A LOAN

TERM AMOUNT	24 YEARS	25 YEARS	26 YEARS	27 YEARS	28 YEARS	29 YEARS	30 YEARS	35 YEARS	40 YEARS
$ 25	.30	.30	.30	.30	.30	.29	.29	.29	.29
50	.59	.59	.59	.59	.59	.58	.58	.58	.57
75	.89	.89	.88	.88	.88	.87	.87	.86	.86
100	1.18	1.18	1.17	1.17	1.17	1.16	1.16	1.15	1.14
200	2.36	2.35	2.34	2.33	2.33	2.32	2.31	2.29	2.28
300	3.54	3.53	3.51	3.50	3.49	3.48	3.47	3.44	3.42
400	4.72	4.70	4.68	4.66	4.65	4.63	4.62	4.58	4.56
500	5.90	5.87	5.85	5.83	5.81	5.79	5.77	5.73	5.70
600	7.08	7.05	7.02	6.99	6.97	6.95	6.93	6.87	6.84
700	8.26	8.22	8.19	8.15	8.13	8.11	8.08	8.01	7.98
800	9.44	9.40	9.35	9.32	9.29	9.26	9.24	9.16	9.12
900	10.62	10.57	10.52	10.48	10.45	10.42	10.39	10.30	10.26
1000	11.80	11.74	11.69	11.65	11.61	11.57	11.54	11.45	11.40
2000	23.60	23.48	23.38	23.29	23.21	23.14	23.08	22.89	22.79
3000	35.40	35.22	35.07	34.93	34.81	34.71	34.62	34.33	34.18
4000	47.20	46.96	46.75	46.57	46.42	46.28	46.16	45.77	45.57
5000	59.00	58.70	58.44	58.21	58.02	57.85	57.70	57.21	56.96
6000	70.80	70.44	70.13	69.86	69.62	69.42	69.24	68.65	68.35
7000	82.60	82.18	81.81	81.50	81.22	80.99	80.78	80.09	79.74
8000	94.40	93.92	93.50	93.14	92.83	92.56	92.32	91.53	91.13
9000	106.19	105.65	105.19	104.78	104.43	104.12	103.86	102.97	102.52
10000	117.99	117.39	116.87	116.42	116.03	115.69	115.40	114.41	113.92
15000	176.99	176.09	175.31	174.63	174.05	173.54	173.10	171.61	170.87
20000	235.98	234.78	233.74	232.84	232.06	231.38	230.79	228.82	227.83
25000	294.98	293.47	292.17	291.05	290.07	289.23	288.49	286.02	284.78
30000	353.97	352.17	350.61	349.26	348.09	347.07	346.19	343.22	341.74
35000	412.96	410.86	409.04	407.47	406.10	404.91	403.88	400.43	398.69
36000	424.76	422.60	420.73	419.11	417.70	416.48	415.42	411.87	410.08
37000	436.56	434.34	432.42	430.75	429.31	428.05	426.96	423.31	421.47
38000	448.36	446.08	444.10	442.39	440.91	439.62	438.50	434.75	432.87
39000	460.16	457.82	455.79	454.03	452.51	451.19	450.04	446.19	444.26
40000	471.96	469.56	467.48	465.68	464.11	462.76	461.58	457.63	455.65
41000	483.76	481.29	479.16	477.32	475.72	474.33	473.12	469.07	467.04
42000	495.56	493.03	490.85	488.96	487.32	485.90	484.66	480.51	478.43
43000	507.36	504.77	502.54	500.60	498.92	497.46	496.20	491.95	489.82
44000	519.15	516.51	514.22	512.24	510.52	509.03	507.74	503.39	501.21
45000	530.95	528.25	525.91	523.88	522.13	520.60	519.28	514.83	512.60
46000	542.75	539.99	537.60	535.53	533.73	532.17	530.82	526.27	523.99
47000	554.55	551.73	549.28	547.17	545.33	543.74	542.36	537.71	535.38
48000	566.35	563.47	560.97	558.81	556.94	555.31	553.90	549.16	546.78
49000	578.15	575.20	572.66	570.45	568.54	566.88	565.44	560.60	558.17
50000	589.95	586.94	584.34	582.09	580.14	578.45	576.97	572.04	569.56
51000	601.75	598.68	596.03	593.74	591.74	590.02	588.51	583.48	580.95
52000	613.54	610.42	607.72	605.38	603.35	601.58	600.05	594.92	592.34
53000	625.34	622.16	619.40	617.02	614.95	613.15	611.59	606.36	603.73
54000	637.14	633.90	631.09	628.66	626.55	624.72	623.13	617.80	615.12
55000	648.94	645.64	642.78	640.30	638.15	636.29	634.67	629.24	626.51
56000	660.74	657.38	654.47	651.94	649.76	647.86	646.21	640.68	637.90
57000	672.54	669.11	666.15	663.59	661.36	659.43	657.75	652.12	649.30
58000	684.34	680.85	677.84	675.23	672.96	671.00	669.29	663.56	660.69
59000	696.14	692.59	689.53	686.87	684.57	682.57	680.83	675.00	672.08
60000	707.94	704.33	701.21	698.51	696.17	694.14	692.37	686.44	683.47
61000	719.73	716.07	712.90	710.15	707.77	705.70	703.91	697.88	694.86
62000	731.53	727.81	724.59	721.79	719.37	717.27	715.45	709.32	706.25
63000	743.33	739.55	736.27	733.44	730.98	728.84	726.99	720.76	717.64
64000	755.13	751.29	747.96	745.08	742.58	740.41	738.53	732.21	729.03
65000	766.93	763.02	759.65	756.72	754.18	751.98	750.07	743.65	740.42
66000	778.73	774.76	771.33	768.36	765.78	763.55	761.61	755.09	751.81
67000	790.53	786.50	783.02	780.00	777.39	775.12	773.14	766.53	763.21
68000	802.33	798.24	794.71	791.65	788.99	786.69	784.68	777.97	774.60
69000	814.13	809.98	806.39	803.29	800.59	798.25	796.22	789.41	785.99
70000	825.92	821.72	818.08	814.93	812.20	809.82	807.76	800.85	797.38
75000	884.92	880.41	876.51	873.14	870.21	867.67	865.46	858.05	854.33
80000	943.91	939.11	934.95	931.35	928.22	925.51	923.16	915.26	911.29
100000	1179.89	1173.88	1168.68	1164.18	1160.28	1156.89	1153.94	1144.07	1139.11

14¼%   MONTHLY PAYMENT
NECESSARY TO AMORTIZE A LOAN

TERM AMOUNT	1 YEAR	1½ YEARS	2 YEARS	2½ YEARS	3 YEARS	3½ YEARS	4 YEARS	4½ YEARS	5 YEARS
$ 25	2.25	1.55	1.20	1.00	.86	.76	.69	.63	.58
50	4.49	3.10	2.40	1.99	1.71	1.51	1.37	1.25	1.16
75	6.73	4.64	3.60	2.98	2.56	2.27	2.05	1.88	1.74
100	8.98	6.19	4.80	3.97	3.42	3.02	2.73	2.50	2.32
200	17.95	12.37	9.59	7.93	6.83	6.04	5.45	5.00	4.64
300	26.92	18.56	14.39	11.89	10.24	9.06	8.18	7.50	6.96
400	35.89	24.74	19.18	15.85	13.65	12.08	10.90	10.00	9.28
500	44.86	30.93	23.97	19.82	17.06	15.09	13.63	12.50	11.60
600	53.83	37.11	28.77	23.78	20.47	18.11	16.35	15.00	13.92
700	62.80	43.29	33.56	27.74	23.88	21.13	19.08	17.49	16.24
800	71.78	49.48	38.36	31.70	27.29	24.15	21.80	19.99	18.56
900	80.75	55.66	43.15	35.67	30.70	27.16	24.53	22.49	20.87
1000	89.72	61.85	47.94	39.63	34.11	30.18	27.25	24.99	23.19
2000	179.43	123.69	95.88	79.25	68.21	60.36	54.50	49.98	46.38
3000	269.15	185.53	143.82	118.88	102.31	90.53	81.75	74.96	69.57
4000	358.86	247.37	191.76	158.50	136.41	120.71	109.00	99.95	92.76
5000	448.57	309.22	239.70	198.12	170.52	150.89	136.25	124.93	115.94
6000	538.29	371.06	287.64	237.75	204.62	181.06	163.50	149.92	139.13
7000	628.00	432.90	335.58	277.37	238.72	211.24	190.74	174.90	162.32
8000	717.72	494.74	383.52	317.00	272.82	241.42	217.99	199.89	185.51
9000	807.43	556.59	431.46	356.62	306.92	271.59	245.24	224.87	208.69
10000	897.14	618.43	479.40	396.24	341.03	301.77	272.49	249.86	231.88
15000	1345.71	927.64	719.10	594.36	511.54	452.65	408.73	374.79	347.82
20000	1794.28	1236.85	958.79	792.48	682.05	603.54	544.98	499.71	463.76
25000	2242.85	1546.06	1198.49	990.60	852.56	754.42	681.22	624.64	579.70
30000	2691.42	1855.27	1438.19	1188.72	1023.07	905.30	817.46	749.57	695.64
35000	3139.99	2164.49	1677.89	1386.84	1193.58	1056.18	953.70	874.50	811.57
36000	3229.71	2226.33	1725.83	1426.47	1227.68	1086.36	980.95	899.48	834.76
37000	3319.42	2288.17	1773.76	1466.09	1261.78	1116.54	1008.20	924.47	857.95
38000	3409.14	2350.01	1821.70	1505.72	1295.89	1146.71	1035.45	949.45	881.14
39000	3498.85	2411.86	1869.64	1545.34	1329.99	1176.89	1062.70	974.44	904.33
40000	3588.56	2473.70	1917.58	1584.96	1364.09	1207.07	1089.95	999.42	927.51
41000	3678.28	2535.54	1965.52	1624.59	1398.19	1237.24	1117.19	1024.41	950.70
42000	3767.99	2597.38	2013.46	1664.21	1432.30	1267.42	1144.44	1049.39	973.89
43000	3857.71	2659.23	2061.40	1703.84	1466.40	1297.60	1171.69	1074.38	997.08
44000	3947.42	2721.07	2109.34	1743.46	1500.50	1327.77	1198.94	1099.36	1020.26
45000	4037.13	2782.91	2157.28	1783.08	1534.60	1357.95	1226.19	1124.35	1043.45
46000	4126.85	2844.75	2205.22	1822.71	1568.70	1388.13	1253.44	1149.34	1066.64
47000	4216.56	2906.59	2253.16	1862.33	1602.81	1418.30	1280.69	1174.32	1089.83
48000	4306.28	2968.44	2301.10	1901.96	1636.91	1448.48	1307.93	1199.31	1113.01
49000	4395.99	3030.28	2349.04	1941.58	1671.01	1478.66	1335.18	1224.29	1136.20
50000	4485.70	3092.12	2396.98	1981.20	1705.11	1508.83	1362.43	1249.28	1159.39
51000	4575.42	3153.96	2444.92	2020.83	1739.21	1539.01	1389.68	1274.26	1182.58
52000	4665.13	3215.81	2492.86	2060.45	1773.32	1569.19	1416.93	1299.25	1205.77
53000	4754.85	3277.65	2540.80	2100.08	1807.42	1599.36	1444.18	1324.23	1228.95
54000	4844.56	3339.49	2588.74	2139.70	1841.52	1629.54	1471.43	1349.22	1252.14
55000	4934.27	3401.33	2636.67	2179.32	1875.62	1659.72	1498.67	1374.20	1275.33
56000	5023.99	3463.18	2684.61	2218.95	1909.73	1689.89	1525.92	1399.19	1298.52
57000	5113.70	3525.02	2732.55	2258.57	1943.83	1720.07	1553.17	1424.18	1321.70
58000	5203.41	3586.86	2780.49	2298.20	1977.93	1750.25	1580.42	1449.16	1344.89
59000	5293.13	3648.70	2828.43	2337.82	2012.03	1780.42	1607.67	1474.15	1368.08
60000	5382.84	3710.54	2876.37	2377.44	2046.13	1810.60	1634.92	1499.13	1391.27
61000	5472.56	3772.39	2924.31	2417.07	2080.24	1840.78	1662.17	1524.12	1414.46
62000	5562.27	3834.23	2972.25	2456.69	2114.34	1870.95	1689.41	1549.10	1437.64
63000	5651.98	3896.07	3020.19	2496.32	2148.44	1901.13	1716.66	1574.09	1460.83
64000	5741.70	3957.91	3068.13	2535.94	2182.54	1931.30	1743.91	1599.07	1484.02
65000	5831.41	4019.76	3116.07	2575.56	2216.64	1961.48	1771.16	1624.06	1507.21
66000	5921.13	4081.60	3164.01	2615.19	2250.75	1991.66	1798.41	1649.04	1530.39
67000	6010.84	4143.44	3211.95	2654.81	2284.85	2021.83	1825.66	1674.03	1553.58
68000	6100.55	4205.28	3259.89	2694.44	2318.95	2052.01	1852.91	1699.02	1576.77
69000	6190.27	4267.13	3307.83	2734.06	2353.05	2082.19	1880.15	1724.00	1599.96
70000	6279.98	4328.97	3355.77	2773.68	2387.16	2112.36	1907.40	1748.99	1623.14
75000	6728.55	4638.18	3595.46	2971.80	2557.67	2263.25	2043.64	1873.11	1739.08
80000	7177.12	4947.39	3835.16	3169.92	2728.18	2414.13	2179.89	1998.84	1855.02
100000	8971.40	6184.24	4793.95	3962.40	3410.22	3017.66	2724.86	2498.55	2318.78

120

MONTHLY PAYMENT 14¼%
NECESSARY TO AMORTIZE A LOAN

TERM AMOUNT	6 YEARS	7 YEARS	8 YEARS	9 YEARS	10 YEARS	11 YEARS	12 YEARS	13 YEARS	14 YEARS
$ 25	.52	.47	.44	.41	.39	.37	.36	.35	.34
50	1.03	.94	.87	.82	.78	.74	.72	.70	.68
75	1.54	1.40	1.30	1.22	1.16	1.11	1.08	1.04	1.02
100	2.06	1.87	1.73	1.63	1.55	1.48	1.43	1.39	1.36
200	4.11	3.74	3.46	3.25	3.09	2.96	2.86	2.78	2.71
300	6.16	5.60	5.19	4.88	4.63	4.44	4.29	4.16	4.06
400	8.21	7.47	6.92	6.50	6.18	5.92	5.71	5.55	5.41
500	10.27	9.33	8.65	8.13	7.72	7.40	7.14	6.93	6.76
600	12.32	11.20	10.37	9.75	9.26	8.88	8.57	8.32	8.11
700	14.37	13.06	12.10	11.37	10.81	10.36	10.00	9.70	9.46
800	16.42	14.93	13.83	13.00	12.35	11.84	11.42	11.09	10.81
900	18.48	16.79	15.56	14.62	13.89	13.32	12.85	12.47	12.16
1000	20.53	18.66	17.29	16.25	15.44	14.80	14.28	13.86	13.51
2000	41.05	37.31	34.57	32.49	30.87	29.59	28.55	27.71	27.01
3000	61.57	55.97	51.85	48.73	46.30	44.38	42.82	41.56	40.51
4000	82.10	74.62	69.14	64.98	61.74	59.17	57.10	55.41	54.02
5000	102.62	93.28	86.42	81.22	77.17	73.96	71.37	69.26	67.52
6000	123.14	111.93	103.70	97.46	92.60	88.75	85.64	83.11	81.02
7000	143.66	130.58	120.99	113.70	108.04	103.54	99.92	96.96	94.52
8000	164.19	149.24	138.27	129.95	123.47	118.33	114.19	110.81	108.03
9000	184.71	167.89	155.55	146.19	138.90	133.12	128.46	124.66	121.53
10000	205.23	186.55	172.84	162.43	154.34	147.91	142.74	138.51	135.03
15000	307.84	279.82	259.25	243.65	231.50	221.87	214.10	207.77	202.54
20000	410.46	373.09	345.67	324.86	308.67	295.82	285.47	277.02	270.06
25000	513.07	466.36	432.08	406.07	385.84	369.78	356.84	346.28	337.57
30000	615.68	559.63	518.50	487.29	463.00	443.73	428.20	415.53	405.08
35000	718.29	652.90	604.91	568.50	540.17	517.69	499.57	484.78	472.60
36000	738.82	671.56	622.20	584.75	555.60	532.48	513.84	498.63	486.10
37000	759.34	690.21	639.48	600.99	571.04	547.27	528.12	512.48	499.60
38000	779.86	708.87	656.76	617.23	586.47	562.06	542.39	526.34	513.10
39000	800.38	727.52	674.05	633.47	601.90	576.85	556.66	540.19	526.61
40000	820.91	746.17	691.33	649.72	617.34	591.64	570.93	554.04	540.11
41000	841.43	764.83	708.61	665.96	632.77	606.43	585.21	567.89	553.61
42000	861.95	783.48	725.90	682.20	648.20	621.22	599.48	581.74	567.11
43000	882.48	802.14	743.18	698.45	663.64	636.01	613.75	595.59	580.62
44000	903.00	820.79	760.46	714.69	679.07	650.81	628.03	609.44	594.12
45000	923.52	839.44	777.75	730.93	694.50	665.60	642.30	623.29	607.62
46000	944.04	858.10	795.03	747.17	709.94	680.39	656.57	637.14	621.12
47000	964.57	876.75	812.31	763.42	725.37	695.18	670.85	650.99	634.63
48000	985.09	895.41	829.59	779.66	740.80	709.97	685.12	664.84	648.13
49000	1005.61	914.06	846.88	795.90	756.24	724.76	699.39	678.69	661.63
50000	1026.13	932.72	864.16	812.14	771.67	739.55	713.67	692.55	675.13
51000	1046.66	951.37	881.44	828.39	787.10	754.34	727.94	706.40	688.64
52000	1067.18	970.02	898.73	844.63	802.54	769.13	742.21	720.25	702.14
53000	1087.70	988.68	916.01	860.87	817.97	783.92	756.49	734.10	715.64
54000	1108.22	1007.33	933.29	877.12	833.40	798.71	770.76	747.95	729.14
55000	1128.75	1025.99	950.58	893.36	848.84	813.51	785.03	761.80	742.65
56000	1149.27	1044.64	967.86	909.60	864.27	828.30	799.31	775.65	756.15
57000	1169.79	1063.30	985.14	925.84	879.70	843.09	813.58	789.50	769.65
58000	1190.31	1081.95	1002.43	942.09	895.14	857.88	827.85	803.35	783.15
59000	1210.84	1100.60	1019.71	958.33	910.57	872.67	842.13	817.20	796.66
60000	1231.36	1119.26	1036.99	974.57	926.00	887.46	856.40	831.05	810.16
61000	1251.88	1137.91	1054.28	990.82	941.44	902.25	870.67	844.90	823.66
62000	1272.40	1156.57	1071.56	1007.06	956.87	917.04	884.95	858.76	837.16
63000	1292.93	1175.22	1088.84	1023.30	972.30	931.83	899.22	872.61	850.67
64000	1313.45	1193.87	1106.12	1039.54	987.73	946.62	913.49	886.46	864.17
65000	1333.97	1212.53	1123.41	1055.79	1003.17	961.41	927.77	900.31	877.67
66000	1354.49	1231.18	1140.69	1072.03	1018.60	976.21	942.04	914.16	891.18
67000	1375.02	1249.84	1157.97	1088.27	1034.03	991.00	956.31	928.01	904.68
68000	1395.54	1268.49	1175.26	1104.51	1049.47	1005.79	970.59	941.86	918.18
69000	1416.06	1287.15	1192.54	1120.76	1064.90	1020.58	984.86	955.71	931.68
70000	1436.58	1305.80	1209.82	1137.00	1080.33	1035.37	999.13	969.56	945.19
75000	1539.20	1399.07	1296.24	1218.21	1157.50	1109.32	1070.50	1038.82	1012.70
80000	1641.81	1492.34	1382.65	1299.43	1234.67	1183.28	1141.86	1108.07	1080.21
100000	2052.26	1865.43	1728.32	1624.28	1543.33	1479.10	1427.33	1385.09	1350.26

121

14¼% MONTHLY PAYMENT
NECESSARY TO AMORTIZE A LOAN

TERM AMOUNT	15 YEARS	16 YEARS	17 YEARS	18 YEARS	19 YEARS	20 YEARS	21 YEARS	22 YEARS	23 YEARS
$ 25	.34	.33	.32	.32	.32	.31	.31	.31	.31
50	.67	.65	.64	.63	.63	.62	.62	.61	.61
75	1.00	.98	.96	.95	.94	.93	.92	.91	.91
100	1.33	1.30	1.28	1.26	1.25	1.24	1.23	1.22	1.21
200	2.65	2.60	2.56	2.52	2.49	2.47	2.45	2.43	2.41
300	3.97	3.90	3.84	3.78	3.74	3.70	3.67	3.64	3.62
400	5.29	5.19	5.11	5.04	4.98	4.93	4.89	4.85	4.82
500	6.61	6.49	6.39	6.30	6.23	6.17	6.11	6.07	6.03
600	7.93	7.79	7.67	7.56	7.47	7.40	7.33	7.28	7.23
700	9.25	9.08	8.94	8.82	8.72	8.63	8.56	8.49	8.44
800	10.58	10.38	10.22	10.08	9.96	9.86	9.78	9.70	9.64
900	11.90	11.68	11.50	11.34	11.21	11.10	11.00	10.92	10.85
1000	13.22	12.98	12.77	12.60	12.45	12.33	12.22	12.13	12.05
2000	26.43	25.95	25.54	25.19	24.90	24.65	24.44	24.25	24.10
3000	39.64	38.92	38.31	37.79	37.35	36.97	36.65	36.38	36.14
4000	52.86	51.89	51.07	50.38	49.79	49.29	48.87	48.50	48.19
5000	66.07	64.86	63.84	62.98	62.24	61.62	61.08	60.62	60.23
6000	79.28	77.83	76.61	75.57	74.69	73.94	73.30	72.75	72.28
7000	92.50	90.80	89.37	88.16	87.14	86.26	85.51	84.87	84.32
8000	105.71	103.77	102.14	100.76	99.58	98.58	97.73	97.00	96.37
9000	118.92	116.74	114.91	113.35	112.03	110.91	109.94	109.12	108.41
10000	132.14	129.71	127.67	125.95	124.48	123.23	122.16	121.24	120.46
15000	198.20	194.57	191.51	188.92	186.72	184.84	183.24	181.86	180.68
20000	264.27	259.42	255.34	251.89	248.95	246.45	244.31	242.48	240.91
25000	330.33	324.27	319.17	314.86	311.19	308.07	305.39	303.10	301.13
30000	396.40	389.13	383.01	377.83	373.43	369.68	366.47	363.72	361.36
35000	462.46	453.98	446.84	440.80	435.67	431.29	427.55	424.34	421.58
36000	475.68	466.95	459.61	453.39	448.11	443.61	439.76	436.46	433.63
37000	488.89	479.92	472.37	465.99	460.56	455.93	451.98	448.59	445.67
38000	502.10	492.89	485.14	478.58	473.01	468.26	464.19	460.71	457.72
39000	515.32	505.87	497.91	491.18	485.46	480.58	476.41	472.83	469.76
40000	528.53	518.84	510.68	503.77	497.90	492.90	488.62	484.96	481.81
41000	541.74	531.81	523.44	516.36	510.35	505.22	500.84	497.08	493.85
42000	554.96	544.78	536.21	528.96	522.80	517.55	513.06	509.21	505.90
43000	568.17	557.75	548.98	541.55	535.25	529.87	525.27	521.33	517.94
44000	581.38	570.72	561.74	554.15	547.69	542.19	537.49	533.45	529.99
45000	594.59	583.69	574.51	566.74	560.14	554.51	549.70	545.58	542.03
46000	607.81	596.66	587.28	579.34	572.59	566.84	561.92	557.70	554.08
47000	621.02	609.63	600.04	591.93	585.04	579.16	574.13	569.82	566.12
48000	634.23	622.60	612.81	604.52	597.48	591.48	586.35	581.95	578.17
49000	647.45	635.57	625.58	617.12	609.93	603.80	598.56	594.07	590.21
50000	660.66	648.54	638.34	629.71	622.38	616.13	610.78	606.20	602.26
51000	673.87	661.51	651.11	642.31	634.83	628.45	623.00	618.32	614.30
52000	687.09	674.49	663.88	654.90	647.27	640.77	635.21	630.44	626.35
53000	700.30	687.46	676.64	667.49	659.72	653.09	647.43	642.57	638.39
54000	713.51	700.43	689.41	680.09	672.17	665.42	659.64	654.69	650.44
55000	726.73	713.40	702.18	692.68	684.62	677.74	671.86	666.81	662.48
56000	739.94	726.37	714.94	705.28	697.06	690.06	684.07	678.94	674.53
57000	753.15	739.34	727.71	717.87	709.51	702.38	696.29	691.06	686.57
58000	766.36	752.31	740.48	730.46	721.96	714.71	708.50	703.19	698.62
59000	779.58	765.28	753.24	743.06	734.41	727.03	720.72	715.31	710.66
60000	792.79	778.25	766.01	755.65	746.85	739.35	732.93	727.43	722.71
61000	806.00	791.22	778.78	768.25	759.30	751.67	745.15	739.56	734.75
62000	819.22	804.19	791.54	780.84	771.75	764.00	757.37	751.68	746.80
63000	832.43	817.16	804.31	793.44	784.20	776.32	769.58	763.81	758.84
64000	845.64	830.13	817.08	806.03	796.64	788.64	781.80	775.93	770.89
65000	858.86	843.11	829.84	818.62	809.09	800.96	794.01	788.05	782.93
66000	872.07	856.08	842.61	831.22	821.54	813.29	806.23	800.18	794.98
67000	885.28	869.05	855.38	843.81	833.99	825.61	818.44	812.30	807.02
68000	898.50	882.02	868.14	856.41	846.43	837.93	830.66	824.42	819.07
69000	911.71	894.99	880.91	869.00	858.88	850.25	842.87	836.55	831.11
70000	924.92	907.96	893.68	881.59	871.33	862.57	855.09	848.67	843.16
75000	990.99	972.81	957.51	944.56	933.57	924.19	916.17	909.29	903.38
80000	1057.05	1037.67	1021.35	1007.54	995.80	985.80	977.24	969.91	963.61
100000	1321.31	1297.08	1276.68	1259.42	1244.75	1232.25	1221.55	1212.39	1204.51

122

MONTHLY PAYMENT 14¼%
NECESSARY TO AMORTIZE A LOAN

TERM AMOUNT	24 YEARS	25 YEARS	26 YEARS	27 YEARS	28 YEARS	29 YEARS	30 YEARS	35 YEARS	40 YEARS
$ 25	.30	.30	.30	.30	.30	.30	.30	.30	.29
50	.60	.60	.60	.60	.59	.59	.59	.59	.58
75	.90	.90	.90	.89	.89	.89	.88	.88	.87
100	1.20	1.20	1.19	1.19	1.18	1.18	1.18	1.17	1.16
200	2.40	2.39	2.38	2.37	2.36	2.36	2.35	2.33	2.32
300	3.60	3.58	3.57	3.55	3.54	3.53	3.52	3.49	3.48
400	4.80	4.77	4.75	4.73	4.72	4.71	4.70	4.66	4.64
500	5.99	5.96	5.94	5.92	5.90	5.88	5.87	5.82	5.80
600	7.19	7.16	7.13	7.10	7.08	7.06	7.04	6.98	6.96
700	8.39	8.35	8.31	8.28	8.26	8.23	8.21	8.15	8.11
800	9.59	9.54	9.50	9.46	9.43	9.41	9.39	9.31	9.27
900	10.78	10.73	10.69	10.65	10.61	10.58	10.50	10.47	10.43
1000	11.98	11.92	11.87	11.83	11.79	11.76	11.73	11.64	11.59
2000	23.96	23.84	23.74	23.65	23.58	23.51	23.46	23.27	23.17
3000	35.94	35.76	35.61	35.48	35.37	35.27	35.18	34.90	34.76
4000	47.91	47.68	47.48	47.30	47.15	47.02	46.91	46.53	46.34
5000	59.89	59.60	59.35	59.13	58.94	58.78	58.63	58.16	57.93
6000	71.87	71.52	71.21	70.95	70.73	70.53	70.36	69.79	69.51
7000	83.85	83.44	83.08	82.78	82.51	82.28	82.09	81.42	81.09
8000	95.82	95.35	94.95	94.60	94.30	94.04	93.81	93.05	92.68
9000	107.80	107.27	106.82	106.43	106.09	105.79	105.54	104.68	104.26
10000	119.78	119.19	118.69	118.25	117.87	117.55	117.26	116.32	115.85
15000	179.66	178.79	178.03	177.37	176.81	176.32	175.89	174.47	173.77
20000	239.55	238.38	237.37	236.50	235.74	235.09	234.52	232.63	231.69
25000	299.44	297.97	296.71	295.62	294.68	293.86	293.15	290.78	289.61
30000	359.32	357.57	356.05	354.74	353.61	352.63	351.78	348.94	347.53
35000	419.21	417.16	415.39	413.87	412.54	411.40	410.41	407.09	405.45
36000	431.18	429.08	427.26	425.69	424.33	423.15	422.13	418.72	417.03
37000	443.16	441.00	439.13	437.52	436.12	434.91	433.86	430.36	428.62
38000	455.14	452.92	451.00	449.34	447.90	446.66	445.58	441.99	440.20
39000	467.12	464.84	462.87	461.16	459.69	458.42	457.31	453.62	451.79
40000	479.09	476.75	474.74	472.99	471.48	470.17	469.03	465.25	463.37
41000	491.07	488.67	486.60	484.81	483.26	481.92	480.76	476.88	474.95
42000	503.05	500.59	498.47	496.64	495.05	493.68	492.49	488.51	486.54
43000	515.03	512.51	510.34	508.46	506.84	505.43	504.21	500.14	498.12
44000	527.00	524.43	522.21	520.29	518.63	517.19	515.94	511.77	509.71
45000	538.98	536.35	534.08	532.11	530.41	528.94	527.66	523.40	521.29
46000	550.96	548.27	545.94	543.94	542.20	540.69	539.39	535.04	532.87
47000	562.93	560.19	557.81	555.76	553.99	552.45	551.11	546.67	544.46
48000	574.91	572.10	569.68	567.59	565.77	564.20	562.84	558.30	556.04
49000	586.89	584.02	581.55	579.41	577.56	575.96	574.57	569.93	567.63
50000	598.87	595.94	593.42	591.24	589.35	587.71	586.29	581.56	579.21
51000	610.84	607.86	605.29	603.06	601.13	599.46	598.02	593.19	590.80
52000	622.82	619.78	617.15	614.88	612.92	611.22	609.74	604.82	602.38
53000	634.80	631.70	629.02	626.71	624.71	622.97	621.47	616.45	613.96
54000	646.77	643.62	640.89	638.53	636.49	634.73	633.20	628.08	625.55
55000	658.75	655.54	652.76	650.36	648.28	646.48	644.92	639.72	637.13
56000	670.73	667.45	664.63	662.18	660.07	658.23	656.65	651.35	648.72
57000	682.71	679.37	676.50	674.01	671.85	669.99	668.37	662.98	660.30
58000	694.68	691.29	688.36	685.83	683.64	681.74	680.10	674.61	671.88
59000	706.66	703.21	700.23	697.66	695.43	693.50	691.82	686.24	683.47
60000	718.64	715.13	712.10	709.48	707.21	705.25	703.55	697.87	695.05
61000	730.62	727.05	723.97	721.31	719.00	717.01	715.28	709.50	706.64
62000	742.59	738.97	735.84	733.13	730.79	728.76	727.00	721.13	718.22
63000	754.57	750.89	747.71	744.96	742.58	740.51	738.73	732.76	729.81
64000	766.55	762.80	759.57	756.78	754.36	752.27	750.45	744.40	741.39
65000	778.52	774.72	771.44	768.60	766.15	764.02	762.18	756.03	752.97
66000	790.50	786.64	783.31	780.43	777.94	775.78	773.90	767.66	764.56
67000	802.48	798.56	795.18	792.25	789.72	787.53	785.63	779.29	776.14
68000	814.46	810.48	807.05	804.08	801.51	799.28	797.36	790.92	787.73
69000	826.43	822.40	818.91	815.90	813.30	811.04	809.08	802.55	799.31
70000	838.41	834.32	830.78	827.73	825.08	822.79	820.81	814.18	810.89
75000	898.30	893.91	890.12	886.85	884.02	881.56	879.44	872.34	868.81
80000	958.18	953.50	949.47	945.97	942.95	940.33	938.06	930.49	926.74
100000	1197.73	1191.88	1186.83	1182.47	1178.69	1175.42	1172.58	1163.12	1158.42

123

14½% MONTHLY PAYMENT
NECESSARY TO AMORTIZE A LOAN

TERM / AMOUNT	1 YEAR	1½ YEARS	2 YEARS	2½ YEARS	3 YEARS	3½ YEARS	4 YEARS	4½ YEARS	5 YEARS
$ 25	2.25	1.55	1.21	1.00	.86	.76	.69	.63	.59
50	4.50	3.10	2.41	1.99	1.72	1.52	1.37	1.26	1.17
75	6.74	4.65	3.61	2.99	2.57	2.28	2.06	1.89	1.75
100	8.99	6.20	4.81	3.98	3.43	3.03	2.74	2.52	2.34
200	17.97	12.40	9.62	7.95	6.85	6.06	5.48	5.03	4.67
300	26.95	18.59	14.42	11.93	10.27	9.09	8.22	7.54	7.00
400	35.93	24.79	19.23	15.90	13.69	12.12	10.95	10.05	9.33
500	44.92	30.98	24.03	19.87	17.11	15.15	13.69	12.56	11.66
600	53.90	37.18	28.84	23.85	20.54	18.18	16.43	15.07	13.99
700	62.88	43.37	33.64	27.82	23.96	21.21	19.16	17.58	16.32
800	71.86	49.57	38.45	31.79	27.38	24.24	21.90	20.09	18.65
900	80.85	55.76	43.25	35.77	30.80	27.27	24.64	22.60	20.98
1000	89.83	61.96	48.06	39.74	34.22	30.30	27.37	25.11	23.31
2000	179.65	123.91	96.11	79.48	68.44	60.59	54.74	50.22	46.62
3000	269.48	185.86	144.16	119.22	102.66	90.88	82.11	75.32	69.93
4000	359.30	247.82	192.21	158.95	136.87	121.18	109.47	100.43	93.24
5000	449.13	309.77	240.26	198.69	171.09	151.47	136.84	125.53	116.55
6000	538.95	371.72	288.31	238.43	205.31	181.76	164.21	150.64	139.86
7000	628.78	433.68	336.36	278.16	239.52	212.06	191.57	175.75	163.17
8000	718.60	495.63	384.41	317.90	273.74	242.35	218.94	200.85	186.48
9000	808.43	557.58	432.46	357.64	307.96	272.64	246.31	225.96	209.79
10000	898.25	619.53	480.51	397.37	342.17	302.93	273.67	251.06	233.10
15000	1347.38	929.30	720.77	596.06	513.26	454.40	410.51	376.59	349.65
20000	1796.50	1239.06	961.02	794.74	684.34	605.86	547.34	502.12	466.20
25000	2245.63	1548.83	1201.28	993.43	855.42	757.33	684.18	627.65	582.75
30000	2694.75	1858.59	1441.53	1192.11	1026.51	908.79	821.01	753.18	699.30
35000	3143.88	2168.36	1681.79	1390.80	1197.59	1060.26	957.84	878.71	815.85
36000	3233.70	2230.31	1729.84	1430.53	1231.81	1090.55	985.21	903.81	839.16
37000	3323.53	2292.26	1777.89	1470.27	1266.02	1120.84	1012.58	928.92	862.47
38000	3413.35	2354.21	1825.94	1510.01	1300.24	1151.14	1039.95	954.02	885.78
39000	3503.18	2416.17	1873.99	1549.74	1334.46	1181.43	1067.31	979.13	909.09
40000	3593.00	2478.12	1922.04	1589.48	1368.67	1211.72	1094.68	1004.23	932.40
41000	3682.83	2540.07	1970.09	1629.22	1402.89	1242.02	1122.05	1029.34	955.71
42000	3772.65	2602.03	2018.14	1668.95	1437.11	1272.31	1149.41	1054.45	979.02
43000	3862.48	2663.98	2066.19	1708.69	1471.32	1302.60	1176.78	1079.55	1002.33
44000	3952.30	2725.93	2114.24	1748.43	1505.54	1332.90	1204.15	1104.66	1025.64
45000	4042.13	2787.88	2162.30	1788.16	1539.76	1363.19	1231.51	1129.76	1048.95
46000	4131.95	2849.84	2210.35	1827.90	1573.97	1393.48	1258.88	1154.87	1072.26
47000	4221.78	2911.79	2258.40	1867.64	1608.19	1423.77	1286.25	1179.97	1095.57
48000	4311.60	2973.74	2306.45	1907.37	1642.41	1454.07	1313.61	1205.08	1118.88
49000	4401.43	3035.70	2354.50	1947.11	1676.62	1484.36	1340.98	1230.19	1142.19
50000	4491.25	3097.65	2402.55	1986.85	1710.84	1514.65	1368.35	1255.29	1165.50
51000	4581.08	3159.60	2450.60	2026.59	1745.06	1544.95	1395.71	1280.40	1188.81
52000	4670.90	3221.55	2498.65	2066.32	1779.27	1575.24	1423.08	1305.50	1212.12
53000	4760.73	3283.51	2546.70	2106.06	1813.49	1605.53	1450.45	1330.61	1235.43
54000	4850.55	3345.46	2594.75	2145.80	1847.71	1635.82	1477.81	1355.71	1258.74
55000	4940.38	3407.41	2642.80	2185.53	1881.92	1666.12	1505.18	1380.82	1282.05
56000	5030.20	3469.37	2690.86	2225.27	1916.14	1696.41	1532.55	1405.93	1305.36
57000	5120.03	3531.32	2738.91	2265.01	1950.36	1726.70	1559.92	1431.03	1328.67
58000	5209.85	3593.27	2786.96	2304.74	1984.57	1757.00	1587.28	1456.14	1351.98
59000	5299.68	3655.22	2835.01	2344.48	2018.79	1787.29	1614.65	1481.24	1375.29
60000	5389.50	3717.18	2883.06	2384.22	2053.01	1817.58	1642.02	1506.35	1398.60
61000	5479.33	3779.13	2931.11	2423.95	2087.22	1847.88	1669.38	1531.45	1421.91
62000	5569.15	3841.08	2979.16	2463.69	2121.44	1878.17	1696.75	1556.56	1445.22
63000	5658.98	3903.04	3027.21	2503.43	2155.66	1908.46	1724.12	1581.67	1468.53
64000	5748.80	3964.99	3075.26	2543.16	2189.87	1938.75	1751.48	1606.77	1491.84
65000	5838.63	4026.94	3123.31	2582.90	2224.09	1969.05	1778.85	1631.88	1515.15
66000	5928.45	4088.89	3171.36	2622.64	2258.31	1999.34	1806.22	1656.98	1538.46
67000	6018.28	4150.85	3219.41	2662.37	2292.52	2029.63	1833.58	1682.09	1561.77
68000	6108.10	4212.80	3267.47	2702.11	2326.74	2059.93	1860.95	1707.19	1585.08
69000	6197.93	4274.75	3315.52	2741.85	2360.96	2090.22	1888.32	1732.30	1608.39
70000	6287.75	4336.71	3363.57	2781.59	2395.17	2120.51	1915.68	1757.41	1631.70
75000	6736.88	4646.47	3603.82	2980.27	2566.26	2271.98	2052.52	1882.93	1748.25
80000	7186.00	4956.24	3844.08	3178.95	2737.34	2423.44	2189.35	2008.46	1864.80
100000	8982.50	6195.29	4805.09	3973.69	3421.68	3029.30	2736.69	2510.58	2331.00

124

MONTHLY PAYMENT 14½%
NECESSARY TO AMORTIZE A LOAN

TERM AMOUNT	6 YEARS	7 YEARS	8 YEARS	9 YEARS	10 YEARS	11 YEARS	12 YEARS	13 YEARS	14 YEARS
$ 25	.52	.47	.44	.41	.39	.38	.37	.36	.35
50	1.04	.94	.88	.82	.78	.75	.73	.71	.69
75	1.55	1.41	1.31	1.23	1.17	1.13	1.09	1.06	1.03
100	2.07	1.88	1.75	1.64	1.56	1.50	1.45	1.41	1.37
200	4.13	3.76	3.49	3.28	3.12	2.99	2.89	2.81	2.74
300	6.20	5.64	5.23	4.92	4.68	4.49	4.33	4.21	4.10
400	8.26	7.52	6.97	6.56	6.24	5.98	5.77	5.61	5.47
500	10.33	9.40	8.71	8.20	7.79	7.47	7.22	7.01	6.83
600	12.39	11.28	10.46	9.83	9.35	8.97	8.66	8.41	8.20
700	14.46	13.15	12.20	11.47	10.91	10.46	10.10	9.81	9.57
800	16.52	15.03	13.94	13.11	12.47	11.95	11.54	11.21	10.93
900	18.59	16.91	15.68	14.75	14.02	13.45	12.98	12.61	12.30
1000	20.65	18.79	17.42	16.39	15.58	14.94	14.43	14.01	13.66
2000	41.30	37.57	34.84	32.77	31.16	29.88	28.85	28.01	27.32
3000	61.95	56.36	52.26	49.15	46.73	44.81	43.27	42.01	40.98
4000	82.60	75.14	69.67	65.53	62.31	59.75	57.69	56.02	54.64
5000	103.25	93.93	87.09	81.91	77.88	74.69	72.12	70.02	68.29
6000	123.90	112.71	104.51	98.29	93.46	89.62	86.54	84.02	81.95
7000	144.55	131.50	121.93	114.67	109.03	104.56	100.96	98.03	95.61
8000	165.20	150.28	139.34	131.05	124.61	119.50	115.38	112.03	109.27
9000	185.84	169.07	156.76	147.43	140.18	134.43	129.80	126.03	122.93
10000	206.49	187.85	174.18	163.81	155.76	149.37	144.23	140.03	136.58
15000	309.74	281.77	261.26	245.72	233.63	224.05	216.34	210.05	204.87
20000	412.98	375.69	348.35	327.62	311.51	298.73	288.45	280.06	273.16
25000	516.23	469.62	435.44	409.53	389.38	373.41	360.56	350.08	341.45
30000	619.47	563.54	522.52	491.43	467.26	448.09	432.67	420.09	409.74
35000	722.71	657.46	609.61	573.33	545.13	522.78	504.78	490.11	478.03
36000	743.36	676.25	627.03	589.71	560.71	537.71	519.20	504.11	491.69
37000	764.01	695.03	644.45	606.10	576.28	552.65	533.62	518.12	505.35
38000	784.66	713.82	661.86	622.48	591.86	567.58	548.04	532.12	519.01
39000	805.31	732.60	679.28	638.86	607.43	582.52	562.47	546.12	532.67
40000	825.96	751.38	696.70	655.24	623.01	597.46	576.89	560.12	546.32
41000	846.61	770.17	714.11	671.62	638.58	612.39	591.31	574.13	559.98
42000	867.26	788.95	731.53	688.00	654.16	627.33	605.73	588.13	573.64
43000	887.91	807.74	748.95	704.38	669.73	642.27	620.16	602.13	587.30
44000	908.55	826.52	766.37	720.76	685.31	657.20	634.58	616.14	600.95
45000	929.20	845.31	783.78	737.14	700.88	672.14	649.00	630.14	614.61
46000	949.85	864.09	801.20	753.52	716.46	687.07	663.42	644.14	628.27
47000	970.50	882.88	818.62	769.90	732.03	702.01	677.84	658.15	641.93
48000	991.15	901.66	836.04	786.28	747.61	716.95	692.27	672.15	655.59
49000	1011.80	920.44	853.45	802.67	763.18	731.88	706.69	686.15	669.24
50000	1032.45	939.23	870.87	819.05	778.76	746.82	721.11	700.15	682.90
51000	1053.10	958.01	888.29	835.43	794.33	761.76	735.53	714.16	696.56
52000	1073.74	976.80	905.71	851.81	809.91	776.69	749.95	728.16	710.22
53000	1094.39	995.58	923.12	868.19	825.48	791.63	764.38	742.16	723.88
54000	1115.04	1014.37	940.54	884.57	841.06	806.57	778.80	756.17	737.53
55000	1135.69	1033.15	957.96	900.95	856.63	821.50	793.22	770.17	751.19
56000	1156.34	1051.94	975.37	917.33	872.21	836.44	807.64	784.17	764.85
57000	1176.99	1070.72	992.79	933.71	887.78	851.37	822.06	798.18	778.51
58000	1197.64	1089.50	1010.21	950.09	903.36	866.31	836.49	812.18	792.17
59000	1218.29	1108.29	1027.63	966.47	918.93	881.25	850.91	826.18	805.82
60000	1238.94	1127.07	1045.04	982.85	934.51	896.18	865.33	840.18	819.48
61000	1259.58	1145.86	1062.46	999.24	950.08	911.12	879.75	854.19	833.14
62000	1280.23	1164.64	1079.88	1015.62	965.66	926.06	894.18	868.19	846.80
63000	1300.88	1183.43	1097.30	1032.00	981.23	940.99	908.60	882.19	860.46
64000	1321.53	1202.21	1114.71	1048.38	996.81	955.93	923.02	896.20	874.11
65000	1342.18	1221.00	1132.13	1064.76	1012.38	970.86	937.44	910.20	887.77
66000	1362.83	1239.78	1149.55	1081.14	1027.96	985.80	951.86	924.20	901.43
67000	1383.48	1258.56	1166.96	1097.52	1043.53	1000.74	966.29	938.21	915.09
68000	1404.13	1277.35	1184.38	1113.90	1059.11	1015.67	980.71	952.21	928.75
69000	1424.77	1296.13	1201.80	1130.28	1074.68	1030.61	995.13	966.21	942.40
70000	1445.42	1314.92	1219.22	1146.66	1090.26	1045.55	1009.55	980.21	956.06
75000	1548.67	1408.84	1306.30	1228.57	1168.13	1120.23	1081.66	1050.23	1024.35
80000	1651.91	1502.76	1393.39	1310.47	1246.01	1194.91	1153.77	1120.24	1092.64
100000	2064.89	1878.45	1741.74	1638.09	1557.51	1493.63	1442.21	1400.30	1365.80

14½% MONTHLY PAYMENT
NECESSARY TO AMORTIZE A LOAN

TERM AMOUNT	15 YEARS	16 YEARS	17 YEARS	18 YEARS	19 YEARS	20 YEARS	21 YEARS	22 YEARS	23 YEARS
$ 25	.34	.33	.33	.32	.32	.32	.31	.31	.31
50	.67	.66	.65	.64	.64	.63	.62	.62	.62
75	1.01	.99	.97	.96	.95	.94	.93	.93	.92
100	1.34	1.32	1.30	1.28	1.27	1.25	1.24	1.23	1.23
200	2.68	2.63	2.59	2.56	2.53	2.50	2.48	2.46	2.45
300	4.02	3.94	3.88	3.83	3.79	3.75	3.72	3.69	3.67
400	5.35	5.26	5.18	5.11	5.05	5.00	4.96	4.92	4.89
500	6.69	6.57	6.47	6.39	6.31	6.25	6.20	6.15	6.12
600	8.03	7.88	7.76	7.66	7.57	7.50	7.44	7.38	7.34
700	9.37	9.20	9.06	8.94	8.84	8.75	8.68	8.61	8.56
800	10.70	10.51	10.35	10.21	10.10	10.00	9.92	9.84	9.78
900	12.04	11.82	11.64	11.49	11.36	11.25	11.15	11.07	11.00
1000	13.38	13.14	12.94	12.77	12.62	12.50	12.39	12.30	12.23
2000	26.75	26.27	25.87	25.53	25.24	24.99	24.78	24.60	24.45
3000	40.12	39.40	38.80	38.29	37.85	37.49	37.17	36.90	36.67
4000	53.49	52.53	51.73	51.05	50.47	49.98	49.56	49.20	48.89
5000	66.86	65.67	64.66	63.81	63.09	62.47	61.95	61.50	61.12
6000	80.23	78.80	77.59	76.57	75.70	74.97	74.34	73.80	73.34
7000	93.61	91.93	90.52	89.33	88.32	87.46	86.73	86.10	85.56
8000	106.98	105.06	103.45	102.09	100.94	99.95	99.12	98.40	97.78
9000	120.35	118.19	116.38	114.85	113.55	112.45	111.50	110.70	110.00
10000	133.72	131.33	129.31	127.61	126.17	124.94	123.89	123.00	122.23
15000	200.58	196.99	193.97	191.42	189.25	187.41	185.84	184.49	183.34
20000	267.44	262.65	258.62	255.22	252.33	249.88	247.78	245.99	244.45
25000	334.29	328.31	323.27	319.02	315.42	312.35	309.73	307.48	305.56
30000	401.15	393.97	387.93	382.83	378.50	374.82	371.67	368.98	366.67
35000	468.01	459.63	452.58	446.63	441.58	437.28	433.62	430.48	427.78
36000	481.38	472.76	465.51	459.39	454.20	449.78	446.00	442.77	440.00
37000	494.75	485.89	478.44	472.15	466.81	462.27	458.39	455.07	452.23
38000	508.12	499.02	491.37	484.91	479.43	474.76	470.78	467.37	464.45
39000	521.49	512.16	504.30	497.67	492.05	487.26	483.17	479.67	476.67
40000	534.87	525.29	517.24	510.43	504.66	499.75	495.56	491.97	488.89
41000	548.24	538.42	530.17	523.19	517.28	512.25	507.95	504.27	501.12
42000	561.61	551.55	543.10	535.95	529.90	524.74	520.34	516.57	513.34
43000	574.98	564.68	556.03	548.72	542.51	537.23	532.73	528.87	525.56
44000	588.35	577.82	568.96	561.48	555.13	549.73	545.11	541.17	537.78
45000	601.72	590.95	581.89	574.24	567.75	562.22	557.50	553.47	550.00
46000	615.09	604.08	594.82	587.00	580.36	574.71	569.89	565.77	562.23
47000	628.47	617.21	607.75	599.76	592.98	587.21	582.28	578.07	574.45
48000	641.84	630.34	620.68	612.52	605.59	599.70	594.67	590.36	586.67
49000	655.21	643.48	633.61	625.28	618.21	612.20	607.06	602.66	598.89
50000	668.58	656.61	646.54	638.04	630.83	624.69	619.45	614.96	611.12
51000	681.95	669.74	659.47	650.80	643.44	637.18	631.84	627.26	623.34
52000	695.32	682.87	672.40	663.56	656.06	649.68	644.23	639.56	635.56
53000	708.69	696.00	685.34	676.32	668.68	662.17	656.61	651.86	647.78
54000	722.07	709.14	698.27	689.08	681.29	674.66	669.00	664.16	660.00
55000	735.44	722.27	711.20	701.84	693.91	687.16	681.39	676.46	672.23
56000	748.81	735.40	724.13	714.60	706.53	699.65	693.78	688.76	684.45
57000	762.18	748.53	737.06	727.37	719.14	712.14	706.17	701.06	696.67
58000	775.55	761.66	749.99	740.13	731.76	724.64	718.56	713.36	708.89
59000	788.92	774.80	762.92	752.89	744.38	737.13	730.95	725.65	721.12
60000	802.30	787.93	775.85	765.65	756.99	749.63	743.34	737.95	733.34
61000	815.67	801.06	788.78	778.41	769.61	762.12	755.73	750.25	745.56
62000	829.04	814.19	801.71	791.17	782.23	774.61	768.11	762.55	757.78
63000	842.41	827.32	814.64	803.93	794.84	787.11	780.50	774.85	770.00
64000	855.78	840.46	827.57	816.69	807.46	799.60	792.89	787.15	782.23
65000	869.15	853.59	840.50	829.45	820.07	812.09	805.28	799.45	794.45
66000	882.52	866.72	853.44	842.21	832.69	824.59	817.67	811.75	806.67
67000	895.90	879.85	866.37	854.97	845.31	837.08	830.06	824.05	818.89
68000	909.27	892.99	879.30	867.73	857.92	849.57	842.45	836.35	831.12
69000	922.64	906.12	892.23	880.49	870.54	862.07	854.84	848.65	843.34
70000	936.01	919.25	905.16	893.25	883.16	874.56	867.23	860.95	855.56
75000	1002.87	984.91	969.81	957.06	946.24	937.03	929.17	922.44	916.67
80000	1069.73	1050.57	1034.47	1020.86	1009.32	999.50	991.11	983.94	977.78
100000	1337.16	1313.21	1293.08	1276.08	1261.65	1249.37	1238.89	1229.92	1222.23

TERM AMOUNT	24 YEARS	25 YEARS	26 YEARS	27 YEARS	28 YEARS	29 YEARS	30 YEARS	35 YEARS	40 YEARS
$ 25	.31	.31	.31	.31	.30	.30	.30	.30	.30
50	.61	.61	.61	.61	.60	.60	.60	.60	.59
75	.92	.91	.91	.91	.90	.90	.90	.89	.89
100	1.22	1.21	1.21	1.21	1.20	1.20	1.20	1.19	1.18
200	2.44	2.42	2.42	2.41	2.40	2.39	2.39	2.37	2.36
300	3.65	3.63	3.62	3.61	3.60	3.59	3.58	3.55	3.54
400	4.87	4.84	4.83	4.81	4.79	4.78	4.77	4.73	4.72
500	6.08	6.05	6.03	6.01	5.99	5.97	5.96	5.92	5.89
600	7.30	7.26	7.24	7.21	7.19	7.17	7.15	7.10	7.07
700	8.51	8.47	8.44	8.41	8.38	8.36	8.34	8.28	8.25
800	9.73	9.68	9.65	9.61	9.58	9.56	9.53	9.46	9.43
900	10.95	10.89	10.85	10.81	10.78	10.75	10.73	10.64	10.60
1000	12.16	12.10	12.06	12.01	11.98	11.94	11.92	11.83	11.78
2000	24.32	24.20	24.11	24.02	23.95	23.88	23.83	23.65	23.56
3000	36.47	36.30	36.16	36.03	35.92	35.82	35.74	35.47	35.34
4000	48.63	48.40	48.21	48.04	47.89	47.76	47.65	47.29	47.11
5000	60.79	60.50	60.26	60.04	59.86	59.70	59.57	59.11	58.89
6000	72.94	72.60	72.31	72.05	71.83	71.64	71.48	70.94	70.67
7000	85.10	84.70	84.36	84.06	83.80	83.58	83.39	82.76	82.45
8000	97.25	96.80	96.41	96.07	95.78	95.52	95.30	94.58	94.22
9000	109.41	108.90	108.46	108.08	107.75	107.46	107.22	106.40	106.00
10000	121.57	121.00	120.51	120.08	119.72	119.40	119.13	118.22	117.78
15000	182.35	181.49	180.76	180.12	179.57	179.10	178.69	177.33	176.66
20000	243.13	241.99	241.01	240.16	239.43	238.80	238.25	236.44	235.55
25000	303.91	302.49	301.26	300.20	299.29	298.50	297.82	295.55	294.44
30000	364.69	362.98	361.51	360.24	359.14	358.20	357.38	354.66	353.32
35000	425.47	423.48	421.76	420.28	419.00	417.90	416.94	413.77	412.21
36000	437.62	435.58	433.81	432.29	430.97	429.84	428.85	425.59	423.99
37000	449.78	447.68	445.86	444.30	442.94	441.78	440.76	437.41	435.76
38000	461.94	459.77	457.91	456.30	454.92	453.72	452.68	449.23	447.54
39000	474.09	471.87	469.96	468.31	466.89	465.65	464.59	461.05	459.32
40000	486.25	483.97	482.01	480.32	478.86	477.59	476.50	472.88	471.10
41000	498.41	496.07	494.06	492.33	490.83	489.53	488.41	484.70	482.87
42000	510.56	508.17	506.11	504.34	502.80	501.47	500.33	496.52	494.65
43000	522.72	520.27	518.16	516.34	514.77	513.41	512.24	508.34	506.43
44000	534.87	532.37	530.21	528.35	526.74	525.35	524.15	520.16	518.21
45000	547.03	544.47	542.26	540.36	538.71	537.29	536.06	531.99	529.98
46000	559.19	556.57	554.31	552.37	550.69	549.23	547.98	543.81	541.76
47000	571.34	568.67	566.36	564.37	562.66	561.17	559.89	555.63	553.54
48000	583.50	580.77	578.41	576.38	574.63	573.11	571.80	567.45	565.31
49000	595.65	592.87	590.46	588.39	586.60	585.05	583.71	579.27	577.09
50000	607.81	604.97	602.51	600.40	598.57	596.99	595.63	591.09	588.87
51000	619.97	617.06	614.56	612.41	610.54	608.93	607.54	602.92	600.65
52000	632.12	629.16	626.61	624.41	622.51	620.87	619.45	614.74	612.42
53000	644.28	641.26	638.66	636.42	634.49	632.81	631.36	626.56	624.20
54000	656.43	653.36	650.71	648.43	646.46	644.75	643.28	638.38	635.98
55000	668.59	665.46	662.76	660.44	658.43	656.69	655.19	650.20	647.76
56000	680.75	677.56	674.81	672.45	670.40	668.63	667.10	662.02	659.53
57000	692.90	689.66	686.86	684.45	682.37	680.57	679.01	673.85	671.31
58000	705.06	701.76	698.91	696.46	694.34	692.51	690.93	685.67	683.09
59000	717.21	713.86	710.97	708.47	706.31	704.45	702.84	697.49	694.86
60000	729.37	725.96	723.02	720.48	718.28	716.39	714.75	709.31	706.64
61000	741.53	738.06	735.07	732.48	730.26	728.33	726.66	721.13	718.42
62000	753.68	750.16	747.12	744.49	742.23	740.27	738.57	732.96	730.20
63000	765.84	762.25	759.17	756.50	754.20	752.21	750.49	744.78	741.97
64000	778.00	774.35	771.22	768.51	766.17	764.15	762.40	756.60	753.75
65000	790.15	786.45	783.27	780.52	778.14	776.09	774.31	768.42	765.53
66000	802.31	798.55	795.32	792.52	790.11	788.03	786.22	780.24	777.31
67000	814.46	810.65	807.37	804.53	802.08	799.97	798.14	792.06	789.08
68000	826.62	822.75	819.42	816.54	814.06	811.91	810.05	803.89	800.86
69000	838.78	834.85	831.47	828.55	826.03	823.85	821.96	815.71	812.64
70000	850.93	846.95	843.52	840.56	838.00	835.79	833.87	827.53	824.41
75000	911.71	907.45	903.77	900.59	897.85	895.49	893.44	886.64	883.30
80000	972.49	967.94	964.02	960.63	957.71	955.18	953.00	945.75	942.19
100000	1215.62	1209.93	1205.02	1200.79	1197.14	1193.98	1191.25	1182.18	1177.73

14¾% MONTHLY PAYMENT
NECESSARY TO AMORTIZE A LOAN

TERM AMOUNT	1 YEAR	1½ YEARS	2 YEARS	2½ YEARS	3 YEARS	3½ YEARS	4 YEARS	4½ YEARS	5 YEARS
$ 25	2.25	1.56	1.21	1.00	.86	.77	.69	.64	.59
50	4.50	3.11	2.41	2.00	1.72	1.53	1.38	1.27	1.18
75	6.75	4.66	3.62	2.99	2.58	2.29	2.07	1.90	1.76
100	9.00	6.21	4.82	3.99	3.44	3.05	2.75	2.53	2.35
200	17.99	12.42	9.64	7.97	6.87	6.09	5.50	5.05	4.69
300	26.99	18.62	14.45	11.96	10.30	9.13	8.25	7.57	7.03
400	35.98	24.83	19.27	15.94	13.74	12.17	11.00	10.10	9.38
500	44.97	31.04	24.09	19.93	17.17	15.21	13.75	12.62	11.72
600	53.97	37.24	28.90	23.91	20.60	18.25	16.50	15.14	14.06
700	62.96	43.45	33.72	27.90	24.04	21.29	19.24	17.66	16.41
800	71.95	49.66	38.53	31.88	27.47	24.33	21.99	20.19	18.75
900	80.95	55.86	43.35	35.87	30.90	27.37	24.74	22.71	21.09
1000	89.94	62.07	48.17	39.85	34.34	30.41	27.49	25.23	23.44
2000	179.88	124.13	96.33	79.70	68.67	60.82	54.98	50.46	46.87
3000	269.81	186.20	144.49	119.55	103.00	91.23	82.46	75.68	70.30
4000	359.75	248.26	192.65	159.40	137.33	121.64	109.95	100.91	93.73
5000	449.68	310.32	240.82	199.25	171.66	152.05	137.43	126.14	117.17
6000	539.62	372.39	288.98	239.10	205.99	182.46	164.92	151.36	140.60
7000	629.56	434.45	337.14	278.95	240.32	212.87	192.40	176.59	164.03
8000	719.49	496.51	385.30	318.80	274.66	243.28	219.89	201.81	187.46
9000	809.43	558.58	433.47	358.65	308.99	273.69	247.37	227.04	210.90
10000	899.36	620.64	481.63	398.50	343.32	304.10	274.86	252.27	234.33
15000	1349.04	930.96	722.44	597.75	514.98	456.15	412.29	378.40	351.49
20000	1798.72	1241.27	963.25	797.00	686.63	608.20	549.71	504.53	468.65
25000	2248.40	1551.59	1204.06	996.25	858.29	760.24	687.14	630.66	585.82
30000	2698.08	1861.91	1444.88	1195.50	1029.95	912.29	824.57	756.79	702.98
35000	3147.76	2172.23	1685.69	1394.75	1201.60	1064.34	961.99	882.92	820.14
36000	3237.70	2234.29	1733.85	1434.60	1235.93	1094.75	989.48	908.15	843.57
37000	3327.63	2296.35	1782.01	1474.45	1270.27	1125.16	1016.96	933.37	867.01
38000	3417.57	2358.42	1830.18	1514.30	1304.60	1155.57	1044.45	958.60	890.44
39000	3507.51	2420.48	1878.34	1554.15	1338.93	1185.98	1071.93	983.83	913.87
40000	3597.44	2482.54	1926.50	1594.00	1373.26	1216.39	1099.42	1009.05	937.30
41000	3687.38	2544.61	1974.66	1633.85	1407.59	1246.79	1126.90	1034.28	960.74
42000	3777.31	2606.67	2022.82	1673.70	1441.92	1277.20	1154.39	1059.51	984.17
43000	3867.25	2668.73	2070.99	1713.55	1476.25	1307.61	1181.87	1084.73	1007.60
44000	3957.19	2730.80	2119.15	1753.40	1510.59	1338.02	1209.36	1109.96	1031.03
45000	4047.12	2792.86	2167.31	1793.25	1544.92	1368.43	1236.85	1135.18	1054.47
46000	4137.06	2854.92	2215.47	1833.10	1579.25	1398.84	1264.33	1160.41	1077.90
47000	4226.99	2916.99	2263.64	1872.95	1613.58	1429.25	1291.82	1185.64	1101.33
48000	4316.93	2979.05	2311.80	1912.80	1647.91	1459.66	1319.30	1210.86	1124.76
49000	4406.87	3041.11	2359.96	1952.65	1682.24	1490.07	1346.79	1236.09	1148.20
50000	4496.80	3103.18	2408.12	1992.50	1716.57	1520.48	1374.27	1261.32	1171.63
51000	4586.74	3165.24	2456.29	2032.35	1750.91	1550.89	1401.76	1286.54	1195.06
52000	4676.67	3227.30	2504.45	2072.20	1785.24	1581.30	1429.24	1311.77	1218.49
53000	4766.61	3289.37	2552.61	2112.05	1819.57	1611.71	1456.73	1336.99	1241.93
54000	4856.55	3351.43	2600.77	2151.89	1853.90	1642.12	1484.21	1362.22	1265.36
55000	4946.48	3413.49	2648.94	2191.74	1888.23	1672.53	1511.70	1387.45	1288.79
56000	5036.42	3475.56	2697.10	2231.59	1922.56	1702.94	1539.18	1412.67	1312.22
57000	5126.35	3537.62	2745.26	2271.44	1956.89	1733.35	1566.67	1437.90	1335.66
58000	5216.29	3599.68	2793.42	2311.29	1991.23	1763.76	1594.15	1463.13	1359.09
59000	5306.23	3661.75	2841.59	2351.14	2025.56	1794.17	1621.64	1488.35	1382.52
60000	5396.16	3723.81	2889.75	2390.99	2059.89	1824.58	1649.13	1513.58	1405.95
61000	5486.10	3785.87	2937.91	2430.84	2094.22	1854.98	1676.61	1538.80	1429.39
62000	5576.03	3847.94	2986.07	2470.69	2128.55	1885.39	1704.10	1564.03	1452.82
63000	5665.97	3910.00	3034.23	2510.54	2162.88	1915.80	1731.58	1589.26	1476.25
64000	5755.91	3972.06	3082.40	2550.39	2197.21	1946.21	1759.07	1614.48	1499.68
65000	5845.84	4034.13	3130.56	2590.24	2231.55	1976.62	1786.55	1639.71	1523.12
66000	5935.78	4096.19	3178.72	2630.09	2265.88	2007.03	1814.04	1664.93	1546.55
67000	6025.71	4158.25	3226.88	2669.94	2300.21	2037.44	1841.52	1690.16	1569.98
68000	6115.65	4220.32	3275.05	2709.79	2334.54	2067.85	1869.01	1715.39	1593.41
69000	6205.59	4282.38	3323.21	2749.64	2368.87	2098.26	1896.49	1740.61	1616.85
70000	6295.52	4344.45	3371.37	2789.49	2403.20	2128.67	1923.98	1765.84	1640.28
75000	6745.20	4654.76	3612.18	2988.74	2574.86	2280.72	2061.41	1891.97	1757.44
80000	7194.88	4965.08	3853.00	3187.99	2746.52	2432.77	2198.83	2018.10	1874.60
100000	8993.60	6206.35	4816.24	3984.99	3433.14	3040.96	2748.54	2522.63	2343.25

128

TERM AMOUNT	6 YEARS	7 YEARS	8 YEARS	9 YEARS	10 YEARS	11 YEARS	12 YEARS	13 YEARS	14 YEARS
$ 25	.52	.48	.44	.42	.40	.38	.37	.36	.35
50	1.04	.95	.88	.83	.79	.76	.73	.71	.70
75	1.56	1.42	1.32	1.24	1.18	1.14	1.10	1.07	1.04
100	2.08	1.90	1.76	1.66	1.58	1.51	1.46	1.42	1.39
200	4.16	3.79	3.52	3.31	3.15	3.02	2.92	2.84	2.77
300	6.24	5.68	5.27	4.96	4.72	4.53	4.38	4.25	4.15
400	8.32	7.57	7.03	6.61	6.29	6.04	5.83	5.67	5.53
500	10.39	9.46	8.78	8.26	7.86	7.55	7.29	7.08	6.91
600	12.47	11.35	10.54	9.92	9.44	9.05	8.75	8.50	8.29
700	14.55	13.25	12.29	11.57	11.01	10.56	10.21	9.91	9.67
800	16.63	15.14	14.05	13.22	12.58	12.07	11.66	11.33	11.06
900	18.70	17.03	15.80	14.87	14.16	13.58	13.12	12.75	12.44
1000	20.78	18.92	17.56	16.52	15.72	15.09	14.58	14.16	13.82
2000	41.56	37.84	35.11	33.04	31.44	30.17	29.15	28.32	27.63
3000	62.33	56.75	52.66	49.56	47.16	45.25	43.72	42.47	41.45
4000	83.11	75.67	70.21	66.08	62.87	60.33	58.29	56.63	55.26
5000	103.88	94.58	87.76	82.60	78.59	75.42	72.86	70.78	69.07
6000	124.66	113.50	105.32	99.12	94.31	90.50	87.43	84.94	82.89
7000	145.43	132.41	122.87	115.64	110.03	105.58	102.01	99.10	96.70
8000	166.21	151.33	140.42	132.16	125.74	120.66	116.58	113.25	110.52
9000	186.98	170.24	157.97	148.68	141.46	135.74	131.15	127.41	124.33
10000	207.76	189.16	175.52	165.20	157.18	150.83	145.72	141.56	138.14
15000	311.64	283.73	263.28	247.79	235.76	226.24	218.58	212.34	207.21
20000	415.51	378.31	351.04	330.39	314.35	301.65	291.43	283.12	276.28
25000	519.39	472.88	438.80	412.99	392.94	377.06	364.29	353.90	345.35
30000	623.27	567.46	526.56	495.58	471.52	452.47	437.15	424.68	414.42
35000	727.14	662.03	614.32	578.18	550.11	527.88	510.01	495.46	483.49
36000	747.92	680.95	631.87	594.70	565.83	542.96	524.58	509.61	497.31
37000	768.70	699.86	649.43	611.22	581.55	558.05	539.15	523.77	511.12
38000	789.47	718.78	666.98	627.74	597.26	573.13	553.72	537.92	524.93
39000	810.25	737.69	684.53	644.26	612.98	588.21	568.29	552.08	538.75
40000	831.02	756.61	702.08	660.78	628.70	603.29	582.86	566.24	552.56
41000	851.80	775.52	719.63	677.30	644.41	618.38	597.44	580.39	566.38
42000	872.57	794.44	737.19	693.82	660.13	633.46	612.01	594.55	580.19
43000	893.35	813.35	754.74	710.34	675.85	648.54	626.58	608.70	594.00
44000	914.12	832.27	772.29	726.85	691.57	663.62	641.15	622.86	607.82
45000	934.90	851.18	789.84	743.37	707.28	678.70	655.72	637.01	621.63
46000	955.67	870.10	807.39	759.89	723.00	693.79	670.29	651.17	635.44
47000	976.45	889.01	824.94	776.41	738.72	708.87	684.87	665.33	649.26
48000	997.22	907.93	842.50	792.93	754.44	723.95	699.44	679.48	663.07
49000	1018.00	926.84	860.05	809.45	770.15	739.03	714.01	693.64	676.89
50000	1038.78	945.76	877.60	825.97	785.87	754.11	728.58	707.79	690.70
51000	1059.55	964.68	895.15	842.49	801.59	769.20	743.15	721.95	704.51
52000	1080.33	983.59	912.70	859.01	817.30	784.28	757.72	736.10	718.33
53000	1101.10	1002.51	930.26	875.53	833.02	799.36	772.29	750.26	732.14
54000	1121.88	1021.42	947.81	892.05	848.74	814.44	786.87	764.42	745.96
55000	1142.65	1040.34	965.36	908.57	864.46	829.53	801.44	778.57	759.77
56000	1163.43	1059.25	982.91	925.09	880.17	844.61	816.01	792.73	773.58
57000	1184.20	1078.17	1000.46	941.61	895.89	859.69	830.58	806.88	787.40
58000	1204.98	1097.08	1018.02	958.13	911.61	874.77	845.15	821.04	801.21
59000	1225.75	1116.00	1035.57	974.64	927.33	889.85	859.72	835.19	815.03
60000	1246.53	1134.91	1053.12	991.16	943.04	904.94	874.29	849.35	828.84
61000	1267.31	1153.83	1070.67	1007.68	958.76	920.02	888.87	863.51	842.65
62000	1288.08	1172.74	1088.22	1024.20	974.48	935.10	903.44	877.66	856.47
63000	1308.86	1191.66	1105.78	1040.72	990.20	950.18	918.01	891.82	870.28
64000	1329.63	1210.57	1123.33	1057.24	1005.91	965.27	932.58	905.97	884.09
65000	1350.41	1229.49	1140.88	1073.76	1021.63	980.35	947.15	920.13	897.91
66000	1371.18	1248.40	1158.43	1090.28	1037.35	995.43	961.72	934.28	911.72
67000	1391.96	1267.32	1175.98	1106.80	1053.06	1010.51	976.30	948.44	925.54
68000	1412.73	1286.23	1193.54	1123.32	1068.78	1025.59	990.87	962.60	939.35
69000	1433.51	1305.15	1211.09	1139.84	1084.50	1040.68	1005.44	976.75	953.16
70000	1454.28	1324.06	1228.64	1156.36	1100.22	1055.76	1020.01	990.91	966.98
75000	1558.16	1418.64	1316.40	1238.95	1178.80	1131.17	1092.87	1061.69	1036.05
80000	1662.04	1513.21	1404.16	1321.55	1257.39	1206.58	1165.72	1132.47	1105.12
100000	2077.55	1891.51	1755.20	1651.94	1571.74	1508.22	1457.15	1415.58	1381.40

14¾% MONTHLY PAYMENT
NECESSARY TO AMORTIZE A LOAN

TERM AMOUNT	15 YEARS	16 YEARS	17 YEARS	18 YEARS	19 YEARS	20 YEARS	21 YEARS	22 YEARS	23 YEARS
$ 25	.34	.34	.33	.33	.32	.32	.32	.32	.31
50	.68	.67	.66	.65	.64	.64	.63	.63	.62
75	1.02	1.00	.99	.97	.96	.95	.95	.94	.93
100	1.36	1.33	1.31	1.30	1.28	1.27	1.26	1.25	1.24
200	2.71	2.66	2.62	2.59	2.56	2.54	2.52	2.50	2.48
300	4.06	3.99	3.93	3.88	3.84	3.80	3.77	3.75	3.72
400	5.42	5.32	5.24	5.18	5.12	5.07	5.03	5.00	4.96
500	6.77	6.65	6.55	6.47	6.40	6.34	6.29	6.24	6.20
600	8.12	7.98	7.86	7.76	7.68	7.60	7.54	7.49	7.44
700	9.48	9.31	9.17	9.05	8.96	8.87	8.80	8.74	8.68
800	10.83	10.64	10.48	10.35	10.23	10.14	10.06	9.99	9.92
900	12.18	11.97	11.79	11.64	11.51	11.40	11.31	11.23	11.16
1000	13.54	13.30	13.10	12.93	12.79	12.67	12.57	12.48	12.40
2000	27.07	26.59	26.20	25.86	25.58	25.34	25.13	24.96	24.80
3000	40.60	39.89	39.29	38.79	38.36	38.00	37.69	37.43	37.20
4000	54.13	53.18	52.39	51.72	51.15	50.67	50.26	49.91	49.60
5000	67.66	66.47	65.48	64.64	63.94	63.33	62.82	62.38	62.00
6000	81.19	79.77	78.58	77.57	76.72	76.00	75.38	74.86	74.40
7000	94.72	93.06	91.67	90.50	89.51	88.66	87.94	87.33	86.80
8000	108.25	106.36	104.77	103.43	102.29	101.33	100.51	99.81	99.20
9000	121.78	119.65	117.86	116.36	115.08	113.99	113.07	112.28	111.60
10000	135.31	132.94	130.96	129.28	127.87	126.66	125.63	124.76	124.00
15000	202.96	199.41	196.44	193.92	191.80	189.99	188.45	187.13	186.00
20000	270.61	265.88	261.91	258.56	255.73	253.31	251.26	249.51	248.00
25000	338.27	332.35	327.39	323.20	319.66	316.64	314.07	311.88	310.00
30000	405.92	398.82	392.87	387.84	383.59	379.97	376.89	374.26	372.00
35000	473.57	465.29	458.34	452.48	447.52	443.30	439.70	436.63	434.00
36000	487.10	478.59	471.44	465.41	460.30	455.96	452.26	449.11	446.40
37000	500.63	491.88	484.53	478.34	473.09	468.63	464.83	461.58	458.80
38000	514.16	505.17	497.63	491.26	485.87	481.29	477.39	474.06	471.20
39000	527.69	518.47	510.72	504.19	498.66	493.96	489.95	486.53	483.60
40000	541.22	531.76	523.82	517.12	511.45	506.62	502.52	499.01	496.00
41000	554.76	545.06	536.91	530.05	524.23	519.29	515.08	511.48	508.40
42000	568.29	558.35	550.01	542.98	537.02	531.96	527.64	523.96	520.80
43000	581.82	571.64	563.11	555.90	549.80	544.62	540.20	536.43	533.20
44000	595.35	584.94	576.20	568.83	562.59	557.29	552.77	548.91	545.60
45000	608.88	598.23	589.30	581.76	575.38	569.95	565.33	561.38	558.00
46000	622.41	611.53	602.39	594.69	588.16	582.62	577.89	573.86	570.40
47000	635.94	624.82	615.49	607.61	600.95	595.28	590.46	586.33	582.80
48000	649.47	638.11	628.58	620.54	613.73	607.95	603.02	598.81	595.20
49000	663.00	651.41	641.68	633.47	626.52	620.61	615.58	611.28	607.60
50000	676.53	664.70	654.77	646.40	639.31	633.28	628.14	623.76	620.00
51000	690.06	678.00	667.87	659.33	652.09	645.94	640.71	636.23	632.40
52000	703.59	691.29	680.96	672.25	664.88	658.61	653.27	648.71	644.80
53000	717.12	704.58	694.06	685.18	677.66	671.28	665.83	661.18	657.20
54000	730.65	717.88	707.15	698.11	690.45	683.94	678.39	673.66	669.60
55000	744.18	731.17	720.25	711.04	703.24	696.61	690.96	686.13	682.00
56000	757.71	744.47	733.35	723.97	716.02	709.27	703.52	698.61	694.40
57000	771.24	757.76	746.44	736.89	728.81	721.94	716.08	711.08	706.80
58000	784.77	771.05	759.54	749.82	741.59	734.60	728.65	723.56	719.20
59000	798.30	784.35	772.63	762.75	754.38	747.27	741.21	736.03	731.60
60000	811.83	797.64	785.73	775.68	767.17	759.93	753.77	748.51	744.00
61000	825.37	810.94	798.82	788.60	779.95	772.60	766.33	760.98	756.40
62000	838.90	824.23	811.92	801.53	792.74	785.27	778.90	773.46	768.80
63000	852.43	837.52	825.01	814.46	805.52	797.93	791.46	785.93	781.20
64000	865.96	850.82	838.11	827.39	818.31	810.60	804.02	798.41	793.60
65000	879.49	864.11	851.20	840.32	831.10	823.26	816.58	810.88	806.00
66000	893.02	877.41	864.30	853.24	843.88	835.93	829.15	823.36	818.40
67000	906.55	890.70	877.39	866.17	856.67	848.59	841.71	835.83	830.80
68000	920.08	903.99	890.49	879.10	869.45	861.26	854.27	848.31	843.20
69000	933.61	917.29	903.58	892.03	882.24	873.92	866.84	860.78	855.60
70000	947.14	930.58	916.68	904.96	895.03	886.59	879.40	873.26	868.00
75000	1014.79	997.05	982.16	969.59	958.96	949.92	942.21	935.63	930.00
80000	1082.44	1063.52	1047.63	1034.23	1022.89	1013.24	1005.03	998.01	992.00
100000	1353.05	1329.40	1309.54	1292.79	1278.61	1266.55	1256.28	1247.51	1239.99

130

MONTHLY PAYMENT 14¾%
NECESSARY TO AMORTIZE A LOAN

TERM AMOUNT	24 YEARS	25 YEARS	26 YEARS	27 YEARS	28 YEARS	29 YEARS	30 YEARS	35 YEARS	40 YEARS
$ 25	.31	.31	.31	.31	.31	.31	.31	.31	.30
50	.62	.62	.62	.61	.61	.61	.61	.61	.60
75	.93	.93	.92	.92	.92	.91	.91	.91	.90
100	1.24	1.23	1.23	1.22	1.22	1.22	1.21	1.21	1.20
200	2.47	2.46	2.45	2.44	2.44	2.43	2.42	2.41	2.40
300	3.71	3.69	3.67	3.66	3.65	3.64	3.63	3.61	3.60
400	4.94	4.92	4.90	4.88	4.87	4.86	4.84	4.81	4.79
500	6.17	6.15	6.12	6.10	6.08	6.07	6.05	6.01	5.99
600	7.41	7.37	7.34	7.32	7.30	7.28	7.26	7.21	7.19
700	8.64	8.60	8.57	8.54	8.51	8.49	8.47	8.41	8.38
800	9.87	9.83	9.79	9.76	9.73	9.71	9.68	9.62	9.58
900	11.11	11.06	11.01	10.98	10.95	10.92	10.89	10.82	10.78
1000	12.34	12.29	12.24	12.20	12.16	12.13	12.10	12.02	11.98
2000	24.68	24.57	24.47	24.39	24.32	24.26	24.20	24.03	23.95
3000	37.01	36.85	36.70	36.58	36.47	36.38	36.30	36.04	35.92
4000	49.35	49.13	48.94	48.77	48.63	48.51	48.40	48.06	47.89
5000	61.68	61.41	61.17	60.96	60.79	60.63	60.50	60.07	59.86
6000	74.02	73.69	73.40	73.15	72.94	72.76	72.60	72.08	71.83
7000	86.35	85.97	85.63	85.35	85.10	84.89	84.70	84.09	83.80
8000	98.69	98.25	97.87	97.54	97.25	97.01	96.80	96.11	95.77
9000	111.02	110.53	110.10	109.73	109.41	109.14	108.90	108.12	107.74
10000	123.36	122.81	122.33	121.92	121.57	121.26	121.00	120.13	119.71
15000	185.04	184.21	183.49	182.88	182.35	181.89	181.50	180.19	179.56
20000	246.71	245.61	244.66	243.84	243.13	242.52	241.99	240.26	239.41
25000	308.39	307.01	305.82	304.79	303.91	303.15	302.49	300.32	299.27
30000	370.07	368.41	366.98	365.75	364.69	363.78	362.99	360.38	359.12
35000	431.75	429.81	428.14	426.71	425.47	424.41	423.48	420.45	418.97
36000	444.08	442.09	440.38	438.90	437.63	436.53	435.58	432.46	430.94
37000	456.42	454.37	452.61	451.09	449.78	448.66	447.68	444.47	442.91
38000	468.75	466.65	464.84	463.28	461.94	460.78	459.78	456.48	454.88
39000	481.09	478.93	477.07	475.47	474.10	472.91	471.88	468.50	466.85
40000	493.42	491.21	489.31	487.67	486.25	485.03	483.98	480.51	478.82
41000	505.76	503.49	501.54	499.86	498.41	497.16	496.08	492.52	490.79
42000	518.09	515.77	513.77	512.05	510.57	509.29	508.18	504.54	502.77
43000	530.43	528.05	526.00	524.24	522.72	521.41	520.28	516.55	514.74
44000	542.77	540.33	538.24	536.43	534.88	533.54	532.38	528.56	526.71
45000	555.10	552.61	550.47	548.62	547.03	545.66	544.48	540.57	538.68
46000	567.44	564.89	562.70	560.82	559.19	557.79	556.58	552.59	550.65
47000	579.77	577.17	574.93	573.01	571.35	569.91	568.68	564.60	562.62
48000	592.11	589.45	587.17	585.20	583.50	582.04	580.78	576.61	574.59
49000	604.44	601.73	599.40	597.39	595.66	594.17	592.88	588.62	586.56
50000	616.78	614.01	611.63	609.58	607.81	606.29	604.98	600.64	598.53
51000	629.11	626.29	623.86	621.77	619.97	618.42	617.07	612.65	610.50
52000	641.45	638.57	636.10	633.96	632.13	630.54	629.17	624.66	622.47
53000	653.78	650.85	648.33	646.16	644.28	642.67	641.27	636.67	634.44
54000	666.12	663.13	660.56	658.35	656.44	654.79	653.37	648.69	646.41
55000	678.46	675.41	672.79	670.54	668.60	666.92	665.47	660.70	658.38
56000	690.79	687.69	685.03	682.73	680.75	679.05	677.57	672.71	670.35
57000	703.13	699.97	697.26	694.92	692.91	691.17	689.67	684.72	682.32
58000	715.46	712.25	709.49	707.11	705.06	703.30	701.77	696.74	694.29
59000	727.80	724.53	721.72	719.30	717.22	715.42	713.87	708.75	706.26
60000	740.13	736.81	733.96	731.50	729.38	727.55	725.97	720.76	718.23
61000	752.47	749.09	746.19	743.69	741.53	739.67	738.07	732.78	730.20
62000	764.80	761.37	758.42	755.88	753.69	751.80	750.17	744.79	742.18
63000	777.14	773.65	770.65	768.07	765.85	763.93	762.27	756.80	754.15
64000	789.47	785.93	782.89	780.26	778.00	776.05	774.37	768.81	766.12
65000	801.81	798.21	795.12	792.45	790.16	788.18	786.47	780.83	778.09
66000	814.15	810.49	807.35	804.65	802.31	800.30	798.57	792.84	790.06
67000	826.48	822.77	819.58	816.84	814.47	812.43	810.66	804.85	802.03
68000	838.82	835.05	831.82	829.03	826.63	824.55	822.76	816.86	814.00
69000	851.15	847.33	844.05	841.22	838.78	836.68	834.86	828.88	825.97
70000	863.49	859.61	856.28	853.41	850.94	848.81	846.96	840.89	837.94
75000	925.16	921.01	917.44	914.37	911.72	909.43	907.46	900.95	897.79
80000	986.84	982.41	978.61	975.33	972.50	970.06	967.96	961.02	957.64
100000	1233.55	1228.02	1223.26	1219.16	1215.62	1212.58	1209.95	1201.27	1197.05

15% MONTHLY PAYMENT
NECESSARY TO AMORTIZE A LOAN

TERM AMOUNT	1 YEAR	1½ YEARS	2 YEARS	2½ YEARS	3 YEARS	3½ YEARS	4 YEARS	4½ YEARS	5 YEARS
$ 25	2.26	1.56	1.21	1.00	.87	.77	.70	.64	.59
50	4.51	3.11	2.42	2.00	1.73	1.53	1.39	1.27	1.18
75	6.76	4.67	3.63	3.00	2.59	2.29	2.08	1.91	1.77
100	9.01	6.22	4.83	4.00	3.45	3.06	2.77	2.54	2.36
200	18.01	12.44	9.66	8.00	6.89	6.11	5.53	5.07	4.72
300	27.02	18.66	14.49	11.99	10.34	9.16	8.29	7.61	7.07
400	36.02	24.87	19.31	15.99	13.78	12.22	11.05	10.14	9.43
500	45.03	31.09	24.14	19.99	17.23	15.27	13.81	12.68	11.78
600	54.03	37.31	28.97	23.98	20.67	18.32	16.57	15.21	14.14
700	63.04	43.53	33.80	27.98	24.12	21.37	19.33	17.75	16.49
800	72.04	49.74	38.62	31.98	27.56	24.43	22.09	20.28	18.85
900	81.05	55.96	43.45	35.97	31.01	27.48	24.85	22.82	21.20
1000	90.05	62.18	48.28	39.97	34.45	30.53	27.61	25.35	23.56
2000	180.10	124.35	96.55	79.93	68.90	61.06	55.21	50.70	47.12
3000	270.15	186.53	144.83	119.89	103.34	91.58	82.82	76.05	70.67
4000	360.19	248.70	193.10	159.86	137.79	122.11	110.42	101.39	94.23
5000	450.24	310.87	241.37	199.82	172.24	152.64	138.03	126.74	117.78
6000	540.29	373.05	289.65	239.78	206.68	183.16	165.63	152.09	141.34
7000	630.33	435.22	337.92	279.74	241.13	213.69	193.23	177.43	164.89
8000	720.38	497.40	386.20	319.71	275.57	244.21	220.84	202.78	188.45
9000	810.43	559.57	434.47	359.67	310.02	274.74	248.44	228.13	212.00
10000	900.47	621.74	482.74	399.63	344.47	305.27	276.05	253.47	235.56
15000	1350.71	932.61	724.11	599.45	516.70	457.90	414.07	380.21	353.33
20000	1800.94	1243.48	965.48	799.26	688.93	610.53	552.09	506.94	471.11
25000	2251.18	1554.35	1206.85	999.08	861.16	763.16	690.11	633.68	588.89
30000	2701.41	1865.22	1448.22	1198.89	1033.39	915.79	828.13	760.41	706.66
35000	3151.65	2176.09	1689.59	1398.70	1205.62	1068.42	966.15	887.15	824.44
36000	3241.69	2238.27	1737.87	1438.67	1240.07	1098.95	993.75	912.49	847.99
37000	3331.74	2300.44	1786.14	1478.63	1274.51	1129.47	1021.35	937.84	871.55
38000	3421.79	2362.62	1834.41	1518.59	1308.96	1160.00	1048.96	963.19	895.10
39000	3511.83	2424.79	1882.69	1558.56	1343.41	1190.53	1076.56	988.53	918.66
40000	3601.88	2486.96	1930.96	1598.52	1377.85	1221.05	1104.17	1013.88	942.21
41000	3691.93	2549.14	1979.24	1638.48	1412.30	1251.58	1131.77	1039.23	965.77
42000	3781.97	2611.31	2027.51	1678.44	1446.74	1282.10	1159.37	1064.58	989.32
43000	3872.02	2673.49	2075.78	1718.41	1481.19	1312.63	1186.98	1089.92	1012.88
44000	3962.07	2735.66	2124.06	1758.37	1515.64	1343.16	1214.58	1115.27	1036.44
45000	4052.11	2797.83	2172.33	1798.33	1550.08	1373.68	1242.19	1140.62	1059.99
46000	4142.16	2860.01	2220.60	1838.30	1584.53	1404.21	1269.79	1165.96	1083.55
47000	4232.21	2922.18	2268.88	1878.26	1618.98	1434.74	1297.39	1191.31	1107.10
48000	4322.26	2984.36	2317.15	1918.22	1653.42	1465.26	1325.00	1216.66	1130.66
49000	4412.30	3046.53	2365.43	1958.18	1687.87	1495.79	1352.60	1242.00	1154.21
50000	4502.35	3108.70	2413.70	1998.15	1722.31	1526.31	1380.21	1267.35	1177.77
51000	4592.40	3170.88	2461.97	2038.11	1756.76	1556.84	1407.81	1292.70	1201.32
52000	4682.44	3233.05	2510.25	2078.07	1791.21	1587.37	1435.41	1318.04	1224.88
53000	4772.49	3295.23	2558.52	2118.04	1825.65	1617.89	1463.02	1343.39	1248.43
54000	4862.54	3357.40	2606.80	2158.00	1860.10	1648.42	1490.62	1368.74	1271.99
55000	4952.58	3419.57	2655.07	2197.96	1894.54	1678.95	1518.23	1394.08	1295.54
56000	5042.63	3481.75	2703.34	2237.92	1928.99	1709.47	1545.83	1419.43	1319.10
57000	5132.68	3543.92	2751.62	2277.89	1963.44	1740.00	1573.43	1444.78	1342.65
58000	5222.72	3606.10	2799.89	2317.85	1997.88	1770.52	1601.04	1470.13	1366.21
59000	5312.77	3668.27	2848.17	2357.81	2032.33	1801.05	1628.64	1495.47	1389.76
60000	5402.82	3730.44	2896.44	2397.78	2066.78	1831.58	1656.25	1520.82	1413.32
61000	5492.87	3792.62	2944.71	2437.74	2101.22	1862.10	1683.85	1546.17	1436.87
62000	5582.91	3854.79	2992.99	2477.70	2135.67	1892.63	1711.45	1571.51	1460.43
63000	5672.96	3916.97	3041.26	2517.66	2170.11	1923.15	1739.06	1596.86	1483.98
64000	5763.01	3979.14	3089.53	2557.63	2204.56	1953.68	1766.66	1622.21	1507.54
65000	5853.05	4041.31	3137.81	2597.59	2239.01	1984.21	1794.27	1647.55	1531.10
66000	5943.10	4103.49	3186.08	2637.55	2273.45	2014.73	1821.87	1672.90	1554.65
67000	6033.15	4165.66	3234.36	2677.52	2307.90	2045.26	1849.47	1698.25	1578.21
68000	6123.19	4227.84	3282.63	2717.48	2342.34	2075.79	1877.08	1723.59	1601.76
69000	6213.24	4290.01	3330.90	2757.44	2376.79	2106.31	1904.68	1748.94	1625.32
70000	6303.29	4352.18	3379.18	2797.40	2411.24	2136.84	1932.29	1774.29	1648.87
75000	6753.52	4663.05	3620.55	2997.22	2583.47	2289.47	2070.31	1901.02	1766.65
80000	7203.76	4973.92	3861.92	3197.03	2755.70	2442.10	2208.33	2027.76	1884.42
100000	9004.69	6217.40	4827.40	3996.29	3444.62	3052.62	2760.41	2534.70	2355.53

132

MONTHLY PAYMENT 15%
NECESSARY TO AMORTIZE A LOAN

TERM AMOUNT	6 YEARS	7 YEARS	8 YEARS	9 YEARS	10 YEARS	11 YEARS	12 YEARS	13 YEARS	14 YEARS
$ 25	.53	.48	.45	.42	.40	.39	.37	.36	.35
50	1.05	.96	.89	.84	.80	.77	.74	.72	.70
75	1.57	1.43	1.33	1.25	1.19	1.15	1.11	1.08	1.05
100	2.10	1.91	1.77	1.67	1.59	1.53	1.48	1.44	1.40
200	4.19	3.81	3.54	3.34	3.18	3.05	2.95	2.87	2.80
300	6.28	5.72	5.31	5.00	4.76	4.57	4.42	4.30	4.20
400	8.37	7.62	7.08	6.67	6.35	6.10	5.89	5.73	5.59
500	10.46	9.53	8.85	8.33	7.94	7.62	7.37	7.16	6.99
600	12.55	11.43	10.62	10.00	9.52	9.14	8.84	8.59	8.39
700	14.64	13.34	12.39	11.67	11.11	10.67	10.31	10.02	9.78
800	16.73	15.24	14.15	13.33	12.69	12.19	11.78	11.45	11.18
900	18.82	17.15	15.92	15.00	14.28	13.71	13.25	12.88	12.58
1000	20.91	19.05	17.69	16.66	15.87	15.23	14.73	14.31	13.98
2000	41.81	38.10	35.38	33.32	31.73	30.46	29.45	28.62	27.95
3000	62.71	57.14	53.07	49.98	47.59	45.69	44.17	42.93	41.92
4000	83.61	76.19	70.75	66.64	63.45	60.92	58.89	57.24	55.89
5000	104.52	95.24	88.44	83.30	79.31	76.15	73.61	71.55	69.86
6000	125.42	114.28	106.13	99.95	95.17	91.38	88.33	85.86	83.83
7000	146.32	133.33	123.81	116.61	111.03	106.61	103.06	100.17	97.80
8000	167.22	152.37	141.50	133.27	126.89	121.83	117.78	114.48	111.77
9000	188.13	171.42	159.19	149.93	142.75	137.06	132.50	128.79	125.74
10000	209.03	190.47	176.87	166.59	158.61	152.29	147.22	143.10	139.71
15000	313.54	285.70	265.31	249.88	237.91	228.43	220.83	214.64	209.56
20000	418.05	380.93	353.74	333.17	317.21	304.58	294.43	286.19	279.41
25000	522.56	476.16	442.18	416.46	396.51	380.72	368.04	357.73	349.27
30000	627.07	571.39	530.61	499.75	475.81	456.86	441.65	429.28	419.12
35000	731.59	666.62	619.05	583.04	555.11	533.01	515.26	500.82	488.97
36000	752.49	685.66	636.73	599.70	570.97	548.23	529.98	515.13	502.94
37000	773.39	704.71	654.42	616.36	586.83	563.46	544.70	529.44	516.91
38000	794.29	723.76	672.11	633.02	602.69	578.69	559.42	543.75	530.88
39000	815.19	742.80	689.79	649.68	618.55	593.92	574.14	558.06	544.85
40000	836.10	761.85	707.48	666.33	634.41	609.15	588.86	572.37	558.82
41000	857.00	780.89	725.17	682.99	650.27	624.38	603.58	586.68	572.79
42000	877.90	799.94	742.86	699.65	666.13	639.61	618.31	600.99	586.76
43000	898.80	818.99	760.54	716.31	681.99	654.84	633.03	615.29	600.73
44000	919.71	838.03	778.23	732.97	697.85	670.06	647.75	629.60	614.70
45000	940.61	857.08	795.92	749.63	713.71	685.29	662.47	643.91	628.67
46000	961.51	876.12	813.60	766.28	729.57	700.52	677.19	658.22	642.64
47000	982.41	895.17	831.29	782.94	745.43	715.75	691.91	672.53	656.62
48000	1003.32	914.22	848.98	799.60	761.29	730.98	706.63	686.84	670.59
49000	1024.22	933.26	866.66	816.26	777.15	746.21	721.36	701.15	684.56
50000	1045.12	952.31	884.35	832.92	793.01	761.44	736.08	715.46	698.53
51000	1066.02	971.35	902.04	849.58	808.87	776.66	750.80	729.77	712.50
52000	1086.92	990.40	919.72	866.23	824.73	791.89	765.52	744.08	726.47
53000	1107.83	1009.45	937.41	882.89	840.59	807.12	780.24	758.39	740.44
54000	1128.73	1028.49	955.10	899.55	856.45	822.35	794.96	772.69	754.41
55000	1149.63	1047.54	972.79	916.21	872.31	837.58	809.68	787.00	768.38
56000	1170.53	1066.59	990.47	932.87	888.17	852.81	824.41	801.31	782.35
57000	1191.44	1085.63	1008.16	949.52	904.03	868.04	839.13	815.62	796.32
58000	1212.34	1104.68	1025.85	966.18	919.89	883.26	853.85	829.93	810.29
59000	1233.24	1123.72	1043.53	982.84	935.75	898.49	868.57	844.24	824.26
60000	1254.14	1142.77	1061.22	999.50	951.61	913.72	883.29	858.55	838.23
61000	1275.04	1161.82	1078.91	1016.16	967.47	928.95	898.01	872.86	852.20
62000	1295.95	1180.86	1096.59	1032.82	983.33	944.18	912.73	887.17	866.17
63000	1316.85	1199.91	1114.28	1049.47	999.19	959.41	927.46	901.48	880.14
64000	1337.75	1218.95	1131.97	1066.13	1015.05	974.64	942.18	915.79	894.11
65000	1358.65	1238.00	1149.65	1082.79	1030.91	989.86	956.90	930.09	908.08
66000	1379.56	1257.05	1167.34	1099.45	1046.77	1005.09	971.62	944.40	922.05
67000	1400.46	1276.09	1185.03	1116.11	1062.63	1020.32	986.34	958.71	936.02
68000	1421.36	1295.14	1202.72	1132.77	1078.49	1035.55	1001.06	973.02	949.99
69000	1442.26	1314.18	1220.40	1149.42	1094.35	1050.78	1015.78	987.33	963.96
70000	1463.17	1333.23	1238.09	1166.08	1110.21	1066.01	1030.51	1001.64	977.94
75000	1567.68	1428.46	1326.52	1249.37	1189.51	1142.15	1104.11	1073.18	1047.79
80000	1672.19	1523.69	1414.96	1332.66	1268.81	1218.29	1177.72	1144.73	1117.64
100000	2090.23	1904.61	1768.70	1665.83	1586.01	1522.87	1472.15	1430.91	1397.05

133

15%

MONTHLY PAYMENT
NECESSARY TO AMORTIZE A LOAN

TERM AMOUNT	15 YEARS	16 YEARS	17 YEARS	18 YEARS	19 YEARS	20 YEARS	21 YEARS	22 YEARS	23 YEARS
$ 25	.35	.34	.34	.33	.33	.33	.32	.32	.32
50	.69	.68	.67	.66	.65	.65	.64	.64	.63
75	1.03	1.01	1.00	.99	.98	.97	.96	.95	.95
100	1.37	1.35	1.33	1.31	1.30	1.29	1.28	1.27	1.26
200	2.74	2.70	2.66	2.62	2.60	2.57	2.55	2.54	2.52
300	4.11	4.04	3.98	3.93	3.89	3.86	3.83	3.80	3.78
400	5.48	5.39	5.31	5.24	5.19	5.14	5.10	5.07	5.04
500	6.85	6.73	6.64	6.55	6.48	6.42	6.37	6.33	6.29
600	8.22	8.08	7.96	7.86	7.78	7.71	7.65	7.60	7.55
700	9.59	9.42	9.29	9.17	9.07	8.99	8.92	8.86	8.81
800	10.96	10.77	10.61	10.48	10.37	10.28	10.19	10.13	10.07
900	12.33	12.12	11.94	11.79	11.67	11.56	11.47	11.39	11.33
1000	13.70	13.46	13.27	13.10	12.96	12.84	12.74	12.66	12.58
2000	27.39	26.92	26.53	26.20	25.92	25.68	25.48	25.31	25.16
3000	41.08	40.37	39.79	39.29	38.87	38.52	38.22	37.96	37.74
4000	54.77	53.83	53.05	52.39	51.83	51.36	50.95	50.61	50.32
5000	68.46	67.29	66.31	65.48	64.79	64.19	63.69	63.26	62.90
6000	82.15	80.74	79.57	78.58	77.74	77.03	76.43	75.91	75.47
7000	95.84	94.20	92.83	91.67	90.70	89.87	89.17	88.56	88.05
8000	109.53	107.66	106.09	104.77	103.65	102.71	101.90	101.22	100.63
9000	123.22	121.11	119.35	117.87	116.61	115.55	114.64	113.87	113.21
10000	136.91	134.57	132.61	130.96	129.57	128.38	127.38	126.52	125.79
15000	205.36	201.85	198.91	196.44	194.35	192.57	191.06	189.78	188.68
20000	273.81	269.13	265.22	261.92	259.13	256.76	254.75	253.03	251.57
25000	342.26	336.41	331.52	327.39	323.91	320.95	318.44	316.29	314.46
30000	410.71	403.70	397.82	392.87	388.69	385.14	382.12	379.55	377.35
35000	479.16	470.98	464.12	458.35	453.47	449.33	445.81	442.80	440.24
36000	492.85	484.44	477.38	471.45	466.43	462.17	458.54	455.45	452.81
37000	506.54	497.89	490.64	484.54	479.38	475.01	471.28	468.11	465.39
38000	520.23	511.35	503.91	497.64	492.34	487.84	484.02	480.76	477.97
39000	533.92	524.80	517.17	510.73	505.29	500.68	496.76	493.41	490.55
40000	547.61	538.26	530.43	523.83	518.25	513.52	509.49	506.06	503.13
41000	561.30	551.72	543.69	536.92	531.21	526.36	522.23	518.71	515.71
42000	574.99	565.17	556.95	550.02	544.16	539.19	534.97	531.36	528.28
43000	588.68	578.63	570.21	563.12	557.12	552.03	547.70	544.01	540.86
44000	602.37	592.09	583.47	576.21	570.08	564.87	560.44	556.67	553.44
45000	616.06	605.54	596.73	589.31	583.03	577.71	573.18	569.32	566.02
46000	629.75	619.00	609.99	602.40	595.99	590.55	585.92	581.97	578.60
47000	643.44	632.46	623.25	615.50	608.94	603.38	598.66	594.62	591.17
48000	657.13	645.91	636.51	628.59	621.90	616.22	611.39	607.27	603.75
49000	670.82	659.37	649.77	641.69	634.86	629.06	624.13	619.92	616.33
50000	684.51	672.82	663.03	654.78	647.81	641.90	636.87	632.57	628.91
51000	698.20	686.28	676.29	667.88	660.77	654.74	649.60	645.23	641.49
52000	711.89	699.74	689.55	680.98	673.72	667.57	662.34	657.88	654.06
53000	725.58	713.19	702.81	694.07	686.68	680.41	675.08	670.53	666.64
54000	739.27	726.65	716.07	707.17	699.64	693.25	687.81	683.18	679.22
55000	752.96	740.11	729.33	720.26	712.59	706.09	700.55	695.83	691.80
56000	766.65	753.56	742.60	733.36	725.55	718.92	713.29	708.48	704.38
57000	780.34	767.02	755.86	746.45	738.51	731.76	726.03	721.13	716.95
58000	794.03	780.48	769.12	759.55	751.46	744.60	738.76	733.79	729.53
59000	807.72	793.93	782.38	772.65	764.42	757.44	751.50	746.44	742.11
60000	821.41	807.39	795.64	785.74	777.37	770.28	764.24	759.09	754.69
61000	835.10	820.85	808.90	798.84	790.33	783.11	776.97	771.74	767.27
62000	848.79	834.30	822.16	811.93	803.29	795.95	789.71	784.39	779.84
63000	862.48	847.76	835.42	825.03	816.24	808.79	802.45	797.04	792.42
64000	876.17	861.21	848.68	838.12	829.20	821.63	815.19	809.69	805.00
65000	889.86	874.67	861.94	851.22	842.15	834.46	827.92	822.35	817.58
66000	903.55	888.13	875.20	864.31	855.11	847.30	840.66	835.00	830.16
67000	917.24	901.58	888.46	877.41	868.07	860.14	853.40	847.65	842.73
68000	930.93	915.04	901.72	890.51	881.02	872.98	866.14	860.30	855.31
69000	944.62	928.50	914.98	903.60	893.98	885.82	878.87	872.95	867.89
70000	958.31	941.95	928.24	916.70	906.93	898.65	891.61	885.60	880.47
75000	1026.76	1009.23	994.55	982.17	971.72	962.84	955.30	948.86	943.36
80000	1095.21	1076.52	1060.85	1047.65	1036.50	1027.03	1018.98	1012.12	1006.25
100000	1369.01	1345.64	1326.06	1309.56	1295.62	1283.79	1273.73	1265.14	1257.81

134

MONTHLY PAYMENT **15%**
NECESSARY TO AMORTIZE A LOAN

TERM AMOUNT	24 YEARS	25 YEARS	26 YEARS	27 YEARS	28 YEARS	29 YEARS	30 YEARS	35 YEARS	40 YEARS
$ 25	.32	.32	.32	.31	.31	.31	.31	.31	.31
50	.63	.63	.63	.62	.62	.62	.62	.62	.61
75	.94	.94	.94	.93	.93	.93	.93	.92	.92
100	1.26	1.25	1.25	1.24	1.24	1.24	1.23	1.23	1.22
200	2.51	2.50	2.49	2.48	2.47	2.47	2.46	2.45	2.44
300	3.76	3.74	3.73	3.72	3.71	3.70	3.69	3.67	3.65
400	5.01	4.99	4.97	4.96	4.94	4.93	4.92	4.89	4.87
500	6.26	6.24	6.21	6.19	6.18	6.16	6.15	6.11	6.09
600	7.51	7.48	7.45	7.43	7.41	7.39	7.38	7.33	7.30
700	8.77	8.73	8.70	8.67	8.64	8.62	8.61	8.55	8.52
800	10.02	9.97	9.94	9.91	9.88	9.85	9.83	9.77	9.74
900	11.27	11.22	11.18	11.14	11.11	11.09	11.06	10.99	10.95
1000	12.52	12.47	12.42	12.38	12.35	12.32	12.29	12.21	12.17
2000	25.04	24.93	24.84	24.76	24.69	24.63	24.58	24.41	24.33
3000	37.55	37.39	37.25	37.13	37.03	36.94	36.87	36.62	36.50
4000	50.07	49.85	49.67	49.51	49.37	49.25	49.15	48.82	48.66
5000	62.58	62.31	62.08	61.88	61.71	61.57	61.44	61.02	60.82
6000	75.10	74.77	74.50	74.26	74.05	73.88	73.73	73.23	72.99
7000	87.61	87.24	86.91	86.63	86.39	86.19	86.01	85.43	85.15
8000	100.13	99.70	99.33	99.01	98.74	98.50	98.30	97.63	97.31
9000	112.64	112.16	111.74	111.39	111.08	110.81	110.59	109.84	109.48
10000	125.15	124.62	124.16	123.76	123.42	123.13	122.87	122.04	121.64
15000	187.73	186.93	186.23	185.64	185.13	184.69	184.31	183.06	182.46
20000	250.31	249.23	248.31	247.52	246.83	246.25	245.74	244.08	243.28
25000	312.89	311.54	310.39	309.39	308.54	307.81	307.17	305.10	304.10
30000	375.46	373.85	372.46	371.27	370.25	369.37	368.61	366.11	364.92
35000	438.04	436.16	434.54	433.15	431.95	430.93	430.04	427.13	425.74
36000	450.55	448.62	446.95	445.53	444.30	443.24	442.33	439.34	437.90
37000	463.07	461.08	459.37	457.90	456.64	455.55	454.61	451.54	450.06
38000	475.59	473.54	471.78	470.28	468.98	467.86	466.90	463.74	462.23
39000	488.10	486.00	484.20	482.65	481.32	480.17	479.19	475.95	474.39
40000	500.62	498.46	496.62	495.03	493.66	492.49	491.47	488.15	486.55
41000	513.13	510.92	509.03	507.40	506.00	504.80	503.76	500.35	498.72
42000	525.65	523.39	521.45	519.78	518.34	517.11	516.05	512.56	510.88
43000	538.16	535.85	533.86	532.15	530.69	529.42	528.33	524.76	523.05
44000	550.68	548.31	546.28	544.53	543.03	541.73	540.62	536.96	535.21
45000	563.19	560.77	558.69	556.91	555.37	554.05	552.91	549.17	547.37
46000	575.71	573.23	571.11	569.28	567.71	566.36	565.19	561.37	559.54
47000	588.22	585.69	583.52	581.66	580.05	578.67	577.48	573.58	571.70
48000	600.74	598.15	595.94	594.03	592.39	590.98	589.77	585.78	583.86
49000	613.25	610.62	608.35	606.41	604.73	603.29	602.05	597.98	596.03
50000	625.77	623.08	620.77	618.78	617.08	615.61	614.34	610.19	608.19
51000	638.28	635.54	633.18	631.16	629.42	627.92	626.63	622.39	620.36
52000	650.80	648.00	645.60	643.53	641.76	640.23	638.91	634.59	632.52
53000	663.31	660.46	658.01	655.91	654.10	652.54	651.20	646.80	644.68
54000	675.83	672.92	670.43	668.29	666.44	664.85	663.49	659.00	656.85
55000	688.35	685.39	682.84	680.66	678.78	677.17	675.77	671.20	669.01
56000	700.86	697.85	695.26	693.04	691.12	689.48	688.06	683.41	681.17
57000	713.38	710.31	707.67	705.41	703.47	701.79	700.35	695.61	693.34
58000	725.89	722.77	720.09	717.79	715.81	714.10	712.63	707.82	705.50
59000	738.41	735.23	732.51	730.16	728.15	726.41	724.92	720.02	717.67
60000	750.92	747.69	744.92	742.54	740.49	738.73	737.21	732.22	729.83
61000	763.44	760.15	757.34	754.91	752.83	751.04	749.49	744.43	741.99
62000	775.95	772.62	769.75	767.29	765.17	763.35	761.78	756.63	754.16
63000	788.47	785.08	782.17	779.67	777.51	775.66	774.07	768.83	766.32
64000	800.98	797.54	794.58	792.04	789.85	787.97	786.35	781.04	778.48
65000	813.50	810.00	807.00	804.42	802.20	800.29	798.64	793.24	790.65
66000	826.01	822.46	819.41	816.79	814.54	812.60	810.93	805.44	802.81
67000	838.53	834.92	831.83	829.17	826.88	824.91	823.21	817.65	814.98
68000	851.04	847.38	844.24	841.54	839.22	837.22	835.50	829.85	827.14
69000	863.56	859.85	856.66	853.92	851.56	849.53	847.79	842.06	839.30
70000	876.07	872.31	869.07	866.29	863.90	861.85	860.07	854.26	851.47
75000	938.65	934.61	931.15	928.17	925.61	923.41	921.51	915.28	912.29
80000	1001.23	996.92	993.23	990.05	987.32	984.97	982.94	976.30	973.10
100000	1251.53	1246.15	1241.53	1237.56	1234.15	1231.21	1228.67	1220.37	1216.38

135

15¼% MONTHLY PAYMENT
NECESSARY TO AMORTIZE A LOAN

TERM AMOUNT	1 YEAR	1½ YEARS	2 YEARS	2½ YEARS	3 YEARS	3½ YEARS	4 YEARS	4½ YEARS	5 YEARS
$ 25	2.26	1.56	1.21	1.01	.87	.77	.70	.64	.60
50	4.51	3.12	2.42	2.01	1.73	1.54	1.39	1.28	1.19
75	6.77	4.68	3.63	3.01	2.60	2.30	2.08	1.92	1.78
100	9.02	6.23	4.84	4.01	3.46	3.07	2.78	2.55	2.37
200	18.04	12.46	9.68	8.02	6.92	6.13	5.55	5.10	4.74
300	27.05	18.69	14.52	12.03	10.37	9.20	8.32	7.65	7.11
400	36.07	24.92	19.36	16.04	13.83	12.26	11.09	10.19	9.48
500	45.08	31.15	24.20	20.04	17.29	15.33	13.87	12.74	11.84
600	54.10	37.38	29.04	24.05	20.74	18.39	16.64	15.29	14.21
700	63.12	43.60	33.87	28.06	24.20	21.46	19.41	17.83	16.58
800	72.13	49.83	38.71	32.07	27.65	24.52	22.18	20.38	18.95
900	81.15	56.06	43.55	36.07	31.11	27.58	24.96	22.93	21.32
1000	90.16	62.29	48.39	40.08	34.57	30.65	27.73	25.47	23.68
2000	180.32	124.57	96.78	80.16	69.13	61.29	55.45	50.94	47.36
3000	270.48	186.86	145.16	120.23	103.69	91.93	83.17	76.41	71.04
4000	360.64	249.14	193.55	160.31	138.25	122.58	110.90	101.88	94.72
5000	450.79	311.43	241.93	200.38	172.81	153.22	138.62	127.34	118.40
6000	540.95	373.71	290.32	240.46	207.37	183.86	166.34	152.81	142.07
7000	631.11	436.00	338.70	280.54	241.93	214.51	194.06	178.28	165.75
8000	721.27	498.28	387.09	320.61	276.49	245.15	221.79	203.75	189.43
9000	811.43	560.57	435.47	360.69	311.05	275.79	249.51	229.22	213.11
10000	901.58	622.85	483.86	400.76	345.62	306.44	277.23	254.68	236.79
15000	1352.37	934.27	725.79	601.14	518.42	459.65	415.85	382.02	355.18
20000	1803.16	1245.70	967.71	801.52	691.23	612.87	554.46	509.36	473.57
25000	2253.95	1557.12	1209.64	1001.90	864.03	766.08	693.08	636.70	591.96
30000	2704.74	1868.54	1451.57	1202.28	1036.84	919.30	831.69	764.04	710.35
35000	3155.53	2179.96	1693.50	1402.66	1209.64	1072.51	970.30	891.38	828.74
36000	3245.69	2242.25	1741.88	1442.74	1244.20	1103.15	998.03	916.85	852.42
37000	3335.84	2304.53	1790.27	1482.81	1278.76	1133.80	1025.75	942.31	876.10
38000	3426.00	2366.82	1838.65	1522.89	1313.33	1164.44	1053.47	967.78	899.78
39000	3516.16	2429.10	1887.04	1562.97	1347.89	1195.08	1081.20	993.25	923.46
40000	3606.32	2491.39	1935.42	1603.04	1382.45	1225.73	1108.92	1018.72	947.13
41000	3696.47	2553.67	1983.81	1643.12	1417.01	1256.37	1136.64	1044.19	970.81
42000	3786.63	2615.96	2032.19	1683.19	1451.57	1287.01	1164.36	1069.65	994.49
43000	3876.79	2678.24	2080.58	1723.27	1486.13	1317.65	1192.09	1095.12	1018.17
44000	3966.95	2740.53	2128.97	1763.35	1520.69	1348.30	1219.81	1120.59	1041.85
45000	4057.11	2802.81	2177.35	1803.42	1555.25	1378.94	1247.53	1146.06	1065.53
46000	4147.26	2865.09	2225.74	1843.50	1589.81	1409.58	1275.26	1171.52	1089.20
47000	4237.42	2927.38	2274.12	1883.57	1624.38	1440.23	1302.98	1196.99	1112.88
48000	4327.58	2989.66	2322.51	1923.65	1658.94	1470.87	1330.70	1222.46	1136.56
49000	4417.74	3051.95	2370.89	1963.73	1693.50	1501.51	1358.42	1247.93	1160.24
50000	4507.89	3114.23	2419.28	2003.80	1728.06	1532.16	1386.15	1273.40	1183.92
51000	4598.05	3176.52	2467.66	2043.88	1762.62	1562.80	1413.87	1298.86	1207.59
52000	4688.21	3238.80	2516.05	2083.95	1797.18	1593.44	1441.59	1324.33	1231.27
53000	4778.37	3301.09	2564.43	2124.03	1831.74	1624.09	1469.32	1349.80	1254.95
54000	4868.53	3363.37	2612.82	2164.11	1866.30	1654.73	1497.04	1375.27	1278.63
55000	4958.68	3425.66	2661.21	2204.18	1900.86	1685.37	1524.76	1400.73	1302.31
56000	5048.84	3487.94	2709.59	2244.26	1935.43	1716.01	1552.48	1426.20	1325.99
57000	5139.00	3550.22	2757.98	2284.33	1969.99	1746.66	1580.21	1451.67	1349.66
58000	5229.16	3612.51	2806.36	2324.41	2004.55	1777.30	1607.93	1477.14	1373.34
59000	5319.31	3674.79	2854.75	2364.49	2039.11	1807.94	1635.65	1502.61	1397.02
60000	5409.47	3737.08	2903.13	2404.56	2073.67	1838.59	1663.38	1528.07	1420.70
61000	5499.63	3799.36	2951.52	2444.64	2108.23	1869.23	1691.10	1553.54	1444.38
62000	5589.79	3861.65	2999.90	2484.71	2142.79	1899.87	1718.82	1579.01	1468.06
63000	5679.95	3923.93	3048.29	2524.79	2177.35	1930.52	1746.54	1604.48	1491.73
64000	5770.10	3986.22	3096.68	2564.87	2211.91	1961.16	1774.27	1629.95	1515.41
65000	5860.26	4048.50	3145.06	2604.94	2246.47	1991.80	1801.99	1655.41	1539.09
66000	5950.42	4110.79	3193.45	2645.02	2281.04	2022.44	1829.71	1680.88	1562.77
67000	6040.58	4173.07	3241.83	2685.09	2315.60	2053.09	1857.44	1706.35	1586.45
68000	6130.74	4235.35	3290.22	2725.17	2350.16	2083.73	1885.16	1731.82	1610.12
69000	6220.89	4297.64	3338.60	2765.25	2384.72	2114.37	1912.88	1757.28	1633.80
70000	6311.05	4359.92	3386.99	2805.32	2419.28	2145.02	1940.60	1782.75	1657.48
75000	6761.84	4671.35	3628.92	3005.70	2592.09	2298.23	2079.22	1910.09	1775.87
80000	7212.63	4982.77	3870.84	3206.08	2764.89	2451.45	2217.83	2037.43	1894.26
100000	9015.78	6228.46	4838.55	4007.60	3456.11	3064.31	2772.29	2546.79	2367.83

136

MONTHLY PAYMENT 15¼%
NECESSARY TO AMORTIZE A LOAN

TERM AMOUNT	6 YEARS	7 YEARS	8 YEARS	9 YEARS	10 YEARS	11 YEARS	12 YEARS	13 YEARS	14 YEARS
$ 25	.53	.48	.45	.42	.41	.39	.38	.37	.36
50	1.06	.96	.90	.84	.81	.77	.75	.73	.71
75	1.58	1.44	1.34	1.26	1.21	1.16	1.12	1.09	1.06
100	2.11	1.92	1.79	1.68	1.61	1.54	1.49	1.45	1.42
200	4.21	3.84	3.57	3.36	3.21	3.08	2.98	2.90	2.83
300	6.31	5.76	5.35	5.04	4.81	4.62	4.47	4.34	4.24
400	8.42	7.68	7.13	6.72	6.41	6.16	5.95	5.79	5.66
500	10.52	9.59	8.92	8.40	8.01	7.69	7.44	7.24	7.07
600	12.62	11.51	10.70	10.08	9.61	9.23	8.93	8.68	8.48
700	14.73	13.43	12.48	11.76	11.21	10.77	10.42	10.13	9.89
800	16.83	15.35	14.26	13.44	12.81	12.31	11.90	11.58	11.31
900	18.93	17.26	16.05	15.12	14.41	13.84	13.39	13.02	12.72
1000	21.03	19.18	17.83	16.80	16.01	15.38	14.88	14.47	14.13
2000	42.06	38.36	35.65	33.60	32.01	30.76	29.75	28.93	28.26
3000	63.09	57.54	53.47	50.40	48.01	46.13	44.62	43.39	42.39
4000	84.12	76.71	71.29	67.20	64.02	61.51	59.49	57.86	56.52
5000	105.15	95.89	89.12	83.99	80.02	76.88	74.36	72.32	70.64
6000	126.18	115.07	106.94	100.79	96.02	92.26	89.24	86.78	84.77
7000	147.21	134.25	124.76	117.59	112.03	107.63	104.11	101.25	98.90
8000	168.24	153.42	142.58	134.39	128.03	123.01	118.98	115.71	113.03
9000	189.27	172.60	160.41	151.18	144.03	138.38	133.85	130.17	127.15
10000	210.30	191.78	178.23	167.98	160.04	153.76	148.72	144.63	141.28
15000	315.45	287.67	267.34	251.97	240.05	230.64	223.08	216.95	211.92
20000	420.59	383.55	356.45	335.96	320.07	307.52	297.44	289.26	282.56
25000	525.74	479.44	445.56	419.95	400.09	384.39	371.80	361.58	353.19
30000	630.89	575.33	534.67	503.93	480.10	461.27	446.16	433.89	423.83
35000	736.04	671.21	623.79	587.92	560.12	538.15	520.52	506.21	494.47
36000	757.07	690.39	641.61	604.72	576.12	553.52	535.39	520.67	508.60
37000	778.10	709.57	659.43	621.52	592.13	568.90	550.27	535.13	522.72
38000	799.12	728.75	677.25	638.31	608.13	584.28	565.14	549.60	536.85
39000	820.15	747.92	695.08	655.11	624.13	599.65	580.01	564.06	550.98
40000	841.18	767.10	712.90	671.91	640.14	615.03	594.88	578.52	565.11
41000	862.21	786.28	730.72	688.71	656.14	630.40	609.75	592.98	579.23
42000	883.24	805.46	748.54	705.50	672.14	645.78	624.63	607.45	593.36
43000	904.27	824.63	766.36	722.30	688.15	661.15	639.50	621.91	607.49
44000	925.30	843.81	784.19	739.10	704.15	676.53	654.37	636.37	621.62
45000	946.33	862.99	802.01	755.90	720.15	691.90	669.24	650.84	635.74
46000	967.36	882.17	819.83	772.70	736.15	707.28	684.11	665.30	649.87
47000	988.39	901.34	837.65	789.49	752.16	722.65	698.98	679.76	664.00
48000	1009.42	920.52	855.48	806.29	768.16	738.03	713.86	694.23	678.13
49000	1030.45	939.70	873.30	823.09	784.16	753.41	728.73	708.69	692.25
50000	1051.48	958.88	891.12	839.89	800.17	768.78	743.60	723.15	706.38
51000	1072.51	978.05	908.94	856.68	816.17	784.16	758.47	737.61	720.51
52000	1093.54	997.23	926.77	873.48	832.17	799.53	773.34	752.08	734.64
53000	1114.57	1016.41	944.59	890.28	848.18	814.91	788.22	766.54	748.76
54000	1135.60	1035.58	962.41	907.08	864.18	830.28	803.09	781.00	762.89
55000	1156.63	1054.76	980.23	923.87	880.18	845.66	817.96	795.47	777.02
56000	1177.66	1073.94	998.05	940.67	896.19	861.03	832.83	809.93	791.15
57000	1198.68	1093.12	1015.88	957.47	912.19	876.41	847.70	824.39	805.27
58000	1219.71	1112.29	1033.70	974.27	928.19	891.79	862.58	838.85	819.40
59000	1240.74	1131.47	1051.52	991.06	944.20	907.16	877.45	853.32	833.53
60000	1261.77	1150.65	1069.34	1007.86	960.20	922.54	892.32	867.78	847.66
61000	1282.80	1169.83	1087.17	1024.66	976.20	937.91	907.19	882.24	861.78
62000	1303.83	1189.00	1104.99	1041.46	992.21	953.29	922.06	896.71	875.91
63000	1324.86	1208.18	1122.81	1058.25	1008.21	968.66	936.94	911.17	890.04
64000	1345.89	1227.36	1140.63	1075.05	1024.21	984.04	951.81	925.63	904.17
65000	1366.92	1246.54	1158.46	1091.85	1040.22	999.41	966.68	940.10	918.29
66000	1387.95	1265.71	1176.28	1108.65	1056.22	1014.79	981.55	954.56	932.42
67000	1408.98	1284.89	1194.10	1125.45	1072.22	1030.17	996.42	969.02	946.55
68000	1430.01	1304.07	1211.92	1142.24	1088.23	1045.54	1011.29	983.48	960.68
69000	1451.04	1323.25	1229.74	1159.04	1104.23	1060.92	1026.17	997.95	974.80
70000	1472.07	1342.42	1247.57	1175.84	1120.23	1076.29	1041.04	1012.41	988.93
75000	1577.22	1438.31	1336.68	1259.83	1200.25	1153.17	1115.40	1084.72	1059.57
80000	1682.36	1534.20	1425.79	1343.81	1280.27	1230.05	1189.76	1157.04	1130.21
100000	2102.95	1917.75	1782.24	1679.77	1600.33	1537.56	1487.20	1446.30	1412.76

137

15¼% MONTHLY PAYMENT
NECESSARY TO AMORTIZE A LOAN

TERM AMOUNT	15 YEARS	16 YEARS	17 YEARS	18 YEARS	19 YEARS	20 YEARS	21 YEARS	22 YEARS	23 YEARS
$ 25	.35	.35	.34	.34	.33	.33	.33	.33	.32
50	.70	.69	.68	.67	.66	.66	.65	.65	.64
75	1.04	1.03	1.01	1.00	.99	.98	.97	.97	.96
100	1.39	1.37	1.35	1.33	1.32	1.31	1.30	1.29	1.28
200	2.78	2.73	2.69	2.66	2.63	2.61	2.59	2.57	2.56
300	4.16	4.09	4.03	3.98	3.94	3.91	3.88	3.85	3.83
400	5.55	5.45	5.38	5.31	5.26	5.21	5.17	5.14	5.11
500	6.93	6.81	6.72	6.64	6.57	6.51	6.46	6.42	6.38
600	8.32	8.18	8.06	7.96	7.88	7.81	7.75	7.70	7.66
700	9.70	9.54	9.40	9.29	9.19	9.11	9.04	8.98	8.93
800	11.09	10.90	10.75	10.62	10.51	10.41	10.33	10.27	10.21
900	12.47	12.26	12.09	11.94	11.82	11.71	11.63	11.55	11.49
1000	13.86	13.62	13.43	13.27	13.13	13.02	12.92	12.83	12.76
2000	27.71	27.24	26.86	26.53	26.26	26.03	25.83	25.66	25.52
3000	41.56	40.86	40.28	39.80	39.39	39.04	38.74	38.49	38.28
4000	55.41	54.48	53.71	53.06	52.51	52.05	51.65	51.32	51.03
5000	69.26	68.10	67.14	66.32	65.64	65.06	64.57	64.15	63.79
6000	83.11	81.72	80.56	79.59	78.77	78.07	77.48	76.97	76.55
7000	96.96	95.34	93.99	92.85	91.89	91.08	90.39	89.80	89.30
8000	110.81	108.96	107.42	106.12	105.02	104.09	103.30	102.63	102.06
9000	124.66	122.58	120.84	119.38	118.15	117.10	116.21	115.46	114.82
10000	138.51	136.20	134.27	132.64	131.27	130.11	129.13	128.29	127.57
15000	207.76	204.30	201.40	198.96	196.91	195.17	193.69	192.43	191.36
20000	277.01	272.39	268.53	265.28	262.54	260.22	258.25	256.57	255.14
25000	346.26	340.49	335.66	331.60	328.18	325.27	322.81	320.71	318.92
30000	415.51	408.59	402.79	397.92	393.81	390.32	387.37	384.85	382.71
35000	484.76	476.68	469.92	464.24	459.44	455.38	451.93	448.99	446.49
36000	498.61	490.30	483.35	477.50	472.57	468.39	464.84	461.82	459.25
37000	512.46	503.92	496.78	490.77	485.70	481.40	477.75	474.65	472.00
38000	526.31	517.54	510.20	504.03	498.82	494.41	490.67	487.48	484.76
39000	540.16	531.16	523.63	517.30	511.95	507.42	503.58	500.31	497.52
40000	554.01	544.78	537.06	530.56	525.08	520.43	516.49	513.13	510.27
41000	567.86	558.40	550.48	543.82	538.20	533.44	529.40	525.96	523.03
42000	581.71	572.02	563.91	557.09	551.33	546.46	542.32	538.79	535.79
43000	595.56	585.64	577.33	570.35	564.46	559.47	555.23	551.62	548.54
44000	609.41	599.26	590.76	583.62	577.58	572.48	568.14	564.45	561.30
45000	623.26	612.88	604.19	596.88	590.71	585.49	581.05	577.28	574.06
46000	637.11	626.50	617.61	610.14	603.84	598.50	593.96	590.10	586.81
47000	650.97	640.12	631.04	623.41	616.96	611.51	606.88	602.93	599.57
48000	664.82	653.74	644.47	636.67	630.09	624.52	619.79	615.76	612.33
49000	678.67	667.36	657.89	649.94	643.22	637.53	632.70	628.59	625.08
50000	692.52	680.98	671.32	663.20	656.35	650.54	645.61	641.42	637.84
51000	706.37	694.60	684.75	676.46	669.47	663.55	658.52	654.25	650.60
52000	720.22	708.22	698.17	689.73	682.60	676.56	671.44	667.07	663.35
53000	734.07	721.83	711.60	702.99	695.73	689.57	684.35	679.90	676.11
54000	747.92	735.45	725.02	716.25	708.85	702.58	697.26	692.73	688.87
55000	761.77	749.07	738.45	729.52	721.98	715.60	710.17	705.56	701.62
56000	775.62	762.69	751.88	742.78	735.11	728.61	723.09	718.39	714.38
57000	789.47	776.31	765.30	756.05	748.23	741.62	736.00	731.21	727.14
58000	803.32	789.93	778.73	769.31	761.36	754.63	748.91	744.04	739.89
59000	817.17	803.55	792.16	782.57	774.49	767.64	761.82	756.87	752.65
60000	831.02	817.17	805.58	795.84	787.61	780.65	774.73	769.70	765.41
61000	844.87	830.79	819.01	809.10	800.74	793.66	787.65	782.53	778.16
62000	858.72	844.41	832.43	822.37	813.87	806.67	800.56	795.36	790.92
63000	872.57	858.03	845.86	835.63	826.99	819.68	813.47	808.18	803.68
64000	886.42	871.65	859.29	848.89	840.12	832.69	826.38	821.01	816.43
65000	900.27	885.27	872.71	862.16	853.25	845.70	839.29	833.84	829.19
66000	914.12	898.89	886.14	875.42	866.37	858.71	852.21	846.67	841.95
67000	927.97	912.51	899.57	888.69	879.50	871.72	865.12	859.50	854.70
68000	941.82	926.13	912.99	901.95	892.63	884.73	878.03	872.33	867.46
69000	955.67	939.75	926.42	915.21	905.75	897.75	890.94	885.15	880.22
70000	969.52	953.36	939.84	928.48	918.88	910.76	903.86	897.98	892.97
75000	1038.77	1021.46	1006.98	994.80	984.51	975.81	968.42	962.12	956.76
80000	1108.02	1089.56	1074.11	1061.12	1050.15	1040.86	1032.98	1026.26	1020.54
100000	1385.03	1361.95	1342.63	1326.39	1312.69	1301.08	1291.22	1282.83	1275.67

TERM AMOUNT	24 YEARS	25 YEARS	26 YEARS	27 YEARS	28 YEARS	29 YEARS	30 YEARS	35 YEARS	40 YEARS
$ 25	.32	.32	.32	.32	.32	.32	.32	.31	.31
50	.64	.64	.63	.63	.63	.63	.63	.62	.62
75	.96	.95	.95	.95	.94	.94	.94	.93	.93
100	1.27	1.27	1.26	1.26	1.26	1.25	1.25	1.24	1.24
200	2.54	2.53	2.52	2.52	2.51	2.50	2.50	2.48	2.48
300	3.81	3.80	3.78	3.77	3.76	3.75	3.75	3.72	3.71
400	5.08	5.06	5.04	5.03	5.02	5.00	4.99	4.96	4.95
500	6.35	6.33	6.30	6.28	6.27	6.25	6.24	6.20	6.18
600	7.62	7.59	7.56	7.54	7.52	7.50	7.49	7.44	7.42
700	8.89	8.86	8.82	8.80	8.77	8.75	8.74	8.68	8.65
800	10.16	10.12	10.08	10.05	10.03	10.00	9.98	9.92	9.89
900	11.43	11.38	11.34	11.31	11.28	11.25	11.23	11.16	11.13
1000	12.70	12.65	12.60	12.56	12.53	12.50	12.48	12.40	12.36
2000	25.40	25.29	25.20	25.12	25.06	25.00	24.95	24.79	24.72
3000	38.09	37.93	37.80	37.68	37.59	37.50	37.43	37.19	37.08
4000	50.79	50.58	50.40	50.24	50.11	50.00	49.90	49.58	49.43
5000	63.48	63.22	63.00	62.80	62.64	62.50	62.38	61.98	61.79
6000	76.18	75.86	75.60	75.36	75.17	75.00	74.85	74.37	74.15
7000	88.87	88.51	88.19	87.92	87.69	87.50	87.32	86.77	86.50
8000	101.57	101.15	100.79	100.48	100.22	99.99	99.80	99.16	98.86
9000	114.26	113.79	113.39	113.04	112.75	112.49	112.27	111.56	111.22
10000	126.96	126.44	125.99	125.60	125.27	124.99	124.75	123.95	123.58
15000	190.44	189.65	188.98	188.40	187.91	187.48	187.12	185.93	185.36
20000	253.92	252.87	251.97	251.20	250.54	249.98	249.49	247.90	247.15
25000	317.39	316.09	314.96	314.00	313.18	312.47	311.86	309.87	308.93
30000	380.87	379.30	377.96	376.80	375.81	374.96	374.23	371.85	370.72
35000	444.35	442.52	440.95	439.60	438.45	437.46	436.60	433.82	432.50
36000	457.04	455.16	453.55	452.16	450.97	449.95	449.08	446.22	444.86
37000	469.74	467.80	466.15	464.72	463.50	462.45	461.55	458.61	457.21
38000	482.44	480.45	478.74	477.28	476.03	474.95	474.03	471.01	469.57
39000	495.13	493.09	491.34	489.84	488.56	487.45	486.50	483.40	481.93
40000	507.83	505.73	503.94	502.40	501.08	499.95	498.97	495.80	494.29
41000	520.52	518.38	516.54	514.96	513.61	512.45	511.45	508.19	506.64
42000	533.22	531.02	529.14	527.52	526.14	524.95	523.92	520.59	519.00
43000	545.91	543.66	541.74	540.08	538.66	537.44	536.40	532.98	531.36
44000	558.61	556.31	554.33	552.64	551.19	549.94	548.87	545.37	543.71
45000	571.30	568.95	566.93	565.20	563.72	562.44	561.34	557.77	556.07
46000	584.00	581.59	579.53	577.76	576.24	574.94	573.82	570.16	568.43
47000	596.69	594.24	592.13	590.32	588.77	587.44	586.29	582.56	580.78
48000	609.39	606.88	604.73	602.88	601.30	599.94	598.77	594.95	593.14
49000	622.09	619.52	617.33	615.44	613.83	612.44	611.24	607.35	605.50
50000	634.78	632.17	629.92	628.00	626.35	624.93	623.72	619.74	617.86
51000	647.48	644.81	642.52	640.56	638.88	637.43	636.19	632.14	630.21
52000	660.17	657.45	655.12	653.12	651.41	649.93	648.66	644.53	642.57
53000	672.87	670.09	667.72	665.68	663.93	662.43	661.14	656.93	654.93
54000	685.56	682.74	680.32	678.24	676.46	674.93	673.61	669.32	667.28
55000	698.26	695.38	692.92	690.80	688.99	687.43	686.09	681.72	679.64
56000	710.95	708.02	705.51	703.36	701.51	699.93	698.56	694.11	692.00
57000	723.65	720.67	718.11	715.92	714.04	712.42	711.04	706.51	704.35
58000	736.35	733.31	730.71	728.48	726.57	724.92	723.51	718.90	716.71
59000	749.04	745.95	743.31	741.04	739.09	737.42	735.98	731.30	729.07
60000	761.74	758.60	755.91	753.60	751.62	749.92	748.46	743.69	741.43
61000	774.43	771.24	768.51	766.16	764.15	762.42	760.93	756.09	753.78
62000	787.13	783.88	781.10	778.72	776.68	774.92	773.41	768.48	766.14
63000	799.82	796.53	793.70	791.28	789.20	787.42	785.88	780.88	778.50
64000	812.52	809.17	806.30	803.84	801.73	799.91	798.35	793.27	790.85
65000	825.21	821.81	818.90	816.40	814.26	812.41	810.83	805.66	803.21
66000	837.91	834.46	831.50	828.96	826.78	824.91	823.30	818.06	815.57
67000	850.61	847.10	844.10	841.52	839.31	837.41	835.78	830.45	827.93
68000	863.30	859.74	856.70	854.08	851.84	849.91	848.25	842.85	840.28
69000	876.00	872.39	869.29	866.64	864.36	862.41	860.73	855.24	852.64
70000	888.69	885.03	881.89	879.20	876.89	874.91	873.20	867.64	865.00
75000	952.17	948.25	944.88	942.00	939.53	937.40	935.57	929.61	926.78
80000	1015.65	1011.46	1007.88	1004.80	1002.16	999.89	997.94	991.59	988.57
100000	1269.56	1264.33	1259.84	1256.00	1252.70	1249.86	1247.43	1239.48	1235.71

15½% MONTHLY PAYMENT
NECESSARY TO AMORTIZE A LOAN

TERM AMOUNT	1 YEAR	1½ YEARS	2 YEARS	2½ YEARS	3 YEARS	3½ YEARS	4 YEARS	4½ YEARS	5 YEARS
$ 25	2.26	1.56	1.22	1.01	.87	.77	.70	.64	.60
50	4.52	3.12	2.43	2.01	1.74	1.54	1.40	1.28	1.20
75	6.78	4.68	3.64	3.02	2.61	2.31	2.09	1.92	1.79
100	9.03	6.24	4.85	4.02	3.47	3.08	2.79	2.56	2.39
200	18.06	12.48	9.70	8.04	6.94	6.16	5.57	5.12	4.77
300	27.09	18.72	14.55	12.06	10.41	9.23	8.36	7.68	7.15
400	36.11	24.96	19.40	16.08	13.88	12.31	11.14	10.24	9.53
500	45.14	31.20	24.25	20.10	17.34	15.38	13.93	12.80	11.91
600	54.17	37.44	29.10	24.12	20.81	18.46	16.71	15.36	14.29
700	63.19	43.68	33.95	28.14	24.28	21.54	19.49	17.92	16.67
800	72.22	49.92	38.80	32.16	27.75	24.61	22.28	20.48	19.05
900	81.25	56.16	43.65	36.18	31.21	27.69	25.06	23.04	21.43
1000	90.27	62.40	48.50	40.19	34.68	30.76	27.85	25.59	23.81
2000	180.54	124.80	97.00	80.38	69.36	61.52	55.69	51.18	47.61
3000	270.81	187.19	145.50	120.57	104.03	92.28	83.53	76.77	71.41
4000	361.08	249.59	193.99	160.76	138.71	123.04	111.37	102.36	95.21
5000	451.35	311.98	242.49	200.95	173.39	153.80	139.21	127.95	119.01
6000	541.62	374.38	290.99	241.14	208.06	184.56	167.06	153.54	142.81
7000	631.89	436.77	339.48	281.33	242.74	215.32	194.90	179.13	166.62
8000	722.15	499.17	387.98	321.52	277.41	246.08	222.74	204.72	190.42
9000	812.42	561.56	436.48	361.71	312.09	276.84	250.58	230.31	214.22
10000	902.69	623.96	484.98	401.90	346.77	307.60	278.42	255.89	238.02
15000	1354.04	935.93	727.46	602.84	520.15	461.40	417.63	383.84	357.03
20000	1805.38	1247.91	969.95	803.79	693.53	615.20	556.84	511.78	476.03
25000	2256.72	1559.88	1212.43	1004.73	866.91	769.00	696.05	639.73	595.04
30000	2708.07	1871.86	1454.92	1205.68	1040.29	922.80	835.26	767.67	714.05
35000	3159.41	2183.83	1697.40	1406.62	1213.67	1076.60	974.47	895.62	833.06
36000	3249.68	2246.23	1745.90	1446.81	1248.34	1107.36	1002.31	921.21	856.86
37000	3339.95	2308.62	1794.40	1487.00	1283.02	1138.12	1030.15	946.80	880.66
38000	3430.21	2371.02	1842.89	1527.19	1317.70	1168.88	1058.00	972.38	904.46
39000	3520.48	2433.41	1891.39	1567.38	1352.37	1199.64	1085.84	997.97	928.26
40000	3610.75	2495.81	1939.89	1607.57	1387.05	1230.40	1113.68	1023.56	952.06
41000	3701.02	2558.20	1988.39	1647.76	1421.72	1261.16	1141.52	1049.15	975.86
42000	3791.29	2620.60	2036.88	1687.95	1456.40	1291.92	1169.36	1074.74	999.67
43000	3881.56	2683.00	2085.38	1728.14	1491.08	1322.68	1197.21	1100.33	1023.47
44000	3971.83	2745.39	2133.88	1768.33	1525.75	1353.44	1225.05	1125.92	1047.27
45000	4062.10	2807.79	2182.37	1808.52	1560.43	1384.20	1252.89	1151.51	1071.07
46000	4152.36	2870.18	2230.87	1848.70	1595.10	1414.96	1280.73	1177.10	1094.87
47000	4242.63	2932.58	2279.37	1888.89	1629.78	1445.72	1308.57	1202.68	1118.67
48000	4332.90	2994.97	2327.86	1929.08	1664.46	1476.48	1336.42	1228.27	1142.47
49000	4423.17	3057.37	2376.36	1969.27	1699.13	1507.24	1364.26	1253.86	1166.28
50000	4513.44	3119.76	2424.86	2009.46	1733.81	1538.00	1392.10	1279.45	1190.08
51000	4603.71	3182.16	2473.36	2049.65	1768.49	1568.76	1419.94	1305.04	1213.88
52000	4693.98	3244.55	2521.85	2089.84	1803.16	1599.52	1447.78	1330.63	1237.68
53000	4784.24	3306.95	2570.35	2130.03	1837.84	1630.28	1475.62	1356.22	1261.48
54000	4874.51	3369.34	2618.85	2170.22	1872.51	1661.04	1503.47	1381.81	1285.28
55000	4964.78	3431.74	2667.34	2210.41	1907.19	1691.80	1531.31	1407.40	1309.09
56000	5055.05	3494.13	2715.84	2250.60	1941.87	1722.56	1559.15	1432.99	1332.89
57000	5145.32	3556.53	2764.34	2290.79	1976.54	1753.32	1586.99	1458.57	1356.69
58000	5235.59	3618.92	2812.84	2330.97	2011.22	1784.08	1614.83	1484.16	1380.49
59000	5325.86	3681.32	2861.33	2371.16	2045.89	1814.84	1642.68	1509.75	1404.29
60000	5416.13	3743.31	2909.83	2411.35	2080.57	1845.60	1670.52	1535.34	1428.09
61000	5506.39	3806.11	2958.33	2451.54	2115.25	1876.36	1698.36	1560.93	1451.89
62000	5596.66	3868.50	3006.82	2491.73	2149.92	1907.12	1726.20	1586.52	1475.70
63000	5686.93	3930.90	3055.32	2531.92	2184.60	1937.88	1754.04	1612.11	1499.50
64000	5777.20	3993.29	3103.82	2572.11	2219.27	1968.64	1781.89	1637.70	1523.30
65000	5867.47	4055.69	3152.32	2612.30	2253.95	1999.40	1809.73	1663.29	1547.10
66000	5957.74	4118.08	3200.81	2652.49	2288.63	2030.16	1837.57	1688.87	1570.90
67000	6048.01	4180.48	3249.31	2692.68	2323.30	2060.92	1865.41	1714.46	1594.70
68000	6138.27	4242.87	3297.81	2732.87	2357.98	2091.68	1893.25	1740.05	1618.50
69000	6228.54	4305.27	3346.30	2773.05	2392.65	2122.44	1921.09	1765.64	1642.31
70000	6318.81	4367.66	3394.80	2813.24	2427.33	2153.20	1948.94	1791.23	1666.11
75000	6770.16	4679.64	3637.29	3014.19	2600.71	2307.00	2088.15	1919.17	1785.11
80000	7221.50	4991.61	3879.77	3215.13	2774.09	2460.80	2227.36	2047.12	1904.12
100000	9026.87	6239.52	4849.71	4018.92	3467.61	3076.00	2784.19	2558.90	2380.15

140

MONTHLY PAYMENT 15½%
NECESSARY TO AMORTIZE A LOAN

TERM AMOUNT	6 YEARS	7 YEARS	8 YEARS	9 YEARS	10 YEARS	11 YEARS	12 YEARS	13 YEARS	14 YEARS
$ 25	.53	.49	.45	.43	.41	.39	.38	.37	.36
50	1.06	.97	.90	.85	.81	.78	.76	.74	.72
75	1.59	1.45	1.35	1.28	1.22	1.17	1.13	1.10	1.08
100	2.12	1.94	1.80	1.70	1.62	1.56	1.51	1.47	1.43
200	4.24	3.87	3.60	3.39	3.23	3.11	3.01	2.93	2.86
300	6.35	5.80	5.39	5.09	4.85	4.66	4.51	4.39	4.29
400	8.47	7.73	7.19	6.78	6.46	6.21	6.01	5.85	5.72
500	10.58	9.66	8.98	8.47	8.08	7.77	7.52	7.31	7.15
600	12.70	11.59	10.78	10.17	9.69	9.32	9.02	8.78	8.58
700	14.81	13.52	12.58	11.86	11.31	10.87	10.52	10.24	10.00
800	16.93	15.45	14.37	13.55	12.92	12.42	12.02	11.70	11.43
900	19.05	17.38	16.17	15.25	14.54	13.98	13.53	13.16	12.86
1000	21.16	19.31	17.96	16.94	16.15	15.53	15.03	14.62	14.29
2000	42.32	38.62	35.92	33.88	32.30	31.05	30.05	29.24	28.58
3000	63.48	57.93	53.88	50.82	48.45	46.57	45.07	43.86	42.86
4000	84.63	77.24	71.84	67.75	64.59	62.10	60.10	58.47	57.15
5000	105.79	96.55	89.80	84.69	80.74	77.62	75.12	73.09	71.43
6000	126.95	115.86	107.75	101.63	96.89	93.14	90.14	87.71	85.72
7000	148.10	135.17	125.71	118.57	113.03	108.67	105.17	102.33	100.00
8000	169.26	154.48	143.67	135.50	129.18	124.19	120.19	116.94	114.29
9000	190.42	173.79	161.63	152.44	145.33	139.71	135.21	131.56	128.57
10000	211.57	193.10	179.59	169.38	161.47	155.23	150.23	146.18	142.86
15000	317.36	289.64	269.38	254.07	242.21	232.85	225.35	219.26	214.28
20000	423.14	386.19	359.17	338.75	322.94	310.46	300.46	292.35	285.71
25000	528.93	482.73	448.96	423.44	403.68	388.08	375.58	365.44	357.13
30000	634.71	579.28	538.75	508.13	484.41	465.69	450.69	438.52	428.56
35000	740.50	675.82	628.54	592.81	565.15	543.31	525.81	511.61	499.99
36000	761.65	695.13	646.50	609.75	581.29	558.83	540.83	526.23	514.27
37000	782.81	714.44	664.46	626.69	597.44	574.35	555.85	540.85	528.56
38000	803.97	733.75	682.41	643.63	613.59	589.88	570.88	555.46	542.84
39000	825.13	753.06	700.37	660.56	629.74	605.40	585.90	570.08	557.13
40000	846.28	772.37	718.33	677.50	645.88	620.92	600.92	584.70	571.41
41000	867.44	791.68	736.29	694.44	662.03	636.45	615.94	599.32	585.70
42000	888.60	810.99	754.25	711.38	678.18	651.97	630.97	613.93	599.98
43000	909.75	830.30	772.20	728.31	694.32	667.49	645.99	628.55	614.27
44000	930.91	849.60	790.16	745.25	710.47	683.01	661.01	643.17	628.55
45000	952.07	868.91	808.12	762.19	726.62	698.54	676.04	657.78	642.84
46000	973.22	888.22	826.08	779.13	742.76	714.06	691.06	672.40	657.12
47000	994.38	907.53	844.04	796.06	758.91	729.58	706.08	687.02	671.41
48000	1015.54	926.84	861.99	813.00	775.06	745.11	721.10	701.64	685.69
49000	1036.69	946.15	879.95	829.94	791.21	760.63	736.13	716.25	699.98
50000	1057.85	965.46	897.91	846.88	807.35	776.15	751.15	730.87	714.26
51000	1079.01	984.77	915.87	863.81	823.50	791.68	766.17	745.49	728.55
52000	1100.17	1004.08	933.83	880.75	839.65	807.20	781.20	760.11	742.83
53000	1121.32	1023.39	951.78	897.69	855.79	822.72	796.22	774.72	757.12
54000	1142.48	1042.70	969.74	914.63	871.94	838.24	811.24	789.34	771.40
55000	1163.64	1062.00	987.70	931.56	888.09	853.77	826.26	803.96	785.69
56000	1184.79	1081.31	1005.66	948.50	904.23	869.29	841.29	818.58	799.97
57000	1205.95	1100.62	1023.62	965.44	920.38	884.81	856.31	833.19	814.26
58000	1227.11	1119.93	1041.58	982.38	936.53	900.34	871.33	847.81	828.54
59000	1248.26	1139.24	1059.53	999.31	952.67	915.86	886.36	862.43	842.83
60000	1269.42	1158.55	1077.49	1016.25	968.82	931.38	901.38	877.04	857.11
61000	1290.58	1177.86	1095.45	1033.19	984.97	946.90	916.40	891.66	871.40
62000	1311.74	1197.17	1113.41	1050.13	1001.12	962.43	931.42	906.28	885.68
63000	1332.89	1216.48	1131.37	1067.06	1017.26	977.95	946.45	920.90	899.97
64000	1354.05	1235.79	1149.32	1084.00	1033.41	993.47	961.47	935.51	914.25
65000	1375.21	1255.09	1167.28	1100.94	1049.56	1009.00	976.49	950.13	928.54
66000	1396.36	1274.40	1185.24	1117.87	1065.70	1024.52	991.52	964.75	942.83
67000	1417.52	1293.71	1203.20	1134.81	1081.85	1040.04	1006.54	979.37	957.11
68000	1438.68	1313.02	1221.16	1151.75	1098.00	1055.57	1021.56	993.98	971.40
69000	1459.83	1332.33	1239.11	1168.69	1114.14	1071.09	1036.59	1008.60	985.68
70000	1480.99	1351.64	1257.07	1185.62	1130.29	1086.61	1051.61	1023.22	999.97
75000	1586.78	1448.19	1346.86	1270.31	1211.03	1164.23	1126.72	1096.30	1071.39
80000	1692.56	1544.73	1436.65	1355.00	1291.76	1241.84	1201.84	1169.39	1142.82
100000	2115.70	1930.91	1795.82	1693.75	1614.70	1552.30	1502.30	1461.74	1428.52

141

15½% MONTHLY PAYMENT
NECESSARY TO AMORTIZE A LOAN

TERM AMOUNT	15 YEARS	16 YEARS	17 YEARS	18 YEARS	19 YEARS	20 YEARS	21 YEARS	22 YEARS	23 YEARS
$ 25	.36	.35	.34	.34	.34	.33	.33	.33	.33
50	.71	.69	.68	.68	.67	.66	.66	.66	.65
75	1.06	1.04	1.02	1.01	1.00	.99	.99	.98	.98
100	1.41	1.38	1.36	1.35	1.33	1.32	1.31	1.31	1.30
200	2.81	2.76	2.72	2.69	2.66	2.64	2.62	2.61	2.59
300	4.21	4.14	4.08	4.03	3.99	3.96	3.93	3.91	3.89
400	5.61	5.52	5.44	5.38	5.32	5.28	5.24	5.21	5.18
500	7.01	6.90	6.80	6.72	6.65	6.60	6.55	6.51	6.47
600	8.41	8.27	8.16	8.06	7.98	7.92	7.86	7.81	7.77
700	9.81	9.65	9.52	9.41	9.31	9.23	9.17	9.11	9.06
800	11.21	11.03	10.88	10.75	10.64	10.55	10.48	10.41	10.35
900	12.61	12.41	12.24	12.09	11.97	11.87	11.78	11.71	11.65
1000	14.02	13.79	13.60	13.44	13.30	13.19	13.09	13.01	12.94
2000	28.03	27.57	27.19	26.87	26.60	26.37	26.18	26.02	25.88
3000	42.04	41.35	40.78	40.30	39.90	39.56	39.27	39.02	38.81
4000	56.05	55.14	54.38	53.74	53.20	52.74	52.36	52.03	51.75
5000	70.06	68.92	67.97	67.17	66.50	65.93	65.44	65.03	64.68
6000	84.07	82.70	81.56	80.60	79.79	79.11	78.53	78.04	77.62
7000	98.08	96.49	95.15	94.03	93.09	92.29	91.62	91.04	90.56
8000	112.09	110.27	108.75	107.47	106.39	105.48	104.71	104.05	103.49
9000	126.10	124.05	122.34	120.90	119.69	118.66	117.79	117.06	116.43
10000	140.11	137.84	135.93	134.33	132.99	131.85	130.88	130.06	129.36
15000	210.17	206.75	203.89	201.50	199.48	197.77	196.32	195.09	194.04
20000	280.22	275.67	271.86	268.66	265.97	263.69	261.76	260.12	258.72
25000	350.28	344.58	339.82	335.82	332.46	329.61	327.19	325.14	323.40
30000	420.33	413.50	407.78	402.99	398.95	395.53	392.63	390.17	388.08
35000	490.39	482.41	475.74	470.15	465.44	461.45	458.07	455.20	452.76
36000	504.40	496.19	489.34	483.58	478.73	474.63	471.16	468.21	465.69
37000	518.41	509.98	502.93	497.02	492.03	487.82	484.25	481.21	478.63
38000	532.42	523.76	516.52	510.45	505.33	501.00	497.33	494.22	491.56
39000	546.43	537.54	530.12	523.88	518.63	514.19	510.42	507.22	504.50
40000	560.44	551.33	543.71	537.31	531.93	527.37	523.51	520.23	517.43
41000	574.45	565.11	557.30	550.75	545.22	540.55	536.60	533.23	530.37
42000	588.46	578.89	570.89	564.18	558.52	553.74	549.68	546.24	543.31
43000	602.47	592.67	584.49	577.61	571.82	566.92	562.77	559.24	556.24
44000	616.49	606.46	598.08	591.04	585.12	580.11	575.86	572.25	569.18
45000	630.50	620.24	611.67	604.48	598.42	593.29	588.95	585.26	582.11
46000	644.51	634.02	625.26	617.91	611.71	606.47	602.03	598.26	595.05
47000	658.52	647.81	638.86	631.34	625.01	619.66	615.12	611.27	607.98
48000	672.53	661.59	652.45	644.77	638.31	632.84	628.21	624.27	620.92
49000	686.54	675.37	666.04	658.21	651.61	646.03	641.30	637.28	633.86
50000	700.55	689.16	679.63	671.64	664.91	659.21	654.38	650.28	646.79
51000	714.56	702.94	693.23	685.07	678.20	672.40	667.47	663.29	659.73
52000	728.57	716.72	706.82	698.51	691.50	685.58	680.56	676.29	672.66
53000	742.58	730.50	720.41	711.94	704.80	698.76	693.65	689.30	685.60
54000	756.59	744.29	734.00	725.37	718.10	711.95	706.73	702.31	698.53
55000	770.61	758.07	747.60	738.80	731.40	725.13	719.82	715.31	711.47
56000	784.62	771.85	761.19	752.24	744.69	738.32	732.91	728.32	724.41
57000	798.63	785.64	774.78	765.67	757.99	751.50	746.00	741.32	737.34
58000	812.64	799.42	788.37	779.10	771.29	764.68	759.09	754.33	750.28
59000	826.65	813.20	801.97	792.53	784.59	777.87	772.17	767.33	763.21
60000	840.66	826.99	815.56	805.97	797.89	791.05	785.26	780.34	776.15
61000	854.67	840.77	829.15	819.40	811.18	804.24	798.35	793.34	789.09
62000	868.68	854.55	842.74	832.83	824.48	817.42	811.44	806.35	802.02
63000	882.69	868.33	856.34	846.27	837.78	830.60	824.52	819.36	814.96
64000	896.70	882.12	869.93	859.70	851.08	843.79	837.61	832.36	827.89
65000	910.71	895.90	883.52	873.13	864.38	856.97	850.70	845.37	840.83
66000	924.73	909.68	897.11	886.56	877.67	870.16	863.79	858.37	853.76
67000	938.74	923.47	910.71	900.00	890.97	883.34	876.87	871.38	866.70
68000	952.75	937.25	924.30	913.43	904.27	896.53	889.96	884.38	879.64
69000	966.76	951.03	937.89	926.86	917.57	909.71	903.05	897.39	892.57
70000	980.77	964.82	951.48	940.29	930.87	922.89	916.14	910.39	905.51
75000	1050.82	1033.73	1019.45	1007.46	997.36	988.81	981.57	975.42	970.19
80000	1120.88	1102.65	1087.41	1074.62	1063.85	1054.73	1047.01	1040.45	1034.86
100000	1401.10	1378.31	1359.26	1343.28	1329.81	1318.42	1308.76	1300.56	1293.58

NECESSARY TO AMORTIZE A LOAN

TERM AMOUNT	24 YEARS	25 YEARS	26 YEARS	27 YEARS	28 YEARS	29 YEARS	30 YEARS	35 YEARS	40 YEARS
$ 25	.33	.33	.32	.32	.32	.32	.32	.32	.32
50	.65	.65	.64	.64	.64	.64	.64	.63	.63
75	.97	.97	.96	.96	.96	.96	.95	.95	.95
100	1.29	1.29	1.28	1.28	1.28	1.27	1.27	1.26	1.26
200	2.58	2.57	2.56	2.55	2.55	2.54	2.54	2.52	2.52
300	3.87	3.85	3.84	3.83	3.82	3.81	3.80	3.78	3.77
400	5.16	5.14	5.12	5.10	5.09	5.08	5.07	5.04	5.03
500	6.44	6.42	6.40	6.38	6.36	6.35	6.34	6.30	6.28
600	7.73	7.70	7.67	7.65	7.63	7.62	7.60	7.56	7.54
700	9.02	8.98	8.95	8.93	8.90	8.88	8.87	8.82	8.79
800	10.31	10.27	10.23	10.20	10.18	10.15	10.13	10.07	10.05
900	11.59	11.55	11.51	11.48	11.45	11.42	11.40	11.33	11.30
1000	12.88	12.83	12.79	12.75	12.72	12.69	12.67	12.59	12.56
2000	25.76	25.66	25.57	25.49	25.43	25.38	25.33	25.18	25.11
3000	38.63	38.48	38.35	38.24	38.14	38.06	37.99	37.76	37.66
4000	51.51	51.31	51.13	50.98	50.86	50.75	50.65	50.35	50.21
5000	64.39	64.13	63.91	63.73	63.57	63.43	63.31	62.94	62.76
6000	77.26	76.96	76.70	76.47	76.28	76.12	75.98	75.52	75.31
7000	90.14	89.78	89.48	89.22	88.99	88.80	88.64	88.11	87.86
8000	103.01	102.61	102.26	101.96	101.71	101.49	101.30	100.69	100.41
9000	115.89	115.43	115.04	114.71	114.42	114.17	113.96	113.28	112.96
10000	128.77	128.26	127.82	127.45	127.13	126.86	126.62	125.87	125.51
15000	193.15	192.39	191.73	191.17	190.70	190.29	189.93	188.80	188.26
20000	257.53	256.51	255.64	254.90	254.26	253.71	253.24	251.73	251.01
25000	321.91	320.64	319.55	318.62	317.82	317.14	316.55	314.66	313.76
30000	386.29	384.77	383.46	382.34	381.39	380.57	379.86	377.59	376.51
35000	450.67	448.89	447.37	446.07	444.95	444.00	443.17	440.52	439.27
36000	463.55	461.72	460.15	458.81	457.66	456.68	455.84	453.10	451.82
37000	476.42	474.54	472.93	471.56	470.38	469.37	468.50	465.69	464.37
38000	489.30	487.37	485.72	484.30	483.09	482.05	481.16	478.27	476.92
39000	502.18	500.19	498.50	497.05	495.80	494.74	493.82	490.86	489.47
40000	515.05	513.02	511.28	509.79	508.52	507.42	506.48	503.45	502.02
41000	527.93	525.84	524.06	522.54	521.23	520.11	519.15	516.03	514.57
42000	540.81	538.67	536.84	535.28	533.94	532.79	531.81	528.62	527.12
43000	553.68	551.49	549.63	548.03	546.65	545.48	544.47	541.20	539.67
44000	566.56	564.32	562.41	560.77	559.37	558.16	557.13	553.79	552.22
45000	579.43	577.15	575.19	573.51	572.08	570.85	569.79	566.38	564.77
46000	592.31	589.97	587.97	586.26	584.79	583.54	582.46	578.96	577.32
47000	605.19	602.80	600.75	599.00	597.51	596.22	595.12	591.55	589.87
48000	618.06	615.62	613.53	611.75	610.22	608.91	607.78	604.13	602.42
49000	630.94	628.45	626.32	624.49	622.93	621.59	620.44	616.72	614.97
50000	643.81	641.27	639.10	637.24	635.64	634.28	633.10	629.31	627.52
51000	656.69	654.10	651.88	649.98	648.36	646.96	645.77	641.89	640.07
52000	669.57	666.92	664.66	662.73	661.07	659.65	658.43	654.48	652.62
53000	682.44	679.75	677.44	675.47	673.78	672.33	671.09	667.06	665.17
54000	695.32	692.57	690.23	688.22	686.49	685.02	683.75	679.65	677.72
55000	708.20	705.40	703.01	700.96	699.21	697.70	696.41	692.24	690.27
56000	721.07	718.22	715.79	713.71	711.92	710.39	709.08	704.82	702.82
57000	733.95	731.05	728.57	726.45	724.63	723.08	721.74	717.41	715.37
58000	746.82	743.87	741.35	739.19	737.35	735.76	734.40	729.99	727.92
59000	759.70	756.70	754.14	751.94	750.06	748.45	747.06	742.58	740.47
60000	772.58	769.53	766.92	764.68	762.77	761.13	759.72	755.17	753.02
61000	785.45	782.35	779.70	777.43	775.48	773.82	772.39	767.75	765.57
62000	798.33	795.18	792.48	790.17	788.20	786.50	785.05	780.34	778.12
63000	811.21	808.00	805.26	802.92	800.91	799.19	797.71	792.92	790.67
64000	824.08	820.83	818.04	815.66	813.62	811.87	810.37	805.51	803.22
65000	836.96	833.65	830.83	828.41	826.34	824.56	823.03	818.10	815.77
66000	849.83	846.48	843.61	841.15	839.05	837.24	835.70	830.68	828.33
67000	862.71	859.30	856.39	853.90	851.76	849.93	848.36	843.27	840.88
68000	875.59	872.13	869.17	866.64	864.47	862.62	861.02	855.85	853.43
69000	888.46	884.95	881.95	879.39	877.19	875.30	873.68	868.44	865.98
70000	901.34	897.78	894.74	892.13	889.90	887.99	886.34	881.03	878.53
75000	965.72	961.91	958.64	955.85	953.46	951.41	949.65	943.96	941.28
80000	1030.10	1026.03	1022.55	1019.58	1017.03	1014.84	1012.96	1006.89	1004.03
100000	1287.62	1282.54	1278.19	1274.47	1271.28	1268.55	1266.20	1258.61	1255.04

15¾% MONTHLY PAYMENT
NECESSARY TO AMORTIZE A LOAN

TERM AMOUNT	1 YEAR	1½ YEARS	2 YEARS	2½ YEARS	3 YEARS	3½ YEARS	4 YEARS	4½ YEARS	5 YEARS
$ 25	2.26	1.57	1.22	1.01	.87	.78	.70	.65	.60
50	4.52	3.13	2.44	2.02	1.74	1.55	1.40	1.29	1.20
75	6.78	4.69	3.65	3.03	2.61	2.32	2.10	1.93	1.80
100	9.04	6.26	4.87	4.04	3.48	3.09	2.80	2.58	2.40
200	18.08	12.51	9.73	8.07	6.96	6.18	5.60	5.15	4.79
300	27.12	18.76	14.59	12.10	10.44	9.27	8.39	7.72	7.18
400	36.16	25.01	19.45	16.13	13.92	12.36	11.19	10.29	9.57
500	45.19	31.26	24.31	20.16	17.40	15.44	13.99	12.86	11.97
600	54.23	37.51	29.17	24.19	20.88	18.53	16.78	15.43	14.36
700	63.27	43.76	34.03	28.22	24.36	21.62	19.58	18.00	16.75
800	72.31	50.01	38.89	32.25	27.84	24.71	22.37	20.57	19.14
900	81.35	56.26	43.75	36.28	31.32	27.79	25.17	23.14	21.54
1000	90.38	62.51	48.61	40.31	34.80	30.88	27.97	25.72	23.93
2000	180.76	125.02	97.22	80.61	69.59	61.76	55.93	51.43	47.85
3000	271.14	187.52	145.83	120.91	104.38	92.64	83.89	77.14	71.78
4000	361.52	250.03	194.44	161.21	139.17	123.51	111.85	102.85	95.70
5000	451.90	312.53	243.05	201.52	173.96	154.39	139.81	128.56	119.63
6000	542.28	375.04	291.66	241.82	208.75	185.27	167.77	154.27	143.55
7000	632.66	437.54	340.27	282.12	243.54	216.14	195.73	179.98	167.48
8000	723.04	500.05	388.87	322.42	278.33	247.02	223.69	205.69	191.40
9000	813.42	562.56	437.48	362.73	313.13	277.90	251.65	231.40	215.33
10000	903.80	625.06	486.09	403.03	347.92	308.78	279.62	257.11	239.25
15000	1355.70	937.59	729.14	604.54	521.87	463.16	419.42	385.66	358.88
20000	1807.60	1250.12	972.18	806.05	695.83	617.55	559.23	514.21	478.50
25000	2259.49	1562.65	1215.22	1007.56	869.78	771.93	699.03	642.76	598.13
30000	2711.39	1875.18	1458.27	1209.08	1043.74	926.32	838.84	771.31	717.75
35000	3163.29	2187.70	1701.31	1410.59	1217.70	1080.70	978.64	899.86	837.38
36000	3253.67	2250.21	1749.92	1450.89	1252.49	1111.58	1006.60	925.57	861.30
37000	3344.05	2312.72	1798.53	1491.19	1287.28	1142.46	1034.56	951.28	885.23
38000	3434.43	2375.22	1847.14	1531.50	1322.07	1173.34	1062.53	976.99	909.15
39000	3524.81	2437.73	1895.75	1571.80	1356.86	1204.21	1090.49	1002.70	933.08
40000	3615.19	2500.23	1944.35	1612.10	1391.65	1235.09	1118.45	1028.42	957.00
41000	3705.57	2562.74	1992.96	1652.40	1426.44	1265.97	1146.41	1054.13	980.93
42000	3795.94	2625.24	2041.57	1692.70	1461.24	1296.84	1174.37	1079.84	1004.85
43000	3886.32	2687.75	2090.18	1733.01	1496.03	1327.72	1202.33	1105.55	1028.78
44000	3976.70	2750.26	2138.79	1773.31	1530.82	1358.60	1230.29	1131.26	1052.70
45000	4067.08	2812.76	2187.40	1813.61	1565.61	1389.48	1258.25	1156.97	1076.63
46000	4157.46	2875.27	2236.01	1853.91	1600.40	1420.35	1286.21	1182.68	1100.55
47000	4247.84	2937.77	2284.62	1894.22	1635.19	1451.23	1314.18	1208.39	1124.48
48000	4338.22	3000.28	2333.22	1934.52	1669.98	1482.11	1342.14	1234.10	1148.40
49000	4428.60	3062.78	2381.83	1974.82	1704.77	1512.98	1370.10	1259.81	1172.33
50000	4518.98	3125.29	2430.44	2015.12	1739.56	1543.86	1398.06	1285.52	1196.25
51000	4609.36	3187.80	2479.05	2055.43	1774.36	1574.74	1426.02	1311.23	1220.18
52000	4699.74	3250.30	2527.66	2095.73	1809.15	1605.62	1453.98	1336.94	1244.10
53000	4790.12	3312.81	2576.27	2136.03	1843.94	1636.49	1481.94	1362.65	1268.03
54000	4880.50	3375.31	2624.88	2176.33	1878.73	1667.37	1509.90	1388.36	1291.95
55000	4970.88	3437.82	2673.49	2216.64	1913.52	1698.25	1537.86	1414.07	1315.88
56000	5061.26	3500.32	2722.09	2256.94	1948.31	1729.12	1565.83	1439.78	1339.80
57000	5151.64	3562.83	2770.70	2297.24	1983.10	1760.00	1593.79	1465.49	1363.73
58000	5242.02	3625.34	2819.31	2337.54	2017.89	1790.88	1621.75	1491.20	1387.65
59000	5332.40	3687.84	2867.92	2377.85	2052.69	1821.75	1649.71	1516.91	1411.58
60000	5422.78	3750.35	2916.53	2418.15	2087.48	1852.63	1677.67	1542.62	1435.50
61000	5513.16	3812.85	2965.14	2458.45	2122.27	1883.51	1705.63	1568.33	1459.43
62000	5603.54	3875.36	3013.75	2498.75	2157.06	1914.39	1733.59	1594.04	1483.35
63000	5693.91	3937.86	3062.35	2539.05	2191.85	1945.26	1761.55	1619.75	1507.28
64000	5784.29	4000.37	3110.96	2579.36	2226.64	1976.14	1789.51	1645.46	1531.20
65000	5874.67	4062.88	3159.57	2619.66	2261.43	2007.02	1817.48	1671.17	1555.12
66000	5965.05	4125.38	3208.18	2659.96	2296.22	2037.89	1845.44	1696.88	1579.05
67000	6055.43	4187.89	3256.79	2700.26	2331.02	2068.77	1873.40	1722.59	1602.97
68000	6145.81	4250.39	3305.40	2740.57	2365.81	2099.65	1901.36	1748.30	1626.90
69000	6236.19	4312.90	3354.01	2780.87	2400.60	2130.53	1929.32	1774.01	1650.82
70000	6326.57	4375.40	3402.62	2821.17	2435.39	2161.40	1957.28	1799.72	1674.75
75000	6778.47	4687.93	3645.66	3022.68	2609.34	2315.79	2097.09	1928.27	1794.37
80000	7230.37	5000.46	3888.70	3224.20	2783.30	2470.17	2236.89	2056.83	1914.00
100000	9037.96	6250.57	4860.88	4030.24	3479.12	3087.72	2796.11	2571.03	2392.50

144

MONTHLY PAYMENT 15¾%
NECESSARY TO AMORTIZE A LOAN

TERM AMOUNT	6 YEARS	7 YEARS	8 YEARS	9 YEARS	10 YEARS	11 YEARS	12 YEARS	13 YEARS	14 YEARS
$ 25	.54	.49	.46	.43	.41	.40	.38	.37	.37
50	1.07	.98	.91	.86	.82	.79	.76	.74	.73
75	1.60	1.46	1.36	1.29	1.23	1.18	1.14	1.11	1.09
100	2.13	1.95	1.81	1.71	1.63	1.57	1.52	1.48	1.45
200	4.26	3.89	3.62	3.42	3.26	3.14	3.04	2.96	2.89
300	6.39	5.84	5.43	5.13	4.89	4.71	4.56	4.44	4.34
400	8.52	7.78	7.24	6.84	6.52	6.27	6.07	5.91	5.78
500	10.65	9.73	9.05	8.54	8.15	7.84	7.59	7.39	7.23
600	12.78	11.67	10.86	10.25	9.78	9.41	9.11	8.87	8.67
700	14.90	13.61	12.67	11.96	11.41	10.97	10.63	10.35	10.12
800	17.03	15.56	14.48	13.67	13.04	12.54	12.14	11.82	11.56
900	19.16	17.50	16.29	15.37	14.67	14.11	13.66	13.30	13.00
1000	21.29	19.45	18.10	17.08	16.30	15.68	15.18	14.78	14.45
2000	42.57	38.89	36.19	34.16	32.59	31.35	30.35	29.55	28.89
3000	63.86	58.33	54.29	51.24	48.88	47.02	45.53	44.32	43.33
4000	85.14	77.77	72.38	68.32	65.17	62.69	60.70	59.09	57.78
5000	106.43	97.21	90.48	85.39	81.46	78.36	75.88	73.87	72.22
6000	127.71	116.65	108.57	102.47	97.75	94.03	91.05	88.64	86.66
7000	149.00	136.09	126.67	119.55	114.04	109.70	106.23	103.41	101.11
8000	170.28	155.53	144.76	136.63	130.33	125.37	121.40	118.18	115.55
9000	191.57	174.97	162.85	153.70	146.62	141.04	136.57	132.96	129.99
10000	212.85	194.42	180.95	170.78	162.92	156.71	151.75	147.73	144.44
15000	319.28	291.62	271.42	256.17	244.37	235.07	227.62	221.59	216.65
20000	425.70	388.83	361.89	341.56	325.83	313.42	303.49	295.45	288.87
25000	532.12	486.03	452.36	426.95	407.28	391.78	379.37	369.31	361.09
30000	638.55	583.24	542.83	512.33	488.74	470.13	455.24	443.17	433.30
35000	744.97	680.44	633.31	597.72	570.19	548.49	531.11	517.03	505.52
36000	766.25	699.88	651.40	614.80	586.48	564.16	546.28	531.81	519.96
37000	787.54	719.33	669.49	631.88	602.78	579.83	561.46	546.58	534.41
38000	808.82	738.77	687.59	648.96	619.07	595.50	576.63	561.35	548.85
39000	830.11	758.21	705.68	666.03	635.36	611.17	591.81	576.12	563.29
40000	851.39	777.65	723.78	683.11	651.65	626.84	606.98	590.90	577.74
41000	872.68	797.09	741.87	700.19	667.94	642.51	622.16	605.67	592.18
42000	893.96	816.53	759.97	717.27	684.23	658.18	637.33	620.44	606.62
43000	915.25	835.97	778.06	734.34	700.52	673.85	652.50	635.21	621.07
44000	936.53	855.41	796.15	751.42	716.81	689.52	667.68	649.98	635.51
45000	957.82	874.85	814.25	768.50	733.10	705.19	682.85	664.76	649.95
46000	979.10	894.30	832.34	785.58	749.40	720.86	698.03	679.53	664.40
47000	1000.39	913.74	850.44	802.66	765.69	736.54	713.20	694.30	678.84
48000	1021.67	933.18	868.53	819.73	781.98	752.21	728.38	709.07	693.28
49000	1042.96	952.62	886.63	836.81	798.27	767.88	743.55	723.85	707.73
50000	1064.24	972.06	904.72	853.89	814.56	783.55	758.73	738.62	722.17
51000	1085.52	991.50	922.81	870.97	830.85	799.22	773.90	753.39	736.61
52000	1106.81	1010.94	940.91	888.04	847.14	814.89	789.07	768.16	751.06
53000	1128.09	1030.38	959.00	905.12	863.43	830.56	804.25	782.93	765.50
54000	1149.38	1049.82	977.10	922.20	879.72	846.23	819.42	797.71	779.94
55000	1170.66	1069.27	995.19	939.28	896.02	861.90	834.60	812.48	794.39
56000	1191.95	1088.71	1013.29	956.35	912.31	877.57	849.77	827.25	808.83
57000	1213.23	1108.15	1031.38	973.43	928.60	893.24	864.95	842.02	823.27
58000	1234.52	1127.59	1049.47	990.51	944.89	908.91	880.12	856.80	837.72
59000	1255.80	1147.03	1067.57	1007.59	961.18	924.59	895.30	871.57	852.16
60000	1277.09	1166.47	1085.66	1024.66	977.47	940.26	910.47	886.34	866.60
61000	1298.37	1185.91	1103.76	1041.74	993.76	955.93	925.64	901.11	881.05
62000	1319.66	1205.35	1121.85	1058.82	1010.05	971.60	940.82	915.88	895.49
63000	1340.94	1224.79	1139.95	1075.90	1026.34	987.27	955.99	930.66	909.93
64000	1362.23	1244.24	1158.04	1092.98	1042.64	1002.94	971.17	945.43	924.38
65000	1383.51	1263.68	1176.13	1110.05	1058.93	1018.61	986.34	960.20	938.82
66000	1404.80	1283.12	1194.23	1127.13	1075.22	1034.28	1001.52	974.97	953.26
67000	1426.08	1302.56	1212.32	1144.21	1091.51	1049.95	1016.69	989.75	967.71
68000	1447.36	1322.00	1230.42	1161.29	1107.80	1065.62	1031.86	1004.52	982.15
69000	1468.65	1341.44	1248.51	1178.36	1124.09	1081.29	1047.04	1019.29	996.59
70000	1489.93	1360.88	1266.61	1195.44	1140.38	1096.97	1062.21	1034.06	1011.04
75000	1596.36	1458.09	1357.08	1280.83	1221.84	1175.32	1138.09	1107.92	1083.25
80000	1702.78	1555.29	1447.55	1366.22	1303.29	1253.67	1213.96	1181.79	1155.47
100000	2128.48	1944.11	1809.44	1707.77	1629.11	1567.09	1517.45	1477.23	1444.34

145

TERM AMOUNT	15 YEARS	16 YEARS	17 YEARS	18 YEARS	19 YEARS	20 YEARS	21 YEARS	22 YEARS	23 YEARS
$ 25	.36	.35	.35	.35	.34	.34	.34	.33	.33
50	.71	.70	.69	.69	.68	.67	.67	.66	.66
75	1.07	1.05	1.04	1.03	1.02	1.01	1.00	.99	.99
100	1.42	1.40	1.38	1.37	1.35	1.34	1.33	1.32	1.32
200	2.84	2.79	2.76	2.73	2.70	2.68	2.66	2.64	2.63
300	4.26	4.19	4.13	4.09	4.05	4.01	3.98	3.96	3.94
400	5.67	5.58	5.51	5.45	5.39	5.35	5.31	5.28	5.25
500	7.09	6.98	6.88	6.81	6.74	6.68	6.64	6.60	6.56
600	8.51	8.37	8.26	8.17	8.09	8.02	7.96	7.92	7.87
700	9.93	9.77	9.64	9.53	9.43	9.36	9.29	9.23	9.19
800	11.34	11.16	11.01	10.89	10.78	10.69	10.62	10.55	10.50
900	12.76	12.56	12.39	12.25	12.13	12.03	11.94	11.87	11.81
1000	14.18	13.95	13.76	13.61	13.47	13.36	13.27	13.19	13.12
2000	28.35	27.90	27.52	27.21	26.94	26.72	26.53	26.37	26.24
3000	42.52	41.85	41.28	40.81	40.41	40.08	39.80	39.56	39.35
4000	56.69	55.79	55.04	54.41	53.88	53.44	53.06	52.74	52.47
5000	70.87	69.74	68.80	68.02	67.35	66.80	66.32	65.92	65.58
6000	85.04	83.69	82.56	81.62	80.82	80.15	79.59	79.11	78.70
7000	99.21	97.63	96.32	95.22	94.29	93.51	92.85	92.29	91.81
8000	113.38	111.58	110.08	108.82	107.76	106.87	106.11	105.47	104.93
9000	127.55	125.53	123.84	122.42	121.23	120.23	119.38	118.66	118.04
10000	141.73	139.48	137.60	136.03	134.70	133.59	132.64	131.84	131.16
15000	212.59	209.21	206.40	204.04	202.05	200.38	198.96	197.76	196.73
20000	283.45	278.95	275.19	272.05	269.40	267.17	265.27	263.67	262.31
25000	354.31	348.68	343.99	340.06	336.75	333.96	331.59	329.59	327.89
30000	425.17	418.42	412.79	408.07	404.10	400.75	397.91	395.51	393.46
35000	496.03	488.15	481.58	476.08	471.44	467.54	464.23	461.42	459.04
36000	510.20	502.10	495.34	489.68	484.91	480.89	477.49	474.61	472.15
37000	524.37	516.05	509.10	503.28	498.38	494.25	490.75	487.79	485.27
38000	538.55	530.00	522.86	516.88	511.85	507.61	504.02	500.97	498.38
39000	552.72	543.94	536.62	530.49	525.32	520.97	517.28	514.16	511.50
40000	566.89	557.89	550.38	544.09	538.79	534.33	530.54	527.34	524.61
41000	581.06	571.84	564.14	557.69	552.26	547.68	543.81	540.52	537.73
42000	595.24	585.78	577.90	571.29	565.73	561.04	557.07	553.71	550.84
43000	609.41	599.73	591.66	584.89	579.20	574.40	570.34	566.89	563.96
44000	623.58	613.68	605.42	598.50	592.67	587.76	583.60	580.07	577.07
45000	637.75	627.63	619.18	612.10	606.14	601.12	596.86	593.26	590.19
46000	651.92	641.57	632.94	625.70	619.61	614.47	610.13	606.44	603.31
47000	666.10	655.52	646.70	639.30	633.08	627.83	623.39	619.62	616.42
48000	680.27	669.47	660.46	652.90	646.55	641.19	636.65	632.81	629.54
49000	694.44	683.41	674.22	666.51	660.02	654.55	649.92	645.99	642.65
50000	708.61	697.36	687.97	680.11	673.49	667.91	663.18	659.17	655.77
51000	722.78	711.31	701.73	693.71	686.96	681.26	676.44	672.36	668.88
52000	736.96	725.26	715.49	707.31	700.43	694.62	689.71	685.54	682.00
53000	751.13	739.20	729.25	720.91	713.90	707.98	702.97	698.72	695.11
54000	765.30	753.15	743.01	734.52	727.37	721.34	716.23	711.91	708.23
55000	779.47	767.10	756.77	748.12	740.84	734.70	729.50	725.09	721.34
56000	793.65	781.04	770.53	761.72	754.31	748.05	742.76	738.27	734.46
57000	807.82	794.99	784.29	775.32	767.78	761.41	756.02	751.46	747.57
58000	821.99	808.94	798.05	788.92	781.25	774.77	769.29	764.64	760.69
59000	836.16	822.89	811.81	802.53	794.72	788.13	782.55	777.82	773.80
60000	850.33	836.83	825.57	816.13	808.19	801.49	795.81	791.01	786.92
61000	864.51	850.78	839.33	829.73	821.66	814.84	809.08	804.19	800.03
62000	878.68	864.73	853.09	843.33	835.13	828.20	822.34	817.37	813.15
63000	892.85	878.67	866.85	856.93	848.60	841.56	835.60	830.56	826.26
64000	907.02	892.62	880.61	870.54	862.07	854.92	848.87	843.74	839.38
65000	921.19	906.57	894.37	884.14	875.54	868.28	862.13	856.92	852.49
66000	935.37	920.52	908.12	897.74	889.01	881.63	875.40	870.11	865.61
67000	949.54	934.46	921.88	911.34	902.48	894.99	888.66	883.29	878.73
68000	963.71	948.41	935.64	924.94	915.94	908.35	901.92	896.47	891.84
69000	977.88	962.36	949.40	938.55	929.41	921.71	915.19	909.66	904.96
70000	992.06	976.30	963.16	952.15	942.88	935.07	928.45	922.84	918.07
75000	1062.92	1046.04	1031.96	1020.16	1010.23	1001.86	994.77	988.76	983.65
80000	1133.78	1115.78	1100.76	1088.17	1077.58	1068.65	1061.08	1054.67	1049.22
100000	1417.22	1394.72	1375.94	1360.21	1346.98	1335.81	1326.35	1318.34	1311.53

MONTHLY PAYMENT 15¾%
NECESSARY TO AMORTIZE A LOAN

TERM AMOUNT	24 YEARS	25 YEARS	26 YEARS	27 YEARS	28 YEARS	29 YEARS	30 YEARS	35 YEARS	40 YEARS
$ 25	.33	.33	.33	.33	.33	.33	.33	.32	.32
50	.66	.66	.65	.65	.65	.65	.65	.64	.64
75	.98	.98	.98	.97	.97	.97	.97	.96	.96
100	1.31	1.31	1.30	1.30	1.29	1.29	1.29	1.28	1.28
200	2.62	2.61	2.60	2.59	2.58	2.58	2.58	2.56	2.55
300	3.92	3.91	3.89	3.88	3.87	3.87	3.86	3.84	3.83
400	5.23	5.21	5.19	5.18	5.16	5.15	5.15	5.12	5.10
500	6.53	6.51	6.49	6.47	6.45	6.44	6.43	6.39	6.38
600	7.84	7.81	7.78	7.76	7.74	7.73	7.72	7.67	7.65
700	9.15	9.11	9.08	9.06	9.03	9.02	9.00	8.95	8.93
800	10.45	10.41	10.38	10.35	10.32	10.30	10.29	10.23	10.20
900	11.76	11.71	11.67	11.64	11.61	11.59	11.57	11.50	11.47
1000	13.06	13.01	12.97	12.93	12.90	12.88	12.86	12.78	12.75
2000	26.12	26.02	25.94	25.86	25.80	25.75	25.71	25.56	25.49
3000	39.18	39.03	38.90	38.79	38.70	38.62	38.56	38.34	38.24
4000	52.23	52.04	51.87	51.72	51.60	51.50	51.41	51.11	50.98
5000	65.29	65.04	64.83	64.65	64.50	64.37	64.26	63.89	63.72
6000	78.35	78.05	77.80	77.58	77.40	77.24	77.11	76.67	76.47
7000	91.41	91.06	90.76	90.51	90.30	90.11	89.96	89.45	89.21
8000	104.46	104.07	103.73	103.44	103.20	102.99	102.81	102.22	101.95
9000	117.52	117.08	116.70	116.37	116.10	115.86	115.66	115.00	114.70
10000	130.58	130.08	129.66	129.30	128.99	128.73	128.51	127.78	127.44
15000	195.86	195.12	194.49	193.95	193.49	193.09	192.76	191.67	191.16
20000	261.15	260.16	259.32	258.60	257.98	257.46	257.01	255.55	254.88
25000	326.44	325.20	324.15	323.25	322.48	321.82	321.26	319.44	318.59
30000	391.72	390.24	388.98	387.90	386.97	386.18	385.51	383.33	382.31
35000	457.01	455.28	453.80	452.54	451.47	450.54	449.76	447.21	446.03
36000	470.07	468.29	466.77	465.47	464.37	463.42	462.61	459.99	458.77
37000	483.12	481.30	479.74	478.40	477.26	476.29	475.46	472.77	471.52
38000	496.18	494.30	492.70	491.33	490.16	489.16	488.31	485.54	484.26
39000	509.24	507.31	505.67	504.26	503.06	502.03	501.16	498.32	497.01
40000	522.30	520.32	518.63	517.19	515.96	514.91	514.01	511.10	509.75
41000	535.35	533.33	531.60	530.12	528.86	527.78	526.86	523.88	522.49
42000	548.41	546.33	544.56	543.05	541.76	540.65	539.71	536.65	535.24
43000	561.47	559.34	557.53	555.98	554.66	553.52	552.56	549.43	547.98
44000	574.52	572.35	570.50	568.91	567.56	566.40	565.41	562.21	560.72
45000	587.58	585.36	583.46	581.84	580.46	579.27	578.26	574.99	573.47
46000	600.64	598.37	596.43	594.77	593.35	592.14	591.11	587.76	586.21
47000	613.70	611.37	609.39	607.70	606.25	605.02	603.96	600.54	598.95
48000	626.75	624.38	622.36	620.63	619.15	617.89	616.81	613.32	611.70
49000	639.81	637.39	635.32	633.56	632.05	630.76	629.66	626.10	624.44
50000	652.87	650.40	648.29	646.49	644.95	643.63	642.51	638.87	637.18
51000	665.92	663.41	661.26	659.42	657.85	656.51	655.36	651.65	649.93
52000	678.98	676.41	674.22	672.35	670.75	669.38	668.21	664.43	662.67
53000	692.04	689.42	687.19	685.28	683.65	682.25	681.06	677.20	675.42
54000	705.10	702.43	700.15	698.21	696.55	695.12	693.91	689.98	688.16
55000	718.15	715.44	713.12	711.14	709.44	708.00	706.76	702.76	700.90
56000	731.21	728.44	726.08	724.07	722.34	720.87	719.61	715.54	713.65
57000	744.27	741.45	739.05	737.00	735.24	733.74	732.46	728.31	726.39
58000	757.33	754.46	752.01	749.93	748.14	746.61	745.31	741.09	739.13
59000	770.38	767.47	764.98	762.86	761.04	759.49	758.16	753.87	751.88
60000	783.44	780.48	777.95	775.79	773.94	772.36	771.01	766.65	764.62
61000	796.50	793.48	790.91	788.72	786.84	785.23	783.86	779.42	777.36
62000	809.55	806.49	803.88	801.65	799.74	798.10	796.71	792.20	790.11
63000	822.61	819.50	816.84	814.57	812.64	810.98	809.56	804.98	802.85
64000	835.67	832.51	829.81	827.50	825.53	823.85	822.41	817.76	815.60
65000	848.73	845.52	842.77	840.43	838.43	836.72	835.26	830.53	828.34
66000	861.78	858.52	855.74	853.36	851.33	849.59	848.11	843.31	841.08
67000	874.84	871.53	868.71	866.29	864.23	862.47	860.96	856.09	853.83
68000	887.90	884.54	881.67	879.22	877.13	875.34	873.81	868.87	866.57
69000	900.96	897.55	894.64	892.15	890.03	888.21	886.66	881.64	879.31
70000	914.01	910.55	907.60	905.08	902.93	901.08	899.51	894.42	892.06
75000	979.30	975.59	972.43	969.73	967.42	965.45	963.76	958.31	955.77
80000	1044.59	1040.63	1037.26	1034.38	1031.92	1029.81	1028.01	1022.19	1019.49
100000	1305.73	1300.79	1296.57	1292.97	1289.89	1287.26	1285.01	1277.74	1274.36

147

16% MONTHLY PAYMENT
NECESSARY TO AMORTIZE A LOAN

TERM AMOUNT	1 YEAR	1½ YEARS	2 YEARS	2½ YEARS	3 YEARS	3½ YEARS	4 YEARS	4½ YEARS	5 YEARS
$ 25	2.27	1.57	1.22	1.02	.88	.78	.71	.65	.61
50	4.53	3.14	2.44	2.03	1.75	1.55	1.41	1.30	1.21
75	6.79	4.70	3.66	3.04	2.62	2.33	2.11	1.94	1.81
100	9.05	6.27	4.88	4.05	3.50	3.10	2.81	2.59	2.41
200	18.10	12.53	9.75	8.09	6.99	6.20	5.62	5.17	4.81
300	27.15	18.79	14.62	12.13	10.48	9.30	8.43	7.75	7.22
400	36.20	25.05	19.49	16.17	13.97	12.40	11.24	10.34	9.62
500	45.25	31.31	24.37	20.21	17.46	15.50	14.05	12.92	12.03
600	54.30	37.57	29.24	24.25	20.95	18.60	16.85	15.50	14.43
700	63.35	43.84	34.11	28.30	24.44	21.70	19.66	18.09	16.84
800	72.40	50.10	38.98	32.34	27.93	24.80	22.47	20.67	19.24
900	81.45	56.36	43.85	36.38	31.42	27.90	25.28	23.25	21.65
1000	90.50	62.62	48.73	40.42	34.91	31.00	28.09	25.84	24.05
2000	180.99	125.24	97.45	80.84	69.82	61.99	56.17	51.67	48.10
3000	271.48	187.85	146.17	121.25	104.72	92.99	84.25	77.50	72.15
4000	361.97	250.47	194.89	161.67	139.63	123.98	112.33	103.33	96.20
5000	452.46	313.09	243.61	202.08	174.54	154.98	140.41	129.16	120.25
6000	542.95	375.70	292.33	242.50	209.44	185.97	168.49	155.00	144.30
7000	633.44	438.32	341.05	282.91	244.35	216.97	196.57	180.83	168.35
8000	723.93	500.94	389.77	323.33	279.26	247.96	224.65	206.66	192.39
9000	814.42	563.55	438.49	363.75	314.16	278.95	252.73	232.49	216.44
10000	904.91	626.17	487.21	404.16	349.07	309.95	280.81	258.32	240.49
15000	1357.36	939.25	730.81	606.24	523.60	464.92	421.21	387.48	360.73
20000	1809.81	1252.33	974.41	808.32	698.13	619.89	561.61	516.64	480.98
25000	2262.26	1565.41	1218.02	1010.40	872.67	774.86	702.02	645.80	601.22
30000	2714.71	1878.49	1461.62	1212.48	1047.20	929.84	842.42	774.96	721.46
35000	3167.17	2191.57	1705.22	1414.55	1221.73	1084.81	982.82	904.12	841.71
36000	3257.66	2254.19	1753.94	1454.97	1256.64	1115.80	1010.90	929.95	865.76
37000	3348.15	2316.81	1802.66	1495.39	1291.54	1146.80	1038.98	955.78	889.80
38000	3438.64	2379.42	1851.38	1535.80	1326.45	1177.79	1067.06	981.61	913.85
39000	3529.13	2442.04	1900.10	1576.22	1361.36	1208.79	1095.14	1007.44	937.90
40000	3619.62	2504.66	1948.82	1616.63	1396.26	1239.78	1123.22	1033.28	961.95
41000	3710.11	2567.27	1997.54	1657.05	1431.17	1270.77	1151.30	1059.11	986.00
42000	3800.60	2629.89	2046.26	1697.46	1466.07	1301.77	1179.38	1084.94	1010.05
43000	3891.09	2692.50	2094.98	1737.88	1500.98	1332.76	1207.46	1110.77	1034.10
44000	3981.58	2755.12	2143.70	1778.30	1535.89	1363.76	1235.54	1136.60	1058.14
45000	4072.07	2817.74	2192.42	1818.71	1570.79	1394.75	1263.63	1162.43	1082.19
46000	4162.56	2880.35	2241.14	1859.13	1605.70	1425.75	1291.71	1188.27	1106.24
47000	4253.05	2942.97	2289.86	1899.54	1640.61	1456.74	1319.79	1214.10	1130.29
48000	4343.54	3005.59	2338.59	1939.96	1675.51	1487.74	1347.87	1239.93	1154.34
49000	4434.03	3068.20	2387.31	1980.37	1710.42	1518.73	1375.95	1265.76	1178.39
50000	4524.52	3130.82	2436.03	2020.79	1745.33	1549.72	1404.03	1291.59	1202.44
51000	4615.01	3193.43	2484.75	2061.21	1780.23	1580.72	1432.11	1317.43	1226.48
52000	4705.50	3256.05	2533.47	2101.62	1815.14	1611.71	1460.19	1343.26	1250.53
53000	4795.99	3318.67	2582.19	2142.04	1850.05	1642.71	1488.27	1369.09	1274.58
54000	4886.48	3381.28	2630.91	2182.45	1884.95	1673.70	1516.35	1394.92	1298.63
55000	4976.97	3443.90	2679.63	2222.87	1919.86	1704.70	1544.43	1420.75	1322.68
56000	5067.46	3506.52	2728.35	2263.28	1954.76	1735.69	1572.51	1446.58	1346.73
57000	5157.95	3569.13	2777.07	2303.70	1989.67	1766.68	1600.59	1472.42	1370.78
58000	5248.44	3631.75	2825.79	2344.12	2024.58	1797.68	1628.67	1498.25	1394.83
59000	5338.93	3694.37	2874.51	2384.53	2059.48	1828.67	1656.75	1524.08	1418.87
60000	5429.42	3756.98	2923.23	2424.95	2094.39	1859.67	1684.83	1549.91	1442.92
61000	5519.92	3819.60	2971.95	2465.36	2129.30	1890.66	1712.91	1575.74	1466.97
62000	5610.41	3882.21	3020.67	2505.78	2164.20	1921.66	1740.99	1601.58	1491.02
63000	5700.90	3944.83	3069.39	2546.19	2199.11	1952.65	1769.07	1627.41	1515.07
64000	5791.39	4007.45	3118.11	2586.61	2234.02	1983.65	1797.15	1653.24	1539.12
65000	5881.88	4070.06	3166.83	2627.03	2268.92	2014.64	1825.23	1679.07	1563.17
66000	5972.37	4132.68	3215.55	2667.44	2303.83	2045.63	1853.31	1704.90	1587.21
67000	6062.86	4195.30	3264.27	2707.86	2338.74	2076.63	1881.40	1730.73	1611.26
68000	6153.35	4257.91	3312.99	2748.27	2373.64	2107.62	1909.48	1756.57	1635.31
69000	6243.84	4320.53	3361.71	2788.69	2408.55	2138.62	1937.56	1782.40	1659.36
70000	6334.33	4383.14	3410.43	2829.10	2443.45	2169.61	1965.64	1808.23	1683.41
75000	6786.78	4696.23	3654.04	3031.18	2617.99	2324.58	2106.04	1937.39	1803.65
80000	7239.23	5009.31	3897.64	3233.26	2792.52	2479.56	2246.44	2066.55	1923.89
100000	9049.04	6261.63	4872.05	4041.58	3490.65	3099.44	2808.05	2583.18	2404.87

148

NECESSARY TO AMORTIZE A LOAN

TERM AMOUNT	6 YEARS	7 YEARS	8 YEARS	9 YEARS	10 YEARS	11 YEARS	12 YEARS	13 YEARS	14 YEARS
$ 25	.54	.49	.46	.44	.42	.40	.39	.38	.37
50	1.08	.98	.92	.87	.83	.80	.77	.75	.74
75	1.61	1.47	1.37	1.30	1.24	1.19	1.15	1.12	1.10
100	2.15	1.96	1.83	1.73	1.65	1.59	1.54	1.50	1.47
200	4.29	3.92	3.65	3.45	3.29	3.17	3.07	2.99	2.93
300	6.43	5.88	5.47	5.17	4.94	4.75	4.60	4.48	4.39
400	8.57	7.83	7.30	6.89	6.58	6.33	6.14	5.98	5.85
500	10.71	9.79	9.12	8.61	8.22	7.91	7.67	7.47	7.31
600	12.85	11.75	10.94	10.34	9.87	9.50	9.20	8.96	8.77
700	14.99	13.71	12.77	12.06	11.51	11.08	10.73	10.45	10.23
800	17.14	15.66	14.59	13.78	13.15	12.66	12.27	11.95	11.69
900	19.28	17.62	16.41	15.50	14.80	14.24	13.80	13.44	13.15
1000	21.42	19.58	18.24	17.22	16.44	15.82	15.33	14.93	14.61
2000	42.83	39.15	36.47	34.44	32.88	31.64	30.66	29.86	29.21
3000	64.24	58.73	54.70	51.66	49.31	47.46	45.98	44.79	43.81
4000	85.66	78.30	72.93	68.88	65.75	63.28	61.31	59.72	58.41
5000	107.07	97.87	91.16	86.10	82.18	79.10	76.64	74.64	73.02
6000	128.48	117.45	109.39	103.31	98.62	94.92	91.96	89.57	87.62
7000	149.89	137.02	127.62	120.53	115.05	110.74	107.29	104.50	102.22
8000	171.31	156.59	145.85	137.75	131.49	126.56	122.62	119.43	116.82
9000	192.72	176.17	164.08	154.97	147.93	142.38	137.94	134.35	131.42
10000	214.13	195.74	182.31	172.19	164.36	158.20	153.27	149.28	146.03
15000	321.20	293.61	273.47	258.28	246.54	237.29	229.90	223.92	219.04
20000	428.26	391.47	364.62	344.37	328.72	316.39	306.53	298.56	292.05
25000	535.32	489.34	455.78	430.46	410.90	395.49	383.17	373.20	365.06
30000	642.39	587.21	546.93	516.55	493.08	474.58	459.80	447.84	438.07
35000	749.45	685.08	638.09	602.65	575.25	553.68	536.43	522.47	511.08
36000	770.86	704.65	656.32	619.86	591.69	569.50	551.76	537.40	525.68
37000	792.28	724.22	674.55	637.08	608.13	585.32	567.08	552.33	540.28
38000	813.69	743.80	692.78	654.30	624.56	601.14	582.41	567.26	554.88
39000	835.10	763.37	711.01	671.52	641.00	616.96	597.74	582.19	569.48
40000	856.52	782.94	729.24	688.74	657.43	632.78	613.06	597.11	584.09
41000	877.93	802.52	747.47	705.96	673.87	648.59	628.39	612.04	598.69
42000	899.34	822.09	765.70	723.17	690.30	664.41	643.71	626.97	613.29
43000	920.75	841.66	783.93	740.39	706.74	680.23	659.04	641.90	627.89
44000	942.17	861.24	802.16	757.61	723.18	696.05	674.37	656.82	642.49
45000	963.58	880.81	820.39	774.83	739.61	711.87	689.69	671.75	657.10
46000	984.99	900.38	838.63	792.05	756.05	727.69	705.02	686.68	671.70
47000	1006.40	919.96	856.86	809.27	772.48	743.51	720.35	701.61	686.30
48000	1027.82	939.53	875.09	826.48	788.92	759.33	735.67	716.54	700.90
49000	1049.23	959.10	893.32	843.70	805.35	775.15	751.00	731.46	715.50
50000	1070.64	978.68	911.55	860.92	821.79	790.97	766.33	746.39	730.11
51000	1092.06	998.25	929.78	878.14	838.23	806.79	781.65	761.32	744.71
52000	1113.47	1017.82	948.01	895.36	854.66	822.61	796.98	776.25	759.31
53000	1134.88	1037.40	966.24	912.58	871.10	838.43	812.31	791.17	773.91
54000	1156.29	1056.97	984.47	929.79	887.53	854.25	827.63	806.10	788.51
55000	1177.71	1076.55	1002.70	947.01	903.97	870.06	842.96	821.03	803.12
56000	1199.12	1096.12	1020.93	964.23	920.40	885.88	858.28	835.96	817.72
57000	1220.53	1115.69	1039.16	981.45	936.84	901.70	873.61	850.88	832.32
58000	1241.94	1135.27	1057.40	998.67	953.28	917.52	888.94	865.81	846.92
59000	1263.36	1154.84	1075.63	1015.89	969.71	933.34	904.26	880.74	861.52
60000	1284.77	1174.41	1093.86	1033.10	986.15	949.16	919.59	895.67	876.13
61000	1306.18	1193.99	1112.09	1050.32	1002.58	964.98	934.92	910.60	890.73
62000	1327.60	1213.56	1130.32	1067.54	1019.02	980.80	950.24	925.52	905.33
63000	1349.01	1233.13	1148.55	1084.76	1035.45	996.62	965.57	940.45	919.93
64000	1370.42	1252.71	1166.78	1101.98	1051.89	1012.44	980.90	955.38	934.54
65000	1391.83	1272.28	1185.01	1119.20	1068.33	1028.26	996.22	970.31	949.14
66000	1413.25	1291.85	1203.24	1136.41	1084.76	1044.08	1011.55	985.23	963.74
67000	1434.66	1311.43	1221.47	1153.63	1101.20	1059.90	1026.88	1000.16	978.34
68000	1456.07	1331.00	1239.70	1170.85	1117.63	1075.71	1042.20	1015.09	992.94
69000	1477.49	1350.57	1257.94	1188.07	1134.07	1091.53	1057.53	1030.02	1007.55
70000	1498.90	1370.15	1276.17	1205.29	1150.50	1107.35	1072.85	1044.94	1022.15
75000	1605.96	1468.01	1367.32	1291.38	1232.68	1186.45	1149.49	1119.58	1095.16
80000	1713.03	1565.88	1458.48	1377.47	1314.86	1265.55	1226.12	1194.22	1168.17
100000	2141.28	1957.35	1823.09	1721.84	1643.58	1581.93	1532.65	1492.78	1460.21

16%

MONTHLY PAYMENT
NECESSARY TO AMORTIZE A LOAN

TERM AMOUNT	15 YEARS	16 YEARS	17 YEARS	18 YEARS	19 YEARS	20 YEARS	21 YEARS	22 YEARS	23 YEARS
$ 25	.36	.36	.35	.35	.35	.34	.34	.34	.34
50	.72	.71	.70	.69	.69	.68	.68	.67	.67
75	1.08	1.06	1.05	1.04	1.03	1.02	1.01	1.01	1.00
100	1.44	1.42	1.40	1.38	1.37	1.36	1.35	1.34	1.33
200	2.87	2.83	2.79	2.76	2.73	2.71	2.69	2.68	2.66
300	4.31	4.24	4.18	4.14	4.10	4.06	4.04	4.01	3.99
400	5.74	5.65	5.58	5.51	5.46	5.42	5.38	5.35	5.32
500	7.17	7.06	6.97	6.89	6.83	6.77	6.72	6.69	6.65
600	8.61	8.47	8.36	8.27	8.19	8.12	8.07	8.02	7.98
700	10.04	9.88	9.75	9.65	9.55	9.48	9.41	9.36	9.31
800	11.47	11.29	11.15	11.02	10.92	10.83	10.76	10.69	10.64
900	12.91	12.71	12.54	12.40	12.28	12.18	12.10	12.03	11.97
1000	14.34	14.12	13.93	13.78	13.65	13.54	13.44	13.37	13.30
2000	28.67	28.23	27.86	27.55	27.29	27.07	26.88	26.73	26.60
3000	43.01	42.34	41.79	41.32	40.93	40.60	40.32	40.09	39.89
4000	57.34	56.45	55.71	55.09	54.57	54.13	53.76	53.45	53.19
5000	71.67	70.56	69.64	68.86	68.21	67.67	67.20	66.81	66.48
6000	86.01	84.68	83.57	82.64	81.86	81.20	80.64	80.17	79.78
7000	100.34	98.79	97.49	96.41	95.50	94.73	94.08	93.54	93.07
8000	114.68	112.90	111.42	110.18	109.14	108.26	107.52	106.90	106.37
9000	129.01	127.01	125.35	123.95	122.78	121.80	120.96	120.26	119.66
10000	143.34	141.12	139.27	137.72	136.42	135.33	134.40	133.62	132.96
15000	215.01	211.68	208.91	206.58	204.63	202.99	201.60	200.43	199.43
20000	286.68	282.24	278.54	275.44	272.84	270.65	268.80	267.24	265.91
25000	358.35	352.80	348.17	344.30	341.05	338.31	336.00	334.04	332.38
30000	430.02	423.36	417.81	413.16	409.26	405.98	403.20	400.85	398.86
35000	501.69	493.92	487.44	482.02	477.47	473.64	470.40	467.66	465.33
36000	516.03	508.03	501.37	495.79	491.11	487.17	483.84	481.02	478.63
37000	530.36	522.14	515.29	509.57	504.76	500.70	497.28	494.38	491.92
38000	544.69	536.25	529.22	523.34	518.40	514.23	510.72	507.74	505.22
39000	559.03	550.36	543.15	537.11	532.04	527.77	524.16	521.10	518.51
40000	573.36	564.48	557.07	550.88	545.68	541.30	537.60	534.47	531.81
41000	587.70	578.59	571.00	564.65	559.32	554.83	551.04	547.83	545.10
42000	602.03	592.70	584.93	578.43	572.96	568.36	564.48	561.19	558.40
43000	616.36	606.81	598.85	592.20	586.61	581.90	577.92	574.55	571.69
44000	630.70	620.92	612.78	605.97	600.25	595.43	591.36	587.91	584.99
45000	645.03	635.04	626.71	619.74	613.89	608.96	604.80	601.27	598.29
46000	659.37	649.15	640.64	633.51	627.53	622.49	618.24	614.64	611.58
47000	673.70	663.26	654.56	647.29	641.17	636.03	631.68	628.00	624.88
48000	688.03	677.37	668.49	661.06	654.82	649.56	645.12	641.36	638.17
49000	702.37	691.48	682.42	674.83	668.46	663.09	658.56	654.72	651.47
50000	716.70	705.59	696.34	688.60	682.10	676.62	672.00	668.08	664.76
51000	731.04	719.71	710.27	702.37	695.74	690.16	685.44	681.44	678.06
52000	745.37	733.82	724.20	716.14	709.38	703.69	698.88	694.80	691.35
53000	759.70	747.93	738.12	729.92	723.03	717.22	712.32	708.17	704.65
54000	774.04	762.04	752.05	743.69	736.67	730.75	725.76	721.53	717.94
55000	788.37	776.15	765.98	757.46	750.31	744.29	739.20	734.89	731.24
56000	802.70	790.26	779.90	771.23	763.95	757.82	752.64	748.25	744.53
57000	817.04	804.38	793.83	785.00	777.59	771.35	766.08	761.61	757.83
58000	831.37	818.49	807.76	798.78	791.24	784.88	779.52	774.97	771.12
59000	845.71	832.60	821.68	812.55	804.88	798.41	792.96	788.34	784.42
60000	860.04	846.71	835.61	826.32	818.52	811.95	806.40	801.70	797.71
61000	874.37	860.82	849.54	840.09	832.16	825.48	819.84	815.06	811.01
62000	888.71	874.94	863.46	853.86	845.80	839.01	833.28	828.42	824.30
63000	903.04	889.05	877.39	867.64	859.44	852.54	846.72	841.78	837.60
64000	917.38	903.16	891.32	881.41	873.09	866.08	860.16	855.14	850.89
65000	931.71	917.27	905.24	895.18	886.73	879.61	873.60	868.50	864.19
66000	946.04	931.38	919.17	908.95	900.37	893.14	887.04	881.87	877.48
67000	960.38	945.49	933.10	922.72	914.01	906.67	900.47	895.23	890.78
68000	974.71	959.61	947.02	936.50	927.65	920.21	913.91	908.59	904.07
69000	989.05	973.72	960.95	950.27	941.30	933.74	927.35	921.95	917.37
70000	1003.38	987.83	974.88	964.04	954.94	947.27	940.79	935.31	930.66
75000	1075.05	1058.39	1044.51	1032.90	1023.15	1014.93	1007.99	1002.12	997.14
80000	1146.72	1128.95	1114.14	1101.76	1091.36	1082.59	1075.19	1068.93	1063.61
100000	1433.40	1411.18	1392.68	1377.20	1364.19	1353.24	1343.99	1336.16	1329.52

MONTHLY PAYMENT 16%
NECESSARY TO AMORTIZE A LOAN

TERM AMOUNT	24 YEARS	25 YEARS	26 YEARS	27 YEARS	28 YEARS	29 YEARS	30 YEARS	35 YEARS	40 YEARS
$ 25	.34	.33	.33	.33	.33	.33	.33	.33	.33
50	.67	.66	.66	.66	.66	.66	.66	.65	.65
75	1.00	.99	.99	.99	.99	.98	.98	.98	.98
100	1.33	1.32	1.32	1.32	1.31	1.31	1.31	1.30	1.30
200	2.65	2.64	2.63	2.63	2.62	2.62	2.61	2.60	2.59
300	3.98	3.96	3.95	3.94	3.93	3.92	3.92	3.90	3.89
400	5.30	5.28	5.26	5.25	5.24	5.23	5.22	5.19	5.18
500	6.62	6.60	6.58	6.56	6.55	6.53	6.52	6.49	6.47
600	7.95	7.92	7.89	7.87	7.86	7.84	7.83	7.79	7.77
700	9.27	9.24	9.21	9.19	9.19	9.15	9.13	9.08	9.06
800	10.60	10.50	10.52	10.50	10.47	10.45	10.44	10.38	10.35
900	11.92	11.88	11.84	11.81	11.78	11.76	11.74	11.68	11.65
1000	13.24	13.20	13.15	13.12	13.09	13.06	13.04	12.97	12.94
2000	26.48	26.39	26.30	26.23	26.18	26.12	26.08	25.94	25.88
3000	39.72	39.58	39.45	39.35	39.26	39.18	39.12	38.91	38.82
4000	52.96	52.77	52.60	52.46	52.35	52.24	52.16	51.88	51.75
5000	66.20	65.96	65.75	65.58	65.43	65.30	65.20	64.85	64.69
6000	79.44	79.15	78.90	78.69	78.52	78.36	78.23	77.82	77.63
7000	92.68	92.34	92.05	91.81	91.60	91.42	91.27	90.79	90.56
8000	105.91	105.53	105.20	104.92	104.69	104.48	104.31	103.76	103.50
9000	119.15	118.72	118.35	118.04	117.77	117.54	117.35	116.72	116.44
10000	132.39	131.91	131.50	131.15	130.86	130.60	130.39	129.69	129.37
15000	198.59	197.87	197.25	196.73	196.28	195.90	195.58	194.54	194.06
20000	264.78	263.82	263.00	262.30	261.71	261.20	260.77	259.38	258.74
25000	330.97	329.77	328.75	327.88	327.14	326.50	325.96	324.22	323.43
30000	397.17	395.73	394.50	393.45	392.56	391.80	391.15	389.07	388.11
35000	463.36	461.68	460.25	459.03	457.99	457.10	456.34	453.91	452.80
36000	476.60	474.87	473.40	472.14	471.07	470.16	469.38	466.88	465.73
37000	489.84	488.06	486.55	485.26	484.16	483.22	482.42	479.85	478.67
38000	503.08	501.25	499.70	498.37	497.25	496.28	495.46	492.82	491.60
39000	516.31	514.44	512.85	511.49	510.33	509.34	508.50	505.79	504.54
40000	529.55	527.63	526.00	524.60	523.42	522.40	521.53	518.76	517.48
41000	542.79	540.82	539.15	537.72	536.50	535.46	534.57	531.73	530.42
42000	556.03	554.01	552.30	550.83	549.59	548.52	547.61	544.69	543.35
43000	569.27	567.21	565.45	563.95	562.67	561.58	560.65	557.66	556.29
44000	582.51	580.40	578.60	577.06	575.76	574.64	573.69	570.63	569.23
45000	595.75	593.59	591.75	590.18	588.84	587.70	586.72	583.60	582.16
46000	608.98	606.78	604.90	603.29	601.93	600.76	599.76	596.57	595.10
47000	622.22	619.97	618.05	616.41	615.01	613.82	612.80	609.54	608.04
48000	635.46	633.16	631.20	629.52	628.10	626.88	625.84	622.51	620.97
49000	648.70	646.35	644.35	642.64	641.18	639.94	638.88	635.48	633.91
50000	661.94	659.54	657.50	655.75	654.27	653.00	651.92	648.44	646.85
51000	675.18	672.73	670.65	668.87	667.35	666.06	664.95	661.41	659.79
52000	688.42	685.92	683.80	681.98	680.44	679.12	677.99	674.38	672.72
53000	701.66	699.11	696.95	695.10	693.52	692.18	691.03	687.35	685.66
54000	714.89	712.30	710.10	708.21	706.61	705.24	704.07	700.32	698.60
55000	728.13	725.49	723.25	721.33	719.69	718.30	717.11	713.29	711.53
56000	741.37	738.68	736.40	734.44	732.78	731.36	730.15	726.26	724.47
57000	754.61	751.87	749.55	747.56	745.87	744.42	743.18	739.23	737.41
58000	767.85	765.07	762.70	760.67	758.95	757.48	756.22	752.19	750.34
59000	781.09	778.26	775.84	773.79	772.04	770.54	769.26	765.16	763.28
60000	794.33	791.45	788.99	786.90	785.12	783.60	782.30	778.13	776.22
61000	807.57	804.64	802.14	800.02	798.21	796.66	795.34	791.10	789.15
62000	820.80	817.83	815.29	813.13	811.29	809.72	808.37	804.07	802.09
63000	834.04	831.02	828.44	826.25	824.38	822.78	821.41	817.04	815.03
64000	847.28	844.21	841.59	839.36	837.46	835.84	834.45	830.01	827.96
65000	860.52	857.40	854.74	852.48	850.55	848.90	847.49	842.98	840.90
66000	873.76	870.59	867.89	865.59	863.63	861.96	860.53	855.94	853.84
67000	887.00	883.78	881.04	878.71	876.72	875.02	873.57	868.91	866.78
68000	900.24	896.97	894.19	891.82	889.80	888.08	886.60	881.88	879.71
69000	913.47	910.16	907.34	904.94	902.89	901.14	899.64	894.85	892.65
70000	926.71	923.35	920.49	918.05	915.97	914.20	912.68	907.82	905.59
75000	992.91	989.31	986.24	983.63	981.40	979.50	977.87	972.66	970.27
80000	1059.10	1055.26	1051.99	1049.20	1046.83	1044.80	1043.06	1037.51	1034.95
100000	1323.87	1319.07	1314.99	1311.50	1308.53	1305.99	1303.83	1296.88	1293.69

151

16¼% MONTHLY PAYMENT
NECESSARY TO AMORTIZE A LOAN

TERM AMOUNT	1 YEAR	1½ YEARS	2 YEARS	2½ YEARS	3 YEARS	3½ YEARS	4 YEARS	4½ YEARS	5 YEARS
$ 25	2.27	1.57	1.23	1.02	.88	.78	.71	.65	.61
50	4.54	3.14	2.45	2.03	1.76	1.56	1.41	1.30	1.21
75	6.80	4.71	3.67	3.04	2.63	2.34	2.12	1.95	1.82
100	9.07	6.28	4.89	4.06	3.51	3.12	2.82	2.60	2.42
200	18.13	12.55	9.77	8.11	7.01	6.23	5.64	5.20	4.84
300	27.19	18.82	14.65	12.16	10.51	9.34	8.46	7.79	7.26
400	36.25	25.10	19.54	16.22	14.01	12.45	11.28	10.39	9.67
500	45.31	31.37	24.42	20.27	17.52	15.56	14.10	12.98	12.09
600	54.37	37.64	29.30	24.32	21.02	18.67	16.92	15.58	14.51
700	63.43	43.91	34.19	28.38	24.52	21.78	19.74	18.17	16.93
800	72.49	50.19	39.07	32.43	28.02	24.89	22.56	20.77	19.34
900	81.55	56.46	43.95	36.48	31.52	28.01	25.38	23.36	21.76
1000	90.61	62.73	48.84	40.53	35.03	31.12	28.20	25.96	24.18
2000	181.21	125.46	97.67	81.06	70.05	62.23	56.40	51.91	48.35
3000	271.81	188.19	146.50	121.59	105.07	93.34	84.60	77.87	72.52
4000	362.41	250.91	195.33	162.12	140.09	124.45	112.80	103.82	96.70
5000	453.01	313.64	244.17	202.65	175.11	155.56	141.00	129.77	120.87
6000	543.61	376.37	293.00	243.18	210.14	186.68	169.20	155.73	145.04
7000	634.21	439.09	341.83	283.71	245.16	217.79	197.40	181.68	169.21
8000	724.81	501.82	390.66	324.24	280.18	248.90	225.60	207.63	193.39
9000	815.41	564.55	439.49	364.77	315.20	280.01	253.80	233.59	217.56
10000	906.02	627.27	488.33	405.30	350.22	311.12	282.00	259.54	241.73
15000	1359.02	940.91	732.49	607.94	525.33	466.68	423.00	389.31	362.59
20000	1812.03	1254.54	976.65	810.59	700.44	622.24	564.00	519.08	483.46
25000	2265.03	1568.18	1220.81	1013.23	875.55	777.80	705.00	648.84	604.32
30000	2718.04	1881.81	1464.97	1215.88	1050.66	933.36	846.00	778.61	725.18
35000	3171.04	2195.45	1709.13	1418.52	1225.77	1088.92	987.00	908.38	846.04
36000	3261.64	2258.17	1757.96	1459.05	1260.79	1120.03	1015.20	934.33	870.22
37000	3352.25	2320.90	1806.79	1499.58	1295.81	1151.14	1043.40	960.28	894.39
38000	3442.85	2383.63	1855.63	1540.11	1330.83	1182.25	1071.60	986.24	918.56
39000	3533.45	2446.35	1904.46	1580.64	1365.85	1213.36	1099.80	1012.19	942.73
40000	3624.05	2509.08	1953.29	1621.17	1400.88	1244.48	1128.00	1038.15	966.91
41000	3714.65	2571.81	2002.12	1661.70	1435.90	1275.59	1156.20	1064.10	991.08
42000	3805.25	2634.53	2050.96	1702.23	1470.92	1306.70	1184.40	1090.05	1015.25
43000	3895.85	2697.26	2099.79	1742.76	1505.94	1337.81	1212.60	1116.01	1039.42
44000	3986.45	2759.99	2148.62	1783.29	1540.96	1368.92	1240.80	1141.96	1063.60
45000	4077.05	2822.71	2197.45	1823.82	1575.98	1400.04	1269.00	1167.91	1087.77
46000	4167.66	2885.44	2246.28	1864.34	1611.01	1431.15	1297.20	1193.87	1111.94
47000	4258.26	2948.17	2295.12	1904.87	1646.03	1462.26	1325.40	1219.82	1136.12
48000	4348.86	3010.89	2343.95	1945.40	1681.05	1493.37	1353.60	1245.77	1160.29
49000	4439.46	3073.62	2392.78	1985.93	1716.07	1524.48	1381.80	1271.73	1184.46
50000	4530.06	3136.35	2441.61	2026.46	1751.09	1555.59	1410.00	1297.68	1208.63
51000	4620.66	3199.07	2490.44	2066.99	1786.11	1586.71	1438.20	1323.63	1232.81
52000	4711.26	3261.80	2539.28	2107.52	1821.14	1617.82	1466.40	1349.59	1256.98
53000	4801.86	3324.53	2588.11	2148.05	1856.16	1648.93	1494.60	1375.54	1281.15
54000	4892.46	3387.26	2636.94	2188.58	1891.18	1680.04	1522.80	1401.49	1305.32
55000	4983.07	3449.98	2685.77	2229.11	1926.20	1711.15	1551.00	1427.45	1329.50
56000	5073.67	3512.71	2734.61	2269.64	1961.22	1742.26	1579.20	1453.40	1353.67
57000	5164.27	3575.44	2783.44	2310.16	1996.25	1773.38	1607.40	1479.35	1377.84
58000	5254.87	3638.16	2832.27	2350.69	2031.27	1804.49	1635.60	1505.31	1402.01
59000	5345.47	3700.89	2881.10	2391.22	2066.29	1835.60	1663.80	1531.26	1426.19
60000	5436.07	3763.62	2929.93	2431.75	2101.31	1866.71	1692.00	1557.22	1450.36
61000	5526.67	3826.34	2978.77	2472.28	2136.33	1897.82	1720.20	1583.17	1474.53
62000	5617.27	3889.07	3027.60	2512.81	2171.35	1928.94	1748.40	1609.12	1498.70
63000	5707.87	3951.80	3076.43	2553.34	2206.38	1960.05	1776.60	1635.08	1522.88
64000	5798.48	4014.52	3125.26	2593.87	2241.40	1991.16	1804.80	1661.03	1547.05
65000	5889.08	4077.25	3174.09	2634.40	2276.42	2022.27	1833.00	1686.98	1571.22
66000	5979.68	4139.98	3222.93	2674.93	2311.44	2053.38	1861.20	1712.94	1595.39
67000	6070.28	4202.70	3271.76	2715.46	2346.46	2084.49	1889.40	1738.89	1619.57
68000	6160.88	4265.43	3320.59	2755.98	2381.48	2115.61	1917.60	1764.84	1643.74
69000	6251.48	4328.16	3369.42	2796.51	2416.51	2146.72	1945.80	1790.80	1667.91
70000	6342.08	4390.89	3418.26	2837.04	2451.53	2177.83	1974.00	1816.75	1692.08
75000	6795.09	4704.52	3662.42	3039.69	2626.64	2333.39	2115.00	1946.52	1812.95
80000	7248.09	5018.15	3906.58	3242.33	2801.75	2488.95	2256.00	2076.29	1933.81
100000	9060.12	6272.69	4883.22	4052.92	3502.18	3111.18	2820.00	2595.36	2417.26

152

MONTHLY PAYMENT 16¼%
NECESSARY TO AMORTIZE A LOAN

TERM AMOUNT	6 YEARS	7 YEARS	8 YEARS	9 YEARS	10 YEARS	11 YEARS	12 YEARS	13 YEARS	14 YEARS
$ 25	.54	.50	.46	.44	.42	.40	.39	.38	.37
50	1.08	.99	.92	.87	.83	.80	.78	.76	.74
75	1.62	1.48	1.38	1.31	1.25	1.20	1.17	1.14	1.11
100	2.16	1.98	1.84	1.74	1.66	1.60	1.55	1.51	1.48
200	4.31	3.95	3.68	3.48	3.32	3.20	3.10	3.02	2.96
300	6.47	5.92	5.52	5.21	4.98	4.80	4.65	4.53	4.43
400	8.62	7.89	7.35	6.95	6.64	6.39	6.20	6.04	5.91
500	10.78	9.86	9.19	8.68	8.30	7.99	7.74	7.55	7.39
600	12.93	11.83	11.03	10.42	9.95	9.59	9.29	9.06	8.86
700	15.08	13.80	12.86	12.16	11.61	11.18	10.84	10.56	10.34
800	17.24	15.77	14.70	13.89	13.27	12.78	12.39	12.07	11.81
900	19.39	17.74	16.54	15.63	14.93	14.38	13.94	13.58	13.29
1000	21.55	19.71	18.37	17.36	16.59	15.97	15.48	15.09	14.77
2000	43.09	39.42	36.74	34.72	33.17	31.94	30.96	30.17	29.53
3000	64.63	59.12	55.11	52.08	49.75	47.91	46.44	45.26	44.29
4000	86.17	78.83	73.48	69.44	66.33	63.88	61.92	60.34	59.05
5000	107.71	98.54	91.84	86.80	82.91	79.85	77.40	75.42	73.81
6000	129.25	118.24	110.21	104.16	99.49	95.81	92.88	90.51	88.57
7000	150.79	137.95	128.58	121.52	116.07	111.78	108.36	105.59	103.33
8000	172.33	157.65	146.95	138.88	132.65	127.75	123.84	120.67	118.10
9000	193.87	177.36	165.32	156.24	149.23	143.72	139.32	135.76	132.86
10000	215.42	197.07	183.68	173.60	165.81	159.69	154.79	150.84	147.62
15000	323.12	295.60	275.52	260.40	248.72	239.53	232.19	226.26	221.42
20000	430.83	394.13	367.36	347.19	331.62	319.37	309.58	301.68	295.23
25000	538.53	492.66	459.20	433.99	414.52	399.21	386.98	377.10	369.04
30000	646.24	591.19	551.04	520.79	497.43	479.05	464.37	452.52	442.84
35000	753.94	689.72	642.88	607.58	580.33	558.89	541.77	527.93	516.65
36000	775.48	709.43	661.25	624.94	596.91	574.86	557.25	543.02	531.41
37000	797.03	729.13	679.61	642.30	613.49	590.83	572.73	558.10	546.17
38000	818.57	748.84	697.98	659.66	630.07	606.79	588.20	573.18	560.93
39000	840.11	768.55	716.35	677.02	646.66	622.76	603.68	588.27	575.69
40000	861.65	788.25	734.72	694.38	663.24	638.73	619.16	603.35	590.46
41000	883.19	807.96	753.09	711.74	679.82	654.70	634.64	618.44	605.22
42000	904.73	827.66	771.45	729.10	696.40	670.67	650.12	633.52	619.98
43000	926.27	847.37	789.82	746.46	712.98	686.63	665.60	648.60	634.74
44000	947.81	867.08	808.19	763.82	729.56	702.60	681.08	663.69	649.50
45000	969.35	886.78	826.56	781.18	746.14	718.57	696.56	678.77	664.26
46000	990.90	906.49	844.93	798.54	762.72	734.54	712.04	693.85	679.02
47000	1012.44	926.19	863.29	815.90	779.30	750.51	727.52	708.94	693.78
48000	1033.98	945.90	881.66	833.26	795.88	766.48	742.99	724.02	708.55
49000	1055.52	965.61	900.03	850.62	812.46	782.44	758.47	739.10	723.31
50000	1077.06	985.31	918.40	867.98	829.04	798.41	773.95	754.19	738.07
51000	1098.60	1005.02	936.76	885.34	845.62	814.38	789.43	769.27	752.83
52000	1120.14	1024.73	955.13	902.69	862.21	830.35	804.91	784.36	767.59
53000	1141.68	1044.43	973.50	920.05	878.79	846.32	820.39	799.44	782.35
54000	1163.22	1064.14	991.87	937.41	895.37	862.28	835.87	814.52	797.11
55000	1184.77	1083.84	1010.24	954.77	911.95	878.25	851.35	829.61	811.87
56000	1206.31	1103.55	1028.60	972.13	928.53	894.22	866.83	844.69	826.64
57000	1227.85	1123.26	1046.97	989.49	945.11	910.19	882.30	859.77	841.40
58000	1249.39	1142.96	1065.34	1006.85	961.69	926.16	897.78	874.86	856.16
59000	1270.93	1162.67	1083.71	1024.21	978.27	942.13	913.26	889.94	870.92
60000	1292.47	1182.37	1102.08	1041.57	994.85	958.09	928.74	905.03	885.68
61000	1314.01	1202.08	1120.44	1058.93	1011.43	974.06	944.22	920.11	900.44
62000	1335.55	1221.79	1138.81	1076.29	1028.01	990.03	959.70	935.19	915.20
63000	1357.09	1241.49	1157.18	1093.65	1044.59	1006.00	975.18	950.28	929.96
64000	1378.64	1261.20	1175.55	1111.01	1061.17	1021.97	990.66	965.36	944.73
65000	1400.18	1280.91	1193.91	1128.37	1077.76	1037.93	1006.14	980.44	959.49
66000	1421.72	1300.61	1212.28	1145.73	1094.34	1053.90	1021.61	995.53	974.25
67000	1443.26	1320.32	1230.65	1163.09	1110.92	1069.87	1037.09	1010.61	989.01
68000	1464.80	1340.02	1249.02	1180.45	1127.50	1085.84	1052.57	1025.69	1003.77
69000	1486.34	1359.73	1267.39	1197.80	1144.08	1101.81	1068.05	1040.78	1018.53
70000	1507.88	1379.44	1285.75	1215.16	1160.66	1117.77	1083.53	1055.86	1033.29
75000	1615.59	1477.97	1377.59	1301.96	1243.56	1197.62	1160.93	1131.28	1107.10
80000	1723.29	1576.50	1469.43	1388.76	1326.47	1277.46	1238.32	1206.70	1180.91
100000	2154.12	1970.62	1836.79	1735.95	1658.08	1596.82	1547.90	1508.37	1476.13

153

16¼% MONTHLY PAYMENT
NECESSARY TO AMORTIZE A LOAN

TERM AMOUNT	15 YEARS	16 YEARS	17 YEARS	18 YEARS	19 YEARS	20 YEARS	21 YEARS	22 YEARS	23 YEARS
$ 25	.37	.36	.36	.35	.35	.35	.35	.34	.34
50	.73	.72	.71	.70	.70	.69	.69	.68	.68
75	1.09	1.08	1.06	1.05	1.04	1.03	1.03	1.02	1.02
100	1.45	1.43	1.41	1.40	1.39	1.38	1.37	1.36	1.35
200	2.90	2.86	2.82	2.79	2.77	2.75	2.73	2.71	2.70
300	4.35	4.29	4.23	4.19	4.15	4.12	4.09	4.07	4.05
400	5.80	5.72	5.64	5.58	5.53	5.49	5.45	5.42	5.40
500	7.25	7.14	7.05	6.98	6.91	6.86	6.81	6.78	6.74
600	8.70	8.57	8.46	8.37	8.29	8.23	8.17	8.13	8.09
700	10.15	10.00	9.87	9.76	9.68	9.60	9.54	9.48	9.44
800	11.60	11.43	11.28	11.16	11.06	10.97	10.90	10.84	10.79
900	13.05	12.85	12.69	12.55	12.44	12.34	12.26	12.19	12.13
1000	14.50	14.28	14.10	13.95	13.82	13.71	13.62	13.55	13.48
2000	29.00	28.56	28.19	27.89	27.63	27.42	27.24	27.09	26.96
3000	43.49	42.84	42.29	41.83	41.45	41.13	40.85	40.63	40.43
4000	57.99	57.11	56.38	55.77	55.26	54.83	54.47	54.17	53.91
5000	72.49	71.39	70.48	69.72	69.08	68.54	68.09	67.71	67.38
6000	86.98	85.67	84.57	83.66	82.89	82.25	81.70	81.25	80.86
7000	101.48	99.94	98.67	97.60	96.71	95.96	95.32	94.79	94.33
8000	115.97	114.22	112.76	111.54	110.52	109.66	108.94	108.33	107.81
9000	130.47	128.50	126.86	125.49	124.34	123.37	122.55	121.87	121.28
10000	144.97	142.77	140.95	139.43	138.15	137.08	136.17	135.41	134.76
15000	217.45	214.16	211.42	209.14	207.22	205.61	204.25	203.11	202.14
20000	289.93	285.54	281.90	278.85	276.30	274.15	272.34	270.81	269.51
25000	362.41	356.93	352.37	348.56	345.37	342.68	340.42	338.51	336.89
30000	434.89	428.31	422.84	418.27	414.44	411.22	408.50	406.21	404.27
35000	507.37	499.70	493.32	487.98	483.51	479.76	476.59	473.91	471.64
36000	521.87	513.98	507.41	501.93	497.33	493.46	490.20	487.45	485.12
37000	536.36	528.25	521.50	515.87	511.14	507.17	503.82	500.99	498.59
38000	550.86	542.53	535.60	529.81	524.96	520.88	517.44	514.53	512.07
39000	565.36	556.81	549.69	543.75	538.77	534.59	531.05	528.07	525.54
40000	579.85	571.08	563.79	557.70	552.59	548.29	544.67	541.61	539.02
41000	594.35	585.36	577.88	571.64	566.40	562.00	558.29	555.15	552.50
42000	608.85	599.64	591.98	585.58	580.22	575.71	571.90	568.69	565.97
43000	623.34	613.91	606.07	599.52	594.03	589.41	585.52	582.23	579.45
44000	637.84	628.19	620.17	613.46	607.85	603.12	599.14	595.77	592.92
45000	652.33	642.47	634.26	627.41	621.66	616.83	612.75	609.31	606.40
46000	666.83	656.74	648.36	641.35	635.48	630.54	626.37	622.85	619.87
47000	681.33	671.02	662.45	655.29	649.29	644.24	639.99	636.39	633.35
48000	695.82	685.30	676.55	669.23	663.10	657.95	653.60	649.93	646.82
49000	710.32	699.58	690.64	683.18	676.92	671.66	667.22	663.47	660.30
50000	724.82	713.85	704.73	697.12	690.73	685.36	680.84	677.01	673.77
51000	739.31	728.13	718.83	711.06	704.55	699.07	694.45	690.55	687.25
52000	753.81	742.41	732.92	725.00	718.36	712.78	708.07	704.09	700.72
53000	768.30	756.68	747.02	738.95	732.18	726.49	721.69	717.63	714.20
54000	782.80	770.96	761.11	752.89	745.99	740.19	735.30	731.17	727.68
55000	797.30	785.24	775.21	766.83	759.81	753.90	748.92	744.71	741.15
56000	811.79	799.51	789.30	780.77	773.62	767.61	762.54	758.25	754.63
57000	826.29	813.79	803.40	794.71	787.44	781.31	776.15	771.79	768.10
58000	840.79	828.07	817.49	808.66	801.25	795.02	789.77	785.33	781.58
59000	855.28	842.34	831.59	822.60	815.06	808.73	803.39	798.87	795.05
60000	869.78	856.62	845.68	836.54	828.88	822.44	817.00	812.41	808.53
61000	884.27	870.90	859.78	850.48	842.69	836.14	830.62	825.95	822.00
62000	898.77	885.18	873.87	864.43	856.51	849.85	844.24	839.49	835.48
63000	913.27	899.45	887.96	878.37	870.32	863.56	857.85	853.03	848.95
64000	927.76	913.73	902.06	892.31	884.14	877.26	871.47	866.57	862.43
65000	942.26	928.01	916.15	906.25	897.95	890.97	885.09	880.11	875.90
66000	956.76	942.28	930.25	920.19	911.77	904.68	898.70	893.65	889.38
67000	971.25	956.56	944.34	934.14	925.58	918.39	912.32	907.19	902.86
68000	985.75	970.84	958.44	948.08	939.40	932.09	925.94	920.73	916.33
69000	1000.24	985.11	972.53	962.02	953.21	945.80	939.55	934.27	929.81
70000	1014.74	999.39	986.63	975.96	967.02	959.51	953.17	947.81	943.28
75000	1087.22	1070.78	1057.10	1045.68	1036.10	1028.04	1021.25	1015.52	1010.66
80000	1159.70	1142.16	1127.57	1115.39	1105.17	1096.58	1089.34	1083.22	1078.04
100000	1449.63	1427.70	1409.46	1394.23	1381.46	1370.72	1361.67	1354.02	1347.54

MONTHLY PAYMENT 16¼%
NECESSARY TO AMORTIZE A LOAN

TERM AMOUNT	24 YEARS	25 YEARS	26 YEARS	27 YEARS	28 YEARS	29 YEARS	30 YEARS	35 YEARS	40 YEARS
$ 25	.34	.34	.34	.34	.34	.34	.34	.33	.33
50	.68	.67	.67	.67	.67	.67	.67	.66	.66
75	1.01	1.01	1.01	1.00	1.00	1.00	1.00	.99	.99
100	1.35	1.34	1.34	1.34	1.33	1.33	1.33	1.32	1.32
200	2.69	2.68	2.67	2.67	2.66	2.65	2.65	2.64	2.63
300	4.03	4.02	4.01	4.00	3.99	3.98	3.97	3.95	3.94
400	5.37	5.35	5.34	5.33	5.31	5.30	5.30	5.27	5.26
500	6.72	6.69	6.67	6.66	6.64	6.63	6.62	6.59	6.57
600	8.06	8.03	8.01	7.99	7.97	7.95	7.94	7.90	7.88
700	9.40	9.37	9.34	9.32	9.30	9.28	9.26	9.22	9.20
800	10.74	10.70	10.67	10.65	10.62	10.60	10.59	10.53	10.51
900	12.08	12.04	12.01	11.98	11.95	11.93	11.91	11.85	11.82
1000	13.43	13.38	13.34	13.31	13.28	13.25	13.23	13.17	13.14
2000	26.85	26.75	26.67	26.61	26.55	26.50	26.46	26.33	26.27
3000	40.27	40.13	40.01	39.91	39.82	39.75	39.68	39.49	39.40
4000	53.69	53.50	53.34	53.21	53.09	52.99	52.91	52.65	52.53
5000	67.11	66.87	66.68	66.51	66.36	66.24	66.14	65.81	65.66
6000	80.53	80.25	80.01	79.81	79.64	79.49	79.36	78.97	78.79
7000	93.95	93.62	93.34	93.11	92.91	92.74	92.59	92.13	91.92
8000	107.37	107.00	106.68	106.41	106.18	105.98	105.82	105.29	105.05
9000	120.79	120.37	120.01	119.71	119.45	119.23	119.04	118.45	118.18
10000	134.21	133.74	133.35	133.01	132.72	132.48	132.27	131.61	131.31
15000	201.31	200.61	200.02	199.51	199.08	198.72	198.40	197.41	196.96
20000	268.41	267.48	266.69	266.02	265.44	264.95	264.54	263.21	262.61
25000	335.52	334.35	333.36	332.52	331.80	331.19	330.67	329.01	328.26
30000	402.62	401.22	400.03	399.02	398.16	397.43	396.80	394.81	393.91
35000	469.72	468.09	466.70	465.53	464.52	463.67	462.94	460.61	459.56
36000	483.14	481.46	480.04	478.83	477.79	476.91	476.16	473.77	472.69
37000	496.56	494.84	493.37	492.13	491.06	490.16	489.39	486.94	485.82
38000	509.98	508.21	506.71	505.43	504.34	503.41	502.62	500.10	498.95
39000	523.40	521.59	520.04	518.73	517.61	516.66	515.84	513.26	512.08
40000	536.82	534.96	533.38	532.03	530.88	529.90	529.07	526.42	525.21
41000	550.24	548.33	546.71	545.33	544.15	543.15	542.30	539.58	538.34
42000	563.67	561.71	560.04	558.63	557.42	556.40	555.52	552.74	551.47
43000	577.09	575.08	573.38	571.93	570.70	569.65	568.75	565.90	564.60
44000	590.51	588.46	586.71	585.23	583.97	582.89	581.98	579.06	577.73
45000	603.93	601.83	600.05	598.53	597.24	596.14	595.20	592.22	590.86
46000	617.35	615.20	613.38	611.83	610.51	609.39	608.43	605.38	603.99
47000	630.77	628.58	626.72	625.13	623.78	622.64	621.66	618.54	617.12
48000	644.19	641.95	640.05	638.43	637.06	635.88	634.88	631.70	630.25
49000	657.61	655.33	653.38	651.73	650.33	649.13	648.11	644.86	643.38
50000	671.03	668.70	666.72	665.03	663.60	662.38	661.34	658.02	656.51
51000	684.45	682.07	680.05	678.33	676.87	675.63	674.56	671.18	669.64
52000	697.87	695.45	693.39	691.63	690.14	688.87	687.79	684.34	682.77
53000	711.29	708.82	706.72	704.94	703.42	702.12	701.02	697.50	695.90
54000	724.71	722.19	720.06	718.24	716.69	715.37	714.24	710.66	709.03
55000	738.13	735.57	733.39	731.54	729.96	728.61	727.47	723.82	722.16
56000	751.55	748.94	746.72	744.84	743.23	741.86	740.70	736.98	735.29
57000	764.97	762.32	760.06	758.14	756.50	755.11	753.92	750.14	748.42
58000	778.39	775.69	773.39	771.44	769.77	768.36	767.15	763.30	761.55
59000	791.81	789.06	786.73	784.74	783.05	781.60	780.38	776.46	774.68
60000	805.23	802.44	800.06	798.04	796.32	794.85	793.60	789.62	787.81
61000	818.65	815.81	813.40	811.34	809.59	808.10	806.83	802.78	800.94
62000	832.07	829.19	826.73	824.64	822.86	821.35	820.06	815.94	814.07
63000	845.50	842.56	840.06	837.94	836.13	834.59	833.28	829.10	827.20
64000	858.92	855.93	853.40	851.24	849.41	847.84	846.51	842.26	840.33
65000	872.34	869.31	866.73	864.54	862.68	861.09	859.74	855.42	853.46
66000	885.76	882.68	880.07	877.84	875.95	874.34	872.96	868.58	866.59
67000	899.18	896.05	893.40	891.14	889.22	887.58	886.19	881.74	879.72
68000	912.60	909.43	906.74	904.44	902.49	900.83	899.42	894.90	892.85
69000	926.02	922.80	920.07	917.74	915.77	914.08	912.64	908.06	905.98
70000	939.44	936.18	933.40	931.05	929.04	927.33	925.87	921.22	919.11
75000	1006.54	1003.05	1000.08	997.55	995.40	993.56	992.00	987.03	984.76
80000	1073.64	1069.92	1066.75	1064.05	1061.76	1059.80	1058.13	1052.83	1050.41
100000	1342.05	1337.39	1333.43	1330.06	1327.19	1324.75	1322.67	1316.03	1313.02

155

16½% MONTHLY PAYMENT
NECESSARY TO AMORTIZE A LOAN

TERM AMOUNT	1 YEAR	1½ YEARS	2 YEARS	2½ YEARS	3 YEARS	3½ YEARS	4 YEARS	4½ YEARS	5 YEARS
$ 25	2.27	1.58	1.23	1.02	.88	.79	.71	.66	.61
50	4.54	3.15	2.45	2.04	1.76	1.57	1.42	1.31	1.22
75	6.81	4.72	3.68	3.05	2.64	2.35	2.13	1.96	1.83
100	9.08	6.29	4.90	4.07	3.52	3.13	2.84	2.61	2.43
200	18.15	12.57	9.79	8.13	7.03	6.25	5.67	5.22	4.86
300	27.22	18.86	14.69	12.20	10.55	9.37	8.50	7.83	7.29
400	36.29	25.14	19.58	16.26	14.06	12.50	11.33	10.44	9.72
500	45.36	31.42	24.48	20.33	17.57	15.62	14.16	13.04	12.15
600	54.43	37.71	29.37	24.39	21.09	18.74	17.00	15.65	14.58
700	63.50	43.99	34.27	28.45	24.60	21.87	19.83	18.26	17.01
800	72.57	50.27	39.16	32.52	28.11	24.99	22.66	20.87	19.44
900	81.65	56.56	44.05	36.58	31.63	28.11	25.49	23.47	21.87
1000	90.72	62.84	48.95	40.65	35.14	31.23	28.32	26.08	24.30
2000	181.43	125.68	97.89	81.29	70.28	62.46	56.64	52.16	48.60
3000	272.14	188.52	146.84	121.93	105.42	93.69	84.96	78.23	72.90
4000	362.85	251.35	195.78	162.58	140.55	124.92	113.28	104.31	97.19
5000	453.56	314.19	244.72	203.22	175.69	156.15	141.60	130.38	121.49
6000	544.28	377.03	293.67	243.86	210.83	187.38	169.92	156.46	145.79
7000	634.99	439.87	342.61	284.50	245.97	218.61	198.24	182.53	170.08
8000	725.70	502.70	391.56	325.15	281.10	249.84	226.56	208.61	194.38
9000	816.41	565.54	440.50	365.79	316.24	281.07	254.88	234.68	218.68
10000	907.12	628.38	489.44	406.43	351.38	312.30	283.20	260.76	242.97
15000	1360.68	942.57	734.16	609.64	527.06	468.44	424.80	391.14	364.46
20000	1814.24	1256.75	978.88	812.86	702.75	624.59	566.40	521.51	485.94
25000	2267.80	1570.94	1223.60	1016.07	878.44	780.74	708.00	651.89	607.42
30000	2721.36	1885.13	1468.32	1219.28	1054.12	936.88	849.60	782.27	728.91
35000	3174.92	2199.32	1713.04	1422.50	1229.81	1093.03	991.20	912.65	850.39
36000	3265.63	2262.15	1761.99	1463.14	1264.94	1124.26	1019.51	938.72	874.69
37000	3356.34	2324.99	1810.93	1503.78	1300.08	1155.49	1047.83	964.80	898.98
38000	3447.06	2387.83	1859.87	1544.42	1335.22	1186.72	1076.15	990.87	923.28
39000	3537.77	2450.67	1908.82	1585.07	1370.36	1217.95	1104.47	1016.95	947.58
40000	3628.48	2513.50	1957.76	1625.71	1405.49	1249.18	1132.79	1043.02	971.87
41000	3719.19	2576.34	2006.71	1666.35	1440.63	1280.41	1161.11	1069.10	996.17
42000	3809.90	2639.18	2055.65	1706.99	1475.77	1311.64	1189.43	1095.17	1020.47
43000	3900.61	2702.02	2104.59	1747.64	1510.90	1342.87	1217.75	1121.25	1044.76
44000	3991.33	2764.85	2153.54	1788.28	1546.04	1374.10	1246.07	1147.32	1069.06
45000	4082.04	2827.69	2202.48	1828.92	1581.18	1405.32	1274.39	1173.40	1093.36
46000	4172.75	2890.53	2251.43	1869.56	1616.32	1436.55	1302.71	1199.48	1117.65
47000	4263.46	2953.37	2300.37	1910.21	1651.45	1467.78	1331.03	1225.55	1141.95
48000	4354.17	3016.20	2349.31	1950.85	1686.59	1499.01	1359.35	1251.63	1166.25
49000	4444.89	3079.04	2398.26	1991.49	1721.73	1530.24	1387.67	1277.70	1190.54
50000	4535.60	3141.88	2447.20	2032.13	1756.87	1561.47	1415.99	1303.78	1214.84
51000	4626.31	3204.71	2496.15	2072.78	1792.00	1592.70	1444.31	1329.85	1239.14
52000	4717.02	3267.55	2545.09	2113.42	1827.14	1623.93	1472.63	1355.93	1263.43
53000	4807.73	3330.39	2594.03	2154.06	1862.28	1655.16	1500.95	1382.00	1287.73
54000	4898.45	3393.23	2642.98	2194.71	1897.41	1686.39	1529.27	1408.08	1312.03
55000	4989.16	3456.06	2691.92	2235.35	1932.55	1717.62	1557.59	1434.15	1336.32
56000	5079.87	3518.90	2740.86	2275.99	1967.69	1748.85	1585.91	1460.23	1360.62
57000	5170.58	3581.74	2789.81	2316.63	2002.83	1780.08	1614.23	1486.31	1384.92
58000	5261.29	3644.58	2838.75	2357.28	2037.96	1811.31	1642.55	1512.38	1409.21
59000	5352.00	3707.41	2887.70	2397.92	2073.10	1842.54	1670.87	1538.46	1433.51
60000	5442.72	3770.25	2936.64	2438.56	2108.24	1873.76	1699.19	1564.53	1457.81
61000	5533.43	3833.09	2985.58	2479.20	2143.37	1904.99	1727.51	1590.61	1482.11
62000	5624.14	3895.93	3034.53	2519.85	2178.51	1936.22	1755.83	1616.68	1506.40
63000	5714.85	3958.76	3083.47	2560.49	2213.65	1967.45	1784.15	1642.76	1530.70
64000	5805.56	4021.60	3132.42	2601.13	2248.79	1998.68	1812.47	1668.83	1555.00
65000	5896.28	4084.44	3181.36	2641.77	2283.92	2029.91	1840.79	1694.91	1579.29
66000	5986.99	4147.28	3230.30	2682.42	2319.06	2061.14	1869.11	1720.98	1603.59
67000	6077.70	4210.11	3279.25	2723.06	2354.20	2092.37	1897.43	1747.06	1627.89
68000	6168.41	4272.95	3328.19	2763.70	2389.34	2123.60	1925.75	1773.13	1652.18
69000	6259.12	4335.79	3377.14	2804.34	2424.47	2154.83	1954.07	1799.21	1676.48
70000	6349.83	4398.63	3426.08	2844.99	2459.61	2186.06	1982.39	1825.29	1700.78
75000	6803.39	4712.81	3670.80	3048.20	2635.30	2342.20	2123.98	1955.66	1822.26
80000	7256.95	5027.00	3915.52	3251.41	2810.98	2498.35	2265.58	2086.04	1943.74
100000	9071.19	6283.75	4894.40	4064.26	3513.73	3122.94	2831.98	2607.55	2429.68

156

MONTHLY PAYMENT 16½%
NECESSARY TO AMORTIZE A LOAN

TERM AMOUNT	6 YEARS	7 YEARS	8 YEARS	9 YEARS	10 YEARS	11 YEARS	12 YEARS	13 YEARS	14 YEARS
$ 25	.55	.50	.47	.44	.42	.41	.40	.39	.38
50	1.09	1.00	.93	.88	.84	.81	.79	.77	.75
75	1.63	1.49	1.39	1.32	1.26	1.21	1.18	1.15	1.12
100	2.17	1.99	1.86	1.76	1.68	1.62	1.57	1.53	1.50
200	4.34	3.97	3.71	3.51	3.35	3.23	3.13	3.05	2.99
300	6.51	5.96	5.56	5.26	5.02	4.84	4.69	4.58	4.48
400	8.67	7.94	7.41	7.01	6.70	6.45	6.26	6.10	5.97
500	10.84	9.92	9.26	8.76	8.37	8.06	7.82	7.63	7.47
600	13.01	11.91	11.11	10.51	10.04	9.68	9.38	9.15	8.96
700	15.17	13.89	12.96	12.26	11.71	11.29	10.95	10.67	10.45
800	17.34	15.88	14.81	14.01	13.39	12.90	12.51	12.20	11.94
900	19.51	17.86	16.66	15.76	15.06	14.51	14.07	13.72	13.43
1000	21.67	19.84	18.51	17.51	16.73	16.12	15.64	15.25	14.93
2000	43.34	39.68	37.02	35.01	33.46	32.24	31.27	30.49	29.85
3000	65.01	59.52	55.52	52.51	50.18	48.36	46.90	45.73	44.77
4000	86.68	79.36	74.03	70.01	66.91	64.47	62.53	60.97	59.69
5000	108.35	99.20	92.53	87.51	83.64	80.59	78.16	76.21	74.61
6000	130.02	119.04	111.04	105.01	100.36	96.71	93.80	91.45	89.53
7000	151.69	138.88	129.54	122.51	117.09	112.83	109.43	106.69	104.45
8000	173.36	158.72	148.05	140.01	133.82	128.94	125.06	121.93	119.37
9000	195.03	178.56	166.55	157.51	150.54	145.06	140.69	137.17	134.29
10000	216.70	198.40	185.06	175.01	167.27	161.18	156.32	152.41	149.21
15000	325.05	297.59	277.58	262.52	250.90	241.77	234.48	228.61	223.82
20000	433.40	396.79	370.11	350.02	334.53	322.35	312.64	304.81	298.42
25000	541.75	495.98	462.63	437.53	418.16	402.94	390.80	381.01	373.03
30000	650.10	595.18	555.16	525.03	501.79	483.53	468.96	457.21	447.63
35000	758.45	694.38	647.69	612.54	585.43	564.12	547.12	533.41	522.24
36000	780.12	714.22	666.19	630.04	602.15	580.23	562.75	548.65	537.16
37000	801.79	734.06	684.70	647.54	618.88	596.35	578.39	563.89	552.08
38000	823.45	753.89	703.20	665.04	635.60	612.47	594.02	579.13	567.00
39000	845.12	773.73	721.71	682.54	652.33	628.59	609.65	594.37	581.92
40000	866.79	793.57	740.21	700.04	669.06	644.70	625.28	609.61	596.84
41000	888.46	813.41	758.72	717.54	685.78	660.82	640.91	624.85	611.77
42000	910.13	833.25	777.22	735.04	702.51	676.94	656.55	640.09	626.69
43000	931.80	853.09	795.73	752.54	719.24	693.06	672.18	655.33	641.61
44000	953.47	872.93	814.23	770.05	735.96	709.17	687.81	670.57	656.53
45000	975.14	892.77	832.74	787.55	752.69	725.29	703.44	685.81	671.45
46000	996.81	912.61	851.24	805.05	769.41	741.41	719.07	701.05	686.37
47000	1018.48	932.45	869.75	822.55	786.14	757.53	734.71	716.29	701.29
48000	1040.15	952.29	888.25	840.05	802.87	773.64	750.34	731.53	716.21
49000	1061.82	972.13	906.76	857.55	819.59	789.76	765.97	746.77	731.13
50000	1083.49	991.96	925.26	875.05	836.32	805.88	781.60	762.01	746.05
51000	1105.16	1011.80	943.77	892.55	853.05	822.00	797.23	777.25	760.98
52000	1126.83	1031.64	962.27	910.05	869.77	838.11	812.87	792.49	775.90
53000	1148.50	1051.48	980.78	927.55	886.50	854.23	828.50	807.73	790.82
54000	1170.17	1071.32	999.28	945.05	903.22	870.35	844.13	822.97	805.74
55000	1191.84	1091.16	1017.79	962.56	919.95	886.47	859.76	838.21	820.66
56000	1213.51	1111.00	1036.29	980.06	936.68	902.58	875.39	853.45	835.58
57000	1235.18	1130.84	1054.80	997.56	953.40	918.70	891.03	868.69	850.50
58000	1256.85	1150.68	1073.31	1015.06	970.13	934.82	906.66	883.93	865.42
59000	1278.52	1170.52	1091.81	1032.56	986.86	950.94	922.29	899.17	880.34
60000	1300.19	1190.36	1110.32	1050.06	1003.58	967.05	937.92	914.41	895.26
61000	1321.86	1210.20	1128.82	1067.56	1020.31	983.17	953.55	929.65	910.19
62000	1343.53	1230.04	1147.33	1085.06	1037.04	999.29	969.19	944.89	925.11
63000	1365.20	1249.87	1165.83	1102.56	1053.76	1015.41	984.82	960.13	940.03
64000	1386.87	1269.71	1184.34	1120.06	1070.49	1031.52	1000.45	975.37	954.95
65000	1408.54	1289.55	1202.84	1137.56	1087.21	1047.64	1016.08	990.61	969.87
66000	1430.21	1309.39	1221.35	1155.07	1103.94	1063.76	1031.71	1005.85	984.79
67000	1451.88	1329.23	1239.85	1172.57	1120.67	1079.88	1047.35	1021.09	999.71
68000	1473.55	1349.07	1258.36	1190.07	1137.39	1095.99	1062.98	1036.33	1014.63
69000	1495.22	1368.91	1276.86	1207.57	1154.12	1112.11	1078.61	1051.57	1029.55
70000	1516.89	1388.75	1295.37	1225.07	1170.85	1128.23	1094.24	1066.81	1044.47
75000	1625.24	1487.94	1387.89	1312.57	1254.48	1208.82	1172.40	1143.02	1119.08
80000	1733.58	1587.14	1480.42	1400.08	1338.11	1289.40	1250.56	1219.22	1193.68
100000	2166.98	1983.92	1850.52	1750.10	1672.63	1611.75	1563.20	1524.02	1492.10

157

16½% MONTHLY PAYMENT
NECESSARY TO AMORTIZE A LOAN

TERM AMOUNT	15 YEARS	16 YEARS	17 YEARS	18 YEARS	19 YEARS	20 YEARS	21 YEARS	22 YEARS	23 YEARS
$ 25	.37	.37	.36	.36	.35	.35	.35	.35	.35
50	.74	.73	.72	.71	.70	.70	.69	.69	.69
75	1.10	1.09	1.07	1.06	1.05	1.05	1.04	1.03	1.03
100	1.47	1.45	1.43	1.42	1.40	1.39	1.38	1.38	1.37
200	2.94	2.89	2.86	2.83	2.80	2.78	2.76	2.75	2.74
300	4.40	4.34	4.28	4.24	4.20	4.17	4.14	4.12	4.10
400	5.87	5.78	5.71	5.65	5.60	5.56	5.52	5.49	5.47
500	7.33	7.23	7.14	7.06	7.00	6.95	6.90	6.86	6.83
600	8.80	8.67	8.56	8.47	8.40	8.33	8.28	8.24	8.20
700	10.27	10.11	9.99	9.88	9.80	9.72	9.66	9.61	9.56
800	11.73	11.56	11.42	11.30	11.20	11.11	11.04	10.98	10.93
900	13.20	13.00	12.84	12.71	12.59	12.50	12.42	12.35	12.30
1000	14.66	14.45	14.27	14.12	13.99	13.89	13.80	13.72	13.66
2000	29.32	28.89	28.53	28.23	27.98	27.77	27.59	27.44	27.32
3000	43.98	43.33	42.79	42.34	41.97	41.65	41.39	41.16	40.97
4000	58.64	57.78	57.06	56.46	55.96	55.53	55.18	54.88	54.63
5000	73.30	72.22	71.32	70.57	69.94	69.42	68.97	68.60	68.29
6000	87.96	86.66	85.58	84.68	83.93	83.30	82.77	82.32	81.94
7000	102.62	101.10	99.85	98.80	97.92	97.18	96.56	96.04	95.60
8000	117.28	115.55	114.11	112.91	111.91	111.06	110.36	109.76	109.25
9000	131.94	129.99	128.37	127.02	125.89	124.95	124.15	123.48	122.91
10000	146.60	144.43	142.63	141.14	139.88	138.83	137.94	137.20	136.57
15000	219.89	216.64	213.95	211.70	209.82	208.24	206.91	205.79	204.85
20000	293.19	288.86	285.26	282.27	279.76	277.65	275.88	274.39	273.13
25000	366.48	361.07	356.58	352.83	349.70	347.07	344.85	342.98	341.41
30000	439.78	433.28	427.89	423.40	419.64	416.48	413.82	411.58	409.69
35000	513.07	505.50	499.21	493.96	489.57	485.89	482.79	480.17	477.97
36000	527.73	519.94	513.47	508.08	503.56	499.77	496.58	493.89	491.62
37000	542.39	534.38	527.73	522.19	517.55	513.66	510.38	507.61	505.28
38000	557.05	548.82	542.00	536.30	531.54	527.54	524.17	521.33	518.93
39000	571.71	563.27	556.26	550.42	545.53	541.42	537.97	535.05	532.59
40000	586.37	577.71	570.52	564.53	559.51	555.30	551.76	548.77	546.25
41000	601.02	592.15	584.79	578.64	573.50	569.18	565.55	562.49	559.90
42000	615.68	606.59	599.05	592.76	587.49	583.07	579.35	576.21	573.56
43000	630.34	621.04	613.31	606.87	601.48	596.95	593.14	589.93	587.21
44000	645.00	635.48	627.57	620.98	615.46	610.83	606.93	603.65	600.87
45000	659.66	649.92	641.84	635.09	629.45	624.71	620.73	617.37	614.53
46000	674.32	664.37	656.10	649.21	643.44	638.60	634.52	631.09	628.18
47000	688.98	678.81	670.36	663.32	657.43	652.48	648.32	644.80	641.84
48000	703.64	693.25	684.63	677.43	671.41	666.36	662.11	658.52	655.49
49000	718.30	707.69	698.89	691.55	685.40	680.24	675.90	672.24	669.15
50000	732.96	722.14	713.15	705.66	699.39	694.13	689.70	685.96	682.81
51000	747.61	736.58	727.41	719.77	713.38	708.01	703.49	699.68	696.46
52000	762.27	751.02	741.68	733.89	727.37	721.89	717.29	713.40	710.12
53000	776.93	765.46	755.94	748.00	741.35	735.77	731.08	727.12	723.77
54000	791.59	779.91	770.20	762.11	755.34	749.66	744.87	740.84	737.43
55000	806.25	794.35	784.47	776.23	769.33	763.54	758.67	754.56	751.09
56000	820.91	808.79	798.73	790.34	783.32	777.42	772.46	768.28	764.74
57000	835.57	823.23	812.99	804.45	797.30	791.30	786.25	782.00	778.40
58000	850.23	837.68	827.26	818.56	811.29	805.19	800.05	795.72	792.05
59000	864.89	852.12	841.52	832.68	825.28	819.07	813.84	809.43	805.71
60000	879.55	866.56	855.78	846.79	839.27	832.95	827.64	823.15	819.37
61000	894.20	881.00	870.04	860.90	853.25	846.83	841.43	836.87	833.02
62000	908.86	895.45	884.31	875.02	867.24	860.72	855.22	850.59	846.68
63000	923.52	909.89	898.57	889.13	881.23	874.60	869.02	864.31	860.33
64000	938.18	924.33	912.83	903.24	895.22	888.48	882.81	878.03	873.99
65000	952.84	938.78	927.10	917.36	909.21	902.36	896.61	891.75	887.65
66000	967.50	953.22	941.36	931.47	923.19	916.25	910.40	905.47	901.30
67000	982.16	967.66	955.62	945.58	937.18	930.13	924.19	919.19	914.96
68000	996.82	982.10	969.88	959.70	951.17	944.01	937.99	932.91	928.61
69000	1011.48	996.55	984.15	973.81	965.16	957.89	951.78	946.63	942.27
70000	1026.14	1010.99	998.41	987.92	979.14	971.78	965.57	960.34	955.93
75000	1099.43	1083.20	1069.73	1058.49	1049.08	1041.19	1034.54	1028.94	1024.21
80000	1172.73	1155.41	1141.04	1129.05	1119.02	1110.60	1103.51	1097.54	1092.49
100000	1465.91	1444.27	1426.30	1411.32	1398.78	1388.25	1379.39	1371.92	1365.61

158

MONTHLY PAYMENT 16½%
NECESSARY TO AMORTIZE A LOAN

TERM AMOUNT	24 YEARS	25 YEARS	26 YEARS	27 YEARS	28 YEARS	29 YEARS	30 YEARS	35 YEARS	40 YEARS
$ 25	.35	.34	.34	.34	.34	.34	.34	.34	.34
50	.69	.68	.68	.68	.68	.68	.68	.67	.67
75	1.03	1.02	1.02	1.02	1.01	1.01	1.01	1.01	1.00
100	1.37	1.36	1.36	1.36	1.35	1.35	1.35	1.34	1.34
200	2.73	2.72	2.71	2.70	2.70	2.69	2.69	2.68	2.67
300	4.09	4.07	4.06	4.05	4.04	4.04	4.03	4.01	4.00
400	5.45	5.43	5.41	5.40	5.39	5.38	5.37	5.35	5.33
500	6.81	6.78	6.76	6.75	6.73	6.72	6.71	6.68	6.67
600	8.17	8.14	8.12	8.10	8.08	8.07	8.05	8.02	8.00
700	9.53	9.50	9.47	9.45	9.43	9.41	9.40	9.35	9.33
800	10.89	10.85	10.82	10.79	10.77	10.75	10.74	10.69	10.66
900	12.25	12.21	12.17	12.14	12.12	12.10	12.08	12.02	12.00
1000	13.61	13.56	13.52	13.49	13.46	13.44	13.42	13.36	13.33
2000	27.21	27.12	27.04	26.98	26.92	26.88	26.84	26.71	26.65
3000	40.81	40.68	40.56	40.46	40.38	40.31	40.25	40.06	39.97
4000	54.42	54.23	54.08	53.95	53.84	53.75	53.67	53.41	53.30
5000	68.02	67.79	67.60	67.44	67.30	67.18	67.08	66.76	66.62
6000	81.62	81.35	81.12	80.92	80.76	80.62	80.50	80.12	79.94
7000	95.22	94.91	94.64	94.41	94.22	94.05	93.91	93.47	93.27
8000	108.83	108.46	108.16	107.90	107.67	107.49	107.33	106.82	106.59
9000	122.43	122.02	121.68	121.38	121.13	120.92	120.74	120.17	119.91
10000	136.03	135.58	135.19	134.87	134.59	134.36	134.16	133.52	133.24
15000	204.04	203.37	202.79	202.30	201.89	201.53	201.23	200.28	199.85
20000	272.06	271.15	270.38	269.73	269.18	268.71	268.31	267.04	266.47
25000	340.07	338.94	337.98	337.17	336.47	335.89	335.38	333.80	333.09
30000	408.08	406.73	405.57	404.60	403.77	403.06	402.46	400.56	399.70
35000	476.10	474.51	473.17	472.03	471.06	470.24	469.54	467.32	466.32
36000	489.70	488.07	486.69	485.52	484.52	483.67	482.95	480.67	479.64
37000	503.30	501.63	500.21	499.00	497.98	497.11	496.37	494.02	492.97
38000	516.90	515.18	513.73	512.49	511.44	510.54	509.78	507.37	506.29
39000	530.51	528.74	527.25	525.98	524.90	523.98	523.20	520.73	519.61
40000	544.11	542.30	540.76	539.46	538.35	537.41	536.61	534.08	532.94
41000	557.71	555.86	554.28	552.95	551.81	550.85	550.03	547.43	546.26
42000	571.31	569.41	567.80	566.43	565.27	564.28	563.44	560.78	559.58
43000	584.92	582.97	581.32	579.92	578.73	577.72	576.86	574.13	572.91
44000	598.52	596.53	594.84	593.41	592.19	591.15	590.27	587.48	586.23
45000	612.12	610.09	608.36	606.89	605.65	604.59	603.69	600.84	599.55
46000	625.73	623.64	621.88	620.38	619.11	618.02	617.10	614.19	612.88
47000	639.33	637.20	635.40	633.87	632.57	631.46	630.52	627.54	626.20
48000	652.93	650.76	648.92	647.35	646.02	644.89	643.93	640.89	639.52
49000	666.53	664.32	662.44	660.84	659.48	658.33	657.35	654.24	652.85
50000	680.14	677.87	675.95	674.33	672.94	671.77	670.76	667.60	666.17
51000	693.74	691.43	689.47	687.81	686.40	685.20	684.18	680.95	679.49
52000	707.34	704.99	702.99	701.30	699.86	698.64	697.59	694.30	692.82
53000	720.94	718.55	716.51	714.78	713.32	712.07	711.01	707.65	706.14
54000	734.55	732.10	730.03	728.27	726.78	725.51	724.43	721.00	719.46
55000	748.15	745.66	743.55	741.76	740.24	738.94	737.84	734.35	732.79
56000	761.75	759.22	757.07	755.24	753.69	752.38	751.26	747.71	746.11
57000	775.35	772.77	770.59	768.73	767.15	765.81	764.67	761.06	759.43
58000	788.96	786.33	784.11	782.22	780.61	779.25	778.09	774.41	772.76
59000	802.56	799.89	797.63	795.70	794.07	792.68	791.50	787.76	786.08
60000	816.16	813.45	811.14	809.19	807.53	806.12	804.92	801.11	799.40
61000	829.76	827.00	824.66	822.68	820.99	819.55	818.33	814.47	812.73
62000	843.37	840.56	838.18	836.16	834.45	832.99	831.75	827.82	826.05
63000	856.97	854.12	851.70	849.65	847.91	846.42	845.16	841.17	839.37
64000	870.57	867.68	865.22	863.14	861.36	859.86	858.58	854.52	852.70
65000	884.17	881.23	878.74	876.62	874.82	873.29	871.99	867.87	866.02
66000	897.78	894.79	892.26	890.11	888.28	886.73	885.41	881.22	879.34
67000	911.38	908.35	905.78	903.59	901.74	900.16	898.82	894.58	892.67
68000	924.98	921.91	919.30	917.08	915.20	913.60	912.24	907.93	905.99
69000	938.59	935.46	932.82	930.57	928.66	927.03	925.65	921.28	919.31
70000	952.19	949.02	946.33	944.05	942.12	940.47	939.07	934.63	932.64
75000	1020.20	1016.81	1013.93	1011.49	1009.41	1007.65	1006.14	1001.39	999.25
80000	1088.21	1084.59	1081.52	1078.92	1076.70	1074.82	1073.22	1068.15	1065.87
100000	1360.27	1355.74	1351.90	1348.65	1345.88	1343.53	1341.52	1335.19	1332.34

159

16¾% MONTHLY PAYMENT
NECESSARY TO AMORTIZE A LOAN

TERM AMOUNT	1 YEAR	1½ YEARS	2 YEARS	2½ YEARS	3 YEARS	3½ YEARS	4 YEARS	4½ YEARS	5 YEARS
$ 25	2.28	1.58	1.23	1.02	.89	.79	.72	.66	.62
50	4.55	3.15	2.46	2.04	1.77	1.57	1.43	1.31	1.23
75	6.82	4.73	3.68	3.06	2.65	2.36	2.14	1.97	1.84
100	9.09	6.30	4.91	4.08	3.53	3.14	2.85	2.62	2.45
200	18.17	12.59	9.82	8.16	7.06	6.27	5.69	5.24	4.89
300	27.25	18.89	14.72	12.23	10.58	9.41	8.54	7.86	7.33
400	36.33	25.18	19.63	16.31	14.11	12.54	11.38	10.48	9.77
500	45.42	31.48	24.53	20.38	17.63	15.68	14.22	13.10	12.22
600	54.50	37.77	29.44	24.46	21.16	18.81	17.07	15.72	14.66
700	63.58	44.07	34.34	28.53	24.68	21.95	19.91	18.34	17.10
800	72.66	50.36	39.25	32.61	28.21	25.08	22.76	20.96	19.54
900	81.75	56.66	44.16	36.69	31.73	28.22	25.60	23.58	21.98
1000	90.83	62.95	49.06	40.76	35.26	31.35	28.44	26.20	24.43
2000	181.65	125.90	98.12	81.52	70.51	62.70	56.88	52.40	48.85
3000	272.47	188.85	147.17	122.27	105.76	94.05	85.32	78.60	73.27
4000	363.30	251.80	196.23	163.03	141.02	125.39	113.76	104.80	97.69
5000	454.12	314.75	245.28	203.79	176.27	156.74	142.20	130.99	122.11
6000	544.94	377.69	294.34	244.54	211.52	188.09	170.64	157.19	146.53
7000	635.76	440.64	343.40	285.30	246.77	219.43	199.08	183.39	170.95
8000	726.59	503.59	392.45	326.05	282.03	250.78	227.52	209.59	195.37
9000	817.41	566.54	441.51	366.81	317.28	282.13	255.96	235.78	219.80
10000	908.23	629.49	490.56	407.57	352.53	313.48	284.40	261.98	244.22
15000	1362.34	944.23	735.84	611.35	528.80	470.21	426.60	392.97	366.32
20000	1816.46	1258.97	981.12	815.13	705.06	626.95	568.80	523.96	488.43
25000	2270.57	1573.71	1226.40	1018.91	881.32	783.68	711.00	654.94	610.53
30000	2724.68	1888.45	1471.68	1222.69	1057.59	940.42	853.19	785.93	732.64
35000	3178.79	2203.19	1716.96	1426.47	1233.85	1097.15	995.39	916.92	854.74
36000	3269.62	2266.13	1766.01	1467.23	1269.10	1128.50	1023.83	943.12	879.17
37000	3360.44	2329.08	1815.07	1507.98	1304.36	1159.84	1052.27	969.32	903.59
38000	3451.26	2392.03	1864.12	1548.74	1339.61	1191.19	1080.71	995.51	928.01
39000	3542.09	2454.98	1913.18	1589.49	1374.86	1222.54	1109.15	1021.71	952.43
40000	3632.91	2517.93	1962.23	1630.25	1410.12	1253.89	1137.59	1047.91	976.85
41000	3723.73	2580.87	2011.29	1671.01	1445.37	1285.23	1166.03	1074.11	1001.27
42000	3814.55	2643.82	2060.35	1711.76	1480.62	1316.58	1194.47	1100.30	1025.69
43000	3905.38	2706.77	2109.40	1752.52	1515.87	1347.93	1222.91	1126.50	1050.11
44000	3996.20	2769.72	2158.46	1793.28	1551.13	1379.27	1251.35	1152.70	1074.53
45000	4087.02	2832.67	2207.51	1834.03	1586.38	1410.62	1279.79	1178.90	1098.96
46000	4177.84	2895.61	2256.57	1874.79	1621.63	1441.97	1308.23	1205.09	1123.38
47000	4268.67	2958.56	2305.62	1915.54	1656.88	1473.31	1336.67	1231.29	1147.80
48000	4359.49	3021.51	2354.68	1956.30	1692.14	1504.66	1365.11	1257.49	1172.22
49000	4450.31	3084.46	2403.74	1997.06	1727.39	1536.01	1393.55	1283.69	1196.64
50000	4541.13	3147.41	2452.79	2037.81	1762.64	1567.36	1421.99	1309.88	1221.06
51000	4631.96	3210.36	2501.85	2078.57	1797.90	1598.70	1450.42	1336.08	1245.48
52000	4722.78	3273.30	2550.90	2119.32	1833.15	1630.05	1478.86	1362.28	1269.90
53000	4813.60	3336.25	2599.96	2160.08	1868.40	1661.40	1507.30	1388.48	1294.32
54000	4904.42	3399.20	2649.01	2200.84	1903.65	1692.74	1535.74	1414.67	1318.75
55000	4995.25	3462.15	2698.07	2241.59	1938.91	1724.09	1564.18	1440.87	1343.17
56000	5086.07	3525.10	2747.13	2282.35	1974.16	1755.44	1592.62	1467.07	1367.59
57000	5176.89	3588.04	2796.18	2323.11	2009.41	1786.78	1621.06	1493.27	1392.01
58000	5267.71	3650.99	2845.24	2363.86	2044.67	1818.13	1649.50	1519.46	1416.43
59000	5358.54	3713.94	2894.29	2404.62	2079.92	1849.48	1677.94	1545.66	1440.85
60000	5449.36	3776.89	2943.35	2445.37	2115.17	1880.83	1706.38	1571.86	1465.27
61000	5540.18	3839.84	2992.40	2486.13	2150.42	1912.17	1734.82	1598.06	1489.69
62000	5631.00	3902.78	3041.46	2526.89	2185.68	1943.52	1763.26	1624.25	1514.11
63000	5721.83	3965.73	3090.52	2567.64	2220.93	1974.87	1791.70	1650.45	1538.54
64000	5812.65	4028.68	3139.57	2608.40	2256.18	2006.21	1820.14	1676.65	1562.96
65000	5903.47	4091.63	3188.63	2649.15	2291.43	2037.56	1848.58	1702.85	1587.38
66000	5994.29	4154.58	3237.68	2689.91	2326.69	2068.91	1877.02	1729.04	1611.80
67000	6085.12	4217.52	3286.74	2730.67	2361.94	2100.25	1905.46	1755.24	1636.22
68000	6175.94	4280.47	3335.79	2771.42	2397.19	2131.60	1933.90	1781.44	1660.64
69000	6266.76	4343.42	3384.85	2812.18	2432.45	2162.95	1962.34	1807.64	1685.06
70000	6357.58	4406.37	3433.91	2852.94	2467.70	2194.30	1990.78	1833.84	1709.48
75000	6811.70	4721.11	3679.18	3056.72	2643.96	2351.03	2132.98	1964.82	1831.59
80000	7265.81	5035.85	3924.46	3260.50	2820.23	2507.77	2275.17	2095.81	1953.69
100000	9082.26	6294.81	4905.58	4075.62	3525.28	3134.71	2843.97	2619.76	2442.12

160

MONTHLY PAYMENT 16¾%
NECESSARY TO AMORTIZE A LOAN

TERM AMOUNT	6 YEARS	7 YEARS	8 YEARS	9 YEARS	10 YEARS	11 YEARS	12 YEARS	13 YEARS	14 YEARS
$ 25	.55	.50	.47	.45	.43	.41	.40	.39	.38
50	1.09	1.00	.94	.89	.85	.82	.79	.77	.76
75	1.64	1.50	1.40	1.33	1.27	1.23	1.19	1.16	1.14
100	2.18	2.00	1.87	1.77	1.69	1.63	1.58	1.54	1.51
200	4.36	4.00	3.73	3.53	3.38	3.26	3.16	3.08	3.02
300	6.54	6.00	5.60	5.30	5.07	4.89	4.74	4.62	4.53
400	8.72	7.99	7.46	7.06	6.75	6.51	6.32	6.16	6.04
500	10.90	9.99	9.33	8.83	8.44	8.14	7.90	7.70	7.55
600	13.08	11.99	11.19	10.59	10.13	9.77	9.48	9.24	9.05
700	15.26	13.99	13.06	12.35	11.82	11.39	11.05	10.78	10.56
800	17.44	15.98	14.92	14.12	13.50	13.02	12.63	12.32	12.07
900	19.62	17.98	16.78	15.88	15.19	14.65	14.21	13.86	13.58
1000	21.80	19.98	18.65	17.65	16.88	16.27	15.79	15.40	15.09
2000	43.60	39.95	37.29	35.29	33.75	32.54	31.58	30.80	30.17
3000	65.40	59.92	55.93	52.93	50.62	48.81	47.36	46.20	45.25
4000	87.20	79.90	74.58	70.58	67.49	65.07	63.15	61.59	60.33
5000	109.00	99.87	93.22	88.22	84.37	81.34	78.93	76.99	75.41
6000	130.80	119.84	111.86	105.86	101.24	97.61	94.72	92.39	90.49
7000	152.60	139.81	130.51	123.50	118.11	113.88	110.50	107.78	105.57
8000	174.39	159.79	149.15	141.15	134.98	130.14	126.29	123.18	120.65
9000	196.19	179.76	167.79	158.79	151.86	146.41	142.07	138.58	135.74
10000	217.99	199.73	186.43	176.43	168.73	162.68	157.86	153.98	150.82
15000	326.98	299.59	279.65	264.65	253.09	244.01	236.79	230.96	226.22
20000	435.98	399.46	372.86	352.86	337.45	325.35	315.71	307.95	301.63
25000	544.97	499.32	466.08	441.08	421.81	406.69	394.64	384.93	377.04
30000	653.96	599.18	559.29	529.29	506.17	488.02	473.57	461.92	452.44
35000	762.96	699.04	652.51	617.50	590.53	569.36	552.50	538.90	527.85
36000	784.76	719.02	671.15	635.15	607.41	585.63	568.28	554.30	542.93
37000	806.56	738.99	689.79	652.79	624.28	601.90	584.07	569.70	558.01
38000	828.35	758.96	708.43	670.43	641.15	618.16	599.85	585.09	573.09
39000	850.15	778.94	727.08	688.08	658.02	634.43	615.64	600.49	588.17
40000	871.95	798.91	745.72	705.72	674.89	650.70	631.42	615.89	603.25
41000	893.75	818.88	764.36	723.36	691.77	666.96	647.21	631.29	618.33
42000	915.55	838.85	783.01	741.00	708.64	683.23	662.99	646.68	633.42
43000	937.35	858.83	801.65	758.65	725.51	699.50	678.78	662.08	648.50
44000	959.15	878.80	820.29	776.29	742.38	715.77	694.56	677.48	663.58
45000	980.94	898.77	838.94	793.93	759.26	732.03	710.35	692.87	678.66
46000	1002.74	918.74	857.58	811.58	776.13	748.30	726.13	708.27	693.74
47000	1024.54	938.72	876.22	829.22	793.00	764.57	741.92	723.67	708.82
48000	1046.34	958.69	894.86	846.86	809.87	780.84	757.71	739.07	723.90
49000	1068.14	978.66	913.51	864.50	826.75	797.10	773.49	754.46	738.98
50000	1089.94	998.63	932.15	882.15	843.62	813.37	789.28	769.86	754.07
51000	1111.74	1018.61	950.79	899.79	860.49	829.64	805.06	785.26	769.15
52000	1133.53	1038.58	969.44	917.43	877.36	845.91	820.85	800.65	784.23
53000	1155.33	1058.55	988.08	935.08	894.23	862.17	836.63	816.05	799.31
54000	1177.13	1078.52	1006.72	952.72	911.11	878.44	852.42	831.45	814.39
55000	1198.93	1098.50	1025.36	970.36	927.98	894.71	868.20	846.85	829.47
56000	1220.73	1118.47	1044.01	988.00	944.85	910.97	883.99	862.24	844.55
57000	1242.53	1138.44	1062.65	1005.65	961.72	927.24	899.77	877.64	859.63
58000	1264.33	1158.41	1081.29	1023.29	978.60	943.51	915.56	893.04	874.72
59000	1286.13	1178.39	1099.94	1040.93	995.47	959.78	931.35	908.43	889.80
60000	1307.92	1198.36	1118.58	1058.58	1012.34	976.04	947.13	923.83	904.88
61000	1329.72	1218.33	1137.22	1076.22	1029.21	992.31	962.92	939.23	919.96
62000	1351.52	1238.30	1155.86	1093.86	1046.08	1008.58	978.70	954.63	935.04
63000	1373.32	1258.28	1174.51	1111.50	1062.96	1024.85	994.49	970.02	950.12
64000	1395.12	1278.25	1193.15	1129.15	1079.83	1041.11	1010.27	985.42	965.20
65000	1416.92	1298.22	1211.79	1146.79	1096.70	1057.38	1026.06	1000.82	980.28
66000	1438.72	1318.19	1230.44	1164.43	1113.57	1073.65	1041.84	1016.21	995.37
67000	1460.51	1338.17	1249.08	1182.08	1130.45	1089.91	1057.63	1031.61	1010.45
68000	1482.31	1358.14	1267.72	1199.72	1147.32	1106.18	1073.41	1047.01	1025.53
69000	1504.11	1378.11	1286.36	1217.36	1164.19	1122.45	1089.20	1062.40	1040.61
70000	1525.91	1398.08	1305.01	1235.00	1181.06	1138.72	1104.99	1077.80	1055.69
75000	1634.90	1497.95	1398.22	1323.22	1265.42	1220.05	1183.91	1154.79	1131.10
80000	1743.90	1597.81	1491.44	1411.43	1349.78	1301.39	1262.84	1231.77	1206.50
100000	2179.87	1997.26	1864.29	1764.29	1687.23	1626.74	1578.55	1539.71	1508.13

16¾% MONTHLY PAYMENT
NECESSARY TO AMORTIZE A LOAN

TERM AMOUNT	15 YEARS	16 YEARS	17 YEARS	18 YEARS	19 YEARS	20 YEARS	21 YEARS	22 YEARS	23 YEARS
$ 25	.38	.37	.37	.36	.36	.36	.35	.35	.35
50	.75	.74	.73	.72	.71	.71	.70	.70	.70
75	1.12	1.10	1.09	1.08	1.07	1.06	1.05	1.05	1.04
100	1.49	1.47	1.45	1.43	1.42	1.41	1.40	1.39	1.39
200	2.97	2.93	2.89	2.86	2.84	2.82	2.80	2.78	2.77
300	4.45	4.39	4.33	4.29	4.25	4.22	4.20	4.17	4.16
400	5.93	5.85	5.78	5.72	5.67	5.63	5.59	5.56	5.54
500	7.42	7.31	7.22	7.15	7.09	7.03	6.99	6.95	6.92
600	8.90	8.77	8.66	8.58	8.50	8.44	8.39	8.34	8.31
700	10.38	10.23	10.11	10.00	9.92	9.85	9.79	9.73	9.69
800	11.86	11.69	11.55	11.43	11.33	11.25	11.18	11.12	11.07
900	13.35	13.15	12.99	12.86	12.75	12.66	12.58	12.51	12.46
1000	14.83	14.61	14.44	14.29	14.17	14.06	13.98	13.90	13.84
2000	29.65	29.22	28.87	28.57	28.33	28.12	27.95	27.80	27.68
3000	44.47	43.83	43.30	42.86	42.49	42.18	41.92	41.70	41.52
4000	59.29	58.44	57.73	57.14	56.65	56.24	55.89	55.60	55.35
5000	74.12	73.05	72.16	71.43	70.81	70.30	69.86	69.50	69.19
6000	88.94	87.66	86.60	85.71	84.97	84.35	83.83	83.40	83.03
7000	103.76	102.27	101.03	100.00	99.13	98.41	97.81	97.29	96.86
8000	118.58	116.88	115.46	114.28	113.30	112.47	111.78	111.19	110.70
9000	133.41	131.48	129.89	128.56	127.46	126.53	125.75	125.09	124.54
10000	148.23	146.09	144.32	142.85	141.62	140.59	139.72	138.99	138.38
15000	222.34	219.14	216.48	214.27	212.42	210.88	209.58	208.48	207.56
20000	296.45	292.18	288.64	285.69	283.23	281.17	279.43	277.98	276.75
25000	370.56	365.22	360.80	357.11	354.04	351.46	349.29	347.47	345.93
30000	444.67	438.27	432.96	428.54	424.84	421.75	419.15	416.96	415.12
35000	518.79	511.31	505.12	499.96	495.65	492.04	489.01	486.45	484.30
36000	533.61	525.92	519.55	514.24	509.81	506.10	502.98	500.35	498.14
37000	548.43	540.53	533.98	528.53	523.97	520.16	516.95	514.25	511.97
38000	563.25	555.14	548.41	542.81	538.13	534.21	530.92	528.15	525.81
39000	578.08	569.75	562.84	557.10	552.29	548.27	544.89	542.05	539.65
40000	592.90	584.36	577.28	571.38	566.46	562.33	558.86	555.95	553.49
41000	607.72	598.96	591.71	585.67	580.62	576.39	572.83	569.84	567.32
42000	622.54	613.57	606.14	599.95	594.78	590.45	586.81	583.74	581.16
43000	637.36	628.18	620.57	614.23	608.94	604.50	600.78	597.64	595.00
44000	652.19	642.79	635.00	628.52	623.10	618.56	614.75	611.54	608.83
45000	667.01	657.40	649.43	642.80	637.26	632.62	628.72	625.44	622.67
46000	681.83	672.01	663.87	657.09	651.42	646.68	642.69	639.34	636.51
47000	696.65	686.62	678.30	671.37	665.59	660.74	656.66	653.24	650.34
48000	711.48	701.23	692.73	685.66	679.75	674.79	670.63	667.13	664.18
49000	726.30	715.84	707.16	699.94	693.91	688.85	684.61	681.03	678.02
50000	741.12	730.44	721.59	714.22	708.07	702.91	698.58	694.93	691.86
51000	755.94	745.05	736.02	728.51	722.23	716.97	712.55	708.83	705.69
52000	770.77	759.66	750.46	742.79	736.39	731.03	726.52	722.73	719.53
53000	785.59	774.27	764.89	757.08	750.55	745.09	740.49	736.63	733.37
54000	800.41	788.88	779.32	771.36	764.71	759.14	754.46	750.52	747.20
55000	815.23	803.49	793.75	785.65	778.88	773.20	768.44	764.42	761.04
56000	830.05	818.10	808.18	799.93	793.04	787.26	782.41	778.32	774.88
57000	844.88	832.71	822.62	814.22	807.20	801.32	796.38	792.22	788.71
58000	859.70	847.31	837.05	828.50	821.36	815.38	810.35	806.12	802.55
59000	874.52	861.92	851.48	842.78	835.52	829.43	824.32	820.02	816.39
60000	889.34	876.53	865.91	857.07	849.68	843.49	838.29	833.92	830.23
61000	904.17	891.14	880.34	871.35	863.84	857.55	852.26	847.81	844.06
62000	918.99	905.75	894.77	885.64	878.00	871.61	866.24	861.71	857.90
63000	933.81	920.36	909.21	899.92	892.17	885.67	880.21	875.61	871.74
64000	948.63	934.97	923.64	914.21	906.33	899.72	894.18	889.51	885.57
65000	963.46	949.58	938.07	928.49	920.49	913.78	908.15	903.41	899.41
66000	978.28	964.18	952.50	942.78	934.65	927.84	922.12	917.31	913.25
67000	993.10	978.79	966.93	957.06	948.81	941.90	936.09	931.21	927.08
68000	1007.92	993.40	981.36	971.34	962.97	955.96	950.06	945.10	940.92
69000	1022.74	1008.01	995.80	985.63	977.13	970.01	964.04	959.00	954.76
70000	1037.57	1022.62	1010.23	999.91	991.29	984.07	978.01	972.90	968.60
75000	1111.68	1095.66	1082.39	1071.33	1062.10	1054.36	1047.86	1042.39	1037.78
80000	1185.79	1168.71	1154.55	1142.76	1132.91	1124.65	1117.72	1111.89	1106.97
100000	1482.24	1460.88	1443.18	1428.44	1416.13	1405.82	1397.15	1389.86	1383.71

MONTHLY PAYMENT 16¾%
NECESSARY TO AMORTIZE A LOAN

TERM AMOUNT	24 YEARS	25 YEARS	26 YEARS	27 YEARS	28 YEARS	29 YEARS	30 YEARS	35 YEARS	40 YEARS
$ 25	.35	.35	.35	.35	.35	.35	.35	.34	.34
50	.69	.69	.69	.69	.69	.69	.69	.68	.68
75	1.04	1.04	1.03	1.03	1.03	1.03	1.03	1.02	1.02
100	1.38	1.38	1.38	1.37	1.37	1.37	1.37	1.36	1.36
200	2.76	2.75	2.75	2.74	2.73	2.73	2.73	2.71	2.71
300	4.14	4.13	4.12	4.11	4.10	4.09	4.09	4.07	4.06
400	5.52	5.50	5.49	5.47	5.46	5.45	5.45	5.42	5.41
500	6.90	6.88	6.86	6.84	6.83	6.82	6.81	6.78	6.76
600	8.28	8.25	8.23	8.21	8.19	8.18	8.17	8.13	8.11
700	9.65	9.62	9.60	9.58	9.56	9.54	9.53	9.49	9.47
800	11.03	11.00	10.97	10.94	10.92	10.90	10.89	10.84	10.82
900	12.41	12.37	12.34	12.31	12.29	12.27	12.25	12.19	12.17
1000	13.79	13.75	13.71	13.68	13.65	13.63	13.61	13.55	13.52
2000	27.58	27.49	27.41	27.35	27.30	27.25	27.21	27.09	27.04
3000	41.36	41.23	41.12	41.02	40.94	40.87	40.82	40.64	40.55
4000	55.15	54.97	54.82	54.69	54.59	54.50	54.42	54.18	54.07
5000	68.93	68.71	68.52	68.37	68.23	68.12	68.02	67.72	67.59
6000	82.72	82.45	82.23	82.04	81.88	81.74	81.63	81.27	81.10
7000	96.50	96.19	95.93	95.71	95.53	95.37	95.23	94.81	94.62
8000	110.29	109.93	109.64	109.38	109.17	108.99	108.84	108.35	108.14
9000	124.07	123.68	123.34	123.06	122.82	122.61	122.44	121.90	121.65
10000	137.86	137.42	137.04	136.73	136.46	136.24	136.04	135.44	135.17
15000	206.78	206.12	205.56	205.09	204.69	204.35	204.06	203.16	202.75
20000	275.71	274.83	274.08	273.45	272.92	272.47	272.08	270.87	270.33
25000	344.63	343.53	342.60	341.82	341.15	340.58	340.10	338.59	337.92
30000	413.56	412.24	411.12	410.18	409.38	408.70	408.12	406.31	405.50
35000	482.48	480.95	479.64	478.54	477.61	476.81	476.14	474.02	473.08
36000	496.27	494.69	493.35	492.21	491.25	490.44	489.75	487.57	486.60
37000	510.05	508.43	507.05	505.89	504.90	504.06	503.35	501.11	500.12
38000	523.84	522.17	520.76	519.56	518.54	517.68	516.95	514.65	513.63
39000	537.62	535.91	534.46	533.23	532.19	531.31	530.56	528.20	527.15
40000	551.41	549.65	548.16	546.90	545.84	544.93	544.16	541.74	540.66
41000	565.19	563.39	561.87	560.58	559.48	558.55	557.77	555.28	554.18
42000	578.98	577.13	575.57	574.25	573.13	572.18	571.37	568.83	567.70
43000	592.76	590.87	589.28	587.92	586.77	585.80	584.97	582.37	581.21
44000	606.55	604.62	602.98	601.59	600.42	599.42	598.58	595.91	594.73
45000	620.33	618.36	616.68	615.27	614.07	613.05	612.18	609.46	608.25
46000	634.12	632.10	630.39	628.94	627.71	626.67	625.78	623.00	621.76
47000	647.90	645.84	644.09	642.61	641.36	640.29	639.39	636.54	635.28
48000	661.69	659.58	657.80	656.28	655.00	653.92	652.99	650.09	648.80
49000	675.47	673.32	671.50	669.96	668.65	667.54	666.60	663.63	662.31
50000	689.26	687.06	685.20	683.63	682.29	681.16	680.20	677.17	675.83
51000	703.04	700.80	698.91	697.30	695.94	694.78	693.80	690.72	689.35
52000	716.83	714.54	712.61	710.97	709.59	708.41	707.41	704.26	702.86
53000	730.61	728.29	726.32	724.65	723.23	722.03	721.01	717.80	716.38
54000	744.40	742.03	740.02	738.32	736.88	735.65	734.62	731.35	729.90
55000	758.18	755.77	753.72	751.99	750.52	749.28	748.22	744.89	743.41
56000	771.97	769.51	767.43	765.66	764.17	762.90	761.82	758.43	756.93
57000	785.75	783.25	781.13	779.34	777.81	776.52	775.43	771.98	770.44
58000	799.54	796.99	794.84	793.01	791.46	790.15	789.03	785.52	783.96
59000	813.32	810.73	808.54	806.68	805.11	803.77	802.64	799.07	797.48
60000	827.11	824.47	822.24	820.35	818.75	817.39	816.24	812.61	810.99
61000	840.89	838.21	835.95	834.03	832.40	831.02	829.84	826.15	824.51
62000	854.68	851.96	849.65	847.70	846.04	844.64	843.45	839.70	838.03
63000	868.46	865.70	863.36	861.37	859.69	858.26	857.05	853.24	851.54
64000	882.25	879.44	877.06	875.04	873.34	871.89	870.66	866.78	865.06
65000	896.03	893.18	890.76	888.72	886.98	885.51	884.26	880.33	878.58
66000	909.82	906.92	904.47	902.39	900.63	899.13	897.86	893.87	892.09
67000	923.60	920.66	918.17	916.06	914.27	912.75	911.47	907.41	905.61
68000	937.39	934.40	931.88	929.73	927.92	926.38	925.07	920.96	919.13
69000	951.17	948.14	945.58	943.41	941.56	940.00	938.67	934.50	932.64
70000	964.96	961.89	959.28	957.08	955.21	953.62	952.28	948.04	946.16
75000	1033.88	1030.59	1027.80	1025.44	1023.44	1021.74	1020.30	1015.76	1013.74
80000	1102.81	1099.30	1096.32	1093.80	1091.67	1089.86	1088.32	1083.48	1081.32
100000	1378.51	1374.12	1370.40	1367.25	1364.58	1362.32	1360.40	1354.34	1351.65

163

17% MONTHLY PAYMENT
NECESSARY TO AMORTIZE A LOAN

TERM AMOUNT	1 YEAR	1½ YEARS	2 YEARS	2½ YEARS	3 YEARS	3½ YEARS	4 YEARS	4½ YEARS	5 YEARS
$ 25	2.28	1.58	1.23	1.03	.89	.79	.72	.66	.62
50	4.55	3.16	2.46	2.05	1.77	1.58	1.43	1.32	1.23
75	6.82	4.73	3.69	3.07	2.66	2.36	2.15	1.98	1.85
100	9.10	6.31	4.92	4.09	3.54	3.15	2.86	2.64	2.46
200	18.19	12.62	9.84	8.18	7.08	6.30	5.72	5.27	4.91
300	27.28	18.92	14.76	12.27	10.62	9.44	8.57	7.90	7.37
400	36.38	25.23	19.67	16.35	14.15	12.59	11.43	10.53	9.82
500	45.47	31.53	24.59	20.44	17.69	15.74	14.28	13.16	12.28
600	54.56	37.84	29.51	24.53	21.23	18.88	17.14	15.80	14.73
700	63.66	44.15	34.42	28.61	24.76	22.03	20.00	18.43	17.19
800	72.75	50.45	39.34	32.70	28.30	25.18	22.85	21.06	19.64
900	81.84	56.76	44.26	36.79	31.84	28.32	25.71	23.69	22.10
1000	90.94	63.06	49.17	40.87	35.37	31.47	28.56	26.32	24.55
2000	181.87	126.12	98.34	81.74	70.74	62.93	57.12	52.64	49.10
3000	272.80	189.18	147.51	122.61	106.11	94.40	85.68	78.96	73.64
4000	363.74	252.24	196.68	163.48	141.48	125.86	114.24	105.28	98.19
5000	454.67	315.30	245.84	204.35	176.85	157.33	142.80	131.60	122.73
6000	545.60	378.36	295.01	245.22	212.22	188.79	171.36	157.92	147.28
7000	636.54	441.42	344.18	286.09	247.58	220.26	199.92	184.24	171.83
8000	727.47	504.47	393.35	326.96	282.95	251.72	228.48	210.56	196.37
9000	818.40	567.53	442.51	367.83	318.32	283.19	257.04	236.88	220.92
10000	909.34	630.59	491.68	408.70	353.69	314.65	285.60	263.20	245.46
15000	1364.00	945.88	737.52	613.05	530.53	471.98	428.40	394.80	368.19
20000	1818.67	1261.18	983.36	817.40	707.37	629.30	571.20	526.40	490.92
25000	2273.34	1576.47	1229.19	1021.75	884.22	786.63	714.00	658.00	613.65
30000	2728.00	1891.76	1475.03	1226.10	1061.06	943.95	856.79	789.60	736.38
35000	3182.67	2207.06	1720.87	1430.45	1237.90	1101.27	999.59	921.20	859.11
36000	3273.60	2270.12	1770.04	1471.32	1273.27	1132.74	1028.15	947.52	883.65
37000	3364.54	2333.17	1819.21	1512.19	1308.64	1164.20	1056.71	973.84	908.20
38000	3455.47	2396.23	1868.37	1553.06	1344.00	1195.67	1085.27	1000.16	932.74
39000	3546.40	2459.29	1917.54	1593.93	1379.37	1227.13	1113.83	1026.48	957.29
40000	3637.33	2522.35	1966.71	1634.80	1414.74	1258.60	1142.39	1052.80	981.83
41000	3728.27	2585.41	2015.88	1675.67	1450.11	1290.06	1170.95	1079.12	1006.38
42000	3819.20	2648.47	2065.04	1716.54	1485.48	1321.53	1199.51	1105.44	1030.93
43000	3910.13	2711.53	2114.21	1757.41	1520.85	1352.99	1228.07	1131.76	1055.47
44000	4001.07	2774.59	2163.38	1798.28	1556.22	1384.46	1256.63	1158.08	1080.02
45000	4092.00	2837.64	2212.55	1839.15	1591.58	1415.92	1285.19	1184.40	1104.56
46000	4182.93	2900.70	2261.71	1880.01	1626.95	1447.39	1313.75	1210.72	1129.11
47000	4273.87	2963.76	2310.88	1920.88	1662.32	1478.85	1342.31	1237.04	1153.65
48000	4364.80	3026.82	2360.05	1961.75	1697.69	1510.32	1370.87	1263.36	1178.20
49000	4455.73	3089.88	2409.22	2002.62	1733.06	1541.78	1399.43	1289.68	1202.75
50000	4546.67	3152.94	2458.38	2043.49	1768.43	1573.25	1427.99	1316.00	1227.29
51000	4637.60	3216.00	2507.55	2084.36	1803.79	1604.71	1456.55	1342.32	1251.84
52000	4728.53	3279.05	2556.72	2125.23	1839.16	1636.18	1485.11	1368.64	1276.38
53000	4819.47	3342.11	2605.89	2166.10	1874.53	1667.64	1513.67	1394.96	1300.93
54000	4910.40	3405.17	2655.05	2206.97	1909.90	1699.11	1542.23	1421.28	1325.48
55000	5001.33	3468.23	2704.22	2247.84	1945.27	1730.57	1570.79	1447.60	1350.02
56000	5092.27	3531.29	2753.39	2288.71	1980.64	1762.04	1599.35	1473.92	1374.57
57000	5183.20	3594.35	2802.56	2329.58	2016.00	1793.50	1627.91	1500.24	1399.11
58000	5274.13	3657.41	2851.72	2370.45	2051.37	1824.97	1656.47	1526.56	1423.66
59000	5365.07	3720.46	2900.89	2411.32	2086.74	1856.43	1685.03	1552.88	1448.20
60000	5456.00	3783.52	2950.06	2452.19	2122.11	1887.89	1713.58	1579.20	1472.75
61000	5546.93	3846.58	2999.23	2493.06	2157.48	1919.36	1742.14	1605.52	1497.30
62000	5637.87	3909.64	3048.40	2533.93	2192.85	1950.82	1770.70	1631.84	1521.84
63000	5728.80	3972.70	3097.56	2574.80	2228.22	1982.29	1799.26	1658.16	1546.39
64000	5819.73	4035.76	3146.73	2615.67	2263.58	2013.75	1827.82	1684.48	1570.93
65000	5910.67	4098.82	3195.90	2656.54	2298.95	2045.22	1856.38	1710.80	1595.48
66000	6001.60	4161.88	3245.07	2697.41	2334.32	2076.68	1884.94	1737.12	1620.02
67000	6092.53	4224.93	3294.23	2738.28	2369.69	2108.15	1913.50	1763.44	1644.57
68000	6183.47	4287.99	3343.40	2779.15	2405.06	2139.61	1942.06	1789.76	1669.12
69000	6274.40	4351.05	3392.57	2820.02	2440.43	2171.08	1970.62	1816.08	1693.66
70000	6365.33	4414.11	3441.74	2860.89	2475.79	2202.54	1999.18	1842.40	1718.21
75000	6820.00	4729.40	3687.57	3065.24	2652.64	2359.87	2141.98	1974.00	1840.94
80000	7274.66	5044.70	3933.41	3269.59	2829.48	2517.19	2284.78	2105.60	1963.66
100000	9093.33	6305.87	4916.76	4086.98	3536.85	3146.49	2855.97	2632.00	2454.58

164

TERM AMOUNT	6 YEARS	7 YEARS	8 YEARS	9 YEARS	10 YEARS	11 YEARS	12 YEARS	13 YEARS	14 YEARS
$ 25	.55	.51	.47	.45	.43	.42	.40	.39	.39
50	1.10	1.01	.94	.89	.86	.83	.80	.78	.77
75	1.65	1.51	1.41	1.34	1.28	1.24	1.20	1.17	1.15
100	2.20	2.02	1.88	1.78	1.71	1.65	1.60	1.56	1.53
200	4.39	4.03	3.76	3.56	3.41	3.29	3.19	3.12	3.05
300	6.58	6.04	5.64	5.34	5.11	4.93	4.79	4.67	4.58
400	8.78	8.05	7.52	7.12	6.81	6.57	6.38	6.23	6.10
500	10.97	10.06	9.40	8.90	8.51	8.21	7.97	7.78	7.63
600	13.16	12.07	11.27	10.68	10.22	9.86	9.57	9.34	9.15
700	15.35	14.08	13.15	12.45	11.92	11.50	11.16	10.89	10.67
800	17.55	16.09	15.03	14.23	13.62	13.14	12.76	12.45	12.20
900	19.74	18.10	16.91	16.01	15.32	14.78	14.35	14.00	13.72
1000	21.93	20.11	18.79	17.79	17.02	16.42	15.94	15.56	15.25
2000	43.86	40.22	37.57	35.58	34.04	32.84	31.88	31.11	30.49
3000	65.79	60.32	56.35	53.36	51.06	49.26	47.82	46.67	45.73
4000	87.72	80.43	75.13	71.15	68.08	65.68	63.76	62.22	60.97
5000	109.64	100.54	93.91	88.93	85.10	82.09	79.70	77.78	76.21
6000	131.57	120.64	112.69	106.72	102.12	98.51	95.64	93.33	91.46
7000	153.50	140.75	131.47	124.50	119.14	114.93	111.58	108.89	106.70
8000	175.43	160.86	150.25	142.29	136.15	131.35	127.52	124.44	121.94
9000	197.36	180.96	169.03	160.07	153.17	147.76	143.46	140.00	137.18
10000	219.28	201.07	187.81	177.86	170.19	164.18	159.40	155.55	152.42
15000	328.92	301.60	281.72	266.78	255.28	246.27	239.10	233.32	228.63
20000	438.56	402.13	375.62	355.71	340.38	328.36	318.79	311.10	304.84
25000	548.20	502.66	469.53	444.63	425.47	410.44	398.49	388.87	381.05
30000	657.84	603.19	563.43	533.56	510.56	492.53	478.19	466.64	457.26
35000	767.48	703.72	657.34	622.49	595.66	574.62	557.88	544.41	533.47
36000	789.41	723.83	676.12	640.27	612.68	591.04	573.82	559.97	548.71
37000	811.34	743.94	694.90	658.06	629.69	607.46	589.76	575.52	563.96
38000	833.26	764.04	713.68	675.84	646.71	623.87	605.70	591.08	579.20
39000	855.19	784.15	732.46	693.63	663.73	640.29	621.64	606.63	594.44
40000	877.12	804.26	751.24	711.41	680.75	656.71	637.58	622.19	609.68
41000	899.05	824.36	770.03	729.20	697.77	673.13	653.52	637.74	624.92
42000	920.97	844.47	788.81	746.98	714.79	689.54	669.46	653.30	640.17
43000	942.90	864.57	807.59	764.77	731.81	705.96	685.40	668.85	655.41
44000	964.83	884.68	826.37	782.55	748.83	722.38	701.34	684.40	670.65
45000	986.76	904.79	845.15	800.34	765.84	738.80	717.28	699.96	685.89
46000	1008.69	924.89	863.93	818.12	782.86	755.21	733.22	715.51	701.13
47000	1030.61	945.00	882.71	835.91	799.88	771.63	749.16	731.07	716.38
48000	1052.54	965.11	901.49	853.69	816.90	788.05	765.10	746.62	731.62
49000	1074.47	985.21	920.27	871.48	833.92	804.47	781.04	762.18	746.86
50000	1096.40	1005.32	939.05	889.26	850.94	820.88	796.97	777.73	762.10
51000	1118.33	1025.42	957.84	907.05	867.96	837.30	812.91	793.29	777.34
52000	1140.25	1045.53	976.62	924.83	884.97	853.72	828.85	808.84	792.59
53000	1162.18	1065.64	995.40	942.62	901.99	870.14	844.79	824.40	807.83
54000	1184.11	1085.74	1014.18	960.40	919.01	886.55	860.73	839.95	823.07
55000	1206.04	1105.85	1032.96	978.19	936.03	902.97	876.67	855.50	838.31
56000	1227.96	1125.96	1051.74	995.97	953.05	919.39	892.61	871.06	853.55
57000	1249.89	1146.06	1070.52	1013.76	970.07	935.81	908.55	886.61	868.80
58000	1271.82	1166.17	1089.30	1031.54	987.09	952.23	924.49	902.17	884.04
59000	1293.75	1186.27	1108.08	1049.33	1004.11	968.64	940.43	917.72	899.28
60000	1315.68	1206.38	1126.86	1067.12	1021.12	985.06	956.37	933.28	914.52
61000	1337.60	1226.49	1145.64	1084.90	1038.14	1001.48	972.31	948.83	929.76
62000	1359.53	1246.59	1164.43	1102.69	1055.16	1017.90	988.25	964.39	945.00
63000	1381.46	1266.70	1183.21	1120.47	1072.18	1034.31	1004.19	979.94	960.25
64000	1403.39	1286.81	1201.99	1138.26	1089.20	1050.73	1020.13	995.50	975.49
65000	1425.32	1306.91	1220.77	1156.04	1106.22	1067.15	1036.07	1011.05	990.73
66000	1447.24	1327.02	1239.55	1173.83	1123.24	1083.57	1052.00	1026.60	1005.97
67000	1469.17	1347.13	1258.33	1191.61	1140.25	1099.98	1067.94	1042.16	1021.21
68000	1491.10	1367.23	1277.11	1209.40	1157.27	1116.40	1083.88	1057.71	1036.46
69000	1513.03	1387.34	1295.89	1227.18	1174.29	1132.82	1099.82	1073.27	1051.70
70000	1534.95	1407.44	1314.67	1244.97	1191.31	1149.24	1115.76	1088.82	1066.94
75000	1644.59	1507.98	1408.58	1333.89	1276.40	1231.32	1195.46	1166.60	1143.15
80000	1754.23	1608.51	1502.48	1422.82	1361.50	1313.41	1275.16	1244.37	1219.36
100000	2192.79	2010.63	1878.10	1778.52	1701.87	1641.76	1593.94	1555.46	1524.20

17%

MONTHLY PAYMENT
NECESSARY TO AMORTIZE A LOAN

TERM AMOUNT	15 YEARS	16 YEARS	17 YEARS	18 YEARS	19 YEARS	20 YEARS	21 YEARS	22 YEARS	23 YEARS
$ 25	.38	.37	.37	.37	.36	.36	.36	.36	.36
50	.75	.74	.74	.73	.72	.72	.71	.71	.71
75	1.13	1.11	1.10	1.09	1.08	1.07	1.07	1.06	1.06
100	1.50	1.48	1.47	1.45	1.44	1.43	1.42	1.41	1.41
200	3.00	2.96	2.93	2.90	2.87	2.85	2.83	2.82	2.81
300	4.50	4.44	4.39	4.34	4.31	4.28	4.25	4.23	4.21
400	6.00	5.92	5.85	5.79	5.74	5.70	5.66	5.64	5.61
500	7.50	7.39	7.31	7.23	7.17	7.12	7.08	7.04	7.01
600	9.00	8.87	8.77	8.68	8.61	8.55	8.49	8.45	8.42
700	10.50	10.35	10.23	10.12	10.04	9.97	9.91	9.86	9.82
800	11.99	11.83	11.69	11.57	11.47	11.39	11.32	11.27	11.22
900	13.49	13.30	13.15	13.02	12.91	12.82	12.74	12.68	12.62
1000	14.99	14.78	14.61	14.46	14.34	14.24	14.15	14.08	14.02
2000	29.98	29.56	29.21	28.92	28.68	28.47	28.30	28.16	28.04
3000	44.96	44.33	43.81	43.37	43.01	42.71	42.45	42.24	42.06
4000	59.95	59.11	58.41	57.83	57.35	56.94	56.60	56.32	56.08
5000	74.94	73.88	73.01	72.29	71.68	71.18	70.75	70.40	70.10
6000	89.92	88.66	87.61	86.74	86.02	85.41	84.90	84.47	84.11
7000	104.91	103.43	102.21	101.20	100.35	99.64	99.05	98.55	98.13
8000	119.89	118.21	116.81	115.65	114.69	113.88	113.20	112.63	112.15
9000	134.88	132.98	131.41	130.11	129.02	128.11	127.35	126.71	126.17
10000	149.87	147.76	146.02	144.57	143.36	142.35	141.50	140.79	140.19
15000	224.80	221.64	219.02	216.85	215.03	213.52	212.25	211.18	210.28
20000	299.73	295.51	292.03	289.13	286.71	284.69	282.99	281.57	280.37
25000	374.66	369.39	365.03	361.41	358.39	355.86	353.74	351.96	350.46
30000	449.59	443.27	438.04	433.69	430.06	427.03	424.49	422.35	420.55
35000	524.52	517.14	511.04	505.97	501.74	498.20	495.24	492.74	490.65
36000	539.50	531.92	525.64	520.43	516.08	512.44	509.39	506.82	504.66
37000	554.49	546.70	540.24	534.88	530.41	526.67	523.53	520.90	518.68
38000	569.48	561.47	554.85	549.34	544.75	540.90	537.68	534.98	532.70
39000	584.46	576.25	569.45	563.79	559.08	555.14	551.83	549.06	546.72
40000	599.45	591.02	584.05	578.25	573.42	569.37	565.98	563.13	560.74
41000	614.43	605.80	598.65	592.71	587.75	583.61	580.13	577.21	574.76
42000	629.42	620.57	613.25	607.16	602.09	597.84	594.28	591.29	588.77
43000	644.41	635.35	627.85	621.62	616.42	612.08	608.43	605.37	602.79
44000	659.39	650.12	642.45	636.08	630.76	626.31	622.58	619.45	616.81
45000	674.38	664.90	657.05	650.53	645.09	640.54	636.73	633.53	630.83
46000	689.37	679.67	671.65	664.99	659.43	654.78	650.88	647.60	644.85
47000	704.35	694.45	686.25	679.44	673.76	669.01	665.03	661.68	658.87
48000	719.34	709.22	700.86	693.90	688.10	683.25	679.18	675.76	672.88
49000	734.32	724.00	715.46	708.36	702.43	697.48	693.33	689.84	686.90
50000	749.31	738.78	730.06	722.81	716.77	711.72	707.48	703.92	700.92
51000	764.30	753.55	744.66	737.27	731.10	725.95	721.63	718.00	714.94
52000	779.28	768.33	759.26	751.72	745.44	740.18	735.78	732.07	728.96
53000	794.27	783.10	773.86	766.18	759.78	754.42	749.93	746.15	742.98
54000	809.25	797.88	788.46	780.64	774.11	768.65	764.08	760.23	756.99
55000	824.24	812.65	803.06	795.09	788.45	782.89	778.22	774.31	771.01
56000	839.23	827.43	817.66	809.55	802.78	797.12	792.37	788.39	785.03
57000	854.21	842.20	832.27	824.01	817.12	811.35	806.52	802.46	799.05
58000	869.20	856.98	846.87	838.46	831.45	825.59	820.67	816.54	813.07
59000	884.18	871.75	861.47	852.92	845.79	839.82	834.82	830.62	827.09
60000	899.17	886.53	876.07	867.37	860.12	854.06	848.97	844.70	841.10
61000	914.16	901.31	890.67	881.83	874.46	868.29	863.12	858.78	855.12
62000	929.14	916.08	905.27	896.29	888.79	882.53	877.27	872.86	869.14
63000	944.13	930.86	919.87	910.74	903.13	896.76	891.42	886.93	883.16
64000	959.11	945.63	934.47	925.20	917.46	910.99	905.57	901.01	897.18
65000	974.10	960.41	949.07	939.65	931.80	925.23	919.72	915.09	911.20
66000	989.09	975.18	963.67	954.11	946.13	939.46	933.87	929.17	925.21
67000	1004.07	989.96	978.28	968.57	960.47	953.70	948.02	943.25	939.23
68000	1019.06	1004.73	992.88	983.02	974.80	967.93	962.17	957.33	953.25
69000	1034.05	1019.51	1007.48	997.48	989.14	982.16	976.32	971.40	967.27
70000	1049.03	1034.28	1022.08	1011.93	1003.48	996.40	990.47	985.48	981.29
75000	1123.96	1108.16	1095.08	1084.22	1075.15	1067.57	1061.21	1055.87	1051.38
80000	1198.89	1182.04	1168.09	1156.50	1146.83	1138.74	1131.96	1126.26	1121.47
100000	1498.61	1477.55	1460.11	1445.62	1433.53	1423.43	1414.95	1407.83	1401.84

MONTHLY PAYMENT 17%
NECESSARY TO AMORTIZE A LOAN

TERM AMOUNT	24 YEARS	25 YEARS	26 YEARS	27 YEARS	28 YEARS	29 YEARS	30 YEARS	35 YEARS	40 YEARS
$ 25	.35	.35	.35	.35	.35	.35	.35	.35	.35
50	.70	.70	.70	.70	.70	.70	.70	.69	.69
75	1.05	1.05	1.05	1.04	1.04	1.04	1.04	1.04	1.03
100	1.40	1.40	1.39	1.39	1.39	1.39	1.39	1.38	1.38
200	2.80	2.79	2.78	2.78	2.77	2.77	2.76	2.75	2.75
300	4.20	4.18	4.17	4.16	4.15	4.15	4.14	4.13	4.12
400	5.59	5.58	5.56	5.55	5.54	5.53	5.52	5.50	5.49
500	6.99	6.97	6.95	6.93	6.92	6.91	6.90	6.87	6.86
600	8.39	8.36	8.34	8.32	8.30	8.29	8.28	8.25	8.23
700	9.78	9.75	9.73	9.71	9.69	9.67	9.66	9.62	9.60
800	11.18	11.15	11.12	11.09	11.07	11.05	11.04	10.99	10.97
900	12.58	12.54	12.51	12.48	12.45	12.44	12.42	12.37	12.34
1000	13.97	13.93	13.89	13.86	13.84	13.82	13.80	13.74	13.71
2000	27.94	27.86	27.78	27.72	27.67	27.63	27.59	27.47	27.42
3000	41.91	41.78	41.67	41.58	41.50	41.44	41.38	41.21	41.13
4000	55.88	55.71	55.56	55.44	55.34	55.25	55.18	54.94	54.84
5000	69.84	69.63	69.45	69.30	69.17	69.06	68.97	68.68	68.55
6000	83.81	83.56	83.34	83.16	83.00	82.87	82.76	82.41	82.26
7000	97.78	97.48	97.23	97.02	96.84	96.68	96.55	96.15	95.97
8000	111.75	111.41	111.12	110.88	110.67	110.49	110.35	109.88	109.68
9000	125.72	125.33	125.01	124.73	124.50	124.31	124.14	123.62	123.39
10000	139.68	139.26	138.90	138.59	138.34	138.12	137.93	137.35	137.10
15000	209.52	208.88	208.34	207.89	207.50	207.17	206.90	206.03	205.65
20000	279.36	278.51	277.79	277.18	276.67	276.23	275.86	274.70	274.20
25000	349.20	348.13	347.23	346.47	345.83	345.29	344.82	343.38	342.74
30000	419.04	417.76	416.68	415.77	415.00	414.34	413.79	412.05	411.29
35000	488.88	487.39	486.13	485.06	484.16	483.40	482.75	480.73	479.84
36000	502.85	501.31	500.02	498.92	497.99	497.21	496.54	494.46	493.55
37000	516.81	515.24	513.91	512.78	511.83	511.02	510.34	508.20	507.26
38000	530.78	529.16	527.79	526.64	525.66	524.83	524.13	521.93	520.97
39000	544.75	543.09	541.68	540.50	539.49	538.64	537.92	535.67	534.68
40000	558.72	557.01	555.57	554.36	553.33	552.45	551.72	549.40	548.39
41000	572.69	570.94	569.46	568.21	567.16	566.27	565.51	563.14	562.10
42000	586.65	584.86	583.35	582.07	580.99	580.08	579.30	576.87	575.81
43000	600.62	598.79	597.24	595.93	594.82	593.89	593.09	590.61	589.52
44000	614.59	612.71	611.13	609.79	608.66	607.70	606.89	604.34	603.23
45000	628.56	626.64	625.02	623.65	622.49	621.51	620.68	618.08	616.94
46000	642.52	640.56	638.91	637.51	636.32	635.32	634.47	631.81	630.65
47000	656.49	654.49	652.80	651.37	650.16	649.13	648.26	645.55	644.36
48000	670.46	668.41	666.69	665.23	663.99	662.94	662.06	659.28	658.07
49000	684.43	682.34	680.58	679.08	677.82	676.75	675.85	673.02	671.78
50000	698.40	696.26	694.46	692.94	691.66	690.57	689.64	686.75	685.48
51000	712.36	710.19	708.35	706.80	705.49	704.38	703.44	700.49	699.19
52000	726.33	724.12	722.24	720.66	719.32	718.19	717.23	714.22	712.90
53000	740.30	738.04	736.13	734.52	733.16	732.00	731.02	727.96	726.61
54000	754.27	751.97	750.02	748.38	746.99	745.81	744.81	741.69	740.32
55000	768.23	765.89	763.91	762.24	760.82	759.62	758.61	755.43	754.03
56000	782.20	779.82	777.80	776.10	774.65	773.43	772.40	769.16	767.74
57000	796.17	793.74	791.69	789.95	788.49	787.24	786.19	782.90	781.45
58000	810.14	807.67	805.58	803.81	802.32	801.05	799.99	796.63	795.16
59000	824.11	821.59	819.47	817.67	816.15	814.87	813.78	810.37	808.87
60000	838.07	835.52	833.36	831.53	829.99	828.68	827.57	824.10	822.58
61000	852.04	849.44	847.25	845.39	843.82	842.49	841.36	837.84	836.29
62000	866.01	863.37	861.14	859.25	857.65	856.30	855.16	851.57	850.00
63000	879.98	877.29	875.02	873.11	871.49	870.11	868.95	865.31	863.71
64000	893.94	891.22	888.91	886.97	885.32	883.92	882.74	879.04	877.42
65000	907.91	905.14	902.80	900.82	899.15	897.73	896.53	892.78	891.13
66000	921.88	919.07	916.69	914.68	912.98	911.55	910.33	906.51	904.84
67000	935.85	932.99	930.58	928.54	926.82	925.36	924.12	920.25	918.55
68000	949.82	946.92	944.47	942.40	940.65	939.17	937.91	933.98	932.26
69000	963.78	960.84	958.36	956.26	954.48	952.98	951.71	947.72	945.97
70000	977.75	974.77	972.25	970.12	968.32	966.79	965.50	961.45	959.68
75000	1047.59	1044.39	1041.69	1039.41	1037.48	1035.85	1034.46	1030.13	1028.22
80000	1117.43	1114.02	1111.14	1108.71	1106.65	1104.90	1103.43	1098.80	1096.77
100000	1396.79	1392.52	1388.92	1385.88	1383.31	1381.13	1379.28	1373.50	1370.96

167

17¼% MONTHLY PAYMENT
NECESSARY TO AMORTIZE A LOAN

TERM AMOUNT	1 YEAR	1½ YEARS	2 YEARS	2½ YEARS	3 YEARS	3½ YEARS	4 YEARS	4½ YEARS	5 YEARS
$ 25	2.28	1.58	1.24	1.03	.89	.79	.72	.67	.62
50	4.56	3.16	2.47	2.05	1.78	1.58	1.44	1.33	1.24
75	6.83	4.74	3.70	3.08	2.67	2.37	2.16	1.99	1.86
100	9.11	6.32	4.93	4.10	3.55	3.16	2.87	2.65	2.47
200	18.21	12.64	9.86	8.20	7.10	6.32	5.74	5.29	4.94
300	27.32	18.96	14.79	12.30	10.65	9.48	8.61	7.94	7.41
400	36.42	25.27	19.72	16.40	14.20	12.64	11.48	10.58	9.87
500	45.53	31.59	24.64	20.50	17.75	15.80	14.34	13.23	12.34
600	54.63	37.91	29.57	24.60	21.30	18.95	17.21	15.87	14.81
700	63.74	44.22	34.50	28.69	24.84	22.11	20.08	18.51	17.27
800	72.84	50.54	39.43	32.79	28.39	25.27	22.95	21.16	19.74
900	81.94	56.86	44.36	36.89	31.94	28.43	25.82	23.80	22.21
1000	91.05	63.17	49.28	40.99	35.49	31.59	28.68	26.45	24.68
2000	182.09	126.34	98.56	81.97	70.97	63.17	57.36	52.89	49.35
3000	273.14	189.51	147.84	122.96	106.46	94.75	86.04	79.33	74.02
4000	364.18	252.68	197.12	163.94	141.94	126.34	114.72	105.77	98.69
5000	455.22	315.85	246.40	204.92	177.43	157.92	143.40	132.22	123.36
6000	546.27	379.02	295.68	245.91	212.91	189.50	172.08	158.66	148.03
7000	637.31	442.19	344.96	286.89	248.39	221.08	200.76	185.10	172.70
8000	728.36	505.36	394.24	327.87	283.88	252.67	229.44	211.54	197.37
9000	819.40	568.53	443.52	368.86	319.36	284.25	258.12	237.99	222.04
10000	910.44	631.70	492.80	409.84	354.85	315.83	286.80	264.43	246.71
15000	1365.66	947.54	739.20	614.76	532.27	473.75	430.20	396.64	370.06
20000	1820.88	1263.39	985.59	819.67	709.69	631.66	573.60	528.85	493.42
25000	2276.10	1579.24	1231.99	1024.59	887.11	789.57	717.00	661.07	616.77
30000	2731.32	1895.08	1478.39	1229.51	1064.53	947.49	860.40	793.28	740.12
35000	3186.54	2210.93	1724.79	1434.43	1241.95	1105.40	1003.80	925.49	863.48
36000	3277.59	2274.10	1774.07	1475.41	1277.44	1136.99	1032.48	951.93	888.15
37000	3368.63	2337.27	1823.35	1516.39	1312.92	1168.57	1061.16	978.38	912.82
38000	3459.67	2400.44	1872.62	1557.38	1348.40	1200.15	1089.84	1004.82	937.49
39000	3550.72	2463.61	1921.90	1598.36	1383.89	1231.73	1118.52	1031.26	962.16
40000	3641.76	2526.77	1971.18	1639.34	1419.37	1263.32	1147.20	1057.70	986.83
41000	3732.80	2589.94	2020.46	1680.33	1454.86	1294.90	1175.88	1084.15	1011.50
42000	3823.85	2653.11	2069.74	1721.31	1490.34	1326.48	1204.56	1110.59	1036.17
43000	3914.89	2716.28	2119.02	1762.29	1525.82	1358.07	1233.24	1137.03	1060.84
44000	4005.94	2779.45	2168.30	1803.28	1561.31	1389.65	1261.92	1163.47	1085.51
45000	4096.98	2842.62	2217.58	1844.26	1596.79	1421.23	1290.60	1189.91	1110.18
46000	4188.02	2905.79	2266.86	1885.25	1632.28	1452.81	1319.28	1216.36	1134.85
47000	4279.07	2968.96	2316.14	1926.23	1667.76	1484.40	1347.96	1242.80	1159.52
48000	4370.11	3032.13	2365.42	1967.21	1703.25	1515.98	1376.64	1269.24	1184.19
49000	4461.16	3095.30	2414.70	2008.20	1738.73	1547.56	1405.32	1295.68	1208.86
50000	4552.20	3158.47	2463.98	2049.18	1774.21	1579.14	1434.00	1322.13	1233.53
51000	4643.24	3221.64	2513.26	2090.16	1809.70	1610.73	1462.68	1348.57	1258.21
52000	4734.29	3284.81	2562.54	2131.15	1845.18	1642.31	1491.36	1375.01	1282.88
53000	4825.33	3347.97	2611.82	2172.13	1880.67	1673.89	1520.04	1401.45	1307.55
54000	4916.38	3411.14	2661.10	2213.11	1916.15	1705.48	1548.72	1427.90	1332.22
55000	5007.42	3474.31	2710.38	2254.10	1951.63	1737.06	1577.40	1454.34	1356.89
56000	5098.46	3537.48	2759.66	2295.08	1987.12	1768.64	1606.08	1480.78	1381.56
57000	5189.51	3600.65	2808.93	2336.06	2022.60	1800.22	1634.76	1507.22	1406.23
58000	5280.55	3663.82	2858.21	2377.05	2058.09	1831.81	1663.44	1533.67	1430.90
59000	5371.59	3726.99	2907.49	2418.03	2093.57	1863.39	1692.12	1560.11	1455.57
60000	5462.64	3790.16	2956.77	2459.01	2129.06	1894.97	1720.80	1586.55	1480.24
61000	5553.68	3853.33	3006.05	2500.00	2164.54	1926.56	1749.48	1612.99	1504.91
62000	5644.73	3916.50	3055.33	2540.98	2200.02	1958.14	1778.16	1639.44	1529.58
63000	5735.77	3979.67	3104.61	2581.96	2235.51	1989.72	1806.84	1665.88	1554.25
64000	5826.81	4042.84	3153.89	2622.95	2270.99	2021.30	1835.52	1692.32	1578.92
65000	5917.86	4106.01	3203.17	2663.93	2306.48	2052.89	1864.20	1718.76	1603.59
66000	6008.90	4169.17	3252.45	2704.91	2341.96	2084.47	1892.88	1745.21	1628.26
67000	6099.95	4232.34	3301.73	2745.90	2377.45	2116.05	1921.56	1771.65	1652.94
68000	6190.99	4295.51	3351.01	2786.88	2412.93	2147.63	1950.24	1798.09	1677.61
69000	6282.03	4358.68	3400.29	2827.87	2448.41	2179.22	1978.92	1824.53	1702.28
70000	6373.08	4421.85	3449.57	2868.85	2483.90	2210.80	2007.60	1850.98	1726.95
75000	6828.30	4737.70	3695.97	3073.77	2661.32	2368.71	2151.00	1983.19	1850.30
80000	7283.52	5053.54	3942.36	3278.68	2838.74	2526.63	2294.40	2115.40	1973.65
100000	9104.39	6316.93	4927.95	4098.35	3548.42	3158.28	2867.99	2644.25	2467.06

168

TERM AMOUNT	6 YEARS	7 YEARS	8 YEARS	9 YEARS	10 YEARS	11 YEARS	12 YEARS	13 YEARS	14 YEARS
$ 25	.56	.51	.48	.45	.43	.42	.41	.40	.39
50	1.11	1.02	.95	.90	.86	.83	.81	.79	.78
75	1.66	1.52	1.42	1.35	1.29	1.25	1.21	1.18	1.16
100	2.21	2.03	1.90	1.80	1.72	1.66	1.61	1.58	1.55
200	4.42	4.05	3.79	3.59	3.44	3.32	3.22	3.15	3.09
300	6.62	6.08	5.68	5.38	5.15	4.98	4.83	4.72	4.63
400	8.83	8.10	7.57	7.18	6.87	6.63	6.44	6.29	6.17
500	11.03	10.13	9.46	8.97	8.59	8.29	8.05	7.86	7.71
600	13.24	12.15	11.36	10.76	10.30	9.95	9.66	9.43	9.25
700	15.45	14.17	13.25	12.55	12.02	11.60	11.27	11.00	10.79
800	17.65	16.20	15.14	14.35	13.74	13.26	12.88	12.57	12.33
900	19.86	18.22	17.03	16.14	15.45	14.92	14.49	14.15	13.87
1000	22.06	20.25	18.92	17.93	17.17	16.57	16.10	15.72	15.41
2000	44.12	40.49	37.84	35.86	34.34	33.14	32.19	31.43	30.81
3000	66.18	60.73	56.76	53.79	51.50	49.71	48.29	47.14	46.21
4000	88.23	80.97	75.68	71.72	68.67	66.28	64.38	62.85	61.62
5000	110.29	101.21	94.60	89.64	85.83	82.85	80.47	78.57	77.02
6000	132.35	121.45	113.52	107.57	103.00	99.41	96.57	94.28	92.42
7000	154.41	141.69	132.44	125.50	120.16	115.98	112.66	109.99	107.83
8000	176.46	161.93	151.36	143.43	137.33	132.55	128.76	125.70	123.23
9000	198.52	182.17	170.28	161.36	154.49	149.12	144.85	141.42	138.63
10000	220.58	202.41	189.20	179.28	171.66	165.69	160.94	157.13	154.04
15000	330.86	303.61	283.80	268.92	257.49	248.53	241.41	235.69	231.05
20000	441.15	404.81	378.39	358.56	343.31	331.37	321.88	314.25	308.07
25000	551.44	506.01	472.99	448.20	429.14	414.21	402.35	392.82	385.08
30000	661.72	607.21	567.59	537.84	514.97	497.05	482.82	471.38	462.10
35000	772.01	708.42	662.19	627.48	600.80	579.90	563.29	549.94	539.11
36000	794.07	728.66	681.10	645.41	617.96	596.46	579.38	565.65	554.52
37000	816.13	748.90	700.02	663.34	635.13	613.03	595.48	581.37	569.92
38000	838.18	769.14	718.94	681.27	652.29	629.60	611.57	597.08	585.32
39000	860.24	789.38	737.86	699.19	669.46	646.17	627.66	612.79	600.73
40000	882.30	809.62	756.78	717.12	686.62	662.74	643.76	628.50	616.13
41000	904.36	829.86	775.70	735.05	703.79	679.31	659.85	644.22	631.53
42000	926.41	850.10	794.62	752.98	720.95	695.87	675.95	659.93	646.94
43000	948.47	870.34	813.54	770.90	738.12	712.44	692.04	675.64	662.34
44000	970.53	890.58	832.46	788.83	755.29	729.01	708.13	691.35	677.74
45000	992.58	910.82	851.38	806.76	772.45	745.58	724.23	707.07	693.15
46000	1014.64	931.06	870.30	824.69	789.62	762.15	740.32	722.78	708.55
47000	1036.70	951.30	889.22	842.62	806.78	778.72	756.41	738.49	723.95
48000	1058.76	971.54	908.14	860.54	823.95	795.28	772.51	754.20	739.36
49000	1080.81	991.78	927.06	878.47	841.11	811.85	788.60	769.92	754.76
50000	1102.87	1012.02	945.98	896.40	858.28	828.42	804.70	785.63	770.16
51000	1124.93	1032.26	964.90	914.33	875.44	844.99	820.79	801.34	785.56
52000	1146.99	1052.50	983.82	932.26	892.61	861.56	836.88	817.05	800.97
53000	1169.04	1072.74	1002.74	950.18	909.78	878.13	852.98	832.77	816.37
54000	1191.10	1092.98	1021.65	968.11	926.94	894.69	869.07	848.48	831.77
55000	1213.16	1113.22	1040.57	986.04	944.11	911.26	885.17	864.19	847.18
56000	1235.22	1133.46	1059.49	1003.97	961.27	927.83	901.26	879.90	862.58
57000	1257.27	1153.70	1078.41	1021.90	978.44	944.40	917.35	895.62	877.98
58000	1279.33	1173.94	1097.33	1039.82	995.60	960.97	933.45	911.33	893.39
59000	1301.39	1194.18	1116.25	1057.75	1012.77	977.54	949.54	927.04	908.79
60000	1323.44	1214.42	1135.17	1075.68	1029.93	994.10	965.63	942.75	924.19
61000	1345.50	1234.66	1154.09	1093.61	1047.10	1010.67	981.73	958.47	939.60
62000	1367.56	1254.90	1173.01	1111.53	1064.26	1027.24	997.82	974.18	955.00
63000	1389.62	1275.14	1191.93	1129.46	1081.43	1043.81	1013.92	989.89	970.40
64000	1411.67	1295.38	1210.85	1147.39	1098.60	1060.38	1030.01	1005.60	985.81
65000	1433.73	1315.62	1229.77	1165.32	1115.76	1076.95	1046.10	1021.31	1001.21
66000	1455.79	1335.86	1248.69	1183.25	1132.93	1093.51	1062.20	1037.03	1016.61
67000	1477.85	1356.11	1267.61	1201.17	1150.09	1110.08	1078.29	1052.74	1032.01
68000	1499.90	1376.35	1286.53	1219.10	1167.26	1126.65	1094.38	1068.45	1047.42
69000	1521.96	1396.59	1305.45	1237.03	1184.42	1143.22	1110.48	1084.16	1062.82
70000	1544.02	1416.83	1324.37	1254.96	1201.59	1159.79	1126.57	1099.88	1078.22
75000	1654.30	1518.03	1418.96	1344.60	1287.42	1242.63	1207.04	1178.44	1155.24
80000	1764.59	1619.23	1513.56	1434.24	1373.24	1325.47	1287.51	1257.00	1232.26
100000	2205.74	2024.04	1891.95	1792.79	1716.55	1656.84	1609.39	1571.25	1540.32

17¼% MONTHLY PAYMENT
NECESSARY TO AMORTIZE A LOAN

TERM AMOUNT	15 YEARS	16 YEARS	17 YEARS	18 YEARS	19 YEARS	20 YEARS	21 YEARS	22 YEARS	23 YEARS
$ 25	.38	.38	.37	.37	.37	.37	.36	.36	.36
50	.76	.75	.74	.74	.73	.73	.72	.72	.71
75	1.14	1.13	1.11	1.10	1.09	1.09	1.08	1.07	1.07
100	1.52	1.50	1.48	1.47	1.46	1.45	1.44	1.43	1.42
200	3.04	2.99	2.96	2.93	2.91	2.89	2.87	2.86	2.84
300	4.55	4.49	4.44	4.39	4.36	4.33	4.30	4.28	4.26
400	6.07	5.98	5.91	5.86	5.81	5.77	5.74	5.71	5.68
500	7.58	7.48	7.39	7.32	7.26	7.21	7.17	7.13	7.10
600	9.10	8.97	8.87	8.78	8.71	8.65	8.60	8.56	8.52
700	10.61	10.46	10.34	10.24	10.16	10.09	10.03	9.99	9.94
800	12.13	11.96	11.82	11.71	11.61	11.53	11.47	11.41	11.36
900	13.64	13.45	13.30	13.17	13.06	12.97	12.90	12.84	12.78
1000	15.16	14.95	14.78	14.63	14.51	14.42	14.33	14.26	14.20
2000	30.31	29.89	29.55	29.26	29.02	28.83	28.66	28.52	28.40
3000	45.46	44.83	44.32	43.89	43.53	43.24	42.99	42.78	42.60
4000	60.61	59.78	59.09	58.52	58.04	57.65	57.32	57.04	56.80
5000	75.76	74.72	73.86	73.15	72.55	72.06	71.64	71.30	71.00
6000	90.91	89.66	88.63	87.77	87.06	86.47	85.97	85.55	85.20
7000	106.06	104.60	103.40	102.40	101.57	100.88	100.30	99.81	99.40
8000	121.21	119.55	118.17	117.03	116.08	115.29	114.63	114.07	113.60
9000	136.36	134.49	132.94	131.66	130.59	129.70	128.96	128.33	127.80
10000	151.51	149.43	147.71	146.29	145.10	144.11	143.28	142.59	142.00
15000	227.26	224.14	221.57	219.43	217.65	216.17	214.92	213.88	213.00
20000	303.01	298.86	295.42	292.57	290.20	288.22	286.56	285.17	284.00
25000	378.76	373.57	369.27	365.71	362.75	360.27	358.20	356.46	355.00
30000	454.52	448.28	443.13	438.85	435.30	432.33	429.84	427.75	426.00
35000	530.27	522.99	516.98	512.00	507.84	504.38	501.48	499.05	497.00
36000	545.42	537.94	531.75	526.62	522.35	518.79	515.81	513.30	511.20
37000	560.57	552.88	546.52	541.25	536.86	533.20	530.13	527.56	525.40
38000	575.72	567.82	561.30	555.88	551.37	547.61	544.46	541.82	539.60
39000	590.87	582.76	576.07	570.51	565.88	562.02	558.79	556.08	553.80
40000	606.02	597.71	590.84	585.14	580.39	576.43	573.12	570.34	568.00
41000	621.17	612.65	605.61	599.77	594.90	590.84	587.45	584.60	582.20
42000	636.32	627.59	620.38	614.39	609.41	605.25	601.77	598.85	596.40
43000	651.47	642.53	635.15	629.02	623.92	619.66	616.10	613.11	610.60
44000	666.62	657.48	649.92	643.65	638.43	634.07	630.43	627.37	624.80
45000	681.77	672.42	664.69	658.28	652.94	648.49	644.76	641.63	639.00
46000	696.92	687.36	679.46	672.91	667.45	662.90	659.08	655.89	653.20
47000	712.07	702.30	694.23	687.54	681.96	677.31	673.41	670.15	667.40
48000	727.22	717.25	709.00	702.16	696.47	691.72	687.74	684.40	681.60
49000	742.37	732.19	723.77	716.79	710.98	706.13	702.07	698.66	695.80
50000	757.52	747.13	738.54	731.42	725.49	720.54	716.40	712.92	710.00
51000	772.67	762.07	753.32	746.05	740.00	734.95	730.72	727.18	724.20
52000	787.82	777.02	768.09	760.68	754.51	749.36	745.05	741.44	738.40
53000	802.97	791.96	782.86	775.31	769.02	763.77	759.38	755.70	752.60
54000	818.12	806.90	797.63	789.93	783.53	778.18	773.71	769.95	766.80
55000	833.27	821.84	812.40	804.56	798.04	792.59	788.03	784.21	781.00
56000	848.42	836.79	827.17	819.19	812.55	807.00	802.36	798.47	795.20
57000	863.57	851.73	841.94	833.82	827.06	821.41	816.69	812.73	809.40
58000	878.72	866.67	856.71	848.45	841.57	835.82	831.02	826.99	823.60
59000	893.88	881.61	871.48	863.08	856.08	850.24	845.35	841.25	837.80
60000	909.03	896.56	886.25	877.70	870.59	864.65	859.67	855.50	852.00
61000	924.18	911.50	901.02	892.33	885.10	879.06	874.00	869.76	866.20
62000	939.33	926.44	915.79	906.96	899.61	893.47	888.33	884.02	880.40
63000	954.48	941.38	930.57	921.59	914.12	907.88	902.66	898.28	894.60
64000	969.63	956.33	945.34	936.22	928.63	922.29	916.98	912.54	908.80
65000	984.78	971.27	960.11	950.85	943.14	936.70	931.31	926.80	923.00
66000	999.93	986.21	974.88	965.47	957.65	951.11	945.64	941.05	937.20
67000	1015.08	1001.15	989.65	980.10	972.16	965.52	959.97	955.31	951.40
68000	1030.23	1016.10	1004.42	994.73	986.67	979.93	974.30	969.57	965.60
69000	1045.38	1031.04	1019.19	1009.36	1001.18	994.34	988.62	983.83	979.80
70000	1060.53	1045.98	1033.96	1023.99	1015.68	1008.75	1002.95	998.09	994.00
75000	1136.28	1120.69	1107.81	1097.13	1088.23	1080.81	1074.59	1069.38	1065.00
80000	1212.03	1195.41	1181.67	1170.27	1160.78	1152.86	1146.23	1140.67	1136.00
100000	1515.04	1494.26	1477.08	1462.84	1450.98	1441.07	1432.79	1425.84	1420.00

MONTHLY PAYMENT 17¼%
NECESSARY TO AMORTIZE A LOAN

TERM AMOUNT	24 YEARS	25 YEARS	26 YEARS	27 YEARS	28 YEARS	29 YEARS	30 YEARS	35 YEARS	40 YEARS
$ 25	.36	.36	.36	.36	.36	.35	.35	.35	.35
50	.71	.71	.71	.71	.71	.70	.70	.70	.70
75	1.07	1.06	1.06	1.06	1.06	1.05	1.05	1.05	1.05
100	1.42	1.42	1.41	1.41	1.41	1.40	1.40	1.40	1.40
200	2.84	2.83	2.82	2.81	2.81	2.80	2.80	2.79	2.79
300	4.25	4.24	4.23	4.22	4.21	4.20	4.20	4.18	4.18
400	5.67	5.65	5.63	5.62	5.61	5.60	5.60	5.58	5.57
500	7.08	7.06	7.04	7.03	7.02	7.00	7.00	6.97	6.96
600	8.50	8.47	8.45	8.43	8.42	8.40	8.39	8.36	8.35
700	9.91	9.88	9.86	9.84	9.82	9.80	9.79	9.75	9.74
800	11.33	11.29	11.26	11.24	11.22	11.20	11.19	11.15	11.13
900	12.74	12.70	12.67	12.65	12.62	12.60	12.59	12.54	12.52
1000	14.16	14.11	14.08	14.05	14.03	14.00	13.99	13.93	13.91
2000	28.31	28.22	28.15	28.10	28.05	28.00	27.97	27.86	27.81
3000	42.46	42.33	42.23	42.14	42.07	42.00	41.95	41.78	41.71
4000	56.61	56.44	56.30	56.19	56.09	56.00	55.93	55.71	55.62
5000	70.76	70.55	70.38	70.23	70.11	70.00	69.91	69.64	69.52
6000	84.91	84.66	84.45	84.28	84.13	84.00	83.90	83.56	83.42
7000	99.06	98.77	98.53	98.32	98.15	98.00	97.88	97.49	97.32
8000	113.21	112.88	112.60	112.37	112.17	112.00	111.86	111.42	111.23
9000	127.36	126.99	126.68	126.41	126.19	126.00	125.84	125.34	125.13
10000	141.51	141.10	140.75	140.46	140.21	140.00	139.82	139.27	139.03
15000	212.27	211.65	211.12	210.68	210.31	210.00	209.73	208.90	208.54
20000	283.02	282.20	281.50	280.91	280.41	279.99	279.64	278.54	278.06
25000	353.78	352.74	351.87	351.14	350.52	349.99	349.55	348.17	347.57
30000	424.53	423.29	422.24	421.36	420.62	419.99	419.46	417.80	417.08
35000	495.28	493.84	492.62	491.59	490.72	489.99	489.37	487.44	486.60
36000	509.44	507.95	506.69	505.63	504.74	503.99	503.35	501.36	500.50
37000	523.59	522.06	520.77	519.68	518.76	517.99	517.33	515.29	514.40
38000	537.74	536.17	534.84	533.72	532.78	531.98	531.31	529.22	528.31
39000	551.89	550.28	548.92	547.77	546.80	545.98	545.29	543.14	542.21
40000	566.04	564.39	562.99	561.82	560.82	559.98	559.27	557.07	556.11
41000	580.19	578.49	577.07	575.86	574.84	573.98	573.26	571.00	570.01
42000	594.34	592.60	591.14	589.91	588.86	587.98	587.24	584.92	583.92
43000	608.49	606.71	605.22	603.95	602.88	601.98	601.22	598.85	597.82
44000	622.64	620.82	619.29	618.00	616.90	615.98	615.20	612.78	611.72
45000	636.79	634.93	633.36	632.04	630.92	629.98	629.18	626.70	625.62
46000	650.94	649.04	647.44	646.09	644.94	643.98	643.17	640.63	639.53
47000	665.09	663.15	661.51	660.13	658.97	657.97	657.15	654.56	653.43
48000	679.25	677.26	675.59	674.18	672.99	671.97	671.13	668.48	667.33
49000	693.40	691.37	689.66	688.22	687.01	685.98	685.11	682.41	681.23
50000	707.55	705.48	703.74	702.27	701.03	699.98	699.09	696.34	695.14
51000	721.70	719.59	717.81	716.31	715.05	713.98	713.07	710.26	709.04
52000	735.85	733.70	731.89	730.36	729.07	727.98	727.06	724.19	722.94
53000	750.00	747.81	745.96	744.40	743.09	741.98	741.04	738.11	736.84
54000	764.15	761.92	760.04	758.45	757.11	755.98	755.02	752.04	750.75
55000	778.30	776.03	774.11	772.49	771.13	769.98	769.00	765.97	764.65
56000	792.45	790.14	788.19	786.54	785.15	783.97	782.98	779.89	778.55
57000	806.60	804.25	802.26	800.58	799.17	797.97	796.96	793.82	792.46
58000	820.75	818.36	816.33	814.63	813.19	811.97	810.95	807.75	806.36
59000	834.90	832.47	830.41	828.67	827.21	825.97	824.93	821.67	820.26
60000	849.06	846.58	844.48	842.72	841.23	839.97	838.91	835.60	834.16
61000	863.21	860.68	858.56	856.77	855.25	853.97	852.89	849.53	848.07
62000	877.36	874.79	872.63	870.81	869.27	867.97	866.87	863.45	861.97
63000	891.51	888.90	886.71	884.86	883.29	881.97	880.85	877.38	875.87
64000	905.66	903.01	900.78	898.90	897.31	895.97	894.84	891.31	889.77
65000	919.81	917.12	914.86	912.95	911.33	909.97	908.82	905.23	903.68
66000	933.96	931.23	928.93	926.99	925.35	923.97	922.80	919.16	917.58
67000	948.11	945.34	943.01	941.04	939.37	937.97	936.78	933.09	931.48
68000	962.26	959.45	957.08	955.08	953.39	951.97	950.76	947.01	945.38
69000	976.41	973.56	971.16	969.13	967.41	965.97	964.75	960.94	959.29
70000	990.56	987.67	985.23	983.17	981.44	979.97	978.73	974.87	973.19
75000	1061.32	1058.22	1055.60	1053.40	1051.54	1049.96	1048.64	1044.50	1042.70
80000	1132.07	1128.77	1125.98	1123.63	1121.64	1119.96	1118.54	1114.13	1112.22
100000	1415.09	1410.96	1407.47	1404.53	1402.05	1399.95	1398.18	1392.67	1390.27

17½% MONTHLY PAYMENT
NECESSARY TO AMORTIZE A LOAN

TERM AMOUNT	1 YEAR	1½ YEARS	2 YEARS	2½ YEARS	3 YEARS	3½ YEARS	4 YEARS	4½ YEARS	5 YEARS
$ 25	2.28	1.59	1.24	1.03	.90	.80	.73	.67	.62
50	4.56	3.17	2.47	2.06	1.79	1.59	1.45	1.33	1.24
75	6.84	4.75	3.71	3.09	2.68	2.38	2.17	2.00	1.86
100	9.12	6.33	4.94	4.11	3.57	3.18	2.89	2.66	2.48
200	18.24	12.66	9.88	8.22	7.13	6.35	5.77	5.32	4.96
300	27.35	18.99	14.82	12.33	10.69	9.52	8.65	7.97	7.44
400	36.47	25.32	19.76	16.44	14.25	12.69	11.53	10.63	9.92
500	45.58	31.64	24.70	20.55	17.81	15.86	14.41	13.29	12.40
600	54.70	37.97	29.64	24.66	21.37	19.03	17.29	15.94	14.88
700	63.81	44.30	34.58	28.77	24.93	22.20	20.17	18.60	17.36
800	72.93	50.63	39.52	32.88	28.49	25.37	23.05	21.26	19.84
900	82.04	56.96	44.46	36.99	32.05	28.54	25.93	23.91	22.32
1000	91.16	63.28	49.40	41.10	35.61	31.71	28.81	26.57	24.80
2000	182.31	126.56	98.79	82.20	71.21	63.41	57.61	53.14	49.60
3000	273.47	189.84	148.18	123.30	106.81	95.11	86.41	79.70	74.39
4000	364.62	253.12	197.57	164.39	142.41	126.81	115.21	106.27	99.19
5000	455.78	316.40	246.96	205.49	178.01	158.51	144.01	132.83	123.98
6000	546.93	379.68	296.35	246.59	213.61	190.21	172.81	159.40	148.78
7000	638.09	442.96	345.74	287.69	249.21	221.91	201.61	185.96	173.57
8000	729.24	506.24	395.14	328.78	284.81	253.61	230.41	212.53	198.37
9000	820.40	569.52	444.53	369.88	320.41	285.31	259.21	239.09	223.17
10000	911.55	632.80	493.92	410.98	356.01	317.01	288.01	265.66	247.96
15000	1367.32	949.20	740.88	616.46	534.01	475.52	432.01	398.48	371.94
20000	1823.10	1265.60	987.83	821.95	712.01	634.02	576.01	531.31	495.92
25000	2278.87	1582.00	1234.79	1027.44	890.01	792.53	720.01	664.13	619.90
30000	2734.64	1898.40	1481.75	1232.92	1068.01	951.03	864.01	796.96	743.88
35000	3190.41	2214.80	1728.70	1438.41	1246.01	1109.54	1008.02	929.79	867.85
36000	3281.57	2278.08	1778.10	1479.51	1281.61	1141.24	1036.82	956.35	892.65
37000	3372.72	2341.36	1827.49	1520.60	1317.21	1172.94	1065.62	982.92	917.45
38000	3463.88	2404.64	1876.88	1561.70	1352.81	1204.64	1094.42	1009.48	942.24
39000	3555.03	2467.92	1926.27	1602.80	1388.41	1236.34	1123.22	1036.05	967.04
40000	3646.19	2531.20	1975.66	1643.90	1424.01	1268.04	1152.02	1062.61	991.83
41000	3737.34	2594.48	2025.05	1684.99	1459.61	1299.74	1180.82	1089.18	1016.63
42000	3828.49	2657.76	2074.44	1726.09	1495.21	1331.44	1209.62	1115.74	1041.42
43000	3919.65	2721.04	2123.84	1767.19	1530.81	1363.14	1238.42	1142.31	1066.22
44000	4010.80	2784.32	2173.23	1808.28	1566.41	1394.84	1267.22	1168.87	1091.01
45000	4101.96	2847.60	2222.62	1849.38	1602.01	1426.55	1296.02	1195.44	1115.81
46000	4193.11	2910.88	2272.01	1890.48	1637.61	1458.25	1324.82	1222.00	1140.61
47000	4284.27	2974.16	2321.40	1931.58	1673.21	1489.95	1353.62	1248.57	1165.40
48000	4375.42	3037.44	2370.79	1972.67	1708.81	1521.65	1382.42	1275.13	1190.20
49000	4466.58	3100.72	2420.18	2013.77	1744.41	1553.35	1411.22	1301.70	1214.99
50000	4557.73	3164.00	2469.58	2054.87	1780.01	1585.05	1440.02	1328.26	1239.79
51000	4648.88	3227.28	2518.97	2095.96	1815.61	1616.75	1468.82	1354.83	1264.58
52000	4740.04	3290.56	2568.36	2137.06	1851.21	1648.45	1497.62	1381.39	1289.38
53000	4831.19	3353.84	2617.75	2178.16	1886.81	1680.15	1526.42	1407.96	1314.18
54000	4922.35	3417.12	2667.14	2219.26	1922.41	1711.85	1555.22	1434.52	1338.97
55000	5013.50	3480.40	2716.53	2260.35	1958.01	1743.55	1584.02	1461.09	1363.77
56000	5104.66	3543.68	2765.92	2301.45	1993.61	1775.25	1612.82	1487.65	1388.56
57000	5195.81	3606.96	2815.31	2342.55	2029.21	1806.96	1641.62	1514.22	1413.36
58000	5286.97	3670.24	2864.71	2383.65	2064.81	1838.66	1670.42	1540.79	1438.15
59000	5378.12	3733.52	2914.10	2424.74	2100.41	1870.36	1699.22	1567.35	1462.95
60000	5469.28	3796.80	2963.49	2465.84	2136.01	1902.06	1728.02	1593.92	1487.75
61000	5560.43	3860.08	3012.88	2506.94	2171.61	1933.76	1756.82	1620.48	1512.54
62000	5651.58	3923.36	3062.27	2548.03	2207.21	1965.46	1785.62	1647.05	1537.34
63000	5742.74	3986.64	3111.66	2589.13	2242.81	1997.16	1814.42	1673.61	1562.13
64000	5833.89	4049.92	3161.05	2630.23	2278.41	2028.86	1843.22	1700.18	1586.93
65000	5925.05	4113.19	3210.45	2671.33	2314.01	2060.56	1872.02	1726.74	1611.72
66000	6016.20	4176.47	3259.84	2712.42	2349.61	2092.26	1900.82	1753.31	1636.52
67000	6107.36	4239.75	3309.23	2753.52	2385.21	2123.96	1929.62	1779.87	1661.32
68000	6198.51	4303.03	3358.62	2794.62	2420.81	2155.67	1958.42	1806.44	1686.11
69000	6289.67	4366.31	3408.01	2835.72	2456.41	2187.37	1987.22	1833.00	1710.91
70000	6380.82	4429.59	3457.40	2876.81	2492.01	2219.07	2016.03	1859.57	1735.70
75000	6836.59	4745.99	3704.36	3082.30	2670.01	2377.57	2160.03	1992.39	1859.68
80000	7292.37	5062.39	3951.32	3287.79	2848.01	2536.08	2304.03	2125.22	1983.66
100000	9115.46	6327.99	4939.15	4109.73	3560.01	3170.09	2880.03	2656.52	2479.57

MONTHLY PAYMENT 17½%
NECESSARY TO AMORTIZE A LOAN

TERM AMOUNT	6 YEARS	7 YEARS	8 YEARS	9 YEARS	10 YEARS	11 YEARS	12 YEARS	13 YEARS	14 YEARS
$ 25	.56	.51	.48	.46	.44	.42	.41	.40	.39
50	1.11	1.02	.96	.91	.87	.84	.82	.80	.78
75	1.67	1.53	1.43	1.36	1.30	1.26	1.22	1.20	1.17
100	2.22	2.04	1.91	1.81	1.74	1.68	1.63	1.59	1.56
200	4.44	4.08	3.82	3.62	3.47	3.35	3.25	3.18	3.12
300	6.66	6.12	5.72	5.43	5.20	5.02	4.88	4.77	4.67
400	8.88	8.15	7.63	7.23	6.93	6.69	6.50	6.35	6.23
500	11.10	10.19	9.53	9.04	8.66	8.36	8.13	7.94	7.79
600	13.32	12.23	11.44	10.85	10.39	10.04	9.75	9.53	9.34
700	15.54	14.27	13.35	12.65	12.12	11.71	11.38	11.11	10.90
800	17.75	16.30	15.25	14.46	13.86	13.38	13.00	12.70	12.46
900	19.97	18.34	17.16	16.27	15.59	15.05	14.63	14.29	14.01
1000	22.19	20.38	19.06	18.08	17.32	16.72	16.25	15.88	15.57
2000	44.38	40.75	38.12	36.15	34.63	33.44	32.50	31.75	31.13
3000	66.57	61.13	57.18	54.22	51.94	50.16	48.75	47.62	46.70
4000	88.75	81.50	76.24	72.29	69.26	66.88	65.00	63.49	62.26
5000	110.94	101.88	95.30	90.36	86.57	83.60	81.25	79.36	77.83
6000	133.13	122.25	114.35	108.43	103.88	100.32	97.50	95.23	93.39
7000	155.31	142.63	133.41	126.50	121.19	117.04	113.75	111.10	108.96
8000	177.50	163.00	152.47	144.57	138.51	133.76	129.99	126.97	124.52
9000	199.69	183.38	171.53	162.64	155.82	150.48	146.24	142.84	140.09
10000	221.88	203.75	190.59	180.72	173.13	167.20	162.49	158.71	155.65
15000	332.81	305.62	285.88	271.07	259.70	250.80	243.74	238.07	233.48
20000	443.75	407.50	381.17	361.43	346.26	334.39	324.98	317.42	311.30
25000	554.68	509.37	476.46	451.78	432.82	417.99	406.22	396.78	389.12
30000	665.62	611.24	571.75	542.14	519.39	501.59	487.47	476.13	466.95
35000	776.55	713.12	667.04	632.49	605.95	585.19	568.71	555.48	544.77
36000	798.74	733.49	686.10	650.56	623.26	601.91	584.96	571.36	560.34
37000	820.93	753.87	705.16	668.63	640.58	618.63	601.21	587.23	575.90
38000	843.11	774.24	724.22	686.70	657.89	635.35	617.46	603.10	591.47
39000	865.30	794.62	743.28	704.78	675.20	652.07	633.70	618.97	607.03
40000	887.49	814.99	762.34	722.85	692.51	668.78	649.95	634.84	622.60
41000	909.68	835.37	781.39	740.92	709.83	685.50	666.20	650.71	638.16
42000	931.86	855.74	800.45	758.99	727.14	702.22	682.45	666.58	653.73
43000	954.05	876.12	819.51	777.06	744.45	718.94	698.70	682.45	669.29
44000	976.24	896.49	838.57	795.13	761.76	735.66	714.95	698.32	684.86
45000	998.42	916.86	857.63	813.20	779.08	752.38	731.20	714.19	700.42
46000	1020.61	937.24	876.69	831.27	796.39	769.10	747.45	730.06	715.99
47000	1042.80	957.61	895.74	849.34	813.70	785.82	763.69	745.93	731.55
48000	1064.99	977.99	914.80	867.41	831.02	802.54	779.94	761.81	747.11
49000	1087.17	998.36	933.86	885.49	848.33	819.26	796.19	777.68	762.68
50000	1109.36	1018.74	952.92	903.56	865.64	835.98	812.44	793.55	778.24
51000	1131.55	1039.11	971.98	921.63	882.95	852.70	828.69	809.42	793.81
52000	1153.73	1059.49	991.03	939.70	900.27	869.42	844.94	825.29	809.37
53000	1175.92	1079.86	1010.09	957.77	917.58	886.14	861.19	841.16	824.94
54000	1198.11	1100.24	1029.15	975.84	934.89	902.86	877.44	857.03	840.50
55000	1220.29	1120.61	1048.21	993.91	952.20	919.58	893.68	872.90	856.07
56000	1242.48	1140.99	1067.27	1011.98	969.52	936.30	909.93	888.77	871.63
57000	1264.67	1161.36	1086.33	1030.05	986.83	953.02	926.18	904.64	887.20
58000	1286.86	1181.74	1105.38	1048.12	1004.14	969.74	942.43	920.51	902.76
59000	1309.04	1202.11	1124.44	1066.20	1021.46	986.46	958.68	936.38	918.33
60000	1331.23	1222.48	1143.50	1084.27	1038.77	1003.17	974.93	952.26	933.89
61000	1353.42	1242.86	1162.56	1102.34	1056.08	1019.89	991.18	968.13	949.46
62000	1375.60	1263.23	1181.62	1120.41	1073.39	1036.61	1007.43	984.00	965.02
63000	1397.79	1283.61	1200.68	1138.48	1090.71	1053.33	1023.67	999.87	980.59
64000	1419.98	1303.98	1219.73	1156.55	1108.02	1070.05	1039.92	1015.74	996.15
65000	1442.17	1324.36	1238.79	1174.62	1125.33	1086.77	1056.17	1031.61	1011.72
66000	1464.35	1344.73	1257.85	1192.69	1142.64	1103.49	1072.42	1047.48	1027.28
67000	1486.54	1365.11	1276.91	1210.76	1159.96	1120.21	1088.67	1063.35	1042.85
68000	1508.73	1385.48	1295.97	1228.84	1177.27	1136.93	1104.92	1079.22	1058.41
69000	1530.91	1405.86	1315.03	1246.91	1194.58	1153.65	1121.17	1095.09	1073.98
70000	1553.10	1426.23	1334.08	1264.98	1211.90	1170.37	1137.41	1110.96	1089.54
75000	1664.04	1528.10	1429.37	1355.33	1298.46	1253.97	1218.66	1190.32	1167.36
80000	1774.97	1629.98	1524.67	1445.69	1385.02	1337.56	1299.90	1269.67	1245.19
100000	2218.71	2037.47	1905.83	1807.11	1731.28	1671.95	1624.88	1587.09	1556.48

173

17½% MONTHLY PAYMENT
NECESSARY TO AMORTIZE A LOAN

TERM AMOUNT	15 YEARS	16 YEARS	17 YEARS	18 YEARS	19 YEARS	20 YEARS	21 YEARS	22 YEARS	23 YEARS
$ 25	.39	.38	.38	.38	.37	.37	.37	.37	.36
50	.77	.76	.75	.75	.74	.73	.73	.73	.72
75	1.15	1.14	1.13	1.12	1.11	1.10	1.09	1.09	1.08
100	1.54	1.52	1.50	1.49	1.47	1.46	1.46	1.45	1.44
200	3.07	3.03	2.99	2.97	2.94	2.92	2.91	2.89	2.88
300	4.60	4.54	4.49	4.45	4.41	4.38	4.36	4.34	4.32
400	6.13	6.05	5.98	5.93	5.88	5.84	5.81	5.78	5.76
500	7.66	7.56	7.48	7.41	7.35	7.30	7.26	7.22	7.20
600	9.19	9.07	8.97	8.89	8.82	8.76	8.71	8.67	8.63
700	10.73	10.58	10.46	10.37	10.28	10.22	10.16	10.11	10.07
800	12.26	12.09	11.96	11.85	11.75	11.68	11.61	11.56	11.51
900	13.79	13.60	13.45	13.33	13.22	13.13	13.06	13.00	12.95
1000	15.32	15.12	14.95	14.81	14.69	14.59	14.51	14.44	14.39
2000	30.64	30.23	29.89	29.61	29.37	29.18	29.02	28.88	28.77
3000	45.95	45.34	44.83	44.41	44.06	43.77	43.52	43.32	43.15
4000	61.27	60.45	59.77	59.21	58.74	58.36	58.03	57.76	57.53
5000	76.58	75.56	74.71	74.01	73.43	72.94	72.54	72.20	71.91
6000	91.90	90.67	89.65	88.81	88.11	87.53	87.04	86.64	86.30
7000	107.21	105.78	104.59	103.61	102.80	102.12	101.55	101.08	100.68
8000	122.53	120.89	119.53	118.41	117.48	116.71	116.06	115.51	115.06
9000	137.84	136.00	134.47	133.21	132.17	131.29	130.56	129.95	129.44
10000	153.16	151.11	149.41	148.01	146.85	145.88	145.07	144.39	143.82
15000	229.73	226.66	224.12	222.02	220.27	218.82	217.60	216.59	215.73
20000	306.31	302.21	298.82	296.02	293.70	291.76	290.14	288.78	287.64
25000	382.88	377.76	373.53	370.03	367.12	364.69	362.67	360.97	359.55
30000	459.46	453.31	448.23	444.03	440.54	437.63	435.20	433.17	431.46
35000	536.03	528.86	522.94	518.04	513.96	510.57	507.73	505.36	503.37
36000	551.35	543.97	537.88	532.84	528.65	525.16	522.24	519.80	517.75
37000	566.66	559.08	552.82	547.64	543.33	539.74	536.75	534.24	532.13
38000	581.98	574.19	567.76	562.44	558.02	554.33	551.25	548.68	546.52
39000	597.29	589.30	582.70	577.24	572.70	568.92	565.76	563.11	560.90
40000	612.61	604.41	597.64	592.04	587.39	583.51	580.27	577.55	575.28
41000	627.92	619.52	612.59	606.84	602.07	598.09	594.77	591.99	589.66
42000	643.24	634.63	627.53	621.64	616.76	612.68	609.28	606.43	604.04
43000	658.55	649.74	642.47	636.44	631.44	627.27	623.79	620.87	618.43
44000	673.87	664.85	657.41	651.25	646.12	641.86	638.29	635.31	632.81
45000	689.18	679.96	672.35	666.05	660.81	656.44	652.80	649.75	647.19
46000	704.50	695.07	687.29	680.85	675.49	671.03	667.30	664.19	661.57
47000	719.81	710.18	702.23	695.65	690.18	685.62	681.81	678.62	675.95
48000	735.13	725.29	717.17	710.45	704.86	700.21	696.32	693.06	690.33
49000	750.44	740.40	732.11	725.25	719.55	714.79	710.82	707.50	704.72
50000	765.76	755.51	747.05	740.05	734.23	729.38	725.33	721.94	719.10
51000	781.07	770.62	761.99	754.85	748.92	743.97	739.84	736.38	733.48
52000	796.39	785.73	776.94	769.65	763.60	758.56	754.34	750.82	747.86
53000	811.70	800.84	791.88	784.45	778.29	773.14	768.85	765.26	762.24
54000	827.02	815.95	806.82	799.25	792.97	787.73	783.36	779.70	776.63
55000	842.33	831.06	821.76	814.06	807.65	802.32	797.86	794.13	791.01
56000	857.65	846.17	836.70	828.86	822.34	816.91	812.37	808.57	805.39
57000	872.96	861.28	851.64	843.66	837.02	831.49	826.88	823.01	819.77
58000	888.28	876.39	866.58	858.46	851.71	846.08	841.38	837.45	834.15
59000	903.59	891.50	881.52	873.26	866.39	860.67	855.89	851.89	848.54
60000	918.91	906.61	896.46	888.06	881.08	875.26	870.40	866.33	862.92
61000	934.22	921.72	911.40	902.86	895.76	889.84	884.90	880.77	877.30
62000	949.54	936.83	926.35	917.66	910.45	904.43	899.41	895.20	891.68
63000	964.85	951.94	941.29	932.46	925.13	919.02	913.92	909.64	906.06
64000	980.17	967.05	956.23	947.26	939.82	933.61	928.42	924.08	920.44
65000	995.48	982.16	971.17	962.07	954.50	948.19	942.93	938.52	934.83
66000	1010.80	997.27	986.11	976.87	969.18	962.78	957.44	952.96	949.21
67000	1026.11	1012.38	1001.05	991.67	983.87	977.37	971.94	967.40	963.59
68000	1041.43	1027.49	1015.99	1006.47	998.55	991.96	986.45	981.84	977.97
69000	1056.74	1042.60	1030.93	1021.27	1013.24	1006.55	1000.95	996.28	992.35
70000	1072.06	1057.71	1045.87	1036.07	1027.92	1021.13	1015.46	1010.71	1006.74
75000	1148.63	1133.26	1120.58	1110.07	1101.34	1094.07	1087.99	1082.91	1078.64
80000	1225.21	1208.81	1195.28	1184.08	1174.77	1167.01	1160.53	1155.10	1150.55
100000	1531.51	1511.01	1494.10	1480.10	1468.46	1458.76	1450.66	1443.88	1438.19

TERM / AMOUNT	24 YEARS	25 YEARS	26 YEARS	27 YEARS	28 YEARS	29 YEARS	30 YEARS	35 YEARS	40 YEARS
$ 25	.36	.36	.36	.36	.36	.36	.36	.36	.36
50	.72	.72	.72	.72	.72	.71	.71	.71	.71
75	1.08	1.08	1.07	1.07	1.07	1.07	1.07	1.06	1.06
100	1.44	1.43	1.43	1.43	1.43	1.42	1.42	1.42	1.41
200	2.87	2.86	2.86	2.85	2.85	2.84	2.84	2.83	2.82
300	4.31	4.29	4.28	4.27	4.27	4.26	4.26	4.24	4.23
400	5.74	5.72	5.71	5.70	5.69	5.68	5.67	5.65	5.64
500	7.17	7.15	7.14	7.12	7.11	7.10	7.09	7.06	7.05
600	8.61	8.58	8.56	8.54	8.53	8.52	8.51	8.48	8.46
700	10.04	10.01	9.99	9.97	9.95	9.94	9.92	9.89	9.87
800	11.47	11.44	11.47	11.39	11.37	11.36	11.34	11.30	11.28
900	12.91	12.87	12.84	12.81	12.79	12.77	12.76	12.71	12.69
1000	14.34	14.30	14.27	14.24	14.21	14.19	14.18	14.12	14.10
2000	28.67	28.59	28.53	28.47	28.42	28.38	28.35	28.24	28.20
3000	43.01	42.89	42.79	42.70	42.63	42.57	42.52	42.36	42.29
4000	57.34	57.18	57.05	56.93	56.84	56.76	56.69	56.48	56.39
5000	71.68	71.48	71.31	71.16	71.04	70.94	70.86	70.60	70.48
6000	86.01	85.77	85.57	85.40	85.25	85.13	85.03	84.71	84.58
7000	100.34	100.06	99.83	99.63	99.46	99.32	99.20	98.83	98.67
8000	114.68	114.36	114.09	113.86	113.67	113.51	113.37	112.95	112.77
9000	129.01	128.65	128.35	128.09	127.88	127.70	127.54	127.07	126.87
10000	143.35	142.95	142.61	142.32	142.08	141.88	141.71	141.19	140.96
15000	215.02	214.42	213.91	213.48	213.12	212.82	212.57	211.78	211.44
20000	286.69	285.89	285.21	284.64	284.16	283.76	283.42	282.37	281.92
25000	358.36	357.36	356.51	355.80	355.20	354.70	354.28	352.96	352.39
30000	430.03	428.83	427.81	426.96	426.24	425.64	425.13	423.55	422.87
35000	501.70	500.30	499.12	498.12	497.28	496.58	495.98	494.14	493.35
36000	516.03	514.59	513.38	512.35	511.49	510.77	510.15	508.26	507.45
37000	530.37	528.88	527.64	526.59	525.70	524.95	524.33	522.38	521.54
38000	544.70	543.18	541.90	540.82	539.91	539.14	538.50	536.49	535.63
39000	559.04	557.47	556.16	555.05	554.12	553.33	552.67	550.62	549.73
40000	573.37	571.77	570.42	569.28	568.32	567.52	566.84	564.73	563.83
41000	587.71	586.06	584.68	583.51	582.53	581.71	581.01	578.85	577.92
42000	602.04	600.36	598.94	597.75	596.74	595.89	595.18	592.97	592.02
43000	616.37	614.65	613.20	611.98	610.95	610.08	609.35	607.09	606.12
44000	630.71	628.94	627.46	626.21	625.16	624.27	623.52	621.21	620.21
45000	645.04	643.24	641.72	640.44	639.36	638.46	637.69	635.32	634.31
46000	659.38	657.53	655.98	654.67	653.57	652.65	651.86	649.44	648.40
47000	673.71	671.83	670.24	668.91	667.78	666.83	666.03	663.56	662.50
48000	688.04	686.12	684.50	683.14	681.99	681.02	680.20	677.68	676.59
49000	702.38	700.41	698.76	697.37	696.20	695.21	694.38	691.80	690.69
50000	716.71	714.71	713.02	711.60	710.40	709.40	708.55	705.92	704.78
51000	731.05	729.00	727.28	725.83	724.61	723.58	722.72	720.03	718.88
52000	745.38	743.30	741.54	740.06	738.82	737.77	736.89	734.15	732.98
53000	759.71	757.59	755.80	754.30	753.03	751.96	751.06	748.27	747.07
54000	774.05	771.88	770.06	768.53	767.24	766.15	765.23	762.39	761.17
55000	788.38	786.18	784.32	782.76	781.44	780.34	779.40	776.51	775.26
56000	802.72	800.47	798.58	796.99	795.65	794.52	793.57	790.62	789.36
57000	817.05	814.77	812.84	811.22	809.86	808.71	807.74	804.74	803.45
58000	831.39	829.06	827.10	825.46	824.07	822.90	821.91	818.86	817.55
59000	845.72	843.35	841.36	839.69	838.28	837.09	836.08	832.98	831.65
60000	860.05	857.65	855.62	853.92	852.48	851.27	850.25	847.10	845.74
61000	874.39	871.94	869.88	868.15	866.69	865.46	864.43	861.22	859.84
62000	888.72	886.24	884.14	882.38	880.90	879.65	878.60	875.33	873.93
63000	903.06	900.53	898.40	896.62	895.11	893.84	892.77	889.45	888.03
64000	917.39	914.82	912.67	910.85	909.32	908.03	906.94	903.57	902.12
65000	931.72	929.12	926.93	925.08	923.52	922.21	921.11	917.69	916.22
66000	946.06	943.41	941.19	939.31	937.73	936.40	935.28	931.81	930.31
67000	960.39	957.71	955.45	953.54	951.94	950.59	949.45	945.93	944.41
68000	974.73	972.00	969.71	967.78	966.15	964.78	963.62	960.04	958.51
69000	989.06	986.29	983.97	982.01	980.36	978.97	977.79	974.16	972.60
70000	1003.40	1000.59	998.23	996.24	994.56	993.15	991.96	988.28	986.70
75000	1075.07	1072.06	1069.53	1067.40	1065.60	1064.09	1062.82	1058.87	1057.17
80000	1146.74	1143.53	1140.83	1138.56	1136.64	1135.03	1133.67	1129.46	1127.65
100000	1433.42	1429.41	1426.04	1423.20	1420.80	1418.79	1417.09	1411.83	1409.56

MONTHLY PAYMENT
NECESSARY TO AMORTIZE A LOAN

TERM AMOUNT	1 YEAR	1½ YEARS	2 YEARS	2½ YEARS	3 YEARS	3½ YEARS	4 YEARS	4½ YEARS	5 YEARS
$ 25	2.29	1.59	1.24	1.04	.90	.80	.73	.67	.63
50	4.57	3.17	2.48	2.07	1.79	1.60	1.45	1.34	1.25
75	6.85	4.76	3.72	3.10	2.68	2.39	2.17	2.01	1.87
100	9.13	6.34	4.96	4.13	3.58	3.19	2.90	2.67	2.50
200	18.26	12.68	9.91	8.25	7.15	6.37	5.79	5.34	4.99
300	27.38	19.02	14.86	12.37	10.72	9.55	8.68	8.01	7.48
400	36.51	25.36	19.81	16.49	14.29	12.73	11.57	10.68	9.97
500	45.64	31.70	24.76	20.61	17.86	15.91	14.47	13.35	12.47
600	54.76	38.04	29.71	24.73	21.43	19.10	17.36	16.02	14.96
700	63.89	44.38	34.66	28.85	25.01	22.28	20.25	18.69	17.45
800	73.02	50.72	39.61	32.97	28.58	25.46	23.14	21.36	19.94
900	82.14	57.06	44.56	37.09	32.15	28.64	26.03	24.02	22.43
1000	91.27	63.40	49.51	41.22	35.72	31.82	28.93	26.69	24.93
2000	182.54	126.79	99.01	82.43	71.44	63.64	57.85	53.38	49.85
3000	273.80	190.18	148.52	123.64	107.15	95.46	86.77	80.07	74.77
4000	365.07	253.57	198.02	164.85	142.87	127.28	115.69	106.76	99.69
5000	456.33	316.96	247.52	206.06	178.59	159.10	144.61	133.45	124.61
6000	547.60	380.35	297.03	247.27	214.30	190.92	173.53	160.13	149.53
7000	638.86	443.74	346.53	288.48	250.02	222.74	202.45	186.82	174.45
8000	730.13	507.13	396.03	329.69	285.73	254.56	231.37	213.51	199.37
9000	821.39	570.52	445.54	370.90	321.45	286.38	260.29	240.20	224.29
10000	912.66	633.91	495.04	412.12	357.17	318.20	289.21	266.89	249.21
15000	1368.98	950.86	742.56	618.17	535.75	477.29	433.82	400.33	373.82
20000	1825.31	1267.81	990.07	824.23	714.33	636.39	578.42	533.77	498.42
25000	2281.63	1584.77	1237.59	1030.28	892.91	795.48	723.03	667.21	623.03
30000	2737.96	1901.72	1485.11	1236.34	1071.49	954.58	867.63	800.65	747.63
35000	3194.28	2218.67	1732.62	1442.39	1250.07	1113.67	1012.23	934.09	872.24
36000	3285.55	2282.06	1782.13	1483.60	1285.78	1145.49	1041.16	960.78	897.16
37000	3376.81	2345.45	1831.63	1524.82	1321.50	1177.31	1070.08	987.46	922.08
38000	3468.08	2408.84	1881.13	1566.03	1357.21	1209.13	1099.00	1014.15	947.00
39000	3559.34	2472.23	1930.64	1607.24	1392.93	1240.95	1127.92	1040.84	971.92
40000	3650.61	2535.62	1980.14	1648.45	1428.65	1272.77	1156.84	1067.53	996.84
41000	3741.87	2599.01	2029.64	1689.66	1464.36	1304.59	1185.76	1094.22	1021.77
42000	3833.14	2662.40	2079.15	1730.87	1500.08	1336.41	1214.68	1120.91	1046.69
43000	3924.40	2725.79	2128.65	1772.08	1535.79	1368.23	1243.60	1147.59	1071.61
44000	4015.67	2789.18	2178.15	1813.29	1571.51	1400.05	1272.52	1174.28	1096.53
45000	4106.93	2852.58	2227.66	1854.50	1607.23	1431.87	1301.44	1200.97	1121.45
46000	4198.20	2915.97	2277.16	1895.72	1642.94	1463.68	1330.36	1227.66	1146.37
47000	4289.46	2979.36	2326.66	1936.93	1678.66	1495.50	1359.29	1254.35	1171.29
48000	4380.73	3042.75	2376.17	1978.14	1714.37	1527.32	1388.21	1281.03	1196.21
49000	4471.99	3106.14	2425.67	2019.35	1750.09	1559.14	1417.13	1307.72	1221.13
50000	4563.26	3169.53	2475.17	2060.56	1785.81	1590.96	1446.05	1334.41	1246.05
51000	4654.52	3232.92	2524.68	2101.77	1821.52	1622.78	1474.97	1361.10	1270.98
52000	4745.79	3296.31	2574.18	2142.98	1857.24	1654.60	1503.89	1387.79	1295.90
53000	4837.05	3359.70	2623.68	2184.19	1892.95	1686.42	1532.81	1414.47	1320.82
54000	4928.32	3423.09	2673.19	2225.40	1928.67	1718.24	1561.73	1441.16	1345.74
55000	5019.59	3486.48	2722.69	2266.62	1964.39	1750.06	1590.65	1467.85	1370.66
56000	5110.85	3549.87	2772.19	2307.83	2000.10	1781.88	1619.57	1494.54	1395.58
57000	5202.12	3613.26	2821.70	2349.04	2035.82	1813.70	1648.49	1521.23	1420.50
58000	5293.38	3676.65	2871.20	2390.25	2071.53	1845.51	1677.41	1547.91	1445.42
59000	5384.65	3740.04	2920.70	2431.46	2107.25	1877.33	1706.34	1574.60	1470.34
60000	5475.91	3803.43	2970.21	2472.67	2142.97	1909.15	1735.26	1601.29	1495.26
61000	5567.18	3866.82	3019.71	2513.88	2178.68	1940.97	1764.18	1627.98	1520.18
62000	5658.44	3930.21	3069.21	2555.09	2214.40	1972.79	1793.10	1654.67	1545.11
63000	5749.71	3993.60	3118.72	2596.30	2250.11	2004.61	1822.02	1681.36	1570.03
64000	5840.97	4056.99	3168.22	2637.52	2285.83	2036.43	1850.94	1708.04	1594.95
65000	5932.24	4120.38	3217.72	2678.73	2321.55	2068.25	1879.86	1734.73	1619.87
66000	6023.50	4183.77	3267.23	2719.94	2357.26	2100.07	1908.78	1761.42	1644.79
67000	6114.77	4247.17	3316.73	2761.15	2392.98	2131.89	1937.70	1788.11	1669.71
68000	6206.03	4310.56	3366.23	2802.36	2428.69	2163.71	1966.62	1814.80	1694.63
69000	6297.30	4373.95	3415.74	2843.57	2464.41	2195.52	1995.54	1841.48	1719.55
70000	6388.56	4437.34	3465.24	2884.78	2500.13	2227.34	2024.46	1868.17	1744.47
75000	6844.89	4754.29	3712.76	3090.84	2678.71	2386.44	2169.07	2001.61	1869.08
80000	7301.21	5071.24	3960.27	3296.89	2857.29	2545.54	2313.67	2135.05	1993.68
100000	9126.51	6339.05	4950.34	4121.12	3571.61	3181.92	2892.09	2668.82	2492.10

176

TERM AMOUNT	6 YEARS	7 YEARS	8 YEARS	9 YEARS	10 YEARS	11 YEARS	12 YEARS	13 YEARS	14 YEARS
$ 25	.56	.52	.48	.46	.44	.43	.42	.41	.40
50	1.12	1.03	.96	.92	.88	.85	.83	.81	.79
75	1.68	1.54	1.44	1.37	1.31	1.27	1.24	1.21	1.18
100	2.24	2.06	1.92	1.83	1.75	1.69	1.65	1.61	1.58
200	4.47	4.11	3.84	3.65	3.50	3.38	3.29	3.21	3.15
300	6.70	6.16	5.76	5.47	5.24	5.07	4.93	4.81	4.72
400	8.93	8.21	7.68	7.29	6.99	6.75	6.57	6.42	6.30
500	11.16	10.26	9.60	9.11	8.74	8.44	8.21	8.02	7.87
600	13.40	12.31	11.52	10.93	10.48	10.13	9.85	9.62	9.44
700	15.63	14.36	13.44	12.76	12.23	11.81	11.49	11.23	11.01
800	17.06	16.41	15.36	14.58	13.97	13.50	13.13	12.83	12.59
900	20.09	18.46	17.28	16.40	15.72	15.19	14.77	14.43	14.16
1000	22.32	20.51	19.20	18.22	17.47	16.88	16.41	16.03	15.73
2000	44.64	41.02	38.40	36.43	34.93	33.75	32.81	32.06	31.46
3000	66.96	61.53	57.60	54.65	52.39	50.62	49.22	48.09	47.19
4000	89.27	82.04	76.79	72.86	69.85	67.49	65.62	64.12	62.91
5000	111.59	102.55	95.99	91.08	87.31	84.36	82.03	80.15	78.64
6000	133.91	123.06	115.19	109.29	104.77	101.23	98.43	96.18	94.37
7000	156.22	143.57	134.39	127.51	122.23	118.10	114.83	112.21	110.09
8000	178.54	164.08	153.58	145.72	139.69	134.97	131.24	128.24	125.82
9000	200.86	184.59	172.78	163.94	157.15	151.84	147.64	144.27	141.55
10000	223.18	205.10	191.98	182.15	174.61	168.72	164.05	160.30	157.27
15000	334.76	307.65	287.97	273.22	261.91	253.07	246.07	240.45	235.91
20000	446.35	410.19	383.95	364.30	349.21	337.43	328.09	320.60	314.54
25000	557.93	512.74	479.94	455.37	436.52	421.78	410.11	400.75	393.18
30000	669.52	615.29	575.93	546.44	523.82	506.14	492.13	480.90	471.81
35000	781.10	717.83	671.92	637.51	611.12	590.49	574.15	561.04	550.45
36000	803.42	738.34	691.11	655.73	628.58	607.36	590.55	577.07	566.17
37000	825.74	758.85	710.31	673.94	646.04	624.24	606.95	593.10	581.90
38000	848.06	779.36	729.51	692.16	663.50	641.11	623.36	609.13	597.63
39000	870.37	799.87	748.71	710.37	680.96	657.98	639.76	625.16	613.35
40000	892.69	820.38	767.90	728.59	698.42	674.85	656.17	641.19	629.08
41000	915.01	840.89	787.10	746.80	715.88	691.72	672.57	657.22	644.81
42000	937.32	861.40	806.30	765.02	733.34	708.59	688.98	673.25	660.53
43000	959.64	881.91	825.50	783.23	750.80	725.46	705.38	689.28	676.26
44000	981.96	902.42	844.69	801.45	768.26	742.33	721.78	705.31	691.99
45000	1004.28	922.93	863.89	819.66	785.72	759.20	738.19	721.34	707.72
46000	1026.59	943.43	883.09	837.87	803.18	776.08	754.59	737.37	723.44
47000	1048.91	963.94	902.29	856.09	820.64	792.95	771.00	753.40	739.17
48000	1071.23	984.45	921.48	874.30	838.10	809.82	787.40	769.43	754.90
49000	1093.54	1004.96	940.68	892.52	855.56	826.69	803.80	785.46	770.62
50000	1115.86	1025.47	959.88	910.73	873.03	843.56	820.21	801.49	786.35
51000	1138.18	1045.98	979.08	928.95	890.49	860.43	836.61	817.52	802.08
52000	1160.50	1066.49	998.27	947.16	907.95	877.30	853.02	833.55	817.80
53000	1182.81	1087.00	1017.47	965.38	925.41	894.17	869.42	849.58	833.53
54000	1205.13	1107.51	1036.67	983.59	942.87	911.04	885.82	865.61	849.26
55000	1227.45	1128.02	1055.86	1001.81	960.33	927.92	902.23	881.64	864.98
56000	1249.76	1148.53	1075.06	1020.02	977.79	944.79	918.63	897.67	880.71
57000	1272.08	1169.04	1094.26	1038.23	995.25	961.66	935.04	913.70	896.44
58000	1294.40	1189.55	1113.46	1056.45	1012.71	978.53	951.44	929.73	912.17
59000	1316.72	1210.06	1132.65	1074.66	1030.17	995.40	967.84	945.76	927.89
60000	1339.03	1230.57	1151.85	1092.88	1047.63	1012.27	984.25	961.79	943.62
61000	1361.35	1251.07	1171.05	1111.09	1065.09	1029.14	1000.65	977.82	959.35
62000	1383.67	1271.58	1190.25	1129.31	1082.55	1046.01	1017.06	993.85	975.07
63000	1405.98	1292.09	1209.44	1147.52	1100.01	1062.88	1033.46	1009.88	990.80
64000	1428.30	1312.60	1228.64	1165.74	1117.47	1079.76	1049.86	1025.91	1006.53
65000	1450.62	1333.11	1247.84	1183.95	1134.93	1096.63	1066.27	1041.93	1022.25
66000	1472.94	1353.62	1267.04	1202.17	1152.39	1113.50	1082.67	1057.96	1037.98
67000	1495.25	1374.13	1286.23	1220.38	1169.85	1130.37	1099.08	1073.99	1053.71
68000	1517.57	1394.64	1305.43	1238.59	1187.31	1147.24	1115.48	1090.02	1069.43
69000	1539.89	1415.15	1324.63	1256.81	1204.77	1164.11	1131.88	1106.05	1085.16
70000	1562.20	1435.66	1343.83	1275.02	1222.23	1180.98	1148.29	1122.08	1100.89
75000	1673.79	1538.21	1439.81	1366.10	1309.54	1265.34	1230.31	1202.23	1179.52
80000	1785.37	1640.75	1535.80	1457.17	1396.84	1349.69	1312.33	1282.38	1258.16
100000	2231.72	2050.94	1919.75	1821.46	1746.05	1687.12	1640.41	1602.97	1572.70

17¾% MONTHLY PAYMENT
NECESSARY TO AMORTIZE A LOAN

TERM AMOUNT	15 YEARS	16 YEARS	17 YEARS	18 YEARS	19 YEARS	20 YEARS	21 YEARS	22 YEARS	23 YEARS
$ 25	.39	.39	.38	.38	.38	.37	.37	.37	.37
50	.78	.77	.76	.75	.75	.74	.74	.74	.73
75	1.17	1.15	1.14	1.13	1.12	1.11	1.11	1.10	1.10
100	1.55	1.53	1.52	1.50	1.49	1.48	1.47	1.47	1.46
200	3.10	3.06	3.03	3.00	2.98	2.96	2.94	2.93	2.92
300	4.65	4.59	4.54	4.50	4.46	4.43	4.41	4.39	4.37
400	6.20	6.12	6.05	5.99	5.95	5.91	5.88	5.85	5.83
500	7.75	7.64	7.56	7.49	7.43	7.39	7.35	7.31	7.29
600	9.29	9.17	9.07	8.99	8.92	8.86	8.82	8.78	8.74
700	10.84	10.70	10.58	10.49	10.41	10.34	10.28	10.24	10.20
800	12.39	12.23	12.09	11.98	11.89	11.82	11.75	11.70	11.66
900	13.94	13.76	13.61	13.48	13.38	13.29	13.22	13.16	13.11
1000	15.49	15.28	15.12	14.98	14.86	14.77	14.69	14.62	14.57
2000	30.97	30.56	30.23	29.95	29.72	29.53	29.38	29.24	29.13
3000	46.45	45.84	45.34	44.93	44.58	44.30	44.06	43.86	43.70
4000	61.93	61.12	60.45	59.90	59.44	59.06	58.75	58.48	58.26
5000	77.41	76.40	75.56	74.87	74.30	73.83	73.43	73.10	72.83
6000	92.89	91.67	90.67	89.85	89.16	88.59	88.12	87.72	87.39
7000	108.37	106.95	105.79	104.82	104.02	103.36	102.80	102.34	101.95
8000	123.85	122.23	120.90	119.80	118.88	118.12	117.49	116.96	116.52
9000	139.33	137.51	136.01	134.77	133.74	132.89	132.18	131.58	131.08
10000	154.81	152.79	151.12	149.74	148.60	147.65	146.86	146.20	145.65
15000	232.21	229.18	226.68	224.61	222.90	221.48	220.29	219.30	218.47
20000	309.61	305.57	302.24	299.48	297.20	295.30	293.72	292.39	291.29
25000	387.01	381.96	377.79	374.35	371.50	369.12	367.14	365.49	364.11
30000	464.41	458.35	453.35	449.22	445.80	442.95	440.57	438.59	436.93
35000	541.81	534.74	528.91	524.09	520.10	516.77	514.00	511.68	509.75
36000	557.29	550.02	544.02	539.07	534.96	531.54	528.69	526.30	524.31
37000	572.77	565.29	559.13	554.04	549.82	546.30	543.37	540.92	538.88
38000	588.25	580.57	574.25	569.01	564.68	561.07	558.06	555.54	553.44
39000	603.73	595.85	589.36	583.99	579.53	575.83	572.74	570.16	568.01
40000	619.21	611.13	604.47	598.96	594.39	590.60	587.43	584.78	582.57
41000	634.69	626.41	619.58	613.94	609.25	605.36	602.11	599.40	597.13
42000	650.17	641.68	634.69	628.91	624.11	620.12	616.80	614.02	611.70
43000	665.65	656.96	649.80	643.88	638.97	634.89	631.48	628.64	626.26
44000	681.14	672.24	664.91	658.86	653.83	649.65	646.17	643.26	640.82
45000	696.62	687.52	680.03	673.83	668.69	664.42	660.86	657.88	655.39
46000	712.10	702.80	695.14	688.81	683.55	679.18	675.54	672.50	669.95
47000	727.58	718.07	710.25	703.78	698.41	693.95	690.23	687.12	684.52
48000	743.06	733.35	725.36	718.75	713.27	708.71	704.91	701.74	699.08
49000	758.54	748.63	740.47	733.73	728.13	723.48	719.60	716.36	713.64
50000	774.02	763.91	755.58	748.70	742.99	738.24	734.28	730.98	728.21
51000	789.50	779.19	770.70	763.68	757.85	753.01	748.97	745.60	742.77
52000	804.98	794.46	785.81	778.65	772.71	767.77	763.65	760.21	757.34
53000	820.46	809.74	800.92	793.62	787.57	782.54	778.34	774.83	771.90
54000	835.94	825.02	816.03	808.60	802.43	797.30	793.03	789.45	786.46
55000	851.42	840.30	831.14	823.57	817.29	812.07	807.71	804.07	801.03
56000	866.90	855.58	846.25	838.55	832.15	826.83	822.40	818.69	815.59
57000	882.38	870.85	861.37	853.52	847.01	841.60	837.08	833.31	830.16
58000	897.86	886.13	876.48	868.49	861.87	856.36	851.77	847.93	844.72
59000	913.34	901.41	891.59	883.47	876.73	871.13	866.45	862.55	859.29
60000	928.82	916.69	906.70	898.44	891.59	885.89	881.14	877.17	873.85
61000	944.30	931.97	921.81	913.41	906.45	900.66	895.82	891.79	888.41
62000	959.78	947.25	936.92	928.39	921.31	915.42	910.51	906.41	902.98
63000	975.26	962.52	952.03	943.36	936.17	930.18	925.20	921.03	917.54
64000	990.74	977.80	967.15	958.34	951.03	944.95	939.88	935.65	932.11
65000	1006.22	993.08	982.26	973.31	965.89	959.71	954.57	950.27	946.67
66000	1021.70	1008.36	997.37	988.28	980.75	974.48	969.25	964.89	961.23
67000	1037.18	1023.64	1012.48	1003.26	995.61	989.24	983.94	979.51	975.80
68000	1052.66	1038.91	1027.59	1018.23	1010.47	1004.01	998.62	994.13	990.36
69000	1068.14	1054.19	1042.70	1033.21	1025.33	1018.77	1013.31	1008.74	1004.93
70000	1083.62	1069.47	1057.82	1048.18	1040.19	1033.54	1027.99	1023.36	1019.49
75000	1161.02	1145.86	1133.37	1123.05	1114.49	1107.36	1101.42	1096.46	1092.31
80000	1238.42	1222.25	1208.93	1197.92	1188.78	1181.19	1174.85	1169.56	1165.13
100000	1548.03	1527.81	1511.16	1497.40	1485.98	1476.48	1468.56	1461.95	1456.41

178

MONTHLY PAYMENT 17¾%
NECESSARY TO AMORTIZE A LOAN

TERM AMOUNT	24 YEARS	25 YEARS	26 YEARS	27 YEARS	28 YEARS	29 YEARS	30 YEARS	35 YEARS	40 YEARS
$ 25	.37	.37	.37	.37	.36	.36	.36	.36	.36
50	.73	.73	.73	.73	.72	.72	.72	.72	.72
75	1.09	1.09	1.09	1.09	1.08	1.08	1.08	1.08	1.08
100	1.46	1.45	1.45	1.45	1.44	1.44	1.44	1.44	1.43
200	2.91	2.90	2.89	2.89	2.88	2.88	2.88	2.87	2.86
300	4.36	4.35	4.34	4.33	4.32	4.32	4.31	4.30	4.29
400	5.81	5.80	5.78	5.77	5.76	5.76	5.75	5.73	5.72
500	7.26	7.24	7.23	7.21	7.20	7.19	7.18	7.16	7.15
600	8.72	8.69	8.67	8.66	8.64	8.63	8.62	8.59	8.58
700	10.17	10.14	10.12	10.10	10.08	10.07	10.06	10.02	10.01
800	11.62	11.59	11.56	11.54	11.52	11.51	11.49	11.45	11.44
900	13.07	13.04	13.01	12.98	12.96	12.94	12.93	12.88	12.80
1000	14.52	14.48	14.45	14.42	14.40	14.38	14.36	14.31	14.29
2000	29.04	28.96	28.90	28.84	28.80	28.76	28.72	28.62	28.58
3000	43.56	43.44	43.34	43.26	43.19	43.13	43.08	42.93	42.87
4000	58.08	57.92	57.79	57.68	57.59	57.51	57.44	57.24	57.16
5000	72.59	72.40	72.24	72.10	71.98	71.89	71.80	71.55	71.45
6000	87.11	86.88	86.68	86.52	86.38	86.26	86.16	85.86	85.74
7000	101.63	101.36	101.13	100.94	100.77	100.64	100.52	100.17	100.02
8000	116.15	115.84	115.57	115.36	115.17	115.02	114.88	114.48	114.31
9000	130.66	130.31	130.02	129.77	129.57	129.39	129.24	128.79	128.60
10000	145.18	144.79	144.47	144.19	143.96	143.77	143.60	143.10	142.89
15000	217.77	217.19	216.70	216.29	215.94	215.65	215.40	214.65	214.33
20000	290.36	289.58	288.93	288.38	287.92	287.53	287.20	286.20	285.77
25000	362.95	361.98	361.16	360.47	359.90	359.41	359.00	357.75	357.22
30000	435.54	434.37	433.39	432.57	431.88	431.29	430.80	429.30	428.66
35000	508.12	506.76	505.62	504.66	503.85	503.18	502.60	500.85	500.10
36000	522.64	521.24	520.07	519.08	518.25	517.55	516.96	515.16	514.39
37000	537.16	535.72	534.51	533.50	532.65	531.93	531.32	529.47	528.68
38000	551.68	550.20	548.96	547.92	547.04	546.30	545.68	543.78	542.97
39000	566.20	564.68	563.41	562.34	561.44	560.68	560.04	558.09	557.26
40000	580.71	579.16	577.85	576.76	575.83	575.06	574.40	572.40	571.54
41000	595.23	593.64	592.30	591.17	590.23	589.43	588.76	586.71	585.83
42000	609.75	608.12	606.74	605.59	604.62	603.81	603.12	601.02	600.12
43000	624.27	622.59	621.19	620.01	619.02	618.19	617.48	615.33	614.41
44000	638.78	637.07	635.64	634.43	633.42	632.56	631.84	629.64	628.70
45000	653.30	651.55	650.08	648.85	647.81	646.94	646.20	643.95	642.99
46000	667.82	666.03	664.53	663.27	662.21	661.32	660.56	658.26	657.28
47000	682.34	680.51	678.98	677.69	676.60	675.69	674.92	672.57	671.56
48000	696.85	694.99	693.42	692.11	691.00	690.07	689.28	686.88	685.85
49000	711.37	709.47	707.87	706.52	705.39	704.44	703.64	701.19	700.14
50000	725.89	723.95	722.31	720.94	719.79	718.82	718.00	715.50	714.43
51000	740.41	738.42	736.76	735.36	734.19	733.20	732.36	729.81	728.72
52000	754.93	752.90	751.21	749.78	748.58	747.57	746.72	744.12	743.01
53000	769.44	767.38	765.65	764.20	762.98	761.95	761.08	758.43	757.29
54000	783.96	781.86	780.10	778.62	777.37	776.33	775.44	772.73	771.58
55000	798.48	796.34	794.54	793.04	791.77	790.70	789.80	787.04	785.87
56000	813.00	810.82	808.99	807.46	806.16	805.08	804.16	801.35	800.16
57000	827.51	825.30	823.44	821.87	820.56	819.45	818.52	815.66	814.45
58000	842.03	839.78	837.88	836.29	834.96	833.83	832.88	829.97	828.74
59000	856.55	854.26	852.33	850.71	849.35	848.21	847.24	844.28	843.03
60000	871.07	868.73	866.78	865.13	863.75	862.58	861.60	858.59	857.31
61000	885.58	883.21	881.22	879.55	878.14	876.96	875.96	872.90	871.60
62000	900.10	897.69	895.67	893.97	892.54	891.34	890.32	887.21	885.89
63000	914.62	912.17	910.11	908.39	906.93	905.71	904.68	901.52	900.18
64000	929.14	926.65	924.56	922.81	921.33	920.09	919.04	915.83	914.47
65000	943.66	941.13	939.01	937.22	935.73	934.47	933.40	930.14	928.76
66000	958.17	955.61	953.45	951.64	950.12	948.84	947.76	944.45	943.04
67000	972.69	970.09	967.90	966.06	964.52	963.22	962.12	958.76	957.33
68000	987.21	984.56	982.35	980.48	978.91	977.59	976.48	973.07	971.62
69000	1001.73	999.04	996.79	994.90	993.31	991.97	990.84	987.38	985.91
70000	1016.24	1013.52	1011.24	1009.32	1007.70	1006.35	1005.20	1001.69	1000.20
75000	1088.83	1085.92	1083.47	1081.41	1079.68	1078.23	1077.00	1073.24	1071.64
80000	1161.42	1158.31	1155.70	1153.51	1151.66	1150.11	1148.80	1144.79	1143.08
100000	1451.78	1447.89	1444.62	1441.88	1439.58	1437.64	1436.00	1430.99	1428.85

179

18% MONTHLY PAYMENT
NECESSARY TO AMORTIZE A LOAN

TERM AMOUNT	1 YEAR	1½ YEARS	2 YEARS	2½ YEARS	3 YEARS	3½ YEARS	4 YEARS	4½ YEARS	5 YEARS
$ 25	2.29	1.59	1.25	1.04	.90	.80	.73	.68	.63
50	4.57	3.18	2.49	2.07	1.80	1.60	1.46	1.35	1.26
75	6.86	4.77	3.73	3.10	2.69	2.40	2.18	2.02	1.88
100	9.14	6.36	4.97	4.14	3.59	3.20	2.91	2.69	2.51
200	18.28	12.71	9.93	8.27	7.17	6.39	5.81	5.37	5.01
300	27.42	19.06	14.89	12.40	10.75	9.59	8.72	8.05	7.52
400	36.56	25.41	19.85	16.54	14.34	12.78	11.62	10.73	10.02
500	45.69	31.76	24.81	20.67	17.92	15.97	14.53	13.41	12.53
600	54.83	38.11	29.77	24.80	21.50	19.17	17.43	16.09	15.03
700	63.97	44.46	34.74	28.93	25.09	22.36	20.33	18.77	17.54
800	73.11	50.81	39.70	33.07	28.67	25.55	23.24	21.45	20.04
900	82.24	57.16	44.66	37.20	32.25	28.75	26.14	24.14	22.55
1000	91.38	63.51	49.62	41.33	35.84	31.94	29.05	26.82	25.05
2000	182.76	127.01	99.24	82.66	71.67	63.88	58.09	53.63	50.10
3000	274.13	190.51	148.85	123.98	107.50	95.82	87.13	80.44	75.14
4000	365.51	254.01	198.47	165.31	143.33	127.75	116.17	107.25	100.19
5000	456.88	317.51	248.08	206.63	179.17	159.69	145.21	134.06	125.24
6000	548.26	381.01	297.70	247.96	215.00	191.63	174.25	160.87	150.28
7000	639.63	444.51	347.31	289.28	250.83	223.57	203.30	187.68	175.33
8000	731.01	508.01	396.93	330.61	286.66	255.50	232.34	214.49	200.38
9000	822.39	571.51	446.54	371.93	322.49	287.44	261.38	241.31	225.42
10000	913.76	635.02	496.16	413.26	358.33	319.38	290.42	268.12	250.47
15000	1370.64	952.52	744.24	619.88	537.49	479.07	435.63	402.17	375.70
20000	1827.52	1270.03	992.31	826.51	716.65	638.75	580.84	536.23	500.94
25000	2284.40	1587.53	1240.39	1033.13	895.81	798.44	726.04	670.29	626.17
30000	2741.27	1905.04	1488.47	1239.76	1074.97	958.13	871.25	804.34	751.40
35000	3198.15	2222.54	1736.54	1446.38	1254.13	1117.82	1016.46	938.40	876.63
36000	3289.53	2286.04	1786.16	1487.71	1289.96	1149.75	1045.50	965.21	901.68
37000	3380.90	2349.54	1835.77	1529.03	1325.79	1181.69	1074.54	992.02	926.73
38000	3472.28	2413.05	1885.39	1570.36	1361.63	1213.63	1103.59	1018.83	951.77
39000	3563.66	2476.55	1935.00	1611.68	1397.46	1245.57	1132.63	1045.64	976.82
40000	3655.03	2540.05	1984.62	1653.01	1433.29	1277.50	1161.67	1072.45	1001.87
41000	3746.41	2603.55	2034.24	1694.33	1469.12	1309.44	1190.71	1099.27	1026.91
42000	3837.78	2667.05	2083.85	1735.66	1504.95	1341.38	1219.75	1126.08	1051.96
43000	3929.16	2730.55	2133.47	1776.98	1540.79	1373.32	1248.79	1152.89	1077.00
44000	4020.53	2794.05	2183.08	1818.31	1576.62	1405.25	1277.83	1179.70	1102.05
45000	4111.91	2857.55	2232.70	1859.63	1612.45	1437.19	1306.88	1206.51	1127.10
46000	4203.28	2921.05	2282.31	1900.96	1648.28	1469.13	1335.92	1233.32	1152.14
47000	4294.66	2984.56	2331.93	1942.28	1684.11	1501.07	1364.96	1260.13	1177.19
48000	4386.04	3048.06	2381.54	1983.61	1719.95	1533.00	1394.00	1286.94	1202.24
49000	4477.41	3111.56	2431.16	2024.93	1755.78	1564.94	1423.04	1313.76	1227.28
50000	4568.79	3175.06	2480.77	2066.26	1791.61	1596.88	1452.08	1340.57	1252.33
51000	4660.16	3238.56	2530.39	2107.58	1827.44	1628.82	1481.13	1367.38	1277.38
52000	4751.54	3302.06	2580.00	2148.91	1863.27	1660.75	1510.17	1394.19	1302.42
53000	4842.91	3365.56	2629.62	2190.23	1899.11	1692.69	1539.21	1421.00	1327.47
54000	4934.29	3429.06	2679.24	2231.56	1934.94	1724.63	1568.25	1447.81	1352.52
55000	5025.67	3492.56	2728.85	2272.88	1970.77	1756.57	1597.29	1474.62	1377.56
56000	5117.04	3556.06	2778.47	2314.21	2006.60	1788.50	1626.33	1501.43	1402.61
57000	5208.42	3619.57	2828.08	2355.53	2042.44	1820.44	1655.38	1528.24	1427.66
58000	5299.79	3683.07	2877.70	2396.86	2078.27	1852.38	1684.42	1555.06	1452.70
59000	5391.17	3746.57	2927.31	2438.18	2114.10	1884.32	1713.46	1581.87	1477.75
60000	5482.54	3810.07	2976.93	2479.51	2149.93	1916.25	1742.50	1608.68	1502.80
61000	5573.92	3873.57	3026.54	2520.83	2185.76	1948.19	1771.54	1635.49	1527.84
62000	5665.29	3937.07	3076.16	2562.16	2221.60	1980.13	1800.58	1662.30	1552.89
63000	5756.67	4000.57	3125.77	2603.48	2257.43	2012.07	1829.62	1689.11	1577.93
64000	5848.05	4064.07	3175.39	2644.81	2293.26	2044.00	1858.67	1715.92	1602.98
65000	5939.42	4127.57	3225.00	2686.13	2329.09	2075.94	1887.71	1742.73	1628.03
66000	6030.80	4191.08	3274.62	2727.46	2364.92	2107.88	1916.75	1769.55	1653.07
67000	6122.17	4254.58	3324.24	2768.78	2400.76	2139.82	1945.79	1796.36	1678.12
68000	6213.55	4318.08	3373.85	2810.11	2436.59	2171.75	1974.83	1823.17	1703.17
69000	6304.92	4381.58	3423.47	2851.43	2472.42	2203.69	2003.87	1849.98	1728.21
70000	6396.30	4445.08	3473.08	2892.76	2508.25	2235.63	2032.92	1876.79	1753.26
75000	6853.18	4762.59	3721.16	3099.38	2687.41	2395.32	2178.12	2010.85	1878.49
80000	7310.06	5080.09	3969.23	3306.01	2866.57	2555.00	2323.33	2144.90	2003.73
100000	9137.57	6350.11	4961.54	4132.51	3583.22	3193.75	2904.16	2681.13	2504.66

180

MONTHLY PAYMENT 18%
NECESSARY TO AMORTIZE A LOAN

TERM AMOUNT	6 YEARS	7 YEARS	8 YEARS	9 YEARS	10 YEARS	11 YEARS	12 YEARS	13 YEARS	14 YEARS
$ 25	.57	.52	.49	.46	.45	.43	.42	.41	.40
50	1.13	1.04	.97	.92	.89	.86	.83	.81	.80
75	1.69	1.55	1.46	1.38	1.33	1.28	1.25	1.22	1.20
100	2.25	2.07	1.94	1.84	1.77	1.71	1.66	1.62	1.59
200	4.49	4.13	3.87	3.68	3.53	3.41	3.32	3.24	3.18
300	6.74	6.20	5.81	5.51	5.29	5.11	4.97	4.86	4.77
400	8.98	8.26	7.74	7.35	7.05	6.81	6.63	6.48	6.36
500	11.23	10.33	9.67	9.18	8.81	8.52	8.28	8.10	7.95
600	13.47	12.39	11.61	11.02	10.57	10.22	9.94	9.72	9.54
700	15.72	14.46	13.54	12.86	12.33	11.92	11.60	11.34	11.13
800	17.96	16.52	15.47	14.69	14.09	13.62	13.25	12.96	12.72
900	20.21	18.58	17.41	16.53	15.85	15.33	14.91	14.58	14.31
1000	22.45	20.65	19.34	18.36	17.61	17.03	16.56	16.19	15.89
2000	44.90	41.29	38.68	36.72	35.22	34.05	33.12	32.38	31.78
3000	67.35	61.94	58.02	55.08	52.83	51.07	49.68	48.57	47.67
4000	89.79	82.58	77.35	73.44	70.44	68.10	66.24	64.76	63.56
5000	112.24	103.23	96.69	91.80	88.05	85.12	82.80	80.95	79.45
6000	134.69	123.87	116.03	110.16	105.66	102.14	99.36	97.14	95.34
7000	157.14	144.52	135.36	128.51	123.26	119.17	115.92	113.33	111.23
8000	179.58	165.16	154.70	146.87	140.87	136.19	132.48	129.52	127.12
9000	202.03	185.80	174.04	165.23	158.48	153.21	149.04	145.71	143.01
10000	224.48	206.45	193.37	183.59	176.09	170.24	165.60	161.89	158.90
15000	336.72	309.67	290.06	275.38	264.13	255.35	248.40	242.84	238.35
20000	448.95	412.89	386.74	367.17	352.17	340.47	331.20	323.78	317.79
25000	561.19	516.11	483.43	458.97	440.22	425.58	414.00	404.73	397.24
30000	673.43	619.34	580.11	550.76	528.26	510.70	496.80	485.67	476.69
35000	785.67	722.56	676.80	642.55	616.30	595.82	579.60	566.62	556.14
36000	808.11	743.20	696.14	660.91	633.91	612.84	596.16	582.81	572.03
37000	830.56	763.85	715.47	679.27	651.52	629.86	612.72	599.00	587.92
38000	853.01	784.49	734.81	697.63	669.13	646.89	629.28	615.19	603.80
39000	875.45	805.13	754.15	715.99	686.74	663.91	645.84	631.38	619.69
40000	897.90	825.78	773.48	734.34	704.34	680.93	662.40	647.56	635.58
41000	920.35	846.42	792.82	752.70	721.95	697.95	678.96	663.75	651.47
42000	942.80	867.07	812.16	771.06	739.56	714.98	695.52	679.94	667.36
43000	965.24	887.71	831.50	789.42	757.17	732.00	712.08	696.13	683.25
44000	987.69	908.36	850.83	807.78	774.78	749.02	728.64	712.32	699.14
45000	1010.14	929.00	870.17	826.14	792.39	766.05	745.20	728.51	715.03
46000	1032.59	949.64	889.51	844.49	810.00	783.07	761.76	744.70	730.92
47000	1055.03	970.29	908.84	862.85	827.60	800.09	778.32	760.89	746.81
48000	1077.48	990.93	928.18	881.21	845.21	817.12	794.88	777.08	762.70
49000	1099.93	1011.58	947.52	899.57	862.82	834.14	811.44	793.26	778.59
50000	1122.38	1032.22	966.85	917.93	880.43	851.16	828.00	809.45	794.48
51000	1144.82	1052.87	986.19	936.29	898.04	868.19	844.56	825.64	810.37
52000	1167.27	1073.51	1005.53	954.65	915.65	885.21	861.12	841.83	826.26
53000	1189.72	1094.15	1024.87	973.00	933.26	902.23	877.68	858.02	842.15
54000	1212.17	1114.80	1044.20	991.36	950.86	919.26	894.24	874.21	858.04
55000	1234.61	1135.44	1063.54	1009.72	968.47	936.28	910.80	890.40	873.93
56000	1257.06	1156.09	1082.88	1028.08	986.08	953.30	927.36	906.59	889.82
57000	1279.51	1176.73	1102.21	1046.44	1003.69	970.33	943.92	922.78	905.70
58000	1301.96	1197.38	1121.55	1064.80	1021.30	987.35	960.48	938.97	921.59
59000	1324.40	1218.02	1140.89	1083.15	1038.91	1004.37	977.00	955.15	937.48
60000	1346.85	1238.67	1160.22	1101.51	1056.51	1021.39	993.60	971.34	953.37
61000	1369.30	1259.31	1179.56	1119.87	1074.12	1038.42	1010.16	987.53	969.26
62000	1391.75	1279.95	1198.90	1138.23	1091.73	1055.44	1026.71	1003.72	985.15
63000	1414.19	1300.60	1218.24	1156.59	1109.34	1072.46	1043.27	1019.91	1001.04
64000	1436.64	1321.24	1237.57	1174.95	1126.95	1089.49	1059.83	1036.10	1016.93
65000	1459.09	1341.89	1256.91	1193.31	1144.56	1106.51	1076.39	1052.29	1032.82
66000	1481.54	1362.53	1276.25	1211.66	1162.17	1123.53	1092.95	1068.48	1048.71
67000	1503.98	1383.18	1295.58	1230.02	1179.77	1140.56	1109.51	1084.67	1064.60
68000	1526.43	1403.82	1314.92	1248.38	1197.38	1157.58	1126.07	1100.86	1080.49
69000	1548.88	1424.46	1334.26	1266.74	1214.99	1174.60	1142.63	1117.04	1096.38
70000	1571.33	1445.11	1353.59	1285.10	1232.60	1191.63	1159.19	1133.23	1112.27
75000	1683.56	1548.33	1450.28	1376.89	1320.64	1276.74	1241.99	1214.18	1191.72
80000	1795.80	1651.55	1546.96	1468.68	1408.68	1361.86	1324.79	1295.12	1271.16
100000	2244.75	2064.44	1933.70	1835.85	1760.85	1702.32	1655.99	1618.90	1588.95

18% MONTHLY PAYMENT
NECESSARY TO AMORTIZE A LOAN

TERM AMOUNT	15 YEARS	16 YEARS	17 YEARS	18 YEARS	19 YEARS	20 YEARS	21 YEARS	22 YEARS	23 YEARS
$ 25	.40	.39	.39	.38	.38	.38	.38	.38	.37
50	.79	.78	.77	.76	.76	.75	.75	.75	.74
75	1.18	1.16	1.15	1.14	1.13	1.13	1.12	1.12	1.11
100	1.57	1.55	1.53	1.52	1.51	1.50	1.49	1.49	1.48
200	3.13	3.09	3.06	3.03	3.01	2.99	2.98	2.97	2.95
300	4.70	4.64	4.59	4.55	4.52	4.49	4.46	4.45	4.43
400	6.26	6.18	6.12	6.06	6.02	5.98	5.95	5.93	5.90
500	7.83	7.73	7.65	7.58	7.52	7.48	7.44	7.41	7.38
600	9.39	9.27	9.17	9.09	9.03	8.97	8.92	8.89	8.85
700	10.96	10.82	10.70	10.61	10.53	10.46	10.41	10.37	10.33
800	12.52	12.36	12.23	12.12	12.03	11.96	11.90	11.85	11.80
900	14.09	13.91	13.76	13.64	13.54	13.45	13.38	13.33	13.28
1000	15.65	15.45	15.29	15.15	15.04	14.95	14.87	14.81	14.75
2000	31.30	30.90	30.57	30.30	30.08	29.89	29.73	29.61	29.50
3000	46.94	46.34	45.85	45.45	45.11	44.83	44.60	44.41	44.24
4000	62.59	61.79	61.14	60.59	60.15	59.77	59.46	59.21	58.99
5000	78.23	77.24	76.42	75.74	75.18	74.72	74.33	74.01	73.74
6000	93.88	92.68	91.70	90.89	90.22	89.66	89.19	88.81	88.48
7000	109.53	108.13	106.98	106.04	105.25	104.60	104.06	103.61	103.23
8000	125.17	123.58	122.27	121.18	120.29	119.54	118.92	118.41	117.98
9000	140.82	139.02	137.55	136.33	135.32	134.49	133.79	133.21	132.72
10000	156.46	154.47	152.83	151.48	150.36	149.43	148.65	148.01	147.47
15000	234.69	231.70	229.24	227.22	225.53	224.14	222.98	222.01	221.20
20000	312.92	308.93	305.66	302.95	300.71	298.85	297.30	296.01	294.94
25000	391.15	386.17	382.07	378.69	375.89	373.56	371.63	370.02	368.67
30000	469.38	463.40	458.48	454.43	451.06	448.27	445.95	444.02	442.40
35000	547.61	540.63	534.90	530.16	526.24	522.99	520.28	518.02	516.13
36000	563.26	556.08	550.18	545.31	541.28	537.93	535.14	532.82	530.88
37000	578.90	571.53	565.46	560.46	556.31	552.87	550.01	547.62	545.63
38000	594.55	586.97	580.74	575.60	571.35	567.81	564.87	562.42	560.37
39000	610.19	602.42	596.03	590.75	586.38	582.76	579.74	577.22	575.12
40000	625.84	617.86	611.31	605.90	601.42	597.70	594.60	592.02	589.87
41000	641.48	633.31	626.59	621.05	616.45	612.64	609.47	606.82	604.61
42000	657.13	648.76	641.87	636.19	631.49	627.58	624.33	621.62	619.36
43000	672.78	664.20	657.16	651.34	646.52	642.52	639.20	636.42	634.11
44000	688.42	679.65	672.44	666.49	661.56	657.47	654.06	651.22	648.85
45000	704.07	695.10	687.72	681.64	676.59	672.41	668.93	666.02	663.60
46000	719.71	710.54	703.00	696.78	691.63	687.35	683.79	680.82	678.35
47000	735.36	725.99	718.29	711.93	706.67	702.29	698.66	695.62	693.09
48000	751.01	741.44	733.57	727.08	721.70	717.24	713.52	710.42	707.84
49000	766.65	756.88	748.85	742.22	736.74	732.18	728.39	725.23	722.59
50000	782.30	772.33	764.14	757.37	751.77	747.12	743.25	740.03	737.33
51000	797.94	787.78	779.42	772.52	766.81	762.06	758.12	754.83	752.08
52000	813.59	803.22	794.70	787.67	781.84	777.01	772.98	769.63	766.82
53000	829.23	818.67	809.98	802.81	796.88	791.95	787.85	784.43	781.57
54000	844.88	834.12	825.27	817.96	811.91	806.89	802.71	799.23	796.32
55000	860.53	849.56	840.55	833.11	826.95	821.83	817.58	814.03	811.06
56000	876.17	865.01	855.83	848.26	841.98	836.77	832.44	828.83	825.81
57000	891.82	880.46	871.11	863.40	857.02	851.72	847.31	843.63	840.56
58000	907.46	895.90	886.40	878.55	872.05	866.66	862.17	858.43	855.30
59000	923.11	911.35	901.68	893.70	887.09	881.60	877.04	873.23	870.05
60000	938.76	926.79	916.96	908.85	902.12	896.54	891.90	888.03	884.80
61000	954.40	942.24	932.24	923.99	917.16	911.49	906.77	902.83	899.54
62000	970.05	957.69	947.53	939.14	932.19	926.43	921.63	917.63	914.29
63000	985.69	973.13	962.81	954.29	947.23	941.37	936.50	932.43	929.04
64000	1001.34	988.58	978.09	969.43	962.27	956.31	951.36	947.23	943.78
65000	1016.98	1004.03	993.37	984.58	977.30	971.26	966.23	962.03	958.53
66000	1032.63	1019.47	1008.66	999.73	992.34	986.20	981.09	976.83	973.28
67000	1048.28	1034.92	1023.94	1014.88	1007.37	1001.14	995.96	991.63	988.02
68000	1063.92	1050.37	1039.22	1030.02	1022.41	1016.08	1010.82	1006.43	1002.77
69000	1079.57	1065.81	1054.50	1045.17	1037.44	1031.03	1025.69	1021.23	1017.52
70000	1095.21	1081.26	1069.79	1060.32	1052.48	1045.97	1040.55	1036.03	1032.26
75000	1173.44	1158.49	1146.20	1136.06	1127.65	1120.68	1114.87	1110.04	1106.00
80000	1251.67	1235.72	1222.61	1211.79	1202.83	1195.39	1189.20	1184.04	1179.73
100000	1564.59	1544.65	1528.27	1514.74	1503.54	1494.24	1486.50	1480.05	1474.66

MONTHLY PAYMENT 18%
NECESSARY TO AMORTIZE A LOAN

TERM AMOUNT	24 YEARS	25 YEARS	26 YEARS	27 YEARS	28 YEARS	29 YEARS	30 YEARS	35 YEARS	40 YEARS
$ 25	.37	.37	.37	.37	.37	.37	.37	.37	.37
50	.74	.74	.74	.74	.73	.73	.73	.73	.73
75	1.11	1.10	1.10	1.10	1.10	1.10	1.10	1.09	1.09
100	1.48	1.47	1.47	1.47	1.46	1.46	1.46	1.46	1.45
200	2.95	2.94	2.93	2.93	2.92	2.92	2.91	2.91	2.90
300	4.42	4.40	4.39	4.39	4.38	4.37	4.37	4.36	4.35
400	5.89	5.87	5.86	5.85	5.84	5.83	5.82	5.81	5.80
500	7.36	7.34	7.32	7.31	7.30	7.29	7.28	7.26	7.25
600	8.83	8.80	8.78	8.77	8.76	8.74	8.73	8.71	8.69
700	10.30	10.27	10.25	10.23	10.21	10.20	10.19	10.16	10.14
800	11.77	11.74	11.71	11.69	11.67	11.66	11.64	11.61	11.59
900	13.24	13.20	13.17	13.15	13.13	13.11	13.10	13.06	13.04
1000	14.71	14.67	14.64	14.61	14.59	14.57	14.55	14.51	14.49
2000	29.41	29.33	29.27	29.22	29.17	29.13	29.10	29.01	28.97
3000	44.11	44.00	43.90	43.82	43.76	43.70	43.65	43.51	43.45
4000	58.81	58.66	58.53	58.43	58.34	58.26	58.20	58.01	57.93
5000	73.51	73.32	73.17	73.03	72.92	72.83	72.75	72.51	72.41
6000	88.21	87.99	87.80	87.64	87.51	87.39	87.30	87.01	86.89
7000	102.92	102.65	102.43	102.25	102.09	101.96	101.85	101.51	101.37
8000	117.62	117.32	117.06	116.85	116.67	116.52	116.40	116.02	115.86
9000	132.32	131.98	131.69	131.46	131.26	131.09	130.95	130.52	130.34
10000	147.02	146.64	146.33	146.06	145.84	145.65	145.50	145.02	144.82
15000	220.53	219.96	219.49	219.09	218.76	218.48	218.24	217.53	217.22
20000	294.03	293.28	292.65	292.12	291.68	291.30	290.99	290.03	289.63
25000	367.54	366.60	365.81	365.15	364.59	364.13	363.74	362.54	362.04
30000	441.05	439.92	438.97	438.18	437.51	436.95	436.48	435.05	434.44
35000	514.56	513.24	512.13	511.21	510.43	509.78	509.23	507.55	506.85
36000	529.26	527.90	526.76	525.81	525.01	524.34	523.78	522.06	521.33
37000	543.96	542.57	541.40	540.42	539.60	538.91	538.33	536.56	535.81
38000	558.66	557.23	556.03	555.02	554.18	553.47	552.88	551.06	550.29
39000	573.36	571.89	570.66	569.63	568.76	568.04	567.43	565.56	564.77
40000	588.06	586.56	585.29	584.23	583.35	582.60	581.97	580.06	579.26
41000	602.77	601.22	599.93	598.84	597.93	597.17	596.52	594.56	593.74
42000	617.47	615.88	614.56	613.45	612.51	611.73	611.07	609.06	608.22
43000	632.17	630.55	629.19	628.05	627.10	626.30	625.62	623.56	622.70
44000	646.87	645.21	643.82	642.66	641.68	640.86	640.17	638.07	637.18
45000	661.57	659.88	658.45	657.26	656.26	655.43	654.72	652.57	651.66
46000	676.27	674.54	673.09	671.87	670.85	669.99	669.27	667.07	666.14
47000	690.98	689.20	687.72	686.48	685.43	684.56	683.82	681.57	680.62
48000	705.68	703.87	702.35	701.08	700.01	699.12	698.37	696.07	695.11
49000	720.38	718.53	716.98	715.69	714.60	713.68	712.92	710.57	709.59
50000	735.08	733.19	731.62	730.29	729.18	728.25	727.47	725.07	724.07
51000	749.78	747.86	746.25	744.90	743.77	742.81	742.02	739.58	738.55
52000	764.48	762.52	760.88	759.50	758.35	757.38	756.57	754.08	753.03
53000	779.18	777.19	775.51	774.11	772.93	771.94	771.11	768.58	767.51
54000	793.89	791.85	790.14	788.72	787.52	786.51	785.66	783.08	781.99
55000	808.59	806.51	804.78	803.32	802.10	801.07	800.21	797.58	796.47
56000	823.29	821.18	819.41	817.93	816.68	815.64	814.76	812.08	810.96
57000	837.99	835.84	834.04	832.53	831.27	830.20	829.31	826.58	825.44
58000	852.69	850.51	848.67	847.14	845.85	844.77	843.86	841.09	839.92
59000	867.39	865.17	863.31	861.74	860.43	859.33	858.41	855.59	854.40
60000	882.09	879.83	877.94	876.35	875.02	873.90	872.96	870.09	868.88
61000	896.80	894.50	892.57	890.96	889.60	888.46	887.51	884.59	883.36
62000	911.50	909.16	907.20	905.56	904.18	903.03	902.06	899.09	897.84
63000	926.20	923.82	921.83	920.17	918.77	917.59	916.61	913.59	912.33
64000	940.90	938.49	936.47	934.77	933.35	932.16	931.16	928.09	926.81
65000	955.60	953.15	951.10	949.38	947.93	946.72	945.71	942.60	941.29
66000	970.30	967.82	965.73	963.98	962.52	961.29	960.26	957.10	955.77
67000	985.01	982.48	980.36	978.59	977.10	975.85	974.80	971.60	970.25
68000	999.71	997.14	995.00	993.20	991.69	990.42	989.35	986.10	984.73
69000	1014.41	1011.81	1009.63	1007.80	1006.27	1004.98	1003.90	1000.60	999.21
70000	1029.11	1026.47	1024.26	1022.41	1020.85	1019.55	1018.45	1015.10	1013.69
75000	1102.62	1099.79	1097.42	1095.44	1093.77	1092.37	1091.20	1087.61	1086.10
80000	1176.12	1173.11	1170.58	1168.46	1166.69	1165.20	1163.94	1160.12	1158.51
100000	1470.15	1466.38	1463.23	1460.58	1458.36	1456.49	1454.93	1450.14	1448.13

18¼%   MONTHLY PAYMENT
NECESSARY TO AMORTIZE A LOAN

TERM AMOUNT	1 YEAR	1½ YEARS	2 YEARS	2½ YEARS	3 YEARS	3½ YEARS	4 YEARS	4½ YEARS	5 YEARS
$ 25	2.29	1.60	1.25	1.04	.90	.81	.73	.68	.63
50	4.58	3.19	2.49	2.08	1.80	1.61	1.46	1.35	1.26
75	6.87	4.78	3.73	3.11	2.70	2.41	2.19	2.03	1.89
100	9.15	6.37	4.98	4.15	3.60	3.21	2.92	2.70	2.52
200	18.30	12.73	9.95	8.29	7.19	6.42	5.84	5.39	5.04
300	27.45	19.09	14.92	12.44	10.79	9.62	8.75	8.09	7.56
400	36.60	25.45	19.90	16.58	14.38	12.83	11.67	10.78	10.07
500	45.75	31.81	24.87	20.72	17.98	16.03	14.59	13.47	12.59
600	54.90	38.17	29.84	24.87	21.57	19.24	17.50	16.17	15.11
700	64.05	44.53	34.81	29.01	25.17	22.44	20.42	18.86	17.63
800	73.19	50.89	39.79	33.16	28.76	25.65	23.33	21.55	20.14
900	82.34	57.26	44.76	37.30	32.36	28.86	26.25	24.25	22.66
1000	91.49	63.62	49.73	41.44	35.95	32.06	29.17	26.94	25.18
2000	182.98	127.23	99.46	82.88	71.90	64.12	58.33	53.87	50.35
3000	274.46	190.84	149.19	124.32	107.85	96.17	87.49	80.81	75.52
4000	365.95	254.45	198.91	165.76	143.80	128.23	116.65	107.74	100.69
5000	457.44	318.06	248.64	207.20	179.75	160.29	145.82	134.68	125.87
6000	548.92	381.68	298.37	248.64	215.69	192.34	174.98	161.61	151.04
7000	640.41	445.29	348.10	290.08	251.64	224.40	204.14	188.55	176.21
8000	731.89	508.90	397.82	331.52	287.59	256.45	233.30	215.48	201.38
9000	823.38	572.51	447.55	372.96	323.54	288.51	262.47	242.42	226.56
10000	914.87	636.12	497.28	414.40	359.49	320.57	291.63	269.35	251.73
15000	1372.30	954.18	745.92	621.59	539.23	480.85	437.44	404.02	377.59
20000	1829.73	1272.24	994.55	828.79	718.97	641.13	583.25	538.70	503.45
25000	2287.16	1590.30	1243.19	1035.98	898.71	801.41	729.07	673.37	629.31
30000	2744.59	1908.36	1491.83	1243.18	1078.45	961.69	874.88	808.04	755.17
35000	3202.02	2226.41	1740.46	1450.37	1258.20	1121.97	1020.69	942.71	881.03
36000	3293.51	2290.03	1790.19	1491.81	1294.14	1154.02	1049.85	969.65	906.21
37000	3384.99	2353.64	1839.92	1533.25	1330.09	1186.08	1079.02	996.58	931.38
38000	3476.48	2417.25	1889.65	1574.69	1366.04	1218.13	1108.18	1023.52	956.55
39000	3567.97	2480.86	1939.37	1616.13	1401.99	1250.19	1137.34	1050.45	981.72
40000	3659.45	2544.47	1989.10	1657.57	1437.94	1282.25	1166.50	1077.39	1006.90
41000	3750.94	2608.08	2038.83	1699.00	1473.88	1314.30	1195.67	1104.32	1032.07
42000	3842.42	2671.70	2088.56	1740.44	1509.83	1346.36	1224.83	1131.26	1057.24
43000	3933.91	2735.31	2138.28	1781.88	1545.78	1378.41	1253.99	1158.19	1082.41
44000	4025.40	2798.92	2188.01	1823.32	1581.73	1410.47	1283.15	1185.12	1107.58
45000	4116.88	2862.53	2237.74	1864.76	1617.68	1442.53	1312.32	1212.06	1132.76
46000	4208.37	2926.14	2287.47	1906.20	1653.63	1474.58	1341.48	1238.99	1157.93
47000	4299.85	2989.75	2337.19	1947.64	1689.57	1506.64	1370.64	1265.93	1183.10
48000	4391.34	3053.37	2386.92	1989.08	1725.52	1538.69	1399.80	1292.86	1208.27
49000	4482.83	3116.98	2436.65	2030.52	1761.47	1570.75	1428.97	1319.80	1233.45
50000	4574.31	3180.59	2486.38	2071.96	1797.42	1602.81	1458.13	1346.73	1258.62
51000	4665.80	3244.20	2536.10	2113.39	1833.37	1634.86	1487.29	1373.67	1283.79
52000	4757.29	3307.81	2585.83	2154.83	1869.32	1666.92	1516.45	1400.60	1308.96
53000	4848.77	3371.42	2635.56	2196.27	1905.26	1698.97	1545.62	1427.54	1334.13
54000	4940.26	3435.04	2685.29	2237.71	1941.21	1731.03	1574.78	1454.47	1359.31
55000	5031.74	3498.65	2735.01	2279.15	1977.16	1763.09	1603.94	1481.40	1384.48
56000	5123.23	3562.26	2784.74	2320.59	2013.11	1795.14	1633.10	1508.34	1409.65
57000	5214.72	3625.87	2834.47	2362.03	2049.06	1827.20	1662.27	1535.27	1434.82
58000	5306.20	3689.48	2884.20	2403.47	2085.01	1859.25	1691.43	1562.21	1460.00
59000	5397.69	3753.09	2933.92	2444.91	2120.95	1891.31	1720.59	1589.14	1485.17
60000	5489.17	3816.71	2983.65	2486.35	2156.90	1923.37	1749.75	1616.08	1510.34
61000	5580.66	3880.32	3033.38	2527.78	2192.85	1955.42	1778.92	1643.01	1535.51
62000	5672.15	3943.93	3083.10	2569.22	2228.80	1987.48	1808.08	1669.95	1560.68
63000	5763.63	4007.54	3132.83	2610.66	2264.75	2019.53	1837.24	1696.88	1585.86
64000	5855.12	4071.15	3182.56	2652.10	2300.70	2051.59	1866.40	1723.82	1611.03
65000	5946.61	4134.76	3232.29	2693.54	2336.64	2083.65	1895.57	1750.75	1636.20
66000	6038.09	4198.38	3282.01	2734.98	2372.59	2115.70	1924.73	1777.68	1661.37
67000	6129.58	4261.99	3331.74	2776.42	2408.54	2147.76	1953.89	1804.62	1686.55
68000	6221.06	4325.60	3381.47	2817.86	2444.49	2179.81	1983.05	1831.55	1711.72
69000	6312.55	4389.21	3431.20	2859.30	2480.44	2211.87	2012.22	1858.49	1736.89
70000	6404.04	4452.82	3480.92	2900.74	2516.39	2243.93	2041.38	1885.42	1762.06
75000	6861.47	4770.88	3729.56	3107.93	2696.13	2404.21	2187.19	2020.10	1887.92
80000	7318.90	5088.94	3978.20	3315.13	2875.87	2564.49	2333.00	2154.77	2013.79
100000	9148.62	6361.17	4972.75	4143.91	3594.83	3205.61	2916.25	2693.46	2517.23

MONTHLY PAYMENT 18¼%
NECESSARY TO AMORTIZE A LOAN

TERM AMOUNT	6 YEARS	7 YEARS	8 YEARS	9 YEARS	10 YEARS	11 YEARS	12 YEARS	13 YEARS	14 YEARS
$ 25	.57	.52	.49	.47	.45	.43	.42	.41	.41
50	1.13	1.04	.98	.93	.89	.86	.84	.82	.81
75	1.70	1.56	1.47	1.39	1.34	1.29	1.26	1.23	1.21
100	2.26	2.08	1.95	1.86	1.78	1.72	1.68	1.64	1.61
200	4.52	4.16	3.90	3.71	3.56	3.44	3.35	3.27	3.22
300	6.78	6.24	5.85	5.56	5.33	5.16	5.02	4.91	4.82
400	9.04	8.32	7.80	7.41	7.11	6.88	6.69	6.54	6.43
500	11.29	10.39	9.74	9.26	8.88	8.59	8.36	8.18	8.03
600	13.55	12.47	11.69	11.11	10.66	10.31	10.03	9.81	9.64
700	15.81	14.55	13.64	12.96	12.43	12.03	11.71	11.45	11.24
800	18.07	16.63	15.59	14.81	14.21	13.75	13.38	13.08	12.85
900	20.33	18.71	17.53	16.66	15.99	15.46	15.05	14.72	14.45
1000	22.58	20.78	19.48	18.51	17.76	17.18	16.72	16.35	16.06
2000	45.16	41.56	38.96	37.01	35.52	34.36	33.44	32.70	32.11
3000	67.74	62.34	58.44	55.51	53.28	51.53	50.15	49.05	48.16
4000	90.32	83.12	77.91	74.02	71.03	68.71	66.87	65.40	64.21
5000	112.90	103.90	97.39	92.52	88.79	85.88	83.59	81.75	80.27
6000	135.47	124.68	116.87	111.02	106.55	103.06	100.30	98.10	96.32
7000	158.05	145.46	136.34	129.52	124.30	120.23	117.02	114.45	112.37
8000	180.63	166.24	155.82	148.03	142.06	137.41	133.73	130.79	128.42
9000	203.21	187.02	175.30	166.53	159.82	154.59	150.45	147.14	144.48
10000	225.79	207.80	194.77	185.03	177.57	171.76	167.17	163.49	160.53
15000	338.68	311.70	292.16	277.55	266.36	257.64	250.75	245.24	240.79
20000	451.57	415.60	389.54	370.06	355.14	343.52	334.33	326.98	321.05
25000	564.46	519.50	486.93	462.57	443.93	429.40	417.91	408.72	401.32
30000	677.35	623.39	584.31	555.09	532.71	515.27	501.49	490.47	481.58
35000	790.24	727.29	681.70	647.60	621.50	601.15	585.07	572.21	561.84
36000	812.81	748.07	701.17	666.10	639.26	618.33	601.78	588.56	577.89
37000	835.39	768.85	720.65	684.61	657.01	635.50	618.50	604.91	593.95
38000	857.97	789.63	740.13	703.11	674.77	652.68	635.22	621.26	610.00
39000	880.55	810.41	759.60	721.61	692.53	669.85	651.93	637.60	626.05
40000	903.13	831.19	779.08	740.12	710.28	687.03	668.65	653.95	642.10
41000	925.70	851.97	798.56	758.62	728.04	704.21	685.36	670.30	658.16
42000	948.28	872.75	818.03	777.12	745.80	721.38	702.08	686.65	674.21
43000	970.86	893.53	837.51	795.62	763.56	738.56	718.80	703.00	690.26
44000	993.44	914.31	856.99	814.13	781.31	755.73	735.51	719.35	706.31
45000	1016.02	935.09	876.47	832.63	799.07	772.91	752.23	735.70	722.37
46000	1038.59	955.87	895.94	851.13	816.83	790.08	768.94	752.05	738.42
47000	1061.17	976.65	915.42	869.64	834.58	807.26	785.66	768.39	754.47
48000	1083.75	997.43	934.90	888.14	852.34	824.44	802.38	784.74	770.52
49000	1106.33	1018.21	954.37	906.64	870.10	841.61	819.09	801.09	786.58
50000	1128.91	1038.99	973.85	925.14	887.85	858.79	835.81	817.44	802.63
51000	1151.48	1059.77	993.33	943.65	905.61	875.96	852.52	833.79	818.68
52000	1174.06	1080.55	1012.80	962.15	923.37	893.14	869.24	850.14	834.73
53000	1196.64	1101.33	1032.28	980.65	941.13	910.31	885.96	866.49	850.79
54000	1219.22	1122.11	1051.76	999.15	958.88	927.49	902.67	882.84	866.84
55000	1241.80	1142.89	1071.23	1017.66	976.64	944.66	919.39	899.18	882.89
56000	1264.37	1163.67	1090.71	1036.16	994.40	961.84	936.10	915.53	898.94
57000	1286.95	1184.45	1110.19	1054.66	1012.15	979.02	952.82	931.88	915.00
58000	1309.53	1205.22	1129.67	1073.17	1029.91	996.19	969.54	948.23	931.05
59000	1332.11	1226.00	1149.14	1091.67	1047.67	1013.37	986.25	964.58	947.10
60000	1354.69	1246.78	1168.62	1110.17	1065.42	1030.54	1002.97	980.93	963.15
61000	1377.26	1267.56	1188.10	1128.67	1083.18	1047.72	1019.68	997.28	979.21
62000	1399.84	1288.34	1207.57	1147.18	1100.94	1064.89	1036.40	1013.62	995.26
63000	1422.42	1309.12	1227.05	1165.68	1118.70	1082.07	1053.12	1029.97	1011.31
64000	1445.00	1329.90	1246.53	1184.18	1136.45	1099.25	1069.83	1046.32	1027.36
65000	1467.58	1350.68	1266.00	1202.69	1154.21	1116.42	1086.55	1062.67	1043.42
66000	1490.15	1371.46	1285.48	1221.19	1171.97	1133.60	1103.26	1079.02	1059.47
67000	1512.73	1392.24	1304.96	1239.69	1189.72	1150.77	1119.98	1095.37	1075.52
68000	1535.31	1413.02	1324.43	1258.19	1207.48	1167.95	1136.70	1111.72	1091.57
69000	1557.89	1433.80	1343.91	1276.70	1225.24	1185.12	1153.41	1128.07	1107.63
70000	1580.47	1454.58	1363.39	1295.20	1242.99	1202.30	1170.13	1144.41	1123.68
75000	1693.36	1558.48	1460.77	1387.71	1331.78	1288.18	1253.71	1226.16	1203.94
80000	1806.25	1662.38	1558.16	1480.23	1420.56	1374.06	1337.29	1307.90	1284.20
100000	2257.81	2077.97	1947.69	1850.28	1775.70	1717.57	1671.61	1634.88	1605.25

18¼% MONTHLY PAYMENT
NECESSARY TO AMORTIZE A LOAN

TERM AMOUNT	15 YEARS	16 YEARS	17 YEARS	18 YEARS	19 YEARS	20 YEARS	21 YEARS	22 YEARS	23 YEARS
$ 25	.40	.40	.39	.39	.39	.38	.38	.38	.38
50	.80	.79	.78	.77	.77	.76	.76	.75	.75
75	1.19	1.18	1.16	1.15	1.15	1.14	1.13	1.13	1.12
100	1.59	1.57	1.55	1.54	1.53	1.52	1.51	1.50	1.50
200	3.17	3.13	3.10	3.07	3.05	3.03	3.01	3.00	2.99
300	4.75	4.69	4.64	4.60	4.57	4.54	4.52	4.50	4.48
400	6.33	6.25	6.19	6.13	6.09	6.05	6.02	6.00	5.98
500	7.91	7.81	7.73	7.67	7.61	7.57	7.53	7.50	7.47
600	9.49	9.37	9.28	9.20	9.13	9.08	9.03	8.99	8.96
700	11.07	10.94	10.82	10.73	10.65	10.59	10.54	10.49	10.46
800	12.65	12.50	12.37	12.26	12.17	12.10	12.04	11.99	11.95
900	14.24	14.06	13.91	13.79	13.70	13.61	13.55	13.49	13.44
1000	15.82	15.62	15.46	15.33	15.22	15.13	15.05	14.99	14.93
2000	31.63	31.24	30.91	30.65	30.43	30.25	30.09	29.97	29.86
3000	47.44	46.85	46.37	45.97	45.64	45.37	45.14	44.95	44.79
4000	63.25	62.47	61.82	61.29	60.85	60.49	60.18	59.93	59.72
5000	79.06	78.08	77.28	76.61	76.06	75.61	75.23	74.91	74.65
6000	94.88	93.70	92.73	91.93	91.27	90.73	90.27	89.90	89.58
7000	110.69	109.31	108.18	107.25	106.48	105.85	105.32	104.88	104.51
8000	126.50	124.93	123.64	122.57	121.70	120.97	120.36	119.86	119.44
9000	142.31	140.54	139.09	137.90	136.91	136.09	135.41	134.84	134.37
10000	158.12	156.16	154.55	153.22	152.12	151.21	150.45	149.82	149.30
15000	237.18	234.24	231.82	229.82	228.17	226.81	225.67	224.73	223.94
20000	316.24	312.31	309.09	306.43	304.23	302.41	300.90	299.64	298.59
25000	395.30	390.39	386.36	383.03	380.29	378.01	376.12	374.55	373.24
30000	474.36	468.47	463.63	459.64	456.34	453.61	451.34	449.46	447.88
35000	553.42	546.54	540.90	536.24	532.40	529.21	526.57	524.36	522.53
36000	569.23	562.16	556.35	551.57	547.61	544.33	541.61	539.35	537.46
37000	585.04	577.77	571.80	566.89	562.82	559.45	556.66	554.33	552.39
38000	600.86	593.39	587.26	582.21	578.03	574.57	571.70	569.31	567.32
39000	616.67	609.00	602.71	597.53	593.24	589.69	586.74	584.29	582.25
40000	632.48	624.62	618.17	612.85	608.46	604.81	601.79	599.27	597.18
41000	648.29	640.23	633.62	628.17	623.67	619.93	616.83	614.25	612.10
42000	664.10	655.85	649.07	643.49	638.88	635.05	631.88	629.24	627.03
43000	679.92	671.46	664.53	658.81	654.09	650.17	646.92	644.22	641.96
44000	695.73	687.08	679.98	674.13	669.30	665.29	661.97	659.20	656.89
45000	711.54	702.70	695.44	689.46	684.51	680.41	677.01	674.18	671.82
46000	727.35	718.31	710.89	704.78	699.72	695.53	692.06	689.16	686.75
47000	743.16	733.93	726.34	720.10	714.93	710.66	707.10	704.14	701.68
48000	758.97	749.54	741.80	735.42	730.15	725.78	722.15	719.13	716.61
49000	774.79	765.16	757.25	750.74	745.36	740.90	737.19	734.11	731.54
50000	790.60	780.77	772.71	766.06	760.57	756.02	752.24	749.09	746.47
51000	806.41	796.39	788.16	781.38	775.78	771.14	767.28	764.07	761.40
52000	822.22	812.00	803.61	796.70	790.99	786.26	782.32	779.05	776.33
53000	838.03	827.62	819.07	812.02	806.20	801.38	797.37	794.03	791.26
54000	853.85	843.23	834.52	827.35	821.41	816.50	812.41	809.02	806.18
55000	869.66	858.85	849.98	842.67	836.62	831.62	827.46	824.00	821.11
56000	885.47	874.46	865.43	857.99	851.84	846.74	842.50	838.98	836.04
57000	901.28	890.08	880.88	873.31	867.05	861.86	857.55	853.96	850.97
58000	917.09	905.69	896.34	888.63	882.26	876.98	872.59	868.94	865.90
59000	932.91	921.31	911.79	903.95	897.47	892.10	887.64	883.92	880.83
60000	948.72	936.93	927.25	919.27	912.68	907.22	902.68	898.91	895.76
61000	964.53	952.54	942.70	934.59	927.89	922.34	917.73	913.89	910.69
62000	980.34	968.16	958.15	949.91	943.10	937.46	932.77	928.87	925.62
63000	996.15	983.77	973.61	965.24	958.31	952.58	947.81	943.85	940.55
64000	1011.96	999.39	989.06	980.56	973.53	967.70	962.86	958.83	955.48
65000	1027.78	1015.00	1004.52	995.88	988.74	982.82	977.90	973.81	970.41
66000	1043.59	1030.62	1019.97	1011.20	1003.95	997.94	992.95	988.80	985.34
67000	1059.40	1046.23	1035.42	1026.52	1019.16	1013.06	1007.99	1003.78	1000.26
68000	1075.21	1061.85	1050.88	1041.84	1034.37	1028.18	1023.04	1018.76	1015.19
69000	1091.02	1077.46	1066.33	1057.16	1049.58	1043.30	1038.08	1033.74	1030.12
70000	1106.84	1093.08	1081.79	1072.48	1064.79	1058.42	1053.13	1048.72	1045.05
75000	1185.90	1171.16	1159.06	1149.09	1140.85	1134.02	1128.35	1123.63	1119.70
80000	1264.95	1249.23	1236.33	1225.69	1216.91	1209.62	1203.57	1198.54	1194.35
100000	1581.19	1561.54	1545.41	1532.12	1521.13	1512.03	1504.47	1498.17	1492.93

TERM AMOUNT	24 YEARS	25 YEARS	26 YEARS	27 YEARS	28 YEARS	29 YEARS	30 YEARS	35 YEARS	40 YEARS
$ 25	.38	.38	.38	.37	.37	.37	.37	.37	.37
50	.75	.75	.75	.74	.74	.74	.74	.74	.74
75	1.12	1.12	1.12	1.11	1.11	1.11	1.11	1.11	1.11
100	1.49	1.49	1.49	1.48	1.48	1.48	1.48	1.47	1.47
200	2.98	2.97	2.97	2.96	2.96	2.96	2.95	2.94	2.94
300	4.47	4.46	4.45	4.44	4.44	4.43	4.43	4.41	4.41
400	5.96	5.94	5.93	5.92	5.91	5.91	5.90	5.88	5.87
500	7.45	7.43	7.41	7.40	7.39	7.38	7.37	7.35	7.34
600	8.94	8.91	8.90	8.88	8.87	8.86	8.85	8.82	8.81
700	10.42	10.40	10.38	10.36	10.35	10.33	10.32	10.29	10.28
800	11.91	11.88	11.86	11.84	11.82	11.81	11.80	11.76	11.74
900	13.40	13.37	13.34	13.32	13.30	13.28	13.27	13.23	13.21
1000	14.89	14.85	14.82	14.80	14.78	14.76	14.74	14.70	14.68
2000	29.78	29.70	29.64	29.59	29.55	29.51	29.48	29.39	29.35
3000	44.66	44.55	44.46	44.38	44.32	44.27	44.22	44.08	44.03
4000	59.55	59.40	59.28	59.18	59.09	59.02	58.96	58.78	58.70
5000	74.43	74.25	74.10	73.97	73.86	73.77	73.70	73.47	73.37
6000	89.32	89.10	88.92	88.76	88.63	88.53	88.44	88.16	88.05
7000	104.20	103.95	103.73	103.56	103.41	103.28	103.17	102.86	102.72
8000	119.09	118.80	118.55	118.35	118.18	118.03	117.91	117.55	117.40
9000	133.97	133.65	133.37	133.14	132.95	132.79	132.65	132.24	132.07
10000	148.86	148.49	148.19	147.93	147.72	147.54	147.39	146.93	146.74
15000	223.29	222.74	222.28	221.90	221.58	221.31	221.08	220.40	220.11
20000	297.72	296.98	296.37	295.86	295.43	295.08	294.78	293.86	293.48
25000	372.14	371.23	370.47	369.83	369.29	368.84	368.47	367.33	366.85
30000	446.57	445.47	444.56	443.79	443.15	442.61	442.16	440.79	440.22
35000	521.00	519.72	518.65	517.76	517.01	516.38	515.85	514.26	513.59
36000	535.88	534.57	533.47	532.55	531.78	531.13	530.59	528.95	528.27
37000	550.77	549.42	548.29	547.34	546.55	545.89	545.33	543.64	542.94
38000	565.65	564.27	563.11	562.13	561.32	560.64	560.07	558.34	557.62
39000	580.54	579.11	577.92	576.93	576.09	575.39	574.81	573.03	572.29
40000	595.43	593.96	592.74	591.72	590.86	590.15	589.55	587.72	586.96
41000	610.31	608.81	607.56	606.51	605.64	604.90	604.29	602.42	601.64
42000	625.20	623.66	622.38	621.31	620.41	619.65	619.02	617.11	616.31
43000	640.08	638.51	637.20	636.10	635.18	634.41	633.76	631.80	630.99
44000	654.97	653.36	652.02	650.89	649.95	649.16	648.50	646.49	645.66
45000	669.85	668.21	666.83	665.68	664.72	663.92	663.24	661.19	660.33
46000	684.74	683.06	681.65	680.48	679.49	678.67	677.98	675.88	675.01
47000	699.62	697.91	696.47	695.27	694.26	693.42	692.72	690.57	689.68
48000	714.51	712.76	711.29	710.06	709.04	708.18	707.46	705.27	704.36
49000	729.39	727.60	726.11	724.86	723.81	722.93	722.19	719.96	719.03
50000	744.28	742.45	740.93	739.65	738.58	737.68	736.93	734.65	733.70
51000	759.17	757.30	755.74	754.44	753.35	752.44	751.67	749.34	748.38
52000	774.05	772.15	770.56	769.23	768.12	767.19	766.41	764.04	763.05
53000	788.94	787.00	785.38	784.03	782.89	781.94	781.15	778.73	777.73
54000	803.82	801.85	800.20	798.82	797.67	796.70	795.89	793.42	792.40
55000	818.71	816.70	815.02	813.61	812.44	811.45	810.63	808.12	807.07
56000	833.59	831.55	829.84	828.41	827.21	826.20	825.36	822.81	821.75
57000	848.48	846.40	844.66	843.20	841.98	840.96	840.10	837.50	836.42
58000	863.36	861.25	859.47	857.99	856.75	855.71	854.84	852.20	851.10
59000	878.25	876.09	874.29	872.78	871.52	870.47	869.58	866.89	865.77
60000	893.14	890.94	889.11	887.58	886.29	885.22	884.32	881.58	880.44
61000	908.02	905.79	903.93	902.37	901.07	899.97	899.06	896.27	895.12
62000	922.91	920.64	918.75	917.16	915.84	914.73	913.80	910.97	909.79
63000	937.79	935.49	933.57	931.96	930.61	929.48	928.53	925.66	924.46
64000	952.68	950.34	948.38	946.75	945.38	944.23	943.27	940.35	939.14
65000	967.56	965.19	963.20	961.54	960.15	958.99	958.01	955.05	953.81
66000	982.45	980.04	978.02	976.33	974.92	973.74	972.75	969.74	968.49
67000	997.33	994.89	992.84	991.13	989.69	988.49	987.49	984.43	983.16
68000	1012.22	1009.74	1007.66	1005.92	1004.47	1003.25	1002.23	999.12	997.83
69000	1027.11	1024.58	1022.48	1020.71	1019.24	1018.00	1016.97	1013.82	1012.51
70000	1041.99	1039.43	1037.29	1035.51	1034.01	1032.75	1031.70	1028.51	1027.18
75000	1116.42	1113.68	1111.39	1109.47	1107.87	1106.52	1105.40	1101.98	1100.55
80000	1190.85	1187.92	1185.48	1183.43	1181.72	1180.29	1179.09	1175.44	1173.92
100000	1488.56	1484.90	1481.85	1479.29	1477.15	1475.36	1473.86	1469.30	1467.40

18½% MONTHLY PAYMENT
NECESSARY TO AMORTIZE A LOAN

TERM AMOUNT	1 YEAR	1½ YEARS	2 YEARS	2½ YEARS	3 YEARS	3½ YEARS	4 YEARS	4½ YEARS	5 YEARS
$ 25	2.29	1.60	1.25	1.04	.91	.81	.74	.68	.64
50	4.58	3.19	2.50	2.08	1.81	1.61	1.47	1.36	1.27
75	6.87	4.78	3.74	3.12	2.71	2.42	2.20	2.03	1.90
100	9.16	6.38	4.99	4.16	3.61	3.22	2.93	2.71	2.53
200	18.32	12.75	9.97	8.32	7.22	6.44	5.86	5.42	5.06
300	27.48	19.12	14.96	12.47	10.82	9.66	8.79	8.12	7.59
400	36.64	25.49	19.94	16.63	14.43	12.87	11.72	10.83	10.12
500	45.80	31.87	24.92	20.78	18.04	16.09	14.65	13.53	12.65
600	54.96	38.24	29.91	24.94	21.64	19.31	17.58	16.24	15.18
700	64.12	44.61	34.89	29.09	25.25	22.53	20.50	18.95	17.71
800	73.28	50.98	39.88	33.25	28.86	25.74	23.43	21.65	20.24
900	82.44	57.36	44.86	37.40	32.46	28.96	26.36	24.36	22.77
1000	91.60	63.73	49.84	41.56	36.07	32.18	29.29	27.06	25.30
2000	183.20	127.45	99.68	83.11	72.13	64.35	58.57	54.12	50.60
3000	274.79	191.17	149.52	124.66	108.20	96.53	87.86	81.18	75.90
4000	366.39	254.89	199.36	166.22	144.26	128.70	117.14	108.24	101.20
5000	457.99	318.62	249.20	207.77	180.33	160.88	146.42	135.30	126.50
6000	549.58	382.34	299.04	249.32	216.39	193.05	175.71	162.35	151.79
7000	641.18	446.06	348.88	290.88	252.46	225.23	204.99	189.41	177.09
8000	732.78	509.78	398.72	332.43	288.52	257.40	234.27	216.47	202.39
9000	824.37	573.51	448.56	373.98	324.59	289.58	263.56	243.53	227.69
10000	915.97	637.23	498.40	415.54	360.65	321.75	292.84	270.59	252.99
15000	1373.95	955.84	747.60	623.30	540.97	482.62	439.26	405.88	379.48
20000	1831.94	1274.45	996.79	831.07	721.30	643.50	585.68	541.17	505.97
25000	2289.92	1593.06	1245.99	1038.83	901.62	804.37	732.09	676.46	632.46
30000	2747.90	1911.67	1495.19	1246.60	1081.94	965.24	878.51	811.75	758.95
35000	3205.89	2230.29	1744.39	1454.36	1262.27	1126.12	1024.93	947.04	885.44
36000	3297.48	2294.01	1794.23	1495.92	1298.33	1158.29	1054.21	974.09	910.74
37000	3389.08	2357.73	1844.07	1537.47	1334.39	1190.47	1083.50	1001.15	936.04
38000	3480.68	2421.45	1893.91	1579.02	1370.46	1222.64	1112.78	1028.21	961.34
39000	3572.27	2485.17	1943.75	1620.57	1406.52	1254.82	1142.06	1055.27	986.64
40000	3663.87	2548.90	1993.58	1662.13	1442.59	1286.99	1171.35	1082.33	1011.93
41000	3755.47	2612.62	2043.42	1703.68	1478.65	1319.17	1200.63	1109.39	1037.23
42000	3847.06	2676.34	2093.26	1745.23	1514.72	1351.34	1229.91	1136.44	1062.53
43000	3938.66	2740.06	2143.10	1786.79	1550.78	1383.51	1259.20	1163.50	1087.83
44000	4030.26	2803.79	2192.94	1828.34	1586.85	1415.69	1288.48	1190.56	1113.13
45000	4121.85	2867.51	2242.78	1869.89	1622.91	1447.86	1317.76	1217.62	1138.43
46000	4213.45	2931.23	2292.62	1911.45	1658.98	1480.04	1347.05	1244.68	1163.72
47000	4305.05	2994.95	2342.46	1953.00	1695.04	1512.21	1376.33	1271.73	1189.02
48000	4396.64	3058.68	2392.30	1994.55	1731.10	1544.39	1405.61	1298.79	1214.32
49000	4488.24	3122.40	2442.14	2036.11	1767.17	1576.56	1434.90	1325.85	1239.62
50000	4579.84	3186.12	2491.98	2077.66	1803.23	1608.74	1464.18	1352.91	1264.92
51000	4671.43	3249.84	2541.82	2119.21	1839.30	1640.91	1493.47	1379.97	1290.21
52000	4763.03	3313.56	2591.66	2160.76	1875.36	1673.09	1522.75	1407.02	1315.51
53000	4854.63	3377.29	2641.50	2202.32	1911.43	1705.26	1552.03	1434.08	1340.81
54000	4946.22	3441.01	2691.34	2243.87	1947.49	1737.44	1581.32	1461.14	1366.11
55000	5037.82	3504.73	2741.18	2285.42	1983.56	1769.61	1610.60	1488.20	1391.41
56000	5129.42	3568.45	2791.02	2326.98	2019.62	1801.78	1639.88	1515.26	1416.71
57000	5221.01	3632.18	2840.86	2368.53	2055.69	1833.96	1669.17	1542.31	1442.00
58000	5312.61	3695.90	2890.70	2410.08	2091.75	1866.13	1698.45	1569.37	1467.30
59000	5404.21	3759.62	2940.54	2451.64	2127.82	1898.31	1727.73	1596.43	1492.60
60000	5495.80	3823.34	2990.37	2493.19	2163.88	1930.48	1757.02	1623.49	1517.90
61000	5587.40	3887.07	3040.21	2534.74	2199.94	1962.66	1786.30	1650.55	1543.20
62000	5679.00	3950.79	3090.05	2576.30	2236.01	1994.83	1815.58	1677.60	1568.49
63000	5770.59	4014.51	3139.89	2617.85	2272.07	2027.01	1844.87	1704.66	1593.79
64000	5862.19	4078.23	3189.73	2659.40	2308.14	2059.18	1874.15	1731.72	1619.09
65000	5953.79	4141.95	3239.57	2700.95	2344.20	2091.36	1903.44	1758.78	1644.39
66000	6045.38	4205.68	3289.41	2742.51	2380.27	2123.53	1932.72	1785.84	1669.69
67000	6136.98	4269.40	3339.25	2784.06	2416.33	2155.71	1962.00	1812.89	1694.99
68000	6228.58	4333.12	3389.09	2825.61	2452.40	2187.88	1991.29	1839.95	1720.28
69000	6320.17	4396.84	3438.93	2867.17	2488.46	2220.06	2020.57	1867.01	1745.58
70000	6411.77	4460.57	3488.77	2908.72	2524.53	2252.23	2049.85	1894.07	1770.88
75000	6869.75	4779.18	3737.97	3116.49	2704.85	2413.10	2196.27	2029.36	1897.37
80000	7327.74	5097.79	3987.16	3324.25	2885.17	2573.98	2342.69	2164.65	2023.86
100000	9159.67	6372.24	4983.95	4155.31	3606.46	3217.47	2928.36	2705.81	2529.83

MONTHLY PAYMENT 18½%
NECESSARY TO AMORTIZE A LOAN

TERM AMOUNT	6 YEARS	7 YEARS	8 YEARS	9 YEARS	10 YEARS	11 YEARS	12 YEARS	13 YEARS	14 YEARS
$ 25	.57	.53	.50	.47	.45	.44	.43	.42	.41
50	1.14	1.05	.99	.94	.90	.87	.85	.83	.82
75	1.71	1.57	1.48	1.40	1.35	1.30	1.27	1.24	1.22
100	2.28	2.10	1.97	1.87	1.80	1.74	1.69	1.66	1.63
200	4.55	4.19	3.93	3.73	3.59	3.47	3.38	3.31	3.25
300	6.82	6.28	5.89	5.60	5.38	5.20	5.07	4.96	4.87
400	9.09	8.37	7.85	7.46	7.17	6.94	6.75	6.61	6.49
500	11.36	10.46	9.81	9.33	8.96	8.67	8.44	8.26	8.11
600	13.63	12.55	11.78	11.19	10.75	10.40	10.13	9.91	9.73
700	15.90	14.65	13.74	13.06	12.54	12.13	11.82	11.56	11.36
800	18.17	16.74	15.70	14.92	14.33	13.87	13.50	13.21	12.98
900	20.44	18.83	17.66	16.79	16.12	15.60	15.19	14.86	14.60
1000	22.71	20.92	19.62	18.65	17.91	17.33	16.88	16.51	16.22
2000	45.42	41.84	39.24	37.30	35.82	34.66	33.75	33.02	32.44
3000	68.13	62.75	58.86	55.95	53.72	51.99	50.62	49.53	48.65
4000	90.84	83.67	78.47	74.59	71.63	69.32	67.50	66.04	64.87
5000	113.55	104.58	98.09	93.24	89.53	86.65	84.37	82.55	81.08
6000	136.26	125.50	117.71	111.89	107.44	103.98	101.24	99.06	97.30
7000	158.97	146.41	137.33	130.54	125.35	121.30	118.11	115.57	113.52
8000	181.68	167.33	156.94	149.18	143.25	138.63	134.99	132.08	129.73
9000	204.38	188.24	176.56	167.83	161.16	155.96	151.86	148.58	145.95
10000	227.09	209.16	196.18	186.48	179.06	173.29	168.73	165.09	162.16
15000	340.64	313.73	294.26	279.72	268.59	259.93	253.10	247.64	243.24
20000	454.18	418.31	392.35	372.95	358.12	346.58	337.46	330.18	324.32
25000	567.73	522.89	490.43	466.19	447.65	433.22	421.82	412.73	405.40
30000	681.27	627.46	588.52	559.43	537.18	519.86	506.19	495.27	486.48
35000	794.82	732.04	686.61	652.67	626.71	606.50	590.55	577.82	567.56
36000	817.52	752.96	706.22	671.31	644.62	623.83	607.42	594.32	583.78
37000	840.23	773.87	725.84	689.96	662.52	641.16	624.30	610.83	599.99
38000	862.94	794.79	745.46	708.61	680.43	658.49	641.17	627.34	616.21
39000	885.65	815.70	765.07	727.26	698.33	675.82	658.04	643.85	632.43
40000	908.36	836.62	784.69	745.90	716.24	693.15	674.91	660.36	648.64
41000	931.07	857.53	804.31	764.55	734.15	710.47	691.79	676.87	664.86
42000	953.78	878.45	823.93	783.20	752.05	727.80	708.66	693.38	681.07
43000	976.49	899.36	843.54	801.85	769.96	745.13	725.53	709.89	697.29
44000	999.20	920.28	863.16	820.49	787.86	762.46	742.40	726.40	713.50
45000	1021.90	941.19	882.78	839.14	805.77	779.79	759.28	742.90	729.72
46000	1044.61	962.11	902.39	857.79	823.68	797.12	776.15	759.41	745.94
47000	1067.32	983.02	922.01	876.44	841.58	814.45	793.02	775.92	762.15
48000	1090.03	1003.94	941.63	895.08	859.49	831.77	809.89	792.43	778.37
49000	1112.74	1024.85	961.25	913.73	877.39	849.10	826.77	808.94	794.58
50000	1135.45	1045.77	980.86	932.38	895.30	866.43	843.64	825.45	810.80
51000	1158.16	1066.68	1000.48	951.03	913.21	883.76	860.51	841.96	827.02
52000	1180.87	1087.60	1020.10	969.67	931.11	901.09	877.39	858.47	843.23
53000	1203.58	1108.52	1039.71	988.32	949.02	918.42	894.26	874.98	859.45
54000	1226.28	1129.43	1059.33	1006.97	966.92	935.75	911.13	891.48	875.66
55000	1248.99	1150.35	1078.95	1025.62	984.83	953.07	928.00	907.99	891.88
56000	1271.70	1171.26	1098.57	1044.26	1002.73	970.40	944.88	924.50	908.10
57000	1294.41	1192.18	1118.18	1062.91	1020.64	987.73	961.75	941.01	924.31
58000	1317.12	1213.09	1137.80	1081.56	1038.55	1005.06	978.62	957.52	940.53
59000	1339.83	1234.01	1157.42	1100.21	1056.45	1022.39	995.49	974.03	956.74
60000	1362.54	1254.92	1177.03	1118.85	1074.36	1039.72	1012.37	990.54	972.96
61000	1385.25	1275.84	1196.65	1137.50	1092.26	1057.05	1029.24	1007.05	989.17
62000	1407.95	1296.75	1216.27	1156.15	1110.17	1074.37	1046.11	1023.55	1005.39
63000	1430.66	1317.67	1235.89	1174.79	1128.08	1091.70	1062.99	1040.06	1021.61
64000	1453.37	1338.58	1255.50	1193.44	1145.98	1109.03	1079.86	1056.57	1037.82
65000	1476.08	1359.50	1275.12	1212.09	1163.89	1126.36	1096.73	1073.08	1054.04
66000	1498.79	1380.41	1294.74	1230.74	1181.79	1143.69	1113.60	1089.59	1070.25
67000	1521.50	1401.33	1314.35	1249.38	1199.70	1161.02	1130.48	1106.10	1086.47
68000	1544.21	1422.24	1333.97	1268.03	1217.61	1178.34	1147.35	1122.61	1102.69
69000	1566.92	1443.16	1353.59	1286.68	1235.51	1195.67	1164.22	1139.12	1118.90
70000	1589.63	1464.07	1373.21	1305.33	1253.42	1213.00	1181.09	1155.63	1135.12
75000	1703.17	1568.65	1471.29	1398.56	1342.95	1299.64	1265.46	1238.17	1216.20
80000	1816.71	1673.23	1569.38	1491.80	1432.48	1386.29	1349.82	1320.71	1297.28
100000	2270.89	2091.53	1961.72	1864.75	1790.59	1732.86	1687.28	1650.89	1621.60

189

18½% MONTHLY PAYMENT
NECESSARY TO AMORTIZE A LOAN

TERM AMOUNT	15 YEARS	16 YEARS	17 YEARS	18 YEARS	19 YEARS	20 YEARS	21 YEARS	22 YEARS	23 YEARS
$ 25	.40	.40	.40	.39	.39	.39	.39	.38	.38
50	.80	.79	.79	.78	.77	.77	.77	.76	.76
75	1.20	1.19	1.18	1.17	1.16	1.15	1.15	1.14	1.14
100	1.60	1.58	1.57	1.55	1.54	1.53	1.53	1.52	1.52
200	3.20	3.16	3.13	3.10	3.08	3.06	3.05	3.04	3.03
300	4.80	4.74	4.69	4.65	4.62	4.59	4.57	4.55	4.54
400	6.40	6.32	6.26	6.20	6.16	6.12	6.09	6.07	6.05
500	7.99	7.90	7.82	7.75	7.70	7.65	7.62	7.59	7.56
600	9.59	9.48	9.38	9.30	9.24	9.18	9.14	9.10	9.07
700	11.19	11.05	10.94	10.85	10.78	10.71	10.66	10.62	10.58
800	12.79	12.63	12.51	12.40	12.32	12.24	12.18	12.14	12.09
900	14.39	14.21	14.07	13.95	13.85	13.77	13.71	13.65	13.61
1000	15.98	15.79	15.63	15.50	15.39	15.30	15.23	15.17	15.12
2000	31.96	31.57	31.26	31.00	30.78	30.60	30.45	30.33	30.23
3000	47.94	47.36	46.88	46.49	46.17	45.90	45.68	45.49	45.34
4000	63.92	63.14	62.51	61.99	61.56	61.20	60.90	60.66	60.45
5000	79.90	78.93	78.13	77.48	76.94	76.50	76.13	75.82	75.57
6000	95.87	94.71	93.76	92.98	92.33	91.80	91.35	90.98	90.68
7000	111.85	110.50	109.39	108.47	107.72	107.09	106.58	106.15	105.79
8000	127.83	126.28	125.01	123.97	123.11	122.39	121.80	121.31	120.90
9000	143.81	142.07	140.64	139.46	138.49	137.69	137.03	136.47	136.01
10000	159.79	157.85	156.26	154.96	153.88	152.99	152.25	151.64	151.13
15000	239.68	236.77	234.39	232.43	230.82	229.48	228.37	227.45	226.69
20000	319.57	315.70	312.52	309.91	307.76	305.97	304.50	303.27	302.25
25000	399.46	394.62	390.65	387.39	384.69	382.47	380.62	379.09	377.81
30000	479.35	473.54	468.78	464.86	461.63	458.96	456.74	454.90	453.37
35000	559.25	552.47	546.91	542.34	538.57	535.45	532.86	530.72	528.93
36000	575.22	568.25	562.53	557.83	553.96	550.75	548.09	545.88	544.04
37000	591.20	584.03	578.16	573.33	569.34	566.05	563.31	561.04	559.16
38000	607.18	599.82	593.79	588.83	584.73	581.35	578.54	576.21	574.27
39000	623.16	615.60	609.41	604.32	600.12	596.64	593.76	591.37	589.38
40000	639.14	631.39	625.04	619.82	615.51	611.94	608.99	606.53	604.49
41000	655.12	647.17	640.66	635.31	630.89	627.24	624.21	621.70	619.61
42000	671.09	662.96	656.29	650.81	646.28	642.54	639.44	636.86	634.72
43000	687.07	678.74	671.92	666.30	661.67	657.84	654.66	652.02	649.83
44000	703.05	694.53	687.54	681.80	677.06	673.14	669.89	667.19	664.94
45000	719.03	710.31	703.17	697.29	692.44	688.43	685.11	682.35	680.05
46000	735.01	726.10	718.79	712.79	707.83	703.73	700.33	697.51	695.17
47000	750.99	741.88	734.42	728.28	723.22	719.03	715.56	712.68	710.28
48000	766.96	757.66	750.04	743.78	738.61	734.33	730.78	727.84	725.39
49000	782.94	773.45	765.67	759.27	753.99	749.63	746.01	743.00	740.50
50000	798.92	789.23	781.30	774.77	769.38	764.93	761.23	758.17	755.62
51000	814.90	805.02	796.92	790.26	784.77	780.22	776.46	773.33	770.73
52000	830.88	820.80	812.55	805.76	800.16	795.52	791.68	788.49	785.84
53000	846.86	836.59	828.17	821.25	815.54	810.82	806.91	803.66	800.95
54000	862.83	852.37	843.80	836.75	830.93	826.12	822.13	818.82	816.06
55000	878.81	868.16	859.43	852.24	846.32	841.42	837.36	833.98	831.18
56000	894.79	883.94	875.05	867.74	861.71	856.72	852.58	849.15	846.29
57000	910.77	899.73	890.68	883.24	877.09	872.02	867.81	864.31	861.40
58000	926.75	915.51	906.30	898.73	892.48	887.31	883.03	879.47	876.51
59000	942.73	931.30	921.93	914.23	907.87	902.61	898.25	894.64	891.63
60000	958.70	947.08	937.55	929.72	923.26	917.91	913.48	909.80	906.74
61000	974.68	962.86	953.18	945.22	938.64	933.21	928.70	924.96	921.85
62000	990.66	978.65	968.81	960.71	954.03	948.51	943.93	940.12	936.96
63000	1006.64	994.43	984.43	976.21	969.42	963.81	959.15	955.29	952.07
64000	1022.62	1010.22	1000.06	991.70	984.81	979.10	974.38	970.45	967.19
65000	1038.60	1026.00	1015.68	1007.20	1000.20	994.40	989.60	985.61	982.30
66000	1054.57	1041.79	1031.31	1022.69	1015.58	1009.70	1004.83	1000.78	997.41
67000	1070.55	1057.57	1046.94	1038.19	1030.97	1025.00	1020.05	1015.94	1012.52
68000	1086.53	1073.36	1062.56	1053.68	1046.36	1040.30	1035.28	1031.10	1027.64
69000	1102.51	1089.14	1078.19	1069.18	1061.75	1055.60	1050.50	1046.27	1042.75
70000	1118.49	1104.93	1093.81	1084.67	1077.13	1070.90	1065.72	1061.43	1057.86
75000	1198.38	1183.85	1171.94	1162.15	1154.07	1147.39	1141.85	1137.25	1133.42
80000	1278.27	1262.77	1250.07	1239.63	1231.01	1223.88	1217.97	1213.06	1208.98
100000	1597.84	1578.46	1562.59	1549.53	1538.76	1529.85	1522.46	1516.33	1511.23

MONTHLY PAYMENT 18½%
NECESSARY TO AMORTIZE A LOAN

TERM AMOUNT	24 YEARS	25 YEARS	26 YEARS	27 YEARS	28 YEARS	29 YEARS	30 YEARS	35 YEARS	40 YEARS
$ 25	.38	.38	.38	.38	.38	.38	.38	.38	.38
50	.76	.76	.76	.75	.75	.75	.75	.75	.75
75	1.14	1.13	1.13	1.13	1.13	1.13	1.12	1.12	1.12
100	1.51	1.51	1.51	1.50	1.50	1.50	1.50	1.49	1.49
200	3.02	3.01	3.01	3.00	3.00	2.99	2.99	2.98	2.98
300	4.53	4.52	4.51	4.50	4.49	4.49	4.48	4.47	4.46
400	6.03	6.02	6.01	6.00	5.99	5.98	5.98	5.96	5.95
500	7.54	7.52	7.51	7.50	7.48	7.48	7.47	7.45	7.44
600	9.05	9.03	9.01	8.99	8.98	8.97	8.96	8.94	8.92
700	10.55	10.53	10.51	10.49	10.48	10.46	10.45	10.42	10.41
800	12.06	12.03	12.01	11.99	11.97	11.96	11.95	11.91	11.90
900	13.57	13.54	13.51	13.49	13.47	13.45	13.44	13.40	13.38
1000	15.07	15.04	15.01	14.99	14.96	14.95	14.93	14.89	14.87
2000	30.14	30.07	30.01	29.97	29.92	29.89	29.86	29.77	29.74
3000	45.21	45.11	45.02	44.95	44.88	44.83	44.79	44.66	44.60
4000	60.28	60.14	60.02	59.93	59.84	59.77	59.72	59.54	59.47
5000	75.35	75.18	75.03	74.91	74.80	74.72	74.64	74.43	74.34
6000	90.42	90.21	90.03	89.89	89.76	89.66	89.57	89.31	89.20
7000	105.49	105.25	105.04	104.87	104.72	104.60	104.50	104.20	104.07
8000	120.56	120.28	120.04	119.85	119.68	119.54	119.43	119.08	118.94
9000	135.63	135.31	135.05	134.83	134.64	134.49	134.36	133.96	133.80
10000	150.70	150.35	150.05	149.81	149.60	149.43	149.28	148.85	148.67
15000	226.05	225.52	225.08	224.71	224.40	224.14	223.92	223.27	223.00
20000	301.40	300.69	300.10	299.61	299.20	298.85	298.56	297.69	297.34
25000	376.75	375.86	375.12	374.51	373.99	373.56	373.20	372.12	371.67
30000	452.10	451.03	450.15	449.41	448.79	448.27	447.84	446.54	446.00
35000	527.45	526.21	525.17	524.31	523.59	522.99	522.48	520.96	520.33
36000	542.52	541.24	540.18	539.29	538.55	537.93	537.41	535.84	535.20
37000	557.58	556.27	555.18	554.27	553.51	552.87	552.34	550.73	550.07
38000	572.65	571.31	570.19	569.25	568.47	567.81	567.27	565.61	564.93
39000	587.72	586.34	585.19	584.23	583.43	582.76	582.19	580.50	579.80
40000	602.79	601.38	600.20	599.21	598.39	597.70	597.12	595.38	594.67
41000	617.86	616.41	615.20	614.19	613.35	612.64	612.05	610.27	609.53
42000	632.93	631.45	630.21	629.17	628.31	627.58	626.98	625.15	624.40
43000	648.00	646.48	645.21	644.15	643.26	642.52	641.91	640.04	639.27
44000	663.07	661.52	660.22	659.13	658.22	657.47	656.83	654.92	654.13
45000	678.14	676.55	675.22	674.11	673.18	672.41	671.76	669.80	669.00
46000	693.21	691.58	690.23	689.09	688.14	687.35	686.69	684.69	683.87
47000	708.28	706.62	705.23	704.07	703.10	702.29	701.62	699.57	698.73
48000	723.35	721.65	720.23	719.05	718.06	717.24	716.55	714.46	713.60
49000	738.42	736.69	735.24	734.03	733.02	732.18	731.47	729.34	728.47
50000	753.49	751.72	750.24	749.01	747.98	747.12	746.40	744.23	743.33
51000	768.56	766.76	765.25	763.99	762.94	762.06	761.33	759.11	758.20
52000	783.63	781.79	780.25	778.97	777.90	777.01	776.26	774.00	773.07
53000	798.70	796.82	795.26	793.95	792.86	791.95	791.19	788.88	787.93
54000	813.77	811.86	810.26	808.93	807.82	806.89	806.11	803.76	802.80
55000	828.84	826.89	825.27	823.91	822.78	821.83	821.04	818.65	817.67
56000	843.91	841.93	840.27	838.89	837.74	836.77	835.97	833.53	832.53
57000	858.98	856.96	855.28	853.87	852.70	851.72	850.90	848.42	847.40
58000	874.05	872.00	870.28	868.85	867.66	866.66	865.82	863.30	862.27
59000	889.12	887.03	885.29	883.83	882.62	881.60	880.75	878.19	877.13
60000	904.19	902.06	900.29	898.81	897.58	896.54	895.68	893.07	892.00
61000	919.26	917.10	915.30	913.79	912.54	911.49	910.61	907.96	906.87
62000	934.33	932.13	930.30	928.77	927.50	926.43	925.54	922.84	921.73
63000	949.40	947.17	945.31	943.75	942.46	941.37	940.46	937.72	936.60
64000	964.47	962.20	960.31	958.73	957.41	956.31	955.39	952.61	951.46
65000	979.54	977.24	975.32	973.71	972.37	971.26	970.32	967.49	966.33
66000	994.61	992.27	990.32	988.69	987.33	986.20	985.25	982.38	981.20
67000	1009.68	1007.30	1005.33	1003.67	1002.29	1001.14	1000.18	997.26	996.06
68000	1024.75	1022.34	1020.33	1018.65	1017.25	1016.08	1015.10	1012.15	1010.93
69000	1039.82	1037.37	1035.34	1033.63	1032.21	1031.02	1030.03	1027.03	1025.80
70000	1054.89	1052.41	1050.34	1048.61	1047.17	1045.97	1044.96	1041.92	1040.66
75000	1130.23	1127.58	1125.36	1123.51	1121.97	1120.68	1119.60	1116.34	1115.00
80000	1205.58	1202.75	1200.39	1198.42	1196.77	1195.39	1194.24	1190.76	1189.33
100000	1506.98	1503.44	1500.48	1498.02	1495.96	1494.24	1492.80	1488.45	1486.66

18¾% MONTHLY PAYMENT
NECESSARY TO AMORTIZE A LOAN

TERM AMOUNT	1 YEAR	1½ YEARS	2 YEARS	2½ YEARS	3 YEARS	3½ YEARS	4 YEARS	4½ YEARS	5 YEARS
$ 25	2.30	1.60	1.25	1.05	.91	.81	.74	.68	.64
50	4.59	3.20	2.50	2.09	1.81	1.62	1.48	1.36	1.28
75	6.88	4.79	3.75	3.13	2.72	2.43	2.21	2.04	1.91
100	9.18	6.39	5.00	4.17	3.62	3.23	2.95	2.72	2.55
200	18.35	12.77	10.00	8.34	7.24	6.46	5.89	5.44	5.09
300	27.52	19.15	14.99	12.51	10.86	9.69	8.83	8.16	7.63
400	36.69	25.54	19.99	16.67	14.48	12.92	11.77	10.88	10.17
500	45.86	31.92	24.98	20.84	18.10	16.15	14.71	13.60	12.71
600	55.03	38.30	29.98	25.01	21.71	19.38	17.65	16.31	15.26
700	64.20	44.69	34.97	29.17	25.33	22.61	20.59	19.03	17.80
800	73.37	51.07	39.97	33.34	28.95	25.84	23.53	21.75	20.34
900	82.54	57.45	44.96	37.51	32.57	29.07	26.47	24.47	22.89
1000	91.71	63.84	49.96	41.67	36.19	32.30	29.41	27.19	25.43
2000	183.42	127.67	99.91	83.34	72.37	64.59	58.81	54.37	50.85
3000	275.13	191.50	149.86	125.01	108.55	96.89	88.22	81.55	76.28
4000	366.83	255.34	199.81	166.67	144.73	129.18	117.62	108.73	101.70
5000	458.54	319.17	249.76	208.34	180.91	161.47	147.03	135.91	127.13
6000	550.25	383.00	299.71	250.01	217.09	193.77	176.43	163.10	152.55
7000	641.95	446.84	349.67	291.68	253.27	226.06	205.84	190.28	177.98
8000	733.66	510.67	399.62	333.34	289.45	258.35	235.24	217.46	203.40
9000	825.37	574.50	449.57	375.01	325.63	290.65	264.65	244.64	228.82
10000	917.08	638.33	499.52	416.68	361.81	322.94	294.05	271.82	254.25
15000	1375.61	957.50	749.28	625.01	542.72	484.41	441.08	407.73	381.37
20000	1834.15	1276.66	999.04	833.35	723.62	645.87	588.10	543.64	508.49
25000	2292.68	1595.83	1248.80	1041.69	904.53	807.34	735.12	679.55	635.62
30000	2751.22	1914.99	1498.55	1250.02	1085.43	968.81	882.15	815.46	762.74
35000	3209.75	2234.16	1748.31	1458.36	1266.34	1130.27	1029.17	951.37	889.86
36000	3301.46	2297.99	1798.26	1500.02	1302.52	1162.57	1058.58	978.55	915.28
37000	3393.17	2361.82	1848.21	1541.69	1338.70	1194.86	1087.98	1005.73	940.71
38000	3484.87	2425.66	1898.17	1583.36	1374.88	1227.15	1117.39	1032.91	966.13
39000	3576.58	2489.49	1948.12	1625.03	1411.06	1259.45	1146.79	1060.09	991.56
40000	3668.29	2553.32	1998.07	1666.69	1447.24	1291.74	1176.20	1087.28	1016.98
41000	3760.00	2617.16	2048.02	1708.36	1483.42	1324.04	1205.60	1114.46	1042.41
42000	3851.70	2680.99	2097.97	1750.03	1519.61	1356.33	1235.00	1141.64	1067.83
43000	3943.41	2744.82	2147.92	1791.69	1555.79	1388.62	1264.41	1168.82	1093.25
44000	4035.12	2808.65	2197.88	1833.36	1591.97	1420.92	1293.81	1196.00	1118.68
45000	4126.82	2872.49	2247.83	1875.03	1628.15	1453.21	1323.22	1223.18	1144.10
46000	4218.53	2936.32	2297.78	1916.70	1664.33	1485.50	1352.62	1250.37	1169.53
47000	4310.24	3000.15	2347.73	1958.36	1700.51	1517.80	1382.03	1277.55	1194.95
48000	4401.95	3063.99	2397.68	2000.03	1736.69	1550.09	1411.43	1304.73	1220.38
49000	4493.65	3127.82	2447.63	2041.70	1772.87	1582.38	1440.84	1331.91	1245.80
50000	4585.36	3191.65	2497.59	2083.37	1809.05	1614.68	1470.24	1359.09	1271.23
51000	4677.07	3255.48	2547.54	2125.03	1845.23	1646.97	1499.65	1386.27	1296.65
52000	4768.77	3319.32	2597.49	2166.70	1881.42	1679.26	1529.05	1413.46	1322.07
53000	4860.48	3383.15	2647.44	2208.37	1917.60	1711.56	1558.46	1440.64	1347.50
54000	4952.19	3446.98	2697.39	2250.03	1953.78	1743.85	1587.86	1467.82	1372.92
55000	5043.90	3510.82	2747.34	2291.70	1989.96	1776.14	1617.27	1495.00	1398.35
56000	5135.60	3574.65	2797.30	2333.37	2026.14	1808.44	1646.67	1522.18	1423.77
57000	5227.31	3638.48	2847.25	2375.04	2062.32	1840.73	1676.08	1549.36	1449.20
58000	5319.02	3702.31	2897.20	2416.70	2098.50	1873.02	1705.48	1576.55	1474.62
59000	5410.72	3766.15	2947.15	2458.37	2134.68	1905.32	1734.89	1603.73	1500.05
60000	5502.43	3829.98	2997.10	2500.04	2170.86	1937.61	1764.29	1630.91	1525.47
61000	5594.14	3893.81	3047.05	2541.70	2207.04	1969.90	1793.70	1658.09	1550.89
62000	5685.84	3957.65	3097.01	2583.37	2243.22	2002.20	1823.10	1685.27	1576.32
63000	5777.55	4021.48	3146.96	2625.04	2279.41	2034.49	1852.50	1712.46	1601.74
64000	5869.26	4085.31	3196.91	2666.71	2315.59	2066.78	1881.91	1739.64	1627.17
65000	5960.97	4149.15	3246.86	2708.37	2351.77	2099.08	1911.31	1766.82	1652.59
66000	6052.67	4212.98	3296.81	2750.04	2387.95	2131.37	1940.72	1794.00	1678.02
67000	6144.38	4276.81	3346.76	2791.71	2424.13	2163.66	1970.12	1821.18	1703.44
68000	6236.09	4340.64	3396.72	2833.37	2460.31	2195.96	1999.53	1848.36	1728.87
69000	6327.79	4404.48	3446.67	2875.04	2496.49	2228.25	2028.93	1875.55	1754.29
70000	6419.50	4468.31	3496.62	2916.71	2532.67	2260.54	2058.34	1902.73	1779.71
75000	6878.04	4787.47	3746.38	3125.05	2713.58	2422.01	2205.36	2038.64	1906.84
80000	7336.57	5106.64	3996.13	3333.38	2894.48	2583.48	2352.39	2174.55	2033.96
100000	9170.71	6383.30	4995.17	4166.73	3618.10	3229.35	2940.48	2718.18	2542.45

192

MONTHLY PAYMENT 18¾%
NECESSARY TO AMORTIZE A LOAN

TERM AMOUNT	6 YEARS	7 YEARS	8 YEARS	9 YEARS	10 YEARS	11 YEARS	12 YEARS	13 YEARS	14 YEARS
$ 25	.58	.53	.50	.47	46	.44	.43	.42	.41
50	1.15	1.06	.99	.94	.91	.88	.86	.84	.82
75	1.72	1.58	1.49	1.41	1.36	1.32	1.28	1.26	1.23
100	2.29	2.11	1.98	1.88	1.81	1.75	1.71	1.67	1.64
200	4.57	4.22	3.96	3.76	3.62	3.50	3.41	3.34	3.28
300	6.86	6.32	5.93	5.64	5.42	5.25	5.11	5.01	4.92
400	9.14	8.43	7.91	7.52	7.23	7.00	6.82	6.67	6.56
500	11.42	10.53	9.88	9.40	9.03	8.75	8.52	8.34	8.19
600	13.71	12.64	11.86	11.28	10.84	10.49	10.22	10.01	9.83
700	15.99	14.74	13.84	13.16	12.64	12.24	11.93	11.67	11.47
800	18.28	16.85	15.81	15.04	14.45	13.99	13.63	13.34	13.11
900	20.56	18.95	17.79	16.92	16.25	15.74	15.33	15.01	14.75
1000	22.84	21.06	19.76	18.80	18.06	17.49	17.03	16.67	16.38
2000	45.68	42.11	39.52	37.59	36.12	34.97	34.06	33.34	32.76
3000	68.52	63.16	59.28	56.38	54.17	52.45	51.09	50.01	49.14
4000	91.36	84.21	79.04	75.18	72.23	69.93	68.12	66.68	65.52
5000	114.20	105.26	98.79	93.97	90.28	87.41	85.15	83.35	81.90
6000	137.04	126.31	118.55	112.76	108.34	104.90	102.18	100.02	98.28
7000	159.88	147.36	138.31	131.55	126.39	122.38	119.21	116.69	114.66
8000	182.72	168.41	158.07	150.35	144.45	139.86	136.24	133.36	131.04
9000	205.56	189.47	177.82	169.14	162.50	157.34	153.27	150.03	147.42
10000	228.40	210.52	197.58	187.93	180.56	174.82	170.30	165.70	163.80
15000	342.60	315.77	296.37	281.89	270.83	262.23	255.45	250.05	245.70
20000	456.80	421.03	395.16	375.86	361.11	349.64	340.60	333.39	327.60
25000	571.00	526.29	493.95	469.82	451.38	437.05	425.75	416.74	409.50
30000	685.20	631.54	592.74	563.78	541.66	524.46	510.90	500.09	491.40
35000	799.40	736.80	691.53	657.74	631.94	611.87	596.05	583.44	573.30
36000	822.24	757.85	711.28	676.54	649.99	629.35	613.08	600.11	589.68
37000	845.08	778.90	731.04	695.33	668.05	646.83	630.11	616.77	606.06
38000	867.92	799.95	750.80	714.12	686.10	664.31	647.14	633.44	622.44
39000	890.76	821.00	770.56	732.91	704.08	681.80	664.17	650.11	638.82
40000	913.60	842.05	790.31	751.71	722.21	699.28	681.20	666.78	655.19
41000	936.44	863.11	810.07	770.50	740.27	716.76	698.23	683.45	671.57
42000	959.28	884.16	829.83	789.29	758.32	734.24	715.26	700.12	687.95
43000	982.12	905.21	849.59	808.08	776.38	751.72	732.29	716.79	704.33
44000	1004.96	926.26	869.35	826.88	794.43	769.21	749.32	733.46	720.71
45000	1027.80	947.31	889.10	845.67	812.49	786.69	766.34	750.13	737.09
46000	1050.64	968.36	908.86	864.46	830.54	804.17	783.37	766.80	753.47
47000	1073.48	989.41	928.62	883.25	848.60	821.65	800.40	783.47	769.85
48000	1096.32	1010.46	948.38	902.05	866.65	839.13	817.43	800.14	786.23
49000	1119.16	1031.52	968.13	920.84	884.71	856.61	834.46	816.81	802.61
50000	1142.00	1052.57	987.89	939.63	902.76	874.10	851.49	833.48	818.99
51000	1164.84	1073.62	1007.65	958.42	920.82	891.58	868.52	850.15	835.37
52000	1187.68	1094.67	1027.41	977.22	938.88	909.06	885.55	866.82	851.75
53000	1210.52	1115.72	1047.17	996.01	956.93	926.54	902.58	883.49	868.13
54000	1233.36	1136.77	1066.92	1014.80	974.99	944.02	919.61	900.16	884.51
55000	1256.20	1157.82	1086.68	1033.59	993.04	961.51	936.64	916.82	900.89
56000	1279.04	1178.87	1106.44	1052.39	1011.10	978.99	953.67	933.49	917.27
57000	1301.88	1199.92	1126.20	1071.18	1029.15	996.47	970.70	950.16	933.65
58000	1324.72	1220.98	1145.95	1089.97	1047.21	1013.95	987.73	966.83	950.03
59000	1347.56	1242.03	1165.71	1108.76	1065.26	1031.43	1004.76	983.50	966.41
60000	1370.40	1263.08	1185.47	1127.56	1083.32	1048.92	1021.79	1000.17	982.79
61000	1393.24	1284.13	1205.23	1146.35	1101.37	1066.40	1038.82	1016.84	999.17
62000	1416.08	1305.18	1224.99	1165.14	1119.43	1083.88	1055.85	1033.51	1015.55
63000	1438.92	1326.23	1244.74	1183.93	1137.48	1101.36	1072.88	1050.18	1031.93
64000	1461.76	1347.28	1264.50	1202.73	1155.54	1118.84	1089.91	1066.85	1048.31
65000	1484.60	1368.33	1284.26	1221.52	1173.59	1136.32	1106.94	1083.52	1064.69
66000	1507.44	1389.39	1304.02	1240.31	1191.65	1153.81	1123.97	1100.19	1081.07
67000	1530.28	1410.44	1323.77	1259.10	1209.70	1171.29	1141.00	1116.86	1097.45
68000	1553.12	1431.49	1343.53	1277.90	1227.76	1188.77	1158.03	1133.53	1113.83
69000	1575.96	1452.54	1363.29	1296.69	1245.81	1206.25	1175.06	1150.20	1130.21
70000	1598.80	1473.59	1383.05	1315.48	1263.87	1223.73	1192.09	1166.87	1146.59
75000	1713.00	1578.85	1481.84	1409.44	1354.14	1311.14	1277.24	1250.21	1228.49
80000	1827.20	1684.10	1580.62	1503.41	1444.42	1398.55	1362.39	1333.56	1310.38
100000	2284.00	2105.13	1975.78	1879.26	1805.52	1748.19	1702.98	1666.95	1637.98

18¾% MONTHLY PAYMENT
NECESSARY TO AMORTIZE A LOAN

TERM AMOUNT	15 YEARS	16 YEARS	17 YEARS	18 YEARS	19 YEARS	20 YEARS	21 YEARS	22 YEARS	23 YEARS
$ 25	.41	.40	.40	.40	.39	.39	.39	.39	.39
50	.81	.80	.79	.79	.78	.78	.78	.77	.77
75	1.22	1.20	1.19	1.18	1.17	1.17	1.16	1.16	1.15
100	1.62	1.60	1.58	1.57	1.56	1.55	1.55	1.54	1.53
200	3.23	3.20	3.16	3.14	3.12	3.10	3.09	3.07	3.06
300	4.85	4.79	4.74	4.71	4.67	4.65	4.63	4.61	4.59
400	6.46	6.39	6.32	6.27	6.23	6.20	6.17	6.14	6.12
500	8.08	7.98	7.90	7.84	7.79	7.74	7.71	7.68	7.65
600	9.69	9.58	9.48	9.41	9.34	9.29	9.25	9.21	9.18
700	11.31	11.17	11.06	10.97	10.90	10.84	10.79	10.75	10.71
800	12.92	12.77	12.64	12.54	12.46	12.39	12.33	12.28	12.24
900	14.54	14.36	14.22	14.11	14.01	13.93	13.87	13.82	13.77
1000	16.15	15.96	15.80	15.67	15.57	15.48	15.41	15.35	15.30
2000	32.30	31.91	31.60	31.34	31.13	30.96	30.81	30.70	30.60
3000	48.44	47.87	47.40	47.01	46.70	46.44	46.22	46.04	45.89
4000	64.59	63.82	63.20	62.68	62.26	61.91	61.62	61.39	61.19
5000	80.73	79.78	79.00	78.35	77.83	77.39	77.03	76.73	76.48
6000	96.88	95.73	94.79	94.02	93.39	92.87	92.43	92.08	91.78
7000	113.02	111.68	110.59	109.69	108.95	108.34	107.84	107.42	107.07
8000	129.17	127.64	126.39	125.36	124.52	123.82	123.24	122.77	122.37
9000	145.31	143.59	142.19	141.03	140.08	139.30	138.65	138.11	137.66
10000	161.46	159.55	157.99	156.70	155.65	154.77	154.05	153.46	152.96
15000	242.18	239.32	236.98	235.05	233.47	232.16	231.08	230.18	229.44
20000	322.91	319.09	315.97	313.40	311.29	309.54	308.10	306.91	305.91
25000	403.63	398.86	394.96	391.75	389.11	386.93	385.13	383.63	382.39
30000	484.36	478.63	473.95	470.10	466.93	464.31	462.15	460.36	458.87
35000	565.09	558.40	552.94	548.45	544.75	541.70	539.17	537.08	535.34
36000	581.23	574.36	568.73	564.12	560.31	557.18	554.58	552.43	550.64
37000	597.38	590.31	584.53	579.79	575.88	572.65	569.98	567.77	565.93
38000	613.52	606.27	600.33	595.46	591.44	588.13	585.39	583.12	581.23
39000	629.67	622.22	616.13	611.13	607.01	603.61	600.79	598.46	596.52
40000	645.81	638.17	631.93	626.80	622.57	619.08	616.20	613.81	611.82
41000	661.96	654.13	647.72	642.47	638.14	634.56	631.60	629.15	627.12
42000	678.10	670.08	663.52	658.14	653.70	650.04	647.01	644.50	642.41
43000	694.25	686.04	679.32	673.80	669.26	665.51	662.41	659.84	657.71
44000	710.39	701.99	695.12	689.47	684.83	680.99	677.82	675.19	673.00
45000	726.54	717.94	710.92	705.14	700.39	696.47	693.22	690.53	688.30
46000	742.68	733.90	726.71	720.81	715.96	711.94	708.63	705.88	703.59
47000	758.83	749.85	742.51	736.48	731.52	727.42	724.03	721.22	718.89
48000	774.97	765.81	758.31	752.15	747.08	742.90	739.44	736.57	734.18
49000	791.12	781.76	774.11	767.82	762.65	758.38	754.84	751.91	749.48
50000	807.26	797.72	789.91	783.49	778.21	773.85	770.25	767.26	764.77
51000	823.41	813.67	805.70	799.16	793.78	789.33	785.65	782.60	780.07
52000	839.56	829.62	821.50	814.83	809.34	804.81	801.05	797.95	795.36
53000	855.70	845.58	837.30	830.50	824.90	820.28	816.46	813.29	810.66
54000	871.85	861.53	853.10	846.17	840.47	835.76	831.86	828.64	825.96
55000	887.99	877.49	868.90	861.84	856.03	851.24	847.27	843.98	841.25
56000	904.14	893.44	884.69	877.51	871.60	866.71	862.67	859.33	856.55
57000	920.28	909.40	900.49	893.18	887.16	882.19	878.08	874.67	871.84
58000	936.43	925.35	916.29	908.85	902.73	897.67	893.48	890.02	887.14
59000	952.57	941.30	932.09	924.52	918.29	913.15	908.89	905.36	902.43
60000	968.72	957.26	947.89	940.19	933.85	928.62	924.29	920.71	917.73
61000	984.86	973.21	963.68	955.86	949.42	944.10	939.70	936.05	933.02
62000	1001.01	989.17	979.48	971.53	964.98	959.58	955.10	951.40	948.32
63000	1017.15	1005.12	995.28	987.20	980.55	975.05	970.51	966.74	963.61
64000	1033.30	1021.08	1011.08	1002.87	996.11	990.53	985.91	982.09	978.91
65000	1049.44	1037.03	1026.88	1018.54	1011.67	1006.01	1001.32	997.43	994.20
66000	1065.59	1052.98	1042.67	1034.21	1027.24	1021.48	1016.72	1012.78	1009.50
67000	1081.73	1068.94	1058.47	1049.88	1042.80	1036.96	1032.13	1028.12	1024.80
68000	1097.88	1084.89	1074.27	1065.55	1058.37	1052.44	1047.53	1043.47	1040.09
69000	1114.02	1100.85	1090.07	1081.22	1073.93	1067.91	1062.94	1058.81	1055.39
70000	1130.17	1116.80	1105.87	1096.89	1089.50	1083.39	1078.34	1074.16	1070.68
75000	1210.89	1196.57	1184.86	1175.24	1167.32	1160.78	1155.37	1150.88	1147.16
80000	1291.62	1276.34	1263.85	1253.59	1245.14	1238.16	1232.39	1227.61	1223.64
100000	1614.52	1595.43	1579.81	1566.98	1556.42	1547.70	1540.49	1534.51	1529.54

194

MONTHLY PAYMENT 18¾%

NECESSARY TO AMORTIZE A LOAN

TERM AMOUNT	24 YEARS	25 YEARS	26 YEARS	27 YEARS	28 YEARS	29 YEARS	30 YEARS	35 YEARS	40 YEARS
$ 25	.39	.39	.38	.38	.38	.38	.38	.38	.38
50	.77	.77	.76	.76	.76	.76	.76	.76	.76
75	1.15	1.15	1.14	1.14	1.14	1.14	1.14	1.14	1.13
100	1.53	1.53	1.52	1.52	1.52	1.52	1.52	1.51	1.51
200	3.06	3.05	3.04	3.04	3.03	3.03	3.03	3.02	3.02
300	4.58	4.57	4.56	4.56	4.55	4.54	4.54	4.53	4.52
400	6.11	6.09	6.08	6.07	6.06	6.06	6.05	6.04	6.03
500	7.63	7.61	7.60	7.59	7.58	7.57	7.56	7.54	7.53
600	9.16	9.14	9.12	9.11	9.09	9.08	9.08	9.05	9.04
700	10.68	10.66	10.64	10.62	10.61	10.60	10.59	10.56	10.55
800	12.21	12.18	12.16	12.14	12.12	12.11	12.10	12.07	12.05
900	13.73	13.70	13.68	13.66	13.64	13.62	13.61	13.57	13.56
1000	15.26	15.22	15.20	15.17	15.15	15.14	15.12	15.08	15.06
2000	30.51	30.44	30.39	30.34	30.30	30.27	30.24	30.16	30.12
3000	45.77	45.66	45.58	45.51	45.45	45.40	45.36	45.23	45.18
4000	61.02	60.88	60.77	60.67	60.60	60.53	60.47	60.31	60.24
5000	76.28	76.10	75.96	75.84	75.74	75.66	75.59	75.38	75.30
6000	91.53	91.32	91.15	91.01	90.89	90.79	90.71	90.46	90.36
7000	106.78	106.54	106.34	106.18	106.04	105.92	105.83	105.54	105.42
8000	122.04	121.76	121.54	121.34	121.19	121.05	120.94	120.61	120.48
9000	137.29	136.98	136.73	136.51	136.33	136.19	136.06	135.69	135.54
10000	152.55	152.20	151.92	151.68	151.48	151.32	151.18	150.76	150.60
15000	228.82	228.30	227.87	227.52	227.22	226.97	226.77	226.14	225.89
20000	305.09	304.40	303.83	303.35	302.96	302.63	302.35	301.52	301.19
25000	381.36	380.50	379.79	379.19	378.70	378.28	377.94	376.90	376.48
30000	457.63	456.60	455.74	455.03	454.43	453.94	453.53	452.28	451.78
35000	533.90	532.70	531.70	530.87	530.17	529.59	529.11	527.66	527.07
36000	549.15	547.92	546.89	546.03	545.32	544.73	544.23	542.74	542.13
37000	564.41	563.14	562.08	561.20	560.47	559.86	559.35	557.81	557.19
38000	579.66	578.36	577.27	576.37	575.62	574.99	574.46	572.89	572.25
39000	594.92	593.58	592.46	591.54	590.76	590.12	589.58	587.96	587.31
40000	610.17	608.80	607.66	606.70	605.91	605.25	604.70	603.04	602.37
41000	625.42	624.02	622.85	621.87	621.06	620.38	619.82	618.12	617.43
42000	640.68	639.24	638.04	637.04	636.21	635.51	634.93	633.19	632.48
43000	655.93	654.46	653.23	652.21	651.35	650.64	650.05	648.27	647.54
44000	671.19	669.68	668.42	667.37	666.50	665.77	665.17	663.34	662.60
45000	686.44	684.90	683.61	682.54	681.65	680.91	680.29	678.42	677.66
46000	701.70	700.12	698.80	697.71	696.80	696.04	695.40	693.50	692.72
47000	716.95	715.34	714.00	712.88	711.95	711.17	710.52	708.57	707.78
48000	732.20	730.56	729.19	728.04	727.09	726.30	725.64	723.65	722.84
49000	747.46	745.78	744.38	743.21	742.24	741.43	740.75	738.72	737.90
50000	762.71	761.00	759.57	758.38	757.39	756.56	755.87	753.80	752.96
51000	777.97	776.22	774.76	773.55	772.54	771.69	770.99	768.88	768.02
52000	793.22	791.44	789.95	788.71	787.68	786.82	786.11	783.95	783.08
53000	808.47	806.66	805.14	803.88	802.83	801.95	801.22	799.03	798.13
54000	823.73	821.88	820.33	819.05	817.98	817.09	816.34	814.10	813.19
55000	838.98	837.10	835.53	834.22	833.13	832.22	831.46	829.18	828.25
56000	854.24	852.32	850.72	849.38	848.27	847.35	846.58	844.26	843.31
57000	869.49	867.54	865.91	864.55	863.42	862.48	861.69	859.33	858.37
58000	884.75	882.76	881.10	879.72	878.57	877.61	876.81	874.41	873.43
59000	900.00	897.98	896.29	894.89	893.72	892.74	891.93	889.48	888.49
60000	915.25	913.20	911.48	910.05	908.86	907.87	907.05	904.56	903.55
61000	930.51	928.42	926.67	925.22	924.01	923.00	922.16	919.63	918.61
62000	945.76	943.63	941.86	940.39	939.16	938.14	937.28	934.71	933.67
63000	961.02	958.85	957.06	955.56	954.31	953.27	952.40	949.79	948.72
64000	976.27	974.07	972.25	970.72	969.46	968.40	967.51	964.86	963.78
65000	991.52	989.29	987.44	985.89	984.60	983.53	982.63	979.94	978.84
66000	1006.78	1004.51	1002.63	1001.06	999.75	998.66	997.75	995.01	993.90
67000	1022.03	1019.73	1017.82	1016.23	1014.90	1013.79	1012.87	1010.09	1008.96
68000	1037.29	1034.95	1033.01	1031.39	1030.05	1028.92	1027.98	1025.17	1024.02
69000	1052.54	1050.17	1048.20	1046.56	1045.19	1044.05	1043.10	1040.24	1039.08
70000	1067.79	1065.39	1063.39	1061.73	1060.34	1059.18	1058.22	1055.32	1054.14
75000	1144.07	1141.49	1139.35	1137.57	1136.08	1134.84	1133.81	1130.70	1129.43
80000	1220.34	1217.59	1215.31	1213.40	1211.82	1210.50	1209.39	1206.08	1204.73
100000	1525.42	1521.99	1519.13	1516.75	1514.77	1513.12	1511.74	1507.59	1505.91

19%

MONTHLY PAYMENT
NECESSARY TO AMORTIZE A LOAN

TERM AMOUNT	1 YEAR	1½ YEARS	2 YEARS	2½ YEARS	3 YEARS	3½ YEARS	4 YEARS	4½ YEARS	5 YEARS
$ 25	2.30	1.60	1.26	1.05	.91	.82	.74	.69	.64
50	4.60	3.20	2.51	2.09	1.82	1.63	1.48	1.37	1.28
75	6.89	4.80	3.76	3.14	2.73	2.44	2.22	2.05	1.92
100	9.19	6.40	5.01	4.18	3.63	3.25	2.96	2.74	2.56
200	18.37	12.79	10.02	8.36	7.26	6.49	5.91	5.47	5.12
300	27.55	19.19	15.02	12.54	10.89	9.73	8.86	8.20	7.67
400	36.73	25.58	20.03	16.72	14.52	12.97	11.82	10.93	10.23
500	45.91	31.98	25.04	20.90	18.15	16.21	14.77	13.66	12.78
600	55.10	38.37	30.04	25.07	21.78	19.45	17.72	16.39	15.34
700	64.28	44.77	35.05	29.25	25.41	22.69	20.67	19.12	17.89
800	73.46	51.16	40.06	33.43	29.04	25.93	23.63	21.85	20.45
900	82.64	57.55	45.06	37.61	32.67	29.18	26.58	24.58	23.00
1000	91.82	63.95	50.07	41.79	36.30	32.42	29.53	27.31	25.56
2000	183.64	127.89	100.13	83.57	72.60	64.83	59.06	54.62	51.11
3000	275.46	191.84	150.20	125.35	108.90	97.24	88.58	81.92	76.66
4000	367.28	255.78	200.26	167.13	145.19	129.65	118.11	109.23	102.21
5000	459.09	319.72	250.32	208.91	181.49	162.07	147.64	136.53	127.76
6000	550.91	383.67	300.39	250.69	217.79	194.48	177.16	163.84	153.31
7000	642.73	447.61	350.45	292.47	254.09	226.89	206.69	191.14	178.86
8000	734.55	511.55	400.52	334.26	290.38	259.30	236.21	218.45	204.41
9000	826.36	575.50	450.58	376.04	326.68	291.72	265.74	245.76	229.96
10000	918.18	639.44	500.64	417.82	362.98	324.13	295.27	273.06	255.51
15000	1377.27	959.16	750.96	626.73	544.47	486.19	442.90	409.59	383.27
20000	1836.36	1278.88	1001.28	835.63	725.95	648.25	590.53	546.12	511.02
25000	2295.44	1598.59	1251.60	1044.54	907.44	810.31	738.16	682.65	638.78
30000	2754.53	1918.31	1501.92	1253.45	1088.93	972.37	885.79	819.17	766.53
35000	3213.62	2238.03	1752.24	1462.35	1270.42	1134.44	1033.42	955.70	894.28
36000	3305.44	2301.97	1802.30	1504.14	1306.71	1166.85	1062.95	983.01	919.83
37000	3397.25	2365.92	1852.36	1545.92	1343.01	1199.26	1092.47	1010.31	945.39
38000	3489.07	2429.86	1902.43	1587.70	1379.31	1231.67	1122.00	1037.62	970.94
39000	3580.89	2493.80	1952.49	1629.48	1415.61	1264.09	1151.52	1064.93	996.49
40000	3672.71	2557.75	2002.56	1671.26	1451.90	1296.50	1181.05	1092.23	1022.04
41000	3764.52	2621.69	2052.62	1713.04	1488.20	1328.91	1210.58	1119.54	1047.59
42000	3856.34	2685.63	2102.68	1754.82	1524.50	1361.32	1240.10	1146.84	1073.14
43000	3948.16	2749.58	2152.75	1796.61	1560.80	1393.73	1269.63	1174.15	1098.69
44000	4039.98	2813.52	2202.81	1838.39	1597.09	1426.15	1299.16	1201.45	1124.24
45000	4131.79	2877.46	2252.87	1880.17	1633.39	1458.56	1328.68	1228.76	1149.79
46000	4223.61	2941.41	2302.94	1921.95	1669.69	1490.97	1358.21	1256.06	1175.34
47000	4315.43	3005.35	2353.00	1963.73	1705.99	1523.38	1387.73	1283.37	1200.89
48000	4407.25	3069.30	2403.07	2005.51	1742.28	1555.80	1417.26	1310.68	1226.44
49000	4499.06	3133.24	2453.13	2047.29	1778.58	1588.21	1446.79	1337.98	1252.00
50000	4590.88	3197.18	2503.19	2089.08	1814.88	1620.62	1476.31	1365.29	1277.55
51000	4682.70	3261.13	2553.26	2130.86	1851.18	1653.03	1505.84	1392.59	1303.10
52000	4774.52	3325.07	2603.32	2172.64	1887.47	1685.45	1535.36	1419.90	1328.65
53000	4866.33	3389.01	2653.39	2214.42	1923.77	1717.86	1564.89	1447.20	1354.20
54000	4958.15	3452.96	2703.45	2256.20	1960.07	1750.27	1594.42	1474.51	1379.75
55000	5049.97	3516.90	2753.51	2297.98	1996.37	1782.68	1623.94	1501.82	1405.30
56000	5141.79	3580.84	2803.58	2339.76	2032.66	1815.09	1653.47	1529.12	1430.85
57000	5233.60	3644.79	2853.64	2381.54	2068.96	1847.51	1683.00	1556.43	1456.40
58000	5325.42	3708.73	2903.70	2423.33	2105.26	1879.92	1712.52	1583.73	1481.95
59000	5417.24	3772.67	2953.77	2465.11	2141.55	1912.33	1742.05	1611.04	1507.50
60000	5509.06	3836.62	3003.83	2506.89	2177.85	1944.74	1771.57	1638.34	1533.05
61000	5600.87	3900.56	3053.90	2548.67	2214.15	1977.16	1801.10	1665.65	1558.60
62000	5692.69	3964.51	3103.96	2590.45	2250.45	2009.57	1830.63	1692.96	1584.16
63000	5784.51	4028.45	3154.02	2632.23	2286.74	2041.98	1860.15	1720.26	1609.71
64000	5876.33	4092.39	3204.09	2674.01	2323.04	2074.39	1889.68	1747.57	1635.26
65000	5968.14	4156.34	3254.15	2715.80	2359.34	2106.81	1919.20	1774.87	1660.81
66000	6059.96	4220.28	3304.21	2757.58	2395.64	2139.22	1948.73	1802.18	1686.36
67000	6151.78	4284.22	3354.28	2799.36	2431.93	2171.63	1978.26	1829.48	1711.91
68000	6243.60	4348.17	3404.34	2841.14	2468.23	2204.04	2007.78	1856.79	1737.46
69000	6335.41	4412.11	3454.41	2882.92	2504.53	2236.46	2037.31	1884.09	1763.01
70000	6427.23	4476.05	3504.47	2924.70	2540.83	2268.87	2066.84	1911.40	1788.56
75000	6886.32	4795.77	3754.79	3133.61	2722.31	2430.93	2214.47	2047.93	1916.32
80000	7345.41	5115.49	4005.11	3342.52	2903.80	2592.99	2362.10	2184.46	2044.07
100000	9181.76	6394.36	5006.38	4178.15	3629.75	3241.24	2952.62	2730.57	2555.09

196

TERM AMOUNT	6 YEARS	7 YEARS	8 YEARS	9 YEARS	10 YEARS	11 YEARS	12 YEARS	13 YEARS	14 YEARS
$ 25	.58	.53	.50	.48	.46	.45	.43	.43	.42
50	1.15	1.06	1.00	.95	.92	.89	.86	.85	.83
75	1.73	1.59	1.50	1.43	1.37	1.33	1.29	1.27	1.25
100	2.30	2.12	1.99	1.90	1.83	1.77	1.72	1.69	1.66
200	4.60	4.24	3.98	3.79	3.65	3.53	3.44	3.37	3.31
300	6.90	6.36	5.97	5.69	5.47	5.30	5.16	5.05	4.97
400	9.19	8.48	7.96	7.58	7.29	7.06	6.88	6.74	6.62
500	11.49	10.60	9.95	9.47	9.11	8.82	8.60	8.42	8.28
600	13.79	12.72	11.94	11.37	10.93	10.59	10.32	10.10	9.93
700	16.08	14.84	13.93	13.26	12.75	12.35	12.04	11.79	11.59
800	18.38	16.95	15.92	15.16	14.57	14.11	13.75	13.47	13.24
900	20.68	19.07	17.91	17.05	16.39	15.88	15.47	15.15	14.89
1000	22.98	21.19	19.90	18.94	18.21	17.64	17.19	16.84	16.55
2000	45.95	42.38	39.80	37.88	36.41	35.28	34.38	33.67	33.09
3000	68.92	63.57	59.70	56.82	54.62	52.91	51.57	50.50	49.64
4000	91.89	84.75	79.60	75.76	72.82	70.55	68.75	67.33	66.18
5000	114.86	105.94	99.50	94.69	91.03	88.18	85.94	84.16	82.73
6000	137.83	127.13	119.40	113.63	109.23	105.82	103.13	100.99	99.27
7000	160.80	148.32	139.30	132.57	127.44	123.45	120.32	117.82	115.81
8000	183.78	169.50	159.19	151.51	145.64	141.09	137.50	134.65	132.36
9000	206.75	190.69	179.09	170.45	163.85	158.72	154.69	151.48	148.90
10000	229.72	211.88	198.99	189.38	182.05	176.36	171.88	168.31	165.45
15000	344.58	317.82	298.49	284.07	273.08	264.54	257.81	252.46	248.17
20000	459.43	423.75	397.98	378.76	364.10	352.72	343.75	336.61	330.89
25000	574.29	529.69	497.47	473.45	455.13	440.89	429.69	420.77	413.61
30000	689.15	635.63	596.97	568.14	546.15	529.07	515.62	504.92	496.33
35000	804.00	741.57	696.46	662.83	637.18	617.25	601.56	589.07	579.05
36000	826.97	762.75	716.36	681.77	655.38	634.88	618.75	605.90	595.59
37000	849.95	783.94	736.26	700.71	673.59	652.52	635.93	622.73	612.13
38000	872.92	805.13	756.16	719.65	691.79	670.16	653.12	639.56	628.68
39000	895.89	826.32	776.05	738.59	710.00	687.79	670.31	656.39	645.22
40000	918.86	847.50	795.95	757.52	728.20	705.43	687.50	673.22	661.77
41000	941.83	868.69	815.85	776.46	746.41	723.06	704.68	690.05	678.31
42000	964.80	889.88	835.75	795.40	764.61	740.70	721.87	706.88	694.85
43000	987.77	911.07	855.65	814.34	782.82	758.33	739.06	723.71	711.40
44000	1010.75	932.25	875.55	833.27	801.02	775.97	756.24	740.54	727.94
45000	1033.72	953.44	895.45	852.21	819.22	793.60	773.43	757.38	744.49
46000	1056.69	974.63	915.34	871.15	837.43	811.24	790.62	774.21	761.03
47000	1079.66	995.82	935.24	890.09	855.63	828.88	807.81	791.04	777.57
48000	1102.63	1017.00	955.14	909.03	873.84	846.51	824.99	807.87	794.12
49000	1125.60	1038.19	975.04	927.96	892.04	864.15	842.18	824.70	810.66
50000	1148.57	1059.38	994.94	946.90	910.25	881.78	859.37	841.53	827.21
51000	1171.55	1080.57	1014.84	965.84	928.45	899.42	876.56	858.36	843.75
52000	1194.52	1101.75	1034.74	984.78	946.66	917.05	893.74	875.19	860.29
53000	1217.49	1122.94	1054.64	1003.72	964.86	934.69	910.93	892.02	876.84
54000	1240.46	1144.13	1074.53	1022.65	983.07	952.32	928.12	908.85	893.38
55000	1263.43	1165.32	1094.43	1041.59	1001.27	969.96	945.30	925.68	909.93
56000	1286.40	1186.50	1114.33	1060.53	1019.48	987.60	962.49	942.51	926.47
57000	1309.37	1207.69	1134.23	1079.47	1037.68	1005.23	979.68	959.34	943.01
58000	1332.34	1228.88	1154.13	1098.41	1055.89	1022.87	996.87	976.17	959.56
59000	1355.32	1250.07	1174.03	1117.34	1074.09	1040.50	1014.05	993.00	976.10
60000	1378.29	1271.25	1193.93	1136.28	1092.30	1058.14	1031.24	1009.83	992.65
61000	1401.26	1292.44	1213.83	1155.22	1110.50	1075.77	1048.43	1026.66	1009.19
62000	1424.23	1313.63	1233.72	1174.16	1128.71	1093.41	1065.62	1043.49	1025.73
63000	1447.20	1334.82	1253.62	1193.10	1146.91	1111.04	1082.80	1060.32	1042.28
64000	1470.17	1356.00	1273.52	1212.03	1165.12	1128.68	1099.99	1077.15	1058.82
65000	1493.14	1377.19	1293.42	1230.97	1183.32	1146.32	1117.18	1093.98	1075.37
66000	1516.12	1398.38	1313.32	1249.91	1201.53	1163.95	1134.36	1110.81	1091.91
67000	1539.09	1419.57	1333.22	1268.85	1219.73	1181.59	1151.55	1127.65	1108.45
68000	1562.06	1440.75	1353.12	1287.79	1237.94	1199.22	1168.74	1144.48	1125.00
69000	1585.03	1461.94	1373.01	1306.72	1256.14	1216.86	1185.93	1161.31	1141.54
70000	1608.00	1483.13	1392.91	1325.66	1274.35	1234.49	1203.11	1178.14	1158.09
75000	1722.86	1589.07	1492.41	1420.35	1365.37	1322.67	1289.05	1262.29	1240.81
80000	1837.72	1695.00	1591.90	1515.04	1456.40	1410.85	1374.99	1346.44	1323.53
100000	2297.14	2118.75	1989.87	1893.80	1820.49	1763.56	1718.73	1683.05	1654.41

197

19% MONTHLY PAYMENT
NECESSARY TO AMORTIZE A LOAN

TERM AMOUNT	15 YEARS	16 YEARS	17 YEARS	18 YEARS	19 YEARS	20 YEARS	21 YEARS	22 YEARS	23 YEARS
$ 25	.41	.41	.40	.40	.40	.40	.39	.39	.39
50	.82	.81	.80	.80	.79	.79	.78	.78	.78
75	1.23	1.21	1.20	1.19	1.19	1.18	1.17	1.17	1.17
100	1.64	1.62	1.60	1.59	1.58	1.57	1.56	1.56	1.55
200	3.27	3.23	3.20	3.17	3.15	3.14	3.12	3.11	3.10
300	4.90	4.84	4.80	4.76	4.73	4.70	4.68	4.66	4.65
400	6.53	6.45	6.39	6.34	6.30	6.27	6.24	6.22	6.20
500	8.16	8.07	7.99	7.93	7.88	7.83	7.80	7.77	7.74
600	9.79	9.68	9.59	9.51	9.45	9.40	9.36	9.32	9.29
700	11.42	11.29	11.18	11.10	11.02	10.96	10.91	10.87	10.84
800	13.05	12.90	12.78	12.68	12.60	12.53	12.47	12.43	12.39
900	14.69	14.52	14.38	14.27	14.17	14.10	14.03	13.98	13.94
1000	16.32	16.13	15.98	15.85	15.75	15.66	15.59	15.53	15.48
2000	32.63	32.25	31.95	31.69	31.49	31.32	31.18	31.06	30.96
3000	48.94	48.38	47.92	47.54	47.23	46.97	46.76	46.59	46.44
4000	65.25	64.50	63.89	63.38	62.97	62.63	62.35	62.11	61.92
5000	81.57	80.63	79.86	79.23	78.71	78.28	77.93	77.64	77.40
6000	97.88	96.75	95.83	95.07	94.45	93.94	93.52	93.17	92.88
7000	114.19	112.87	111.80	110.92	110.19	109.60	109.10	108.69	108.36
8000	130.50	129.00	127.77	126.76	125.93	125.25	124.69	124.22	123.84
9000	146.82	145.12	143.74	142.61	141.67	140.91	140.27	139.75	139.31
10000	163.13	161.25	159.71	158.45	157.42	156.56	155.86	155.28	154.79
15000	244.69	241.87	239.56	237.67	236.12	234.84	233.78	232.91	232.19
20000	326.25	322.49	319.42	316.90	314.83	313.12	311.71	310.55	309.58
25000	407.82	403.11	399.27	396.12	393.53	391.40	389.64	388.18	386.97
30000	489.38	483.73	479.12	475.34	472.24	469.68	467.56	465.82	464.37
35000	570.94	564.35	558.97	554.57	550.94	547.96	545.49	543.45	541.76
36000	587.25	580.48	574.95	570.41	566.68	563.61	561.08	558.98	557.24
37000	603.57	596.60	590.92	586.26	582.42	579.27	576.66	574.51	572.72
38000	619.88	612.73	606.89	602.10	598.17	594.92	592.25	590.03	588.20
39000	636.19	628.85	622.86	617.94	613.91	610.58	607.83	605.56	603.68
40000	652.50	644.97	638.83	633.79	629.65	626.24	623.42	621.09	619.16
41000	668.82	661.10	654.80	649.63	645.39	641.89	639.00	636.61	634.63
42000	685.13	677.22	670.77	665.48	661.13	657.55	654.59	652.14	650.11
43000	701.44	693.35	686.74	681.32	676.87	673.20	670.17	667.67	665.59
44000	717.75	709.47	702.71	697.17	692.61	688.86	685.76	683.19	681.07
45000	734.07	725.60	718.68	713.01	708.35	704.51	701.34	698.72	696.55
46000	750.38	741.72	734.65	728.86	724.09	720.17	716.93	714.25	712.03
47000	766.69	757.84	750.62	744.70	739.84	735.83	732.51	729.78	727.51
48000	783.00	773.97	766.59	760.55	755.58	751.48	748.10	745.30	742.99
49000	799.32	790.09	782.56	776.39	771.32	767.14	763.68	760.83	758.46
50000	815.63	806.22	798.53	792.24	787.06	782.79	779.27	776.36	773.94
51000	831.94	822.34	814.50	808.08	802.80	798.45	794.86	791.88	789.42
52000	848.25	838.47	830.47	823.92	818.54	814.10	810.44	807.41	804.90
53000	864.57	854.59	846.44	839.77	834.28	829.76	826.03	822.94	820.38
54000	880.88	870.71	862.42	855.61	850.02	845.42	841.61	838.46	835.86
55000	897.19	886.84	878.39	871.46	865.76	861.07	857.20	853.99	851.34
56000	913.50	902.96	894.36	887.30	881.51	876.73	872.78	869.52	866.82
57000	929.81	919.09	910.33	903.15	897.25	892.38	888.37	885.05	882.29
58000	946.13	935.21	926.30	918.99	912.99	908.04	903.95	900.57	897.77
59000	962.44	951.34	942.27	934.84	928.73	923.69	919.54	916.10	913.25
60000	978.75	967.46	958.24	950.68	944.47	939.35	935.12	931.63	928.73
61000	995.06	983.58	974.21	966.53	960.21	955.01	950.71	947.15	944.21
62000	1011.38	999.71	990.18	982.37	975.95	970.66	966.29	962.68	959.69
63000	1027.69	1015.83	1006.15	998.22	991.69	986.32	981.88	978.21	975.17
64000	1044.00	1031.96	1022.12	1014.06	1007.43	1001.97	997.46	993.73	990.65
65000	1060.31	1048.08	1038.09	1029.90	1023.18	1017.63	1013.05	1009.26	1006.12
66000	1076.63	1064.21	1054.06	1045.75	1038.92	1033.29	1028.64	1024.79	1021.60
67000	1092.94	1080.33	1070.03	1061.59	1054.66	1048.94	1044.22	1040.32	1037.08
68000	1109.25	1096.45	1086.00	1077.44	1070.40	1064.60	1059.81	1055.84	1052.56
69000	1125.56	1112.58	1101.97	1093.28	1086.14	1080.25	1075.39	1071.37	1068.04
70000	1141.88	1128.70	1117.94	1109.13	1101.88	1095.91	1090.98	1086.90	1083.52
75000	1223.44	1209.32	1197.80	1188.35	1180.59	1174.19	1168.90	1164.53	1160.91
80000	1305.00	1289.94	1277.65	1267.57	1259.29	1252.47	1246.83	1242.17	1238.31
100000	1631.25	1612.43	1597.06	1584.47	1574.11	1565.58	1558.54	1552.71	1547.88

TERM AMOUNT	24 YEARS	25 YEARS	26 YEARS	27 YEARS	28 YEARS	29 YEARS	30 YEARS	35 YEARS	40 YEARS
$ 25	.39	.39	.39	.39	.39	.39	.39	.39	.39
50	.78	.78	.77	.77	.77	.77	.77	.77	.77
75	1.16	1.16	1.16	1.16	1.16	1.15	1.15	1.15	1.15
100	1.55	1.55	1.54	1.54	1.54	1.54	1.54	1.53	1.53
200	3.09	3.09	3.08	3.08	3.07	3.07	3.07	3.06	3.06
300	4.64	4.63	4.62	4.61	4.61	4.60	4.60	4.59	4.58
400	6.18	6.17	6.16	6.15	6.14	6.13	6.13	6.11	6.11
500	7.72	7.71	7.69	7.68	7.67	7.66	7.66	7.64	7.63
600	9.27	9.25	9.23	9.22	9.21	9.20	9.19	9.17	9.16
700	10.81	10.79	10.77	10.75	10.74	10.73	10.72	10.69	10.68
800	12.36	12.33	12.31	12.29	12.27	12.26	12.25	12.22	12.21
900	13.90	13.87	13.85	13.82	13.81	13.79	13.78	13.75	13.73
1000	15.44	15.41	15.38	15.36	15.34	15.32	15.31	15.27	15.26
2000	30.88	30.82	30.76	30.71	30.68	30.64	30.62	30.54	30.51
3000	46.32	46.22	46.14	46.07	46.01	45.96	45.93	45.81	45.76
4000	61.76	61.63	61.52	61.42	61.35	61.28	61.23	61.07	61.01
5000	77.20	77.03	76.89	76.78	76.68	76.60	76.54	76.34	76.26
6000	92.64	92.44	92.27	92.13	92.02	91.92	91.85	91.61	91.51
7000	108.08	107.84	107.65	107.49	107.36	107.24	107.15	106.88	106.76
8000	123.51	123.25	123.03	122.84	122.69	122.56	122.46	122.14	122.02
9000	138.95	138.65	138.41	138.20	138.03	137.88	137.77	137.41	137.27
10000	154.39	154.06	153.78	153.55	153.36	153.20	153.07	152.68	152.52
15000	231.59	231.09	230.67	230.33	230.04	229.80	229.61	229.01	228.78
20000	308.78	308.12	307.56	307.10	306.72	306.40	306.14	305.35	305.03
25000	385.97	385.14	384.45	383.88	383.40	383.00	382.67	381.69	381.29
30000	463.17	462.17	461.34	460.65	460.08	459.60	459.21	458.02	457.55
35000	540.36	539.20	538.23	537.43	536.76	536.20	535.74	534.36	533.80
36000	555.80	554.60	553.61	552.78	552.10	551.52	551.05	549.63	549.06
37000	571.24	570.01	568.99	568.14	567.43	566.84	566.36	564.89	564.31
38000	586.68	585.41	584.37	583.49	582.77	582.16	581.66	580.16	579.56
39000	602.12	600.82	599.74	598.85	598.10	597.48	596.97	595.43	594.81
40000	617.55	616.23	615.12	614.20	613.44	612.80	612.28	610.70	610.06
41000	632.99	631.63	630.50	629.56	628.78	628.12	627.58	625.96	625.31
42000	648.43	647.04	645.88	644.91	644.11	643.44	642.89	641.23	640.56
43000	663.87	662.44	661.25	660.27	659.45	658.76	658.20	656.50	655.82
44000	679.31	677.85	676.63	675.62	674.78	674.08	673.50	671.77	671.07
45000	694.75	693.25	692.01	690.98	690.12	689.40	688.81	687.03	686.32
46000	710.19	708.66	707.39	706.33	705.46	704.72	704.12	702.30	701.57
47000	725.63	724.06	722.77	721.69	720.79	720.04	719.42	717.57	716.82
48000	741.06	739.47	738.14	737.04	736.13	735.36	734.73	732.84	732.07
49000	756.50	754.87	753.52	752.40	751.46	750.68	750.04	748.10	747.32
50000	771.94	770.28	768.90	767.75	766.80	766.00	765.34	763.37	762.58
51000	787.38	785.69	784.28	783.11	782.13	781.32	780.65	778.64	777.83
52000	802.82	801.09	799.66	798.46	797.47	796.64	795.96	793.90	793.08
53000	818.26	816.50	815.03	813.82	812.81	811.96	811.26	809.17	808.33
54000	833.70	831.90	830.41	829.17	828.14	827.28	826.57	824.44	823.58
55000	849.14	847.31	845.79	844.53	843.48	842.60	841.88	839.71	838.83
56000	864.57	862.71	861.17	859.88	858.81	857.92	857.18	854.97	854.08
57000	880.01	878.12	876.55	875.24	874.15	873.24	872.49	870.24	869.34
58000	895.45	893.52	891.92	890.59	889.49	888.56	887.80	885.51	884.59
59000	910.89	908.93	907.30	905.95	904.82	903.88	903.10	900.78	899.84
60000	926.33	924.34	922.68	921.30	920.16	919.20	918.41	916.04	915.09
61000	941.77	939.74	938.06	936.66	935.49	934.52	933.72	931.31	930.34
62000	957.21	955.15	953.43	952.01	950.83	949.84	949.03	946.58	945.59
63000	972.65	970.55	968.81	967.37	966.17	965.16	964.33	961.84	960.84
64000	988.08	985.96	984.19	982.72	981.50	980.48	979.64	977.11	976.10
65000	1003.52	1001.36	999.57	998.08	996.84	995.80	994.95	992.38	991.35
66000	1018.96	1016.77	1014.95	1013.43	1012.17	1011.12	1010.25	1007.65	1006.60
67000	1034.40	1032.17	1030.32	1028.79	1027.51	1026.44	1025.56	1022.91	1021.85
68000	1049.84	1047.58	1045.70	1044.14	1042.84	1041.76	1040.87	1038.18	1037.10
69000	1065.28	1062.98	1061.08	1059.50	1058.18	1057.08	1056.17	1053.45	1052.35
70000	1080.72	1078.39	1076.46	1074.85	1073.52	1072.40	1071.48	1068.72	1067.60
75000	1157.91	1155.42	1153.35	1151.63	1150.20	1149.00	1148.01	1145.05	1143.86
80000	1235.10	1232.45	1230.24	1228.40	1226.87	1225.60	1224.55	1221.39	1220.12
100000	1543.88	1540.56	1537.80	1535.50	1533.59	1532.00	1530.68	1526.73	1525.15

19½% MONTHLY PAYMENT
NECESSARY TO AMORTIZE A LOAN

TERM AMOUNT	1 YEAR	1½ YEARS	2 YEARS	2½ YEARS	3 YEARS	3½ YEARS	4 YEARS	4½ YEARS	5 YEARS
$ 25	2.31	1.61	1.26	1.06	.92	.82	.75	.69	.65
50	4.61	3.21	2.52	2.11	1.83	1.64	1.49	1.38	1.30
75	6.91	4.82	3.78	3.16	2.74	2.45	2.24	2.07	1.94
100	9.21	6.42	5.03	4.21	3.66	3.27	2.98	2.76	2.59
200	18.41	12.84	10.06	8.41	7.31	6.54	5.96	5.52	5.17
300	27.62	19.25	15.09	12.61	10.96	9.80	8.94	8.27	7.75
400	36.82	25.67	20.12	16.81	14.62	13.07	11.91	11.03	10.33
500	46.02	32.09	25.15	21.01	18.27	16.33	14.89	13.78	12.91
600	55.23	38.50	30.18	25.21	21.92	19.60	17.87	16.54	15.49
700	64.43	44.92	35.21	29.41	25.58	22.86	20.84	19.29	18.07
800	73.64	51.34	40.24	33.61	29.23	26.13	23.82	22.05	20.65
900	82.84	57.75	45.26	37.81	32.88	29.39	26.80	24.80	23.23
1000	92.04	64.17	50.29	42.02	36.54	32.66	29.77	27.56	25.81
2000	184.08	128.33	100.58	84.03	73.07	65.31	59.54	55.11	51.61
3000	276.12	192.50	150.87	126.04	109.60	97.96	89.31	82.67	77.42
4000	368.16	256.66	201.16	168.05	146.13	130.61	119.08	110.22	103.22
5000	460.20	320.83	251.45	210.06	182.66	163.26	148.85	137.77	129.03
6000	552.23	384.99	301.73	252.07	219.19	195.91	178.62	165.33	154.83
7000	644.27	449.16	352.02	294.08	255.72	228.56	208.39	192.88	180.63
8000	736.31	513.32	402.31	336.09	292.25	261.21	238.16	220.44	206.44
9000	828.35	577.49	452.60	378.10	328.78	293.86	267.93	247.99	232.24
10000	920.39	641.65	502.89	420.11	365.31	326.51	297.70	275.54	258.05
15000	1380.58	962.48	754.33	630.16	547.97	489.76	446.55	413.31	387.07
20000	1840.77	1283.30	1005.77	840.21	730.62	653.02	595.39	551.08	516.09
25000	2300.96	1604.13	1257.21	1050.26	913.27	816.27	744.24	688.85	645.11
30000	2761.15	1924.95	1508.65	1260.31	1095.93	979.52	893.09	826.62	774.13
35000	3221.34	2245.77	1760.09	1470.36	1278.58	1142.77	1041.93	964.39	903.15
36000	3313.38	2309.94	1810.38	1512.37	1315.11	1175.42	1071.70	991.95	928.96
37000	3405.42	2374.10	1860.67	1554.38	1351.64	1208.07	1101.47	1019.50	954.76
38000	3497.46	2438.27	1910.96	1596.39	1388.17	1240.73	1131.24	1047.06	980.57
39000	3589.50	2502.43	1961.24	1638.40	1424.70	1273.38	1161.01	1074.61	1006.37
40000	3681.54	2566.60	2011.53	1680.41	1461.23	1306.03	1190.78	1102.16	1032.18
41000	3773.57	2630.76	2061.82	1722.42	1497.77	1338.68	1220.55	1129.72	1057.98
42000	3865.61	2694.93	2112.11	1764.43	1534.30	1371.33	1250.32	1157.27	1083.78
43000	3957.65	2759.09	2162.40	1806.44	1570.83	1403.98	1280.09	1184.83	1109.59
44000	4049.69	2823.26	2212.69	1848.45	1607.36	1436.63	1309.86	1212.38	1135.39
45000	4141.73	2887.42	2262.97	1890.46	1643.89	1469.28	1339.63	1239.93	1161.20
46000	4233.76	2951.59	2313.26	1932.47	1680.42	1501.93	1369.40	1267.49	1187.00
47000	4325.80	3015.75	2363.55	1974.48	1716.95	1534.58	1399.17	1295.04	1212.81
48000	4417.84	3079.92	2413.84	2016.49	1753.48	1567.23	1428.94	1322.60	1238.61
49000	4509.88	3144.08	2464.13	2058.50	1790.01	1599.88	1458.71	1350.15	1264.41
50000	4601.92	3208.25	2514.41	2100.51	1826.54	1632.53	1488.47	1377.70	1290.22
51000	4693.96	3272.41	2564.70	2142.52	1863.07	1665.18	1518.24	1405.26	1316.02
52000	4785.99	3336.58	2614.99	2184.53	1899.60	1697.83	1548.01	1432.81	1341.83
53000	4878.03	3400.74	2665.28	2226.54	1936.13	1730.48	1577.78	1460.37	1367.63
54000	4970.07	3464.91	2715.57	2268.55	1972.67	1763.13	1607.55	1487.92	1393.44
55000	5062.11	3529.07	2765.86	2310.56	2009.20	1795.78	1637.32	1515.47	1419.24
56000	5154.15	3593.23	2816.14	2352.57	2045.73	1828.43	1667.09	1543.03	1445.04
57000	5246.19	3657.40	2866.43	2394.58	2082.26	1861.09	1696.86	1570.58	1470.85
58000	5338.22	3721.56	2916.72	2436.59	2118.79	1893.74	1726.63	1598.14	1496.65
59000	5430.26	3785.73	2967.01	2478.60	2155.32	1926.39	1756.40	1625.69	1522.46
60000	5522.30	3849.89	3017.30	2520.61	2191.85	1959.04	1786.17	1653.24	1548.26
61000	5614.34	3914.06	3067.59	2562.62	2228.38	1991.69	1815.94	1680.80	1574.07
62000	5706.38	3978.22	3117.87	2604.63	2264.91	2024.34	1845.71	1708.35	1599.87
63000	5798.41	4042.39	3168.16	2646.64	2301.44	2056.99	1875.48	1735.91	1625.67
64000	5890.45	4106.55	3218.45	2688.65	2337.97	2089.64	1905.25	1763.46	1651.48
65000	5982.49	4170.72	3268.74	2730.66	2374.50	2122.29	1935.02	1791.01	1677.28
66000	6074.53	4234.88	3319.03	2772.67	2411.03	2154.94	1964.79	1818.57	1703.09
67000	6166.57	4299.05	3369.31	2814.68	2447.56	2187.59	1994.55	1846.12	1728.89
68000	6258.61	4363.21	3419.60	2856.69	2484.10	2220.24	2024.32	1873.68	1754.70
69000	6350.64	4427.38	3469.89	2898.70	2520.63	2252.89	2054.09	1901.23	1780.50
70000	6442.68	4491.54	3520.18	2940.71	2557.16	2285.54	2083.86	1928.78	1806.30
75000	6902.87	4812.37	3771.62	3150.76	2739.81	2448.79	2232.71	2066.55	1935.33
80000	7363.07	5133.19	4023.06	3360.81	2922.46	2612.05	2381.56	2204.32	2064.35
100000	9203.83	6416.49	5028.82	4201.01	3653.08	3265.06	2976.94	2755.40	2580.43

MONTHLY PAYMENT 19½%
NECESSARY TO AMORTIZE A LOAN

TERM AMOUNT	6 YEARS	7 YEARS	8 YEARS	9 YEARS	10 YEARS	11 YEARS	12 YEARS	13 YEARS	14 YEARS
$ 25	.59	.54	.51	.49	.47	.45	.44	.43	.43
50	1.17	1.08	1.01	.97	.93	.90	.88	.86	.85
75	1.75	1.61	1.52	1.45	1.39	1.35	1.32	1.29	1.27
100	2.33	2.15	2.02	1.93	1.86	1.80	1.76	1.72	1.69
200	4.65	4.30	4.04	3.85	3.71	3.59	3.51	3.44	3.38
300	6.98	6.44	6.06	5.77	5.56	5.39	5.26	5.15	5.07
400	9.30	8.59	8.08	7.70	7.41	7.18	7.01	6.87	6.75
500	11.62	10.74	10.10	9.62	9.26	8.98	8.76	8.58	8.44
600	13.95	12.88	12.11	11.54	11.11	10.77	10.51	10.30	10.13
700	16.27	15.03	14.13	13.47	12.96	12.57	12.26	12.01	11.82
800	18.59	17.17	16.15	15.39	14.81	14.36	14.01	13.73	13.50
900	20.92	19.32	18.17	17.31	16.66	16.15	15.76	15.44	15.19
1000	23.24	21.47	20.19	19.23	18.51	17.95	17.51	17.16	16.88
2000	46.47	42.93	40.37	38.46	37.02	35.89	35.01	34.31	33.75
3000	69.71	64.39	60.55	57.69	55.52	53.84	52.52	51.47	50.63
4000	92.94	85.85	80.73	76.92	74.03	71.78	70.02	68.62	67.50
5000	116.18	107.31	100.91	96.15	92.53	89.73	87.52	85.77	84.37
6000	139.41	128.77	121.09	115.38	111.04	107.67	105.03	102.93	101.25
7000	162.65	150.23	141.28	134.61	129.54	125.61	122.53	120.08	118.12
8000	185.88	171.69	161.46	153.84	148.05	143.56	140.03	137.23	134.99
9000	209.12	193.15	181.64	173.07	166.55	161.50	157.54	154.39	151.87
10000	232.35	214.61	201.82	192.30	185.06	179.45	175.04	171.54	168.74
15000	348.53	321.92	302.73	288.45	277.59	269.17	262.56	257.31	253.11
20000	464.70	429.22	403.64	384.60	370.11	358.89	350.07	343.08	337.48
25000	580.88	536.53	504.54	480.75	462.64	448.61	437.59	428.85	421.85
30000	697.05	643.83	605.45	576.90	555.17	538.33	525.11	514.61	506.22
35000	813.23	751.14	706.36	673.05	647.70	628.05	612.63	600.38	590.58
36000	836.46	772.60	726.54	692.28	666.20	646.00	630.13	617.54	607.46
37000	859.70	794.06	746.72	711.51	684.71	663.94	647.63	634.69	624.33
38000	882.93	815.52	766.91	730.74	703.21	681.88	665.14	651.84	641.21
39000	906.11	836.98	787.09	749.97	721.72	699.83	682.64	669.00	658.08
40000	929.40	858.44	807.27	769.20	740.22	717.77	700.14	686.15	674.95
41000	952.64	879.90	827.45	788.43	758.73	735.72	717.65	703.30	691.83
42000	975.87	901.36	847.63	807.66	777.23	753.66	735.15	720.46	708.70
43000	999.11	922.82	867.81	826.89	795.74	771.60	752.65	737.61	725.57
44000	1022.34	944.28	888.00	846.12	814.24	789.55	770.16	754.77	742.45
45000	1045.58	965.75	908.18	865.35	832.75	807.49	787.66	771.92	759.32
46000	1068.81	987.21	928.36	884.58	851.25	825.44	805.16	789.07	776.20
47000	1092.05	1008.67	948.54	903.81	869.76	843.38	822.67	806.23	793.07
48000	1115.28	1030.13	968.72	923.04	888.27	861.33	840.17	823.38	809.94
49000	1138.52	1051.59	988.90	942.27	906.77	879.27	857.67	840.53	826.82
50000	1161.75	1073.05	1009.08	961.50	925.28	897.21	875.18	857.69	843.69
51000	1184.99	1094.51	1029.27	980.73	943.78	915.16	892.68	874.84	860.56
52000	1208.22	1115.97	1049.45	999.96	962.29	933.10	910.18	891.99	877.44
53000	1231.46	1137.43	1069.63	1019.19	980.79	951.05	927.69	909.15	894.31
54000	1254.69	1158.89	1089.81	1038.42	999.30	968.99	945.19	926.30	911.18
55000	1277.93	1180.35	1109.99	1057.65	1017.80	986.93	962.69	943.46	928.06
56000	1301.16	1201.81	1130.17	1076.88	1036.31	1004.88	980.20	960.61	944.93
57000	1324.40	1223.28	1150.36	1096.11	1054.81	1022.82	997.70	977.76	961.81
58000	1347.63	1244.74	1170.54	1115.34	1073.32	1040.77	1015.20	994.92	978.68
59000	1370.87	1266.20	1190.72	1134.57	1091.83	1058.71	1032.71	1012.07	995.55
60000	1394.10	1287.66	1210.90	1153.80	1110.33	1076.66	1050.21	1029.22	1012.43
61000	1417.34	1309.12	1231.08	1173.03	1128.84	1094.60	1067.71	1046.38	1029.30
62000	1440.57	1330.58	1251.26	1192.26	1147.34	1112.54	1085.22	1063.53	1046.17
63000	1463.81	1352.04	1271.45	1211.49	1165.85	1130.49	1102.72	1080.68	1063.05
64000	1487.04	1373.50	1291.63	1230.72	1184.35	1148.43	1120.22	1097.84	1079.92
65000	1510.28	1394.96	1311.81	1249.95	1202.86	1166.38	1137.73	1114.99	1096.80
66000	1533.51	1416.42	1331.99	1269.18	1221.36	1184.32	1155.23	1132.15	1113.67
67000	1556.75	1437.88	1352.17	1288.41	1239.87	1202.26	1172.74	1149.30	1130.54
68000	1579.98	1459.35	1372.35	1307.64	1258.37	1220.21	1190.24	1166.45	1147.42
69000	1603.22	1480.81	1392.53	1326.87	1276.88	1238.15	1207.74	1183.61	1164.29
70000	1626.45	1502.27	1412.72	1346.10	1295.39	1256.10	1225.25	1200.76	1181.16
75000	1742.63	1609.57	1513.62	1442.25	1387.91	1345.82	1312.76	1286.53	1265.53
80000	1858.80	1716.88	1614.53	1538.40	1480.44	1435.54	1400.28	1372.30	1349.90
100000	2323.50	2146.09	2018.16	1923.00	1850.55	1794.42	1750.35	1715.37	1687.37

19½% MONTHLY PAYMENT
NECESSARY TO AMORTIZE A LOAN

TERM AMOUNT	15 YEARS	16 YEARS	17 YEARS	18 YEARS	19 YEARS	20 YEARS	21 YEARS	22 YEARS	23 YEARS
$ 25	.42	.42	.41	.41	.41	.41	.40	.40	.40
50	.84	.83	.82	.81	.81	.81	.80	.80	.80
75	1.25	1.24	1.23	1.22	1.21	1.21	1.20	1.20	1.19
100	1.67	1.65	1.64	1.62	1.61	1.61	1.60	1.59	1.59
200	3.33	3.30	3.27	3.24	3.22	3.21	3.19	3.18	3.17
300	5.00	4.94	4.90	4.86	4.83	4.81	4.79	4.77	4.76
400	6.66	6.59	6.53	6.48	6.44	6.41	6.38	6.36	6.34
500	8.33	8.24	8.16	8.10	8.05	8.01	7.98	7.95	7.93
600	9.99	9.88	9.80	9.72	9.66	9.61	9.57	9.54	9.51
700	11.66	11.53	11.43	11.34	11.27	11.21	11.17	11.13	11.10
800	13.32	13.18	13.06	12.96	12.88	12.82	12.76	12.72	12.68
900	14.99	14.82	14.69	14.58	14.49	14.42	14.36	14.31	14.27
1000	16.65	16.47	16.32	16.20	16.10	16.02	15.95	15.90	15.85
2000	33.30	32.94	32.64	32.40	32.20	32.03	31.90	31.79	31.70
3000	49.95	49.40	48.96	48.59	48.29	48.05	47.85	47.68	47.54
4000	66.60	65.87	65.27	64.79	64.39	64.06	63.79	63.57	63.39
5000	83.25	82.33	81.59	80.98	80.48	80.08	79.74	79.46	79.24
6000	99.89	98.80	97.91	97.18	96.58	96.09	95.69	95.36	95.08
7000	116.54	115.26	114.22	113.37	112.68	112.10	111.63	111.25	110.93
8000	133.19	131.73	130.54	129.57	128.77	128.12	127.58	127.14	126.77
9000	149.84	148.19	146.86	145.76	144.87	144.13	143.53	143.03	142.62
10000	166.49	164.66	163.17	161.96	160.96	160.15	159.48	158.92	158.47
15000	249.73	246.99	244.76	242.93	241.44	240.22	239.21	238.38	237.70
20000	332.97	329.31	326.34	323.91	321.92	320.29	318.95	317.84	316.93
25000	416.21	411.64	407.92	404.89	402.40	400.36	398.68	397.30	396.16
30000	499.45	493.97	489.51	485.86	482.88	480.43	478.42	476.76	475.39
35000	582.69	576.29	571.09	566.84	563.36	560.50	558.15	556.22	554.62
36000	599.34	592.76	587.41	583.03	579.45	576.52	574.10	572.11	570.46
37000	615.99	609.22	603.72	599.23	595.55	592.53	590.05	588.00	586.31
38000	632.63	625.69	620.04	615.43	611.65	608.54	606.00	603.89	602.16
39000	649.28	642.16	636.36	631.62	627.74	624.56	621.94	619.78	618.00
40000	665.93	658.62	652.67	647.82	643.84	640.57	637.89	635.67	633.85
41000	682.58	675.09	668.99	664.01	659.93	656.59	653.83	651.57	649.69
42000	699.23	691.55	685.31	680.21	676.03	672.60	669.78	667.46	665.54
43000	715.87	708.02	701.62	696.40	692.13	688.62	685.73	683.35	681.39
44000	732.52	724.48	717.94	712.60	708.22	704.63	701.68	699.24	697.23
45000	749.17	740.95	734.26	728.79	724.32	720.64	717.62	715.13	713.08
46000	765.82	757.41	750.57	744.99	740.41	736.66	733.57	731.02	728.93
47000	782.47	773.88	766.89	761.18	756.51	752.67	749.52	746.92	744.77
48000	799.12	790.34	783.21	777.38	772.60	768.69	765.46	762.81	760.62
49000	815.76	806.81	799.52	793.57	788.70	784.70	781.41	778.70	776.46
50000	832.41	823.27	815.84	809.77	804.80	800.71	797.36	794.59	792.31
51000	849.06	839.74	832.16	825.96	820.89	816.73	813.30	810.48	808.16
52000	865.71	856.21	848.47	842.16	836.99	832.74	829.25	826.37	824.00
53000	882.36	872.67	864.79	858.35	853.08	848.76	845.20	842.27	839.85
54000	899.00	889.14	881.11	874.55	869.18	864.77	861.15	858.16	855.69
55000	915.65	905.60	897.42	890.75	885.28	880.79	877.09	874.05	871.54
56000	932.30	922.07	913.74	906.94	901.37	896.80	893.04	889.94	887.39
57000	948.95	938.53	930.06	923.14	917.47	912.81	908.99	905.83	903.23
58000	965.60	955.00	946.37	939.33	933.56	928.83	924.93	921.73	919.08
59000	982.24	971.46	962.69	955.53	949.66	944.84	940.88	937.62	934.92
60000	998.89	987.93	979.01	971.72	965.75	960.86	956.83	953.51	950.77
61000	1015.54	1004.39	995.32	987.92	981.85	976.87	972.77	969.40	966.62
62000	1032.19	1020.86	1011.64	1004.11	997.95	992.89	988.72	985.29	982.46
63000	1048.84	1037.32	1027.96	1020.31	1014.04	1008.90	1004.67	1001.18	998.31
64000	1065.49	1053.79	1044.27	1036.50	1030.14	1024.91	1020.62	1017.08	1014.15
65000	1082.13	1070.26	1060.59	1052.70	1046.23	1040.93	1036.56	1032.97	1030.00
66000	1098.78	1086.72	1076.91	1068.89	1062.33	1056.94	1052.51	1048.86	1045.85
67000	1115.43	1103.19	1093.22	1085.09	1078.43	1072.96	1068.46	1064.75	1061.69
68000	1132.08	1119.65	1109.54	1101.28	1094.52	1088.97	1084.40	1080.64	1077.54
69000	1148.73	1136.12	1125.86	1117.48	1110.62	1104.98	1100.35	1096.53	1093.39
70000	1165.37	1152.58	1142.17	1133.67	1126.71	1121.00	1116.30	1112.43	1109.23
75000	1248.61	1234.91	1223.76	1214.65	1207.19	1201.07	1196.03	1191.88	1188.46
80000	1331.86	1317.24	1305.34	1295.63	1287.67	1281.14	1275.77	1271.34	1267.69
100000	1664.82	1646.54	1631.67	1619.53	1609.59	1601.42	1594.71	1589.18	1584.61

202

MONTHLY PAYMENT 19½%
NECESSARY TO AMORTIZE A LOAN

TERM AMOUNT	24 YEARS	25 YEARS	26 YEARS	27 YEARS	28 YEARS	29 YEARS	30 YEARS	35 YEARS	40 YEARS
$ 25	.40	.40	.40	.40	.40	.40	.40	.40	.40
50	.80	.79	.79	.79	.79	.79	.79	.79	.79
75	1.19	1.19	1.19	1.18	1.18	1.18	1.18	1.18	1.18
100	1.59	1.58	1.58	1.58	1.58	1.57	1.57	1.57	1.57
200	3.17	3.16	3.16	3.15	3.15	3.14	3.14	3.13	3.13
300	4.75	4.74	4.73	4.72	4.72	4.71	4.71	4.70	4.70
400	6.33	6.32	6.31	6.30	6.29	6.28	6.28	6.26	6.26
500	7.91	7.89	7.88	7.87	7.86	7.85	7.85	7.83	7.82
600	9.49	9.47	9.46	9.44	9.43	9.42	9.42	9.39	9.39
700	11.07	11.05	11.03	11.02	11.00	10.99	10.98	10.96	10.95
800	12.65	12.63	12.61	12.59	12.57	12.56	12.55	12.52	12.51
900	14.23	14.20	14.18	14.16	14.15	14.13	14.12	14.09	14.08
1000	15.81	15.78	15.76	15.74	15.72	15.70	15.69	15.65	15.64
2000	31.62	31.56	31.51	31.47	31.43	31.40	31.38	31.30	31.28
3000	47.43	47.34	47.26	47.20	47.14	47.10	47.06	46.95	46.91
4000	63.24	63.11	63.01	62.93	62.85	62.80	62.75	62.60	62.55
5000	79.05	78.89	78.76	78.66	78.57	78.49	78.43	78.25	78.18
6000	94.86	94.67	94.51	94.39	94.28	94.19	94.12	93.90	93.82
7000	110.66	110.45	110.27	110.12	109.99	109.89	109.80	109.55	109.46
8000	126.47	126.22	126.02	125.85	125.70	125.59	125.49	125.20	125.09
9000	142.28	142.00	141.77	141.58	141.42	141.29	141.18	140.85	140.73
10000	158.09	157.78	157.52	157.31	157.13	156.98	156.86	156.50	156.36
15000	237.13	236.66	236.28	235.96	235.69	235.47	235.29	234.75	234.54
20000	316.17	315.55	315.03	314.61	314.25	313.96	313.72	313.00	312.72
25000	395.21	394.44	393.79	393.26	392.82	392.45	392.15	391.25	390.90
30000	474.26	473.32	472.55	471.91	471.38	470.94	470.58	469.50	469.08
35000	553.30	552.21	551.31	550.56	549.94	549.43	549.00	547.75	547.26
36000	569.11	567.99	567.06	566.29	565.65	565.13	564.69	563.40	562.89
37000	584.92	583.76	582.81	582.02	581.37	580.82	580.38	579.05	578.53
38000	600.72	599.54	598.56	597.75	597.08	596.52	596.06	594.70	594.17
39000	616.53	615.32	614.31	613.48	612.79	612.22	611.75	610.35	609.80
40000	632.34	631.09	630.06	629.21	628.50	627.92	627.43	626.00	625.44
41000	648.15	646.87	645.82	644.94	644.22	643.62	643.12	641.65	641.07
42000	663.96	662.65	661.57	660.67	659.93	659.31	658.80	657.30	656.71
43000	679.77	678.43	677.32	676.40	675.64	675.01	674.49	672.95	672.34
44000	695.57	694.20	693.07	692.13	691.35	690.71	690.18	688.60	687.98
45000	711.38	709.98	708.82	707.86	707.07	706.41	705.86	704.25	703.62
46000	727.19	725.76	724.57	723.59	722.78	722.11	721.55	719.90	719.25
47000	743.00	741.54	740.32	739.32	738.49	737.80	737.23	735.55	734.89
48000	758.81	757.31	756.08	755.05	754.20	753.50	752.92	751.20	750.52
49000	774.62	773.09	771.83	770.78	769.92	769.20	768.60	766.85	766.16
50000	790.42	788.87	787.58	786.51	785.63	784.90	784.29	782.50	781.80
51000	806.23	804.64	803.33	802.24	801.34	800.59	799.98	798.15	797.43
52000	822.04	820.42	819.08	817.97	817.05	816.29	815.66	813.80	813.07
53000	837.85	836.20	834.83	833.70	832.77	831.99	831.35	829.45	828.70
54000	853.66	851.98	850.58	849.43	848.48	847.69	847.03	845.10	844.34
55000	869.47	867.75	866.34	865.16	864.19	863.39	862.72	860.75	859.97
56000	885.28	883.53	882.09	880.89	879.90	879.08	878.40	876.40	875.61
57000	901.08	899.31	897.84	896.62	895.62	894.78	894.09	892.05	891.25
58000	916.89	915.09	913.59	912.35	911.33	910.48	909.78	907.70	906.88
59000	932.70	930.86	929.34	928.08	927.04	926.18	925.46	923.35	922.52
60000	948.51	946.64	945.09	943.81	942.75	941.87	941.15	939.00	938.15
61000	964.32	962.42	960.84	959.54	958.47	957.57	956.83	954.65	953.79
62000	980.13	978.19	976.60	975.27	974.18	973.27	972.52	970.30	969.43
63000	995.93	993.97	992.35	991.00	989.89	988.97	988.20	985.95	985.06
64000	1011.74	1009.75	1008.10	1006.73	1005.60	1004.67	1003.89	1001.60	1000.70
65000	1027.55	1025.53	1023.85	1022.46	1021.32	1020.36	1019.58	1017.25	1016.33
66000	1043.36	1041.30	1039.60	1038.19	1037.03	1036.06	1035.26	1032.90	1031.97
67000	1059.17	1057.08	1055.35	1053.92	1052.74	1051.76	1050.95	1048.55	1047.60
68000	1074.98	1072.86	1071.10	1069.65	1068.45	1067.46	1066.63	1064.20	1063.24
69000	1090.78	1088.63	1086.86	1085.38	1084.17	1083.16	1082.32	1079.85	1078.88
70000	1106.59	1104.41	1102.61	1101.11	1099.88	1098.85	1098.00	1095.50	1094.51
75000	1185.63	1183.30	1181.37	1179.77	1178.44	1177.34	1176.43	1173.75	1172.69
80000	1264.68	1262.18	1260.12	1258.42	1257.00	1255.83	1254.86	1252.00	1250.87
100000	1580.84	1577.73	1575.15	1573.02	1571.25	1569.79	1568.58	1564.99	1563.59

203

20% MONTHLY PAYMENT
NECESSARY TO AMORTIZE A LOAN

TERM AMOUNT	1 YEAR	1½ YEARS	2 YEARS	2½ YEARS	3 YEARS	3½ YEARS	4 YEARS	4½ YEARS	5 YEARS
$ 25	2.31	1.61	1.27	1.06	.92	.83	.76	.70	.66
50	4.62	3.22	2.53	2.12	1.84	1.65	1.51	1.40	1.31
75	6.92	4.83	3.79	3.17	2.76	2.47	2.26	2.09	1.96
100	9.23	6.44	5.06	4.23	3.68	3.29	3.01	2.79	2.61
200	18.46	12.88	10.11	8.45	7.36	6.58	6.01	5.57	5.22
300	27.68	19.32	15.16	12.68	11.03	9.87	9.01	8.35	7.82
400	36.91	25.76	20.21	16.90	14.71	13.16	12.01	11.13	10.43
500	46.13	32.20	25.26	21.12	18.39	16.45	15.01	13.91	13.03
600	55.36	38.64	30.31	25.35	22.06	19.74	18.01	16.69	15.64
700	64.59	45.08	35.36	29.57	25.74	23.03	21.01	19.47	18.25
800	73.81	51.51	40.42	33.80	29.42	26.32	24.02	22.25	20.85
900	83.04	57.95	45.47	38.02	33.09	29.61	27.02	25.03	23.46
1000	92.26	64.39	50.52	42.24	36.77	32.89	30.02	27.81	26.06
2000	184.52	128.78	101.03	84.48	73.53	65.78	60.03	55.61	52.12
3000	276.78	193.16	151.54	126.72	110.30	98.67	90.04	83.41	78.18
4000	369.04	257.55	202.06	168.96	147.06	131.56	120.06	111.22	104.24
5000	461.30	321.94	252.57	211.20	183.83	164.45	150.07	139.02	130.30
6000	553.56	386.32	303.08	253.44	220.59	197.34	180.08	166.82	156.36
7000	645.82	450.71	353.59	295.68	257.36	230.23	210.10	194.63	182.42
8000	738.08	515.09	404.11	337.92	294.12	263.12	240.11	222.43	208.47
9000	830.33	579.48	454.62	380.16	330.88	296.01	270.12	250.23	234.53
10000	922.59	643.87	505.13	422.39	367.65	328.90	300.14	278.04	260.59
15000	1383.89	965.80	757.70	633.59	551.47	493.34	450.20	417.05	390.88
20000	1845.18	1287.73	1010.26	844.78	735.29	657.79	600.27	556.07	521.18
25000	2306.48	1609.66	1262.82	1055.98	919.12	822.24	750.34	695.08	651.47
30000	2767.77	1931.59	1515.39	1267.17	1102.94	986.68	900.40	834.10	781.76
35000	3229.07	2253.52	1767.95	1478.37	1286.76	1151.13	1050.47	973.11	912.06
36000	3321.32	2317.90	1818.46	1520.61	1323.52	1184.02	1080.48	1000.92	938.11
37000	3413.58	2382.29	1868.98	1562.84	1360.29	1216.91	1110.50	1028.72	964.17
38000	3505.84	2446.68	1919.49	1605.08	1397.05	1249.80	1140.51	1056.52	990.23
39000	3598.10	2511.06	1970.00	1647.32	1433.82	1282.69	1170.52	1084.33	1016.29
40000	3690.36	2575.45	2020.52	1689.56	1470.58	1315.58	1200.54	1112.13	1042.35
41000	3782.62	2639.83	2071.03	1731.80	1507.35	1348.46	1230.55	1139.93	1068.41
42000	3874.88	2704.22	2121.54	1774.04	1544.11	1381.35	1260.56	1167.73	1094.47
43000	3967.14	2768.61	2172.05	1816.28	1580.88	1414.24	1290.58	1195.54	1120.52
44000	4059.39	2832.99	2222.57	1858.52	1617.64	1447.13	1320.59	1223.34	1146.58
45000	4151.65	2897.38	2273.08	1900.76	1654.40	1480.02	1350.60	1251.14	1172.64
46000	4243.91	2961.77	2323.59	1942.99	1691.17	1512.91	1380.62	1278.95	1198.70
47000	4336.17	3026.15	2374.11	1985.23	1727.93	1545.80	1410.63	1306.75	1224.76
48000	4428.43	3090.54	2424.62	2027.47	1764.70	1578.69	1440.64	1334.55	1250.82
49000	4520.69	3154.92	2475.13	2069.71	1801.46	1611.58	1470.66	1362.36	1276.88
50000	4612.95	3219.31	2525.64	2111.95	1838.23	1644.47	1500.67	1390.16	1302.93
51000	4705.21	3283.70	2576.16	2154.19	1874.99	1677.36	1530.68	1417.96	1328.99
52000	4797.47	3348.08	2626.67	2196.43	1911.76	1710.25	1560.70	1445.77	1355.05
53000	4889.72	3412.47	2677.18	2238.67	1948.52	1743.14	1590.71	1473.57	1381.11
54000	4981.98	3476.85	2727.69	2280.91	1985.28	1776.02	1620.72	1501.37	1407.17
55000	5074.24	3541.24	2778.21	2323.14	2022.05	1808.91	1650.74	1529.18	1433.23
56000	5166.50	3605.63	2828.72	2365.38	2058.81	1841.80	1680.75	1556.98	1459.29
57000	5258.76	3670.01	2879.23	2407.62	2095.58	1874.69	1710.76	1584.78	1485.34
58000	5351.02	3734.40	2929.75	2449.86	2132.34	1907.58	1740.78	1612.58	1511.40
59000	5443.28	3798.78	2980.26	2492.10	2169.11	1940.47	1770.79	1640.39	1537.46
60000	5535.54	3863.17	3030.77	2534.34	2205.87	1973.36	1800.80	1668.19	1563.52
61000	5627.80	3927.56	3081.28	2576.58	2242.64	2006.25	1830.82	1695.99	1589.58
62000	5720.05	3991.94	3131.80	2618.82	2279.40	2039.14	1860.83	1723.80	1615.64
63000	5812.31	4056.33	3182.31	2661.05	2316.16	2072.03	1890.84	1751.60	1641.70
64000	5904.57	4120.71	3232.82	2703.29	2352.93	2104.92	1920.86	1779.40	1667.75
65000	5996.83	4185.10	3283.33	2745.53	2389.69	2137.81	1950.87	1807.21	1693.81
66000	6089.09	4249.49	3333.85	2787.77	2426.46	2170.70	1980.88	1835.01	1719.87
67000	6181.35	4313.87	3384.36	2830.01	2463.22	2203.59	2010.90	1862.81	1745.93
68000	6273.61	4378.26	3434.87	2872.25	2499.99	2236.47	2040.91	1890.62	1771.99
69000	6365.87	4442.65	3485.39	2914.49	2536.75	2269.36	2070.92	1918.42	1798.05
70000	6458.13	4507.03	3535.90	2956.73	2573.52	2302.25	2100.94	1946.22	1824.11
75000	6919.42	4828.96	3788.46	3167.92	2757.34	2466.70	2251.00	2085.24	1954.40
80000	7380.71	5150.89	4041.03	3379.12	2941.16	2631.15	2401.07	2224.25	2084.69
100000	9225.89	6438.61	5051.28	4223.90	3676.45	3288.93	3001.33	2780.31	2605.86

MONTHLY PAYMENT   20%
NECESSARY TO AMORTIZE A LOAN

TERM AMOUNT	6 YEARS	7 YEARS	8 YEARS	9 YEARS	10 YEARS	11 YEARS	12 YEARS	13 YEARS	14 YEARS
$ 25	.59	.55	.52	.49	.48	.46	.45	.44	.44
50	1.18	1.09	1.03	.98	.95	.92	.90	.88	.87
75	1.77	1.64	1.54	1.47	1.42	1.37	1.34	1.32	1.30
100	2.35	2.18	2.05	1.96	1.89	1.83	1.79	1.75	1.73
200	4.70	4.35	4.10	3.91	3.77	3.66	3.57	3.50	3.45
300	7.05	6.53	6.14	5.86	5.65	5.48	5.35	5.25	5.17
400	9.40	8.70	8.19	7.81	7.53	7.31	7.13	7.00	6.89
500	11.75	10.87	10.24	9.77	9.41	9.13	8.92	8.74	8.61
600	14.10	13.05	12.28	11.72	11.29	10.96	10.70	10.49	10.33
700	16.45	15.22	14.33	13.67	13.17	12.78	12.48	12.24	12.05
800	18.80	17.39	16.38	15.62	15.05	14.61	14.26	13.99	13.77
900	21.15	19.57	18.42	17.58	16.93	16.43	16.04	15.74	15.49
1000	23.50	21.74	20.47	19.53	18.81	18.26	17.83	17.48	17.21
2000	47.00	43.48	40.94	39.05	37.62	36.51	35.65	34.96	34.41
3000	70.50	65.21	61.40	58.57	56.43	54.77	53.47	52.44	51.62
4000	94.00	86.95	81.87	78.10	75.23	73.02	71.29	69.92	68.82
5000	117.50	108.68	102.33	97.62	94.04	91.28	89.11	87.40	86.03
6000	141.00	130.42	122.80	117.14	112.85	109.53	106.93	104.88	103.23
7000	164.50	152.15	143.27	136.67	131.66	127.79	124.75	122.35	120.44
8000	188.00	173.89	163.73	156.19	150.46	146.04	142.57	139.83	137.64
9000	211.50	195.62	184.20	175.71	169.27	164.29	160.40	157.31	154.85
10000	235.00	217.36	204.66	195.24	188.08	182.55	178.22	174.79	172.05
15000	352.50	326.04	306.99	292.85	282.12	273.82	267.32	262.18	258.08
20000	470.00	434.72	409.32	390.47	376.15	365.09	356.43	349.57	344.10
25000	587.49	543.39	511.65	488.09	470.19	456.36	445.53	436.97	430.13
30000	704.99	652.07	613.98	585.70	564.23	547.64	534.64	524.36	516.15
35000	822.49	760.75	716.31	683.32	658.27	638.91	623.75	611.75	602.18
36000	845.99	782.48	736.77	702.84	677.07	657.16	641.57	629.23	619.38
37000	869.49	804.22	757.24	722.37	695.88	675.42	659.39	646.71	636.59
38000	892.99	825.95	777.71	741.89	714.69	693.67	677.21	664.18	653.79
39000	916.49	847.69	798.17	761.41	733.50	711.92	695.03	681.66	671.00
40000	939.99	869.43	818.64	780.94	752.30	730.18	712.85	699.14	688.20
41000	963.49	891.16	839.10	800.46	771.11	748.43	730.67	716.62	705.41
42000	986.99	912.90	859.57	819.98	789.92	766.69	748.49	734.10	722.61
43000	1010.49	934.63	880.04	839.51	808.73	784.94	766.32	751.58	739.82
44000	1033.99	956.37	900.50	859.03	827.53	803.20	784.14	769.05	757.02
45000	1057.48	978.10	920.97	878.55	846.34	821.45	801.96	786.53	774.23
46000	1080.98	999.84	941.43	898.08	865.15	839.70	819.78	804.01	791.43
47000	1104.48	1021.57	961.90	917.60	883.96	857.96	837.60	821.49	808.64
48000	1127.98	1043.31	982.36	937.12	902.76	876.21	855.42	838.97	825.84
49000	1151.48	1065.04	1002.83	956.65	921.57	894.47	873.24	856.45	843.05
50000	1174.98	1086.78	1023.30	976.17	940.38	912.72	891.06	873.93	860.25
51000	1198.48	1108.52	1043.76	995.69	959.19	930.98	908.88	891.40	877.46
52000	1221.98	1130.25	1064.23	1015.22	977.99	949.23	926.71	908.88	894.66
53000	1245.48	1151.99	1084.69	1034.74	996.80	967.49	944.53	926.36	911.87
54000	1268.98	1173.72	1105.16	1054.26	1015.61	985.74	962.35	943.84	929.07
55000	1292.48	1195.46	1125.63	1073.79	1034.42	1003.99	980.17	961.32	946.28
56000	1315.98	1217.19	1146.09	1093.31	1053.22	1022.25	997.99	978.80	963.48
57000	1339.48	1238.93	1166.56	1112.83	1072.03	1040.50	1015.81	996.27	980.69
58000	1362.98	1260.66	1187.02	1132.36	1090.84	1058.76	1033.63	1013.75	997.89
59000	1386.48	1282.40	1207.49	1151.88	1109.65	1077.01	1051.45	1031.23	1015.09
60000	1409.98	1304.14	1227.95	1171.40	1128.45	1095.27	1069.28	1048.71	1032.30
61000	1433.48	1325.87	1248.42	1190.93	1147.26	1113.52	1087.10	1066.19	1049.50
62000	1456.98	1347.61	1268.89	1210.45	1166.07	1131.77	1104.92	1083.67	1066.71
63000	1480.48	1369.34	1289.35	1229.97	1184.88	1150.03	1122.74	1101.14	1083.91
64000	1503.98	1391.08	1309.82	1249.50	1203.68	1168.28	1140.56	1118.62	1101.12
65000	1527.48	1412.81	1330.28	1269.02	1222.49	1186.54	1158.38	1136.10	1118.32
66000	1550.98	1434.55	1350.75	1288.54	1241.30	1204.79	1176.20	1153.58	1135.53
67000	1574.47	1456.28	1371.22	1308.07	1260.11	1223.05	1194.02	1171.06	1152.73
68000	1597.97	1478.02	1391.68	1327.59	1278.91	1241.30	1211.84	1188.54	1169.94
69000	1621.47	1499.75	1412.15	1347.11	1297.72	1259.55	1229.67	1206.01	1187.14
70000	1644.97	1521.49	1432.61	1366.64	1316.53	1277.81	1247.49	1223.49	1204.35
75000	1762.47	1630.17	1534.94	1464.25	1410.57	1369.08	1336.59	1310.89	1290.37
80000	1879.97	1738.85	1637.27	1561.87	1504.60	1460.35	1425.70	1398.28	1376.40
100000	2349.96	2173.56	2046.59	1952.34	1880.75	1825.44	1782.12	1747.85	1720.50

MONTHLY PAYMENT
NECESSARY TO AMORTIZE A LOAN

TERM AMOUNT	15 YEARS	16 YEARS	17 YEARS	18 YEARS	19 YEARS	20 YEARS	21 YEARS	22 YEARS	23 YEARS
$ 25	.43	.43	.42	.42	.42	.41	.41	.41	.41
50	.85	.85	.84	.83	.83	.82	.82	.82	.82
75	1.28	1.27	1.25	1.25	1.24	1.23	1.23	1.22	1.22
100	1.70	1.69	1.67	1.66	1.65	1.64	1.64	1.63	1.63
200	3.40	3.37	3.34	3.31	3.30	3.28	3.27	3.26	3.25
300	5.10	5.05	5.00	4.97	4.94	4.92	4.90	4.88	4.87
400	6.80	6.73	6.67	6.62	6.59	6.55	6.53	6.51	6.49
500	8.50	8.41	8.34	8.28	8.23	8.19	8.16	8.13	8.11
600	10.20	10.09	10.00	9.93	9.88	9.83	9.79	9.76	9.73
700	11.89	11.77	11.67	11.59	11.52	11.47	11.42	11.39	11.35
800	13.59	13.45	13.34	13.24	13.17	13.10	13.05	13.01	12.98
900	15.29	15.13	15.00	14.90	14.81	14.74	14.68	14.64	14.60
1000	16.99	16.81	16.67	16.55	16.46	16.38	16.31	16.26	16.22
2000	33.98	33.62	33.33	33.10	32.91	32.75	32.62	32.52	32.43
3000	50.96	50.43	50.00	49.65	49.36	49.13	48.93	48.78	48.65
4000	67.95	67.24	66.66	66.19	65.81	65.50	65.24	65.03	64.86
5000	84.93	84.04	83.33	82.74	82.26	81.87	81.55	81.29	81.08
6000	101.92	100.85	99.99	99.29	98.72	98.25	97.86	97.55	97.29
7000	118.90	117.66	116.65	115.84	115.17	114.62	114.17	113.81	113.50
8000	135.89	134.47	133.32	132.38	131.62	130.99	130.48	130.06	129.72
9000	152.87	151.28	149.98	148.93	148.07	147.37	146.79	146.32	145.93
10000	169.86	168.08	166.65	165.48	164.52	163.74	163.10	162.58	162.15
15000	254.78	252.12	249.97	248.21	246.78	245.61	244.65	243.86	243.22
20000	339.71	336.16	333.29	330.95	329.04	327.48	326.20	325.15	324.29
25000	424.64	420.20	416.61	413.68	411.30	409.35	407.75	406.44	405.36
30000	509.56	504.24	499.93	496.42	493.56	491.21	489.30	487.72	486.43
35000	594.49	588.28	583.25	579.16	575.81	573.08	570.84	569.01	567.50
36000	611.47	605.09	599.91	595.70	592.27	589.46	587.15	585.26	583.71
37000	628.46	621.90	616.58	612.25	608.72	605.83	603.46	601.52	599.93
38000	645.45	638.71	633.24	628.80	625.17	622.20	619.77	617.78	616.14
39000	662.43	655.51	649.91	645.34	641.62	638.58	636.08	634.04	632.35
40000	679.42	672.32	666.57	661.89	658.07	654.95	652.39	650.29	648.57
41000	696.40	689.13	683.23	678.44	674.52	671.32	668.70	666.55	664.78
42000	713.39	705.94	699.90	694.99	690.98	687.70	685.01	682.81	681.00
43000	730.37	722.75	716.56	711.53	707.43	704.07	701.32	699.06	697.21
44000	747.36	739.55	733.23	728.08	723.88	720.45	717.63	715.32	713.42
45000	764.34	756.36	749.89	744.63	740.33	736.82	733.94	731.58	729.64
46000	781.33	773.17	766.56	761.17	756.78	753.19	750.25	747.84	745.85
47000	798.31	789.98	783.22	777.72	773.23	769.57	766.56	764.09	762.07
48000	815.30	806.79	799.88	794.27	789.69	785.94	782.87	780.35	778.28
49000	832.28	823.59	816.55	810.82	806.14	802.31	799.18	796.61	794.50
50000	849.27	840.40	833.21	827.36	822.59	818.69	815.49	812.87	810.71
51000	866.25	857.21	849.88	843.91	839.04	835.06	831.80	829.12	826.92
52000	883.24	874.02	866.54	860.46	855.49	851.43	848.11	845.38	843.14
53000	900.22	890.83	883.20	877.00	871.95	867.81	864.42	861.64	859.35
54000	917.21	907.63	899.87	893.55	888.40	884.18	880.73	877.89	875.57
55000	934.19	924.44	916.53	910.10	904.85	900.56	897.04	894.15	891.78
56000	951.18	941.25	933.20	926.65	921.30	916.93	913.35	910.41	907.99
57000	968.17	958.06	949.86	943.19	937.75	933.30	929.66	926.67	924.21
58000	985.15	974.87	966.53	959.74	954.20	949.68	945.97	942.92	940.42
59000	1002.14	991.67	983.19	976.29	970.66	966.05	962.28	959.18	956.64
60000	1019.12	1008.48	999.85	992.83	987.11	982.42	978.59	975.44	972.85
61000	1036.11	1025.29	1016.52	1009.38	1003.56	998.80	994.90	991.69	989.06
62000	1053.09	1042.10	1033.18	1025.93	1020.01	1015.17	1011.21	1007.95	1005.28
63000	1070.08	1058.90	1049.85	1042.48	1036.46	1031.54	1027.52	1024.21	1021.49
64000	1087.06	1075.71	1066.51	1059.02	1052.91	1047.92	1043.82	1040.47	1037.71
65000	1104.05	1092.52	1083.17	1075.57	1069.37	1064.29	1060.13	1056.72	1053.92
66000	1121.03	1109.33	1099.84	1092.12	1085.82	1080.67	1076.44	1072.98	1070.13
67000	1138.02	1126.14	1116.50	1108.66	1102.27	1097.04	1092.75	1089.24	1086.35
68000	1155.00	1142.94	1133.17	1125.21	1118.72	1113.41	1109.06	1105.50	1102.56
69000	1171.99	1159.75	1149.83	1141.76	1135.17	1129.79	1125.37	1121.75	1118.78
70000	1188.97	1176.56	1166.50	1158.31	1151.62	1146.16	1141.68	1138.01	1134.99
75000	1273.90	1260.60	1249.82	1241.04	1233.88	1228.03	1223.23	1219.30	1216.06
80000	1358.83	1344.64	1333.14	1323.78	1316.14	1309.90	1304.78	1300.58	1297.13
100000	1698.53	1680.80	1666.42	1654.72	1645.18	1637.37	1630.97	1625.73	1621.41

MONTHLY PAYMENT 20%
NECESSARY TO AMORTIZE A LOAN

TERM AMOUNT	24 YEARS	25 YEARS	26 YEARS	27 YEARS	28 YEARS	29 YEARS	30 YEARS	35 YEARS	40 YEARS
$ 25	.41	.41	.41	.41	.41	.41	.41	.41	.41
50	.81	.81	.81	.81	.81	.81	.81	.81	.81
75	1.22	1.22	1.21	1.21	1.21	1.21	1.21	1.21	1.21
100	1.62	1.62	1.62	1.62	1.61	1.61	1.61	1.61	1.61
200	3.24	3.23	3.23	3.23	3.22	3.22	3.22	3.21	3.21
300	4.86	4.85	4.84	4.84	4.83	4.83	4.82	4.81	4.81
400	6.48	6.46	6.46	6.45	6.44	6.44	6.43	6.42	6.41
500	8.09	8.08	8.07	8.06	8.05	8.04	8.04	8.02	8.01
600	9.71	9.69	9.68	9.67	9.66	9.65	9.64	9.62	9.62
700	11.33	11.31	11.29	11.28	11.27	11.26	11.25	11.23	11.22
800	12.95	12.92	12.91	12.89	12.88	12.87	12.86	12.83	12.82
900	14.57	14.54	14.52	14.50	14.49	14.47	14.46	14.43	14.42
1000	16.18	16.15	16.13	16.11	16.09	16.08	16.07	16.04	16.02
2000	32.36	32.30	32.26	32.22	32.18	32.16	32.13	32.07	32.04
3000	48.54	48.45	48.38	48.32	48.27	48.23	48.20	48.10	48.06
4000	64.72	64.60	64.51	64.43	64.36	64.31	64.26	64.13	64.08
5000	80.90	80.75	80.63	80.53	80.45	80.38	80.33	80.17	80.10
6000	97.08	96.90	96.76	96.64	96.54	96.46	96.39	96.20	96.12
7000	113.26	113.05	112.88	112.74	112.63	112.54	112.46	112.23	112.14
8000	129.43	129.20	129.01	128.85	128.72	128.61	128.52	128.26	128.16
9000	145.61	145.35	145.13	144.96	144.81	144.69	144.59	144.29	144.18
10000	161.79	161.50	161.26	161.06	160.90	160.76	160.65	160.33	160.20
15000	242.68	242.25	241.89	241.59	241.34	241.14	240.97	240.49	240.30
20000	323.58	322.99	322.51	322.12	321.79	321.52	321.30	320.65	320.40
25000	404.47	403.74	403.14	402.64	402.24	401.90	401.62	400.81	400.50
30000	485.36	484.49	483.77	483.17	482.68	482.28	481.94	480.97	480.60
35000	566.26	565.24	564.39	563.70	563.13	562.66	562.27	561.13	560.69
36000	582.44	581.38	580.52	579.81	579.22	578.73	578.33	577.16	576.71
37000	598.61	597.53	596.64	595.91	595.31	594.81	594.40	593.20	592.73
38000	614.79	613.68	612.77	612.02	611.40	610.88	610.46	609.23	608.75
39000	630.97	629.83	628.90	628.12	627.49	626.96	626.53	625.26	624.77
40000	647.15	645.98	645.02	644.23	643.57	643.04	642.59	641.29	640.79
41000	663.33	662.13	661.15	660.33	659.66	659.11	658.65	657.32	656.81
42000	679.51	678.28	677.27	676.44	675.75	675.19	674.72	673.36	672.83
43000	695.69	694.43	693.40	692.54	691.84	691.26	690.78	689.39	688.85
44000	711.86	710.58	709.52	708.65	707.93	707.34	706.85	705.42	704.87
45000	728.04	726.73	725.65	724.76	724.02	723.41	722.91	721.45	720.89
46000	744.22	742.88	741.77	740.86	740.11	739.49	738.98	737.48	736.91
47000	760.40	759.03	757.90	756.97	756.20	755.57	755.04	753.52	752.93
48000	776.58	775.18	774.02	773.07	772.29	771.64	771.11	769.55	768.95
49000	792.76	791.33	790.15	789.18	788.38	787.72	787.17	785.58	784.97
50000	808.94	807.48	806.27	805.28	804.47	803.79	803.24	801.61	800.99
51000	825.12	823.63	822.40	821.39	820.56	819.87	819.30	817.65	817.01
52000	841.29	839.78	838.53	837.49	836.65	835.94	835.37	833.68	833.03
53000	857.47	855.93	854.65	853.60	852.73	852.02	851.43	849.71	849.05
54000	873.65	872.07	870.78	869.71	868.82	868.10	867.49	865.74	865.07
55000	889.83	888.22	886.90	885.81	884.91	884.17	883.56	881.77	881.09
56000	906.01	904.37	903.03	901.92	901.00	900.25	899.62	897.81	897.11
57000	922.19	920.52	919.15	918.02	917.09	916.32	915.69	913.84	913.13
58000	938.37	936.67	935.28	934.13	933.18	932.40	931.75	929.87	929.15
59000	954.54	952.82	951.40	950.23	949.27	948.47	947.82	945.90	945.17
60000	970.72	968.97	967.53	966.34	965.36	964.55	963.88	961.94	961.19
61000	986.90	985.12	983.65	982.45	981.45	980.63	979.95	977.97	977.21
62000	1003.08	1001.27	999.78	998.55	997.54	996.70	996.01	994.00	993.23
63000	1019.26	1017.42	1015.90	1014.66	1013.63	1012.78	1012.08	1010.03	1009.25
64000	1035.44	1033.57	1032.03	1030.76	1029.72	1028.85	1028.14	1026.06	1025.27
65000	1051.62	1049.72	1048.16	1046.87	1045.81	1044.93	1044.21	1042.10	1041.28
66000	1067.79	1065.87	1064.28	1062.97	1061.89	1061.00	1060.27	1058.13	1057.30
67000	1083.97	1082.02	1080.41	1079.08	1077.98	1077.08	1076.34	1074.16	1073.32
68000	1100.15	1098.17	1096.53	1095.18	1094.07	1093.16	1092.40	1090.19	1089.34
69000	1116.33	1114.32	1112.66	1111.29	1110.16	1109.23	1108.46	1106.22	1105.36
70000	1132.51	1130.47	1128.78	1127.40	1126.25	1125.31	1124.53	1122.26	1121.38
75000	1213.40	1211.21	1209.41	1207.92	1206.70	1205.69	1204.85	1202.42	1201.48
80000	1294.30	1291.96	1290.04	1288.45	1287.14	1286.07	1285.18	1282.58	1281.58
100000	1617.87	1614.95	1612.54	1610.56	1608.93	1607.58	1606.47	1603.22	1601.97

207

20½%   MONTHLY PAYMENT
NECESSARY TO AMORTIZE A LOAN

TERM AMOUNT	1 YEAR	1½ YEARS	2 YEARS	2½ YEARS	3 YEARS	3½ YEARS	4 YEARS	4½ YEARS	5 YEARS
$ 25	2.32	1.62	1.27	1.07	.93	.83	.76	.71	.66
50	4.63	3.24	2.54	2.13	1.85	1.66	1.52	1.41	1.32
75	6.94	4.85	3.81	3.19	2.78	2.49	2.27	2.11	1.98
100	9.25	6.47	5.08	4.25	3.70	3.32	3.03	2.81	2.64
200	18.50	12.93	10.15	8.50	7.40	6.63	6.06	5.62	5.27
300	27.75	19.39	15.23	12.75	11.10	9.94	9.08	8.42	7.90
400	37.00	25.85	20.30	16.99	14.80	13.26	12.11	11.23	10.53
500	46.24	32.31	25.37	21.24	18.50	16.57	15.13	14.03	13.16
600	55.49	38.77	30.45	25.49	22.20	19.88	18.16	16.84	15.79
700	64.74	45.23	35.52	29.73	25.90	23.19	21.19	19.64	18.42
800	73.99	51.69	40.59	33.98	29.60	26.51	24.21	22.45	21.06
900	83.24	58.15	45.67	38.23	33.30	29.82	27.24	25.25	23.69
1000	92.48	64.61	50.74	42.47	37.00	33.13	30.26	28.06	26.32
2000	184.96	129.22	101.48	84.94	74.00	66.26	60.52	56.11	52.63
3000	277.44	193.83	152.22	127.41	111.00	99.39	90.78	84.16	78.95
4000	369.92	258.43	202.95	169.88	148.00	132.52	121.04	112.22	105.26
5000	462.40	323.04	253.69	212.35	185.00	165.65	151.29	140.27	131.57
6000	554.88	387.65	304.43	254.81	222.00	198.78	181.55	168.32	157.89
7000	647.36	452.26	355.17	297.28	258.99	231.90	211.81	196.38	184.20
8000	739.84	516.86	405.90	339.75	295.99	265.03	242.07	224.43	210.51
9000	832.32	581.47	456.64	382.22	332.99	298.16	272.33	252.48	236.83
10000	924.80	646.08	507.38	424.69	369.99	331.29	302.58	280.53	263.14
15000	1387.19	969.12	761.07	637.03	554.98	496.93	453.87	420.80	394.71
20000	1849.59	1292.15	1014.75	849.37	739.98	662.58	605.16	561.06	526.28
25000	2311.98	1615.19	1268.44	1061.71	924.97	828.22	756.45	701.33	657.85
30000	2774.38	1938.23	1522.13	1274.05	1109.96	993.86	907.74	841.59	789.42
35000	3236.78	2261.26	1775.82	1486.39	1294.95	1159.50	1059.03	981.86	920.99
36000	3329.26	2325.87	1826.55	1528.86	1331.95	1192.63	1089.29	1009.91	947.30
37000	3421.74	2390.48	1877.29	1571.32	1368.95	1225.76	1119.54	1037.96	973.61
38000	3514.22	2455.09	1928.03	1613.79	1405.95	1258.89	1149.80	1066.02	999.93
39000	3606.70	2519.69	1978.77	1656.26	1442.95	1292.02	1180.06	1094.07	1026.24
40000	3699.18	2584.30	2029.50	1698.73	1479.95	1325.15	1210.32	1122.12	1052.55
41000	3791.66	2648.91	2080.24	1741.20	1516.94	1358.27	1240.58	1150.18	1078.87
42000	3884.14	2713.51	2130.98	1783.66	1553.94	1391.40	1270.83	1178.23	1105.18
43000	3976.62	2778.12	2181.72	1826.13	1590.94	1424.53	1301.09	1206.28	1131.50
44000	4069.10	2842.73	2232.45	1868.60	1627.94	1457.66	1331.35	1234.33	1157.81
45000	4161.57	2907.34	2283.19	1911.07	1664.94	1490.79	1361.61	1262.39	1184.12
46000	4254.05	2971.94	2333.93	1953.54	1701.94	1523.92	1391.86	1290.44	1210.44
47000	4346.53	3036.55	2384.67	1996.00	1738.94	1557.04	1422.12	1318.49	1236.75
48000	4439.01	3101.16	2435.40	2038.47	1775.93	1590.17	1452.38	1346.55	1263.06
49000	4531.49	3165.77	2486.14	2080.94	1812.93	1623.30	1482.64	1374.60	1289.38
50000	4623.97	3230.37	2536.88	2123.41	1849.93	1656.43	1512.90	1402.65	1315.69
51000	4716.45	3294.98	2587.62	2165.88	1886.93	1689.56	1543.15	1430.70	1342.00
52000	4808.93	3359.59	2638.35	2208.34	1923.93	1722.69	1573.41	1458.76	1368.32
53000	4901.41	3424.20	2689.09	2250.81	1960.93	1755.82	1603.67	1486.81	1394.63
54000	4993.89	3488.80	2739.83	2293.28	1997.92	1788.94	1633.93	1514.86	1420.95
55000	5086.37	3553.41	2790.57	2335.75	2034.92	1822.07	1664.18	1542.92	1447.26
56000	5178.85	3618.02	2841.30	2378.22	2071.92	1855.20	1694.44	1570.97	1473.57
57000	5271.33	3682.63	2892.04	2420.68	2108.92	1888.33	1724.70	1599.02	1499.89
58000	5363.81	3747.23	2942.78	2463.15	2145.92	1921.46	1754.96	1627.07	1526.20
59000	5456.29	3811.84	2993.52	2505.62	2182.92	1954.59	1785.22	1655.13	1552.51
60000	5548.76	3876.45	3044.25	2548.09	2219.92	1987.72	1815.47	1683.18	1578.83
61000	5641.24	3941.05	3094.99	2590.56	2256.91	2020.84	1845.73	1711.23	1605.14
62000	5733.72	4005.66	3145.73	2633.02	2293.91	2053.97	1875.99	1739.29	1631.46
63000	5826.20	4070.27	3196.47	2675.49	2330.91	2087.10	1906.25	1767.34	1657.77
64000	5918.68	4134.88	3247.20	2717.96	2367.91	2120.23	1936.50	1795.39	1684.08
65000	6011.16	4199.48	3297.94	2760.43	2404.91	2153.36	1966.76	1823.45	1710.40
66000	6103.64	4264.09	3348.68	2802.90	2441.91	2186.49	1997.02	1851.50	1736.71
67000	6196.12	4328.70	3399.42	2845.37	2478.91	2219.61	2027.28	1879.55	1763.02
68000	6288.60	4393.31	3450.15	2887.83	2515.90	2252.74	2057.54	1907.60	1789.34
69000	6381.08	4457.91	3500.89	2930.30	2552.90	2285.87	2087.79	1935.66	1815.65
70000	6473.56	4522.52	3551.63	2972.77	2589.90	2319.00	2118.05	1963.71	1841.97
75000	6935.95	4845.56	3805.32	3185.11	2774.89	2484.64	2269.34	2103.97	1973.53
80000	7398.35	5168.59	4059.00	3397.45	2959.89	2650.29	2420.63	2244.24	2105.10
100000	9247.94	6460.74	5073.75	4246.81	3699.86	3312.86	3025.79	2805.30	2631.38

MONTHLY PAYMENT 20½%
NECESSARY TO AMORTIZE A LOAN

TERM AMOUNT	6 YEARS	7 YEARS	8 YEARS	9 YEARS	10 YEARS	11 YEARS	12 YEARS	13 YEARS	14 YEARS
$ 25	.60	.56	.52	.50	.48	.47	.46	.45	.44
50	1.19	1.11	1.04	1.00	.96	.93	.91	.90	.88
75	1.79	1.66	1.56	1.49	1.44	1.40	1.37	1.34	1.32
100	2.38	2.21	2.08	1.99	1.92	1.86	1.82	1.79	1.76
200	4.76	4.41	4.16	3.97	3.83	3.72	3.63	3.57	3.51
300	7.13	6.61	6.23	5.95	5.74	5.57	5.45	5.35	5.27
400	9.51	8.81	8.31	7.93	7.65	7.43	7.26	7.13	7.02
500	11.89	11.01	10.38	9.91	9.56	9.29	9.08	8.91	8.77
600	14.26	13.21	12.46	11.90	11.47	11.14	10.89	10.69	10.53
700	16.64	15.41	14.53	13.88	13.38	13.00	12.70	12.47	12.28
800	19.02	17.61	16.61	15.86	15.29	14.86	14.52	14.25	14.04
900	21.39	19.82	18.68	17.84	17.20	16.71	16.33	16.03	15.79
1000	23.77	22.02	20.76	19.82	19.12	18.57	18.15	17.81	17.54
2000	47.54	44.03	41.51	39.64	38.23	37.14	36.29	35.61	35.08
3000	71.30	66.04	62.26	59.46	57.34	55.70	54.43	53.42	52.62
4000	95.07	88.05	83.01	79.28	76.45	74.27	72.57	71.22	70.16
5000	118.83	110.06	103.76	99.10	95.56	92.84	90.71	89.03	87.69
6000	142.60	132.07	124.51	118.91	114.67	111.40	108.85	106.83	105.23
7000	166.36	154.08	145.26	138.73	133.78	129.97	126.99	124.64	122.77
8000	190.13	176.10	166.02	158.55	152.89	148.53	145.13	142.44	140.31
9000	213.89	198.11	186.77	178.37	172.00	167.10	163.27	160.25	157.84
10000	237.66	220.12	207.52	198.19	191.11	185.67	181.41	178.05	175.38
15000	356.48	330.17	311.28	297.28	286.67	278.50	272.11	267.07	263.07
20000	475.31	440.23	415.03	396.37	382.22	371.33	362.81	356.10	350.76
25000	594.13	550.29	518.79	495.46	477.78	464.16	453.52	445.12	438.44
30000	712.96	660.34	622.55	594.55	573.33	556.99	544.22	534.14	526.13
35000	831.79	770.40	726.30	693.64	668.89	649.82	634.92	623.17	613.82
36000	855.55	792.41	747.05	713.46	688.00	668.38	653.06	640.97	631.36
37000	879.32	814.42	767.81	733.27	707.11	686.95	671.20	658.78	648.90
38000	903.08	836.43	788.56	753.09	726.22	705.51	689.34	676.58	666.43
39000	926.85	858.45	809.31	772.91	745.33	724.08	707.48	694.39	683.97
40000	950.61	880.46	830.06	792.73	764.44	742.65	725.62	712.19	701.51
41000	974.38	902.47	850.81	812.55	783.56	761.21	743.76	730.00	719.05
42000	998.14	924.48	871.56	832.37	802.67	779.78	761.90	747.80	736.58
43000	1021.91	946.49	892.31	852.18	821.78	798.34	780.04	765.60	754.12
44000	1045.67	968.50	913.07	872.00	840.89	816.91	798.18	783.41	771.66
45000	1069.44	990.51	933.82	891.82	860.00	835.48	816.32	801.21	789.20
46000	1093.20	1012.52	954.57	911.64	879.11	854.04	834.46	819.02	806.73
47000	1116.97	1034.54	975.32	931.46	898.22	872.61	852.60	836.82	824.27
48000	1140.73	1056.55	996.07	951.27	917.33	891.17	870.74	854.63	841.81
49000	1164.50	1078.56	1016.82	971.09	936.44	909.74	888.89	872.43	859.35
50000	1188.26	1100.57	1037.57	990.91	955.55	928.31	907.03	890.24	876.88
51000	1212.03	1122.58	1058.32	1010.73	974.67	946.87	925.17	908.04	894.42
52000	1235.79	1144.59	1079.08	1030.55	993.78	965.44	943.31	925.85	911.96
53000	1259.56	1166.60	1099.83	1050.36	1012.89	984.00	961.45	943.65	929.50
54000	1283.32	1188.62	1120.58	1070.18	1032.00	1002.57	979.59	961.46	947.03
55000	1307.09	1210.63	1141.33	1090.00	1051.11	1021.14	997.73	979.26	964.57
56000	1330.85	1232.64	1162.08	1109.82	1070.22	1039.70	1015.87	997.06	982.11
57000	1354.62	1254.65	1182.83	1129.64	1089.33	1058.27	1034.01	1014.87	999.65
58000	1378.39	1276.66	1203.58	1149.45	1108.44	1076.83	1052.15	1032.67	1017.18
59000	1402.15	1298.67	1224.34	1169.27	1127.55	1095.40	1070.29	1050.48	1034.72
60000	1425.92	1320.68	1245.09	1189.09	1146.66	1113.97	1088.43	1068.28	1052.26
61000	1449.68	1342.69	1265.84	1208.91	1165.78	1132.53	1106.57	1086.09	1069.80
62000	1473.45	1364.71	1286.59	1228.73	1184.89	1151.10	1124.71	1103.89	1087.33
63000	1497.21	1386.72	1307.34	1248.55	1204.00	1169.66	1142.85	1121.70	1104.87
64000	1520.98	1408.73	1328.09	1268.36	1223.11	1188.23	1160.99	1139.50	1122.41
65000	1544.74	1430.74	1348.84	1288.18	1242.22	1206.80	1179.13	1157.31	1139.95
66000	1568.51	1452.75	1369.60	1308.00	1261.33	1225.36	1197.27	1175.11	1157.48
67000	1592.27	1474.76	1390.35	1327.82	1280.44	1243.93	1215.41	1192.92	1175.02
68000	1616.04	1496.77	1411.10	1347.64	1299.55	1262.49	1233.55	1210.72	1192.56
69000	1639.80	1518.78	1431.85	1367.45	1318.66	1281.06	1251.69	1228.53	1210.10
70000	1663.57	1540.80	1452.60	1387.27	1337.77	1299.63	1269.83	1246.33	1227.64
75000	1782.39	1650.85	1556.36	1486.36	1433.33	1392.46	1360.54	1335.35	1315.32
80000	1901.22	1760.91	1660.11	1585.45	1528.88	1485.29	1451.24	1424.38	1403.01
100000	2376.52	2201.13	2075.14	1981.81	1911.10	1856.61	1814.05	1780.47	1753.76

20½% MONTHLY PAYMENT
NECESSARY TO AMORTIZE A LOAN

TERM / AMOUNT	15 YEARS	16 YEARS	17 YEARS	18 YEARS	19 YEARS	20 YEARS	21 YEARS	22 YEARS	23 YEARS
$ 25	.44	.43	.43	.43	.43	.42	.42	.42	.42
50	.87	.86	.86	.85	.85	.84	.84	.84	.83
75	1.30	1.29	1.28	1.27	1.27	1.26	1.26	1.25	1.25
100	1.74	1.72	1.71	1.70	1.69	1.68	1.67	1.67	1.66
200	3.47	3.44	3.41	3.39	3.37	3.35	3.34	3.33	3.32
300	5.20	5.15	5.11	5.08	5.05	5.03	5.01	4.99	4.98
400	6.93	6.87	6.81	6.77	6.73	6.70	6.67	6.65	6.64
500	8.67	8.58	8.51	8.46	8.41	8.37	8.34	8.32	8.30
600	10.40	10.30	10.21	10.15	10.09	10.05	10.01	9.98	9.95
700	12.13	12.01	11.91	11.84	11.77	11.72	11.68	11.64	11.61
800	13.86	13.73	13.62	13.53	13.45	13.39	13.34	13.30	13.27
900	15.60	15.44	15.32	15.22	15.13	15.07	15.01	14.97	14.93
1000	17.33	17.16	17.02	16.91	16.81	16.74	16.68	16.63	16.59
2000	34.65	34.31	34.03	33.81	33.62	33.47	33.35	33.25	33.17
3000	51.98	51.46	51.04	50.71	50.43	50.21	50.02	49.88	49.75
4000	69.30	68.61	68.06	67.61	67.24	66.94	66.70	66.50	66.34
5000	86.62	85.76	85.07	84.51	84.05	83.67	83.37	83.12	82.92
6000	103.95	102.92	102.08	101.41	100.86	100.41	100.04	99.75	99.50
7000	121.27	120.07	119.09	118.31	117.67	117.14	116.72	116.37	116.08
8000	138.60	137.22	136.11	135.21	134.47	133.88	133.39	132.99	132.67
9000	155.92	154.37	153.12	152.11	151.28	150.61	150.06	149.62	149.25
10000	173.24	171.52	170.13	169.01	168.09	167.34	166.74	166.24	165.83
15000	259.86	257.28	255.20	253.51	252.13	251.01	250.10	249.36	248.75
20000	346.48	343.04	340.26	338.01	336.18	334.68	333.47	332.47	331.66
25000	433.10	428.80	425.33	422.51	420.22	418.35	416.83	415.59	414.57
30000	519.72	514.56	510.39	507.01	504.26	502.02	500.20	498.71	497.49
35000	606.34	600.32	595.45	591.51	588.31	585.69	583.56	581.82	580.40
36000	623.66	617.47	612.47	608.41	605.11	602.43	600.24	598.45	596.98
37000	640.99	634.62	629.48	625.31	621.92	619.16	616.91	615.07	613.56
38000	658.31	651.77	646.49	642.21	638.73	635.90	633.58	631.69	630.15
39000	675.63	668.92	663.50	659.11	655.54	652.63	650.26	648.32	646.73
40000	692.96	686.08	680.52	676.01	672.35	669.36	666.93	664.94	663.31
41000	710.28	703.23	697.53	692.91	689.16	686.10	683.60	681.56	679.89
42000	727.60	720.38	714.54	709.81	705.97	702.83	700.28	698.19	696.48
43000	744.93	737.53	731.56	726.71	722.77	719.57	716.95	714.81	713.06
44000	762.25	754.68	748.57	743.61	739.58	736.30	733.62	731.43	729.64
45000	779.58	771.84	765.58	760.51	756.39	753.03	750.30	748.06	746.23
46000	796.90	788.99	782.59	777.41	773.20	769.77	766.97	764.68	762.81
47000	814.22	806.14	799.61	794.31	790.01	786.50	783.64	781.30	779.39
48000	831.55	823.29	816.62	811.21	806.82	803.24	800.31	797.93	795.97
49000	848.87	840.44	833.63	828.11	823.63	819.97	816.99	814.55	812.56
50000	866.19	857.59	850.65	845.01	840.43	836.70	833.66	831.17	829.14
51000	883.52	874.75	867.66	861.91	857.24	853.44	850.33	847.80	845.72
52000	900.84	891.90	884.67	878.81	874.05	870.17	867.01	864.42	862.30
53000	918.17	909.05	901.68	895.71	890.86	886.91	883.68	881.04	878.89
54000	935.49	926.20	918.70	912.61	907.67	903.64	900.35	897.67	895.47
55000	952.81	943.35	935.71	929.51	924.48	920.37	917.03	914.29	912.05
56000	970.14	960.51	952.72	946.41	941.29	937.11	933.70	930.91	928.63
57000	987.46	977.66	969.74	963.31	958.09	953.84	950.37	947.54	945.22
58000	1004.79	994.81	986.75	980.21	974.90	970.58	967.05	964.16	961.80
59000	1022.11	1011.96	1003.76	997.11	991.71	987.31	983.72	980.78	978.38
60000	1039.43	1029.11	1020.77	1014.01	1008.52	1004.04	1000.39	997.41	994.97
61000	1056.76	1046.26	1037.79	1030.91	1025.33	1020.78	1017.07	1014.03	1011.55
62000	1074.08	1063.42	1054.80	1047.81	1042.14	1037.51	1033.74	1030.65	1028.13
63000	1091.40	1080.57	1071.81	1064.72	1058.95	1054.25	1050.41	1047.28	1044.71
64000	1108.73	1097.72	1088.83	1081.62	1075.75	1070.98	1067.08	1063.90	1061.30
65000	1126.05	1114.87	1105.84	1098.52	1092.56	1087.71	1083.76	1080.52	1077.88
66000	1143.38	1132.02	1122.85	1115.42	1109.37	1104.45	1100.43	1097.15	1094.46
67000	1160.70	1149.17	1139.86	1132.32	1126.18	1121.18	1117.10	1113.77	1111.04
68000	1178.02	1166.33	1156.88	1149.22	1142.99	1137.92	1133.78	1130.39	1127.63
69000	1195.35	1183.48	1173.89	1166.12	1159.80	1154.65	1150.45	1147.02	1144.21
70000	1212.67	1200.63	1190.90	1183.02	1176.61	1171.38	1167.12	1163.64	1160.79
75000	1299.29	1286.39	1275.97	1267.52	1260.65	1255.05	1250.49	1246.76	1243.71
80000	1385.91	1372.15	1361.03	1352.02	1344.69	1338.72	1333.85	1329.88	1326.62
100000	1732.38	1715.18	1701.29	1690.02	1680.86	1673.40	1667.32	1662.34	1658.27

MONTHLY PAYMENT 20½%
NECESSARY TO AMORTIZE A LOAN

TERM AMOUNT	24 YEARS	25 YEARS	26 YEARS	27 YEARS	28 YEARS	29 YEARS	30 YEARS	35 YEARS	40 YEARS
$ 25	.42	.42	.42	.42	.42	.42	.42	.42	.42
50	.83	.83	.83	.83	.83	.83	.83	.83	.83
75	1.25	1.24	1.24	1.24	1.24	1.24	1.24	1.24	1.24
100	1.66	1.66	1.65	1.65	1.65	1.65	1.65	1.65	1.65
200	3.31	3.31	3.30	3.30	3.30	3.30	3.29	3.29	3.29
300	4.97	4.96	4.95	4.95	4.94	4.94	4.94	4.93	4.93
400	6.62	6.61	6.60	6.60	6.59	6.59	6.58	6.57	6.57
500	8.28	8.27	8.25	8.25	8.24	8.23	8.23	8.21	8.21
600	9.93	9.92	9.90	9.89	9.88	9.88	9.87	9.85	9.85
700	11.59	11.57	11.55	11.54	11.53	11.52	11.52	11.49	11.49
800	13.24	13.22	13.20	13.19	13.18	13.17	13.16	13.14	13.13
900	14.90	14.87	14.85	14.84	14.82	14.81	14.80	14.78	14.77
1000	16.55	16.53	16.50	16.49	16.47	16.46	16.45	16.42	16.41
2000	33.10	33.05	33.00	32.97	32.94	32.91	32.89	32.83	32.81
3000	49.65	49.57	49.50	49.45	49.40	49.37	49.34	49.25	49.21
4000	66.20	66.09	66.00	65.93	65.87	65.82	65.78	65.66	65.62
5000	82.75	82.61	82.50	82.41	82.34	82.27	82.22	82.08	82.02
6000	99.30	99.14	99.00	98.89	98.80	98.73	98.67	98.49	98.42
7000	115.85	115.66	115.50	115.37	115.27	115.18	115.11	114.90	114.83
8000	132.40	132.18	132.00	131.85	131.73	131.63	131.55	131.32	131.23
9000	148.95	148.70	148.50	148.34	148.20	148.09	148.00	147.73	147.63
10000	165.50	165.22	165.00	164.82	164.67	164.54	164.44	164.15	164.04
15000	248.24	247.83	247.50	247.22	247.00	246.81	246.66	246.22	246.05
20000	330.99	330.44	330.00	329.63	329.33	329.08	328.87	328.29	328.07
25000	413.74	413.05	412.49	412.03	411.66	411.35	411.09	410.36	410.08
30000	496.48	495.66	494.99	494.44	493.99	493.62	493.31	492.43	492.10
35000	579.23	578.27	577.49	576.85	576.32	575.88	575.53	574.50	574.11
36000	595.78	594.80	593.99	593.33	592.78	592.34	591.97	590.91	590.51
37000	612.33	611.32	610.49	609.81	609.25	608.79	608.41	607.33	606.92
38000	628.88	627.84	626.99	626.29	625.72	625.24	624.86	623.74	623.32
39000	645.43	644.36	643.49	642.77	642.18	641.70	641.30	640.15	639.72
40000	661.98	660.88	659.99	659.25	658.65	658.15	657.74	656.57	656.13
41000	678.53	677.41	676.49	675.73	675.11	674.61	674.19	672.98	672.53
42000	695.08	693.93	692.99	692.21	691.58	691.06	690.63	689.40	688.93
43000	711.63	710.45	709.49	708.70	708.05	707.51	707.07	705.81	705.34
44000	728.18	726.97	725.99	725.18	724.51	723.97	723.52	722.22	721.74
45000	744.72	743.49	742.49	741.66	740.98	740.42	739.96	738.64	738.14
46000	761.27	760.02	758.99	758.14	757.44	756.87	756.41	755.05	754.54
47000	777.82	776.54	775.49	774.62	773.91	773.33	772.85	771.47	770.95
48000	794.37	793.06	791.98	791.10	790.38	789.78	789.29	787.88	787.35
49000	810.92	809.58	808.48	807.58	806.84	806.24	805.74	804.30	803.75
50000	827.47	826.10	824.98	824.06	823.31	822.69	822.18	820.71	820.16
51000	844.02	842.63	841.48	840.55	839.78	839.14	838.62	837.12	836.56
52000	860.57	859.15	857.98	857.03	856.24	855.60	855.07	853.54	852.96
53000	877.12	875.67	874.48	873.51	872.71	872.05	871.51	869.95	869.37
54000	893.67	892.19	890.98	889.99	889.17	888.50	887.95	886.37	885.77
55000	910.22	908.71	907.48	906.47	905.64	904.96	904.40	902.78	902.17
56000	926.77	925.24	923.98	922.95	922.11	921.41	920.84	919.19	918.57
57000	943.32	941.76	940.48	939.43	938.57	937.86	937.28	935.61	934.98
58000	959.87	958.28	956.98	955.91	955.04	954.32	953.73	952.02	951.38
59000	976.42	974.80	973.48	972.39	971.50	970.77	970.17	968.44	967.78
60000	992.96	991.32	989.98	988.88	987.97	987.23	986.61	984.85	984.19
61000	1009.51	1007.85	1006.48	1005.36	1004.44	1003.68	1003.06	1001.26	1000.59
62000	1026.06	1024.37	1022.98	1021.84	1020.90	1020.13	1019.50	1017.68	1016.99
63000	1042.61	1040.89	1039.48	1038.32	1037.37	1036.59	1035.94	1034.09	1033.40
64000	1059.16	1057.41	1055.98	1054.80	1053.83	1053.04	1052.39	1050.51	1049.80
65000	1075.71	1073.93	1072.48	1071.28	1070.30	1069.49	1068.83	1066.92	1066.20
66000	1092.26	1090.46	1088.98	1087.76	1086.77	1085.95	1085.27	1083.33	1082.61
67000	1108.81	1106.98	1105.48	1104.24	1103.23	1102.40	1101.72	1099.75	1099.01
68000	1125.36	1123.50	1121.98	1120.73	1119.70	1118.86	1118.16	1116.16	1115.41
69000	1141.91	1140.02	1138.48	1137.21	1136.16	1135.31	1134.61	1132.58	1131.81
70000	1158.46	1156.54	1154.98	1153.69	1152.63	1151.76	1151.05	1148.99	1148.22
75000	1241.20	1239.15	1237.47	1236.09	1234.96	1234.03	1233.27	1231.06	1230.23
80000	1323.95	1321.76	1319.97	1318.50	1317.29	1316.30	1315.48	1313.13	1312.25
100000	1654.94	1652.20	1649.96	1648.12	1646.61	1645.37	1644.35	1641.41	1640.31

21% MONTHLY PAYMENT
NECESSARY TO AMORTIZE A LOAN

TERM AMOUNT	1 YEAR	1½ YEARS	2 YEARS	2½ YEARS	3 YEARS	3½ YEARS	4 YEARS	4½ YEARS	5 YEARS
$ 25	2.32	1.63	1.28	1.07	.94	.84	.77	.71	.67
50	4.64	3.25	2.55	2.14	1.87	1.67	1.53	1.42	1.33
75	6.96	4.87	3.83	3.21	2.80	2.51	2.29	2.13	2.00
100	9.27	6.49	5.10	4.27	3.73	3.34	3.06	2.84	2.66
200	18.54	12.97	10.20	8.54	7.45	6.68	6.11	5.67	5.32
300	27.81	19.45	15.29	12.81	11.17	10.02	9.16	8.50	7.98
400	37.08	25.94	20.39	17.08	14.90	13.35	12.21	11.33	10.63
500	46.35	32.42	25.49	21.35	18.62	16.69	15.26	14.16	13.29
600	55.62	38.90	30.58	25.62	22.34	20.03	18.31	16.99	15.95
700	64.89	45.39	35.68	29.89	26.07	23.36	21.36	19.82	18.60
800	74.16	51.87	40.77	34.16	29.79	26.70	24.41	22.65	21.26
900	83.43	58.35	45.87	38.43	33.51	30.04	27.46	25.48	23.92
1000	92.70	64.83	50.97	42.70	37.24	33.37	30.51	28.31	26.57
2000	185.40	129.66	101.93	85.40	74.47	66.74	61.01	56.61	53.14
3000	278.10	194.49	152.89	128.10	111.70	100.11	91.51	84.92	79.71
4000	370.80	259.32	203.85	170.79	148.94	133.48	122.02	113.22	106.28
5000	463.50	324.15	254.82	213.49	186.17	166.85	152.52	141.52	132.85
6000	556.20	388.98	305.78	256.19	223.40	200.21	183.02	169.83	159.42
7000	648.90	453.81	356.74	298.89	260.64	233.58	213.53	198.13	185.99
8000	741.60	518.63	407.70	341.58	297.87	266.95	244.03	226.43	212.56
9000	834.30	583.46	458.67	384.28	335.10	300.32	274.53	254.74	239.13
10000	927.00	648.29	509.63	426.98	372.33	333.69	305.03	283.04	265.70
15000	1390.50	972.43	764.44	640.47	558.50	500.53	457.55	424.56	398.55
20000	1854.00	1296.58	1019.25	853.95	744.66	667.37	610.06	566.07	531.40
25000	2317.50	1620.72	1274.06	1067.44	930.83	834.21	762.58	707.59	664.25
30000	2781.00	1944.86	1528.88	1280.93	1116.99	1001.05	915.09	849.11	797.10
35000	3244.49	2269.01	1783.69	1494.42	1303.16	1167.89	1067.61	990.63	929.94
36000	3337.19	2333.84	1834.65	1537.11	1340.39	1201.26	1098.11	1018.93	956.51
37000	3429.89	2398.67	1885.61	1579.81	1377.63	1234.63	1128.61	1047.23	983.08
38000	3522.59	2463.49	1936.57	1622.51	1414.86	1268.00	1159.12	1075.54	1009.65
39000	3615.29	2528.32	1987.54	1665.21	1452.09	1301.31	1189.62	1103.84	1036.22
40000	3707.99	2593.15	2038.50	1707.90	1489.32	1334.74	1220.12	1132.14	1062.79
41000	3800.69	2657.98	2089.46	1750.60	1526.56	1368.10	1250.63	1160.45	1089.36
42000	3893.39	2722.81	2140.42	1793.30	1563.79	1401.47	1281.13	1188.75	1115.93
43000	3986.09	2787.64	2191.39	1836.00	1601.02	1434.84	1311.63	1217.06	1142.50
44000	4078.79	2852.47	2242.35	1878.69	1638.26	1468.21	1342.13	1245.36	1169.07
45000	4171.49	2917.29	2293.31	1921.39	1675.49	1501.58	1372.64	1273.66	1195.64
46000	4264.19	2982.12	2344.27	1964.09	1712.72	1534.94	1403.14	1301.97	1222.21
47000	4356.89	3046.95	2395.23	2006.79	1749.96	1568.31	1433.64	1330.27	1248.78
48000	4449.59	3111.78	2446.20	2049.48	1787.19	1601.68	1464.15	1358.57	1275.35
49000	4542.29	3176.61	2497.16	2092.18	1824.42	1635.05	1494.65	1386.88	1301.92
50000	4634.99	3241.44	2548.12	2134.88	1861.65	1668.42	1525.15	1415.18	1328.49
51000	4727.69	3306.27	2599.08	2177.58	1898.89	1701.79	1555.66	1443.48	1355.06
52000	4820.39	3371.10	2650.05	2220.27	1936.12	1735.15	1586.16	1471.79	1381.63
53000	4913.09	3435.92	2701.01	2262.97	1973.35	1768.52	1616.66	1500.09	1408.20
54000	5005.79	3500.75	2751.97	2305.67	2010.59	1801.89	1647.16	1528.39	1434.77
55000	5098.49	3565.58	2802.93	2348.37	2047.82	1835.26	1677.67	1556.70	1461.34
56000	5191.19	3630.41	2853.90	2391.06	2085.05	1868.63	1708.17	1585.00	1487.91
57000	5283.89	3695.24	2904.86	2433.76	2122.29	1902.00	1738.67	1613.30	1514.48
58000	5376.59	3760.07	2955.82	2476.46	2159.52	1935.36	1769.18	1641.61	1541.05
59000	5469.29	3824.90	3006.78	2519.16	2196.75	1968.73	1799.68	1669.91	1567.62
60000	5561.99	3889.72	3057.75	2561.85	2233.98	2002.10	1830.18	1698.21	1594.19
61000	5654.69	3954.55	3108.71	2604.55	2271.22	2035.47	1860.68	1726.52	1620.76
62000	5747.38	4019.38	3159.67	2647.25	2308.45	2068.84	1891.19	1754.82	1647.33
63000	5840.08	4084.21	3210.63	2689.95	2345.68	2102.21	1921.69	1783.12	1673.90
64000	5932.78	4149.04	3261.59	2732.64	2382.92	2135.57	1952.19	1811.43	1700.47
65000	6025.48	4213.87	3312.56	2775.34	2420.15	2168.94	1982.70	1839.73	1727.04
66000	6118.18	4278.70	3363.52	2818.04	2457.38	2202.31	2013.20	1868.04	1753.60
67000	6210.88	4343.53	3414.48	2860.74	2494.62	2235.68	2043.70	1896.34	1780.17
68000	6303.58	4408.35	3465.44	2903.43	2531.85	2269.05	2074.21	1924.64	1806.74
69000	6396.28	4473.18	3516.41	2946.13	2569.08	2302.41	2104.71	1952.95	1833.31
70000	6488.98	4538.01	3567.37	2988.83	2606.31	2335.78	2135.21	1981.25	1859.88
75000	6952.48	4862.15	3822.18	3202.32	2792.48	2502.62	2287.73	2122.77	1992.73
80000	7415.98	5186.30	4076.99	3415.80	2978.64	2669.47	2440.24	2264.28	2125.58
100000	9269.97	6482.87	5096.24	4269.75	3723.30	3336.83	3050.30	2830.35	2656.97

212

TERM AMOUNT	6 YEARS	7 YEARS	8 YEARS	9 YEARS	10 YEARS	11 YEARS	12 YEARS	13 YEARS	14 YEARS
$ 25	.61	.56	.53	.51	.49	.48	.47	.46	.45
50	1.21	1.12	1.06	1.01	.98	.95	.93	.91	.90
75	1.81	1.68	1.58	1.51	1.46	1.42	1.39	1.36	1.35
100	2.41	2.23	2.11	2.02	1.95	1.89	1.85	1.82	1.79
200	4.81	4.46	4.21	4.03	3.89	3.78	3.70	3.63	3.58
300	7.21	6.69	6.32	6.04	5.83	5.67	5.54	5.44	5.37
400	9.62	8.92	8.42	8.05	7.77	7.56	7.39	7.26	7.15
500	12.02	11.15	10.52	10.06	9.71	9.44	9.24	9.07	8.94
600	14.47	13.38	12.63	12.07	11.65	11.33	11.08	10.88	10.73
700	16.83	15.61	14.73	14.08	13.60	13.22	12.93	12.70	12.52
800	19.23	17.84	16.84	16.10	15.54	15.11	14.77	14.51	14.30
900	21.63	20.06	18.94	18.11	17.48	17.00	16.62	16.32	16.09
1000	24.04	22.29	21.04	20.12	19.42	18.88	18.47	18.14	17.88
2000	48.07	44.58	42.08	40.23	38.84	37.76	36.93	36.27	35.75
3000	72.10	66.87	63.12	60.35	58.25	56.64	55.39	54.40	53.62
4000	96.13	89.16	84.16	80.46	77.67	75.52	73.85	72.53	71.49
5000	120.16	111.45	105.20	100.58	97.08	94.40	92.31	90.67	89.36
6000	144.20	133.73	126.23	120.69	116.50	113.28	110.77	108.80	107.23
7000	168.23	156.02	147.27	140.80	135.92	132.16	129.23	126.93	125.11
8000	192.26	178.31	168.31	160.92	155.33	151.04	147.69	145.06	142.98
9000	216.29	200.60	189.35	181.03	174.75	169.92	166.15	163.20	160.85
10000	240.32	222.89	210.39	201.15	194.16	188.80	184.62	181.33	178.72
15000	360.48	334.33	315.58	301.72	291.24	283.19	276.92	271.99	268.08
20000	480.64	445.77	420.77	402.29	388.32	377.59	369.23	362.65	357.44
25000	600.80	557.21	525.96	502.86	485.40	471.98	461.53	453.31	446.80
30000	720.96	668.65	631.15	603.43	582.48	566.38	553.84	543.97	536.15
35000	841.12	780.09	736.34	704.00	679.56	660.77	646.14	634.64	625.51
36000	865.15	802.38	757.38	724.12	698.98	679.65	664.60	652.77	643.38
37000	889.18	824.67	778.42	744.23	718.39	698.53	683.07	670.90	661.25
38000	913.21	846.96	799.46	764.35	737.81	717.41	701.53	689.03	679.13
39000	937.25	869.25	820.49	784.46	757.23	736.29	719.99	707.16	697.00
40000	961.28	891.53	841.53	804.58	776.64	755.17	738.45	725.30	714.87
41000	985.31	913.82	862.57	824.69	796.06	774.05	756.91	743.43	732.74
42000	1009.34	936.11	883.61	844.80	815.47	792.93	775.37	761.56	750.61
43000	1033.37	958.40	904.65	864.92	834.89	811.81	793.83	779.69	768.48
44000	1057.40	980.69	925.68	885.03	854.31	830.69	812.29	797.83	786.36
45000	1081.44	1002.98	946.72	905.15	873.72	849.57	830.75	815.96	804.23
46000	1105.47	1025.26	967.76	925.26	893.14	868.44	849.22	834.09	822.10
47000	1129.50	1047.55	988.80	945.37	912.55	887.32	867.68	852.22	839.97
48000	1153.53	1069.84	1009.84	965.49	931.97	906.20	886.14	870.36	857.84
49000	1177.56	1092.13	1030.88	985.60	951.39	925.08	904.60	888.49	875.71
50000	1201.60	1114.42	1051.91	1005.72	970.80	943.96	923.06	906.62	893.59
51000	1225.63	1136.71	1072.95	1025.83	990.22	962.84	941.52	924.75	911.46
52000	1249.66	1158.99	1093.99	1045.95	1009.63	981.72	959.98	942.88	929.33
53000	1273.69	1181.28	1115.03	1066.06	1029.05	1000.60	978.44	961.02	947.20
54000	1297.72	1203.57	1136.07	1086.17	1048.46	1019.48	996.90	979.15	965.07
55000	1321.75	1225.86	1157.10	1106.29	1067.88	1038.36	1015.37	997.28	982.94
56000	1345.79	1248.15	1178.14	1126.40	1087.30	1057.24	1033.83	1015.41	1000.82
57000	1369.82	1270.44	1199.18	1146.52	1106.71	1076.11	1052.29	1033.55	1018.69
58000	1393.85	1292.72	1220.22	1166.63	1126.13	1094.99	1070.75	1051.68	1036.56
59000	1417.88	1315.01	1241.26	1186.75	1145.54	1113.87	1089.21	1069.81	1054.43
60000	1441.91	1337.30	1262.30	1206.86	1164.96	1132.75	1107.67	1087.94	1072.30
61000	1465.95	1359.59	1283.33	1226.97	1184.38	1151.63	1126.13	1106.08	1090.17
62000	1489.98	1381.88	1304.37	1247.09	1203.79	1170.51	1144.59	1124.21	1108.04
63000	1514.01	1404.16	1325.41	1267.20	1223.21	1189.39	1163.05	1142.34	1125.92
64000	1538.04	1426.45	1346.45	1287.32	1242.62	1208.27	1181.52	1160.47	1143.79
65000	1562.07	1448.74	1367.49	1307.43	1262.04	1227.15	1199.98	1178.60	1161.66
66000	1586.10	1471.03	1388.52	1327.55	1281.46	1246.03	1218.44	1196.74	1179.53
67000	1610.14	1493.32	1409.56	1347.66	1300.87	1264.91	1236.90	1214.87	1197.40
68000	1634.17	1515.61	1430.60	1367.77	1320.29	1283.78	1255.36	1233.00	1215.27
69000	1658.20	1537.89	1451.64	1387.89	1339.70	1302.66	1273.82	1251.13	1233.15
70000	1682.23	1560.18	1472.68	1408.00	1359.12	1321.54	1292.28	1269.27	1251.02
75000	1802.39	1671.62	1577.87	1508.57	1456.20	1415.94	1384.59	1359.93	1340.38
80000	1922.55	1783.06	1683.06	1609.15	1553.28	1510.33	1476.89	1450.59	1429.73
100000	2403.19	2228.83	2103.82	2011.43	1941.60	1887.92	1846.12	1813.23	1787.17

MONTHLY PAYMENT
NECESSARY TO AMORTIZE A LOAN

TERM AMOUNT	15 YEARS	16 YEARS	17 YEARS	18 YEARS	19 YEARS	20 YEARS	21 YEARS	22 YEARS	23 YEARS
$ 25	.45	.44	.44	.44	.43	.43	.43	.43	.43
50	.89	.88	.87	.87	.86	.86	.86	.85	.85
75	1.33	1.32	1.31	1.30	1.29	1.29	1.28	1.28	1.28
100	1.77	1.75	1.74	1.73	1.72	1.71	1.71	1.70	1.70
200	3.54	3.50	3.48	3.46	3.44	3.42	3.41	3.40	3.40
300	5.30	5.25	5.21	5.18	5.15	5.13	5.12	5.10	5.09
400	7.07	7.00	6.95	6.91	6.87	6.84	6.82	6.80	6.79
500	8.84	8.75	8.69	8.63	8.59	8.55	8.52	8.50	8.48
600	10.60	10.50	10.42	10.36	10.30	10.26	10.23	10.20	10.18
700	12.37	12.25	12.16	12.08	12.02	11.97	11.93	11.90	11.87
800	14.14	14.00	13.90	13.81	13.74	13.68	13.63	13.60	13.57
900	15.90	15.75	15.63	15.53	15.45	15.39	15.34	15.30	15.26
1000	17.67	17.50	17.37	17.26	17.17	17.10	17.04	17.00	16.96
2000	35.33	35.00	34.73	34.51	34.34	34.20	34.08	33.99	33.91
3000	53.00	52.50	52.09	51.77	51.50	51.29	51.12	50.98	50.86
4000	70.66	69.99	69.46	69.02	68.67	68.39	68.15	67.97	67.81
5000	88.32	87.49	86.82	86.28	85.84	85.48	85.19	84.96	84.76
6000	105.99	104.99	104.18	103.53	103.00	102.58	102.23	101.95	101.72
7000	123.65	122.48	121.54	120.78	120.17	119.67	119.27	118.94	118.67
8000	141.31	139.98	138.91	138.04	137.34	136.77	136.30	135.93	135.62
9000	158.98	157.48	156.27	155.29	154.50	153.86	153.34	152.92	152.57
10000	176.64	174.97	173.63	172.55	171.67	170.96	170.38	169.91	169.52
15000	264.96	262.46	260.44	258.82	257.50	256.43	255.56	254.86	254.28
20000	353.28	349.94	347.26	345.09	343.33	341.91	340.75	339.81	339.04
25000	441.60	437.43	434.07	431.36	429.17	427.38	425.94	424.76	423.80
30000	529.91	524.91	520.88	517.63	515.00	512.86	511.12	509.71	508.56
35000	618.23	612.40	607.70	603.90	600.83	598.34	596.31	594.66	593.32
36000	635.90	629.89	625.06	621.16	618.00	615.43	613.35	611.65	610.27
37000	653.56	647.39	642.42	638.41	635.16	632.53	630.38	628.64	627.22
38000	671.22	664.89	659.78	655.66	652.33	649.62	647.42	645.63	644.17
39000	688.89	682.38	677.15	672.92	669.49	666.72	664.46	662.62	661.12
40000	706.55	699.88	694.51	690.17	686.66	683.81	681.50	679.61	678.07
41000	724.21	717.38	711.87	707.43	703.83	700.91	698.53	696.60	695.03
42000	741.88	734.87	729.24	724.68	720.99	718.00	715.57	713.59	711.98
43000	759.54	752.37	746.60	741.94	738.16	735.10	732.61	730.58	728.93
44000	777.20	769.87	763.96	759.19	755.33	752.19	749.64	747.57	745.88
45000	794.87	787.36	781.32	776.44	772.49	769.29	766.68	764.56	762.83
46000	812.53	804.86	798.69	793.70	789.66	786.38	783.72	781.55	779.78
47000	830.20	822.36	816.05	810.95	806.83	803.48	800.76	798.54	796.74
48000	847.86	839.85	833.41	828.21	823.99	820.57	817.79	815.53	813.69
49000	865.52	857.35	850.77	845.46	841.16	837.67	834.83	832.52	830.64
50000	883.19	874.85	868.14	862.72	858.33	854.76	851.87	849.51	847.59
51000	900.85	892.35	885.50	879.97	875.49	871.86	868.91	866.50	864.54
52000	918.51	909.84	902.86	897.22	892.66	888.95	885.94	883.49	881.50
53000	936.18	927.34	920.22	914.48	909.82	906.05	902.98	900.48	898.45
54000	953.84	944.84	937.59	931.73	926.99	923.14	920.02	917.47	915.40
55000	971.50	962.33	954.95	948.99	944.16	940.24	937.05	934.46	932.35
56000	989.17	979.83	972.31	966.24	961.32	957.33	954.09	951.45	949.30
57000	1006.83	997.33	989.67	983.49	978.49	974.43	971.13	968.44	966.25
58000	1024.50	1014.82	1007.04	1000.75	995.66	991.52	988.17	985.43	983.21
59000	1042.16	1032.32	1024.40	1018.00	1012.82	1008.62	1005.20	1002.42	1000.16
60000	1059.82	1049.82	1041.76	1035.26	1029.99	1025.72	1022.24	1019.41	1017.11
61000	1077.49	1067.31	1059.12	1052.51	1047.16	1042.81	1039.28	1036.40	1034.06
62000	1095.15	1084.81	1076.49	1069.77	1064.32	1059.91	1056.32	1053.39	1051.01
63000	1112.81	1102.31	1093.85	1087.02	1081.49	1077.00	1073.35	1070.38	1067.96
64000	1130.48	1119.80	1111.21	1104.27	1098.66	1094.10	1090.39	1087.37	1084.92
65000	1148.14	1137.30	1128.58	1121.53	1115.82	1111.19	1107.43	1104.36	1101.87
66000	1165.80	1154.80	1145.94	1138.78	1132.99	1128.29	1124.46	1121.35	1118.82
67000	1183.47	1172.30	1163.30	1156.04	1150.15	1145.38	1141.50	1138.34	1135.77
68000	1201.13	1189.79	1180.66	1173.29	1167.32	1162.48	1158.54	1155.33	1152.72
69000	1218.80	1207.29	1198.03	1190.54	1184.49	1179.57	1175.58	1172.32	1169.67
70000	1236.46	1224.79	1215.39	1207.80	1201.65	1196.67	1192.61	1189.31	1186.63
75000	1324.78	1312.27	1302.20	1294.07	1287.49	1282.14	1277.80	1274.27	1271.38
80000	1413.10	1399.75	1389.01	1380.34	1373.32	1367.62	1362.99	1359.22	1356.14
100000	1766.37	1749.69	1736.27	1725.43	1716.65	1709.52	1703.73	1699.02	1695.18

TERM AMOUNT	24 YEARS	25 YEARS	26 YEARS	27 YEARS	28 YEARS	29 YEARS	30 YEARS	35 YEARS	40 YEARS
$ 25	.43	.43	.43	43	.43	.43	.43	.42	.42
50	.85	.85	.85	.85	.85	.85	.85	.84	.84
75	1.27	1.27	1.27	1.27	1.27	1.27	1.27	1.26	1.26
100	1.70	1.69	1.69	1.69	1.69	1.69	1.69	1.68	1.68
200	3.39	3.38	3.38	3.38	3.37	3.37	3.37	3.36	3.36
300	5.08	5.07	5.07	5.06	5.06	5.05	5.05	5.04	5.04
400	6.77	6.76	6.75	6.75	6.74	6.74	6.73	6.72	6.72
500	8.47	8.45	8.44	8.43	8.43	8.42	8.42	8.40	8.40
600	10.16	10.14	10.13	10.12	10.11	10.10	10.10	10.08	10.08
700	11.85	11.83	11.82	11.80	11.80	11.79	11.78	11.76	11.76
800	13.54	13.52	13.50	13.49	13.48	13.47	13.46	13.44	13.43
900	15.23	15.21	15.19	15.18	15.16	15.15	15.14	15.12	15.11
1000	16.93	16.90	16.88	16.86	16.85	16.84	16.83	16.80	16.79
2000	33.85	33.79	33.75	33.72	33.69	33.67	33.65	33.60	33.58
3000	50.77	50.69	50.63	50.58	50.53	50.50	50.47	50.39	50.36
4000	67.69	67.58	67.50	67.43	67.38	67.33	67.29	67.19	67.15
5000	84.61	84.48	84.37	84.29	84.22	84.16	84.12	83.99	83.93
6000	101.53	101.37	101.25	101.15	101.06	100.99	100.94	100.78	100.72
7000	118.45	118.27	118.12	118.00	117.91	117.83	117.76	117.57	117.51
8000	135.37	135.16	135.00	134.86	134.75	134.66	134.58	134.37	134.29
9000	152.29	152.06	151.87	151.72	151.59	151.49	151.40	151.17	151.08
10000	169.21	168.95	168.74	168.57	168.43	168.32	168.23	167.96	167.86
15000	253.81	253.43	253.11	252.86	252.65	252.48	252.34	251.94	251.79
20000	338.41	337.90	337.48	337.14	336.86	336.64	336.45	335.92	335.72
25000	423.02	422.38	421.85	421.43	421.08	420.79	420.56	419.90	419.65
30000	507.62	506.85	506.22	505.71	505.29	504.95	504.67	503.87	503.58
35000	592.22	591.32	590.59	590.00	589.51	589.11	588.78	587.85	587.51
36000	609.14	608.22	607.47	606.85	606.35	605.94	605.60	604.65	604.29
37000	626.06	625.11	624.34	623.71	623.19	622.77	622.43	621.44	621.08
38000	642.98	642.01	641.22	640.57	640.04	639.60	639.25	638.24	637.87
39000	659.90	658.90	658.09	657.42	656.88	656.43	656.07	655.03	654.65
40000	676.82	675.80	674.96	674.28	673.72	673.27	672.89	671.83	671.44
41000	693.74	692.69	691.84	691.14	690.57	690.10	689.72	688.62	688.22
42000	710.66	709.59	708.71	707.99	707.41	706.93	706.54	705.42	705.01
43000	727.58	726.48	725.59	724.85	724.25	723.76	723.36	722.22	721.80
44000	744.50	743.38	742.46	741.71	741.09	740.59	740.18	739.01	738.58
45000	761.42	760.27	759.33	758.57	757.94	757.42	757.00	755.81	755.37
46000	778.34	777.17	776.21	775.42	774.78	774.26	773.83	772.60	772.15
47000	795.26	794.06	793.08	792.28	791.62	791.09	790.65	789.40	788.94
48000	812.18	810.96	809.95	809.14	808.47	807.92	807.47	806.19	805.72
49000	829.11	827.85	826.83	825.99	825.31	824.75	824.29	822.99	822.51
50000	846.03	844.75	843.70	842.85	842.15	841.58	841.12	839.79	839.30
51000	862.95	861.64	860.58	859.71	859.00	858.41	857.94	856.58	856.08
52000	879.87	878.54	877.45	876.56	875.84	875.24	874.76	873.38	872.87
53000	896.79	895.43	894.32	893.42	892.68	892.08	891.58	890.17	889.65
54000	913.71	912.33	911.20	910.28	909.52	908.91	908.40	906.97	906.44
55000	930.63	929.22	928.07	927.13	926.37	925.74	925.23	923.76	923.23
56000	947.55	946.12	944.95	943.99	943.21	942.57	942.05	940.56	940.01
57000	964.47	963.01	961.82	960.85	960.05	959.40	958.87	957.35	956.80
58000	981.39	979.91	978.69	977.70	976.90	976.23	975.69	974.15	973.58
59000	998.31	996.80	995.57	994.56	993.74	993.07	992.52	990.95	990.37
60000	1015.23	1013.70	1012.44	1011.42	1010.58	1009.90	1009.34	1007.74	1007.15
61000	1032.15	1030.59	1029.32	1028.28	1027.42	1026.73	1026.16	1024.54	1023.94
62000	1049.07	1047.49	1046.19	1045.13	1044.27	1043.56	1042.98	1041.33	1040.73
63000	1065.99	1064.38	1063.06	1061.99	1061.11	1060.39	1059.80	1058.13	1057.51
64000	1082.91	1081.27	1079.94	1078.85	1077.95	1077.22	1076.63	1074.92	1074.30
65000	1099.83	1098.17	1096.81	1095.70	1094.80	1094.05	1093.45	1091.72	1091.08
66000	1116.75	1115.06	1113.69	1112.56	1111.64	1110.89	1110.27	1108.51	1107.87
67000	1133.67	1131.96	1130.56	1129.42	1128.48	1127.72	1127.09	1125.31	1124.66
68000	1150.59	1148.85	1147.43	1146.27	1145.33	1144.55	1143.92	1142.11	1141.44
69000	1167.51	1165.75	1164.31	1163.13	1162.17	1161.38	1160.74	1158.90	1158.23
70000	1184.43	1182.64	1181.18	1179.99	1179.01	1178.21	1177.56	1175.70	1175.01
75000	1269.04	1267.12	1265.55	1264.27	1263.23	1262.37	1261.67	1259.68	1258.94
80000	1353.64	1351.59	1349.92	1348.56	1347.44	1346.53	1345.78	1343.65	1342.87
100000	1692.05	1689.49	1687.40	1685.69	1684.30	1683.16	1682.23	1679.57	1678.59

21½% MONTHLY PAYMENT
NECESSARY TO AMORTIZE A LOAN

TERM AMOUNT	1 YEAR	1½ YEARS	2 YEARS	2½ YEARS	3 YEARS	3½ YEARS	4 YEARS	4½ YEARS	5 YEARS
$ 25	2.33	1.63	1.28	1.08	.94	.85	.77	.72	.68
50	4.65	3.26	2.56	2.15	1.88	1.69	1.54	1.43	1.35
75	6.97	4.88	3.84	3.22	2.82	2.53	2.31	2.15	2.02
100	9.30	6.51	5.12	4.30	3.75	3.37	3.08	2.86	2.69
200	18.59	13.01	10.24	8.59	7.50	6.73	6.15	5.72	5.37
300	27.88	19.52	15.36	12.88	11.25	10.09	9.23	8.57	8.05
400	37.17	26.02	20.48	17.18	14.99	13.45	12.30	11.43	10.74
500	46.46	32.53	25.60	21.47	18.74	16.81	15.38	14.28	13.42
600	55.76	39.03	30.72	25.76	22.49	20.17	18.45	17.14	16.10
700	65.05	45.54	35.84	30.05	26.23	23.53	21.53	19.99	18.78
800	74.34	52.04	40.95	34.35	29.98	26.89	24.60	22.85	21.47
900	83.63	58.55	46.07	38.64	33.73	30.25	27.68	25.70	24.15
1000	92.92	65.05	51.19	42.93	37.47	33.61	30.75	28.56	26.83
2000	185.84	130.10	102.38	85.86	74.94	67.22	61.50	57.11	53.66
3000	278.76	195.15	153.57	128.79	112.41	100.83	92.25	85.67	80.48
4000	371.68	260.20	204.75	171.71	149.88	134.44	123.00	114.22	107.31
5000	464.60	325.25	255.94	214.64	187.34	168.05	153.75	142.78	134.14
6000	557.52	390.30	307.13	257.57	224.81	201.66	184.50	171.33	160.96
7000	650.44	455.35	358.32	300.50	262.28	235.26	215.25	199.89	187.79
8000	743.36	520.40	409.50	343.42	299.75	268.87	245.99	228.44	214.62
9000	836.28	585.45	460.69	386.35	337.22	302.48	276.74	257.00	241.44
10000	929.20	650.50	511.88	429.28	374.68	336.09	307.49	285.55	268.27
15000	1393.80	975.75	767.81	643.91	562.02	504.13	461.24	428.33	402.40
20000	1858.40	1301.00	1023.75	858.55	749.36	672.18	614.98	571.10	536.53
25000	2323.00	1626.25	1279.69	1073.18	936.70	840.22	768.72	713.87	670.67
30000	2787.60	1951.50	1535.62	1287.82	1124.04	1008.26	922.47	856.65	804.80
35000	3252.20	2276.75	1791.56	1502.46	1311.38	1176.30	1076.21	999.42	938.93
36000	3345.12	2341.80	1842.75	1545.38	1348.85	1209.91	1106.96	1027.98	965.76
37000	3438.04	2406.85	1893.94	1588.31	1386.32	1243.52	1137.71	1056.53	992.58
38000	3530.96	2471.90	1945.12	1631.24	1423.78	1277.13	1168.46	1085.09	1019.41
39000	3623.88	2536.95	1996.31	1674.17	1461.25	1310.74	1199.20	1113.64	1046.24
40000	3716.80	2602.00	2047.50	1717.09	1498.72	1344.35	1229.95	1142.20	1073.06
41000	3809.72	2667.05	2098.69	1760.02	1536.19	1377.95	1260.70	1170.75	1099.89
42000	3902.64	2732.10	2149.87	1802.95	1573.65	1411.56	1291.45	1199.31	1126.72
43000	3995.56	2797.15	2201.06	1845.87	1611.12	1445.17	1322.20	1227.86	1153.54
44000	4088.48	2862.20	2252.25	1888.80	1648.59	1478.78	1352.95	1256.41	1180.37
45000	4181.40	2927.25	2303.43	1931.73	1686.06	1512.39	1383.70	1284.97	1207.20
46000	4274.32	2992.30	2354.62	1974.66	1723.53	1546.00	1414.45	1313.52	1234.02
47000	4367.24	3057.35	2405.81	2017.58	1760.99	1579.60	1445.19	1342.08	1260.85
48000	4460.16	3122.40	2457.00	2060.51	1798.46	1613.21	1475.94	1370.63	1287.68
49000	4553.08	3187.45	2508.18	2103.44	1835.93	1646.82	1506.69	1399.19	1314.50
50000	4646.00	3252.50	2559.37	2146.36	1873.40	1680.43	1537.44	1427.74	1341.33
51000	4738.92	3317.55	2610.56	2189.29	1910.87	1714.04	1568.19	1456.30	1368.16
52000	4831.84	3382.60	2661.75	2232.22	1948.33	1747.65	1598.94	1484.85	1394.98
53000	4924.76	3447.65	2712.93	2275.15	1985.80	1781.26	1629.69	1513.41	1421.81
54000	5017.68	3512.70	2764.12	2318.07	2023.27	1814.86	1660.43	1541.96	1448.63
55000	5110.60	3577.75	2815.31	2361.00	2060.74	1848.47	1691.18	1570.52	1475.46
56000	5203.52	3642.80	2866.50	2403.93	2098.20	1882.08	1721.93	1599.07	1502.29
57000	5296.44	3707.85	2917.68	2446.85	2135.67	1915.69	1752.68	1627.63	1529.11
58000	5389.36	3772.90	2968.87	2489.78	2173.14	1949.30	1783.43	1656.18	1555.94
59000	5482.28	3837.95	3020.06	2532.71	2210.61	1982.91	1814.18	1684.74	1582.77
60000	5575.20	3903.00	3071.24	2575.64	2248.08	2016.51	1844.93	1713.29	1609.59
61000	5668.12	3968.05	3122.43	2618.56	2285.54	2050.12	1875.68	1741.85	1636.42
62000	5761.04	4033.10	3173.62	2661.49	2323.01	2083.73	1906.42	1770.40	1663.25
63000	5853.96	4098.15	3224.81	2704.42	2360.48	2117.34	1937.17	1798.96	1690.07
64000	5946.88	4163.20	3275.99	2747.35	2397.95	2150.95	1967.92	1827.51	1716.90
65000	6039.80	4228.25	3327.18	2790.27	2435.42	2184.56	1998.67	1856.06	1743.73
66000	6132.72	4293.30	3378.37	2833.20	2472.88	2218.17	2029.42	1884.62	1770.55
67000	6225.64	4358.35	3429.56	2876.13	2510.35	2251.78	2060.17	1913.17	1797.38
68000	6318.56	4423.40	3480.74	2919.05	2547.82	2285.38	2090.92	1941.73	1824.21
69000	6411.48	4488.45	3531.93	2961.98	2585.29	2318.99	2121.67	1970.28	1851.03
70000	6504.40	4553.50	3583.12	3004.91	2622.75	2352.60	2152.41	1998.84	1877.86
75000	6969.00	4878.75	3839.05	3219.54	2810.09	2520.64	2306.16	2141.61	2011.99
80000	7433.60	5204.00	4094.99	3434.18	2997.43	2688.69	2459.90	2284.39	2146.12
100000	9291.99	6505.00	5118.74	4292.72	3746.79	3360.86	3074.87	2855.48	2682.65

216

MONTHLY PAYMENT 21½%
NECESSARY TO AMORTIZE A LOAN

TERM AMOUNT	6 YEARS	7 YEARS	8 YEARS	9 YEARS	10 YEARS	11 YEARS	12 YEARS	13 YEARS	14 YEARS
$ 25	.61	.57	.54	.52	.50	.48	.47	.47	.46
50	1.22	1.13	1.07	1.03	.99	.96	.94	.93	.92
75	1.83	1.70	1.60	1.54	1.48	1.44	1.41	1.39	1.37
100	2.43	2.26	2.14	2.05	1.98	1.92	1.88	1.85	1.83
200	4.86	4.52	4.27	4.09	3.95	3.84	3.76	3.70	3.65
300	7.29	6.77	6.40	6.13	5.92	5.76	5.64	5.54	5.47
400	9.72	9.03	8.54	8.17	7.89	7.68	7.52	7.39	7.29
500	12.15	11.29	10.67	10.21	9.87	9.60	9.40	9.24	9.11
600	14.58	13.54	12.80	12.25	11.84	11.52	11.27	11.08	10.93
700	17.01	15.80	14.93	14.29	13.81	13.44	13.15	12.93	12.75
800	19.44	18.06	17.07	16.33	15.78	15.36	15.03	14.77	14.57
900	21.87	20.31	19.20	18.38	17.76	17.28	16.91	16.62	16.39
1000	24.30	22.57	21.33	20.42	19.73	19.20	18.79	18.47	18.21
2000	48.60	45.14	42.66	40.83	39.45	38.39	37.57	36.93	36.42
3000	72.90	67.70	63.98	61.24	59.17	57.59	56.35	55.39	54.63
4000	97.20	90.27	85.31	81.65	78.89	76.78	75.14	73.85	72.83
5000	121.50	112.84	106.64	102.06	98.62	95.97	93.92	92.31	91.04
6000	145.80	135.40	127.96	122.48	118.34	115.17	112.70	110.77	109.25
7000	170.10	157.97	149.29	142.89	138.06	134.36	131.49	129.23	127.45
8000	194.40	180.54	170.61	163.30	157.78	153.55	150.27	147.70	145.66
9000	218.70	203.10	191.94	183.71	177.51	172.75	169.05	166.16	163.87
10000	243.00	225.67	213.27	204.12	197.23	191.94	187.84	184.62	182.07
15000	364.50	338.50	319.90	306.18	295.84	287.91	281.75	276.92	273.11
20000	485.99	451.33	426.53	408.24	394.45	383.88	375.67	369.23	364.14
25000	607.49	564.16	533.16	510.30	493.06	479.85	469.58	461.54	455.18
30000	728.99	676.99	639.79	612.36	591.67	575.81	563.50	553.84	546.21
35000	850.49	789.83	746.42	714.42	690.28	671.78	657.42	646.15	637.25
36000	874.78	812.39	767.75	734.83	710.01	690.98	676.20	664.61	655.46
37000	899.08	834.96	789.08	755.24	729.73	710.17	694.98	683.07	673.66
38000	923.38	857.53	810.40	775.65	749.45	729.36	713.77	701.53	691.87
39000	947.68	880.09	831.73	796.06	769.17	748.56	732.55	720.00	710.08
40000	971.98	902.66	853.05	816.47	788.89	767.75	751.33	738.46	728.28
41000	996.28	925.22	874.38	836.89	808.62	786.94	770.12	756.92	746.49
42000	1020.58	947.79	895.71	857.30	828.34	806.14	788.90	775.38	764.70
43000	1044.88	970.36	917.03	877.71	848.06	825.33	807.68	793.84	782.90
44000	1069.18	992.92	938.36	898.12	867.78	844.52	826.46	812.30	801.11
45000	1093.48	1015.49	959.69	918.53	887.51	863.72	845.25	830.76	819.32
46000	1117.78	1038.06	981.01	938.94	907.23	882.91	864.03	849.23	837.52
47000	1142.08	1060.62	1002.34	959.36	926.95	902.11	882.81	867.69	855.73
48000	1166.38	1083.19	1023.66	979.77	946.67	921.30	901.60	886.15	873.94
49000	1190.68	1105.76	1044.99	1000.18	966.39	940.49	920.38	904.61	892.15
50000	1214.98	1128.32	1066.32	1020.59	986.12	959.69	939.16	923.07	910.35
51000	1239.28	1150.89	1087.64	1041.00	1005.84	978.88	957.95	941.53	928.56
52000	1263.58	1173.45	1108.97	1061.42	1025.56	998.07	976.73	959.99	946.77
53000	1287.87	1196.02	1130.30	1081.83	1045.28	1017.27	995.51	978.45	964.97
54000	1312.17	1218.59	1151.62	1102.24	1065.01	1036.46	1014.30	996.92	983.18
55000	1336.47	1241.15	1172.95	1122.65	1084.73	1055.65	1033.08	1015.38	1001.39
56000	1360.77	1263.72	1194.27	1143.06	1104.45	1074.85	1051.86	1033.84	1019.59
57000	1385.07	1286.29	1215.60	1163.47	1124.17	1094.04	1070.65	1052.30	1037.80
58000	1409.37	1308.85	1236.93	1183.89	1143.89	1113.24	1089.43	1070.76	1056.01
59000	1433.67	1331.42	1258.25	1204.30	1163.62	1132.43	1108.21	1089.22	1074.21
60000	1457.97	1353.98	1279.58	1224.71	1183.34	1151.62	1127.00	1107.68	1092.42
61000	1482.27	1376.55	1300.91	1245.12	1203.06	1170.82	1145.78	1126.15	1110.63
62000	1506.57	1399.12	1322.23	1265.53	1222.78	1190.01	1164.56	1144.61	1128.84
63000	1530.87	1421.68	1343.56	1285.94	1242.51	1209.20	1183.35	1163.07	1147.04
64000	1555.17	1444.25	1364.88	1306.36	1262.23	1228.40	1202.13	1181.53	1165.25
65000	1579.47	1466.82	1386.21	1326.77	1281.95	1247.59	1220.91	1199.99	1183.46
66000	1603.77	1489.38	1407.54	1347.18	1301.67	1266.78	1239.69	1218.45	1201.66
67000	1628.07	1511.95	1428.86	1367.59	1321.39	1285.98	1258.48	1236.91	1219.87
68000	1652.37	1534.52	1450.19	1388.00	1341.12	1305.17	1277.26	1255.37	1238.08
69000	1676.67	1557.08	1471.52	1408.41	1360.84	1324.36	1296.04	1273.84	1256.28
70000	1700.97	1579.65	1492.84	1428.83	1380.56	1343.56	1314.83	1292.30	1274.49
75000	1822.46	1692.48	1599.47	1530.89	1479.17	1439.53	1408.74	1384.60	1365.53
80000	1943.96	1805.31	1706.10	1632.94	1577.78	1535.49	1502.66	1476.91	1456.56
100000	2429.95	2256.64	2132.63	2041.18	1972.23	1919.37	1878.32	1846.14	1820.70

21½% MONTHLY PAYMENT
NECESSARY TO AMORTIZE A LOAN

TERM AMOUNT	15 YEARS	16 YEARS	17 YEARS	18 YEARS	19 YEARS	20 YEARS	21 YEARS	22 YEARS	23 YEARS
$ 25	.46	.45	.45	.45	.44	.44	.44	.44	.44
50	.91	.90	.89	.89	.88	.88	.88	.87	.87
75	1.36	1.34	1.33	1.33	1.32	1.31	1.31	1.31	1.30
100	1.81	1.79	1.78	1.77	1.76	1.75	1.75	1.74	1.74
200	3.61	3.57	3.55	3.53	3.51	3.50	3.49	3.48	3.47
300	5.41	5.36	5.32	5.29	5.26	5.24	5.23	5.21	5.20
400	7.21	7.14	7.09	7.05	7.02	6.99	6.97	6.95	6.93
500	9.01	8.93	8.86	8.81	8.77	8.73	8.71	8.68	8.67
600	10.81	10.71	10.63	10.57	10.52	10.48	10.45	10.42	10.40
700	12.61	12.50	12.40	12.33	12.27	12.22	12.19	12.16	12.13
800	14.41	14.28	14.18	14.09	14.03	13.97	13.93	13.89	13.86
900	16.21	16.06	15.95	15.85	15.78	15.72	15.67	15.63	15.59
1000	18.01	17.85	17.72	17.61	17.53	17.46	17.41	17.36	17.33
2000	36.01	35.69	35.43	35.22	35.06	34.92	34.81	34.72	34.65
3000	54.02	53.53	53.15	52.83	52.58	52.38	52.21	52.08	51.97
4000	72.02	71.38	70.86	70.44	70.11	69.83	69.61	69.43	69.29
5000	90.03	89.22	88.57	88.05	87.63	87.29	87.02	86.79	86.61
6000	108.03	107.06	106.29	105.66	105.16	104.75	104.42	104.15	103.93
7000	126.04	124.91	124.00	123.27	122.68	122.20	121.82	121.51	121.25
8000	144.04	142.75	141.71	140.88	140.21	139.66	139.22	138.86	138.57
9000	162.05	160.59	159.43	158.49	157.73	157.12	156.62	156.22	155.90
10000	180.05	178.44	177.14	176.10	175.26	174.58	174.03	173.58	173.22
15000	270.08	267.65	265.71	264.14	262.88	261.86	261.04	260.37	259.82
20000	360.10	356.87	354.27	352.19	350.51	349.15	348.05	347.15	346.43
25000	450.12	446.08	442.84	440.23	438.13	436.43	435.06	433.94	433.04
30000	540.15	535.30	531.41	528.28	525.76	523.72	522.07	520.73	519.64
35000	630.17	624.51	619.98	616.33	613.38	611.00	609.08	607.51	606.25
36000	648.17	642.36	637.69	633.94	630.91	628.46	626.48	624.87	623.57
37000	666.18	660.20	655.40	651.55	648.43	645.92	643.88	642.23	640.89
38000	684.18	678.04	673.12	669.15	665.96	663.37	661.28	659.59	658.21
39000	702.19	695.89	690.83	686.76	683.48	680.83	678.68	676.94	675.53
40000	720.19	713.73	708.54	704.37	701.01	698.29	696.09	694.30	692.85
41000	738.20	731.57	726.26	721.98	718.53	715.75	713.49	711.66	710.17
42000	756.20	749.42	743.97	739.59	736.06	733.20	730.89	729.02	727.50
43000	774.21	767.26	761.68	757.20	753.58	750.66	748.29	746.37	744.82
44000	792.21	785.10	779.40	774.81	771.11	768.12	765.69	763.73	762.14
45000	810.22	802.94	797.11	792.42	788.63	785.57	783.10	781.09	779.46
46000	828.22	820.79	814.83	810.03	806.16	803.03	800.50	798.45	796.78
47000	846.23	838.63	832.54	827.64	823.68	820.49	817.90	815.80	814.10
48000	864.23	856.47	850.25	845.25	841.21	837.94	835.30	833.16	831.42
49000	882.24	874.32	867.97	862.86	858.73	855.40	852.70	850.52	848.74
50000	900.24	892.16	885.68	880.46	876.26	872.86	870.11	867.88	866.07
51000	918.24	910.00	903.39	898.07	893.78	890.32	887.51	885.23	883.39
52000	936.25	927.85	921.11	915.68	911.31	907.77	904.91	902.59	900.71
53000	954.25	945.69	938.82	933.29	928.83	925.23	922.31	919.95	918.03
54000	972.26	963.53	956.53	950.90	946.36	942.69	939.71	937.31	935.35
55000	990.26	981.38	974.25	968.51	963.88	960.14	957.12	954.66	952.67
56000	1008.27	999.22	991.96	986.12	981.41	977.60	974.52	972.02	969.99
57000	1026.27	1017.06	1009.67	1003.73	998.93	995.06	991.92	989.38	987.31
58000	1044.28	1034.90	1027.39	1021.34	1016.46	1012.52	1009.32	1006.73	1004.63
59000	1062.28	1052.75	1045.10	1038.95	1033.98	1029.97	1026.72	1024.09	1021.96
60000	1080.29	1070.59	1062.81	1056.56	1051.51	1047.43	1044.13	1041.45	1039.28
61000	1098.29	1088.43	1080.53	1074.17	1069.03	1064.89	1061.53	1058.81	1056.60
62000	1116.30	1106.28	1098.24	1091.77	1086.56	1082.34	1078.93	1076.16	1073.92
63000	1134.30	1124.12	1115.95	1109.38	1104.08	1099.80	1096.33	1093.52	1091.24
64000	1152.31	1141.96	1133.67	1126.99	1121.61	1117.26	1113.73	1110.88	1108.56
65000	1170.31	1159.81	1151.38	1144.60	1139.13	1134.71	1131.14	1128.24	1125.88
66000	1188.32	1177.65	1169.09	1162.21	1156.66	1152.17	1148.54	1145.59	1143.20
67000	1206.32	1195.49	1186.81	1179.82	1174.18	1169.63	1165.94	1162.95	1160.53
68000	1224.32	1213.34	1204.52	1197.43	1191.71	1187.09	1183.34	1180.31	1177.85
69000	1242.33	1231.18	1222.24	1215.04	1209.23	1204.54	1200.75	1197.67	1195.17
70000	1260.33	1249.02	1239.95	1232.65	1226.76	1222.00	1218.15	1215.02	1212.49
75000	1350.36	1338.24	1328.52	1320.69	1314.39	1309.29	1305.16	1301.81	1299.10
80000	1440.38	1427.45	1417.08	1408.74	1402.01	1396.57	1392.17	1388.60	1385.70
100000	1800.47	1784.32	1771.35	1760.92	1752.51	1745.71	1740.21	1735.75	1732.13

MONTHLY PAYMENT 21½%
NECESSARY TO AMORTIZE A LOAN

TERM AMOUNT	24 YEARS	25 YEARS	26 YEARS	27 YEARS	28 YEARS	29 YEARS	30 YEARS	35 YEARS	40 YEARS
$ 25	.44	.44	.44	.44	.44	.44	.44	.43	.43
50	.87	.87	.87	.87	.87	.87	.87	.86	.86
75	1.30	1.30	1.30	1.30	1.30	1.30	1.30	1.29	1.29
100	1.73	1.73	1.73	1.73	1.73	1.73	1.73	1.72	1.72
200	3.46	3.46	3.45	3.45	3.45	3.45	3.45	3.44	3.44
300	5.19	5.19	5.18	5.17	5.17	5.17	5.17	5.16	5.16
400	6.92	6.91	6.90	6.90	6.89	6.89	6.89	6.88	6.87
500	8.65	8.64	8.63	8.62	8.61	8.61	8.61	8.59	8.59
600	10.38	10.37	10.35	10.34	10.34	10.33	10.33	10.31	10.31
700	12.11	12.09	12.08	12.07	12.06	12.05	12.05	12.03	12.02
800	13.84	13.82	13.80	13.79	13.78	13.77	13.77	13.75	13.74
900	15.57	15.55	15.53	15.51	15.50	15.49	15.49	15.46	15.46
1000	17.30	17.27	17.25	17.24	17.22	17.21	17.21	17.18	17.17
2000	34.59	34.54	34.50	34.47	34.44	34.42	34.41	34.36	34.34
3000	51.88	51.81	51.75	51.70	51.66	51.63	51.61	51.54	51.51
4000	69.17	69.08	69.00	68.94	68.88	68.84	68.81	68.71	68.68
5000	86.46	86.34	86.25	86.17	86.10	86.05	86.01	85.89	85.85
6000	103.76	103.61	103.50	103.40	103.32	103.26	103.21	103.07	103.01
7000	121.05	120.88	120.74	120.63	120.54	120.47	120.41	120.24	120.18
8000	138.34	138.15	137.99	137.87	137.76	137.68	137.61	137.42	137.35
9000	155.63	155.42	155.24	155.10	154.98	154.89	154.81	154.60	154.52
10000	172.92	172.68	172.49	172.33	172.20	172.10	172.01	171.77	171.69
15000	259.38	259.02	258.73	258.49	258.30	258.14	258.02	257.66	257.53
20000	345.84	345.36	344.97	344.66	344.40	344.19	344.02	343.54	343.37
25000	432.30	431.70	431.22	430.82	430.50	430.24	430.02	429.42	429.21
30000	518.76	518.04	517.46	516.98	516.60	516.28	516.03	515.31	515.05
35000	605.22	604.38	603.70	603.15	602.70	602.33	602.03	601.19	600.89
36000	622.51	621.65	620.95	620.38	619.92	619.54	619.23	618.37	618.05
37000	639.80	638.92	638.20	637.61	637.14	636.75	636.43	635.54	635.22
38000	657.09	656.18	655.45	654.84	654.36	653.96	653.63	652.72	652.39
39000	674.38	673.45	672.69	672.08	671.58	671.17	670.83	669.90	669.56
40000	691.68	690.72	689.94	689.31	688.80	688.38	688.03	687.07	686.73
41000	708.97	707.99	707.19	706.54	706.01	705.59	705.24	704.25	703.89
42000	726.26	725.26	724.44	723.78	723.23	722.79	722.44	721.43	721.06
43000	743.55	742.52	741.69	741.01	740.45	740.00	739.64	738.60	738.23
44000	760.84	759.79	758.94	758.24	757.67	757.21	756.84	755.78	755.40
45000	778.14	777.06	776.19	775.47	774.89	774.42	774.04	772.96	772.57
46000	795.43	794.33	793.43	792.71	792.11	791.63	791.24	790.13	789.73
47000	812.72	811.60	810.68	809.94	809.33	808.84	808.44	807.31	806.90
48000	830.01	828.86	827.93	827.17	826.55	826.05	825.64	824.49	824.07
49000	847.30	846.13	845.18	844.40	843.77	843.26	842.84	841.66	841.24
50000	864.59	863.40	862.43	861.64	860.99	860.47	860.04	858.84	858.41
51000	881.89	880.67	879.68	878.87	878.21	877.68	877.24	876.02	875.57
52000	899.18	897.94	896.92	896.10	895.43	894.89	894.44	893.19	892.74
53000	916.47	915.20	914.17	913.33	912.65	912.10	911.64	910.37	909.91
54000	933.76	932.47	931.42	930.57	929.87	929.31	928.84	927.55	927.08
55000	951.05	949.74	948.67	947.80	947.09	946.52	946.05	944.72	944.25
56000	968.35	967.01	965.92	965.03	964.31	963.72	963.25	961.90	961.41
57000	985.64	984.27	983.17	982.26	981.53	980.93	980.45	979.08	978.58
58000	1002.93	1001.54	1000.41	999.50	998.75	998.14	997.65	996.25	995.75
59000	1020.22	1018.81	1017.66	1016.73	1015.97	1015.35	1014.85	1013.43	1012.92
60000	1037.51	1036.08	1034.91	1033.96	1033.19	1032.56	1032.05	1030.61	1030.09
61000	1054.80	1053.35	1052.16	1051.20	1050.41	1049.77	1049.25	1047.78	1047.25
62000	1072.10	1070.61	1069.41	1068.43	1067.63	1066.98	1066.45	1064.96	1064.42
63000	1089.39	1087.88	1086.66	1085.66	1084.85	1084.19	1083.65	1082.14	1081.59
64000	1106.68	1105.15	1103.91	1102.89	1102.07	1101.40	1100.85	1099.31	1098.76
65000	1123.97	1122.42	1121.15	1120.13	1119.29	1118.61	1118.05	1116.49	1115.93
66000	1141.26	1139.69	1138.40	1137.36	1136.51	1135.82	1135.25	1133.67	1133.09
67000	1158.55	1156.95	1155.65	1154.59	1153.73	1153.03	1152.45	1150.84	1150.26
68000	1175.85	1174.22	1172.90	1171.82	1170.95	1170.24	1169.66	1168.02	1167.43
69000	1193.14	1191.49	1190.15	1189.06	1188.17	1187.44	1186.86	1185.20	1184.60
70000	1210.43	1208.76	1207.40	1206.29	1205.39	1204.65	1204.06	1202.37	1201.77
75000	1296.89	1295.10	1293.64	1292.45	1291.49	1290.70	1290.06	1288.26	1287.61
80000	1383.35	1381.44	1379.88	1378.62	1377.59	1376.75	1376.06	1374.14	1373.45
100000	1729.18	1726.79	1724.85	1723.27	1721.98	1720.93	1720.08	1717.67	1716.81

MONTHLY PAYMENT
NECESSARY TO AMORTIZE A LOAN

TERM AMOUNT	1 YEAR	1½ YEARS	2 YEARS	2½ YEARS	3 YEARS	3½ YEARS	4 YEARS	4½ YEARS	5 YEARS
$ 25	2.33	1.64	1.29	1.08	.95	.85	.78	.73	.68
50	4.66	3.27	2.58	2.16	1.89	1.70	1.55	1.45	1.36
75	6.99	4.90	3.86	3.24	2.83	2.54	2.33	2.17	2.04
100	9.32	6.53	5.15	4.32	3.78	3.39	3.10	2.89	2.71
200	18.63	13.06	10.29	8.64	7.55	6.77	6.20	5.77	5.42
300	27.95	19.59	15.43	12.95	11.32	10.16	9.30	8.65	8.13
400	37.26	26.11	20.57	17.27	15.09	13.54	12.40	11.53	10.84
500	46.57	32.64	25.71	21.58	18.86	16.93	15.50	14.41	13.55
600	55.89	39.17	30.85	25.90	22.63	20.31	18.60	17.29	16.26
700	65.20	45.69	35.99	30.22	26.40	23.70	21.70	20.17	18.96
800	74.52	52.22	41.13	34.53	30.17	27.08	24.80	23.05	21.67
900	83.83	58.75	46.28	38.85	33.94	30.47	27.90	25.93	24.38
1000	93.14	65.28	51.42	43.16	37.71	33.85	31.00	28.81	27.09
2000	186.28	130.55	102.83	86.32	75.41	67.70	62.00	57.62	54.17
3000	279.42	195.82	154.24	129.48	113.11	101.55	92.99	86.43	81.26
4000	372.56	261.09	205.65	172.63	150.82	135.40	123.99	115.23	108.34
5000	465.70	326.36	257.07	215.79	188.52	169.25	154.98	144.04	135.43
6000	558.84	391.63	308.48	258.95	226.22	203.10	185.98	172.85	162.51
7000	651.98	456.90	359.89	302.11	263.93	236.95	216.97	201.65	189.59
8000	745.12	522.18	411.30	345.26	301.63	270.80	247.97	230.46	216.68
9000	838.26	587.45	462.72	388.42	339.33	304.65	278.96	259.27	243.76
10000	931.40	652.72	514.13	431.58	377.04	338.50	309.96	288.07	270.85
15000	1397.10	979.07	771.19	647.36	565.55	507.74	464.93	432.11	406.27
20000	1862.80	1305.43	1028.25	863.15	754.07	676.99	619.91	576.14	541.69
25000	2328.50	1631.79	1285.32	1078.93	942.58	846.24	774.88	720.17	677.11
30000	2794.20	1958.14	1542.38	1294.72	1131.10	1015.48	929.86	864.21	812.53
35000	3259.90	2284.50	1799.44	1510.51	1319.61	1184.73	1084.83	1008.24	947.95
36000	3353.04	2349.77	1850.85	1553.66	1357.32	1218.58	1115.83	1037.05	975.03
37000	3446.18	2415.04	1902.27	1596.82	1395.02	1252.43	1146.82	1065.85	1002.12
38000	3539.32	2480.31	1953.68	1639.98	1432.72	1286.28	1177.82	1094.66	1029.20
39000	3632.46	2545.58	2005.09	1683.13	1470.43	1320.13	1208.81	1123.47	1056.28
40000	3725.60	2610.86	2056.50	1726.29	1508.13	1353.98	1239.81	1152.28	1083.37
41000	3818.74	2676.13	2107.92	1769.45	1545.83	1387.82	1270.80	1181.08	1110.45
42000	3911.88	2741.40	2159.33	1812.61	1583.53	1421.67	1301.80	1209.89	1137.54
43000	4005.02	2806.67	2210.74	1855.76	1621.24	1455.52	1332.79	1238.70	1164.62
44000	4098.16	2871.94	2262.15	1898.92	1658.94	1489.37	1363.79	1267.50	1191.70
45000	4191.30	2937.21	2313.57	1942.08	1696.64	1523.22	1394.78	1296.31	1218.79
46000	4284.44	3002.48	2364.98	1985.23	1734.35	1557.07	1425.78	1325.12	1245.87
47000	4377.58	3067.75	2416.39	2028.39	1772.05	1590.92	1456.77	1353.92	1272.96
48000	4470.72	3133.03	2467.80	2071.55	1809.75	1624.77	1487.77	1382.73	1300.04
49000	4563.86	3198.30	2519.22	2114.71	1847.46	1658.62	1518.76	1411.54	1327.12
50000	4657.00	3263.57	2570.63	2157.86	1885.16	1692.47	1549.76	1440.34	1354.21
51000	4750.14	3328.84	2622.04	2201.02	1922.86	1726.32	1580.75	1469.15	1381.29
52000	4843.28	3394.11	2673.45	2244.18	1960.57	1760.17	1611.75	1497.96	1408.38
53000	4936.42	3459.38	2724.87	2287.33	1998.27	1794.02	1642.74	1526.76	1435.46
54000	5029.56	3524.65	2776.28	2330.49	2035.97	1827.87	1673.74	1555.57	1462.54
55000	5122.70	3589.93	2827.69	2373.65	2073.68	1861.71	1704.73	1584.38	1489.63
56000	5215.84	3655.20	2879.10	2416.81	2111.38	1895.56	1735.73	1613.18	1516.71
57000	5308.98	3720.47	2930.52	2459.96	2149.08	1929.41	1766.72	1641.99	1543.80
58000	5402.12	3785.74	2981.93	2503.12	2186.78	1963.26	1797.72	1670.80	1570.88
59000	5495.26	3851.01	3033.34	2546.28	2224.49	1997.11	1828.71	1699.60	1597.97
60000	5588.40	3916.28	3084.75	2589.43	2262.19	2030.96	1859.71	1728.41	1625.05
61000	5681.54	3981.55	3136.17	2632.59	2299.89	2064.81	1890.70	1757.22	1652.13
62000	5774.68	4046.82	3187.58	2675.75	2337.60	2098.66	1921.70	1786.02	1679.22
63000	5867.82	4112.10	3238.99	2718.91	2375.30	2132.51	1952.69	1814.83	1706.30
64000	5960.96	4177.37	3290.40	2762.06	2413.00	2166.36	1983.69	1843.64	1733.39
65000	6054.10	4242.64	3341.82	2805.22	2450.71	2200.21	2014.68	1872.44	1760.47
66000	6147.24	4307.91	3393.23	2848.38	2488.41	2234.06	2045.68	1901.25	1787.55
67000	6240.38	4373.18	3444.64	2891.53	2526.11	2267.91	2076.67	1930.06	1814.64
68000	6333.52	4438.45	3496.05	2934.69	2563.82	2301.75	2107.67	1958.86	1841.72
69000	6426.66	4503.72	3547.46	2977.85	2601.52	2335.60	2138.66	1987.67	1868.81
70000	6519.80	4568.99	3598.88	3021.01	2639.22	2369.45	2169.66	2016.48	1895.89
75000	6985.50	4895.35	3855.94	3236.79	2827.74	2538.70	2324.63	2160.51	2031.31
80000	7451.20	5221.71	4113.00	3452.58	3016.25	2707.95	2479.61	2304.55	2166.73
100000	9314.00	6527.13	5141.25	4315.72	3770.31	3384.93	3099.51	2880.68	2708.41

TERM AMOUNT	6 YEARS	7 YEARS	8 YEARS	9 YEARS	10 YEARS	11 YEARS	12 YEARS	13 YEARS	14 YEARS
$ 25	.62	.58	.55	.52	.51	.49	.48	.47	.47
50	1.23	1.15	1.09	1.04	1.01	.98	.96	.94	.93
75	1.85	1.72	1.63	1.56	1.51	1.47	1.44	1.41	1.40
100	2.46	2.29	2.17	2.08	2.01	1.96	1.92	1.88	1.86
200	4.92	4.57	4.33	4.15	4.01	3.91	3.83	3.76	3.71
300	7.38	6.86	6.49	6.22	6.01	5.86	5.74	5.64	5.57
400	9.83	9.14	8.65	8.29	8.02	7.81	7.65	7.52	7.42
500	12.29	11.43	10.81	10.36	10.02	9.76	9.56	9.40	9.28
600	14.75	13.71	12.97	12.43	12.02	11.71	11.47	11.28	11.13
700	17.20	16.00	15.14	14.50	14.03	13.66	13.38	13.16	12.99
800	19.66	18.28	17.30	16.57	16.03	15.61	15.29	15.04	14.84
900	22.12	20.57	19.46	18.64	18.03	17.56	17.20	16.92	16.69
1000	24.57	22.85	21.62	20.72	20.03	19.51	19.11	18.80	18.55
2000	49.14	45.70	43.24	41.43	40.06	39.02	38.22	37.59	37.09
3000	73.71	68.54	64.85	62.14	60.09	58.53	57.32	56.38	55.64
4000	98.28	91.39	86.47	82.85	80.12	78.04	76.43	75.17	74.18
5000	122.85	114.23	108.08	103.56	100.15	97.55	95.54	93.96	92.72
6000	147.41	137.08	129.70	124.27	120.18	117.06	114.64	112.75	111.27
7000	171.98	159.92	151.31	144.98	140.21	136.57	133.75	131.55	129.81
8000	196.55	182.77	172.93	165.69	160.24	156.08	152.86	150.34	148.35
9000	221.12	205.61	194.54	186.40	180.27	175.59	171.96	169.13	166.90
10000	245.69	228.46	216.16	207.11	200.30	195.10	191.07	187.92	185.44
15000	368.53	342.69	324.24	310.66	300.45	292.65	286.60	281.88	278.16
20000	491.37	456.92	432.32	414.22	400.60	390.19	382.14	375.84	370.88
25000	614.21	571.14	540.39	517.77	500.75	487.74	477.67	469.80	463.59
30000	737.05	685.37	648.47	621.32	600.90	585.29	573.20	563.75	556.31
35000	859.89	799.60	756.55	724.87	701.05	682.84	668.74	657.71	649.03
36000	884.45	822.44	778.16	745.58	721.08	702.35	687.84	676.50	667.57
37000	909.02	845.29	799.78	766.29	741.11	721.86	706.95	695.29	686.12
38000	933.59	868.13	821.39	787.00	761.14	741.37	726.06	714.09	704.66
39000	958.16	890.98	843.01	807.71	781.17	760.87	745.16	732.88	723.20
40000	982.73	913.83	864.63	828.43	801.20	780.38	764.27	751.67	741.75
41000	1007.29	936.67	886.24	849.14	821.23	799.89	783.37	770.46	760.29
42000	1031.86	959.52	907.86	869.85	841.26	819.40	802.48	789.25	778.83
43000	1056.43	982.36	929.47	890.56	861.29	838.91	821.59	808.04	797.38
44000	1081.00	1005.21	951.09	911.27	881.32	858.42	840.69	826.84	815.92
45000	1105.57	1028.05	972.70	931.98	901.35	877.93	859.80	845.63	834.46
46000	1130.13	1050.90	994.32	952.69	921.38	897.44	878.91	864.42	853.01
47000	1154.70	1073.74	1015.93	973.40	941.41	916.95	898.01	883.21	871.55
48000	1179.27	1096.59	1037.55	994.11	961.44	936.46	917.12	902.00	890.09
49000	1203.84	1119.44	1059.17	1014.82	981.47	955.97	936.23	920.79	908.64
50000	1228.41	1142.28	1080.78	1035.53	1001.50	975.48	955.33	939.59	927.18
51000	1252.97	1165.13	1102.40	1056.24	1021.53	994.99	974.44	958.38	945.72
52000	1277.54	1187.97	1124.01	1076.95	1041.56	1014.50	993.55	977.17	964.27
53000	1302.11	1210.82	1145.63	1097.66	1061.59	1034.01	1012.65	995.96	982.81
54000	1326.68	1233.66	1167.24	1118.37	1081.62	1053.52	1031.76	1014.75	1001.36
55000	1351.25	1256.51	1188.86	1139.08	1101.65	1073.03	1050.87	1033.54	1019.90
56000	1375.81	1279.35	1210.47	1159.79	1121.68	1092.54	1069.97	1052.34	1038.44
57000	1400.38	1302.20	1232.09	1180.50	1141.71	1112.05	1089.08	1071.13	1056.99
58000	1424.95	1325.05	1253.70	1201.21	1161.74	1131.55	1108.19	1089.92	1075.53
59000	1449.52	1347.89	1275.32	1221.92	1181.77	1151.06	1127.29	1108.71	1094.07
60000	1474.09	1370.74	1296.94	1242.64	1201.80	1170.57	1146.40	1127.50	1112.62
61000	1498.65	1393.58	1318.55	1263.35	1221.83	1190.08	1165.51	1146.29	1131.16
62000	1523.22	1416.43	1340.17	1284.06	1241.86	1209.59	1184.61	1165.09	1149.70
63000	1547.79	1439.27	1361.78	1304.77	1261.89	1229.10	1203.72	1183.88	1168.25
64000	1572.36	1462.12	1383.40	1325.48	1281.92	1248.61	1222.83	1202.67	1186.79
65000	1596.93	1484.96	1405.01	1346.19	1301.95	1268.12	1241.93	1221.46	1205.33
66000	1621.49	1507.81	1426.63	1366.90	1321.98	1287.63	1261.04	1240.25	1223.88
67000	1646.06	1530.66	1448.24	1387.61	1342.01	1307.14	1280.15	1259.04	1242.42
68000	1670.63	1553.50	1469.86	1408.32	1362.04	1326.65	1299.25	1277.84	1260.96
69000	1695.20	1576.35	1491.48	1429.03	1382.07	1346.16	1318.36	1296.63	1279.51
70000	1719.77	1599.19	1513.09	1449.74	1402.10	1365.67	1337.47	1315.42	1298.05
75000	1842.61	1713.42	1621.17	1553.29	1502.24	1463.22	1433.00	1409.38	1390.77
80000	1965.45	1827.65	1729.25	1656.85	1602.39	1560.76	1528.53	1503.33	1483.49
100000	2456.81	2284.56	2161.56	2071.06	2002.99	1950.95	1910.66	1879.17	1854.36

22% MONTHLY PAYMENT
NECESSARY TO AMORTIZE A LOAN

TERM AMOUNT	15 YEARS	16 YEARS	17 YEARS	18 YEARS	19 YEARS	20 YEARS	21 YEARS	22 YEARS	23 YEARS
$ 25	.46	.46	.46	.45	.45	.45	.45	.45	.45
50	.92	.91	.91	.90	.90	.90	.89	.89	.89
75	1.38	1.37	1.36	1.35	1.35	1.34	1.34	1.33	1.33
100	1.84	1.82	1.81	1.80	1.79	1.79	1.78	1.78	1.77
200	3.67	3.64	3.62	3.60	3.58	3.57	3.56	3.55	3.54
300	5.51	5.46	5.42	5.39	5.37	5.35	5.34	5.32	5.31
400	7.34	7.28	7.23	7.19	7.16	7.13	7.11	7.10	7.08
500	9.18	9.10	9.04	8.99	8.95	8.91	8.89	8.87	8.85
600	11.01	10.92	10.84	10.78	10.74	10.70	10.67	10.64	10.62
700	12.85	12.74	12.65	12.58	12.52	12.48	12.44	12.41	12.39
800	14.68	14.56	14.46	14.38	14.31	14.26	14.22	14.19	14.16
900	16.52	16.38	16.26	16.17	16.10	16.04	16.00	15.96	15.93
1000	18.35	18.20	18.07	17.97	17.89	17.82	17.77	17.73	17.70
2000	36.70	36.39	36.14	35.94	35.77	35.64	35.54	35.46	35.39
3000	55.05	54.58	54.20	53.90	53.66	53.46	53.31	53.18	53.08
4000	73.39	72.77	72.27	71.87	71.54	71.28	71.07	70.91	70.77
5000	91.74	90.96	90.33	89.83	89.43	89.10	88.84	88.63	88.46
6000	110.09	109.15	108.40	107.80	107.31	106.92	106.61	106.36	106.15
7000	128.43	127.34	126.46	125.76	125.20	124.74	124.38	124.08	123.84
8000	146.78	145.53	144.53	143.73	143.08	142.56	142.14	141.81	141.53
9000	165.13	163.72	162.59	161.69	160.97	160.38	159.91	159.53	159.22
10000	183.47	181.91	180.66	179.66	178.85	178.20	177.68	177.26	176.91
15000	275.21	272.86	270.98	269.48	268.27	267.30	266.51	265.88	265.37
20000	366.94	363.81	361.31	359.31	357.69	356.40	355.35	354.51	353.82
25000	458.68	454.77	451.64	449.13	447.12	445.50	444.19	443.13	442.28
30000	550.41	545.72	541.96	538.96	536.54	534.59	533.02	531.76	530.73
35000	642.15	636.67	632.29	628.78	625.96	623.69	621.86	620.38	619.19
36000	660.49	654.86	650.36	646.75	643.85	641.51	639.63	638.11	636.88
37000	678.84	673.05	668.42	664.71	661.73	659.33	657.40	655.83	654.57
38000	697.19	691.24	686.49	682.68	679.62	677.15	675.16	673.56	672.26
39000	715.54	709.43	704.55	700.64	697.50	694.97	692.93	691.28	689.95
40000	733.88	727.62	722.62	718.61	715.38	712.79	710.70	709.01	707.64
41000	752.23	745.81	740.68	736.57	733.27	730.61	728.47	726.73	725.34
42000	770.58	764.00	758.75	754.54	751.15	748.43	746.23	744.46	743.03
43000	788.92	782.19	776.81	772.50	769.04	766.25	764.00	762.18	760.72
44000	807.27	800.38	794.88	790.47	786.92	784.07	781.77	779.91	778.41
45000	825.62	818.57	812.94	808.43	804.81	801.89	799.53	797.63	796.10
46000	843.96	836.76	831.01	826.40	822.69	819.71	817.30	815.36	813.79
47000	862.31	854.95	849.07	844.36	840.58	837.53	835.07	833.09	831.48
48000	880.66	873.14	867.14	862.33	858.46	855.35	852.84	850.81	849.17
49000	899.00	891.33	885.21	880.29	876.34	873.17	870.60	868.54	866.86
50000	917.35	909.53	903.27	898.26	894.23	890.99	888.37	886.26	884.55
51000	935.70	927.72	921.34	916.22	912.11	908.81	906.14	903.99	902.25
52000	954.05	945.91	939.40	934.19	930.00	926.63	923.91	921.71	919.94
53000	972.39	964.10	957.47	952.15	947.88	944.45	941.67	939.44	937.63
54000	990.74	982.29	975.53	970.12	965.77	962.26	959.44	957.16	955.32
55000	1009.09	1000.48	993.60	988.08	983.65	980.08	977.21	974.89	973.01
56000	1027.43	1018.67	1011.66	1006.05	1001.54	997.90	994.98	992.61	990.70
57000	1045.78	1036.86	1029.73	1024.01	1019.42	1015.72	1012.74	1010.34	1008.39
58000	1064.13	1055.05	1047.79	1041.98	1037.31	1033.54	1030.51	1028.06	1026.08
59000	1082.47	1073.24	1065.86	1059.94	1055.19	1051.36	1048.28	1045.79	1043.77
60000	1100.82	1091.43	1083.92	1077.91	1073.07	1069.18	1066.04	1063.51	1061.46
61000	1119.17	1109.62	1101.99	1095.87	1090.96	1087.00	1083.81	1081.24	1079.16
62000	1137.51	1127.81	1120.05	1113.84	1108.84	1104.82	1101.58	1098.96	1096.85
63000	1155.86	1146.00	1138.12	1131.80	1126.73	1122.64	1119.35	1116.69	1114.54
64000	1174.21	1164.19	1156.19	1149.77	1144.61	1140.46	1137.11	1134.41	1132.23
65000	1192.56	1182.38	1174.25	1167.73	1162.50	1158.28	1154.88	1152.14	1149.92
66000	1210.90	1200.57	1192.32	1185.70	1180.38	1176.10	1172.65	1169.86	1167.61
67000	1229.25	1218.76	1210.38	1203.66	1198.27	1193.92	1190.42	1187.59	1185.30
68000	1247.60	1236.95	1228.45	1221.63	1216.15	1211.74	1208.18	1205.31	1202.99
69000	1265.94	1255.14	1246.51	1239.59	1234.03	1229.56	1225.95	1223.04	1220.68
70000	1284.29	1273.33	1264.58	1257.56	1251.92	1247.38	1243.72	1240.76	1238.37
75000	1376.02	1364.29	1354.90	1347.38	1341.34	1336.48	1332.55	1329.39	1326.83
80000	1467.76	1455.24	1445.23	1437.21	1430.76	1425.58	1421.39	1418.01	1415.28
100000	1834.70	1819.05	1806.54	1796.51	1788.45	1781.97	1776.74	1772.52	1769.10

222

MONTHLY PAYMENT 22%
NECESSARY TO AMORTIZE A LOAN

TERM AMOUNT	24 YEARS	25 YEARS	26 YEARS	27 YEARS	28 YEARS	29 YEARS	30 YEARS	35 YEARS	40 YEARS
$ 25	.45	.45	.45	.45	.44	.44	.44	.44	.44
50	.89	.89	.89	.89	.88	.88	.88	.88	.88
75	1.33	1.33	1.33	1.33	1.32	1.32	1.32	1.32	1.32
100	1.77	1.77	1.77	1.77	1.76	1.76	1.76	1.76	1.76
200	3.54	3.53	3.53	3.53	3.52	3.52	3.52	3.52	3.51
300	5.30	5.30	5.29	5.29	5.28	5.28	5.28	5.27	5.27
400	7.07	7.06	7.05	7.05	7.04	7.04	7.04	7.03	7.02
500	8.84	8.83	8.82	8.81	8.80	8.80	8.79	8.78	8.78
600	10.60	10.59	10.58	10.57	10.56	10.56	10.55	10.54	10.53
700	12.37	12.35	12.34	12.34	12.32	12.32	12.31	12.30	12.29
800	14.14	14.12	14.10	14.09	14.00	14.07	14.07	14.05	14.04
900	15.90	15.88	15.87	15.85	15.84	15.83	15.83	15.81	15.80
1000	17.67	17.65	17.63	17.61	17.60	17.59	17.58	17.56	17.55
2000	35.33	35.29	35.25	35.22	35.20	35.18	35.16	35.12	35.10
3000	53.00	52.93	52.87	52.83	52.79	52.77	52.74	52.68	52.65
4000	70.66	70.57	70.50	70.44	70.39	70.35	70.32	70.23	70.20
5000	88.32	88.21	88.12	88.05	87.99	87.94	87.90	87.79	87.75
6000	105.99	105.85	105.74	105.65	105.58	105.53	105.48	105.35	105.30
7000	123.65	123.49	123.37	123.26	123.18	123.11	123.06	122.91	122.85
8000	141.31	141.13	140.99	140.87	140.78	140.70	140.64	140.46	140.40
9000	158.98	158.77	158.61	158.48	158.37	158.29	158.22	158.02	157.95
10000	176.64	176.42	176.23	176.09	175.97	175.87	175.80	175.58	175.50
15000	264.96	264.62	264.35	264.13	263.95	263.81	263.69	263.36	263.25
20000	353.27	352.83	352.46	352.17	351.93	351.74	351.59	351.15	351.00
25000	441.59	441.03	440.58	440.21	439.92	439.68	439.48	438.94	438.75
30000	529.91	529.24	528.69	528.25	527.90	527.61	527.38	526.72	526.49
35000	618.22	617.44	616.81	616.30	615.88	615.54	615.27	614.51	614.24
36000	635.89	635.08	634.43	633.90	633.48	633.13	632.85	632.07	631.79
37000	653.55	652.72	652.06	651.51	651.07	650.72	650.43	649.62	649.34
38000	671.21	670.37	669.68	669.12	668.67	668.30	668.01	667.18	666.89
39000	688.88	688.01	687.30	686.73	686.27	685.89	685.59	684.74	684.44
40000	706.54	705.65	704.92	704.34	703.86	703.48	703.17	702.30	701.99
41000	724.20	723.29	722.55	721.95	721.46	721.06	720.75	719.85	719.54
42000	741.87	740.93	740.17	739.55	739.06	738.65	738.32	737.41	737.09
43000	759.53	758.57	757.79	757.16	756.65	756.24	755.90	754.97	754.64
44000	777.19	776.21	775.42	774.77	774.25	773.83	773.48	772.53	772.19
45000	794.86	793.85	793.04	792.38	791.85	791.41	791.06	790.08	789.74
46000	812.52	811.49	810.66	809.99	809.44	809.00	808.64	807.64	807.29
47000	830.18	829.13	828.28	827.60	827.04	826.59	826.22	825.20	824.84
48000	847.85	846.78	845.91	845.20	844.63	844.17	843.80	842.75	842.39
49000	865.51	864.42	863.53	862.81	862.23	861.76	861.38	860.31	859.94
50000	883.17	882.06	881.15	880.42	879.83	879.35	878.96	877.87	877.49
51000	900.84	899.70	898.78	898.03	897.42	896.93	896.54	895.43	895.04
52000	918.50	917.34	916.40	915.64	915.02	914.52	914.11	912.98	912.59
53000	936.17	934.98	934.02	933.25	932.62	932.11	931.69	930.54	930.14
54000	953.83	952.62	951.65	950.85	950.21	949.69	949.27	948.10	947.69
55000	971.49	970.26	969.27	968.46	967.81	967.28	966.85	965.66	965.23
56000	989.16	987.90	986.89	986.07	985.41	984.87	984.43	983.21	982.78
57000	1006.82	1005.55	1004.51	1003.68	1003.00	1002.45	1002.01	1000.77	1000.33
58000	1024.48	1023.19	1022.14	1021.29	1020.60	1020.04	1019.59	1018.33	1017.88
59000	1042.15	1040.83	1039.76	1038.90	1038.20	1037.63	1037.17	1035.88	1035.43
60000	1059.81	1058.47	1057.38	1056.50	1055.79	1055.21	1054.75	1053.44	1052.98
61000	1077.47	1076.11	1075.01	1074.11	1073.39	1072.80	1072.33	1071.00	1070.53
62000	1095.14	1093.75	1092.63	1091.72	1090.99	1090.39	1089.90	1088.56	1088.08
63000	1112.80	1111.39	1110.25	1109.33	1108.58	1107.98	1107.48	1106.11	1105.63
64000	1130.46	1129.03	1127.88	1126.94	1126.18	1125.56	1125.06	1123.67	1123.18
65000	1148.13	1146.67	1145.50	1144.55	1143.77	1143.15	1142.64	1141.23	1140.73
66000	1165.79	1164.32	1163.12	1162.15	1161.37	1160.74	1160.22	1158.79	1158.28
67000	1183.45	1181.96	1180.74	1179.76	1178.97	1178.32	1177.80	1176.34	1175.83
68000	1201.12	1199.60	1198.37	1197.37	1196.56	1195.91	1195.38	1193.90	1193.38
69000	1218.78	1217.24	1215.99	1214.98	1214.16	1213.50	1212.96	1211.46	1210.93
70000	1236.44	1234.88	1233.61	1232.59	1231.76	1231.08	1230.54	1229.01	1228.48
75000	1324.76	1323.08	1321.73	1320.63	1319.74	1319.02	1318.43	1316.80	1316.23
80000	1413.08	1411.29	1409.84	1408.67	1407.72	1406.95	1406.33	1404.59	1403.98
100000	1766.34	1764.11	1762.30	1760.84	1759.65	1758.69	1757.91	1755.73	1754.97

223

22½% MONTHLY PAYMENT
NECESSARY TO AMORTIZE A LOAN

TERM AMOUNT	1 YEAR	1½ YEARS	2 YEARS	2½ YEARS	3 YEARS	3½ YEARS	4 YEARS	4½ YEARS	5 YEARS
$ 25	2.34	1.64	1.30	1.09	.95	.86	.79	.73	.69
50	4.67	3.28	2.59	2.17	1.90	1.71	1.57	1.46	1.37
75	7.01	4.92	3.88	3.26	2.85	2.56	2.35	2.18	2.06
100	9.34	6.55	5.17	4.34	3.80	3.41	3.13	2.91	2.74
200	18.68	13.10	10.33	8.68	7.59	6.82	6.25	5.82	5.47
300	28.01	19.65	15.50	13.02	11.39	10.23	9.38	8.72	8.21
400	37.35	26.20	20.66	17.36	15.18	13.64	12.50	11.63	10.94
500	46.68	32.75	25.82	21.70	18.97	17.05	15.63	14.53	13.68
600	56.02	39.30	30.99	26.04	22.77	20.46	18.75	17.44	16.41
700	65.36	45.85	36.15	30.38	26.56	23.87	21.87	20.35	19.14
800	74.69	52.40	41.32	34.71	30.36	27.28	25.00	23.25	21.88
900	84.03	58.95	46.48	39.05	34.15	30.69	28.12	26.16	24.61
1000	93.36	65.50	51.64	43.39	37.94	34.10	31.25	29.06	27.35
2000	186.72	130.99	103.28	86.78	75.88	68.19	62.49	58.12	54.69
3000	280.08	196.48	154.92	130.17	113.82	102.28	93.73	87.18	82.03
4000	373.44	261.98	206.56	173.55	151.76	136.37	124.97	116.24	109.37
5000	466.80	327.47	258.19	216.94	189.70	170.46	156.21	145.30	136.72
6000	560.16	392.96	309.83	260.33	227.64	204.55	187.46	174.36	164.06
7000	653.52	458.45	361.47	303.72	265.58	238.64	218.70	203.42	191.40
8000	746.88	523.95	413.11	347.10	303.51	272.73	249.94	232.48	218.74
9000	840.24	589.44	464.74	390.49	341.45	306.82	281.18	261.54	246.09
10000	933.60	654.93	516.38	433.88	379.39	340.91	312.43	290.60	273.43
15000	1400.40	982.39	774.57	650.82	569.09	511.36	468.64	435.90	410.14
20000	1867.20	1309.86	1032.76	867.75	758.78	681.82	624.85	581.19	546.85
25000	2334.00	1637.32	1290.95	1084.69	948.47	852.27	781.06	726.49	683.57
30000	2800.80	1964.78	1549.14	1301.63	1138.17	1022.72	937.27	871.79	820.28
35000	3267.60	2292.25	1807.33	1518.56	1327.86	1193.17	1093.48	1017.09	956.99
36000	3360.96	2357.74	1858.96	1561.95	1365.80	1227.26	1124.72	1046.14	984.33
37000	3454.32	2423.23	1910.60	1605.34	1403.74	1261.35	1155.96	1075.20	1011.68
38000	3547.68	2488.72	1962.24	1648.72	1441.68	1295.44	1187.20	1104.26	1039.02
39000	3641.04	2554.22	2013.88	1692.11	1479.61	1329.53	1218.44	1133.32	1066.36
40000	3734.40	2619.71	2065.51	1735.50	1517.55	1363.63	1249.69	1162.38	1093.70
41000	3827.76	2685.20	2117.15	1778.89	1555.49	1397.72	1280.93	1191.44	1121.05
42000	3921.12	2750.69	2168.79	1822.27	1593.43	1431.81	1312.17	1220.50	1148.39
43000	4014.48	2816.19	2220.43	1865.66	1631.37	1465.90	1343.41	1249.56	1175.73
44000	4107.84	2881.68	2272.07	1909.05	1669.31	1499.99	1374.65	1278.62	1203.07
45000	4201.20	2947.17	2323.70	1952.44	1707.25	1534.08	1405.90	1307.68	1230.42
46000	4294.56	3012.66	2375.34	1995.82	1745.19	1568.17	1437.14	1336.74	1257.76
47000	4387.92	3078.16	2426.98	2039.21	1783.12	1602.26	1468.38	1365.80	1285.10
48000	4481.28	3143.65	2478.62	2082.60	1821.06	1636.35	1499.62	1394.86	1312.44
49000	4574.64	3209.14	2530.25	2125.99	1859.00	1670.44	1530.86	1423.92	1339.79
50000	4668.00	3274.63	2581.89	2169.37	1896.94	1704.53	1562.11	1452.98	1367.13
51000	4761.36	3340.13	2633.53	2212.76	1934.88	1738.62	1593.35	1482.04	1394.47
52000	4854.72	3405.62	2685.17	2256.15	1972.82	1772.71	1624.59	1511.10	1421.81
53000	4948.08	3471.11	2736.80	2299.54	2010.76	1806.80	1655.83	1540.16	1449.15
54000	5041.44	3536.60	2788.44	2342.92	2048.70	1840.89	1687.07	1569.21	1476.50
55000	5134.80	3602.10	2840.08	2386.31	2086.63	1874.98	1718.32	1598.27	1503.84
56000	5228.16	3667.59	2891.72	2429.70	2124.57	1909.07	1749.56	1627.33	1531.18
57000	5321.52	3733.08	2943.36	2473.08	2162.51	1943.16	1780.80	1656.39	1558.52
58000	5414.88	3798.57	2994.99	2516.47	2200.45	1977.25	1812.04	1685.45	1585.87
59000	5508.24	3864.07	3046.63	2559.86	2238.39	2011.34	1843.28	1714.51	1613.21
60000	5601.60	3929.56	3098.27	2603.25	2276.33	2045.44	1874.53	1743.57	1640.55
61000	5694.96	3995.05	3149.91	2646.63	2314.27	2079.53	1905.77	1772.63	1667.89
62000	5788.32	4060.55	3201.54	2690.02	2352.21	2113.62	1937.01	1801.69	1695.24
63000	5881.68	4126.04	3253.18	2733.41	2390.14	2147.71	1968.25	1830.75	1722.58
64000	5975.04	4191.53	3304.82	2776.80	2428.08	2181.80	1999.49	1859.81	1749.92
65000	6068.40	4257.02	3356.46	2820.18	2466.02	2215.89	2030.74	1888.87	1777.26
66000	6161.76	4322.52	3408.10	2863.57	2503.96	2249.98	2061.98	1917.93	1804.61
67000	6255.12	4388.01	3459.73	2906.96	2541.90	2284.07	2093.22	1946.99	1831.95
68000	6348.48	4453.50	3511.37	2950.35	2579.84	2318.16	2124.46	1976.05	1859.29
69000	6441.84	4518.99	3563.01	2993.73	2617.78	2352.25	2155.70	2005.11	1886.63
70000	6535.20	4584.49	3614.65	3037.12	2655.72	2386.34	2186.95	2034.17	1913.98
75000	7002.00	4911.95	3872.83	3254.06	2845.41	2556.79	2343.16	2179.46	2050.69
80000	7468.80	5239.41	4131.02	3470.99	3035.10	2727.25	2499.37	2324.76	2187.40
100000	9336.00	6549.26	5163.78	4338.74	3793.88	3409.06	3124.21	2905.95	2734.25

224

MONTHLY PAYMENT $22\frac{1}{2}\%$
NECESSARY TO AMORTIZE A LOAN

TERM / AMOUNT	6 YEARS	7 YEARS	8 YEARS	9 YEARS	10 YEARS	11 YEARS	12 YEARS	13 YEARS	14 YEARS
$ 25	.63	.58	.55	.53	.51	.50	.49	.48	.48
50	1.25	1.16	1.10	1.06	1.02	1.00	.98	.96	.95
75	1.87	1.74	1.65	1.58	1.53	1.49	1.46	1.44	1.42
100	2.49	2.32	2.20	2.11	2.04	1.99	1.95	1.92	1.89
200	4.97	4.63	4.39	4.21	4.07	3.97	3.89	3.83	3.78
300	7.46	6.94	6.58	6.31	6.11	5.95	5.83	5.74	5.67
400	9.94	9.26	8.77	8.41	8.14	7.94	7.78	7.65	7.56
500	12.42	11.57	10.96	10.51	10.17	9.92	9.72	9.57	9.45
600	14.91	13.88	13.15	12.61	12.21	11.90	11.66	11.48	11.33
700	17.39	16.19	15.34	14.71	14.24	13.88	13.61	13.39	13.22
800	19.88	18.51	17.53	16.81	16.28	15.87	15.55	15.30	15.11
900	22.36	20.82	19.72	18.91	18.31	17.85	17.49	17.22	17.00
1000	24.84	23.13	21.91	21.02	20.34	19.83	19.44	19.13	18.89
2000	49.68	46.26	43.82	42.03	40.68	39.66	38.87	38.25	37.77
3000	74.52	69.38	65.72	63.04	61.02	59.48	58.30	57.37	56.65
4000	99.36	92.51	87.63	84.05	81.36	79.31	77.73	76.50	75.53
5000	124.19	115.63	109.53	105.06	101.70	99.14	97.16	95.62	94.41
6000	149.03	138.76	131.44	126.07	122.04	118.96	116.59	114.74	113.29
7000	173.87	161.89	153.35	147.08	142.38	138.79	136.02	133.87	132.17
8000	198.71	185.01	175.25	168.09	162.72	158.62	155.46	152.99	151.06
9000	223.54	208.14	197.16	189.10	183.05	178.44	174.89	172.11	169.94
10000	248.38	231.26	219.06	210.11	203.39	198.27	194.32	191.24	188.82
15000	372.57	346.89	328.59	315.16	305.09	297.40	291.47	286.85	283.22
20000	496.76	462.52	438.12	420.22	406.78	396.54	388.63	382.47	377.63
25000	620.94	578.15	547.65	525.27	508.47	495.67	485.79	478.08	472.04
30000	745.13	693.78	657.18	630.32	610.17	594.80	582.94	573.70	566.44
35000	869.32	809.41	766.71	735.37	711.86	693.94	680.10	669.32	660.85
36000	894.16	832.53	788.62	756.38	732.20	713.76	699.53	688.44	679.73
37000	919.00	855.66	810.53	777.39	752.54	733.59	718.96	707.56	698.61
38000	943.83	878.79	832.43	798.41	772.88	753.42	738.39	726.69	717.49
39000	968.67	901.91	854.34	819.42	793.22	773.24	757.82	745.81	736.37
40000	993.51	925.04	876.24	840.43	813.56	793.07	777.26	764.93	755.26
41000	1018.35	948.16	898.15	861.44	833.90	812.90	796.69	784.05	774.14
42000	1043.18	971.29	920.06	882.45	854.23	832.72	816.12	803.18	793.02
43000	1068.02	994.41	941.96	903.46	874.57	852.55	835.55	822.30	811.90
44000	1092.86	1017.54	963.87	924.47	894.91	872.38	854.98	841.42	830.78
45000	1117.70	1040.67	985.77	945.48	915.25	892.20	874.41	860.55	849.66
46000	1142.53	1063.79	1007.68	966.49	935.59	912.03	893.84	879.67	868.54
47000	1167.37	1086.92	1029.59	987.50	955.93	931.86	913.27	898.79	887.42
48000	1192.21	1110.04	1051.49	1008.51	976.27	951.68	932.71	917.92	906.31
49000	1217.05	1133.17	1073.40	1029.52	996.61	971.51	952.14	937.04	925.19
50000	1241.88	1156.30	1095.30	1050.53	1016.94	991.34	971.57	956.16	944.07
51000	1266.72	1179.42	1117.21	1071.54	1037.28	1011.16	991.00	975.29	962.95
52000	1291.56	1202.55	1139.12	1092.55	1057.62	1030.99	1010.43	994.41	981.83
53000	1316.40	1225.67	1161.02	1113.56	1077.96	1050.82	1029.86	1013.53	1000.71
54000	1341.23	1248.80	1182.93	1134.57	1098.30	1070.64	1049.29	1032.66	1019.59
55000	1366.07	1271.92	1204.83	1155.58	1118.64	1090.47	1068.72	1051.78	1038.47
56000	1390.91	1295.05	1226.74	1176.59	1138.98	1110.30	1088.16	1070.90	1057.36
57000	1415.75	1318.18	1248.65	1197.61	1159.32	1130.12	1107.59	1090.03	1076.24
58000	1440.58	1341.30	1270.55	1218.62	1179.65	1149.95	1127.02	1109.15	1095.12
59000	1465.42	1364.43	1292.46	1239.63	1199.99	1169.78	1146.45	1128.27	1114.00
60000	1490.26	1387.55	1314.36	1260.64	1220.33	1189.60	1165.88	1147.39	1132.88
61000	1515.10	1410.68	1336.27	1281.65	1240.67	1209.43	1185.31	1166.52	1151.76
62000	1539.93	1433.81	1358.18	1302.66	1261.01	1229.26	1204.74	1185.64	1170.64
63000	1564.77	1456.93	1380.08	1323.67	1281.35	1249.08	1224.17	1204.76	1189.52
64000	1589.61	1480.06	1401.99	1344.68	1301.69	1268.91	1243.61	1223.89	1208.41
65000	1614.45	1503.18	1423.89	1365.69	1322.03	1288.74	1263.04	1243.01	1227.29
66000	1639.29	1526.31	1445.80	1386.70	1342.37	1308.56	1282.47	1262.13	1246.17
67000	1664.12	1549.43	1467.71	1407.71	1362.70	1328.39	1301.90	1281.26	1265.05
68000	1688.96	1572.56	1489.61	1428.72	1383.04	1348.22	1321.33	1300.38	1283.93
69000	1713.80	1595.69	1511.52	1449.73	1403.38	1368.04	1340.76	1319.50	1302.81
70000	1738.64	1618.81	1533.42	1470.74	1423.72	1387.87	1360.19	1338.63	1321.69
75000	1862.82	1734.44	1642.95	1575.79	1525.41	1487.00	1457.35	1434.24	1416.10
80000	1987.01	1850.07	1752.48	1680.85	1627.11	1586.13	1554.51	1529.86	1510.51
100000	2483.76	2312.59	2190.60	2101.06	2033.88	1982.67	1943.13	1912.32	1888.13

22½%

MONTHLY PAYMENT
NECESSARY TO AMORTIZE A LOAN

TERM AMOUNT	15 YEARS	16 YEARS	17 YEARS	18 YEARS	19 YEARS	20 YEARS	21 YEARS	22 YEARS	23 YEARS
$ 25	.47	.47	.47	.46	.46	.46	.46	.46	.46
50	.94	.93	.93	.92	.92	.91	.91	.91	.91
75	1.41	1.40	1.39	1.38	1.37	1.37	1.36	1.36	1.36
100	1.87	1.86	1.85	1.84	1.83	1.82	1.82	1.81	1.81
200	3.74	3.71	3.69	3.67	3.65	3.64	3.63	3.62	3.62
300	5.61	5.57	5.53	5.50	5.48	5.46	5.44	5.43	5.42
400	7.48	7.42	7.37	7.33	7.30	7.28	7.26	7.24	7.23
500	9.35	9.27	9.21	9.17	9.13	9.10	9.07	9.05	9.04
600	11.22	11.13	11.06	11.00	10.95	10.91	10.88	10.86	10.84
700	13.09	12.98	12.90	12.83	12.78	12.73	12.70	12.67	12.65
800	14.96	14.84	14.74	14.66	14.60	14.55	14.51	14.48	14.45
900	16.83	16.69	16.58	16.49	16.43	16.37	16.32	16.29	16.26
1000	18.70	18.54	18.42	18.33	18.25	18.19	18.14	18.10	18.07
2000	37.39	37.08	36.84	36.65	36.49	36.37	36.27	36.19	36.13
3000	56.08	55.62	55.26	54.97	54.74	54.55	54.40	54.28	54.19
4000	74.77	74.16	73.68	73.29	72.98	72.74	72.54	72.38	72.25
5000	93.46	92.70	92.10	91.61	91.23	90.92	90.67	90.47	90.31
6000	112.15	111.24	110.51	109.94	109.47	109.10	108.80	108.56	108.37
7000	130.84	129.78	128.93	128.26	127.72	127.28	126.94	126.66	126.43
8000	149.53	148.31	147.35	146.58	145.96	145.47	145.07	144.75	144.49
9000	168.22	166.85	165.77	164.90	164.21	163.65	163.20	162.84	162.55
10000	186.91	185.39	184.19	183.22	182.45	181.83	181.34	180.94	180.62
15000	280.36	278.09	276.28	274.83	273.67	272.75	272.00	271.40	270.92
20000	373.81	370.78	368.37	366.44	364.90	363.66	362.67	361.87	361.23
25000	467.26	463.47	460.46	458.05	456.12	454.57	453.33	452.33	451.53
30000	560.71	556.17	552.55	549.66	547.34	545.49	544.00	542.80	541.84
35000	654.16	648.86	644.64	641.26	638.57	636.40	634.66	633.27	632.14
36000	672.85	667.40	663.05	659.59	656.81	654.58	652.80	651.36	650.20
37000	691.54	685.94	681.47	677.91	675.05	672.77	670.93	669.45	668.26
38000	710.23	704.48	699.89	696.23	693.30	690.95	689.06	687.55	686.32
39000	728.92	723.01	718.31	714.55	711.54	709.13	707.20	705.64	704.39
40000	747.61	741.55	736.73	732.87	729.79	727.31	725.33	723.73	722.45
41000	766.30	760.09	755.14	751.19	748.03	745.50	743.46	741.82	740.51
42000	785.00	778.63	773.56	769.52	766.28	763.68	761.59	759.92	758.57
43000	803.69	797.17	791.98	787.84	784.52	781.86	779.73	778.01	776.63
44000	822.38	815.71	810.40	806.16	802.77	800.05	797.86	796.10	794.69
45000	841.07	834.25	828.82	824.48	821.01	818.23	815.99	814.20	812.75
46000	859.76	852.79	847.23	842.80	839.26	836.41	834.13	832.29	830.81
47000	878.45	871.32	865.65	861.12	857.50	854.59	852.26	850.38	848.87
48000	897.14	889.86	884.07	879.45	875.74	872.78	870.39	868.48	866.93
49000	915.83	908.40	902.49	897.77	893.99	890.96	888.53	886.57	885.00
50000	934.52	926.94	920.91	916.09	912.23	909.14	906.66	904.66	903.06
51000	953.21	945.48	939.33	934.41	930.48	927.32	924.79	922.76	921.12
52000	971.90	964.02	957.74	952.73	948.72	945.51	942.93	940.85	939.18
53000	990.59	982.56	976.16	971.05	966.97	963.69	961.06	958.94	957.24
54000	1009.28	1001.09	994.58	989.38	985.21	981.87	979.19	977.04	975.30
55000	1027.97	1019.63	1013.00	1007.70	1003.46	1000.06	997.32	995.13	993.36
56000	1046.66	1038.17	1031.42	1026.02	1021.70	1018.24	1015.46	1013.22	1011.42
57000	1065.35	1056.71	1049.83	1044.34	1039.95	1036.42	1033.59	1031.32	1029.48
58000	1084.04	1075.25	1068.25	1062.66	1058.19	1054.60	1051.72	1049.41	1047.54
59000	1102.73	1093.79	1086.67	1080.98	1076.44	1072.79	1069.86	1067.50	1065.61
60000	1121.42	1112.33	1105.09	1099.31	1094.68	1090.97	1087.99	1085.59	1083.67
61000	1140.11	1130.87	1123.51	1117.63	1112.92	1109.15	1106.12	1103.69	1101.73
62000	1158.80	1149.40	1141.92	1135.95	1131.17	1127.33	1124.26	1121.78	1119.79
63000	1177.49	1167.94	1160.34	1154.27	1149.41	1145.52	1142.39	1139.87	1137.85
64000	1196.18	1186.48	1178.76	1172.59	1167.66	1163.70	1160.52	1157.97	1155.91
65000	1214.87	1205.02	1197.18	1190.91	1185.90	1181.88	1178.66	1176.06	1173.97
66000	1233.56	1223.56	1215.60	1209.24	1204.15	1200.07	1196.79	1194.15	1192.03
67000	1252.25	1242.10	1234.01	1227.56	1222.39	1218.25	1214.92	1212.25	1210.09
68000	1270.94	1260.64	1252.43	1245.88	1240.64	1236.43	1233.05	1230.34	1228.16
69000	1289.63	1279.18	1270.85	1264.20	1258.88	1254.61	1251.19	1248.43	1246.22
70000	1308.32	1297.71	1289.27	1282.52	1277.13	1272.80	1269.32	1266.53	1264.28
75000	1401.77	1390.41	1381.36	1374.13	1368.35	1363.71	1359.99	1356.99	1354.58
80000	1495.22	1483.10	1473.45	1465.74	1459.57	1454.62	1450.65	1447.46	1444.89
100000	1869.03	1853.88	1841.81	1832.17	1824.46	1818.28	1813.31	1809.32	1806.11

226

MONTHLY PAYMENT 22½%
NECESSARY TO AMORTIZE A LOAN

TERM AMOUNT	24 YEARS	25 YEARS	26 YEARS	27 YEARS	28 YEARS	29 YEARS	30 YEARS	35 YEARS	40 YEARS
$ 25	.46	.46	.45	.45	.45	.45	.45	.45	.45
50	.91	.91	.90	.90	.90	.90	.90	.90	.90
75	1.36	1.36	1.35	1.35	1.35	1.35	1.35	1.35	1.35
100	1.81	1.81	1.80	1.80	1.80	1.80	1.80	1.80	1.80
200	3.61	3.61	3.60	3.60	3.60	3.60	3.60	3.59	3.59
300	5.42	5.41	5.40	5.40	5.40	5.39	5.39	5.39	5.38
400	7.22	7.21	7.20	7.20	7.19	7.19	7.19	7.18	7.18
500	9.02	9.01	9.00	9.00	8.99	8.99	8.98	8.97	8.97
600	10.83	10.81	10.80	10.80	10.79	10.78	10.78	10.77	10.76
700	12.63	12.62	12.60	12.59	12.59	12.58	12.57	12.56	12.56
800	14.43	14.42	14.40	14.39	14.30	14.38	14.37	14.35	14.35
900	16.24	16.22	16.20	16.19	16.18	16.17	16.17	16.15	16.14
1000	18.04	18.02	18.00	17.99	17.98	17.97	17.96	17.94	17.94
2000	36.08	36.03	36.00	35.97	35.95	35.93	35.92	35.88	35.87
3000	54.11	54.05	54.00	53.96	53.92	53.90	53.88	53.82	53.80
4000	72.15	72.06	71.99	71.94	71.90	71.86	71.83	71.75	71.73
5000	90.18	90.08	89.99	89.92	89.87	89.83	89.79	89.69	89.66
6000	108.22	108.09	107.99	107.91	107.84	107.79	107.75	107.63	107.59
7000	126.25	126.11	125.99	125.89	125.82	125.75	125.70	125.57	125.52
8000	144.29	144.12	143.98	143.88	143.79	143.72	143.66	143.50	143.45
9000	162.32	162.13	161.98	161.86	161.76	161.68	161.62	161.44	161.38
10000	180.36	180.15	179.98	179.84	179.73	179.65	179.58	179.38	179.31
15000	270.53	270.22	269.97	269.76	269.60	269.47	269.36	269.07	268.96
20000	360.71	360.29	359.95	359.68	359.46	359.29	359.15	358.75	358.62
25000	450.88	450.36	449.94	449.60	449.33	449.11	448.93	448.44	448.27
30000	541.06	540.43	539.93	539.52	539.19	538.93	538.72	538.13	537.92
35000	631.24	630.51	629.92	629.44	629.06	628.75	628.50	627.81	627.58
36000	649.27	648.52	647.91	647.43	647.03	646.71	646.46	645.75	645.51
37000	667.31	666.53	665.91	665.41	665.01	664.68	664.41	663.69	663.44
38000	685.34	684.55	683.91	683.39	682.98	682.64	682.37	681.63	681.37
39000	703.38	702.56	701.91	701.38	700.95	700.61	700.33	699.56	699.30
40000	721.41	720.58	719.90	719.36	718.92	718.57	718.29	717.50	717.23
41000	739.45	738.59	737.90	737.35	736.90	736.54	736.24	735.44	735.16
42000	757.48	756.61	755.90	755.33	754.87	754.50	754.20	753.38	753.09
43000	775.52	774.62	773.90	773.31	772.84	772.46	772.16	771.31	771.02
44000	793.55	792.63	791.89	791.30	790.82	790.43	790.11	789.25	788.95
45000	811.59	810.65	809.89	809.28	808.79	808.39	808.07	807.19	806.88
46000	829.62	828.66	827.89	827.27	826.76	826.36	826.03	825.12	824.81
47000	847.66	846.68	845.89	845.25	844.74	844.32	843.99	843.06	842.74
48000	865.69	864.69	863.88	863.23	862.71	862.28	861.94	861.00	860.68
49000	883.73	882.71	881.88	881.22	880.68	880.25	879.90	878.94	878.61
50000	901.76	900.72	899.88	899.20	898.65	898.21	897.86	896.87	896.54
51000	919.80	918.73	917.88	917.19	916.63	916.18	915.81	914.81	914.47
52000	937.83	936.75	935.87	935.17	934.60	934.14	933.77	932.75	932.40
53000	955.87	954.76	953.87	953.15	952.57	952.11	951.73	950.69	950.33
54000	973.90	972.78	971.87	971.14	970.55	970.07	969.68	968.62	968.26
55000	991.94	990.79	989.87	989.12	988.52	988.03	987.64	986.56	986.19
56000	1009.97	1008.81	1007.86	1007.10	1006.49	1006.00	1005.60	1004.50	1004.12
57000	1028.01	1026.82	1025.86	1025.09	1024.47	1023.96	1023.56	1022.44	1022.05
58000	1046.04	1044.83	1043.86	1043.07	1042.44	1041.93	1041.51	1040.37	1039.98
59000	1064.08	1062.85	1061.86	1061.06	1060.41	1059.89	1059.47	1058.31	1057.91
60000	1082.11	1080.86	1079.85	1079.04	1078.38	1077.85	1077.43	1076.25	1075.84
61000	1100.15	1098.88	1097.85	1097.02	1096.36	1095.82	1095.38	1094.19	1093.77
62000	1118.18	1116.89	1115.85	1115.01	1114.33	1113.78	1113.34	1112.12	1111.70
63000	1136.22	1134.91	1133.85	1132.99	1132.30	1131.75	1131.30	1130.06	1129.63
64000	1154.26	1152.92	1151.84	1150.98	1150.28	1149.71	1149.25	1148.00	1147.57
65000	1172.29	1170.93	1169.84	1168.96	1168.25	1167.67	1167.21	1165.93	1165.50
66000	1190.33	1188.95	1187.84	1186.94	1186.22	1185.64	1185.17	1183.87	1183.43
67000	1208.36	1206.96	1205.84	1204.93	1204.19	1203.60	1203.13	1201.81	1201.36
68000	1226.40	1224.98	1223.83	1222.91	1222.17	1221.57	1221.08	1219.75	1219.29
69000	1244.43	1242.99	1241.83	1240.90	1240.14	1239.53	1239.04	1237.68	1237.22
70000	1262.47	1261.01	1259.83	1258.88	1258.11	1257.50	1257.00	1255.62	1255.15
75000	1352.64	1351.08	1349.82	1348.80	1347.98	1347.32	1346.78	1345.31	1344.80
80000	1442.82	1441.15	1439.80	1438.72	1437.84	1437.14	1436.57	1435.00	1434.46
100000	1803.52	1801.44	1799.75	1798.40	1797.30	1796.42	1795.71	1793.74	1793.07

23% MONTHLY PAYMENT
NECESSARY TO AMORTIZE A LOAN

TERM / AMOUNT	1 YEAR	1½ YEARS	2 YEARS	2½ YEARS	3 YEARS	3½ YEARS	4 YEARS	4½ YEARS	5 YEARS
$ 25	2.34	1.65	1.30	1.10	.96	.86	.79	.74	.70
50	4.68	3.29	2.60	2.19	1.91	1.72	1.58	1.47	1.39
75	7.02	4.93	3.89	3.28	2.87	2.58	2.37	2.20	2.08
100	9.36	6.58	5.19	4.37	3.82	3.44	3.15	2.94	2.77
200	18.72	13.15	10.38	8.73	7.64	6.87	6.30	5.87	5.53
300	28.08	19.72	15.56	13.09	11.46	10.30	9.45	8.80	8.29
400	37.44	26.29	20.75	17.45	15.27	13.74	12.60	11.73	11.05
500	46.79	32.86	25.94	21.81	19.09	17.17	15.75	14.66	13.81
600	56.15	39.43	31.12	26.18	22.91	20.60	18.90	17.59	16.57
700	65.51	46.00	36.31	30.54	26.73	24.04	22.05	20.52	19.33
800	74.87	52.58	41.50	34.90	30.54	27.47	25.20	23.46	22.09
900	84.23	59.15	46.68	39.26	34.36	30.90	28.35	26.39	24.85
1000	93.58	65.72	51.87	43.62	38.18	34.34	31.49	29.32	27.61
2000	187.16	131.43	103.73	87.24	76.35	68.67	62.98	58.63	55.21
3000	280.74	197.15	155.59	130.86	114.53	103.00	94.47	87.94	82.81
4000	374.32	262.86	207.46	174.48	152.70	137.33	125.96	117.26	110.41
5000	467.90	328.57	259.32	218.09	190.88	171.67	157.45	146.57	138.01
6000	561.48	394.29	311.18	261.71	229.05	206.00	188.94	175.88	165.61
7000	655.06	460.00	363.05	305.33	267.23	240.33	220.43	205.19	193.22
8000	748.64	525.72	414.91	348.95	305.40	274.66	251.92	234.51	220.82
9000	842.22	591.43	466.77	392.57	343.58	309.00	283.41	263.82	248.42
10000	935.80	657.14	518.64	436.18	381.75	343.33	314.90	293.13	276.02
15000	1403.70	985.71	777.95	654.27	572.63	514.99	472.35	439.70	414.03
20000	1871.60	1314.28	1037.27	872.36	763.50	686.65	629.80	586.26	552.04
25000	2339.50	1642.85	1296.58	1090.45	954.37	858.31	787.24	732.83	690.05
30000	2807.40	1971.42	1555.90	1308.54	1145.25	1029.97	944.69	879.39	828.05
35000	3275.30	2299.99	1815.21	1526.63	1336.12	1201.63	1102.14	1025.95	966.06
36000	3368.88	2365.71	1867.08	1570.25	1374.29	1235.97	1133.63	1055.27	993.66
37000	3462.46	2431.42	1918.94	1613.86	1412.47	1270.30	1165.12	1084.58	1021.26
38000	3556.03	2497.13	1970.80	1657.48	1450.64	1304.63	1196.61	1113.89	1048.87
39000	3649.61	2562.85	2022.67	1701.10	1488.82	1338.96	1228.10	1143.20	1076.47
40000	3743.19	2628.56	2074.53	1744.72	1526.99	1373.29	1259.59	1172.52	1104.07
41000	3836.77	2694.27	2126.39	1788.34	1565.17	1407.63	1291.08	1201.83	1131.67
42000	3930.35	2759.99	2178.26	1831.95	1603.34	1441.96	1322.57	1231.14	1159.27
43000	4023.93	2825.70	2230.12	1875.57	1641.52	1476.29	1354.06	1260.46	1186.87
44000	4117.51	2891.42	2281.98	1919.19	1679.69	1510.62	1385.55	1289.77	1214.48
45000	4211.09	2957.13	2333.85	1962.81	1717.87	1544.96	1417.04	1319.08	1242.08
46000	4304.67	3022.84	2385.71	2006.43	1756.04	1579.29	1448.52	1348.39	1269.68
47000	4398.25	3088.56	2437.57	2050.04	1794.22	1613.62	1480.01	1377.71	1297.28
48000	4491.83	3154.27	2489.44	2093.66	1832.39	1647.95	1511.50	1407.02	1324.88
49000	4585.41	3219.99	2541.30	2137.28	1870.57	1682.28	1542.99	1436.33	1352.48
50000	4678.99	3285.70	2593.16	2180.90	1908.74	1716.62	1574.48	1465.65	1380.09
51000	4772.57	3351.41	2645.02	2224.51	1946.92	1750.95	1605.97	1494.96	1407.69
52000	4866.15	3417.13	2696.89	2268.13	1985.09	1785.28	1637.46	1524.27	1435.29
53000	4959.73	3482.84	2748.75	2311.75	2023.26	1819.61	1668.95	1553.58	1462.89
54000	5053.31	3548.56	2800.61	2355.37	2061.44	1853.95	1700.44	1582.90	1490.49
55000	5146.89	3614.27	2852.48	2398.99	2099.61	1888.28	1731.93	1612.21	1518.09
56000	5240.47	3679.98	2904.34	2442.60	2137.79	1922.61	1763.42	1641.52	1545.70
57000	5334.05	3745.70	2956.20	2486.22	2175.96	1956.94	1794.91	1670.84	1573.30
58000	5427.63	3811.41	3008.07	2529.84	2214.14	1991.27	1826.40	1700.15	1600.90
59000	5521.21	3877.13	3059.93	2573.46	2252.31	2025.61	1857.89	1729.46	1628.50
60000	5614.79	3942.84	3111.79	2617.08	2290.49	2059.94	1889.38	1758.77	1656.10
61000	5708.37	4008.55	3163.66	2660.69	2328.66	2094.27	1920.87	1788.09	1683.70
62000	5801.95	4074.27	3215.52	2704.31	2366.84	2128.60	1952.36	1817.40	1711.30
63000	5895.53	4139.98	3267.38	2747.93	2405.01	2162.94	1983.85	1846.71	1738.91
64000	5989.11	4205.69	3319.25	2791.55	2443.19	2197.27	2015.34	1876.03	1766.51
65000	6082.69	4271.41	3371.11	2835.16	2481.36	2231.60	2046.83	1905.34	1794.11
66000	6176.27	4337.12	3422.97	2878.78	2519.54	2265.93	2078.32	1934.65	1821.71
67000	6269.85	4402.84	3474.83	2922.40	2557.71	2300.26	2109.81	1963.96	1849.31
68000	6363.43	4468.55	3526.70	2966.02	2595.89	2334.60	2141.30	1993.28	1876.91
69000	6457.01	4534.26	3578.56	3009.64	2634.06	2368.93	2172.78	2022.59	1904.52
70000	6550.59	4599.98	3630.42	3053.25	2672.23	2403.26	2204.27	2051.90	1932.12
75000	7018.49	4928.55	3889.74	3271.34	2863.11	2574.92	2361.72	2198.47	2070.13
80000	7486.38	5257.12	4149.06	3489.43	3053.98	2746.58	2519.17	2345.03	2208.13
100000	9357.98	6571.40	5186.32	4361.79	3817.48	3433.23	3148.96	2931.29	2760.17

228

MONTHLY PAYMENT 23%
NECESSARY TO AMORTIZE A LOAN

TERM AMOUNT	6 YEARS	7 YEARS	8 YEARS	9 YEARS	10 YEARS	11 YEARS	12 YEARS	13 YEARS	14 YEARS
$ 25	.63	.59	.56	.54	.52	.51	.50	49	49
50	1.26	1.18	1.11	1.07	1.04	1.01	.99	.98	.97
75	1.89	1.76	1.67	1.60	1.55	1.52	1.49	1.46	1.45
100	2.52	2.35	2.22	2.14	2.07	2.02	1.98	1.95	1.93
200	5.03	4.69	4.44	4.27	4.13	4.03	3.96	3.90	3.85
300	7.54	7.03	6.66	6.40	6.20	6.05	5.93	5.84	5.77
400	10.05	9.37	8.88	8.53	8.26	8.06	7.91	7.79	7.69
500	12.56	11.71	11.10	10.66	10.33	10.08	9.88	9.73	9.62
600	15.07	14.05	13.32	12.79	12.39	12.09	11.86	11.68	11.54
700	17.58	16.39	15.54	14.92	14.46	14.11	13.84	13.62	13.46
800	20.09	18.73	17.76	17.05	16.52	16.12	15.81	15.57	15.38
900	22.60	21.07	19.98	19.19	18.59	18.14	17.79	17.52	17.30
1000	25.11	23.41	22.20	21.32	20.65	20.15	19.76	19.46	19.23
2000	50.22	46.82	44.40	42.63	41.30	40.30	39.52	38.92	38.45
3000	75.33	70.23	66.60	63.94	61.95	60.44	59.28	58.37	57.67
4000	100.44	93.63	88.80	85.25	82.60	80.59	79.03	77.83	76.89
5000	125.55	117.04	110.99	106.56	103.25	100.73	98.79	97.28	96.11
6000	150.65	140.45	133.19	127.88	123.90	120.88	118.55	116.74	115.33
7000	175.76	163.86	155.39	149.19	144.55	141.02	138.31	136.20	134.55
8000	200.87	187.26	177.59	170.50	165.20	161.17	158.06	155.65	153.77
9000	225.98	210.67	199.78	191.81	185.85	181.31	177.82	175.11	172.99
10000	251.09	234.08	221.98	213.12	206.49	201.46	197.58	194.56	192.21
15000	376.63	351.11	332.97	319.68	309.74	302.18	296.36	291.84	288.31
20000	502.17	468.15	443.96	426.24	412.98	402.91	395.15	389.12	384.41
25000	627.71	585.18	554.95	532.80	516.23	503.63	493.93	486.40	480.51
30000	753.25	702.22	665.93	639.36	619.47	604.36	592.72	583.68	576.61
35000	878.79	819.26	776.92	745.92	722.72	705.08	691.51	680.96	672.71
36000	903.90	842.66	799.12	767.23	743.37	725.23	711.26	700.42	691.93
37000	929.00	866.07	821.32	788.54	764.02	745.37	731.02	719.87	711.15
38000	954.11	889.48	843.51	809.85	784.67	765.52	750.78	739.33	730.37
39000	979.22	912.88	865.71	831.16	805.31	785.66	770.53	758.78	749.59
40000	1004.33	936.29	887.91	852.48	825.96	805.81	790.29	778.24	768.81
41000	1029.44	959.70	910.11	873.79	846.61	825.95	810.05	797.70	788.03
42000	1054.54	983.11	932.30	895.10	867.26	846.10	829.81	817.15	807.25
43000	1079.65	1006.51	954.50	916.41	887.91	866.24	849.56	836.61	826.47
44000	1104.76	1029.92	976.70	937.72	908.56	886.39	869.32	856.06	845.69
45000	1129.87	1053.33	998.90	959.04	929.21	906.53	889.08	875.52	864.91
46000	1154.98	1076.73	1021.09	980.35	949.86	926.68	908.83	894.98	884.13
47000	1180.08	1100.14	1043.29	1001.66	970.51	946.82	928.59	914.43	903.35
48000	1205.19	1123.55	1065.49	1022.97	991.16	966.97	948.35	933.89	922.57
49000	1230.30	1146.96	1087.69	1044.28	1011.80	987.11	968.11	953.34	941.79
50000	1255.41	1170.36	1109.89	1065.59	1032.45	1007.26	987.86	972.80	961.01
51000	1280.52	1193.77	1132.08	1086.91	1053.10	1027.40	1007.62	992.25	980.23
52000	1305.62	1217.18	1154.28	1108.22	1073.75	1047.55	1027.38	1011.71	999.45
53000	1330.73	1240.58	1176.48	1129.53	1094.40	1067.69	1047.14	1031.17	1018.67
54000	1355.84	1263.99	1198.68	1150.84	1115.05	1087.84	1066.89	1050.62	1037.89
55000	1380.95	1287.40	1220.87	1172.15	1135.70	1107.98	1086.65	1070.08	1057.11
56000	1406.06	1310.81	1243.07	1193.46	1156.35	1128.13	1106.41	1089.53	1076.33
57000	1431.16	1334.21	1265.27	1214.78	1177.00	1148.27	1126.16	1108.99	1095.55
58000	1456.27	1357.62	1287.47	1236.09	1197.65	1168.42	1145.92	1128.45	1114.77
59000	1481.38	1381.03	1309.66	1257.40	1218.29	1188.56	1165.68	1147.90	1133.99
60000	1506.49	1404.43	1331.86	1278.71	1238.94	1208.71	1185.44	1167.36	1153.21
61000	1531.60	1427.84	1354.06	1300.02	1259.59	1228.85	1205.19	1186.81	1172.43
62000	1556.71	1451.25	1376.26	1321.34	1280.24	1249.00	1224.95	1206.27	1191.65
63000	1581.81	1474.66	1398.45	1342.65	1300.89	1269.14	1244.71	1225.73	1210.87
64000	1606.92	1498.06	1420.65	1363.96	1321.54	1289.29	1264.46	1245.18	1230.09
65000	1632.03	1521.47	1442.85	1385.27	1342.19	1309.43	1284.22	1264.64	1249.31
66000	1657.14	1544.88	1465.05	1406.58	1362.84	1329.58	1303.98	1284.09	1268.53
67000	1682.25	1568.28	1487.24	1427.89	1383.49	1349.72	1323.74	1303.55	1287.75
68000	1707.35	1591.69	1509.44	1449.21	1404.14	1369.87	1343.49	1323.00	1306.97
69000	1732.46	1615.10	1531.64	1470.52	1424.78	1390.01	1363.25	1342.46	1326.19
70000	1757.57	1638.51	1553.84	1491.83	1445.43	1410.16	1383.01	1361.92	1345.41
75000	1883.11	1755.54	1664.83	1598.39	1548.68	1510.88	1481.79	1459.20	1441.51
80000	2008.65	1872.58	1775.81	1704.95	1651.92	1611.61	1580.58	1556.47	1537.61
100000	2510.81	2340.72	2219.77	2131.18	2064.90	2014.51	1975.72	1945.59	1922.02

229

23% MONTHLY PAYMENT
NECESSARY TO AMORTIZE A LOAN

TERM AMOUNT	15 YEARS	16 YEARS	17 YEARS	18 YEARS	19 YEARS	20 YEARS	21 YEARS	22 YEARS	23 YEARS
$ 25	.48	.48	.47	.47	.47	.47	.47	.47	.47
50	.96	.95	.94	.94	.94	.93	.93	.93	.93
75	1.43	1.42	1.41	1.41	1.40	1.40	1.39	1.39	1.39
100	1.91	1.89	1.88	1.87	1.87	1.86	1.85	1.85	1.85
200	3.81	3.78	3.76	3.74	3.73	3.71	3.70	3.70	3.69
300	5.72	5.67	5.64	5.61	5.59	5.57	5.55	5.54	5.53
400	7.62	7.56	7.51	7.48	7.45	7.42	7.40	7.39	7.38
500	9.52	9.45	9.39	9.34	9.31	9.28	9.25	9.24	9.22
600	11.43	11.34	11.27	11.21	11.17	11.13	11.10	11.08	11.06
700	13.33	13.23	13.15	13.08	13.03	12.99	12.95	12.93	12.91
800	15.23	15.12	15.02	14.95	14.89	14.84	14.80	14.77	14.75
900	17.14	17.00	16.90	16.82	16.75	16.70	16.65	16.62	16.59
1000	19.04	18.89	18.78	18.68	18.61	18.55	18.50	18.47	18.44
2000	38.07	37.78	37.55	37.36	37.22	37.10	37.00	36.93	36.87
3000	57.11	56.67	56.32	56.04	55.82	55.64	55.50	55.39	55.30
4000	76.14	75.56	75.09	74.72	74.43	74.19	74.00	73.85	73.73
5000	95.18	94.44	93.86	93.40	93.03	92.74	92.50	92.31	92.16
6000	114.21	113.33	112.63	112.08	111.64	111.28	111.00	110.77	110.59
7000	133.25	132.22	131.41	130.76	130.24	129.83	129.50	129.24	129.02
8000	152.28	151.11	150.18	149.44	148.85	148.38	148.00	147.70	147.46
9000	171.32	170.00	168.95	168.12	167.45	166.92	166.50	166.16	165.89
10000	190.35	188.88	187.72	186.80	186.06	185.47	185.00	184.62	184.32
15000	285.52	283.32	281.58	280.19	279.08	278.20	277.49	276.93	276.47
20000	380.70	377.76	375.44	373.59	372.11	370.93	369.99	369.23	368.63
25000	475.87	472.20	469.29	466.98	465.14	463.66	462.49	461.54	460.79
30000	571.04	566.64	563.15	560.38	558.16	556.40	554.98	553.85	552.94
35000	666.22	661.08	657.01	653.77	651.19	649.13	647.48	646.16	645.10
36000	685.25	679.97	675.78	672.45	669.79	667.67	665.98	664.62	663.53
37000	704.28	698.86	694.55	691.13	688.40	686.22	684.48	683.08	681.96
38000	723.32	717.75	713.33	709.81	707.01	704.77	702.98	701.54	700.39
39000	742.35	736.63	732.10	728.49	725.61	723.31	721.47	720.00	718.82
40000	761.39	755.52	750.87	747.17	744.22	741.86	739.97	738.46	737.26
41000	780.42	774.41	769.64	765.85	762.82	760.41	758.47	756.93	755.69
42000	799.46	793.30	788.41	784.52	781.43	778.95	776.97	775.39	774.12
43000	818.49	812.19	807.18	803.20	800.03	797.50	795.47	793.85	792.55
44000	837.53	831.07	825.95	821.88	818.64	816.04	813.97	812.31	810.98
45000	856.56	849.96	844.73	840.56	837.24	834.59	832.47	830.77	829.41
46000	875.60	868.85	863.50	859.24	855.85	853.14	850.97	849.23	847.84
47000	894.63	887.74	882.27	877.92	874.45	871.68	869.47	867.70	866.27
48000	913.66	906.63	901.04	896.60	893.06	890.23	887.97	886.16	884.71
49000	932.70	925.51	919.81	915.28	911.66	908.78	906.47	904.62	903.14
50000	951.73	944.40	938.58	933.96	930.27	927.32	924.97	923.08	921.57
51000	970.77	963.29	957.36	952.64	948.87	945.87	943.47	941.54	940.00
52000	989.80	982.18	976.13	971.32	967.48	964.42	961.96	960.00	958.43
53000	1008.84	1001.06	994.90	989.99	986.08	982.96	980.46	978.46	976.86
54000	1027.87	1019.95	1013.67	1008.67	1004.69	1001.51	998.96	996.93	995.29
55000	1046.91	1038.84	1032.44	1027.35	1023.29	1020.05	1017.46	1015.39	1013.72
56000	1065.94	1057.73	1051.21	1046.03	1041.90	1038.60	1035.96	1033.85	1032.16
57000	1084.98	1076.62	1069.99	1064.71	1060.51	1057.15	1054.46	1052.31	1050.59
58000	1104.01	1095.50	1088.76	1083.39	1079.11	1075.69	1072.96	1070.77	1069.02
59000	1123.05	1114.39	1107.53	1102.07	1097.72	1094.24	1091.46	1089.23	1087.45
60000	1142.08	1133.28	1126.30	1120.75	1116.32	1112.79	1109.96	1107.69	1105.88
61000	1161.11	1152.17	1145.07	1139.43	1134.93	1131.33	1128.46	1126.16	1124.31
62000	1180.15	1171.06	1163.84	1158.11	1153.53	1149.88	1146.96	1144.62	1142.74
63000	1199.18	1189.94	1182.61	1176.78	1172.14	1168.43	1165.46	1163.08	1161.17
64000	1218.22	1208.83	1201.39	1195.46	1190.74	1186.97	1183.96	1181.54	1179.61
65000	1237.25	1227.72	1220.16	1214.14	1209.35	1205.52	1202.45	1200.00	1198.04
66000	1256.29	1246.61	1238.93	1232.82	1227.95	1224.06	1220.95	1218.46	1216.47
67000	1275.32	1265.50	1257.70	1251.50	1246.56	1242.61	1239.45	1236.93	1234.90
68000	1294.36	1284.38	1276.47	1270.18	1265.16	1261.16	1257.95	1255.39	1253.33
69000	1313.39	1303.27	1295.24	1288.86	1283.77	1279.70	1276.45	1273.85	1271.76
70000	1332.43	1322.16	1314.02	1307.54	1302.37	1298.25	1294.95	1292.31	1290.19
75000	1427.60	1416.60	1407.87	1400.93	1395.40	1390.98	1387.45	1384.62	1382.35
80000	1522.77	1511.04	1501.73	1494.33	1488.43	1483.71	1479.94	1476.92	1474.51
100000	1903.46	1888.80	1877.16	1867.91	1860.53	1854.64	1849.93	1846.15	1843.13

MONTHLY PAYMENT 23%
NECESSARY TO AMORTIZE A LOAN

TERM AMOUNT	24 YEARS	25 YEARS	26 YEARS	27 YEARS	28 YEARS	29 YEARS	30 YEARS	35 YEARS	40 YEARS
$ 25	.47	.46	.46	.46	.46	.46	.46	.46	.46
50	.93	.92	.92	.92	.92	.92	.92	.92	.92
75	1.39	1.38	1.38	1.38	1.38	1.38	1.38	1.38	1.38
100	1.85	1.84	1.84	1.84	1.84	1.84	1.84	1.84	1.84
200	3.69	3.68	3.68	3.68	3.67	3.67	3.67	3.67	3.67
300	5.53	5.52	5.52	5.51	5.51	5.51	5.51	5.50	5.50
400	7.37	7.36	7.35	7.35	7.34	7.34	7.34	7.33	7.33
500	9.21	9.20	9.19	9.18	9.18	9.18	9.17	9.16	9.16
600	11.05	11.04	11.03	11.02	11.01	11.01	11.01	11.00	10.99
700	12.89	12.88	12.87	12.86	12.85	12.84	12.84	12.83	12.82
800	14.73	14.72	14.70	14.69	14.68	14.68	14.07	14.66	14.65
900	16.57	16.55	16.54	16.53	16.52	16.51	16.51	16.49	16.48
1000	18.41	18.39	18.38	18.36	18.35	18.35	18.34	18.32	18.32
2000	36.82	36.78	36.75	36.72	36.70	36.69	36.67	36.64	36.63
3000	55.23	55.17	55.12	55.08	55.05	55.03	55.01	54.96	54.94
4000	73.63	73.56	73.49	73.44	73.40	73.37	73.34	73.27	73.25
5000	92.04	91.94	91.86	91.80	91.75	91.71	91.68	91.59	91.56
6000	110.45	110.33	110.24	110.16	110.10	110.05	110.01	109.91	109.87
7000	128.85	128.72	128.61	128.52	128.45	128.39	128.35	128.22	128.18
8000	147.26	147.11	146.98	146.88	146.80	146.73	146.68	146.54	146.49
9000	165.67	165.49	165.35	165.24	165.15	165.08	165.02	164.86	164.80
10000	184.08	183.88	183.72	183.60	183.50	183.42	183.35	183.17	183.11
15000	276.11	275.82	275.58	275.40	275.24	275.12	275.03	274.76	274.67
20000	368.15	367.76	367.44	367.19	366.99	366.83	366.70	366.34	366.22
25000	460.18	459.69	459.30	458.99	458.74	458.54	458.37	457.93	457.78
30000	552.22	551.63	551.16	550.79	550.48	550.24	550.05	549.51	549.33
35000	644.25	643.57	643.02	642.58	642.23	641.95	641.72	641.10	640.89
36000	662.66	661.96	661.39	660.94	660.58	660.29	660.05	659.42	659.20
37000	681.06	680.34	679.77	679.30	678.93	678.63	678.39	677.73	677.51
38000	699.47	698.73	698.14	697.66	697.28	696.97	696.72	696.05	695.82
39000	717.88	717.12	716.51	716.02	715.63	715.31	715.06	714.37	714.13
40000	736.29	735.51	734.88	734.38	733.98	733.65	733.39	732.68	732.44
41000	754.69	753.89	753.25	752.74	752.33	751.99	751.73	751.00	750.76
42000	773.10	772.28	771.63	771.10	770.68	770.34	770.06	769.32	769.07
43000	791.51	790.67	790.00	789.46	789.02	788.68	788.40	787.63	787.38
44000	809.91	809.06	808.37	807.82	807.37	807.02	806.73	805.95	805.69
45000	828.32	827.44	826.74	826.18	825.72	825.36	825.07	824.27	824.00
46000	846.73	845.83	845.11	844.54	844.07	843.70	843.40	842.59	842.31
47000	865.13	864.22	863.49	862.90	862.42	862.04	861.74	860.90	860.62
48000	883.54	882.61	881.86	881.26	880.77	880.38	880.07	879.22	878.93
49000	901.95	900.99	900.23	899.61	899.12	898.72	898.40	897.54	897.24
50000	920.36	919.38	918.60	917.97	917.47	917.07	916.74	915.85	915.55
51000	938.76	937.77	936.97	936.33	935.82	935.41	935.07	934.17	933.87
52000	957.17	956.16	955.35	954.69	954.17	953.75	953.41	952.49	952.18
53000	975.58	974.55	973.72	973.05	972.52	972.09	971.74	970.80	970.49
54000	993.98	992.93	992.09	991.41	990.87	990.43	990.08	989.12	988.80
55000	1012.39	1011.32	1010.46	1009.77	1009.22	1008.77	1008.41	1007.44	1007.11
56000	1030.80	1029.71	1028.83	1028.13	1027.57	1027.11	1026.75	1025.75	1025.42
57000	1049.20	1048.10	1047.20	1046.49	1045.92	1045.45	1045.08	1044.07	1043.73
58000	1067.61	1066.48	1065.58	1064.85	1064.26	1063.79	1063.42	1062.39	1062.04
59000	1086.02	1084.87	1083.95	1083.21	1082.61	1082.14	1081.75	1080.71	1080.35
60000	1104.43	1103.26	1102.32	1101.57	1100.96	1100.48	1100.09	1099.02	1098.66
61000	1122.83	1121.65	1120.69	1119.93	1119.31	1118.82	1118.42	1117.34	1116.98
62000	1141.24	1140.03	1139.06	1138.29	1137.66	1137.16	1136.76	1135.66	1135.29
63000	1159.65	1158.42	1157.44	1156.65	1156.01	1155.50	1155.09	1153.97	1153.60
64000	1178.05	1176.81	1175.81	1175.01	1174.36	1173.84	1173.43	1172.29	1171.91
65000	1196.46	1195.20	1194.18	1193.36	1192.71	1192.18	1191.76	1190.61	1190.22
66000	1214.87	1213.58	1212.55	1211.72	1211.06	1210.52	1210.09	1208.92	1208.53
67000	1233.27	1231.97	1230.92	1230.08	1229.41	1228.86	1228.43	1227.24	1226.84
68000	1251.68	1250.36	1249.30	1248.44	1247.76	1247.21	1246.76	1245.56	1245.15
69000	1270.09	1268.75	1267.67	1266.80	1266.11	1265.55	1265.10	1263.88	1263.46
70000	1288.50	1287.13	1286.04	1285.16	1284.46	1283.89	1283.43	1282.19	1281.77
75000	1380.53	1379.07	1377.90	1376.96	1376.20	1375.60	1375.11	1373.78	1373.33
80000	1472.57	1471.01	1469.76	1468.76	1467.95	1467.30	1466.78	1465.36	1464.88
100000	1840.71	1838.76	1837.20	1835.94	1834.94	1834.13	1833.47	1831.70	1831.10

23½% MONTHLY PAYMENT
NECESSARY TO AMORTIZE A LOAN

TERM AMOUNT	1 YEAR	1½ YEARS	2 YEARS	2½ YEARS	3 YEARS	3½ YEARS	4 YEARS	4½ YEARS	5 YEARS
$ 25	2.35	1.65	1.31	1.10	.97	.87	.80	.74	.70
50	4.69	3.30	2.61	2.20	1.93	1.73	1.59	1.48	1.40
75	7.04	4.95	3.91	3.29	2.89	2.60	2.39	2.22	2.09
100	9.38	6.60	5.21	4.39	3.85	3.46	3.18	2.96	2.79
200	18.76	13.19	10.42	8.77	7.69	6.92	6.35	5.92	5.58
300	28.14	19.79	15.63	13.16	11.53	10.38	9.53	8.88	8.36
400	37.52	26.38	20.84	17.54	15.37	13.83	12.70	11.83	11.15
500	46.90	32.97	26.05	21.93	19.21	17.29	15.87	14.79	13.94
600	56.28	39.57	31.26	26.31	23.05	20.75	19.05	17.75	16.72
700	65.66	46.16	36.47	30.70	26.89	24.21	22.22	20.70	19.51
800	75.04	52.75	41.68	35.08	30.73	27.66	25.40	23.66	22.29
900	84.42	59.35	46.88	39.47	34.57	31.12	28.57	26.62	25.08
1000	93.80	65.94	52.09	43.85	38.42	34.58	31.74	29.57	27.87
2000	187.60	131.88	104.18	87.70	76.83	69.15	63.48	59.14	55.73
3000	281.40	197.81	156.27	131.55	115.24	103.73	95.22	88.71	83.59
4000	375.20	263.75	208.36	175.40	153.65	138.30	126.96	118.27	111.45
5000	469.00	329.68	260.45	219.25	192.06	172.88	158.69	147.84	139.31
6000	562.80	395.62	312.54	263.10	230.47	207.45	190.43	177.41	167.17
7000	656.60	461.55	364.63	306.94	268.88	242.03	222.17	206.97	195.04
8000	750.40	527.49	416.71	350.79	307.29	276.60	253.91	236.54	222.90
9000	844.20	593.42	468.80	394.64	345.70	311.17	285.64	266.11	250.76
10000	938.00	659.36	520.89	438.49	384.12	345.75	317.38	295.67	278.62
15000	1407.00	989.03	781.33	657.73	576.17	518.62	476.07	443.51	417.93
20000	1875.99	1318.71	1041.78	876.98	768.23	691.49	634.76	591.34	557.24
25000	2344.99	1648.39	1302.22	1096.22	960.28	864.37	793.45	739.18	696.54
30000	2813.99	1978.06	1562.66	1315.46	1152.34	1037.24	952.14	887.01	835.85
35000	3282.98	2307.74	1823.11	1534.70	1344.39	1210.11	1110.82	1034.85	975.16
36000	3376.78	2373.67	1875.20	1578.55	1382.80	1244.68	1142.56	1064.41	1003.02
37000	3470.58	2439.61	1927.29	1622.40	1421.21	1279.26	1174.30	1093.98	1030.88
38000	3564.38	2505.54	1979.37	1666.25	1459.63	1313.83	1206.04	1123.55	1058.74
39000	3658.18	2571.48	2031.46	1710.10	1498.04	1348.41	1237.77	1153.11	1086.61
40000	3751.98	2637.41	2083.55	1753.95	1536.45	1382.98	1269.51	1182.68	1114.47
41000	3845.78	2703.35	2135.64	1797.80	1574.86	1417.56	1301.25	1212.25	1142.33
42000	3939.58	2769.28	2187.73	1841.64	1613.27	1452.13	1332.99	1241.81	1170.19
43000	4033.38	2835.22	2239.82	1885.49	1651.68	1486.71	1364.73	1271.38	1198.05
44000	4127.18	2901.15	2291.91	1929.34	1690.09	1521.28	1396.46	1300.95	1225.91
45000	4220.98	2967.09	2343.99	1973.19	1728.50	1555.85	1428.20	1330.51	1253.77
46000	4314.78	3033.03	2396.08	2017.04	1766.91	1590.43	1459.94	1360.08	1281.64
47000	4408.58	3098.96	2448.17	2060.89	1805.33	1625.00	1491.68	1389.65	1309.50
48000	4502.38	3164.90	2500.26	2104.74	1843.74	1659.58	1523.41	1419.21	1337.36
49000	4596.18	3230.83	2552.35	2148.58	1882.15	1694.15	1555.15	1448.78	1365.22
50000	4689.98	3296.77	2604.44	2192.43	1920.56	1728.73	1586.89	1478.35	1393.08
51000	4783.78	3362.70	2656.53	2236.28	1958.97	1763.30	1618.63	1507.92	1420.94
52000	4877.57	3428.64	2708.62	2280.13	1997.38	1797.88	1650.36	1537.48	1448.81
53000	4971.37	3494.57	2760.70	2323.98	2035.79	1832.45	1682.10	1567.05	1476.67
54000	5065.17	3560.51	2812.79	2367.83	2074.20	1867.02	1713.84	1596.62	1504.53
55000	5158.97	3626.44	2864.88	2411.68	2112.61	1901.60	1745.58	1626.18	1532.39
56000	5252.77	3692.38	2916.97	2455.52	2151.03	1936.17	1777.32	1655.75	1560.25
57000	5346.57	3758.31	2969.06	2499.37	2189.44	1970.75	1809.05	1685.32	1588.11
58000	5440.37	3824.25	3021.15	2543.22	2227.85	2005.32	1840.79	1714.88	1615.97
59000	5534.17	3890.18	3073.24	2587.07	2266.26	2039.90	1872.53	1744.45	1643.84
60000	5627.97	3956.12	3125.32	2630.92	2304.67	2074.47	1904.27	1774.02	1671.70
61000	5721.77	4022.05	3177.41	2674.77	2343.08	2109.05	1936.00	1803.58	1699.56
62000	5815.57	4087.99	3229.50	2718.62	2381.49	2143.62	1967.74	1833.15	1727.42
63000	5909.37	4153.92	3281.59	2762.46	2419.90	2178.19	1999.48	1862.72	1755.28
64000	6003.17	4219.86	3333.68	2806.31	2458.31	2212.77	2031.22	1892.28	1783.14
65000	6096.97	4285.79	3385.77	2850.16	2496.72	2247.34	2062.95	1921.85	1811.01
66000	6190.77	4351.73	3437.86	2894.01	2535.14	2281.92	2094.69	1951.42	1838.87
67000	6284.57	4417.66	3489.95	2937.86	2573.55	2316.49	2126.43	1980.98	1866.73
68000	6378.37	4483.60	3542.03	2981.71	2611.96	2351.07	2158.17	2010.55	1894.59
69000	6472.16	4549.54	3594.12	3025.56	2650.37	2385.64	2189.91	2040.12	1922.45
70000	6565.96	4615.47	3646.21	3069.40	2688.78	2420.22	2221.64	2069.69	1950.31
75000	7034.96	4945.15	3906.65	3288.65	2880.84	2593.09	2380.33	2217.52	2089.62
80000	7503.96	5274.82	4167.10	3507.89	3072.89	2765.96	2539.02	2365.35	2228.93
100000	9379.95	6593.53	5208.87	4384.86	3841.11	3457.45	3173.77	2956.69	2786.16

TERM AMOUNT	6 YEARS	7 YEARS	8 YEARS	9 YEARS	10 YEARS	11 YEARS	12 YEARS	13 YEARS	14 YEARS
$ 25	.64	.60	.57	.55	.53	.52	.51	.50	.49
50	1.27	1.19	1.13	1.09	1.05	1.03	1.01	.99	.98
75	1.91	1.78	1.69	1.63	1.58	1.54	1.51	1.49	1.47
100	2.54	2.37	2.25	2.17	2.10	2.05	2.01	1.98	1.96
200	5.08	4.74	4.50	4.33	4.20	4.10	4.02	3.96	3.92
300	7.62	7.11	6.75	6.49	6.29	6.14	6.03	5.94	5.87
400	10.16	9.48	9.00	8.65	8.39	8.19	8.04	7.92	7.83
500	12.69	11.85	11.25	10.81	10.49	10.24	10.05	9.90	9.78
600	15.23	14.22	13.50	12.97	12.58	12 28	12.06	11.88	11.74
700	17.77	16.59	15.75	15.13	14.68	14.33	14.06	13.86	13.70
800	20.31	18.96	18.00	17.30	16.77	16.38	16.07	15.84	15.65
900	22.85	21.33	20.25	19.46	18.87	18.42	18.08	17.82	17.61
1000	25.38	23.69	22.50	21.62	20.97	20.47	20.09	19.79	19.56
2000	50.76	47.38	44.99	43.23	41.93	40.93	40.17	39.58	39.12
3000	76.14	71.07	67.48	64.85	62.89	61.40	60.26	59.37	58.68
4000	101.52	94.76	89.97	86.46	83.85	81.86	80.34	79.16	78.24
5000	126.90	118.45	112.46	108.08	104.81	102.33	100.43	98.95	97.80
6000	152.28	142.14	134.95	129.69	125.77	122.79	120.51	118.74	117.36
7000	177.66	165.83	157.44	151.30	146.73	143.26	140.59	138.53	136.92
8000	203.04	189.52	179.93	172.92	167.69	163.72	160.68	158.32	156.48
9000	228.42	213.21	202.42	194.53	188.65	184.19	180.76	178.11	176.04
10000	253.80	236.90	224.91	216.15	209.61	204.65	200.85	197.90	195.60
15000	380.70	355.35	337.36	324.22	314.41	306.97	301.27	296.85	293.40
20000	507.59	473.80	449.81	432.29	419.21	409.30	401.69	395.80	391.20
25000	634.49	592.24	562.26	540.36	524.01	511.62	502.11	494.75	489.00
30000	761.39	710.69	674.72	648.43	628.82	613.94	602.53	593.70	586.80
35000	888.29	829.14	787.17	756.50	733.62	716.27	702.95	692.64	684.60
36000	913.67	852.83	809.66	778.12	754.58	736.73	723.04	712.43	704.16
37000	939.05	876.52	832.15	799.73	775.54	757.20	743.12	732.22	723.72
38000	964.43	900.21	854.64	821.35	796.50	777.66	763.21	752.01	743.28
39000	989.80	923.90	877.13	842.96	817.46	798.13	783.29	771.80	762.84
40000	1015.18	947.59	899.62	864.57	838.42	818.59	803.37	791.59	782.40
41000	1040.56	971.28	922.11	886.19	859.38	839.05	823.46	811.38	801.96
42000	1065.94	994.97	944.60	907.80	880.34	859.52	843.54	831.17	821.52
43000	1091.32	1018.66	967.09	929.42	901.30	879.98	863.63	850.96	841.08
44000	1116.70	1042.35	989.58	951.03	922.26	900.45	883.71	870.75	860.64
45000	1142.08	1066.03	1012.07	972.64	943.22	920.91	903.80	890.54	880.20
46000	1167.46	1089.72	1034.56	994.26	964.18	941.38	923.88	910.33	899.76
47000	1192.84	1113.41	1057.05	1015.87	985.14	961.84	943.96	930.12	919.32
48000	1218.22	1137.10	1079.54	1037.49	1006.10	982.31	964.05	949.91	938.88
49000	1243.60	1160.79	1102.03	1059.10	1027.06	1002.77	984.13	969.70	958.44
50000	1268.98	1184.48	1124.52	1080.72	1048.02	1023.24	1004.22	989.49	978.00
51000	1294.36	1208.17	1147.01	1102.33	1068.98	1043.70	1024.30	1009.28	997.56
52000	1319.74	1231.86	1169.50	1123.94	1089.94	1064.17	1044.39	1029.07	1017.12
53000	1345.12	1255.55	1191.99	1145.56	1110.90	1084.63	1064.47	1048.86	1036.68
54000	1370.50	1279.24	1214.48	1167.17	1131.86	1105.09	1084.55	1068.65	1056.24
55000	1395.88	1302.93	1236.97	1188.79	1152.82	1125.56	1104.64	1088.44	1075.80
56000	1421.26	1326.62	1259.47	1210.40	1173.79	1146.02	1124.72	1108.23	1095.36
57000	1446.64	1350.31	1281.96	1232.02	1194.75	1166.49	1144.81	1128.02	1114.92
58000	1472.01	1374.00	1304.45	1253.63	1215.71	1186.95	1164.89	1147.81	1134.48
59000	1497.39	1397.69	1326.94	1275.24	1236.67	1207.42	1184.98	1167.60	1154.04
60000	1522.77	1421.38	1349.43	1296.86	1257.63	1227.88	1205.06	1187.39	1173.60
61000	1548.15	1445.07	1371.92	1318.47	1278.59	1248.35	1225.14	1207.18	1193.16
62000	1573.53	1468.76	1394.41	1340.09	1299.55	1268.81	1245.23	1226.97	1212.72
63000	1598.91	1492.45	1416.90	1361.70	1320.51	1289.28	1265.31	1246.76	1232.28
64000	1624.29	1516.14	1439.39	1383.31	1341.47	1309.74	1285.40	1266.55	1251.84
65000	1649.67	1539.83	1461.88	1404.93	1362.43	1330.21	1305.48	1286.34	1271.40
66000	1675.05	1563.52	1484.37	1426.54	1383.39	1350.67	1325.57	1306.13	1290.96
67000	1700.43	1587.20	1506.86	1448.16	1404.35	1371.13	1345.65	1325.91	1310.52
68000	1725.81	1610.89	1529.35	1469.77	1425.31	1391.60	1365.73	1345.70	1330.08
69000	1751.19	1634.58	1551.84	1491.39	1446.27	1412.06	1385.82	1365.49	1349.64
70000	1776.57	1658.27	1574.33	1513.00	1467.23	1432.53	1405.90	1385.28	1369.20
75000	1903.47	1776.72	1686.78	1621.07	1572.03	1534.85	1506.32	1484.23	1467.00
80000	2030.36	1895.17	1799.23	1729.14	1676.83	1637.17	1606.74	1583.18	1564.80
100000	2537.95	2368.96	2249.04	2161.43	2096.04	2046.47	2008.43	1978.98	1956.00

233

23½% MONTHLY PAYMENT
NECESSARY TO AMORTIZE A LOAN

TERM AMOUNT	15 YEARS	16 YEARS	17 YEARS	18 YEARS	19 YEARS	20 YEARS	21 YEARS	22 YEARS	23 YEARS
$ 25	.49	.49	.48	.48	.48	.48	.48	.48	.48
50	.97	.97	.96	.96	.95	.95	.95	.95	.95
75	1.46	1.45	1.44	1.43	1.43	1.42	1.42	1.42	1.42
100	1.94	1.93	1.92	1.91	1.90	1.90	1.89	1.89	1.89
200	3.88	3.85	3.83	3.81	3.80	3.79	3.78	3.77	3.77
300	5.82	5.78	5.74	5.72	5.69	5.68	5.66	5.65	5.65
400	7.76	7.70	7.66	7.62	7.59	7.57	7.55	7.54	7.53
500	9.69	9.62	9.57	9.52	9.49	9.46	9.44	9.42	9.41
600	11.63	11.55	11.48	11.43	11.38	11.35	11.32	11.30	11.29
700	13.57	13.47	13.39	13.33	13.28	13.24	13.21	13.19	13.17
800	15.51	15.40	15.31	15.23	15.18	15.13	15.10	15.07	15.05
900	17.45	17.32	17.22	17.14	17.07	17.02	16.98	16.95	16.93
1000	19.38	19.24	19.13	19.04	18.97	18.92	18.87	18.84	18.81
2000	38.76	38.48	38.26	38.08	37.94	37.83	37.74	37.67	37.61
3000	58.14	57.72	57.38	57.12	56.91	56.74	56.60	56.50	56.41
4000	77.52	76.96	76.51	76.15	75.87	75.65	75.47	75.33	75.21
5000	96.90	96.19	95.63	95.19	94.84	94.56	94.33	94.16	94.01
6000	116.28	115.43	114.76	114.23	113.80	113.47	113.20	112.99	112.81
7000	135.66	134.67	133.89	133.26	132.77	132.38	132.06	131.82	131.62
8000	155.04	153.91	153.01	152.30	151.74	151.29	150.93	150.65	150.42
9000	174.42	173.15	172.14	171.34	170.70	170.20	169.80	169.48	169.22
10000	193.80	192.38	191.26	190.38	189.67	189.11	188.66	188.31	188.02
15000	290.70	288.57	286.89	285.56	284.50	283.66	282.99	282.46	282.03
20000	387.60	384.76	382.52	380.75	379.33	378.21	377.32	376.61	376.04
25000	484.50	480.95	478.15	475.93	474.17	472.76	471.65	470.76	470.05
30000	581.40	577.14	573.78	571.12	569.00	567.32	565.98	564.91	564.05
35000	678.30	673.33	669.41	666.30	663.83	661.87	660.30	659.06	658.06
36000	697.68	692.57	688.54	685.34	682.80	680.78	679.17	677.89	676.86
37000	717.06	711.81	707.66	704.38	701.77	699.69	698.04	696.72	695.66
38000	736.44	731.05	726.79	723.41	720.73	718.60	716.90	715.55	714.47
39000	755.82	750.29	745.91	742.45	739.70	737.51	735.77	734.38	733.27
40000	775.20	769.52	765.04	761.49	758.66	756.42	754.63	753.21	752.07
41000	794.58	788.76	784.17	780.52	777.63	775.33	773.50	772.04	770.87
42000	813.96	808.00	803.29	799.56	796.60	794.24	792.36	790.87	789.67
43000	833.34	827.24	822.42	818.60	815.56	813.15	811.23	809.70	808.47
44000	852.72	846.48	841.54	837.63	834.53	832.06	830.10	828.53	827.28
45000	872.10	865.71	860.67	856.67	853.50	850.97	848.96	847.36	846.08
46000	891.48	884.95	879.80	875.71	872.46	869.88	867.83	866.19	864.88
47000	910.86	904.19	898.92	894.75	891.43	888.79	886.69	885.02	883.68
48000	930.24	923.43	918.05	913.78	910.40	907.70	905.56	903.85	902.48
49000	949.62	942.67	937.17	932.82	929.36	926.61	924.42	922.68	921.28
50000	969.00	961.90	956.30	951.86	948.33	945.52	943.29	941.51	940.09
51000	988.38	981.14	975.42	970.89	967.30	964.43	962.15	960.34	958.89
52000	1007.76	1000.38	994.55	989.93	986.26	983.34	981.02	979.17	977.69
53000	1027.14	1019.62	1013.68	1008.97	1005.23	1002.26	999.89	998.00	996.49
54000	1046.52	1038.86	1032.80	1028.01	1024.20	1021.17	1018.75	1016.83	1015.29
55000	1065.90	1058.09	1051.93	1047.04	1043.16	1040.08	1037.62	1035.66	1034.09
56000	1085.28	1077.33	1071.05	1066.08	1062.13	1058.99	1056.48	1054.49	1052.89
57000	1104.66	1096.57	1090.18	1085.12	1081.10	1077.90	1075.35	1073.32	1071.70
58000	1124.04	1115.81	1109.31	1104.15	1100.06	1096.81	1094.21	1092.15	1090.50
59000	1143.42	1135.05	1128.43	1123.19	1119.03	1115.72	1113.08	1110.98	1109.30
60000	1162.80	1154.28	1147.56	1142.23	1137.99	1134.63	1131.95	1129.81	1128.10
61000	1182.18	1173.52	1166.68	1161.26	1156.96	1153.54	1150.81	1148.64	1146.90
62000	1201.56	1192.76	1185.81	1180.30	1175.93	1172.45	1169.68	1167.47	1165.70
63000	1220.94	1212.00	1204.94	1199.34	1194.89	1191.36	1188.54	1186.30	1184.51
64000	1240.32	1231.24	1224.06	1218.38	1213.86	1210.27	1207.41	1205.13	1203.31
65000	1259.70	1250.47	1243.19	1237.41	1232.83	1229.18	1226.27	1223.96	1222.11
66000	1279.08	1269.71	1262.31	1256.45	1251.79	1248.09	1245.14	1242.79	1240.91
67000	1298.46	1288.95	1281.44	1275.49	1270.76	1267.00	1264.01	1261.62	1259.71
68000	1317.84	1308.19	1300.56	1294.52	1289.73	1285.91	1282.87	1280.45	1278.51
69000	1337.22	1327.43	1319.69	1313.56	1308.69	1304.82	1301.74	1299.28	1297.32
70000	1356.60	1346.66	1338.82	1332.60	1327.66	1323.73	1320.60	1318.11	1316.12
75000	1453.49	1442.85	1434.45	1427.78	1422.49	1418.28	1414.93	1412.26	1410.13
80000	1550.39	1539.04	1530.08	1522.97	1517.32	1512.84	1509.26	1506.41	1504.13
100000	1937.99	1923.80	1912.59	1903.71	1896.65	1891.04	1886.57	1883.01	1880.17

MONTHLY PAYMENT 23½%
NECESSARY TO AMORTIZE A LOAN

TERM AMOUNT	24 YEARS	25 YEARS	26 YEARS	27 YEARS	28 YEARS	29 YEARS	30 YEARS	35 YEARS	40 YEARS
$ 25	.47	.47	.47	.47	.47	.47	.47	.47	.47
50	.94	.94	.94	.94	.94	.94	.94	.94	.94
75	1.41	1.41	1.41	1.41	1.41	1.41	1.41	1.41	1.41
100	1.88	1.88	1.88	1.88	1.88	1.88	1.88	1.87	1.87
200	3.76	3.76	3.75	3.75	3.75	3.75	3.75	3.74	3.74
300	5.64	5.63	5.63	5.63	5.62	5.62	5.62	5.61	5.61
400	7.52	7.51	7.50	7.50	7.50	7.49	7.49	7.48	7.48
500	9.39	9.39	9.38	9.37	9.37	9.36	9.36	9.35	9.35
600	11.27	11.26	11.25	11.25	11.24	11.24	11.23	11.22	11.22
700	13.15	13.14	13.13	13.12	13.11	13.11	13.10	13.09	13.09
800	15.03	15.01	15.00	14.99	14.99	14.98	14.97	14.96	14.96
900	16.91	16.89	16.88	16.87	16.86	16.85	16.85	16.83	16.83
1000	18.78	18.77	18.75	18.74	18.73	18.72	18.72	18.70	18.70
2000	37.56	37.53	37.50	37.47	37.46	37.44	37.43	37.40	37.39
3000	56.34	56.29	56.24	56.21	56.18	56.16	56.14	56.09	56.08
4000	75.12	75.05	74.99	74.94	74.91	74.88	74.85	74.79	74.77
5000	93.90	93.81	93.74	93.68	93.63	93.59	93.56	93.48	93.46
6000	112.68	112.57	112.48	112.41	112.36	112.31	112.28	112.18	112.15
7000	131.46	131.33	131.23	131.15	131.08	131.03	130.99	130.88	130.84
8000	150.24	150.09	149.97	149.88	149.81	149.75	149.70	149.57	149.53
9000	169.02	168.85	168.72	168.62	168.53	168.47	168.41	168.27	168.22
10000	187.79	187.61	187.47	187.35	187.26	187.18	187.12	186.96	186.91
15000	281.69	281.42	281.20	281.02	280.89	280.77	280.68	280.44	280.37
20000	375.58	375.22	374.93	374.70	374.51	374.36	374.24	373.92	373.82
25000	469.48	469.02	468.66	468.37	468.14	467.95	467.80	467.40	467.27
30000	563.37	562.83	562.39	562.04	561.77	561.54	561.36	560.88	560.73
35000	657.27	656.63	656.12	655.72	655.39	655.13	654.92	654.36	654.18
36000	676.05	675.39	674.87	674.45	674.12	673.85	673.64	673.06	672.87
37000	694.82	694.15	693.62	693.19	692.84	692.57	692.35	691.76	691.56
38000	713.60	712.91	712.36	711.92	711.57	711.29	711.06	710.45	710.25
39000	732.38	731.67	731.11	730.66	730.29	730.00	729.77	729.15	728.94
40000	751.16	750.43	749.85	749.39	749.02	748.72	748.48	747.84	747.63
41000	769.94	769.20	768.60	768.12	767.74	767.44	767.20	766.54	766.33
42000	788.72	787.96	787.35	786.86	786.47	786.16	785.91	785.24	785.02
43000	807.50	806.72	806.09	805.59	805.20	804.88	804.62	803.93	803.71
44000	826.28	825.48	824.84	824.33	823.92	823.59	823.33	822.63	822.40
45000	845.06	844.24	843.59	843.06	842.65	842.31	842.04	841.32	841.09
46000	863.83	863.00	862.33	861.80	861.37	861.03	860.76	860.02	859.78
47000	882.61	881.76	881.08	880.53	880.10	879.75	879.47	878.72	878.47
48000	901.39	900.52	899.82	899.27	898.82	898.47	898.18	897.41	897.16
49000	920.17	919.28	918.57	918.00	917.55	917.18	916.89	916.11	915.85
50000	938.95	938.04	937.32	936.74	936.27	935.90	935.60	934.80	934.54
51000	957.73	956.80	956.06	955.47	955.00	954.62	954.32	953.50	953.23
52000	976.51	975.56	974.81	974.21	973.72	973.34	973.03	972.20	971.92
53000	995.29	994.32	993.56	992.94	992.45	992.06	991.74	990.89	990.61
54000	1014.07	1013.09	1012.30	1011.68	1011.17	1010.77	1010.45	1009.59	1009.30
55000	1032.84	1031.85	1031.05	1030.41	1029.90	1029.49	1029.16	1028.28	1028.00
56000	1051.62	1050.61	1049.79	1049.14	1048.62	1048.21	1047.88	1046.98	1046.69
57000	1070.40	1069.37	1068.54	1067.88	1067.35	1066.93	1066.59	1065.68	1065.38
58000	1089.18	1088.13	1087.29	1086.61	1086.08	1085.64	1085.30	1084.37	1084.07
59000	1107.96	1106.89	1106.03	1105.35	1104.80	1104.36	1104.01	1103.07	1102.76
60000	1126.74	1125.65	1124.78	1124.08	1123.53	1123.08	1122.72	1121.76	1121.45
61000	1145.52	1144.41	1143.53	1142.82	1142.25	1141.80	1141.44	1140.46	1140.14
62000	1164.30	1163.17	1162.27	1161.55	1160.98	1160.52	1160.15	1159.16	1158.83
63000	1183.08	1181.93	1181.02	1180.29	1179.70	1179.23	1178.86	1177.85	1177.52
64000	1201.85	1200.69	1199.76	1199.02	1198.43	1197.95	1197.57	1196.55	1196.21
65000	1220.63	1219.45	1218.51	1217.76	1217.15	1216.67	1216.28	1215.24	1214.90
66000	1239.41	1238.21	1237.26	1236.49	1235.88	1235.39	1235.00	1233.94	1233.59
67000	1258.19	1256.97	1256.00	1255.23	1254.60	1254.11	1253.71	1252.64	1252.28
68000	1276.97	1275.74	1274.75	1273.96	1273.33	1272.82	1272.42	1271.33	1270.97
69000	1295.75	1294.50	1293.50	1292.69	1292.05	1291.54	1291.13	1290.03	1289.67
70000	1314.53	1313.26	1312.24	1311.43	1310.78	1310.26	1309.84	1308.72	1308.36
75000	1408.42	1407.06	1405.97	1405.10	1404.41	1403.85	1403.40	1402.20	1401.81
80000	1502.32	1500.86	1499.70	1498.78	1498.03	1497.44	1496.96	1495.68	1495.26
100000	1877.89	1876.08	1874.63	1873.47	1872.54	1871.80	1871.20	1869.60	1869.08

235

24%

MONTHLY PAYMENT
NECESSARY TO AMORTIZE A LOAN

TERM AMOUNT	1 YEAR	1½ YEARS	2 YEARS	2½ YEARS	3 YEARS	3½ YEARS	4 YEARS	4½ YEARS	5 YEARS
$ 25	2.36	1.66	1.31	1.11	.97	.88	.80	.75	.71
50	4.71	3.31	2.62	2.21	1.94	.75	1.60	1.50	1.41
75	7.06	4.97	3.93	3.31	2.90	2.62	2.40	2.24	2.11
100	9.41	6.62	5.24	4.41	3.87	3.49	3.20	2.99	2.82
200	18.81	13.24	10.47	8.82	7.73	6.97	6.40	5.97	5.63
300	28.21	19.85	15.70	13.23	11.60	10.45	9.60	8.95	8.44
400	37.61	26.47	20.93	17.64	15.46	13.93	12.80	11.93	11.25
500	47.01	33.08	26.16	22.04	19.33	17.41	16.00	14.92	14.07
600	56.42	39.70	31.39	26.45	23.19	20.90	19.20	17.90	16.88
700	65.82	46.31	36.63	30.86	27.06	24.38	22.40	20.88	19.69
800	75.22	52.93	41.86	35.27	30.92	27.86	25.59	23.86	22.50
900	84.62	59.55	47.09	39.68	34.79	31.34	28.79	26.84	25.32
1000	94.02	66.16	52.32	44.08	38.65	34.82	31.99	29.83	28.13
2000	188.04	132.32	104.63	88.16	77.30	69.64	63.98	59.65	56.25
3000	282.06	198.47	156.95	132.24	115.95	104.46	95.96	89.47	84.37
4000	376.08	264.63	209.26	176.32	154.60	139.27	127.95	119.29	112.49
5000	470.10	330.79	261.58	220.40	193.24	174.09	159.94	149.11	140.62
6000	564.12	396.94	313.89	264.48	231.89	208.91	191.92	178.93	168.74
7000	658.14	463.10	366.21	308.56	270.54	243.72	223.91	208.76	196.86
8000	752.16	529.26	418.52	352.64	309.19	278.54	255.90	238.58	224.98
9000	846.18	595.41	470.83	396.72	347.84	313.36	287.88	268.40	253.11
10000	940.19	661.57	523.15	440.80	386.48	348.18	319.87	298.22	281.23
15000	1410.29	992.35	784.72	661.20	579.72	522.26	479.80	447.33	421.84
20000	1880.38	1323.14	1046.29	881.60	772.96	696.35	639.73	596.44	562.45
25000	2350.48	1653.92	1307.86	1101.99	966.20	870.43	799.66	745.54	703.06
30000	2820.57	1984.70	1569.43	1322.39	1159.44	1044.52	959.60	894.65	843.67
35000	3290.67	2315.48	1831.01	1542.79	1352.68	1218.60	1119.53	1043.76	984.28
36000	3384.69	2381.64	1883.32	1586.87	1391.33	1253.42	1151.52	1073.58	1012.41
37000	3478.71	2447.80	1935.63	1630.95	1429.97	1288.24	1183.50	1103.40	1040.53
38000	3572.73	2513.95	1987.95	1675.03	1468.62	1323.06	1215.49	1133.23	1068.65
39000	3666.74	2580.11	2040.26	1719.11	1507.27	1357.87	1247.47	1163.05	1096.77
40000	3760.76	2646.27	2092.58	1763.19	1545.92	1392.69	1279.46	1192.87	1124.89
41000	3854.78	2712.42	2144.89	1807.27	1584.56	1427.51	1311.45	1222.69	1153.02
42000	3948.80	2778.58	2197.21	1851.35	1623.21	1462.32	1343.43	1252.51	1181.14
43000	4042.82	2844.74	2249.52	1895.43	1661.86	1497.14	1375.42	1282.33	1209.26
44000	4136.84	2910.89	2301.83	1939.50	1700.51	1531.96	1407.41	1312.15	1237.38
45000	4230.86	2977.05	2354.15	1983.58	1739.16	1566.78	1439.39	1341.98	1265.51
46000	4324.88	3043.21	2406.46	2027.66	1777.80	1601.59	1471.38	1371.80	1293.63
47000	4418.90	3109.36	2458.78	2071.74	1816.45	1636.41	1503.37	1401.62	1321.75
48000	4512.92	3175.52	2511.09	2115.82	1855.10	1671.23	1535.35	1431.44	1349.87
49000	4606.93	3241.68	2563.41	2159.90	1893.75	1706.04	1567.34	1461.26	1377.99
50000	4700.95	3307.83	2615.72	2203.98	1932.40	1740.86	1599.32	1491.08	1406.12
51000	4794.97	3373.99	2668.04	2248.06	1971.04	1775.68	1631.31	1520.91	1434.24
52000	4888.99	3440.15	2720.35	2292.14	2009.69	1810.50	1663.30	1550.73	1462.36
53000	4983.01	3506.30	2772.66	2336.22	2048.34	1845.31	1695.28	1580.55	1490.48
54000	5077.03	3572.46	2824.98	2380.30	2086.99	1880.13	1727.27	1610.37	1518.61
55000	5171.05	3638.61	2877.29	2424.38	2125.63	1914.95	1759.26	1640.19	1546.73
56000	5265.07	3704.77	2929.61	2468.46	2164.28	1949.76	1791.24	1670.01	1574.85
57000	5359.09	3770.93	2981.92	2512.54	2202.93	1984.58	1823.23	1699.84	1602.97
58000	5453.11	3837.08	3034.24	2556.62	2241.58	2019.40	1855.22	1729.66	1631.09
59000	5547.12	3903.24	3086.55	2600.70	2280.23	2054.22	1887.20	1759.48	1659.22
60000	5641.14	3969.40	3138.86	2644.78	2318.87	2089.03	1919.19	1789.30	1687.34
61000	5735.16	4035.55	3191.18	2688.86	2357.52	2123.85	1951.17	1819.12	1715.46
62000	5829.18	4101.71	3243.49	2732.94	2396.17	2158.67	1983.16	1848.94	1743.58
63000	5923.20	4167.87	3295.81	2777.02	2434.82	2193.48	2015.15	1878.76	1771.71
64000	6017.22	4234.02	3348.12	2821.10	2473.46	2228.30	2047.13	1908.59	1799.83
65000	6111.24	4300.18	3400.44	2865.17	2512.11	2263.12	2079.12	1938.41	1827.95
66000	6205.26	4366.34	3452.75	2909.25	2550.76	2297.93	2111.11	1968.23	1856.07
67000	6299.28	4432.49	3505.06	2953.33	2589.41	2332.75	2143.09	1998.05	1884.19
68000	6393.30	4498.65	3557.38	2997.41	2628.06	2367.57	2175.08	2027.87	1912.32
69000	6487.31	4564.81	3609.69	3041.49	2666.70	2402.39	2207.07	2057.69	1940.44
70000	6581.33	4630.96	3662.01	3085.57	2705.35	2437.20	2239.05	2087.52	1968.56
75000	7051.43	4961.75	3923.58	3305.97	2898.59	2611.29	2398.98	2236.62	2109.17
80000	7521.52	5292.53	4185.15	3526.37	3091.83	2785.37	2558.92	2385.73	2249.78
100000	9401.90	6615.66	5231.44	4407.96	3864.79	3481.72	3198.64	2982.16	2812.23

236

TERM AMOUNT	6 YEARS	7 YEARS	8 YEARS	9 YEARS	10 YEARS	11 YEARS	12 YEARS	13 YEARS	14 YEARS
$ 25	.65	.60	.57	.55	.54	.52	.52	.51	.50
50	1.29	1.20	1.14	1.10	1.07	1.04	1.03	1.01	1.00
75	1.93	1.80	1.71	1.65	1.60	1.56	1.54	1.51	1.50
100	2.57	2.40	2.28	2.20	2.13	2.08	2.05	2.02	2.00
200	5.14	4.80	4.56	4.39	4.26	4.16	4.09	4.03	3.99
300	7.70	7.20	6.84	6.58	6.39	6.24	6.13	6.04	5.98
400	10.27	9.59	9.12	8.77	8.51	8.32	8.17	8.05	7.97
500	12.83	11.99	11.40	10.96	10.64	10.40	10.21	10.07	9.96
600	15.40	14.39	13.68	13.16	12.77	12.48	12.25	12.08	11.95
700	17.96	16.79	15.95	15.35	14.90	14.55	14.29	14.09	13.94
800	20.53	19.18	18.23	17.54	17.02	16.63	16.33	16.10	15.93
900	23.09	21.58	20.51	19.73	19.15	18.71	18.38	18.12	17.92
1000	25.66	23.98	22.79	21.92	21.28	20.79	20.42	20.13	19.91
2000	51.31	47.95	45.57	43.84	42.55	41.58	40.83	40.25	39.81
3000	76.96	71.92	68.36	65.76	63.82	62.36	61.24	60.38	59.71
4000	102.61	95.90	91.14	87.68	85.10	83.15	81.65	80.50	79.61
5000	128.26	119.87	113.93	109.59	106.37	103.93	102.07	100.63	99.51
6000	153.92	143.84	136.71	131.51	127.64	124.72	122.48	120.75	119.41
7000	179.57	167.82	159.49	153.43	148.92	145.50	142.89	140.88	139.31
8000	205.22	191.79	182.28	175.35	170.19	166.29	163.30	161.00	159.21
9000	230.87	215.76	205.06	197.27	191.46	187.07	183.72	181.13	179.11
10000	256.52	239.73	227.85	219.18	212.73	207.86	204.13	201.25	199.01
15000	384.78	359.60	341.77	328.77	319.10	311.79	306.19	301.87	298.52
20000	513.04	479.46	455.69	438.36	425.46	415.71	408.25	402.50	398.02
25000	641.30	599.33	569.61	547.95	531.83	519.64	510.32	503.12	497.53
30000	769.56	719.19	683.53	657.54	638.19	623.57	612.38	603.74	597.03
35000	897.82	839.06	797.45	767.13	744.56	727.49	714.44	704.37	696.54
36000	923.47	863.03	820.24	789.05	765.83	748.28	734.85	724.49	716.44
37000	949.12	887.00	843.02	810.96	787.10	769.06	755.27	744.61	736.34
38000	974.77	910.98	865.81	832.88	808.38	789.85	775.68	764.74	756.24
39000	1000.43	934.95	888.59	854.80	829.65	810.63	796.09	784.86	776.14
40000	1026.08	958.92	911.37	876.72	850.92	831.42	816.50	804.99	796.04
41000	1051.73	982.90	934.16	898.64	872.19	852.21	836.91	825.11	815.94
42000	1077.38	1006.87	956.94	920.55	893.47	872.99	857.33	845.24	835.84
43000	1103.03	1030.84	979.73	942.47	914.74	893.78	877.74	865.36	855.74
44000	1128.68	1054.82	1002.51	964.39	936.01	914.56	898.15	885.49	875.64
45000	1154.34	1078.79	1025.30	986.31	957.29	935.35	918.56	905.61	895.54
46000	1179.99	1102.76	1048.08	1008.22	978.56	956.13	938.98	925.74	915.44
47000	1205.64	1126.73	1070.86	1030.14	999.83	976.92	959.39	945.86	935.35
48000	1231.29	1150.71	1093.65	1052.06	1021.11	997.70	979.80	965.98	955.25
49000	1256.94	1174.68	1116.43	1073.98	1042.38	1018.49	1000.21	986.11	975.15
50000	1282.60	1198.65	1139.22	1095.90	1063.65	1039.27	1020.63	1006.23	995.05
51000	1308.25	1222.63	1162.00	1117.81	1084.92	1060.06	1041.04	1026.36	1014.95
52000	1333.90	1246.60	1184.78	1139.73	1106.20	1080.84	1061.45	1046.48	1034.85
53000	1359.55	1270.57	1207.57	1161.65	1127.47	1101.63	1081.86	1066.61	1054.75
54000	1385.20	1294.55	1230.35	1183.57	1148.74	1122.42	1102.28	1086.73	1074.65
55000	1410.85	1318.52	1253.14	1205.48	1170.02	1143.20	1122.69	1106.86	1094.55
56000	1436.51	1342.49	1275.92	1227.40	1191.29	1163.99	1143.10	1126.98	1114.45
57000	1462.16	1366.46	1298.71	1249.32	1212.56	1184.77	1163.51	1147.11	1134.35
58000	1487.81	1390.44	1321.49	1271.24	1233.83	1205.56	1183.93	1167.23	1154.25
59000	1513.46	1414.41	1344.27	1293.16	1255.11	1226.34	1204.34	1187.36	1174.16
60000	1539.11	1438.38	1367.06	1315.07	1276.38	1247.13	1224.75	1207.48	1194.06
61000	1564.76	1462.36	1389.84	1336.99	1297.65	1267.91	1245.16	1227.60	1213.96
62000	1590.42	1486.33	1412.63	1358.91	1318.93	1288.70	1265.58	1247.73	1233.86
63000	1616.07	1510.30	1435.41	1380.83	1340.20	1309.48	1285.99	1267.85	1253.76
64000	1641.72	1534.27	1458.20	1402.74	1361.47	1330.27	1306.40	1287.98	1273.66
65000	1667.37	1558.25	1480.98	1424.66	1382.74	1351.05	1326.81	1308.10	1293.56
66000	1693.02	1582.22	1503.76	1446.58	1404.02	1371.84	1347.23	1328.23	1313.46
67000	1718.68	1606.19	1526.55	1468.50	1425.29	1392.63	1367.64	1348.35	1333.36
68000	1744.33	1630.17	1549.33	1490.42	1446.56	1413.41	1388.05	1368.48	1353.26
69000	1769.98	1654.14	1572.12	1512.33	1467.84	1434.20	1408.46	1388.60	1373.16
70000	1795.63	1678.11	1594.90	1534.25	1489.11	1454.98	1428.88	1408.73	1393.07
75000	1923.89	1797.98	1708.82	1643.84	1595.47	1558.91	1530.94	1509.35	1492.57
80000	2052.15	1917.84	1822.74	1753.43	1701.84	1662.84	1633.00	1609.97	1592.07
100000	2565.19	2397.30	2278.43	2191.79	2127.30	2078.54	2041.25	2012.46	1990.09

24% MONTHLY PAYMENT
NECESSARY TO AMORTIZE A LOAN

TERM AMOUNT	15 YEARS	16 YEARS	17 YEARS	18 YEARS	19 YEARS	20 YEARS	21 YEARS	22 YEARS	23 YEARS
$ 25	.50	.49	.49	.49	.49	.49	.49	.48	.48
50	.99	.98	.98	.97	.97	.97	.97	.96	.96
75	1.48	1.47	1.47	1.46	1.45	1.45	1.45	1.44	1.44
100	1.98	1.96	1.95	1.94	1.94	1.93	1.93	1.92	1.92
200	3.95	3.92	3.90	3.88	3.87	3.86	3.85	3.84	3.84
300	5.92	5.88	5.85	5.82	5.80	5.79	5.77	5.76	5.76
400	7.90	7.84	7.80	7.76	7.74	7.71	7.70	7.68	7.67
500	9.87	9.80	9.75	9.70	9.67	9.64	9.62	9.60	9.59
600	11.84	11.76	11.69	11.64	11.60	11.57	11.54	11.52	11.51
700	13.81	13.72	13.64	13.58	13.53	13.50	13.47	13.44	13.43
800	15.79	15.68	15.59	15.52	15.47	15.42	15.39	15.36	15.34
900	17.76	17.63	17.54	17.46	17.40	17.35	17.31	17.28	17.26
1000	19.73	19.59	19.49	19.40	19.33	19.28	19.24	19.20	19.18
2000	39.46	39.18	38.97	38.80	38.66	38.55	38.47	38.40	38.35
3000	59.18	58.77	58.45	58.19	57.99	57.83	57.70	57.60	57.52
4000	78.91	78.36	77.93	77.59	77.32	77.10	76.93	76.80	76.69
5000	98.64	97.95	97.41	96.98	96.65	96.38	96.17	96.00	95.87
6000	118.36	117.54	116.89	116.38	115.97	115.65	115.40	115.20	115.04
7000	138.09	137.13	136.37	135.77	135.30	134.93	134.63	134.40	134.21
8000	157.81	156.72	155.85	155.17	154.63	154.20	153.86	153.59	153.38
9000	177.54	176.30	175.33	174.57	173.96	173.48	173.10	172.79	172.55
10000	197.27	195.89	194.81	193.96	193.29	192.75	192.33	191.99	191.73
15000	295.90	293.84	292.22	290.94	289.93	289.13	288.49	287.99	287.59
20000	394.53	391.78	389.62	387.92	386.57	385.50	384.65	383.98	383.45
25000	493.16	489.73	487.03	484.90	483.21	481.87	480.81	479.97	479.31
30000	591.79	587.67	584.43	581.87	579.85	578.25	576.98	575.97	575.17
35000	690.42	685.61	681.83	678.85	676.49	674.62	673.14	671.96	671.03
36000	710.14	705.20	701.32	698.25	695.82	693.90	692.37	691.16	690.20
37000	729.87	724.79	720.80	717.64	715.15	713.17	711.60	710.36	709.37
38000	749.59	744.38	740.28	737.04	734.48	732.45	730.84	729.56	728.54
39000	769.32	763.97	759.76	756.43	753.80	751.72	750.07	748.76	747.71
40000	789.05	783.56	779.24	775.83	773.13	771.00	769.30	767.95	766.89
41000	808.77	803.15	798.72	795.22	792.46	790.27	788.53	787.15	786.06
42000	828.50	822.74	818.20	814.62	811.79	809.55	807.77	806.35	805.23
43000	848.22	842.33	837.68	834.02	831.12	828.82	827.00	825.55	824.40
44000	867.95	861.91	857.16	853.41	850.45	848.09	846.23	844.75	843.57
45000	887.68	881.50	876.64	872.81	869.77	867.37	865.46	863.95	862.75
46000	907.40	901.09	896.12	892.20	889.10	886.64	884.70	883.15	881.92
47000	927.13	920.68	915.61	911.60	908.43	905.92	903.93	902.35	901.09
48000	946.85	940.27	935.09	930.99	927.76	925.19	923.16	921.54	920.26
49000	966.58	959.86	954.57	950.39	947.09	944.47	942.39	940.74	939.43
50000	986.31	979.45	974.05	969.79	966.41	963.74	961.62	959.94	958.61
51000	1006.03	999.04	993.53	989.18	985.74	983.02	980.86	979.14	977.78
52000	1025.76	1018.63	1013.01	1008.58	1005.07	1002.29	1000.09	998.34	996.95
53000	1045.48	1038.21	1032.49	1027.97	1024.40	1021.57	1019.32	1017.54	1016.12
54000	1065.21	1057.80	1051.97	1047.37	1043.73	1040.84	1038.55	1036.74	1035.29
55000	1084.94	1077.39	1071.45	1066.76	1063.06	1060.12	1057.79	1055.94	1054.47
56000	1104.66	1096.98	1090.93	1086.16	1082.38	1079.39	1077.02	1075.13	1073.64
57000	1124.39	1116.57	1110.41	1105.55	1101.71	1098.67	1096.25	1094.33	1092.81
58000	1144.12	1136.16	1129.89	1124.95	1121.04	1117.94	1115.48	1113.53	1111.98
59000	1163.84	1155.75	1149.38	1144.35	1140.37	1137.22	1134.72	1132.73	1131.15
60000	1183.57	1175.34	1168.86	1163.74	1159.70	1156.49	1153.95	1151.93	1150.33
61000	1203.29	1194.93	1188.34	1183.14	1179.02	1175.77	1173.18	1171.13	1169.50
62000	1223.02	1214.51	1207.82	1202.53	1198.35	1195.04	1192.41	1190.33	1188.67
63000	1242.75	1234.10	1227.30	1221.93	1217.68	1214.32	1211.65	1209.53	1207.84
64000	1262.47	1253.69	1246.78	1241.32	1237.01	1233.59	1230.88	1228.72	1227.01
65000	1282.20	1273.28	1266.26	1260.72	1256.34	1252.86	1250.11	1247.92	1246.18
66000	1301.92	1292.87	1285.74	1280.12	1275.67	1272.14	1269.34	1267.12	1265.36
67000	1321.65	1312.46	1305.22	1299.51	1294.99	1291.41	1288.58	1286.32	1284.53
68000	1341.38	1332.05	1324.70	1318.91	1314.32	1310.69	1307.81	1305.52	1303.70
69000	1361.10	1351.64	1344.18	1338.30	1333.65	1329.96	1327.04	1324.72	1322.87
70000	1380.83	1371.22	1363.66	1357.70	1352.98	1349.24	1346.27	1343.92	1342.05
75000	1479.46	1469.17	1461.07	1454.68	1449.62	1445.61	1442.43	1439.91	1437.91
80000	1578.09	1567.11	1558.47	1551.65	1546.26	1541.99	1538.60	1535.90	1533.77
100000	1972.61	1958.89	1948.09	1939.57	1932.82	1927.48	1923.24	1919.88	1917.21

238

MONTHLY PAYMENT **24%**
NECESSARY TO AMORTIZE A LOAN

TERM AMOUNT	24 YEARS	25 YEARS	26 YEARS	27 YEARS	28 YEARS	29 YEARS	30 YEARS	35 YEARS	40 YEARS
$ 25	.48	.48	.48	.48	.48	.48	.48	.48	.48
50	.96	.96	.96	.96	.96	.96	.96	.96	.96
75	1.44	1.44	1.44	1.44	1.44	1.44	1.44	1.44	1.44
100	1.92	1.92	1.92	1.92	1.92	1.91	1.91	1.91	1.91
200	3.84	3.83	3.83	3.83	3.83	3.82	3.82	3.82	3.82
300	5.75	5.75	5.74	5.74	5.74	5.73	5.73	5.73	5.73
400	7.67	7.66	7.65	7.65	7.65	7.64	7.64	7.63	7.63
500	9.58	9.57	9.57	9.57	9.56	9.55	9.55	9.54	9.54
600	11.50	11.49	11.48	11.47	11.47	11.46	11.46	11.45	11.45
700	13.41	13.40	13.39	13.38	13.38	13.37	13.37	13.36	13.35
800	15.33	15.31	15.30	15.29	15.29	15.28	15.28	15.26	15.26
900	17.24	17.23	17.21	17.20	17.20	17.19	17.19	17.17	17.17
1000	19.16	19.14	19.13	19.11	19.11	19.10	19.09	19.08	19.07
2000	38.31	38.27	38.25	38.22	38.21	38.19	38.18	38.15	38.14
3000	57.46	57.41	57.37	57.33	57.31	57.29	57.27	57.23	57.21
4000	76.61	76.54	76.49	76.44	76.41	76.38	76.36	76.30	76.28
5000	95.76	95.67	95.61	95.55	95.51	95.48	95.45	95.38	95.35
6000	114.91	114.81	114.73	114.66	114.61	114.57	114.54	114.45	114.42
7000	134.06	133.94	133.85	133.77	133.71	133.67	133.63	133.53	133.49
8000	153.21	153.08	152.97	152.88	152.81	152.76	152.72	152.60	152.56
9000	172.36	172.21	172.09	171.99	171.91	171.85	171.81	171.68	171.63
10000	191.51	191.34	191.21	191.10	191.02	190.95	190.89	190.75	190.70
15000	287.27	287.01	286.81	286.65	286.52	286.42	286.34	286.12	286.05
20000	383.02	382.68	382.41	382.20	382.03	381.89	381.78	381.49	381.40
25000	478.77	478.35	478.01	477.75	477.53	477.36	477.23	476.87	476.75
30000	574.53	574.02	573.62	573.29	573.04	572.83	572.67	572.24	572.10
35000	670.28	669.69	669.22	668.84	668.54	668.31	668.12	667.61	667.45
36000	689.43	688.82	688.34	687.95	687.64	687.40	687.21	686.69	686.52
37000	708.58	707.96	707.46	707.06	706.75	706.49	706.29	705.76	705.59
38000	727.73	727.09	726.58	726.17	725.85	725.59	725.38	724.83	724.66
39000	746.88	746.22	745.70	745.28	744.95	744.68	744.47	743.91	743.73
40000	766.03	765.36	764.82	764.39	764.05	763.78	763.56	762.98	762.80
41000	785.19	784.49	783.94	783.50	783.15	782.87	782.65	782.06	781.87
42000	804.34	803.63	803.06	802.61	802.25	801.97	801.74	801.13	800.94
43000	823.49	822.76	822.18	821.72	821.35	821.06	820.83	820.21	820.01
44000	842.64	841.89	841.30	840.83	840.45	840.15	839.92	839.28	839.08
45000	861.79	861.03	860.42	859.94	859.55	859.25	859.01	858.36	858.15
46000	880.94	880.16	879.54	879.05	878.66	878.34	878.09	877.43	877.22
47000	900.09	899.29	898.66	898.16	897.76	897.44	897.18	896.50	896.29
48000	919.24	918.43	917.78	917.27	916.86	916.53	916.27	915.58	915.36
49000	938.39	937.56	936.90	936.38	935.96	935.63	935.36	934.65	934.43
50000	957.54	956.70	956.02	955.49	955.06	954.72	954.45	953.73	953.50
51000	976.69	975.83	975.14	974.60	974.16	973.81	973.54	972.80	972.57
52000	995.84	994.96	994.26	993.71	993.26	992.91	992.63	991.88	991.64
53000	1014.99	1014.10	1013.38	1012.82	1012.36	1012.00	1011.72	1010.95	1010.71
54000	1034.15	1033.23	1032.50	1031.93	1031.46	1031.10	1030.81	1030.03	1029.78
55000	1053.30	1052.37	1051.63	1051.04	1050.57	1050.19	1049.89	1049.10	1048.85
56000	1072.45	1071.50	1070.75	1070.15	1069.67	1069.29	1068.98	1068.18	1067.92
57000	1091.60	1090.63	1089.87	1089.25	1088.77	1088.38	1088.07	1087.25	1086.99
58000	1110.75	1109.77	1108.99	1108.36	1107.87	1107.47	1107.16	1106.32	1106.05
59000	1129.90	1128.90	1128.11	1127.47	1126.97	1126.57	1126.25	1125.40	1125.12
60000	1149.05	1148.03	1147.23	1146.58	1146.07	1145.66	1145.34	1144.47	1144.19
61000	1168.20	1167.17	1166.35	1165.69	1165.17	1164.76	1164.43	1163.55	1163.26
62000	1187.35	1186.30	1185.47	1184.80	1184.27	1183.85	1183.52	1182.62	1182.33
63000	1206.50	1205.44	1204.59	1203.91	1203.37	1202.95	1202.61	1201.70	1201.40
64000	1225.65	1224.57	1223.71	1223.02	1222.48	1222.04	1221.69	1220.77	1220.47
65000	1244.80	1243.70	1242.83	1242.13	1241.58	1241.13	1240.78	1239.85	1239.54
66000	1263.95	1262.84	1261.95	1261.24	1260.68	1260.23	1259.87	1258.92	1258.61
67000	1283.10	1281.97	1281.07	1280.35	1279.78	1279.32	1278.96	1277.99	1277.68
68000	1302.26	1301.11	1300.19	1299.46	1298.88	1298.42	1298.05	1297.07	1296.75
69000	1321.41	1320.24	1319.31	1318.57	1317.98	1317.51	1317.14	1316.14	1315.82
70000	1340.56	1339.37	1338.43	1337.68	1337.08	1336.61	1336.23	1335.22	1334.89
75000	1436.31	1435.04	1434.03	1433.23	1432.59	1432.08	1431.67	1430.59	1430.24
80000	1532.06	1530.71	1529.63	1528.78	1528.09	1527.55	1527.12	1525.96	1525.59
100000	1915.08	1913.39	1912.04	1910.97	1910.12	1909.44	1908.89	1907.45	1906.99

239

SUPPLEMENTARY TABLES

LOAN PROGRESS CHARTS

MONTHLY PAYMENT FACTOR TABLES

BASIC PAYMENT FACTOR TABLES

MONTHLY INTEREST FACTORS

LOAN PROGRESS CHART

Showing the dollar balance remaining on a $1,000 loan

INTEREST RATE	ORIG TERM	ELAPSED TERM IN YEARS									
		2	3	4	5	8	10	12	15	20	25
7%	10	851	768	680	585	258					
	15	918	873	825	773	594	452	290			
	20	950	923	893	861	752	666	566	389		
	25	968	950	931	910	840	784	720	606	355	
	30	979	967	954	940	893	856	813	737	570	333
7¼%	10	853	771	683	588	261					
	15	920	875	827	776	598	456	293			
	20	951	925	896	864	757	671	572	395		
	25	969	952	933	913	844	789	726	613	360	
	30	980	968	956	943	897	861	819	744	578	340
7½%	10	854	773	685	591	263					
	15	921	877	830	779	602	461	296			
	20	953	926	898	868	761	676	578	400		
	25	970	953	935	916	849	795	732	619	366	
	30	980	970	958	945	901	866	825	751	585	346
7¾%	10	856	775	688	594	265					
	15	923	880	833	783	607	465	300			
	20	954	928	901	871	766	681	583	405		
	25	971	955	938	919	853	800	738	626	372	
	30	981	971	960	947	905	870	830	758	593	352
8%	10	857	777	691	597	267					
	15	924	882	836	786	611	469	303			
	20	955	930	903	874	770	687	589	410		
	25	972	957	940	921	857	805	744	633	378	
	30	982	972	961	950	908	875	836	764	601	359
8¼%	10	859	779	693	600	269					
	15	926	884	838	789	615	473	307			
	20	957	932	905	877	775	692	594	415		
	25	973	958	942	924	861	810	750	639	383	
	30	983	973	963	952	912	879	841	771	608	365
8½%	10	861	782	696	603	271					
	15	927	886	841	792	619	477	310			
	20	958	934	908	880	779	697	600	420		
	25	974	960	944	926	865	815	755	646	389	
	30	984	975	965	954	915	884	846	777	616	371
8¾%	10	862	784	698	605	274					
	15	929	888	844	795	623	482	313			
	20	959	936	910	882	783	702	605	425		
	25	975	962	946	929	869	820	761	652	395	
	30	985	976	966	956	918	888	851	783	623	377
9%	10	864	786	701	608	276					
	15	930	890	846	799	628	486	317			
	20	960	937	912	885	788	707	610	430		
	25	976	962	947	931	873	824	766	658	400	
	30	985	977	968	958	922	892	856	789	630	383
9¼%	10	865	788	704	611	278					
	15	931	892	849	802	632	490	320			
	20	961	939	915	888	792	712	616	435		
	25	977	964	949	933	876	829	772	664	406	
	30	986	978	969	959	925	896	861	795	637	390
9½%	10	867	790	706	614	280					
	15	933	894	851	805	636	494	323			
	20	962	941	917	891	796	717	621	440		
	25	978	965	951	936	880	833	777	671	412	
	30	987	979	970	961	928	899	865	801	645	396

LOAN PROGRESS CHART

Showing the dollar balance remaining on a $1,000 loan

INTEREST RATE	ORIG TERM	ELAPSED TERM IN YEARS									
		2	3	4	5	8	10	12	15	20	25
9¾%	10	868	792	709	617	282					
	15	934	896	854	808	640	498	327			
	20	963	942	919	893	800	722	626	445		
	25	979	966	953	938	884	838	782	677	417	
	30	987	980	972	963	930	903	870	807	651	402
10%	10	870	794	711	620	285					
	15	935	898	856	811	644	502	330			
	20	964	944	921	896	804	726	632	450		
	25	979	968	054	940	887	842	787	683	423	
	30	988	981	974	964	933	906	874	812	658	400
10¼%	10	871	796	714	622	287					
	15	936	899	859	814	648	506	334			
	20	965	945	923	898	808	731	637	455		
	25	980	969	956	942	890	846	792	689	429	
	30	988	982	976	966	936	910	878	817	665	414
10½%	10	873	798	716	625	289					
	15	938	901	861	817	652	510	337			
	20	966	947	925	901	812	736	642	460		
	25	981	970	958	944	894	850	797	694	434	
	30	989	983	975	967	938	913	882	823	672	420
10¾%	10	874	800	719	628	291					
	15	939	903	863	819	656	515	340			
	20	967	948	927	903	816	740	647	465		
	25	982	971	959	946	897	854	802	700	440	
	30	989	983	976	969	941	916	886	828	678	426
11%	10	875	802	721	631	293					
	15	940	905	866	822	660	519	344			
	20	968	950	929	906	820	745	652	470		
	25	982	972	961	948	900	858	807	706	445	
	30	990	984	978	970	943	920	890	833	685	432
11¼%	10	877	804	724	633	296					
	15	941	907	868	825	664	523	347			
	20	969	951	931	908	823	749	657	475		
	25	983	973	962	950	903	862	812	711	451	
	30	990	985	979	972	945	923	894	838	691	438
11½%	10	878	806	726	636	298					
	15	942	908	870	828	668	527	350			
	20	970	952	933	910	827	754	662	479		
	25	984	974	963	951	906	866	816	717	456	
	30	991	986	980	973	948	925	898	843	697	444
11¾%	10	880	808	729	639	300					
	15	944	910	873	831	671	531	354			
	20	971	954	934	913	831	758	667	484		
	25	984	975	965	953	909	870	821	722	462	
	30	991	986	981	974	950	928	901	847	704	450
12%	10	881	810	731	642	302					
	15	945	912	875	833	675	535	357			
	20	972	955	936	915	834	762	672	489		
	25	985	976	966	955	912	873	825	728	467	
	30	992	987	982	975	952	931	905	852	710	455
12¼%	10	882	812	733	644	304					
	15	946	913	877	836	679	539	361			
	20	973	956	938	917	838	767	676	494		
	25	986	977	967	956	914	877	829	733	472	
	30	992	988	982	976	954	934	908	856	716	461

LOAN PROGRESS CHART

Showing the dollar balance remaining on a $1,000 loan

INTEREST RATE	ORIG TERM	ELAPSED TERM IN YEARS									
		2	3	4	5	8	10	12	15	20	25
12½%	10	884	814	736	647	307					
	15	947	915	879	839	683	543	364			
	20	973	957	939	919	841	771	681	499		
	25	986	978	968	958	917	880	833	738	478	
	30	993	988	983	977	956	936	911	860	722	467
12¾%	10	885	816	738	650	309					
	15	948	917	881	841	687	547	367			
	20	974	959	941	921	844	775	686	503		
	25	987	979	970	959	920	884	838	743	483	
	30	993	989	984	978	958	939	914	865	727	473
13%	10	886	818	740	652	311					
	15	949	918	883	844	690	551	371			
	20	975	960	943	923	848	779	691	508		
	25	987	979	971	961	922	887	842	748	488	
	30	993	989	985	979	959	941	917	869	733	478
13¼%	10	888	820	743	655	313					
	15	950	920	885	846	694	554	374			
	20	976	961	944	925	851	783	695	513		
	25	988	980	972	962	924	890	846	753	493	
	30	994	990	985	980	961	943	920	873	739	484
13½%	10	889	822	745	658	315					
	15	951	921	887	849	698	558	377			
	20	976	962	946	927	854	787	700	518		
	25	988	981	973	963	927	893	849	758	499	
	30	994	990	986	981	963	945	923	876	744	489
13¾%	10	890	824	747	660	318					
	15	952	923	889	851	701	562	381			
	20	977	963	947	929	857	791	704	522		
	25	989	982	974	965	929	896	853	763	504	
	30	994	991	987	982	964	948	926	880	749	495
14%	10	892	826	750	663	320					
	15	953	924	891	854	705	566	384			
	20	978	964	949	931	860	795	709	527		
	25	989	982	975	966	931	899	857	768	509	
	30	995	991	987	983	966	950	928	884	755	500
14¼%	10	893	827	752	666	322					
	15	954	926	893	856	708	570	387			
	20	978	965	950	933	863	798	713	531		
	25	990	983	976	967	934	902	861	772	514	
	30	995	992	988	984	967	952	931	887	760	506
14½%	10	894	829	754	668	324					
	15	955	927	895	859	712	574	391			
	20	979	966	951	934	866	802	717	536		
	25	990	984	977	968	936	905	864	777	519	
	30	995	992	989	985	969	953	934	891	765	511
14¾%	10	895	831	757	671	326					
	15	956	929	897	861	715	577	394			
	20	980	967	953	936	869	806	722	541		
	25	990	984	978	970	938	908	868	781	524	
	30	995	992	989	985	970	955	936	894	770	516
15%	10	897	833	759	673	329					
	15	957	930	899	863	719	581	397			
	20	980	968	954	938	872	809	726	545		
	25	991	985	978	971	940	910	871	786	529	
	30	996	993	990	986	971	957	938	897	775	522

LOAN PROGRESS CHART

Showing the dollar balance remaining on a $1,000 loan

INTEREST RATE	ORIG TERM	ELAPSED TERM IN YEARS									
		2	3	4	5	8	10	12	15	20	25
15¼%	10	898	834	761	676	331					
	15	958	931	901	865	722	585	401			
	20	981	969	955	939	875	813	730	549		
	25	991	986	979	972	942	913	874	790	534	
	30	996	993	990	987	972	959	940	901	779	527
15½%	10	899	836	763	678	333					
	15	959	933	903	868	726	589	404			
	20	981	970	957	941	878	817	734	554		
	25	991	986	980	973	944	916	877	794	539	
	30	996	994	991	987	974	960	943	904	784	532
15¾%	10	900	838	765	681	335					
	15	959	934	904	870	729	592	407			
	20	982	971	958	943	880	820	738	558		
	25	992	987	981	974	945	918	881	798	544	
	30	996	994	991	988	975	962	945	907	789	537
16%	10	902	840	768	683	337					
	15	960	935	906	872	732	596	411			
	20	983	972	959	944	883	823	742	563		
	25	992	987	981	975	947	920	884	803	549	
	30	996	994	992	988	976	963	947	910	793	542
16¼%	10	903	841	770	686	340					
	15	961	937	908	874	736	600	414			
	20	983	973	960	946	886	827	746	567		
	25	992	988	982	976	949	923	887	807	553	
	30	997	994	992	989	977	965	949	912	798	547
16½%	10	904	843	772	688	342					
	15	962	938	910	876	739	603	417			
	20	984	973	961	947	888	830	750	571		
	25	993	988	983	977	951	925	890	811	558	
	30	997	995	992	990	978	966	951	915	802	552
16¾%	10	905	845	774	691	344					
	15	963	939	911	879	742	607	420			
	20	984	974	962	948	891	833	754	576		
	25	993	989	984	977	952	927	892	814	563	
	30	997	995	993	990	979	968	952	918	806	557
17%	10	906	846	776	693	346					
	15	963	940	913	881	745	611	424			
	20	985	975	963	950	893	836	758	580		
	25	993	989	984	978	954	929	895	818	567	
	30	997	995	994	993	980	969	954	920	810	562
17¼%	10	907	848	778	696	348					
	15	964	941	914	883	749	614	427			
	20	985	976	964	951	895	840	762	584		
	25	994	990	985	979	955	931	898	822	572	
	30	997	995	993	992	981	970	956	923	815	567
17½%	10	908	850	780	698	351					
	15	965	943	916	885	752	618	430			
	20	986	976	965	952	898	843	765	588		
	25	994	990	985	980	957	933	901	826	576	
	30	997	996	994	991	981	971	957	925	819	572
17¾%	10	910	851	782	701	353					
	15	966	944	918	887	755	621	433			
	20	986	977	966	954	900	846	769	592		
	25	994	990	986	981	958	935	903	829	581	
	30	998	996	994	992	982	973	959	928	822	576

LOAN PROGRESS CHART

Showing the dollar balance remaining on a $1,000 loan

INTEREST RATE	ORIG TERM	ELAPSED TERM IN YEARS									
		2	3	4	5	8	10	12	15	20	25
18%	10	911	853	784	703	355					
	15	966	945	919	889	758	625	437			
	20	986	978	967	955	902	849	773	597		
	25	994	991	986	981	960	937	906	833	585	
	30	998	996	994	992	983	974	961	930	826	581
18¼%	10	912	855	786	705	357					
	15	967	946	921	890	761	628	440			
	20	987	978	968	956	905	852	776	601		
	25	995	991	987	982	961	939	908	836	590	
	30	998	996	995	993	984	975	962	932	830	586
18½%	10	913	856	788	708	359					
	15	968	947	922	892	764	632	443			
	20	987	979	969	957	907	854	780	605		
	25	995	991	988	983	962	941	911	840	594	
	30	998	997	995	993	984	976	963	934	834	590
18¾%	10	914	858	791	710	361					
	15	969	948	924	894	767	635	446			
	20	988	980	970	959	909	857	783	609		
	25	995	992	988	983	963	943	913	843	599	
	30	998	997	995	993	985	977	965	936	837	595
19%	10	915	859	793	712	364					
	15	969	949	925	896	770	638	449			
	20	988	980	971	960	911	860	787	613		
	25	995	992	988	984	965	944	915	846	603	
	30	998	997	995	994	986	978	966	938	841	599
19½%	10	917	862	796	717	368					
	15	971	951	928	900	776	645	456			
	20	989	981	973	962	915	865	794	621		
	25	996	993	989	985	967	948	920	853	611	
	30	998	997	996	994	987	979	969	942	848	608
20%	10	919	865	800	722	372					
	15	972	953	930	903	781	652	462			
	20	990	983	974	964	919	871	800	628		
	25	996	993	990	986	969	951	924	859	620	
	30	998	997	996	995	988	981	971	946	854	616
20½%	10	921	868	804	726	377					
	15	973	955	933	906	787	658	468			
	20	990	984	976	966	922	876	806	636		
	25	996	994	991	987	971	954	928	865	628	
	30	999	998	997	995	989	983	973	949	860	625
21%	10	923	871	808	731	381					
	15	974	957	936	910	793	665	474			
	20	991	985	977	968	926	880	813	643		
	25	997	994	992	989	973	956	932	870	636	
	30	999	998	997	996	990	984	975	952	866	633
21½%	10	925	874	812	735	385					
	15	975	959	938	913	798	671	481			
	20	991	986	978	970	929	885	819	651		
	25	997	995	992	989	975	959	935	876	644	
	30	999	998	997	996	991	985	977	955	872	641
22%	10	927	877	815	740	390					
	15	976	960	940	916	803	677	487			
	20	992	986	980	971	933	890	824	658		
	25	997	995	993	990	977	962	939	881	651	
	30	999	998	998	996	992	986	979	958	878	649

LOAN PROGRESS CHART

Showing the dollar balance remaining on a $1,000 loan

INTEREST RATE	ORIG TERM	ELAPSED TERM IN YEARS									
		2	3	4	5	8	10	12	15	20	25
22½%	10	928	879	819	744	394					
	15	977	962	943	919	808	684	493			
	20	992	987	981	973	936	894	830	665		
	25	997	996	993	991	978	964	942	886	659	
	30	999	999	998	997	992	988	980	961	883	657
23%	10	930	882	822	748	398					
	15	978	963	046	922	813	690	499			
	20	993	988	982	974	939	898	836	672		
	25	998	996	994	991	980	966	945	890	666	
	30	999	999	998	997	993	989	982	963	888	664
23½%	10	932	885	826	752	402					
	15	979	965	947	925	818	696	505			
	20	993	989	983	976	942	902	841	679		
	25	998	996	994	992	981	968	948	895	673	
	30	999	999	998	998	994	990	983	966	893	672
24%	10	934	887	829	756	407					
	15	980	966	949	927	823	701	510			
	20	994	989	984	977	944	906	846	685		
	25	998	997	995	993	982	970	951	899	680	
	30	999	999	998	998	994	990	984	968	897	679

MONTHLY PAYMENT
NECESSARY TO AMORTIZE A LOAN OF $1000

RATE	1 YEAR	2 YEARS	3 YEARS	4 YEARS	5 YEARS	6 YEARS	7 YEARS	8 YEARS
7	86.49	44.73	30.84	23.90	19.76	17.01	15.05	13.59
7 1/8	86.54	44.79	30.89	23.96	19.82	17.06	15.11	13.65
7 1/4	86.60	44.84	30.95	24.02	19.87	17.12	15.17	13.71
7 3/8	86.65	44.90	31.00	24.07	19.93	17.18	15.23	13.77
7 1/2	86.71	44.95	31.06	24.13	19.99	17.24	15.29	13.83
7 5/8	86.77	45.01	31.11	24.19	20.05	17.30	15.35	13.89
7 3/4	86.82	45.06	31.17	24.24	20.10	17.36	15.41	13.95
7 7/8	86.88	45.12	31.23	24.30	20.16	17.42	15.47	14.01
8	86.93	45.17	31.28	24.36	20.22	17.47	15.53	14.08
8 1/8	86.99	45.23	31.34	24.41	20.28	17.53	15.59	14.14
8 1/4	87.05	45.28	31.39	24.47	20.33	17.59	15.65	14.20
8 3/8	87.10	45.34	31.45	24.53	20.39	17.65	15.71	14.26
8 1/2	87.16	45.39	31.50	24.58	20.45	17.71	15.77	14.32
8 5/8	87.21	45.45	31.56	24.64	20.51	17.77	15.83	14.38
8 3/4	87.27	45.50	31.62	24.70	20.57	17.83	15.89	14.45
8 7/8	87.32	45.56	31.67	24.76	20.63	17.89	15.95	14.51
9	87.38	45.61	31.73	24.81	20.68	17.95	16.01	14.57
9 1/8	87.44	45.67	31.78	24.87	20.74	18.01	16.07	14.63
9 1/4	87.49	45.72	31.84	24.93	20.80	18.07	16.13	14.69
9 3/8	87.55	45.78	31.90	24.98	20.86	18.13	16.19	14.76
9 1/2	87.60	45.84	31.95	25.04	20.92	18.19	16.26	14.82
9 5/8	87.66	45.89	32.01	25.10	20.98	18.25	16.32	14.88
9 3/4	87.72	45.95	32.06	25.16	21.04	18.31	16.38	14.95
9 7/8	87.77	46.00	32.12	25.21	21.10	18.37	16.44	15.01
10	87.83	46.06	32.18	25.27	21.15	18.43	16.50	15.07
10 1/8	87.88	46.11	32.23	25.33	21.21	18.49	16.56	15.14
10 1/4	87.94	46.17	32.29	25.39	21.27	18.55	16.63	15.20
10 3/8	87.99	46.22	32.35	25.44	21.33	18.61	16.69	15.26
10 1/2	88.05	46.28	32.40	25.50	21.39	18.67	16.75	15.33
10 5/8	88.11	46.33	32.46	25.56	21.45	18.73	16.81	15.39
10 3/4	88.16	46.39	32.52	25.62	21.51	18.79	16.87	15.45
10 7/8	88.22	46.44	32.57	25.67	21.57	18.85	16.94	15.52
11	88.27	46.50	32.63	25.73	21.63	18.91	17.00	15.58
11 1/8	88.33	46.56	32.68	25.79	21.69	18.98	17.06	15.65
11 1/4	88.38	46.61	32.74	25.85	21.74	19.04	17.12	15.71
11 3/8	88.44	46.67	32.80	25.91	21.80	19.10	17.19	15.78
11 1/2	88.50	46.72	32.85	25.96	21.86	19.16	17.25	15.84
11 5/8	88.55	46.78	32.91	26.02	21.92	19.22	17.31	15.90
11 3/4	88.61	46.83	32.97	26.08	21.98	19.28	17.38	15.97
11 7/8	88.66	46.89	33.02	26.14	22.04	19.34	17.44	16.03
12	88.72	46.94	33.08	26.20	22.10	19.40	17.50	16.10
12 1/8	88.77	47.00	33.14	26.26	22.16	19.47	17.57	16.16
12 1/4	88.83	47.05	33.19	26.31	22.22	19.53	17.63	16.23
12 3/8	88.89	47.11	33.25	26.37	22.28	19.59	17.69	16.29
12 1/2	88.94	47.17	33.31	26.43	22.34	19.65	17.76	16.36
12 5/8	89.00	47.22	33.37	26.49	22.40	19.71	17.82	16.43
12 3/4	89.05	47.28	33.42	26.55	22.46	19.78	17.89	16.49
12 7/8	89.11	47.33	33.48	26.61	22.52	19.84	17.95	16.56
13	89.16	47.39	33.54	26.66	22.59	19.90	18.01	16.62
13 1/8	89.22	47.44	33.59	26.72	22.65	19.96	18.08	16.69
13 1/4	89.27	47.50	33.65	26.78	22.71	20.03	18.14	16.76
13 3/8	89.33	47.55	33.71	26.84	22.77	20.09	18.21	16.82
13 1/2	89.39	47.61	33.76	26.90	22.83	20.15	18.27	16.89
13 5/8	89.44	47.67	33.82	26.96	22.89	20.21	18.34	16.95
13 3/4	89.50	47.72	33.88	27.02	22.95	20.28	18.40	17.02
13 7/8	89.55	47.78	33.94	27.08	23.01	20.34	18.46	17.09
14	89.61	47.83	33.99	27.14	23.07	20.40	18.53	17.15
14 1/8	89.66	47.89	34.05	27.19	23.13	20.46	18.59	17.22
14 1/4	89.72	47.94	34.11	27.25	23.19	20.53	18.66	17.29
14 3/8	89.77	48.00	34.16	27.31	23.25	20.59	18.72	17.36

MONTHLY PAYMENT
NECESSARY TO AMORTIZE A LOAN OF $1000

RATE	1 YEAR	2 YEARS	3 YEARS	4 YEARS	5 YEARS	6 YEARS	7 YEARS	8 YEARS
14 1/2	89.83	48.06	34.22	27.37	23.31	20.65	18.79	17.42
14 5/8	89.89	48.11	34.28	27.43	23.38	20.72	18.85	17.49
14 3/4	89.94	48.17	34.34	27.49	23.44	20.78	18.92	17.56
14 7/8	90.00	48.22	34.39	27.55	23.50	20.84	18.99	17.62
15	90.05	48.28	34.45	27.61	23.56	20.91	19.05	17.69
15 1/8	90.11	48.33	34.51	27.67	23.62	20.97	19.12	17.76
15 1/4	90.16	48.39	34.57	27.73	23.68	21.03	19.18	17.83
15 3/8	90.22	48.45	34.62	27.79	23.74	21.10	19.25	17.90
1b 1/2	90.27	48.50	34.68	27.85	23.81	21.16	19.31	17.96
15 5/8	90.33	48.56	34.74	27.91	23.87	21.23	19.38	10.03
15 3/4	90.38	48.61	34.80	27.97	23.93	21.29	19.45	18.10
15 7/8	90.44	48.67	34.85	28.03	23.99	21.35	19.51	18.17
16	90.50	48.73	34.91	28.09	24.05	21.42	19.58	18.24
16 1/8	90.55	48.78	34.97	28.15	24.12	21.48	19.64	18.30
16 1/4	90.61	48.84	35.03	28.20	24.18	21.55	19.71	18.37
16 3/8	90.66	48.89	35.08	28.26	24.24	21.61	19.78	18.44
16 1/2	90.72	48.95	35.14	28.32	24.30	21.67	19.84	18.51
16 5/8	90.77	49.00	35.20	28.38	24.36	21.74	19.91	18.58
16 3/4	90.83	49.06	35.26	28.44	24.43	21.80	19.98	18.65
16 7/8	90.88	49.12	35.32	28.50	24.49	21.87	20.04	18.72
17	90.94	49.17	35.37	28.56	24.55	21.93	20.11	18.79
17 1/8	90.99	49.23	35.43	28.62	24.61	22.00	20.18	18.86
17 1/4	91.05	49.28	35.49	28.68	24.68	22.06	20.25	18.92
17 3/8	91.10	49.34	35.55	28.75	24.74	22.13	20.31	18.99
17 1/2	91.16	49.40	35.61	28.81	24.80	22.19	20.38	19.06
17 5/8	91.21	49.45	35.66	28.87	24.86	22.26	20.45	19.13
17 3/4	91.27	49.51	35.72	28.93	24.93	22.32	20.51	19.20
17 7/8	91.33	49.56	35.78	28.99	24.99	22.39	20.58	19.27
18	91.38	49.62	35.84	29.05	25.05	22.45	20.65	19.34
18 1/8	91.44	49.68	35.90	29.11	25.11	22.52	20.72	19.41
18 1/4	91.49	49.73	35.95	29.17	25.18	22.58	20.78	19.48
18 3/8	91.55	49.79	36.01	29.23	25.24	22.65	20.85	19.55
18 1/2	91.60	49.84	36.07	29.29	25.30	22.71	20.92	19.62
18 5/8	91.66	49.90	36.13	29.35	25.37	22.78	20.99	19.69
18 3/4	91.71	49.96	36.19	29.41	25.43	22.84	21.06	19.76
18 7/8	91.77	50.01	36.24	29.47	25.49	22.91	21.12	19.83
19	91.82	50.07	36.30	29.53	25.56	22.98	21.19	19.90
19 1/8	91.88	50.12	36.36	29.59	25.62	23.04	21.26	19.97
19 1/4	91.93	50.18	36.42	29.65	25.68	23.11	21.33	20.04
19 3/8	91.99	50.24	36.48	29.71	25.75	23.17	21.40	20.12
19 1/2	92.04	50.29	36.54	29.77	25.81	23.24	21.47	20.19
19 5/8	92.10	50.35	36.59	29.84	25.87	23.31	21.53	20.26
19 3/4	92.15	50.41	36.65	29.90	25.94	23.37	21.60	20.33
19 7/8	92.21	50.46	36.71	29.96	26.00	23.44	21.67	20.40
20	92.26	50.52	36.77	30.02	26.06	23.50	21.74	20.47
20 1/4	92.37	50.63	36.89	30.14	26.19	23.64	21.88	20.61
20 1/2	92.48	50.74	37.00	30.26	26.32	23.77	22.02	20.76
20 3/4	92.59	50.85	37.12	30.39	26.45	23.90	22.15	20.90
21	92.70	50.97	37.24	30.51	26.57	24.04	22.29	21.04
21 1/4	92.81	51.08	37.36	30.63	26.70	24.17	22.43	21.19
21 1/2	92.92	51.19	37.47	30.75	26.83	24.30	22.57	21.33
21 3/4	93.03	51.30	37.59	30.88	26.96	24.44	22.71	21.48
22	93.14	51.42	37.71	31.00	27.09	24.57	22.85	21.62
22 1/4	93.25	51.53	37.83	31.12	27.22	24.71	22.99	21.77
22 1/2	93.36	51.64	37.94	31.25	27.35	24.84	23.13	21.91
22 3/4	93.47	51.76	38.06	31.37	27.48	24.98	23.27	22.06
23	93.58	51.87	38.18	31.49	27.61	25.11	23.41	22.20
23 1/4	93.69	51.98	38.30	31.62	27.74	25.25	23.55	22.35
23 1/2	93.80	52.09	38.42	31.74	27.87	25.38	23.69	22.50
23 3/4	93.91	52.21	38.53	31.87	28.00	25.52	23.84	22.64
24	94.02	52.32	38.65	31.99	28.13	25.66	23.98	22.79

MONTHLY PAYMENT
NECESSARY TO AMORTIZE A LOAN OF $1000

RATE		9 YEARS	10 YEARS	11 YEARS	12 YEARS	13 YEARS	14 YEARS	15 YEARS	16 YEARS
7		12.46	11.56	10.84	10.24	9.73	9.30	8.94	8.62
7	1/8	12.52	11.63	10.90	10.30	9.80	9.37	9.01	8.69
7	1/4	12.58	11.69	10.96	10.37	9.86	9.44	9.07	8.76
7	3/8	12.65	11.75	11.03	10.43	9.93	9.51	9.14	8.83
7	1/2	12.71	11.82	11.09	10.50	10.00	9.57	9.21	8.90
7	5/8	12.77	11.88	11.16	10.56	10.06	9.64	9.28	8.97
7	3/4	12.83	11.94	11.22	10.63	10.13	9.71	9.35	9.04
7	7/8	12.89	12.01	11.29	10.69	10.20	9.78	9.42	9.11
8		12.96	12.07	11.35	10.76	10.26	9.84	9.49	9.18
8	1/8	13.02	12.13	11.42	10.82	10.33	9.91	9.56	9.25
8	1/4	13.08	12.20	11.48	10.89	10.40	9.98	9.63	9.32
8	3/8	13.14	12.26	11.55	10.96	10.47	10.05	9.70	9.39
8	1/2	13.21	12.33	11.61	11.02	10.53	10.12	9.77	9.46
8	5/8	13.27	12.39	11.68	11.09	10.60	10.19	9.84	9.53
8	3/4	13.33	12.45	11.74	11.16	10.67	10.26	9.91	9.61
8	7/8	13.40	12.52	11.81	11.23	10.74	10.33	9.98	9.68
9		13.46	12.58	11.88	11.29	10.81	10.40	10.05	9.75
9	1/8	13.52	12.65	11.94	11.36	10.88	10.47	10.12	9.82
9	1/4	13.59	12.71	12.01	11.43	10.95	10.54	10.19	9.90
9	3/8	13.65	12.78	12.07	11.50	11.02	10.61	10.27	9.97
9	1/2	13.72	12.84	12.14	11.56	11.08	10.68	10.34	10.04
9	5/8	13.78	12.91	12.21	11.63	11.15	10.75	10.41	10.12
9	3/4	13.85	12.98	12.28	11.70	11.22	10.82	10.48	10.19
9	7/8	13.91	13.04	12.34	11.77	11.29	10.89	10.55	10.26
10		13.97	13.11	12.41	11.84	11.36	10.97	10.63	10.34
10	1/8	14.04	13.17	12.48	11.91	11.44	11.04	10.70	10.41
10	1/4	14.10	13.24	12.55	11.98	11.51	11.11	10.77	10.49
10	3/8	14.17	13.31	12.61	12.05	11.58	11.18	10.85	10.56
10	1/2	14.23	13.37	12.68	12.12	11.65	11.25	10.92	10.64
10	5/8	14.30	13.44	12.75	12.19	11.72	11.33	11.00	10.71
10	3/4	14.37	13.51	12.82	12.26	11.79	11.40	11.07	10.79
10	7/8	14.43	13.58	12.89	12.33	11.86	11.47	11.14	10.86
11		14.50	13.64	12.96	12.40	11.93	11.55	11.22	10.94
11	1/8	14.56	13.71	13.03	12.47	12.01	11.62	11.29	11.02
11	1/4	14.63	13.78	13.09	12.54	12.08	11.69	11.37	11.09
11	3/8	14.69	13.84	13.16	12.61	12.15	11.77	11.44	11.17
11	1/2	14.76	13.91	13.23	12.68	12.22	11.84	11.52	11.24
11	5/8	14.83	13.98	13.30	12.75	12.29	11.91	11.59	11.32
11	3/4	14.89	14.05	13.37	12.82	12.37	11.99	11.67	11.40
11	7/8	14.96	14.12	13.44	12.89	12.44	12.06	11.75	11.48
12		15.03	14.19	13.51	12.96	12.51	12.14	11.82	11.55
12	1/8	15.09	14.25	13.58	13.04	12.59	12.21	11.90	11.63
12	1/4	15.16	14.32	13.65	13.11	12.66	12.29	11.97	11.71
12	3/8	15.23	14.39	13.72	13.18	12.73	12.36	12.05	11.79
12	1/2	15.29	14.46	13.79	13.25	12.81	12.44	12.13	11.86
12	5/8	15.36	14.53	13.86	13.32	12.88	12.51	12.20	11.94
12	3/4	15.43	14.60	13.93	13.40	12.96	12.59	12.28	12.02
12	7/8	15.50	14.67	14.01	13.47	13.03	12.66	12.36	12.10
13		15.56	14.74	14.08	13.54	13.10	12.74	12.44	12.18
13	1/8	15.63	14.81	14.15	13.62	13.18	12.82	12.51	12.26
13	1/4	15.70	14.88	14.22	13.69	13.25	12.89	12.59	12.34
13	3/8	15.77	14.95	14.29	13.76	13.33	12.97	12.67	12.42
13	1/2	15.84	15.02	14.36	13.84	13.40	13.05	12.75	12.50
13	5/8	15.90	15.09	14.43	13.91	13.48	13.12	12.82	12.58
13	3/4	15.97	15.16	14.51	13.98	13.55	13.20	12.90	12.66
13	7/8	16.04	15.23	14.58	14.06	13.63	13.28	12.98	12.74
14		16.11	15.30	14.65	14.13	13.70	13.35	13.06	12.82
14	1/8	16.18	15.37	14.72	14.20	13.78	13.43	13.14	12.90
14	1/4	16.25	15.44	14.80	14.28	13.86	13.51	13.22	12.98
14	3/8	16.32	15.51	14.87	14.35	13.93	13.59	13.30	13.06

MONTHLY PAYMENT
NECESSARY TO AMORTIZE A LOAN OF $1000

RATE	9 YEARS	10 YEARS	11 YEARS	12 YEARS	13 YEARS	14 YEARS	15 YEARS	16 YEARS
14 1/2	16.39	15.58	14.94	14.43	14.01	13.66	13.38	13.14
14 5/8	16.46	15.65	15.01	14.50	14.08	13.74	13.46	13.22
14 3/4	16.52	15.72	15.09	14.58	14.16	13.82	13.54	13.30
14 7/8	16.59	15.79	15.16	14.65	14.24	13.90	13.62	13.38
15	16.66	15.87	15.23	14.73	14.31	13.98	13.70	13.46
15 1/8	16.73	15.94	15.31	14.80	14.39	14.05	13.78	13.54
15 1/4	16.80	16.01	15.38	14.88	14.47	14.13	13.86	13.62
15 3/8	16.87	16.08	15.45	14.95	14.55	14.21	13.94	13.71
15 1/2	16.94	16.15	15.53	15.03	14.62	14.29	14.02	13.79
15 5/8	17.01	16.22	15.60	15.10	14.70	14.37	14.10	13.87
15 3/4	17.08	16.30	15.68	15.18	14.78	14.45	14.18	13.95
15 7/8	17.15	16.37	15.75	15.26	14.85	14.53	14.26	14.03
16	17.22	16.44	15.82	15.33	14.93	14.61	14.34	14.12
16 1/8	17.29	16.51	15.90	15.41	15.01	14.69	14.42	14.20
16 1/4	17.36	16.59	15.97	15.48	15.09	14.77	14.50	14.28
16 3/8	17.44	16.66	16.05	15.56	15.17	14.85	14.58	14.36
16 1/2	17.51	16.73	16.12	15.64	15.25	14.93	14.66	14.45
16 5/8	17.58	16.80	16.20	15.71	15.32	15.01	14.75	14.53
16 3/4	17.65	16.88	16.27	15.79	15.40	15.09	14.83	14.61
16 7/8	17.72	16.95	16.35	15.87	15.48	15.17	14.91	14.70
17	17.79	17.02	16.42	15.94	15.56	15.25	14.99	14.78
17 1/8	17.86	17.10	16.50	16.02	15.64	15.33	15.07	14.86
17 1/4	17.93	17.17	16.57	16.10	15.72	15.41	15.16	14.95
17 3/8	18.00	17.24	16.65	16.18	15.80	15.49	15.24	15.03
17 1/2	18.08	17.32	16.72	16.25	15.88	15.57	15.32	15.12
17 5/8	18.15	17.39	16.80	16.33	15.96	15.65	15.40	15.20
17 3/4	18.22	17.47	16.88	16.41	16.03	15.73	15.49	15.28
17 7/8	18.29	17.54	16.95	16.49	16.11	15.81	15.57	15.37
18	18.36	17.61	17.03	16.56	16.19	15.89	15.65	15.45
18 1/8	18.44	17.69	17.10	16.64	16.27	15.98	15.73	15.54
18 1/4	18.51	17.76	17.18	16.72	16.35	16.06	15.82	15.62
18 3/8	18.58	17.84	17.26	16.80	16.43	16.14	15.90	15.70
18 1/2	18.65	17.91	17.33	16.88	16.51	16.22	15.98	15.79
18 5/8	18.72	17.99	17.41	16.96	16.59	16.30	16.07	15.87
18 3/4	18.80	18.06	17.49	17.03	16.67	16.38	16.15	15.96
18 7/8	18.87	18.13	17.56	17.11	16.75	16.47	16.23	16.04
19	18.94	18.21	17.64	17.19	16.84	16.55	16.32	16.13
19 1/8	19.02	18.28	17.72	17.27	16.92	16.63	16.40	16.21
19 1/4	19.09	18.36	17.79	17.35	17.00	16.71	16.49	16.30
19 3/8	19.16	18.44	17.87	17.43	17.08	16.80	16.57	16.38
19 1/2	19.23	18.51	17.95	17.51	17.16	16.88	16.65	16.47
19 5/8	19.31	18.59	18.03	17.59	17.24	16.96	16.74	16.56
19 3/4	19.38	18.66	18.10	17.67	17.32	17.04	16.82	16.64
19 7/8	19.45	18.74	18.18	17.75	17.40	17.13	16.91	16.73
20	19.53	18.81	18.26	17.83	17.48	17.21	16.99	16.81
20 1/4	19.68	18.96	18.41	17.99	17.65	17.38	17.16	16.98
20 1/2	19.82	19.12	18.57	18.15	17.81	17.54	17.33	17.16
20 3/4	19.97	19.27	18.73	18.31	17.97	17.71	17.50	17.33
21	20.12	19.42	18.88	18.47	18.14	17.88	17.67	17.50
21 1/4	20.27	19.57	19.04	18.63	18.30	18.04	17.84	17.67
21 1/2	20.42	19.73	19.20	18.79	18.47	18.21	18.01	17.85
21 3/4	20.57	19.88	19.36	18.95	18.63	18.38	18.18	18.02
22	20.72	20.03	19.51	19.11	18.80	18.55	18.35	18.20
22 1/4	20.87	20.19	19.67	19.27	18.96	18.72	18.52	18.37
22 1/2	21.02	20.34	19.83	19.44	19.13	18.89	18.70	18.54
22 3/4	21.17	20.50	19.99	19.60	19.29	19.06	18.87	18.72
23	21.32	20.65	20.15	19.76	19.46	19.23	19.04	18.89
23 1/4	21.47	20.81	20.31	19.93	19.63	19.39	19.21	19.07
23 1/2	21.62	20.97	20.47	20.09	19.79	19.56	19.38	19.24
23 3/4	21.77	21.12	20.63	20.25	19.96	19.74	19.56	19.42
24	21.92	21.28	20.79	20.42	20.13	19.91	19.73	19.59

MONTHLY PAYMENT
NECESSARY TO AMORTIZE A LOAN OF $1000

RATE	17 YEARS	18 YEARS	19 YEARS	20 YEARS	25 YEARS	30 YEARS	35 YEARS	40 YEARS
7	8.34	8.10	7.89	7.70	7.01	6.59	6.32	6.15
7 1/8	8.41	8.17	7.96	7.77	7.09	6.67	6.41	6.23
7 1/4	8.48	8.24	8.03	7.84	7.16	6.75	6.49	6.32
7 3/8	8.55	8.32	8.10	7.92	7.24	6.84	6.58	6.41
7 1/2	8.63	8.39	8.18	7.99	7.32	6.92	6.67	6.50
7 5/8	8.70	8.46	8.25	8.06	7.40	7.00	6.75	6.59
7 3/4	8.77	8.53	8.32	8.14	7.48	7.08	6.84	6.68
7 7/8	8.84	8.60	8.40	8.21	7.56	7.17	6.93	6.77
8	8.91	8.68	8.47	8.29	7.64	7.25	7.01	6.86
8 1/8	8.98	8.75	8.54	8.36	7.72	7.34	7.10	6.95
8 1/4	9.05	8.82	8.62	8.44	7.80	7.42	7.19	7.04
8 3/8	9.13	8.90	8.69	8.51	7.88	7.51	7.28	7.13
8 1/2	9.20	8.97	8.77	8.59	7.96	7.59	7.37	7.22
8 5/8	9.27	9.04	8.84	8.67	8.04	7.68	7.45	7.32
8 3/4	9.35	9.12	8.92	8.74	8.12	7.76	7.54	7.41
8 7/8	9.42	9.19	8.99	8.82	8.20	7.85	7.63	7.50
9	9.49	9.27	9.07	8.90	8.28	7.93	7.72	7.59
9 1/8	9.57	9.34	9.15	8.97	8.37	8.02	7.81	7.68
9 1/4	9.64	9.42	9.22	9.05	8.45	8.11	7.90	7.78
9 3/8	9.71	9.49	9.30	9.13	8.53	8.19	7.99	7.87
9 1/2	9.79	9.57	9.38	9.21	8.62	8.28	8.08	7.96
9 5/8	9.86	9.64	9.45	9.29	8.70	8.37	8.17	8.06
9 3/4	9.94	9.72	9.53	9.36	8.78	8.46	8.26	8.15
9 7/8	10.01	9.80	9.61	9.44	8.87	8.54	8.36	8.24
10	10.09	9.87	9.69	9.52	8.95	8.63	8.45	8.34
10 1/8	10.17	9.95	9.76	9.60	9.03	8.72	8.54	8.43
10 1/4	10.24	10.03	9.84	9.68	9.12	8.81	8.63	8.53
10 3/8	10.32	10.11	9.92	9.76	9.20	8.90	8.72	8.62
10 1/2	10.39	10.18	10.00	9.84	9.29	8.99	8.81	8.71
10 5/8	10.47	10.26	10.08	9.92	9.37	9.08	8.91	8.81
10 3/4	10.55	10.34	10.16	10.00	9.46	9.17	9.00	8.90
10 7/8	10.62	10.42	10.24	10.08	9.54	9.25	9.09	9.00
11	10.70	10.49	10.32	10.16	9.63	9.34	9.18	9.09
11 1/8	10.78	10.57	10.40	10.24	9.72	9.43	9.28	9.19
11 1/4	10.86	10.65	10.48	10.32	9.80	9.52	9.37	9.28
11 3/8	10.93	10.73	10.56	10.40	9.89	9.61	9.46	9.38
11 1/2	11.01	10.81	10.64	10.49	9.98	9.71	9.56	9.47
11 5/8	11.09	10.89	10.72	10.57	10.06	9.80	9.65	9.57
11 3/4	11.17	10.97	10.80	10.65	10.15	9.89	9.74	9.67
11 7/8	11.25	11.05	10.88	10.73	10.24	9.98	9.84	9.76
12	11.32	11.13	10.96	10.81	10.32	10.07	9.93	9.86
12 1/8	11.40	11.21	11.04	10.90	10.41	10.16	10.03	9.95
12 1/4	11.48	11.29	11.12	10.98	10.50	10.25	10.12	10.05
12 3/8	11.56	11.37	11.21	11.06	10.59	10.34	10.21	10.14
12 1/2	11.64	11.45	11.29	11.15	10.68	10.43	10.31	10.24
12 5/8	11.72	11.53	11.37	11.23	10.76	10.53	10.40	10.34
12 3/4	11.80	11.61	11.45	11.31	10.85	10.62	10.50	10.43
12 7/8	11.88	11.69	11.53	11.40	10.94	10.71	10.59	10.53
13	11.96	11.78	11.62	11.48	11.03	10.80	10.69	10.62
13 1/8	12.04	11.86	11.70	11.56	11.12	10.90	10.78	10.72
13 1/4	12.12	11.94	11.78	11.65	11.21	10.99	10.88	10.82
13 3/8	12.20	12.02	11.87	11.73	11.30	11.08	10.97	10.91
13 1/2	12.28	12.10	11.95	11.82	11.39	11.17	11.07	11.01
13 5/8	12.36	12.19	12.03	11.90	11.47	11.27	11.16	11.11
13 3/4	12.45	12.27	12.12	11.99	11.56	11.36	11.26	11.20
13 7/8	12.53	12.35	12.20	12.07	11.65	11.45	11.35	11.30
14	12.61	12.43	12.28	12.16	11.74	11.54	11.45	11.40
14 1/8	12.69	12.52	12.37	12.24	11.83	11.64	11.54	11.49
14 1/4	12.77	12.60	12.45	12.33	11.92	11.73	11.64	11.59
14 3/8	12.85	12.68	12.54	12.41	12.01	11.82	11.73	11.69

MONTHLY PAYMENT
NECESSARY TO AMORTIZE A LOAN OF $1000

RATE	17 YEARS	18 YEARS	19 YEARS	20 YEARS	25 YEARS	30 YEARS	35 YEARS	40 YEARS
14	12.94	12.77	12.62	12.50	12.10	11.92	11.83	11.78
14 5/8	13.02	12.85	12.71	12.58	12.19	12.01	11.92	11.88
14 3/4	13.10	12.93	12.79	12.67	12.29	12.10	12.02	11.98
14 7/8	13.18	13.02	12.88	12.76	12.38	12.20	12.11	12.07
15	13.27	13.10	12.96	12.84	12.47	12.29	12.21	12.17
15 1/8	13.35	13.18	13.05	12.93	12.56	12.39	12.30	12.27
15 1/4	13.43	13.27	13.13	13.02	12.65	12.48	12.40	12.36
15 3/8	13.51	13.35	13.22	13.10	12.74	12.57	12.50	12.46
15 1/2	13.60	13.44	13.30	13.19	12.83	12.67	12.59	12.56
15 5/8	13.68	13.52	13.39	13.28	12.92	12.76	12.69	12.65
15 3/4	13.76	13.61	13.47	13.36	13.01	12.86	12.78	12.75
15 7/8	13.85	13.69	13.56	13.45	13.10	12.95	12.88	12.85
16	13.93	13.78	13.65	13.54	13.20	13.04	12.97	12.94
16 1/8	14.02	13.86	13.73	13.62	13.29	13.14	13.07	13.04
16 1/4	14.10	13.95	13.82	13.71	13.38	13.23	13.17	13.14
16 3/8	14.18	14.03	13.91	13.80	13.47	13.33	13.26	13.23
16 1/2	14.27	14.12	13.99	13.89	13.56	13.42	13.36	13.33
16 5/8	14.35	14.20	14.08	13.98	13.65	13.51	13.45	13.42
16 3/4	14.44	14.29	14.17	14.06	13.75	13.61	13.55	13.52
16 7/8	14.52	14.38	14.25	14.15	13.84	13.70	13.64	13.62
17	14.61	14.46	14.34	14.24	13.93	13.80	13.74	13.71
17 1/8	14.69	14.55	14.43	14.33	14.02	13.89	13.84	13.81
17 1/4	14.78	14.63	14.51	14.42	14.11	13.99	13.93	13.91
17 3/8	14.86	14.72	14.60	14.50	14.21	14.08	14.03	14.00
17 1/2	14.95	14.81	14.69	14.59	14.30	14.18	14.12	14.10
17 5/8	15.03	14.89	14.78	14.68	14.39	14.27	14.22	14.20
17 3/4	15.12	14.98	14.86	14.77	14.48	14.36	14.31	14.29
17 7/8	15.20	15.07	14.95	14.86	14.58	14.46	14.41	14.39
18	15.29	15.15	15.04	14.95	14.67	14.55	14.51	14.49
18 1/8	15.37	15.24	15.13	15.04	14.76	14.65	14.60	14.58
18 1/4	15.46	15.33	15.22	15.13	14.85	14.74	14.70	14.68
18 3/8	15.54	15.41	15.30	15.21	14.95	14.84	14.79	14.78
18 1/2	15.63	15.50	15.39	15.30	15.04	14.93	14.89	14.87
18 5/8	15.72	15.59	15.48	15.39	15.13	15.03	14.99	14.97
18 3/4	15.80	15.67	15.57	15.48	15.22	15.12	15.08	15.06
18 7/8	15.89	15.76	15.66	15.57	15.32	15.22	15.18	15.16
19	15.98	15.85	15.75	15.66	15.41	15.31	15.27	15.26
19 1/8	16.06	15.94	15.83	15.75	15.50	15.41	15.37	15.35
19 1/4	16.15	16.02	15.92	15.84	15.60	15.50	15.46	15.45
19 3/8	16.24	16.11	16.01	15.93	15.69	15.60	15.56	15.54
19 1/2	16.32	16.20	16.10	16.02	15.78	15.69	15.65	15.64
19 5/8	16.41	16.29	16.19	16.11	15.88	15.79	15.75	15.74
19 3/4	16.50	16.38	16.28	16.20	15.97	15.88	15.85	15.83
19 7/8	16.58	16.46	16.37	16.29	16.06	15.97	15.94	15.93
20	16.67	16.55	16.46	16.38	16.15	16.07	16.04	16.02
20 1/4	16.84	16.73	16.64	16.56	16.34	16.26	16.23	16.22
20 1/2	17.02	16.91	16.81	16.74	16.53	16.45	16.42	16.41
20 3/4	17.19	17.08	16.99	16.92	16.71	16.64	16.61	16.60
21	17.37	17.26	17.17	17.10	16.90	16.83	16.80	16.79
21 1/4	17.54	17.44	17.35	17.28	17.09	17.02	16.99	16.98
21 1/2	17.72	17.61	17.53	17.46	17.27	17.21	17.18	17.17
21 3/4	17.89	17.79	17.71	17.64	17.46	17.39	17.37	17.36
22	18.07	17.97	17.89	17.82	17.65	17.58	17.56	17.55
22 1/4	18.25	18.15	18.07	18.01	17.83	17.77	17.75	17.75
22 1/2	18.42	18.33	18.25	18.19	18.02	17.96	17.94	17.94
22 3/4	18.60	18.51	18.43	18.37	18.21	18.15	18.13	18.13
23	18.78	18.68	18.61	18.55	18.39	18.34	18.32	18.32
23 1/4	18.95	18.86	18.79	18.73	18.58	18.53	18.51	18.51
23 1/2	19.13	19.04	18.97	18.92	18.77	18.72	18.70	18.70
23 3/4	19.31	19.22	19.15	19.10	18.95	18.91	18.89	18.89
24	19.49	19.40	19.33	19.28	19.14	19.09	19.08	19.07

WEEKLY PAYMENT
NECCESSARY TO AMORTIZE A LOAN OF $1000

RATE		5 YEARS	TERM 10 YEARS	15 YEARS
7		4.548 585 0143	2.661 674 1403	2.056 801 4864
7	1/8	4.561 593 3947	2.675 967 3896	2.072 333 7544
7	1/4	4.574 617 3001	2.690 296 8344	2.087 919 8343
7	3/8	4.587 656 6887	2.704 662 3308	2.103 559 3902
7	1/2	4.600 711 5187	2.719 063 7338	2.119 252 0842
7	5/8	4.613 781 7481	2.733 500 8981	2.134 997 5768
7	3/4	4.626 867 3351	2.747 973 6775	2.150 795 5266
7	7/8	4.639 968 2376	2.762 481 9253	2.166 645 5904
8		4.653 084 4136	2.777 025 4940	2.182 547 4237
8	1/8	4.666 215 8210	2.791 604 2355	2.198 500 6803
8	1/4	4.679 362 4175	2.806 218 0012	2.214 505 0122
8	3/8	4.692 524 1611	2.820 866 6417	2.230 560 0705
8	1/2	4.705 701 0095	2.835 550 0072	2.246 665 5044
8	5/8	4.718 892 9203	2.850 267 9470	2.262 820 9621
8	3/4	4.732 099 8513	2.865 020 3102	2.279 026 0904
8	7/8	4.745 321 7601	2.879 806 9450	2.295 280 5350
9		4.758 558 6042	2.894 627 6994	2.311 583 9403
9	1/8	4.771 810 3412	2.909 482 4206	2.327 935 9499
9	1/4	4.785 076 9287	2.924 370 9553	2.344 336 2060
9	3/8	4.798 358 3239	2.939 293 1497	2.360 784 3502
9	1/2	4.811 654 4844	2.954 248 8497	2.377 280 0229
9	5/8	4.824 965 3676	2.969 237 9005	2.393 822 8638
9	3/4	4.838 290 9307	2.984 260 1468	2.410 412 5118
9	7/8	4.851 631 1311	2.999 315 4329	2.427 048 6051
10		4.864 985 9261	3.014 403 6028	2.443 730 7811
10	1/8	4.878 355 2728	3.029 524 4999	2.460 458 6768
10	1/4	4.891 739 1286	3.044 677 9672	2.477 231 9283
10	3/8	4.905 137 4504	3.059 863 8472	2.494 050 1715
10	1/2	4.918 550 1955	3.075 081 9822	2.510 913 0417
10	5/8	4.931 977 3210	3.090 332 2139	2.527 820 1738
10	3/4	4.945 418 7839	3.105 614 3839	2.544 771 2024
10	7/8	4.958 874 5413	3.120 928 3331	2.561 765 7617
11		4.972 344 5502	3.136 273 9023	2.578 803 4859
11	1/8	4.985 828 7675	3.151 650 9319	2.595 884 0087
11	1/4	4.999 327 1502	3.167 059 2619	2.613 006 9639
11	3/8	5.012 839 6553	3.182 498 7321	2.630 171 9851
11	1/2	5.026 366 2396	3.197 969 1819	2.647 378 7058
11	5/8	5.039 906 8600	3.213 470 4503	2.664 626 7596
11	3/4	5.053 461 4733	3.229 002 3764	2.681 915 7803
11	7/8	5.067 030 0365	3.244 564 7986	2.699 245 4016
12		5.080 612 5062	3.260 157 5554	2.716 615 2573
12	1/8	5.094 208 8392	3.275 780 4847	2.734 024 9816
12	1/4	5.107 818 9924	3.291 433 4245	2.751 474 2090
12	3/8	5.121 442 9224	3.307 116 2124	2.768 962 5739
12	1/2	5.135 080 5860	3.322 828 6857	2.786 489 7116
12	5/8	5.148 731 9399	3.338 570 6819	2.804 055 2573
12	3/4	5.162 396 9407	3.354 342 0378	2.821 658 8470
12	7/8	5.176 075 5452	3.370 142 5903	2.839 300 1168
13		5.189 767 7099	3.385 972 1761	2.856 978 7037
13	1/8	5.203 473 3915	3.401 830 6318	2.874 694 2450
13	1/4	5.217 192 5466	3.417 717 7938	2.892 446 3788
13	3/8	5.230 925 1319	3.433 633 4983	2.910 234 7435
13	1/2	5.244 671 1038	3.449 577 5815	2.928 058 9786
13	5/8	5.258 430 4190	3.465 549 8793	2.945 918 7241
13	3/4	5.272 203 0341	3.481 550 2278	2.963 813 6208

WEEKLY PAYMENT
NECCESSARY TO AMORTIZE A LOAN OF $1000

RATE		5 YEARS	TERM 10 YEARS	15 YEARS
13	7/8	5.285 988 9056	3.497 578 4627	2.981 743 3102
14		5.299 787 9900	3.513 634 4199	2.999 707 4349
14	1/8	5.313 600 2439	3.529 717 9350	3.017 705 6380
14	1/4	5.327 425 6238	3.545 828 8436	3.035 737 5638
14	3/8	5.341 264 0862	3.561 966 9814	3.053 802 8575
14	1/2	5.355 115 5877	3.578 132 1838	3.071 901 1652
14	5/8	5.368 980 0846	3.594 324 2865	3.090 032 1340
14	3/4	5.382 857 5337	3.610 543 1250	3.108 195 4121
14	7/8	5.396 747 8912	3.626 788 5346	3.126 390 6489
15		5.410 651 1137	3.643 060 3510	3.144 617 4947
15	1/8	5.424 567 1577	3.659 358 4096	3.162 875 6010
15	1/4	5.438 495 9797	3.675 682 5460	3.181 164 6205
15	3/8	5.452 437 5362	3.692 032 5958	3.199 484 2072
15	1/2	5.466 391 7836	3.708 408 3945	3.217 834 0161
15	5/8	5.480 358 6784	3.724 809 7779	3.236 213 7038
15	3/4	5.494 338 1770	3.741 236 5816	3.254 622 9279
15	7/8	5.508 330 2361	3.757 688 6415	3.273 061 3473
16		5.522 334 8119	3.774 165 7935	3.291 528 6226
16	1/8	5.536 351 8611	3.790 667 8734	3.310 024 4153
16	1/4	5.550 381 3401	3.807 194 7174	3.328 548 3887
16	3/8	5.564 423 2054	3.823 746 1616	3.347 100 2072
16	1/2	5.578 477 4134	3.840 322 0424	3.365 679 5369
16	5/8	5.592 543 9208	3.856 922 1960	3.384 286 0453
16	3/4	5.606 622 6839	3.873 546 4592	3.402 919 4013
16	7/8	5.620 713 6593	3.890 194 6685	3.421 579 2753
17		5.634 816 8035	3.906 866 6609	3.440 265 3394
17	1/8	5.648 932 0730	3.923 562 2733	3.458 977 2671
17	1/4	5.663 059 4244	3.940 281 3428	3.477 714 7336
17	3/8	5.677 198 8142	3.957 023 7068	3.496 477 4157
17	1/2	5.691 350 1989	3.973 789 2030	3.515 264 9916
17	5/8	5.705 513 5351	3.990 577 6688	3.534 077 1413
17	3/4	5.719 688 7794	4.007 388 9424	3.552 913 5466
17	7/8	5.733 875 8884	4.024 222 8618	3.571 773 8907
18		5.748 074 8186	4.041 079 2654	3.590 657 8587
18	1/4	5.776 507 9693	4.074 858 8796	3.628 495 4145
18	1/2	5.804 987 8844	4.108 726 4965	3.666 423 7286
18	3/4	5.833 514 2174	4.142 680 8314	3.704 440 3431
19		5.862 086 6216	4.176 720 6039	3.742 542 8290
19	1/4	5.890 704 7509	4.210 844 5380	3.780 728 7856
19	1/2	5.919 368 2595	4.245 051 3624	3.818 995 8417
19	3/4	5.948 076 8017	4.279 339 8105	3.857 341 6556
20		5.976 830 0324	4.313 708 6210	3.895 763 9153
20	1/4	6.005 627 6065	4.348 156 5378	3.934 260 3390
20	1/2	6.034 469 1798	4.382 682 3103	3.972 828 6751
20	3/4	6.063 354 4079	4.417 284 6935	4.011 466 7026
21		6.092 282 9474	4.451 962 4485	4.050 172 2312
21	1/4	6.121 254 4549	4.486 714 3422	4.088 943 1014
21	1/2	6.150 268 5875	4.521 539 1479	4.127 777 1849
21	3/4	6.179 325 0031	4.556 435 6454	4.166 672 3841
22		6.208 423 3597	4.591 402 6209	4.205 626 6330
22	1/4	6.237 563 3160	4.626 438 8673	4.244 637 8965
22	1/2	6.266 744 5312	4.661 543 1847	4.283 704 1707
22	3/4	6.295 966 6651	4.696 714 3801	4.322 823 4831
23		6.325 229 3778	4.731 951 2675	4.361 993 8924
24		6.442 679 2440	4.873 532 2817	4.519 148 7588

WEEKLY PAYMENT
NECCESSARY TO AMORTIZE A LOAN OF $1000

RATE		20 YEARS	25 YEARS	30 YEARS
7		1.771 419 2555	1.612 781 4901	1.516 503 8906
7	1/8	1.788 109 3128	1.630 527 9966	1.535 193 8212
7	1/4	1.804 866 7513	1.648 350 9079	1.553 964 6310
7	3/8	1.821 690 9416	1.666 249 2151	1.572 814 8823
7	1/2	1.838 581 2520	1.684 221 9087	1.591 743 1422
7	5/8	1.855 537 0484	1.702 267 9787	1.610 747 9833
7	3/4	1.872 557 6944	1.720 386 4147	1.629 827 9841
7	7/8	1.889 642 5520	1.738 576 2070	1.648 981 7298
8		1.906 790 9811	1.756 836 3463	1.668 207 8130
8	1/8	1.924 002 3400	1.775 165 8242	1.687 506 8339
8	1/4	1.941 275 9858	1.793 563 6341	1.706 871 4014
8	3/8	1.958 611 2741	1.812 028 7706	1.726 306 1328
8	1/2	1.976 007 5595	1.830 560 2308	1.745 807 6553
8	5/8	1.993 464 1957	1.849 157 0139	1.765 374 6055
8	3/4	2.010 980 5356	1.867 818 1219	1.785 005 6305
8	7/8	2.028 555 9317	1.886 542 5599	1.804 699 3883
9		2.046 189 7359	1.905 329 3363	1.824 454 5478
9	1/8	2.063 881 2998	1.924 177 4631	1.844 269 7896
9	1/4	2.081 629 9751	1.943 085 9562	1.864 143 8061
9	3/8	2.099 435 1134	1.962 053 8357	1.884 075 3021
9	1/2	2.117 296 0665	1.981 080 1263	1.904 062 9950
9	5/8	2.135 212 1867	2.000 163 8573	1.924 105 6150
9	3/4	2.153 182 8268	2.019 304 0630	1.944 201 9057
9	7/8	2.171 207 3401	2.038 499 7830	1.964 350 6239
10		2.189 285 0809	2.057 750 0624	1.984 550 5404
10	1/8	2.207 415 4042	2.077 053 9519	2.004 800 4399
10	1/4	2.225 597 6663	2.096 410 5083	2.025 099 1211
10	3/8	2.243 831 2247	2.115 818 7942	2.045 445 3975
10	1/2	2.262 115 4381	2.135 277 8788	2.065 838 0967
10	5/8	2.280 449 6668	2.154 786 8379	2.086 276 0613
10	3/4	2.298 833 2727	2.174 344 7538	2.106 758 1488
10	7/8	2.317 265 6194	2.193 950 7159	2.127 283 2317
11		2.335 746 0724	2.213 603 8204	2.147 850 1974
11	1/8	2.354 273 9990	2.233 303 1711	2.168 457 9489
11	1/4	2.372 848 7689	2.253 047 8788	2.189 105 4043
11	3/8	2.391 469 7537	2.272 837 0621	2.209 791 4972
11	1/2	2.410 136 3275	2.292 669 8471	2.230 515 1764
11	5/8	2.428 847 8668	2.312 545 3679	2.251 275 4067
11	3/4	2.447 603 7504	2.332 462 7663	2.272 071 1679
11	7/8	2.466 403 3601	2.352 421 1923	2.292 901 4557
12		2.485 246 0801	2.372 419 8039	2.313 765 2813
12	1/8	2.504 131 2976	2.392 457 7675	2.334 661 6713
12	1/4	2.523 058 4027	2.412 534 2577	2.355 589 6680
12	3/8	2.542 026 7884	2.432 648 4577	2.376 548 3291
12	1/2	2.561 035 8508	2.452 799 5590	2.397 536 7280
12	5/8	2.580 084 9894	2.472 986 7618	2.418 553 9534
12	3/4	2.599 173 6068	2.493 209 2750	2.439 599 1092
12	7/8	2.618 301 1087	2.513 466 3161	2.460 671 3148
13		2.637 466 9047	2.533 757 1114	2.481 769 7050
13	1/8	2.656 670 4076	2.554 080 8961	2.502 893 4295
13	1/4	2.675 911 0337	2.574 436 9140	2.524 041 6532
13	3/8	2.695 188 2031	2.594 824 4182	2.545 213 5558
13	1/2	2.714 501 3395	2.615 242 6705	2.566 408 3322
13	5/8	2.733 849 8705	2.635 690 9414	2.587 625 1918
13	3/4	2.753 233 2273	2.656 168 5109	2.608 863 3588

256

WEEKLY PAYMENT
NECCESSARY TO AMORTIZE A LOAN OF $1000

RATE		20 YEARS	25 YEARS	30 YEARS
		TERM		
13	7/8	2.772 650 8451	2.676 674 6676	2.630 122 0717
14		2.792 102 1631	2.697 208 7092	2.651 400 5838
14	1/8	2.811 586 6244	2.717 769 9424	2.672 698 1622
14	1/4	2.831 103 6762	2.738 357 6830	2.694 014 0884
14	3/8	2.850 652 7696	2.758 971 2557	2.715 347 6579
14	1/2	2.870 233 3601	2.779 609 9942	2.736 698 1800
14	5/8	2.889 844 9072	2.800 273 2411	2.758 064 9775
14	3/4	2.909 486 8748	2.820 960 3482	2.779 447 3871
14	7/8	2.920 158 7308	2.841 670 6760	2.800 844 7587
15		2.948 859 9476	2.862 403 5940	2.822 256 4552
15	1/8	2.968 590 0018	2.883 158 4808	2.843 681 8529
15	1/4	2.988 348 3745	2.903 934 7235	2.865 120 3408
15	3/8	3.008 134 5511	2.924 731 7182	2.886 571 3208
15	1/2	3.027 948 0214	2.945 548 8698	2.908 034 2070
15	5/8	3.047 788 2797	2.966 385 5920	2.929 508 4263
15	3/4	3.067 654 8247	2.987 241 3070	2.950 993 4176
15	7/8	3.087 547 1598	3.008 115 4458	2.972 488 6318
16		3.107 464 7926	3.029 007 4481	2.993 993 5317
16	1/8	3.127 407 2355	3.049 916 7620	3.015 507 5919
16	1/4	3.147 374 0053	3.070 842 8440	3.037 030 2983
16	3/8	3.167 364 6234	3.091 785 1593	3.058 561 1483
16	1/2	3.187 378 6157	3.112 743 1813	3.080 099 6504
16	5/8	3.207 415 5128	3.133 716 3917	3.101 645 3241
16	3/4	3.227 474 8499	3.154 704 2806	3.123 197 6996
16	7/8	3.247 556 1667	3.175 706 3461	3.144 756 3178
17		3.267 659 0075	3.196 722 0946	3.166 320 7301
17	1/8	3.287 782 9213	3.217 751 0405	3.187 890 4980
17	1/4	3.307 927 4617	3.238 792 7060	3.209 465 1933
17	3/8	3.328 092 1869	3.259 846 6214	3.231 044 3975
17	1/2	3.348 276 6597	3.280 912 3248	3.252 627 7021
17	5/8	3.368 480 4474	3.301 989 3621	3.274 214 7078
17	3/4	3.388 703 1222	3.323 077 2867	3.295 805 0251
17	7/8	3.408 944 2605	3.344 175 6597	3.317 398 2733
18		3.429 203 4437	3.365 284 0498	3.338 994 0812
18	1/8	3.469 774 2924	3.407 529 1930	3.382 191 9345
18	1/2	3.510 412 4094	3.449 809 4126	3.425 395 7880
18	3/4	3.551 114 6091	3.492 121 5204	3.468 602 9792
19		3.591 877 7781	3.534 462 4405	3.511 810 9746
19	1/4	3.632 698 8752	3.576 829 2071	3.555 017 3645
19	1/2	3.673 574 9306	3.619 218 9612	3.598 219 8580
19	3/4	3.714 503 0454	3.661 628 9487	3.641 416 2784
20		3.755 480 3908	3.704 056 5167	3.684 604 5586
20	1/4	3.796 504 2074	3.746 499 1117	3.727 782 7359
20	1/2	3.837 571 8049	3.788 954 2761	3.770 948 9481
20	3/4	3.878 680 5603	3.831 419 6461	3.814 101 4292
21		3.919 827 9181	3.873 892 9488	3.857 238 5046
21	1/4	3.961 011 3887	3.916 371 9992	3.900 358 5880
21	1/2	4.002 228 5477	3.958 854 6981	3.943 460 1766
21	3/4	4.043 477 0351	4.001 339 0292	3.986 541 8478
22		4.084 754 5540	4.043 823 0565	4.029 602 2554
22	1/4	4.126 058 8699	4.086 304 9220	4.072 640 1263
22	1/2	4.167 387 8094	4.128 782 8428	4.115 654 2568
22	3/4	4.208 739 2594	4.171 255 1090	4.158 643 5095
23		4.250 111 1657	4.213 720 0814	4.201 606 8101
24		4.415 764 2831	4.383 476 5796	4.373 181 0544

BIWEEKLY PAYMENT
NECCESSARY TO AMORTIZE A LOAN OF $1000

RATE	5 YEARS	TERM 10 YEARS	15 YEARS
7	9.103 192 3893	5.326 872 3571	4.116 326 1934
7 1/8	9.129 332 4283	5.355 539 9952	4.147 459 4752
7 1/4	9.155 504 0819	5.384 280 7023	4.178 701 1485
7 3/8	9.181 707 2668	5.413 094 1920	4.210 050 5443
7 1/2	9.207 941 9002	5.441 980 1767	4.241 506 9895
7 5/8	9.234 207 8986	5.470 938 3672	4.273 069 8077
7 3/4	9.260 505 1788	5.499 968 4729	4.304 738 3185
7 7/8	9.286 833 6572	5.529 070 2020	4.336 511 8384
8	9.313 193 2505	5.558 243 2614	4.368 389 6806
8 1/8	9.339 583 8748	5.587 487 3566	4.400 371 1551
8 1/4	9.366 005 4464	5.616 802 1919	4.432 455 5687
8 3/8	9.392 457 8815	5.646 187 4702	4.464 642 2255
8 1/2	9.418 941 0961	5.675 642 8934	4.496 930 4267
8 5/8	9.445 455 0062	5.705 168 1620	4.529 319 4707
8 3/4	9.471 999 5276	5.734 762 9757	4.561 808 6536
8 7/8	9.498 574 5760	5.764 427 0325	4.594 397 2688
9	9.525 180 0672	5.794 160 0299	4.627 084 6076
9 1/8	9.551 815 9167	5.823 961 6638	4.659 869 9590
9 1/4	9.578 482 0400	5.853 831 6293	4.692 752 6098
9 3/8	9.605 178 3526	5.883 769 6203	4.725 731 8450
9 1/2	9.631 904 7697	5.913 775 3300	4.758 806 9478
9 5/8	9.658 661 2066	5.943 848 4502	4.791 977 1995
9 3/4	9.685 447 5784	5.973 988 6720	4.825 241 8798
9 7/8	9.712 263 8003	6.004 195 6854	4.858 600 2669
10	9.739 109 7873	6.034 469 1798	4.892 051 6379
10 1/8	9.765 985 4542	6.064 808 8432	4.925 595 2681
10 1/4	9.792 890 7160	6.095 214 3632	4.959 230 4320
10 3/8	9.819 825 4874	6.125 685 4264	4.992 956 4030
10 1/2	9.846 789 6832	6.156 221 7184	5.026 772 4535
10 5/8	9.873 783 2180	6.186 822 9243	5.060 677 8550
10 3/4	9.900 806 0063	6.217 488 7282	5.094 671 8783
10 7/8	9.927 857 9628	6.248 218 8136	5.128 753 7937
11	9.954 939 0019	6.279 012 8632	5.162 922 8708
11 1/8	9.982 049 0379	6.309 870 5591	5.197 178 3789
11 1/4	10.009 187 9852	6.340 791 5826	5.231 519 5870
11 3/8	10.036 355 7580	6.371 775 6144	5.265 945 7636
11 1/2	10.063 552 2707	6.402 822 3347	5.300 456 1776
11 5/8	10.090 777 4372	6.433 931 4230	5.335 050 0975
11 3/4	10.118 031 1719	6.465 102 5581	5.369 726 7920
11 7/8	10.145 313 3887	6.496 335 4184	5.404 485 5299
12	10.172 624 0016	6.527 629 6817	5.439 325 5805
12 1/8	10.199 962 9246	6.558 985 0254	5.474 246 2132
12 1/4	10.227 330 0716	6.590 401 1264	5.509 246 6981
12 3/8	10.254 725 3565	6.621 877 6609	5.544 326 3057
12 1/2	10.282 148 6930	6.653 414 3050	5.579 484 3072
12 5/8	10.309 599 9951	6.685 010 7341	5.614 719 9747
12 3/4	10.337 079 1763	6.716 666 6235	5.650 032 5807
12 7/8	10.364 586 1505	6.748 381 6478	5.685 421 3991
13	10.392 120 8313	6.780 155 4815	5.720 885 7046
13 1/8	10.419 683 1323	6.811 987 7987	5.756 424 7728
13 1/4	10.447 272 9671	6.843 878 2731	5.792 037 8808
13 3/8	10.474 890 2493	6.875 826 5784	5.827 724 3068
13 1/2	10.502 534 8924	6.907 832 3876	5.863 483 3303
13 5/8	10.530 206 8099	6.939 895 3739	5.899 314 2322
13 3/4	10.557 905 9153	6.972 015 2100	5.935 216 2950

BIWEEKLY PAYMENT
NECCESSARY TO AMORTIZE A LOAN OF $1000

RATE		5 YEARS	TERM 10 YEARS	15 YEARS
13	7/8	10.585 632 1220	7.004 191 5686	5.971 188 8027
14		10.613 385 3435	7.036 424 1220	6.007 231 0409
14	1/8	10.641 165 4931	7.068 712 5425	6.043 342 2970
14	1/4	10.668 972 4843	7.101 056 5022	6.079 521 8600
14	3/8	10.696 806 2303	7.133 455 6733	6.115 769 0211
14	1/2	10.724 666 6446	7.165 909 7276	6.152 083 0731
14	5/8	10.752 553 6404	7.198 418 3369	6.188 463 3109
14	3/4	10.780 467 1310	7.230 981 1732	6.224 909 0316
14	7/8	10.808 407 0298	7.263 597 9081	6.261 419 5343
15		10.836 373 2500	7.296 268 2136	6.297 994 1202
15	1/8	10.864 365 7049	7.328 991 7613	6.334 632 0929
15	1/4	10.892 384 3077	7.361 768 2230	6.371 332 7584
15	3/8	10.920 428 9718	7.394 597 2707	6.408 095 4249
15	1/2	10.948 499 6102	7.427 478 5763	6.444 919 4031
15	5/8	10.976 596 1363	7.460 411 8117	6.481 804 0062
15	3/4	11.004 718 4633	7.493 396 6492	6.518 748 5500
15	7/8	11.032 866 5043	7.526 432 7610	6.555 752 3529
16		11.061 040 1728	7.559 519 8194	6.592 814 7358
16	1/8	11.089 239 3818	7.592 657 4971	6.629 935 0225
16	1/4	11.117 464 0445	7.625 845 4667	6.667 112 5395
16	3/8	11.145 714 0744	7.659 083 4013	6.704 346 6161
16	1/2	11.173 989 3844	7.692 370 9740	6.741 636 5846
16	5/8	11.202 289 8880	7.725 707 8581	6.778 981 7801
16	3/4	11.230 615 4983	7.759 093 7273	6.816 381 5405
16	7/8	11.258 966 1286	7.792 528 2556	6.853 835 2070
17		11.287 341 6922	7.826 011 1171	6.891 342 1237
17	1/8	11.315 742 1023	7.859 541 9864	6.928 901 6377
17	1/4	11.344 167 2722	7.893 120 5383	6.966 513 0995
17	3/8	11.372 617 1153	7.926 746 4479	7.004 175 8624
17	1/2	11.401 091 5448	7.960 419 3907	7.041 889 2833
17	5/8	11.429 590 4741	7.994 139 0427	7.079 652 7220
17	3/4	11.458 113 8166	8.027 905 0802	7.117 465 5418
17	7/8	11.486 661 4856	8.061 717 1798	7.155 327 1093
18		11.515 233 3945	8.095 575 0186	7.193 236 7944
18	1/4	11.572 449 5856	8.163 426 6245	7.269 198 0137
18	1/2	11.629 761 6977	8.231 457 3237	7.345 344 2272
18	3/4	11.687 169 0387	8.299 664 5497	7.421 670 5181
19		11.744 670 9172	8.368 045 7441	7.498 172 0259
19	1/4	11.802 266 6420	8.436 598 3573	7.574 843 9473
19	1/2	11.859 955 5227	8.505 319 8487	7.651 681 5373
19	3/4	11.917 736 8694	8.574 207 6870	7.728 680 1094
20		11.975 609 9928	8.643 259 3512	7.805 835 0365
20	1/4	12.033 574 2042	8.712 472 3305	7.883 141 7513
20	1/2	12.091 628 8157	8.781 844 1249	7.960 595 7469
20	3/4	12.149 773 1401	8.851 372 2455	8.038 192 5773
21		12.208 006 4909	8.921 054 2152	8.115 927 8573
21	1/4	12.266 328 1824	8.990 887 5685	8.193 797 2634
21	1/2	12.324 737 5299	9.060 869 8525	8.271 796 5340
21	3/4	12.383 233 8495	9.130 998 6267	8.349 921 4689
22		12.441 816 4581	9.201 271 4636	8.428 167 9305
22	1/4	12.500 484 6737	9.271 685 9492	8.506 531 8429
22	1/2	12.559 237 8151	9.342 239 6829	8.585 009 1928
22	3/4	12.618 075 2025	9.412 930 2782	8.663 596 0288
23		12.676 996 1567	9.483 755 3627	8.742 288 4620
24		12.913 502 1014	9.768 353 6580	9.058 038 5555

BIWEEKLY PAYMENT
NECCESSARY TO AMORTIZE A LOAN OF $1000

RATE	TERM 20 YEARS	25 YEARS	30 YEARS
7	3.545 183 8834	3.227 698 3150	3.035 015 6438
7 1/8	3.578 627 6685	3.263 259 7336	3.072 455 9431
7 1/4	3.612 207 0600	3.298 960 8693	3.110 058 9598
7 3/8	3.645 920 8025	3.334 820 7080	3.147 821 8215
7 1/2	3.679 767 6355	3.370 830 2334	3.185 741 6650
7 5/8	3.713 746 2939	3.406 987 4286	3.223 815 6380
7 3/4	3.747 855 5080	3.443 290 2759	3.262 040 9002
7 7/8	3.782 094 0044	3.479 736 7585	3.300 414 6244
8	3.816 460 5059	3.516 324 8606	3.338 933 9980
8 1/8	3.850 953 7320	3.553 052 5683	3.377 596 2236
8 1/4	3.885 572 3993	3.589 917 8705	3.416 398 5208
8 3/8	3.920 315 2219	3.626 918 7592	3.455 338 1265
8 1/2	3.955 180 9115	3.664 053 2307	3.494 412 2963
8 5/8	3.990 168 1781	3.701 319 2859	3.533 618 3055
8 3/4	4.025 275 7300	3.738 714 9308	3.572 953 4499
8 7/8	4.060 502 2743	3.776 238 1778	3.612 415 0466
9	4.095 846 5172	3.813 887 0454	3.652 000 4349
9 1/8	4.131 307 1643	3.851 659 5598	3.691 706 9772
9 1/4	4.166 882 9211	3.889 553 7545	3.731 532 0595
9 3/8	4.202 572 4929	3.927 567 6715	3.771 473 0924
9 1/2	4.238 374 5856	3.965 699 3616	3.811 527 5115
9 5/8	4.274 287 9056	4.003 946 8852	3.851 692 7781
9 3/4	4.310 311 1604	4.042 308 3123	3.891 966 3800
9 7/8	4.346 443 0585	4.080 781 7236	3.932 345 8317
10	4.382 682 3103	4.119 365 2103	3.972 828 6751
10 1/8	4.419 027 6277	4.158 056 8753	4.013 412 4800
10 1/4	4.455 477 7250	4.196 854 8329	4.054 094 8446
10 3/8	4.492 031 3186	4.235 757 2100	4.094 873 3955
10 1/2	4.528 687 1278	4.274 762 1457	4.135 745 7886
10 5/8	4.565 443 8745	4.313 867 7925	4.176 709 7092
10 3/4	4.602 300 2840	4.353 072 3158	4.217 762 8721
10 7/8	4.639 255 0849	4.392 373 8951	4.258 903 0221
11	4.676 307 0096	4.431 770 7239	4.300 127 9345
11 1/8	4.713 454 7941	4.471 261 0098	4.341 435 4146
11 1/4	4.750 697 1787	4.510 842 9755	4.382 823 2985
11 3/8	4.788 032 9082	4.550 514 8585	4.424 289 4530
11 1/2	4.825 460 7315	4.590 274 9115	4.465 831 7756
11 5/8	4.862 979 4029	4.630 121 4029	4.507 448 1949
11 3/4	4.900 587 6811	4.670 052 6167	4.549 136 6706
11 7/8	4.938 284 3305	4.710 066 8530	4.590 895 1931
12	4.976 068 1205	4.750 162 4282	4.632 721 7842
12 1/8	5.013 937 8263	4.790 337 6750	4.674 614 4966
12 1/4	5.051 892 2288	4.830 590 9429	4.716 571 4140
12 3/8	5.089 930 1151	4.870 920 5980	4.758 590 6513
12 1/2	5.128 050 2779	4.911 325 0234	4.800 670 3540
12 5/8	5.166 251 5168	4.951 802 6195	4.842 808 6986
12 3/4	5.204 532 6375	4.992 351 8037	4.885 003 8924
12 7/8	5.242 892 4525	5.032 971 0109	4.927 254 1732
13	5.281 329 7809	5.073 658 6935	4.969 557 8091
13 1/8	5.319 843 4490	5.114 413 3214	5.011 913 0987
13 1/4	5.358 432 2899	5.155 233 3822	5.054 318 3705
13 3/8	5.397 095 1441	5.196 117 3812	5.096 771 9832
13 1/2	5.435 830 8594	5.237 063 8415	5.139 272 3250
13 5/8	5.474 638 2911	5.278 071 3043	5.181 817 8135
13 3/4	5.513 516 3021	5.319 138 3283	5.224 406 8959

BIWEEKLY PAYMENT
NECCESSARY TO AMORTIZE A LOAN OF $1000

RATE		20 YEARS	25 YEARS	30 YEARS
13	7/8	5.552 463 7629	5.360 263 4904	5.267 038 0481
14		5.591 479 5519	5.401 445 3854	5.309 709 7749
14	1/8	5.630 562 5556	5.442 682 6261	5.352 420 6096
14	1/4	5.669 711 6682	5.483 973 8431	5.395 169 1137
14	3/8	5.708 925 7925	5.525 317 6852	5.437 953 8767
14	1/2	5.748 203 8390	5.566 712 8190	5.480 773 5158
14	5/8	5.787 544 7268	5.608 157 9290	5.523 626 6753
14	3/4	5.826 947 3835	5.649 651 7177	5.566 512 0268
14	7/8	5.866 410 7451	5.691 192 9054	5.609 428 2685
15		5.905 933 7559	5.732 780 2302	5.652 374 1252
15	1/8	5.945 515 3691	5.774 412 4479	5.695 348 3476
15	1/4	5.985 154 5467	5.816 088 3322	5.738 349 7122
15	3/8	6.024 850 2590	5.857 806 6741	5.781 377 0210
15	1/2	6.064 601 4856	5.899 566 2824	5.824 429 1010
15	5/8	6.104 407 2146	5.941 365 9832	5.867 504 8041
15	3/4	6.144 266 4432	5.983 204 6201	5.910 603 0064
15	7/8	6.184 178 1774	6.025 081 0538	5.953 722 6082
16		6.224 141 4324	6.066 994 1625	5.996 862 5335
16	1/8	6.264 155 2324	6.108 942 8411	6.040 021 7296
16	1/4	6.304 218 6103	6.150 926 0018	6.083 199 1668
16	3/8	6.344 330 6086	6.192 942 5734	6.126 393 8381
16	1/2	6.384 490 2787	6.234 991 5015	6.169 604 7588
16	5/8	6.424 696 6809	6.277 071 7483	6.212 830 9661
16	3/4	6.464 948 8851	6.319 182 2927	6.256 071 5188
16	7/8	6.505 245 9701	6.361 322 1296	6.299 325 4969
17		6.545 587 0239	6.403 490 2704	6.342 592 0015
17	1/8	6.585 971 1437	6.445 685 7425	6.385 870 1538
17	1/4	6.626 397 4361	6.487 907 5890	6.429 159 0956
17	3/8	6.666 865 0166	6.530 154 8692	6.472 457 9883
17	1/2	6.707 373 0100	6.572 426 6578	6.515 766 0127
17	5/8	6.747 920 5504	6.614 722 0449	6.559 082 3690
17	3/4	6.788 506 7810	6.657 040 1363	6.602 406 2760
17	7/8	6.829 130 8542	6.699 380 0526	6.645 736 9710
18		6.869 791 9316	6.741 740 9298	6.689 073 7092
18	1/4	6.951 221 7909	6.826 522 1837	6.775 762 4257
18	1/2	7.032 789 8343	6.911 377 2792	6.862 466 8177
18	3/4	7.114 489 6825	6.996 299 8274	6.949 181 5458
19		7.196 315 1010	7.081 283 6644	7.035 901 5283
19	1/4	7.278 259 9991	7.166 322 8468	7.122 621 9317
19	1/2	7.360 318 4286	7.251 411 6415	7.209 338 1600
19	3/4	7.442 484 5830	7.336 544 5300	7.296 045 8456
20		7.524 752 7957	7.421 716 1933	7.382 740 8396
20	1/4	7.607 117 5388	7.506 921 5109	7.469 419 2028
20	1/2	7.689 577 4216	7.592 155 5553	7.556 077 1968
20	3/4	7.772 115 1891	7.677 413 5855	7.642 711 2749
21		7.854 737 7199	7.762 691 0424	7.729 318 0747
21	1/4	7.937 436 0250	7.847 983 5434	7.815 894 4090
21	1/2	8.020 205 2453	7.933 286 8766	7.902 437 2585
21	3/4	8.103 040 6502	8.018 596 9964	7.988 943 7644
22		8.185 937 6355	8.103 910 0176	8.075 411 2206
22	1/4	8.268 891 7214	8.189 222 2108	8.161 831 0670
22	1/2	8.351 898 5504	8.274 529 9973	8.248 218 8827
22	3/4	8.434 953 8851	8.359 829 9442	8.334 554 3797
23		8.518 053 6065	8.445 118 7595	8.420 841 3960
24		8.850 817 9888	8.786 101 5392	8.765 465 5148

SEMI-MONTHLY PAYMENT
NECCESSARY TO AMORTIZE A LOAN OF $1000

RATE		5 YEARS	10 YEARS	15 YEARS
7		9.862 879 6855	5.771 415 0060	4.459 845 3219
7	1/8	9.891 220 3412	5.802 486 2775	4.493 585 4672
7	1/4	9.919 595 3482	5.833 636 8299	4.527 443 1756
7	3/8	9.948 004 6169	5.864 866 3532	4.561 417 7227
7	1/2	9.976 448 0571	5.896 174 5360	4.595 508 3800
7	5/8	10.004 925 5789	5.927 561 0655	4.629 714 4150
7	3/4	10.033 437 0920	5.959 025 6272	4.664 035 0912
7	7/8	10.061 982 5062	5.990 567 9053	4.698 469 6686
8		10.090 561 7310	6.022 187 5824	4.733 017 4036
8	1/8	10.119 174 6759	6.053 884 3400	4.767 677 5491
8	1/4	10.147 821 2503	6.085 657 8578	4.802 449 3546
8	3/8	10.176 501 3633	6.117 507 8145	4.837 332 0666
8	1/2	10.205 214 9242	6.149 433 8874	4.872 324 9286
8	5/8	10.233 961 8421	6.181 435 7524	4.907 427 1809
8	3/4	10.262 742 0257	6.213 513 0842	4.942 638 0614
8	7/8	10.291 555 3840	6.245 665 5562	4.977 956 8050
9		10.320 401 8257	6.277 892 8407	5.013 382 6442
9	1/8	10.349 281 2594	6.310 194 6089	5.048 914 8093
9	1/4	10.378 193 5938	6.342 570 5305	5.084 552 5281
9	3/8	10.407 138 7371	6.375 020 2743	5.120 295 0263
9	1/2	10.436 116 5979	6.407 543 5081	5.156 141 5277
9	5/8	10.465 127 0844	6.440 139 8984	5.192 091 2542
9	3/4	10.494 170 1047	6.472 809 1107	5.228 143 4257
9	7/8	10.523 245 5670	6.505 550 8097	5.264 297 2608
10		10.552 353 3792	6.538 364 6588	5.300 551 9765
10	1/8	10.581 493 4494	6.571 250 3205	5.336 906 7881
10	1/4	10.610 665 6853	6.604 207 4566	5.373 360 9101
10	3/8	10.639 869 9947	6.637 235 7277	5.409 913 5555
10	1/2	10.669 106 2854	6.670 334 7937	5.446 563 9365
10	5/8	10.698 374 4649	6.703 504 3134	5.483 311 2641
10	3/4	10.727 674 4408	6.736 743 9451	5.520 154 7489
10	7/8	10.757 006 1206	6.770 053 3460	5.557 093 6003
11		10.786 369 4116	6.803 432 1727	5.594 127 0276
11	1/8	10.815 764 2213	6.836 880 0809	5.631 254 2394
11	1/4	10.845 190 4569	6.870 396 7258	5.668 474 4441
11	3/8	10.874 648 0257	6.903 981 7615	5.705 786 8496
11	1/2	10.904 136 8347	6.937 634 8419	5.743 190 6639
11	5/8	10.933 656 7910	6.971 355 6198	5.780 685 0950
11	3/4	10.963 207 8017	7.005 143 7478	5.818 269 3509
11	7/8	10.992 789 7738	7.038 998 8774	5.855 942 6397
12		11.022 402 6142	7.072 920 6601	5.893 704 1700
12	1/8	11.052 046 2297	7.106 908 7463	5.931 553 1506
12	1/4	11.081 720 5271	7.140 962 7863	5.969 488 7909
12	3/8	11.111 425 4133	7.175 082 4296	6.007 510 3010
12	1/2	11.141 160 7949	7.209 267 3253	6.045 616 8915
12	5/8	11.170 926 5787	7.243 517 1223	6.083 807 7740
12	3/4	11.200 722 6711	7.277 831 4687	6.122 082 1607
12	7/8	11.230 548 9789	7.312 210 0123	6.160 439 2651
13		11.260 405 4085	7.346 652 4007	6.198 878 3016
13	1/8	11.290 291 8665	7.381 158 2810	6.237 398 4858
13	1/4	11.320 208 2592	7.415 727 3000	6.275 999 0346
13	3/8	11.350 154 4933	7.450 359 1041	6.314 679 1663
13	1/2	11.380 130 4749	7.485 053 3395	6.353 438 1004
13	5/8	11.410 136 1105	7.519 809 6522	6.392 275 0582
13	3/4	11.440 171 3065	7.554 627 6879	6.431 189 2625

SEMI-MONTHLY PAYMENT
NECCESSARY TO AMORTIZE A LOAN OF $1000

RATE		5 YEARS	10 YEARS	15 YEARS
13	7/8	11.470 235 9691	7.589 507 0921	6.470 179 9377
14		11.500 330 0046	7.624 447 5100	6.509 246 3100
14	1/8	11.530 453 3192	7.659 448 5867	6.548 387 6077
14	1/4	11.560 605 8191	7.694 509 9674	6.587 603 0608
14	3/8	11.590 787 4106	7.729 631 2967	6.626 891 9012
14	1/2	11.620 997 9999	7.764 812 2195	6.666 253 3631
14	5/8	11.651 237 4930	7.800 052 3804	6.705 686 6828
14	3/4	11.681 505 7962	7.835 351 4240	6.745 191 0988
14	7/8	11.711 802 8154	7.870 708 9950	6.784 765 8520
15		11.742 128 4570	7.906 124 7378	6.824 410 1854
15	1/8	11.772 482 6269	7.941 598 2971	6.864 123 3448
15	1/4	11.802 865 2312	7.977 129 3175	6.903 904 5783
15	3/8	11.833 276 1760	8.012 717 4437	6.943 753 1366
15	1/2	11.863 715 3673	8.048 362 3423	6.983 668 2730
15	5/8	11.894 182 7113	8.084 063 5921	7.023 649 2435
15	3/4	11.924 678 1140	8.119 820 9041	7.063 695 3071
15	7/8	11.955 201 4814	8.155 633 9015	7.103 805 7253
16		11.985 752 7195	8.191 502 2293	7.143 979 7626
16	1/8	12.016 331 7344	8.227 425 5330	7.184 216 6865
16	1/4	12.046 938 4322	8.263 403 4581	7.224 515 7674
16	3/8	12.077 572 7189	8.299 435 6506	7.264 876 2788
16	1/2	12.108 234 5006	8.335 521 7563	7.305 297 4973
16	5/8	12.138 923 6832	8.371 661 4216	7.345 778 7025
16	3/4	12.169 640 1730	8.407 854 2930	7.386 319 1775
16	7/8	12.200 383 8758	8.444 100 0174	7.426 918 2083
17		12.231 154 6980	8.480 398 2419	7.467 575 0846
17	1/8	12.261 952 5454	8.516 748 6140	7.508 289 0990
17	1/4	12.292 777 3242	8.553 150 7816	7.549 059 5478
17	3/8	12.323 628 9407	8.589 604 3927	7.589 885 7307
17	1/2	12.354 507 3008	8.626 109 0961	7.630 766 9507
17	5/8	12.385 412 3107	8.662 664 5406	7.671 702 5144
17	3/4	12.416 343 8767	8.699 270 3756	7.712 691 7320
17	7/8	12.447 301 9048	8.735 926 2510	7.753 733 9173
18		12.478 286 3014	8.772 631 8170	7.794 828 3877
18	1/4	12.540 333 8249	8.846 190 6244	7.877 171 4714
18	1/2	12.602 485 6972	8.919 944 0096	7.959 715 5961
18	3/4	12.664 741 1690	8.993 889 1927	8.042 455 4349
19		12.727 099 4915	9.068 023 4028	8.125 385 7218
19	1/4	12.789 559 9162	9.142 343 8779	8.208 501 2531
19	1/2	12.852 121 6955	9.216 847 8663	8.291 796 8878
19	3/4	12.914 784 0821	9.291 532 6262	8.375 267 5484
20		12.977 546 3296	9.366 395 4267	8.458 908 2216
20	1/4	13.040 407 6920	9.441 433 5480	8.542 713 9590
20	1/2	13.103 367 4244	9.516 644 2822	8.626 679 8774
20	3/4	13.166 424 7825	9.592 024 9332	8.710 801 1594
21		13.229 579 0227	9.667 572 8174	8.795 073 0539
21	1/4	13.292 829 4025	9.743 285 2642	8.879 490 8763
21	1/2	13.356 175 1801	9.819 159 6162	8.964 050 0086
21	3/4	13.419 615 6149	9.895 193 2297	9.048 745 9002
22		13.483 149 9669	9.971 383 4751	9.133 574 0674
22	1/4	13.546 777 4975	10.047 727 7370	9.218 530 0938
22	1/2	13.610 497 4690	10.124 223 4147	9.303 609 6306
22	3/4	13.674 309 1447	10.200 867 9229	9.388 808 3960
23		13.738 211 7892	10.277 658 6912	9.474 122 1759
24		13.994 717 3868	10.586 233 5178	9.816 445 5055

SEMI-MONTHLY PAYMENT
NECCESSARY TO AMORTIZE A LOAN OF $1000

RATE		20 YEARS	25 YEARS	30 YEARS
		TERM		
7		3.841 039 5616	3.497 058 9196	3.288 296 3314
7	1/8	3.877 281 8348	3.535 587 3028	3.328 867 5711
7	1/4	3.913 671 1676	3.574 282 3771	3.369 615 2735
7	3/8	3.950 206 2005	3.613 141 9610	3.410 536 3091
7	1/2	3.986 885 5686	3.652 163 8709	3.451 627 5829
7	5/8	4.023 707 9019	3.691 345 9222	3.492 886 0052
7	3/4	4.060 671 8255	3.730 685 9298	3.534 308 4995
7	7/8	4.097 775 9604	3.770 181 7092	3.575 892 0036
8		4.135 018 9235	3.809 831 0771	3.617 633 4707
8	1/8	4.172 399 3280	3.849 631 8523	3.659 529 8709
8	1/4	4.209 915 7841	3.889 581 8566	3.701 578 1922
8	3/8	4.247 566 8993	3.929 678 9151	3.743 775 4418
8	1/2	4.285 351 2783	3.969 920 8575	3.786 118 6468
8	5/8	4.323 267 5241	4.010 305 5186	3.828 604 8559
8	3/4	4.361 314 2377	4.050 830 7386	3.871 231 1397
8	7/8	4.399 490 0191	4.091 494 3646	3.913 994 5919
9		4.437 793 4669	4.132 294 2505	3.956 892 3306
9	1/8	4.476 223 1795	4.173 228 2581	3.999 921 4984
9	1/4	4.514 777 7547	4.214 294 2575	4.043 079 2638
9	3/8	4.553 455 7904	4.255 490 1279	4.086 362 8217
9	1/2	4.592 255 8849	4.296 813 7580	4.129 769 3942
9	5/8	4.631 176 6373	4.338 263 0467	4.173 296 2313
9	3/4	4.670 216 6477	4.379 835 9035	4.216 940 6114
9	7/8	4.709 374 5174	4.421 530 2493	4.260 699 8421
10		4.748 648 8495	4.463 344 0167	4.304 571 2606
10	1/8	4.788 038 2491	4.505 275 1505	4.348 552 2343
10	1/4	4.827 541 3235	4.547 321 6084	4.392 640 1611
10	3/8	4.867 156 6825	4.589 481 3610	4.436 832 4700
10	1/2	4.906 882 9389	4.631 752 3929	4.481 126 6217
10	5/8	4.946 718 7084	4.674 132 7024	4.525 520 1085
10	3/4	4.986 662 6105	4.716 620 3025	4.570 010 4548
10	7/8	5.026 713 2679	4.759 213 2211	4.614 595 2176
11		5.066 869 3076	4.801 909 5010	4.659 271 9865
11	1/8	5.107 129 3607	4.844 707 2010	4.704 038 3842
11	1/4	5.147 492 0626	4.887 604 3955	4.748 892 0662
11	3/8	5.187 956 0537	4.930 599 1751	4.793 830 7215
11	1/2	5.228 519 9790	4.973 689 6473	4.838 852 0725
11	5/8	5.269 182 4890	5.016 873 9361	4.883 953 8750
11	3/4	5.309 942 2393	5.060 150 1825	4.929 133 9185
11	7/8	5.350 797 8914	5.103 516 5452	4.974 390 0260
12		5.391 748 1125	5.146 971 2002	5.019 720 0542
12	1/8	5.432 791 5757	5.190 512 3412	5.065 121 8935
12	1/4	5.473 926 9605	5.234 138 1803	5.110 593 4677
12	3/8	5.515 152 9531	5.277 846 9474	5.156 132 7345
12	1/2	5.556 468 2458	5.321 636 8909	5.201 737 6848
12	5/8	5.597 871 5381	5.365 506 2777	5.247 406 3429
12	3/4	5.639 361 5364	5.409 453 3936	5.293 136 7665
12	7/8	5.680 936 9543	5.453 476 5428	5.338 927 0464
13		5.722 596 5127	5.497 574 0487	5.384 775 3062
13	1/8	5.764 338 9401	5.541 744 2537	5.430 679 7025
13	1/4	5.806 162 9724	5.585 985 5194	5.476 638 4245
13	3/8	5.848 067 3537	5.630 296 2263	5.522 649 6936
13	1/2	5.890 050 8357	5.674 674 7745	5.568 711 7637
13	5/8	5.932 112 1783	5.719 119 5833	5.614 822 9203
13	3/4	5.974 250 1499	5.763 629 0915	5.660 981 4809

SEMI-MONTHLY PAYMENT
NECCESSARY TO AMORTIZE A LOAN OF $1000

RATE		20 YEARS	25 YEARS	30 YEARS
		TERM		
13	7/8	6.016 463 5268	5.808 201 7572	5.707 185 7942
14		6.058 751 0940	5.852 836 0579	5.753 434 2402
14	1/8	6.101 111 6451	5.897 530 4906	5.799 725 2297
14	1/4	6.143 543 9825	5.942 283 5720	5.846 057 2040
14	3/8	6.186 046 9171	5.987 093 8378	5.892 428 6350
14	1/2	6.228 619 2689	6.031 959 8435	5.938 838 0241
14	5/8	6.271 259 8671	6.076 880 1640	5.985 283 9027
14	3/4	6.313 967 5496	6.121 853 3932	6.031 764 8312
14	7/8	6.356 741 1637	6.166 878 1448	6.078 270 3003
15		6.399 579 5659	6.211 953 0516	6.124 826 2249
15	1/8	6.442 481 6222	6.257 076 7655	6.171 403 9546
15	1/4	6.485 446 2077	6.302 247 9576	6.218 011 2626
15	3/8	6.528 472 2073	6.347 465 3184	6.264 646 8508
15	1/2	6.571 558 5151	6.392 727 5569	6.311 309 4481
15	5/8	6.614 704 0351	6.438 033 4014	6.357 997 8104
15	3/4	6.657 907 6808	6.483 381 5988	6.404 710 7199
15	7/8	6.701 168 3753	6.528 770 9148	6.451 446 9850
16		6.744 485 0516	6.574 200 1337	6.498 205 4397
16	1/8	6.787 856 6524	6.619 668 0583	6.544 984 9433
16	1/4	6.831 282 1303	6.665 173 5097	6.591 784 3799
16	3/8	6.874 760 4476	6.710 715 3274	6.638 602 6584
16	1/2	6.918 290 5765	6.756 292 3690	6.685 438 7117
16	5/8	6.961 871 4993	6.801 903 5098	6.732 291 4965
16	3/4	7.005 502 2078	6.847 547 6434	6.779 159 9927
16	7/8	7.049 181 7042	6.893 223 6808	6.826 043 2036
17		7.092 909 0003	6.938 930 5508	6.872 940 1547
17	1/8	7.136 683 1181	6.984 667 1992	6.919 849 8940
17	1/4	7.180 503 0893	7.030 432 5896	6.966 771 4913
17	3/8	7.224 367 9558	7.076 225 7022	7.013 704 0377
17	1/2	7.268 276 7694	7.122 045 5347	7.060 646 6458
17	5/8	7.312 228 5917	7.167 891 1010	7.107 598 4484
17	3/4	7.356 222 4945	7.213 761 4320	7.154 558 5992
17	7/8	7.400 257 5593	7.259 655 5749	7.201 526 2713
18		7.444 332 8778	7.305 572 5933	7.248 500 6579
18	1/4	7.532 600 6913	7.397 471 5909	7.342 466 4422
18	1/2	7.621 018 8653	7.489 451 2521	7.436 449 8745
18	3/4	7.709 580 4877	7.581 504 6536	7.530 445 1678
19		7.798 278 8030	7.673 625 1155	7.624 446 8146
19	1/4	7.887 107 2115	7.765 806 1960	7.718 449 5758
19	1/2	7.976 059 2678	7.858 041 6850	7.812 448 4699
19	3/4	8.065 128 6798	7.950 325 5989	7.906 438 7628
20		8.154 309 3072	8.042 652 1739	8.000 415 9573
20	1/4	8.243 595 1599	8.135 015 8609	8.094 375 7835
20	1/2	8.332 980 3962	8.227 411 3190	8.188 314 1887
20	3/4	8.422 459 3215	8.319 833 4102	8.282 227 3284
21		8.512 026 3858	8.412 277 1929	8.376 111 5573
21	1/4	8.601 676 1825	8.504 737 9170	8.469 963 4203
21	1/2	8.691 403 4458	8.597 211 0173	8.563 779 6439
21	3/4	8.781 203 0491	8.689 692 1087	8.657 557 1285
22		8.871 070 0026	8.782 176 9798	8.751 292 9401
22	1/4	8.960 999 4513	8.874 661 5882	8.844 984 3029
22	1/2	9.050 986 6725	8.967 142 0546	8.938 628 5919
22	3/4	9.141 027 0739	9.059 614 6575	9.032 223 3258
23		9.231 116 1911	9.152 075 8284	9.125 766 1603
24		9.591 874 8781	9.521 739 8818	9.499 376 0546

MONTHLY PAYMENT
NECCESSARY TO AMORTIZE A LOAN OF $1000

RATE		5 YEARS	10 YEARS	15 YEARS
		TERM		
7		19.754 074 6996	11.559 399 1600	8.932 494 4081
7	1/8	19.811 336 4116	11.621 923 6558	9.000 298 2722
7	1/4	19.868 669 5114	11.684 609 9214	9.068 340 8979
7	3/8	19.926 073 8221	11.747 457 3455	9.136 620 8377
7	1/2	19.983 549 1669	11.810 465 3141	9.205 136 6512
7	5/8	20.041 095 3683	11.873 633 2097	9.273 886 8857
7	3/4	20.098 712 2487	11.936 960 4120	9.342 870 0809
7	7/8	20.156 399 6304	12.000 446 2974	9.412 084 7689
8		20.214 157 3353	12.064 090 2398	9.481 529 4745
8	1/8	20.271 985 1851	12.127 891 6099	9.551 202 7153
8	1/4	20.329 883 0011	12.191 849 7757	9.621 103 0023
8	3/8	20.387 850 6047	12.255 964 1022	9.691 228 8397
8	1/2	20.445 887 8167	12.320 233 9521	9.761 578 7258
8	5/8	20.503 994 4579	12.384 658 6849	9.832 151 1526
8	3/4	20.562 170 3489	12.449 237 6581	9.902 944 6065
8	7/8	20.620 415 3099	12.513 970 2261	9.973 957 5684
9		20.678 729 1610	12.578 855 7411	10.045 188 5141
9	1/8	20.737 111 7220	12.643 893 5527	10.116 635 9142
9	1/4	20.795 562 8126	12.709 083 0083	10.188 298 2348
9	3/8	20.854 082 2523	12.774 423 4528	10.260 173 9375
9	1/2	20.912 669 8602	12.839 914 2288	10.332 261 4796
9	5/8	20.971 325 4554	12.905 554 6767	10.404 559 3147
9	3/4	21.030 048 8567	12.971 344 1349	10.477 065 8924
9	7/8	21.088 839 8829	13.037 281 9395	10.549 779 6591
10		21.147 698 3522	13.103 367 4244	10.622 699 0578
10	1/8	21.206 624 0831	13.169 599 9218	10.695 822 5287
10	1/4	21.265 616 8937	13.235 978 7618	10.769 148 5092
10	3/8	21.324 676 6017	13.302 503 2724	10.842 675 4342
10	1/2	21.383 803 0250	13.369 172 7801	10.916 401 7365
10	5/8	21.442 995 9811	13.435 986 6093	10.990 325 8468
10	3/4	21.502 255 2874	13.502 944 0829	11.064 446 1939
10	7/8	21.561 580 7613	13.570 044 5219	11.138 761 2053
11		21.620 972 2196	13.637 287 2456	11.213 269 3069
11	1/8	21.680 429 4795	13.704 671 5721	11.287 968 9239
11	1/4	21.739 952 3576	13.772 196 8175	11.362 858 4803
11	3/8	21.799 540 6706	13.839 862 2966	11.437 936 3995
11	1/2	21.859 194 2349	13.907 667 3229	11.513 201 1047
11	5/8	21.918 912 8669	13.975 611 2082	11.588 651 0187
11	3/4	21.978 696 3828	14.043 693 2633	11.664 284 5643
11	7/8	22.038 544 5987	14.111 912 7976	11.740 100 1645
12		22.098 457 3304	14.180 269 1191	11.816 096 2429
12	1/8	22.158 434 3938	14.248 761 5348	11.892 271 2237
12	1/4	22.218 475 6046	14.317 389 3504	11.968 623 5317
12	3/8	22.278 580 7783	14.386 151 8709	12.045 151 5930
12	1/2	22.338 749 7304	14.455 048 3998	12.121 853 8347
12	5/8	22.398 982 2762	14.524 078 2398	12.198 728 6857
12	3/4	22.459 278 2310	14.593 240 6928	12.275 774 5761
12	7/8	22.519 637 4098	14.662 535 0596	12.352 989 9380
13		22.580 059 6276	14.731 960 6403	12.430 373 2056
13		22.640 544 6995	14.801 516 7342	12.507 922 8152
13	1/4	22.701 092 4401	14.871 202 6397	12.585 637 2053
13	3/8	22.761 702 6642	14.941 017 6548	12.663 514 8172
13	1/2	22.822 375 1865	15.010 961 0766	12.741 554 0948
13	5/8	22.883 109 8215	15.081 032 2017	12.819 753 4849
13	3/4	22.943 906 3836	15.151 230 3261	12.898 111 4373

MONTHLY PAYMENT
NECCESSARY TO AMORTIZE A LOAN OF $1000

RATE		TERM		
		5 YEARS	10 YEARS	15 YEARS
13	7/8	23.004 764 6874	15.221 554 7454	12.976 626 4052
14		23.065 684 5469	15.292 004 7546	13.055 296 8450
14	1/8	23.126 665 7766	15.362 579 6485	13.134 121 2169
14	1/4	23.187 708 1906	15.433 278 7212	13.213 097 9845
14	3/8	23.248 811 6029	15.504 101 2668	13.292 225 6154
14	1/2	23.309 975 8276	15.575 046 5789	13.371 502 5814
14	5/8	23.371 200 6788	15.646 113 9510	13.450 927 3583
14	3/4	23.432 485 9702	15.717 302 6764	13.530 498 4261
14	7/8	23.493 831 5159	15.788 612 0482	13.610 214 2095
15		23.555 237 1296	15.860 041 3594	13.690 073 3777
15	1/8	23.616 702 6251	15.931 589 9030	13.770 074 2447
15	1/4	23.678 227 8161	16.003 256 9719	13.850 215 3692
15	3/8	23.739 812 5163	16.075 041 8591	13.930 495 2551
15	1/2	23.801 456 5395	16.146 943 8576	14.010 912 4113
15	5/8	23.863 159 6991	16.218 962 2606	14.091 465 3522
15	3/4	23.924 921 8088	16.291 096 3614	14.172 152 5972
15	7/8	23.986 742 6822	16.363 345 4534	14.252 972 6716
16		24.048 622 1328	16.435 708 8305	14.333 924 1061
16	1/8	24.110 559 9741	16.508 185 7866	14.415 005 4373
16	1/4	24.172 556 0197	16.580 775 6160	14.496 215 2074
16	3/8	24.234 610 0830	16.653 477 6135	14.577 551 9647
16	1/2	24.296 721 9774	16.726 291 0740	14.659 014 2638
16	5/8	24.358 891 5166	16.799 215 2931	14.740 600 6651
16	3/4	24.421 118 5138	16.872 249 5667	14.822 309 7355
16	7/8	24.483 402 7826	16.945 393 1914	14.904 140 0483
17		24.545 744 1365	17.018 645 4641	14.986 090 1830
17	1/8	24.608 142 3889	17.092 005 6824	15.068 158 7260
17	1/4	24.670 597 3532	17.165 473 1447	15.150 344 2702
17	3/8	24.733 108 8430	17.239 047 1497	15.232 645 4153
17	1/2	24.795 676 6718	17.312 726 9970	15.315 060 7677
17	5/8	24.858 300 6529	17.386 511 9871	15.397 588 9408
17	3/4	24.920 980 6001	17.460 401 4208	15.480 228 5550
17	7/8	24.983 716 3268	17.534 394 6002	15.562 978 2378
18		25.046 507 6466	17.608 490 8278	15.645 836 6237
18	1/4	25.172 256 3199	17.756 989 6433	15.811 874 0795
18	1/2	25.298 225 1291	17.905 892 3070	15.978 330 1448
18	3/4	25.424 412 5841	18.055 193 2740	16.145 194 1604
19		25.550 817 1951	18.204 887 0161	16.312 455 5879
19	1/4	25.677 437 4733	18.354 968 0226	16.480 104 0112
19	1/2	25.804 271 9308	18.505 430 8013	16.648 129 1383
19	3/4	25.931 319 0803	18.656 269 8797	16.816 520 8028
20		26.058 577 4359	18.807 479 8057	16.985 268 9653
20	1/4	26.186 045 5126	18.959 055 1486	17.154 363 7143
20	1/2	26.313 721 8266	19.110 990 4999	17.323 795 2678
20	3/4	26.441 604 8953	19.263 280 4743	17.493 553 9741
21		26.569 693 2377	19.415 919 7107	17.663 630 3124
21	1/4	26.697 985 3739	19.568 902 8724	17.834 014 8937
21	1/2	26.826 479 8259	19.722 224 6488	18.004 698 4614
21	3/4	26.955 175 1170	19.875 879 7553	18.175 671 8918
22		27.084 069 7722	20.029 862 9347	18.346 926 1944
22	1/4	27.213 162 3185	20.184 168 9573	18.518 452 5122
22	1/2	27.342 451 2844	20.338 792 6224	18.690 242 1217
22	3/4	27.471 935 2006	20.493 728 7582	18.862 286 4334
23		27.601 612 5996	20.648 972 2228	19.034 576 9911
24		28.122 227 7491	21.272 917 6134	19.726 037 2297

MONTHLY PAYMENT
NECCESSARY TO AMORTIZE A LOAN OF $1000

RATE		20 YEARS	25 YEARS	30 YEARS
7		7.693 106 3588	7.004 157 5411	6.586 033 0285
7	1/8	7.765 890 5719	7.081 503 2981	6.667 459 9458
7	1/4	7.838 972 8890	7.159 186 7206	6.749 244 2885
7	3/8	7.912 350 6064	7.237 203 4611	6.831 379 8481
7	1/2	7.986 021 0093	7.315 549 1676	6.913 860 4354
7	5/8	8.059 981 3721	7.394 219 4852	6.996 679 8842
7	3/4	8.134 228 9595	7.473 210 0581	7.079 832 0534
7	7/8	8.208 761 0273	7.552 516 5306	7.163 310 8302
8		8.283 574 8228	7.632 134 5497	7.247 110 1320
8	1/8	8.358 667 5862	7.712 059 7655	7.331 223 9094
8	1/4	8.434 036 5508	7.792 287 8337	7.415 646 1482
8	3/8	8.509 678 9440	7.872 814 4167	7.500 370 8719
8	1/2	8.585 591 9882	7.953 635 1852	7.585 392 1439
8	5/8	8.661 772 9010	8.034 745 8195	7.670 704 0693
8	3/4	8.738 218 8967	8.116 142 0109	7.756 300 7970
8	7/8	8.814 927 1864	8.197 819 4634	7.842 176 5219
9		8.891 894 9790	8.279 773 8947	7.928 325 4863
9	1/8	8.969 119 4817	8.362 001 0376	8.014 741 9818
9	1/4	9.046 597 9010	8.444 496 6411	8.101 420 3509
9	3/8	9.124 327 4431	8.527 256 4720	8.188 354 9887
9	1/2	9.202 305 3147	8.610 276 3157	8.275 540 3439
9	5/8	9.280 528 7235	8.693 551 9778	8.362 970 9207
9	3/4	9.358 994 8792	8.777 079 2846	8.450 641 2798
9	7/8	9.437 700 9938	8.860 854 0845	8.538 546 0396
10		9.516 644 2822	8.944 872 2494	8.626 679 8774
10	1/8	9.595 821 9632	9.029 129 6749	8.715 037 5303
10	1/4	9.675 231 2596	9.113 622 2820	8.803 613 7965
10	3/8	9.754 869 3993	9.198 346 0176	8.892 403 5356
10	1/2	9.834 733 6154	9.283 296 8555	8.981 401 6700
10	5/8	9.914 821 1472	9.368 470 7973	9.070 603 1853
10	3/4	9.995 129 2402	9.453 863 8732	9.160 003 1309
10	7/8	10.075 655 1474	9.539 472 1427	9.249 596 6209
11		10.156 396 1292	9.625 291 6955	9.339 378 8345
11		10.237 349 4540	9.711 318 6521	9.429 345 0162
11	1/4	10.318 512 3992	9.797 549 1644	9.519 490 4764
11	3/8	10.399 882 2511	9.883 979 4166	9.609 810 5920
11	1/2	10.481 456 3055	9.970 605 6255	9.700 300 8060
11	5/8	10.563 231 8687	10.057 424 0413	9.790 956 6286
11	3/4	10.645 206 2571	10.144 430 9480	9.881 773 6363
11	7/8	10.727 376 7983	10.231 622 6641	9.972 747 4731
12		10.809 740 8314	10.318 995 5429	10.063 873 8495
12	1/8	10.892 295 7073	10.406 545 9729	10.155 148 5436
12	1/4	10.975 038 7890	10.494 270 3784	10.246 567 3998
12	3/8	11.057 967 4523	10.582 165 2199	10.338 126 3300
12	1/2	11.141 079 0861	10.670 226 9942	10.429 821 3123
12	5/8	11.224 371 0925	10.758 452 2351	10.521 648 3917
12	3/4	11.307 840 8876	10.846 837 5132	10.613 603 6793
12	7/8	11.391 485 9015	10.935 379 4367	10.705 683 3523
13		11.475 303 5787	11.024 074 6513	10.797 883 6537
13	1/8	11.559 291 3787	11.112 919 8406	10.890 200 8918
13	1/4	11.643 446 7759	11.201 911 7263	10.982 631 4400
13	3/8	11.727 767 2602	11.291 047 0681	11.075 171 7362
13	1/2	11.812 250 3371	11.380 322 6641	11.167 818 2826
13	5/8	11.896 893 5283	11.469 735 3510	11.260 567 6452
13	3/4	11.981 694 3714	11.559 282 0039	11.353 416 4531

MONTHLY PAYMENT
NECCESSARY TO AMORTIZE A LOAN OF $1000

RATE		20 YEARS	25 YEARS	30 YEARS
13	7/8	12.066 650 4208	11.648 959 5367	11.446 361 3980
14		12.151 759 2475	11.738 764 9017	11.539 399 2340
14	1/8	12.237 018 4395	11.828 695 0902	11.632 526 7766
14	1/4	12.322 425 6020	11.918 747 1321	11.725 740 9026
14	3/8	12.407 978 3578	12.008 918 0961	11.819 038 5488
14	1/2	12.493 674 3471	12.099 205 0896	11.912 416 7121
14	5/8	12.579 511 2279	12.189 605 2585	12.005 872 4485
14	3/4	12.665 486 6764.	12.280 115 7874	12.099 402 8723
14	7/8	12.751 598 3070	12.370 733 8995	12.193 005 1558
15		12.837 844 0721	12.461 456 8563	12.286 676 5284
15	1/8	12.924 221 4630	12.552 281 9575	12.380 414 2758
15	1/4	13.010 728 3094	12.643 206 5411	12.474 215 7396
15	3/8	13.097 362 3800	12.734 227 9831	12.568 078 3163
15	1/2	13.184 121 4620	12.825 343 6974	12.661 999 4566
15	5/8	13.271 003 3621	12.916 551 1354	12.755 976 6650
15	3/4	13.358 005 9059	13.007 847 7863	12.850 007 4985
15	7/8	13.445 126 9381	13.099 231 1763	12.944 089 5662
16		13.532 364 3231	13.190 698 8689	13.038 220 5288
16	1/8	13.619 715 9442	13.282 248 4644	13.132 398 0972
16	1/4	13.707 179 7046	13.373 877 5997	13.226 620 0321
16	3/8	13.794 753 5269	13.465 583 9482	13.320 884 1434
16	1/2	13.882 435 3533	13.557 365 2194	13.415 188 2893
16	5/8	13.970 223 1456	13.649 219 1586	13.509 530 3751
16	3/4	14.058 114 8854	13.741 143 5467	13.603 908 3534
16	7/8	14.146 108 5739	13.833 136 2001	13.698 320 2222
17		14.234 202 2323	13.925 194 9702	13.792 764 0250
17	1/8	14.322 393 9013	14.017 317 7429	13.887 237 8498
17	1/4	14.410 681 6415	14.109 502 4388	13.981 739 8281
17	3/8	14.499 063 5334	14.201 747 0125	14.076 268 1344
17	1/2	14.587 537 6773	14.294 049 4525	14.170 820 9854
17	5/8	14.676 102 1931	14.386 407 7808	14.265 396 6392
17	3/4	14.764 755 2207	14.478 820 0524	14.359 993 3944
17	7/8	14.853 494 9197	14.571 284 3554	14.454 609 5899
18		14.942 319 4695	14.663 798 8102	14.549 243 6035
18	1/4	15.120 215 9373	14.848 970 8174	14.738 558 7884
18	1/2	15.298 430 4527	15.034 321 6746	14.927 926 7287
18	3/4	15.476 949 1578	15.219 837 4802	15.117 335 7856
19		15.655 758 5069	15.405 504 8192	15.306 774 8786
19	1/4	15.834 845 2640	15.591 310 7514	15.496 233 4647
19	1/2	16.014 196 5006	15.777 242 7999	15.685 701 5159
19	3/4	16.193 799 5935	15.963 288 9397	15.875 169 4990
20		16.373 642 6042	16.149 437 5856	16.064 628 3549
20	1/4	16.553 712 3641	16.335 677 5808	16.254 069 4791
20	1/2	16.733 998 2945	16.521 998 1848	16.443 484 7021
20	3/4	16.914 488 5802	16.708 389 0624	16.632 866 2708
21		17.095 172 0772	16.894 840 2714	16.822 206 8307
21	1/4	17.276 037 9267	17.081 342 2516	17.011 499 4081
21	1/2	17.457 075 5514	17.267 885 8135	17.200 737 3931
21	3/4	17.638 274 6510	17.454 462 1265	17.389 914 5237
22		17.819 625 1984	17.641 062 7084	17.579 024 8694
22	1/4	18.001 117 4353	17.827 679 4141	17.768 062 8167
22	1/2	18.182 741 8675	18.014 304 4253	17.957 023 0538
22	3/4	18.364 489 2610	18.200 930 2393	18.145 900 5569
23		18.546 350 6371	18.387 549 6589	18.334 690 5766
24		19.274 765 0708	19.133 829 5817	19.088 889 7216

MONTHLY INTEREST FACTORS

Interest for one month at nominal annual rates shown, based upon interest compounded semiannually.

7 %	-	.005 750 0395	12½%	-	.010 155 3225
7⅛%	-	.005 851 2369	12⅝%	-	.010 254 3331
7¼%	-	.005 952 3834	12¾%	-	.010 353 2952
7⅜%	-	.006 053 4791	12⅞%	-	.010 452 2088
7½%	-	.006 154 5240	13 %	-	.010 551 0740
7⅝%	-	.006 255 5182	13⅛%	-	.010 649 8909
7¾%	-	.006 356 4617	13¼%	-	.010 748 6596
7⅞%	-	.006 457 3546	13⅜%	-	.010 847 3799
8 %	-	.006 558 1970	13½%	-	.010 946 0522
8⅛%	-	.006 658 9889	13⅝%	-	.011 044 6762
8¼%	-	.006 759 7303	13¾%	-	.011 143 2522
8⅜%	-	.006 860 4214	13⅞%	-	.011 241 7802
8½%	-	.006 961 0622	14 %	-	.010 340 2602
8⅝%	-	.007 061 6527	14⅛%	-	.011 438 6923
8¾%	-	.007 162 1929	14¼%	-	.011 537 0764
8⅞%	-	.007 262 6831	14⅜%	-	.011 635 4128
9 %	-	.007 363 1231	14½%	-	.011 733 7014
9⅛%	-	.007 463 5130	14⅝%	-	.011 831 9423
9¼%	-	.007 563 8530	14¾%	-	.011 930 1355
9⅜%	-	.007 664 1431	14⅞%	-	.012 028 2811
9½%	-	.007 764 3832	15 %	-	.012 126 3791
9⅝%	-	.007 864 5735	15⅛%	-	.012 224 4297
9¾%	-	.007 964 7141	15¼%	-	.012 322 4327
9⅞%	-	.008 064 8049	15⅜%	-	.012 420 3883
10 %	-	.008 164 8461	15½%	-	.012 518 2966
10⅛%	-	.008 264 8377	15⅝%	-	.012 616 1575
10¼%	-	.008 364 7797	15¾%	-	.012 713 9712
10⅜%	-	.008 464 6722	15⅞%	-	.012 811 7377
10½%	-	.008 564 5152	16 %	-	.012 909 4570
10⅝%	-	.008 664 3089	16⅛%	-	.013 007 1292
10¾%	-	.008 764 0532	16¼%	-	.013 104 7543
10⅞%	-	.008 863 7482	16⅜%	-	.013 202 3325
11 %	-	.008 963 3940	16½%	-	.013 299 8636
11⅛%	-	.009 062 9906	16⅝%	-	.013 397 3478
11¼%	-	.009 162 5381	16¾%	-	.013 494 7852
11⅜%	-	.009 262 0365	16⅞%	-	.013 592 1758
11½%	-	.009 361 4858	17 %	-	.013 689 5196
11⅝%	-	.009 460 8863	17⅛%	-	.013 786 8166
11¾%	-	.009 560 2378	17¼%	-	.013 884 0670
11⅞%	-	.009 659 5404	17⅜%	-	.013 981 2708
12 %	-	.009 758 7942	17½%	-	.014 078 4280
12⅛%	-	.009 857 9993	17⅝%	-	.014 175 5387
12¼%	-	.009 957 1557	17¾%	-	.014 272 6030
12⅜%	-	.010 056 2634	17⅞%	-	.014 369 6208

Interest for one month on any amount may be obtained by multiplying that amount by this factor.

MONTHLY INTEREST FACTORS

Interest for one month at nominal annual rates shown,
based upon interest compounded semiannually.

18 %	-	.014 466 5922	23½%	-	.018 688 1526
18⅛%	-	.014 563 5173	23⅝%	-	.018 783 0865
18¼%	-	.014 660 3961	23¾%	-	.018 877 9762
18⅜%	-	.014 757 2287	23⅞%	-	.018 972 8217
18½%	-	.014 854 0152	24 %	-	.019 067 6231
18⅝%	-	.014 950 7554	24⅛%	-	.019 162 3804
18¾%	-	.015 047 4497	24¼%	-	.019 257 0937
18⅞%	-	.015 144 0978	24⅜%	-	.019 351 7630
19 %	-	.015 240 7000	24½%	-	.019 446 3884
19⅛%	-	.015 337 2563	24⅝%	-	.019 540 9699
19¼%	-	.015 433 7666	24¾%	-	.019 635 5075
19⅜%	-	.015 530 2312	24⅞%	-	.019 730 0013
19½%	-	.015 626 6499	25 %	-	.019 824 4514
19⅝%	-	.015 723 0229	25⅛%	-	.019 918 8577
19¾%	-	.015 819 3502	25¼%	-	.020 013 2204
19⅞%	-	.015 915 6318	25⅜%	-	.020 107 5394
20 %	-	.016 011 8678	25½%	-	.020 201 8149
20⅛%	-	.016 108 0583	25⅝%	-	.020 296 0468
20¼%	-	.016 204 2033	25¾%	-	.020 390 2352
20⅜%	-	.016 300 3028	25⅞%	-	.020 484 3802
20½%	-	.016 396 3569	26 %	-	.020 578 4817
20⅝%	-	.016 492 3656	26⅛%	-	.020 672 5399
20¾%	-	.016 588 3290	26¼%	-	.020 766 5548
20⅞%	-	.016 684 2471	26⅜%	-	.020 860 5264
21 %	-	.016 780 1200	26½%	-	.020 954 4548
21⅛%	-	.016 875 9478	26⅝%	-	.021 048 3400
21¼%	-	.016 971 7304	26¾%	-	.021 142 1820
21⅜%	-	.017 067 4679	26⅞%	-	.021 235 9810
21½%	-	.017 163 1604	27 %	-	.021 329 7369
21⅝%	-	.017 258 8079	27⅛%	-	.021 423 4498
21¾%	-	.017 354 4104	27¼%	-	.021 517 1197
21⅞%	-	.017 449 9680	27⅜%	-	.021 610 7466
22 %	-	.017 545 4808	27½%	-	.021 704 3307
22⅛%	-	.017 640 9488	27⅝%	-	.021 797 8720
22¼%	-	.017 736 3720	27¾%	-	.021 891 3704
22⅜%	-	.017 831 7505	27⅞%	-	.021 984 8261
22½%	-	.017 927 0844	28 %	-	.022 078 2391
22⅝%	-	.018 022 3736	28⅛%	-	.022 171 6095
22¾%	-	.018 117 6183	28¼%	-	.022 264 9372
22⅞%	-	.018 212 8184	28⅜%	-	.022 358 2223
23 %	-	.018 307 9740	28½%	-	.022 451 4649
23⅛%	-	.018 403 0852	28⅝%	-	.022 544 6649
23¼%	-	.018 498 1520	28¾%	-	.022 637 8226
23⅜%	-	.018 593 1745	28⅞%	-	.022 730 9378

Interest for one month on any amount may be obtained
by multiplying that amount by this factor.